T0238658

Lecture Notes in Computer Science   8424

Commenced Publication in 1973
Founding and Former Series Editors:
Gerhard Goos, Juris Hartmanis, and Jan van Leeuwen

For further volumes:
http://www.springer.com/series/7410

Shiho Moriai (Ed.)

Fast
Software Encryption

20th International Workshop, FSE 2013
Singapore, March 11–13, 2013
Revised Selected Papers

 Springer

Editor
Shiho Moriai
Network Security Research Institute
National Institute of Information and
    Communications Technology (NICT)
Tokyo
Japan

ISSN 0302-9743   ISSN 1611-3349   (electronic)
ISBN 978-3-662-43932-6   ISBN 978-3-662-43933-3   (eBook)
DOI 10.1007/978-3-662-43933-3
Springer Heidelberg New York Dordrecht London

Library of Congress Control Number: 2014942655

Printed on acid-free paper

Springer is part of Springer Science+Business Media (www.springer.com)

Preface

The 20th International Workshop on Fast Software Encryption (FSE 2013) was held at Novotel Singapore Clarke Quay, Singapore, during March 11–13, 2013. The workshop was sponsored by the International Association for Cryptologic Research. FSE 2013 received 97 submissions from 24 countries. The 21 members of the Program Committee were assisted by more than 90 external reviewers. In total, they delivered 337 reviews. Each submission was reviewed by at least three Program Committee members. Submissions by Program Committee members received at least five reviews. The review process was double-blind, and conflicts of interest were carefully handled. The review process was handled through an online review system that supported discussions among Program Committee members. Over the entire review period, more than 200 messages were exchanged between Program Committee members. Eventually, the Program Committee selected 30 papers (a 31 % acceptance rate) for publication in the proceedings.

The program also included two invited talks, by Serge Vaudenay from Ecole Polytechnique Federale de Lausanne, Switzerland, and by Daniel Bernstein from University of Illinois at Chicago, USA, and Technische Universiteit Eindhoven, The Netherlands.

The Program Committee also identified the best submissions from FSE for their scientific quality, their originality, and their clarity. The FSE 2013 Best Paper Award went to Gordon Procter and Carlos Cid from Royal Holloway, University of London, United Kingdom. Their paper, "On Weak Keys and Forgery Attacks against Polynomial-based MAC Schemes", identifies some properties of hash functions based on polynomial evaluation that arise from the underlying algebraic structure.

Many people contributed to FSE 2013. We thank the authors for contributing their excellent research. We thank the Program Committee members, and their external reviewers, for making a significant effort to select for the program. We particularly thank Dmitry Khovratovich, Subhamoy Maitra, Florian Mendel, and Christian Rechberger for shepherding papers. Finally, we thank Jian Guo and Thomas Peyrin, the general co-chairs, and the FSE Steering Committee members, who worked so hard for the event and helped me a lot.

FSE 2013 collected a diversity of recent results in symmetric cryptography, from theory to practical aspects, from design to cryptanalysis. We feel privileged for the opportunity to develop the FSE 2013 program. We hope that the papers in these proceedings will continue to inspire, guide, and clarify your academic and professional endeavors.

May 2014   Shiho Moriai

FSE 2013

Workshop on Fast Software Encryption
Singapore, 11–13 March, 2013
Sponsored by the International Association
for Cryptologic Research

General Co-chairs

Jian Guo   Institute for Infocomm Research, Singapore
Thomas Peyrin   Nanyang Technological University, Singapore

Program Chairs

Shiho Moriai   NICT, Japan

Program Committee

Kazumaro Aoki   NTT Corporation, Japan
Jean-Philippe Aumasson   Kudelski Security, Switzerland
Alex Biryukov   University of Luxembourg, Luxembourg
Anne Canteaut   Inria Paris-Rocquencourt, France
Orr Dunkelman   University of Haifa and Weizmann Institute, Israel
Martin Hell   Lund University, Sweden
Tetsu Iwata   Nagoya University, Japan
John Kelsey   NIST, USA
Dmitry Khovratovich   University of Luxembourg, Luxembourg
Gregor Leander   Technical University of Denmark, Denmark
Subhamoy Maitra   ISI Kolkata, India
Florian Mendel   K.U. Leuven, Belgium
Maria Naya-Plasencia   Inria, France
Elisabeth Oswald   University of Bristol, UK
Christian Rechberger   Technical University of Denmark, Denmark
Vincent Rijmen   K.U. Leuven, Belgium and TU Graz, Austria
Matt Robshaw   Impinj, USA
Kyoji Shibutani   Sony Corporation, Japan
François-Xavier Standaert   Universite catholique de Louvain, Belgium
Gilles Van Assche   STMicroelectronics, Belgium

External Reviewers

Aagren, Martin
Ahmed Abdelraheem, Mohamed
Akishita, Toru
Albrecht, Martin
Arnab, Roy
Banciu, Valentina
Banik, Subhadeep
Bay, Asli
Bertoni, Guido
Bhattacharya, Srimanta
Bilgin, Begul
Blondeau, Céline
Bogdanov, Andrey
Borghoff, Julia
Boura, Christina
Burr, Bill
Carlet, Claude
Chattopadhyay, Anupam
Collard, Baudoin
Daemen, Joan
De Mulder, Yoni
Duc, Alexandre
Durvaux, François
Dworkin, Morris
Fuhr, Thomas
Gangopadhyay, Sugata
Gaëtan, Leurent
Gérard, Benoît
Grosso, Vincent
Gérard, Benoît
Güneysu, Tim
Hiwatari, Harunaga
Isobe, Takanori
Junod, Pascal
Kerckhof, Stéphanie
Kizhvatov, Ilya
Knellwolf, Simon
Kucuk, Ozgul
Lamberger, Mario
Lange, Tanja

Leurent, Gaetan
Lucks, Stefan
Luykx, Atul
Macchetti, Marco
Medwed, Marcel
Mehl Lauridsen, Martin
Meier, Willi
Melzani, Filippo
Mennink, Bart
Minier, Marine
Mironov, Ilya
Misoczki, Rafael
Mitsuda, Atsushi
Moradi, Amir
Nad, Tomislav
Nakahara Jr, Jorge
Nandi, Mridul
Nikolic, Ivica
Paul, Goutam
Peeters, Michaël
Perlner, Ray
Petit, Christophe
Peyrin, Thomas
Pietrzak, Krzysztof
Prouff, Emmanuel
Ralf-Philipp, Weinmann
Regazzoni, Francesco
Reinhard, Jean-René
Reyhanitabar, Reza
Ristenpart, Thomas
Sarkar, Palash
Sasaki, Yu
Schläffer, Martin
Schmidt, Joern-Marc
Sen Gupta, Sourav
Shimoyama, Takeshi
Shirai, Taizo
Sonmez Turan, Meltem
Stankovski, Paul
Susil, Petr

Tillich, Stefan
Tischhauser, Elmar
Todo, Yosuke
Toz, Deniz
Tunstall, Michael
Varici, Kerem

Vesselin, Velichkov
Veyrat-Charvillon, Nicolas
Whitnall, Carolyn
Wyseur, Brecht
Xagawa, Keita

Contents

Block Ciphers

Complementing Feistel Ciphers

Alex Biryukov[1] and Ivica Nikolić[2] (✉)

[1] University of Luxembourg, Luxembourg, Luxembourg
alex.biryukov@uni.lu
[2] Nanyang Technological University, Singapore, Singapore
inikolic@ntu.edu.sg

Abstract. In this paper, we propose related-key differential distinguishers based on the complementation property of Feistel ciphers. We show that with relaxed requirements on the complementation, i.e. the property does not have to hold for all keys and the complementation does not have to be on all bits, one can obtain a variety of distinguishers. We formulate criteria sufficient for attacks based on the complementation property. To stress the importance of our findings we provide analysis of the *full-round* primitives:

– For the hash mode of *Camellia-128* without FL, FL^{-1} layers, differential multicollisions with 2^{112} time.
– For GOST, practical recovery of the full key with 31 related keys and 2^{38} time/data.

Keywords: Complementation · Feistel · Camellia · GOST

1 Introduction

It is a well established fact that the effective key size of DES [9] is 55 instead of 56 bits. The reduction of one bit is due to the complementation property of DES, i.e. by flipping all the bits in the key and in the plaintext, all the bits of the ciphertext will flip as well. Hence in an exhaustive key search, one has to try only half of the possible values for the key – the other complemented half would produce related ciphertexts. This property applies to all Feistel ciphers with round keys obtained as permutations of the master key bits/words, and with a round function that starts with an XOR of a single round key.

The complementation property can be seen as a simple related-key distinguisher applicable to all of the keys and detectable with a single pair of plaintexts and a corresponding pair of ciphertexts. The difference in the round keys, plaintexts and the ciphertexts is always −1, i.e. it is in all of the bits. In this paper we investigate the cases of ciphers with complementation properties applicable not necessarily to all of the keys, but only to a subset i.e. weak-key class, and with round key differences other than −1. We are aware of only one published result that analyzes the complementation property – the work of Bouillaguet et al. [3]. Even there the focus in not on the original property – the authors

S. Moriai (Ed.): FSE 2013, LNCS 8424, pp. 3–18, 2014.
DOI: 10.1007/978-3-662-43933-3_1, © Springer-Verlag Berlin Heidelberg 2014

examine the generalizations of the complementation property, and exploit self-similarity of the rounds in the ciphers. Our work however targets exclusively the cases of complementation and only Feistel ciphers.

The starting point of our analysis is the observation that if instead of the requirement that the complementation property holds for all keys (as in the case of DES), we can examine only a subset of keys for which it applies. This leads to the problem of constructing a high probability differential in the key schedule of the cipher. We give the conditions on the output difference in the differential and obtain quite simple criteria for existence of related-key attacks based on the complementation property. The importance of our findings is shown on the example of two full-round Feistel ciphers: Camellia-128 [1] and GOST [5]. We analyze Camellia-128 without the non-linear layers FL, FL^{-1} and show how to find a pair of keys that follow the low probability differential in the key schedule constructed to exploit the complementation – this allows us to attack the hash mode of this version of the cipher. Thus we obtain the first analysis on the full-round Camellia without the FL, FL^{-1} in the hash mode – it requires around 2^{112} encryptions. Complementation property of GOST has been known (see [4,7]), however all of the proposed key recovery attacks require impractical time complexity. We show that if one uses several similar complementation properties, an efficient key recovery attack on GOST exists. Our attack requires 31 related-key pair, and only 2^{38} time and data complexities to recover the full 256-bit key. Thus we are able to perform the first experimental cryptanalysis of GOST on a computer.

2 Complementation Property of Feistel Constructions

The complementation property was first observed in DES. It is based on the observation that if one flips all of the bits of the master key and the plaintext, then all of the bits of the ciphertext will flip as well. The foundation of these observations for Feistel ciphers is given below. Without loss of generality we assume that the Feistel is balanced as the case for unbalanced Feistels can be examined similarly.

A balanced Feistel with r rounds is defined as:

$$L_{n+1} = F(L_n, K_n) \oplus R_n$$
$$R_{n+1} = L_n,$$

where K_n is the n-th round key, $P = L_0||R_0$ is the plaintext, and $C = L_r||R_r$ is the ciphertext. In the vast majority of Feistel ciphers, the round function $F(L, K)$ can be decomposed as[1]:

$$F(L, K) = G(L \oplus K),$$

---

[1] The round function of DES does not strictly follow this definition due to the expansion of the initial input from 32 bits to 48 bits, nonetheless our reasoning can still be applied to DES.

i.e. first the round key is bitwise added to the state L, followed by some additional non-linear and linear transformations (G is usually a Substitution-Permutation network). We use the term *classical Feistels* for the ciphers that have such an F function.

Let $KS(K)$ be the key schedule function of the cipher, i.e. given the master key K, the function produces $K_i, i = 1, \ldots, r$ round keys:

$$KS(K) = (K_1, \ldots, K_r)$$

Further assume that all of the round keys K_i are obtained by (possibly different) bit permutations of the master key K (as in the case of DES). If one has two related master keys K^1, K^2 such that $K^1 \oplus K^2 = -1$ (with -1 we denote the difference in all of the bits) then the following holds for all i: $K_i^1 \oplus K_i^2 = -1$. Let P^1, P^2 be two related plaintexts such that $P^1 \oplus P^2 = -1$, i.e. $L_0^1 \oplus L_0^2 = -1$ and $R_0^1 \oplus R_0^2 = -1$. Then by induction for each i we get:

$$L_{i+1}^1 \oplus L_{i+1}^2 = F(L_i^1, K_i^1) \oplus R_i^1 \oplus F(L_i^1, K_i^1) \oplus R_i^1 =$$
$$G(L_i^1 \oplus K_i^1) \oplus R_i^1 \oplus G(L_i^1 \oplus -1 \oplus K_i^1 \oplus -1) \oplus R_i^1 = R_i^1 \oplus R_i^2 = -1$$
$$R_{i+1}^1 \oplus R_{i+1}^2 = L_i^1 \oplus L_i^2 = -1$$

Therefore $L_r^1 \oplus L_r^2 = -1, R_r^1 \oplus R_r^2 = -1$ and hence there is a difference in all of the bits of the ciphertext.

The complementation property of such ciphers allows reduction of the key space by one bit as for the brute force of the whole key space it is sufficient to try only one half of all possible keys – the other half will produce a compliment ciphertext under a compliment plaintext.

The complementation property can be observed for ciphers that not necessarily have a key schedule composed of bit permutations. Notice, the only requirement on the key schedule is to produce complemented round keys.

Lemma 1 (Classical Feistel complementation). *Let for an n-bit classical Feistel cipher $E_K(P)$ with k-bit keys and a key schedule $KS(K)$ exist a differential with probability p for $KS(K)$ with output difference in all of the bits in all of the round keys, i.e.*

$$\exists \Delta : KS(K \oplus \Delta) \oplus KS(K) \xrightarrow{p} (-1, \ldots, -1)$$

Then, if $p > 2^{-k}$, distinguisher for a weak-key class of size $p \cdot 2^k$ exists for the cipher $E_K(P)$.

Proof. Once the difference in all of the round keys is -1, the complementation property can be applied, i.e. the differential in the state holds with probability 1. Therefore if the attacker can build a differential with the input difference in the master keys Δ, and output difference -1 in all of the round keys, then the differential $(-1, \Delta) \rightarrow (-1)$ for the cipher $E_K(P)$ holds with probability p. To find the right key pair that follows the differential in the key schedule one has to try around $1/p$ pairs of randomly chosen master keys with input difference

Δ, therefore the size of this weak key class is $2^k \cdot p$. For any cipher, to produce a pair of complemented plaintexts that result in complemented ciphertexts, one has to try around 2^n pairs, however even when $p < 2^{-n}$, a false positive (i.e. a complementation pair of plaintexts-ciphertexts that indicate belonging of a key to the weak-key class) can be easily detected by trying a few more pairs of complementing plaintexts. $\square$

Remark 1. *The complementation property holds regardless of the number of rounds in the cipher, by increasing the number of rounds one cannot expect to get a better resistance against this type of attacks.*

Remark 2. *The additional key whitenings at the beginning and at the end of the Feistel do not influence the attack complexities, but merely change the input difference in the plaintext and the output difference in the ciphertext.*

The requirement of having the difference -1 in all of the round keys can be replaced with the requirement of having some difference Δ which is not necessarily -1. We call this property *a partial complementation*. Also, instead of a single difference Δ one can require two differences Δ_1, Δ_2 that alternate, i.e. the first round key has Δ_1, the second Δ_2, the third Δ_1, etc. – this is *an alternating complementation*.

Lemma 2 (Classical Feistel partial alternating complementation). *Let for an n-bit classical Feistel cipher $E_K(P)$ with k-bit keys and a key schedule $KS(K)$ exist a differential with probability p for $KS(K)$ with alternating differences in the round keys, i.e.*

$$\exists \Delta : KS(K \oplus \Delta) \oplus KS(K) \xrightarrow{p} (\Delta_1, \Delta_2, \Delta_1, \Delta_2, \ldots, \Delta_1, \Delta_2)$$

Then, if $p > 2^{-k}$, distinguisher for a weak-key class of size $p \cdot 2^k$ exists for the cipher $E_K(P)$.

Proof. We can follow the same logic as in the proof of Lemma 1 with one exception – the initial difference in the plaintext should be (Δ_1, Δ_2). Then in each round, in the XOR the difference from the round key (either Δ_1 or Δ_2) would cancel the difference in the state. As they alternate with the same period of two rounds, the XOR will always produce zero difference, hence the probability of the differential in the state would be 1. Depending if the number of rounds is even or odd, the difference in the ciphertext would be either (Δ_1, Δ_2) for even rounds, or (Δ_2, Δ_1) for odd rounds. $\square$

Remark 3. *Lemma 2 is more general then Lemma 1, as the later is a particular case of the former for $\Delta_1 = \Delta_2 = -1$.*

The round function of some Feistel ciphers instead of an XOR applies modular addition of the round key, i.e. $F(L, K) = G(L + K)$. We call this type of ciphers, *modular Feistels*. The (complementary) differential in the state of a modular Feistel not necessarily holds with probability 1 – the precise probability depends on the differences in the round key K_i and the state word L_i as well as on the number of rounds.

An efficient algorithm for computing the differential probability of modular addition was presented by Limpaa and Moriai in [8]. Our further analysis is based on this algorithm, however, due to space constraints we would not provide its description. Let $(X)_m$ be the m rightmost (least significant) bits of an n-bit word X and let $|X|$ be the Hamming weight, i.e. the number of bits with value 1, of the word X.

Lemma 3 (Modular Feistel alternating complementation[2]). *Let for an r-round n-bit modular Feistel cipher $E_K(P)$ with k-bit keys and a key schedule $KS(K)$ exist a differential with probability p for $KS(K)$ with alternating differences in the round keys, i.e.*

$$\exists \Delta : KS(K \oplus \Delta) \oplus KS(K) \xrightarrow{p} (\Delta_1, \Delta_2, \Delta_1, \Delta_2, \ldots, \Delta_1, \Delta_2)$$

Then, if $p \cdot 2^{-\lceil \frac{r}{2} \rceil (|(\Delta_1)_{n-1}| + |(\Delta_2)_{n-1}|)} > 2^{-k}$ and $2^{-\lceil \frac{r}{2} \rceil (|(\Delta_1)_{n-1}| + |(\Delta_2)_{n-1}|)} > 2^{-n}$, distinguisher for a weak-key class of size $p \cdot 2^k$ exists for the cipher $E_K(P)$.

Proof. In modular ciphers, we have to compute the probability of the differential in the state as well. As in r rounds, there are[3] $\lceil \frac{r}{2} \rceil$ round keys with Δ_1 difference, and the same number of keys with difference Δ_2, it is sufficient to find only the probability of one round (with both Δ_1 and Δ_2). The differences from the incoming round key and the state word should cancel, thus avoid any incoming difference in the SP network of the round function. Hence, by Algorithm 2 of [8], γ should be equal to zero, and the maximal probability of one round is reached when the incoming differences in the round key K_i and the state word L_i (or in the notation from [8], $\alpha = \beta$) are the same – in this case the probability of modular addition is $2^{-|(\Delta_1)_{n-1}|}$ or $2^{-|(\Delta_2)_{n-1}|}$. Taking into account the number of rounds, one obtains the claimed probability. The second requirement in the Lemma is to ensure that the probability of the differential in the state is not bellow 2^{-n}.   □

The variations of the complementation property presented above are indeed related-key differential distinguishers for ciphers. In both classical and modular Feistels, the size of the weak-key class depends only on the probability of the differential in the key schedule. However, to find and detect if a specific key belongs to the weak-key class differs between these two families, as for classical Feistels, the probability of the differential in the state is 1, whereas for modular Feistels, this probability might be lower. Hence, in the case of former one has to try around 2^P different pairs of keys and encrypt one pair of plaintexts, while in the case of modular Feistels, for each of the 2^P pairs of related-key has to encrypt 2^Q pairs of plaintexts ($2^{-P}, 2^{-Q}$ are the probabilities of the differential in the key schedule and in the state).

---

[2] One of our anonymous reviewers has informed us that a similar idea was used against DESX in Kelsey et al. [6]

[3] When r is odd, there are $\lceil \frac{r}{2} \rceil$ round keys with difference Δ_1, and $\lceil \frac{r}{2} \rceil - 1$ round keys with Δ_2.

3   The Case of Camellia-128

In this section we show how to apply the complementation property (Lemma 1) to Camellia-128 [1] in the hash mode. We analyze the full-round *Camellia-128* without the non-linear layers, i.e. we assume FL, FL^{-1} to be identity functions.

3.1   Description

Camellia is a classical Feistel cipher with a non-linear key schedule defined as follows. The 128-bit master key K_L is split into two keys L, R, i.e. $K_L = L\|R$ – both L and R are seen as 8-byte vectors. Further, these keys are fed to a 4-round Feistel-like transformation with an additional keys feedback after the second round (see Fig. 1). Formally, the key schedule can be described as:

$$L_1\|R_1 = K_L \tag{1}$$

$$L_2 = F(L_1 \oplus \Sigma_1) \oplus R_1; \qquad R_2 = L_1 \tag{2}$$

$$L_3 = F(L_2 \oplus \Sigma_2) \oplus R_2; \qquad R_3 = L_2 \tag{3}$$

$$\overline{L_3} = L_3 \oplus L_1; \qquad \overline{R_3} = R_3 \oplus R_1 \tag{4}$$

$$L_4 = F(\overline{L_3} \oplus \Sigma_3) \oplus \overline{R_3}; \qquad R_4 = \overline{L_3} \tag{5}$$

$$L_5 = F(L_4 \oplus \Sigma_4) \oplus R_4; \qquad R_5 = L_4 \tag{6}$$

$$K_A = L_5\|R_5 \tag{7}$$

where Σ_i are word constants. In the sequel, we omit the addition of the constants as they play no role in our analysis. The function F is an SP network, with the S-layer defined as application of eight 8×8 S-boxes, and P-layer is a multiplication of the eight-byte input with 8×8 byte matrix P. All the round keys K_i used in the state are obtained from the two keys K_L and K_A with rotations on various amounts, e.g. $K_4 = K_L \lll_{15}, K_{15} = K_A \lll_{95}$, etc.

3.2   Complementing *Camellia-128*

From the description of Camellia-128 it follows that two different keys K_L, K_A are used, the first key being also the only input to the key schedule. Since the round keys are produced from these two keys with various rotations it follows that the differences in K_L, K_A have to be invariant of rotations and thus -1. Therefore, we need the differential $\Delta K_L \rightarrow (\Delta K_L, \Delta K_A)$ to be $(-1) \rightarrow (-1, -1)$.

The easiest way to build such differential is by providing a differential trail, i.e. besides specifying the input and output differences, fixing as well the intermediate differences after each transformation in the key schedule. Note that from the condition on the differential it follows that $\Delta L_1 = \Delta R_1 = \Delta L_5 = \Delta R_5 = -1$, i.e. each byte of these words has the fixed difference -1 (or ff in the hexadecimal representation). Therefore, in the first and the fourth round of the key schedule, the number of active bytes has to be maximal, i.e. eight active bytes will enter the S-layer. It is tempting to go with a trail that has no active bytes (or one active byte) in both the second and third round, hence obtain a trail of the form (we write only the round-by-round active bytes entering the F function):

$$8 \to 0 \to 0 \to 8 \text{ or } 8 \to 1 \to 1 \to 8$$

However, these types of trails are not possible due to the matrix multiplication P, i.e. P-layer. For example, if we require no active bytes in the second round, then this means the output of the F function in the first round has canceled with the -1 difference in R_1, i.e. if we denote with $\tilde{a} = (a_1, \ldots, a_8)$ the output difference of the S-boxes in the function F of the first round, then the above condition can be expressed as:

$$P \cdot \tilde{a} \oplus (-1) = 0 \Rightarrow \tilde{a} = (0, 0, 0, 0, -1, -1, -1, -1)$$

The solution vector $\tilde{a}$ has difference only in 4 bytes out of 8, while all the bijective S-boxes are active, i.e. we get a contradiction. Therefore, the second round of the key schedule cannot have zero active bytes. A similar situation can be observed when the second (or the third) round has only 1 active byte.

The above result suggests that the minimal number of active bytes in the key schedule is $8+2+2+8 = 20$. Theoretically, this can lead to a trail with probability $2^{-6 \cdot 20} = 2^{-120} > 2^{-128}$ when all the active S-boxes hold with probability 2^{-6}. Due to the specific input and output differences in the active S-boxes in the first and the fourth rounds, this is not achievable – the differential probability of these S-boxes is 2^{-7}. Therefore if we assume the differential is composed of a single trail only, its probability would always be lower than 2^{-128}.

Further we try to find the actual probability of the differential taking into account all possible differential trails that compose it. All the trails can be divided into two groups: trails that have the same path (i.e. they have the same position of the active bytes, but different values for the differences), and trails that have different path.

Let $\tilde{S}_i$ be a possible output difference of the S-layer at round i, and $\tilde{F}_i$ be an output difference of the F function at round i. Note, both $\tilde{S}_i, \tilde{F}_i$ are 8 byte vectors – $\tilde{S}_i = (s_i^1, \ldots, s_i^8), \tilde{F}_i = (f_i^1, \ldots, f_i^8)$. Also, let F_i be the actual output of the F function at round i. We will use $S(x)$ to denote the S-layer, and ΔL_i to denote the difference of the left state at round i, hence $S(\Delta L_i) = \tilde{S}_i$. From the definition of the round function it holds $F(\Delta L_i) = P \cdot S(\Delta L_i) = P \cdot \tilde{S}_i = \tilde{F}_i$.

For $\tilde{S}_1, \tilde{S}_2, \tilde{S}_3$ the following conditions apply (see Fig. 1):

- $\tilde{S}_1$ is produced when -1 difference in L_1 goes through the S-layer:

$$\tilde{S}_1 = S(-1) \tag{8}$$

- $\tilde{S}_2$ is produced with an XOR of $\tilde{F}_1$ and the difference -1 in R_1, followed by the S-layer:

$$\tilde{S}_2 = S(\tilde{F}_1 \oplus (-1)) = S(P \cdot \tilde{S}_1 \oplus (-1)) \tag{9}$$

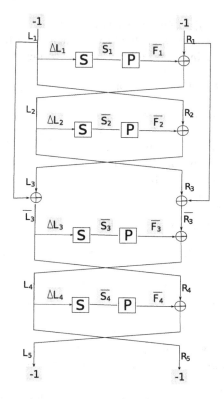

Fig. 1. The key schedule of *Camellia-128* with the $(-1,-1) \rightarrow (-1,-1)$ differential. The gray values are the differences.

- $\tilde{S}_3$ is produced with application of the S-layer to $\Delta \overline{L_3}$:

$$\tilde{S}_3 = S(\Delta \overline{L_3})) = S(P \cdot \tilde{S}_2) \qquad (10)$$

Additionally, when $\tilde{F}_3$ is XOR-ed to $\Delta \overline{R_3}$, the output difference -1 is obtained in R_5:

$$\tilde{F}_3 \oplus \Delta \overline{R_3} = P \cdot \tilde{S}_3 \oplus P \cdot \tilde{S}_1 = -1 \qquad (11)$$

- $\tilde{S}_4$ is produced when -1 difference in R_5 goes through the S-layer:

$$\tilde{S}_4 = S(-1) \qquad (12)$$

Additionally, when $\tilde{F}_4$ is XOR-ed to $\Delta \overline{L_3}$, the output difference -1 is obtained in L_5:

$$\tilde{F}_4 \oplus \Delta \overline{L_3} = P \cdot \tilde{S}_4 \oplus P \cdot \tilde{S}_2 = -1 \qquad (13)$$

The probability of the differential can be computed as the sum of probabilities of all differential trails defined with 4 intermediate differences:

$$\sum_{(\tilde{S}_1, \tilde{S}_2, \tilde{S}_3, \tilde{S}_4) \mid (8),(9),(10),(11),(12),(13) \text{ are satisfied}} 2^{-7(|\tilde{S}_1|+|\tilde{S}_2|+|\tilde{S}_3|+|\tilde{S}_4|)} \qquad (14)$$

where $|\tilde{S}_i|$ denotes the number of active bytes in $\tilde{S}_i$. In the following, we try to simplify the conditions and to achieve formula for computing the above probability.

Note that although both $\tilde{S}_1 = S(-1)$ and $\tilde{S}_4 = S(-1)$ are produced when (-1) goes through the S-layer, a randomly chosen difference $\tilde{S}_1$ and a difference $\tilde{S}_4$ are not necessarily the same (in fact they are different with a very high probability). To distinguish them we will use $S(-1)_{L_1}$ for the former and $S(-1)_{R_5}$ for the later.

Further we reduce the conditions on all $\tilde{S}_i$ to conditions only on $\tilde{S}_2, \tilde{S}_3$. From (11) and the linearity of the matrix multiplication P it follows that

$$P \cdot \tilde{S}_3 \oplus P \cdot \tilde{S}_1 = P \cdot (\tilde{S}_3 \oplus \tilde{S}_1) = -1$$

This leads to:

$$\tilde{S}_3 = P^{-1}(-1) \oplus \tilde{S}_1 \tag{15}$$

Similarly, from (12) and (13) we get:

$$\tilde{S}_2 = P^{-1}(-1) \oplus S(-1)_{R_5} \tag{16}$$

Taking into account (15), the condition (9) can be expressed as:

$$\tilde{S}_2 = S(P \cdot \tilde{S}_1 \oplus (-1)) = S(P \cdot (\tilde{S}_3 \oplus P^{-1}(-1)) \oplus (-1)) \tag{17}$$
$$= S(P \cdot \tilde{S}_3 \oplus (-1) \oplus (-1)) = S(P \cdot \tilde{S}_3) \tag{18}$$

Let us summarize our findings. We get that for $\tilde{S}_2, \tilde{S}_3$ defined as:

$$\tilde{S}_2 = P^{-1}(-1) \oplus S(-1)_{R_5} \tag{19}$$
$$\tilde{S}_3 = P^{-1}(-1) \oplus S(-1)_{L_1} \tag{20}$$

two additional conditions have to hold:

$$\tilde{S}_2 = S(P \cdot \tilde{S}_3) \tag{21}$$
$$\tilde{S}_3 = S(P \cdot \tilde{S}_2) \tag{22}$$

In $\tilde{S}_1, \tilde{S}_4$ there are always 8 active S-boxes. The number of active S-boxes in $\tilde{S}_2, \tilde{S}_3$ is defined by the above conditions. As P is linear, we can compute the value of the vector $P^{-1}(-1)$, i.e.

$$P^{-1}(-1) = (0, 0, 0, 0, ff, ff, ff, ff) \tag{23}$$

Since the S-boxes in Camellia are bijective, the vector $S(-1)$ always has 8 active S-boxes. Therefore from (19), (20) we can conclude that the first 4 elements of $\tilde{S}_2, \tilde{S}_3$ have to be non-zero, thus the number of active S-boxes in round 2 and 3 is at least 4 (the first 4 bytes must be active). Additionally, regarding the number and position of the active S-boxes, since there are always at least 4 active S-boxes in $\tilde{S}_2$ and $\tilde{S}_3$, the conditions (21), (22) can always be satisfied (the branch number of P is 4).

Finally, we can give the probability of the differential $(-1, -1) \rightarrow (-1, -1)$:

$$\sum_{(\tilde{S}_2, \tilde{S}_3) \text{ satisfy } (19), (20), (21), (22)} 2^{-7(8+|\tilde{S}_2|+|\tilde{S}_3|+8)} \qquad (24)$$

Recall that a differential is a collection of trails that take the same path (have the same position of the active bytes) and trails that take different path. We group all trails that take the same path into one single *truncated trail*. Then a differential is a collection of truncated trails and hence its probability is the sum of probabilities of the truncated trails. To define a truncated trail we just have to fix the position of the actives S-boxes in the four rounds of the key schedule. With T_i we denote the truncated difference entering the round function of round i. Then a truncated trail can be defined as T_1, T_2, T_3, T_4. An actual trail with $\tilde{S}_1, \ldots, \tilde{S}_4$ belongs to a truncated trail if the position of the active S-boxes in S_i coincide with the position of the active S-boxes in T_i. Obviously $T_1 = T_4 = (1, 1, \ldots, 1)$ as all the S-boxes in the first and the fourth round are active. For the probability of the differential we get:

$$\sum_{(T_2, T_3)} 2^{-7(8+|T_2|+|T_3|+8)} \#\{(\tilde{S}_2, \tilde{S}_3) | \tilde{S}_2 \in T_2, \tilde{S}_3 \in T_3, \tilde{S}_1, \tilde{S}_2$$

$$\text{satisfy } (19), (20), (21), (22)\} \qquad (25)$$

Hence, to find the probability of the differential, we only have to count the number of possible differential trails (that satisfy a set of conditions) in all possible truncated trails T_2, T_3 of the form $(1, 1, 1, 1, x_5, x_6, x_7, x_8), x_i \in \{0, 1\}$. To proceed further we define the notion of compliance.

Definition 1. *Two differences Δ_1, Δ_2 comply through the function $f(x)$ if there exist x such that $f(x \oplus \Delta_1) \oplus f(x) = \Delta_2$.*

This notion is introduced to check if some input difference Δ_1 at function $f(x)$ can produce output difference Δ_2.

Observation 1. *Two randomly chosen differences Δ_1, Δ_2 comply through the S-boxes of Camellia with probability $\frac{127}{255} \approx 2^{-1}$.*

Every input difference to the S-box can go to 127 output differences or approximately to 2^7 out of $2^8 - 1$ possible, which is around 2^{-1}.

As an example, let us compute the number of possible trails for the case when T_2, T_3 have all 8 active bytes. From the properties of the S-boxes used in *Camellia* we have that each input byte difference (including the difference ff) can go to 127 or approximately[4] 2^7 distinct output differences. Since we have

---

[4] We can approximate with 2^7 as one of the output differences happens twice, which means that although we increase the number from 127 to 128, on the other hand we decrease the probability for this difference from 2^{-6} to 2^{-7}, hence the two rounding errors compensate one another. This fact can easily be checked if one takes instead of bytes, 7-bit nibbles. Then the maximal differential probability of 7×7 S-box can be 2^6.

8 active input bytes in $S(-1)_{L_1}$ and in $S(-1)_{R_5}$, there are in total $2^{7 \cdot 8} = 2^{56}$ differences for $\tilde{S}_2$ and $\tilde{S}_3$ (see the definitions (19), (20)). As $\tilde{S}_2$ has 8 active bytes, the following condition has to hold:

$$(d_1, \ldots, d_8) = P^{-1}(-1) \oplus (s^1_{R_5}, \ldots, s^8_{R_5}) \tag{26}$$

$$= (0, 0, 0, 0, ff, ff, ff, ff) \oplus (s^1_{R_5}, \ldots, s^8_{R_5}), \tag{27}$$

where all d_i are non-zero. Hence, out of all 2^{56} this condition satisfy $2^{56} \cdot (1 - 127^{-4}) \approx 2^{56}$ differences, or approximately all. A similar conclusion can be obtained regarding (20).

Now let us focus on (21), (22). The probability that $\tilde{S}_2$ comply with $\tilde{S}_3$ from (21) can be computed as:

1. the probability that $P \cdot \tilde{S}_3$ is 8 byte difference – it is approximately 1. In the general case, when $\tilde{S}_2$ has i active bytes, the probability is approximately $2^{-8 \cdot (8-i)}$.
2. the probability that each of the differences in 8 bytes of $\tilde{S}_2$ and $P \cdot \tilde{S}_3$ comply. This is 2^{-8}, while in the general case it is 2^{-i} for differences in i bytes.

Therefore, for a randomly chosen differences the probability of (21) is 2^{-8}. A similar reasoning can be applied to (22). Hence, out of all possible $\tilde{S}_2, \tilde{S}_3$ there are $2^{56} \cdot 2^{56} \cdot 2^{-8} \cdot 2^{-8} = 2^{96}$ differences that satisfy all four conditions. Therefore, for $T_2 = T_3 = (1, 1, 1, 1, 1, 1, 1, 1)$, the probability of the differential is at least:

$$2^{96} \cdot 2^{-7(8+8+8+8)} = 2^{96} \cdot 2^{-224} = 2^{-128} \tag{28}$$

If we take into account all possible T_2, T_3 for the probability of the differential we get:

$$\sum_{i,j} 2^{-7(8+i+j+8)} C_4^{i-4} \cdot C_4^{j-4} 2^{112-8 \cdot (8-i)-8 \cdot (8-j)} 2^{-8(8-i)-i} 2^{-8(8-j)-j} \tag{29}$$

$$\approx 2^{-128} \tag{30}$$

Thus, by Lemma 1, the size of the weak key class is $2^{128} \cdot 2^{-128} = 1$. For this key K, the complementation property holds, i.e. $KS(K \oplus (-1)) \oplus KS(K) = -1$, and taking into account the whitening keys, we get that for any plaintext P, it holds

$$E_{K \oplus (-1)}(P) = E_K(P).$$

Note that the size of the weak key class is too small for any attack on the cipher, however it is sufficient for an attack on the hash function mode of the cipher. As a compression function, we can choose the standard Davies-Meyer compression mode:

$$C(H, M) = E_M(H) \oplus H \tag{31}$$

Let K be the key value for which the $(-1, -1) \rightarrow (-1, -1)$ differential in the key schedule holds. For the compression function we get that for any H the following holds:

$$C(H, K \oplus (-1)) \oplus C(H, K) = E_{K \oplus (-1)}(H) \oplus H \oplus E_K(H) \oplus H = 0 \tag{32}$$

Therefore if we can find the correct key K (which is indeed the correct message M, as $M = K$ in the hash mode), we can produce collisions for the compression function of *Camellia*. Note, as H can be arbitrary, this leads to collisions for the whole hash function. To find the exact value of the key K we use the conditions (19)–(22) combined into the algorithm:

1. Create a set $\tilde{S}$ of all possible differences $P^{-1}(-1) \oplus S(-1)$ – the size of the set is 2^{56}.
2. Create a set S^R of pairs of differences $(\delta_2, \delta_3), \delta_2, \delta_3 \in \tilde{S}$ such that δ_2 complies with $P \cdot \delta_3$ and δ_3 complies with $P \cdot \delta_2$ - the size of this set is 2^{96}.
3. Choose a random pair (δ_2, δ_3) from S^R.
4. Produce the value of L_1 (and the corresponding F_1) that converts -1 into the $\delta_3 \oplus P^{-1}(-1)$, i.e. $S(L_1 \oplus (-1)) \oplus S(L_1) = \delta_3 \oplus P^{-1}(-1)$. As δ_3 has 8 active S-boxes, and for each active S-box there are 2 different values (A and $A \oplus (-1)$), for a fixed δ_3 there are 2^8 possible values of (L_1, F_1).
5. Produce similarly the values of (L_4, F_4) from δ_2.
6. Produce $F_3 = L_4 \oplus \overline{F_3} = L_4 \oplus F_1$, and $\overline{L_3} = F^{-1}(F_3)$. Check if $F(\overline{L_3} \oplus P \cdot \delta_2) \oplus F(\overline{L_3}) = P \cdot \delta_3$. If not, go to step 3.
7. Produce $F_2 = \overline{L_3}$, and $L_2 = F^{-1}(F_2)$. Check if $F(L_2 \oplus P \cdot \delta_3) \oplus F(L_2) = P \cdot \delta_2$. If not, go to step 3.
8. Output the key $(L_1, R_1) = (L_1, F(L_1) \oplus L_2)$.

The probability of steps 6, 7 is 2^{-56} each and there are $2^{2(48+8)}$ possible (L_1, F_1) and (L_4, F_4). Hence, after repeating step three 2^{96} times and steps four-five 2^{112} times, one key candidate will be produced. Thus the complexity of the algorithm is 2^{112}.

Note that with an effort of 2^{112} we can produce one collision for the compression function of *Camellia-128* (without FL, FL^{-1}). Once we have the correct message M, we can produce collision for any input chaining value. This means that for any messages M_1, M_3 (the M_3 block is used as message padding), we can produce a collision for the hash function of *Camellia-128*. The colliding pairs are $(M_1 || M \oplus (-1) || M_3)$ and $(M_1 || M || M_3)$. Therefore, to produce q collisions with the same fixed difference between the message words (the difference is $(0|| -1||0)$ we need 2^{112} calls to the hash function[5]. On the other hand, for the generic case, producing such collisions (they are indeed called differential q multicollisions, see [2]), one needs around $q2^{\frac{q-2}{q+2}128}$ calls to the hash function. Hence, producing 256 differential multicollisions requires $2^8 \cdot 2^{\frac{254}{258}128} \approx 2^{134}$ encryptions whereas for the hash function of *Camellia-128* without the non-linear layers FL, FL^{-1} in the Davies-Meyer mode, they can be produced with 2^{112} calls to the hash function.

4 The Case of GOST

In this section we show how the partial complementation property (Lemma 3) of GOST can be used to launch a practical related-key recovery attack on the

---

[5] Actually, the number is smaller, as one hash function call requires much larger number of operations compared to the steps of our algorithm.

full-round cipher. We note that the mentioned below complementation properties have been known and exploited in attacks on GOST [4, 7]. However, to the best of our knowledge, all the attacks on GOST that recover the full key, are impractical.

4.1   Description of GOST

GOST is a modular 32-round Feistel cipher with 256-bit key. The key schedule of GOST is trivial. The master key K is divided into eight 32-bit words $K_i, i = 1, \ldots, 8$ and in each of the four groups of 8 rounds, the round keys $RK_j, j = 1, \ldots, 32$ are permutation of the key words K_i, i.e.

$$(RK_1, \ldots, RK_8) = (K_1, \ldots, K_8) \tag{33}$$
$$(RK_9, \ldots, RK_{16}) = (K_1, \ldots, K_8) \tag{34}$$
$$(RK_{17}, \ldots, RK_{24}) = (K_1, \ldots, K_8) \tag{35}$$
$$(RK_{25}, \ldots, RK_{32}) = (K_8, \ldots, K_1) \tag{36}$$

4.2   Complementing GOST

As GOST is a modular Feistel, Lemma 3 can be applied to this cipher. The round keys do not allow the choice of different alternating Δ_1, Δ_2 as each of the key words K_i is used in both even and odd rounds. For example, K_1 is used in rounds 1, 9, 17, and *32*. Therefore, one has to choose $\Delta_1 = \Delta_2 = \Delta$, i.e. all of the keys K_i have the same difference Δ. The differential in the key schedule holds with probability $p = 1$. To maximize the probability of the differential in the state, one has to choose $\Delta = 2^{31}$ – in this case the size of the class is 2^{256}, i.e. the complementation is applicable to all of the keys.

One can maintain the same size of the weak-key class (all keys), but reduce the probability of the differential in the state. For example, when $\Delta_1 = \Delta_2 = \Delta = 2^i, i = 0, \ldots, 30$, then the partial complementation property is still applicable to all keys, but detecting this property requires more data, i.e. instead of the previous one pair of plaintexts and ciphertexts, by Lemma 3 now one needs $1/2^{-16(1+1)} = 2^{32}$ pairs. This weakens the distinguisher, but allows key recovery attacks. Let $\Delta = 2^m, m < 31$. If in some round i, one knows the value of the state S that is modularly added to the round key RK_i (in the state/key pair, the m-th bit has the difference 1), then under the assumption that the differences have canceled, one can find the exact value RK_i^m of the m-bit of the round key RK_i, i.e. if S is known, and

$$(S + RK_i) \oplus ((S \oplus 2^m) + (RK_i \oplus 2^m)) = 0,$$

then the value RK_i^m of the m-th bit of RK_i can be computed as:

$$RK_i^m = S^m \oplus 1. \tag{37}$$

It is trivial to check that only under such values of RK_i^m and S^m the differences would cancel. For $m = 31$, i.e. when the difference is in the most significant bit, then the cancellation always occurs, hence one cannot find the exact value of the most significant bit with this approach.

The above single-bit recovery can be applied sequentially to all the bits of the round key RK_i, thus the whole RK_i can be recovered. Once the i-th round key is known, one can compute the state of the cipher in the next round and thus repeat the same process but for the round key RK_{i+1}. Hence this domino effect allows to recover all of the round keys resulting in a full key recovery of the master key. The attack presented below is a related-key attack with 31 related-key pairs. For the secret master key K with the key words K_i, $K = (K_1, \ldots, K_8)$, the related keys K^i are defined as $K^i = (K_1 \oplus 2^i, \ldots, K_8 \oplus 2^i), i = 0, \ldots, 30$. The algorithm can be formulated as:

1. For each of the 31 related-key pairs $(K, K^i), i = 0, \ldots, 30$ create 2^{32} pairs of plaintexts $(P_j^i, P_j^i \oplus 2^i)$ and obtain the corresponding ciphertexts $(C_j^i, \tilde{C}_j^i), j = 0, \ldots, 2^{32} - 1$.
2. For each $i, i = 0, \ldots, 30$, find the pair of ciphertexts that have the required difference 2^i, i.e. find j_i, such that $C_{j_i}^i \oplus \tilde{C}_{j_i}^i = 2^i, i = 0, \ldots, 30$. The corresponding plaintext pairs are $(P_{j_i}^i, P_{j_i}^i \oplus 2^i)$. In total there are 31 such pairs.
3. For each round $r = 1, \ldots 8$, recover the key word K_r.
   (a) For each $k, k = 0, \ldots, 30$, the k-bit of K_r can be recovered from the knowledge of incoming state. In the first round, the value of the state is known, i.e. $P_{j_k}^k$, and therefore $K_r^k = P_{j_k}^k \oplus 1$ (see (37)). In total, 31 out of 32 bits of K_r are recovered.
   (b) Guess the most significant bit of K_r, and compute the values of the 31 states for the next round – this can be performed as one knows both the state and the round key.

The encryption of the initial 2^{32} pairs of plaintexts for each i, guarantees that with a high probability one can find a pair of ciphertexts with the same difference – hence this pair follows the differential in the state. For each round, one has to guess only a single bit (the most significant bit) of the round key, thus step 3 has to be repeated at most 2^8 times. Therefore the time complexity of the full key-recovery attack is $2 \cdot (31 \cdot 2^{32} + 2^8) \approx 2^{38}$ encryptions and a similar data complexity of 2^{38} chosen plaintexts.

The low complexities allow to perform an experimental cryptanalysis of GOST on a computer. We have followed the attack algorithm described above and were able to verify our approach by recovering the full 256-bit key – our unoptimized implementation ran for one day on a single Intel i5 core. As the key recovery can be parallelized, another implementation was able to recover the full key in around 7 h using four Intel i5 cores.

5 Conclusion

We have shown a potential vulnerability in Feistel ciphers based on the complementation property that results in relatively easily detectable related-key differential attacks. Two such attacks on full-round Feistel primitives, the hash mode of *Camellia-128* without FL, FL^{-1}, and the block cipher GOST, have been presented in this paper.

We have deduced a simple criteria for cryptanalysis of classical Feistel ciphers: *if for the key schedule there exists a high probability differential that produces alternating differences in the round keys then the cipher is vulnerable to related-key attacks, regardless of the number of rounds in the state.* Moreover, from the analysis of *Camellia-128* without FL, FL^{-1}, one can conclude that even if such differential has a low probability, but a pair of keys following the differential could be found, the hash mode of the cipher is still vulnerable.

The Feistel ciphers that use modular addition of the round keys in the state are less susceptible to this type of attacks as the data required to detect the complementation property depends on the number of rounds as well. However, from the analysis of GOST one can see that, *when the alternating differences in the round keys have a low Hamming weight, such ciphers are potential targets of complementation weaknesses as well.* Our related-key attack on GOST was confirmed experimentally.

We believe that our attacks based on the complementation property might be launched on several other existing Feistel primitives, i.e. this paper does not exhaust the possible targets. Thus the approach presented here can be seen as simple tool for cryptanalysis of current Feistel primitives, but also an important security threat that should be taken into account when designing new primitives based on Feistel.

Acknowledgement. The authors would like to thank anonymous reviewers of FSE 2013 for their helpful comments. Ivica Nikolić is supported by the Singapore National Research Foundation under Research Grant NRF-CRP2-2007-03.

References

1. Aoki, K., Ichikawa, T., Kanda, M., Matsui, M., Moriai, S., Nakajima, J., Tokita, T.: *Camellia*: a 128-bit block cipher suitable for multiple platforms - design and analysis. In: Stinson, D.R., Tavares, S. (eds.) SAC 2000. LNCS, vol. 2012, pp. 39–56. Springer, Heidelberg (2001)
2. Biryukov, A., Khovratovich, D., Nikolić, I.: Distinguisher and related-key attack on the full AES-256. In: Halevi, S. (ed.) CRYPTO 2009. LNCS, vol. 5677, pp. 231–249. Springer, Heidelberg (2009)
3. Bouillaguet, C., Dunkelman, O., Leurent, G., Fouque, P.-A.: Another look at complementation properties. In: Hong, S., Iwata, T. (eds.) FSE 2010. LNCS, vol. 6147, pp. 347–364. Springer, Heidelberg (2010)
4. Dinur, I., Dunkelman, O., Shamir, A.: Improved attacks on full GOST. In: Canteaut, A. (ed.) FSE 2012. LNCS, vol. 7549, pp. 9–28. Springer, Heidelberg (2012)
5. Government Committee of the USSR for Standards. GOST, Gosudarstvennyi Standard 28147-89, Cryptographic Protection for Data Processing Systems (1989)
6. Kelsey, J., Schneier, B., Wagner, D.: Related-key cryptanalysis of 3-WAY, Biham-DES, CAST, DES-X, NewDES, RC2, and TEA. In: Han, Y., Quing, S. (eds.) ICICS 1997. LNCS, vol. 1334, pp. 233–246. Springer, Heidelberg (1997)

7. Ko, Y., Hong, S., Lee, W., Lee, S., Kang, J.-S.: Related key differential attacks on 27 rounds of XTEA and full-round GOST. In: Roy, B., Meier, W. (eds.) FSE 2004. LNCS, vol. 3017, pp. 299–316. Springer, Heidelberg (2004)
8. Lipmaa, H., Moriai, S.: Efficient algorithms for computing differential properties of addition. In: Matsui, M. (ed.) FSE 2001. LNCS, vol. 2355, p. 336. Springer, Heidelberg (2002)
9. National Bureau of Standards. Data Encryption Standard. U.S. Department of Commerce, FIPS pub. 46, January 1977

On the Wrong Key Randomisation and Key Equivalence Hypotheses in Matsui's Algorithm 2

Andrey Bogdanov[1](✉) and Elmar Tischhauser[2]

[1] Technical University of Denmark, Kongens Lyngby, Denmark
anbog@dtu.dk
[2] KU Leuven and iMinds, Leuven, Belgium
elmar.tischhauser@esat.kuleuven.be

Abstract. This paper aims to improve the understanding of the complexities for Matsui's Algorithm 2 — one of the most well-studied and powerful cryptanalytic techniques available for block ciphers today.

We start with the observation that the standard interpretation of the wrong key randomisation hypothesis needs adjustment. We show that it systematically neglects the varying bias for wrong keys. Based on that, we propose an adjusted statistical model and derive more accurate estimates for the success probability and data complexity of linear attacks which are demonstrated to deviate from all known estimates. Our study suggests that the efficiency of Matsui's Algorithm 2 has been previously somewhat overestimated in the cases where the adversary attempts to use a linear approximation with a low bias, to attain a high computational advantage over brute force, or both. These cases are typical since cryptanalysts always try to break as many rounds of the cipher as possible by pushing the attack to its limit.

Surprisingly, our approach also reveals the fact that the success probability is *not* a monotonously increasing function of the data complexity, and can decrease if more data is used. Using less data can therefore result in a more powerful attack.

A second assumption usually made in linear cryptanalysis is the key equivalence hypothesis, even though due to the linear hull effect, the bias can heavily depend on the key. As a further contribution of this paper, we propose a practical technique that aims to take this into account. All theoretical observations and techniques are accompanied by experiments with small-scale ciphers.

Keywords: Block ciphers · Linear cryptanalysis · Data complexity · Wrong key randomisation hypothesis · Key equivalence · Linear hull effect

1 Introduction

Linear cryptanalysis proposed by Matsui [25,26], besides differential cryptanalysis [5], has been a seminal cryptanalytic technique used to attack block ciphers

S. Moriai (Ed.): FSE 2013, LNCS 8424, pp. 19–38, 2014.
DOI: 10.1007/978-3-662-43933-3_2, © Springer-Verlag Berlin Heidelberg 2014

since two decades now. It was linear cryptanalysis that both theoretically and practically broke the former U.S. encryption standard DES. This might suggest that NSA could have been unaware of the entire power of this attack, at least at the design time of DES back in the 1970s.

Numerous papers investigated the questions of how to improve linear cryptanalysis on the one hand and how to design ciphers resistant to linear cryptanalysis on the other. With the establishment of such block cipher design approaches as the wide-trail design strategy [9], which eventually lead to the design of the current U.S. encryption standard AES [9], the cryptographers were given reliable tools to construct ciphers that are arguably resistant against the classical flavours of linear cryptanalysis.

The extension of linear cryptanalysis to take advantage of multiple approximations revived the field [16–18,32]. Lately, increasingly more works [23,27,32] have been dedicated to the study of the linear hull effect [28,29] – the fact that depending on the key, the efficiency of linear cryptanalysis may significantly vary. Also in terms of the success probability and data complexity estimation, a lot of detailed works have been published [2,3,6,19–21,33]. The fact that many published attacks have data and time requirements beyond practical reach implies that the question of how to accurately estimate their complexity (and hence determine which attack actually is a valid attack) is of great importance to the security of block ciphers.

Our Contributions. In this paper, we aim to obtain a more accurate estimation of success probability and data complexity of linear attacks using Matsui's Algorithm 2 — a question fundamental to symmetric-key cryptanalysis. Our contributions are as follows:

- **New wrong key randomisation hypothesis:** Informally speaking, the wrong key randomisation hypothesis says that by partially decrypting/encrypting with a wrong key up to the boundary of the linear approximation, the adversary faces a randomly drawn permutation instead of the expected cipher structure with rounds peeled off. The standard interpretation of this hypothesis in linear cryptanalysis seems to have been to replace a randomly drawn permutation which varies for every wrong key candidate with the expected behaviour among all permutations. We demonstrate that this can be misleading and result in underestimated complexity in some cases. Those cases are likely to occur when the adversary tries to exploit a linear approximation with low bias, or to attain a high advantage over the brute force, or both. These cases are actually very typical since cryptanalysts always try to break as many rounds of the cipher as possible by pushing the attack to the limit.
- **More data does not necessarily mean higher probability of success:** As a surprising consequence of the adjusted wrong key randomisation hypothesis, our analysis reveals that the success probability in general is not a monotonous function of the data complexity. This means that sometimes, using less

data can result in a better success probability of a linear attack. This is backed up by experimental results confirming the non-monotonous behaviour of the success rate.

- **Linear hull vs. linear trails:** The general methodologies to evaluate the complexity of linear attacks at hand assume the exact bias or its good estimate is given to the adversary. Practically speaking, however, this is never the case for almost any real-world cipher. This is due to the fact that for a relatively large block size (e.g. longer 50 bits) it is challenging to exactly evaluate the bias even for one known key. That is why most linear attacks base their complexity estimates on one or several known trails[1] (rather than on the entire linear hull bias). In this context, we make two observations in this paper. First, we propose to split the linear hull into a signal part and a noise part. The signal part is then sampled for random cipher keys to obtain a more reliable evaluation of the impact of those trails. Second, we statistically model the noise part to make the estimation of complexity more realistic.

The remainder of the paper is organized as follows. Some brief background on block ciphers, linear cryptanalysis and previous work in this direction is given in Sect. 2. In Sect. 3, the new model for the data complexity of linear attacks based on the new wrong key randomisation hypothesis is developed. The non-monotonicity of the success rate as function of data complexity is studied in Sect. 4. Section 5 proposes a method of computing the data complexity of a linear attack and presents experimental results. Our refined key equivalence hypothesis is presented in Sect. 6. Section 7 proposes a practical algorithm implementing the new key equivalence hypothesis for key-alternating ciphers. We conclude in Sect. 8.

2   Preliminaries

2.1   Notation

We denote by $\mathbb{F}_2 = \{0, 1\}$ the finite field with two elements and the n-dimensional vector space over $\mathbb{F}_2$ by $\mathbb{F}_2^n$. The canonical scalar product of two vectors $a, b \in \mathbb{F}_2^n$ is denoted by $a^T b$.

We denote by $\mathcal{N}(\mu, \sigma^2)$ the normal distribution with mean μ and variance σ^2. The probability density and cumulative distribution function of the standard normal distribution $\mathcal{N}(0, 1)$ are denoted by $\phi(x)$ and $\Phi(x)$, respectively.

2.2   Block Ciphers and Linear Cryptanalysis

Block Ciphers. A *block cipher* is a mapping $E : \mathbb{F}_2^n \times \mathbb{F}_2^\kappa \to \mathbb{F}_2^n$ with the property that $E_k \stackrel{\text{def}}{=} E(\cdot, k)$ is a bijection of $\mathbb{F}_2^n$ for every $k \in \mathbb{F}_2^\kappa$. If $y = E_k(x)$,

---

[1] We are aware of the earlier term *linear characteristic* [4] but prefer to use the term *linear trail* throughout the paper.

we refer to x as the *plaintext*, k as the *key* and y as the *ciphertext* of x under the key k. We call n the *block length* and κ the *key size* of the cipher.

Block ciphers are often constructed as iterated mappings based on round functions $\rho_i[k_i]$. Let R denote the number of rounds. A key scheduling algorithm expands the encryption key k into R round keys $K \stackrel{\text{def}}{=} (k_0, \ldots, k_{R-1})$. The ciphertext y of $x_0 = x$ is then obtained as $y = x_R$ with $x_{i+1} = \rho_i[k_i](x_i)$. If the iteration can be written as a sequence of unkeyed rounds and bitwise addition of the round keys by XOR, the cipher is called a *key-alternating cipher* [8,9].

Note that ciphers following the substitution-permutation network design are key-alternating by definition. However, also some Feistel ciphers [13] can be written as key-alternating ciphers [10]. This includes the well-known Feistel ciphers CLEFIA [35], CAMELLIA [1], Piccolo [34], SMS4 [24], KASUMI [14].

Linear Cryptanalysis and Matsui's Algorithm 2. A *linear approximation* (α, β) of a vectorial Boolean function $f : \mathbb{F}_2^n \to \mathbb{F}_2^n$ is an ordered pair of n-bit *masks* α and β. It is said to hold with probability $p \stackrel{\text{def}}{=} \text{Pr}_{x \in \mathbb{F}_2^n}(\alpha^T x = \beta^T f(x))$. The deviation of p from $1/2$ is called the *bias* $\epsilon \stackrel{\text{def}}{=} p - 1/2$. The *correlation* of a linear approximation (α, β) is $C \stackrel{\text{def}}{=} 2p - 1 = 2\epsilon$. The quantity $LP \stackrel{\text{def}}{=} C^2$ is called the *linear probability* of (α, β).

Linear cryptanalysis [25,26] is a known plaintext attack exploiting linear relations between bits of the plaintext and ciphertext holding with absolute bias $|\epsilon| > 0$. Note that in the known plaintext model, the plaintexts are assumed to be sampled independently and uniformly at random from the plaintext space, which implies that repetitions can occur [20,33].

In this paper, we consider linear attacks using Matsui's Algorithm 2. We describe the attack for the case where subkey bits of the last round are attacked. The adversary observes a number N of plaintext/ciphertext pairs encrypted under the same cipher key k and chooses a linear approximation (α, β) with $|\epsilon| > 0$ for the remaining first $R - 1$ rounds. Suppose that the bits of $x_{R-1} = \rho[k_R]^{-1}(y)$ selected by β depend on M bits of k_R and the attacker wants to recover a subset of $m \leq M$ of them. For each of the 2^m possible values of the target subkey bits, the adversary (partially) decrypts the N ciphertexts and tests whether the linear approximation $\alpha^T x = \beta^T \rho[k_R]^{-1}(y)$ holds. In this way, a counter T_i is maintained for each key candidate k_i, $0 \leq i < 2^m$. After this step, the key candidates are ranked in increasing order of the absolute value of the sample bias $|\widehat{\epsilon}_i| \stackrel{\text{def}}{=} |T_i/N - 1/2|$. Following [33], if the correct key k_r is ranked among the highest 2^l out of the 2^m key candidates with probability P_S, we say that the attack provides an *advantage* of $a \stackrel{\text{def}}{=} m - l$ bits over exhaustive search with *success probability* P_S.

Linear Trails and Hulls. A linear approximation (α, β) for an iterative block cipher of R rounds with round functions ρ_i can actually be decomposed into R connecting linear approximations for the intermediate steps: $U = [(\alpha, u_1),$

$(u_1, u_2), \ldots, (u_{R-1}, \beta)]$ with $u_i \in \mathbb{F}_2^n$. For each fixed value of the u_i, such a sequence is called a *linear trail* [9] or *linear characteristic* [25,26]. The approximation (α, β) can permit many trails with the same input mask α and output mask β, but different intermediate masks. The collection of all such trails is called the *linear hull* (α, β) [28,29].

2.3   Previous Analyses of the Data Complexity of Linear Attacks

The data complexity of both Matsui's Algorithm 2 and the more general problem of distinguishing the distributions for the right and the wrong keys have been extensively studied in the literature [2,3,6,19–21,25,26,33].

In his original papers, using a normal approximation to the binomial distribution, Matsui [25,26] estimates the data complexity to be of the order $|2\epsilon|^{-2}$ and gives estimations which multiple of this is required to obtain a certain success probability. This analysis has been systematized and deepened by Junod [19]. Furthermore, Junod and Vaudenay [21] have proven that Matsui's key ranking procedure is optimal for the case of Algorithm 2 using a single linear approximation.

In his important work, Selçuk [33] presented a thorough statistical analysis of the data complexity of linear and differential attacks based on a model of Junod [19] and a normal approximation for order statistics. This yields practical closed formulas for the success probability P_S and data complexity N of a linear attack when an advantage of a bits is sought:

Theorem 1 ([33, Theorem 2]). *Let P_S be the probability that a linear attack on an m-bit subkey, with a linear approximation of probability p, with N known plaintext blocks, delivers an a-bit or higher advantage. Assuming that the linear approximation's probability to hold is independent for each key tried and is equal to $1/2$ for all wrong keys, one has for sufficiently large m and N:*

$$P_S = \Phi\left(2\sqrt{N}|p - 1/2| - \Phi^{-1}(1 - 2^{-a-1})\right). \tag{1}$$

Corollary 1 ([33, Corollary 1]). *With the assumptions of Theorem 1,*

$$N = \left((\Phi^{-1}(P_S) + \Phi^{-1}(1 - 2^{-a-1}))/2\right)^2 \cdot |p - 1/2|^{-2} \tag{2}$$

plaintext blocks are needed in a linear attack to accomplish an a-bit advantage with a success probability of P_S.

Other published estimates include analyses by Junod [20], Baignères, Junod and Vaudenay [2], Baignères and Vaudenay [3], and Blondeau, Gérard and Tillich [6]. Those estimates are summarised in Table 1, with $D(p||q)$ denoting the Kullback-Leibler divergence between two binomial distributions with probabilities p and q.

Note that throughout the literature, the assumption is made that decrypting with a wrong key results in a zero bias for the linear approximation. As we will see, this constitutes a simplified view of the problem.

Table 1. Estimates for the data complexity of a linear attack based on a linear approximation with probability p, success probability P_S and advantage a

Estimate for data complexity N	Reference
$N \approx \dfrac{2\Phi^{-1}\left(\frac{(1-P_S)+2^{-a-1}}{2}\right)^2}{D(p||0.5)}$	Baignères, Junod and Vaudenay [2], Theorem 6
$N \approx -\dfrac{\ln \max\{1-P_S, 2^{-a-1}\}}{D(p||0.5)}$	Baignères and Vaudenay [3], Corollary 4
$N' = -\dfrac{\ln\left(\frac{\nu \cdot 2^{-a-1}}{\sqrt{D(p||0.5)}}\right)+0.5\ln\left(-\ln\left(\nu \cdot 2^{-a-1}\right)\right)}{D(p||0.5)}$ with $\nu = \left((p-0.5)\sqrt{2\pi(1-p)}\right)/\left(\sqrt{p}/2\right)$	Blondeau, Gérard and Tillich [6], Theorem 2

2.4 Distribution of Biases in Boolean Permutations

Daemen and Rijmen [11] have proved the following characterisation of the distribution of correlation of a fixed linear approximation over the set of all n-bit permutations:

Fact 1 ([11, Theorem 4.7]). *Consider a fixed nontrivial linear approximation* (α, β) *with* $\alpha, \beta \neq 0$. *When* $n \geq 5$, *the distribution of the correlation* $C_{\alpha,\beta}$ *over all n-bit permutations can be approximated by the following distribution up to continuity correction:*

$$C_{\alpha,\beta} \sim \mathcal{N}(0, 2^{-n}). \tag{3}$$

Since $C = 2\epsilon$, this immediately implies

Corollary 2. *With the assumptions of Fact 1,*

$$\epsilon_{\alpha,\beta} \sim \mathcal{N}(0, 2^{-n-2}). \tag{4}$$

3   Improved Key Randomisation Hypothesis and Success Rate

3.1   More Accurate Wrong Key Randomisation

In Matsui's Algorithm 2 using a linear approximation (α, β) and N known plaintexts, a counter T_i is maintained for each key candidate k_i. For each of the N texts, the counter T_i is incremented if the approximation holds for a text when performing a trial decryption with the key k_i.

The distribution of T_i has a crucial impact on the precision of estimating the data complexity of Matsui's Algorithm 2. First of all, the distribution of the T_i for the wrong keys has to be determined. It has been generally assumed that once the ciphertext is partially decrypted using a wrong key, the resulting permutation – over which the linear approximation is checked – turns into a randomly chosen permutation. This is called *the wrong key randomisation hypothesis* [15,19].

Multiple works have used this hypothesis and it usually proves to reflect the reality. However, in its basic formulation it does not explicitly specify which distribution to assume for the T_i. In the sequel, we argue that this is exactly the point where the standard interpretation of the wrong key randomisation hypothesis needs adjustment.

To the best of our knowledge, all previous complexity evaluations of Matsui's Algorithm 2 have used the hypothesis that for all wrong keys k_w, $0 \leq w \neq r < 2^m$, the approximation (α, β) will hold with probability of exactly $1/2$, that is with bias zero. This constitutes the best scenario from the attacker's point of view:

Hypothesis 1 (Standard wrong key randomisation hypothesis). *Consider a nontrivial linear approximation* $\mathcal{L} = (\alpha, \beta)$ *with absolute bias* $|\epsilon| \gg 0$ *for virtually all possible cipher keys. Let* k_r *be the right subkey guess. Then, for virtually all cipher keys and for all wrong subkey guesses* $k_w \neq k_r$:

$$\left| \Pr(\mathcal{L} \text{ holds} \mid k_w) - \frac{1}{2} \right| = 0.$$

In this case, making the usual independence assumption, the distribution of the wrong key counters T_w is given by a binomial distribution with probability $p = 1/2$ and N repetitions. For sufficiently large N, this can be very closely approximated by a normal distribution with mean $Np = N/2$ and variance $Np(1 - p) = N/4$. The sample bias $\widehat{\epsilon}_w = T_w/N - 1/2$ of the wrong keys is therefore assumed to be approximately distributed as $\mathcal{N}(0, 1/(4N))$.

Though the standard formulation of the wrong key randomisation hypothesis is inspired by the intention to make the approximation (α, β) behave as for a randomly drawn n-bit permutation, the distribution of the $\widehat{\epsilon}_w$ is not completely adequate. In fact, it is known (see Fact 1 and Corollary 2) that the bias of (α, β) over the n-bit permutations is not constantly zero, but instead follows a known distribution over the wrong keys. We therefore postulate:

Hypothesis 2 (Adjusted wrong key randomisation hypothesis). *Consider a nontrivial linear approximation* $\mathcal{L} = (\alpha, \beta)$ *with absolute bias* $|\epsilon| \gg 0$ *for virtually all possible cipher keys. Let* k_r *be the right subkey guess. Then, for virtually all cipher keys and for all wrong subkey guesses* $k_w \neq k_r$:

$$\left| \Pr(\mathcal{L} \text{ holds} \mid k_w) - \frac{1}{2} \right| = \mathcal{N}(0, 2^{-n-2}).$$

The following lemma, which is a new result, takes this into account.

Lemma 1. *In a linear attack with Matsui's Algorithm 2 on an n-bit block cipher using N known plaintexts, the sample bias $\widehat{\epsilon}_w$ of the wrong keys approximately follows a normal distribution with mean zero and variance $1/4 \cdot (1/N + 1/2^n)$:*

$$\widehat{\epsilon}_w \sim \mathcal{N}\left(0, 1/4 \left(\frac{1}{N} + \frac{1}{2^n} \right) \right). \tag{5}$$

Proof. See the full version [7] of this paper for the proof.

Previous interpretations of the wrong key randomisation hypothesis have therefore used the mean zero instead of the full distribution $\mathcal{N}(0, 2^{-n-2})$ for the bias when decrypting with a wrong key. For the sample bias of the wrong keys, this resulted in using $\mathcal{N}(0, 1/(4N))$ instead of $\mathcal{N}(0, 1/4\left(\frac{1}{N} + \frac{1}{2^n}\right))$, implying that the distributions for the right key and the wrong keys were assumed to only differ in the mean, but had the same variance. While this arguably simplifies the analysis, the possible impact of this simplification has to be investigated.

Experimental Verification. Even in the new form presented in Lemma 1, the wrong key randomisation hypothesis remains an idealisation. In order to verify that it reflects the reality with reasonable accuracy, we have experimentally determined the distribution of the sample bias over 2^{16} wrong keys for two structurally very different small-scale ciphers with a block length of 20 bits: SMALLPRESENT-20 [22] with 8 rounds, and RC6-5/6/10 [31] with four 5-bit words, 6 rounds and an 80-bit key. In both cases, the number of samples was $N = 2^{16}$. As illustrated in Fig. 1 the resulting distributions follow the theoretical estimate of (5) quite closely in both cases. Note that the scattering of data points occurs due to the fact that we are basically using a histogram with bin size one, and deal with raw data instead of averaging.

3.2   Probability of Success

In this section, we study the implications of Lemma 1 for the success probability in linear cryptanalysis with Matsui's Algorithm 2. This leads to a new formula for the success probability of a linear attack.

Theorem 2. *Consider a linear attack with Matsui's Algorithm 2 on an n-bit block cipher (n ≥ 5) using a linear approximation with bias $\epsilon \neq 0$ and sufficiently*

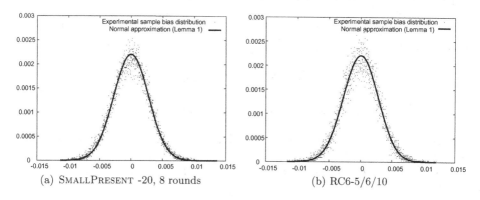

(a) SMALLPRESENT -20, 8 rounds   (b) RC6-5/6/10

Fig. 1. Experimental distribution of the sample bias over 2^{16} wrong keys and 2^{16} texts for SMALLPRESENT and small-scale RC6.

large $N \leq 2^n$ known plaintexts. Denote by P_S the probability that this attack succeeds with an advantage of $a > 0$ bits over exhaustive key search. Then

$$P_S \approx \Phi \left(2\sqrt{N}|\epsilon| - \sqrt{1 + \frac{N}{2^n}} \Phi^{-1}(1 - 2^{-a-1}) \right). \tag{6}$$

Proof. See the full version of this paper [7] for the proof.

Note that the difference between (6) and Selçuk's formula (1) lies in the factor $\sqrt{1 + \frac{N}{2^n}}$ of the term $\Phi^{-1}(1 - 2^{-a-1})$. Since Φ is monotonously increasing, our estimate for P_S is always smaller or equal to (1), and the resulting data complexity required for a certain advantage and P_S will always be at least as big as the one of (2).

The biggest deviations between both models occur when the influence of the second term $\sqrt{1 + \frac{N}{2^n}} \cdot \Phi^{-1}(1 - 2^{-a-1})$ grows. This can happen if the adversary seeks a particularly big advantage a, or when the number of known plaintexts gets close to 2^n. Both cases typically occur when the cryptanalyst is aiming for the maximum possible number of rounds that can be broken by his respective linear attack.

4   Non-monotonicity of Success Rate as Function of Data Complexity

Consider any fixed given combination of the bias ϵ, the block length n and the advantage a. The success probability of a linear attack is then a function of the number of known plaintexts N only and can hence be expressed as $P_S(N)$. Even though our estimate for $P_S(N)$ given by Theorem 2 is always smaller or equal to Selçuk's formula (1), the addition of the second term results in a function that is not necessarily monotonously increasing in N anymore.

From (6), we can derive

Proposition 1. *For fixed ϵ, a and n, the success probability $P_S(N)$ with respect to the data complexity as given by Eq. (6) attains a relative maximum at*

$$\widehat{N} \stackrel{\text{def}}{=} \frac{4|\epsilon|^2 \cdot 2^{2n}}{\left(\Phi^{-1}(1 - 2^{-a-1})\right)^2 - 4|\epsilon|^2 \cdot 2^{2n}}. \tag{7}$$

Proposition 1 implies that our model can in certain cases predict a decrease in success probability for an increased number of known plaintexts. While this may seem counterintuitive at first, one has to take into account that the success probability depends on the overlapping area between two approximately normal distributions, namely $\mathcal{N}(\epsilon, \frac{1}{4N})$ for the right key and $\mathcal{N}(0, \frac{1}{4}(\frac{1}{N} + \frac{1}{2^n}))$ for the wrong keys. In the context of small ϵ and large N of the order 2^n, increasing N can actually result in increasing the overlapping area, and hence decrease the success probability. This can be seen as a direct consequence of linear cryptanalysis being a known plaintext attack: Since the observed plaintexts are sampled

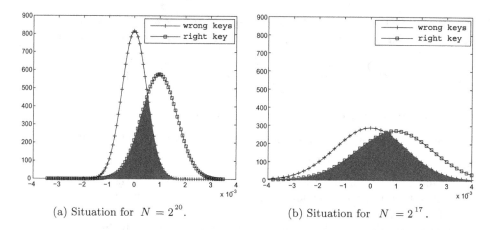

(a) Situation for $N = 2^{20}$.   (b) Situation for $N = 2^{17}$.

Fig. 2. Example of an equal overlapping area between $\mathcal{N}(\epsilon, \frac{1}{4N})$ and $\mathcal{N}(0, \frac{1}{4}\left(\frac{1}{N} + \frac{1}{2^n}\right))$ for $n = 20, \epsilon = 2^{-10}$ and different values of N.

independently and uniformly at random from the plaintext space, the probability of duplicates increases with N, up to a point where adding more samples to the statistic only amplifies the noise. An attack exploiting a fixed linear approximation with fewer known plaintexts could therefore be more efficient than with more given samples.

A given advantage a corresponds to a fixed threshold T for distinguishing the distributions, with the type I error $\mathcal{E}_I = 1 - P_S$ varying with N, and fixed type II error $\mathcal{E}_{II} = 2^{-a-1}$. Having $P_S(N) = P_S(N')$ for $N \neq N'$ is therefore equivalent to having the same overlapping area $\mathcal{E}_I + \mathcal{E}_{II}$ between the distributions for N and N' samples. This is depicted in Fig. 2: the overlapping area $\mathcal{E}_I + \mathcal{E}_{II}$ between the two Gaussian distributions in Fig. 2a and b is the same for different values of N.

We note that two conditions have to be fulfilled to be able to speak of meaningful (i.e., practically relevant) non-monotonous behaviour: First, the condition $\widehat{N} < 2^n$ has to be satisfied (since N cannot exceed 2^n); and second, one must have $P_S \geq 2^{-a}$, i.e. the success probability of the attack must be higher than two times the false positive rate. Otherwise, the adversary would have to repeat the attack $1/P_S > 2^a$ times and gain only a bits advantage over the exhaustive search.

An example of a parameter combination fulfilling both conditions is $|\epsilon| = 2^{-10}, n = 20$ and $a = 12$, i.e., seeking a large advantage out of an approximation with only marginal bias. In this case, $\widehat{N} \approx 2^{18.75} < 2^{20}$, and $P_S(\widehat{N}) \approx 2^{-9.89} > 2^{-12} = 2^{-a}$. With $P_S(2^{20}) \approx 2^{-10.45}$, this constitutes a meaningful example where using more samples actually decreases the success probability. This theoretical prediction has been verified in the real world using experiments with SMALLPRESENT-20. The recovery of 10000 keys exhibiting exactly the bias $\epsilon = 2^{-10}$ was attempted for different values of N. The results given in Fig. 3 confirm the non-monotonous behaviour.

N	theor. P_S	exp. P_S
2^{17}	0.00072	0.0006
2^{18}	0.00096	0.0009
$2^{18.5}$	0.00104	0.0009
$2^{18.75}$	0.00105	0.0011
2^{19}	0.00104	0.0010
$2^{19.5}$	0.00093	0.0009
2^{20}	0.00071	0.0007

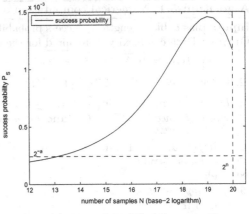

(a) Experimental success probability.   (b) Plot of $P_S(N)$ (Theorem 2).

Fig. 3. Experimental verification of non-monotonous behaviour for SMALLPRESENT-20 with $\epsilon = 2^{-10}$ and $a = 12$.

5   Evaluation of the Data Complexity

In practice, when evaluating a particular linear attack (where n and ϵ are fixed), it is often interesting to determine the number N of required known plaintexts for certain success probabilities and advantages that are sought by the attacker. In the case of $P_S = 1/2$ and an arbitrary fixed advantage of $a \geq 1$ bits, Eq. (6) yields a closed formula for N:

Corollary 3. *With the assumptions of Theorem 2, using a linear approxima-tion with bias $|\epsilon| > \Phi^{-1}(1 - 2^{-a-1})/2^{n/2-1}$, the number N of known plaintexts required to obtain an advantage of $a \geq 1$ bits with success probability $P_S = 1/2$ is given by*

$$N \approx 1/\left(\left(2\epsilon/\Phi^{-1}(1 - 2^{-a-1})\right)^2 - 2^{-n} \right). \qquad (8)$$

The condition $|\epsilon| > \Phi^{-1}(1 - 2^{-a-1})/2^{n/2-1}$ in Corollary 3 basically prevents the estimate for N from becoming negative. This happens if the sought advantage a is too big for the given bias $|\epsilon|$, resulting in a data requirement of $N > 2^n$ texts, which is clearly impossible and a step outside the model.

For values of P_S different from $1/2$, we can determine N by means of an efficient numerical procedure for given $P_S, a, |\epsilon|$ and n. Note that this procedure is equally applicable to the case $P_S = 1/2$.

Proposition 2. *With the assumptions of Theorem 2, for fixed ϵ, P_S, n and a, the data complexity N can be determined numerically using Algorithm 5.1 up to an absolute error of $1 - 2^{-n}$ in linear time in the block length n.*

Proof. See the full version of the paper [7] for the proof.

Algorithm 5.1. Numerical computation of the data complexity N

Input: Bias ϵ, block length n, success probability $P_S \geq 2^{-a}$, precision bound ν (*)
Output: Data complexity N required for the given parameters.

1: Define $f(N) = 2\sqrt{N}|\epsilon| - \sqrt{1 + \frac{N}{2^n}}\Phi^{-1}(1 - 2^{-a-1})$

2: Calculate $\widehat{N} \leftarrow \left(4|\epsilon|^2 \cdot 2^{2n}\right) / \left(\left(\Phi^{-1}(1 - 2^{-a-1})\right)^2 - 4|\epsilon|^2 \cdot 2^{2n}\right)$

3: $lower \leftarrow 1$, $upper \leftarrow \min\{\widehat{N}, 2^n\}$, $i \leftarrow 0$
4: **while** $|f(lower) - P_S| > 10^{-\nu}$ **and** $i < n$ **do**
5:     $mid \leftarrow \frac{lower+upper}{2}$
6:     **if** $f(mid) < P_S$ **then**
7:         $lower \leftarrow mid$
8:     **else**
9:         $upper \leftarrow mid$
10:     **end if**
11:     $i \leftarrow i + 1$
12: **end while**
13: **return** $lower$

*The value of ν in step 4 is used to early-abort fast-converging iterations as soon as an adequate precision is reached. A recommended value is $\nu = 15$.

Algorithm 5.1 runs very efficiently even for large block sizes. For instance, a straightforward Matlab implementation computes the value $N = 2^{126.76}$ for $n = 128$, $|\epsilon| = 2^{-61.9}$, $a = 10$ and $P_S = 0.95$ in about 0.09 seconds on an Intel Core2 Duo E8400.

5.1 Experimental Results

In this section, we summarise the results of experiments carried out to verify the accuracy of the estimate given by Theorem 2 and Proposition 2 and compare it to other models.

The experiments were first carried out on SMALLPRESENT-20, a small-scale variant [22] of the block cipher PRESENT with block size $n = 20$ bits. The original key schedule algorithm was used. In all experiments, we fixed a linear approximation with a certain bias ϵ and success probability P_S and then analysed the data complexity N which is required to obtain different levels of advantage with this P_S. Each experiment for a certain combination of N and a was averaged over 1000 times to obtain a reliable relation between N and a for this fixed P_S. To verify the independence of our experimental findings from the structure of SMALLPRESENT, all experiments were repeated with RC6-5/r/10, an instantiation of RC6 [31] with a block size of 20 bits and an 80-bit key. The results on this small-scale variant of RC6 indicate that our model is equally applicable to this substantially different block cipher structure.

In the first experiment on SMALLPRESENT, a linear approximation with bias $\epsilon = 2^{-8.22}$ was used. The success probability was fixed at 0.95. From (6), the influence of the new model for wrong keys is expected to manifest itself already for small advantages given this relatively high P_S and low ϵ (compared to the

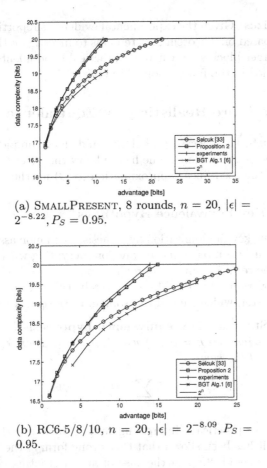

(a) SMALLPRESENT, 8 rounds, $n = 20$, $|\epsilon| = 2^{-8.22}$, $P_S = 0.95$.

(b) RC6-5/8/10, $n = 20$, $|\epsilon| = 2^{-8.09}$, $P_S = 0.95$.

Fig. 4. Theoretical and experimental evaluation of the data complexity estimate of Proposition 2 for different levels of advantage.

block length). The results are depicted in Fig. 4a. The curve with squares was obtained using Proposition 2 with an estimation of the hull bias averaged over 200 random keys. We can see that the experiments follow the theoretical prediction very closely. The difference to the estimate of [33] is also apparent as soon as $a \geq 6$. For $a = 11$, Selçuk's formula can result in an underestimation of N of factor two. The line with crosses represents the estimate based on Algorithm 1 of [6]. The results of an analogous experiment on RC6-5/8/10 are given in Fig. 4b.

Additional experimental results for different levels of ϵ and a are given the full version of the paper [7].

Our experiments indicate that Theorem 2 and its derivatives are unlikely to decrease the precision in comparison to previous work, since our estimates are more realistic for large a and/or low ϵ but very close to Selçuk's for small advantages and/or high biases. They can hence be used as a universal replacement.

Larger Block Sizes. Given the experimental evidence supporting the accuracy of the estimates based on Theorem 2, it remains to investigate the impact of the new model for larger block sizes where no practical experiments can be carried out. This is detailed in the full version of the paper [7].

6   Towards a More Realistic Key Equivalence Hypothesis

In order to evaluate the success probability and data complexity of a linear attack using Matsui's Algorithm 2, one has to know the exact (absolute value of the) bias $\epsilon(k_r)$ of the used linear approximation (α, β) for the right key k_r.

6.1   Standard Key Equivalence Hypothesis

Dually to the wrong key randomisation hypothesis, a common assumption for the statistical behaviour when partially de- and/or encrypting with the right key is that the bias of the resulting linear approximation does not deviate significantly from its average over all keys [19]. More concretely, this is usually interpreted in the following way [15], which we call the *standard key equivalence hypothesis*:

Hypothesis 3 (Standard key equivalence hypothesis). *Consider a nontrivial linear approximation* $\mathcal{L} = (\alpha, \beta)$ *with bias* $\epsilon(k_r)$. *Then* $|\epsilon(k_r)|$ *is independent of the choice of the key:*

$$|\epsilon(k_r)| = 2^{-\kappa} \sum_{k \in \mathbb{F}_2^\kappa} |\epsilon(k)| \qquad \forall k_r.$$

However, for most practically interesting designs (including the AES, Serpent and PRESENT), it has been shown that this strong form of the key equivalence hypothesis does not hold [8,9]. In the case of key-alternating ciphers (or Feistel ciphers which can be written as such), the contributions of the biases of the individual trails to the bias of the hull for a fixed key k_r can be explicitly computed [8,9] as:

$$\epsilon(k_r) = \sum_{u_0 = \alpha, u_r = \beta} (-1)^{d_U \oplus U^T K} |\epsilon_U|, \tag{9}$$

with K denoting the key expansion of the key k_r. This is known as the *linear hull*, which causes the trail biases to be added or subtracted depending on the value of the key [18,23,27,32]. As a consequence, it usually becomes infeasible to compute the exact value of $|\epsilon_r|$ or even its average over all keys.

Since the standard key equivalence hypothesis does not hold in most cases, the question arises *which value of* ϵ_r *to take for the evaluation of the attack complexity*. For instance, the work [30] fixes the expanded key of PRESENT to zero to estimate ϵ_r. We note, though, that using a different key for this estimation will result in a different value of ϵ_r and hence change the estimated attack complexity.

In order to address this issue, we need to refine the usual key equivalence hypothesis by taking the influence of linear hulls into account.

To this end, we propose to decompose the linear hull into two parts: a signal part (corresponding to the known dominant trails) and a noise part (consisting of the unknown remainder of the hull). The signal part is then sampled for random cipher keys to obtain a more reliable evaluation of the impact of those dominant trails. We then model the noise part statistically to make the estimation of complexity more realistic.

Previous approaches have omitted the influence of the unknown trails completely, and as has been demonstrated [23, 27], the influence of the unknown part of the hull can be very significant. Additionally, we average the data complexity estimate over a number of randomly drawn master keys, as opposed to fixing one specific expanded key. This leads to a refined formulation of the key equivalence hypothesis.

6.2   Refined Key Equivalence Hypothesis

Assume that only one or a small number of dominant trails with high contribution to the absolute bias of the hull (α, β) are known. In a linear attack, to recover (part of) the key k_r, this hull has an unknown bias $\epsilon_r(k_r)$, potentially varying from key to key. For each fixed value of the key, the actual value of $\epsilon_r(k_r)$ can be decomposed into the contributions that stem from the biases of the known trails and the biases of the remaining unknown trails in the hull. We define the former to be the *signal* and the latter the *noise*:

Definition 1. *Consider the linear approximation* (α, β) *over an R-round iterative block cipher and a fixed cipher key* k_r. *The bias* $\epsilon_r(k_r)$ *of the hull* (α, β) *is given by*

$$\epsilon_r(k_r) = \sum_{u_0 = \alpha, u_R = \beta} \epsilon_U(k_r),$$

with $\epsilon_U(k_r)$ *denoting the bias of the trail* U *with key* k_r. *Suppose some* t *dominant trails* $\mathcal{U} = \{U_1, \dots, U_t\}$ *of the hull* (α, β) *are known. By defining*

$$\epsilon_{U_{signal}}(k_r) \stackrel{\text{def}}{=} \sum_{U \in \mathcal{U}} \epsilon_U(k_r) \tag{10}$$

$$\epsilon_{U_{noise}}(k_r) \stackrel{\text{def}}{=} \sum_{(\alpha, \beta) \backslash \mathcal{U}} \epsilon_U(k_r), \tag{11}$$

we obtain a repartitioning of the above sum as follows:

$$\epsilon_r(k_r) = \epsilon_{U_{signal}}(k_r) + \epsilon_{U_{noise}}(k_r). \tag{12}$$

In contrast to our approach, Röck and Nyberg [32] mention the concept of considering a subset of dominant trails, but do not consider the remainder of the hull.

Based on Corollary 2, the noise part $\epsilon_{U_{noise}}(k_r)$ of the trail contributions can now be modeled to approximately follow a normal distribution $\mathcal{N}(0, 2^{-n-2})$ over the right keys. This leads to our refined key equivalence hypothesis:

Hypothesis 4 (Refined key equivalence hypothesis). *In the setting of Definition 1, the key-dependent bias of a linear approximation in a key-alternating cipher is given by*

$$\epsilon(k_r) = \epsilon_{U_{signal}}(k_r) + \epsilon_{U_{noise}}(k_r)$$

$$= \sum_{j=1}^{t} (-1)^{d_{U_j} \oplus U_j^T k_r} |\epsilon_{U_j}| + \mathcal{N}(0, 2^{-n-2}).$$

Here, d_{U_j} is either 0 or 1, standing for the key-independent part of the sign of the linear trail contribution $|\epsilon_{U_j}|$, while $U_j^T k_r$ deals with the key-dependent part of it.

7 Constructive Key Equivalence in Key-Alternating Ciphers

This leads to the following algorithm for estimating the data complexity N of a linear attack on an n-bit block cipher using the linear approximation (α, β): We know t trails from the hull and sample $\epsilon_{U_{signal}}$ over a number of keys by means of (9), each time adding $\epsilon_{U_{noise}}$ sampled from $\mathcal{N}(0, 2^{-n-2})$. For each tried key, we compute an estimate for N based on this value of ϵ_r. Then the average over all tried keys is taken as the final estimate for N. This procedure is described in Algorithm 7.1.

Algorithm 7.1. Computation of N using the signal-noise decomposition of the hull for key-alternating ciphers.

Input: Trails $U_j, 1 \leq j \leq t$ from the hull (α, β), their absolute biases $|\epsilon_{U_j}|$, number of keys ℓ to sample.
Input: Block length n, success probability $P_S \geq 2^{-a}$.
Output: Estimate of the data complexity N required for the given parameters.
1: **for** $i = 1, \ldots, \ell$ **do**
2:    Select the master key k_i uniformly at random and compute the expanded key.
3:    Sample $noise(k_i)$ from $\mathcal{N}(0, 2^{-n-2})$.
4:    Compute

$$\epsilon(k_i) = \epsilon_{U_{\text{signal}}}(k_i) + \epsilon_{U_{\text{noise}}}(k_i)$$

$$= \sum_{j=1}^{t} (-1)^{d_{U_j} \oplus U_j^T K_i} |\epsilon_{U_j}| + noise(k_i).$$

5:    Compute $N(k_i)$ based on $\epsilon(k_i)$ with Algorithm 5.1.
6: **end for**
7: **return** Average $\overline{N} = \frac{1}{\ell} \sum_{i=1}^{\ell} N(k_i)$.

7.1 Experimenting the Signal/Noise Decomposition

We have performed experiments on SMALLPRESENT-20 to illustrate the effect of the signal/noise decomposition of a linear hull. With a block length of $n = 20$ bits, and an 80-bit key space, it is not feasible to compute the exact distribution or even only the exact average bias of a hull (α, β) over the keys. Since n is small, sampling and averaging over some keys is possible here, but this is not the case anymore for realistic block lengths.

Consider the hull $(\alpha, \beta) = (0x20400, 0x20000)$ over 3 rounds. A branch-and-bound search for trails with $|\epsilon| \geq 2^{-11}$ yields 8 trails from the hull: three with absolute bias $|\epsilon| = 2^{-10}$ and five with $|\epsilon| = 2^{-11}$. Based on this data, the following estimates for the data complexities of a linear attack with $P_S = 0.95$ and varying advantages were computed based on Proposition 2:

1. N for $\epsilon_r(k_r)$ of the known trails for one cipher key k_r;
2. N determined with Algorithm 7.1 with $\ell = 200$ keys, but without the noise part;
3. N determined with Algorithm 7.1 with $\ell = 200$ keys;
4. N for an estimation of the hull bias by means of the expected linear probability (ELP), averaged over all keys [28].

Additionally, the actual data complexity was determined experimentally. Each experiment for a certain combination of N and a was averaged over 1000 times to obtain a reliable relation between N and a for this fixed P_S.

The results are depicted in Fig. 5. One observes that summing the trail biases for one key results in a far too optimistic estimation. Averaging the data complexity estimates for the signal trails for 200 keys (but without the noise part)

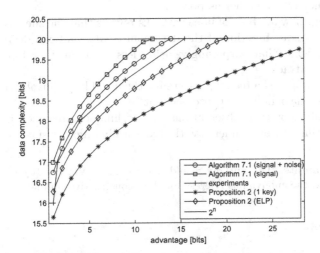

Fig. 5. Theoretical and experimental evaluation of the data complexity with the signal-noise decomposition of Algorithm 7.1. Cipher is SMALLPRESENT with 5 rounds, $n = 20, P_S = 0.95$, the signal part contains 8 trails U_j with $2^{-10} \leq |\epsilon_{U_j}| \leq 2^{-11}$. Experimental value of ϵ is $2^{-8.02}$.

improves the accuracy, but yields an overestimate here. This can be attributed to the impact of two factors: First, the hull must contain more signal trails that are missing in our set of eight trails; and second, the noise impact of the remainder of the hull is not accounted for. Additionally taking the noise into account yields a more realistic estimate. In this specific case though, it is still an overestimate since here obviously the remainder of the hull constructively helps to increase the bias for many keys.

Figure 5 also compares our approach to the estimate based on the ELP, obtained as the sum of the trail ELPs [28]. Note that computing the ELP exactly is infeasible for realistic block ciphers, in contrast to our decomposition approach where only a limited number of dominant trails have to be known.

8   Conclusions

In this paper, we proposed an approach to improving the accuracy of estimating the data complexity and success probability of Matsui's Algorithm 2.

First, we demonstrated that the standard interpretation of the wrong key randomisation hypothesis in linear cryptanalysis implies a simplification that can result in significant overestimations of the attack efficiency. Our adjusted interpretation results in more precise estimates for the success probability and data complexity of linear attacks. The largest improvements compared to previous results occur in the cases where the adversary attempts to use a linear approximation with a low bias, or to attain a high computational advantage over brute force, or both. These cases are particularly relevant in practice since attacks are usually pushed to the limit by recovering many key bits or covering as many rounds of the cipher as possible.

Second, our new analysis of linear attacks reveals that the success probability is not a monotonous function of the data complexity, and can decrease if more data is used. Somewhat surprisingly, using less data can therefore result in a more powerful attack.

Third, we proposed a technique to refine the usual key equivalence hypothesis by taking the linear hull effect into account.

Finally, all theoretical observations and techniques presented in this paper have been verified by experiments with structurally different small-scale ciphers.

Acknowledgments. The authors would like to thank Vincent Rijmen for fruitful discussions and the anonymous referees for their constructive comments.

References

1. Aoki, K., Ichikawa, T., Kanda, M., Matsui, M., Moriai, S., Nakajima, J., Tokita, T.: *Camellia*: A 128-bit block cipher suitable for multiple platforms - design and analysis. In: Stinson, D.R., Tavares, S. (eds.) SAC 2000. LNCS, vol. 2012, pp. 39–56. Springer, Heidelberg (2001)

2. Baignères, T., Junod, P., Vaudenay, S.: How far can we go beyond linear crypt-analysis? In: Lee, P.J. (ed.) ASIACRYPT 2004. LNCS, vol. 3329, pp. 432–450. Springer, Heidelberg (2004)
3. Baignères, T., Vaudenay, S.: The complexity of distinguishing distributions (invited talk). In: Safavi-Naini, R. (ed.) ICITS 2008. LNCS, vol. 5155, pp. 210–222. Springer, Heidelberg (2008)
4. Biham, E.: On Matsui's linear cryptanalysis. In: De Santis [12], pp. 341–355
5. Biham, E., Shamir, A.: Differential cryptanalysis of DES-like cryptosystems. J. Cryptology 4(1), 3–72 (1991)
6. Blondeau, C., Gérard, B., Tillich, J.P.: Accurate estimates of the data complexity and success probability for various cryptanalyses. Des. Codes Crypt. 59(1–3), 3–34 (2011)
7. Bogdanov, A., Tischhauser, E.: On the wrong key randomisation and key equivalence hypotheses in Matsuis algorithm 2. IACR ePrint Archive (2013)
8. Daemen, J., Govaerts, R., Vandewalle, J.: Correlation matrices. In: Preneel, B. (ed.) FSE 1994. LNCS, vol. 1008, pp. 275–285. Springer, Heidelberg (1995)
9. Daemen, J., Rijmen, V.: The Design of Rijndael: AES - The Advanced Encryption Standard. Springer, New York (2002)
10. Daemen, J., Rijmen, V.: Probability distributions of correlation and differentials in block ciphers. Technical report 212, IACR eprint Report 2005/212 (2005). http://eprint.iacr.org/2005/212
11. Daemen, J., Rijmen, V.: Probability distributions of correlations and differentials in block ciphers. J. Math. Cryptology 1(3), 221–242 (2007)
12. De Santis, A. (ed.): EUROCRYPT 1994. LNCS, vol. 950. Springer, Heidelberg (1995)
13. Feistel, H.: Cryptography and computer privacy. Sci. Am. 228, 15–23 (1973)
14. 3rd Generation Partnership Project: Technical specification group services and system aspects, 3G security, specification of the 3GPP confidentiality and integrity algorithms; document 2: KASUMI specification, v3.1.1 (2001)
15. Harpes, C., Kramer, G.G., Massey, J.L.: A generalization of linear cryptanalysis and the applicability of Matsui's piling-up lemma. In: Guillou, L.C., Quisquater, J.-J. (eds.) EUROCRYPT 1995. LNCS, vol. 921, pp. 24–38. Springer, Heidelberg (1995)
16. Hermelin, M., Cho, J.Y., Nyberg, K.: Multidimensional extension of Matsui's algorithm 2. In: Dunkelman, O. (ed.) FSE 2009. LNCS, vol. 5665, pp. 209–227. Springer, Heidelberg (2009)
17. Hermelin, M., Nyberg, K.: Dependent linear approximations: the algorithm of Biryukov and others revisited. In: Pieprzyk, J. (ed.) CT-RSA 2010. LNCS, vol. 5985, pp. 318–333. Springer, Heidelberg (2010)
18. Hermelin, M., Nyberg, K.: Linear cryptanalysis using multiple linear approxima-tions. In: Junod, P., Canteaut, A. (eds.) Advanced Linear Cryptanalysis of Block and Stream Ciphers. IOS Press (2011)
19. Junod, P.: On the complexity of Matsui's attack. In: Vaudenay, S., Youssef, A.M. (eds.) SAC 2001. LNCS, vol. 2259, pp. 199–211. Springer, Heidelberg (2001)
20. Junod, P.: On the optimality of linear, differential, and sequential distinguishers. In: Biham, E. (ed.) EUROCRYPT 2003. LNCS, vol. 2656, pp. 17–32. Springer, Heidelberg (2003)
21. Junod, P., Vaudenay, S.: Optimal key ranking procedures in a statistical crypt-analysis. In: Johansson, T. (ed.) FSE 2003. LNCS, vol. 2887, pp. 235–246. Springer, Heidelberg (2003)

22. Leander, G.: Small scale variants of the block cipher PRESENT. Technical report 143, IACR eprint Report 2010/143 (2010). http://eprint.iacr.org/2010/143
23. Leander, G.: On linear hulls, statistical saturation attacks, PRESENT and a cryptanalysis of PUFFIN. In: Paterson, K.G. (ed.) EUROCRYPT 2011. LNCS, vol. 6632, pp. 303–322. Springer, Heidelberg (2011)
24. Beijing Data Security Technology Co. Ltd: Specification of SMS4 (in Chinese) (2006). http://www.oscca.gov.cn/UpFile/200621016423197990.pdf
25. Matsui, M.: Linear cryptanalysis method for DES cipher. In: Helleseth, T. (ed.) EUROCRYPT 1993. LNCS, vol. 765, pp. 386–397. Springer, Heidelberg (1994)
26. Matsui, M.: The first experimental cryptanalysis of the data encryption standard. In: Desmedt, Y.G. (ed.) CRYPTO 1994. LNCS, vol. 839, pp. 1–11. Springer, Heidelberg (1994)
27. Murphy, S.: The effectiveness of the linear hull effect. Technical report RHUL-MA-2009-19, Royal Holloway (2009)
28. Nyberg, K.: Linear approximations of block ciphers. In: De Santis [12], pp. 439–444
29. Nyberg, K.: Correlation theorems in cryptanalysis. Discrete Appl. Math. 111(1–2), 177–188 (2001)
30. Ohkuma, K.: Weak keys of reduced-round PRESENT for linear cryptanalysis. In: Jacobson Jr, M.J., Rijmen, V., Safavi-Naini, R. (eds.) SAC 2009. LNCS, vol. 5867, pp. 249–265. Springer, Heidelberg (2009)
31. Rivest, R., Robshaw, M., Sidney, R., Yin, Y.L.: The RC6 block cipher. In: First Advanced Encryption Standard (AES) Conference, p. 16 (1998)
32. Röck, A., Nyberg, K.: Exploiting linear hull in Matsui's Algorithm 1. In: The Seventh International Workshop on Coding and Cryptography, WCC, April 2011 (to appear)
33. Selçuk, A.A.: On probability of success in linear and differential cryptanalysis. J. Cryptology 21(1), 131–147 (2008)
34. Shibutani, K., Isobe, T., Hiwatari, H., Mitsuda, A., Akishita, T., Shirai, T.: *Piccolo*: an ultra-lightweight blockcipher. In: Preneel, B., Takagi, T. (eds.) CHES 2011. LNCS, vol. 6917, pp. 342–357. Springer, Heidelberg (2011)
35. Shirai, T., Shibutani, K., Akishita, T., Moriai, S., Iwata, T.: The 128-Bit blockcipher CLEFIA (extended abstract). In: Biryukov, A. (ed.) FSE 2007. LNCS, vol. 4593, pp. 181–195. Springer, Heidelberg (2007)

Cryptanalysis of WIDEA

Gaëtan Leurent[(✉)]

UCL Crypto Group, Louvain-la-Neuve, Belgium
Gaetan.Leurent@uclouvain.be

Abstract. WIDEA is a family of block ciphers designed by Junod and Macchetti in 2009 as an extension of IDEA to larger block sizes (256 and 512 bits for the main instances WIDEA-4 and WIDEA-8) and larger key sizes (512 and 1024 bits, respectively). WIDEA-w is composed of w parallel copies of the IDEA block cipher, with an MDS matrix to provide diffusion between them. An important motivation was to use WIDEA to design a hash function.

In this paper we present low complexity attacks on WIDEA based on truncated differentials. We show a distinguisher for the full WIDEA with complexity only 2^{65}, and we use the distinguisher in a key-recovery attack with complexity $w \cdot 2^{68}$. We also show a collision attack on WIDEA-8 if it is used to build a hash function using the Merkle-Damgård mode of operation.

The attacks exploit the parallel structure of WIDEA and the limited diffusion between the IDEA instances, using differential trails where the MDS diffusion layer is never active. In addition, we use structures of plaintext to reduce the data complexity.

Keywords: Cryptanalysis · Block cipher · Hash function · Truncated differential · IDEA · WIDEA · HIDEA

1 Introduction

Block ciphers are one of the most useful and versatile primitive in symmetric cryptography. Their basic use is to encrypt data and provide confidentiality, but they can also be used to build MAC algorithms (e.g. CBC-MAC), stream ciphers (e.g. in counter mode) and hash functions (e.g. using the Davies-Meyer or Matyas-Meyer-Oseas mode). Block ciphers are relatively well understood and we have well-established ciphers suitable for most uses such as DES, AES, IDEA, RC5, or Blowfish. However, there are still some new proposals to accommodate specific needs such as large block size, low resources, reduced leakage, or high speed on a particular platform. All these designs must be studied in depth before they can be trusted and used in actual products. In this paper we study the recent proposal WIDEA, which is based on IDEA.

S. Moriai (Ed.): FSE 2013, LNCS 8424, pp. 39–51, 2014.
DOI: 10.1007/978-3-662-43933-3_3, © Springer-Verlag Berlin Heidelberg 2014

IDEA. The "International Data Encryption Standard" (IDEA) is a block cipher designed by Lai and Massey in 1991 [12]. IDEA is a modification of their earlier "Proposed Encryption Standard" (PES) [11] and was initially called Improved PES (IPES). IDEA uses 8.5 rounds of the so-called Lai-Massey scheme [16], and mixes operations from incompatible structures ($\oplus$, $\boxplus$, and $\odot$). It is well-considered in the cryptographic community, and used in some products (e.g. in PGP), but its adoption has been limited by IP restrictions.

After years of cryptanalysis, most of the known cryptanalytic techniques have been used against IDEA: differential, linear, differential-linear, boomerang, impossible differentials, bicliques, weak-keys, related-keys, ... Still, the best attacks in a block cipher scenario do not really affect the security of IDEA: attack with a significant margin only reach 6 rounds [1,3,10,14] and only marginal attacks have been shown on the full version [3,10]. On the other hand, the key schedule has been shown to be weak, and this gives classes of weak keys [4–6], related-key attacks [2], and attacks in various hashing modes [17].

WIDEA. At FSE 2009 Junod and Macchetti proposed to revisit the IDEA philosophy [9] in the light of modern CPU architectures. They gave a wordslice implementation of IDEA using the vector instructions available in many current CPU (*SSE* on x86, *Altivec* on PowerPC, *NEON* on ARM ...) and design a new wide block cipher based on IDEA: WIDEA.

WIDEA-w is built from w parallel IDEA instances, using MDS matrices for the diffusion across the parallel instances. WIDEA is quite fast on CPU with vector instructions because the IDEA instances can be computed simultaneously. WIDEA was expected to retain the good security properties of IDEA because it follows the same design criteria: it mixes operations from incompatible structures ($\oplus$, $\boxplus$, $\odot$, and $\otimes$) and full diffusion is achieved after one round.

WIDEA-w has a blocksize of $64 \cdot w$ bits and a key size of $128 \cdot w$ bits. The main versions considered by the designers are WIDEA-4 and WIDEA-8; the large block size and key size are justified with the idea of using them to design a hash function.

Previous Analysis of WIDEA. Recently, Nakahara [7] and Mendel *et al.* [13] found weak keys for WIDEA, similar to the weak keys of IDEA [5]. Mendel *et al.* used the weak key property to create a free-start collision attack when WIDEA is used in hash function mode.

1.1 Our Results

In this paper, we study the security of WIDEA as a block cipher, and when used in a hashing mode. Our main result is a key recovery attack with complexity 2^{70} or 2^{71} which shows that WIDEA is very far from the expected strength of a 512-bit or 1024-bit cipher. The large gap between the security of IDEA and WIDEA is due to the insufficient diffusion across the parallel IDEA instances.

Table 1. Comparision of attacks on WIDEA

Attack	Version	Data	Time	Mem.	Ref, notes
CF collisions	HIDEA-512 ($w = 8$)		2^{14}		[13], free-start
Distinguisher	WIDEA-w	2^{65} CP	2^{65}	2^{64}	3
Success: 63 %	$w \geq 4$	2^{65} CP	2^{71}	2^{64}	5.1, Seq. M
		$5 \cdot 2^{65+t/2}$ ACP	$5 \cdot 2^{65+t/2}$	2^{64-t}	5.2
Key recovery	WIDEA-w	$w \cdot 2^{68}$ CP	$w \cdot 2^{68}$	2^{64}	4
	$w \geq 4$	$w \cdot 2^{68}$ CP	$w \cdot 2^{74}$	2^{64}	5.1, Seq. M
		$5w \cdot 2^{68+t/2}$ ACP	$5w \cdot 2^{68+t/2}$	2^{64-t}	5.2
Hash collisions	HIDEA-512 ($w = 8$)		2^{224}		6

We describe a simple truncated differential trail in Sect. 2, where the MDS diffusion layer is never active. This allows to keep a single IDEA instance active and to have a relatively high probability for the trail. We show how to build a distinguisher for WIDEA using structures of plaintext in Sect. 3. We give a full key recovery attack in Sect. 4, and we discuss some techniques to reduce the memory cost in Sect. 5. Finally, we study WIDEA used as a hash function, and give a collision attack based on the same differential trail in Sect. 6.

Attack Settings. A block cipher is expected to behave like a family of pseudo-random permutations: for an unknown key K, E_K should be indistinguishable from a truly random permutation. In this paper, we consider two different settings, and our results are listed in Table 1:

Chosen Plaintext Attack: The adversary builds a list of plaintext P_i, and receives the corresponding ciphertexts $C_i = E_K(P_i)$ under an unknown key K.

Adaptively Chosen Plaintext Attack: The adversary is given black-box access to a block cipher E_K with an unknown key K. He can ask for the encryption of any plaintext, and the choice of the plaintext can depend on previous answers.

1.2   Description of WIDEA

We give a brief description of WIDEA, but our attack is independent of most low-level details of the design. WIDEA, like IDEA, is a 16-bit oriented cipher, and combines operations from several algebraic structures of size 2^{16}. The elements of these structures are all mapped to 16-bit words, and the cipher uses the operations alternatively. We use the following notations:

E	Block cipher	*Operations on 16-bit words:*	
P	Plaintext	⊞	Addition modulo 2^{16}
C	Ciphertext	⊙	Multiplication modulo $2^{16} + 1$
X	State		(0x0000 represents 2^{16})
K	Master Key	⊕	Boolean exclusive or (xor)
Z_i	Round keys	⊗	Multiplication in $GF(2^{16})$

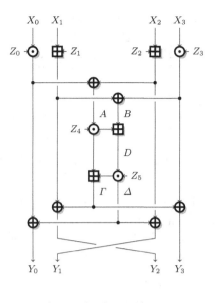

$$A \leftarrow (X_0 \odot Z_0) \oplus (X_2 \boxplus Z_2)$$
$$B \leftarrow (X_1 \boxplus Z_1) \oplus (X_3 \odot Z_3)$$
$$D \leftarrow (A \odot Z_4) \boxplus B$$

$$\Delta \leftarrow D \odot Z_5$$
$$\Gamma \leftarrow \Delta \boxplus (A \odot Z_4)$$
$$Y_0 \leftarrow (X_0 \odot Z_0) \oplus \Delta$$
$$Y_1 \leftarrow (X_2 \boxplus Z_2) \oplus \Delta$$
$$Y_2 \leftarrow (X_1 \boxplus Z_1) \oplus \Gamma$$
$$Y_3 \leftarrow (X_3 \odot Z_3) \oplus \Gamma$$

for $0 \leq i < w$ do
$$A_i \leftarrow (X_{0,i} \odot Z_{0,i}) \oplus (X_{2,i} \boxplus Z_{2,i})$$
$$B_i \leftarrow (X_{1,i} \boxplus Z_{1,i}) \oplus (X_{3,i} \odot Z_{3,i})$$
$$D_i \leftarrow (A_i \odot Z_{4,i}) \boxplus B_i$$
end for
$$D \leftarrow M \cdot D \qquad \triangleright M \text{ is an MDS matrix}$$
for $0 \leq i < w$ do
$$\Delta_i \leftarrow D_i \odot Z_{5,i}$$
$$\Gamma_i \leftarrow \Delta_i \boxplus (A_i \odot Z_{4,i})$$
$$Y_{0,i} \leftarrow (X_{0,i} \odot Z_{0,i}) \oplus \Delta_i$$
$$Y_{1,i} \leftarrow (X_{2,i} \boxplus Z_{2,i}) \oplus \Delta_i$$
$$Y_{2,i} \leftarrow (X_{1,i} \boxplus Z_{1,i}) \oplus \Gamma_i$$
$$Y_{3,i} \leftarrow (X_{3,i} \odot Z_{3,i}) \oplus \Gamma_i$$
end for

Fig. 1. IDEA round function   **Fig. 2.** WIDEA round function

The round functions of IDEA and WIDEA are given in Figs. 1 and 2. The important difference between the two is the multiplication by an MDS matrix M over the field $(\mathrm{GF}(2^{16}), \oplus, \otimes)$. This operation is similar to the AES MixColumn operation; it is used for diffusion between the parallel IDEA instances of WIDEA. WIDEA iterates 8 rounds (for all values of w) plus a final half-round for key-whitening:

$$C_{0,i} = X_{0,i} \odot K_{48,i} \quad C_{1,i} = X_{2,i} \odot K_{49,i} \quad C_{2,i} = X_{1,i} \odot K_{50,i} \quad C_{3,i} = X_{3,i} \odot K_{51,i}$$

The key schedule is described over $64 \cdot w$ words. The first 8 words are loaded with the master key K, and the expanded words are computed as:

$$K_i = \left(\left(\left((K_{i-1} \oplus K_{i-8}) \overset{16}{\boxplus} K_{i-5} \right) \overset{16}{\lll} 5 \right) \lll 24 \right) \oplus R_i,$$

where R_i are round constants. The round keys used for round r are $Z_{i,j} = K_{6r+i,j}$.

2   Truncated Differential Trail

Our attacks are based on a differential trail. We consider a pair of messages P, P' with a small difference encrypted through IDEA under the same key K, and we study the difference in the state X, X' after each round. However, we don't specify exactly the difference: we only specify for each word whether the difference is zero or non-zero, giving a truncated differential trail.

We start with a pair of states with only one IDEA instance active, such as (with instance 0 active):

$$X_{0,0} \neq X_{0,0}' \quad X_{1,0} \neq X_{1,0}' \quad X_{2,0} \neq X_{2,0}' \quad X_{3,0} \neq X_{3,0}'$$
$$X_{0,i} = X_{0,i}' \quad X_{1,i} = X_{1,i}' \quad X_{2,i} = X_{2,i}' \quad X_{3,i} = X_{3,i}' \quad \text{for } 1 \leq i < w$$

When we compute the round function, we have $D_i = D_i'$ for $i \neq 0$, and with probability 2^{-16}, we also have $D_0 = D_0'$. In this case, the input of the MDS matrix will be inactive, and the difference does not propagate to the other IDEA instances. This leads to:

$$Y_{0,0} \neq Y_{0,0}' \quad Y_{1,0} \neq Y_{1,0}' \quad Y_{2,0} \neq Y_{2,0}' \quad Y_{3,0} \neq Y_{3,0}'$$
$$Y_{0,i} = Y_{0,i}' \quad Y_{1,i} = Y_{1,i}' \quad Y_{2,i} = Y_{2,i}' \quad Y_{3,i} = Y_{3,i}' \quad \text{for } 1 \leq i < w$$

Graphically, we can represent the state X as a matrix of 16-words, with active words in black and inactive words in white:

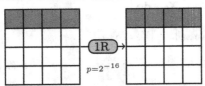

The trail inside the Multiply/Add/Diffuse box is:

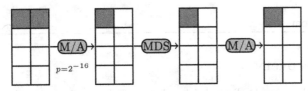

The MDS matrix is applied to the right column, and all inputs are inactive.

We iterate this trail for 8 rounds of WIDEA, and the final half round does not affect which words are active. This gives a truncated differential trail with probability 2^{-128} for the full 8.5 rounds of WIDEA:

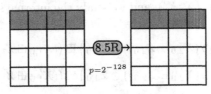

For a random permutation over $64 \cdot w$ bits, a pair would follow this trail with probability $2^{-64 \cdot (w-1)}$. Therefore, we have an efficient distinguisher for WIDEA-w as soon as $w \geq 3$. If $w \geq 4$, the distinguisher is very strong, and we do not expect to have any false positives.

3   Distinguisher

To exploit this property, we use structures of 2^{64} plaintext, where one slice takes all possible values, and the other slices are fixed to a constant value. This structure gives $2^{64} \times (2^{64} - 1)/2 \approx 2^{127}$ pairs of plaintext; each pair has only one active slice and is a potential candidate for the differential trail. If we take two such structures, this gives about 2^{128} plaintext pairs, and with a probability of $1 - 1/e \approx 63\%$, at least one pair will follow the truncated trail.

We can efficiently test if such pairs are present by inserting all the ciphertexts in a hash table indexed by the slices that are expected to be inactive. This gives a chosen-plaintext distinguisher for WIDEA with complexity 2^{65} as shown in Algorithm 1.

Algorithm 1. Distinguish WIDEA from a random permutation

Input: E
   for $0 \leq t < 2$ **do**
      $T \leftarrow \varnothing$
      $X \leftarrow \mathsf{Rand}()$
      for all $X_{0,0}, X_{0,1}, X_{0,2}, X_{0,3}$ **do**
         $Y \leftarrow E(X)$
         $Y' \leftarrow Y_{1,0\ldots3} \| Y_{2,0\ldots3} \| \ldots \| Y_{w-1,0\ldots3}$
         if $Y' \in T$ **then**
            return WIDEA $\triangleright$ $(T\{Y'\}, X)$ is a right pair.
         end if
         $T\{Y'\} \leftarrow X$
      end for
   end for
   return Random

---

4   Key Recovery

We can turn this simple distinguisher into a full key recovery with some more effort.

4.1   First-Round Key

We consider a right pair (X, X'), and we study the internal state; we can express D_0, D_0':

$$D_0 = \Big(\big((X_{0,0} \odot Z_{0,0}) \oplus (X_{2,0} \boxplus Z_{2,0}) \big) \odot Z_{4,0} \Big) \boxplus \big((X_{1,0} \boxplus Z_{1,0}) \oplus (X_{3,0} \odot Z_{3,0}) \big)$$

$$D_0' = \Big(\big((X_{0,0}' \odot Z_{0,0}) \oplus (X_{2,0}' \boxplus Z_{2,0}) \big) \odot Z_{4,0} \Big) \boxplus \big((X_{1,0}' \boxplus Z_{1,0}) \oplus (X_{3,0}' \odot Z_{3,0}) \big)$$

Since the pair follows the trail, we have $D_0 = D_0'$, or equivalently:

$$\left(\left((X_{0,0} \odot Z_{0,0}) \oplus (X_{2,0} \boxplus Z_{2,0}) \right) \odot Z_{4,0} \right) \boxminus \left(\left((X_{0,0}' \odot Z_{0,0}) \oplus (X_{2,0}' \boxplus Z_{2,0}) \right) \odot Z_{4,0} \right)$$
$$= \left((X_{1,0}' \boxplus Z_{1,0}) \oplus (X_{3,0}' \odot Z_{3,0}) \right) \boxminus \left((X_{1,0} \boxplus Z_{1,0}) \oplus (X_{3,0} \odot Z_{3,0}) \right) \tag{1}$$

In this equation, the left hand side is a function of $Z_{0,0}, Z_{2,0}, Z_{4,0}$ only, while the right hand size is a function of $Z_{1,0}, Z_{3,0}$ only. We denote them as:

$$F_i(X, X', Z_{0,i}, Z_{2,i}, Z_{4,i}) = \left(\left((X_{0,i} \odot Z_{0,i}) \oplus (X_{2,i} \boxplus Z_{2,i}) \right) \odot Z_{4,i} \right)$$
$$\boxminus \left(\left((X_{0,i}' \odot Z_{0,i}) \oplus (X_{2,i}' \boxplus Z_{2,i}) \right) \odot Z_{4,i} \right) \tag{2}$$
$$G_i(X, X', Z_{1,i}, Z_{3,i}) = \left((X_{1,i}' \boxplus Z_{1,i}) \oplus (X_{3,i}' \odot Z_{3,i}) \right)$$
$$\boxminus \left((X_{1,i} \boxplus Z_{1,i}) \oplus (X_{3,i} \odot Z_{3,i}) \right). \tag{3}$$

We can recover the key efficiently using a meet-in-the-middle technique. On the one hand, we compute $F_0(X, X', k_0, k_2, k_4)$ for all k_0, k_2, k_4, and on the other hand, we compute $G_0(X, X', k_1, k_3)$ for all k_1, k_3. Then we look for matches in the list because the correct key satisfies $F_0(X, X', Z_{0,0}, Z_{2,0}, Z_{4,0}) = G_0(X, X', Z_{1,0}, Z_{3,0})$ for a right pair X, X'.

In order to achieve a strong filtering, we use several right pairs $X^{(j)}, X'^{(j)}$ and we look for simultaneous matches between all the F's and G's, i.e. matches in the concatenations $\|_{j=0}^{k} F_0(X^{(j)}, X'^{(j)}, k_0, k_2, k_4)$ and $\|_{j=0}^{k} G_0(X^{(j)}, X'^{(j)}, k_1, k_3)$. Unfortunately, this filtering cannot distinguish the real key K, and the key K' where the most significant bit of $Z_{1,0}$ is flipped, because the effect of this bit on D is linear.

Each pair gives a 16-bit filtering and we are recovering 79 key bits, so we expect that 5 pairs would be sufficient. However, when implementing the attack, we found out that the filtering given by each pair is not independent, and we need more than 5 pairs; our experiments show that using $k = 8$ pairs is enough to isolate a single key pair most of time.

Therefore we can recover the correct value of $Z_{0\ldots4,0}$ (up to one bit) with complexity $2^{3\cdot16} = 2^{51}$ (we consider that the computation of 8 F and G functions costs about the same as one evaluation of WIDEA). We can also recover the keys $Z_{0\ldots4,i}$ used in the other IDEA instances in the same way: we just need different pairs following a path with another active slice.

4.2   Second-Round Key

We can now compute all the inputs to the MDS matrix in the first round, since we know the keys used in each IDEA instance. Then we compute the output of the MDS matrix, and we can again consider the parallel IDEA instances independently. First, we guess $Z_{5,i}$ in order to compute the state after the end of the first round. Then we apply the same meet-in-the-middle strategy as for the first round, in order to recover the second round key $Z_{6\ldots10,i}$. Finally, we know that the master key is $Z_{0...7}$ according to the key expansion algorithm. If several key candidates remain, we test them with one of the plaintext/ciphertext pairs. This would give a key-recovery with complexity $w \cdot 2^{16} \cdot 2^{48} = w \cdot 2^{64}$.

Missing Key Bits. In fact, we have 2^w key candidates for the first round, because the most significant bits of the $Z_{1,i}$'s can not be recovered by testing collisions in D. Instead of running the analysis for the second round with all these candidates, we use the fact that the unknown bits have a linear effect on the MDS operation. Moreover, the coefficients of the MDS matrix given in [9] for WIDEA-8 are all between 1 and 9; therefore any linear combination is between 0 and 15. For WIDEA-4, the coefficients are between 1 and 3; any linear combination is between 0 and 3. Instead of guessing the w missing bits of the key, we can guess the effect on the MDS output, which is of the form $t \otimes \texttt{0x8000}$, with $0 \leq t < 4$ for WIDEA-4 and $0 \leq t < 16$ for WIDEA-8 (i.e. a 2-bit guess and a 4-bit guess, respectively). Therefore the actual complexity of the key-recovery attack will be $4 \cdot 2^2 \cdot 2^{64} = 2^{68}$ for WIDEA-4, and $8 \cdot 2^4 \cdot 2^{64} = 2^{71}$ for WIDEA-8. The attack is described in Algorithms 2 and 3.

4.3 Complexity

We can slightly reduce the complexity using properties of the key schedule. More precisely, when $K_{6...10,0}$ has been recovered in the first IDEA instance, we can use the key scheduling algorithm to compute some bits of K_8, so that recovering the key of the next instance become negligible compared to the first key recovery. This reduces the complexity by a factor w.

Therefore, the analysis step has a complexity of only 2^{66} memory accesses to a table of size 2^{32} for WIDEA-4 (2^{68} accesses to a similar table for WIDEA8). The computation of the F's and G's will likely be negligible before the cost of memory accesses. As a rough estimation we can assume that a memory access to a table of size 2^{32} takes about the same time as the computation of the block cipher.

Data Complexity. The data complexity of the attack is $w \cdot 2^{68}$: we need $8 \cdot w$ right pairs, and each pair is found after 2^{65} chosen plaintexts. The data filtering step to isolate right pairs is actually the most expensive step of the attack: it requires $w \cdot 2^{68}$ memory accesses to a table of size 2^{64}.

5 Reducing the Memory Cost

Since the complexity of the key-recovery attacks on WIDEA is rather low, we briefly discuss practical aspects of the attack, in addition to the complexity figures which don't account for the cost of the memory. The bottleneck of the attack is the filtering of right pairs. If we use a hash table to find collisions in each structures as explained in Sect. 3, we need a random access memory of size 2^{64}, which is probably less practical than the time complexity of 2^{66} or 2^{68} for the analysis step.

Algorithm 2. Recover the Key from WIDEA

Input: $(X^{(i,j)}, X'^{(i,j)})$ right pairs with slice i active $0 \leq i < w, 0 \leq j < k = 8$
▷ First step: recover $K_{0\ldots4}$
for $0 \leq i < w$ **do**
    $T \leftarrow \varnothing$
    for all k_1, k_3 **do**
        $G \leftarrow ||_{j=0}^{k} G_i(X^{(i,j)}, X'^{(i,j)}, k_1, k_3)$
        $T\{G\} \leftarrow (k_1, k_3)$
    end for
    for all k_0, k_2, k_4 **do**
        $F \leftarrow ||_{j=0}^{k} F_i(X^{(i,j)}, X'^{(i,j)}, k_0, k_2, k_4)$
        if $F \in T$ **then**
            $k_1, k_3 \leftarrow T\{F\}$
            $K_{0\ldots4,i} \leftarrow k_0, k_1, k_2, k_3, k_4$
        end if
    end for
end for
▷ Second step: recover $K_{5\ldots10}$
for $0 \leq i < w$ **do**
    for all $k_5, 0 \leq t < 16$ **do**
        $K_{5,i} \leftarrow k_5$
        for all i, k **do**
            $Y^{i,k} \leftarrow \text{RoundTweak}(X^{(i,k)}, K, i, t \otimes \text{0x8000})$
            $Y'^{i,k} \leftarrow \text{RoundTweak}(X'^{(i,k)}, K, i, t \otimes \text{0x8000})$
        end for
        $T \leftarrow \varnothing$
        for all k_1, k_3 **do**
            $G \leftarrow ||_{j=0}^{k} G_i(Y^{(i,j)}, Y'^{(i,j)}, k_1, k_3)$
            $T\{G\} \leftarrow (k_1, k_3)$
        end for
        for all k_0, k_2, k_4 **do**
            $F \leftarrow ||_{j=0}^{k} F_i(Y^{(i,j)}, Y'^{(i,j)}, k_0, k_2, k_4)$
            if $F \in T$ **then**
                $k_1, k_3 \leftarrow T\{F\}$
                $K_{6\ldots10,i} \leftarrow k_0, k_1, k_2, k_3, k_4$
            end if
        end for
    end for
end for

Algorithm 3. WIDEA round with a tweak (ι, t) after the MDS step

---

▷ t is the effect of the missing bits of Z_1 on D_ι

function ROUNDTWEAK(X, Z, ι, t)

    for $0 \leq i < w$ **do**

        $A_i \leftarrow (X_{0,i} \odot Z_{0,i}) \oplus (X_{2,i} \boxplus Z_{2,i})$

        $B_i \leftarrow (X_{1,i} \boxplus Z_{1,i}) \oplus (X_{3,i} \odot Z_{3,i})$

        $D_i \leftarrow (A_i \odot Z_{4,i}) \boxplus B_i$

    end for

    $D \leftarrow M \cdot D$

    $D_\iota \leftarrow D_\iota \oplus t$

    for $0 \leq i < w$ **do**

        $\Delta_i \leftarrow D_i \odot Z_{5,i}$

        $\Gamma_i \leftarrow \Delta_i \boxplus (A_i \odot Z_{4,i})$

        $Y_{0,i} \leftarrow (X_{0,i} \odot Z_{0,i}) \oplus \Delta_i$

        $Y_{1,i} \leftarrow (X_{2,i} \boxplus Z_{2,i}) \oplus \Delta_i$

        $Y_{2,i} \leftarrow (X_{1,i} \boxplus Z_{1,i}) \oplus \Gamma_i$

        $Y_{3,i} \leftarrow (X_{3,i} \odot Z_{3,i}) \oplus \Gamma_i$

    end for

    return Y

end function

5.1 Sorting

A first way to avoid this problem is to store all the ciphertexts from a structure sequentially, and to run a sorting algorithm to find collisions. This still requires a memory of size 2^{64}, but we only make sequential accesses to this huge memory, and we can use disk or tape storage. The sorting algorithm increases the cost of the attack by a logarithmic factor, but the resulting attack will be much easier to carry out in practice.

The storage needed for the attack will be about 2^{64} elements of 16 bytes each (4 16-bit words for the active input slice, and the output can be restricted to 4 16-bit words if we use an extra pass to check that the rest of the state collides). This amounts to 2^{68} bytes, or 256 exabytes.

5.2 Time-Memory Trade-Offs

We can also use a time-memory trade-off to reduce the memory requirement of the attack. The filtering step of the attack is essentially a collision search for the function

$$\phi_r \colon \{0,1\}^{64} \to \{0,1\}^{64 \cdot (w-1)}$$

$$x \mapsto \text{Trunc}_{64 \cdot (w-1)}(E_K(x\|r))$$

with a random $r \in \{0,1\}^{64 \cdot (w-1)}$. If we truncate the output of ϕ_r to 64 bits, we can find collisions with a memory-less algorithm for a complexity of 2^{32}, using adaptively chosen inputs. However, we expect on average that 2^{63} collisions exists for this function, but only 0.5 collisions correspond to a right pair for the differential trail. Therefore the total complexity to find a right pair without memory will be 2^{96}.

More generally, we can store distinguished points so that finding N collisions costs less than $N \cdot 2^{32}$. Using the analysis of [15], we know that we can find a "golden collision" with a complexity of $2 \cdot 2.5 \cdot 2^{64+t/2}$ if we have a memory of size 2^{64-t} (with $0 < t < 64$).

6   Hash Function Collisions

One important use case of WIDEA as envisioned by the designers is to build a hash function. Hash function benchmarks are given in [9], and a more complete description of a hash function (named HIDEA) was presented in the ESC seminar [8]. HIDEA uses WIDEA to build a compression function with the Davies-Meyer mode, and iterates it with the Merkle-Damgård and HAIFA modes of operation. We note that the presentation of HIDEA in [8] suggests to use a 10.5-round WIDEA, instead of the 8.5-round version of [9].

To find collisions for HIDEA, we first look for a pair of messages M, M' so that the internal state X, X' reached after processing them satisfies $X_{0...3,i} = X'_{0...3,i}$ for $i \neq 0$. This is equivalent to finding a collision in a truncated function with an output of $64 \cdot (w - 1)$ bits. For this step we can store the hash of $2^{32 \cdot (w-1)}$ random messages, or use a memory-less collision finding algorithm. This step has a complexity of $2^{32 \cdot (w-1)}$, i.e. 2^{224} for WIDEA-8. We note that we can just as easily have two pre-specified prefixes P and P' and look for M, M' such that the state X, X' reached after processing $P\|M$ and $P'\|M'$ satisfies $X_{0...3,i} = X'_{0...3,i}$ for $i \neq 0$.

We assume that $P\|M$ and $P'\|M'$ both have the same length, and this length is an integral number of blocks. When we append a random block N to $P\|M$ and $P'\|M'$, the compression function is computed as:

$$h(X, N) = Y \oplus X, \qquad\qquad Y = E_N(X)$$
$$h(X', N) = Y' \oplus X', \qquad\qquad Y' = E_N(X').$$

We have $X_{0...3,i} = X'_{0...3,i}$ for $i \neq 0$, and we know that with probability 2^{-128} (2^{-160} for a 10.5-round WIDEA), this gives $Y_{0...3,i} = Y'_{0...3,i}$ for $i \neq 0$. Additionally, we have $Y_{0...3,0} \oplus X_{0...3,0} = Y'_{0...3,0} \oplus X'_{0...3,0}$ with probability 2^{-64}. Therefore we have $h(X, N) = h(X', N)$ with probability 2^{-192} (2^{-224} for a 10.5-round WIDEA).

When combining both steps, we have a collision attack with complexity 2^{224} for WIDEA-8 with up to 10.5 rounds. The attack is described by Algorithm 4.

Surprisingly, this attack doesn't use any property of the key schedule, and can use arbitrary messages. This allows to build meaningful collisions easily. On the other hand, a few more rounds can be attacked using message modification techniques, if needed.

Algorithm 4. Find collisions for HIDEA-512

Input: P, P' chosen prefix

Find M, M' with $\text{Trunc}_{64(w-1)}(H(P\|M)) = \text{Trunc}_{64(w-1)}(H(P'\|M'))$
▷ Complexity 2^{224}
repeat
$\quad N \leftarrow \text{Rand}()$
until $H(P\|M\|N) = H(P'\|M'\|N)$
▷ Complexity 2^{224}

---

7 Conclusion

In this paper we show devastating attacks on the WIDEA block cipher. Our main result is a key-recovery attack with complexity $w \cdot 2^{68}$ for the WIDEA family with $w \geq 4$. In particular this affects the main instances considered in the WIDEA paper: WIDEA-4 (256-bit block and 512-bit key) and WIDEA-8 (512-bit block and 1024-bit key). We also show a collision attack when WIDEA is used to build a hash function, as was proposed by the designers. The collision attack affects instances with $w \geq 8$: we can build collisions for HIDEA-512 (based on WIDEA-8) with a complexity of 2^{224}.

The attacks exploit the limited diffusion between the IDEA instances by building trails where the MDS diffusion layer is never active. Since the input of the MDS layer is only 16-bit for one IDEA instance, such trails have a probability of $2^{-16 \cdot r}$ for an r-round WIDEA. In addition, we use structures of plaintext to reduce the data complexity of the block-cipher attacks. The attacks don't depend on low-level details of the design (such as the key schedule, the MDS matrix, or the exact computational graph of IDEA). The complexity is almost independent of the width w, and can even break extended version of WIDEA with more than 8.5 rounds.

We have implemented the key-recovery attack with a reduced WIDEA using 8-bit words, and all the steps of the attack worked as expected.

Acknowledgment. We would like to thanks the anonymous reviewers for very detailed comments. In particular, they noticed a mistake in our description of IDEA and WIDEA (our implementation of the attack used the correct algorithm, though).

The author is supported by the ERC project CRASH. Part of this work was done while the author was at the university of Luxembourg, supported by the AFR grant PDR-10-022 of the FNR.

References

1. Biham, E., Dunkelman, O., Keller, N.: A new attack on 6-round IDEA. In: Biryukov, A. (ed.) FSE 2007. LNCS, vol. 4593, pp. 211–224. Springer, Heidelberg (2007)
2. Biham, E., Dunkelman, O., Keller, N.: A unified approach to related-key attacks. In: Nyberg, K. (ed.) FSE 2008. LNCS, vol. 5086, pp. 73–96. Springer, Heidelberg (2008)

3. Biham, E., Dunkelman, O., Keller, N., Shamir, A.: New data-efficient attacks on 6-round IDEA. Cryptology ePrint Archive, Report 2011/417 (2011). http://eprint. iacr.org/

4. Biryukov, A., Nakahara Jr, J., Preneel, B., Vandewalle, J.: New weak-key classes of IDEA. In: Deng, R.H., Qing, S., Bao, F., Zhou, J. (eds.) ICICS 2002. LNCS, vol. 2513, pp. 315–326. Springer, Heidelberg (2002)

5. Daemen, J., Govaerts, R., Vandewalle, J.: Weak keys for IDEA. In: Stinson, D.R. (ed.) CRYPTO 1993. LNCS, vol. 773, pp. 224–231. Springer, Heidelberg (1994)

6. Hawkes, P.: Differential-linear weak key classes of IDEA. In: Nyberg, K. (ed.) EUROCRYPT 1998. LNCS, vol. 1403, pp. 112–126. Springer, Heidelberg (1998)

7. Nakahara Jr, J.: Differential and linear attacks on the full WIDEA-n block ciphers (under Weak Keys). In: Pieprzyk, J., Sadeghi, A.-R., Manulis, M. (eds.) CANS 2012. LNCS, vol. 7712, pp. 56–71. Springer, Heidelberg (2012)

8. Junod, P.: IDEA: past, present, and future. Early Symmetric Crypto (2010). https://www.cryptolux.org/esc2010/Pascal_Junod

9. Junod, P., Macchetti, M.: Revisiting the IDEA Philosophy. In: Dunkelman, O. (ed.) FSE 2009. LNCS, vol. 5665, pp. 277–295. Springer, Heidelberg (2009)

10. Khovratovich, D., Leurent, G., Rechberger, C.: Narrow-Bicliques: cryptanalysis of full IDEA. In: Pointcheval, D., Johansson, T. (eds.) EUROCRYPT 2012. LNCS, vol. 7237, pp. 392–410. Springer, Heidelberg (2012)

11. Lai, X., Massey, J.L.: A proposal for a new block encryption standard. In: Damgård, I.B. (ed.) EUROCRYPT 1990. LNCS, vol. 473, pp. 389–404. Springer, Heidelberg (1991)

12. Lai, X., Massey, J.L.: Markov ciphers and differential cryptanalysis. In: Davies, D.W. (ed.) EUROCRYPT 1991. LNCS, vol. 547, pp. 17–38. Springer, Heidelberg (1991)

13. Mendel, F., Rijmen, V., Toz, D., Varıcı, K.: Collisions for the WIDEA-8 compression function. In: Dawson, E. (ed.) CT-RSA 2013. LNCS, vol. 7779, pp. 162–173. Springer, Heidelberg (2013)

14. Sun, X., Lai, X.: The key-dependent attack on block ciphers. In: Matsui, M. (ed.) ASIACRYPT 2009. LNCS, vol. 5912, pp. 19–36. Springer, Heidelberg (2009)

15. van Oorschot, P.C., Wiener, M.J.: Parallel collision search with application to hash functions and discrete logarithms. In: Denning, D.E., Pyle, R., Ganesan, R., Sandhu, R.S. (eds.) ACM Conference on Computer and Communications Security, pp. 210–218. ACM (1994)

16. Vaudenay, S.: On the Lai-Massey scheme. In: Lam, K.-Y., Okamoto, E., Xing, Ch. (eds.) ASIACRYPT 1999. LNCS, vol. 1716, pp. 8–19. Springer, Heidelberg (1999)

17. Wei, L., Peyrin, T., Sokołowski, P., Ling, S., Pieprzyk, J., Wang, H.: On the (In)security of IDEA in various hashing modes. In: Canteaut, A. (ed.) FSE 2012. LNCS, vol. 7549, pp. 163–179. Springer, Heidelberg (2012)

Invited Talk

Towards Secure Distance Bounding

Ioana Boureanu[1], Aikaterini Mitrokotsa[2], and Serge Vaudenay[1]([⊠])

[1] EPFL, 1015 Lausanne, Switzerland
serge.vaudenay@epfl.ch
http://lasec.epfl.ch
[2] University of Applied Sciences of Western Switzerland (HES-SO),
1227 Geneva, Switzerland
katerina.mitrokotsa@hesge.ch

Abstract. Relay attacks (and, more generally, man-in-the-middle attacks) are a serious threat against many access control and payment schemes. In this work, we present distance-bounding protocols, how these can deter relay attacks, and the security models formalizing these protocols. We show several pitfalls making existing protocols insecure (or at least, vulnerable, in some cases). Then, we introduce the SKI protocol which enjoys resistance to all popular attack-models and features provable security. As far as we know, this is the first protocol with such all-encompassing security guarantees.

1 Why Distance-Bounding?

It is well known that a chess beginner can win against a chess grand-master easily by defeating two grand-masters concurrently, taking different colors in both games, and relaying the move of one master to the other. This is a pure *relay attack* where two masters play against each other while each of them thinks he is playing against a beginner.

In real life, relay attacks find applications in access control. For instance, a car with a wireless key can be opened by relaying the communication between the key (the token) and the car. RFID-based access control to buildings can also be subject to relay attacks [21]. The same goes for (contactless) credit-card payments: a customer may try to pay for something on a malicious terminal which relays to a fake card paying for something more expensive [15].

To defeat relay attacks, Brands and Chaum [9] introduced the notion of *distance bounding protocol*. This relies on the fact that information is local and it cannot travel faster than light. So, an RFID reader can identify when participants are close enough because the round-trip communication time has been small enough. The idea is that a *prover* holding a key x proves to a *verifier* that he is close to him. Ideally, this notion should behave like a traditional interactive proof system in the sense that it must satisfy:

This invited paper summarizes results from [4–8].

S. Moriai (Ed.): FSE 2013, LNCS 8424, pp. 55–67, 2014.
DOI: 10.1007/978-3-662-43933-3_4, © Springer-Verlag Berlin Heidelberg 2014

- completeness (i.e., an honest prover close to the verifier will pass the protocol with high probability)
- soundness (i.e., if the verifier accepts the protocol, then it must be the case that the information held by all close participants includes x)
- security (i.e., if the prover honestly runs the protocol, the provided information does not provide any advantage to defeat soundness).

The last property is weaker than zero-knowledge and is generally required in *identification protocols*. In practice, the literature does not define distance-bounding like this but rather considers several popular threat models, as per the following summary.

- *Distance fraud* [9]: a far-away malicious prover tries to pass the protocol.
- *Mafia fraud* [14]: an adversary between a far-away honest prover and a verifier tries to get advantage of his position to make the verifier accept. (This generalizes relay attacks as the adversary may also modify messages.)
- *Terrorist fraud* [14]: a far-away malicious prover, with the help of an adversary, tries to make the verifier accept, but without giving the adversary any advantage to later pass the protocol alone. For instance, the malicious prover wants to make the verifier accept, although he is far away, but does not want to give his secret x to the adversary.
- *Impersonation fraud* [3]: An adversary tries to impersonate the prover and make the verifier accept.
- *Distance hijacking* [13]: A far-away prover takes advantage of some honest provers running the protocol to make the verifier accept.

In our model [8], we factor all these common threats into three possible frauds.

- *Distance fraud*: this is the classical notion in which we also consider concurrency with many other participants. I.e., we include other possible provers (with other secrets) and verifiers. Consequently, our generalized distance fraud also includes distance hijacking.
- *Man-in-the-middle*: we consider an adversary (maybe at several locations) who can interact with many honest provers (possibly with different keys) and verifiers during a *learning phase*. Then, the *attack phase* contains honest provers with the key x, far away from a verifier V, and possibly many other honest provers (with other keys) and other verifiers. The goal of the adversary is to make V accept the prover holding x. Clearly, this generalizes mafia fraud and includes impersonation fraud.
- *Collusion fraud*: A far-away prover holding x helps an adversary to make the verifier accept the proof. This might be in the presence of many other honest participants. However, there should be no man-in-the-middle attack constructed based on this malicious prover. I.e., the adversary should not extract from him any advantage to run (later) a man-in-the-middle attack.

Ideally, we could just keep this last notion which includes all others and is closer to the soundness and the security notion in the interactive proof system.

Table 1. Best attack results on existing distance-bounding Protocols [7]

Protocol	Success probability			
	Distance-fraud	MIM		Collusion-fraud
Brands & Chaum [9]	$(1/2)^n$ [18]	$(1/2)^n$	[25]	1 [25]
Bussard & Bagga [10]	1 [4]	$(1/2)^n$	[10]	1 [4]
Čapkun et al. (SECTOR) [11]	$(1/2)^n$ [18]	$(1/2)^n$	[25]	1 [25]
Hancke & Kuhn [20]	$(3/4)^n$ [18]	$(3/4)^n$	[25]	1 [25]
Reid et al. [34]	$(3/4)^n$ [18]	$(3/4)^n$ or 1	[4,26]	$(3/4)^\nu$ [25]
Singelée & Preneel [35]	$(1/2)^n$ [18]	$(1/2)^n$	[25]	1 [25]
Tu & Piramuthu [36]	$(3/4)^n$ [30]	1	[25]	$(3/4)^\nu$ [30]
Munilla & Peinado [29]	$(3/4)^n$ [18]	$(3/5)^n$	[18]	1 [18]
Swiss-Knife [25]	$(3/4)^n$ [25]	$(1/2)^n$	[25]	$(3/4)^\nu$ [25]
Kim & Avoine [24]	$(7/8)^n$ [18]	$(1/2)^n$	[18]	1 [18]
Nikov & Vauclair [31]	$1/k^a$ [25]	$(1/2)^n$	[25]	1 [25]
Avoine et al. [2]	$(3/4)^n$ [2]	$(2/3)^n$	[2]	$(2/3)^\nu$ [2]

[a] k is an additional parameter in this protocol

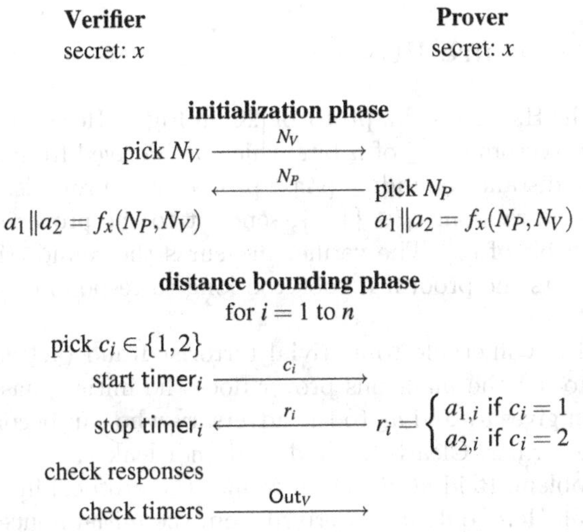

Verifier	Prover
secret: x	secret: x

initialization phase

pick N_V $\xrightarrow{\quad N_V \quad}$

$\xleftarrow{\quad N_P \quad}$ pick N_P

$a_1 \| a_2 = f_x(N_P, N_V)$ $a_1 \| a_2 = f_x(N_P, N_V)$

distance bounding phase
for $i = 1$ to n

pick $c_i \in \{1, 2\}$

start timer$_i$ $\xrightarrow{\quad c_i \quad}$

stop timer$_i$ $\xleftarrow{\quad r_i \quad}$ $r_i = \begin{cases} a_{1,i} & \text{if } c_i = 1 \\ a_{2,i} & \text{if } c_i = 2 \end{cases}$

check responses

check timers $\xrightarrow{\quad Out_V \quad}$

Fig. 1. The Hancke-Kuhn distance-bounding protocol [20]

We summarize the best security results for many existing distance-bounding protocols. Table 1 gives the probability of success of the best known attacks. This table does not consider possibly bad pseudorandom function (PRF) instances [5] nor any terrorist fraud based on noise tolerance [19]. These aspects will be discussed later in the present paper. For collusion-frauds, we consider a prover leaking all but ν bits of his secret.

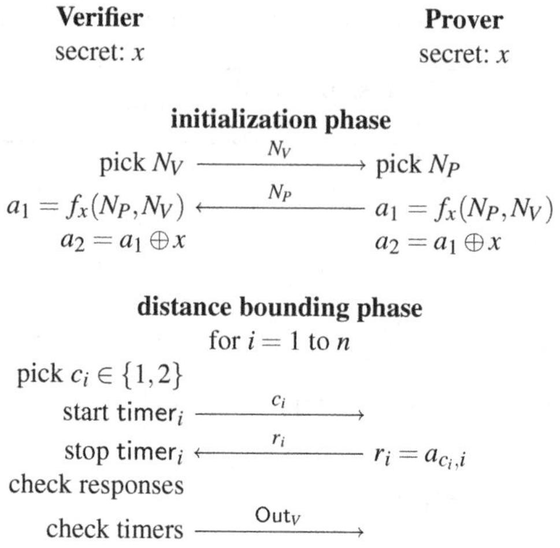

Verifier
secret: x

Prover
secret: x

initialization phase

$$\text{pick } N_V \xrightarrow{\quad N_V \quad} \text{pick } N_P$$

$$a_1 = f_x(N_P, N_V) \xleftarrow{\quad N_P \quad} a_1 = f_x(N_P, N_V)$$

$$a_2 = a_1 \oplus x \qquad\qquad a_2 = a_1 \oplus x$$

distance bounding phase

for $i = 1$ to n

pick $c_i \in \{1, 2\}$

$$\text{start timer}_i \xrightarrow{\quad c_i \quad}$$

$$\text{stop timer}_i \xleftarrow{\quad r_i \quad} r_i = a_{c_i, i}$$

check responses

$$\text{check timers} \xrightarrow{\quad \text{Out}_V \quad}$$

Fig. 2. The DBENC distance-bounding protocol [5,34]

2 Towards a Secure Protocol

We first look at the Hancke-Kuhn protocol [20] in Fig. 1. Here, we use a symmetric key x and two vectors a_1, a_2 of n bits which are derived from an exchange of nonces. Then, the distance bounding phase proceeds in n rounds. In each round, the verifier selects a random $c_i \in \{1, 2\}$, sends it to the prover and expects to receive r_i, the ith bit of a_{c_i}. The verifier measures the round-trip communication time and rejects the proof if it took too long to respond or the response is incorrect.

This protocol is vulnerable to a trivial terrorist fraud (actually, it was not meant to resist to it): the malicious prover does the initial phase which is not time-critical, then gives a_1 and a_2 to the adversary who can become a proxy for the prover to the verifier. Clearly, a_1 and a_2 do not leak x.

To fix this problem, Reid *et al.* [34] introduce the protocol in Fig. 2 which we call DBENC in [5]. Here, only a_1 is derived from the initial nonces and a_2 is set to $a_1 \oplus x$. So, a malicious prover providing a_1 and a_2 to an adversary would also leak x.

First of all, we stress that nonces must really be "numbers once used", as their name suggests. I.e., they shall not repeat. Otherwise, this protocol (as well as many others) would leak some sensitive information, as noticed in [28].

Second, we observe that this protocol unfortunately becomes vulnerable to a man-in-the-middle attack [25]. The idea of the attack is that the adversary relays, during a learning phase, the communication between a close prover and a verifier, but flips one challenge c_j. The value r_j which is sent as a response to the verifier is selected at random. So, from the prover, the adversary learns the response to c_j, and by the final output of the verifier (acceptance or rejection), the adversary deduces what is the correct answer to $1 - c_j$. So, he learns the jth

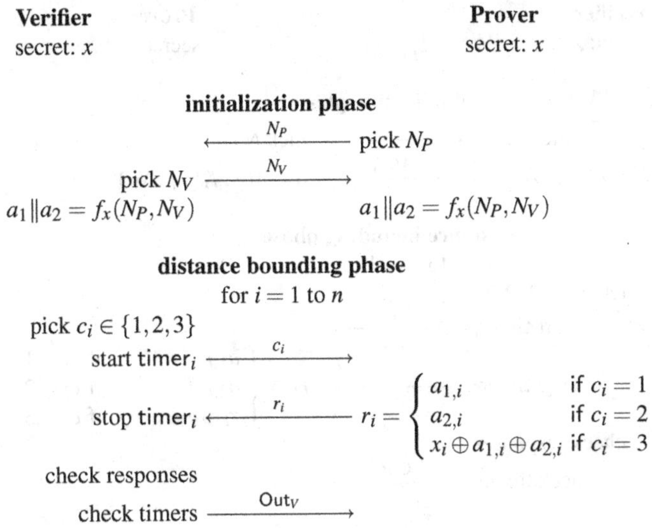

Verifier		Prover
secret: x		secret: x

initialization phase

$\xleftarrow{\quad N_P \quad}$ pick N_P

pick N_V $\xrightarrow{\quad N_V \quad}$

$a_1 \| a_2 = f_x(N_P, N_V)$ $\qquad\qquad$ $a_1 \| a_2 = f_x(N_P, N_V)$

distance bounding phase
for $i = 1$ to n

pick $c_i \in \{1, 2, 3\}$

start timer$_i$ $\xrightarrow{\quad c_i \quad}$

stop timer$_i$ $\xleftarrow{\quad r_i \quad}$ $r_i = \begin{cases} a_{1,i} & \text{if } c_i = 1 \\ a_{2,i} & \text{if } c_i = 2 \\ x_i \oplus a_{1,i} \oplus a_{2,i} & \text{if } c_i = 3 \end{cases}$

check responses

check timers $\xrightarrow{\quad \text{Out}_V \quad}$

Fig. 3. The TDB distance-bounding protocol [2]

bit of a_1 and a_2 and deduces x_j. He can repeat this for each j and infer x. Then, the attack phase just impersonates the prover to the verifier, thanks to x. Other instances of DBENC where $a_2 = a_1 \oplus x$ are replaced by addition modulo some q or addition with a random factor, can also be broken, as shown in [4].

In [28], it was suggested to replace $a_1 = f_x(N_P, N_V)$ and $a_2 = a_1 \oplus x$ by $a_1 \| a_2 = f_x(N_P, N_V)$ and a release of $(R, x \oplus h_R(a_1, a_2))$ for some random R, where h is a universal hash function. However, proving the security of such a protocol does not seem to be easy.

The problem seems more easily amended by considering the TDB protocol [2] in Fig. 3. Now, there are three possible challenges $c_i \in \{1, 2, 3\}$. The answer to 1 and to 2 consists of bits from a_1 and a_2, respectively. Both a_1 and a_2 are derived from the nonces. The answer to 3 is a bit from $a_3 = a_1 \oplus a_2 \oplus x$. The main idea is that we use a threshold secret-sharing scheme to split x_i into three shares, so that two shares alone leak no information.

The security of TDB assumes that f is a PRF. Unfortunately, this assumption alone is not enough to guarantee the security and some related security results from the literature are incorrect. Indeed, as shown in [5], we can artificially construct PRFs which make the protocol insecure. The PRF construction is done by *PRF programming*. For instance, given a PRF g, we construct a new function f defined by the following instances:

$$f_x(N_P, N_V) = \begin{cases} x \| x & \text{if } N_P = x \\ g_x(N_P, N_V) & \text{otherwise} \end{cases}$$

We can easily show that f is also a PRF [5]. When the TDB protocol is instantiated with this f, a malicious prover can mount a distance fraud by selecting

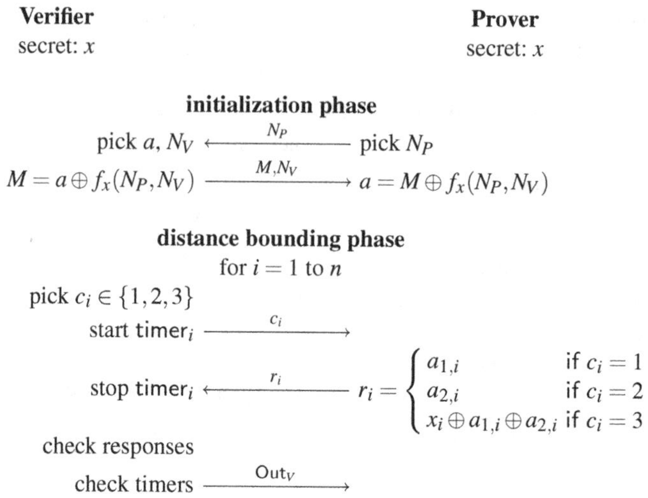

Verifier	Prover
secret: x	secret: x

initialization phase

$$\text{pick } a, N_V \xleftarrow{\quad N_P \quad} \text{pick } N_P$$

$$M = a \oplus f_x(N_P, N_V) \xrightarrow{\quad M, N_V \quad} a = M \oplus f_x(N_P, N_V)$$

distance bounding phase
for $i = 1$ to n

pick $c_i \in \{1, 2, 3\}$

$$\text{start timer}_i \xrightarrow{\quad c_i \quad}$$

$$\text{stop timer}_i \xleftarrow{\quad r_i \quad} r_i = \begin{cases} a_{1,i} & \text{if } c_i = 1 \\ a_{2,i} & \text{if } c_i = 2 \\ x_i \oplus a_{1,i} \oplus a_{2,i} & \text{if } c_i = 3 \end{cases}$$

check responses

$$\text{check timers} \xrightarrow{\quad \text{Out}_V \quad}$$

Fig. 4. The TDB distance-bounding protocol with PRF masking [5]

$N_P = x$. Indeed, we would have $a_1 = a_2 = a_3$. So, the response r_i is predicted before receiving the challenge c_i. Consequently, the prover can make sure that the response arrives on time, without even knowing c_i: he just replies before receiving c_i.

We fix this PRF-based problem by using PRF masking [5,7,8] as shown in Fig. 4. There, the vectors a are chosen by the verifier. So, the malicious prover cannot induce some properties onto a to mount distance frauds.

But, we can also mount a man-in-the-middle attack by PRF programming. Given a PRF g, we first define a predicate $\text{trapdoor}_x(\bar{\alpha}\|t) \iff t = g_x(\bar{\alpha}) \oplus \text{right\_half}(x)$. It must be hard, by playing with a g_x oracle, to construct a string satisfying this predicate. However, when playing with the prover in a learning phase, and using the challenges $c = (1, \ldots, 1, 3, \ldots, 3)$, the adversary obtains such a string $\bar{\alpha}$. We define

$$f_x(N_P, N_V) = \begin{cases} a_1\|a_2 = \alpha \| \beta \| \gamma \| \beta \oplus g_x(\alpha) & \text{if } \neg\text{trapdoor}_x(N_V) \\ & \text{where } (\alpha, \beta, \gamma) = g_x(N_P, N_V) \\ a_1\|a_2 = x\|x & \text{otherwise} \end{cases}$$

We can easily see that f is a PRF. Then, the learning phase works as follows:

1: play with P and send $c = (1, \ldots, 1, 3, \ldots, 3)$ to obtain from the responses $\bar{\alpha}\|t$ satisfying trapdoor_x
2: play with P again with $N_V = \bar{\alpha}\|t$ and get x

Based on x, the adversary can impersonate the prover.

In [5], we report other protocols which are weak, with respect to PRF programming (see Table 2).

Table 2. Protocol which can be broken by PRF programming techniques [5]

Protocol	Distance-Fraud	MIM
TDB Avoine-Lauradoux-Martin [2]	$\checkmark$	$\checkmark$
Dürholz-Fischlin-Kasper-Onete [17]	$\checkmark$	–
Hancke-Kuhn [20]	$\checkmark$	–
Avoine-Tchamkerten [3]	$\checkmark$	–
Reid-Nieto-Tang-Senadji [34]	$\checkmark$	$\checkmark$
Swiss-Knife Kim-Avoine-Koeune-Standaert-Pereira [25]	–	$\checkmark$

We do not fix this problem by primarily proposing another protocol but by firstly requiring a new security assumption on the PRF f. Indeed, we somehow require that leaking $f_x(y)$, sometimes $f_x(y) \oplus x$, and sometimes a mixture of both, does not compromise the security. More precisely, we require the (ε, T)-*circular keying* property [8]. This assumes that an adversary $\mathcal{A}$ of complexity at most T making queries of the form (y_i, a_i, b_i) to an oracle

$$y, a, b \mapsto (a \cdot x') + (b \cdot f_x(y))$$

cannot distinguish (up to an advantage ε) whether x and x' have been selected by having $x = x'$ or x and x' are independent. To make it possible, the adversary must follow the constraint that for each $i_1, \ldots, i_q, c_1, \ldots, c_q$ satisfying $y_{i_1} = \cdots = y_{i_q}$ and $\sum_{j=1}^{q} c_j b_{i_j} = 0$, we have that $\sum_{j=1}^{q} c_j a_{i_j} = 0$. As a sanity check, we prove that this notion makes sense by constructing a circular-keying secure PRF in the random oracle model [8]. Furthermore, this property excludes programmed PRFs as per mentioned before.

All the previous protocols assume that there is no noise to harm the protocol execution. However, the distance bounding phase is subject to high constraints. Indeed, an allowed error of one microsecond in the time measurement will correspond to an imprecision of 300 meters in the distance estimate, due to the speed of light. Clearly, this may not defeat relay attacks. To reach a precision of 10 meters, the prover shall not spend more than 33 nanoseconds for receiving c_i, computing r_i, and sending r_i. So, computation or transmission will eventually be subject to noise. To keep the completeness property, we need to tolerate a linear number of errors, depending on the noise level. Thus, in the following protocol (depicted on Fig. 5), only τ out of n rounds should be correct for a successful run of the protocol.

As noticed by Hancke [19], this introduces a new vulnerability to terrorist fraud. The idea of his attack is that the malicious prover will run the initialization phase, then for τ out of n values of i he will reveal the response function $c_i \mapsto r_i$ to the adversary. This will only leak τ bits of x which is not enough to impersonate the prover. Then, the adversary will be able to correctly answer τ rounds to pass the protocol. (To make the attack work, the selection of the τ out of n values of i must be fixed.)

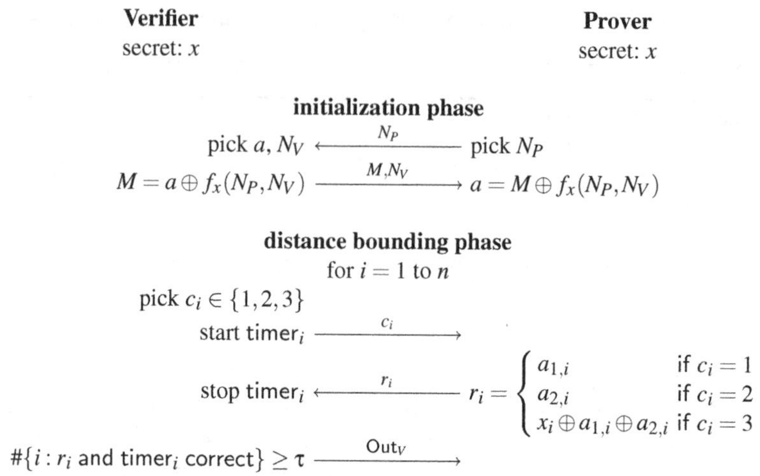

Verifier	Prover
secret: x	secret: x

initialization phase

$$\text{pick } a, N_V \xleftarrow{\quad N_P \quad} \text{pick } N_P$$

$$M = a \oplus f_x(N_P, N_V) \xrightarrow{\quad M, N_V \quad} a = M \oplus f_x(N_P, N_V)$$

distance bounding phase

for $i = 1$ to n

pick $c_i \in \{1, 2, 3\}$

$$\text{start timer}_i \xrightarrow{\quad c_i \quad}$$

$$\text{stop timer}_i \xleftarrow{\quad r_i \quad} r_i = \begin{cases} a_{1,i} & \text{if } c_i = 1 \\ a_{2,i} & \text{if } c_i = 2 \\ x_i \oplus a_{1,i} \oplus a_{2,i} & \text{if } c_i = 3 \end{cases}$$

$$\#\{i : r_i \text{ and timer}_i \text{ correct}\} \geq \tau \xrightarrow{\quad \text{Out}_V \quad}$$

Fig. 5. The TDB distance-bounding protocol with PRF masking and noise tolerance

3   The SKI Protocol

To address all previously noticed vulnerabilities, we introduce the SKI protocol.[1] This protocol appeared in [7,8]. It enjoys provable security. The protocol is depicted in Fig. 6. There, the function f must be a PRF with circular-keying security.

Given a vector μ, the linear function L_μ is defined by

$$L_\mu(x) = (\mu \cdot x, \ldots, \mu \cdot x)$$

Namely, all bits are set to the dot product between μ and x. With $x' = L_\mu(x)$, Hancke's terrorist fraud would reveal a majority of the bits of x' thus leaking $L_\mu(x)$. Since L_μ is not chosen by the prover, by repeating the attack, we can collect enough information about x to reconstruct x. So, Hancke's terrorist fraud is prevented.

We let s denote the bit-length of the secret x. I.e., it is no longer necessarily equal to n, the number of rounds.

We define the following function:

$$B(n, \tau, q) = \sum_{i=\tau}^{n} \binom{n}{i} q^i (1 - q)^{n-i}$$

To study *completeness*, we assume that there is a probability of p_{noise} that one round is incorrectly executed by honest players. The probability that an honest

---

[1] The name *SKI* comes from the first names of the authors: Serge, Katerina, and Ioana.

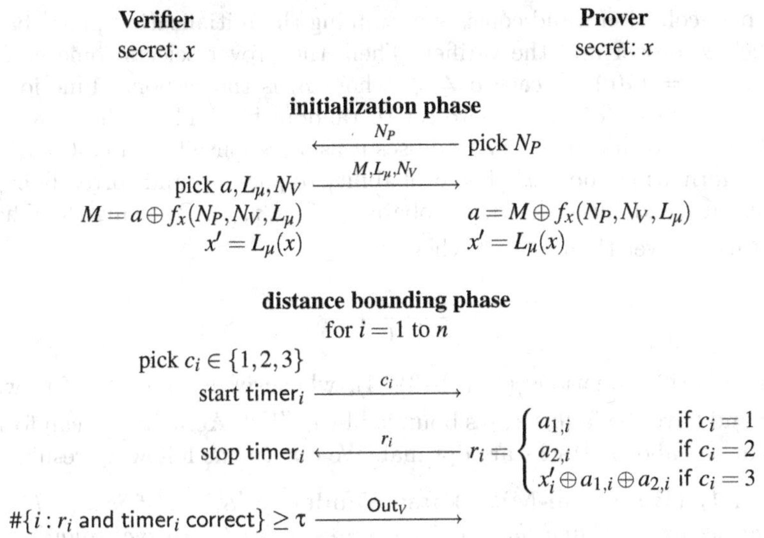

Verifier		Prover
secret: x		secret: x

initialization phase

$$\xleftarrow{\quad N_P \quad} \text{pick } N_P$$

pick a, L_μ, N_V $\xrightarrow{\quad M, L_\mu, N_V \quad}$

$M = a \oplus f_x(N_P, N_V, L_\mu)$ $\qquad a = M \oplus f_x(N_P, N_V, L_\mu)$

$x' = L_\mu(x)$ $\qquad x' = L_\mu(x)$

distance bounding phase

for $i = 1$ to n

pick $c_i \in \{1, 2, 3\}$

start timer$_i$ $\xrightarrow{\quad c_i \quad}$

stop timer$_i$ $\xleftarrow{\quad r_i \quad}$ $r_i = \begin{cases} a_{1,i} & \text{if } c_i = 1 \\ a_{2,i} & \text{if } c_i = 2 \\ x'_i \oplus a_{1,i} \oplus a_{2,i} & \text{if } c_i = 3 \end{cases}$

$\#\{i : r_i \text{ and timer}_i \text{ correct}\} \geq \tau$ $\xrightarrow{\quad \text{Out}_V \quad}$

Fig. 6. The SKI distance-bounding protocol [7,8]

prover, close to the verifier, passes the protocol is $B(n, \tau, 1 - p_{\text{noise}})$. By using the Chernoff bound [12], this is greater than $1 - e^{-2\varepsilon^2 n}$ for

$$\frac{\tau}{n} < 1 - p_{\text{noise}} - \varepsilon \tag{1}$$

We now describe the best distance fraud against SKI. The malicious prover just runs the initialization phase. During the distance-bounding phase, he anticipates the challenge c_i by sending some r_i such that r_i has the largest preimage set by the $c_i \mapsto r_i$ response function. This maximizes the chances to win. We can easily see that a single round will pass with probability $\frac{3}{4}$. So, the distance fraud succeeds with probability $B(n, \tau, \frac{3}{4})$. By using the Chernoff bound, this is lower than $e^{-2\varepsilon^2 n}$ when

$$\frac{\tau}{n} > \frac{3}{4} + \varepsilon \tag{2}$$

The best man-in-the-middle attack runs as follows: the adversary first relays messages between the prover and the verifier in the initialization phase. Then, he plays with the prover a distance-bounding phase to learn some answers. He can then play with the verifier, with the responses that he has learnt, or with random ones if he ignores the correct one. The probability to pass a round correctly is $\frac{2}{3}$. So, the man-in-the-middle attack succeeds with probability $B(n, \tau, \frac{2}{3})$. By using the Chernoff bound, this is lower than $e^{-2\varepsilon^2 n}$ when

$$\frac{\tau}{n} > \frac{2}{3} + \varepsilon \tag{3}$$

The best collusion fraud consists of running the initialization phase between the malicious prover and the verifier. Then, the prover selects some $c_1^*, \ldots, c_n^*$ and set $F_i^*(c) = F_i(c)$ for each $c \neq c_i^*$, where F_i is the response function $c_i \mapsto F_i(c_i) = r_i$. The $F_i^*(c_i^*)$ values are set to random bits. Then, the prover gives the table of F^* to the adversary who uses it as a response function. Clearly, this leaks no information about x'. The probability to pass a round correctly is $\frac{5}{6}$. So, the collusion fraud succeeds with probability $B(n, \tau, \frac{5}{6})$. By using the Chernoff bound, this is lower than $e^{-2\varepsilon^2 n}$ when

$$\frac{\tau}{n} > \frac{5}{6} + \varepsilon \tag{4}$$

To summarize equations (1)-(2)-(3)-(4), whenever $p_{\mathsf{noise}} < \frac{1}{6} - 2\varepsilon$, we can adjust τ and have the failure cases bounded by $e^{-2\varepsilon^2 n}$. Actually, we can formally prove that the above attacks are optimal. We obtain the following result.

Theorem 1. (Boureanu-Mitrokotsa-Vaudenay [8]). *If f is a (ε, T)-circular-keying secure PRF and the verifier requires at least τ correct rounds,*

- *all distance frauds (with complexity bounded by T) have a success probability bounded by $\Pr[\mathsf{success}] \geq B(n, \tau, \frac{3}{4}) + \varepsilon$;*
- *all man-in-the-middle attacks (with complexity bounded by T) have a success probability bounded by $\Pr[\mathsf{success}] \geq B(n, \tau, \frac{2}{3}) + \frac{r^2}{2}2^{-k} + \varepsilon$, where k is the nonce length and r is the number of participants in the experiment;*
- *for all collusion frauds such that $p = \Pr[\mathsf{CF\ succeeds}] \geq B(\frac{n}{2}, \tau - \frac{n}{2}, \frac{2}{3})^{1-c}$ and p^{-1} polynomially bounded, there is an associated man-in-the-middle attack with P^* such that $\Pr[\mathsf{MiM\ succeeds}] \geq \left(1 - B(\frac{n}{2}, \tau - \frac{n}{2}, \frac{2}{3})^c\right)^s$, for any c.*

Although it does not explicitly appear for distance-fraud and man-in-the-middle, we note that s plays a role in the ε anyway: if s is too small, f cannot be a secure PRF so ε cannot be negligible.

To optimize τ with respect to the expected loss in the case of a failed authentication or of an attack, we can follow the method in [16]. It requires to quantify all possible types of losses.

There exist several variants of SKI with different properties. Namely, we can consider secret sharing schemes other than the one in Fig. 6. We can consider other leakage schemes L_μ as well. We refer to [7,8] for details.

4   Conclusion

Modeling the different types of frauds for distance-bounding is not easy. When adopting an appropriate model, we can see that none of the existing distance-bounding protocols in the literature resist all frauds, with the exception of SKI. SKI is very lightweight, with several possible variants, of which herein we showed two. Under the assumption that the underlying primitive is a PRF with circular-keying security and that the level of noise in each round (in honest executions) is lower than $\frac{1}{6}$, we can achieve provable secure distance-bounding.

As future work, we will optimize the protocol to adjust the key sizes and number of rounds in an adequate way. We also leave open the problem of making a secure protocol without the $p_{\mathsf{noise}} < \frac{1}{6}$ limitation. For instance, we could try to defeat man-in-the-middle attacks in a different way than by introducing a secret sharing scheme [2]. Namely, we could use a challenge set of two elements and authenticate the received challenges at the end, as done in the Swiss-Knife protocol [25]. This way, we could reach a level of noise p_{noise} close to $\frac{1}{4}$. One problem with this option is that proving security does not seem easy and, finally, it may be weak against PRF programming [5].

Another line of research consists of adding privacy preservation. People already suggested to protect *location privacy* [33], but this suffers from severe limitations as shown in [1,27]. Anonymity could also be considered in a way similar to RFID protocols [23,32,37]. One proposal is made in [22] but without terrorist fraud protection.

Acknowledgments. We warmly thank Shiho Moriai, program chair of FSE'13, and her program committee, for inviting us to present our results on distance bounding.

This work was partially supported by

- the National Competence Center in Research on Mobile Information and Communication Systems (NCCR-MICS), under the Swiss National Science Foundation;
- the Marie Curie IEF Project Grant No. 252323 "PPIDR: Privacy-Preserving Intrusion Detection and Response in Wireless Communications".

References

1. Aumasson, J.-P., Mitrokotsa, A., Peris-Lopez, P.: A note on a privacy-preserving distance-bounding protocol. In: Qing, S., Susilo, W., Wang, G., Liu, D. (eds.) ICICS 2011. LNCS, vol. 7043, pp. 78–92. Springer, Heidelberg (2011)
2. Avoine, G., Lauradoux, C., Martin, B.: How secret-sharing can defeat terrorist fraud. In: ACM Conference on Wireless Network Security WISEC'11, Hamburg, Germany, pp. 145–156. ACM (2011)
3. Avoine, G., Tchamkerten, A.: An efficient distance bounding RFID authentication protocol: balancing false-acceptance rate and memory requirement. In: Samarati, P., Yung, M., Martinelli, F., Ardagna, C.A. (eds.) ISC 2009. LNCS, vol. 5735, pp. 250–261. Springer, Heidelberg (2009)
4. Bay, A., Boureanu, I., Mitrokotsa, A., Spulber, I., Vaudenay, S.: The Bussard-Bagga and other distance-bounding protocols under attacks. In: Kutyłowski, M., Yung, M. (eds.) Inscrypt 2012. LNCS, vol. 7763, pp. 371–391. Springer, Heidelberg (2013)
5. Boureanu, I., Mitrokotsa, A., Vaudenay, S.: On the pseudorandom function assumption in (secure) distance-bounding protocols - PRF-ness alone does not stop the frauds!. In: Hevia, A., Neven, G. (eds.) LATINCRYPT 2012. LNCS, vol. 7533, pp. 100–120. Springer, Heidelberg (2012)
6. Boureanu, I., Mitrokotsa, A., Vaudenay, S.: On the Need for Secure Distance-Bounding. In: Proceedings of ESC'13 (to appear)

7. Boureanu, I., Mitrokotsa, A., Vaudenay, S.: Secure and lightweight distance-bounding. In: Avoine, G., Kara, O. (eds.) LightSec 2013. LNCS, vol. 8162, pp. 97–113. Springer, Heidelberg (2013)

8. Boureanu, I., Mitrokotsa, A., Vaudenay, S.: Practical provably secure distance-bounding. In: Proceedings of ISC 13 (to appear)

9. Brands, S., Chaum, D.: Distance bounding protocols (extended abstract). In: Helleseth, T. (ed.) EUROCRYPT 1993. LNCS, vol. 765, pp. 344–359. Springer, Heidelberg (1994)

10. Bussard, L., Bagga, W.: Distance-Bounding Proof of Knowledge to Avoid Real-Time Attacks. In: Sasaki, R., Qing, S., Okamoto, E., Yoshiura, H. (eds.) SEC 2005. IFIP AICT, vol. 181, pp. 223–238. Springer, Heidelberg (2005)

11. Čapkun, S., Buttyán, L., Hubaux, J.P.: SECTOR: secure tracking of node encounters in multi-hop wireless networks. In: ACM Workshop on Security of Ad Hoc and Sensor Networks SASN'03, Fairfax VA, USA, pp. 21–32. ACM (2003)

12. Chernoff, H.: A measure of asymptotic efficiency for tests of a hypothesis based on the sum of observations. Ann. Math. Stat. 23(4), 493–507 (1952)

13. Cremers, C.J. F., Rasmussen, K.B., Schmidt, B., Čapkun, S.: Distance hijacking attacks on distance bounding protocols. In: IEEE Symposium on Security and Privacy S&P'12, San Francisco CA, USA, pp. 113–127. IEEE Computer Society (2012)

14. Desmedt, Y.: Major security problems with the "Unforgeable" (Feige-)Fiat-Shamir Proofs of Identity and how to overcome them. In: Congress on Computer and Communication Security and Protection Securicom'88, Paris, France, pp. 147–159. SEDEP, Paris, France (1988)

15. Drimer, S., Murdoch, S.J.: Keep your enemies close: distance bounding gainst smartcard relay attacks. In: USENIX Security Symposium, Boston MA, USA, pp. 87–102. USENIX (2007)

16. Dimitrakakis, C., Mitrokotsa, A., Vaudenay, S.: Expected loss bounds for authentication in constrained channels. In: Proceedings of the IEEE INFOCOM'12, Orlando FL, USA, pp. 478–485. IEEE (2012)

17. Dürholz, U., Fischlin, M., Kasper, M., Onete, C.: A formal approach to distance-bounding RFID protocols. In: Lai, X., Zhou, J., Li, H. (eds.) ISC 2011. LNCS, vol. 7001, pp. 47–62. Springer, Heidelberg (2011)

18. Özhan Gürel, A., Arslan, A., Akgün, M.: Non-uniform stepping approach to RFID Distance bounding problem. In: Garcia-Alfaro, J., Navarro-Arribas, G., Cavalli, A., Leneutre, J. (eds.) DPM 2010 and SETOP 2010. LNCS, vol. 6514, pp. 64–78. Springer, Heidelberg (2011)

19. Hancke, G.P.: Distance bounding for RFID: effectiveness of terrorist fraud. In: Conference on RFID-Technologies and Applications RFID-TA'12, Nice, France, pp. 91–96. IEEE (2012)

20. Hancke, G.P., Kuhn, M.G.: An RFID distance bounding protocol. In: Conference on Security and Privacy for Emerging Areas in Communications Networks SecureComm'05, Athens, Greece, pp. 67–73. IEEE (2005)

21. Hancke, G.P., Mayes, K., Markantonakis, K.: Confidence in smart token proximity: relay attacks revisited. Comput. Secur. 28, 615–627 (2009)

22. Hermans, J., Onete, C., Peeters, R.: Efficient, secure, private distance bounding without key updates. In: ACM Conference on Security and Privacy in Wireless and Mobile Networks WISEC'13, Budapest, Hungary, pp. 207–218. ACM (2013)

23. Hermans, J., Pashalidis, A., Vercauteren, F., Preneel, B.: A new RFID privacy model. In: Atluri, V., Diaz, C. (eds.) ESORICS 2011. LNCS, vol. 6879, pp. 568–587. Springer, Heidelberg (2011)

24. Kim, C.H., Avoine, G.: RFID distance bounding protocol with mixed challenges to prevent relay attacks. In: Garay, J.A., Miyaji, A., Otsuka, A. (eds.) CANS 2009. LNCS, vol. 5888, pp. 119–133. Springer, Heidelberg (2009)
25. Kim, C.H., Avoine, G., Koeune, F., Standaert, F.-X., Pereira, O.: The swiss-knife RFID distance bounding protocol. In: Lee, P.J., Cheon, J.H. (eds.) ICISC 2008. LNCS, vol. 5461, pp. 98–115. Springer, Heidelberg (2009)
26. Mitrokotsa, A., Dimitrakakis, C., Peris-Lopez, P., Hermandez-Castro, J.C.: Reid et al'.s distance bounding protocol and mafia fraud attacks over noisy channels. IEEE Commun. Lett. **14**, 121–123 (2010)
27. Mitrokotsa, A., Onete, C., Vaudenay, S.: Mafia fraud attack against the RC distance- bounding protocol. In: Conference on RFID-Technologies and Applications RFID-TA'12, Nice, France, pp. 74–79. IEEE (2012)
28. Mitrokotsa, A., Peris-Lopez, P., Dimitrakakis, C., Vaudenay, S.: On selecting the nonce length in distance-bounding protocols. To appear in the Computer Journal (Oxford), Special Issue on Advanced Semantic and Social Multimedia Technologies for Future Computing Environment (2013). doi:10.1093/comjnl/bxt033
29. Munilla, J., Peinado, A.: Distance bounding protocols for RFID enhanced by using void-challenges and analysis in noisy channels. Wirel. Commun. Mob. Comput. **8**, 1227–1232 (2008)
30. Munilla, J., Peinado, A.: Security analysis of Tu and Piramuthu's protocol. In: Conference on New Technologies, Mobility and Security NTMS'08, Tangier, Morocco, pp. 1–5. IEEE (2008)
31. Nikov, V., Vauclair, M.: Yet another secure distance-bounding protocol. In: International Conference on Security and Cryptography Porto, Portugal, pp. 218-221. INSTICC Press (2008)
32. Ouafi, K., Vaudenay, S.: Strong privacy for RFID systems from plaintext-aware encryption. In: Pieprzyk, J., Sadeghi, A.-R., Manulis, M. (eds.) CANS 2012. LNCS, vol. 7712, pp. 247–262. Springer, Heidelberg (2012)
33. Rasmussen, K.B., Capkun, S.: Location privacy of distance bounding protocols. In: 15th ACM Conference on Computer and Communications Security, Alexandria VA, USA, pp. 149–160. ACM Press (2008)
34. Reid, J., Nieto, J.M.G., Tang, T., Senadji, B.: Detecting Relay Attacks with Timing-Based Protocols. In: ACM Symposium on Information, Computer and Communications Security ASIACCS'07, Singapore, pp. 204–213. ACM (2007)
35. Singelée, D., Preneel, B.: Distance bounding in noisy environments. In: Stajano, F., Meadows, C., Capkun, S., Moore, T. (eds.) ESAS 2007. LNCS, vol. 4572, pp. 101–115. Springer, Heidelberg (2007)
36. Tu, Y.J., Piramuthu, S.: RFID distance bounding protocols. In: EURASIP Workshop on RFID Technology, Vienna, Austria (2007)
37. Vaudenay, S.: On privacy models for RFID. In: Kurosawa, K. (ed.) ASIACRYPT 2007. LNCS, vol. 4833, pp. 68–87. Springer, Heidelberg (2007)

Lightweight Block Ciphers

Reflection Cryptanalysis
of PRINCE-Like Ciphers

Hadi Soleimany[1]([✉]), Céline Blondeau[1], Xiaoli Yu[2,3], Wenling Wu[2],
Kaisa Nyberg[1], Huiling Zhang[2], Lei Zhang[2], and Yanfeng Wang[2]

[1] Department of Information and Computer Science,
Aalto University School of Science, Espoo, Finland
{hadi.soleimany,celine.blondeau}@aalto.fi
[2] TCA, Institute of Software, Chinese Academy of Sciences,
Beijing, People's Republic of China
[3] Graduate University of Chinese Academy of Sciences,
Beijing, People's Republic of China
{yuxiaoli,wwl}@is.iscas.ac.cn

Abstract. PRINCE is a low-latency block cipher presented at ASIACRYPT 2012. The cipher was designed with a property called α-reflection which reduces the definition of the decryption with a given key to an encryption with a different but related key determined by α. In the design document, it was shown that PRINCE is secure against known attacks independently of the value of α, and the design criteria for α remained open.

In this paper, we introduce new generic distinguishers on PRINCE-like ciphers. First, we show that, by folding the cipher in the middle, the number of rounds can be halved due to the α-reflection property. Furthermore, we investigate many classes of α and find the best differential characteristic for the folded cipher. For such α there exist an efficient key-recovery attack on the full 12-round cipher with the data complexity of $2^{57.98}$ known plaintexts and time complexity of $2^{72.39}$ encryptions. With the original value of α we can attack a reduced six-round version of PRINCE. As a result of the new cryptanalysis method presented in this paper, new design criteria concerning the selection of the value of α for PRINCE-like ciphers are obtained.

Keywords: Block cipher · α-reflection property · PRINCE · Statistical attack · Reflection attack

1 Introduction

Recently, important applications in special constrained environments such as RFID tags and sensors have received a lot of attention by the cryptographic community. The new secure primitives should provide the best security possible while under tight constraints. Traditionally, cryptographic algorithms have been designed with large security margin to be on the secure side even when exposed

S. Moriai (Ed.): FSE 2013, LNCS 8424, pp. 71–91, 2014.
DOI: 10.1007/978-3-662-43933-3_5, © Springer-Verlag Berlin Heidelberg 2014

to new and unknown vulnerabilities. Since lightweight ciphers must be as small and power-efficient as possible, it is of utmost importance to analyze and understand the security of cryptographic designs to reduce the superfluous margins. New innovative and unconventional designs pose new challenges. For instance, to reduce the power consumption of the encryption algorithm, new cipher proposals, such as PRINTcipher [7] and LED [5] with very simple key-schedule or even without key-schedule, have been developed. With the emergence of such constructions, new attacks have emerged.

PRINCE is a low-latency block cipher proposed at ASIACRYPT 2012 [2]. In order to reduce the cost of implementation of decryption, this iterated cipher uses a property called α-reflection. As the key-schedule of the encryption is almost non-existent, the round constants play crucial role in preventing self-similarity attacks like slide attacks. The α-reflection property is built in the cipher by selecting the round constants in pairs. The constants that form a pair have a difference equal to α, and if one of them is used on round r then the other one is used on round $2R - r + 1$, where $r = 1, 2, \ldots, 2R$, and $2R$ is the total number of rounds of the cipher. As the round functions at round r and $2R - r + 1$, $r < R$, are selected to be inverses of each other, it follows that decryption with round key K is identical to encryption with round key $K \oplus \alpha$.

In the original proposal, the security of PRINCE and the effects of the α-reflection were studied extensively. In particular, it was shown that the cipher is secure against known attacks with reasonable security margin. For instance, it was shown that any differential or linear characteristic over 4 consecutive rounds has at least 16 active S-boxes. This holds independently of the selection of the non-zero parameter α.

In this paper, we study PRINCE in a more general setting of PRINCE-like ciphers by allowing freedom in the selection of the value of α and of some other components of the cipher. We identify new types of relations over the cipher, and show that they can be used as distinguishers over PRINCE, but that their effectivity depends crucially on the properties of α. We call these new relations *reflection characteristics*. They are constructed by feeding input data of round r, $r \leq R$, forward over $2(R - r + 1)$ rounds and comparing it with the corresponding output data of round $2R - r + 1$ by exclusive-or differences. We investigate distributions of these reflection differences. Their non-uniformity properties crucially depend on the relationships between the differential properties of the round function, fixed points of the middle linear layer and the reflection parameter α.

The starting point of the reflection cryptanalysis is a probabilistic relation on the middle rounds of the cipher. The extracted relations starting from the middle of the cipher share some similarities with some attacks on Feistel ciphers. Self-similarity properties can be used to determine classes of weak keys as for instance for the DES [8]. The reflection attack [6] and its modifications for hash functions [3] take advantage of involution properties when classes of fixed points exist in some intermediate rounds. In this paper, the involution property is replaced by the α-reflection property, and the resulting reflection characteristics are not necessarily deterministic, but evaluated in terms of differential probabilities. The resulting attacks require known plaintext only.

In sharp contrast to differential and linear characteristics on PRINCE-like ciphers, the number of active S-boxes in a reflection characteristic strongly depends on the value of α. In particular, we show that for some values of α the key-recovery attack using reflection characteristic works for the full cipher. We present a known-plaintext single-key attack with the data complexity of $2^{57.95}$ plaintexts and time complexity of $2^{72.37}$. For the original α specified in [2], the key recovery attack using a reflection distinguisher found in this paper breaks reduced-round versions of the cipher only up to 6 rounds and hence does not threaten the security of full 12-round version of PRINCE. Nevertheless, we believe that the introduction of the new distinguishers will shed light on the security of PRINCE-like ciphers and can be taken into consideration when designing ciphers according to the model of PRINCE.

The paper is organized as follows. In Sect. 2, we define a family of ciphers called PRINCE-like ciphers. In Sect. 3, different characteristics for the ciphers in this family are described and their probabilities determined. Concatenations of these characteristics are also studied in order to provide characteristics on a larger number of rounds. In Sect. 4, we show how reflection characteristics over $2R - 2$ rounds of the cipher can be converted to distinguishers and used for key recovery attacks on the full $2R$ rounds of the cipher. In Sect. 5, we evaluate the complexity of the best reflection attacks and identify classes of the weakest α using the original S-layer and M-layer of PRINCE.

2   Brief Description of PRINCE

Distinguishers and attacks presented in this paper focus not only on the original PRINCE but are more general and can be applied to all ciphers with similar reflection structure. To this aim, let us start by describing what we call a PRINCE-like cipher.

2.1   PRINCE-Like Cipher

A PRINCE-like cipher encrypts messages of n-bit blocks by iterating $2R$ times a round function. We denote by E_k^α the encryption function parametrized with a $2n$-bit key $k = (k_0||k_1) \in \mathbb{F}_2^{2n}$ and the reflection parameter $\alpha \in \mathbb{F}_2^{n*}$.

The key schedule of a PRINCE-like cipher is simple. The $2n$-bit key is split into two n-bit parts k_0 and k_1. From k_0, a key k_0' is derived using a rotation and a shift as follows

$$k_0' = (k_0 \ggg 1) \oplus (k_0 \gg (n - 1)). \tag{1}$$

The keys k_0 and k_0' are used as whitening keys in the encryption operation that follows the FX structure. The n-bit key k_1 is added to the state in the $2R$ rounds of the cipher.

The core function $G_{k_1}^\alpha$ of this cipher (denoted by PRINCE$_{core}$ in the original proposal) is defined as an iteration of the $2R$ rounds. To keep it as general as possible, we assume that we have a non-linear S-layer composed of a set of parallel Sboxes and two different linear layers, defined by $n \times n$ matrices M' and M, where M' is an involution matrix.

The first $R - 1$ rounds $\mathfrak{R}_r : \mathbb{F}_2^n \to \mathbb{F}_2^n$, $1 \leq r \leq R - 1$, are identical and are composed (in this order) of addition of the round constant RC_r and the key k_1, the non-linear layer S and the linear permutation layer M. The $R-1$ last rounds $\mathfrak{R}_r : \mathbb{F}_2^n \to \mathbb{F}_2^n$, $R + 2 \leq r \leq 2R$ are, in the reverse order, equal to inverses of the first $R - 1$ rounds except that the round constants are modified by α so that the following holds:

$$RC_{2R-r+1} = RC_r \oplus \alpha, \text{ for all } r = 1, \ldots, 2R. \tag{2}$$

We call these rounds with $r \leq R - 1$ or $r \geq R + 2$ the external rounds of the PRINCE-like cipher.

The symmetry is broken by specifying the two middle rounds R and $R+1$ to be different from each other and from the external rounds. Below we summarize the definitions for all rounds.

$$
\begin{aligned}
\mathfrak{R}_r(x) &= M(S(x \oplus RC_r \oplus k_1)) && \text{if } 1 \leq r \leq R - 1 \\
\mathfrak{R}_r(x) &= M'(S(x \oplus RC_r \oplus k_1)) && \text{if } r = R \\
\mathfrak{R}_r(x) &= S^{-1}(x) \oplus RC_r \oplus k_1 && \text{if } r = R + 1 \\
\mathfrak{R}_r(x) &= S^{-1}(M^{-1}(x)) \oplus RC_r \oplus k_1 && \text{if } R + 2 \leq r \leq 2R
\end{aligned}
\tag{3}
$$

The function $G_{k_1}^{\alpha}(x)$ is then defined as the composition of these $2R$ round functions. The structure of the cipher is depicted in Fig. 1. The family of PRINCE-like ciphers have been designed, like for the original cipher, such that decryption can be obtained from encryption with a different key. If we denote by P a plaintext, the corresponding ciphertext is computed as $C = E_k^{\alpha}(P)$ with $k = (k_0||k_0'||k_1)$. Decryption of C can be obtained by computing the encryption over a related key: $D_k^{\alpha}(C) = E_{k'}^{\alpha}(C)$ with $k' = (k_0'||k_0||k_1 \oplus \alpha)$.

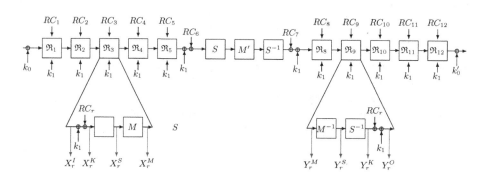

Fig. 1. Description of a $2R = 12$ rounds PRINCE-like cipher

2.2   Description of PRINCE

The full specification of PRINCE is given in [2]. It is a PRINCE-like cipher with $n = 64$ and $R = 6$. The reflection constant is defined as $\alpha = \text{C0AC29B7C97C50DD}$. The function $G_{k_1}^{\alpha}$ is called PRINCE$_{core}$. The S-layer is a non-linear layer where each nibble is processed by the same Sbox. The action of this Sbox is given in Table 5, in Appendix A.1. To construct the linear layers, first two 16×16 binary involution matrices $\hat{M}_0, \hat{M}_1$ are defined. Definition of these components can be found in Appendix A.1. Then the 64×64 block diagonal matrix M' is generated by setting its diagonal equal to $(\hat{M}_0, \hat{M}_1, \hat{M}_1, \hat{M}_0)$. Then M' is an involution. The second linear matrix M for PRINCE is obtained by composition of M' and a permutation SR of nibbles by setting $M = SR \circ M'$. The permutation SR is analogous to the AES shift row operation, but instead of bytes, it operates on nibbles.

Definition of the original round constants can be found in [2]. Exact values of these round constants are not used in the analysis presented in this paper. However, our attacks exploit the α-reflection of the round constants RC_r, $r = 1, \ldots, 12$, given in (2).

The description of the round functions given in Sect. 2.1 differs slightly from the original. Nevertheless, it is easy to see that both descriptions are equivalent.

3   Distinguishers for PRINCE-Like Ciphers

In this section, different reflection characteristics on PRINCE-like ciphers are constructed and investigated. The necessary notations for describing these characteristics are depicted in Fig. 1 and explained next in more detail.

Given the round number r, $1 \leq r \leq R$, we denote by X_r^I the input state of the round number r, and by X_r^K, X_r^S and X_r^M, the states *after* the key and round constant addition, the S-layer, and the M-layer, respectively. In order to exploit the symmetry of the cipher, we give different definitions for $R + 1 \leq r \leq 2R$. For these rounds, we denote by Y_r^O the output state of the round number r, and by Y_r^K, Y_r^S and Y_r^M, the states *before* the key and round constant addition, the S-layer, and the M-layer, respectively.

To build a distinguisher on a PRINCE-like cipher, we introduce two types of characteristics. First we focus on the middle rounds of the cipher which are different from the external ones. Characteristics on the middle rounds depend on the property of the matrix M'. Then by using a folded view of the cipher and the α-reflection property, we extend these characteristics to the external rounds of the cipher.

3.1   Characteristics on the Middle Rounds

We identify two kinds of characteristics on 2 or 4 middle rounds of the cipher. The first characteristic on the 2 midmost rounds is independent of the reflection parameter. The second one is defined on 4 rounds and extends over one round before and one round after the midmost rounds. It behaves differently depending of the reflection parameter. Probability of both of these characteristics is related to the number of fixed points of the matrix M'.

Definition 1. *Let $f : A \to A$ be a function on a set A. A point $x \in A$ is called a fixed point of the function f if and only if $f(x) = x$.*

In [2] it is stated based on the result of [4] that the number of fixed points of an involution $f : \mathbb{F}_2^n \to \mathbb{F}_2^n$ is on the average equal to $2^{n/2}$. While the result of [4] holds in general, restricting to the case of linear involutions f over $\mathbb{F}_2$ gives the following result.

Lemma 1. *Let $f : \mathbb{F}_2^n \to \mathbb{F}_2^n$ be a linear involution. Then the number of fixed points of f is greater than or equal to $2^{n/2}$.*

Proof. Let us denote $B = f \oplus I$, where I is the $n \times n$ identity matrix over $\mathbb{F}_2$. Then $B^2 = 0$, which means that $\mathrm{Im}(B) \subset \mathrm{Ker}(B)$. As $\dim(\mathrm{Ker}(B)) + \dim(\mathrm{Im}(B)) = n$, we have $\dim(\mathrm{Ker}(B)) \geq \frac{n}{2}$. As $\mathrm{Ker}(B)$ is the set of fixed points of f, the claim follows.

In what follows, we denote by $F_{M'}$, the set of fixed points of the matrix M' and by $|F_{M'}|$ the size of this set, which by Lemma 1 is larger than or equal to $2^{n/2}$.

Characteristic $\mathcal{I}_1$. The characteristic

$$Y_{R+1}^O \oplus X_R^I = \alpha$$

over two rounds $\mathfrak{R}_{R+1} \circ \mathfrak{R}_R$ of a PRINCE-like cipher holds with probability

$$\mathcal{P}_{\mathcal{I}_1} = \mathcal{P}_{F_{M'}} = \frac{|F_{M'}|}{2^n}.$$

Characteristic $\mathcal{I}_1$ is depicted in Fig. 2(a). By Lemma 1 we have that $\mathcal{P}_{\mathcal{I}_1} \geq 2^{-n/2}$. As the matrix M' of PRINCE has exactly $2^{32} = 2^{n/2}$ fixed points, it minimizes the probability of characteristic $\mathcal{I}_1$.

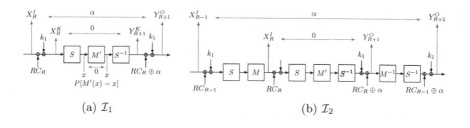

(a) $\mathcal{I}_1$ (b) $\mathcal{I}_2$

Fig. 2. Middle-round characteristics

Characteristic $\mathcal{I}_2$. The characteristic

$$Y^O_{R+2} \oplus X^I_{R-1} = \alpha$$

over four rounds $\mathfrak{R}_{R+2} \circ \mathfrak{R}_{R+1} \circ \mathfrak{R}_R \circ \mathfrak{R}_{R-1}$ of a PRINCE-like cipher holds with probability

$$\mathcal{P}_{\mathcal{I}_2} = 2^{-n} \# \left\{ x \in \mathbb{F}_2^n \mid S^{-1}\left(M'(S(x))\right) \oplus x = \alpha \right\}.$$

Characteristic $\mathcal{I}_2$ is depicted in Fig. 2(b). Next we show that $\mathcal{P}_{\mathcal{I}_2}$ can be computed efficiently. We write

$$\mathcal{P}_{\mathcal{I}_2} = 2^{-n} \sum_{\Delta \in \mathbb{F}_2^n} \# \left\{ x \in \mathbb{F}_2^n \mid M'(S(x)) \oplus S(x) = \Delta, S(x \oplus \alpha) \oplus S(x) = \Delta \right\}.$$

The set on the right hand side of the equality is not empty only if $\Delta \in \mathrm{Im}(M' \oplus I)$. We then deduce as in the proof of Lemma 1 that $\Delta \in F_{M'}$, and obtain

$$\mathcal{P}_{\mathcal{I}_2} = 2^{-n} \sum_{\Delta \in F_{M'}} \# \{ x \in \mathbb{F}_2^n \mid M'(S(x)) \oplus S(x) = \Delta, S(x \oplus \alpha) \oplus S(x) = \Delta \}.$$

Assuming that the fixed point properties of M' and differential properties of S are independent we obtain

$$\mathcal{P}_{\mathcal{I}_2} \approx \mathcal{P}_{F_{M'}} \sum_{\Delta \in F_{M'}} \mathrm{Pr}_{\mathbf{X}} \left[S(\mathbf{X}) \oplus S(\mathbf{X} \oplus \alpha)) = \Delta \right]. \qquad (4)$$

The exact expression of the probability can be efficiently evaluated as the summation is taken over the fixed points only. In the case where M' is a block-diagonal matrix, the probability $\mathcal{P}_{\mathcal{I}_2}$ can be computed by decomposing the probabilities over the different blocks, and will be shown in detail in the case of PRINCE in Sect. 5.

This characteristic is useful for building a distinguisher if $\mathcal{P}_{\mathcal{I}_2} > 2^{-n}$. But depending on M' and the value of α, it is also possible that $\mathcal{P}_{\mathcal{I}_2} = 0$. In this case we get an *impossible reflection characteristic*. We will show in Sect. 4.2 how characteristic $\mathcal{I}_2$, even if impossible, can be used for a distinguisher. Such a situation occurs if $S(x \oplus \alpha) \oplus S(x)$ is never equal to a fixed point of M'.

3.2   External Characteristic

When the probabilities $\mathcal{P}_{\mathcal{I}_1}$ and $\mathcal{P}_{\mathcal{I}_2}$ are large, it is useful to extend the characteristics $\mathcal{I}_1$ and $\mathcal{I}_2$ to more rounds. In what follows, we denote these characteristics by $\mathcal{I}_v$, $v = 1, 2$. The structure of PRINCE-like ciphers is such that the first and the last external rounds are symmetrical. One of the main ideas in this paper is to use this specific property to extend the distinguishers $\mathcal{I}_v$, which cover $2v$ middle rounds, to external rounds. This idea is illustrated in Fig. 3, which gives another view of the cipher. In this representation, the $2R$-round cipher can be viewed as composed of two parallel copies of a $(R - v)$-round cipher connected together by $2v$ rounds. Then characteristics on $2u$ external rounds, $1 \le u \le R-v$, are built as ordinary related key differential characteristics with input data difference equal to α and the key difference or round constant difference equal to α.

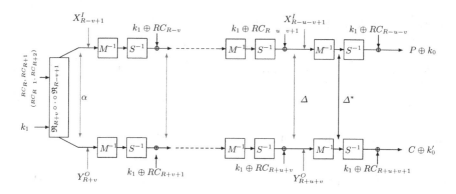

Fig. 3. A folded view of a PRINCE-like cipher: the external characteristic

Characteristic $\mathcal{C}_u$. Suppose that the characteristic $Y^O_{R+v} \oplus X^I_{R-v+1} = \alpha$ holds. The characteristic

$$Y^O_{R+u+v} \oplus X^I_{R-u-v+1} = \Delta$$

on the $2u$ external rounds is denoted by $\mathcal{C}_u$. It holds with probability

$$\mathcal{P}_{\mathcal{C}_v} = \text{Pr}_{\mathbf{X}} \left[F^u_0(x) \oplus F^u_\alpha(x \oplus \alpha) = \Delta \right],$$

where $F^u_0 = \mathfrak{R}^{-1}_{R-v-u+1} \circ \cdots \circ \mathfrak{R}^{-1}_{R-v}$ and $F^u_\alpha = \mathfrak{R}^{-1}_{R+v+u} \circ \cdots \circ \mathfrak{R}^{-1}_{R+v+1}$.

The probability of this characteristic can be computed by using techniques similar to the ones used in classical differential cryptanalysis. In particular, using the Branch and Bound algorithm, it is possible to find the best characteristics for a fixed reflection parameter α. Description of this method for PRINCE is detailed in Sect. 5.

In comparison with differential cryptanalysis, the characteristic $\mathcal{C}_u$ benefits from the related constant α. Similarly to related key differential attacks, zero differences between states are possible. Then two parallel rounds, say $\mathfrak{R}_{R-z+1}$ and $\mathfrak{R}_{R+z}$, can for some characteristics be passed with probability equal to 1. This happens when the data difference is cancelled by the key or round constant difference. Examples of such situations will be given in Sect. 5. Even when the difference is non-zero, two rounds of the cipher can be passed at the cost of one non-linear layer, where the classical differential cryptanalysis on PRINCE-like ciphers must consider differential probabilities over two non-linear layers.

Distinguishers over several rounds of the cipher, can then be built using a combination of the external characteristic $\mathcal{C}_u$ with $\mathcal{I}_v$, $v = 1, 2$. If $\mathcal{P}_{\mathcal{I}_v} \times \mathcal{P}_{\mathcal{C}_u} > 2^{-n}$, then $2v + 2u$ rounds of the cipher are distinguishable from random. In Sect. 5 we identify classes of parameters α such that 4, 6, 8 and 10 rounds of a PRINCE-like cipher can be distinguished from random.

4   Key Recovery

The characteristics constructed in the previous section can be used to build either a probabilistic or a deterministic distinguisher. The combination of $\mathcal{I}_v$

and $\mathcal{C}_u$ gives a *probabilistic reflection distinguisher*. Then the relation

$$Y^O_{R+i} \oplus X^I_{R-i+1} = \Delta, \tag{5}$$

for some $i = u + v$, holds with a positive probability p.

A deterministic distinguisher over 4 rounds exists for those values of α such that $\mathcal{P}_{\mathcal{I}_2} = 0$. Then we have an *impossible reflection distinguisher* such that the relation

$$Y^O_{R+2} \oplus X^I_{R-1} \neq \alpha, \tag{6}$$

holds with probability 1.

In this section we describe how to convert these distinguishers on $2i$ rounds to a key recovery attack on a cipher of $2R = 2i + 2$ rounds.

4.1   Probabilistic Reflection Setting

Assuming a probabilistic distinguisher on $2i$ rounds of a PRINCE-like cipher as described in Sect. 3, a key recovery attack can be derived by counting the number of plaintext-ciphertext pairs such that the difference between X^I_2 and Y^O_{2i+1} is equal to Δ.

In what follows, we denote by 2^m the data complexity of the attack. This value can be computed using Algorithm 1 of [1]. If we denote by a the advantage of this attack, the corresponding false alarm probability is $p_{\text{fa}} = 2^{-a}$.

Key Recovery Attack for $2R = 2i + 2$ Rounds. Let us assume that a characteristic $Y^O_{2i+1} \oplus X^I_2 = \Delta$ over the midmost $2i$ rounds holds with probability p, $0 < p \leq 1$. Without modification of the probability, this characteristic can be extended in both sides over linear layer M^{-1} to obtain a characteristic $Y^S_{2i+2} \oplus X^S_1 = M^{-1}(\Delta) = \Delta^*$ depicted in Fig. 4.

To find the values of X^S_1 and Y^S_{2i+2} for all pairs (P, C), the whole key $(k_0\|k_1)$ needs to be guessed. The procedure makes use of the word-oriented structure of the non-linear layer. We assume that the S-layer is nibble-oriented like in the original PRINCE.

We present the n-bit state with $n/4$ nibbles and number them from 1 to $n/4$. The j-th nibble of any n-bit word X is denoted by $X(j)$. The complexity of the attack depends of the number of non-zero nibbles of Δ^*. In what follows, we denote by $w(\Delta^*)$, the number of non-zero nibbles of the difference Δ^*.

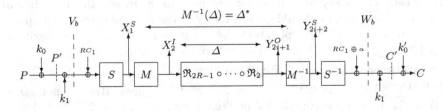

Fig. 4. Key recovery principle when $2R = 2i + 2$

As depicted in Fig. 4, the following property holds for all $1 \leq j \leq n/4$:

$$\Delta^*(j) = S\big(P(j) \oplus k_0(j) \oplus k_1(j) \oplus RC_1(j)\big) \oplus S\big(C(j) \oplus k_0'(j) \oplus k_1(j) \oplus RC_{2R}(j)\big).$$

We denote the number of nibbles of Δ^* that are equal to zero by $\ell = n/4 - w(\Delta^*)$. Indices of these nibbles are stored in a list L. Hence $|L| = \ell$. Then the property

$$P(j) \oplus k_0(j) \oplus C(j) \oplus k_0'(j) \oplus \alpha(j) = 0,$$

holds for all $j \in L$, and can be used to reduce the time complexity of the attack. For these nibbles, the value of $k_1(j)$ need not be guessed. Guessing $k_0 \oplus k_0'$ and computing $P(j) \oplus k_0(j) \oplus C(j) \oplus k_0'(j)$ allows us to discard already a large number of (P, C) pairs.

Let us assume that the attacker has 2^m plaintexts with corresponding ciphertexts. Then the attack proceeds as follows:

1. For $2^{4\ell}$ values of K_0 such that $K_0(j) = k_0(j) \oplus k_0'(j)$ holds for all $j \in L$
   1.0 Take all 2^m plaintext ciphertext pairs
   1.1 For all $j \in L$
        Among the remaining pairs discard the ones such that
        $P(j) \oplus C(j) \oplus K_0(j) \oplus \alpha(j) \neq 0$.
   1.2 For $2^{4w(\Delta^*)} = 2^{n-4\ell}$ values of K_1 such that $K_1(j) = k_0(j) \oplus k_1(j)$ holds
        for all $j \notin L$ and for all $2^{n-4\ell}$ completions of K_0
        1.2.1 For all $j \notin L$
              Compute $K_1'(j) = K_0(j) \oplus K_1(j) = k_0'(j) \oplus k_1(j)$
              Among the remaining pairs discard the ones such that
              $S(P(j) \oplus K_1(j) \oplus RC_1(j)) \oplus S(C(j) \oplus K_1'(j) \oplus RC_{2R}(j)) \neq \Delta^*(j)$.
        1.2.2 Count the number of remaining pairs.
              Store this number to a counter indexed by $(K_0 \| K_1)$.
2. Keep a list of $(K_0 \| K_1)$ ordered according to the counter values with the highest value on top. Compute the corresponding keys k_0 from K_0 according to the key expansion. Also compute $k_1(j)$ for $j \notin L$.
3. For the $2^{2n-4\ell-a}$ top candidates of k_0 on the list and the $2^{4\ell}$ remaining bits of k_1, do an exhaustive search to find the whole key $(k_0 \| k_1)$.

For each j in Step 1.1, only 4 bits out of $2^{4\ell}$ of key K_0 are involved. The first time we do this loop, we have to check the equality of 2^m plaintexts, among which 2^{m-4} pairs are expected to remain. After z iterations of the loop in Step 1.1, for each $4z - 4$ key bits guessed in the previous steps and the 4 key bits of the current iteration, we should guess a nibble of the key and check the property for all remaining $2^{m-4(z-1)}$ plaintext-ciphertext pairs. The time complexity of Step 1.1 is $\sum_{z=1}^{\ell} 2^{m-4z+4} \cdot 2^{4z} = \ell \cdot 2^{m+4}$ simple operations.

Using the same arguments, Step 1.2 is iterated $2^{4\ell} \sum_{z=\ell+1}^{n/4} 2^{m-4z+4} \cdot 2^{8(z-\ell)} = 2^{m-4\ell+4} \sum_{z=\ell+1}^{n/4} 2^{4z} \simeq 2^{m+n+4-4\ell} = 2^{m+4w(\Delta^*)+4}$ times. If we denote $\omega = w(\Delta^*)$, the total time complexity of Step 1 corresponds to $2^{m+4\omega+4}$ double S-box evaluations, which is equivalent to $\frac{2^{m+5+4\omega}}{(n/4)\cdot(2R)} = \frac{2^{m+6+4\omega}}{n \cdot R}$ full encryptions.

Step 3 corresponds to 2^{2n-a} full encryptions, where $0 \leq a \leq 2n - 4\ell$. Step 2, is negligible compared to Step 1 and 3 and the total complexity of the algorithm is $2^{2n-a} + \frac{1}{n \cdot R} \times 2^{m+6+4w(\Delta^*)}$ full encryptions. When the advantage is large, the second term dominates.

To perform the described attack, storage of the 2^m plaintext-ciphertext pairs is necessary, as well as storage of all the 2^{2n-l} counters, one per guessed key. Nevertheless, the memory complexity can be reduced by keeping only keys for which the number of remaining pairs is above some fixed bound.

4.2   Impossible Reflection Setting

In this attack we make use of $\mathcal{I}_2$ and assume that the parameter α is such that $\mathcal{I}_2$ holds with probability equal to zero. Then a deterministic reflection distinguisher with probability equal to one can be built. A guessed key can be discarded if it gives a data pair such that the difference is equal to α.

Key Recovery for $2R = 2i + 2$ Rounds. In the case of $\mathcal{I}_2$ we have $i = 2$, but the attack works for any i, if an impossible characteristic over $2i$ rounds can be built. To reduce the time complexity, we precompute certain values from the states of the second round and the second to last round of the cipher. We denote by $P' = P \oplus k_0$ and $C' = C \oplus k'_0$ the states after modification of the plaintext and ciphertext by the whitening keys. For all $0 \leq b \leq 2^n - 1$, we denote by (V_b, W_b) the following values:

$$V_b = S^{-1}(b) \oplus RC_1,$$
$$W_b = S^{-1}(b \oplus M^{-1}(\alpha)) \oplus RC_{2R}. \tag{7}$$

Then, as depicted in Fig. 4, the following properties hold for the pairs (P', C') and the corresponding (V_b, W_b):

$$P' \oplus V_b = k_1,$$
$$P' \oplus C' = V_b \oplus W_b.$$

Assume again we have 2^m known pairs (P, C) of plaintexts with corresponding ciphertexts. The goal is to find for as many key candidates k_1 as possible a (P', C') such that $(P' \oplus k_1, C' \oplus k_1)$ is equal to some pair (V_b, W_b). Then we can conclude that the key k_1 is a wrong key and discard it. After pre-computation, the attack works as follows.

Attack Procedure when (k_0, k'_0) is known

1. Consider a list of all keys k_1.
2. For each 2^m pairs (P', C')
   Compute $\Lambda = P' \oplus C'$.
   For all V_b in the row Λ in the hash table T compute the value $k_1 = P' \oplus V_b$ and discard it from the list.

3. If there is still a key in the list of key k_1, consider $k = (k_0||k_1)$ as a key candidate.

On average, there is one V_b in each row of T. So by using 2^m known plaintexts and by considering the collisions, the number of remaining wrong keys k_1 is about $2^n(1 - 2^{-n})^{2^m} = 2^n(1 - 2^{-n})^{2^n 2^{m-n}} \approx 2^n e^{-2^{m-n}} = 2^{n-1.44 \times 2^{m-n}}$, for each fixed k_0. The remaining keys are then searched exhaustively.

The impossible characteristic $\mathcal{I}_2$ holds for the involution matrix M', the non-linear layer S and the reflection parameter value α specified for the original PRINCE. In Sect. 5.4, many more such values of α are shown to exist. For all these α, by using the full codebook, the right key can be found after $2^{126.56}$ encryptions. In total 2^{67} bytes are necessary for the storage of the hash table. Considering only PRINCE$_{core}$, using the full codebook, the right key k_1 can be found after $2^{62.56}$ encryptions.

5   Various Classes of α-Reflection

In [2], the security of PRINCE and the effects of the α-reflection were studied extensively. In particular, it was shown that the cipher is secure against known attacks with reasonable security margin. For instance, it was shown that any differential or linear characteristic over 4 consecutive rounds has at least 16 active Sboxes. This holds independently of the selection of the non-zero parameter α.

In this section, we focus on a sub-family of PRINCE-like ciphers using the same S-layer and the same linear layers M and M' as in the original PRINCE. Definition of these components as given in [2] are recalled in Sect. A.1. We compute the probabilities $\mathcal{P}_{\mathcal{I}_1}$, $\mathcal{P}_{\mathcal{I}_2}$, and $\mathcal{P}_{\mathcal{C}_u}$ ($1 \leq u \leq 4$) of the distinguishers proposed in Sect. 3, for various classes of values of α. Then we use these distinguishers for key-recovery attacks on PRINCE presented in Sect. 4, determine the maximum number of rounds that can be attacked, and give complexities of these attacks. The key-recovery attacks in Sect. 4, can be modified to apply on PRINCE$_{core}$, in which case their complexities will be reduced. We will give these complexities for comparison, but omit the descriptions of the actual attacks on PRINCE$_{core}$ due to lack of space.

5.1   Probability of the Characteristics: Computation

The difference between $\mathcal{I}_1$ and $\mathcal{I}_2$ is noticeable, since the probability of the former is independent of the value of α, which is not the case for $\mathcal{I}_2$ on the 4 midmost rounds. Next we describe how to compute the probability of these characteristics for PRINCE.

Characteristic $\mathcal{I}_1$. The involution matrix M' of the original PRINCE is such that $|F'_M| = 2^{32}$. The probability of the characteristic $\mathcal{I}_1$ is then $\mathcal{P}_{\mathcal{I}_1} = \frac{2^{32}}{2^{64}} = 2^{-32}$.

Characteristic $\mathcal{I}_2$. As M' is a block-diagonal matrix constructed from the 16×16 matrices $\hat{M}_0$ and $\hat{M}_1$, probability $\mathcal{P}_{\mathcal{I}_2}$ can be computed exactly by computing the following probabilities:

$$\mathcal{P}_{\hat{M}_0}^{(\beta)} = 2^{-16} \# \left\{ x \in \mathbb{F}_2^{16} | S^{-1}\left(\hat{M}_0\left(S(x)\right) \right) \oplus x = \beta \right\}$$

$$\mathcal{P}_{\hat{M}_1}^{(\beta)} = 2^{-16} \# \left\{ x \in \mathbb{F}_2^{16} | S^{-1}\left(\hat{M}_1\left(S(x)\right) \right) \oplus x = \beta \right\}$$

where β is a 16-bits word and S is the application of 4 Sboxes. Then if $\alpha = (\alpha_0, \alpha_1, \alpha_2, \alpha_3)$, we have

$$\mathcal{P}_{\mathcal{I}_2} = \mathcal{P}_{\hat{M}_0}^{(\alpha_0)} \times \mathcal{P}_{\hat{M}_1}^{(\alpha_1)} \times \mathcal{P}_{\hat{M}_1}^{(\alpha_2)} \times \mathcal{P}_{\hat{M}_0}^{(\alpha_3)}. \tag{8}$$

Characteristic $\mathcal{C}_u$. As presented in Sect. 3.2, characteristics on the external rounds can be seen as a differential characteristics with input difference α and related constant difference α, see Fig. 3. As PRINCE is a 64-bit cipher with 12 rounds, only 3 or 4 external rounds must be considered, and therefore computation of the best characteristics for a fixed α is possible by the Branch and Bound algorithm. Finding the weakest α for such a characteristic remains nevertheless a challenging task. When aiming at a combination with $\mathcal{I}_2$, focusing on the best α for $\mathcal{I}_2$ gives a good starting point, whereas $\mathcal{I}_1$ is independent of α, a more complex analysis should be done to find the values of α for which an attack on the full 12 rounds of PRINCE_{core} is possible.

5.2 Maximizing $\mathcal{P}_{\mathcal{C}_u}$ for Combination of $\mathcal{C}_u$ with $\mathcal{I}_1$

We describe here the method we use to derive the α for which 12 rounds of the cipher can be attacked using a combination of $\mathcal{I}_1$ and $\mathcal{C}_4$. As we have seen in Sect. 4, a key-recovery attack on 12 rounds can be derived using a distinguisher on 10 rounds. Hence we are interested in finding values of α which maximize $\mathcal{P}_{\mathcal{C}_4}$.

Maximizing $\mathcal{P}_{\mathcal{C}_4}$. We start by the analysis of the properties of the S-box and permutation layer M of PRINCE. Indeed, the values of α for which a minimal number of Sboxes are active (that is, have non-zero differences) at each round and the differential probabilities of the Sbox are maximal. To this aim, we first express some properties of the matrices $\hat{M}_0$ and $\hat{M}_1$.

To maximize $\mathcal{P}_{\mathcal{C}_u}$, we want to minimize the weight of $\alpha = (\alpha_0, \alpha_1, \alpha_2, \alpha_3)$ and $M^{-1}(\alpha)$. Since $\hat{M}_\epsilon$, $\epsilon = 0, 1$, have a branch number 4, $w(\beta) + w(\hat{M}_\epsilon(\beta)) \geq 4$ and we have only 61 out of the total of 2^{16} values β such that $w(\beta) + w(\hat{M}_\epsilon(\beta)) = 4$ for both $\epsilon = 1$ and $\epsilon = 2$. Among these 61 values, 57 are such that $\beta = (a_1, a_2, a_3, a_4)$, where $a_i \in \{0, 1, 2, 4, 8\}$. Differential probabilities of the inverse Sbox for single-bit differences are given in Table 1. Based on this table and experiments, we assume that α with some nibble equal to 2 is not likely to maximize $\mathcal{P}_{\mathcal{C}_4}$. To find the best distinguisher on 10 rounds, we reduce the search space of α using

Table 1. Differential probabilities of the inverse Sbox for single-bit differences.

$a\backslash b$	1	2	4	8
1	2^{-2}	2^{-3}	2^{-3}	0
2	0	0	2^{-3}	2^{-3}
4	2^{-3}	0	2^{-3}	2^{-2}
8	2^{-2}	2^{-3}	2^{-3}	2^{-3}

the following procedure: For $\alpha = (a_1, a_2, \cdots, a_{15}, a_{16})$, where $a_i \in \{0, 1, 4, 8\}$ (2^{32} values), we select the ones such that there exists a characteristic $\mathcal{C}_2$ with $\mathcal{P}_{\mathcal{C}_2} \geq 2^{-12}$ (there are more than 300 values of α of this sort). Among the remaining ones, check if there is a characteristic $\mathcal{C}_4$ with $\mathcal{P}_{\mathcal{C}_4} \geq 2^{-28}$.

In Tables 2 and 3, we present some values of α, for which we obtain a distinguisher on 10 rounds. Estimated time and data complexities of a key recovery attack on the 12-round cipher are also shown in the same tables. These estimates have been computed under the assumption that the right key maximizes the number of remaining pairs in Step 4 of the key recovery attack, meaning that the advantage is $a = n + 4w(\Delta^*)$. The success probability is taken equal to 95 %. The data complexity is derived using Algorithm 1 of [1] and the time complexity is derived as for the key recovery attack presented in Sect. 4.1.

Iterative Characteristic. For the α in Table 2, which maximize the probability $\mathcal{P}_{\mathcal{C}_4} \times \mathcal{P}_{\mathcal{I}_1}$, the characteristic $\mathcal{C}_4$ is particular since a cancellation of the difference occurs every second round. For instance, we can have $Y^O_{R+1} \oplus X^I_R = \alpha$, $Y^O_{R+2} \oplus X^I_{R-1} = 0$, $Y^O_{R+3} \oplus X^I_{R-2} = \alpha$, $Y^O_{R+4} \oplus X^I_{R-3} = 0$, and $Y^O_{R+5} \oplus X^I_{R-4} = \alpha$. Then every second folded round can be passed with probability one, and it can be applied iteratively to minimize the probability of the characteristic. Such characteristic are easily found even by hand. We just look for α such that α and $M^{-1}(\alpha)$ are non-zero on exactly the same nibble position. Such a cancellation property occurs for some particular values of α. When $w(\alpha) = 4$, the cancellation property leads to an attack on 12 rounds of the cipher. No α with less than 4

Table 2. The weakest α with attack on 12 rounds (using $\mathcal{C}_4 \circ \mathcal{I}_1$). Iterative characteristic based on the cancellation idea.

α	Δ^*	$w(\Delta^*)$	$\mathcal{P}_{\mathcal{C}_4}$	PRINCE$_{core}$ Data/Time	PRINCE Data	Time
8400400800000000	8800400400000000	4	2^{-22}	$2^{56.21}$	$2^{57.98}$	$2^{72.39}$
8040000040800000	8080000040400000	4	2^{-22}	$2^{56.21}$	$2^{57.98}$	$2^{72.39}$
0000408000008040	0000404000008080	4	2^{-22}	$2^{56.21}$	$2^{57.98}$	$2^{72.39}$
0000000048008004	0000000044008008	4	2^{-22}	$2^{56.21}$	$2^{57.98}$	$2^{72.39}$
0000440040040000	0000440040040000	4	2^{-24}	$2^{58.72}$	$2^{60.28}$	$2^{74.69}$
8008000000008800	8008000000008800	4	2^{-24}	$2^{58.72}$	$2^{60.28}$	$2^{74.69}$

Table 3. Example of α with attack on 12 rounds (using $C_4 \circ \mathcal{I}_1$).

α	Δ^*	$w(\Delta^*)$	$\mathcal{P}_{C_4}$	PRINCE$_{core}$ Data/Time	PRINCE Data	Time
0108088088010018	0000001008000495	5	2^{-26}	$2^{61.22}$	$2^{62.80}$	$2^{79.21}$
0088188080018010	00000100C09D0008	5	2^{-26}	$2^{61.22}$	$2^{62.80}$	$2^{79.21}$
0108088088010018	000000100800D8CC	6	2^{-26}	$2^{61.42}$	$2^{62.86}$	$2^{83.27}$
0001111011010011	1101100110000100	7	2^{-28}	$2^{63.57}(\dagger)$	$2^{63.57}(\dagger)$	2^{112}

$\dagger$: complexities computed for an advantage of $a = 16$ bits.

active nibbles or with $w(\alpha) = 5$ can satisfy the cancellation property. Nevertheless some α with 6 active nibbles have characteristic which cancel the difference after two rounds. As for these α, $Y_{R+3}^O \oplus X_{R-2}^I = \alpha$ with probability $\mathcal{P}_{C_2} \leq 2^{-16}$, the iterative characteristic $\mathcal{C}_u$ can be applied only once and a distinguisher on 6 rounds with probability p, where $2^{-49} \leq p \leq 2^{-48}$, leads to a key-recovery attack on 8 rounds.

Non-Iterative Characteristic. In Table 3, we give other values of α, which allow an attack on 12 rounds. While the list is not exhaustive, this table illustrates that also α with larger weight can lead to an attack on 12 rounds. Different characteristic for the same α can be derived. While the weight of Δ^* is larger for these characteristics, the time complexity of this attack is still reasonable. While the list of α with a key recovery attack on 12 rounds is already quite large, the number of α such that attacks on 6, 8, or 10 rounds are possible is even larger. Search for α of this sort can be done by adjusting the constraint of the Branch and Bound algorithm.

5.3 Maximizing $\mathcal{P}_{\mathcal{I}_2}$ for Combination with $\mathcal{C}_u$

Finding the values of α which maximize $\mathcal{P}_{\mathcal{I}_2}$ can be done exhaustively by decomposing over the matrices $\hat{M}_\epsilon$, $\epsilon = 0, 1$, see Sect. 5.1. Computation for 2^{16} values of β gives us the list of best α regarding to this characteristic. In what follows, we focus on $\beta \neq 0$ such that $2^{-12} \leq \mathcal{P}_{\hat{M}_\epsilon}^{(\beta)} \leq 2^{-10.54}$. As $\mathcal{P}_{\hat{M}_\epsilon}^0 \leq 2^{-8}$, we obtain a list of $63^2 \times 73^2 \approx 2^{24.33}$ values of α for which $2^{-48} \leq \mathcal{P}_{C_2} \leq 2^{-34.54}$. Two values of α reach this upper bound. They are $\alpha = 0000111100000000$ and $\alpha = 0000000011110000$.

The values α which maximize $\mathcal{I}_2$ and for which 10 rounds of a PRINCE-like cipher can be distinguished from random also allow a combination of C_4 and $\mathcal{I}_1$. For instance, for $\alpha = 0000408000008040$ we have a characteristic with $\mathcal{P}_{C_3} = 2^{-19}$ and $\mathcal{P}_{\mathcal{I}_2} = 2^{-40}$. None of these characteristics give a better cryptanalysis results than the ones given in Table 2. While for the attacks on 12 rounds all values of α are such that $w(\alpha) \geq 4$, we can find α of smaller nibble weight which

Table 4. Example of α with attack on 10 rounds and $w(\alpha) = 2$ (using $C_2 \circ \mathcal{I}_2$). Computation done for $P_S = 95\%$ and $a = 16$.

α	Δ^*	$w(\Delta^*)$	$\mathcal{P}_{C_2}$	$\mathcal{P}_{\mathcal{I}_2}$	PRINCE$_{core}$ Data/Time	PRINCE Data	Time
0000000001100000	1000111011011101	10	2^{-20}	2^{-36}	$2^{58.17}$	$2^{58.17}$	2^{112}
0000000008040000	9189505500008991	11	2^{-24}	2^{-36}	$2^{63.57}$	$2^{63.57}$	2^{112}
0000000000000804	4C0C18998C0C0000	10	2^{-24}	2^{-36}	$2^{63.57}$	$2^{63.57}$	2^{112}

allow a key recovery attack on a 10-round cipher using a combination of C_2 and $\mathcal{I}_2$ as illustrated in Table 4.

For all the α presented in this section, also other characteristics can be derived. Complexities of our attacks are based on the best characteristic.

5.4 Impossible Attack

If $\mathcal{P}_{\mathcal{I}_2} = 0$, a deterministic distinguisher on 4 rounds of the cipher can be built. It leads to a key-recovery attack for a 6-round cipher described in Sect. 4.2. The time complexity of this attack correspond to $2^{126.56}$ encryptions and 2^{67} bytes are necessary for the storage of the hash table. This attack is efficient, in particular, for $\alpha = \mathtt{C0AC29b7C97C50DD}$ of PRINCE. But we can find many more values of α with $\mathcal{P}_{\mathcal{I}_2} = 0$.

As specified by Eq. (8), the computation of $\mathcal{P}_{C_2}$ can be decomposed over $\hat{M}_0$ and $\hat{M}_1$. For $\hat{M}_0$, the number of $\beta \in \mathbb{F}_2^{16}$ for which $\mathcal{P}_{\hat{M}_0}^{(\beta)} = 0$ is 5940. For $\hat{M}_1$, the number of β for which $\mathcal{P}_{\hat{M}_1}^{(\beta)} = 0$ is 6914. In total, we deduce that the impossible distinguisher is valid for approximately $2 \cdot (2^{12.54}) \times 2^{48} + 2 \cdot (2^{12.76}) \times 2^{48} = 2^{62.65}$ values of α.

Using the fact that $\hat{M}_0$ and $\hat{M}_1$ have no fixed points of weight 1, we conclude that $\mathcal{P}_{C_2} = 0$, for all α with only 1 or 3 non-zero nibbles. Also a large number of α with 2, 4 and 5 non-zero nibbles allow this impossible distinguisher. We also found that for some α with 4 active nibbles we have an attack on 12 rounds, while for some other α the best attack we found is on 6 rounds only. Hence the weight of α alone does not prove anything about security or insecurity against the reflection attacks discussed in this paper.

5.5 Truncated Attack

When the linear layer is defined as in the original proposal, using the shift row operation of the AES, truncated reflection distinguishers can be derived for α such that $M^{-1}(\alpha)$ has a small number of active nibbles. Proof of the characteristic presented below can be found in Appendix A.2.

Lemma 2. *Assume α is such that* $M^{-1}(\alpha) = \begin{bmatrix} * & 0 & 0 & 0 \\ 0 & 0 & 0 & * \\ 0 & 0 & * & 0 \\ 0 & * & 0 & 0 \end{bmatrix}$, *where $*$ can be any*

4-bit value. Then the following truncated characteristic

$$Y^{O}_{R+3} \oplus X^{I}_{R-2} = \begin{bmatrix} * & 0 & 0 & 0 \\ * & 0 & 0 & * \\ * & 0 & * & 0 \\ * & * & 0 & 0 \end{bmatrix} \oplus \alpha, \tag{9}$$

holds on 6 rounds $\mathfrak{R}_{R-2} \circ \cdots \circ \mathfrak{R}_{R+3}$ of the cipher with probability $\mathcal{P}_{F_{M'}} = 2^{-32}$.
Similar characteristics can be obtained for α such that:

$$M^{-1}(\alpha) = \begin{bmatrix} 0 & * & 0 & 0 \\ * & 0 & 0 & 0 \\ 0 & 0 & 0 & * \\ 0 & 0 & * & 0 \end{bmatrix} \; or \; M^{-1}(\alpha) = \begin{bmatrix} 0 & 0 & * & 0 \\ 0 & * & 0 & 0 \\ * & 0 & 0 & 0 \\ 0 & 0 & 0 & * \end{bmatrix} \; or \; M^{-1}(\alpha) = \begin{bmatrix} 0 & 0 & 0 & * \\ 0 & 0 & * & 0 \\ 0 & * & 0 & 0 \\ * & 0 & 0 & 0 \end{bmatrix}.$$

In all four cases of the characteristics, nine nibbles of the data difference are equal to those of α. Hence the probability of such a truncated characteristic is 2^{-36}.

By the previous lemma, such truncated characteristics exist for $4 \times (2^{16} - 1) \approx 2^{18}$ values of α. While distinguisher of Sects. 5.2 and 5.3 focused on α with a small number of active nibbles, this distinguisher is targeted on α, for which $M^{-1}(\alpha)$ has a small number of active nibbles, but α itself can have any number of non-zero nibbles. As an example, we give

$$\alpha = \begin{bmatrix} 7 & 1 & C & B \\ 9 & 5 & 9 & 3 \\ 9 & A & 5 & 9 \\ 3 & 6 & 8 & D \end{bmatrix}, \; M^{-1}(\alpha) = \begin{bmatrix} 7 & 0 & 0 & 0 \\ 0 & 0 & 0 & B \\ 0 & 0 & D & 0 \\ 0 & 9 & 0 & 0 \end{bmatrix}.$$

This truncated distinguisher enables a key-recovery attack for a cipher reduced to eight rounds in the same way that the key recovery attack described in Sect. 4. The keys k_0 and k_1 can then be recovered independently. In Appendix A.2 details of this key recovery attack are explained. This key recovery attack has data complexity $2^{36.85}$, time complexity of $2^{97.8}$ memory accesses and 2^{80} full encryptions. The memory complexity is dominated by the storage of $2^{63.6}$ bytes for the hash table.

Several other kinds of truncated reflection characteristics can be derived for different configuration of $M^{-1}(\alpha)$. For instance, in some configurations, where $M^{-1}(\alpha)$ has up to eight non-zero nibbles a key-recovery attack on a 6-round cipher can be done using a distinguisher on 4 rounds.

6 Conclusion

In this paper, we investigated the security of a family of ciphers, which includes the new design PRINCE. This family is characterized by the α-reflection property. We constructed new types of characteristics for such ciphers starting from a probabilistic or impossible relation on the midmost rounds of the cipher. By using properties of the constant α and the symmetry of the cipher, such reflection characteristics can be considered as differential characteristics over a half of the cipher, and in particular, their probabilities can be computed efficiently using ordinary differential probabilities over the non-linear components of the cipher. In the security analysis of PRINCE given in [2] the properties of α did not receive much attention. In this paper, we show that the security of PRINCE-like ciphers depends strongly on the choice of the value of α. By keeping the other components of PRINCE as in the original design, and by varying the value of α, we identified special classes of α for which reduced-round versions of the cipher can be distinguished from random. The values of α in the weakest class allow an efficient key-recovery attack on 12 rounds of the cipher. These results show that the security of PRINCE is not independent of the value of α. On the other hand, the best attack we could construct using this technique on PRINCE with the original value of the reflection parameter α, was a key recovery attack on a reduced 6-round version of the cipher. While the new technique, which exploits the special reflection structure of the cipher, did not reveal any vulnerabilities in the original design, it provided new information about the security criteria for the selection of the reflection parameter as well as other componenets of the cipher.

Acknowledgments. We wish to thank the anonymous reviewers for helpful comments. The authors from Aalto University wish to acknowledge useful discussions with Gregor Leander during his visits funded by the Aalto Science Institute. The work of Hadi Soleimany is supported by Helsinki Doctoral Program in Computer Science - Advanced Computing and Intelligent Systems (HECSE). The work of Hadi Soleimany and Céline Blondeau is partly supported by European Commission through the ICT program under contract ICT-2007-216676 ECRYPT II. The work of Xiaoli Yu, Wenling Wu, Huiling Zhang, Lei Zhang and Yanfeng Wang is partly supported by the National Basic Research Program of China (No. 2013CB338002) and the National Natural Science Foundation of China (No. 61272476, 61232009, 61202420).

A   Appendix

A.1   Components of PRINCE

The linear layer of PRINCE is defined using four 4×4 matrices M_0, M_1, M_2, M_3 given as follows:

$$M_0 = \begin{pmatrix} 0\,0\,0\,0 \\ 0\,1\,0\,0 \\ 0\,0\,1\,0 \\ 0\,0\,0\,1 \end{pmatrix}, \quad M_1 = \begin{pmatrix} 1\,0\,0\,0 \\ 0\,0\,0\,0 \\ 0\,0\,1\,0 \\ 0\,0\,0\,1 \end{pmatrix}, \quad M_2 = \begin{pmatrix} 1\,0\,0\,0 \\ 0\,1\,0\,0 \\ 0\,0\,0\,0 \\ 0\,0\,0\,1 \end{pmatrix}, \quad M_3 = \begin{pmatrix} 1\,0\,0\,0 \\ 0\,1\,0\,0 \\ 0\,0\,1\,0 \\ 0\,0\,0\,0 \end{pmatrix}.$$

Then the two 16×16 matrices $\hat{M}_0$ and $\hat{M}_1$ are defined as:

$$
\hat{M}_0 = \begin{pmatrix} M_0 & M_1 & M_2 & M_3 \\ M_1 & M_2 & M_3 & M_0 \\ M_2 & M_3 & M_0 & M_1 \\ M_3 & M_0 & M_1 & M_2 \end{pmatrix}, \quad \hat{M}_1 = \begin{pmatrix} M_1 & M_2 & M_3 & M_0 \\ M_2 & M_3 & M_0 & M_1 \\ M_3 & M_0 & M_1 & M_2 \\ M_0 & M_1 & M_2 & M_3 \end{pmatrix}.
$$

The non-linear layer S consists of 16 copies of a 4-to-4-bit Sbox given in Table 5.

Table 5. Sbox of PRINCE

x	0	1	2	3	4	5	6	7	8	9	A	B	C	D	E	F
S[x]	B	F	3	2	A	C	9	1	6	7	8	0	E	5	D	4

A.2   Truncated Reflection Characteristic

Proof of Lemma 2. The 4 types of truncated characteristics given in Lemma 2 differ only by the position of the completely undetermined column of the difference. We present here the proof for the first column. Proofs for the other types are similar.

As described by the characteristic $\mathcal{C}_1$, the probability that $X_R^I \oplus Y_{R+1}^O = \alpha$ is equal to $P_{F_{M'}}$ $(= 2^{-32}$ for PRINCE$)$. For the previous and the next round, we have

$$
Y_{R+2}^O \oplus X_{R-1}^I = S^{-1}\left(M^{-1}(\alpha)\right) \oplus \alpha = \begin{bmatrix} * & 0 & 0 & 0 \\ 0 & 0 & 0 & * \\ 0 & 0 & * & 0 \\ 0 & * & 0 & 0 \end{bmatrix} \oplus \alpha.
$$

Since $M^{-1} = M' \circ SR^{-1}$ is linear and

$$
M^{-1}\left(\begin{bmatrix} * & 0 & 0 & 0 \\ 0 & 0 & 0 & * \\ 0 & 0 & * & 0 \\ 0 & * & 0 & 0 \end{bmatrix} \right) = \begin{bmatrix} * & 0 & 0 & 0 \\ * & 0 & 0 & 0 \\ * & 0 & 0 & 0 \\ * & 0 & 0 & 0 \end{bmatrix},
$$

we have

$$
Y_{R+3}^O \oplus X_{R-2}^I = S^{-1}\left(M^{-1}(\alpha) \oplus \begin{bmatrix} * & 0 & 0 & 0 \\ * & 0 & 0 & 0 \\ * & 0 & 0 & 0 \\ * & 0 & 0 & 0 \end{bmatrix} \right) \oplus \alpha = \begin{bmatrix} * & 0 & 0 & 0 \\ * & 0 & 0 & * \\ * & 0 & * & 0 \\ * & * & 0 & 0 \end{bmatrix} \oplus \alpha.
$$

Key Recovery Attack. For simplicity, we restrict to the characteristic given by Eq. (9). As this characteristic is completely undetermined in the first column, and will stay completely undetermined in the same column after application of the inverse of shift row, it is sufficient to focus on the 12 nibbles corresponding to the three most right columns of the matrix of (9). For a state Z, we denote the truncation of the state to the last three columns by Z_t. Let (P, C) be a plaintext-ciphertext pair. The distinguisher involves only partial encryption of 48 bits of the plaintext P_t and partial decryption of the ciphertext C_t with the key k_0, k_0' and k_1. It means that only up to 49 bits of k_0 and 48 bits of k_1 can be obtained in a similar way to the attack of Sect. 4. An exhaustive search on the remaining bits is then necessary to recover the full key.

The attack procedure is as follows:

Pre-computation

For each possible 2^{60} pairs $(a, b) \in (\mathbb{F}_2^{48})^2$ such that $a \oplus b$ is equal to the truncated state of $\begin{bmatrix} * & 0 & 0 & 0 \\ * & 0 & 0 & * \\ * & 0 & * & 0 \\ * & * & 0 & 0 \end{bmatrix} \oplus \alpha$ compute the pair $(\nu_a, \omega_b) \in (\mathbb{F}_2^{48})^2$ such that

$$\nu_a = S^{-1}\big(M^{-1}(a)\big) \oplus RC_1,$$
$$\omega_b = S^{-1}\big(M^{-1}(b)\big) \oplus RC_8.$$

Store ν_a in the row $\Lambda = \nu_a \oplus \omega_b$ of the hash table T. The hash table T has 2^{48} rows and on average each row have $\frac{2^{60}}{2^{48}} = 2^{12}$ values.

Attack Procedure

1. Guess 49 bits of the key k_0 and extract 48 bits of k_0 and of k_0'.
   (i) Allocate a counter D_{k_1} for each 2^{48} values of k_1.
   (ii) For each 2^m pairs $(P_t', C_t') = (P_t \oplus k_0, C_t \oplus k_0')$
       Compute $\Lambda = P_t' \oplus C_t'$.
       For all ν_a in the row Λ of the hash table T increase the counter $D_{(P_t' \oplus \nu_a)}$ by one.
   (iii) Consider a list of 2^{48-a} of the keys k_1 with highest counter values.
2. Do an exhaustive search on the remaining $128 - a$ bits of key.

The time complexity of the attack without whitening keys (Steps (i) to (iii)) corresponds to 2^{m+12} memory accesses. To obtain k_0, the attack should be repeated for 2^{49} keys k_0. So the time complexity to find the whole key corresponds to 2^{61+m} memory accesses in addition to 2^{128-a} full encryptions. We need $2^{60} \times 48/8 \times 2 \simeq 2^{63.6}$ bytes for the storage of the hash table T and $2^{49+48-a} \times 48/8 = 2^{99.6-a}$ bytes for the storage of the list of keys candidates.

References

1. Blondeau, C., Gérard, B., Tillich, J.-P.: Accurate estimates of the data complexity and success probability for various cryptanalyses. Des. Codes Crypt. 59(1–3), 3–34 (2011)
2. Borghoff, J., et al.: PRINCE – a low-latency block cipher for pervasive computing applications (extended abstract). In: Wang, X., Sako, K. (eds.) ASIACRYPT 2012. LNCS, vol. 7658, pp. 208–225. Springer, Heidelberg (2012)

3. Bouillaguet, C., Dunkelman, O., Leurent, G., Fouque, P.-A.: Another look at complementation properties. In: Hong, S., Iwata, T. (eds.) FSE 2010. LNCS, vol. 6147, pp. 347–364. Springer, Heidelberg (2010)
4. Flajolet, P., Sedgewick, R.: Analytic Combinatorics. Cambridge University Press, New York (2009)
5. Guo, J., Peyrin, T., Poschmann, A., Robshaw, M.: The LED block cipher. In: Preneel, B., Takagi, T. (eds.) CHES 2011. LNCS, vol. 6917, pp. 326–341. Springer, Heidelberg (2011)
6. Kara, O.: Reflection cryptanalysis of some ciphers. In: Chowdhury, D.R., Rijmen, V., Das, A. (eds.) INDOCRYPT 2008. LNCS, vol. 5365, pp. 294–307. Springer, Heidelberg (2008)
7. Knudsen, L., Leander, G., Poschmann, A., Robshaw, M.J.B.: PRINTCIPHER: a block cipher for IC-printing. In: Mangard, S., Standaert, F.-X. (eds.) CHES 2010. LNCS, vol. 6225, pp. 16–32. Springer, Heidelberg (2010)
8. Moore, J.H., Simmons, G.J.: Cycle structure of the DES with weak and semi-weak keys. In: Odlyzko, A.M. (ed.) CRYPTO 1986. LNCS, vol. 263, pp. 9–32. Springer, Heidelberg (1987)

Security Analysis of PRINCE

Jérémy Jean[1]([✉]), Ivica Nikolić[2], Thomas Peyrin[2],
Lei Wang[2], and Shuang Wu[2]

[1] École Normale Supérieure, Paris, France
[2] Division of Mathematical Sciences,
School of Physical and Mathematical Sciences,
Nanyang Technological University, Singapore, Singapore
Jeremy.Jean@ens.fr,
{inikolic,thomas.peyrin,wang.lei,wushuang}@ntu.edu.sg

Abstract. In this article, we provide the first third-party security analysis of the PRINCE lightweight block cipher, and the underlying PRINCE$_{core}$. First, while no claim was made by the authors regarding related-key attacks, we show that one can attack the full cipher with only a single pair of related keys, and then reuse the same idea to derive an attack in the single-key model for the full PRINCE$_{core}$ for several instances of the α parameter (yet not the one randomly chosen by the designers). We also show how to exploit the structural linear relations that exist for PRINCE in order to obtain a key recovery attack that slightly breaks the security claims for the full cipher. We analyze the application of integral attacks to get the best known key-recovery attack on a reduced version of the PRINCE cipher. Finally, we provide time-memory-*data* tradeoffs that require only known plaintext-ciphertext data and that can be applied to full PRINCE.

Keywords: PRINCE · Block cipher · Cryptanalysis · Related-key boomerang · Time-memory-data tradeoff

1 Introduction

Lightweight cryptography is a new, rapidly developing area of symmetric cryptography that has emerged from the needs of constrained devices. The increasing deployment of such devices in the everyday life has captured the attention of the cryptographic community. It became clear that most of the available cryptographic primitives, both ciphers and hash functions, fail to meet the basic requirements of constrained devices – low cost hardware implementation, as well as low power usage and latency. Thus, so-called lightweight primitives, designed only for these type of devices, have been proposed (and some already have been implemented) in the past several years.

This collaborative work was done while the first author was visiting CCRG lab of Nanyang Technological University in Singapore.

S. Moriai (Ed.): FSE 2013, LNCS 8424, pp. 92–111, 2014.
DOI: 10.1007/978-3-662-43933-3_6, © Springer-Verlag Berlin Heidelberg 2014

PRINCE [4] is a lightweight cipher published at Asiacrypt 2012, and optimized with respect to latency when implemented in hardware. It is based on Even-Mansour-like construction (so-called FX construction [2,10]) and it has the interesting feature that one can perform decryption by reusing the encryption process with a slightly different key. This feature, so-called α-reflection property, clearly provides an advantage in implementations requiring both encryption and decryption, but at the same time induces some structure. This structure forced the designers to reduce the security expectations compared to an ideal cipher and they claimed that the security of the cipher is ensured up to 2^{127-n} operations when 2^n encryption/decryption queries are made. This bound is only valid for the single-key model, and the authors made no claim concerning the related-key model (a trivial related-key distinguisher can be built).

Our Contributions. In this article, we provide the first third-party analysis of the PRINCE cipher. First, we analyze in Sect. 3 the resistance of PRINCE in regard to related-key attacks. We emphasize that the designers clearly did not make any claim regarding this attack model. However, the best attack is a trivial related-key distinguisher and moreover, it is not clear up to what extend an attack can be mounted. We show that with a single pair of related keys, one can recover the whole secret key faster than exhaustive search or faster than the claimed single-key security bound.

Furthermore, our related-key attacks are actually interesting not only for the related-key model, but also for the single-key one since we leverage these techniques to show in Sect. 4 that several choices of values for α lead to an insecure version of PRINCE$_{core}$ in the single-key model. It is to be noted that the designers required $\alpha \neq 0$ to enforce their security claims and the value of α was eventually derived from the fraction part of π. We show that the choice of α is actually sensitive for the security of the cipher.

In Sect. 5, we exploit the related-key relations verified with probability 1 that exist for PRINCE in order to mount a key recovery attack, slightly breaking the designers claims in the single-key scenario. Namely, we show that one can generically gain a factor $2^{0.6}$ compared to their claims, by only taking into account that the cipher is using the FX construction and has the α-reflection property. While the gain is quite small, it indicates that more precise security proof (taking in account the α-reflection property) might be an interesting research problem.

We explore the application of integral attacks in Sect. 6 and improve the best known result on a reduced version of PRINCE, providing a 6-round key recovery attack with low complexity.

Finally, in Sect. 7 we propose tradeoffs for PRINCE. We show that due to the specific structure of the cipher, tradeoffs involving data and requiring only known plaintexts-ciphertext are achievable for PRINCE. We start with a Memory-Data tradeoff based on the meet-in-the-middle technique, and improve our results to Time-Memory-Data tradeoff based on the original Hellman's approach.

Our results are summarized in Table 1.

Table 1. Summary of the results on PRINCE and PRINCE$_{core}$.

Cipher	Rounds	Data	Time	Memory	Technique	Ref.
PRINCE	4	2^4	2^{64}	2^4	Integral	Sect. 6
	5	$5 \cdot 2^4$	2^{64}	2^8	Integral	Sect. 6
	6	2^{16}	2^{64}	2^{16}	Integral	Sect. 6
	12	2^1	$2^{125.47}$	negl.	Single-key	Sect. 5
	12 †	2^{33}	2^{64}	2^{33}	Related-key	Sect. 3.1
	12	$MD = N, T = N^{\frac{1}{2}}$			MD TO	Sect. 7
	12	$T(MD)^2 = N^2 N^{\frac{1}{2}}$			TMD TO	Sect. 7
	12	$TMD = NN^{\frac{1}{2}}$			TMD TO	·Sect. 7
PRINCE$_{core}$	4	2^4	2^8	2^4	Integral	Sect. 6
	5	$5 \cdot 2^4$	2^{21}	2^8	Integral	Sect. 6
	6	2^{16}	2^{30}	2^{16}	Integral	Sect. 6
	12 †	2^{39}	2^{39}	2^{39}	RK boomerang	Sect. 3.2
	12	2^{41}	2^{41}	negl.	SK boomerang for chosen α	Sect. 4

†: No security claim for related-key attacks   TO: (Cryptanalytic) Tradeoff
RK: Related-key   MD: Memory-Data
SK: Single-key   TMD: Time-Memory-Data

2 Description of PRINCE

PRINCE [4] is a 64-bit block cipher that uses a 128-bit secret key k. The key expansion first divides k into two parts of 64 bits each $k = (k_0 \| k_1)$, where $\|$ denotes the concatenation, and then extends the key material into 192 bits:

$$k = (k_0 \| k_1) \rightarrow (k_0 \| k_0' \| k_1) = (k_0 \| L(k_0) \| k_1), \tag{1}$$

with $L(x) = (x \ggg 1) \oplus (x \gg 63)$. The 64-bit subkeys k_0 and k_0' are used as input and output whitening keys respectively, while k_1 is used as internal key for the core block cipher PRINCE$_{core}$ (see Fig. 1).

The internal block cipher PRINCE$_{core}$ is a Substitution-Permutation Network composed of 12 rounds. The round function $\mathcal{R}_i$ is defined by the bitwise addition of the 64-bit subkey k_1 and a 64-bit constant RC_i, the application of a 4-bit Sbox S to each of the 16 4-bit nibbles of the internal state, and finally the

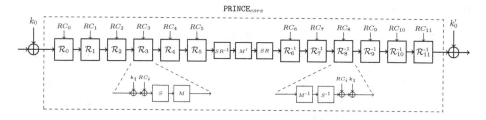

Fig. 1. A schematic view of the PRINCE cipher.

multiplication by a linear diffusion matrix M. The encryption of PRINCE_{core} is then composed of the application of the 6 rounds $\mathcal{R}_0, \ldots, \mathcal{R}_5$, the multiplication by a linear diffusion matrix M_{mid}, and finally the application the 6 inverse rounds $\mathcal{R}_6^{-1}, \ldots, \mathcal{R}_{11}^{-1}$:

$$\text{PRINCE}_{core} = \mathcal{R}_{11}^{-1} \circ \mathcal{R}_{10}^{-1} \circ \mathcal{R}_9^{-1} \circ \mathcal{R}_8^{-1} \circ \mathcal{R}_7^{-1} \circ \mathcal{R}_6^{-1} \circ M_{mid} \circ \mathcal{R}_5 \circ \mathcal{R}_4 \circ \mathcal{R}_3 \circ \mathcal{R}_2 \circ \mathcal{R}_1 \circ \mathcal{R}_0.$$

The 4-bit S-box S has a maximal differential probability of $p_{max} = 2^{-2}$, and is given by (in hexadecimal display) $S[x] = [\text{B}, \text{F}, 3, 2, \text{A}, \text{C}, 9, 1, 6, 7, 8, 0, \text{E}, 5, \text{D}, 4]$. The linear diffusion matrix M is composed of a linear matrix M' and a nibble shifting part SR (similar to a ShiftRows in AES [6]): $M = SR \circ M'$. Then, the linear middle matrix M_{mid} is defined by $M_{mid} = M \circ M' \circ M^{-1} = SR \circ M' \circ SR^{-1}$. We refer to [4] for the complete description of M', but one must remark that its diffusion property ensures that at least 16 Sboxes are active for 4 consecutive round functions.

It is to be noted that $RC_i \oplus RC_{11-i} = \alpha = \text{0xc0ac29b7c97c50dd}$ for all $0 \leq i \leq 11$, and since the matrix M' is an involution, this allows to perform the decryption D of PRINCE by simply encrypting with the key $k_1 \oplus \alpha$ instead of k_1 and flipping the whitening keys k_0 with k_0': $D_{(k_0 \| k_0' \| k_1)}(\cdot) = E_{(k_0' \| k_0 \| k_1 \oplus \alpha)}(\cdot)$.

In this article, we see the internal state s of PRINCE as a 4×4 matrix form, where each cell is a nibble, and if we denote $s[i]$ the i-th nibble, $0 \leq i < 16$ from MSB to LSB, it would be located at row $i \pmod 4$ and column $\lfloor i/4 \rfloor$.

3   Related-Key Attacks

In this section, we describe a related-key attack on the full PRINCE, and a related-key attack on the core block cipher PRINCE_{core}. The first one (Sect. 3.1) uses a single related-key, and the α-reflection property of the core cipher to recover the 128-bit master key with 2^{33} data, 2^{63} operations and 2^{32} memory. The second attack (Sect. 3.2) uses a related-key differential characteristic with high-probability to mount a boomerang distinguisher on the core block cipher, that can be turned into a key-recovery attack for the 64-bit key k_1 of PRINCE_{core}. We have verified experimentally our results – an example of boomerang quartet for the full 12-round PRINCE_{core} is given in Appendix A.

3.1   Related-Key Attack on Full PRINCE with the α-Reflection Property

We denote in the sequel the secret master key that we aim to recover by $k = (k_0, k_1)$. We introduce one related-key $k' = (k_0, k_1 \oplus \alpha)$, where α refers to constant defined in Sect. 2. The attack procedure uses the following distinguisher on the whole core of PRINCE.

Property 1. Let (P, C) be the plaintext/ciphertext pair encrypted under the secret key k of PRINCE, and (P', C') be the plaintext/ciphertext pair obtained from PRINCE with the related key k'. If $C \oplus P' = k_0 \oplus L(k_0)$, then $P \oplus C' = k_0 \oplus L(k_0)$ with probability 1.

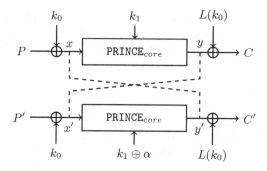

Fig. 2. Related-key distinguisher on full PRINCE.

Proof. As described in Sect. 2, PRINCE transforms a plaintext P into the cipher-text $C = E_{k_1}(k_0 \oplus P) \oplus L(k_0)$, where E_{k_1} instantiates PRINCE$_{core}$ with key k_1. For a second plaintext P', we set $C' = E_{k_1 \oplus \alpha}(k_0 \oplus P') \oplus L(k_0)$ using the related-key. The condition $C \oplus P' = k_0 \oplus L(k_0)$ actually states that the output of PRINCE$_{core}$ in the first message equals the input of PRINCE$_{core}$ in the second one. Namely, $C \oplus P' = k_0 \oplus L(k_0)$ means $x' = y$ from the notations of Fig. 2. Since $y = E_{k_1}(x)$ and $y' = E_{k_1 \oplus \alpha}(x')$, we have $x = y'$, which gives $P \oplus C' = k_0 \oplus L(k_0)$.   □

From this distinguisher, we show how to mount a key-recovery attack on PRINCE.

1. Query 2^{32} ciphertexts to PRINCE with the key $k = (k_0, k_1)$, and obtain plaintext/ciphertext pairs denoted as (P_i, C_i). Store them in a hash table T_c indexed by $X_i = P_i \oplus C_i$.
2. Query 2^{32} plaintexts to PRINCE with the related key $k' = (k_0, k_1 \oplus \alpha)$, and obtain plaintext/ciphertext pairs denoted as (P'_i, C'_i). Store them in a table T_p index by $Y_i = P'_i \oplus C'_i$.
3. Find collisions in the keys of T_p and T_c.
4. For each pair $X_i = Y_j$, compute $Z = C_i \oplus P'_j$. Sample a plaintext P uniformly at random, and obtain the corresponding ciphertext C from the encryption oracle. Check the distinguisher by constructing the ciphertext $C' = P \oplus Z$, querying its corresponding plaintext P' decrypted with the related-key, and check if $P' \oplus C = Z$. If this holds, then $Z = k_0 \oplus L(k_0)$.
5. Retrieve k_0 by inverting the bijection $x \to L(x) \oplus x$, and finish the attack by recovering k_1 exhaustively.

Complexity Analysis. After the two first steps where two structures of 2^{32} independent values have been constructed, by the birthday paradox we expect one collision for step 3. This collision gives a suggestion for k_0 that we check with the previously described distinguisher. This attack requires known plaintexts, but we note that with a chosen plaintext attack, we can pick C_i and P'_j carefully such that $C_i \oplus P'_j$ covers all the possible 2^{64} values. This ensures the value of k_0 to be recover with probability 1 at Step 4.

The total data complexity is about 2^{33} chosen plaintexts to construct the two tables and check the distinguisher, and requires a time complexity equivalent to $2^{33} + 2^{64} \approx 2^{64}$ encryptions. We recall that the security bound for single-key attack with 2^{33} data claimed by the designers equals $127 - 33 = 94$ bits.

3.2 Related-Key Boomerang Attack on PRINCE$_{core}$

In this section, we describe a related-key boomerang attack on PRINCE$_{core}$ with a time complexity equivalent to 2^{48} encryptions. To construct the boomerang distinguisher, we split the core block cipher E of PRINCE into two halves $E = E_1 \circ E_0$, where both E_0 and E_1 consists in 6 non-linear layers. The main observation that makes the distinguisher efficient is the existence of related-key differential characteristics with a very high probability. We start our analysis with an inspection of the S-box of PRINCE.

Property 2. For the S-box of PRINCE, there are 15 differential transitions, i.e. 15 pairs of input-output differences, that hold with probability 2^{-2}.

Further, we introduce three differences $(\Delta, \Delta_M, \nabla)$ that play the main role in our boomerang attacks. Let $\Delta \to \Delta_O$ be one of the 15 transitions with probability 2^{-2}, and let Δ_M be defined as $\Delta_M = M(\Delta_O)$, where M is the linear layer of PRINCE. Finally, let $\nabla = \Delta \oplus \Delta_M$.

Property 3. For PRINCE$_{core}$, there exists one round iterative characteristic $(\Delta_M, \nabla) \to (\Delta_M)$ where Δ_M is the difference in the incoming state and ∇ is the difference in the key, that holds with probability 2^{-2}.

The proof is trivial and is based on the particular values of the differences we have defined above (see Fig. 3).

The related-key boomerang distinguisher uses two independent six-round differential characteristics, produced as concatenation of six copies on the single-round differential characteristic previously described. Thus, we obtain two six-round characteristics with probabilities $p = q = 2^{-2 \times 6} = 2^{-12}$. Consequently,

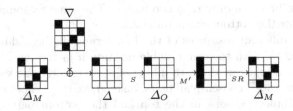

Fig. 3. Iterative differential characteristic on one round of PRINCE$_{core}$ used in the boomerang distinguisher.

the related-key boomerang distinguisher finds a boomerang quartet of plaintexts in $(pq)^{-2} = 2^{48}$ queries to the encryption/decryption oracle. We have implemented the distinguisher on a PC and found out that due to the amplified probability of the boomerang, the actual complexity is lower, i.e. it is somewhere around 2^{36}. Thus, we were able to find a boomerang quartet for the full 12 rounds of PRINCE_{core}. An example of one such quartet is given in Appendix A.

Before we continue, we would like to make a few observations regarding the boomerang:

- the distinguisher is applicable regardless of the choice of the diffusion matrix M,
- the distinguisher is applicable regardless of the position of Δ in the state, i.e. we can choose any of the 16 nibbles,
- the distinguisher is applicable regardless of the choice of Δ in the top and the bottom characteristics,
- for one of the six-round characteristics one can choose differential transition that holds even with probability 2^{-3}. In that case, the probability of the boomerang becomes $2^{6\cdot2\cdot(-3)+6\cdot2\cdot(-2)} = 2^{-60}$.

Thus we can conclude that for PRINCE_{core}, one can launch around $15\cdot16\cdot15\cdot16 \approx 2^{16}$ different related-key boomerang distinguishers that hold with probability 2^{-48}, and around $210 \cdot 16 \cdot 15 \cdot 16 + 15 \cdot 16 \cdot 210 \cdot 16 \approx 2^{21}$ boomerangs with probability 2^{-60}. In the sequel, we denote $\mathcal{A}(i,j)$ the boomerang distinguisher with probability 2^{-48} where the active on the top characteristic is the i-th one, and the j-th one for the bottom characteristic, $0 \le i, j < 16$.

Key-Recovery Attack. We now show how to turn the previous related-key boomerang distinguisher into a key-recovery attack. After the previously described distinguishing algorithm has completed, the attacker has one boomerang structure consisting in two pairs conforming to the first differential characteristic, and two other pairs verifying the second differential characteristic. From the plaintext, we show that the entropy of the nibble from k_1 corresponding to the active nibble in the top characteristic has been reduced to 2 bits. Indeed, as the pair verifies the first round, we know the differential transition of the first active nibble, so that there are only 4 possible values of that particular nibble[1]. Since we know the values in the plaintexts, and we have two pairs that verify this transition, the corresponding key-nibble can only take two values. The same reasoning applies on the ciphertexts for the bottom characteristic.

If we run 16 different instances of the boomerang distinguishing algorithm $\mathcal{A}(n,n)$, $0 \le n < 16$, with the same nibble position n in the two characteristic, each iteration would narrow the n-th nibble of k_1 to exactly one value, but this would also require $16\cdot2^{36}$ chosen-plaintexts. Instead, we run 8 times the algorithm with different nibble positions in the top and the bottom part: $\mathcal{A}(n, n + 8)$,

---

[1] The transitions occurring with probability 2^{-2}, there are two pairs of values that are solution to $S(x) \oplus S(x \oplus \Delta) = \Delta_O$.

$0 \leq n < 8$. Consequently, the information from the top pairs reduces the left half of k_1 to 2^8 values, and the bottom pairs reduces the right half of k_1 to 2^8 values as well. In total, this requires $8 \cdot 2^{36}$ data and time to run the boomerang algorithm $\mathcal{A}$, and an additional 2^{16} time to recover the actual key k_1.

4   A Single-Key Attack on PRINCE$_{core}$ with Chosen α

The related-key boomerang attack presented above does not make use of the α-reflection property, but rather of the high probability one-round iterative characteristic. In this section, we show that the two concepts can be combined into a single-key boomerang attack with a modified value of α, i.e. we show existence of a set of values of $\alpha \neq 0$ for which one can launch key-recovery attack on PRINCE$_{core}$. The idea of our single-key attack is to align encryption with decryption in the boomerang. We note that the possibility of alignment has been discussed in the submission (see Sect. 3.1 of [4]), however the designers did not examine the case of boomerangs.

First, let us assume the encryption Enc of PRINCE$_{core}$ is aligned with decryption Dec, and focus on differential trails. Due to the α-reflection property, these two primitives are identical up the the addition of the round constants RC_i. As pointed by the designers, to build a related-key differential trail between Enc and Dec, one takes difference α in the related keys and since the same difference α is introduced by the round constants, in each round the differences cancel and the trail holds with probability 1. On the other hand in the single-key case, the difference coming from the key is 0, while the constants would still have the predefined α. Recall that in the six-round differential trails used in the related-key boomerang attack, in each round the difference introduced by the key is ∇. Hence, if α would coincide with the difference ∇ in the key from the above related-key boomerang, then a six-round single-key trail between Enc and Dec is precisely the same as the six-round related-key trail between two Enc (or between two Dec), i.e. the keys and constants switch roles. In other words, in the single-key case one can build a six-round trail with probability 2^{-12}.

The single-key boomerang attack for the whole PRINCE$_{core}$ uses the same Δ_M in the top and bottom characteristics, and it can be described as follows:

1. **Aligning encryption with decryption at the beginning:** Take a random plaintext P_1 and compute $C_2 = P_1 \oplus \Delta_M$.
2. **Aligning two encryptions with decryptions at the end:** Encrypt P_1 to produce the ciphertext C_1, and decrypt C_2 to produce the plaintext P_2. Compute $C_3 = C_1 \oplus \Delta_M$ and $P_4 = P_2 \oplus \Delta_M$.
3. **Aligning encryption with decryption at the beginning:** Decrypt C_3 to produce the plaintext P_3. Encrypt P_4 to produce the ciphertext C_4. If $P_3 \oplus C_4 = \Delta_M$ output the boomerang quartet (P_1, C_2, P_3, C_4), otherwise go to step 1.

After repeating 1–3 around 2^{48} times, one finds the quartet with a high probability. The proof of correctness of the above boomerang is similar as in the case of standard boomerangs (where one aligns encryptions with encryptions).

In the single-key case, we cannot choose the position of the active nibble as it is fixed by the value of α. Thus in the key recovery attack, we can recover only a single nibble of the master key. The first boomerang quartet will suggest 4 possible values for this nibble, and an additional quartet will give the exact value. Thus the complexity of recovering 4 bits of the master key is $2 \cdot 2^{48} = 2^{49}$. The remaining 60 bits can be searched exhaustively. Our experimental results suggest that when the top and the bottom characteristic use the same value Δ_M then the probability of the boomerang is somewhat lower, i.e. instead of 2^{-36} obtained in the case of different Δ_M, now we get 2^{-40}. Therefore the actual recovery of the 4 bits is around $2 \cdot 2^{40} = 2^{41}$.

The above attack is applicable only when the value of the constant α coincides with the value of Δ_M defined in the previous section. Therefore, α can take $15 \cdot 16 = 240$ different values. We note that the original value chosen by the designers is not among these 240 values.

5   Exploiting the Extra Linear Relation

In this section, we give an analysis of PRINCE in the single-key model. We show that while the claim of the authors is that no attack can be conducted on PRINCE with less than 2^{127-n} computations with 2^n queries, it is possible to slightly break this bound by leveraging the various linear relations that exist with probability 1 in the cipher. Of course, considering the small gain factor (only about $2^{0.6}$), our attack does not really contradict the claim of the designers. However, it indicates that perhaps it might be worth to tweak the security proof in order to take into account all the linear relations inherent to the structure of PRINCE. We emphasize that the gain factor comes directly from the number of keys tested, and not by computing only parts of the cipher as for biclique attacks [3]. It would be possible to slightly increase the gain by combining with the accelerating tricks from biclique attacks, but our goal is not in this direction as we are analyzing the structural behavior of the cipher.

5.1   The Linear Relations

The idea underlying our attack is that there exist two linear relations for PRINCE cipher that are verified with probability 1:

$$E_{(k_0||k_1)}(P) = E_{(k_0 \oplus \Delta||k_1)}(P \oplus \Delta) \oplus L(\Delta) \tag{2}$$

$$\text{or:} \quad D_{(k_0||k_1)}(C) = D_{(k_0 \oplus \Delta||k_1)}(C \oplus L(\Delta)) \oplus \Delta \tag{3}$$

$$\text{and:} \quad D_{(k_0||k_1)}(C) = E_{(k_0||k_1 \oplus \alpha)}(C \oplus k_0 \oplus L(k_0)) \oplus k_0 \oplus L(k_0) \tag{4}$$

The first Eq. (2) is the simple related-key relation due to the Even-Mansour construction of PRINCE, while the second Eq. (4) is the α relation required for the smooth decryption of PRINCE. Using these two relations, we will be able to test 4 keys at the same time, with only one PRINCE computation, thus leading to a maximal gain factor of 2 over the claimed security (2^{127} with a single query).

First let us assume that we queried some plaintext P to the encryption oracle and we received ciphertext C. By picking a random key $(k_0||k_1)$, the attacker can compute $E_{(k_0||k_1)}(P) = C'$ and directly check if $C' = C$. If not, then he knows that $(k_0||k_1)$ is not the secret key. However, he can deduce more than just this information. Indeed, from (2) and by denoting $C' \oplus C = \delta \neq 0$, we deduce

$$E_{(k_0 \oplus L^{-1}(\delta)||k_1)}(P \oplus L^{-1}(\delta)) = E_{(k_0||k_1)}(P) \oplus L(L^{-1}(\delta))$$
$$= C' \oplus \delta = C$$

and since $\delta \neq 0$, then $L^{-1}(\delta) \neq 0$ and thus the key $(k_0 \oplus L^{-1}(\delta)||k_1)$ encrypts a different plaintext than P to ciphertext C, i.e. it is not a valid key (and it is different from key $(k_0||k_1)$ since $L^{-1}(\delta) \neq 0$).

At this point, the attacker can test two keys with one PRINCE query and one PRINCE offline computation. However, he can deduce even more information by using Eq. (4) and using notation $X = L^{-1}(P \oplus C \oplus k_0)$:

$$D_{(X||k_1 \oplus \alpha)}(C) = E_{(X||k_1)}(C \oplus X \oplus L(X)) \oplus X \oplus L(X)$$
$$= E_{(k_0||k_1)}(C \oplus X \oplus L(X) \oplus k_0 \oplus X) \oplus X \oplus L(X) \oplus L(k_0 \oplus X)$$
$$= E_{(k_0||k_1)}(P) \oplus L(k_0) \oplus X$$
$$= C' \oplus L(k_0) \oplus L^{-1}(P \oplus C \oplus k_0)$$

and if $C' \oplus L(k_0) \oplus L^{-1}(P \oplus C \oplus k_0) \neq P$, then it means that the key $(X||k_1 \oplus \alpha)$ deciphers the ciphertext C to a plaintext different from P, i.e. it is not a valid key. Let us denote $Y = P \oplus C' \oplus L(k_0)$. Then:

$$E_{(Y||k_1 \oplus \alpha)}(P) = D_{(Y||k_1)}(P \oplus Y \oplus L(Y)) \oplus Y \oplus L(Y)$$
$$= D_{(k_0||k_1)}(P \oplus Y \oplus L(Y) \oplus L(k_0 \oplus Y)) \oplus Y \oplus L(Y) \oplus k_0 \oplus Y$$
$$= D_{(k_0||k_1)}(C') \oplus k_0 \oplus L(Y)$$
$$= P \oplus k_0 \oplus L(P \oplus C' \oplus L(k_0))$$

and if $P \oplus k_0 \oplus L(P \oplus C' \oplus L(k_0)) \neq C$, then it means that the key $(Y||k_1 \oplus \alpha)$ encrypts the plaintext P to a ciphertext different from C, i.e. it is not a valid key.

5.2 Speeding Up the Key Recovery with Linear Relations

For previous subsection, it is clear that with only a single query to the encryption oracle, and performing only a single PRINCE offline computation, one can eliminate four keys at a time (namely $K_1 = (k_0||k_1)$, $K_2 = (k_0 \oplus L^{-1}(\delta)||k_1)$, $K_3 = (L^{-1}(P \oplus C \oplus k_0)||k_1 \oplus \alpha)$ and $K_4 = (P \oplus C \oplus \delta \oplus L(k_0)||k_1 \oplus \alpha)$) by testing simple linear relations. However, there is a subtlety here because among the four keys that are tested, some are not controlled by the attacker. Indeed, while K_1 is directly chosen by the attacker, the value of the tested keys K_2 or K_4 depend on δ which is a random value from the view of the attacker. The third key K_3 does not depend on δ and therefore can be chosen by the attacker as well (that is, k_0 and k_1 linearly define K_1 and K_3).

We would like to evaluate the complexity of a brute force key search using this method that tests four keys with only a single PRINCE computation. One can first divide the sets of keys k_1 into 2^{63} independent pairs $(k_1, k_1 \oplus \alpha)$. The attacker will go through the 2^{63} pairs and for each of them test all the possible values of k_0. For each PRINCE computation, he will eliminate two keys for k_1 (i.e. K_1 and K_2) and two keys for $k_1 \oplus \alpha$ (i.e. K_3 and K_4), continuing until he has tested all the keys k_0 for both k_1 and $k_1 \oplus \alpha$, and then going to the next pair $(k_1, k_1 \oplus \alpha)$. To minimize the overall complexity, at each step the attacker will select a value for k_0 such that key K_1 and key K_3 have not been tested yet and this can be done with a good probability[2] as long as the number of untested keys k_0 for both k_1 and $k_1 \oplus \alpha$ is bigger than 2^{32}. The two others keys K_2 and K_4 will randomly hit either a new and untested key or an already tested one, but on average over the whole process about one key will be eliminated. Overall, with one PRINCE computation on average about three new key candidates are removed and the total key recovery complexity is about $2^{128}/3 = 2^{126.4}$ PRINCE evaluations, while with a single query to the encryption oracle the security claim by the designers is 2^{127}. We give in Appendix B a slightly more precise analysis of the attack complexity, leading to $2^{126.47}$ computations.

5.3   Generalization to Several Queries

In the previous subsection, only a single plaintext query was sent to the encryption oracle, but in fact this is not enough to fully recover the PRINCE secret key since at least two 64-bit queries are required to fully determine the 128-bit secret key. Asking one more query to the oracle in order to prune the remaining key candidates will reduce by a factor 2 the security claim given by the designers which will become lower than our key recovery complexity. Therefore, we need to generalize our previous attack to the case of several oracle queries, and we analyze the example of two queries.

Our goal with two queries is now to be able to test 8 keys at a time (instead of 4), using only one offline PRINCE computation. Let us assume that in addition to the first query (P, C), we also ask for the encryption of $P \oplus 1$ and we receive C^{+1}. As before, by choosing a random key $(k_0 || k_1)$ and computing offline $E_{(k_0||k_1)}(P) = C'$, we can test four keys at a time by using (P, C). It is actually straightforward to apply the very same reasoning to $(P \oplus 1, C^{+1})$ as well and get to test four more keys for free. For example, similarly to the first key K_1 we can write:

$$E_{(k_0 \oplus 1 || k_1)}(P \oplus 1) = E_{(k_0||k_1)}(P) \oplus L(1)$$
$$= C' \oplus L(1)$$

and if $C' \oplus L(1) \neq C^{+1}$, then it means that the key $(k_0 \oplus 1 || k_1)$ ciphers the plaintext $P \oplus 1$ to a ciphertext different from C^{+1}, i.e. it is not a valid key.

---

[2] Since there are 2^{64} values of k_0 to test, there will always be at least 2^{32} untested key for both k_1 and $k_1 \oplus \alpha$ except at the very end of the process, but then the effect is negligible since only 2^{32} keys will remain to be tested.

We can apply this kind of transformation to the three other keys K_2, K_3, K_4 and obtain three more free keys.

During the key recovery process, we now get a structure with 8 tested keys, where 4 are for k_1 (two controlled and two uncontrolled) and 4 are for $k_1 \oplus \alpha$ (two controlled and two uncontrolled). With the very same reasoning as before[3], we deduce that 6 new keys are tested on average per offline PRINCE computation, and the final key recovery complexity is $2^{128}/6 = 2^{125.4}$ PRINCE evaluations, while with two queries to the encryption oracle the security claim by the designers is 2^{126}. Using the same reasoning than depicted in Appendix B, we obtain a slightly more precise analysis of the attack complexity, leading to $2^{125.47}$ computations.

6   Integral Attacks for Reduced-Round PRINCE$_{core}$ and PRINCE

In this section, we present key-recovery attacks for reduced variants of 4, 5 and 6 rounds of PRINCE$_{core}$, and show how to extend them to key-recovery attack on the same number of rounds for PRINCE. The basic strategy comes as a direct application of the SQUARE attack proposed in [5]. We begin by describing the context for PRINCE with a 4-round version, and then show how to extend it to 5 and 6 rounds. In the sequel, we use the notations defined in Sect. 2 where the middle layer M_{mid} is linear.

6.1   Attack on 4 Rounds

This small version considers two rounds $\mathcal{R}_0$ and $\mathcal{R}_1$ in the first part of the core block cipher, followed by the middle linear layer M_{mid}, and finally the two last rounds $\mathcal{R}_2$ and $\mathcal{R}_3$. The secret key to recover for PRINCE$_{core}$ is k_1. This attack, as well as the subsequent ones, uses the following 3-round distinguishing property as its core.

Property 4. Let $\mathcal{P}_n$ be a set of 2^4 plaintexts such that a particular nibble n assumes all 2^4 possible values while the 15 other ones are fixed to chosen constants. We call this structure a δ-set. The encryption of the δ-set $\mathcal{P}_n$ through three rounds of PRINCE$_{core}$ produces a set $\mathcal{C}$ where all nibbles are balanced, that is:

$$\forall n \in \{0, \ldots, 15\}, \bigoplus_{c \in \mathcal{C}} c[n] = 0.$$

The proof strictly follows the one from [5] and is due to the wide-trail strategy followed by the designers. Additionally, we can also consider the encryption of $\mathcal{P}_n$

---

[3] We have 4 controlled keys, which can be chosen to be always untested keys as long as the number of untested keys k_0 for both k_1 and $k_1 \oplus \alpha$ is bigger than 2^{48}. Since there are 2^{64} values of k_0 to test, there will always be at least 2^{48} untested key for both k_1 and $k_1 \oplus \alpha$ except at the very end of the process, but then the effect is negligible since only 2^{48} keys will remain to be tested.

under 3.5 rounds of PRINCE_{core}, where we skip the application of the non-linear layer in the fourth round. Applying the S-box destroys this algebraic property of the δ-set, but allows to mount a key-recovery attack.

We begin by constructing a δ-set $\mathcal{P}_0$ of 2^4 plaintexts where nibble at position 0 assumes all 2^4 values, we ask the encryption $\mathcal{P}_0$ under the secret key k_1, and store the ciphertexts in $\mathcal{C}$. Then, for all nibbles n in k_1, guess the value of $k_1[n]$ and compute $\sigma = \bigoplus_{c \in \mathcal{C}} S\Big(c[n] \oplus k_1[n] \oplus RC_4[n]\Big)$. If $\sigma = 0$, then the nibble before the last non-linear layer is balanced, and we get a valid suggestion for the value $k_1[n]$. Otherwise, we discard the guess.

This algorithm requires 2^4 chosen plaintexts and suggests in average one value per nibble of k_1 since each check should remove 1 out of 2^4 guesses. At the end, we recover in sequence all the nibbles of k_1 with a total time complexity of $16 \cdot 2^4 = 2^8$ simple operations, and 2^4 64-bit words of memory.

6.2 Attack on 5 Rounds

Further we show how to add one round at the end of the previous attack, to reach five rounds. We note that this reduced variant of PRINCE_{core} is not symmetric since there are two rounds, $\mathcal{R}_0$ and $\mathcal{R}_1$, before M_{mid} and three rounds after: $\mathcal{R}_2$, $\mathcal{R}_3$ and $\mathcal{R}_4$. The strategy remains the same: we guess particular key nibbles to check the distinguishing property on an encrypted δ-set $\mathcal{C}$. Now we need to guess 4 nibbles of a column of k_1 to partially decrypt the corresponding columns of the ciphertexts and check the balanced property. Note that in the case of PRINCE_{core}, we only need to guess 4 nibbles since there is no key-schedule, whereas for the AES we would need 5.

In comparison to the previous attack where one check suffices to remove all but one key guess, here we need more. Indeed, we expect a single check to behave as a 4-bit filter, so that 4 δ-sets should provide enough information to discard all but 1 key guess. In practice, we measure that the filter is not that strong: we require in average 4.7 δ-set to determine the 4 key nibbles uniquely. In total, the attack requires $5 \cdot 2^4$ chosen plaintexts, $5 \cdot 2^4$ memory to store them, and a time complexity of $4 \cdot 5 \cdot 2^{16} \approx 2^{21}$ simple operations to recover the full k_1.

6.3 Attack on 6 Rounds

On top on the previous attack, we add one additional round at the beginning to reach six rounds. The strategy is the same as the one for the AES: we construct a set of plaintexts $\mathcal{P}$ such that we can construct a δ-set after one round. To do so, we consider a larger structure of 2^{16} plaintexts where the four diagonal nibbles assume all the possible values, and we ask its encryption to get the set of corresponding ciphertexts $\mathcal{C}$. Then, we guess the four diagonal nibbles of k_1 and partially encrypt the associated data under the key guess to find 2^4 plaintexts/ciphertexts pairs defining a δ-set in the second round. We expect 2^{12} δ-sets $\mathcal{P}_i$ for any nibble i, so the data can be reused to replay the attack on a different δ-set. We can now apply the 5-round attack by guessing only 3 additional nibbles: we already know one in each column from the diagonal guess. In total, the attack requires 2^{16} chosen plaintexts of data and same for memory requirements and runs in time equivalent to $4 \cdot 2^{16} \cdot 2^{12} = 2^{30}$ simple operations.

6.4 Extension from PRINCE$_{core}$ to PRINCE

All the three previous attacks on PRINCE$_{core}$ can be extended to attacks on PRINCE by guessing the same nibbles in $L(k_0)$. Namely, if we have an integral attack on r rounds of PRINCE$_{core}$ requiring g precise guesses in the last application k_1, we can deduce an attack recovering $k_1 \oplus L(k_0)$ on the same number r of rounds by guessing the same g nibbles in both k_1 and $L(k_0)$. For each correct final guess g that verifies the balanced property, we deduce the right value for $k_1[g] \oplus L(k_0)[g]$. Hence, for the 6-round attack, we can recover $k_1 \oplus L(k_0)$ with 2^{16} chosen plaintexts and $(2^4)^{4+3+4} = 2^{44}$ simple operations. We first guess the four diagonal nibbles of k_1 to find the δ-set, then we guess 4 nibbles in a column of $L(k_0)$ and three new guesses in the same column of k_1 to partially decrypt the ciphertexts. For the same reason as before, only three guesses are needed in k_1 because we already know one. Finally, we can exhaust the 2^{64} values of either k_0 or k_1 to recover the full 128-bit master key.

7 Time-Memory-Data Tradeoffs

In this section, we present tradeoffs for the construction used in PRINCE, i.e. our approaches work regardless of the cipher used as PRINCE$_{core}$. The proposed tradeoffs are based on a property that the cipher can be divided into two parts, leading to a similar division of the phases of the key recovery attack. Then, one side of the attack is precomputed as it does not depend on the plaintext-ciphertext, while the other side is data-dependent and it is recomputed in the online phase. Depending on the precomputation phase and in particular on the memory used in this phase, our tradeoffs are based either on the meet-in-the-middle (MITM) attacks or on Hellman's tradeoffs [9]. We note that we give time-memory-*data* tradeoffs, i.e. we show that one can achieve tradeoffs involving data as well. This is not the case for the rest of the block ciphers, as the only known generic block cipher tradeoff is the Hellman's tradeoff which does not make use of larger data set.

We assume the reader is familiar with the Hellman's time-memory tradeoff that consists of two phases: (1) precomputation or offline phase, when the attacker encrypts a chosen plaintext under all possible keys and stores part of the results in so-called Hellman's tables, and (2) online phase, in which the attacker recovers the secret key using the tables. A cryptanalytic tradeoff is defined by the following parameters:

- N is the size of the key space (e.g. for PRINCE $N = 2^{128}$)
- P is the time complexity of the precomputation phase
- M is the amount of the memory used in both the precomputation and the online phases

- T is the time required to recover the secret key, i.e. the complexity of the online phase
- D is the amount of data required to recover the secret key

The standard way of presenting a tradeoff is by giving its curve, which is a simple relation between the time, memory, data, and the size of the key. The Hellman's time-memory tradeoff is the only known generic tradeoff for block ciphers, and has the curve $TM^2 = N^2, M > N^{\frac{1}{2}}$ and $P = N$. We use (P, C) to denote the plaintext-ciphertext pair for PRINCE, and (A, B) to denote the pair for $PRINCE_{core}$.

Our tradeoffs exploit the linearity of the addition of k_0. Recall that the addition of the key k_0 is defined as:

$$P \oplus k_0 = A \tag{5}$$
$$B \oplus L(k_0) = C, \tag{6}$$

or equivalently

$$L(P) \oplus L(A) = L(k_0) \tag{7}$$
$$B \oplus C = L(k_0). \tag{8}$$

Thus, the values of P, C, A, B are related as:

$$L(P) \oplus C = L(A) \oplus B \tag{9}$$

Therefore, the separation of (P, C) on one side, and (A, B) on the other is manageable. We note that a similar reduction was presented in [7]. It was applied to the case of single-key Even-Mansour, where $L(k_0) = k_0$, and the inner transformation F is a permutation rather than a cipher as in our case. However, [7] does not examine the possibility of tradeoff attacks.

A MITM Tradeoff. Our first tradeoff is MITM based. It can be described as follows:

1. In the precomputation phase, the attacker fixes 2^{64-d} values of A and for all possible 2^{64} values of the key k_1 computes the corresponding value of $B = PRINCE_{core}(A, k_1)$ and stores the tuple $(L(A) \oplus B, A, B, k_1)$ in a table $\tilde{S}$. The size of $\tilde{S}$ is 2^{128-d}.
2. In the online phase, given 2^d pairs of known plaintexts-ciphertexts, for each pair (P_i, C_i), the attacker computes the value of $L(P) \oplus C$ and checks for a match in the table $\tilde{S}$. For every found match, the outer key k_0 is computed, and a possible candidate $k_0 || k_1$ is checked on a few more pairs of plaintexts-ciphertexts.

As there is 2^d data, the size of the set $\tilde{S}$ is 2^{128-d}, and the matching space is only 64 bits, there would be $2^{d+128-d-64} = 2^{64}$ candidates, thus the correct key would be found with an overwhelming probability.

This tradeoff has the following parameters:

$$N = 2^{128}, P = 2^{128-d}, M = 2^{128-d}, T = 2^{64}, D = 2^d, \qquad (10)$$

and thus the precomputation phase is smaller than N, i.e. $PD = N$, while the resulting memory-data tradeoff curve is of the type:

$$DM = N, T = N^{\frac{1}{2}}, M > N^{\frac{1}{2}}. \qquad (11)$$

Interestingly, this is precisely the curve given by Babbage and Golić [1,8] for stream ciphers. Compared to the Hellman's curve, we get $TM^2 = 2^{64} 2^{4 \cdot 64 - 2d} = 2^{4 \cdot 64} 2^{64 - 2d} = N^2 2^{64 - 2d}$, hence when the data $D > N^{\frac{1}{4}} = 2^{32}$, we get a better tradeoff.

Hellman's Tables Trade-off. Though the time complexity seems attractive as it is only $N^{\frac{1}{2}}$, the memory complexity required by the previous tradeoff is quite large. Hence, it is reasonable to try to reduce the memory by increasing the time. This is achievable by implementing Hellman's tradeoff as intermediate step of the tradeoff for the whole cipher. Hellman's tradeoff satisfies the curve $TM^2 = N^2$, where $N = 2^n$, $T = t^2$, $M = mt$, and $mt^2 = 2^n$. The values t, m are related to the dimension and the number of the tables created during the offline phase. Note that Hellman's tables are computed for a particular plaintext. We call P-*Hellman's tables*, the precomputation phase computed under the plaintext P. Thus P-Hellman's tables can recover the secret key if the supplied plaintext is P.

Our tradeoff based on Hellman's tables can be described as:

1. In the precomputation phase, the attacker creates a set $\tilde{S}$ of 2^{n-d} different values A_i for A and for each value, builds A_i-Hellman's tables for the cipher $PRINCE_{core}(A_i, k_1)$.
2. In the online phase, given 2^d pairs of known plaintexts-ciphertexts, for each pair (P_i, C_i), the attacker performs the following steps:
   - Fixes one value of A_i from the predefined set $\tilde{S}$,
   - Computes the value of $k_0 = P_i \oplus A$,
   - Computes the corresponding value of $B = C_i \oplus L(k_0)$,
   - Uses A_i-Hellman's table, to find a value of k_1 such that $PRINCE_{core}(A_i, k_1) = B$,
   - Checks if the found key $k_0 \| k_1$ is the correct key by testing on a few more pairs of plaintext-ciphertext,
   - If the suggested key is incorrect, repeats all of the above steps.

As there is 2^d data, and 2^{64-d} values of A_i in $\tilde{S}$, in total there are $2^d 2^{64-d} = 2^{64}$ possible values for the key k_0, and for each of them on average one value for the key k_1, or 2^{64} pairs of suggested keys, thus the attacker finds the right key with a high probability. In the precomputation phase, for a single value of A, the attacker uses 2^{64} computations to build Hellman's tables and requires $M = mt$ memory to store each of them. In the online phase, given A and B, the attacker needs $T = t^2$ time to find the correct value of the key k_1. Therefore, the tradeoff has the following parameters:

$$N = 2^{128}, P = 2^{128-d}, M = 2^{64-d}mt, T = 2^{64}t^2, D = 2^d, \qquad (12)$$

and the resulting time-memory-data tradeoff curve is of the type:

$$T(MD)^2 = 2^{64}t^2 2^{2\cdot 64-2d}m^2 t^2 2^{2d} = 2^{3\cdot 64}(t^2 m^2 t^2) = 2^{3\cdot 64}2^{2\cdot 64} = 2^{5\cdot 64} = N^2 N^{\frac{1}{2}}. \qquad (13)$$

Again, our tradeoff compared to the Hellman's tradeoff is better at the points of the curve where $D > N^{\frac{1}{4}}$. We should note that due to the claimed security level of PRINCE, i.e. $TD < N$, an additional requirement $M^2 D > 2^{192}$ is introduced.

Hellman's Single Table Trade-off. In the Hellman's tradeoff, different tables, each with a unique reduction function, are created in order to avoid colliding chains, i.e. if the chains are too long, the probability they will collide is high and therefore either the precomputation time has to be increased or the number of keys that can be recovered in the online phase becomes small. The collisions in the precomputation phase cannot be detected, hence the chains are kept short. However, the situation changes if one can store all of the values. This type of scenario is discarded in the classical Hellman's tradeoff as it requires $M = N$. However, in the case of PRINCE$_{core}$, the required memory is only $M = N^{\frac{1}{2}}$ which is precisely the lower bound on the memory in the Hellman's tradeoff (recall that the memory requirement in the Hellman's tradeoff is $M > N^{\frac{1}{2}} = 2^{64}$). Using 2^{64} memory, one can easily create a single Hellman's table for the whole tradeoff – the table has m chains, each with around t points. The first chain starts with a terminal point (a value that does not have a preimage) and can have a length of up to 2^{32}, i.e. $t < 2^{32}$. If the length t is chosen to be less than 2^{32}, then the starting point of the next chain is the end point of the previous one. This process is repeated until a collision is obtained – such collision can be detected immediately as one has all the values stored. Once a collision occurs, the next chain starts again with a terminal point. Hence, to build the whole table, one needs 2^{64} time and memory, and $mt = 2^{64}$. Only the starting and end points of the chains are stored for the online phase, thus the memory of the online phase is m, while the time complexity is t, and therefore the tradeoff curve becomes $TM = N$. Note that the memory 2^{64} is reusable across different tables, i.e. if one wants to create different tables for tradeoffs with different plaintexts, the same 2^{64} can be used. Also, as the chains can have a maximal length of 2^{32}, if follows that $t \leq 2^{32}$ and $m \geq 2^{32}$.

The tradeoff presented above can be tweaked, and instead of building multiple Hellman's tables with $mt^2 = 2^{128}$, we can use the single table described here with $mt = 2^{64}$. Hence, using this technique, we obtain the following tradeoff:

$$N = 2^{128}, P = 2^{128-d}, M = max(2^{64-d}m, 2^{64}), T = 2^{64}t, D = 2^d, \qquad (14)$$

and the resulting time-memory-data tradeoff curve is of the type:

$$TMD = 2^{64}t2^{64-d}m2^d = 2^{2\cdot 64}(tm) = 2^{2\cdot 64}2^{64} = NN^{\frac{1}{2}}. \qquad (15)$$

Obviously $M > N^{\frac{1}{2}}$ has to hold (same as in the Hellman's tradeoff), but now we get that for any $D > M/N^{\frac{1}{2}}$ our tradeoff is better than Hellman's, that is if one uses 2^{64+d} memory, and can obtain more than 2^d known pairs of plaintext-ciphertext, by implementing our tradeoff he can recover the key with less computations then by implementing the generic Hellman's tradeoff. We emphasize that our tradeoff requires only known data, i.e. it is far more practical requirement, than the one of the generic tradeoff.

Acknowledgement. The authors would like to thank the FSE 2013 reviewers and the PRINCE team for their valuable comments. Ivica Nikolić is supported by the Singapore National Research Foundation under Research Grant NRF-CRP2-2007-03. Thomas Peyrin, Lei Wang and Shuang Wu are supported by the Singapore National Research Foundation Fellowship 2012 NRF-NRFF2012-06.

A   Example of a Boomerang Structure

We present here an example of a boomerang structure found for the attack described in Sect. 3.2 (Table 2).

Table 2. Example of a related-key boomerang structure $\Big((k_i, p_i, c_i)\Big)_{i=1,\ldots,4}$ for the full PRINCE$_{core}$ in hexadecimal values.

$(k_1, k_2, k_1 \oplus k_2)$	91b4e89d2625f1fb	91b5e88d2725f1fa	0001001001000001
$(p_1, p_2, p_1 \oplus p_2)$	0b92a736c9bb91a3	0b93a726c8bb91a3	0001001001000000
$(c_1, c_2, c_1 \oplus c_2)$	2f04603451d1d3df	3846bd541167b633	1742dd6040b665ec
$(k_3, k_4, k_3 \oplus k_4)$	91a4e99d2635f1fa	91a5e98d2735f1fb	0001001001000001
$(p_3, p_4, p_3 \oplus p_4)$	a763296ea531a6b8	a762297ea431a6b8	0001001001000000
$(c_3, c_4, c_3 \oplus c_4)$	2f14613451d1d3de	3856bc541167b632	1742dd6040b665ec
$(k_1, k_3, k_1 \oplus k_3)$	91b4e89d2625f1fb	91a4e99d2635f1fa	0010010000100001
$(p_1, p_3, p_1 \oplus p_3)$	0b92a736c9bb91a3	a763296ea531a6b8	acf18e586c8a371b
$(c_1, c_3, c_1 \oplus c_3)$	2f04603451d1d3df	2f14613451d1d3de	0010010000000001
$(k_2, k_4, k_2 \oplus k_4)$	91b5e88d2725f1fa	91a5e98d2735f1fb	0010010000100001
$(p_2, p_4, p_2 \oplus p_4)$	0b93a726c8bb91a3	a762297ea431a6b8	acf18e586c8a371b
$(c_2, c_4, c_2 \oplus c_4)$	3846bd541167b633	3856bc541167b632	0010010000000001

B   Analysis of the Key Recovery Attack Complexity of Sect. 5

In the cryptanalysis described in Sect. 5, the attacker would like to test the entire set of the 2^k possible keys. At each step, four keys will be tested directly. However, for each step, the attacker can only choose the value of two keys, and the two others are randomly chosen among the set of all possible keys (thus potentially already tested ones). Since the overall complexity of the attack is the number of steps required to test the entire set of keys, we would like to evaluate this quantity precisely.

In order to ease the modeling, we consider the problem where at each step one key is chosen by the attacker (thus always an untested one) and another one is chosen randomly. Let $T_{1/2}$ be the step where half of the keys have already been tested. After $T_{1/2}$, at least one new key will be tested on average, since the attacker can choose one key each step. Before $T_{1/2}$, at least 1.5 new key will be tested on average, since the attacker can choose one key each step and since the randomly chosen key will have a probability greater than 1/2 to be an untested key. We can conclude that the average number of keys tested per step is at least $2/(1 + 1/1.5) = 1.2$.

We further continue the partitioning by denoting $T_{i/x}$ the step where a proportion i/x of all keys have already been tested. Then, with the same reasoning, after $T_{i/x}$ at least $(2 - (i + 1)/x)$ new keys will be tested on average and before $T_{i/x}$ at least $(2 - i/x)$ new keys will be tested on average. The approximation gets more precise as x grows and we obtain that the average number of key tested per step is equal to

$$\lim_{x \to \infty} \frac{x}{\sum_{i=0}^{x-1} (1/(1 + i/x))} = \frac{1}{\ln(2)} \approx 1.443. \tag{16}$$

As a consequence, the average number of steps required to test the entire key space in Sect. 5 is approximately $2^k/(2 \times 1.443) = 2^{k-1.53}$.

References

1. Babbage, S.: A space/time trade-off in exhaustive search attacks on stream ciphers. In: European Convention on Security and Detection, IEE Conference Publication No. 408 (1995)
2. Biryukov, A.: DES-X (or DESX). In: van Tilborg, H.C.A., Jajodia, S. (eds.) Encyclopedia of Cryptography and Security, 2nd edn, p. 331. Springer, New York (2011)
3. Bogdanov, A., Khovratovich, D., Rechberger, C.: Biclique cryptanalysis of the full AES. In: Lee, D.H., Wang, X. (eds.) ASIACRYPT 2011. LNCS, vol. 7073, pp. 344–371. Springer, Heidelberg (2011)
4. Borghoff, J., et al.: PRINCE – a low-latency block cipher for pervasive computing applications. In: Sako, K., Wang, X. (eds.) ASIACRYPT 2012. LNCS, vol. 7658, pp. 208–225. Springer, Heidelberg (2012)
5. Daemen, J., Knudsen, L.R., Rijmen, V.: The block cipher SQUARE. In: Biham, E. (ed.) FSE 1997. LNCS, vol. 1267, pp. 149–165. Springer, Heidelberg (1997)
6. Daemen, J., Rijmen, V.: The Design of Rijndael: AES - The Advanced Encryption Standard. Springer, New York (2002)
7. Dunkelman, O., Keller, N., Shamir, A.: Minimalism in cryptography: the even-mansour scheme revisited. In: Pointcheval, D., Johansson, T. (eds.) EUROCRYPT 2012. LNCS, vol. 7237, pp. 336–354. Springer, Heidelberg (2012)
8. Golić, J.D.: Cryptanalysis of alleged A5 stream cipher. In: Fumy, W. (ed.) EUROCRYPT 1997. LNCS, vol. 1233, pp. 239–255. Springer, Heidelberg (1997)

9. Hellman, M.E.: A cryptanalytic time-memory trade-off. IEEE Trans. Inf. Theory **26**(4), 401–406 (1980)
10. Kilian, J., Rogaway, P.: How to protect DES against exhaustive key search (an analysis of DESX). J. Cryptology **14**(1), 17–35 (2001)

Cryptanalysis of Round-Reduced LED

Ivica Nikolić[(✉)], Lei Wang, and Shuang Wu

Division of Mathematical Sciences, School of Physical and Mathematical Sciences,
Nanyang Technological University, Singapore, Singapore
{inikolic,wang.lei,wushuang}@ntu.edu.sg

Abstract. In this paper we present known-plaintext single-key and chosen-key attacks on round-reduced LED-64 and LED-128. We show that with an application of the recently proposed *slidex* attacks [5], one immediately improves the complexity of the previous single-key 4-step attack on LED-128. Further, we explore the possibility of multicollisions and show single-key attacks on 6 steps of LED-128. A generalization of our multicollision attack leads to the statement that no 6-round cipher with two subkeys that alternate, or 2-round cipher with linearly dependent subkeys, is secure in the single-key model. Next, we exploit the possibility of finding pairs of inputs that follow a certain differential rather than a differential characteristic, and obtain chosen-key differential distinguishers for 5-step LED-64, as well as 8-step and 9-step LED-128. We provide examples of inputs that follow the 8-step differential, i.e. we are able to practically confirm our results on 2/3 of the steps of LED-128. We introduce a new type of chosen-key differential distinguisher, called *random-difference* distinguisher, and successfully penetrate 10 of the total 12 steps of LED-128. We show that this type of attack is generic in the chosen-key model, and can be applied to any 10-round cipher with two alternating subkeys.

Keywords: LED · Lightweight · Multicollision · Single-key attack · Chosen-key attack

1 Introduction

The lightweight block cipher LED was proposed by Guo *et al.* at CHES 2011 [10]. It is a hardware optimized 64-bit cipher, with two main instances LED-64 for 64-bit key support, and LED-128 for 128-bit keys. Based on the AES design, LED uses modified, hardware-friendly operations and a trivial key schedule. As the authors targeted compact design, but as well secure even against related-key attacks, the number of rounds of LED is relatively large, i.e. LED-64 uses 32 rounds grouped in 8 steps of 4 rounds, while LED-128 has 48 rounds, or equivalently 12 steps. A round of LED is similar to a round of AES, with one exception: the addition of the round keys in AES is replaced with an addition of constants in LED. The subkeys are added only after every fourth round, thus

S. Moriai (Ed.): FSE 2013, LNCS 8424, pp. 112–129, 2014.
DOI: 10.1007/978-3-662-43933-3_7, © Springer-Verlag Berlin Heidelberg 2014

one step of LED (which consists of 4 rounds), behaves as 4 rounds of single-key AES – a construction with well analyzed differential and linear properties.

In the submission paper, the designers provide analysis of LED against various attacks – we mention the attacks in the chosen-key model: 15 rounds for LED-64 and 27 rounds for LED-128. Isobe and Shibutani [11] show single-key attacks on LED-64 reduced to 8 rounds, and LED-128 reduced to 16 rounds. Mendel et al. [14] give a supplementary cryptanalysis in different single and related-key models for both versions of the cipher. They are able to penetrate 16 rounds in the related-key model for LED-64, and 24 rounds for LED-128, with an additional single-key attack on 16 rounds of LED-128. An independent work proposed by Bodganov et al. in [2] also introduced similar related-key attacks on the generic structure of two-round SEM [5] with three identical keys.

We start our analysis with a brief overview of the previous results on the scheme used in LED as well as of the techniques applied in the attacks on LED (Sect. 2). The overview would help us to clearly describe our attacks in the single-key model (Sect. 3), and in the chosen-key model (Sect. 4). Our first result is an improvement of the single-key attack on 16-round LED-128 presented in [14]. We show that instead of using Daemen's attack [4] as a preliminary step, one can use the recently proposed slidex attack [5], and end up with an immediate twofold gain in terms of the data requirements: the attack from a chosen plaintext as in [14] becomes a known plaintext, while the data complexity from the whole codebook drops to 2^d, where d can be any value chosen by the attacker. Next, by exploiting the idea of multicollisions, we show a *single-key* attack on 24 rounds of LED-128. We eliminate one of the subkeys by guessing, and then we are able to attack the remaining construction by creating a set of multicollisions which allows to find the second subkey. It is important to note that our technique is applicable to LED for any step function, that is the number of rounds we can attack depends strictly on the number of used subkeys. Moreover, using the same approach one can mount attacks on any two-round construction with three equal (or linearly dependent) subkeys, e.g. SEM [5] with an additional round. The idea of using differentials instead of differential characteristic is examined in our chosen-key attacks on 20-round LED-64, and 32-,36-round LED-128. We show that two consecutive active steps in a differential path, can be threated as a differential. This leads to a significant reduction of the complexity for finding a pair that follows the path. We are able with a complexity of around 2^{32} encryptions to construct a pair that follows our defined path, and give an example of such pair found on a computer for 32 rounds of LED-128, i.e. we can show a practical chosen-key distinguisher for 2/3 of the cipher rounds. We propose a new type of chosen-key distinguishers, called *random-difference distinguishers*, where the attacker is supposed to find a pair of inputs that follow a certain differential, for any input difference. We show that LED-128 is vulnerable to this type of distinguishers for 40 rounds out of the total 48 rounds, i.e. 5/6 of the rounds of LED-128 can be distinguished in the chosen-key model. Furthermore, we show that this distinguisher is generic to all 10-round/step ciphers with two subkeys that alternate. An overview of the results on LED is given in Table 1.

Table 1. Attacks on LED

Cipher	Framework	Type	Steps	Time	Data	Memory	Ideal	Source
LED-64	single-key	Key recovery	2	2^{56}	2^8	2^{11}	2^{64}	[11]
(8 steps)	chosen-key	Distinguiher	3.75	2^{16}	–	2^{16}	2^{32}	[10]
	related-key‡	Key recovery	4	$2^{62.7}$	$2^{62.7}$	$2^{62.7}$	2^{64}	[14]
	chosen-key	Distinguisher	4	$2^{33.5}$	–	2^{32}	$2^{41.4}$	4.1
	chosen-key	Distinguisher	5	$2^{60.2}$	–	$2^{61.5}$	$2^{66.1}$	4.1
LED-128	single-key	Key recovery	4	2^{112}	2^{16}	2^{19}	2^{128}	[11]
(12 steps)	single-key	Key recovery	4	2^{96}	2^{64}	2^{32}	2^{128}	[14]
	single-key	Key recovery	4	2^{96}	2^{32}	2^{32}	2^{128}	3.1
	related-key	Key recovery	6	2^{96}	2^{64}	2^{32}	2^{128}	[14]
	single-key	Key recovery	6	$2^{124.4}$	2^{59}	2^{59}	2^{128}	3.2
	chosen-key	Distinguisher	6.75	2^{16}	–	2^{16}	2^{32}	[10]
	chosen-key	Distinguisher	8	$2^{33.5}$	–	2^{32}	$2^{41.4}$	4.2
	chosen-key	Distinguisher	9	$2^{60.8}$	–	2^{62}	$2^{66.1}$	4.2
	chosen-key	Distinguisher	10	$2^{60.3}$	–	2^{60}	2^{64}	4.3

‡: Complexity is based on the 6 found pairs that follow the iterative characteristic.

2   Specification and Related Works

In this section we give a brief description of LED and present related analysis relevant for understanding our attacks.

2.1   The Block Cipher LED [10]

LED uses a block size of 64 bits and a key size ranging from 64 bits to 128 bits. The two primary instances, LED-64 and LED-128, use a 64-bit key and an 128-bit key, respectively.

The key schedule is trivial and very efficient: LED-64 uses the 64-bit secret key in each step as a subkey, while LED-128 divides the 128-bit secret key K into halves $K_0 \| K_1$ and uses K_0 and K_1 alternatively as the subkeys, i.e. K_0 is used in the even steps, while K_1 is used in the odd steps. LED follows the standard iterative cipher structure and produces a ciphertext C from the plaintext P in t iterations of a so-called step function F_i (see Fig. 1):

$$S_0 \longleftarrow P$$
$$S_{i+1} \longleftarrow F_i(S_i \oplus K_i), 0 \le i \le t - 1$$
$$C \longleftarrow S_t \oplus K_t$$

In LED-64 the number of steps t is 8, while in the other instances including LED-128, t is defined as 12. The step function F_i is a 4-round AES-like permutation where the addition of the subkeys is replaced with an addition of constants. Thus, all the step functions F_i can be seen as public permutations and differ only in the round constants they use. Since most of our attacks can be mounted independently of the specification of the step functions, we omit their description and refer the interested reader to [9, 10] for a full specification.

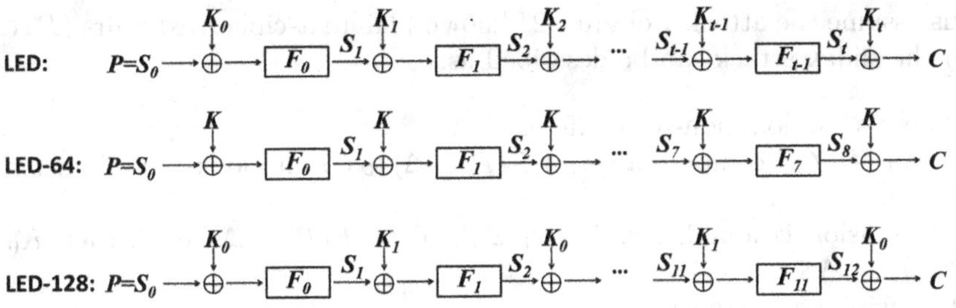

Fig. 1. LED and its two primary instances LED-64 and LED-128

2.2   Related Attacks on the Even-Mansour Scheme

The Even-Mansour scheme [6] uses two secret keys (K_0, K_1) and a public permutation F to construct a cipher $EM_{K_0,K_1}(P) = F(P \oplus K_0) \oplus K_1$ (see Fig. 2). This scheme is very attractive due to its extremely simple design with a provable security margin. Several papers on cryptanalysis of Even-Mansour have been published. This section briefly describes the attacks relevant to our paper.

Daemen's Attack [4]. The chosen-plaintext attack of Daemen can be sketched as:

1. Choose a non-zero difference Δ.
2. Choose 2^d different random values as plaintexts P, query P and $P \oplus \Delta$ to the Even-Mansour scheme to receive the corresponding ciphertexts C and C' respectively, and compute and store $\Delta C = C \oplus C'$.
3. Choose a random value X, compute $\Delta F(X) = F(X) \oplus F(X \oplus \Delta)$, and check if $\Delta F(X)$ is among the stored ΔC computed at step 2. If a match is found, then compute $K_0 = P \oplus X$ and $K_1 = F(X) \oplus C$ and confirm on another pair of plaintext-ciphertext that the values are correct.

After repeating the step 3 around 2^{n-d} times, where n is the block size, the secret keys are expected to be recovered. Thus the overall complexity is 2^d chosen plaintexts and 2^{n-d} encryptions.

Slidex Attack [5]. Dunkelman *et al.* were able to match the complexity of Daemen's attack with only known-plaintexts, using a so-called *slidex attack*.

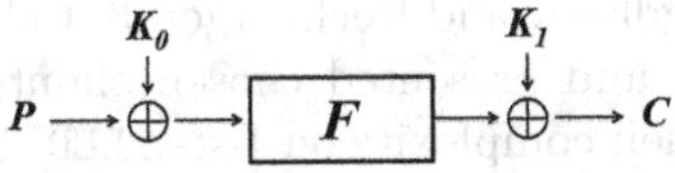

Fig. 2. Even-Mansour scheme

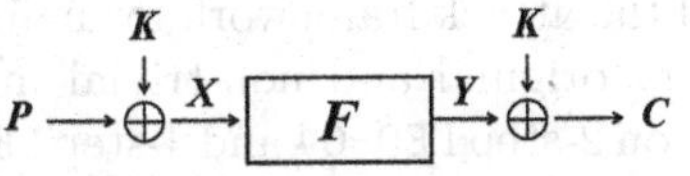

Fig. 3. Single-key Even-Mansour scheme (SEM)

Let us assume the attacker obtains 2^d known plaintext-ciphertext pairs (P_i, C_i). Then the slidex attack can be described as:

1. Choose a random non-zero difference Δ.
2. For all (P_i, C_i) compute a set of $F(P_i \oplus \Delta) \oplus C_i$ and look for a collision in the set.
3. If a collision is found, e.g. $F(P \oplus \Delta) \oplus C = F(P' \oplus \Delta) \oplus C'$, then $K_0 = P \oplus P' \oplus \Delta$.
4. Otherwise, go to step 1.

After repeating the steps $1 - 4$ around 2^{n-2d} times, the correct value of K_0 is expected to be recovered. With the knowledge of K_0, the value of K_1 can be trivially recovered using a single known pair (P, C). Thus the overall complexity is 2^d known plaintexts and 2^{n-d} encryptions.

An Attack on SEM [5]. Dunkelman *et al.* proposed a single-key variant of the Even-Mansour scheme depicted in Fig. 3, which uses the same secret key as both the pre- and the post-whitening keys, i.e. $F(P \oplus K) \oplus K$. Following the notation from [5], we refer to this single-key variant as SEM. Dunkelman *et al.* provided once more a known-plaintext attack on SEM based on the observation that $P \oplus C = X \oplus Y$. Again, we assume the attacker obtains 2^d known plaintext-cihertext pairs (P_i, C_i). The steps of the attack are as follows:

1. Compute a set of $P_i \oplus C_i$ for all 2^d (P_i, C_i).
2. Choose a random value of X, compute $Y = F(X)$ and match $X \oplus Y$ to the values of $P \oplus C$ from the set computed at step 1.
3. If a match is found, $K = P \oplus X$.
4. Otherwise, go to to step 2.

After repeating the steps $2 - 4$ around 2^{n-d} times, the correct value of K is expected to be recovered. Thus the complexity is 2^d known plaintexts and $2^d + 2^{n-d}$ computations.

2.3   Key-Recovery Attacks on LED

Several chosen-plaintext key-recovery attacks on LED have been published. This section briefly describes the attacks related to this paper.

Three-Subset Meet-in-the-Middle Attacks on LED [11]. Isobe and Shibutani applied the attack framework formalized by Bogdanov and Rechberger [3] to LED in a very original and non-trivial manner [11] and presented chosen-plaintext attacks on 2-step LED-64 and 4-step LED-128. Their complexity on 4-step LED-128 is 2^{16} chosen plaintexts and 2^{112} encryptions. We stress that the time complexity of their attacks cannot be reduced when more data is available.

Guess-and-Recover Attacks on LED-128 [14]. Mendel *et al.* published key-recovery attacks on 4-step and 6-step LED-128 in the single-key and the related-key settings, respectively. The main strategy of their attacks is first to guess the value of K_0 in order to peel off the first and the last step functions, and then to efficiently recover the value of K_1 by attacking the shortened cipher. In this paper we call such attack strategy *guess-and-recover*. The attack on 4-step LED-128 (depicted in Fig. 4) starts by guessing the key K_0, thus the 4-step LED-128 is shortened to a cipher E, and moreover G (in Fig. 4) becomes now a public permutation. As E follows the Even-Mansour scheme, Mendel *et al.* adopted Daemen's attack [4] sketched in Sect. 2.2 to recover the key K_1. In particular, for an input S_1 to the cipher E, in order to get the value of $E(S_1)$, the attacker computes $P = F_0^{-1}(S_1) \oplus K_0$, then queries P to LED-128 to receive the corresponding ciphertext C, and finally computes $F_3^{-1}(C \oplus K_0)$ as $E(S_1)$. Note, Mendel *et al.*'s attack is a known/chosen-plaintext attack and since the Daemen's attack procedure is executed for each guess of K_0 (thus repeated 2^{64} times), the data complexity of the attack equals the entire codebook while the time complexity is 2^{96} encryptions. The authors point out that the attacker is able to reduce the data complexity below the entire codebook, however then he has to sacrifice the time complexity, i.e. the time will increase proportionally. We stress that the attack becomes a chosen-plaintext attack if the data complexity is less than the entire codebook, otherwise it can be considered known-plaintext attack (it requires the whole codebook, hence there is no difference between chosen and known plaintext).

Mendel *et al.* were able to extended the above attack on 4 steps to 6 steps of LED-128 in the related key settings. A pictorial view of the guess-and-recover strategy on 6-step LED-128 is given in Fig. 5. The attack uses a related key $K' = K_0 \| K_1'$, where K_1' is $K_1 \oplus \Delta$. Let E' be the shortened cipher under the related key K'. For a random value S_1, inside the computations of $E(S_1)$ and $E'(S_1 \oplus \Delta)$, the difference $\Delta G_1(S_1) = G_1(S_1 \oplus K_1) \oplus G_1(S_1 \oplus \Delta \oplus K_1')$ is always 0. Hence the input difference of G_2 is always Δ. Thus Daemen's attack can be applied to recover the value of K_1 in a straightforward way with the same data and time complexity.

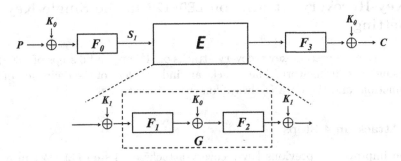

Fig. 4. Guess-and-recover strategy on 4-step LED-128

Attacks on LED-64 Exploiting Differential Characteristics for the Step Functions [14]. Mendel *et al.* proposed as well attacks on 3-step and 4-step LED-64 in the related-key setting, by investigating the differential properties of the step functions of LED, in particular differential characteristics with high height as well as iterative differential characteristics. For the public permutations used in the step function, the authors found differential characteristics with a probability of around 2^{-54}, while theoretically it may go up to 2^{-50} (25 active Sboxes and each with 2^{-2}). In one part of our analysis, we use the results of [14], and in order to provide conservative results, we assume the optimal differential characteristic for the step functions to hold with probability 2^{-54}. However, as pointed out by Mendel *et al.*, differential characteristics with a better probability may exist and if such characteristic is found, our attack complexity will be immediately improved.

2.4   Differential Multicollisions for Block Ciphers [1]

This concept was introduced by Biryukov *et al.* [1]. It can be defined as follows:

Definition 1. *A differential q-multicollision for the block cipher $E_K(\cdot)$ is defined as a set of two differences ΔP and ΔK and q key-plaintext pairs (K_1, P_1), (K_2, P_2), ..., (K_q, P_q) that satisfy the relation:*

$$E_{K_1}(P_1) \oplus E_{K_1 \oplus \Delta K}(P_1 \oplus \Delta P) =$$
$$E_{K_1}(P_2) \oplus E_{K_2 \oplus \Delta K}(P_2 \oplus \Delta P) =$$
$$\cdots =$$
$$E_{K_q}(P_q) \oplus E_{K_q \oplus \Delta K}(P_q \oplus \Delta P),$$

Biryukov *et al.* have proven that it takes at least $q \cdot 2^{\frac{q-2}{q+2}n}$ queries to produce a differential q-multicollision for an *ideal* n-bit block cipher. Thus if an attacker can find a differential q-multicollision on a dedicated block cipher with a complexity less than the lower bound $q \cdot 2^{\frac{q-2}{q+2}n}$, he can distinguish the cipher from ideal in the chosen-key model.

3   Key-Recovery Attacks on LED-128 in the Single-Key Setting

In this section we present key recovery attacks on 4 steps and 6 steps of LED-128 in the single-key framework. The attacks are independent of the definition of the step function, and the data is always known-plaintext.

3.1   Attack on 4 Steps

We can improve the previous key-recovery attacks on 4-step LED-128 in a relatively straightforward way. Our attack follows the guess-and-recover strategy, which is depicted in Fig. 4. First, note that the shortened cipher E is the SEM scheme. Thus after guessing the value K_0, to recover K_1 instead of adopting Daemen's approach [4] as in the previous attack [14], we apply Dunkelman et al.'s slidex attack or their attack approach on SEM [5] sketched in Sect. 2.2. This immediately gives us the first advantage: our attack is a known-plaintext attack. Moreover, based on the complexity evaluation given below, our approach has a second advantage: the complexity also gets improved. Since we will extend the below approach to attack 6-step LED-128 in Sect. 3.2, here we give a detailed description of the complete attack approach. The notations below follow the one from Fig. 4.

Attack Procedure. Suppose the attacker obtains 2^d known plaintext-ciphertext pairs (P, C).

1. Guess the value of K_0.
2. For all 2^d pairs (P, C), compute $S_1 = F_0(K_0 \oplus P)$ and $E(S_1) = F_3^{-1}(K_0 \oplus C)$, then compute $S_1 \oplus E(S_1)$, and store the pairs $(S_1, S_1 \oplus E(S_1))$.
3. Choose 2^{64-d} different random values denoted as X. For each X:
   (a) Compute $G(X) \oplus X$ and match it to $S_1 \oplus E(S_1)$ stored at step 2.
   (b) If a match is found, compute the value $S_1 \oplus X$ as a candidate of K_1. Otherwise, go to step 3(a) with the next value of X.
   (c) Verify the correctness of the candidate for K_1 by using another $(S_1', E(S_1'))$, where S_1' is not equal to S_1. In particular, compute the value for $E(S_1')$ using the current guessed K_0 and the candidate K_1, and check whether it is equal to the value for $E(S_1')$ computed at Step 2. If they are equal, output the currently guessed K_0 and the candidate K_1 as the real key, and terminate the procedure. Otherwise, go to step 3(a) with the next value of X.
4. Change the value of K_0, and repeat steps $1-3$ until all possible values of K_0 are tested.

Complexity. The unit is one computation of the whole 4-step LED-128 consisting of four step functions. The steps $1-3$ are repeated 2^{64} times. One execution of step 2 requires $2^d \times \frac{2}{4} = 2^{d-1}$ computations. In one execution of step 3, step 3(a) is repeated 2^{64-d} times, and therefore the total complexity is $2^{64-d} \times \frac{2}{4} = 2^{63-d}$. At step 3(b), on average there is one match among all the 2^{64-d} repetitions. Hence the complexity of steps 3(b) and 3(c) is 1. Thus the overall time complexity is $2^{64} \cdot (2^{d-1} + 2^{63-d} + 1) \approx 2^{63+d} + 2^{127-d}$, while the data complexity is 2^d known plaintext-ciphertext pairs, and 2^d memory required in step 2.

Success Probability. When the guessed value of K_0 is correct, if one random X at step 3 collides with $S_1 \oplus K_1$ for some S_1 computed at step 2, the value of K_1 will be correctly recovered. The probability of a such collision is $1 - \frac{1}{e} \approx 0.63$.

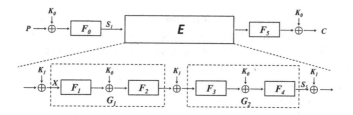

Fig. 5. Guess-and-recover attack on 6-step LED-128

Comparison to Previous Attacks. The optimal time complexity of our attack is 2^{96} by setting d to 32, while the data complexity is 2^{32} known plaintexts. Previous attacks either cannot reach such low time complexity (e.g. [11]) or with a much higher data complexity, i.e. the entire codebook, for the same time complexity (e.g. [14]).

3.2 Attack on 6 Steps

We can extend the above attack to 6-step LED-128 by using multicollisions. As depicted in Fig. 5, the shortened cipher E after guessing K_0 can be regarded as a two-step SEM. The relation $S_1 \oplus E(S_1) = X \oplus S_5$ holds. Suppose we have a q-multicollision on $E(S_1) \oplus S_1$. Namely, we find q values $S_1^{(1)}, S_1^{(2)}, \ldots, S_1^{(q)}$ such that $E(S_1^{(1)}) \oplus S_1^{(1)} = E(S_1^{(2)}) \oplus S_1^{(2)} = \cdots = E(S_1^{(q)}) \oplus S_1^{(q)}$ holds. Denote the value of $E(S_1^{(i)}) \oplus S_1^{(i)}$, $1 \le i \le q$, by Y. Let us select a random value as X, then set S_5 as $X \oplus Y$, and compute the value $G_1(X) \oplus G_2^{-1}(S_5)$ as a candidate value of K_1, which can be verified trivially. Note that if X is equal to any of $S_1^{(i)} \oplus K_1$, $1 \le i \le q$, the computed candidate is the correct value of K_1. Thus after testing $2^{64}/q$ random values as X, the real value of K_1 is expected to be recovered. Recall that such attack procedure needs to be repeated for each guess of K_0, i.e. in total 2^{64} times. Hence the overall complexity is $2^{128}/q$. The details of the attack procedure are given below - for $q = 8$ the attack has the lowest complexity.

Attack Procedure. The attacker obtains 2^{59} known plaintext-ciphertext pairs (P, C).

1. Guess the value of K_0.
2. For all 2^{59} (P, C), compute $S_1 = F_0(P \oplus K_0)$ and $E(S_1) = F_5^{-1}(C \oplus K_0)$. Then compute $S_1 \oplus E(S_1)$ and store $(P, S_1, S_1 \oplus E(S_1))$.
3. Find an 8-multicollision on $S_1 \oplus E(S_1)$, namely a set of $(P^{(1)}, S_1^{(1)}, S_1^{(1)} \oplus E(S_1^{(1)})), \ldots, (P^{(8)}, S_1^{(8)}, S_1^{(8)} \oplus E(S_1^{(8)}))$ such that $S_1^{(1)} \oplus E(S_1^{(1)}) = S_1^{(2)} \oplus E(S_1^{(2)}) = \cdots = S_1^{(8)} \oplus E(S_1^{(8)})$. Denote the value of $S_1^{(i)} \oplus E(S_1^{(i)})$, $1 \le i \le 8$, as Y. If no such 8-multicollision exists, go to step 1 with another guess value as K_0.

4. Choose 2^{61} random values as X. For each value of X:
    (a) Compute $X \oplus Y$ as S_5.
    (b) Compute $G_1(X) \oplus G_2^{-1}(S_5)$ denoted as Z.
    (c) Compute $X \oplus Z$, and match it to $\{S_1^{(1)}, \ldots, S_1^{(8)}\}$. If it coincides with some $S_1^{(i)}$, then Z is regarded as a candidate value of K_1. Otherwise, go to step 4(a) with the next value of X.
    (d) Verify the correctness of Z as K_1 by using another relation $(S_1, E(S_1))$ with $S_1 \neq S_1^{(i)}$. If it is correct, set $K_1 = Z$, then output the current guessed value of K_0 and K_1 as the real key, and terminate the attack procedure. Otherwise, go to step 4(a) with the next value of X.
5. Change the value of K_0, and repeat steps $1 - 4$ until all possible values of K_0 are tested.

Complexity. The unit is one computation of the whole 6-step LED-128. The steps $1 - 4$ are repeated 2^{64} times. One execution of step 2 has the complexity of $2^{59} \times \frac{2}{6} \approx 2^{57.4}$. In one execution of step 4, steps 4(a), 4(b) and 4(c) are repeated 2^{61} times, and the total complexity is $2^{61} \times \frac{4}{6} \approx 2^{60.4}$. On average, there is only one match at step 4(d) among 2^{62} random values. Thus the complexity of step 4(e) is 1. Therefore the overall time complexity is $2^{64} \cdot (2^{59.4} + 2^{60.4} + 1) \approx 2^{124.4}$, while data complexity is 2^{59} known plaintexts. The memory requirement is 2^{59} for step 2.

Success Probability. We focus on the success probability of recovering K_1, when the guessed value of K_0 is correct. First we evaluate the probability of 8-multicollisions at step 2. It has been proven that a q-multicollision among $\sqrt[q]{q!} \times 2^{\frac{q-1}{q}n}$ n-bit random values exists with a probability 0.5 [7,16]. By setting $q = 8$ and $n = 64$, $\sqrt[q]{q!} \times 2^{\frac{q-1}{q}n}$ is smaller than 2^{58}. Since we have in total 2^{59} values, the probability of an 8-multicollision is almost 1. Then we evaluate the probability of a collision between a random value X and a $S_1^{(i)} \oplus K_1$. The probability of such a collision is $1 - \frac{1}{e} \approx 0.63$. Thus the overall success probability is 0.63.

Remark. We emphasize that our attack is not related to the specification of step functions, and thus applicable to any 6-step Even-Mansour scheme with the key schedule of alternating two keys. The advantage of our attack is related to the block size n. A shown above for the case $n = 64$, q is chosen as 8, and the complexity is $2^{3.6}$ times faster than the brute-force attack. In particular, for the common block size $n = 128$, q can be 16, and our attack becomes $2^{4.6}$ times faster than the brute-force attack.

As we can see from the above analysis, the 6-step attack is actually based on a 2-step multicollision-type attack (the permutations G_1, G_2 with subkey additions), that is applicable to any permutations G_1, G_2. Thus we can derive the following interesting fact:

Observation 1. *For any two-round n-bit cipher* $E_K(P) = G_2(G_1(P \oplus K) \oplus L_1(K)) \oplus L_2(K)$, *where* G_1, G_2 *are arbitrary permutations, and* L_1, L_2 *are linear bijective functions, exists a known-plaintext attack a with time complexity of less than* 2^n *encryption queries.*

It is interesting to note that Observation 1 actually answers affirmatively the open problem proposed in [2] if there exist a single-key attack on two-round SEM structure with three identical keys and computational complexity below 2^n.

4   Chosen Key Differential Distinguishers for LED-64 and LED-128

The designers of LED pointed out in the specification document [10], that in order to gain confidence in the cipher, one should study the security of the cipher in the framework where the attacker knows or controls the key. Using the rebound [13] and Super-Sbox [8,12] techniques, they were able to penetrate 15 rounds (3.75 steps) of LED-64, and 27 rounds (6.75 steps) of LED-128. The design strategy underlying LED, in particular the trivial key schedule and fact that the best probability of a differential characteristic in an active step of LED cannot be higher than 2^{-50}, seem to confirm the findings of the designers. As LED-64 has 128-bit input (64-bit key and 64-bit state), it leads that a differential characteristic cannot have more than 2 active steps, otherwise the probability (for 3 steps) would be at most 2^{-150}, and the freedom of the 128-bit input is insufficient to satisfy the characteristic. Similarly, for LED-128, the best characteristic cannot have more than 3 active steps, as the probability of a 4-step characteristic would be at most 2^{-200}, hence the 192-bit input (128-bit key and 64-bit plaintext) is insufficient for this characteristic.

The above reasoning however, applies to the case of *differential character-istics*. Further we show that the situation changes when one investigates the effects of *differentials*. To clarify our reasoning, let us examine the case of a 2-step differential where both steps are active and assume the input and the output difference take some predefined values. The probability of a single differential characteristic that composes the differential is at most 2^{-100}. However, the probability of the differential is much higher, i.e. 2^{-64} for *any* input-output differences. Hence if we can efficiently find a pair of inputs that follow this differential, then we would spend only 64-bits of freedom, instead of 100 bits as in the case of characteristics.

The results presented in this section give solutions for finding such pairs, and use the additional freedom to penetrate more steps of LED.

4.1   Differential Multicollision on 5-Step LED-64

Our distinguisher is based on the differential path given in Fig. 6. The path is built by fixing an optimal differential characteristic in the last step function

F_4: $\Delta \rightarrow \Delta*$, which determines the value of Δ and $\Delta*$, and then the following values are set as well: $\Delta P = \Delta$, $\Delta K = \Delta$ and $\Delta C = \Delta \oplus \Delta*$. Note, the differential characteristic $\Delta \rightarrow \Delta*$ holds with a probability of at least 2^{-54}, following Mendel et al.'s investigation [14] described in Sect. 2.3. After the path is determined, we search for pairs (P, K) satisfying LED-64 $_K(P) \oplus$ LED-64 $_{K \oplus \Delta}(P \oplus \Delta) = \Delta \oplus \Delta*$. The search procedure starts with launching a meet-in-the-middle attack between step functions F_1 and F_2. Note that both the input difference of F_1 and the output difference of F_2 are fixed as Δ. We select random values X and Y, and independently compute $\Delta F_1(X) = F_1(X) \oplus F_1(X \oplus \Delta)$ and $\Delta F_2^{-1}(Y) = F_2^{-1}(Y) \oplus F_2^{-1}(Y \oplus \Delta)$. Then we match between $\Delta F_1(X)$ and $\Delta F_2^{-1}(Y) \oplus \Delta$. For a match, by adaptively selecting two values $F_1(X) \oplus F_2^{-1}(Y)$ and $F_1(X) \oplus F_2^{-1}(Y \oplus \Delta)$ as the key K and computing the corresponding values of P from (K, X), we obtain two pairs (K, P) which can satisfy the path on the first four step functions in Fig. 6. Finally, the differential characteristic on the last step function F_4 is satisfied probabilistically.

Attack Procedure

1. Select 2^s random values X, compute $\Delta F_1(X) = F_1(X) \oplus F_1(X \oplus \Delta)$, and store $(X, \Delta F_1(X))$. The value of s will be determined in the complexity evaluation below.
2. Select 2^s random values Y, compute $\Delta F_2^{-1}(Y) = F_2^{-1}(Y) \oplus F_2^{-1}(Y \oplus \Delta)$ and match $\Delta F_2^{-1}(Y) \oplus \Delta$ to stored ΔF_1 at step 1. On average, there are 2^{2s-64} matches.
3. For each matched pair X and Y,
   (a) Compute two values as K: $K = F_1(X) \oplus F_2^{-1}(Y)$ and $K = F_1(X \oplus \Delta) \oplus F_2^{-1}(Y \oplus \Delta)$.
   (b) Compute C and C' for each pair (K, Y) and $(K \oplus \Delta, Y \oplus \Delta)$ respectively.
   (c) If ΔC is equal to $\Delta \oplus \Delta*$, compute the corresponding value of P, and store the values of (P, K). On average, there are 2^{2s-117} values of (P, K) stored.

Complexity of Finding Differential q-Multicollision. The unit is one computation of the whole 5-step LED-64. The dominant complexity comes from steps 1 and 2, each of them requires $2^s \times \frac{1}{5}$ units, hence the total complexity is approximately $2^{s-1.3}$. To produce a differential q-multicollision, set $2^{2s-117} = q$, which implies $s = 58.5 + \log_2 \sqrt{q}$, and thus the complexity is $\sqrt{q} \cdot 2^{57.2}$. For $q = 2^6$, the overall complexity of our attack is $2^{60.2}$, while the generic attack requires at least $2^{66.1} > 2^{64}$ encryptions.

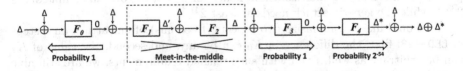

Fig. 6. Distinguisher on 5-step LED-64

Table 2. An example of pair of inputs following the 8-STEP (32 rounds) differential for LED-128. The two rows of each step denote the input and output values/differences of the steps.

	Input 1	Input 2	XOR difference
K_0	63686a8c6ed193f6	63686a8c6ed193f7	0000000000000001
K_1	0000000000000000	0000000000000000	0000000000000000
plaintext	33960e4a40a0f740	33960e4a40a0f740	0000000000000001
step 0	50fe64c62e7164b6	50fe64c62e7164b6	0000000000000000
	e82c1e07da3b4304	e82c1e07da3b4304	0000000000000000
step 1	e82c1e07da3b4304	e82c1e07da3b4304	0000000000000000
	3bb5fd710efb3bba	3bb5fd710efb3bba	0000000000000000
step 2	58dd97fd602aa84c	58dd97fd602aa84d	0000000000000001
	50fdeb1af852210e	56c051f2c88d007a	063dbae830df2174
step 3	50fdeb1af852210e	56c051f2c88d007a	063dbae830df2174
	eb82dccf19e68610	fe5507900afd76ad	15d7db5f131bf0bd
step 4	88eab643773715e6	9d3d6d1c642ce55a	15d7db5f131bf0bc
	c6dbdb083c8dfccb	b688dc44effea528	7053074cd37359e3
step 5	c6dbdb083c8dfccb	b688dc44effea528	7053074cd37359e3
	ef7e6ce5ebb78007	ef7e6ce5ebb78006	0000000000000001
step 6	8c160669856613f1	8c160669856613f1	0000000000000000
	5f2a1e2a6f01e9eb	5f2a1e2a6f01e9eb	0000000000000000
step 7	5f2a1e2a6f01e9eb	5f2a1e2a6f01e9eb	0000000000000000
	337e6d7828ea8fec	337e6d7828ea8fec	0000000000000000
ciphertext	501607f4463b1c1a	501607f4463b1c1b	0000000000000001

4.2   Differential Multicollision for 8-Step and 9-Step LED-128

Our distinguisher on 8-step LED-128 is based on a differential path given in Fig. 7, where Δ can be any non-zero value. We set $\Delta P = \Delta$, $\Delta K = (\Delta K_0 = \Delta, \Delta K_1 = 0)$ and $\Delta C = \Delta$. First we select a random value as K_1, which makes G_1 and G_2 to become two public permutations. Then we carry out a meet-in-the-middle attack between G_1 and G_2. Note both the input differences of G_1 and the output differences of G_2 are fixed as Δ. We adopt the same meet-in-the-middle procedure as the one presented in Sect. 4.1, and adaptively choose the value of K_0. As the rest of the differential path holds with probability 1, the chosen K_0 with previously fixed K_1 and P, which can be computed trivially from X, is the expected solution, namely it satisfy the whole differential path. Following the complexity evaluation as in Sect. 4.1, our attack needs $q \cdot 2^{30.5}$ computations to produce a differential q-multicollision, hence for $q = 8$, the overall complexity is $2^{33.5}$, while the generic attack needs at least $2^{41.4}$.

We would like to emphasize two aspects (freedoms) of our attack on 8 steps of LED-128: first, the difference in K_0 can be any, and second, the value of K_1 can be arbitrary as well. Even with such relaxed requirements, we are still able to find a pair that follows the differential path with a complexity of around $2^{30.5}$.

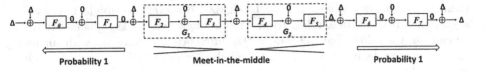

Fig. 7. Distinguisher on 8-step LED-128

8-step encryptions. An example of such pair, found on a computer, is given in Table 2. Note, in the example the difference in K_0 is 1 and the value of K_1 is 0.

Extension to 9 Steps. The above path can be extended with an additional step at the end, thus leading to a 9-step path. First, we find an optimal differential characteristic for the last step function F_9: $\Delta \rightarrow \Delta*$, i.e. we use again the same characteristic that holds with 2^{-54}. Then the differential is defined as $\Delta P = \Delta$, $\Delta K = (\Delta K_0 = \Delta, \Delta K_1 = 0)$, and $\Delta C = \Delta*$. The distinguisher uses a differential path, which is a concatenation of the path on the first 8 step functions from Fig. 7 and the characteristic $\Delta \rightarrow \Delta*$ for the last step function F_9. After selecting a random value as K_1, we apply exactly the same search procedure as in Sect. 4.1. However, this time instead of producing q pairs that follow the 8-step differential, we produce $q2^{54}$ such pairs. Obviously, after the last step, there would be around q pairs that satisfy the whole 9-step differential.

The complexity is dominated by the meet-in-the-middle attack and the generation of $q2^{54}$ pairs for the 8-step differential. To optimize the complexity, we should create $\sqrt{q}2^{59}$ differences for each G_1 and G_2, hence there would be $q2^{118}$ pairs in the middle and $q2^{118-64} = q2^{54}$ that follow the 8-step differential or q pairs for the whole 9-step differential. Thus taking into account that the G_1, G_2 take $\frac{2}{9}$ of the total number of rounds, the overall complexity for $q = 2^6$ is $2 \cdot 2^3 2^{59} \frac{2}{9} = 2^{60.8}$ encryptions of 9-step LED-128. The generic case again requires $2^{66.1}$ encryptions.

4.3 A Differential Distinguisher on 10-Step LED-128

In this section we introduce the concept of chosen-key *random-difference* distinguisher and present such distinguisher for 10 steps of LED-128.

In differential multicollisions, the attacker finds a set of two differences for the key and the plaintext, such that all the differences in the ciphertext of q pairs of keys/plaintexts, are the same. Thus the freedom is three differences: in the key, in the plaintext, and in the ciphertext, and therefore, to prove the distinguisher is not trivial, the attacker has to find many pairs of keys/plaintexts that follow the same differential. Now assume, the freedom is only in one of the input differences, and the other two depend on (or are equal to) this single difference, i.e. the attacker wants to find a key/plaintext (K, P) such that for some given difference Δ, $E_{K \oplus \Delta}(P \oplus \Delta) \oplus E_K(P) = \Delta$ holds. Obviously, if the difference Δ is random, he cannot find the input pair with a complexity lower than 2^n (see below), where n is the block size. However, one might reasonably argue, that if the attacker has to provide a single pair of key/plaintext, then he can use the additional freedom of the difference and come up with his own Δ in time complexity lower than 2^n, and thus achieve such distinguisher. Our distinguisher below thwarts such approach, since it requires the attacker to be able to build the input pair for *any random* difference Δ. This type of problem already has been analyzed in the work of Patarin [15] – he has shown that the xor of two random permutations cannot be distinguished from a pseudo-random function with less than 2^n queries. In our case, the permutations are defined as $P_1(X) = P_1(K, P, \Delta) = E_{K \oplus \Delta}(P \oplus \Delta)$ and $P_2(X) = P_2(K, P, \Delta) = E_K(P) \oplus \Delta$, i.e. they are keyed with both K and Δ, and for fixed values of these two parameters they are two distinct permutations (as long as $\Delta \neq 0$). In the chosen-key scenario discussed below, although the key can be chosen, the difference Δ is still arbitrary and unknown, hence Patarin's proof again applies to the pseudo-random function (PRF) $P_1(X) \oplus P_2(X)$, which can be translated into finding a preimage of 0 for the PRF, as from $E_{K \oplus \Delta}(P \oplus \Delta) \oplus E_K(P) = \Delta$ is follows we are looking at the condition $P_1(X) \oplus P_2(X) = 0$. The complexity of finding such preimage for an n-bit PRF is 2^n queries, and thus encryptions/decryptions. Now we are ready to give a formal definition of this non-trivial distinguisher:

Definition 2. *A random-difference distinguisher exists for the cipher $E_K(P)$, if for any randomly chosen Δ, the attacker with a complexity less than 2^n encryptions/decryptions can find a plaintext P and a key K, such that $E_K(P) \oplus E_{K \oplus \Delta}(P \oplus \Delta) = \Delta$.*

Further, we show that this type of distinguisher can be found for 10-step LED-128, i.e. we show that for a randomly chosen Δ, with less than 2^{64} queries/ encryptions we can find the input P, K_0, K_1 such that $E_{K_0 \oplus \Delta || K_1}(P \oplus \Delta) \oplus E_{K_0 || K_1}(P) = \Delta$. Our analysis is based on a differential path given in Fig. 8, where the step functions denoted in a black color are active, while the white steps are non-active. In Fig. 8 we also sketch the attack procedure. We start with a meet-in-the-middle (MITM) attack between F_2 and F_3. Note that both the input difference of F_2 and the output difference of F_3 are fixed as Δ. We carry out the same MITM procedure as the one in Sect. 4.1, and find pairs (K_1, X), where X is the output value of F_3, satisfying the differential path on the first four step functions. Similarly, we perform MITM on the other side, between F_6 and F_7, and find pairs (K_1, Y) where Y is the input value of F_6, satisfying the differential path on the last four step functions. Next, we match (K_1, X) and (K_1, Y) on the value of K_1, and store (K_1, X, Y) if the value of

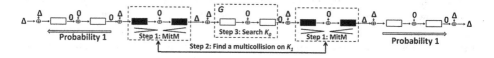

Fig. 8. Distinguisher on 10-step LED-128

K_1 is matched. Then we search for a q-multicollision among (K_1, X, Y) on the value of K_1. Namely we find a set of $(K_1^{(1)}, X^{(1)}, Y^{(1)})$, $(K_1^{(2)}, X^{(2)}, Y^{(2)})$, ..., $(K_1^{(q)}, X^{(q)}, Y^{(q)})$ with $K_1 = K_1^{(1)} = K_2^{(2)} = \cdots = K_1^{(q)}$. For this fixed K_1, G becomes a public permutation. The last step is to find a value of K_0, which links $X^{(i)}$ to $Y^{(i)}$ for some $1 \leq i \leq q$, i.e. $G(X^{(i)} \oplus K_0) \oplus K_0 = Y^{(i)}$. The search procedure is similar to the attack on SEM [5], i.e. if we have q possible values for $(X^{(i)}, Y^{(i)})$, we need only $2^n/q$ values for the inputs/outputs of G in order to find one match. A single match suggests immediately the value of K_0, hence we have fixed as well the second key K_0, and thus finding the input plaintext is trivial.

Attack Procedure. Let Δ be any non-zero value.

1. Choose 2^{60} different random values A. Compute and store $\Delta F_2(A) = F_2(A) \oplus F_2(A \oplus \Delta)$. Then choose 2^{60} different random values X, compute $\Delta F_3^{-1}(X) = F_3^{-1}(X) \oplus F_3^{-1}(X \oplus \Delta)$, and match it to the stored $\Delta F_2(A)$. For each matched $(\Delta F_2(A), \Delta F_3^{-1}(X))$, compute $F_2(A) \oplus F_3^{-1}(X)$ and $F_2(A \oplus \Delta) \oplus F_3^{-1}(X)$ as K_1, and store (K_1, X). On average, there are 2^{57} stored (K_1, X).
2. Launch the same procedure between F_6 and F_7 as in step 1, and store 2^{57} (K_1, Y), where Y is the input value of F_6.
3. Match (K_1, X) and (K_1, Y) on the value of K_1, and store (K_1, X, Y) if (K_1, X) and (K_1, Y) are matched. On average there are 2^{50} (K_1, X, Y).
4. Find a 4-multicollision among (K_1, X, Y) on the value of K_1. Namely, find $(K_1^{(1)}, X_1^{(1)}, Y_1^{(1)})$, $(K_1^{(2)}, X_1^{(2)}, Y_1^{(2)})$, $(K_1^{(3)}, X_1^{(3)}, Y_1^{(3)})$ and $(K_1^{(4)}, X_1^{(4)}, Y_1^{(4)})$ with $K_1^{(1)} = K_1^{(2)} = K_1^{(3)} = K_1^{(4)}$. Compute $X_1^{(1)} \oplus Y_1^{(1)}$, $X_1^{(2)} \oplus Y_1^{(2)}$, $X_1^{(3)} \oplus Y_1^{(3)}$ and $X_1^{(4)} \oplus Y_1^{(4)}$.
5. Choose 2^{62} random value Z, and compute $G(Z) \oplus Z$, where G uses $K_1^{(i)}$, $1 \leq i \leq 4$ as K_1. Match the value of $G(Z) \oplus Z$ to $X_1^{(1)} \oplus Y_1^{(1)}$, $X_1^{(2)} \oplus Y_1^{(2)}$, $X_1^{(3)} \oplus Y_1^{(3)}$ and $X_1^{(4)} \oplus Y_1^{(4)}$. If a match to $(X^{(i)}, Y^{(i)})$ for some $1 \leq i \leq 4$ is found, compute $X^{(i)} \oplus Z$ as K_0, and output it with $K_1^{(i)}$ as K_1 and P, which can be trivially computed from $X_1^{(i)}$.

Complexity. The unit is one computation of the whole 10-step LED–128. Steps 1 and 2 are both with a complexity $2^{60} \times \frac{2}{10} \approx 2^{57.7}$ encryptions. Step 5 requires $2^{62} \times \frac{2}{10} \approx 2^{59.7}$ encryptions. Thus the overall complexity is $2^{57.7} + 2^{57.7} + 2^{59.7} \approx 2^{60.3}$, hence lower than 2^{64}.

Remark. As shown from the analysis above, again our attack is not related to the specification of the step functions, and can be applied to any 10-round construction with subkeys that come one after another, in a form of a chosen-key random-difference distinguisher. Thus we can conclude that:

Observation 2. *For any ten-round n-bit cipher with arbitrary round functions and alternating subkeys, exists a chosen-key distinguisher with time complexity less than 2^n queries.*

5   Conclusion

In this paper, we have presented various attacks on LED in the single-key and chosen-key models. We have improved the data complexity of the single-key attack on 16 rounds of LED-128 in terms of lower and known-plaintext data. We have also shown the first single-key attack on 24 rounds of LED-128. In the chosen-key model, we have given practical results on 32 rounds, and have reached as far as 40 rounds, using a novel chosen-key distinguisher.

The main contribution of this work is actually the idea of multicollisions and their applications. The vast majority of our results/attacks, in particular the attacks that penetrate through the largest number of rounds, are based on creating multicollisions for some intermediate states inside the cipher, thus obtaining a small set of independent values that are used further in meet-in-the-middle attacks. As we have seen from our analysis, the primary advantage of multicollisions is that they can be applied regardless of the specification of the internal rounds/steps. Both Observations 1 and 2 are surprising to a large extend as they state that the round transformation plays no role in the security against 2-round single-key and 10-round chosen-key attacks. This result is indeed due to the multicollisions and their property given above. Another condition for applying the observations is simplicity of the key schedule. Although it seems very compelling to use a trivial key schedule, especially in lightweight primitives, its application leads to a huge reduction of the security margin at least in the chosen-key model.

The two primary instances of LED apply 8, and 12 steps, respectively. However, when K_1 in LED-128 is fixed, then this cipher has only 6 steps, i.e. 2 steps less than LED-64. Although the steps now contain 8 rounds, the security margin of the cipher against attacks (such as most of our attacks presented here) independent of the step function, is less than the one of LED-64. Hence, it seems that an attack on 6-step LED-64, that does not use the structural properties of the step functions, might result in an attack on full-round LED-128. We were not able to trivially extend our 5-round chosen-key attack on LED-64, to 10-step chosen-key attack on LED-128, only because it uses a differential characteristic in the last step. We leave as an open research topic the problem of finding a 6-step attack on LED-64, independent of the step function.

Acknowledgement. The authors would like to thank the FSE 2013 reviewers and the LED team members Jian Guo and Thomas Peyrin for their valuable comments. Ivica Nikolić is supported by the Singapore National Research Foundation under Research Grant NRF-CRP2-2007-03. Lei Wang and Shuang Wu are supported by the Singapore National Research Foundation Fellowship 2012 NRF-NRFF2012-06.

References

1. Biryukov, A., Khovratovich, D., Nikolić, I.: Distinguisher and related-key attack on the full AES-256. In: Halevi, S. (ed.) CRYPTO 2009. LNCS, vol. 5677, pp. 231–249. Springer, Heidelberg (2009)

2. Bogdanov, A., Knudsen, L.R., Leander, G., Standaert, F.-X., Steinberger, J., Tischhauser, E.: Key-alternating ciphers in a provable setting: encryption using a small number of public permutations (extended abstract). In: Pointcheval, D., Johansson, T. (eds.) EUROCRYPT 2012. LNCS, vol. 7237, pp. 45–62. Springer, Heidelberg (2012)

3. Bogdanov, A., Rechberger, C.: A 3-subset meet-in-the-middle attack: cryptanalysis of the lightweight block cipher KTANTAN. In: Biryukov, A., Gong, G., Stinson, D.R. (eds.) SAC 2010. LNCS, vol. 6544, pp. 229–240. Springer, Heidelberg (2011)

4. Daemen, J.: Limitations of the Even-Mansour construction. In: Imai, H., Rivest, R.L., Matsumoto, T. (eds.) ASIACRYPT 1991. LNCS, vol. 739, pp. 495–498. Springer, Heidelberg (1993)

5. Dunkelman, O., Keller, N., Shamir, A.: Minimalism in cryptography: the Even-Mansour scheme revisited. In: Pointcheval, D., Johansson, T. (eds.) EUROCRYPT 2012. LNCS, vol. 7237, pp. 336–354. Springer, Heidelberg (2012)

6. Even, S., Mansour, Y.: A construction of a cipher from a single pseudorandom permutation. J. Cryptology 10(3), 151–162 (1997)

7. Feller, W.: An Introduction to Probability Theory and Its Applications, vol. 1, 3rd edn. Wiley, New York (1968)

8. Gilbert, H., Peyrin, T.: Super-Sbox cryptanalysis: improved attacks for AES-like permutations. In: Hong, S., Iwata, T. (eds.) FSE 2010. LNCS, vol. 6147, pp. 365–383. Springer, Heidelberg (2010)

9. Guo, J., Peyrin, T., Poschmann, A., Robshaw, M.: The LED block cipher. Cryptology ePrint Archive, Report 2012/600 (2012). http://eprint.iacr.org/2012/600

10. Guo, J., Peyrin, T., Poschmann, A., Robshaw, M.: The LED block cipher. In: Preneel, B., Takagi, T. (eds.) CHES 2011. LNCS, vol. 6917, pp. 326–341. Springer, Heidelberg (2011)

11. Isobe, T., Shibutani, K.: Security analysis of the lightweight block ciphers XTEA, LED and piccolo. In: Susilo, W., Mu, Y., Seberry, J. (eds.) ACISP 2012. LNCS, vol. 7372, pp. 71–86. Springer, Heidelberg (2012)

12. Lamberger, M., Mendel, F., Rechberger, C., Rijmen, V., Schläffer, M.: Rebound distinguishers: results on the full whirlpool compression function. In: Matsui, M. (ed.) ASIACRYPT 2009. LNCS, vol. 5912, pp. 126–143. Springer, Heidelberg (2009)

13. Mendel, F., Rechberger, C., Schläffer, M., Thomsen, S.S.: The rebound attack: cryptanalysis of reduced whirlpool and Grøstl. In: Dunkelman, O. (ed.) FSE 2009. LNCS, vol. 5665, pp. 260–276. Springer, Heidelberg (2009)

14. Mendel, F., Rijmen, V., Toz, D., Varici, K.: Differential analysis of the LED block cipher. In: Wang, X., Sako, K. (eds.) ASIACRYPT 2012. LNCS, vol. 7658, pp. 190–207. Springer, Heidelberg (2012)

15. Patarin, J.: A proof of security in $O(2^n)$ for the Xor of two random permutations. In: Safavi-Naini, R. (ed.) ICITS 2008. LNCS, vol. 5155, pp. 232–248. Springer, Heidelberg (2008)

16. Suzuki, K., Tonien, D., Kurosawa, K., Toyota, K.: Birthday paradox for multicollisions. In: Rhee, M.S., Lee, B. (eds.) ICISC 2006. LNCS, vol. 4296, pp. 29–40. Springer, Heidelberg (2006)

Tweakable Block Ciphers

Tweakable Blockciphers with Asymptotically Optimal Security

Rodolphe Lampe[1] and Yannick Seurin[2]($\boxtimes$)

[1] University of Versailles, Versailles, France
rodolphe.lampe@gmail.com
[2] ANSSI, Paris, France
yannick.seurin@m4x.org

Abstract. We consider tweakable blockciphers with beyond the birthday bound security. Landecker, Shrimpton, and Terashima (CRYPTO 2012) gave the first construction with security up to $\mathcal{O}(2^{2n/3})$ adversarial queries (n denotes the block size in bits of the underlying blockcipher), and for which changing the tweak does not require changing the keys for blockcipher calls. In this paper, we extend this construction, which consists of two rounds of a previous proposal by Liskov, Rivest, and Wagner (CRYPTO 2002), by considering larger numbers of rounds $r > 2$. We show that asymptotically, as r increases, the resulting tweakable blockcipher approaches security up to the information bound, namely $\mathcal{O}(2^n)$ queries. Our analysis makes use of a coupling argument, and carries some similarities with the analysis of the iterated Even-Mansour cipher by Lampe, Patarin, and Seurin (ASIACRYPT 2012).

Keywords: Tweakable blockcipher · Beyond birthday bound · Coupling · Message authentication code

1 Introduction

Tweakable Blockciphers. Tweakable blockciphers (TBC), introduced by Liskov, Rivest, and Wagner [12], are families of (efficiently invertible) permutations indexed by two functionally distinct parameters: the key (as usual for a blockcipher) and the *tweak*. Phrased differently, a TBC is a family of blockciphers indexed by a tweak. The tweak is usually seen as a public parameter bringing more versatility to the blockcipher, and in particular is assumed to be under control of the attacker when defining security for a TBC.

There are very few constructions of blockciphers which are tweakable "by-design". The notable examples are the Hasty Pudding cipher [21], Mercy [3],

R. Lampe – This author is partially supported by the French Direction Générale de l'Armement.

Y. Seurin – This author is partially supported by the French National Agency of Research: ANR-11-INS-011.

S. Moriai (Ed.): FSE 2013, LNCS 8424, pp. 133–151, 2014.
DOI: 10.1007/978-3-662-43933-3_8, © Springer-Verlag Berlin Heidelberg 2014

and Threefish, the blockcipher underlying the Skein hash function [6]. See also Goldenberg *et al.* [7] who considered how to incorporate a tweak in a Feistel structure. Most of the time however, proposed constructions start from an existing blockcipher (which is assumed to be a secure strong pseudorandom permutation) and build on top of it (in a black-box way) a new family of permutations admitting a tweak. An important property of a TBC is that changing the tweak should be very efficient (this is required for example for applications such as disk or database encryption). Most of the time, changing the key in a blockcipher is a costly operation. Hence, TBC designs where a change in the tweak implies a change in the keys used for calls to the underlying blockcipher tend to be avoided.

Simple constructions of tweakable blockciphers, such as the two proposals made in the original paper by Liskov *et al.* [12], or the XE and XEX constructions by Rogaway [20], are usually proven secure up to the so-called *birthday bound* (BB), i.e. up to $\mathcal{O}(2^{n/2})$ adversarial queries for a blockcipher with n-bit block length. The first proposal with beyond BB security was made by Minematsu [16], however the construction suffers from a restricted tweak length and requires rekeying the blockcipher when changing the tweak. More recently, Landecker, Shrimpton, and Terashima [11] considered chaining two rounds of the second proposal by [12] (called LRW2 in [11]), which works as follows: given a blockcipher E with keyspace $\mathcal{K}$ and an ε-AXU$_2$ family of functions $\mathcal{H}$, the TBC constructed from E through the LRW2 construction has key space $\mathcal{K} \times \mathcal{H}$, and given a key $k \in \mathcal{K}$ and a function $h \in \mathcal{H}$, the encryption of x with tweak t is given by $\widetilde{E}_{k,h}(t, x) = h(t) \oplus E_k(x \oplus h(t))$. Landecker *et. al.* named CLRW2 the construction resulting from the chaining of two LRW2 constructions, namely:

$$\widetilde{E}_{(k_1,k_2),(h_1,h_2)}(t, x) = h_2(t) \oplus E_{k_2}\Big(h_1(t) \oplus E_{k_1}\big(x \oplus h_1(t)\big) \oplus h_2(t)\Big).$$

They proved that the resulting TBC is secure (against adaptive chosen-plaintexts and ciphertexts attacks) up to $\mathcal{O}(2^{2n/3})$ queries. Moreover it admits arbitrary tweaks (by choosing a suitable family $\mathcal{H}$) and does not require rekeying the blockcipher E when changing the tweak, hence resulting in a very interesting design.

Contributions of This Work. In this paper, we extend the work of Landecker *et al.* [11] by considering longer chains of the LRW2 construction, with the hope that security increases with the number r of rounds (see Fig. 1 for an idea of the construction). We simply call this the CLRW construction with r rounds (r-CLRW for short). And indeed, we show that asymptotically as r goes to $+\infty$, the r-CLRW TBC achieves security up to $\mathcal{O}(2^{(1-\varepsilon)n})$ adversarial queries. More precisely, we show the following:

- first, against non-adaptive chosen-plaintexts (NCPA) adversaries, r-CLRW achieves security up to $\mathcal{O}(2^{rn/(r+1)})$ queries;
- then, we prove a general "two weak make one strong" composition theorem for TBCs stating that, given two TBCs $\widetilde{E}$ and $\widetilde{E}'$ secure against (information-theoretic) NCPA adversaries, the composition $\widetilde{E}'^{-1} \circ \widetilde{E}$ is secure against adaptive chosen-plaintexts and ciphertexts (CCA) adversaries (care must be taken

in how the tweak is handled when composing). We then use this theorem to prove that r-CLRW achieves security up to $\mathcal{O}(2^{rn/(r+2)})$ queries against CCA adversaries (in other words, it is a strong tweakable pseudorandom permutation up to this number of queries).

Our proof technique for the first part (NCPA adversaries) of the proof uses a coupling argument. The coupling technique is a very useful tool for upper bounding the statistical distance of the distribution of the outputs of an iterated structure to the uniform distribution, and was previously used in cryptography in [8,17,18]. More specifically, our analysis carries some similarities with the analysis of the iterated Even-Mansour cipher by Lampe, Patarin, and Seurin [10], with important differences though. The iterated Even-Mansour cipher [2,5] (also called *key-alternating cipher*) is the construction of a blockcipher in the random permutation model defined as follows: given r public permutations $P_1, \ldots, P_r$ on $\{0,1\}^n$, encryption of x is computed as:

$$y = k_r \oplus P_r(k_{r-1} \oplus P_{r-1}(\cdots P_1(k_0 \oplus x) \cdots)),$$

where $k_0, \ldots, k_r$ are $r+1$ keys of n bits.[1] This construction was shown to be secure (against CCA adversaries) up to $\mathcal{O}(2^{n/2})$ queries for $r = 1$ in [5], and up to $\mathcal{O}(2^{2n/3})$ queries for $r = 2$ in [2]. Later, Lampe *et al.* [10] showed, using a coupling argument, that the construction is secure up to $\mathcal{O}(2^{rn/(r+1)})$ queries against NCPA adversaries, and up to $\mathcal{O}(2^{rn/(r+2)})$ queries against CCA adversaries.

Though these results sound similar to ours, the two settings are quite different. Namely, in the Even-Mansour setting, internal permutations $P_1, \ldots, P_r$ are publicly accessible by the adversary, whereas in the CLRW setting, $E_{k_1}, \ldots, E_{k_r}$ remain "hidden" in the construction. On the other hand, in the Even-Mansour setting, keys are drawn at random at the beginning of the security experiment and fixed afterwards, whereas in the CLRW setting, values $h_i(t)$ (which may be seen as the analog of keys in the iterated Even-Mansour cipher) can be "refreshed" by the adversary through the tweak t. Yet, in both settings, problems that have to be handled in the security proof are collisions at the input of the internal permutations (but the way the adversary provokes such events in both settings is quite different).

Application to MAC and Authenticated Encryption. In [11], the authors defined a nonce-based MAC construction from a TBC called TBC-MAC2 (this is a variant of a previous proposal by [12] called TBC-MAC). This construction preserves the security of the underlying TBC. When instantiated with r-CLRW,

---

[1] We remark that the iterated Even-Mansour cipher can be modified to use only r keys $(k_1, \ldots, k_r)$ as follows: the encryption of x is computed as the composition of r rounds of the single-key construction $x \mapsto k_i \oplus P_i(x \oplus k_i)$. The resulting construction is then the strict analog of r-CLRW. Moreover results of [10] carry over to this construction.

this directly yields a secure MAC (i.e. a secure PRF) up to $\mathcal{O}(2^{rn/(r+2)})$ queries.[2] MAC schemes with security beyond the birthday bound are quite rare, and two notable examples have been given by Yasuda [24,25]. Dodis ans Steinberger [4] also gave an example with security close to $\mathcal{O}(2^n)$ queries. Their construction is more complex, but relies only on the weaker assumption that the underlying blockcipher is unpredictable.

Besides MAC schemes, the r-CLRW construction can also be used to obtain an authenticated encryption scheme with security close to the information bound: for example, the OCB1 construction by Rogaway [20] gives an authenticated encryption scheme from a TBC with a tight security bound.

Open Problems. We conjecture that our NCPA bound in fact also holds for CCA adversaries, i.e. that the r-CLRW construction is secure up to $\mathcal{O}(2^{rn/(r+1)})$ queries *against CCA adversaries*. We think that this is probably the main open problem regarding the construction since for r small, this makes a meaningful gap in the bound. For example, we prove security up to $\mathcal{O}(2^{3n/4})$ queries against CCA adversaries only for 6 rounds, but we conjecture that this already holds for 3 rounds. We note that the corresponding problem is equally open for the iterated Even-Mansour cipher. In a recent preprint [23], Steinberger showed that the iterated Even-Mansour cipher with 3 rounds is secure up to $\mathcal{O}(2^{3n/4})$ queries against CCA adversaries. We are currently unable to transfer his proof technique to the r-CLRW construction for $r = 3$.

We also stress that we view our security proofs more as a *feasibility* result than a practical one. Indeed, as soon as r is more than 4 or maybe 5, the key size and the number of blockcipher calls of the resulting construction will become too large to be reasonably practical. We think however that it is interesting to see that a relatively simple construction enables to approach the information bound. Moreover, improvements may come which will make the construction more efficient or even practical for larger values of r.

Organization. We define the notation and give some useful definitions in Sect. 2. Then, in Sect. 3, we prove our security result for r-CLRW against NCPA adversaries. Finally, in Sect. 4, we prove our composition theorem for tweakable blockciphers and apply it to characterize the security of r-CLRW against CCA adversaries.

2   Preliminaries

2.1   Notation and Security Definitions

The set of integers i such that $a \leq i \leq b$ will be denoted $[a; b]$. When S is a non-empty finite set, we write $s \leftarrow_\$ S$ to mean that a value is sampled uniformly

---

[2] The security of TBC-MAC2 relies on the security of the underlying TBC against *adaptive* CPA adversaries. We do not have a better bound for r-CLRW against such adversaries than against adaptive CCA ones.

at random from S and assigned to s. By $\mathcal{A}^{\mathcal{O}_1,\mathcal{O}_2,\cdots}(x,y,\ldots) \Rightarrow z$ we denote the operation of running the (possibly probabilistic) algorithm $\mathcal{A}$ on inputs $x, y, \ldots$ with access to oracles $\mathcal{O}_1, \mathcal{O}_2, \ldots$ (possibly none), and letting z be the output.

For a set $\mathcal{D}$, we note $\mathrm{Perm}(\mathcal{D})$ the set of permutations of $\mathcal{D}$, and we use $\mathrm{Perm}(n)$ to denote the set of permutations of $\mathcal{D} = \{0,1\}^n$. For two sets $\mathcal{D}$ and $\mathcal{K}$, we denote $\mathsf{BC}(\mathcal{K},\mathcal{D})$ the set of blockciphers with domain $\mathcal{D}$ and key space $\mathcal{K}$, i.e. the set of functions $E : \mathcal{K} \times \mathcal{D} \to \mathcal{D}$ such that for all $k \in \mathcal{K}$, $E_k := E(k, \cdot) \in \mathrm{Perm}(\mathcal{D})$. For three sets $\mathcal{D}$, $\mathcal{K}$, and $\mathcal{T}$, we denote $\mathsf{TBC}(\mathcal{K},\mathcal{T},\mathcal{D})$ the set of tweakable blockciphers with domain $\mathcal{D}$, key space $\mathcal{K}$, and tweak space $\mathcal{T}$, i.e. the set of functions $\widetilde{E} : \mathcal{K} \times \mathcal{T} \times \mathcal{D} \to \mathcal{D}$ such that for each tweak $t \in \mathcal{T}$, $\widetilde{E}(\cdot, t, \cdot) \in \mathsf{BC}(\mathcal{K},\mathcal{D})$. We will use $\widetilde{E}_k(\cdot, \cdot)$ as a shorthand for $\widetilde{E}(k, \cdot, \cdot)$. We denote $\mathsf{BC}(\mathcal{K}, n)$ (resp. $\mathsf{TBC}(\mathcal{K}, \mathcal{T}, n)$) the set of blockciphers (resp. tweakable blockciphers) with domain $\mathcal{D} = \{0,1\}^n$. The *perfect cipher* over $\mathcal{D}$ is defined as the (inefficient) blockcipher whose key space is $\mathrm{Perm}(\mathcal{D})$. In the following, when the domain is clear ($\mathcal{D} = \{0,1\}^n$ most of the time), we will simply denote E^* the perfect cipher over $\mathcal{D}$. Sampling a random key for E^* simply means sampling a random permutation over $\mathcal{D}$.

Fix an integer $q \leq |\mathcal{D}|$. Given a tuple $t = (t_1, \ldots, t_q) \in \mathcal{T}^q$, we will denote $\Omega_t \subset \mathcal{D}^q$ the set of possible inputs $x = (x_1, \ldots, x_q) \in \mathcal{D}^q$ such that all pairs (t_i, x_i) are pairwise distinct:

$$\Omega_t = \{x := (x_1, \ldots, x_q) \in \mathcal{D}^q : (x_i, t_i) \neq (x_j, t_j), \forall i \neq j\} \ .$$

Let $\mathcal{D}, \mathcal{K}, \mathcal{T}$ be sets, $E \in \mathsf{BC}(\mathcal{K}, \mathcal{D})$ a blockcipher and $\widetilde{E} \in \mathsf{TBC}(\mathcal{K}, \mathcal{T}, \mathcal{D})$ a tweakable blockcipher. An adversary $\mathcal{A}$ is said to be non-adaptive if it chooses all its queries (possibly randomly) before issuing the first one, and adaptive otherwise. For any q, τ, we define the following advantages (where, depending on the security experiment, one has $k \leftarrow_\$ \mathcal{K}$, $\pi \leftarrow_\$ \mathrm{Perm}(\mathcal{D})$, or $\widetilde{\pi} \leftarrow_\$ \mathsf{BC}(\mathcal{T}, \mathcal{D})$):

$$\mathbf{Adv}_E^{\mathrm{ncpa}}(q, \tau) = \max_{\mathcal{A}} \left| \Pr\left[\mathcal{A}^{E_k(\cdot)} \Rightarrow 1\right] - \Pr\left[\mathcal{A}^{\pi(\cdot)} \Rightarrow 1\right] \right|$$

$$\mathbf{Adv}_E^{\mathrm{cca}}(q, \tau) = \max_{\mathcal{A}} \left| \Pr\left[\mathcal{A}^{E_k(\cdot),E_k^{-1}(\cdot)} \Rightarrow 1\right] - \Pr\left[\mathcal{A}^{\pi(\cdot),\pi^{-1}(\cdot)} \Rightarrow 1\right] \right|$$

$$\mathbf{Adv}_{\widetilde{E}}^{\widetilde{\mathrm{ncpa}}}(q, \tau) = \max_{\mathcal{A}} \left| \Pr\left[\mathcal{A}^{\widetilde{E}_k(\cdot,\cdot)} \Rightarrow 1\right] - \Pr\left[\mathcal{A}^{\widetilde{\pi}(\cdot,\cdot)} \Rightarrow 1\right] \right|$$

$$\mathbf{Adv}_{\widetilde{E}}^{\widetilde{\mathrm{cca}}}(q, \tau) = \max_{\mathcal{A}} \left| \Pr\left[\mathcal{A}^{\widetilde{E}_k(\cdot,\cdot),\widetilde{E}_k^{-1}(\cdot,\cdot)} \Rightarrow 1\right] - \Pr\left[\mathcal{A}^{\widetilde{\pi}(\cdot,\cdot),\widetilde{\pi}^{-1}(\cdot,\cdot)} \Rightarrow 1\right] \right| \ ,$$

where for ncpa and $\widetilde{\mathrm{ncpa}}$ (resp. cca and $\widetilde{\mathrm{cca}}$) the max is taken over non-adaptive (resp. adaptive) adversaries making at most q oracle queries and running in time at most τ. The probabilities are over the random coins of $\mathcal{A}$ and the random draw of k, π or $\widetilde{\pi}$. In the following, we will refer to $\widetilde{\pi}$ as a *tweakable permutation* (though this object is syntactically equivalent to a blockcipher) since it takes the tweak as first input rather than the key.

Definition 1. *Let S be an arbitrary set. A family of functions $\mathcal{H}$ from S to $\{0,1\}^n$ is said to be ε-almost-2-XOR-universal (ε-AXU$_2$) if for all distinct $x, x' \in S$ and all $y \in \{0,1\}^n$, one has $\Pr[h \leftarrow_\$ \mathcal{H} : h(x) \oplus h(x') = y] \leq \varepsilon$.*

Note that there exists very efficient and well-studied constructions of ε-AXU$_2$ function families with $\varepsilon \simeq 2^{-n}$ [22], with short descriptions (i.e. keys). We will stick to the convention of using a notation where the key is implicit in the remaining of the paper.

2.2   Statistical Distance and Coupling

Given a finite event space Ω and two probability distributions μ and ν defined on Ω, the *statistical distance* (or total variation distance) between μ and ν, denoted $\|\mu - \nu\|$ is defined as:

$$\|\mu - \nu\| = \frac{1}{2} \sum_{x \in \Omega} |\mu(x) - \nu(x)|.$$

The following definitions can easily be seen equivalent:

$$\|\mu - \nu\| = \max_{S \subset \Omega} \{\mu(S) - \nu(S)\} = \max_{S \subset \Omega} \{\nu(S) - \mu(S)\} = \max_{S \subset \Omega} \{|\mu(S) - \nu(S)|\}.$$

A *coupling* of μ and ν is a distribution λ on $\Omega \times \Omega$ such that for all $x \in \Omega$, $\sum_{y \in \Omega} \lambda(x, y) = \mu(x)$ and for all $y \in \Omega$, $\sum_{x \in \Omega} \lambda(x, y) = \nu(y)$. In other words, λ is a joint distribution whose marginal distributions are resp. μ and ν. The fundamental result of the coupling technique is the following one. For completeness, we provide the proof in Appendix A.

Lemma 1 (Coupling Lemma). *Let μ and ν be probability distributions on a finite event space Ω, let λ be a coupling of μ and ν, and let $(X, Y) \sim \lambda$ (i.e. (X, Y) is a random variable sampled according to distribution λ). Then $\|\mu - \nu\| \leq \Pr[X \neq Y]$.*

2.3   Description of the r-CLRW Construction

We use and adapt the notation of [11]. Let $\mathcal{K}$ be a set and $E \in \mathsf{BC}(\mathcal{K}, n)$ a blockcipher. Let $\mathcal{T}$ be a set and $\mathcal{H}$ a set of functions from $\mathcal{T}$ to $\{0, 1\}^n$. We define the tweakable blockcipher $\mathsf{LRW}^{E, \mathcal{H}}$ with domain $\{0, 1\}^n$, key space $\widetilde{\mathcal{K}} = \mathcal{K} \times \mathcal{H}$, and tweak space $\mathcal{T}$ as follows. For any $(k_1, h_1) \in \mathcal{K} \times \mathcal{H}$, $t \in \mathcal{T}$, and $x \in \{0, 1\}^n$, let:

$$\mathsf{LRW}^{E, \mathcal{H}}((k_1, h_1), t, x) = E_{k_1}(x \oplus h_1(t)) \oplus h_1(t).$$

We also denote $\mathsf{LRW}^{E, \mathcal{H}}_{k_1, h_1} := \mathsf{LRW}^{E, \mathcal{H}}((k_1, h_1), \cdot, \cdot)$ the mapping taking as input $(t, x) \in \mathcal{T} \times \{0, 1\}^n$ and returning $y \in \{0, 1\}^n$.

This construction was called the LRW2 construction in [11], being the second construction proposed by Liskov *et al.* in [12] to build a tweakable blockcipher. We simply call it the LRW construction in this paper. In [11], the authors proposed to chain two LRW constructions to increase the security beyond the birthday bound, and called the resulting construction CLRW2. In this paper, we will consider chaining r LRW constructions with $r > 2$ to obtain security asymptotically close to the information bound.

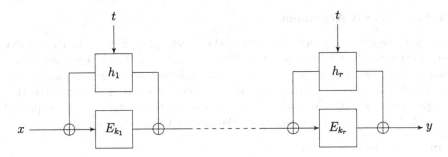

Fig. 1. The $\texttt{CLRW}^{r,E,\mathcal{H}}$ tweakable blockcipher construction.

Let r be a positive integer. We define the tweakable blockcipher $\texttt{CLRW}^{r,E,\mathcal{H}}$ with domain $\{0,1\}^n$, key space $\widetilde{\mathcal{K}} = \mathcal{K}^r \times \mathcal{H}^r$, and tweak space $\mathcal{T}$ as follows. For any $k = (k_1, \ldots, k_r) \in \mathcal{K}^r$, $h = (h_1, \ldots, h_r) \in \mathcal{H}^r$, $t \in \mathcal{T}$, and $x \in \{0,1\}^n$, let $\texttt{CLRW}^{r,E,\mathcal{H}}((k,h),t,x)$ be defined as the value y_r obtained recursively as:

$$\begin{cases} y_0 = x \\ y_i = \texttt{LRW}^{E,\mathcal{H}}((k_i,h_i),t,y_{i-1}) & \text{for } 1 \leq i \leq r. \end{cases}$$

We also denote $\texttt{CLRW}^{r,E,\mathcal{H}}_{k,h} := \texttt{CLRW}^{r,E,\mathcal{H}}((k,h),\cdot,\cdot)$ the mapping taking as input $(t,x) \in \mathcal{T} \times \{0,1\}^n$ and returning $y \in \{0,1\}^n$. The construction is depicted on Fig. 1.

Thereafter, we will need the more ideal construction where the blockcipher E is replaced by the perfect cipher E^* over $\{0,1\}^n$ as defined in Sect. 2.1. The resulting (inefficient) TBC will be denoted $\texttt{CLRW}^{r,E^*,\mathcal{H}}$, and for every $\pi = (\pi_1, \ldots, \pi_r) \in \text{Perm}(n)^r$ and $h = (h_1, \ldots, h_r) \in \mathcal{H}^r$, we denote $\texttt{CLRW}^{r,E^*,\mathcal{H}}_{\pi,h}$ the function defined as $\texttt{CLRW}^{r,E,\mathcal{H}}_{k,h}$ above, where calls to E_{k_i} are replaced by calls to π_i.

3   Security Analysis for Non-adaptive Adversaries

In this section, we first deal with non-adaptive chosen-plaintext (NCPA) adversaries. Using a coupling argument, we will prove the following theorem.

Theorem 1. *Let $\mathcal{K}, \mathcal{T}$ be sets, $E \in \text{BC}(\mathcal{K}, n)$ be a blockcipher, and $\mathcal{H}$ be an ε-AXU$_2$ family of functions from $\mathcal{T}$ to $\{0,1\}^n$. Then one has:*

$$\mathbf{Adv}^{\overline{\text{ncpa}}}_{\texttt{CLRW}^{r,E,\mathcal{H}}}(q,\tau) \leq r \cdot \mathbf{Adv}^{\text{ncpa}}_E(q, \tau + rqT) + \frac{q^{r+1}}{r+1}(2\varepsilon)^r,$$

where T is the time to compute E or E^{-1}.

Using an ε-AXU$_2$ function family with $\varepsilon \simeq 2^{-n}$, one can see that the construction ensures security up to $\mathcal{O}(2^{rn/(r+1)})$ queries (assuming E is sufficiently secure against NCPA adversaries). The remaining of the section is devoted to the proof of Theorem 1.

3.1   An Hybrid Argument

As a first step in the proof, we replace the blockcipher E used in the CLRW construction by the perfect cipher E^*, i.e. we replace calls to E_{k_i} for random and independent keys k_i by calls to uniformly random permutations π_i. If we assume that the blockcipher is a (strong) pseudorandom permutation, the construction using E is only slightly less secure than the construction using E^*, as is captured by the following lemma (we also treat the case of CCA adversaries).

Lemma 2. *For any q, τ, one has:*

$$\mathbf{Adv}^{\widetilde{\mathrm{ncpa}}}_{\mathrm{CLRW}^{r}, E, \mathcal{H}}(q, \tau) \leq r \cdot \mathbf{Adv}^{\mathrm{ncpa}}_{E}(q, \tau + rqT) + \mathbf{Adv}^{\widetilde{\mathrm{ncpa}}}_{\mathrm{CLRW}^{r}, E^*, \mathcal{H}}(q, \tau)$$

$$\mathbf{Adv}^{\widetilde{\mathrm{cca}}}_{\mathrm{CLRW}^{r}, E, \mathcal{H}}(q, \tau) \leq r \cdot \mathbf{Adv}^{\mathrm{cca}}_{E}(q, \tau + rqT) + \mathbf{Adv}^{\widetilde{\mathrm{cca}}}_{\mathrm{CLRW}^{r}, E^*, \mathcal{H}}(q, \tau),$$

where T is the time to compute E or E^{-1}.

Proof. This is a classical hybrid argument. We only prove the NCPA case, the CCA case is similar. Let $\mathcal{A}$ be a NCPA adversary trying to distinguish $\mathrm{CLRW}^{r, E, \mathcal{H}}$ from a random tweakable permutation. For each $i \in [1; r]$, consider the following adversary $\mathcal{A}_i$ trying to distinguish E from a random permutation. $\mathcal{A}_i$ runs $\mathcal{A}$, answering its queries as follows: it computes the r-CLRW construction where the first $i - 1$ permutations are uniformly random permutations, the i-th permutation is computed by querying $\mathcal{A}_i$'s own oracle, and the last $r - i$ permutations correspond to E with randomly drawn keys. Note that $\mathcal{A}_i$ is non-adaptive, makes at most q queries to its own oracle, and runs in time at most $\tau + rqT$. Denote $\mathcal{O}_i$ the oracle defined as the r-CLRW construction where the first i permutations are uniformly random, and the last $r - i$ permutations are E with uniformly random keys. Then, when $\mathcal{A}_i$ is interacting with a random permutation, it answers $\mathcal{A}$'s queries as $\mathcal{O}_{i+1}$, whereas when it is interacting with E_k it implements $\mathcal{O}_i$. Moreover $\mathcal{O}_0 = \mathrm{CLRW}^{r, E, \mathcal{H}}$ and $\mathcal{O}_r = \mathrm{CLRW}^{r, E^*, \mathcal{H}}$. By the triangular inequality:

$$\left| \Pr\left[\mathcal{A}^{\mathrm{CLRW}^{r, E, \mathcal{H}}} \Rightarrow 1 \right] - \Pr\left[\mathcal{A}^{\widetilde{\pi}} \Rightarrow 1 \right] \right| \leq$$

$$\sum_{i=0}^{r-1} \left| \Pr\left[\mathcal{A}^{\mathcal{O}_i} \Rightarrow 1 \right] - \Pr\left[\mathcal{A}^{\mathcal{O}_{i+1}} \Rightarrow 1 \right] \right| +$$

$$\left| \Pr\left[\mathcal{A}^{\mathrm{CLRW}^{r, E^*, \mathcal{H}}} \Rightarrow 1 \right] - \Pr\left[\mathcal{A}^{\widetilde{\pi}} \Rightarrow 1 \right] \right|.$$

The lemma follows by noting that the r first terms are exactly the advantages of adversaries $\mathcal{A}_i$, which are all upper bounded by $\mathbf{Adv}^{\mathrm{ncpa}}_{E}(q, \tau + rqT)$.   □

Hence to study the security of $\mathrm{CLRW}^{r, E, \mathcal{H}}$, we have to study the security of $\mathrm{CLRW}^{r, E^*, \mathcal{H}}$. This is what we do in the remaining of the proof.

3.2   NCPA Advantage and Statistical Distance

A classical result states that the advantage of a (computationally unbounded) NCPA adversary in distinguishing two systems S_1 and S_2 with at most q queries is upper bounded by the max over any q inputs of the statistical distance between the outputs of the two systems. The two systems we consider here are $\mathtt{CLRW}^{r,E^*,\mathcal{H}}$ and a random tweakable permutation $\widetilde{\pi}$, and we want to upper bound the statistical distance between the outputs of $\mathtt{CLRW}^{r,E^*,\mathcal{H}}$ and the outputs of a random tweakable permutation for any q queries to these two systems.

Thereafter, we will consider a NCPA-distinguisher $\mathcal{A}$ which chooses all its (plaintexts) queries in advance. We will denote the i-th query (t_i, x_i). We denote μ_q the distribution of the outputs when the distinguisher is accessing the $\mathtt{CLRW}^{r,E^*,\mathcal{H}}$ construction (the distribution is defined by the random draw of $\pi = (\pi_1, \ldots, \pi_r) \in \mathrm{Perm}(n)^r$ and $h = (h_1, \ldots, h_r) \in \mathcal{H}^r$) and μ_0 the distribution of the outputs when the distinguisher is accessing a uniformly random tweakable permutation $\widetilde{\pi}$. Hence, for any τ (since this holds even for computationally unbounded adversaries):

$$\mathbf{Adv}^{\widetilde{\mathrm{ncpa}}}_{\mathtt{CLRW}^{r,E^*,\mathcal{H}}}(q, \tau) \leq \|\mu_q - \mu_0\|.$$

In the following, we will denote $\tau = +\infty$ in the advantage when it applies to computationally unbounded adversaries.

3.3 Dividing the Problem into q Simpler Problems

We now give another way to describe the distribution μ_0. For any $t \in \mathcal{T}$, we do the following experiment: let I_t be the set of indexes $i \in [1; q]$ such that $t_i = t$ and let $(u_i)_{i \in I_t}$ be uniformly random pairwise distinct elements. We claim that the distribution of the outputs of $(t_1, u_1), \ldots, (t_q, u_q)$ by any (not necessarily uniform) random tweakable permutation $\widetilde{\pi}'$ whose distribution is independent of the distribution of (u_i) is μ_0, i.e. the distribution of the outputs of (t_i, x_i) by a uniformly random tweakable permutation $\widetilde{\pi}$. Indeed, for every t, the values $(\widetilde{\pi}(t_i, x_i))_{i \in I_t}$ and $(\widetilde{\pi}'(t_i, u_i))_{i \in I_t}$ are both uniformly random and pairwise distinct.

Now that we gave this new description of μ_0, we can split the computation of $\|\mu_q - \mu_0\|$ in q simpler computations. The idea is to construct a distribution μ_ℓ for every $\ell \leq q$ such that μ_ℓ is the distribution of the outputs of a random instance of $\mathtt{CLRW}^{r,E^*,\mathcal{H}}$ queried with (t_i, x_i) for $i = 1, \ldots, \ell$ and the last $q - \ell$ queries keep the same tweak t_i as in adversarial queries, but their last coordinate is uniformly random among unqueried values. More precisely, for each $\ell \in [0; q]$, let $((t_1, z_1), \ldots, (t_q, z_q))$ be a tuple of queries such that $z_i = x_i$ for $i \leq \ell$, and z_i is uniformly random in $\{0, 1\}^n \setminus \{z_j \mid t_j = t_i, j < i\}$ for $i > \ell$. This means that the first ℓ queries are the adversary's queries and the remaining z_i are chosen uniformly at random among the possible values (all queries have to be pairwise distinct). Denoting μ_ℓ the distribution of the tuple of q outputs when a random instance of $\mathtt{CLRW}^{r,E^*,\mathcal{H}}$ receives inputs $((t_1, z_1), \ldots, (t_q, z_q))$, we have:

$$\mathbf{Adv}^{\widetilde{\mathrm{ncpa}}}_{\mathtt{CLRW}^{r,E^*,\mathcal{H}}}(q, \tau = +\infty) \leq \|\mu_q - \mu_0\| \leq \sum_{\ell=0}^{q-1} \|\mu_{\ell+1} - \mu_\ell\|. \tag{1}$$

3.4 Coupling of $\mu_{\ell+1}$ and μ_ℓ

Restricting to the First $\ell+1$ Queries
It remains to upper bound the statistical distance between $\mu_{\ell+1}$ and μ_ℓ, for each $\ell \in [0; q-1]$. For this, we will construct a suitable coupling of the two distributions. Note that we only have to consider the first $\ell+1$ elements of the two tuples of outputs since for both distributions, the i-th inputs for $i > \ell+1$ are sampled uniformly at random. In other words,

$$\|\mu_{\ell+1} - \mu_\ell\| = \|\mu'_{\ell+1} - \mu'_\ell\|, \tag{2}$$

where $\mu'_{\ell+1}$ and μ'_ℓ are the respective distributions of the $\ell+1$ first outputs of the r-CLRW construction.

Construction of μ'_ℓ and $\mu'_{\ell+1}$
To define the coupling of $\mu'_{\ell+1}$ and μ'_ℓ, we consider a random $\mathrm{CLRW}^{r,E^*,\mathcal{H}}_{\pi,h}$ (i.e. $\pi = (\pi_1, \ldots, \pi_r)$ and $h = (h_1, \ldots, h_r)$ are uniformly random in respectively $\mathrm{Perm}(n)^r$ and $\mathcal{H}^r$) that receives inputs (t_j, x_j) for $j = 1, \ldots, \ell+1$ so that the outputs are distributed according to $\mu'_{\ell+1}$, and we consider another random $\mathrm{CLRW}^{r,E^*,\mathcal{H}}_{\pi',h'}$ (i.e. $\pi' = (\pi'_1, \ldots, \pi'_r)$ and $h' = (h'_1, \ldots, h'_r)$ are uniformly random in respectively $\mathrm{Perm}(n)^r$ and $\mathcal{H}^r$) with inputs (t_j, z_j) for $j = 1, \ldots, \ell+1$ with $z_j = x_j$ for every $j \le \ell$ and $z_{\ell+1}$ being uniformly random in $\{0,1\}^n \setminus \{x_j \,|\, t_j = t_{\ell+1}, j < \ell+1\}$, so that the outputs are distributed according to μ'_ℓ.

Notation
For every $j \le \ell+1$ and every $i \in [0; r]$, we note x^i_j and z^i_j the values defined by induction:

$$\begin{cases} x^0_j = x_j, z^0_j = z_j \\ x^{i+1}_j = h_i(t_j) \oplus \pi_i(x^i_j \oplus h_i(t_j)) \\ z^{i+1}_j = h'_i(t_j) \oplus \pi'_i(z^i_j \oplus h'_i(t_j)) \,. \end{cases} \tag{3}$$

In order to apply the Coupling Lemma (Lemma 1), we have to find how to correlate (π, h) and (π', h') so that the outputs of both systems $(x^r_1, \ldots, x^r_{\ell+1})$ and $(z^r_1, \ldots, z^r_{\ell+1})$ are equal with high probability. We choose (π, h) uniformly at random and we construct (π', h') as a function of (π, h). We have to pay attention that the distribution of (π', h') remains uniform in order for $(z^r_1, \ldots, z^r_{\ell+1})$ to be distributed according to μ'_ℓ.

Coupling of the First ℓ Queries
For every $j \le \ell$, the j-th queries x^0_j and z^0_j are equal by definition. Considering the system (3), we set $h' = h$ and $\pi'_i(x^i_j \oplus h_i(t_j)) = \pi_i(x^i_j \oplus h_i(t_j))$ for every $j \le \ell$ and $i \le r$. This implies that the first ℓ outputs $(x^r_1, \ldots, x^r_\ell)$ and $(z^r_1, \ldots, z^r_\ell)$ are equal.

Coupling of the $(\ell + 1)$-th Query

For every $i \in [0; r - 1]$ we define the coupling for the $\ell + 1$-th query as follows:

(1) if there exists $j \le \ell$ such that $z_{\ell+1}^i \oplus h_i(t_{\ell+1}) = z_j^i \oplus h_i(t_j)$ then $\pi_i'(z_{\ell+1}^i \oplus h_i(t_{\ell+1}))$ is already defined. Unless we have coupled $z_{\ell+1}^i$ and $x_{\ell+1}^i$ in a previous round, we cannot couple $z_{\ell+1}^{i+1}$ and $x_{\ell+1}^{i+1}$ at this round.

(2) else, if $z_{\ell+1}^i \oplus h_i(t_{\ell+1}) \ne z_j^i \oplus h_i(t_j)$ for all $j \le \ell$, then:

    (a) if there exists $j \le \ell$ such that $x_{\ell+1}^i \oplus h_i(t_{\ell+1}) = x_j^i \oplus h_i(t_j)$ then we choose $\pi_i'(z_{\ell+1}^i \oplus h_i(t_{\ell+1}))$ uniformly at random in $\{0, 1\}^n \setminus \{\pi_i'(z_j^i \oplus h_i(t_j)), j \le \ell\}$. We cannot couple $z_{\ell+1}^{i+1}$ and $x_{\ell+1}^{i+1}$ at this round.

    (b) else, we define $\pi_i'(z_{\ell+1}^i \oplus h_i(t_{\ell+1})) = \pi_i(x_{\ell+1}^i \oplus h_i(t_{\ell+1}))$. This implies that $z_{\ell+1}^{i+1} = x_{\ell+1}^{i+1}$.

Note that once $z_{\ell+1}^{i+1} = x_{\ell+1}^{i+1}$, $z_{\ell+1}^{i'} = x_{\ell+1}^{i'}$ for any subsequent round $i' \ge i+1$, in particular for $i' = r$, so that the coupling is successful.

Verification that (π', h') Is Uniformly Random

We set $h' = h$ and h is uniformly random so h' is uniformly random. During the coupling of the first ℓ queries, we set $\pi_i'(x_j^i \oplus h_i(t_j)) = \pi_i(x_j^i \oplus h_i(t_j))$ for every $j \le \ell$ and $i \le r$ and $\pi_i(x_j^i \oplus h_i(t_j))$ is uniformly random among possible values so $\pi_i'(x_j^i \oplus h_i(t_j))$ is uniformly random among possible values. Rule (1) says that if there is a collision with a previous input of π_i', we cannot choose the value of $\pi_i'(z_j^i \oplus h_i(t_j))$ so this does not change anything to the distribution of π_i'. When conditions of rule (2)(a) are met, we have for some $j \le \ell$:

$$\begin{cases} \pi_i(x_{\ell+1}^i \oplus h_i(t_{\ell+1})) = \pi_i(x_j^i \oplus h_i(t_j)) = \pi_i'(z_j^i \oplus h_i(t_j)) \\ z_{\ell+1}^i \oplus h_i(t_{\ell+1}) \ne z_j^i \oplus h_i(t_j), \end{cases}$$

which implies that $\pi_i'(z_{\ell+1}^i \oplus h_i(t_{\ell+1})) \ne \pi_i(x_j^i \oplus h_i(t_j))$. This means that the coupling is impossible and we choose $\pi_i'(z_{\ell+1}^i \oplus h_i(t_{\ell+1}))$ uniformly at random among possible values to keep π_i' uniformly distributed. Finally, when conditions of rule (2)(b) are met, we have no problem to couple: $\pi_i(x_{\ell+1}^i \oplus h_i(t_{\ell+1}))$ and $\pi_i'(z_{\ell+1}^i \oplus h_i(t_{\ell+1}))$ are both uniformly random among possible values. In conclusion, permutations π_i' are uniformly random and independent as wanted, so that $(z_1^r, \ldots, z_{\ell+1}^r)$ is distributed according to μ_ℓ'.

Failure Probability of the Coupling

It remains to upper bound the probability that the coupling fails, i.e.

$$(z_1^r, \ldots, z_{\ell+1}^r) \ne (x_1^r, \ldots, x_{\ell+1}^r).$$

For every $i \in [0; r - 1]$, we denote $\mathtt{fail}^i$ the event that it exists $j \le \ell$ such that $z_{\ell+1}^i \oplus h_i(t_{\ell+1}) = z_j^i \oplus h_i(t_j)$ or $x_{\ell+1}^i \oplus h_i(t_{\ell+1}) = x_j^i \oplus h_i(t_j)$. This is the event of failing to couple at round i. Then we have:

$$\Pr\left[\texttt{fail}^i\right] \leq \sum_{j \leq \ell} \Pr\left[z^i_{\ell+1} \oplus h_i(t_{\ell+1}) = z^i_j \oplus h_i(t_j)\right.$$

$$\left. \text{or } x^i_{\ell+1} \oplus h_i(t_{\ell+1}) = x^i_j \oplus h_i(t_j)\right]$$

$$= \sum_{j \leq \ell} \Pr\left[h_i(t_j) \oplus h_i(t_{\ell+1}) = z^i_j \oplus z^i_{\ell+1}\right.$$

$$\left. \text{or } h_i(t_j) \oplus h_i(t_{\ell+1}) = x^i_j \oplus x^i_{\ell+1}\right]$$

$$\leq \sum_{j \leq \ell} 2\varepsilon = 2\ell\varepsilon,$$

where the second inequality comes from the ε-AXU$_2$ property of $\mathcal{H}$ (note that when $t_{\ell+1} = t_j$, necessarily $z^i_{\ell+1} \neq z^i_j$ and $x^i_{\ell+1} \neq x^i_j$ since all queries must be distinct, so that the probability is zero). Since the functions h_i are independent, we have:

$$\Pr\left[\bigcap_{i=0}^{r-1} \texttt{fail}^i\right] \leq (2\ell\varepsilon)^r. \tag{4}$$

Using the Coupling Lemma and the fact that $z^r_j = x^r_j$ for all $j \leq \ell$, we have:

$$\|\mu'_{\ell+1} - \mu'_\ell\| \leq \Pr\left[(z^r_1, \ldots, z^r_{\ell+1}) \neq (x^r_1, \ldots, x^r_{\ell+1})\right] \leq \Pr\left[z^r_{\ell+1} \neq x^r_{\ell+1}\right]. \tag{5}$$

If we succeed to couple the last query at some round $i \leq r - 1$, we know that $z^{i'}_{\ell+1}$ and $x^{i'}_{\ell+1}$ remain equal in the subsequent rounds so that:

$$\Pr\left[z^r_{\ell+1} \neq x^r_{\ell+1}\right] \leq \Pr\left[\bigcap_{i=0}^{r-1} \texttt{fail}^i\right]. \tag{6}$$

Using (4), (5) and (6), we have:

$$\|\mu'_{\ell+1} - \mu'_\ell\| \leq (2\ell\varepsilon)^r. \tag{7}$$

Finally, using (1), (2) and (7), we obtain:

$$\mathbf{Adv}^{\widetilde{\text{ncpa}}}_{\text{CLRW}^r, E^*, \mathcal{H}}(q, \tau = +\infty) \leq \sum_{\ell=0}^{q-1} \|\mu'_{\ell+1} - \mu'_\ell\|$$

$$\leq \sum_{\ell=0}^{q-1} (2\ell\varepsilon)^r$$

$$\leq \int_0^q (2\ell\varepsilon)^r dl$$

$$= \frac{q^{r+1}}{r+1}(2\varepsilon)^r.$$

Theorem 1 then follows from the above inequality combined with Lemma 2.

4   Security Analysis for Adaptive Adversaries

In this section, we first prove a general composition theorem for tweakable block-ciphers similar to the "two weak make one strong" theorem for the composition of usual blockciphers. This theorem roughly states that composing two blockciphers secure against NCPA adversaries yields a blockcipher secure against CCA adversaries [14,15]. We prove exactly the same result for TBCs, but we stress that the exact way the tweak is used in composition is important: namely, the *same* tweak must be used in both ciphers. We state this theorem in the information-theoretic setting (i.e. for computationally unbounded adversaries) since we will then apply it to the $\mathtt{CLRW}^{r,E^*\mathcal{H}}$ construction which has information-theoretic security. Corresponding theorems in the computational setting are usually much harder to obtain. Our proof technique is an extension of the "H Coefficients" technique of Patarin [19] to tweakable blockciphers. One could probably use the formalism of random systems [13] to obtain a tight bound in the computational setting as in [15], however subtle problems have been recently found in this proof technique [9] so that we prefer the more simple and straightforward statistical approach. We then apply this result to prove the security of r-CLRW against CCA adversaries up to $\mathcal{O}(2^{rn/(r+2)})$ queries.

4.1   Definitions ans Preliminary Results

Fix $\widetilde{E} \in \mathsf{TBC}(\mathcal{K},\mathcal{T},\mathcal{D})$. For any $t = (t_1,\ldots,t_q) \in \mathcal{T}^q$, and any $x = (x_1,\ldots,x_q) \in \Omega_t$, we denote $\nu_{(t,x)}$ the distribution on Ω_t induced by $\widetilde{E}$ and $\nu_{(t,x)}^*$ the distribution induced by a random tweakable permutation on inputs (t_i,x_i), namely for $y = (y_1,\ldots,y_q) \in \Omega_t$:

$$
\begin{cases}
\nu_{(t,x)}(y) = \Pr\left[k \leftarrow_\$ \mathcal{K} : \widetilde{E}_k(t_i,x_i) = y_i, \forall i \le q\right] \\
\nu_{(t,x)}^*(y) = \Pr[\widetilde{\pi} \leftarrow_\$ \mathsf{BC}(\mathcal{T},\mathcal{D}) : \widetilde{\pi}(t_i,x_i) = y_i, \forall i \le q] .
\end{cases}
$$

Note that $\nu_{(t,x)}^*$ is uniform over Ω_t (the exact cardinality of Ω_t depends on t). For any $\alpha \in [0,1]$, we note $S_{\alpha,(t,x)}$ the set of $y \in \Omega_t$ satisfying $\nu_{(t,x)}(y) \ge (1-\alpha)\nu_{(t,x)}^*(y)$.

We start by proving two lemmas which will be useful for our main result. The first one says that if, for every $t = (t_1,\ldots,t_q)$, $x = (x_1,\ldots,x_q)$, and $y = (y_1,\ldots,y_q)$, the probability that $\widetilde{E}_k$ maps (t_i,x_i) to y_i for all i is close to the corresponding probability for a random tweakable permutation, then the advantage of any adversary in distinguishing $\widetilde{E}$ from a random tweakable permutation with q queries is small.

Lemma 3. *Fix* $\widetilde{E} \in \mathsf{TBC}(\mathcal{K},\mathcal{T},\mathcal{D})$, *and* $q \le |\mathcal{D}|$. *If there exists* $\alpha \in [0,1]$ *such that, for all* $t \in \mathcal{T}^q$ *and for all* $x \in \Omega_t$, $\nu_{(t,x)}^*(S_{\alpha,(t,x)}) = 1$, *then*

$$
\mathbf{Adv}_{\widetilde{E}}^{\mathrm{cca}}(q,\tau = +\infty) \le \alpha .
$$

Proof. Consider a computationally unbounded CCA attacker $\mathcal{A}$ making q queries to an oracle $\mathcal{O}$ acting like $\widetilde{E}$ or like a random tweakable permutation $\widetilde{\pi}$. We assume *wlog* that $\mathcal{A}$ is deterministic. We note $\delta = (\delta_1, \ldots, \delta_q) \in \mathcal{D}^q$ the transcript of the attack, defined as follows. If $\mathcal{A}$ makes a direct query (t_1, x_1) and receives an answer y_1, one has $\delta_1 = y_1$ and then, the attacker continues his attack and receives the next answers $\delta_2, \ldots, \delta_q$. If the attacker makes an inverse query (t_i, y_i) then δ_i is the answer x_i. For each transcript δ, we denote $t(\delta), x(\delta)$ and $y(\delta)$ the corresponding values of $t_1, \ldots, t_q, x_1, \ldots, x_q, y_1, \ldots, y_q$. We denote Σ the set of transcripts δ such that the attacker outputs 1. If the oracle is acting like $\widetilde{E}$ then the probability that the attacker outputs 1 is exactly

$$\sum_{\delta \in \Sigma} \nu_{t(\delta), x(\delta)}(y(\delta)).$$

If the oracle is acting like a random tweakable permutation $\widetilde{\pi}$ then the probability that the attacker outputs 1 is exactly

$$\sum_{\delta \in \Sigma} \nu^*_{t(\delta), x(\delta)}(y(\delta)).$$

We deduce that the advantage of $\mathcal{A}$ equals:

$$\left| \sum_{\delta \in \Sigma} \left(\nu_{t(\delta), x(\delta)}(y(\delta)) - \nu^*_{t(\delta), x(\delta)}(y(\delta)) \right) \right|. \tag{8}$$

Since for every $t \in \mathcal{T}^q$, $x \in \Omega_t$, and $y \in \Omega_t$, one has $\nu_{(t,x)}(y) \geq (1 - \alpha)\nu^*_{(t,x)}(y)$, it follows that:

$$\sum_{\delta \in \Sigma} \left(\nu_{t(\delta), x(\delta)}(y(\delta)) - \nu^*_{t(\delta), x(\delta)}(y(\delta)) \right) \geq -\alpha$$

$$\text{and} \sum_{\delta \notin \Sigma} \left(\nu_{t(\delta), x(\delta)}(y(\delta)) - \nu^*_{t(\delta), x(\delta)}(y(\delta)) \right) \geq -\alpha. \tag{9}$$

Finally, it is easy to verify that

$$\sum_{\delta \in \Sigma} \left(\nu_{t(\delta), x(\delta)}(y(\delta)) - \nu^*_{t(\delta), x(\delta)}(y(\delta)) \right) = \tag{10}$$

$$- \sum_{\delta \notin \Sigma} \left(\nu_{t(\delta), x(\delta)}(y(\delta)) - \nu^*_{t(\delta), x(\delta)}(y(\delta)) \right)$$

because

$$\sum_{\delta} \nu_{t(\delta), x(\delta)}(y(\delta)) = \sum_{\delta} \nu^*_{t(\delta), x(\delta)}(y(\delta)) = 1.$$

Using (8), (9) and (10), we deduce that the advantage of $\mathcal{A}$ is upper bounded by α. □

The second lemma says that if the advantage of the best NCPA adversary is small, then, for all t, x, almost all y are such that the probability of sending (t, x) to y for a random $\widetilde{E}_k$ is close to the probability of sending (t, x) to y for a random tweakable permutation.

Lemma 4. *Fix $\widetilde{E} \in \mathsf{TBC}(\mathcal{K}, \mathcal{T}, \mathcal{D})$ and $q \leq |\mathcal{D}|$. If there exists $\beta \in [0, 1]$ such that*

$$\mathbf{Adv}_{\widetilde{E}}^{\widetilde{\mathsf{ncpa}}}(q, \tau = +\infty) \leq \beta,$$

then, for all $t \in \mathcal{T}^q$ and $x \in \Omega_t$, one has:

$$\nu_{(t,x)}^* \left(S_{\sqrt{\beta},(t,x)} \right) \geq 1 - \sqrt{\beta}.$$

Proof. By contrapositive, suppose there exists $t = (t_1, \ldots, t_q) \in \mathcal{T}^q$ and $x = (x_1, \ldots, x_q) \in \Omega_t$ such that

$$\nu_{(t,x)}^* \left(S_{\sqrt{\beta},(t,x)} \right) < 1 - \sqrt{\beta}.$$

Consider the adversary which queries (t_1, x_1), ..., (t_q, x_q) and outputs 0 if the answers $y = (y_1, \ldots, y_q)$ are such that $y \in S_{\sqrt{\beta},(t,x)}$ and 1 otherwise. His advantage is exactly

$$\left| \sum_{y \notin S_{\sqrt{\beta},(t,x)}} \nu_{(t,x)}(y) - \nu_{(t,x)}^*(y) \right|,$$

and $y \notin S_{\sqrt{\beta},(t,x)}$ means, by definition, that $\nu_{(t,x)}(y) < (1 - \sqrt{\beta})\nu_{(t,x)}^*(y)$, so that the advantage of this adversary is strictly greater than:

$$\sqrt{\beta} \times \left(1 - \nu_{(t,x)}^* \left(S_{\sqrt{\beta},(t,x)} \right) \right) > \beta,$$

hence the result. $\qquad\square$

4.2   A Composition Theorem for Tweakable Blockciphers

Given two TBCs sharing the same set of tweaks and the same domain $\widetilde{E}_1 \in \mathsf{TBC}(\mathcal{K}_1, \mathcal{T}, \mathcal{D})$ and $\widetilde{E}_2 \in \mathsf{TBC}(\mathcal{K}_2, \mathcal{T}, \mathcal{D})$, we define the tweakable blockcipher $\widetilde{E}_2 \circ \widetilde{E}_1 \in \mathsf{TBC}(\mathcal{K}_1 \times \mathcal{K}_2, \mathcal{T}, \mathcal{D})$ as:

$\forall (t, x) \in \mathcal{D} \times \mathcal{T}, (k_1, k_2) \in \mathcal{K}_1 \times \mathcal{K}_2,$

$$\widetilde{E}_2 \circ \widetilde{E}_1((k_1, k_2), t, x) := \widetilde{E}_2(k_2, t, \widetilde{E}_1(k_1, t, x)).$$

Theorem 2. *Let $\widetilde{E}_1 \in \mathsf{TBC}(\mathcal{K}_1, \mathcal{T}, \mathcal{D})$ and $\widetilde{E}_2 \in \mathsf{TBC}(\mathcal{K}_2, \mathcal{T}, \mathcal{D})$ be two TBCs satisfying:*

$$\mathbf{Adv}_{\widetilde{E}_1}^{\widetilde{\mathsf{ncpa}}}(q, \tau = +\infty) \leq \beta_1 \text{ and } \mathbf{Adv}_{\widetilde{E}_2}^{\widetilde{\mathsf{ncpa}}}(q, \tau = +\infty) \leq \beta_2.$$

Then:

$$\mathbf{Adv}_{\widetilde{E}_2^{-1} \circ \widetilde{E}_1}^{\widetilde{\mathsf{cca}}}(q, \tau = +\infty) \leq 2(\sqrt{\beta_1} + \sqrt{\beta_2}).$$

Proof. We denote ν^1, ν^2, and ν^3 the distributions associated respectively to $\widetilde{E}_1, \widetilde{E}_2$ and $\widetilde{E}_2^{-1} \circ \widetilde{E}_1$. For every $t \in \mathcal{T}^q$, $x \in \Omega_t$, and $\alpha \in [0,1]$, we denote $S_{\alpha,(t,x)}^{\widetilde{E}_i}$ the set $S_{\alpha,(t,x)}$ corresponding to $\widetilde{E}_i$, $i = 1, 2$.

By Lemma 4, for all $t \in \mathcal{T}^q$, $x \in \Omega_t$, and $y \in \Omega_t$, we have:

$$\nu_{(t,x)}^* \left(S_{\sqrt{\beta_1},(t,x)}^{\widetilde{E}_1} \right) \geq 1 - \sqrt{\beta_1} \quad \text{and} \quad \nu_{(t,y)}^* \left(S_{\sqrt{\beta_2},(t,y)}^{\widetilde{E}_2} \right) \geq 1 - \sqrt{\beta_2}. \tag{11}$$

Furthermore, for all $(k_1, k_2) \in \mathcal{K}_1 \times \mathcal{K}_2$, $\widetilde{E}_2^{-1} \circ \widetilde{E}_1((k_1, k_2), \cdot, \cdot)$ maps (t,x) to y if and only if for all $i \leq q$, $\widetilde{E}_1(k_1, t_i, x_i) = \widetilde{E}_2(k_2, t_i, y_i)$. Denoting $S' = S_{\sqrt{\beta_1},(t,x)}^{\widetilde{E}_1} \cap S_{\sqrt{\beta_2},(t,y)}^{\widetilde{E}_2}$, one has, for any $y \in \Omega_t$:

$$\begin{aligned}
\nu_{(t,x)}^3(y) &= \sum_{z \in \Omega_t} \nu_{(t,x)}^1(z) \cdot \nu_{(t,y)}^2(z) \\
&\geq \sum_{z \in S'} \nu_{(t,x)}^1(z) \cdot \nu_{(t,y)}^2(z) \\
&\geq \sum_{z \in S'} \left(1 - \sqrt{\beta_1}\right) \nu^*{}_{(t,x)}(z) \cdot \left(1 - \sqrt{\beta_2}\right) \nu^*{}_{(t,y)}(z) \\
&\geq \left(1 - \sqrt{\beta_1}\right) \left(1 - \sqrt{\beta_2}\right) \frac{|S'|}{|\Omega_t|^2} \\
&= \left(1 - \sqrt{\beta_1}\right) \left(1 - \sqrt{\beta_2}\right) \nu_{(t,x)}^*(S') \nu_{(t,x)}^*(y).
\end{aligned}$$

By definition of S' and using Eq. 11, one has $\nu_{(t,x)}^*(S') \geq (1 - \sqrt{\beta_1} - \sqrt{\beta_2})$ (note that ν^* in fact only depends on t), so that:

$$\nu_{(t,x)}^3(y) \geq (1 - 2(\sqrt{\beta_1} + \sqrt{\beta_2}))\nu_{(t,x)}^*(y).$$

Since this holds for any t, x, and y, the theorem follows by applying Lemma 3 with $\alpha = 2(\sqrt{\beta_1} + \sqrt{\beta_2})$. □

4.3 Application to the r-CLRW Construction

Finally, we apply the previous result to prove the security of r-CLRW against CCA adversaries.

Theorem 3. *Let $\mathcal{K}, \mathcal{T}$ be sets, $E \in \mathsf{BC}(\mathcal{K}, n)$ be a blockcipher, and $\mathcal{H}$ be an ε-AXU$_2$ family of functions from $\mathcal{T}$ to $\{0,1\}^n$. Then for any even integer r, one has:*

$$\mathbf{Adv}_{\mathrm{CLRW}^r, E, \mathcal{H}}^{\widetilde{\mathrm{cca}}}(q, \tau) \leq r \cdot \mathbf{Adv}_E^{\mathrm{cca}}(q, \tau + rqT) + \frac{4\sqrt{2}}{\sqrt{r+2}} q^{(r+2)/4} (2\varepsilon)^{r/4},$$

where T is the time to compute E or E^{-1}.

Proof. Noting that the inverse of a $r/2$-CLRW construction is again a $r/2$-CLRW construction, we can apply Theorem 2 to get:

$$\mathbf{Adv}^{\widetilde{cca}}_{\mathrm{CLRW}^r, E^*, \mathcal{H}}(q, \tau = +\infty) \leq 4\sqrt{\alpha},$$

where

$$\alpha := \mathbf{Adv}^{\widetilde{ncpa}}_{\mathrm{CLRW}^{r/2}, E^*, \mathcal{H}}(q, \tau = +\infty) \leq \frac{q^{r/2+1}}{r/2+1}(2\varepsilon)^{r/2}$$

by the results of Sect. 3. The theorem then follows from Lemma 2.   □

Again, using an ε-AXU$_2$ function family with $\varepsilon \simeq 2^{-n}$, the construction achieves security against CCA adversaries up to $\mathcal{O}(2^{rn/(r+2)})$ queries.

A   Proof of the Coupling Lemma

The original statement and proof of the Coupling Lemma is due to Aldous [1]. Here we follow closely a proof by Vigoda.[3]

Let λ be a coupling of μ and ν, and $(X, Y) \sim \lambda$. By definition, we have that for any $z \in \omega$, $\lambda(z, z) \leq \min\{\mu(z), \nu(z)\}$. Moreover, $\Pr[X = Y] = \sum_{z \in \Omega} \lambda(z, z)$. Hence we have:

$$\Pr[X = Y] \leq \sum_{z \in \Omega} \min\{\mu(z), \nu(z)\}.$$

Therefore:

$$\Pr[X \neq Y] \geq 1 - \sum_{z \in \Omega} \min\{\mu(z), \nu(z)\}$$
$$= \sum_{z \in \Omega} (\mu(z) - \min\{\mu(z), \nu(z)\})$$
$$= \sum_{\substack{z \in \Omega \\ \mu(z) \geq \nu(z)}} (\mu(z) - \nu(z))$$
$$= \max_{S \subset \Omega}\{\mu(S) - \nu(S)\}$$
$$= \|\mu - \nu\|.$$

References

1. Aldous, D.J.: Random walks on finite groups and rapidly mixing Markov chains. In: Azéma, J., Yor, M. (eds.) Séminaire de Probabilités XVII. Lecture Notes in Mathematics, vol. 986, pp. 243–297. Springer, Heidelberg (1983)
2. Bogdanov, A., Knudsen, L.R., Leander, G., Standaert, F.-X., Steinberger, J., Tischhauser, E.: Key-alternating ciphers in a provable setting: encryption using a small number of public permutations (extended abstract). In: Pointcheval, D., Johansson, T. (eds.) EUROCRYPT 2012. LNCS, vol. 7237, pp. 45–62. Springer, Heidelberg (2012)

---

[3] Available from www.cc.gatech.edu/~vigoda/MCMC_Course/MC-basics.pdf

3. Crowley, P.: Mercy: a fast large block cipher for disk sector encryption. In: Schneier, B. (ed.) FSE 2000. LNCS, vol. 1978, pp. 49–63. Springer, Heidelberg (2001)
4. Dodis, Y., Steinberger, J.: Domain extension for MACs beyond the birthday barrier. In: Paterson, K.G. (ed.) EUROCRYPT 2011. LNCS, vol. 6632, pp. 323–342. Springer, Heidelberg (2011)
5. Even, S., Mansour, Y.: A construction of a cipher from a single pseudorandom permutation. J. Cryptol. **10**(3), 151–162 (1997)
6. Ferguson, N., Lucks, S., Schneier, B., Whiting, D., Bellare, M., Kohno, T., Callas, J., Walker, J.: The Skein Hash Function Family. SHA3 Submission to NIST (Round 3) (2010)
7. Goldenberg, D., Hohenberger, S., Liskov, M., Schwartz, E.C., Seyalioglu, H.: On tweaking Luby-Rackoff blockciphers. In: Kurosawa, K. (ed.) ASIACRYPT 2007. LNCS, vol. 4833, pp. 342–356. Springer, Heidelberg (2007)
8. Hoang, V.T., Rogaway, P.: On generalized Feistel networks. In: Rabin, T. (ed.) CRYPTO 2010. LNCS, vol. 6223, pp. 613–630. Springer, Heidelberg (2010)
9. Jetchev, D., Özen, O., Stam, M.: Understanding adaptivity: random systems revisited. In: Wang, X., Sako, K. (eds.) ASIACRYPT 2012. LNCS, vol. 7658, pp. 313–330. Springer, Heidelberg (2012)
10. Lampe, R., Patarin, J., Seurin, Y.: An asymptotically tight security analysis of the iterated Even-Mansour cipher. In: Wang, X., Sako, K. (eds.) ASIACRYPT 2012. LNCS, vol. 7658, pp. 278–295. Springer, Heidelberg (2012)
11. Landecker, W., Shrimpton, T., Terashima, R.S.: Tweakable blockciphers with beyond birthday-bound security. In: Safavi-Naini, R., Canetti, R. (eds.) CRYPTO 2012. LNCS, vol. 7417, pp. 14–30. Springer, Heidelberg (2012)
12. Liskov, M., Rivest, R.L., Wagner, D.: Tweakable block ciphers. In: Yung, M. (ed.) CRYPTO 2002. LNCS, vol. 2442, pp. 31–46. Springer, Heidelberg (2002)
13. Maurer, U.M.: Indistinguishability of random systems. In: Knudsen, L.R. (ed.) EUROCRYPT 2002. LNCS, vol. 2332, pp. 110–132. Springer, Heidelberg (2002)
14. Maurer, U.M., Pietrzak, K.: Composition of random systems: when two weak make one strong. In: Naor, M. (ed.) TCC 2004. LNCS, vol. 2951, pp. 410–427. Springer, Heidelberg (2004)
15. Maurer, U.M., Pietrzak, K., Renner, R.S.: Indistinguishability amplification. In: Menezes, A. (ed.) CRYPTO 2007. LNCS, vol. 4622, pp. 130–149. Springer, Heidelberg (2007)
16. Minematsu, K.: Beyond-birthday-bound security based on tweakable block cipher. In: Dunkelman, O. (ed.) FSE 2009. LNCS, vol. 5665, pp. 308–326. Springer, Heidelberg (2009)
17. Mironov, I.: (Not so) Random shuffles of RC4. In: Yung, M. (ed.) CRYPTO 2002. LNCS, vol. 2442, p. 304. Springer, Heidelberg (2002)
18. Morris, B., Rogaway, P., Stegers, T.: How to encipher messages on a small domain. In: Halevi, S. (ed.) CRYPTO 2009. LNCS, vol. 5677, pp. 286–302. Springer, Heidelberg (2009)
19. Patarin, J.: New results on pseudorandom permutation generators based on the DES scheme. In: Feigenbaum, J. (ed.) CRYPTO 1991. LNCS, vol. 576, pp. 301–312. Springer, Heidelberg (1992)
20. Rogaway, P.: Efficient instantiations of tweakable blockciphers and refinements to modes OCB and PMAC. In: Lee, P.J. (ed.) ASIACRYPT 2004. LNCS, vol. 3329, pp. 16–31. Springer, Heidelberg (2004)
21. Schroeppel, R.: The Hasty Pudding Cipher. AES Submission to NIST (1998)

22. Shoup, V.: On fast and provably secure message authentication based on universal hashing. In: Koblitz, N. (ed.) CRYPTO 1996. LNCS, vol. 1109, pp. 313–328. Springer, Heidelberg (1996)
23. Steinberger, J.: Improved security bounds for key-alternating ciphers via Hellinger distance. IACR Cryptology ePrint Archive Report 2012/481 (2012). http://eprint.iacr.org/2012/481.pdf
24. Yasuda, K.: The sum of CBC MACs is a secure PRF. In: Pieprzyk, J. (ed.) CT-RSA 2010. LNCS, vol. 5985, pp. 366–381. Springer, Heidelberg (2010)
25. Yasuda, K.: A new variant of PMAC: beyond the birthday bound. In: Rogaway, P. (ed.) CRYPTO 2011. LNCS, vol. 6841, pp. 596–609. Springer, Heidelberg (2011)

Stream Ciphers I

Smashing WEP in a Passive Attack

Pouyan Sepehrdad[1]([✉]), Petr Sušil[2], Serge Vaudenay[2], and Martin Vuagnoux[3]

[1] Intel CRI-SC at TU-Darmstadt, Darmstadt, Germany
pouyan.sepehrdad@trust.cased.de
[2] EPFL, Lausanne, Switzerland
{petr.susil,serge.vaudenay}@epfl.ch
[3] base23 SA, Geneva, Switzerland
martin@vuagnoux.com

Abstract. In this paper, we report extremely fast and optimised active and passive attacks against the old IEEE 802.11 wireless communication protocol WEP. This was achieved through a huge amount of theoretical and experimental analysis (capturing WiFi packets), refinement and optimisation of all the former known attacks and methodologies against RC4 stream cipher in WEP mode. We support all our claims by providing an implementation of this attack as a publicly available patch on Aircrack-ng. Our new attacks improve its success probability drastically. We adapt our theoretical analysis in Eurocrypt 2011 to real-world scenarios and we perform a slight adjustment to match the empirical observations. Our active attack, based on ARP injection, requires 22 500 packets to gain success probability of 50 % against a 104-bit WEP key, using Aircrack-ng in non-interactive mode. It runs in less than 5 s on an off-the-shelf PC. Using the same number of packets, Aicrack-ng yields around 3 % success rate. Furthermore, we describe very fast passive only attacks by just eavesdropping TCP/IPv4 packets in a WiFi communication. Our passive attack requires 27 500 packets. This is *much less than the number of packets* Aircrack-ng requires in *active mode* (around 37 500), which is a huge improvement. We believe that our analysis brings on further insight to the security of RC4.

1 Introduction

RC4 was designed by Rivest in 1987. It used to be a trade secret until it was anonymously posted on Cypherpunks mailing list in September 1994. Nowadays, due to its simplicity, RC4 is widely used in SSL/TLS, Microsoft Lotus, Oracle Secure SQL and Wi-Fi 802.11 wireless communications. The 802.11 [9] used to be protected by WEP (Wired Equivalent Privacy) which is now being replaced by WPA (Wi-Fi Protected Access) due to security weaknesses.

WEP uses RC4 with a pre-shared key. Each packet is encrypted by an XOR to a keystream generated by RC4. The RC4 key is a pre-shared key prepended with a 3-byte nonce initialisation vector IV. The IV is sent in clear

Supported by a grant of the Swiss National Science Foundation, 200021_134860/1.

S. Moriai (Ed.): FSE 2013, LNCS 8424, pp. 155–178, 2014.
DOI: 10.1007/978-3-662-43933-3_9, © Springer-Verlag Berlin Heidelberg 2014

for self-synchronisation. There have been several attempts to break the full RC4 algorithm, but it has only been devastating so far in this scenario. Indeed, the adversary knows that the key is constant except the IV, which is known. An active adversary can alter the IV. Nowadays, WEP is considered as being terribly weak, since passive attacks can recover the full key easily by assuming that the first bytes of every plaintext frame are known.

Structure of the paper. First, in Sect. 2, we refer to the motivation in this research area, then we present RC4, WEP and Aircrack-ng in Sect. 3. In Sect. 4, we go through all the existing well-known attacks on WEP. Next, we introduce some useful lemmas in Sect. 5. Then, we present all known biases for RC4 in Sect. 6. Subsequently, we elaborate on an optimised attack on WEP in Sect. 7 and, we compare our results with Aircrack-ng 1.1 in Sect. 8. Finally, we discuss some challenges and open problems in Sect. 9.

2   Motivation

For some people, attacking WEP is like beating a dead horse, but this horse is still running wildly in many countries all over the world. Also, some companies are selling hardware using modified versions of the WEP protocol, they claim to be secure [2]. Moreover, the new analysis and biases presented in this paper are related to RC4, which is the most popular stream cipher in the history of symmetric key cryptography. WEP is an example of a practical exploitation of these biases. The cryptanalysis of WEP is one of the most applied cryptographic attacks in practice. Indeed, tools such as Aircrack-ng are massively downloaded to provide a good example of weaknesses in cryptography. Finally, the TKIP protocol used by WPA is not much different from WEP (just a patch over WEP), so that attacks on WEP can affect the security of networks using TKIP, as seen in [2,26]. For instance in [26], the authors used exactly the same biases as in WEP to break WPA. Hence, gaining a better understanding of the behaviour of these biases may lead to a practical breach of WPA security in future.

3   Preliminaries

3.1   Description of RC4 and Notations

The RC4 stream cipher consists of two algorithms: the Key Scheduling Algorithm (KSA) and the Pseudo Random Generator Algorithm (PRGA). The RC4 engine has a state defined by two registers (words) i and j and one array (of N words) S defining a permutation over $\mathbf{Z}/N\mathbf{Z}$. The KSA generates an initial state for the PRGA from a random key K of L words as described in Fig. 1. It starts with an array $\{0, 1, \ldots, N-1\}$, where $N = 2^8$ and swaps N pairs, depending on the value of the secret key K. At the end, we obtain the initial state S_0'.

We define all the operators such as addition, subtraction and multiplication in the ring of integers modulo N represented as $\mathbf{Z}/N\mathbf{Z}$, or $\mathbf{Z}_N$, where $N = 256$ (i.e. *words* are *bytes*). Thus, $x + y$ should be read as $(x + y) \mod N$.

KAS

1: **for** $i = 0$ to $N - 1$ **do**
2:    $S[i] \leftarrow i$
3: **end for**
4: $j \leftarrow 0$
5: **for** $i = 0$ to $N - 1$ **do**
6:    $j \leftarrow j + S[i] + K[i \bmod L]$
7:    swap($S[i]$,$S[j]$)
8: **end for**

PAGR

1: $i \leftarrow 0$
2: $j \leftarrow 0$
3: **loop**
4:    $i \leftarrow i + 1$
5:    $j \leftarrow j + S[i]$
6:    swap($S[i]$,$S[j]$)
7:    output $z_i = S[S[i] + S[j]]$
8: **end loop**

Fig. 1. The KSA and the PRGA algorithms of RC4.

Once the initial state S'_0 is created, it is used by the second algorithm of RC4, the PRGA. Its role is to generate a keystream of words of $\log_2 N$ bits, which will be XORed with the plaintext to obtain the ciphertext. Thus, RC4 computes the loop of the PRGA each time a new keystream word z_i is needed, according to the algorithm in Fig. 1. Note that each time a word of the keystream is generated, the internal state (i, j, S) of RC4 is updated.

Sometimes, we consider an idealised version RC4*(t) of RC4 defined by a parameter t as shown in Fig. 2. Namely, after round t, index j is assigned randomly. This model has been already used in the literature such as in [17,20,22]. In fact, t is the index of the last known state. For instance, since we know $K[0], K[1], K[2]$ in WEP protocol, we can initially assume $t = 2$.

Let $S_i[k]$ (resp. $S'_i[k]$) denote the value of the permutation defined by the array S at index k, after the round i in the KSA (resp. the PRGA). We also denote $S_{N-1} = S'_0$. Let j_i (resp. j'_i) be the value of j after round i of the KSA (resp. PRGA), where the rounds are indexed with respect to i. Thus, the

KSA*(t)

1: **for** $i = 0$ to $N - 1$ **do**
2:    $S[i] \leftarrow i$
3: **end for**
4: $j \leftarrow 0$
5: **for** $i = 0$ to $N - 1$ **do**
6:    **if** $i \leq t$ **then**
7:       $j \leftarrow j + S[i] + K[i \bmod L]$
8:    **else**
9:       $j \leftarrow$ random
10:    **end if**
11:    swap($S[i]$,$S[j]$)
12: **end for**

PRGA*

1: $i \leftarrow 0$
2: $j \leftarrow 0$
3: **loop**
4:    $i \leftarrow i + 1$
5:    $j \leftarrow$ random
6:    swap($S[i]$,$S[j]$)
7:    output $z_i = S[S[i] + S[j]]$
8: **end loop**

Fig. 2. The KSA*(t) and the PRGA* algorithms of RC4*(t).

KSA has rounds $0, 1, \ldots, N-1$ and the PRGA has rounds $1, 2, \ldots$. The KSA and the PRGA are defined by

$$
\begin{array}{c|c}
\textbf{KSA} & \textbf{PRGA} \\
\begin{aligned}
j_{-1} &= 0 \\
j_i &= j_{i-1} + S_{i-1}[i] + K[i \mod L] \\
S_{-1}[k] &= k \\
S_i[k] &= \begin{cases} S_{i-1}[j_i] & \text{if } k = i \\ S_{i-1}[i] & \text{if } k = j_i \\ S_{i-1}[k] & \text{otherwise} \end{cases}
\end{aligned}
&
\begin{aligned}
j'_0 &= 0 \\
j'_i &= j'_{i-1} + S'_{i-1}[i] \\
S'_0[k] &= S_{N-1}[k] \\
S'_i[k] &= \begin{cases} S'_{i-1}[j'_i] & \text{if } k = i \\ S'_{i-1}[i] & \text{if } k = j'_i \\ S'_{i-1}[k] & \text{otherwise} \end{cases} \\
z_i &= S'_i[S'_i[i] + S'_i[j'_i]]
\end{aligned}
\end{array}
$$

Throughout this paper, we denote $\bar{K}[i] \stackrel{\text{def}}{=} K[0] + \cdots + K[i]$. We let z denote the keystream derived from K using RC4. In the applications we are concerned, the first bytes of a plaintext frame are often known (see Fig. 6 in Appendix), as well as the IV, the first 3 bytes of K. That is, we assume that the adversary can use the keystream z and the IV in a known plaintext attack.

We let I_0 be a set of integers, which represents the key byte indices which are already known. We define a set clue which consists of all $\bar{K}$ bytes whose indices are in I_0. To begin with, we have $I_0 = \{0, 1, 2\}$ and clue = IV. Given a set of indices I_0 and an index i, we assume that we have a list $\text{row}_{i|I_0}^{\text{RC4}}$ of $d_{i|I_0}$ vectors $(\bar{f}_j, \bar{g}_j, p_j, q_j)$, $j = 1, \ldots, d_{i|I_0}$ with functions $\bar{f}_j$ and the corresponding predicates $\bar{g}_j$ such that

$$
\Pr\left[\bar{K}[i] = \bar{f}_j(z, \text{clue}) \,|\, \bar{g}_j(z, \text{clue})\right] = p_j
$$

for some probability $p_j \neq \frac{1}{N}$ and

$$
\Pr\left[\bar{g}_j(z, \text{clue})\right] = q_j
$$

where q_j is called the *density* of the bias (for the list of such correlations, see Table 1 in Appendix).

For simplicity, we assume that for some given i, z, and clue, all suggested $\bar{f}_j(z, \text{clue})$ for j's such that $\bar{g}_j(z, \text{clue})$ holds, are pairwise distinct. We further assume that the events $\bar{K}[i] = \bar{f}_j(z, \text{clue})$ with different i's are independent. We will also assume that $\bar{f}_j$ and $\bar{g}_j$ are of the form $\bar{f}_j(z, \text{clue}) = f_j(h(z, \text{clue}))$ and $\bar{g}_j(z, \text{clue}) = g_j(h(z, \text{clue}))$, where $\mu = h(z, \text{clue})$ lies in a domain of size N_μ. In fact, h is just a function compressing the data to the minimum necessary to compute $\bar{f}_j$ and $\bar{g}_j$. The following prominent relation exists between the key bytes of RC4:

$$
\bar{K}[i + 16j] = \bar{K}[i] + j\bar{K}[15] \tag{1}
$$

for $0 \leq i \leq 15$ and $j = 0, 1, 2$. This relation reveals that if $\bar{K}[15]$ is known, the biases for $\bar{K}[i]$ and $\bar{K}[i + 16j]$ can be merged. This relation was initially used in [34] to derive a better success probability. For example, if we know $\bar{K}[15]$, we can use the biases for $\bar{K}[19]$ to vote for $\bar{K}[3]$. Similarly, the biases for $\bar{K}[15], \ldots, \bar{K}[18]$ and $\bar{K}[31], \bar{K}[32]$ can be merged to vote for $\bar{K}[15]$. Consequently, later, we recover $\bar{K}[15]$ before any other byte of the key.

Definition 1. *Let A, B and C be three random variables over $\mathbf{Z}_N$. We say that A is biased towards B with bias p conditioned on an event E and we represent it as $A \overset{p}{\underset{E}{=}} B$ if*

$$\Pr(A - B = x|E) = \begin{cases} p & if \quad x = 0 \\ \\ \frac{1-p}{N-1} & otherwise \end{cases}$$

When $\Pr[E] = 1$, it is denoted as $A \overset{p}{=} B$.

3.2   Description of WEP

WEP [8] uses a 3-byte IV concatenated to a secret key of 40 or 104 bits (5 or 13 bytes) as an RC4 key. Thus, the RC4 key size is either 64 or 128 bits. Since the RC4 design does not accept an IV by default, WEP generates a per packet key for each packet. A devastating problem of WEP is that the 13 bytes of the key do not change for each packet encryption, while the first 3 bytes of the key are changing. Thus, the attacker can run a statistical attack on the key. This was avoided in WPA. In this paper, we do not consider the 40-bit key variant, but a very similar approach can be leveraged to break the 40-bit key version. So, $L = 16$. In fact, we have

$$K = K[0]\|K[1]\|K[2]\|K[3]\| \cdots \|K[15] = \mathsf{IV}_0\|\mathsf{IV}_1\|\mathsf{IV}_2\|K[3]\| \cdots \|K[15]$$

where IV_i represents the $(i + 1)$-th byte of the IV and $K[3]\|...\|K[15]$ represents the fixed secret part of the key. In theory, the value of the IV should be random but in practice, it is a counter, mostly in little-endian and it is incremented by one each time a new 802.11b frame is encrypted. Sometimes, some particular values of the IV are skipped to thwart the specific attacks based on "weak IV's". Thus, each packet uses a slightly different key.

To protect the integrity of the data, a 32-bit long CRC32 check sum called ICV is appended to the data. Similar to other stream ciphers, the resulting stream is XORed with the RC4 keystream and it is sent through the communication channel together with the IV in clear. On the receiver's end, the ciphertext is again XORed with the shared key and the plaintext is recovered. The receiver checks the linear error correcting code and it either accepts the data or declines it.

It is well known [21,31,34] that a relevant portion of the plaintext is practically constant and that some other bytes can be predicted. They correspond to the LLC header and the SNAP header and some bytes of the TCP/IPv4 and ARP encapsulated frames. For example, by XORing the first byte of the ciphertext with the constant value 0xAA, we obtain the first byte of the keystream. Thus, even if these attacks are called known plaintext attacks, they are ciphertext only in practice (see the Appendix for the structure of ARP and TCP/IPv4 packets).

We consider both passive and active adversaries in this paper. For an active attack, the attacker eavesdrops the ARP packets and since the plaintext bytes are known up to the 32-nd byte, she can compute $z_1, \ldots, z_{32}$ values using the ciphertext. It is also possible to inject data into the network. Because the ARP replies expire quickly (resetting the ARP cache), it usually takes only a few seconds or minutes until an attacker can capture an ARP request and start re-injecting it [31]. On the other hand, active attacks are detectable by Intrusion Detection systems (IDS) and also some network cards require extra driver patches to be able to inject data into the traffic, which is not available for all network cards. This is not the case for a passive attack. The attacker can eavesdrop the wireless communication channel for TCP/IPv4 packets, but some of the data frames are not known in this case (see the Appendix). As represented in Table 1, the Klein and the Maitra-Paul attacks require z_i and z_{i+1} to recover $\bar{K}[i]$ respectively. Hence in reality, we are not able to use those attacks to recover some bytes of the key. This is not the case for the Korek attacks, since they only require z_1 and z_2. To summarise, we need more packets in a passive attack compared to an active attack. We are going to elaborate on both types of attacks later.

3.3   Aircrack-ng

Aircrack-ng [5] is a WEP and WPA-PSK keys cracking program that can recover keys once enough data packets have been captured. It is the most widely downloaded cracking software in the world. It implements the standard Fluhrer, Mantin and Shamir's (FMS) attack [7] along with some optimisations like the Korek attacks [13,14], as well as the Physkin, Tews and Weinmann (PTW) attack [31]. In fact, it currently has the implementation of state of the art attacks on WEP and WPA. We applied a patch on Aircrack-ng 1.1 in our implementation.

4   State of the Art Attacks on WEP

WEP key recovery process is harder in practice than in theory. Indeed, some bytes of the keystream are unknown, depending on which type of packets are captured. Moreover, theoretical success probability has often been miscalculated and conditions to recover the secret key are not the same depending on the paper. For example, [2,25,31,34] check 2×10^6 most probable keys instead of the first one as in [7,11,13,14,27,28]. Additionally, IEEE 802.11 standard does not specify how the IV's should be chosen. Thus, some attacks consider randomly picked IV's or incremental IV's (both little-endian and big-endian encoded). Some implementations specifically avoid some classes of IV's which are weak with respect to some attacks.

To unify the results, we consider recovering a random 104-bit long secret key with random IV's. This corresponds to the default IV behaviour of the 802.11 GNU/Linux stack. We compare the previous and the new results using both theoretical and practical analysis:

– In [7], Fluhrer, Mantin and Shamir's (FMS) attack is only theoretically described. The authors postulate that 4 million packets would be sufficient to recover the secret key of WEP with success probability of 50 % with incremental IV's. A practical implementation of this attack has been realised by Stubblefield, Ioannidis and Rubin [27,28]. They showed that indeed between 5 million to 6 million packets are required to recover the secret key using the FMS attack. Note that in 2001, almost all wireless cards were using incremental IV's in big-endian.

– There is no theoretical analysis of the Korek [13,14] key recovery attacks. Only practical implementations such as Aircrack-ng [5] are available. Additionally, Aircrack-ng classifies the most probable secret keys and does a brute-force attack on this list. The success probability of 50 % is obtained when about 100 000 packets are captured with random IV's. Note that the amount of the brute-forced keys depends on the values of the secret key and the *"Fudge"* factor [5] (the highest vote counter is divided by the Fudge factor and all values with votes higher than this value is brute-forced), a parameter chosen by the attacker (often 1, 2 or 3). By default, around one thousand to one million keys are brute-forced.

– The ChopChop attack was introduced in [12,30], which allows an attacker to interactively decrypt the last m bytes of an encrypted packet by sending $128 \times m$ packets in average to the network. The attack does not reveal the main key and is not based on any special property of the RC4 stream cipher.

– In [11], Klein showed theoretically that his new attack needs about 25 000 packets with random IV's to recover the secret key with probability 50 %. Note that, there is no practical implementation of the Klein attack alone, but both PTW [31] and VV07 [34] attacks (using Klein attack by default), which theoretically improve the key recovery process, need more than 25 000 packets. So, the theoretical success probability of the Klein attack was over estimated. We implemented this attack and we obtained the success probability of 50 % with about 60 000 packets (random IV's).

– Physkin, Tews and Weinmann (PTW) showed in [31] that the secret key can be recovered with only 40 000 packets for the same success probability (random IV's). However, this attack brute-forces the 2×10^6 most probable secret keys. Thus, the comparison with previous attacks is less obvious. Moreover, there is no theoretical analysis of this attack, only practical results are provided by the authors. We confirmed this practical result.

– Vaudenay and Vuagnoux [34] showed an improved attack, where the same success probability can be reached with an average of 32 700 packets with random IV's. This attack also tests the 2×10^6 most probable secret keys. Moreover, only practical results are provided by the authors. We confirmed this practical result.

– According to [2], Beck and Tews re-implemented the [34] attack in 2009, obtaining the same success probability with only 24 200 packets using Aircrack-ng in "interactive mode", i.e., the success probability is fixed in this approach and the goal is to derive the least average number of packets for a successful attack. Obviously, this approach requires less packets than the case where we fix the number of packets and compute the success rate. We focus on the latter approach, since this is done often in the literature as a measure of comparison. Since Beck and Tews's attack was implemented on Aircrack-ng, we ran it in non-interactive mode. We observed that 24 200 packets brings about only less that 8 % success rate in non-interactive mode. In fact, it needs more than 36 000 packets to yield the success probability of 50 %. Therefore, it seems this attack does not yield any more success rate than the [34] attack.

– Sepehrdad, Vaudenay and Vuagnoux [25], showed that only 9 800 packets is enough to break WEP with success probability of 50 %, while they used a *class of weak* IV's for their attack. We show in the following that reaching 9 800 packets to break WEP with *random* IV's is extremely ambitious by the currently available biases for RC4.

– In Eurocrypt 2011 [26], we presented an attack on WEP by optimising all the previous known attacks in the literature and by introducing a few new correlations. As a result, we claimed *theoretically* that using 4 000 packets, our analysis provides a success probability of 50 % to break WEP. We did not implement the attack at that time. Only theoretical results were presented. In this paper, we show that some parts of that evaluation is not precise enough and need modification. In fact, we show that our theory needs more than 4 000 packets, due to the imprecise approximation of the variance of the rank of the correct key and an improper estimation of the probability distribution of this random variable.

– In this paper, in an optimised attack, we drop the number of packets to 22 500 for the same success probability by modifying the [26] attack and patching Aircrack-ng in non-interactive mode. It requires only 19 800 packets using Aircrack-ng in interactive mode. In our approach, the 2×10^6 most probable secret keys are brute-forced and we use random IV's.

We are going to construct a precise theory behind the WEP attack in the subsequent sections. All our analysis has been checked precisely through extensive amount of experiments. We show that we can recover a 104-bit long WEP key using 22 500 packets in less than 5 s using an off-the-shelf PC. With less number of packets, the attack will run for a longer period.

5   Some Useful Lemmas

Lemma 1. *Let A, B and C be random variables in $\mathbf{Z}_N$ such that*

$$A \stackrel{p_1}{=} B \qquad B \stackrel{p_2}{=} C$$

then we assume that $A - B$ and $B - C$ are independent. We have $A \stackrel{P}{=} C$, where

$$P = \frac{1}{N} + \left(\frac{N}{N-1}\right)\left(p_1 - \frac{1}{N}\right)\left(p_2 - \frac{1}{N}\right) \stackrel{\text{def}}{=} p_1 \otimes p_2$$

Proof. See Chap. 3 of [24] for the proof.   □

Corollary 1. *Let A, B, C, D and E be random variables in $\mathbf{Z}_N$ such that*

$$A \overset{p_1}{=} B \qquad B \overset{p_2}{=} C \qquad C \overset{p_3}{=} D \qquad D \overset{p_4}{=} E$$

then we assume that $A - B$, $B - C$, $C - D$ and $D - E$ are independent. We have $A \overset{P}{=} E$, where

$$P = p_1 \otimes p_2 \otimes p_3 \otimes p_4 = \frac{1}{N} + \left(\frac{N}{N-1}\right)^3 \cdot \prod_{i=1}^{4}\left(p_i - \frac{1}{N}\right)$$

For $p_4 = 1$, we obtain

$$P = p_1 \otimes p_2 \otimes p_3 = \frac{1}{N} + \left(\frac{N}{N-1}\right)^2 \cdot \prod_{i=1}^{3}\left(p_i - \frac{1}{N}\right)$$

Proof. The $\otimes$ operation is commutative and associative over $[0, 1]$ and 1 is the neutral element. The above statements should be trivial using these properties. $\square$

We can extend the above Corollary by adding new conditions.

Lemma 2. *Let A, B, C, D and E be random variables in $\mathbf{Z}_N$ and* Cond *and* Cond′ *be two events such that*

$$A \overset{p_1}{=} B \qquad B \overset{p_2}{=} C \qquad C \underset{\mathsf{Cond'}}{\overset{p_3}{=}} S[D] \qquad D \overset{p_4}{=} E$$

We assume that $A - B$, $B - C$, $C - S[D]$, $D - E$ and Cond′ *are independent; Furthermore, we assume*

$$(A = S[D] \wedge \mathsf{Cond}) \Leftrightarrow (A = S[D] \wedge \mathsf{Cond'}) \qquad and \quad \Pr[\mathsf{Cond}] = \Pr[\mathsf{Cond'}]$$

Assuming that

$$\Pr[A = S[E] | A \neq S[D], D \neq E, \mathsf{Cond}] = \frac{1}{N-1}$$

we have

$$\Pr[A = S[E] | \mathsf{Cond}] = p_1 \otimes p_2 \otimes p_3 \otimes p_4$$

Proof. See Chap. 3 of [24] for the proof. $\square$

Lemma 3. *To avoid the key byte dependency, the following equation can be extracted to have a better key recovery attack.*

$$\bar{K}[i] = j_i - \sum_{x=1}^{i} S_{x-1}[x]$$

Proof. We prove it by induction on i by using

$$j_i = j_{i-1} + S_{i-1}[i] + K[i]$$

□

Lemma 4. *For $0 \le t < i$, the following five relations hold on $RC4^*(t)$ for any set $(m_1, \ldots, m_b)$ of pairwise different m_j's such that $m_j \le t$ or $m_j > i - 1$.*

$$P_A^b(i,t) \stackrel{\text{def}}{=} \Pr\left[\bigwedge_{j=1}^{b} S_{i-1}[m_j] = \cdots = S_{t+1}[m_j] = S_t[m_j]\right] = \left(\tfrac{N-b}{N}\right)^{i-t-1}$$

$$S_{i-1}[m_j] \stackrel{P_A^1}{=} S_t[m_j]$$

$$\sum_{x=1}^{i} S_{x-1}[x] \stackrel{P_B(i,t)}{=} \sigma_i(t) \quad where$$

$$P_B(i,t) \stackrel{\text{def}}{=} \prod_{k=0}^{i-t-1}\left(\frac{N-k}{N}\right) + \frac{1}{N}\left(1 - \prod_{k=0}^{i-t-1}\left(\frac{N-k}{N}\right)\right)$$

$$P_0 \stackrel{\text{def}}{=} \Pr[S'_{i-1}[i] = \cdots = S'_1[i] = S_{N-1}[i] = \cdots = S_i[i]] = \left(\tfrac{N-1}{N}\right)^{N-2}$$

$$S'_{i-1}[i] \stackrel{P_0}{=} S_i[i]$$

where m_j's are distinct and

$$\sigma_i(t) = \sum_{j=0}^{t} S_{j-1}[j] + \sum_{j=t+1}^{i} S_t[j]$$

Proof. See Chap. 3 of [24] for the proof.   □

6   The List of Biases for RC4

In this section, we only report RC4 correlations which are exploitable against WEP application. All such biases are listed in Table 1 in Appendix, following the notations in Sect. 3.1. This list includes the improved version of the Klein attack in [34] and the improved version of the Maitra-Paul attack in [15]. Furthermore, it includes an improved version of 19 biases by Korek [13,14] and SVV_10, the improved bias of Sepehrdad, Vaudenay and Vuagnoux in [25]. All the probabilities are new. We have proved all the correlations listed in Table 1, but, we have omitted the proofs due to the lack of space[1]. Biases were computed using the formulas represented after Table 1.

As an example, we are going to elaborate and provide a proof for the Klein-Improved attack, since it is fundamental in our WEP attack. The proof of all the other correlations are similar. The interested reader can also look at [4, 24, 26] for more details.

---

[1] See [23] for the proof of SVV_10 bias and for all the others, see Chap. 6 of [24].

6.1   The Klein-Improved Attack

Andreas Klein combined the Jenkins correlation for the PRGA and weaknesses of the KSA and derived a correlation between the key bytes and the keystream. This bias was further improved in [34] by recovering $\bar{K}[i]$'s instead of $K[i]$ to reduce the secret key bytes dependency.

Theorem 1 (Jenkins correlation [10], Sec. 2.3 in [16]). *Assume that the initial permutation $S_0' = S_{N-1}$ is randomly chosen from the set of all the possible permutations over $\{0, \ldots, N-1\}$. Then,*

$$\Pr[S_i'[j_i'] = i - z_i] \approx \tfrac{2}{N} \qquad \Pr[S_i'[i] = j_i' - z_i] \approx \tfrac{2}{N}$$

Proof

$$\begin{aligned}
\Pr[S_i'[j_i'] = i - z_i] &= \Pr[S_i'[j_i'] = i - z_i | S_i'[i] + S_i'[j_i'] = i] \cdot \Pr[S_i'[i] + S_i'[j_i'] = i] \\
&\quad + \Pr[S_i'[j_i'] = i - z_i | S_i'[i] + S_i'[j_i'] \neq i] \cdot \Pr[S_i'[i] + S_i'[j_i'] \neq i] \\
&= \tfrac{1}{N} + \tfrac{1}{N}\left(1 - \tfrac{1}{N}\right) \approx \tfrac{2}{N}
\end{aligned}$$

By symmetry, the other equation can be proved similarly.   □

We use the theorem by Jenkins and explain how it can be merged with the weaknesses of the KSA (see Algorithm 1). In fact, the attacker checks the conditions. If they all hold, she votes for $\bar{K}[i]$ using the key recovery relation. We are only using the assumptions in Algorithm 1 to compute the Klein-Improved attack success probability. More clearly, we do not assume these relations always hold. They are all probabilistic.

Algorithm 1. The Klein-Improved Attack

Success Probability: $P_{KI}(i, t)$
Assumptions: (see Fig. 3)
  1: $S_t[j_i] = \cdots = S_{i-1}[j_i] = S_i[i] = S_{i-1}'[i] = S_i'[j_i'] = i - z_i$
Conditions: $(i - z_i) \notin \{S_t[t+1], \ldots, S_t[i-1]\}$ (Cond)
Key recovery relation: $\bar{K}[i] = S_t^{-1}[i - z_i] - \sigma_i(t)$

Exploiting the Jenkins correlation and the relations in the KSA and the PRGA, we obtain

1. $S_i'[j_i'] \overset{P_J}{=} i - z_i$ (Lemma 1)
2. $S_i'[j_i'] = S_{i-1}'[i]$
3. $S_{i-1}'[i] \overset{P_0}{=} S_i[i]$ (Lemma 4)
4. $S_i[i] = S_{i-1}[j_i]$
5. $S_{i-1}[j_i] \overset{P_1}{\underset{Cond'}{=}} S_t[j_i]$ (where Cond' is the event that $j_i \leq t$ or $j_i > i - 1$.)
6. $j_i = \bar{K}[i] + \displaystyle\sum_{x=1}^{i} S_{x-1}[x]$ (Lemma 3)

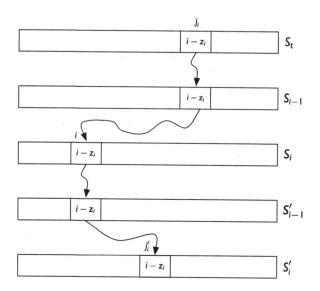

Fig. 3. The RC4 state update in the Klein-Improved attack

7. $\displaystyle\sum_{x=1}^{i} S_{x-1}[x] \stackrel{P_B}{=} \sigma_i$ (Lemma 4)

We make the same heuristic assumptions of independence as in Lemma 2, then using Lemmas 2 and 4, we derive

$$P_{\mathrm{KI}}(i,t) = P_J \otimes P_0 \otimes P_A^1(i,t) \otimes P_B(i,t)$$

conditioned to Cond (see Algorithm 1). Hence, the key recovery relation becomes

$$\bar{K}[i] \stackrel{P_{\mathrm{KI}}}{\underset{\mathsf{Cond}}{=}} S_t^{-1}[i - z_i] - \sigma_i(t)$$

Next, we are going to describe our modifications on Sepehrdad, Vaudenay and Vuagnoux attack [26] to mount a very fast key recovery attack on WEP.

7   An Optimised Attack on WEP

We define an statistical attack using the following mapping:

$$z^m, \mathsf{IV}^m \xrightarrow{\;\;h_i\;\;} \mu_i \xrightarrow[\text{if } g_{\ell_i}(\mu_i)]{f_{\ell_i}(\mu_i)} x_i$$

Our goal is to recover the values of $\bar{K}[i]$'s for $i = \{3, \ldots, 15\}$. For each key candidate value x_i (corresponding to $\bar{K}[i]$), each packet m, and each $\ell_i = 1, \ldots, d_i$ (corresponding to each bias), if the agglomerated condition $g_{\ell_i}(h_i(z^m, \mathsf{IV}^m))$

holds, we define $x_i = f_{\ell_i}(h_i(z^m, \mathsf{IV}^m))$ as the value of the RC4 key byte suggested by the bias ℓ_i on packet m, which is correct with probability p_{ℓ_i}. We let X_{x_i, m, ℓ_i} be some magic coefficient a_{ℓ_i} (to be optimised later) if $f_{\ell_i}(h_i(z^m, \mathsf{IV}^m)) = x_i$ and 0 otherwise. We let

$$Y_{x_i} = \sum_{m=1}^{n} \sum_{\ell_i=1}^{d_i} X_{x_i, m, \ell_i}$$

where n_i is the total number of packets to be used in attacking $\bar{K}[i]$. Clearly, the correct value for x_i is suggested with probability p_{ℓ_i} and others are obtained randomly. We assume the incorrect ones are suggested with the same probability $\frac{1-p_{\ell_i}}{N_{x_i}-1}$. So, the X_{x_i, m, ℓ_i} for the incorrect x_i's are random variables with the expected values $a_{\ell_i} q_{\ell_i} \frac{1-p_{\ell_i}}{N_{x_i}-1}$ if x_i is not the correct value. For the correct x_i, then X_{x_i, m, ℓ_i} are random variables with the expected value $a_{\ell_i} q_{\ell_i} p_{\ell_i}$. The difference between these two expected values is important. This is also the case for the difference of the variances. As every x_i is suggested with probability roughly $\frac{q_{\ell_i}}{N_{x_i}}$, we assume that the variance of a bad X_{x_i, m, ℓ_i} can be approximated by $\frac{q_{\ell_i}}{N_{x_i}}\left(1 - \frac{q_{\ell_i}}{N_{x_i}}\right) a_{\ell_i}^2$. In [26], it was assumed that the variance of a good and a bad counter Y_{x_i} is the same. Our experiments revealed that they are actually very different. Let Δ be the operator making the difference between the distributions of a good x_i and a bad one. We have

$$E(Y_{x_i \text{ bad}}) = \frac{n_i}{N_{x_i} - 1} \sum_{\ell_i} a_{\ell_i} q_{\ell_i} (1 - p_{\ell_i})$$

$$E(Y_{x_i \text{ good}}) = E(Y_{x_i \text{ bad}}) + \Delta E(Y_i)$$

$$\Delta E(Y_i) = \frac{n_i}{1 - \frac{1}{N_{x_i}}} \sum_{\ell_i} a_{\ell_i} q_{\ell_i} \left(p_{\ell_i} - \frac{1}{N_{x_i}}\right)$$

$$V(Y_{x_i \text{ bad}}) \approx n_i \sum_{\ell_i} a_{\ell_i}^2 \frac{q_{\ell_i}}{N_{x_i}}\left(1 - \frac{q_{\ell_i}}{N_{x_i}}\right)$$

$$V(Y_{x_i \text{ good}}) = V(Y_{x_i \text{ bad}}) + \Delta V(Y_i)$$

$$\Delta V(Y_i) \approx \frac{n_i}{1 - \frac{1}{N_{x_i}}} \sum_{\ell_i} a_{\ell_i}^2 q_{\ell_i} \left(p_{\ell_i} - \frac{1}{N_{x_i}}\right)$$

where $E(Y_{x_i \text{ bad}})$ and $V(Y_{x_i \text{ bad}})$ denote the expected value and the variance of a Y_{x_i} variable for any bad x_i respectively. Here, we removed the subscript x_i of Y_{x_i} in $\Delta E(Y_i)$ as this does not depend on a specific value for x_i. Let λ_i be such that $\Delta E(Y_i) = \lambda_i \sqrt{V(Y_{x_i \text{ bad}}) + V(Y_{x_i \text{ good}})}$. The probability that the correct Y_{x_i} is lower than an arbitrary wrong Y_{x_i} is $\rho_i = \varphi(-\lambda_i)$. That is, the expected number of wrong x_i's with larger Y_{x_i} is

$$r_i = (N_{x_i} - 1)\varphi(-\lambda_i) \tag{2}$$

So,

$$
n_i = \frac{\lambda_i^2 \sum_{\ell_i} a_{\ell_i}^2 \left[2 \left(\frac{q_{\ell_i}}{N_{x_i}} \right) \left(1 - \frac{q_{\ell_i}}{N_{x_i}} \right) \left(1 - \frac{1}{N_{x_i}} \right)^2 + q_{\ell_i} \left(p_{\ell_i} - \frac{1}{N_{x_i}} \right) \left(1 - \frac{1}{N_{x_i}} \right) \right]}{\left(\sum_{\ell_i} a_{\ell_i} q_{\ell_i} \left(p_{\ell_i} - \frac{1}{N_{x_i}} \right) \right)^2}
$$

By derivating both terms of the fraction with respect to a_{ℓ_i} and equaling them, we obtain that the optimal value is reached for

$$
a_{\ell_i} = a_{\mathsf{opt}_i} \overset{\text{def}}{=} \frac{\left(p_{\ell_i} - \frac{1}{N_{x_i}} \right)}{\left(p_{\ell_i} - \frac{1}{N_{x_i}} \right) + \frac{2}{N_{x_i}} \left(1 - \frac{1}{N_{x_i}} \right) \left(1 - \frac{q_{\ell_i}}{N_{x_i}} \right)}
$$

The above a_{opt_i} is very different from the one derived in [26]. In fact, a_{opt_i} is the most crucial value to be optimised in the WEP attack. Using the old value of a_{opt_i} in [26], the success probability would be much lower. Hence, we obtain

$$
n_i = n_{\mathsf{opt}} \overset{\text{def}}{=} \frac{\lambda_i^2 \left(1 - \frac{1}{N_{x_i}} \right)}{\sum_{\ell_i} a_{\ell_i} q_{\ell_i} \left(p_{\ell_i} - \frac{1}{N_{x_i}} \right)} \tag{3}
$$

The attack works as in Algorithm 2, where Step 9 is computed using the below algorithm:

1: Set $I = (3, 4, \ldots, 15)$ and $I_0 = \{0, 1, 2\}$.
2: Initialize the Y_{x_i} counters to 0.
3: **for** $m = 1$ to n_i **do**
4:     **for** $\ell_i = 1$ to d_i **do**
5:         **if** $g_{\ell_i}(h_i(z^m, \mathsf{IV}^m))$ holds **then**
6:             Compute $x_i = f_{\ell_i}(h_i(z^m, \mathsf{IV}^m))$, the suggested value for $\bar{K}[i]$.
7:             Increment Y_{x_i} by a_{ℓ_i}.
8:         **end if**
9:     **end for**
10: **end for**
11: Output $x_i = \arg\max_{x_i} Y_{x_i}$.

This attack produces a ranking of possible x_i's (possible $\bar{K}[i]$) in the form of a list $\mathcal{L}_i$ by decreasing order of likelihood. The complexity of voting for each $\bar{K}[i]$ is represented as c_i, where

$$
c_i = n_i d_i \tag{4}
$$

Algorithm 2. An optimised attack against the WEP protocol

1: compute the ranking $\mathcal{L}_{15}$ for $I = (15)$ and $I_0 = \{0, 1, 2\}$
2: truncate $\mathcal{L}_{15}$ to its first ρ_{15} terms
3: **for each** $\bar{k}_{15}$ in $\mathcal{L}_{15}$ **do**
4:   run recursive attack on input $\bar{k}_{15}$
5: **end for**
6: stop: attack failed
recursive attack with input $(\bar{k}_{15}, \bar{k}_3, \ldots, \bar{k}_{i-1})$**:**
7: If input is only $\bar{k}_{15}$, set $i = 3$.
8: **if** $i \leq i_{\max}$ **then**
9:   compute the ranking $\mathcal{L}_i$ for $I = (i)$ and $I_0 = \{0, \ldots, i - 1, 15\}$
10:   truncate $\mathcal{L}_i$ to its first ρ_i terms
11:   **for each** $\bar{k}_i$ in $\mathcal{L}_i$ **do**
12:     run recursive attack on input $(\bar{k}_{15}, \bar{k}_3, \ldots, \bar{k}_{i-1}, \bar{k}_i)$
13:   **end for**
14: **else**
15:   **for each** $\bar{k}_{i_{\max}+1}, \ldots, \bar{k}_{14}$ **do**
16:     test key $(\bar{k}_3, \ldots, \bar{k}_{14}, \bar{k}_{15})$ and stop if correct
17:   **end for**
18: **end if**

Let $N_{x_i} = N$ for all i and r_i, c_i be their parameters following Eqs. (2), (4). Let R_i be the rank of the correct $\bar{k}_i$ value in $\mathcal{L}_i$. Let's define a random variable $U_{ij} = 1_{(Y_{x_i \text{ good}} < Y_{x_i \text{ bad}_j})}$, where $Y_{x_i \text{ bad}_j}$ is the j-th bad counter in attacking $\bar{K}[i]$. Hence, we have

$$R_i = \sum_{j=1}^{N_{x_i} - 1} U_{ij}$$

The expected value and the variance of this random variable can be computed as follows:

$$r_i = E(R_i) = (N_{x_i} - 1)\varphi(-\lambda_i)$$
$$\text{and} \tag{5}$$
$$E(R_i^2) = E(R_i) + (N_{x_i} - 1)(N_{x_i} - 2) \cdot E(U_{i1}.U_{i2})$$

where

$$E(U_{i1}.U_{i2}) = \frac{1}{\sqrt{2\pi V(Y_{x_i \text{ good}})}} \int_{-\infty}^{\infty} e^{-\frac{\left(Y - E(Y_{x_i \text{ good}})\right)^2}{2V(Y_{x_i \text{ good}})}} \left(1 - \varphi\left(\frac{Y - E(Y_{x_i \text{ bad}})}{\sqrt{V(Y_{x_i \text{ bad}})}}\right)^2\right) dY$$

This finally yields

$$V(R_i) = (N_{x_i} - 1)\varphi(-\lambda_i) + (N_{x_i} - 1)(N_{x_i} - 2) \cdot E(U_{i1}.U_{i2}) - (N_{x_i} - 1)^2 \varphi(-\lambda_i)^2 \tag{6}$$

In [26], U_{i1} and U_{i2} were incorrectly assumed to be independent, leading to

$$V(R_i) \approx (N_{x_i} - 1)\varphi(-\lambda_i)(1 - \varphi(\lambda_i)) \approx r_i$$

which did not match our experiment. Now, the fundamental question is what would be the distribution of R_i. This is discussed in the next section.

7.1   Analysis Based on Pólya Distribution

In [26], it was assumed that the distribution of R_i is normal. Running a few experiments, we noticed that in fact it is not normal and it is following a distribution very close to the Poisson distribution. A crucial observation was that the variance of the distribution was much higher than the expected value. A number of distributions have been devised for series in which the variance is significantly larger than the mean [1,6,18], frequently on the basis of more or less complex biological models [3]. The first of these was the negative binomial, which arose in deriving the Poisson series from the point binomial [29,35]. We use a generalised version of negative binomial distribution called the Pólya distribution.

To be more precise, if two events occur with Poisson distribution and their expected values are very low, then it can be assumed that those events are happening independently. On the other hand, for the Poisson events with high expected values (approximated as normal), the occurrence of the former event may increase the probability of the latter. In such cases, the overall distribution would be the Pólya [32,33]. Regarding the current problem, the events $(Y_{x_i \text{ good}} < Y_{x_i \text{ bad}_j})$ and $(Y_{x_i \text{ good}} < Y_{x_i \text{ bad}_{j'}})$ are not independent. Therefore, they tend to follow the Pólya distribution. As $E(R_i)$ and $V(R_i)$ are known from Eqs. (5), (6), the values p_i and r_i for attacking $\bar{K}[i]$ can be simply computed by

$$p_i = \left(1 - \frac{E(R_i)}{V(R_i)}\right) \quad \text{and} \quad r_i = \left(\frac{E(R_i)^2}{V(R_i) - E(R_i)}\right)$$

As a proof of concept, we have sketched the probability distribution of R_3 for 5 000 packets. The corresponding parameters for the Pólya distribution would be $p = 0.9839$ and $r = 0.356$ (see Fig. 4). As can be observed, those two distributions are extremely close. Also,

$$u_i \overset{\text{def}}{=} \Pr[R_i \le \rho_i - 1] = 1 - I_{p_i}(\rho_i, r_i)$$

where I is the regularised incomplete beta function. Overall, the success probability is

$$u = u_{15} \prod_{i=3}^{i_{\max}} u_i$$

and the complexity is

$$c = c_{15} + \rho_{15}\left(c_3 + \rho_3\left(c_4 + \rho_4\left(\cdots c_{i_{\max}} + \rho_{i_{\max}} N^{14-i_{\max}} \cdots\right)\right)\right)$$

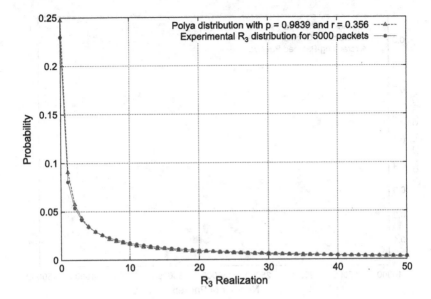

Fig. 4. R_3 distribution using 5 000 packets following the Pólya distribution

To be able to compare our results with the state of the art, we set $u = 50\%$. To approximate the optimal choice of ρ's, let $i_{\max} = 14$. We have to deal with the following optimisation problem:

$$\text{Minimize } c \text{ in terms of } \rho_i\text{'s, limiting } u = \prod_{i=3}^{15}(1 - I_{p_i}(\rho_i, r_i)) = \frac{1}{2}$$

To solve this optimisation problem, we use Lagrange multipliers to find the optimal solution. We used the fmincon function in Matlab with the Sequential Quadratic Programming [19] (SQP) algorithm as the default algorithm to compute the local minimum. As this algorithm needs a starting point x0 for its computations, we used the GlobalSearch class which iterates the fmincon function multiple times using random vectors for x0. Simultaneously, it checks how the results merge towards the global minimum. One can also use Genetic algorithms to find the optimal values.

8   Comparison with Aircrack-ng

Figure 5 represents a comparison between Aircrack-ng and our new attack. The reader can see that our passive attack outperforms Aircrack-ng running in active mode. This gives significant advantage to the attacker, since for some network

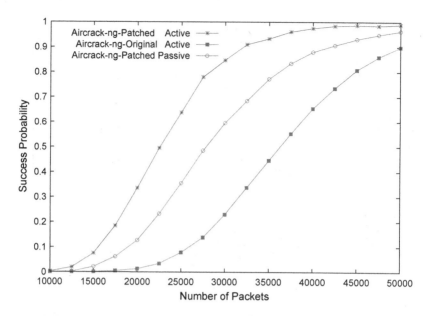

Fig. 5. Our attacks success probability (both active and passive attacks) with respect to the number of packets compared to Aircrack-ng in active attack mode.

cards, the driver has to be patched so that the network card can inject packets, and in some cases such patch is not available at all. Moreover, the active attacks are detectable by intrusion detection systems. Similarly, passive attacks can be performed from much large distance. Moreover, the TCP/IPv4 packets can be captured with much higher rate than ARP packets. As a rule of thumb, in a high traffic network, (for instance the user is downloading a movie), if we consider TCP/IPv4 packets with maximum size around 1500 bytes, in a 20 Mbit/sec wireless network, it takes almost 10 s to capture 22 500 packets. This amount is already enough to find a key with our improved Aircrack-ng in less than 5 s.

9   Challenges and Open Problems

WEP key recovery process is harder in practice than in theory. This is because the biases in RC4 are not independent, and several bytes of the keystream are unknown in ARP and TCP/IP packets. Therefore, the theoretical analysis is more complex if the dependencies are considered. Also, some bytes of the keystream have to be guessed, and the proportion of TCP/IP packets to ARP packets is distinct for every network and attack (passive vs. active). The a priori probability of guessing those bytes correctly can not be precisely determined, and we had to leverage some heuristics to deal with this problem; Since this proportion also depends on the traffic itself, finding the ρ which is optimised for every network is not feasible. We leveraged some heuristics to set the ρ to obtain a high success rate in practice. Moreover, the Aircrack-ng is not an interactive software. The interaction with the user may allow to tweak the ρ and/or wait for more packets to capture. This trade-off should also be considered in real life applications.

The Algorithm 2 is recursive. This recursion is very expensive in practice, since with a wrong guess on a key byte, all the subsequent key bytes with higher indices are recovered incorrectly (in theory), so we need to recompute the vote for each of them again. In practice, we observed that a wrong guess of a key byte *does not* influence the next key bytes recovery significantly. For instance, even with a wrong guess on $\bar{K}[3]$, in many cases, we could still recover all the subsequent bytes correctly. This is because a wrong guess for $\bar{K}[3]$ mandates only 16 wrong swaps out of 256 iterations of the KSA. A further improvement to our work can be to adjust our theory to consider such cases. Hence, in our implementation, we perform a recursive attack to only find the best key candidate, and if it turns out to be a wrong key, we then use the pre-computed voted list to perform an exhaustive search, with no re-voting.

Conclusion

In this paper, we gave a precise theoretical background to improve the state of the art attacks on WEP. As an empirical proof, we updated Aircrack-ng and showed that our attack significantly outperforms the previous versions in all scenarios. We modified the algorithm according to the theoretical results, removed the ad-hoc constants which were initially found empirically in previous papers and implementations. We gave a theoretical background for all constants which affect the performance of the new Aircrack-ng. This result shows the significance of theoretical analysis in practical scenarios, and allows the attacker to break WEP even on constrained devices. As a result, the best attack to date requires 22 500 packets for the success probability of 50 % to break WEP.

Note. The imprecision of distributions and variances also affect our analysis reported for WPA in [26]. But, we recomputed all numerical values with the precise theoretical formulas and observed only a negligible overheard compared to the derived complexity in [26].

Acknowledgment. We would like to sincerely thank Dr. Erik Tews for giving very helpful comments on Aicrack-ng implementation.

A   IEEE 802.11 Data Frames Encapsulating ARP and TCP/IPv4 Protocols

ARP Packet

0xAA	DSAP
0xAA	SSAP
0x03	CTRL
0x00	
0x00	ORG Code
0x00	
0x08	ARP
0x06	
0x00	Ethernet
0x01	
0x08	IP
0x00	
0x06	Hardware size
0x04	Protocol
0x00	Opcode Request/Reply
0x??	
0x??	MAC addr src
0x??	
0x??	
0x??	
0x??	
0x??	
0x??	IP src
0x??	
0x??	
0x??	
0x??	MAC addr dst
0x??	
0x??	
0x??	
0x??	
0x??	

TCP/IPv4 Packet

0xAA	DSAP
0xAA	SSAP
0x03	CTRL
0x00	
0x00	ORG Code
0x00	
0x08	IP
0x00	
0x45	IP Version + Header length
0x00	Type of Service
0x??	Packet length
0x??	
0x??	IP ID RFC815
0x??	
0x40	Fragment type and offset
0x??	
0x??	TTL
0x06	TCP type
0x??	Header checksum
0x??	
0x??	IP src
0x??	
0x??	
0x??	
0x??	IP dst
0x??	
0x??	
0x??	
0x??	Port src
0x??	
0x??	Port dst
0x??	

Fig. 6. The plaintext bytes of the 802.11 data frames encapsulating ARP and TCP/IPv4 protocols [31,34]. The values in white are almost fixed or can be computed dynamically. The values in light Grey can be guessed. The values in dark Grey are not predictable. Often one of Port src or Port dest can be guessed, but not both.

B Computation of Biases

Table 1. The biases for RC4, exploitable against WEP and WPA

row	reference	$\bar{f}$	$\bar{g}$	p
i	Klein − Improved	$S_t^{-1}[-z_i+i]-\sigma_i(t)$	$(i-z_i)\notin\{S_t[t+1],\ldots,S_t[i-1]\}$	$P_{KI}(i,t)$
$i\neq 1$	MP − Improved	$z_{i+1}-\sigma_i(t)$	$i\neq 1, z_{i+1}\geq i, \forall 0\leq i'\leq t: j_{i'}\neq z_{i+1}$	$P_{MPI}(i,t)$
i	A_u15	$2-\sigma_i(t)$	$S_t[i]=0, z_2=0$	$P^1_{fixed-j}$
i	A_s13	$S_t^{-1}[0]-\sigma_i(t)$	$S_t[1]=i, (S_t^{-1}[0]<t+1$ or $S_t^{-1}[0]>i-1), z_1=i$	Kor^2_1
i	A_u13_1	$S_t^{-1}[z_1]-\sigma_i(t)$	$S_t[1]=i, (S_t^{-1}[z_1]<t+1$ or $S_t^{-1}[z_1]>i-1), z_1=1-i$	Kor^2_1
i	A_u13_2	$1-\sigma_i(t)$	$S_t[i]=i, S_t[1]=0, z_1=i$	$P^3_{fixed-j}$
i	A_u13_3	$1-\sigma_i(t)$	$S_t[i]=i, S_t[1]=1-i, z_1=1-i$	$P^3_{fixed-j}$
i	A_s5_1	$S_t^{-1}[z_1]-\sigma_i(t)$	$S_t[1]<t+1, S_t[1]+S_t[S_t[1]]=i, z_1\neq\{S_t[1],S_t[S_t[1]]\}, (S_t^{-1}[z_1]<t+1$ or $S_t^{-1}[z_1]>i-1)$	Kor^3_2
i	A_s5_2	$S_t^{-1}[S_t[1]-S_t[2]]-\sigma_i(t)$	$S_t[2]+S_t[1]=i, S_t^{-1}[S_t[1]-S_t[2]]\neq\{1,2\}, (S_t^{-1}[S_t[1]-S_t[2]]<t+1$ or $S_t^{-1}[S_t[1]-S_t[2]]>i-1), z_2=S_t[1]$	Kor^3_2
i	A_s5_3	$S_t^{-1}[z_2]-\sigma_i(t)$	$S_t[2]+S_t[1]=i, S_t^{-1}[z_2]\neq\{1,2\}, (S_t^{-1}[z_2]<t+1$ or $S_t^{-1}[z_2]>i-1), z_2=2-S_t[2]$	Kor^3_2
i	A_u5_1	$S_t^{-1}[S_t^{-1}[z_1]-i]-\sigma_i(t)$	$S_t[1]=i, S_t^{-1}[z_1]<t+1, S_t^{-1}[S_t^{-1}[z_1]-i]\neq 1, (S_t^{-1}[S_t^{-1}[z_1]-i]<t+1$ or $S_t^{-1}[S_t^{-1}[z_1]-i]>i-1), z_1\neq\{i,1-i,S_t^{-1}[z_1]-i\}, S_t^{-1}[z_1]\neq 2i$	Kor^3_2
i	A_u5_2	$1-\sigma_i(t)$	$S_t[i]=1, z_1=S_t[2]$	$P^2_{fixed-j}$
i	A_u5_3	$1-\sigma_i(t)$	$S_t[i]=i, S_t^{-1}[z_1]\neq 1, S_t^{-1}[z_1]<t+1, z_1=S_t[S_t[1]+i]$	$P^5_{fixed-j}$
i	A_s3	$S_t^{-1}[z_2]-\sigma_i(t)$	$S_t[1]\neq 2, S_t[2]\neq 0, S_t[2]+S_t[1]<t+1, S_t[2]+S_t[S_t[2]+S_t[1]]=i, S_t^{-1}[z_2]\neq\{1,2,S_t[1]+S_t[2]\}, S_t[1]+S_t[2]\neq\{1,2\}, (S_t^{-1}[z_2]<t+1$ or $S_t^{-1}[z_2]>i-1)$	Kor^4_3
4	A_4_s13	$S_t^{-1}[0]-\sigma_4(t)$	$S_t[1]=2, S_t[4]\neq 0, (S_t^{-1}[0]<t+1$ or $S_t^{-1}[0]>i-1), z_2=0$	$P^4_{fixed-j}$
4	A_4_u5_1	$S_t^{-1}[N-2]-\sigma_4(t)$	$S_t[1]=2, z_2\neq 0, z_2=S_t[0], z_2\neq N-2, (S_t^{-1}[N-2]<t+1$ or $S_t^{-1}[N-2]>3)$	Kor^3_2
4	A_4_u5_2	$S_t^{-1}[N-1]-\sigma_4(t)$	$S_t[1]=2, z_2\neq 0, (S_t^{-1}[N-1]<t+1$ or $S_t^{-1}[N-1]>3), z_2=S_t[2]$	Kor^3_2
i	A_neg_1	$1-\sigma_i(t)$ or $2-\sigma_i(t)$	$S_t[2]=0, S_t[1]=2, z_1=2$	$P_{neg}(i,t)$
i	A_neg_2	$2-\sigma_i(t)$	$S_t[2]=0, S_t[1]\neq 2, z_2=0$	$P_{neg}(i,t)$
i	A_neg_3	$1-\sigma_i(t)$ or $2-\sigma_i(t)$	$S_t[1]=1, z_1=S_t[2]$	$P_{neg}(i,t)$
i	A_neg_4	$-\sigma_i(t)$ or $1-\sigma_i(t)$	$S_t[1]=0, S_t[0]=1, z_1=1$	$P_{neg}(i,t)$
16	SVV_10	$S_t^{-1}[0]-\sigma_{16}(t)$	$S_t^{-1}[0]<t+1$ or $S_t^{-1}[0]>15, z_{16}=-16, j_2\notin\{t+1,\ldots,15\}$	$P_{SVV10}(t)$

$$P_{\mathrm{KI}}(i,t) = P_J \otimes P_0 \otimes P_A^1(i,t) \otimes P_B(i,t)$$
$$P_{\mathrm{MPI}}(i,t) = P_D(i) \otimes P_B(i,t)$$
$$\mathsf{Kor}_c^b(i,t) = R_c^b(i,t) \otimes P_B(i,t)$$
$$P_{\mathrm{neg}}(i,t) = \left(\tfrac{1-P_B(i,t)}{N-1} \right)$$
$$P_{\mathsf{SVV}10}(t) = P_{db2} \otimes P_A^1(16,t) \otimes P_B(16,t)$$

$$P_{\mathrm{fixed}-j}^1 = C(i,t) \cdot \left[\tfrac{1}{2} P_A^1(i,t) \left(\tfrac{N-1}{N} \right)^{N-i} + \tfrac{1}{N} \left(1 - P_A^1(i,t) \left(\tfrac{N-1}{N} \right)^{N-i} \right) \right]$$
$$+ P_{\mathrm{neg}}(i,t)$$

$$P_{\mathrm{fixed}-j}^2 = \left[\tfrac{1}{\xi} P_A^2(i,t) \left(\tfrac{N}{N-1} \right)^{t-2} \left(\tfrac{N-2}{N} \right)^{N-1-i} + \left(1 - P_A^2(i,t) \left(\tfrac{N-2}{N} \right)^{N-i-1} \right) \right] \cdot$$
$$\left(\tfrac{1}{N} \right) C(i,t) + P_{\mathrm{neg}}(i,t)$$

$$P_{\mathrm{fixed}-j}^3 = \left[\left(\tfrac{N-1}{N} \right)^{t+1} \left(\tfrac{N-2}{N} \right)^{N-1-i} \cdot P_A^2(i,t) + \tfrac{1}{N} \left(1 - P_A^2(i,t) \left(\tfrac{N-2}{N} \right)^{N-i-1} \right) \right] \cdot$$
$$C(i,t) + P_{\mathrm{neg}}(i,t)$$

$$P_{\mathrm{fixed}-j}^4 = \left[\tfrac{1}{2} \left(\tfrac{N-1}{N} \right)^{t+1} \left(\tfrac{N-2}{N} \right)^{N-1-i} \cdot P_A^2(i,t) + \tfrac{1}{N} \left(1 - P_A^2(i,t) \left(\tfrac{N-2}{N} \right)^{N-i-1} \right) \right] \cdot$$
$$C(i,t) + P_{\mathrm{neg}}(i,t)$$

$$P_{\mathrm{fixed}-j}^5 = \left[\tfrac{ \left(\tfrac{N-1}{N} \right)^{t+1} \left(\tfrac{t}{N} \right) \left(\tfrac{N-3}{N} \right)^{N-1-i} }{ \left(1 - \tfrac{1}{N} \right) \left(\tfrac{N-1}{N} \right)^{t+1} \left(\tfrac{t}{N} \right) + \tfrac{1}{N} } \cdot P_A^3(i,t) + \tfrac{1}{N} \left(1 - P_A^3(i,t) \left(\tfrac{N-3}{N} \right)^{N-i-1} \right) \right] \cdot$$
$$C(i,t) + P_{\mathrm{neg}}(i,t)$$

where $P_J = \tfrac{2}{N}$, $P_0 = \left(\tfrac{N-1}{N} \right)^{N-2}$, $P_{db2} = \tfrac{9.444}{N}$,

$\xi = \tfrac{1}{N} \left[\left(\tfrac{N-1}{N} \right)^N \left(1 - \tfrac{1}{N} + \tfrac{1}{N^2} \right) + \tfrac{1}{N^2} + 1 \right]$.

$$C(i,t) = \left(\tfrac{N P_B(i,t) - 1}{N-1} \right)$$
$$P_A^b(i,t) = \left(\tfrac{N-b}{N} \right)^{i-t-1}$$
$$P_B(i,t) = \prod_{k=0}^{i-t-1} \left(\tfrac{N-k}{N} \right) + \tfrac{1}{N} \left(1 - \prod_{k=0}^{i-t-1} \left(\tfrac{N-k}{N} \right) \right)$$
$$P_D(i) = \tfrac{(N-i-1)(N-i)}{N^3} \left(\tfrac{N-2}{N} \right)^{N-3+i} \left(\tfrac{N-1}{N} \right)^3$$
$$R_c^b(i,t) = r_c(i) P_A^b(i,t) + \tfrac{1}{N} (1 - r_c(i) P_A^b(i,t))$$
$$r_1(i) = \left(\tfrac{N-2}{N} \right)^{N-i-1}$$
$$r_2(i) = \left(\tfrac{N-3}{N} \right)^{N-i-1}$$
$$r_3(i) = \left(\tfrac{N-4}{N} \right)^{N-i-1}$$

References

1. Anscombe, F.J.: Sampling theory of the negative binomial and logarithmic series distributions. Biometrika **37**(3–4), 358–382 (1950)
2. Beck, M., Tews, E.: Practical attacks against WEP and WPA. In: WISEC, pp. 79–86. ACM (2009)
3. Bliss, C.I., Fisher, R.A.: Fitting the negative binomial distribution to biological data. Biometrika **9**, 176–200 (1953)
4. Chaabouni, R.: Break WEP Faster with Statistical Analysis. Semester Project. EPFL, Switzerland (2006)
5. Devine, C., Otreppe, T.: Aircrack-ng. http://www.aircrack-ng.org/. Accessed 22 October 2011
6. Feller, W.: On a general class of "contagious" distributions. Ann. Math. Stat. **14**, 389–400 (1943)
7. Fluhrer, S.R., Mantin, I., Shamir, A.: Weaknesses in the key scheduling algorithm of RC4. In: Vaudenay, S., Youssef, A.M. (eds.) SAC 2001. LNCS, vol. 2259, pp. 1–24. Springer, Heidelberg (2001)
8. IEEE. IEEE Std 802.11, Standards for Local and Metropolitan Area Networks: Wireless Lan Medium Access Control (MAC) and Physical Layer (PHY) Specifications (1999)
9. IEEE. ANSI/IEEE standard 802.11i, Amendment 6 Wireless LAN Medium Access Control (MAC) and Physical Layer (phy) Specifications, Draft 3 (2003)
10. Jenkins, R.: ISAAC and RC4 (1996). http://burtleburtle.net/bob/rand/isaac.html
11. Klein, A.: Attacks on the RC4 Stream Cipher. Des. Codes Crypt. **48**, 269–286 (2008)
12. Korek. chopchop (experimental WEP attacks) (2004). http://www.netstumbler.org/showthread.php?t=12489
13. Korek. Need Security Pointers (2004). http://www.netstumbler.org/showthread.php?postid=89036#post89036
14. Korek. Next Generation of WEP Attacks? (2004). http://www.netstumbler.org/showpost.php?p=93942&postcount=35
15. Maitra, S., Paul, G.: New form of permutation bias and secret key leakage in keystream bytes of RC4. In: Nyberg, K. (ed.) FSE 2008. LNCS, vol. 5086, pp. 253–269. Springer, Heidelberg (2008)
16. Mantin, I.: Analysis of the stream cipher RC4. Master's thesis, Weizmann Institute of Science (2001)
17. Maximov, A.: Two linear distinguishing attacks on VMPC and RC4A and weakness of RC4 family of stream ciphers. In: Gilbert, H., Handschuh, H. (eds.) FSE 2005. LNCS, vol. 3557, pp. 342–358. Springer, Heidelberg (2005)
18. Neyman, J.: On a new class of "contagious" distributions, applicable in entomology and bacteriology. Ann. Math. Stat. **10**, 35–57 (1939)
19. Nocedal, J., Wright, S.J.: Numerical Optimization. Springer Series in Operations Research, 2nd edn. Springer, New York (2006)
20. Paul, G., Maitra, S.: Permutation after RC4 key scheduling reveals the secret key. In: Adams, C., Miri, A., Wiener, M. (eds.) SAC 2007. LNCS, vol. 4876, pp. 360–377. Springer, Heidelberg (2007)
21. Postel, J., Reynolds, J.: A standard for the transmission of IP datagrams over IEEE 802 networks (1988). http://www.cs.berkeley.edu/~daw/my-posts/my-rc4-weak-keys

22. Roos, A.: A Class of Weak Keys in RC4 Stream Cipher (sci.crypt) (1995). http://marcel.wanda.ch/Archive/WeakKeys
23. Gupta, S.S., Maitra, S., Paul, G., Sarkar, S.: (Non)Random sequences from (Non)Random permutations - analysis of RC4 stream cipher. J. Crypt. **27**(1), 67–108 (2012)
24. Sepehrdad, P.: Statistical and Algebraic Cryptanalysis of Lightweight and Ultralightweight Symmetric Primitives. Ph.D. thesis, EPFL, Switzerland (2012)
25. Sepehrdad, P., Vaudenay, S., Vuagnoux, M.: Discovery and exploitation of new biases in RC4. In: Biryukov, A., Gong, G., Stinson, D.R. (eds.) SAC 2010. LNCS, vol. 6544, pp. 74–91. Springer, Heidelberg (2011)
26. Sepehrdad, P., Vaudenay, S., Vuagnoux, M.: Statistical attack on RC4: Distinguishing WPA. In: Paterson, K.G. (ed.) EUROCRYPT 2011. LNCS, vol. 6632, pp. 343–363. Springer, Heidelberg (2011)
27. Stubblefield, A., Ioannidis, J., Rubin, A.D.: Using the Fluhrer, Mantin, and Shamir attack to break WEP. In: Network and Distributed System Security Symposium (NDSS) (2002)
28. Stubblefield, A., Ioannidis, J., Rubin, A.D.: A key recovery attack on the 802.11b wired equivalent privacy protocol (WEP). In: ACM Transactions on Information and System Security (TISSEC), vol. 7(2) (2004)
29. Student. On the error of counting with a haemocytometer. Biometrika 5, 351–360 (1907)
30. Tews, E.: Attacks on the WEP protocol. Cryptology ePrint Archive (2007). http://eprint.iacr.org/2007/471.pdf
31. Tews, E., Weinmann, R.-P., Pyshkin, A.: Breaking 104 bit WEP in less than 60 seconds. In: Kim, S., Yung, M., Lee, H.-W. (eds.) WISA 2007. LNCS, vol. 4867, pp. 188–202. Springer, Heidelberg (2008)
32. Thom, H.C.S.: The frequency of hail occurrence. Theoret. Appl. Climatol. **8**, 185–194 (1957)
33. Thom, H.C.S.: Tornado Probabilities. In: American Meteorological Society, pp. 730–736 (1963)
34. Vaudenay, S., Vuagnoux, M.: Passive–only key recovery attacks on RC4. In: Adams, C., Miri, A., Wiener, M. (eds.) SAC 2007. LNCS, vol. 4876, pp. 344–359. Springer, Heidelberg (2007)
35. Whitaker, L.: On the Poisson law of small numbers. Biometrika **10**, 36–71 (1914)

Full Plaintext Recovery Attack on Broadcast RC4

Takanori Isobe[1] (✉), Toshihiro Ohigashi[2] (✉),
Yuhei Watanabe[1] (✉), and Masakatu Morii[1] (✉)

[1] Kobe University, 1-1 Rokkoudai, Nada-ku, Kobe 657-8501, Japan
Takanori.Isobe@jp.sony.com,
yuheiwatanabe@stu.kobe-u.ac.jp, mmorii@kobe-u.ac.jp
[2] Hiroshima University, 1-4-2 Kagamiyama,
Higashi-Hiroshima, Hiroshima 739-8511, Japan
ohigashi@hiroshima-u.ac.jp

Abstract. This paper investigates the practical security of RC4 in broadcast setting where the same plaintext is encrypted with different user keys. We introduce several new biases in the initial (1st to 257th) bytes of the RC4 keystream, which are substantially stronger than known biases. Combining the new biases with the known ones, a cumulative list of strong biases in the first 257 bytes of the RC4 keystream is constructed. We demonstrate a plaintext recovery attack using our strong bias set of initial bytes by the means of a computer experiment. Almost all of the first 257 bytes of the plaintext can be recovered, with probability more than 0.8, using only 2^{32} ciphertexts encrypted by randomly-chosen keys. We also propose an efficient method to extract later bytes of the plaintext, after the 258th byte. The proposed method exploits our bias set of first 257 bytes in conjunction with the digraph repetition bias proposed by Mantin in EUROCRYPT 2005, and sequentially recovers the later bytes of the plaintext after recovering the first 257 bytes. Once the possible candidates for the first 257 bytes are obtained by our bias set, the later bytes can be recovered from about 2^{34} ciphertexts with probability close to 1.

Keywords: RC4 · Broadcast setting · Plaintext recovery attack · Bias · Experimentally-verified attack · SSL/TLS · Multi-session setting

1 Introduction

RC4, designed by Rivest in 1987, is one of most widely used stream ciphers in the world. It is adopted in many software applications and standard protocols such as SSL/TLS, WEP, Microsoft Lotus and Oracle secure SQL. RC4 consists of a key scheduling algorithm (KSA) and a pseudo-random generation algorithm (PRGA). The KSA converts a user-provided variable-length key (typically, 5–32 bytes) into an initial state S consisting of a permutation of $\{0, 1, 2, \ldots, N - 1\}$, where N is typically 256. The PRGA generates a keystream $Z_1, Z_2, \ldots, Z_r$,

S. Moriai (Ed.): FSE 2013, LNCS 8424, pp. 179–202, 2014.
DOI: 10.1007/978-3-662-43933-3_10, © Springer-Verlag Berlin Heidelberg 2014

... from S, where r is a round number of the PRGA. Z_r is XOR-ed with the r-th plaintext byte P_r to obtain the ciphertext byte C_r. The algorithm of RC4 is shown in Algorithm 1, where $+$ denotes arithmetic addition modulo N, ℓ is the key length, and i and j are used to point to the locations of S, respectively. Then, $S[x]$ denotes the value of S indexed x.

After the disclosure of its algorithm in 1994, RC4 has attracted intensive cryptanalytic efforts over past 20 years. Distinguishing attacks, which attempt to distinguish an RC4 keystream from a random stream, were proposed in [3, 4,8,10,11,14,16]. State recovery attack, which recovers a full state instead of the user-provided key, was shown by Knudsen et al. [7], and it was improved by Maximov and Khovratovich [13]. Other types of attacks are also proposed, e.g., key collision attack [12], keystream predictive attack [10] and key recovery attacks from a state [1,15].

In FSE 2001, Mantin and Shamir presented an attack on RC4 in the broadcast setting where the same plaintext is encrypted with different user keys [11]. The Mantin-Shamir attack can extract the second byte of the plaintext from only $\Omega(N)$ ciphertexts encrypted with randomly-chosen different keys by exploiting a bias of Z_2. Specifically, the event $Z_2 = 0$ occurs with twice the expected probability of a random one. In FSE 2011, Maitra, Paul and Sen Gupta showed that $Z_3, Z_4, \ldots, Z_{255}$ are also biased to 0 [8]. Then the bytes 3 to 255 can also be recovered in the broadcast setting, from $\Omega(N^3)$ ciphertexts.

Although the broadcast attacks were theoretically estimated, we find that three questions are still open in terms of a practical security of broadcast RC4.

1. *Are the biases exploited in the previous attacks the strongest biases for the initial bytes 1 to 255?*
2. *While the previous results [8,11] estimate only lower bounds (Ω), how many ciphertexts encrypted with different keys are actually required for a practical attack on broadcast RC4?*
3. *Is it possible to efficiently recover the later bytes of the plaintext, after byte 256?*

Algorithm 1. RC4 Algorithm

KSA($K[0 \ldots \ell - 1]$):	**PRGA**(K):
for $i = 0$ to $N - 1$ **do**	$i \leftarrow 0$
$\quad S[i] \leftarrow i$	$j \leftarrow 0$
end for	$S \leftarrow KSA(K)$
$j \leftarrow 0$	**loop**
for $i = 0$ to $N - 1$ **do**	$\quad i \leftarrow i + 1$
$\quad j \leftarrow j + S[i] + K[i \bmod \ell]$	$\quad j \leftarrow j + S[i]$
$\quad$Swap $S[i]$ and $S[j]$	$\quad$Swap $S[i]$ and $S[j]$
end for	$\quad$Output $Z \leftarrow S[S[i] + S[j]]$
	end loop

1.1 Our Contribution

In this paper, we provide answers to all the aforesaid questions. To begin with, we introduce a new bias regarding Z_1, which is a conditional bias such that Z_1 is biased to 0 when Z_2 is 0. Using this bias in conjunction with the bias of $Z_2 = 0$ [11], the first byte of a plaintext is extracted from $\Omega(N^2)$ ciphertexts encrypted with different keys. Although the strong bias of the first byte, which is a negative bias towards zero, has already been pointed out in [6,14], it requires $\Omega(N^3)$ ciphertexts to extract the first byte of the plaintext. Thus, the new conditional bias observed by us is very useful, because the number of required ciphertexts to recover the first byte reduces by a factor of $N/2$ compared the straightforward method. Besides, we introduce new strong biases, i.e., $Z_3 = 131$, $Z_r = r$ for $3 \leq r \leq 255$, and extended keylength-dependent biases such that $Z_{x \cdot \ell} = -x \cdot \ell$ for $x = 2, 3, \ldots, 7$ and $\ell = 16$, which are extensions of the keylength-dependent biases in which only the parameter of $x = 1$ is considered [5]. These new biases are substantially stronger than known biases of $Z_r = 0$ in case of certain bytes within $Z_3, Z_4, \ldots, Z_{255}$. After providing theoretical considerations for these biases, we experimentally confirm the validity of the same. Combining the new biases with known biases, we construct a cumulative list of strongest known biases in $Z_1, Z_2, \ldots, Z_{255}$. At the same time, we experimentally show two new biases of Z_{256} and Z_{257}, and add these to our bias set. Note that biases of $Z_2, Z_3, \ldots, Z_{257}$ included in our bias set are *strongest* biases amongst all *single* positive and negative biases of each byte when a 16-byte (128-bit) key is used.

We demonstrate a plaintext recovery attack using our bias set by the computer experiment, and estimate the number of required ciphertexts and success probability when $N = 256$. Almost all first 257 bytes, $P_1, P_2, \ldots, P_{257}$, can be extracted with probability more than 0.8 from 2^{32} ciphertexts encrypted by randomly-chosen keys. Given 2^{34} ciphertexts, all bytes of $P_1, P_2, \ldots, P_{257}$ can be narrowed down to two candidates each with probability one. This is a first practical security evaluation of broadcast RC4 using all known biases of the cipher, and some new ones that we observe.

Finally, an efficient method to extract later bytes of the plaintext, namely bytes after P_{258}, is given. It exploits our bias set of $Z_1, Z_2, \ldots, Z_{257}$ in conjunction with the digraph repetition bias proposed by Mantin [10], and then sequentially recovers bytes of the plaintext. Once the possible candidates for $P_1, P_2, \ldots, P_{257}$ are obtained by our bias set, P_r $(r \geq 258)$ are recovered from about 2^{34} ciphertexts with probability one. Since the digraph repetition bias is a long-term bias, which occurs in any keystream byte, our sequential method is expected to recover any plaintext byte from only ciphertexts produced by different randomly-chosen keys. We show that the first 2^{50} bytes ≈ 1000 T bytes of the plaintext can be recovered from 2^{34} ciphertexts with probability of 0.97170.

Also, the broadcast setting is converted into the multi-session setting of SSL/TLS where the target plaintext block are repeatedly sent in the same position in the plaintexts in multiple sessions.

2   Known Attacks on Broadcast RC4

This section briefly reviews known attacks on RC4 in the broadcast setting where the same plaintext is encrypted with different randomly-chosen keys.

2.1   Mantin-Shamir (MS) Attack

Mantin and Shamir first presented a broadcast RC4 attack exploiting a bias of Z_2 [11].

Theorem 1 [11]. *Assume that the initial permutation S is randomly chosen from the set of all the possible permutations of $\{0, 1, 2, \ldots, N-1\}$. Then the probability that the second output byte of RC4 is 0 is approximately $\frac{2}{N}$.*

This probability is estimated as $\frac{2}{256}$ when $N = 256$. Based on this bias, the broadcast RC4 attack is demonstrated by Theorems 2 and 3.

Theorem 2 [11]. *Let X and Y be two distributions, and suppose that the event e happens in X with probability p and in Y with probability $p \cdot (1 + q)$. Then for small p and q, $O(\frac{1}{p \cdot q^2})$ samples suffice to distinguish X from Y with a constant probability of success.*

In this case, p and q are given as $p = 1/N$ and $q = 1$. The number of samples is about N.

Theorem 3 [11]. *Let P be a plaintext, and let $C^{(1)}, C^{(2)}, \ldots, C^{(k)}$ be the RC4 encryptions of P under k uniformly distributed keys. Then, if $k = \Omega(N)$, the second byte of P can be reliably extracted from $C^{(1)}, C^{(2)}, \ldots, C^{(k)}$.*

According to the relation $C_2^{(i)} = P_2^{(i)} \oplus Z_2^{(i)}$, if $Z_2^{(i)} = 0$ holds, then $C_2^{(i)}$ is same as $P_2^{(i)}$. From Theorem 1, $Z_2 = 0$ occurs with twice the expected probability of a random one. Thus, most frequent byte in amongst $C_2^{(1)}, C_2^{(2)}, \ldots, C_2^{(k)}$ is likely to be P_2 itself. When $N = 256$, it requires more than 2^8 ciphertexts encrypted with randomly-chosen keys.

2.2   Maitra, Paul and Sen Gupta (MPS) Attack

Maitra, Paul and Sen Gupta showed that $Z_3, Z_4, \ldots, Z_{255}$ are also biased to 0 [6,8]. Although the MS attack assumes that an initial permutation S is random, the MPS attack exploits biases of S after the KSA [9]. Let $S_r[x]$ be the value of S indexed x after r round, where S_0 is the initial state of RC4 after the KSA. Biases of the initial state of the PRGA are given as follow.

Proposition 1 [9]. *After the end of KSA, for $0 \leq u \leq N-1, 0 \leq v \leq N-1$,*

$$\Pr(S_0[u] = v) = \begin{cases} \frac{1}{N} \cdot \left((\frac{N-1}{N})^v + (1 - (\frac{N-1}{N})^v) \cdot (\frac{N-1}{N})^{N-u-1} \right) & (v \le u), \\ \frac{1}{N} \cdot \left((\frac{N-1}{N})^{N-u-1} + (\frac{N-1}{N})^v \right) & (v > u). \end{cases}$$

The probability of $S_{r-1}[r]$ in the PRGA are given as the follows.

Theorem 4 [6][1]**.** *For* $3 \le r \le N - 1$*, the probability* $\Pr(S_{r-1}[r] = v)$ *is approximately*

$$\Pr(S_1[r] = v) \cdot \left(1 - \frac{1}{N} \right)^{r-2} + \sum_{t=2}^{r-1} \sum_{w=0}^{r-t} \frac{\Pr(S_1[t] = v)}{w! \cdot N} \cdot \left(\frac{r-t-1}{N} \right)^w \cdot \left(1 - \frac{1}{N} \right)^{r-3-w},$$

where $\Pr(S_1[t] = v)$ *is given as*

$$\Pr(S_1[t] = v) = \begin{cases} \Pr(S_0[1] = 1) + \sum_{X \neq 1} \Pr(S_0[1] = X \land S_0[X] = 1) & (t = 1, v = 1), \\ \sum_{X \neq 1, v} \Pr(S_0[1] = X \land S_0[X] = v) & (t = 1, v \neq 1), \\ \Pr(S_0[1] = t) + \sum_{X \neq t} \Pr(S_0[1] = X \land S_0[t] = t) & (t \neq 1, v = t), \\ \sum_{X \neq t, v} \Pr(S_0[1] = X \land S_0[t] = v) & (t \neq 1, v \neq t). \end{cases}$$

Then, the bias of $\Pr(Z_r = 0)$ is estimated as follows.

Theorem 5 [6]**.** *For* $3 \le r \le N - 1$*,* $\Pr(Z_r = 0)$ *is approximately*

$$\Pr(Z_r = 0) \approx \frac{1}{N} + \frac{c_r}{N^2},$$

where c_r *is given as*

$$c_r = \begin{cases} \frac{N}{N-1} \cdot (N \cdot \Pr(S_{r-1}[r] = r) - 1) - \frac{N-2}{N-1} & (r = 3), \\ \frac{N}{N-1} \cdot (N \cdot \Pr(S_{r-1}[r] = r) - 1) & (r \neq 3). \end{cases}$$

Since the parameters of p and q are given as $p = 1/N$ and $q = c_r/N$, The number of required ciphertexts with different keys for the extraction of $P_3, P_4, \dots, P_{255}$ is roughly estimated as $\Omega(N^3)$.

3   New Biases : Theory and Experiment

This section introduces four new biases in the keystream of RC4. To begin with, we prove a conditional bias of Z_1 towards 0 when $Z_2 = 0$. After that, we present new biases in the events, $Z_3 = 131$, $Z_r = r$, and extended keylength-dependent biases, which are substantially stronger than the known biases such as $Z_r = 0$. Then, we construct a cumulative list of strong biases in $Z_1, Z_2, \dots, Z_{257}$ to mount an efficient plaintext recovery attack on broadcast RC4.

---

[1] The theorems with respect to $Z_r = 0$ in [8] and [6] are slightly different. This paper uses the results from the full version [6].

3.1 Bias of $Z_1 = 0|Z_2 = 0$

A new conditional bias such that Z_1 is biased to 0 when $Z_2 = 0$ is given as Theorem 6.

Theorem 6. $\Pr(Z_1 = 0|Z_2 = 0)$ *is approximately*

$$\Pr(Z_1 = 0|Z_2 = 0) \approx \frac{1}{2} \cdot \left(\Pr(S_0[1] = 1) + (1 - \Pr(S_0[1] = 1)) \cdot \frac{1}{N}\right) + \frac{1}{2} \cdot \frac{1}{N}.$$

Proof. Two cases of $S_0[2] = 0$ and $S_0[2] \neq 0$ are considered. As mentioned in [11], when Z_2 is 0, $S_0[2]$ is also 0 with probability of $\frac{1}{2}$.

– $S_0[2] = 0$
  For $i = 1$, if $S_0[1]$ is 1, the index j is updated as $j = S_0[i] = S_0[1] = 1$. Then the first output byte Z_1 is expressed as follows (see Fig. 1),

$$Z_1 = S_1[S_1[i] + S_1[j]] = S_1[S_1[1] + S_1[1]] = S_1[2] = S_0[2] = 0.$$

Assuming that $Z_1 = 0$ holds with probability of $\frac{1}{N}$ when $S_0[1] \neq 1$, the probability of $\Pr(Z_1 = 0|S_0[2] = 0)$ is estimated as

$$\Pr(Z_1 = 0|S_0[2] = 0) = \Pr(S_0[1] = 1) + (1 - \Pr(S_0[1] = 1)) \cdot \frac{1}{N}.$$

– $S_0[2] \neq 0$
  Suppose that the event of $Z_1 = 0$ occurs with probability of $\frac{1}{N}$. Then $\Pr(Z_1 = 0|S_0[2] = 0)$ is estimated as

$$\Pr(Z_1 = 0|S_0[2] \neq 0) = \frac{1}{N}.$$

Therefore $\Pr(Z_1 = 0|Z_2 = 0)$ is approximately

$$\begin{aligned}
\Pr(Z_1 = 0|Z_2 = 0) &= \Pr(Z_1 = 0|S_0[2] = 0) \cdot \Pr(S_0[2] = 0|Z_2 = 0) \\
&\quad + \Pr(Z_1 = 0|S_0[2] \neq 0) \cdot \Pr(S_0[2] \neq 0|Z_2 = 0) \\
&\approx \frac{1}{2} \cdot \left(\Pr(S_0[1] = 1) + (1 - \Pr(S_0[1] = 1)) \cdot \frac{1}{N}\right) + \frac{1}{2} \cdot \frac{1}{N}.
\end{aligned}$$

$\square$

When $N = 256$, $\Pr(S_0[1] = 1)$ is obtained by Proposition 1.

$$\Pr(S_0[1] = 1) = \frac{1}{256} \cdot \left(\left(\frac{1}{256}\right) + \left(1 - \left(\frac{1}{256}\right)\right)\right) \cdot \left(\frac{1}{256}\right)^{254} = 0.0038966.$$

Then, $\Pr(Z_1 = 0|Z_2 = 0)$ is computed as

$$\begin{aligned}
\Pr(Z_1 = 0|Z_2 = 0) &= \frac{1}{2} \cdot \left(\Pr(S_0[1] = 1) + (1 - \Pr(S_0[1] = 1)) \cdot \frac{1}{256}\right) + \frac{1}{2} \cdot \frac{1}{256} \\
&= 0.0058470 = 2^{-7.418} = 2^{-8} \cdot (1 + 2^{-1.009}).
\end{aligned}$$

Since the experimental value of $\Pr(Z_1 = 0 | Z_2 = 0)$ for 2^{40} randomly-chosen keys is obtained as $0.0058109 = 2^{-8} \cdot (1 + 2^{-1.036})$, the theoretical value is correctly approximated.

From this bias, $\Pr(Z_1 = 0 \wedge Z_2 = 0)$ can also be estimated, as follows.

$$\Pr(Z_1 = 0 \wedge Z_2 = 0) = \Pr(Z_2 = 0) \cdot \Pr(Z_1 = 0 | Z_2 = 0).$$

When $N = 256$, it is estimated as

$$\Pr(Z_1 = 0 \wedge Z_2 = 0) = \frac{2}{256} \cdot 2^{-7.418} = 2^{-14.418} = 2^{-16} \cdot (1 + 2^{0.996}).$$

This type of bias, called digraph bias, was proved as a long term bias by Fluhrer and McGrew [3]. However, such a strong bias in initial bytes was not reported. Specifically, the probability of the general long-term digraph bias is estimated as $2^{-16} \cdot (1 + 2^{-8})$ in [3] when $N = 256$, while that of our bias is $2^{-16} \cdot (1 + 2^{0.996})$. Thus our result reveals that the digraph bias in initial bytes is much stronger than what is estimated in [3].

Note that we searched for the similar form of conditional biases in first 256 bytes of the RC4 keystream. In particular, we check following specific patterns, $(Z_{r-a} = X | Z_r = Y)$ for $0 \leq X, Y \leq 255, 2 \leq r \leq 256, 1 \leq a \leq 8$. However, such a strong bias could not be found in our experiment, while all conditional biases are not covered.

Application to Broadcast RC4 attack. Using this new conditional bias of $Z_1 = 0 | Z_2 = 0$ in conjunction with the bias of $Z_2 = 0$ [11], the first byte of the plaintext can be efficiently extracted, where $N = 256$. After 2^{17} ciphertexts with randomly-chosen keys are collected, following procedures are performed.

Step 1. Extract the second byte of the target plaintext, P_2, from 2^8 ciphertexts [11].

Step 2. Find the ciphertext in which $Z_2 = 0$ is XOR-ed by the computation of $C_2 \oplus P_2$. Then, $2^{10} = 2^{17} \cdot 2/256$ ciphertexts matching this criterion are expected to be obtained.

Step 3. Regard the most frequent byte in the first byte C_1 of these matching 2^{10} ciphertexts as P_1.

In Step 3, using the bias of $\Pr(Z_1 = 0 | Z_2 = 0) = 2^{-8} \cdot (1 + 2^{-1.009})$, P_1 is extracted from remaining $2^{10} (\sim \frac{1}{2^{-8} \cdot (2^{-1.009})^2})$ ciphertexts by Theorems 2 and 3, assuming the relation of $C_1 = P_1 \oplus Z_1 = P_1$ holds. Although the bias of the first byte has already been pointed out in [6,14], it requires 2^{24} ciphertexts to extract the first byte using the known biases, because the probability of the strongest bias, which is a negative bias of Z_1 towards 0, is estimated as about $2^{-8} \cdot (1 - 2^{-8})$ [6]. Thus, the new conditional bias identified by us is very efficient, because the number of required ciphertexts reduces by a factor close to $N/2$ compared to that of the straightforward method.

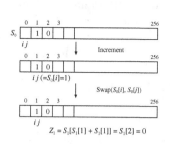

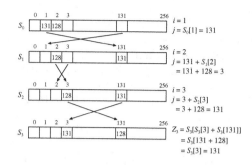

Fig. 1. Event for bias of $Z_1 = 0|Z_2 = 0$ **Fig. 2.** Event for bias of $Z_3 = 131$

3.2   Bias of $Z_3 = 131$

A new bias of $Z_3 = 131$, which is stronger than $Z_3 = 0$ [6,8], is given as Theorem 7.

Theorem 7. $\Pr(Z_3 = 131)$ *is approximately*

$$\Pr(Z_3 = 131) \approx \Pr(S_0[1] = 131) \cdot \Pr(S_0[2] = 128) +$$
$$(1 - \Pr(S_0[1] = 131) \cdot \Pr(S_0[2] = 128)) \cdot 1/N.$$

Proof. Suppose the events $S_0[1] = 131$ and $S_0[2] = 128$ occur after the KSA. For $i = 1$, j is updated as $S_0[1] = 131$. After $S_0[1]$ and $S_0[131]$ are swapped, $S_1[131]$ becomes 131. For $i = 2$, j is updated as $131 + S_1[2] = 131 + S_0[2] = 131 + 128 = 3$, and $S_1[2]$ and $S_1[3]$ are swapped. Then $S_2[3] = 128$ is obtained. Finally, for $i = 3$, j is updated as $3 + S_2[3] = 3 + 128 = 131$. After $S_2[3]$ and $S_2[131]$ are swapped, $S_3[3] = 131$ and $S_3[131] = 128$ holds. Then, a third output byte Z_3 is $Z_3 = S_3[S_3[3] + S_3[131]] = S_3[131 + 128] = S_3[3] = 131$. Thus, when $S_0[1] = 131$ and $S_0[2] = 128$ hold, $Z_3 = 131$ holds with probability one. Figure 2 depicts this event.

Assuming that in other cases, that is when $S_0[1] \neq 131$ or $S_0[2] \neq 128$, the event $Z_3 = 131$ holds with probability of $1/N$, the probability of $\Pr(Z_3 = 131)$ is estimated as

$$\Pr(Z_3 = 131) \approx \Pr(S_0[1] = 131) \cdot \Pr(S_0[2] = 128) +$$
$$(1 - \Pr(S_0[1] = 131) \cdot \Pr(S_0[2] = 128)) \cdot 1/N. \qquad \square$$

When $N = 256$, by Proposition 1, $\Pr(S_0[1] = 131)$ and $\Pr(S_0[2] = 128)$ are estimated as

$$\Pr(S_0[1] = 131) = \frac{1}{256} \cdot \left(\left(\frac{255}{256}\right)^{256-1-1} + \left(\frac{255}{256}\right)^{131} \right) = 0.0037848,$$

$$\Pr(S_0[2] = 128) = \frac{1}{256} \cdot \left(\left(\frac{255}{256}\right)^{256-2-1} + \left(\frac{255}{256}\right)^{128} \right) = 0.0038181.$$

Thus, $\Pr(Z_r = 131)$ is computed as

$$\Pr(Z_3 = 131) \approx 0.0039206 = 2^{-8} \cdot (1 + 2^{-8.089}).$$

Since experimental value of this bias for 2^{40} randomly-chosen keys is obtained as $0.0039204 = 2^{-8} \cdot (1 + 2^{-8.109})$, the theoretical value is correctly approximated.

Let us compare it to the bias of $Z_3 = 0$ of the MPS attack [6,8]. The experimental value for 2^{40} randomly-chosen keys is obtained as

$$\Pr(Z_3 = 0) = 0.0039116 = 2^{-8} \cdot (1 + 2^{-9.512}).$$

Thus, the bias of $Z_3 = 131$ is stronger than that of $Z_3 = 0$.

We should utilize $Z_3 = 131$ instead of $Z_3 = 0$ for the efficient plaintext recovery attack. When $Z_3 = 131$ and $Z_3 = 0$ are jointly used, two candidates of P_3 remain. Thus, in order to detect one correct value of P_3, the only use of $Z_3 = 131$ is more efficient.

3.3   Bias of $Z_r = r$ for $3 \leq r \leq N - 1$

We also present a new bias in the event $Z_r = r$ for $3 \leq r \leq N - 1$, whose probabilities are very close to those of $Z_r = 0$ [8], and the new biases are stronger than those of $Z_r = 0$ in some rounds. Thus, for an efficient attack, we need to carefully consider which biases are stronger in each round. The probability of $Z_r = r$ is given as Theorem 8.

Theorem 8. $\Pr(Z_r = r)$ *for* $3 \leq r \leq N - 1$ *is approximately*

$$\Pr(Z_r = r) \approx p_{r-1,0} \cdot \frac{1}{N} + p_{r-1,r} \cdot \frac{1}{N} \cdot \frac{N-2}{N} +$$
$$(1 - p_{r-1,0} \cdot \frac{1}{N} - p_{r-1,r} \cdot \frac{1}{N} - (1 - p_{r-1,0}) \cdot \frac{1}{N} \cdot 2) \cdot \frac{1}{N},$$

where $p_{r-1,0} = \Pr(S_{r-1}[r] = 0)$ *and* $p_{r-1,r} = \Pr(S_{r-1}[r] = r)$.

Proof. Let i_r and j_r be r-th i and j, respectively. For $i_r = r$, an output Z_r is expressed as

$$Z_r = S_r[S_r[i_r] + S_r[j_r]] = S_r[S_r[r] + S_{r-1}[r]].$$

Then, let us consider four independent cases.

Case 1 : $S_{r-1}[r] = 0 \wedge S_r[r] = r$
Case 2 : $S_{r-1}[r] = r \wedge S_r[r] = j_r - r \wedge j_r \neq r, r + r$
Case 3 : $S_{r-1}[r] \neq 0 \wedge S_r[r] = r - S_{r-1}[r]$
Case 4 : $S_{r-1}[r] \neq 0 \wedge S_r[r] = r$

In Case 1 and Case 2, the output is always $Z_r = r$. On the other hand, in Case 3 and Case 4, the output is not $Z_r = r$.

Case 1 : $S_{r-1}[r] = 0 \land S_r[r] = r$
The output is expressed as $Z_r = S_r[S_r[r] + S_{r-1}[r]] = S_r[r + 0] = S_r[r] = r$ (see Fig. 3). Then, the probability of $Z_r = r$ is one. Here $S_r[r]$ is chosen by pointer j. Since j_r for $r \geq 3$ behaves randomly [8], $S_r[r]$ is assumed to be uniformly random. it is estimated as

$$\Pr(S_{r-1}[r] = 0 \land S_r[r] = r) = p_{r-1,0} \cdot \frac{1}{N}.$$

Case 2 : $S_{r-1}[r] = r \land S_r[r] = j_r - r \land j_r \neq r, r + r$
The output is expressed as $Z_r = S_r[S_r[r] + S_{r-1}[r]] = S_r[j_r - r + r] = S_r[j_r] = S_{r-1}[r] = r$ (see Fig. 4). Then, the probability of $Z_r = r$ is one. Similar to Case 1, $S_r[r]$ is assumed to be uniformly random.

When $j_r = r$, the probability of $Z_r = r$ is zero because of the relation of $Z_r = S_r[S_r[r] + S_{r-1}[r]] = S_r[0 + r] = S_r[r] = 0$. Also, when $j_r = r + r$, since $S_r[r] = r$ and $Z_r = S_r[S_r[r] + S_{r-1}[r]] = S_r[r + r] \neq r$, the probability of $Z_r = r$ is zero. Thus, the conditions of $j_r \neq r, r + r$ are necessary for $Z_r = r$. Then, it is estimated as

$$\Pr(S_{r-1}[r] = r \land S_r[r] = j_r - r \land j_r \neq r, r + r) = p_{r-1,r} \cdot \frac{1}{N} \cdot \frac{N-2}{N}.$$

Case 3 : $S_{r-1}[r] \neq 0 \land S_r[r] = r - S_{r-1}[r]$
The equation of $Z_r = S_r[r - S_{r-1}[r] + S_{r-1}[r]] = S_r[r]$ holds. Then, $S_r[r] = r - S_{r-1}[r]$ is not r, because $S_{r-1}[r]$ is not 0. Thus, it is estimated as

$$\Pr(S_{r-1}[r] \neq 0 \land S_r[r] = r - S_{r-1}[r]) = (1 - p_{r-1,0}) \cdot \frac{1}{N}.$$

Case 4 : $S_{r-1}[r] \neq 0 \land S_r[r] = r$
The output is expressed as $Z_r = S_r[r + S_{r-1}[r]]$. According to the equation of $S_{r-1}[r] \neq 0$, The probability of $Z_r = r$ is zero. Thus, it is estimated as

$$\Pr(S_{r-1}[r] \neq (0, r) \land S_r[r] = r - S_{r-1}[r]) = (1 - p_{r-1,0}) \cdot \frac{1}{N}.$$

Assuming that in other cases, $Z_r = r$ holds with probability of $1/N$, the probability of $\Pr(Z_r = r)$ is estimated as

$$\Pr(Z_r = r) \approx p_{r-1,0} \cdot \frac{1}{N} + p_{r-1,r} \cdot \frac{1}{N} \cdot \frac{N-2}{N} +$$
$$(1 - p_{r-1,0} \cdot \frac{1}{N} - p_{r-1,r} \cdot \frac{1}{N} - (1 - p_{r-1,0}) \cdot \frac{1}{N} \cdot 2) \cdot \frac{1}{N}.$$

$\square$

Here, $p_{r-1,r}$ and $p_{r-1,0}$ are obtained from Theorem 4. Figure 5 shows the comparison of theoretical values and experimental values of $Z_r = r$ for 2^{40} randomly-chosen keys when $N = 256$. Since the theoretical values do not exactly coincide with the experimental values, we do not claim that Theorem 8 completely prove this bias. We guess that several minor events are not covered in our approach. However, the order of the bias seems to be well matched. At least it can be said that the main event causing this bias is discovered.

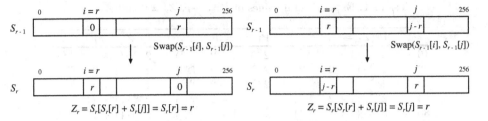

Fig. 3. Event (Case 1) for bias of $Z_r = r$

Fig. 4. Event (Case 2) for bias of $Z_r = r$

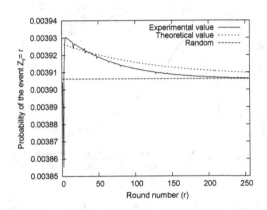

Fig. 5. Theoretical values and experimental values of $Z_r = r$

3.4 Extended Keylength-Dependent Biases

Extended keylength-dependent biases, which are extensions of keylength-dependent biases [5,17], are the bias of $Z_\ell = -\ell$ when the key length is ℓ bytes. For example, when using a 128-bit key (16 bytes), Z_{16} is biased to -16 ($= 240$). In addition to it, we show that when the key length is ℓ bytes, $Z_{x\cdot\ell}$ is also biased to $-x \cdot \ell$ ($x = 2,3,4,5,6,7$), e.g., $Z_r = -r$ for $r = 32,\ 48,\ 64,\ 80,\ 96,\ 112$, assuming $\ell = 16$. Importantly, the extended keylength-dependent biases are much stronger than the other known biases such as $Z_r = 0$ and $Z_r = r$. Table 1 shows experimental values of the extended keylength-dependent bias $Z_r = -r$, $Z_r = 0$, and $Z_r = r$ for 2^{40} randomly-chosen keys, when r is a multiple of the key length, $\ell = 16$ in this case.

The probability of these biases is given as Theorem 9 (the proof is in Appendix A).

Theorem 9. *When $r = x \cdot \ell$ ($x = 1, 2, \ldots, 7$), the probability of $\Pr(Z_r = -r)$ is approximately*

$$\Pr(Z_r = -r) \approx \frac{1}{N^2} + \left(1 - \frac{1}{N^2}\right) \cdot \gamma_r + (1 - \delta_r) \cdot \frac{1}{N},$$

Table 1. Experimental values of $Z_r = -r$, $Z_r = 0$ and $Z_r = r$

r	$\Pr(Z_r = -r)$	$\Pr(Z_r = 0)$	$\Pr(Z_r = r)$
16	$2^{-8} \cdot \left(1 + 2^{-4.811}\right)$	$2^{-8} \cdot \left(1 + 2^{-7.714}\right)$	$2^{-8} \cdot \left(1 + 2^{-7.762}\right)$
32	$2^{-8} \cdot \left(1 + 2^{-5.383}\right)$	$2^{-8} \cdot \left(1 + 2^{-7.880}\right)$	$2^{-8} \cdot \left(1 + 2^{-7.991}\right)$
48	$2^{-8} \cdot \left(1 + 2^{-5.938}\right)$	$2^{-8} \cdot \left(1 + 2^{-8.043}\right)$	$2^{-8} \cdot \left(1 + 2^{-8.350}\right)$
64	$2^{-8} \cdot \left(1 + 2^{-6.496}\right)$	$2^{-8} \cdot \left(1 + 2^{-8.244}\right)$	$2^{-8} \cdot \left(1 + 2^{-8.664}\right)$
80	$2^{-8} \cdot \left(1 + 2^{-7.224}\right)$	$2^{-8} \cdot \left(1 + 2^{-8.407}\right)$	$2^{-8} \cdot \left(1 + 2^{-9.052}\right)$
96	$2^{-8} \cdot \left(1 + 2^{-7.911}\right)$	$2^{-8} \cdot \left(1 + 2^{-8.577}\right)$	$2^{-8} \cdot \left(1 + 2^{-9.351}\right)$
112	$2^{-8} \cdot \left(1 + 2^{-8.666}\right)$	$2^{-8} \cdot \left(1 + 2^{-8.747}\right)$	$2^{-8} \cdot \left(1 + 2^{-9.732}\right)$

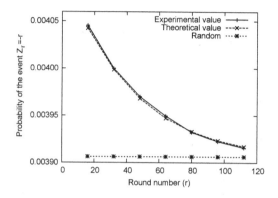

Fig. 6. Experimental values and theoretical values of $Z_r = -r$ when $\ell = 16$ for $r = 16, 32, 48, 64, 80, 96, 112$

where

$$\gamma_r = \frac{1}{N^2} \cdot \left(1 - \frac{r+1}{N}\right)$$

$$\cdot \sum_{y=r+1}^{N-1} \left(1 - \frac{1}{N}\right)^y \cdot \left(1 - \frac{2}{N}\right)^{y-r} \cdot \left(1 - \frac{3}{N}\right)^{N-y+2r-4},$$

and $\delta_r = \Pr(S_r[j_r] = 0) = \Pr(S_{r-1}[r] = 0)$.

Figure 6 shows our experimental values for 2^{40} randomly-chosen keys and theoretical values of these extended keylength-dependent biases. Since theoretical and experimental values have almost the same value, theoretical values are correctly approximated.

3.5 Cumulative Bias Set of First 257 Bytes

When $N = 256$, a set of strong biases in $Z_1, Z_2, \ldots, Z_{255}$ is given in Table 2. Our new biases, namely the ones involving Z_1, Z_3, Z_{32}, Z_{48}, Z_{64}, Z_{80}, Z_{96}, Z_{112}, are included. Here, let us compare between the biases of $Z_r = 0$ [6,8] and

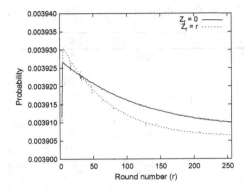

Fig. 7. Comparison between $Z_r = 0$ and $Z_r = r$ for $3 \le r \le 255$

$Z_r = r$, whose probabilities are of the same order, and are very close in the range $3 \le r \le 255$. According to our experiments with 2^{40} randomly-chosen keys (see Fig. 7), $Z_r = r$ is stronger than $Z_r = 0$ in $Z_5, Z_6, \ldots, Z_{31}$. Thus we choose the bias $Z_r = r$ in $Z_5, Z_6, \ldots, Z_{31}$ and the bias $Z_r = 0$ in the other cases as the strongest bias except for the cases involving Z_3, Z_{16}, Z_{32}, Z_{48}, Z_{64}, Z_{80}, Z_{96}, Z_{112}. Besides, we experimentally found two new biases for the events $Z_{256} \ne 0$ and $Z_{257} = 0$, and added these to our bias set, while we could not provide the theoretical proofs. Note that it is experimentally confirmed that biases of $Z_2, Z_3, \ldots, Z_{257}$ included in our bias set are strongest known biases amongst all the positive and negative biases that have been discovered for these bytes.

For the first time, we propose a cumulative list of strongest known biases in the initial bytes of RC4 that can be exploited in a practical attack against the broadcast mode of the cipher.

4   Experimental Results of Plaintext Recovery Attack

We demonstrate a plaintext recovery attack using our cumulative bias set of first 257 bytes by a computer experiment, when $N = 256$, and estimate the number of required ciphertexts and the probability of success for our attack. The details of our experiment are as follows.

Step 1. Randomly generate a target plaintext P.

Step 2. Encrypt P with 2^x randomly-chosen keys, and obtain 2^x ciphertexts C.

Step 3. Find most frequent byte in each byte, and extract P_r, assuming $P_r = C_r \oplus Z_r$ where Z_r is the value of the keystream byte from our bias set.

In the case of P_1, the method mentioned in Sect. 3.1 is used for efficient extraction of P_1. Specifically, after P_2 is recovered, we extract P_1 by using the conditional bias such that $Z_1 = 0$ when $Z_2 = 0$.

We perform the above experiment for 256 different plaintexts in the cases where $2^6, 2^7, \ldots, 2^{35}$ ciphertexts with randomly-chosen keys are given. Figure 8

Table 2. Cumulative bias set of first 257 bytes

r	Strongest known bias of Z_r	Prob.(Theoretical)	Prob.(Experimental)
1	$Z_1 = 0 \| Z_2 = 0$ (Our)	$2^{-8} \cdot (1 + 2^{-1.009})$	$2^{-8} \cdot (1 + 2^{-1.036})$
2	$Z_2 = 0$ [11]	$2^{-8} \cdot (1 + 2^{0})$	$2^{-8} \cdot (1 + 2^{0.002})$
3	$Z_3 = 131$ (Our)	$2^{-8} \cdot (1 + 2^{-8.089})$	$2^{-8} \cdot (1 + 2^{-8.109})$
4	$Z_4 = 0$ [8]	$2^{-8} \cdot (1 + 2^{-7.581})$	$2^{-8} \cdot (1 + 2^{-7.611})$
5–15	$Z_r = r$ (Our)	max: $2^{-8} \cdot (1 + 2^{-7.627})$	max: $2^{-8} \cdot (1 + 2^{-7.335})$
		min: $2^{-8} \cdot (1 + 2^{-7.737})$	min: $2^{-8} \cdot (1 + 2^{-7.535})$
16	$Z_{16} = 240$ [5]	$2^{-8} \cdot (1 + 2^{-4.841})$	$2^{-8} \cdot (1 + 2^{-4.811})$
17–31	$Z_r = r$ (Our)	max: $2^{-8} \cdot (1 + 2^{-7.759})$	max: $2^{-8} \cdot (1 + 2^{-7.576})$
		min: $2^{-8} \cdot (1 + 2^{-7.912})$	min: $2^{-8} \cdot (1 + 2^{-7.839})$
32	$Z_{32} = 224$ (Our)	$2^{-8} \cdot (1 + 2^{-5.404})$	$2^{-8} \cdot (1 + 2^{-5.383})$
33–47	$Z_r = 0$ [8]	max: $2^{-8} \cdot (1 + 2^{-7.897})$	max: $2^{-8} \cdot (1 + 2^{-7.868})$
		min: $2^{-8} \cdot (1 + 2^{-8.050})$	min: $2^{-8} \cdot (1 + 2^{-8.039})$
48	$Z_{48} = 208$ (Our)	$2^{-8} \cdot (1 + 2^{-5.981})$	$2^{-8} \cdot (1 + 2^{-5.938})$
49–63	$Z_r = 0$ [8]	max: $2^{-8} \cdot (1 + 2^{-8.072})$	max: $2^{-8} \cdot (1 + 2^{-8.046})$
		min: $2^{-8} \cdot (1 + 2^{-8.224})$	min: $2^{-8} \cdot (1 + 2^{-8.238})$
64	$Z_{64} = 192$ (Our)	$2^{-8} \cdot (1 + 2^{-6.576})$	$2^{-8} \cdot (1 + 2^{-6.496})$
65–79	$Z_r = 0$ [8]	max: $2^{-8} \cdot (1 + 2^{-8.246})$	max: $2^{-8} \cdot (1 + 2^{-8.223})$
		min: $2^{-8} \cdot (1 + 2^{-8.398})$	min: $2^{-8} \cdot (1 + 2^{-8.376})$
80	$Z_{80} = 176$ (Our)	$2^{-8} \cdot (1 + 2^{-7.192})$	$2^{-8} \cdot (1 + 2^{-7.224})$
81–95	$Z_r = 0$ [8]	max: $2^{-8} \cdot (1 + 2^{-8.420})$	max: $2^{-8} \cdot (1 + 2^{-8.398})$
		min: $2^{-8} \cdot (1 + 2^{-8.571})$	min: $2^{-8} \cdot (1 + 2^{-8.565})$
96	$Z_{96} = 160$ (Our)	$2^{-8} \cdot (1 + 2^{-7.831})$	$2^{-8} \cdot (1 + 2^{-7.911})$
97–111	$Z_r = 0$ [8]	max: $2^{-8} \cdot (1 + 2^{-8.592})$	max: $2^{-8} \cdot (1 + 2^{-8.570})$
		min: $2^{-8} \cdot (1 + 2^{-8.741})$	min: $2^{-8} \cdot (1 + 2^{-8.722})$
112	$Z_{112} = 144$ (Our)	$2^{-8} \cdot (1 + 2^{-8.500})$	$2^{-8} \cdot (1 + 2^{-8.666})$
113–255	$Z_r = 0$ [8]	max: $2^{-8} \cdot (1 + 2^{-8.763})$	max: $2^{-8} \cdot (1 + 2^{-8.760})$
		min: $2^{-8} \cdot (1 + 2^{-10.052})$	min: $2^{-8} \cdot (1 + 2^{-10.041})$
256	$Z_{256} = 0$ (negative bias) (Our)	N/A	$2^{-8} \cdot (1 - 2^{-9.407})$
257	$Z_{257} = 0$ (Our)	N/A	$2^{-8} \cdot (1 + 2^{-9.531})$

shows the probability of successfully recovering the values of P_1, P_2, P_3, P_5, and P_{16} for each amount of ciphertexts. Here, the success probability is estimated by the number of correctly-extracted plaintexts for each byte. For example, if the target byte of only 100 plaintexts out of 256 plaintexts can be correctly recovered, the probability is estimated as 0.39 ($= 100/256$). The second byte of plaintext P_2 can be extracted from 2^{12} ciphertexts with probability one. In previous attacks such as the MS attack [11] and the MPS attack [8], the number of required ciphertexts is theoretically estimated only in terms of the lower bound Ω. Our results first reveal the concrete number of ciphertexts, and the corresponding success probability.

Figure 9 shows that the success probability of extracting each byte P_r ($1 \le r \le 257$) when $2^{24}, 2^{28}, 2^{32}, 2^{35}$ ciphertexts are given. Note that the probability of a random guess is $1/256 = 0.00390625$. Given 2^{32} ciphertexts, all bytes of $P_1, P_2, \ldots, P_{257}$ can be extracted with probability more than 0.5. In addition, most bytes can be extracted with probability more than 0.8. Also, the bytes having stronger bias such as $P_1, P_2, P_{16}, P_{32}, P_{48}, P_{64}$, are extracted from

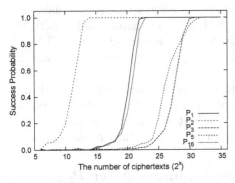

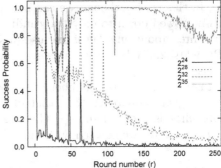

Fig. 8. Relation of the number of ciphertexts and success probability of recovering P_1, P_2, P_3, P_5, and P_{16}

Fig. 9. Success probability of extracting P_r $(1 \leq r \leq 257)$ with different number of samples (one candidate)

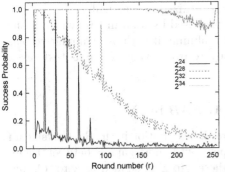

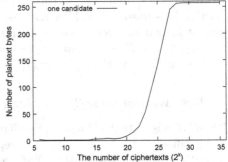

Fig. 10. Success probability of extracting P_r $(1 \leq r \leq 257)$ with different number of samples (two candidates)

Fig. 11. The number of plaintext bytes that are extracted with five times higher than that of a random guess

only 2^{24} ciphertexts with high probability. However, even if 2^{35} ciphertexts are given, the probability does not become one in some bytes. It is guessed that in such bytes, the difference of probability of the strongest known bias (as in our cumulative bias set) and the second one is very small. Thus, more ciphertexts are required for an attack with probability one.

We additionally utilize the second most frequent byte in the ciphertexts for extracting plaintext bytes. In other words, two candidates are obtained by using the relation of $P_r = C_r \oplus Z_r$, where C_r are most and second most frequent ciphertext bytes and Z_r is chosen from our bias set. This result is shown in Fig. 10, and its success probability is estimated as the probability that the guess for the correct plaintext byte is narrowed down to two possible candidates. Note that the probability of a random guess for such a scenario is $2/256 = 0.0078125$. Given 2^{34} ciphertexts, each byte of $P_1, P_2, \ldots, P_{257}$ can be extracted with probability one. In this case, although we can not obtain the correct byte of the plaintext, it is narrowed down to only two candidates. For the experiments of Figs. 9, 10, it requires about one day if one uses a single CPU core (Intel(R) Core(TM) i7 CPU 920@ 2.67 GHz) to obtain the result of one plaintext, where 256 plaintexts are used.

Figure 11 shows the number of plaintext bytes that are extracted with five times higher probability than that of a random guess, i.e., where the success probability is more than $\frac{5}{256}$. Given 2^{29} ciphertexts, all the plaintext bytes $P_1, P_2, \ldots, P_{257}$ are guessed with much higher probability than random guesses.

5   How to Recover Bytes of the Plaintext After P_{258}

In this section, we propose an efficient method to recover later bytes of the plaintext, namely bytes after P_{258}. The method using our bias in initial bytes is not directly applied to extract these bytes, because it exploits biases existing in only the initial keystream. For the extraction of the later bytes, a long-term bias, which occurs in any keystream bytes, is utilized. In particular, the digraph repetition bias (also called $ABSAB$ bias) proposed by Mantin [10], which is the strongest known long-term bias, is used. Combining it with our cumulative bias set of $Z_1, Z_2, \ldots, Z_{257}$, we can sequentially recover bytes of a plaintext, even after P_{258}, given only the ciphertexts.

5.1   Best Known Long-Term Bias ($ABSAB$ bias)

$ABSAB$ bias is statistical biases of the digraph distribution in the RC4 keystream [10]. Specifically, digraphs AB tend to repeat with short gaps S between them, e.g., $ABAB$, $ABCAB$ and $ABCDAB$, where gap S is defined as zero, C, and CD, respectively. The detail of $ABSAB$ bias is expressed as follows,

$$Z_r \;\|\; Z_{r+1} = Z_{r+2+G} \;\|\; Z_{r+3+G} \quad \text{for } G \geq 0, \tag{1}$$

where $\|$ is a concatenation. The probability that Eq. (1) holds is given as Theorem 10.

Theorem 10 [10]. *For small values of G the probability of the pattern $ABSAB$ in RC4 keystream, where S is a G-byte string, is $(1 + e^{(-4-8G)/N}/N) \cdot 1/N^2$.*

For the enhancement of these biases, combining use of $ABSAB$ biases with different G is considered by using the following lemma for the discrimination.

Lemma 1 [10]. *Let X and Y be two distributions and suppose that the independent events $\{E_i\colon 1 \leq i \leq k \}$ occur with probabilities $p_X(E_i) = p_i$ in X and $p_Y(E_i) = (1 + b_i) \cdot p_i$ in Y. Then the discrimination D of the distributions is $\sum_i p_i \cdot b_i^2$.*

The number of required samples for distinguishing the biased distribution from the random distribution with probability of $1 - \alpha$ is given as the following lemma.

Lemma 2 [10]. *The number of samples that is required for distinguishing two distributions that have discrimination D with success rate $1 - \alpha$ (for both directions) is $(1/D) \cdot (1 - 2\alpha) \cdot log_2 \frac{1-\alpha}{\alpha}$.*

This lemma shows that in the broadcast RC4 attack, given D and the number of samples $N_{ciphertext}$, the success probability for distinguishing the distribution of correct candidate plaintext byte (the biased distribution) from the distribution of one wrong candidate of plaintext byte (a random distribution) is a constant. $Pr_{distinguish}$ denotes this probability.

5.2   Plaintext Recovery Method Using $ABSAB$ Bias and Our Bias Set

The following equation allows us to efficiently use $ABSAB$ bias in the broadcast RC4 attack.

$$(C_r \parallel C_{r+1}) \oplus (C_{r+2+G} \parallel C_{r+3+G})$$
$$= (P_r \oplus Z_r \parallel P_{r+1} \oplus Z_{r+1}) \oplus (P_{r+2+G} \oplus Z_{r+2+G} \parallel P_{r+3+G} \oplus Z_{r+3+G})$$
$$= (P_r \oplus P_{r+2+G} \oplus Z_r \oplus Z_{r+2+G} \parallel P_{r+1} \oplus P_{r+3+G} \oplus Z_{r+1} \oplus Z_{r+3+G}). \quad (2)$$

Assuming that Eq. (1) (the event of the $ABSAB$ bias) holds, the relation of plaintexts and ciphertexts without keystreams is obtained, i.e., $(C_r \parallel C_{r+1}) \oplus (C_{r+2+G} \parallel C_{r+3+G}) = (P_r \oplus P_{r+2+G} \parallel P_{r+1} \oplus P_{r+3+G}) = (P_r \parallel P_{r+1}) \oplus (P_{r+2+G} \parallel P_{r+3+G})$.

However, in the straight way, we can not combine these relations with different G to enhance the biases, as we do in the distinguishing attack setting. When the value of G is different, the above equation is surely different even if r is properly chosen. For example, in the cases of (r and $G = 1$) and ($r + 1$ and $G = 0$), right parts of equations are given as $(P_r \parallel P_{r+1}) \oplus (P_{r+3} \parallel P_{r+4})$ and $(P_{r+1} \parallel P_{r+2}) \oplus (P_{r+3} \parallel P_{r+4})$, respectively. Thus, due to independent use of these equations with different G, we are not able to efficiently make use of $ABSAB$ bias in the broadcast setting.

In order to get rid of this problem, we give a method that sequentially recovers the plaintext after P_{258} with the knowledge of pre-guessed plaintext bytes. For example, in the cases of (r and $G = 1$) and ($r + 1$ and $G = 0$), if P_r, P_{r+1}, and P_{r+2} are already known, the two equations with respected to $(P_{r+3} \parallel P_{r+4})$ is obtained by transposing P_r, P_{r+1}, and P_{r+2} to the left part of the equation. Then, these equations with different G can be merged.

Suppose that $P_1, P_2, \ldots, P_{257}$ are guessed by our cumulative bias set of the initial bytes, where the success probability of finding these bytes are evaluated in Sect. 4. Then we aim to sequentially find P_r for $r = 258, 259, \ldots, P_{MAX}$ by using $ABSAB$ biases of $G = 0, 1, \ldots, G_{MAX}$. The detailed procedures are given as follows.

Step 1. Obtain $C_{258-3-G_{MAX}}, C_{258-2-G_{MAX}}, \ldots, C_{P_{MAX}}$ in each ciphertext, and make frequency tables $T_{count}[r][G]$ of $(C_{r-3-G} \parallel C_{r-2-G}) \oplus (C_{r-1} \parallel C_r)$ for all $r = 258, 259, \ldots, P_{MAX}$ and $G = 0, 1, \ldots, G_{MAX}$, where $(C_{r-3-G} \parallel C_{r-2-G}) \oplus (C_{r-1} \parallel C_r) = (P_{r-3-G} \parallel P_{r-2-G}) \oplus (P_{r-1} \parallel P_r)$ only if Eq. (1) holds.

Step 2. Set $r = 258$.

Step 3. Guess the value of P_r.

Step 3.1. For $G = 0, 1, \ldots, G_{MAX}$, convert $T_{count}[r][G]$ into a frequency table $T_{marge}[r]$ of $(P_{r-1} \parallel P_r)$ by using pre-guessed values of $P_{r-3-G_{MAX}}, \ldots, P_{r-2}$, and merge counter values of all tables.

Step 3.2. Make a frequency table $T_{guess}[r]$ indexed by only P_r from $T_{marge}[r]$ with knowledge of the P_{r-1}. To put it more precisely, using a pre-guessed value of P_{r-1}, only Tables $T_{marge}[r]$ corresponding to the value of P_{r-1} is taken into consideration. Finally, regard most frequency one in table $T_{guess}[r]$ as the correct P_r.

Step 4. Increment r. If $r = P_{MAX} + 1$, terminate this algorithm. Otherwise, go to Step 3.

The bytes of the plaintext are correctly extracted from $T_{marge}[r]$ only if it is distinguished from other $N^2 - 1$ wrong candidate distributions. Assuming that wrong candidates are randomly distributed, a probability of the correct extraction from $T_{marge}[r]$ is estimated as $(\mathrm{Pr}_{distingush})^{N^2-1}$. In Step 3.2, our method converts $T_{marge}[r]$ into $T_{guess}[r]$ by using knowledge of P_{r-1}, where $T_{guess}[r]$ has $N-1$ wrong candidates. It enables us to reduce the number of wrong candidates from $N^2 - 1$ to $N - 1$. Then, a probability of the correct extraction from $T_{guess}[r]$ is estimated as $(\mathrm{Pr}_{distingush})^{N-1}$, which is $1/(\mathrm{Pr}_{distingush})^{N+1}$ times higher than that of $T_{marge}[r]$. Therefore, the table reduction technique of Step 3.2 enables us to further optimize the attack.

Experimental Results. We perform practical experiments using our algorithm to find P_{258}, P_{259}, P_{260}, and P_{261} ($P_{MAX} = 261$). As a parameter of $ABSAB$ bias, $G_{MAX} = 63$ is chosen, because the increase of D is converged around $G_{MAX} = 63$. Then, D is estimated as $D = 2^{-28.0}$. The success probability of our algorithm for recovering P_r ($r \geq 258$) when 2^{30} to 2^{34} ciphertexts are given is shown in Table 3, where the number of tests is 256. Note that $P_1, P_2, \ldots, P_{257}$ are obtained by using our bias set (candidate one) with success probability as shown in Fig. 9. For this experiment, it requires about one week if one uses a single CPU core (Intel(R) Core(TM) i7 CPU 920@ 2.67 GHz) to get the result of one plaintext, where 256 plaintexts are used.

Interestingly, given 2^{34} ciphertexts, P_{258}, P_{259}, P_{260}, and P_{261} can be recovered with probability one, while the success probability of some bytes in P_1, $P_2, \ldots, P_{257}$ is not one. Combining multiple biases allows us to omit negative effects of some uncorrected value of $P_1, P_2, \ldots, P_{257}$. Although our experiment is performed until P_{261}, the success probability is expected not to change even in the case of later bytes, because $ABSAB$ bias is a long-term bias.

Table 3. Success Probability of our algorithm for recovering P_r ($r \geq 258$).

# of ciphertexts	P_{258}	P_{259}	P_{260}	P_{261}
2^{30}	0.003906	0.003906	0.000000	0.000000
2^{31}	0.039062	0.007812	0.003906	0.007812
2^{32}	0.386719	0.152344	0.070312	0.027344
2^{33}	0.964844	0.941406	0.921875	0.902344
2^{34}	1.000000	1.000000	1.000000	1.000000

Let us discuss the success probability of extracting bytes after P_{262} when 2^{34} ciphertexts are given. According to Lemma 2 and $D = 2^{-28.0}$, 2^{34} ciphertexts allow us to distinguish an RC4 keystream from a random stream with the probability of $\Pr_{distinguish} = 1 - 10^{-19}$. Then, assuming that wrong candidates are randomly distributed, the probability of correctly extracting the candidate from $(N - 1)$ wrong candidates is estimated as $(\Pr_{distinguish})^{N-1}$. Therefore, our method enables to extract consecutive $(257 + X)$ bytes of a plaintext with the probability of $((\Pr_{distinguish})^{N-1})^X = (\Pr_{distinguish})^{(N-1)\cdot X}$. For instance, when $X = 2^{40}$ and $X = 2^{50}$, the success probabilities are estimated as 0.99997 and 0.97170, respectively.

As a result, by using our sequential method, a large amount of plaintext bytes, e.g., first 2^{50} bytes ≈ 1000 T bytes, is recovered from 2^{34} ciphertext with a probability of almost one. Therefore, it can be said that our attack is a full plaintext recovery attack on broadcast RC4, the first of its kind proposed in the literature.

6 Conclusion

In this paper, we have evaluated the practical security of RC4 in the broadcast setting. After the introduction of four new biases of the keystream of RC4, i.e., the conditional bias of Z_1, the biases of $Z_3 = 131$ and $Z_r = r$ for $3 \leq r \leq 255$, and the extended keylength-dependent biases, a cumulative list of strongest known biases in $Z_1, Z_2, \ldots, Z_{257}$ is given. Then, we demonstrate a practical plaintext recovery attack using our bias set by a computer experiment. As a result, most bytes of $P_1, P_2, \ldots, P_{257}$ could be extracted with probability more than 0.8 using 2^{32} ciphertexts encrypted by randomly-chosen keys. Finally, we have proposed an efficient method to extract bytes of plaintexts after P_{258}. Our attack is able to recover any plaintext byte from only ciphertexts generated using different keys. For example, first 2^{50} bytes of the plaintext are expected to be recovered from 2^{34} ciphertexts with high probability.

Note that our attack on broadcast RC4, as proposed in this paper, utilizes the advantage of sequential recovery of plaintext bytes. If the initial 256/512/768 bytes of the keystream are suppressed in the protocol, as recommended in case of RC4 usages [14], our attack does not work any more. However, widely-used protocols such as SSL/TLS use initial bytes of the keystream. For SSL/TLS, the broadcast setting is converted into the multi-session setting where the target plaintext block are repeatedly sent in the same position in the plaintexts in multiple SSL/TLS sessions [2].

Our evaluation reveals that broadcast RC4 is practically vulnerable to the plaintext recovery attacks as moderate amount of ciphertexts, i.e., 2^{24} to 2^{34} ciphertexts generated by different keys, leaks considerable information about the plaintext. Thus, RC4 is not to be recommended for the encryption in case of the typical broadcast setting and multi-session setting of SSL/TLS.

Acknowledgments. We would like to thank to Sourav Sen Gupta and the anonymous referees for their fruitful comments and suggestions. We also would like to thank to Tubasa Tsukaune and Atsushi Nagao for insightful discussions. This work was supported in part by Grant-in-Aid for Scientific Research (C) (KAKENHI 23560455) for Japan Society for the Promotion of Science and Cryptography Research and Evaluation Committee (CRYPTREC).

A   Proof of Theorem 9

In order to prove Theorem 9, we give following Lemma 3 and Theorem 11, which are extensions of Lemma 2 and Theorem 3 in [6]. Let (S_r^K, i_r^K, j_r^K) be (S, i, j) of the r-th round in the KSA, respectively.

Lemma 3. *When* $r = x \cdot \ell$ $(x = 1, 2, \ldots, 7)$, *the probability of* $\Pr(S_{r+1}^K[r-1] = -r \wedge S_{r+1}^K[r] = 0)$ *is approximately*

$$\Pr(S_{r+1}^K[r-1] = -r \wedge S_{r+1}^K[r] = 0) \approx \frac{1}{N^2} + \left(1 - \frac{1}{N^2}\right) \cdot \alpha_r,$$

where $\alpha_r = \frac{1}{N} \cdot \left(1 - \frac{3}{N}\right)^{r-2} \cdot \left(1 - \frac{r+1}{N}\right)$.

Proof. The event of $(S_{r+1}^K[r-1] = -r \wedge S_{r+1}^K[r] = 0)$ consists of following events. In the first round of the KSA, when $i_1^K = 0$ and $j_1^K = K[0]$, the value 0 is swapped for the value of $S_0^K[K[0]]$ with probability of one. The index j_1^K requires $j_1^K = K[0] \notin \{r-1, r, -r\}$, so that the values $r-1$, r, $-r$ are not swapped in the first round of the KSA, respectively. In addition to it, it is required that $K[0] \notin \{1, 2, \ldots, r-2\}$, so that the value 0 at index $K[0]$ is not touched by these values of i^K during the next $r-2$ rounds of the KSA. This happens with probability of $\left(1 - \frac{r+1}{N}\right)$. From round 2 to $r-1$ of the KSA, $j_2^K, j_3^K, \ldots, j_{r-1}^K$ do not touch the three indices $\{r, -r, K[0]\}$, respectively. This happens with probability of $\left(1 - \frac{3}{N}\right)^{r-2}$. In the r-th round of the KSA, if the index j_r^K has the index $-r$, which happens with probability of $1/N$, the value $-r$ is swapped into the index $r-1$. In the $(r+1)$-th round of the KSA, when $i_{r+1}^K = r$ and $j_{r+1}^K = j_r^K + S_r^K[r] + K[r] = -r + r + K[0] = K[0]$, the value $S_r^K[r]$ is swapped for the value $S_r^K[K[0]]$, and from the above discussion, this index contains the value 0. Considering the above events to be independent, the probability that all of above events happen together is given by $\alpha_r = \frac{1}{N} \cdot \left(1 - \frac{3}{N}\right)^{r-2} \cdot \left(1 - \frac{r+1}{N}\right)$.

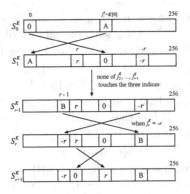

Fig. 12. Event for bias of $S_{r+1}^K[r-1] = -r \wedge S_{r+1}^K[r] = 0$

Assuming that in other cases, $(S_{r+1}^K[r-1] = -r \wedge S_{r+1}^K[r] = 0)$ holds with probability of $1/N^2$, the probability of $\Pr(S_{r+1}^K[r-1] = -r \wedge S_{r+1}^K[r] = 0)$ is estimated as

$$\Pr(S_{r+1}^K[r-1] = -r \wedge S_{r+1}^K[r] = 0) \approx \frac{1}{N^2} + \left(1 - \frac{1}{N^2}\right) \cdot \alpha_r.$$

$\square$

Figure 12 shows the major path of $S_{r+1}^K[r-1] = -r \wedge S_{r+1}^K[r] = 0$.

Theorem 11. *When $r = x \cdot \ell$ ($x = 1, 2, \ldots, 7$), the probability of $\Pr(Z_r = -r \wedge S_r[j_r] = 0)$ is approximately*

$$\Pr(Z_r = -r \wedge S_r[j_r] = 0) \approx \frac{1}{N^2} + \left(1 - \frac{1}{N^2}\right) \cdot \gamma_r,$$

where

$$\gamma_r = \frac{1}{N^2} \cdot \left(1 - \frac{r+1}{N}\right)$$
$$\cdot \sum_{y=r+1}^{N-1} \left(1 - \frac{1}{N}\right)^y \cdot \left(1 - \frac{2}{N}\right)^{y-r} \cdot \left(1 - \frac{3}{N}\right)^{N-y+2r-4}.$$

Proof. From the algorithm of the PRGA, we have $j_r = j_{r-1} + S_{r-1}[r]$. Hence, $S_r[j_r] = S_{r-1}[r] = 0$ implies $j_r = j_{r-1}$. In this case, an output Z_r is expressed as

$$Z_r = S_r[S_r[i_r] + S_r[j_r]] = S_r[S_{r-2}[r-1]].$$

Then, let us consider $\Pr(S_r[S_{r-2}[r-1]] = -r \wedge S_r[j_r] = 0)$.

The major path for the joint event $(S_{r+1}^K[r-1] = -r \wedge S_{r+1}^K[r] = 0)$ constitutes the first part of our main path leading to the target event. The second part can be constructed as follows. In an index $y \in [r + 1, N - 1]$, if the j^K do not touch the index y, we have $S_y^K[y] = y$ with probability of $\left(1 - \frac{1}{N}\right)^y$. From round $r + 2$ to y of the KSA, j^K do not touch the two indices $\{r - 1, r\}$, respectively. This happens with probability of $\left(1 - \frac{2}{N}\right)^{y-r-1}$. In the $(y + 1)$-th round of the KSA, if the index j_{y+1}^K has the index $r - 1$, which happens with probability of $1/N$, the value y is swapped for the value $-r$. Then, the value $-r$ moves to $S_{y+1}^K[y] = S_{y+1}^K[S_{y+1}^K[r - 1]]$. For the remaining $N - y - 1$ rounds of the KSA and for the first $r - 1$ rounds of the PRGA, the j^K or j values should not touch the indices $\{r - 1, S[r - 1], r\}$, respectively. This happens with probability of $\left(1 - \frac{3}{N}\right)^{N-y+r-2}$. Now, we have $(S_{r-1}[S_{r-2}[r - 1]] = -r \wedge S_{r-1}[r] = 0)$. And then, we should also have $j_r \notin \{r-1, y\}$ for $S_r[S_{r-2}[r-1]] = -r$. The probability of this condition is $\left(1 - \frac{2}{N}\right)$. Then, from algorithm of the PRGA, the output is $Z_r = S_r[S_{r-2}[r - 1]] = -r$. Considering the above events to be independent, the probability that the second part events happen together is given by

$$\alpha_r' = \frac{1}{N} \cdot \sum_{y=r+1}^{N-1} \left(1 - \frac{1}{N}\right)^y \cdot \left(1 - \frac{2}{N}\right)^{y-r} \cdot \left(1 - \frac{3}{N}\right)^{N-y+r-2}.$$

Then, the probability that all of the events happen together is estimated as

$$\gamma_r = \alpha_r \cdot \alpha_r'$$
$$= \frac{1}{N^2} \cdot \left(1 - \frac{r+1}{N}\right)$$
$$\cdot \sum_{y=r+1}^{N-1} \left(1 - \frac{1}{N}\right)^y \cdot \left(1 - \frac{2}{N}\right)^{y-r} \cdot \left(1 - \frac{3}{N}\right)^{N-y+2r-4}.$$

Assuming that in other cases, $Z_r = -r \wedge S_r[j_r] = 0$ holds with probability of $1/N^2$, the probability of $\Pr(Z_r = -r \wedge S_r[j_r] = 0)$ is approximately

$$\Pr(Z_r = -r \wedge S_r[j_r] = 0) \approx \frac{1}{N^2} + \left(1 - \frac{1}{N^2}\right) \cdot \gamma_r.$$

□

Figures 13, 14 show the major path of $Z_r = -r \wedge S_r[j_r] = 0$.
Using these extended joint events, the theorem 9 is proved as follows.

Proof. We can write $\Pr(Z_r = -r) = \Pr(Z_r = -r \wedge S_r[j_r] = 0) + \Pr(Z_r = -r \wedge S_r[j_r] \neq 0)$, where the first term is given by Theorem 11. When $S_r[j_r] \neq 0$, the event $Z_r = -r$ can be assumed to hold with probability of $1/N$. Then, the probability of $\Pr(Z_r = -r)$ is estimated as

$$\Pr(Z_r = -r) \approx \frac{1}{N^2} + \left(1 - \frac{1}{N^2}\right) \cdot \gamma_r + (1 - \delta_r) \cdot \frac{1}{N}.$$

□

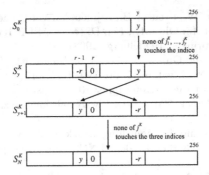

Fig. 13. Event for bias of $Z_r = -r \wedge S_r[j_r] = 0$ on KSA

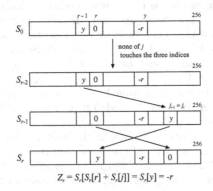

Fig. 14. Event for bias of $Z_r = -r \wedge S_r[j_r] = 0$ on PRGA

References

1. Biham, E., Carmeli, Y.: Efficient reconstruction of RC4 keys from internal states. In: Nyberg, K. (ed.) FSE 2008. LNCS, vol. 5086, pp. 270–288. Springer, Heidelberg (2008)
2. Canvel, B., Hiltgen, A.P., Vaudenay, S., Vuagnoux, M.: Password interception in a SSL/TLS channel. In: Boneh, D. (ed.) CRYPTO 2003. LNCS, vol. 2729, pp. 583–599. Springer, Heidelberg (2003)
3. Fluhrer, S.R., McGrew, D.A.: Statistical analysis of the alleged RC4 keystream generator. In: Schneier, B. (ed.) FSE 2000. LNCS, vol. 1978, p. 19. Springer, Heidelberg (2001)
4. Golić, J.D.: Linear statistical weakness of alleged RC4 keystream generator. In: Fumy, W. (ed.) EUROCRYPT 1997. LNCS, vol. 1233, pp. 226–238. Springer, Heidelberg (1997)
5. Sen Gupta, S., Maitra, S., Paul, G., Sarkar, S.: Proof of empirical RC4 biases and new key correlations. In: Miri, A., Vaudenay, S. (eds.) SAC 2011. LNCS, vol. 7118, pp. 151–168. Springer, Heidelberg (2012)
6. Sen Gupta, S., Maitra, S., Paul, G., Sarkar, S.: (Non-)random sequences from (Non-)random permutations - analysis of RC4 stream cipher. J. Cryptol **27**(1), 67–108 (2014). http://dblp.uni-trier.de/rec/bibtex/journals/joc/GuptaMPS14

7. Knudsen, L.R., Meier, W., Preneel, B., Rijmen, V., Verdoolaege, S.: Analysis methods for (alleged) RC4. In: Ohta, K., Pei, D. (eds.) ASIACRYPT 1998. LNCS, vol. 1514, pp. 327–341. Springer, Heidelberg (1998)

8. Maitra, S., Paul, G., Sen Gupta, S.: Attack on broadcast RC4 revisited. In: Joux, A. (ed.) FSE 2011. LNCS, vol. 6733, pp. 199–217. Springer, Heidelberg (2011)

9. Mantin, I.: Analysis of the stream cipher RC4. Master's Thesis, The Weizmann Institute of Science, Israel (2001). http://www.wisdom.weizmann.ac.il/itsik/RC4/rc4.html

10. Mantin, I.: Predicting and distinguishing attacks on RC4 keystream generator. In: Cramer, R. (ed.) EUROCRYPT 2005. LNCS, vol. 3494, pp. 491–506. Springer, Heidelberg (2005)

11. Mantin, I., Shamir, A.: A practical attack on broadcast RC4. In: Matsui, M. (ed.) FSE 2001. LNCS, vol. 2355, p. 152. Springer, Heidelberg (2002)

12. Matsui, M.: Key collisions of the RC4 stream cipher. In: Dunkelman, O. (ed.) FSE 2009. LNCS, vol. 5665, pp. 38–50. Springer, Heidelberg (2009)

13. Maximov, A., Khovratovich, D.: New state recovery attack on RC4. In: Wagner, D. (ed.) CRYPTO 2008. LNCS, vol. 5157, pp. 297–316. Springer, Heidelberg (2008)

14. Mironov, I.: (Not so) random shuffles of RC4. In: Yung, M. (ed.) CRYPTO 2002. LNCS, vol. 2442, pp. 304–319. Springer, Heidelberg (2002)

15. Paul, G., Maitra, S.: Permutation after RC4 key scheduling reveals the secret key. In: Adams, C., Miri, A., Wiener, M. (eds.) SAC 2007. LNCS, vol. 4876, pp. 360–377. Springer, Heidelberg (2007)

16. Paul, S., Preneel, B.: A new weakness in the RC4 keystream generator and an approach to improve the security of the cipher. In: Roy, B., Meier, W. (eds.) FSE 2004. LNCS, vol. 3017, pp. 245–259. Springer, Heidelberg (2004)

17. Sepehrdad, P., Vaudenay, S., Vuagnoux, M.: Discovery and exploitation of new biases in RC4. In: Biryukov, A., Gong, G., Stinson, D.R. (eds.) SAC 2010. LNCS, vol. 6544, pp. 74–91. Springer, Heidelberg (2011)

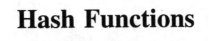

Hash Functions

Time-Memory Trade-Offs for Near-Collisions

Gaëtan Leurent[(✉)]

UCL Crypto Group, Louvain-la-Neuve, Belgium
Gaetan.Leurent@uclouvain.be

Abstract. In this work we consider generic algorithms to find near-collisions for a hash function. If we consider only hash computations, it is easy to compute a lower-bound for the complexity of near-collision algorithms, and to build a matching algorithm. However, this algorithm needs a lot of memory, and makes more than $2^{n/2}$ memory accesses. Recently, several algorithms have been proposed without this memory requirement; they require more hash evaluations, but the attack is actually more practical. They can be divided in two main categories: they are either based on truncation, or based on covering codes.

In this paper, we give a new insight to the generic complexity of a near-collision attack. First, we consider time-memory trade-offs for truncation-based algorithms. For a practical implementation, it seems reasonable to assume that *some* memory is available and we show that taking advantage of this memory can significantly reduce the complexity. Second, we show a new method combining truncation and covering codes. The new algorithm is always at least as good as the previous works, and often gives a significant improvement. We illustrate our results by giving a 10-near collision for MD5: our algorithm has a complexity of $2^{45.4}$ using $1\,\mathrm{TB}$ of memory while the best previous algorithm required $2^{52.5}$ computations.

Keywords: Hash function · Near-collision · Generic attack · Time-memory trade-off

1 Introduction

Hash functions are fundamental cryptographic primitives used in many constructions and protocols. A hash function takes a bitstring of arbitrary length as input, and outputs a digest, a small bitstring of fixed length n:

$$h : \{0,1\}^* \to \{0,1\}^n$$

When used in a cryptographic context, we expect a hash function to resist three major attacks:

Collision attack: Given h, find $x \neq x'$ s.t. $h(x) = h(x')$.
Second-preimage attack: Given h and x, find $x' \neq x$ s.t. $h(x) = h(x')$.
Preimage attack: Given h and $\overline{h}$, find x s.t. $h(x) = \overline{h}$.

S. Moriai (Ed.): FSE 2013, LNCS 8424, pp. 205–218, 2014.
DOI: 10.1007/978-3-662-43933-3_11, © Springer-Verlag Berlin Heidelberg 2014

Due to the birthday paradox, we have a generic collision attack with complexity $2^{n/2}$, while brute force preimage or second-preimage attacks have complexity 2^n: this defines the security requirements of an n-bit hash function.

More generally, we expect a hash function to behave *like a random function*. This requirement can not really be formalized but we expect that any property that can be shown on a given hash function should also be present on a random function.

In particular, we expect that it should be hard to find two messages resulting in a digest with a small difference. This property is called near-collision, and several attacks have been proposed in this setting recently [1–5].

It is relatively easy to give a lower bound on the complexity of near-collision attacks: one needs at least $2^{n/2}/\sqrt{\mathcal{B}_w(n)}$ hash function evaluation. However the only known way to reach this lower bound requires a lot of memory, and more than $2^{n/2}$ memory accesses. In order to bridge this gap, Lamberger *et al.* proposed a memory-less approach based on covering codes [6,7], with a complexity between $2^{n/2}$ and $2^{n/2}/\sqrt{\mathcal{B}_{w/2}(n)}$.

In this work, we revisit the problem of finding near-collisions with an algorithm that can be efficiently implemented in practice. We start from the observation that the machines used to run this kind of large computation (clusters, GPUs, or dedicated hardware) usually have a decent amount of memory readily available, or it can be added at a reasonable cost. Therefore, we do not aim for a *memory-less* algorithm, we only aim for an algorithm with a practical amount of memory, and a practical number of memory accesses. Our results show that we can indeed reach a lower complexity than the memory-less algorithms based on covering codes.

We first review previous collision and near-collision algorithms in Sect. 2. We describe the main idea of our time-memory trade-off applied to truncation-based algorithms in Sect. 3, and we describe a more general algorithm in Sect. 4 that includes previous algorithms as special cases.

We use the following notations through this paper:

n	Hash function output size;
t	Truncated output size;
w	Maximum distance for near-collisions;
M	Memory size (number of chains stored);
$\mathcal{B}_w(n)$	Size of a Hamming ball of radius w.

2   Previous Works

Let us first discuss techniques to find full collisions (i.e. $w = 0$). This allows to explain the basic techniques which will be used later to find near-collisions.

2.1   Finding Full Collisions

The basic approach to find collisions or near-collisions in a generic manner is to evaluate the hash function a large number of times on random inputs, and to compute the Hamming distance for each pair of outputs. After i evaluations of the hash function, one can test $i(i-1)/2$ pairs, and this birthday effect allows to find collisions with only $O(2^{n/2})$ evaluations of the hash function. More precisely, the expected number of computation required is $i = \sqrt{\pi/2} \cdot 2^{n/2}$ [8, Appendix A]. When looking for full collisions, instead of comparing each new output to all the previous ones, which require $\Omega(2^n)$ comparisons in total, one can create a list of all the outputs, and sort the list in time $O(n2^{n/2})$, or use a hash table to reduce the number of comparisons to $O(2^{n/2})$.

Memory-Less Algorithms. Even if we avoid the complexity of $\Omega(2^n)$ comparisons, the memory complexity of this simple approach makes it impractical. Several works have shown that collisions can be found with little or no memory, with a small increase in the time complexity. The main idea was introduced by Pollard as the "rho" algorithm for factorization [9] and discrete logarithms [10], and was later generalized to collision search. The hash function is first restricted from $\{0,1\}^* \to \{0,1\}^n$ to $\{0,1\}^n \to \{0,1\}^n$, so that it can be iterated. After some number of steps, a chain of iterations reaches a cycle, and the graph will have the shape of the greek letter "ρ". On average, the cycle has length $O(2^{n/2})$ and is reached after $O(2^{n/2})$ steps. The point where the tail of the ρ meets with the cycle gives a collision in the hash function. It can be detected in time $O(2^{n/2})$ with little or no memory, using various cycle detection methods, such as Floyd's algorithm [11], Brent's algorithm [12], using distinguished points [13], or several other techniques [14,15]. These techniques mostly differ by the memory requirements (constant or logarithmic), and the constant in the $O(\cdot)$ (between 1 and 3).

In this work we focus on the distinguished point approach because it can be efficiently parallelized, and our focus is on problems with a relatively large complexity. The complexity of finding collisions using distinguished points is analyzed in detail by van Oorschot and Wiener in [8]. The main step of the algorithm is to compute chains of iterations, starting from a random point, and stopping when a *distinguished* point is reached, with an easily recognized feature, such as a number of leading zeroes. The algorithm uses a table to store M such chains (i.e. starting points and ending points) and when the same ending point is seen twice, this most likely corresponds to a collision. To locate the collision, one has to run the computation again from the starting point.

The analysis of van Oorschot and Wiener considers two different situations, depending on i, the number of collision one is looking for. An important parameter in the analysis is the proportion of distinguished points θ.

Finding a small number of collisions i.e. $i \ll M$.
If we have enough memory to store all the chains, we can expect to find i collisions after a workload of $\Theta(\sqrt{2^n i})$, since this covers $\Theta(2^n i)$ pairs of points. More precisely, the complexity given by van Oorschot and Wiener[1] is $C_{small} = \sqrt{\pi/2} \cdot \sqrt{2^n i} + 2.5i/\theta$.

---

[1] In [8], the complexity is given as $\sqrt{\pi/2} \cdot \sqrt{2^n i} + 2.5/\theta$, but this only holds if i is smaller than the number of processors used in the attack.

We choose the distinguishing property so that the memory will just be filled at the end, but we try to avoid overwriting chains, so we use $\theta = M/C_{small}$. This results in $C_{small} = \sqrt{\pi/2} \cdot \sqrt{2^n i}/(1 - 2.5i/M)$. If $i \ll M$, this becomes:

$$C_{small} = \sqrt{\pi/2} \cdot \sqrt{2^n i}.$$

There is a speedup factor of $\sqrt{i}$ compared to finding i collisions independently.

Finding a large number of collisions i.e. $i \gg M$.
In this case, the memory will have to be overwritten. The analysis of [8] shows that when the memory is full, the complexity per collision is roughly $2^n \theta/M + 2/\theta$. This reaches a minimum of $\sqrt{8 \cdot 2^n/M}$ for $\theta = \sqrt{2M/2^n}$. More precisely, van Oorschot and Wiener performed experiments to determine the actual constants, and the optimal complexity, reached with when $\theta = 2.25\sqrt{M/2^n}$, is:

$$C_{large} \approx 5\sqrt{2^n/M} \cdot i.$$

There is a speedup factor of $\sqrt{M}/4$ compared to finding i collisions independently.

Global Bound. More generally, we can express an upper bound on the complexity that works in both situations by summing the two expressions:

$$C \leq \left(\sqrt{\frac{\pi}{2}} + 5\sqrt{\frac{i}{M}} \right) \sqrt{2^n i}. \tag{1}$$

When $i \ll M$ or $i \gg M$, one term is negligible, and this expression is equivalent to C_{small} or C_{large}, respectively. Moreover, we verified experimentally that this is also an upper bound when $i \approx M$, and the bound is relatively tight. In all cases, there is a linear speedup when using several machines in parallel (see [8] for full details).

2.2   Near-Collisions

A w-near-collision is a pair of messages x, x' such that $\|h(x) \oplus h(x')\| \leq w$, where $\| \cdot \|$ is the Hamming weight. Let us first introduce some results regarding the Hamming distance.

Definition 1. *We denote the size of a Hamming ball of radius w by*
$$\mathcal{B}_w(n) = \# \{x \in \{0,1\}^n : \|x\| \leq w\}.$$

Property 1. We have $\mathcal{B}_w(n) = \sum_{i=0}^{w} \binom{n}{i}$.

Property 2. The probability that a random pair x, x' results in a w-near-collisions is $\mathcal{B}_w(n)/2^n$.

Property 3. We have the following relation: $\mathcal{B}_w(n) = \mathcal{B}_w(n-1) + \mathcal{B}_{w-1}(n-1)$.

Lemma 1. *We have the following inequality:*

$$\mathcal{B}_{w-1}(x) \le \binom{x}{w} \frac{w}{x - 2w + 1}$$

Proof. (following [16])

$$\frac{\mathcal{B}_{w-1}(x)}{\binom{x}{w}} = \frac{\binom{x}{w-1} + \binom{x}{w-2} + \binom{x}{w-3} + \cdots}{\binom{x}{w}}$$

$$= \frac{w}{x - w + 1} + \frac{w(w-1)}{(x - w + 1)(x - w + 2)} + \cdots$$

$$\le \frac{w}{x - w + 1} + \left(\frac{w}{x - w + 1}\right)^2 + \cdots$$

$$\le \frac{\frac{w}{x-w+1}}{1 - \frac{w}{x-w+1}} = \frac{w}{x - 2w + 1} \quad \text{using the sum of a geometric series} \quad \square$$

We can now describe algorithms for near-collision attacks.

Memory-Full Algorithm. The obvious method to find near-collisions is to evaluate the hash function a large number of times on random inputs, and to compute the Hamming distance between each pair of outputs. After i evaluations of the hash function, one can test $i(i-1)/2$ pairs, and a pair gives a w-near-collision with probability $\mathcal{B}_w(n)/2^n$. The expected number of hash function computations before finding a near-collision is $i = \sqrt{\pi/2 \cdot 2^n/\mathcal{B}_w(n)}$. This also gives a lower bound on the number of hash evaluations needed for any near-collision algorithm: we need at least $\sqrt{\pi/2 \cdot 2^n/\mathcal{B}_w(n)}$ evaluations in order to have a w-near-collision with a non-negligible probability.

However, this simple approach requires $i \cdot \mathcal{B}_w(n) = \Omega(\sqrt{2^n \cdot \mathcal{B}_w(n)})$ memory access to a table of size $i = \Omega(\sqrt{2^n/\mathcal{B}_w(n)})$, because for every new point, we must check whether a point at distance less than w was reached previously. As opposed to a collision attack, we can not reduce this complexity using a sorting algorithm, a hash table, or chain of iterations; for any practical implementation, this will in fact be the bottleneck. This leads to the study of techniques to find near-collision without this huge memory complexity. Two categories of algorithms have proposed recently to solve this problem by reducing it to finding collision in a related function (which can done in a memory-less way).

Using Collisions in a Truncated Hash Function. A simple approach is to look for collisions in a truncated version of the hash function. In the simplest case, the hash function is truncated to $t = n-w$ bits, and any collision in the truncated version will give a w-near-collision for the full hash function. More interestingly, if the hash function is truncated to $t = n - 2w - 1$ bits, a t-bit collision will give a w-near-collision of the full hash function with probability $1/2$ [7]. This gives a near-collision algorithm with expected complexity $\sqrt{\pi/2} \cdot 2^{(n-2w)/2}$ using a memory-less collision finding algorithm on the truncated function.

This can be represented as:

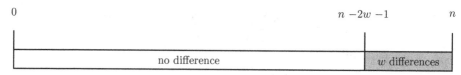

More generally, one can truncate τ bits, find collisions in a $n - \tau$-bit function, and check the Hamming weight of the τ truncated bits. This will give a w-near-collision with probability $\mathcal{B}_w(\tau)/2^\tau$. The optimal value of τ can be found by evaluating the complexity for all choices of τ. This problem is discussed more formally in [17].

Using Covering Codes. A more efficient approach is to use covering codes, as proposed by Lamberger *et al.* [6,7]. The idea is to use a covering code with radius $w/2$, i.e. a set of codewords $\mathcal{C}$ such that for any point $x \in \{0,1\}^n$, there exists a codeword $c(x) \in \mathcal{C}$ with $\|x \oplus c(x)\| \leq w/2$. If the decoding function c is efficient, we can look for collisions in $c \circ h$. If $c(h(x)) = c(h(x'))$, then $h(x)$ and $h(x')$ are decoded to the same codeword c; we have $\|h(x') \oplus h(x)\| \leq \|h(x') \oplus c\| + \|h(x) \oplus c\| \leq w$, which gives a w-near-collision. With a code of dimension k, the attack has a complexity of $\sqrt{\pi/2} \cdot 2^{k/2}$.

This can be represented as:

$$0 \hspace{10cm} n$$

$$\boxed{w = 2R \text{ differences}}$$

Finding the optimal k and building a corresponding code is a hard problem. The sphere covering bound shows that $2^k \geq 2^n/\mathcal{B}_{w/2}(n)$, but there is a gap between the best known codes and this lower bound. This problem is discussed by Lamberger *et al.* in the context of near-collision attacks [6,7] using a concatenation of Hamming codes. With a given length n, and a covering radius of $R = w/2$, the optimal code following their construction has a dimension:

$$k = n - R \cdot \ell - r \tag{2}$$

where $\ell := \lfloor \log_2\left(\frac{n}{R} + 1\right) \rfloor$ and $r := \lfloor \frac{n - R(2^\ell - 1)}{2^\ell} \rfloor$.

This result is listed in Table 2 for some relevant values of the parameters, together with the lower bound implied by the sphere covering bound.

3   Time-Memory Trade-Off with Truncation

Our first algorithm is a simple generalization of the truncation based method described in Sect. 2.2. We observe that if we truncate τ bits with $\tau > 2w - 1$, the probability that a collision in the truncated function is a near-collision of the full hash function decreases rapidly, and we need to find many collisions. In a truly memory-less approach, finding i such collisions require $\sqrt{\pi/2} \cdot \sqrt{2^{n-\tau}} \cdot i$ computations, and there is little to gain by truncating more than $2w - 1$ bits[2] However, with some memory, this can be significantly reduced — by a factor $\sqrt{i}$ if $M \gg i$, or $\sqrt{M}/4$ if $M \ll i$, as detailed in Sect. 2.1.

In the following section, we explore this idea, and study the optimal value of τ and the complexity of the resulting attack, depending on how much memory is available. In a practical implementation of a near-collision attack, it seems reasonable to assume that *some* memory is available, and we show that this leads to significantly better attacks.

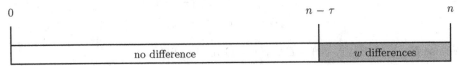

3.1   Complexity

Our algorithm is quite simple: we truncate τ bits of the hash function, and we look for collisions for the remaining $n - \tau$ bits. For each $n - \tau$-bit collision, we compute the Hamming distance in the truncated τ bits. We expect to find a w-near-collision after testing $i = 2^{\tau}/\mathcal{B}_w(\tau)$ collisions.

We observe that $i(\tau)$ is monotonically increasing since $\mathcal{B}_w(\tau) = \mathcal{B}_w(\tau - 1) + \mathcal{B}_{w-1}(\tau - 1) < 2\mathcal{B}_w(\tau - 1)$. With a small τ, we only need a small number of collision, but the collisions are harder to find because the number of non-truncated bit, $n - \tau$ is large. In order to find the best trade-off, we need an accurate evaluation of the complexity of the algorithm, depending on the value of τ and M. We use the analysis of van Oorschot and Wiener [8], as recalled in Sect. 2.1.

3.2   Finding Optimal Parameters

In order to find an algebraic characterization of the optimal τ, we follow the analysis of Sect. 2.1, and we consider two cases for the complexity, depending on the relationship between i and M.

Small τ, small number of collisions i.e. $2^{\tau}/\mathcal{B}_w(\tau) \ll M$
The complexity is

$$C_{small} = \sqrt{\pi/2} \cdot \sqrt{2^{n-\tau} \cdot 2^{\tau}/\mathcal{B}_w(\tau)} = \sqrt{\pi/2} \cdot 2^{n/2}/\sqrt{\mathcal{B}_w(\tau)}.$$

This decreases when τ grows.

---

[2] As shown in [17], the minimal complexity is achieved with $\tau \sim (2 + \sqrt{2})(w - 1)$.

Large τ, large number of collisions i.e. $2^\tau/\mathcal{B}_w(\tau) \gg M$ The complexity is

$$C_{large} = \frac{5\sqrt{2^{n-\tau}/M} \cdot 2^\tau}{\mathcal{B}_w(\tau)} = \frac{5 \cdot 2^{n/2+\tau/2}}{\mathcal{B}_w(\tau)\sqrt{M}}.$$

For most useful values of the parameters, this complexity is increasing when τ grows. More precisely, we prove that C_{large} is increasing when $\tau \geq (\sqrt{2}+2)w$:

$$C_{large} \text{ is increasing} \iff \frac{C_{large}(\tau-1)}{C_{large}(\tau)} \leq 1$$

$$\iff \frac{\mathcal{B}_w(\tau)}{\mathcal{B}_w(\tau-1)} \leq \sqrt{2}$$

We use $\mathcal{B}_w(\tau) = \mathcal{B}_w(\tau-1) + \mathcal{B}_{w-1}(\tau-1)$ to simplify:

$$\iff \frac{\mathcal{B}_w(\tau-1) + \mathcal{B}_{w-1}(\tau-1)}{\mathcal{B}_w(\tau-1)} \leq \sqrt{2}$$

$$\iff \frac{\mathcal{B}_{w-1}(\tau-1)}{\mathcal{B}_w(\tau-1)} \leq \sqrt{2}-1$$

$$\iff \frac{\mathcal{B}_w(\tau-1)}{\mathcal{B}_{w-1}(\tau-1)} \geq \sqrt{2}+1$$

We use $\mathcal{B}_w(\tau-1) = \binom{\tau-1}{w} + \mathcal{B}_{w-1}(\tau-1)$ to further simplify:

$$\iff \frac{\binom{\tau-1}{w} + \mathcal{B}_{w-1}(\tau-1)}{\mathcal{B}_{w-1}(\tau-1)} \geq \sqrt{2}+1$$

$$\iff \frac{\binom{\tau-1}{w}}{\mathcal{B}_{w-1}(\tau-1)} \geq \sqrt{2}$$

Using Lemma 1, we have $\binom{\tau-1}{w}/\mathcal{B}_{w-1}(\tau-1) \geq \frac{\tau-2w}{w}$. When $\tau \geq (\sqrt{2}+2)w$, this gives $\binom{\tau-1}{w}/\mathcal{B}_{w-1}(\tau-1) \geq \sqrt{2}$, and $C_{large}(\tau)$ is increasing. Note that this formula only makes sense when $M \ll 2^\tau/\mathcal{B}_w(\tau)$, i.e. for large values of τ, and the assumption that $\tau \geq (\sqrt{2}+2)w$ will be true in this domain for useful values of the parameters. In particular it is true as soon as $M > 2^{24}$ and $w < 48$.

Optimal τ. When τ is small i.e. $2^\tau/\mathcal{B}_w(\tau) \ll M$, the complexity decreases with τ, but when τ is large, i.e. $2^\tau/\mathcal{B}_w(\tau) \gg M$, it increases with τ. This proves that the optimal choice of τ satisfies

$$2^\tau/\mathcal{B}_w(\tau) \approx M.$$

For this value of τ, the two expressions C_{small} and C_{large} are equal up to a small constant[3], and the complexity is given by

$$C \approx 2^{n/2}/\sqrt{\mathcal{B}_w(\tau)}.$$

This is larger than the optimal complexity reached by the memory-full algorithm of $2^{n/2}/\sqrt{\mathcal{B}_w(n)}$, but for most parameters, it is better than the bound of $2^{n/2}/\sqrt{\mathcal{B}_{w/2}(n)}$ which limits covering-code based algorithms.

Optimal τ in Practice. For given values of n and w, we can find a better estimation of the optimal τ. We use the upper bound of (1), which gives the following upper bound on the complexity:

$$C \leq C_{small} + C_{large} = \left(\sqrt{\frac{\pi}{2}} + 5\sqrt{\frac{2^\tau/\mathcal{B}_w(\tau)}{M}}\right) \cdot \sqrt{\frac{2^n}{\mathcal{B}_w(\tau)}}.$$

To find a good trade-off, we evaluate this bound for all values of τ, and we use the τ that gives the lowest bound. Our experiments show that the upper bound is quite tight, and the τ found in this way is optimal or almost optimal.

4   Combining Truncation and Covering Codes

We can build a better algorithm by combining the truncation approach with the covering-code technique. When we truncate the hash function to $n - \tau$ bits, instead of looking for collisions in the truncated function, we can look for near-collisions using a covering code. More precisely, we use a covering code of radius R, to find $2R$-near-collisions in the truncated hash function. Then we check if one of the near-collisions have less than $w - 2R$ active bits in the truncated part. This approach covers both the truncation based techniques (when $R = 0$), and the previous covering-code based techniques (when $\tau = 0$ and $R = w/2$). This is described by Algorithm 1, and can be represent by the following diagram:

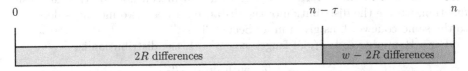

If we use a covering code of dimension k, length $n - \tau$, and radius R, we will have near-collisions with a distance of $2R$. Using the same ideas as in the previous section, we use a time-memory trade-off to find a large number of near-collisions; we can find i near-collisions for a cost of roughly $\sqrt{2^k i}$ if $i \ll M$ or $\sqrt{2^k/M} \cdot i$ if $i \gg M$. On average, we need $i = 2^\tau/\mathcal{B}_{w-2R}(\tau)$ $2R$-near-collisions.

---

[3] Like in Sect. 2.1, the complexity is in fact continuous.

Algorithm 1. Find near-collisions

Input: h, n, w
Parameter: τ, R, k
    Let c be the decoding function of a covering code $[n - \tau, k, R]$
    repeat
        Find a collision x, x' for $c \circ \mathsf{Trunc}_{n-\tau} \circ h$
        ▷ This implies $\|\mathsf{Trunc}_{n-\tau}(h(x)) \oplus \mathsf{Trunc}_{n-\tau}(h(x'))\| \le 2R$
    until $\|h(x) \oplus h(x')\| \le w$

Like in the previous section, we use the bound of (1) to evaluate the complexity of the attack:

$$C \le \left(\sqrt{\frac{\pi}{2}} + 5\sqrt{\frac{2^\tau / \mathcal{B}_{w-2R}(\tau)}{M}} \right) \sqrt{\frac{2^k \cdot 2^\tau}{\mathcal{B}_{w-2R}(\tau)}}$$

It seems quite hard to give of close formula of the optimal choice of R and τ for a given n, w and M. In particular, we note that k is a function of R and τ. However, it is easy to find the optimal parameters by trying all the possibilities for R and τ, and evaluating the resulting complexity using (2) to compute the optimal k. We give the optimal parameters for several cases in Table 2.

Like in the previous section, we observe that the best parameters usually satisfy $2^\tau / \mathcal{B}_w(\tau) \approx M$. Moreover, we note that for many parameters, the optimal choice gives $R = 0$ and we just have a truncation-based attack without any covering code. The covering codes allow to improve the complexity only for large values of n or small values of M.

4.1   Improved Analysis

In the previous analysis, we only consider near-collisions with less than $w - 2R$ active bits in the truncated part. However, the algorithm can find w-near-collisions with more active bits in the truncated part if the distance in the remaining part is strictly smaller than $2R$. In order to compute the probability that a collision in the covering code gives a w-near-collision for the full hash function, we use the distribution of the distance between two messages decoded to the same codeword, as given in [6, Sect. 3.6].

For a Hamming code $\mathcal{H}_r$ of length $n = 2^r - 1$, the distribution is:

$$d(y, y') = \begin{cases} 0 & \text{with prob. } \frac{n+1}{(n+1)^2} \\ 1 & \text{with prob. } \frac{2n}{(n+1)^2} \\ 2 & \text{with prob. } \frac{n(n-1)}{(n+1)^2}. \end{cases}$$

The covering codes used in [6,7] are built as the direct sum of several Hamming codes, and we can compute the distribution of their distance as a convolution of the distribution for a Hamming code. For the truncation, the distribution is

$$d(y, y') = \begin{cases} 0 & \text{with prob. } 1/2^\tau \\ i & \text{with prob. } \binom{\tau}{i}/2^\tau \end{cases}$$

This allows to compute accurately the probability that a collision in the covering code is a near-collision for the hash function. The complexity will still be given by

$$C \leq \left(\sqrt{\frac{\pi}{2}} + 5\sqrt{\frac{i}{M}} \right) \sqrt{2^k \cdot i}$$

but we compute i from the distribution instead of using $i = 2^\tau/\mathcal{B}_{w-2R}(\tau)$. In addition, we can now consider a radius R larger than $w/2$, as suggested in [6]. In this case, most collisions in the covering code will have a distance larger than w, but the time-memory trade-off reduces the cost of finding many collisions.

4.2 Application

Our final algorithm described in Algorithm 1 is quite general, and the behavior will be very different depending on the parameters R and τ. We don't see how to analyze the optimal choice of parameters, but for a given value of n, w and M, we can just evaluate the complexity for all values of the parameters R and τ and select the best ones.

We give the complexity of our algorithm for some values of n, w and M in Table 2, and we provide code to find the optimal parameters in Listing 1 using Sage [18]. We compare several possible trade-offs with previous approaches: the simple memory-full algorithm, the covering code algorithm of [6,7] and the corresponding lower bound, and the simple truncation of $2w-1$ bits. With reasonable amounts of memory, our approach can lead to a significant improvement in the complexity.

We note that the number of memory accesses is relatively limited (in the order of M). The communication cost should not be a bottleneck for a practical implementation. Additionally, the memory does not need to be in a single machine, it can be distributed over the computing nodes. Like previous algorithms, our algorithm scales linearly when using more than one processor. Moreover, it should be noted that even the memory-less algorithms actually need some memory for an efficient parallel implementation.

We implemented this algorithm to verify that it behaves as expected, and we give a 10-near-collision for MD5 in Table 1.

Table 1. 10-near collision for MD5. This was found after a 20 h computation using 1 TB of memory, and 152 cores.

x	x'	$x \oplus x'$
b6 24 ac c6 40 94 08 84	0d 87 0f a4 00 4b 6c bf	bb a3 a3 62 40 df 64 3b
00 00 00 00 00 00 00 00	00 00 00 00 00 00 00 00	00 00 00 00 00 00 00 00
MD5(x)	MD5(x')	MD5(x) $\oplus$ MD5(x')
ac 6b 49 aa fe 42 4f f8	68 79 db a8 fe 52 4f f8	c4 12 92 02 00 10 00 00
8a c9 5d f6 ef 4f 7b 3d	8a c9 5d f6 ef 4f 7b 3d	00 00 00 00 00 00 00 00

Listing 1. Sage code to compute the complexity of a generic near-collision attack.

```
@CachedFunction
def covering_k(n,R):
    if R = = 0:
        return n
    l = floor(log(n/R+1)/log(2))
    r = floor((n-R*(2^l-1))/2^l)
    return n - R*l - r

@CachedFunction
def covering_dist(n,R):
    if R = = 0:
        return [1]
    l = floor(log(n/R+1)/log(2))
    r = floor((n-R*(2^l-1))/2^l)
    d = [1]
    m = 2^l
    for i in [1..R-r]:
        d = convolution(d, [m/m^2,(2*m-2)/m^2,((m-1)*(m-2))/m^2])
    m = 2^(l+1)
    for i in [1..r]:
        d = convolution(d, [m/m^2,(2*m-2)/m^2,((m-1)*(m-2))/m^2])
    return d

@CachedFunction
def binomial_dist(n):
    return [ binomial(n,i)/2^n for i in [0..n] ]

@CachedFunction
def prob_dist(n,t,R):
    return convolution(binomial_dist(t),covering_dist(n-t,R))

def near_complexity(n,mem,maxw):
    best = n
    for t in [0..n]:
        for R in [0..2*maxw]:
            K = prob_dist(n,t,R)
            p = sum(K[0:maxw+1])
            C = (sqrt(pi/2)+5*sqrt(1/p/2^mem)) \
                * sqrt(2^covering_k(n-t,R)/p)
            C = float(log(C)/log(2))
            if C < best:
                best = C
                bestr = R
                bestt = t
        print "Compexity: %.1f (\\tau = %i, R = %i)" \
            % (best , bestt , bestr )
            return best
```

Table 2. Comparison of various approaches: $\log_2$ of the number of hash computations. We omit a factor $\sqrt{\pi/2}$ so that birthday search is listed as $2^{n/2}$.

	M-Full[a]	Time-memory trade-off (τ, R)			Covering codes		Trunc.
128 bits		2^{16} (1 MB)	2^{26} (1 GB)	2^{36} (1 TB)	Bound[b]	[7,8]	$\tau=2w-1$
$w=2$	57.5	60.5 (1,1)	60.0 (25,0)	59.5 (35,0)	60.5	60.5	62.0
$w=4$	52.3	57.6 (17,1)	56.5 (27,1)	55.6 (44,0)	57.5	58.0	60.0
$w=6$	47.8	54.5 (19,2)	53.1 (35,1)	52.0 (46,1)	54.8	56.0	58.0
$w=8$	43.8	51.6 (26,2)	49.8 (43,1)	48.5 (54,1)	52.3	54.0	56.0
$w=10$	40.1	48.7 (33,2)	46.7 (50,1)	45.2 (62,1)	50.0	52.5	54.0
160 bits		2^{16} (1 MB)	2^{26} (1 GB)	2^{36} (1 TB)			
$w=2$	73.2	76.5 (5,1)	76.0 (17,1)	75.5 (35,0)	76.3	76.5	78.0
$w=4$	67.7	73.2 (16,1)	72.2 (26,1)	71.6 (33,1)	73.2	74.0	76.0
$w=6$	62.8	70.2 (24,1)	68.8 (33,1)	68.0 (46,1)	70.3	71.5	74.0
$w=8$	58.5	67.3 (31,1)	65.7 (34,2)	64.5 (54,1)	67.7	69.5	72.0
$w=10$	54.4	64.4 (33,2)	62.7 (45,2)	61.2 (62,1)	65.2	67.5	70.0
512 bits		2^{26} (1 GB)	2^{36} (1 TB)	2^{46} (1 PB)			
$w=2$	247.5	251.5 (2,2)	251.4 (26,1)	251.1 (36,1)	251.5	251.5	254.0
$w=4$	240.3	247.7 (3,4)	247.2 (29,2)	246.7 (39,2)	247.5	248.0	252.0
$w=6$	233.8	244.0 (27,2)	243.2 (38,2)	242.6 (49,2)	243.8	245.0	250.0
$w=8$	227.7	240.5 (23,4)	239.6 (46,2)	238.7 (57,2)	240.3	242.0	248.0
$w=10$	221.9	237.1 (30,4)	236.0 (42,4)	235.0 (65,2)	237.0	239.5	246.0

[a] Number of hash function evaluation needed. The actual complexity is dominated by memory accesses (more than $2^{n/2}$ accesses to a huge table).
[b] Lower bound for covering code approaches (van Wee bound).

5   Conclusion

In this work we present a new generic algorithm to find near-collision, that generalizes both the previous truncation-based algorithms, and the previous covering-code based algorithms. As opposed to previous work, we don't aim for a memory-less algorithm, but we study time-memory trade-offs. The algorithm has been implemented in practice, and we give actual complexity figures including the constants hidden in the analysis.

We show that with a practical amount of memory, this allows to select better parameters than previous works; in most cases we achieve a complexity lower than the sphere covering bound which limits the previous memory-less covering-code based algorithms. The main advantage comes from the parallel collision search algorithm of van Oorschot and Wiener, which can find i collisions in time significantly less than $\sqrt{2^n} \cdot i$ when using some memory.

Acknowledgment. The author is supported by the ERC project CRASH. Part of this work was done while the author was at the university of Luxembourg, supported by the AFR grant PDR-10-022 of the FNR. Experiments presented in this paper were carried out using the HPC facility of the University of Luxembourg.

References

1. Leurent, G., Thomsen, S.S.: Practical near-collisions on the compression function of BMW. In: [19], pp. 238–251
2. Jean, J., Fouque, P.A.: Practical near-collisions and collisions on round-reduced ECHO-256 compression function. In: [19], pp. 107–127
3. Su, B., Wu, W., Wu, S., Dong, L.: Near-collisions on the reduced-round compression functions of skein and BLAKE. In: Heng, S.-H., Wright, R.N., Goi, B.-M. (eds.) CANS 2010. LNCS, vol. 6467, pp. 124–139. Springer, Heidelberg (2010)
4. Kelsey, J., Lucks, S.: Collisions and near-collisions for reduced-round tiger. In: Robshaw, M. (ed.) FSE 2006. LNCS, vol. 4047, pp. 111–125. Springer, Heidelberg (2006)
5. Biham, E., Chen, R.: Near-collisions of SHA-0. In: Franklin, M. (ed.) CRYPTO 2004. LNCS, vol. 3152, pp. 290–305. Springer, Heidelberg (2004)
6. Lamberger, M., Mendel, F., Rijmen, V., Simoens, K.: Memoryless near-collisions via coding theory. Des. Codes Crypt. **62**(1), 1–18 (2012)
7. Lamberger, M., Rijmen, V.: Optimal covering codes for finding near-collisions. In: Biryukov, A., Gong, G., Stinson, D.R. (eds.) SAC 2010. LNCS, vol. 6544, pp. 187–197. Springer, Heidelberg (2011)
8. van Oorschot, P.C., Wiener, M.J.: Parallel collision search with cryptanalytic applications. J. Crypt. **12**(1), 1–28 (1999)
9. Pollard, J.: A monte carlo method for factorization. BIT Numer. Math. **15**(3), 331–334 (1975)
10. Pollard, J.: Monte carlo methods for index computation (mod p). Math. Comput. **32**(143), 918–924 (1978)
11. Knuth, D.: Seminumerical Algorithms. The Art of Computer Programming, vol. 2. Addison-Wesley, Reading (1981)
12. Brent, R.: An improved monte carlo factorization algorithm. BIT Numer. Math. **20**(2), 176–184 (1980)
13. Quisquater, J.-J., Delescaille, J.-P.: How easy is collision search. New results and applications to DES. In: Brassard, G. (ed.) CRYPTO 1989. LNCS, vol. 435, pp. 408–413. Springer, Heidelberg (1990)
14. Sedgewick, R., Szymanski, T., Yao, A.: The complexity of finding cycles in periodic functions. SIAM J. Comput. **11**, 376 (1982)
15. Nivasch, G.: Cycle detection using a stack. Inf. Process. Lett. **90**(3), 135–140 (2004)
16. Lugo, M.: Sum of "the first k" binomial coefficients for fixed n. (MathOverflow). http://mathoverflow.net/questions/17236 (version: 2010-03-05)
17. Lamberger, M., Teufl, E.: Memoryless near-collisions, revisited. Inf. Process. Lett. **113**(3), 60–66 (2013)
18. Stein, W., et al.: Sage Mathematics Software (Version 5.7). The Sage Development Team (2013). http://www.sagemath.org
19. Joux, A. (ed.): FSE 2011. LNCS, vol. 6733. Springer, Heidelberg (2011)

Collision Attacks on Up to 5 Rounds of SHA-3 Using Generalized Internal Differentials

Itai Dinur[1]([⊠]), Orr Dunkelman[1,2], and Adi Shamir[1]

[1] Computer Science Department, The Weizmann Institute, Rehovot, Israel
{itaid,adi.shamir}@weizmann.ac.il
[2] Computer Science Department, University of Haifa, Haifa, Israel
orrd@cs.haifa.ac.il

Abstract. On October 2-nd 2012 NIST announced its selection of the Keccak scheme as the new SHA-3 hash standard. In this paper we present the first published collision finding attacks on reduced-round versions of Keccak-384 and Keccak-512, providing actual collisions for 3-round versions, and describing an attack which is 2^{45} times faster than birthday attacks for 4-round Keccak-384. For Keccak-256, we increase the number of rounds which can be attacked to 5. All these results are based on a generalized *internal differential attack* (introduced by Peyrin at Crypto 2010), and use it to map a large number of Keccak inputs into a relatively small subset of possible outputs with a surprisingly large probability. In such a *squeeze attack* it is easier to find random collisions in the reduced target subset by a standard birthday argument.

Keywords: Hash function · Cryptanalysis · SHA-3 · Keccak · Collisions · Internal differentials · Squeeze attack

1 Introduction

One of the stated reasons for the recent selection of Keccak by NIST as the new SHA-3 hash standard was its exceptional resistance to cryptanalytic attacks [9]. Even though it was a prime target for several years and many cryptanalysts have tried to break it (see [1,2,4,8,10,12–14,16,20,21]), there was very limited progress so far in finding collisions even in greatly simplified versions of its various flavors. In particular, there were no published collision finding attacks *on any number of rounds* of its two largest flavors (Keccak-384 and Keccak-512), and only three published collision finding attacks on Keccak-256 ([16,21] attacked two rounds, and [12] doubled the number of rounds to 4). One of the main reasons for this lack of progress is that the probabilities of the standard differential characteristics of Keccak's internal permutation are extremely small, as was rigorously shown in [10]. We bypass this seemingly insurmountable barrier by using

---

The second author was supported in part by the Israel Science Foundation through grant No. 827/12.

S. Moriai (Ed.): FSE 2013, LNCS 8424, pp. 219–240, 2014.
DOI: 10.1007/978-3-662-43933-3_12, © Springer-Verlag Berlin Heidelberg 2014

a different kind of differential property, whose probability is not bounded by such a proof.[1] By using the new property, we provide in this paper either the first or an improved attack on all these flavors: For Keccak-384 and Keccak-512 we describe practical attacks (with actual collisions) on three rounds, and impractical attacks on four rounds of Keccak-384. For Keccak-256 we increase the number of rounds which can be attacked from 4 to 5. The previous collision attacks and our new results are summarized in Table 1.

Table 1. Collision attacks on round-reduced Keccak: the number of rounds attacked with the corresponding time complexity in parentheses

Reference	Keccak-224	Keccak-256	Keccak-384	Keccak-512
[16,21]	2 (practical)	2 (practical)	-	-
[12]	4 (practical)	4 (practical)	-	-
This paper	-	5 (2^{115})	3 (practical) 4 (2^{147})	3 (practical)

Our new attacks use many ideas which were already known in some limited form, but improves and combines them in new ways. They are a special type of the very general notion of *subset cryptanalysis*, which tries to track the statistical evolution of a certain set of values (which could be single states, pairs of states, or a collection of states with "don't care parts") through the various operations in the cryptographic scheme. In general, the goal in subset cryptanalysis is to find a subset of inputs which are mapped with larger than expected probability to some pre-fixed subset of all possible outputs. This is a widely used technique, which includes as special cases most of our standard cryptanalytic attacks, including differential, integral, and linear attacks, both in the single key and in the related key cases. The first step in subset cryptanalysis is to construct a *subset characteristic* which associates a triplet (input subset, output subset, transition probability) to each internal operation f of the cryptosystem. The transition probability specifies the probability that a random state chosen from the input subset will be a member of the output subset after applying f. Based on standard randomness assumptions, the total probability of the characteristic is calculated by multiplying the various transition probabilities. Subset cryptanalysis is typically used in order to construct a distinguisher, which makes it possible to extract information about the last subkey of a cryptosystem.

Previous examples of subset cryptanalysis include partitioning cryptanalysis [15] which divides the plaintext space and the output space (or the one-before the last round value space) into sets which are related with non-trivial probabilities. Other works track the development of the "subset" through the cryptographic primitive by looking for invariants, e.g., fixed-points or fixed subsets. For example, in [19] a subset of invariant values under the encryption process

---

[1] While we do not actually go beyond the bound mentioned in [10], its proof does not apply to the type of differential properties we consider in this paper.

(in weak key classes) in PRINTcipher are identified. Another example is the subset of special states identified in [18] which contains states whose left half is equal to the right half, and is an invariant of the encryption under keyless AES. We also note the close relationship between our approach and many of the self-similarity properties identified over the years. Slide attacks [6] (as well as the original flavor of related-key attacks [5]) is built over pairs of plaintexts which are shifted versions of each other in the encryption process. In many cases (e.g., Feistel ciphers), it is easy to rewrite the slide requirement as a relation between the slid pairs by defining the subsets according to the slid relation.

Squeeze Attacks. In the case of hash functions, we can use subset characteristic in a different way, which we call a *squeeze attack*. To motivate this attack, assume that the hash function maps a set S of possible inputs into a set D of possible outputs. By the birthday paradox, we have to try a subset $S' \subseteq S$ of size $\sqrt{|D|}$ of inputs before we expect to find the first collision in D. Consider now the variant of this attack in which we discard all the outputs we generate which do not fall into a particular subset $D' \subseteq D$. Since D' is smaller than D we need fewer samples in it in order to find a collision, but finding each sample is more expensive. To find which effect is stronger, assume that the probability of picking an input in S' whose output is in D' is p, and that D' contains a fraction q of the points in D. The number of outputs in D' we need is $\sqrt{|D'|} = \sqrt{q|D|}$, and the number of inputs in S' we have to try is $\sqrt{q|D|}/p$. When the mapping is random, $p = q$ and this variant of the attack is worse than the birthday bound for all D' which are smaller than D. However, if we can exploit some non-random behavior of the hash function in order to find sets S' and D' for which $p^2 > q$, we can get an improved collision finding algorithm. We call it a squeeze attack since we are forcing a larger than expected number of inputs to squeeze into a smaller subset of possible outputs in which collisions are more likely. By memorizing only such outputs and discarding all the other outputs we generate, we can reduce both the time and the space needed to find collisions in the given hash function (see Fig. 1). The analysis above shows that *any* subset characteristic for which $p^2 > q$ suffices for an efficient squeeze attack on a hash function, provided only that we can generate sufficiently many inputs in the initial subset of the characteristic. This is more flexible than standard differential cryptanalysis of hash functions, where a high-probability differential characteristic can be directly used in a collision attack only if it leads to a zero difference in the output value.

The squeeze attack was used in several previous attacks, but usually in cases where p was 1, in which the idea was beneficial for any $q < 1$ (e.g., in [7]). In this paper, we apply the squeeze attack to Keccak with $p \ll 1$. Our starting point is the observation that most of the operations in Keccak have potentially dangerous symmetry properties. The designers of Keccak were fully aware of this fact, and decided to use asymmetric round constants precisely in order to avoid this problem. However, the constants they chose were of very low Hamming

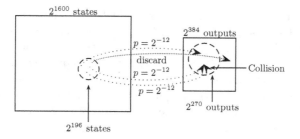

Fig. 1. A squeeze attack with $|S| = 2^{1600}, |S'| = 2^{196}, |D| = 2^{384}, |D'| = 2^{270}, p = 2^{-12}$

weight, and thus their effect was small, changing a fully symmetric state into an almost symmetric state.

Generalized Internal Differential Cryptanalysis. In this paper, we generalize the technique of *internal differential cryptanalysis* developed by Peyrin [22] in the cryptanalysis of the Grøstl hash function. While in standard differential attacks we consider two different plaintexts, and follow the evolution of the difference between them, in internal differential attacks we consider only one plaintext, and follow the statistical evolution of the differences between its parts. In the case of Keccak, we use internal differential cryptanalysis in order to follow the statistical evolution of almost symmetric states through the first few rounds of Keccak. For example, if the symmetry we consider is that the first half of the state should be equal to the second half of the state, then we follow the evolution of small differences between these two parts through the various cryptographic operations. Note that fully symmetric states have a zero internal difference, which remains zero as the state goes through symmetry preserving operations, whereas almost symmetric states have a low Hamming weight internal difference, which in many cases remains low Hamming weight after such operations.

Our approach generalizes and extends the original idea presented in [22] in several ways: first, internal differential cryptanalysis was previously shown to be applicable to hash functions with explicitly defined and completely separate data-paths. In this paper, we show that it is applicable in a much broader setting, where the cryptosystem is not necessarily built using separate data-paths, but still admits differential relations in the internal state that we can follow and control. Second, in [22] Peyrin considers differences between two halves of the state, whereas most of our attacks consider more complex internal structures which divide the state into more than two parts. This approach requires definitions of new objects that capture the notion of these generalized difference relations and allow us to analyze them. In addition to these generalizations, we introduce several new techniques such as aggregating multiple internal differences, which allow us to extend our subset characteristics, and thus attack more rounds of reduced Keccak.

2   Description of Keccak

In this section, we briefly describe the sponge construction and the Keccak hash function. More details can be found in the Keccak specification [4]. The sponge construction [3] works on a state of b bits, which is split into two parts: the first part contains the first r bits of the state (called the outer part) and the second part contains the last $c = b - r$ bits of the state (called the inner part).

Given a message, it is first padded and cut into r-bit blocks, and the b state bits are initialized to zero. The sponge construction then processes the message in two phases: In the absorbing phase, the message blocks are processed iteratively by XORing each block into the first r bits of the current state, and then applying a fixed permutation on the value of the b-bit state. After processing all the blocks, the sponge construction switches to the squeezing phase. In this phase, n output bits are produced iteratively, where in each iteration the first r bits of the state are returned as output and the permutation is applied to the state.

The Keccak hash function uses multi-rate padding: given a message, it first appends a single 1 bit. Then, it appends the minimum number of 0 bits followed by a single 1 bit, such that the length of the result is a multiple of r. Thus, multi-rate padding appends at least 2 bits and at most $r + 1$ bits.

The Keccak versions submitted to the SHA-3 competition have $b = 1600$ and $c = 2n$, where $n \in \{224, 256, 384, 512\}$. The 1600-bit state can be viewed as a 3-dimensional array of bits, a[5][5][64], and each state bit is associated with 3 integer coordinates, a[x][y][z], where x and y are taken modulo 5, and z is taken modulo 64.

The Keccak permutation consists of 24 rounds, which operate on the 1600 state bits. Keccak uses the following naming conventions, which are helpful in describing its round function:

- A row is a set of 5 bits with constant y and z coordinates, i.e. a[*][y][z], or $r(y, z)$.
- A column is a set of 5 bits with constant x and z coordinates, i.e. a[x][*][z].
- A lane is a set of 64 bits with constant x and y coordinates, i.e. a[x][y][*].
- A slice is a set of 25 bits with a constant z coordinate, i.e. a[*][*][z].

Each round of the Keccak permutation consists of five mappings $R = \iota \circ \chi \circ \pi \circ \rho \circ \theta$. The five mappings given below are applied for each x, y, and z (where the state addition operations are over $GF(2)$):

1. θ is a linear map, which adds to each bit in a column, the parity of two other columns.

$$\theta: a[x][y][z] \leftarrow a[x][y][z] + \sum_{y'=0}^{4} a[x-1][y'][z] + \sum_{y'=0}^{4} a[x+1][y'][z-1]$$

2. ρ rotates the bits within each lane by T(x,y), which is a predefined constant for each lane.

$$\rho: a[x][y][z] \leftarrow a[x][y][z + T(x,y)]$$

3. π reorders the lanes.

$$\pi\colon a[x][y][z] \leftarrow a[x'][y'][z], \text{ where } \begin{pmatrix} x \\ y \end{pmatrix} = \begin{pmatrix} 0 & 1 \\ 2 & 3 \end{pmatrix} \cdot \begin{pmatrix} x' \\ y' \end{pmatrix}$$

4. χ is the only non-linear mapping of Keccak, working on each of the 320 rows independently.

$$\chi\colon a[x][y][z] \leftarrow a[x][y][z] + ((\neg a[x+1][y][z]) \wedge a[x+2][y][z])$$

Since χ works on each row independently, it can be viewed as an Sbox layer which simultaneously applies the same 5 bits to 5 bits Sbox to the 320 rows of the state. We note that the Sbox function is an invertible mapping, and some of our techniques are based on the known observation that the algebraic degree the algebraic degree of each output bit of χ as a polynomial in the five input bits is only 2.

5. ι adds a 64-bit round constant to the first lane of the state.

$$\iota\colon a[0][0][*] \leftarrow a[0][0][*] + RC[i_r]$$

Since we analyze in this paper round-reduced variants of Keccak with at most 5 rounds, we are only interested in the first five round constants: 0000000000 000001, 0000000000008082, 800000000000808a, 8000000080008000, 00000000 0000808b (given respectively in hexadecimal using the little-endian format). Note that all five round constants have a low Hamming weight and the first round-constant has a Hamming weight of only 1.

3   Notations

Given a message M, we denote its length in bits by $|M|$. Unless specified otherwise, in this paper we assume that $|M| = r - 2$, namely we consider only single-block messages of maximal length. Given M, we denote the initial state of the Keccak permutation as the 1600-bit word $\overline{M} \triangleq M||11||0^{2n}$, where $||$ denotes concatenation.

The first three operations of Keccak's round function are linear mappings, and we denote their composition by $L \triangleq \rho \circ \pi \circ \theta$. We sometimes refer to L as a "half round" of the Keccak permutation, where $\iota \circ \chi$ represents the other half. We denote the Keccak nonlinear function on 5-bit words defined by varying the first index by $\chi_{|5}$. The difference distribution table (DDT) of this function is a two-dimensional 32×32 integer table, where all the differences are assumed to be over $GF(2)$. The entry $DDT(\delta^{in}, \delta^{out})$ specifies the number of input pairs to this Sbox with difference δ^{in} that produce the output difference δ^{out} (i.e., the size of the set $\{x \in \{0,1\}^5 \mid \chi_{|5}(x) + \chi_{|5}(x + \delta^{in}) = \delta^{out}\}$).

Given a set S of internal states of Keccak, we define the action of each of Keccak's mappings on the set by applying it to every element of the set (e.g., $\theta(S) = \{\theta(u) | u \in S\}$).

4   Description of Our Basic Techniques

Given a subset characteristic for the compression function of a given hash function, we can describe our basic squeeze attack in the following way:

1. Pick an arbitrary message for which the values entering the compression function are in the initial subset of the characteristic.
2. Apply the compression function. If the subset characteristic is satisfied, compute the output of the compression function. Otherwise, discard the message and go back to Step 1.
3. Store the output in a table (along with the message). In case a collision is found, stop and output the collision. Otherwise, go back to Step 1.

If the size of the output set is 2^d (i.e., $|D'| = q|D| = 2^d$ using the notation of the Introduction), then after $2^{d/2}$ messages for which the characteristic is followed, we expect a collision due to the birthday paradox. Hence, when the probability of the subset characteristic is p, the time complexity of finding a collision is $p^{-1} \cdot 2^{d/2}$ and the memory complexity is[2] $2^{d/2}$. To optimize the attack, we need a subset characteristic for which p is as high as possible and d is as small as possible.

4.1   Internal Difference Sets

A very interesting observation concerning Keccak is that four out of its five internal mappings (all but ι), are translation invariant in the direction of the z axis (as was already noted in the Keccak submission paper [4]). Namely, if one state is the rotation of another state with respect to the z-axis (i.e., satisfies $b[x][y][z] = a[x][y][z + i]$, for some value of i), then applying to them any of the θ, ρ, π, χ operations, maintains this property. To exploit this symmetry, we pick subsets which are invariant with respect to the rotation along the z-axis with all the non-trivial possible choices of i. Namely, given a rotation index $i \in \{1, 2, 4, 8, 16, 32\}$, the subsets are all the states for which $a[x][y][z] = a[x][y][z+i]$.

In most of the remainder of this section, we assume for the sake of simplicity that $i = 16$, but note that all of our definitions extend naturally to any $i \in \{1, 2, 4, 8, 16, 32\}$. For $i = 16$, a symmetric state $a[x][y][z]$ is composed of four repetitions of slices 0–15 (see Example 1). Each such sequence of slices (0–15, 16–31, 32–47, 48–63) is called a *consecutive slice set* or *CSS* in short. Applying any of the four operations θ, ρ, π, χ to a symmetric state in which all CSS's are equal, does not disturb its symmetry. The application of ι interferes with this symmetry, since the round constants are not the same among the consecutive slice sets. However, given the low weight of the constants used by ι, the state remains close to being symmetric.

---

[2] Notice that we can use either Floyd's cycle finding algorithm [17] or the parallel collision search algorithm [23] to reduce the memory complexity of the attack, depending on the relative sizes of its domain and range subsets.

169D169D169D169D	A965A965A965A965	3EC73EC73EC73EC7	9025902590259025	C264C264C264C264
A34BA34BA34BA34B	0F330F330F330F33	4902490249024902	3D683D683D683D68	613D613D613D613D
C684C684C684C684	B368B368B368B368	589B589B589B589B	5F335F335F335F33	E27AE27AE27AE27A
22E822E822E822E8	3D583D583D583D58	B37AB37AB37AB37A	1047104710471047	D525D525D525D525
60F360F360F360F3	C3E4C3E4C3E4C3E4	37FA37FA37FA37FA	8193819381938193	69BA69BA69BA69BA

The state is described as a matrix of 5×5 lanes of 64 bits, ordered from left to right, where each lane is given in hexadecimal using the little-endian format. Each lane of the state consists of 4 repetitions of a 16-bit word.

Example 1: A symmetric state with $i = 16$

To deal with ι, we have to extend our point of view, and consider states for which the equality "almost holds". The subsets used in our subset characteristics are *internal differences*, which measure how close the state is to a symmetric state. Generally speaking, this can be done by computing the XOR differences between the first consecutive slice set, and each of the three other ones, denoted by the triplet $(\Delta_1, \Delta_2, \Delta_3)$. We define an internal difference in Keccak to be the set of states with a fixed value of $(\Delta_1, \Delta_2, \Delta_3)$. Obviously, when all 4 CSS's are equal, the differences between them are zero and the subset is called a *zero internal difference*.

Alternatively, we can define an internal difference set as a coset in a group, using a single *representative state* v and adding to it all the fully symmetric states: $\{v + w | w$ is symmetric$\}$. In general, given a rotation index i, we represent an internal difference using the pair $[i, v]$ (or $[16, v]$ in case $i = 16$). Obviously, this representation is redundant as we can select any $u \in [16, v]$ as the representative state. However, as shown in the next subsection, it allows us to describe the evolution of an internal difference $[i, v]$ through Keccak's linear mappings in a very compact way.

Since an internal difference does not place any constraint on the value of the first CSS, it will sometimes be convenient to choose a *canonical representative state* for which this value is zero, and we denote it by $\hat{v}$. Namely, for an internal difference defined by $(\Delta_1, \Delta_2, \Delta_3)$, the *values* of the four CSS's in the canonical representative state are $0, \Delta_1, \Delta_2$ and Δ_3, respectively.

4.2 The Evolution of Internal Differences Through Keccak's Permutation

As in standard differential cryptanalysis, we consider the difference between the CSS's, rather than the actual values. Hence, the zero internal difference passes with probability 1 all the four operations θ, ρ, π, χ, just as a zero difference in a differential characteristic passes through any operation.

Unlike a classical differential characteristic, in an internal differential characteristic, the addition of a constant (i.e., the ι operation) effects the characteristic by introducing a difference between the equal CSS's. This difference then propagates through the other operations, and its development has to be studied and controlled. Luckily, we can construct internal differential characteristics for Keccak (with good probability) that track this evolution of "distance" from a zero internal difference through the various Keccak mappings.

Given the affine nature of an internal difference, tracking its evolution through Keccak's affine mappings is trivial (and does not change the probability of the internal differential characteristic): due to the translation invariance property and the associativity of linear operations, the action of the first three mappings on $[i, v]$ is determined by their action on the representative state, i.e., $\theta([i, v]) = [i, \theta(v)]$, $\rho([i, v]) = [i, \rho(v)]$ and $\pi([i, v]) = [i, \pi(v)]$. Since ι simply adds a constant to each state of the set then $\iota([i, v]) = [i, \iota(v)]$ as well.

The Evolution of Internal Differences Through χ. In contrast to the linear mappings, applying χ, the non-linear mapping, to a randomly selected state from an internal difference, the output internal difference depends on the actual input, i.e., the output can belong to one of several internal differences. Just as in differential cryptanalysis, we can choose a single output internal difference, and then calculate the probability of the transition from the input internal difference to this output internal difference.

When a state of an internal difference which is not symmetric enters the χ function, we have to consider the possible outcomes in terms of "distance" from the zero internal difference. To do so, we consider the rows on which χ operates using an object called a *rotated row set*. For $i = 16$, a rotated row set contains a row $r(y, z)$ in the first CSS, along with its 3 symmetric counterparts $r(y, z + 16), r(y, z + 32)$ and $r(y, z + 48)$ in the other CSS's (see Example 2). We note that given the input internal difference, once the value of $r(y, z)$ is set, we know the value of the remaining rows as well. Hence, given the value of $r(y, z)$ we can compute the corresponding outputs, and check the resulting output internal difference.

Once we perform this operation, we can associate with each input internal difference all the possible output internal differences (and the corresponding probabilities) by trying all 32 possible values for $r(y, z)$. In the particular case where the input internal difference assigns a zero difference to all the rows of a rotated row set, it passes through the χ mapping with probability 1. Similarly to differential cryptanalysis, we call such a rotated row set *inactive* (with respect to the internal difference), whereas a rotated row set with a non-zero difference is called *active*.

For $i = 32$, each rotated row set contains exactly 2 Sboxes (rows), i.e., v specifies a single input difference for the Sbox pair. In this case one can easily use the difference distribution table of the Sbox to determine the distribution of the output difference δ^{out} given the input difference δ^{in}.

In the internal differences that we consider in this paper, most rotated row sets contain at most two distinct input values to the Sbox. We call such a rotated row set *sparse*. In active sparse rotated row sets,[3] one can divide the values $r(y, z), r(y, z + 16), r(y, z + 32)$ and $r(y, z + 48)$ (or $r(y, z), r(y, z + i), \ldots$ for general $i \in \{1, 2, 4, 8, 16, 32\}$) into two groups, each with the same input to the Sbox (see Example 3). Obviously, each group of Sboxes has the same output,

---

[3] For inactive rotated row sets, the output internal difference is necessarily 0.

leading to a sparse output internal difference as well. Since there is only a single input difference between the two groups of Sboxes, we can use the difference distribution table also in the more general case of $i \neq 32$, when a rotated row set is sparse.

| 0001000100010001 | 0001000100010001 | 0001000100010001 | 0001000100010001 | 0001000100010001 |

The first five lanes of a state in which the 20 bits of the first rotated row set for $i = 16$ are set to 1. The lanes are ordered from left to right, where each lane is given in hexadecimal using the little-endian format.

Example 2: A rotated row set

| 0001000100010001 | 0001000000010000 | 0000000000000000 | 0001000100010001 | 0000000100000001 |

The first five lanes (given in the format of Example 2) of a state in an internal difference in which the first rotated row set is sparse for $i = 16$. The (binary) value of $r(0,0)$ and $r(0,32)$ is 10011, while the value of $r(0,16)$ and $r(0,48)$ is 11010. In this example, the internal difference fixes the difference of 01001 between the two groups of rows. The value of the other rows is zero.

Example 3: A sparse rotated row set

The Weight of Internal Differences. Finally, we give a heuristic concerning the "quality" of a given internal difference in a characteristic. The closer the internal difference is to the zero internal difference, its *weight* (i.e., the minimal Hamming weight of a state in the internal difference) is lower.[4] Since the zero internal difference contains the zero state, its weight is zero, and the weight of an internal difference measures the minimal Hamming distance between a state in the internal difference and a symmetric state. In general, a low-weight internal difference has only a few active rotated row sets, and thus passes through χ with high probability. In this paper, we construct characteristics whose internal differences have a low weight (and thus a high probability) by choosing low-weight internal differences as outputs, as well as a few additional techniques which will be described in the rest of this paper. As a preliminary example, consider Characteristic 1 in Appendix A. This characteristic starts from the zero internal difference and extends to 1.5 Keccak rounds with probability 1, where the final internal difference has a weight of 11.

---

[4] While there may be many states with minimal Hamming weight in an internal difference, we can calculate one of them from an arbitrary state w in the internal difference: we iterate over all sets of 4 bits (in case $i = 16$), each containing one bit in the first CSS and its symmetric counterparts in the other 3 CSS's. For each such set, we compute the majority of its bits in w, and complement it if its majority is 1.

5 Exploiting Internal Differential Characteristics in Collision Attacks on Keccak

In this section, we describe optimizations that allow us to devise efficient attacks on round-reduced Keccak using internal differential characteristics.

5.1 Choosing the Value of the Rotation Index

Recall that a subset characteristic maps an input, selected from a subset of inputs to the compression function, to a restricted output set of size 2^d with probability p. In order to find a collision, we have to try about $p^{-1} \cdot 2^{d/2}$ such inputs, and in the case of Keccak, we need the ability to generate $p^{-1} \cdot 2^{d/2}$ single-block messages M, such that $\overline{M}$ is a member of the initial internal difference. In our basic attack, we use a zero internal difference $(i, \mathbf{0})$ for a fixed $i \in \{1, 2, 4, 8, 16, 32\}$ (i.e., we restrict our messages M such that $\overline{M} \in (i, \mathbf{0})$), which implies that we are free to choose the value of the first i bits in each lane of the outer (controllable) part of the initial state, not including the lane containing the padding, in which we can only choose the value of the first $i - 2$ bits.[5] Exploiting the fact that the initialization sets the inner (uncontrollable) part of state to 0, and the fact that we can control the values of $r/64$ lanes when the rate is r, we can generate $2^{r \cdot (i/64) - 2}$ initial states which are symmetric. Hence, we have to ensure that $2^{r \cdot (i/64) - 2} \geq p^{-1} \cdot 2^{d/2}$.

As we decrease the value of i, we increase the number of constraints on the internal differences, leading to a smaller expected output subset size, thus reducing the complexity of the attack. On the other hand, a value of i which is too small leads to an insufficient number of possible messages for a collision attack. Hence, we choose the smallest $i \in \{1, 2, 4, 8, 16, 32\}$ such that $2^{r \cdot (i/64) - 2} \geq p^{-1} \cdot 2^{d/2}$ holds. We note that the value of i determines how a state is partitioned into rotated row sets, and thus it may also affect the probability p of a characteristic (i.e., we need to calculate p separately for each value of i).

5.2 Extending Internal Differential Characteristics

Constructing an internal differential characteristic which spans many rounds of Keccak reduces its probability significantly, leading to an inefficient collision attack which requires the evaluation of many messages. Thus, instead of covering all the attacked rounds, we extend the internal differential characteristic up to some point (in our attacks, one and a half rounds before the output), and continue to exploit Keccak's properties (such as the limited diffusion of its Sbox layer) in order to bound the size of the output subset (which is crucial in squeeze attacks). This is done by extending the internal differential characteristic to a subset characteristic without restricting its subsets to a particular form of $[i, \hat{v}]$.

---

[5] The calculation for the padded lane does not apply for the case of $i = 1$, but we do not use this value in our attacks on Keccak.

In fact, since the output subset is not an internal difference (and actually not even affine), in the final part we use subset cryptanalysis in its most general form.

Aggregating Internal Differences Using Affine Subspaces. Assume that the internal difference part of the subset characteristics ends just before the χ layer with an internal difference $[i, \hat{v}]$. We aggregate all the potential values of $[i, \hat{u}]$, the output internal difference of χ, into an affine subspace by considering each rotated row set independently, and computing $\hat{u}$ in symbolic form (i.e., by allocating linear variables). We then continue and apply L to the symbolic form of $\hat{u}$, and thus maintain the knowledge of the affine subspace up to the χ function of the next round.

Since the computed symbolic form of $\hat{u}$ may include some impossible values, this may increase the bound on the size of the output size. However, due to the limited diffusion properties of χ, it is easy to show explicitly that every single-bit difference in a rotated row set can result in allocation of at most two variables, hence the number of allocated variables for $\hat{u}$ is upper-bounded by twice the weight of $[i, \hat{v}]$. Moreover, when a rotated row set is sparse (with respect to $[i, \hat{v}]$), its Sboxes assume only (at most) two values, with a single input difference which is fixed by $\hat{v}$. Since the algebraic degree of the Keccak Sbox is only 2, all the possible output differences of the Sboxes form an affine subspace (as observed in the Keccak reference document [4]). Thus, when all the rotated row sets with respect to $[i, \hat{v}]$ are sparse, the aggregated internal difference does not include impossible internal differences.

In order to distinguish between explicit binary vectors, and symbolic forms, we denote the explicit vector by $\hat{u}$ and the symbolic form by $\hat{u}$. We note that $[i, \hat{u}]$ still represents an affine subspace whose dimension is increased compared to $[i, \hat{u}]$ by the number of allocated variables.

Bounding the Size of the Output Subset Beyond the Last χ Mapping. Assume that we have an affine subspace of the form $[i, \hat{u}]$ as an input to χ, after which χ and ι are applied, and the state is truncated and sent to the output. Our goal is to upper bound the size of the output subset without reducing its probability (which may happen if we restrict it to an affine subspace).

Clearly, the final application of ι does not affect the size of the output subset, and can be ignored. In order to obtain a good bound, we exploit the limited diffusion of χ which maps each row to itself and in particular, maps each set of 64 rows (320 consecutive bits) of the form $a[*][y][*]$ to itself. As the output consists of the first n bits of the final state, we want to bound the number of its possible values by computing the size of the subset before the last χ mapping when projected to its first $320\lceil n/320 \rceil$ bits. Namely, for output sizes of 224, 256, 384 and 512, it is sufficient to compute the size of the subset before the χ mapping on its first 320, 320, 640 and 640 bits respectively. For $n = 384$ we can achieve a better bound by using a more specific property of χ: each bit $a[x][y][z]$ at the output of χ, depends only on the 3 input bits $a[x][y][z]$, $a[x + 1][y][z]$ and $a[x + 2][y][z]$. Thus, the 64 bits of the lane $a[x][y][*]$ at the output of χ, depend only on the 3 input lanes $a[x][y][*]$, $a[x+1][y][*]$ and $a[x+2][y][*]$. In the case of $n = 384$, the first 320 bits are mapped to themselves by χ, and the remaining 64 bits depend only on 192 bits. Thus, in order to upper bound the output subset size it is sufficient to compute the size of the subset when projected to its first $320 + 192 = 512$ bits.

We now show how to bound the size of the n-bit output subset, given that it depends only on the first n' bits before the χ mapping, and the affine subspace at the entry to χ is represented by $[i, \hat{u}]$. We first assign the variables of $\hat{u}$ an arbitrary value (e.g., zero). We denote the resultant binary vector by $\hat{u}$, and obtain a basic bound in this simplified case, where $[i, \hat{u}]$ is an internal difference: recall that each rotated row set can assume at most 32 values, hence each set of 320 bits of the form $a[*][y][*]$ can assume at most $32^i = 2^{5i}$ values. Thus, for $n = 224$ and $n = 256$ we obtain a basic bound of 2^{5i}, and for $n = 512$ we obtain a basic bound of $2^{2(5i)}$. For $n = 384$, the computation can be split into two parts: the 320 LSBs of the output can assume at most 2^{5i} values, and the 64 MSBs depend on 3 input lanes and can assume at most $min(2^{64}, 2^{3i})$ values. This gives a basic bound of $2^{5i} \cdot min(2^{64}, 2^{3i})$ for $n = 384$. In all cases, we emphasize that the bound only depends on i and n (which determines n'), rather than on the actual values of the n' bits of $\hat{u}$.

In the symbolic case, the n' bits of $\hat{u}$ are expressions, and the basic bound applies independently for each possible value of these n' bits. Consequently, in order to upper bound the output subset size, we need to multiply the basic bound by the number of possible values that the n' expressions can assume. Since the expressions are affine, we can easily compute their number of possible values by computing their dimension using simple linear algebra.

In order to minimize the dimension of the n' expressions at the output, we have to minimize the number of variables allocated in the previous round, when extending the internal differential characteristic. Since we do not allocate any variables to inactive rotated row sets, this can be assured if the final internal difference of the characteristic (before the variable allocation) is of low weight. Thus, in addition to the influence of the weight of the internal differences on the probability p of a characteristic, the weight also plays a role in bounding the size of the output subset 2^d.

6   Collision Attacks on Round-Reduced Keccak-384 and Keccak-512

In this section, we present the details of our practical 3-round collision attacks on Keccak-384 and Keccak-512 and our non-practical 4-round attack on Keccak-384. Although our techniques can be applied to all variants of Keccak, actual collisions were already presented for 4 rounds of Keccak-224 and Keccak-256 in [12], and thus we focus first on Keccak-384 and Keccak-512, for which there are no previously published collision attacks on any number of rounds.

6.1   Practical Collisions in 3-Round Keccak-512

In order to find actual collisions in 3-round Keccak-512, we used the internal differential characteristic given in Characteristic 1 in Appendix A. This characteristic spans only the first Keccak round and the L mapping of the second round (i.e., the first 1.5 rounds), and has a probability of 1. in our attack, we choose $i = 4$, and we use the techniques of Sect. 5.2 in order to bound the size of the output subset: we apply the variable allocation technique to the final internal difference of the characteristic (whose weight is 11) to allocate 22 variables and to extend the characteristic beyond the χ mapping of the second round. The basic bound on the size of the output subset is $2^{2 \cdot 5 \cdot i} = 2^{40}$, and the dimension of the first $n' = 640$ linear expressions is 22 (the maximal possible dimension of linear expressions with 22 variables). This gives a bound of $2^{40+22} = 2^{62}$ on the size of the output subset. Since the probability of the characteristic is 1, we have to try about 2^{31} single-block messages which give initial states in the zero internal difference $[4, \mathbf{0}]$, in order to find a collision with good probability. Since $n = 512$, in this case we have $r = 576$ and we can choose a sufficient number of $2^{r \cdot (i/64) - 2} = 2^{34}$ messages that satisfy the constraints. We implemented the attack and obtained actual collisions in 3-round Keccak-512. A concrete example (found in less than an hour on a single PC) is given in Collision 1 in Appendix B.

6.2   Practical Collisions in 3-Round Keccak-384

For Keccak-384, we can easily use the same characteristic (Characteristic 1 from Appendix A). However, we prefer to use a different characteristic which leads to a more efficient attack, and is also used as a basis for our 4-round attack of Keccak-384 (described in the next section). The idea is to choose a low-weight initial internal difference that limits the increase in the weight caused by the second-round θ mapping, and thus reduces the weight of the internal difference at the entry to the second-round χ mapping.[6] In particular, we make sure that θ acts as the identity on some low Hamming weight vector in the internal difference after the first round.

Searching for Internal Differential Characteristics. The most interesting set of states which are fixed-points of θ is the *column parity kernel* or *CP-kernel*, which was defined in the Keccak submission document [4]: a 1600-bit state is in the CP-kernel if all of its columns have an even parity, which makes such a state a fixed-point of θ. Denote the initial internal difference in our characteristic by $[i, v_0]$ and the internal difference obtained after one round by $[i, v_1]$. We require that there exists some low Hamming weight state $u_1 \in [i, v_1]$ in the CP-kernel, and also set a similar constraint on $[i, v_0]$, which (unlike the attack on Keccak-512) is not zero. Namely, we require that there exists a low Hamming

---

[6] We note that the rate r of Keccak-384 is much larger than the rate of Keccak-512, and thus we could not choose a similar initial internal difference for Keccak-512.

weight state $u_0 \in [i, v_0]$ in the CP-kernel (otherwise θ will significantly increase the weight of the internal difference already in the first round).

Techniques to find state differences that stay in the CP-kernel for two consecutive rounds were described in [10,14,21] in order to construct low Hamming weight classical differential characteristics. Here, we use these techniques in a straightforward way in order to construct low Hamming weight internal differential characteristics that fulfill the two constraints: As done in several previous paper which analyze standard differential characteristics of Keccak, we first assume that the χ mappings act as an identity on the input internal differences (this is typically possible when the input internal difference is of low weight). As a result, the evolution of the internal differential characteristic is completely linear and deterministic, and if we ignore the ι constants, then it is identical to the evolution of a standard differential characteristic with the same initial state-difference (which in our case represents an internal difference). Thus, we can use the previous techniques to find good internal differential characteristics which ignore the ι constants. Finally, we post-filter these characteristics by trying to cancel the ι constants using the additional degrees of freedom offered by the χ mappings.

The best internal differential characteristic that we found for Keccak-384 (which spans 1.5 rounds) is given in Characteristic 2 in Appendix A. Note that its final internal difference has a weight of 6, which is lower compared to the weight of 11 of the final internal difference in Characteristic 1. On the other hand, the characteristic has a probability of 2^{-12} due to the transition through the first χ mapping, whereas Characteristic 1 has probability 1. However, we can easily reduce the workload of finding initial states that conform to this characteristic from the trivial 2^{12} to 1 (as described next), while losing only 12 degree of freedom.

Reducing the Workload of Finding Messages Conforming to the First χ Transition. When the input to the first χ mapping is a state which belongs to a non-zero internal difference $[i, \hat{v}]$, this transition is associated which a probability which is lower than 1. However, we can reduce the workload of finding messages conforming to the first χ transition: we analyze each rotated row set independently and restrict its inputs to an affine subspace for which the first χ transition occurs with probability 1. Due to the fact that L is affine, we can compute an affine subspace of initial states in the first internal difference of the characteristic that satisfy the first χ transition.

Note that we restrict the initial states to an affine subspace that may not include all the values which guarantee the first χ transition. Thus, this optimization can also be detrimental by reducing the available degrees of freedom further compared to the non-optimized method of trying arbitrary states in the initial internal difference. Nevertheless, due to the limited diffusion properties of χ, the transition of every single-bit difference in a rotated row set of $\hat{v}$ depends on the values of at most two state bits. Hence, the total number of state bits whose values we restrict (and the total number of degrees of freedom that we lose as a result) in order to guarantee the first χ transition is upper-bounded by twice the weight of $[i, \hat{v}]$. Indeed, in Characteristic 2 the weight of the internal difference at the input to the first χ mapping is 6, and we lose 12 degree of freedom.

The Full Attack. In our 3-round attack on Keccak-384, we choose $i = 4$, and calculate the bound on the output subset as follows: we use the variable allocation technique to allocate 12 variables (which is the maximal number since the final internal difference has a weight of 6) and extend the characteristic beyond the χ mapping of the second round. The basic bound on the size of the output subset is $2^{8 \cdot 4} = 2^{32}$, and the dimension of the first $n' = 512$ linear expressions is 12. This gives a bound of $2^{32+12} = 2^{44}$ on the size of the output subset. Since the workload to find initial states that conform to Characteristic 2 is 1, we have to try (at most) 2^{22} such initial states in order to find a collision with high probability. For $n = 384$, we have $r = 832$ and we can choose a sufficient number of $2^{-12} \cdot 2^{r \cdot (i/64)-2} = 2^{38}$ messages that satisfy the constraints. We implemented the attack and obtained actual collisions in 3-round Keccak-384. A concrete example (found in less than a minute on a single PC) is given in Collision 2 in Appendix B.

6.3   A Collision Attack on 4-Round Keccak-384

In this subsection, we briefly present a collision attack on 4-round Keccak-384. The attack is based on the 2.5-round internal differential characteristic given in Characteristic 3 in Appendix A, which is an extension by one round of the 1.5-round characteristic used in the 3-round attack on Keccak-384. The analysis of the attack is given in the full version of this paper [11], and shows that the expected time complexity of the attack is bounded by 2^{147}. This is non-practical, but 2^{45} times faster than the birthday bound of 2^{192}.

7   A Collision Attack on 5-Round Keccak-256

The target difference algorithm (TDA) was developed in [12] as a technique to link a differential characteristic (which starts from an arbitrary state difference) to the initial state of the Keccak permutation, using one permutation round. More precisely, the initial state difference of the characteristic is called the target difference, and the algorithm outputs many single-block message pairs which satisfy the target difference after one permutation round. Hence, a differential characteristic leading to a collision at the output after k rounds can be leveraged to a collision attack on $k + 1$ rounds of Keccak.

In this section, we present a 5-round collision attack on Keccak-256 which is based on an analogous variant of the TDA for internal differential cryptanalysis, and is called a *target internal difference algorithm* (TIDA). Analogously to the TDA, the TIDA is a technique that links an internal differential characteristic (which starts from an arbitrary internal difference) to the initial state of the Keccak permutation, using one permutation round. Thus, the initial internal difference of the internal differential characteristic is called the *target internal difference*, and the algorithm outputs single-block messages whose internal state belongs to the target internal difference after one permutation round.

Both the TDA, and the TIDA proposed in this paper are heuristic randomized algorithms, and we cannot formally prove their success. Given a subset characteristic (which is an extension of an internal differential characteristic) spanning k rounds of the Keccak permutation, a collision attack on $k+1$ rounds of Keccak consists of the following steps:

1. Run the TIDA on the target internal difference (derived from the first internal difference of the characteristic) with fresh randomness until it succeeds to output single-block messages satisfying the target internal difference after one permutation round.
2. Let M be the next message outputted by the TIDA (if no more messages remain, return to Step 1):
   (a) Run the Keccak permutation on $\overline{M}$. If the evolution of the state from the second round conforms with the internal differential characteristic, continue and calculate the output of the hash function. Otherwise, discard M and go to Step 2.
   (b) Store the output in a hash table next to M, and check if it collides with an output of a different message. If a collision is found, output the colliding message pair, otherwise go to Step 2.

In order to analyze the time complexity of the attack, we have to estimate the amortized time complexity of finding one message that satisfies the target internal difference after one permutation round. The amortized time is calculated as the ratio between the execution time of the TIDA and the number of messages that it returns in a single execution. If we assume that the amortized time is smaller than 1 (i.e., the amortized time is less than the execution time of the Keccak permutation), and the time of a single execution of the TIDA in Step 1 is not too large, then the time complexity analysis of the attack is similar to the analysis of the basic attack given in Sect. 4. Given that the size of the output set is 2^d values, then the memory complexity of the attack is $2^{d/2}$, similarly to the basic attack given in Sect. 4.

Our 5-round collision attack on Keccak uses the internal differential characteristic given in the full version of this paper [11], which covers rounds 1–3.5. This characteristic is leveraged in order to attack 5 rounds using the techniques of Sect. 5, while the TIDA is used to find messages in the initial internal difference of the characteristic (after 1 Keccak round). The full details and analysis of the attack are given in the full version of this paper [11]. Based on extensive simulations of the critical part of the attack, its estimated time complexity is at most 2^{115}, which is 2^{13} times faster than the birthday bound of 2^{128}.

8   Conclusions and Future Work

In this paper, we presented the first collision attacks on round-reduced Keccak-384 and Keccak-512, and for Keccak-256, we increased the number of rounds which can be attacked from 4 to 5. Our algorithms are based on a squeeze attack which uses internal differential cryptanalysis (which is a special case of subset cryptanalysis) in order to map a large subset of inputs into a small pre-fixed subset of all possible outputs, for which the birthday bound is significantly reduced.

Internal differential cryptanalysis is also very useful in attack scenarios which are different than the squeeze attack. For example, it is possible to use internal differential cryptanalysis in preimage attacks on hash functions, given that the target output is contained in a specific subset of outputs. Moreover, one can think of several other attacks based on internal differential cryptanalysis (such as impossible internal differential cryptanalysis and rebound attacks), which are analogous to attacks in the standard differential setting.

An important future item is to construct better internal differential charac-teristics for Keccak, or prove that they do not exist (and thus extend the work of [10]). More generally, subset cryptanalysis, and in particular internal differential cryptanalysis, seems to be a fruitful research direction. It may improve the crypt-analytic toolbox, suggest better attacks on various schemes, and shed some light on the types of constants which are hazardous to the security of cryptosystems.

Acknowledgements. The authors would like to thank the anonymous referees for their very helpful comments on the preliminary version of this paper.

A   Appendix: Internal Differential Characteristics for Keccak

We provide the precise internal differential characteristics (labeled as Charac-teristics 1–3) which we use in our collision attacks on round-reduced Keccak.

An internal difference $[i, v]$ is represented by a state with the lowest Hamming weight. Each state is given as a matrix of 5×5 lanes of 64 bits, ordered from left to right, where each lane is given in hexadecimal using the little-endian format. The symbol '-' is used in order to denote a zero 4-bit value.

The internal differential characteristics are given as a sequence of internal differences. The operation performed in each transition is specified between the representative states and round numbers are specified to the right of the states.

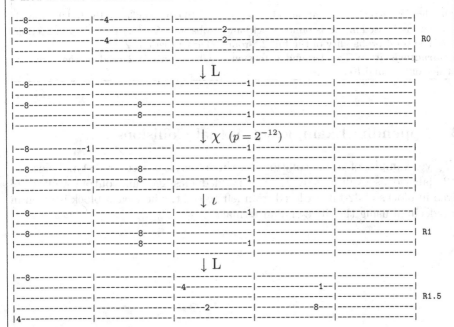

The characteristic has a rotation index value of $i = 4$, as described in Section 6.1.

Characteristic 1: The 1.5-round internal differential characteristic with probability 1 used in order to find collisions in 3-round Keccak-512

The characteristic has a rotation index value of $i = 4$ for the 3-round attack on Keccak-384, as described in Section 6.2.

Characteristic 2: The 1.5-round internal differential characteristic with probability 2^{-12} used in order to find collisions in 3-round Keccak-384

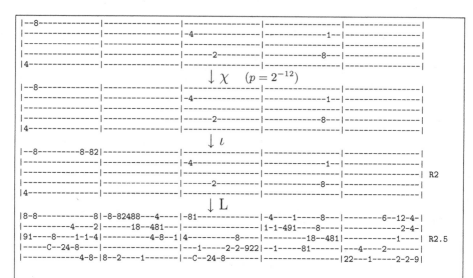

The characteristic has a rotation index value of $i = 16$ (this applies to the full 2.5-round characteristic used in the 4-round attack) and probability 2^{-12}, as described in Section 6.3. The total probability of the full 2.5-round characteristic is 2^{-24}.

Characteristic 3: The 1-round extension of Characteristic 2 used in the collision attack on 4-round Keccak-384

B   Appendix: Examples of Actual Collisions

We give examples of actual collisions for three rounds of Keccak-384 and Keccak-512 (labeled as Collisions 1, 2). The padded messages and output values are given in blocks of 32-bits ordered from left to right, where each block is given in hexadecimal using the little-endian format.

```
M1=

88888888 88888888 66666666 66666666 AAAAAAAA AAAAAAAA 77777777 77777777 BBBBBBBB BBBBBBBB
BBBBBBBB BBBBBBBB 11111111 11111111 88888888 88888888 CCCCCCCC CCCCCCCC

M2=

AAAAAAAA AAAAAAAA 88888888 88888888 EEEEEEEE EEEEEEEE 99999999 99999999 99999999 99999999
99999999 99999999 88888888 88888888 CCCCCCCC CCCCCCCC CCCCCCCC CCCCCCCC

Output=

56BCC94B C4445644 D7655451 5DD96555 71FA7332 3BA30B23 958408C5 64407664 41805414 11190901
6ABAA8BA A8ABAEFA 7EF8AEEE ECCE68DC 4EC8ACEC DD5D5CCC
```

The messages were found using Characteristic 1.

Collision 1: A collision in 3-round Keccak-512

```
M1=

FFFFFFFF FF7FFFFF BBBBBBBB BBFBBBBB 44444444 44444444 FFFFFFFF FFFFFFFF 99999999 99999999
44444444 44C44444 44444444 44444444 44644444 44444444 AAAAAAAA AAAAAAAA 66666666 66666666
44444444 44444444 DDDDDDDD DD9DDDDD DDFDDDDD DDDDDDDD

M2=

33333333 33B33333 55555555 55155555 AAAAAAAA AAAAAAAA 77777777 77777777 44444444 44444444
66666666 66E66666 EEEEEEEE EEEEEEEE 11311111 11111111 CCCCCCCC CCCCCCCC FFFFFFFF FFFFFFFF
11111111 11111111 99999999 99D99999 DDFDDDDD DDDDDDDD

Output=

99999991 11199999 4440C444 405C60DC 00000000 0C100010 777677F7 73F77767 3550F597 55D57155
66666664 66666666
```

The messages were found using Characteristic 2.

Collision 2: A collision in 3-round Keccak-384

References

1. Aumasson, J.-P., Meier, W.: Zero-sum distinguishers for reduced Keccak-f and for the core functions of Luffa and Hamsi. NIST mailing list (2009)
2. Bernstein, D.J.: Second preimages for 6 (7? (8??)) rounds of keccak? NIST mailing list (2010)
3. Bertoni, G., Daemen, J., Peeters, M., Van Assche, G.: On the indifferentiability of the sponge construction. In: Smart, N.P. (ed.) EUROCRYPT 2008. LNCS, vol. 4965, pp. 181–197. Springer, Heidelberg (2008)
4. Bertoni, G., Daemen, J., Peeters, M., Van Assche, G.: The Keccak SHA-3 submission. Submission to NIST (Round 3) (2011)
5. Biham, E.: New types of cryptanalytic attacks using related keys. J. Cryptology 7(4), 229–246 (1994)
6. Biryukov, A., Wagner, D.: Slide attacks. In: Knudsen, L.R. (ed.) FSE 1999. LNCS, vol. 1636, pp. 245–259. Springer, Heidelberg (1999)

7. Bouillaguet, C., Dunkelman, O., Leurent, G., Fouque, P.-A.: Another look at complementation properties. In: Hong, S., Iwata, T. (eds.) FSE 2010. LNCS, vol. 6147, pp. 347–364. Springer, Heidelberg (2010)

8. Boura, C., Canteaut, A.: Zero-sum distinguishers for iterated permutations and application to KECCAK-f and Hamsi-256. In: Biryukov, A., Gong, G., Stinson, D.R. (eds.) SAC 2010. LNCS, vol. 6544, pp. 1–17. Springer, Heidelberg (2011)

9. Chang, S.-J., Perlner, R., Burr, W.E., Turan, M.S., Kelsey, J.M., Paul, S., Bassham, L.E.: Third-Round Report of the SHA-3 Cryptographic Hash Algorithm Competition (2012). http://csrc.nist.gov/groups/ST/hash/sha-3/Round3/documents/Round3_Report_NISTIR_7896.pdf

10. Daemen, J., Van Assche, G.: Differential propagation analysis of Keccak. In: Canteaut, A. (ed.) FSE 2012. LNCS, vol. 7549, pp. 422–441. Springer, Heidelberg (2012)

11. Dinur, I., Dunkelman, O., Shamir, A.: Collision attacks on Up to 5 rounds of SHA-3 using generalized internal differentials. Cryptology ePrint Archive, Report 2012/672 (2012). http://eprint.iacr.org/

12. Dinur, I., Dunkelman, O., Shamir, A.: New attacks on Keccak-224 and Keccak-256. In: Canteaut, A. (ed.) FSE 2012. LNCS, vol. 7549, pp. 442–461. Springer, Heidelberg (2012)

13. Duan, M., Lai, X.: Improved zero-sum distinguisher for full round Keccak-f Permutation. Cryptology ePrint Archive, Report 2011/023 (2011)

14. Duc, A., Guo, J., Peyrin, T., Wei, L.: Unaligned rebound attack: application to Keccak. In: Canteaut, A. (ed.) FSE 2012. LNCS, vol. 7549, pp. 402–421. Springer, Heidelberg (2012)

15. Harpes, C., Massey, J.L.: Partitioning cryptanalysis. In: Biham, E. (ed.) FSE 1997. LNCS, vol. 1267, pp. 13–27. Springer, Heidelberg (1997)

16. Homsirikamol, E., Morawiecki, P., Rogawski, M., Srebrny, M.: Security margin evaluation of SHA-3 contest finalists through SAT-Based attacks. In: Cortesi, A., Chaki, N., Saeed, K., Wierzchoń, S. (eds.) CISIM 2012. LNCS, vol. 7564, pp. 56–67. Springer, Heidelberg (2012)

17. Knuth, D.E.: The Art of Computer Programming. Seminumerical algorithms, vol. 2, 2nd edn. Addison-Wesley, Reading (1981)

18. Van Le, T., Sparr, R., Wernsdorf, R., Desmedt, Y.G.: Complementation-like and cyclic properties of AES round functions. In: Dobbertin, H., Rijmen, V., Sowa, A. (eds.) AES 2005. LNCS, vol. 3373, pp. 128–141. Springer, Heidelberg (2005)

19. Leander, G., Abdelraheem, M.A., AlKhzaimi, H., Zenner, E.: A Cryptanalysis of PRINTCIPHER: The Invariant Subspace Attack. In: Rogaway, P. (ed.) CRYPTO 2011. LNCS, vol. 6841, pp. 206–221. Springer, Heidelberg (2011)

20. Morawiecki, P., Pieprzyk, J., Srebrny, M.: Rotational cryptanalysis of round-reduced Keccak. Cryptology ePrint Archive, Report 2012/546 (2012). http://eprint.iacr.org/

21. Naya-Plasencia, M., Röck, A., Meier, W.: Practical analysis of reduced-round KECCAK. In: Bernstein, D.J., Chatterjee, S. (eds.) INDOCRYPT 2011. LNCS, vol. 7107, pp. 236–254. Springer, Heidelberg (2011)

22. Peyrin, T.: Improved differential attacks for ECHO and Grøstl. In: Rabin, T. (ed.) CRYPTO 2010. LNCS, vol. 6223, pp. 370–392. Springer, Heidelberg (2010)

23. van Oorschot, P.C., Wiener, M.: Improving implementable meet-in-the-middle attacks by orders of magnitude. In: Koblitz, N. (ed.) CRYPTO 1996. LNCS, vol. 1109, pp. 229–236. Springer, Heidelberg (1996)

Rotational Cryptanalysis of Round-Reduced KECCAK

Paweł Morawiecki[1,3]($\boxtimes$), Josef Pieprzyk[2], and Marian Srebrny[1,3]

[1] Section of Informatics, University of Commerce, Kielce, Poland
pawelm@wsh-kielce.edu.pl
[2] Department of Computing, Macquarie University, Sydney, Australia
josef.pieprzyk@mq.edu.au
[3] Institute of Computer Science, Polish Academy of Sciences, Warsaw, Poland
marians@ipipan.waw.pl

Abstract. In this paper we attack round-reduced KECCAK hash function with a technique called rotational cryptanalysis. We focus on KEC-CAK variants proposed as SHA-3 candidates in the NIST's contest for a new standard of cryptographic hash function. Our main result is a preimage attack on 4-round KECCAK and a 5-round distinguisher on KECCAK-f[1600] permutation — the main building block of KECCAK hash function.

Keywords: Preimage attack · KECCAK · Rotational cryptanalysis · SHA-3

1 Introduction

In 2007, the U.S. National Institute of Standards and Technology (NIST) announced a public contest aiming at the selection of a new standard for a cryptographic hash function. The main motivation behind starting the contest has been the security flaws identified in the SHA-1 standard in 2005. Similarities between SHA-1 and the most recent standard SHA-2 were worrisome and NIST decided that a new, stronger hash function would be needed. Overall, 51 functions were submitted to the first round of the contest. In July 2009 out of the submitted functions, 14 were selected to the second round. At the end of 2010, the five finalists were announced and eventually in October 2012 the winner has been selected. The new SHA-3 standard will be KECCAK hash function [5]. In this paper we analyze KECCAK using a technique called rotational cryptanalysis.

Rotational analysis is a relatively new type of attack. The technique was mentioned and applied in [2,14,16], and formally introduced in [12]. Unlike the differential analysis, where for a pair (x, y) the attacker follows the propagation of the difference $x \oplus y$ through the cryptographic system, in the rotational analysis, the adversary investigates the propagation of the rotational relations through the cryptographic transformations. Khovratovich and Nikolić in [12] analyze the primitives composed of only three operations: addition, rotation, xor (ARX).

S. Moriai (Ed.): FSE 2013, LNCS 8424, pp. 241–262, 2014.
DOI: 10.1007/978-3-662-43933-3_13, © Springer-Verlag Berlin Heidelberg 2014

For these primitives, they prove that the probability that a rotational pair of inputs will produce a rotational pair on the output depends on the number of additions only. In [17] a rotational distinguisher was designed for the keyed permutation of the Shabal hash function. Rotational cryptanalysis was combined with the rebound attack and applied to the compression function of the SHA-3 candidate Skein and its underlying cipher Threefish [13].

The known cryptanalytic results on KECCAK can be divided into two types. The first type is showing a non-random behaviour, weakness in the KECCAK's internal permutation, such as our rotational distinguishers. The second type is attacking the core security properties of the whole function (a preimage attack and a collision attack). The distinguisher of Keccak's permutation with the highest number of rounds is the zero-sum distinguisher proposed in [1] and later improved in [6,9]. However, the complexity of these distinguishers is very high. For example, the zero-sum distinguisher for all 24 rounds has the complexity of 2^{1579}. A differential analysis of KECCAK's internal permutation, given in [10], leads to distinguishers up to 8 rounds with complexity of $2^{491.47}$ and for 5 rounds with complexity of 2^8. Among the attacks on the KECCAK hash function, the most rounds were reached by Bernstein in his 8-round preimage attack [3]. However, the attack is much slower than parallel exhaustive search and it is inherently memory-intensive. Also with the aid of differential analysis, Naya-Plasencia et al. mounted the preimage and collision attacks on 2-round KECCAK [15]. In [11] the same result (2-round preimage and 2-round collision attacks) were obtained through the SAT-based attacks. The most successful collision attack was given in [8] where 4-round collisions were presented.

In this paper we focus our analysis on the KECCAK variants proposed as SHA-3 candidates. First we analyze the permutation KECCAK-f[1600]. We mount the 4-round rotational distinguisher and then enhance it with a correlation analysis which improves the result to 5 rounds. We implement the distinguishers and verify the experimental results. Unlike the other rotational analysis we treat rotational relations between bits independently and we operate on probabilities of rotational relations. Our rotational cryptanalysis not only serves as a mean to show a non-random behaviour in the cryptographic primitive, but also for the first time the technique is used for mounting the preimage attack. A family of 4-round distinguishers is the base for our 4-round preimage attack with the complexity 64 times lower than exhaustive search. This is also the first 4-round preimage attack with a negligible amount of memory needed for the attack.

2 KECCAK

In this section we provide a description of KECCAK to the extent necessary for understanding the attack described in the paper. For a complete specification, we refer the interested reader to the original specification [5] (Table 1).

KECCAK uses the sponge construction and hence is a member of the sponge function family [4]. Figure 1 shows the construction. It can be used as a hash function but also can be applied for generating infinite bit stream, making it

Table 1. Best known preimage attacks on the KECCAK variants proposed as SHA-3 candidates. The number in the column 'Variant' denotes a hash length.

Rounds	Variant	Time	Memory	Reference
6/7/8	512	$2^{506}/2^{507}/2^{511.5}$	$2^{176}/2^{320}/2^{508}$	[3]
4	224/256	$2^{217.3}/2^{249.3}$	2^{61}	[3]*
4	384/512	$2^{377.3}/2^{505.3}$	2^{61}	[3]*
4	512	2^{506}	Negligible	Sect. 4.2
4	384	2^{378}	Negligible	Sect. 4.2
4	256	2^{252}	Negligible	Sect. 4.2
4	224	2^{221}	Negligible	Sect. 4.2

*These results were provided for us by the author of the attack. Originally in [3] the results are given only for 6, 7 and 8 rounds

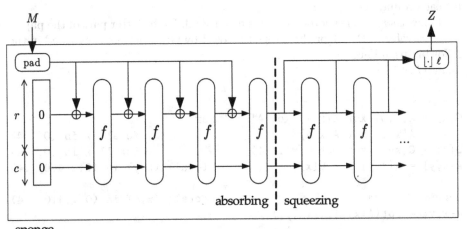

Fig. 1. Sponge construction [4]

suitable as a stream cipher or a pseudorandom bit generator. In this paper we focus on the sponge construction for cryptographic hashing. KECCAK has two main parameters r and c, which are called bitrate and capacity, respectively. The sum of those two makes the state size, which KECCAK operates on. For the SHA-3 proposal, the state size is 1600 bits. Different values for bitrate and capacity give the trade-off between speed and security. The higher bitrate gives the faster function that is less secure. KECCAK follows the sponge two-phase processing.

The initial 1600-bit state is filled with 0's. In the first phase (also called the absorbing phase), interleaved with applications of the permutation f (called KECCAK-f in the specification). The absorbing phase is finished when all message blocks have been processed. In the second phase (also called the squeezing phase), the first r bits of the state are returned as part of the output bits, interleaved with applications of the function f. The squeezing phase is finished after the desired length of output digest has been produced.

For the variants proposed as SHA-3 candidates, the value of the parameter c is equal to a hash length multiplied by 2. For example, the SHA-3 candidate with 512-bit hash length is KECCAK with $c = 1024$ and $r = 576$ ($r + c = 1600$). In this paper we denote variants proposed as SHA-3 candidates by KECCAK-512, KECCAK-384, KECCAK-256, and KECCAK-224. (The number is a hash length for a given variant.)

KECCAK can also operate on smaller states but through the whole paper we always refer to the default variant with 1600-bit state. The state can be visualised as an array of 5×5 lanes, each lane is 64-bit long. The state size determines the number of rounds in KECCAK-f function. For the default 1600-bit state there are 24 rounds. All rounds are the same except for constants which are different for each round.

Below there is a pseudo-code of a single round. In the latter part of the paper, we often refer to the algorithm steps (denoted by Greek letters) described in the following pseudo-code.

```
Round(A,RC) {

θ step
C[x] = A[x,0] xor A[x,1] xor A[x,2] xor
       A[x,3] xor A[x,4],              forall x in (0...4)
D[x] = C[x-1] xor rot(C[x+1],1),       forall x in (0...4)
A[x,y] = A[x,y] xor D[x],        forall (x,y) in (0...4,0...4)

ρ step                           forall (x,y) in (0...4,0...4)
A[x,y] = rot(A[x,y], r[x,y]),

π step                           forall (x,y) in (0...4,0...4)
B[y,2*x+3*y] = A[x,y],

χ step                           forall (x,y) in (0...4,0...4)
A[x,y] = B[x,y] xor ((not B[x+1,y]) and B[x+2,y]),

ι step
A[0,0] = A[0,0] xor RC

return A    }
```

All the operations on the indices shown in the pseudo-code are done modulo 5. A denotes the complete permutation state array and A[x,y] denotes a particular lane in that state. B[x,y], C[x], D[x] are 64-bit intermediate variables. The constants r[x,y] are the rotation offsets, while RC are the round constants. rot(W,m) is the usual bitwise rotation operation, moving bit at position i into position $i+m$ in lane W ($i+m$ are done modulo 64 – note that 64 is the lane size for the default variant of KECCAK). θ is the linear operation intends to provide diffusion for the state. ρ is a permutation between bits in the lanes and π is a permutation between the whole lanes. The only non-linear operation is χ which can be treated as a layer of 5-bit Sboxes. Finally, ι xores the round constant with the first lane. The constants play a vital role in our analysis and it is worth mentioning that they have the very low Hamming weight. The constants for the first 5 rounds are: 0000000000000001, 0000000000008082, 800000000000808a, 8000000080008000, 000000000000808b (given respectively in hexadecimal using the little-endian format).

In our work we often need to refer to a particular bit of the state and we do that by $A_{(x,y,z)}$. The coordinates x, y range from 0 to 4 specifying the lane in the state and the coordinate z ranges from 0 to 63 specifying the bit number in the given lane. With this notation we can refer to a state by A, to a lane by $A_{(3,2)}$, to a value of a single bit by $A_{(1,4,6)}$, or to a position of a single bit by $(3, 1, 60)$.

3   Rotational Distinguishers for the Keccak-f[1600] Permutation

In our analysis we follow the relation between two states $(A, A^{\leftarrow})$ which change through subsequent steps of KECCAK-f[1600] permutation. In particular we are interested in evolution of a rotational pair of states. Let us define the rotational pair in the context of the KECCAK-f[1600] permutation.

Definition 1. *A pair of two 1600-bit states $(A, A^{\leftarrow})$ is called a rotational pair when each lane in the state $A^{\leftarrow}$ is created by bitwise rotation operation of the corresponding lane in the state A. The operation moves the bit from the position (x, y, z) to the position $(x, y, z + n)$, where $z + n$ is done modulo 64. The coordinates x, y range from 0 to 4 specifying the lane in the state and the coordinate z ranges from 0 to 63 specifying the bit number in the given lane. n is called a rotational number and is the same for every lane. Thus in the rotational pair $\forall(x, y, z) : A_{(x,y,z)} = A^{\leftarrow}_{(x,y,z+n)}$.*

Remark 1. Following Definition 1, there are up to 64 possible rotational pairs including a pair, where A and $A^{\leftarrow}$ are the same (having $n = 0$). We will use this fact in the preimage attack described later in the paper.

In some parts of this work we are interested in the probability that a given pair is a rotational one or a given pair of corresponding bits preserve the rotational relation. Two following definitions help to formally define this probability.

Definition 2. *Set S_n is a set of 2^{1600} pairs of states which are created by an operation (some number of steps of KECCAK-f[1600] or their inverse) applied to all possible rotational pairs. (All possible means 2^{1600} possible rotational pairs for a chosen rotational number n.)*

Definition 3. *Probability $p^n_{(x,y,z)}$ is the probability that for a pair of states $(A,$ $A^{\leftarrow})$ randomly selected from the set S_n we have $A_{(x,y,z)} \neq A^{\leftarrow}_{(x,y,z+n)}$. $p^n_{(x,y,z)}$ can be expressed as $p^n_{(x,y,z)} = 1/2 + \epsilon^n_{(x,y,z)}$. Therefore if $\epsilon^n_{(x,y,z)} = 1/2$, the corresponding bits have opposite values and if $\epsilon^n_{(x,y,z)} = -1/2$, the corresponding bits are equal. In case $\epsilon^n_{(x,y,z)} = 0$, the bits are independent (Fig. 2).*

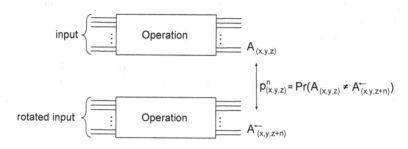

Fig. 2. Probabilistic relation between bits in a pair of states $(A,\ A^{\leftarrow})$

When mounting distinguishers we refer to a random permutation which now we define formally.

Given a permutation of n-bit sequences, i.e. $p : \{0,1\}^n \to \{0,1\}^n$. The collection of all permutations over n bit sequences is denoted by $\mathcal{P}_n$. The cardinality of the set $\mathcal{P}_n$ is $n!$.

Definition 4. *Given a probability distribution $\mathcal{D}_n$ that assigns the probability $\frac{1}{n!}$ for each permutation $p \in \mathcal{P}_n$. A permutation is called random if it is chosen according to the (uniform) distribution $\mathcal{D}_n$.*

For a random permutation we assume that $p^n_{(x,y,z)}$ follows the binomial distribution $\mathcal{B}(t, s)$ where t is a number of trials and s is a probability of success and is equal to 0.5. The mean for the binomial distribution equals $s \cdot t$ and the standard deviation $\sigma = \sqrt{(1-s)s \cdot t}$.

To distinguish KECCAK-$f[1600]$ permutation from a random permutation we check whether the experimental results (for a chosen $p_{(x,y,z)}$) follow the binomial distribution $\mathcal{B}(t, 0.5)$. We choose a typical 95 % confidence interval and hence the mean from the experimental sample should be within the range $0.5t \pm 2\sigma$. If the mean is beyond that range we conclude that experimental results do not follow the binomial distribution $\mathcal{B}(t, 0.5)$ and hence KECCAK-$f[1600]$ can be distinguished from a random permutation.

To calculate how the probabilities change through the successive steps of the algorithm, let us first analyze two basic bitwise operations used in KECCAK.

For the following Lemmas it is assumed that each $p_{(x,y,z)}$ is independent. Also we assume that if corresponding bits from $(A, A^{\leftarrow})$ are equal, both combinations ('00' or '11') have the same probability to be the actual values. The same applies for combinations with opposite bits ('01' or '10').

Lemma 1 (AND). *Given the bitwise AND operation, its input bits a, b and the output bit out. Then the probability*

$$P_{out} = \frac{1}{2}(p_a + p_b - p_a p_b),$$

where the probabilities p_a and p_b are defined according to Definition 3.

Lemma 2 (XOR). *Given the bitwise XOR operation, its input bits a, b and the output bit out. Then the probability*

$$P_{out} = p_a + p_b - 2p_a p_b,$$

where the probabilities p_a and p_b are defined according to Definition 3.

Proofs of the lemmas are given in Appendix.

There is also the bitwise NOT operation in the algorithm but it does not affect the probabilities. NOT flips the values of the corresponding bits $A_{(x,y,z)}$ and $A^{\leftarrow}_{(x,y,z+n)}$ but their relation (or precisely speaking the probability of relation $p^n_{(x,y,z)}$) remains unchanged. Also the bitwise rotation operation (denoted in the pseudo-code as `rot(W,n)`) does not change the values of probabilities. It rotates the bits in the lane so their positions (coordinates z in $p^n_{(x,y,z)}$) change while their probabilities $p^n_{(x,y,z)}$ are not changed.

Having explained how the basic bitwise operations change the rotation probabilities, the analysis of the KECCAK-$f[1600]$ steps remains mostly straightforward. In the transformation θ, there is the XOR operation only, applied a number of times. Due to the linearity of the XOR operation, the repeated application of Lemma 2 will give the correct results of calculated probabilities. For the permutations ρ and π, nothing needs to be calculated as only the positions of bits change. In the transformation χ, the two Lemma 1 and Lemma 2 are applied. The last step is the transformation ι, where the lane $(0,0)$ is xored with a constant. Xoring with '0' does not change anything. However, if there is '1' at position m in the constant and a rotational number $n > 0$, then xoring with a constant change the probabilities as follows

$$p^n_{(0,0,m)} := 1 - p^n_{(0,0,m)} \text{ and}$$
$$p^n_{(0,0,m-n)} := 1 - p^n_{(0,0,m-n)}$$

Example 1. Let us consider two 8-bit lanes $A_{(0,0)}$ and $A^{\leftarrow}_{(0,0)}$ with the rotational number $n = 3$. The lanes have the following binary values: $A_{(0,0)} = 00000010$ and $A^{\leftarrow}_{(0,0)} = 00010000$. Because $\forall z: A_{(0,0,z)} = A^{\leftarrow}_{(0,0,z+3)}$, then $\forall z: p^3_{(x,y,z)} = 0$ (according to Definition 3). Now if both lanes are xored with 8-bit constant $C = 00000001$, new values of lanes are $A_{(0,0)} = 00000011$ and $A^{\leftarrow}_{(0,0)} = 00010001$. Rotational relation has been spoilt at two positions (0 and 5), therefore the probabilities $p^3_{(0,0,0)}$ and $p^3_{(0,0,5)}$ are now equal to 1. In KECCAK-$f[1600]$ the constants are 64-bit long but the reasoning shown above is still valid.

3.1   4-Round Distinguishers

We build a 4-round rotational distinguisher and show that after 4 rounds, there are some coordinates (x, y, z) and the rotational number n for which $p^n_{(x,y,z)}$ does not follow the binomial distribution $\mathcal{B}(t, 0.5)$. Figure 3 illustrates an evolution of rotation probabilities. A single square represents a value (or a range of values) of the probability $p^n_{(x,y,z)}$. Usually in this paper, we refer to a lane by its two coordinates (x, y). However here for the sake of diagram readability instead of 5×5 matrix of lanes there are 25 rows, each representing a single lane. For example, a value of $p^n_{(0,1,0)}$ is represented by the leftmost square in the sixth row and $p^n_{(4,4,63)}$ is represented by the rightmost square in the last (25th) row.

In the beginning, all corresponding bits from a rotational pair are equal so $\forall(x, y, z)\ p^n_{(x,y,z)} = 0$. After the first application of ι, some probabilities $p^n_{(x,y,z)}$ change and in the subsequent steps these changes propagate and influence other bits. For most rotational numbers n, there are some probabilities $p^n_{(x,y,z)}$ deviating from 0.5 until the end of the 4th round. According to our calculations, at the end of 4th round the probability $p^{54}_{(4,4,14)} = 0.5625$. To verify the distinguisher we chose randomly 10000 rotational pairs and ran them on the 4-round KECCAK-$f[1600]$. The mean from that sample was equal to 5682 (for 5682 rotational pairs bits had different values). For a random permutation which follows the binomial distribution $\mathcal{B}(10000, 0.5)$, the mean equals 5000 and the standard deviation equals 50. Thus the mean from the experiment on the 4-round KECCAK-$f[1600]$ should be within the range $5000 \pm 2 \cdot 50$ and clearly 5682 is beyond that range. Hence we conclude we have a distinguisher for the 4-round KECCAK-$f[1600]$ permutation.

We could not directly extend the distinguisher to 5 rounds because after θ in the 5th round all $p^n_{(x,y,z)} = 0.5$.

3.2   Extension to 5-Round Distinguisher

To extend the distinguisher to 5 rounds, we show that correlation between some corresponding bits from A and $A^{\leftarrow}$ deviates from what is expected from random permutation. Let us first give an observation which helps to mount the 5-round distinguisher.

Observation 1. Consider two bits $(A_{(x,y,z)}, A_{(x,y',z)})$ from state A which are in the same column and let us assume that we know the probability that $A_{(x,y,z)} \neq A_{(x,y',z)})$. Our point is that θ does not change this probability. It is because θ treats each bit within a column in the same way: either it flips all 5 of them or it leaves them unchanged.

We can use this observation in our rotational analysis. The difference is that now we look at relations in one pair $(A_{(x,y,z)}, A^{\leftarrow}_{(x,y,z+n)})$ and the second pair $(A_{(x,y',z)}, A^{\leftarrow}_{(x,y',z+n)})$. Each of these two pairs has the relation between its bits (that is bits have either the same or opposite values). We are interested whether

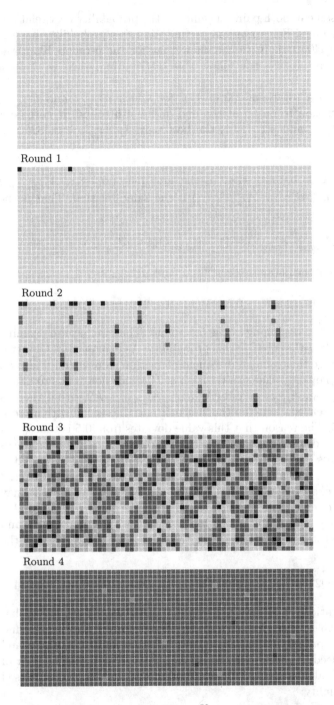

$p = 0$
$0.4 \geq p > 0$
$0.5 > p > 0.4$
$p = 0.5$
$0.6 \geq p > 0.5$
$1 > p > 0.6$
$p = 1$

Round 1

Round 2

Round 3

Round 4

Fig. 3. Evolution of probabilities $p^{53}_{(x,y,z)}$ through 4 rounds of KECCAK-$f[1600]$.

the relations are the same in both pairs, specifically the probability that relations are the same in both pairs. For a random permutation this probability has the binomial distribution $\mathcal{B}(t, 0.5)$. If we can show that for the 5-round KECCAK-$f[1600]$ experimental results do not follow this distribution, then we have a distinguisher.

First we determine a rotational number n for which $p^n_{(x,y,z)}$ and $p^n_{(x,y',z)}$ have the highest deviation from 0.5 at the end of the 4th round. It turns out that for $n = 63$, $p^{63}_{(2,1,37)}$ and $p^{63}_{(2,2,37)}$ is the best pair[1] ($p^{63}_{(2,1,37)} = 0.5625$ and $p^{63}_{(2,2,37)} = 0.49219$).

Now let P_c denotes a probability that in the first pair $(A_{(x,y,z)}, A^{\leftarrow}_{(x,y,z+n)})$ and in the second pair $(A_{(x,y',z)}, A^{\leftarrow}_{(x,y',z+n)})$ is the same relation. That is the probability:

$$P_c = p^n_{(x,y,z)} \cdot p^n_{(x,y',z)} + (1 - p^n_{(x,y,z)})(1 - p^n_{(x,y',z)})$$

We can calculate P_c for the chosen pair $p^{63}_{(2,1,37)}$ and $p^{63}_{(2,2,37)}$.

$$P_c = 0.5625 \cdot 0.49219 + (1 - 0.5625)(1 - 0.49219) = 0.49902375$$

This is the P_c value at the beginning of the 5th round. Then we have to examine how the steps in the algorithm change this probability. As explained in Observation 1, θ does not change this value. Subsequent algorithm steps ρ and π also do not change P_c value, they only change a position of P_c which now refers to different pairs of bits $(A_{(1,2,43)}, A^{\leftarrow}_{(1,2,44)})$ and $(A_{(2,0,16)}, A^{\leftarrow}_{(2,0,17)})$. After that there is χ which preserves the relation between the first pair and the second with a probability equals 0.53125. The reason that this value deviates from 0.5 is that χ is a non-linear operation and precisely the bitwise AND operation which introduces the bias. All the details on how this value is calculated are given in Appendix. Finally, ι does not affect our analysis here. Therefore, to have our pairs with the same relation at the end of the 5th round, there are two ways this event may occur. Either the pairs enter into the 5th round with the same relation and χ does not spoil it or they enter into the 5th round with the opposite relation and χ 'fixes' it. Then the total probability P_c for the chosen pair at the end of the 5th round is:

$$P_c = 0.53125 \cdot 0.49902375 + (1 - 0.53125) \cdot (1 - 0.49902375) = 0.499938984$$

For a random permutation, P_c follows the binomial distribution with the probability of success $s = 0.5$ — very close to 0.499938984. Then the bias for 5-round KECCAK-$f[1600]$ is expected to be very small. To experimentally verify and observe the bias we need to check many rotational pairs. A sufficient number of rotational pairs m is calculated from Chernoff bound [7] and can be expressed as the following inequality:

---

[1] An anonymous reviewer pointed that a better pair can be found, that is $p^{31}_{(0,0,3)}$ and $p^{31}_{(0,2,3)}$. It improves the distinguisher by a factor of 4.

$$m \geq \frac{1}{(P_c - 0.5)^2} \ln \frac{1}{\sqrt{\epsilon}},$$

where ϵ is the probability of an error of the bound (typically set to 0.05). From the inequality we have $m \geq 402\,332\,890 \approx 2^{28.6}$ and in the experiment we checked $403\,000\,000$ rotational pairs. The distinguisher we implemented can be described in a few short steps:

1. Generate randomly $403\,000\,000$ rotational pairs
2. **For each** pair
   (a) Run 5-round KECCAK-$f[1600]$ on the state A and the state $A^{\leftarrow}$;
   (b) **if** $(A_{(1,2,43)} \oplus A^{\leftarrow}_{(1,2,44)} \oplus A_{(2,0,16)} \oplus A^{\leftarrow}_{(2,0,17)} = 0)$ **then**
   $mean := mean + 1$.

The mean from the experiment was equal to $201\,450\,503$. For a random permutation which follows the binomial distribution $\mathcal{B}(403\,000\,000, 0.5)$, the mean equals $201\,500\,000$ and the standard deviation equals $10\,037$. Thus the mean from the experiment on the 5-round KECCAK-$f[1600]$ should be within the range $201\,500\,000 \pm 2 \cdot 10\,037$ and $201\,450\,503$ is beyond that range. Hence we conclude we have a distinguisher for the 5-round KECCAK-$f[1600]$ permutation.

3.3   5-Round Distinguisher with Lower Complexity

The idea allowing us to reduce the complexity of the 5-round distinguisher is to start not from a rotational pair of states but from the pair of states (called 'good' states) which after one round gives the rotational pair. First diagram in Fig. 4 shows the structure which is used to generate a pair of 'good' states. Now we explain how we construct this structure. (A rotational number n is set to 63 in the following explanation but for any other n the logic of construction stays the same.)

On the way to the rotational pair from a pair of 'good' states the following should happen:

- ι from the first round flips the value of $p^{63}_{(0,0,0)}$ and $p^{63}_{(0,0,1)}$. Thus to get the rotational pair after ι, there have to be $p^{63}_{(0,0,0)} = 1$, $p^{63}_{(0,0,1)} = 1$ and for all other $p^{63}_{(x,y,z)} = 0$ before ι step.
- We want that $p^{63}_{(0,0,0)} = 1$, $p^{63}_{(0,0,1)} = 1$ and all other $p^{63}_{(x,y,z)} = 0$ are going to χ and χ does not change any of $p^{63}_{(x,y,z)}$. This way ι gets the right $p^{63}_{(x,y,z)}$ to produce the rotational pair.

However χ is a non-linear operation and to have the condition fulfilled, some $A_{(x,y,z)}$ and $A^{\leftarrow}_{(x,y,z+n)}$ have to be fixed. To have values fixed at this point it has to be taken under consideration at the beginning of the first round. Once we know the relation of the states A and $A^{\leftarrow}$ before χ step, it is easy to go back till the beginning of the round. It is because π, ρ and θ are all linear operations and they change the rotational relation with probability 1. Thus we simply invert these three operations to get the rotational relation at the beginning of the

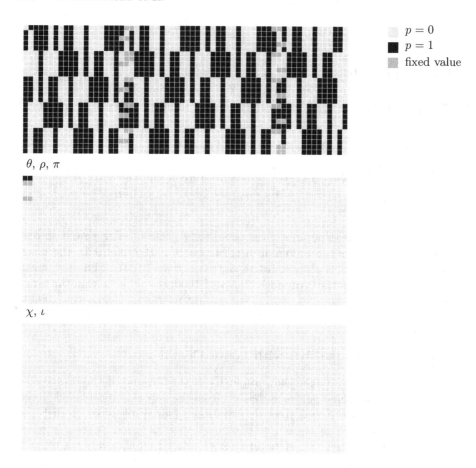

$p = 0$
$p = 1$
fixed value

θ, ρ, π

χ, ι

Fig. 4. 1-round transition to a rotational pair. A rotational number n set to 63.

first round. Figure 4 shows a 1-round transition to a rotational pair where exact positions of the fixed bits are marked. The values of fixed bits which lead to this transition are given in Appendix.

We hoped that this 1-round transition to a rotational pair would give one more round in the distinguisher. However it is not the case and the problem is that the constant of the second round has the Hamming weight 3 (and not 1 as for the first round). More 1's in the round constant introduce more $p^n_{(x,y,z)} = 1$ which subsequently cause more $p^n_{(x,y,z)}$ with undesirable value of 0.5. Yet this 1-round transition can be used to lower the complexity of the 5-round distinguisher. Similarly as in the distinguisher from the previous section, we are interested in the pair of $p^n_{(x,y,z)}$ at the end of 4th round which are in the same column and whose values deviate from 0.5. For a rotational number n set to 63, we find an excellent pair where both $p^{63}_{(4,3,22)}$ and $p^{63}_{(4,4,22)}$ are equal to 0. We calculate P_c in exactly the same way as in Sect. 3.2 but this time the total probability

P_c is much higher and is equal to 0.53125. Putting this value to the Chernoff inequality, we calculate the number of pairs m needed to detect the bias and obtain $m \geq 1534 \approx 2^{11}$. Around 2^{11} needed pairs make the complexity of the distinguisher roughly equal 2^{12}.

Trying to win more rounds by 'going backwards' by 2 (or more) rounds is problematic. Either we end up with all fixed bits at the beginning of the distinguisher (then in fact is not a structural distinguisher any more), or if we assume that transitions can be probabilistic the complexity of the distinguisher becomes much higher than the complexity of the generic 'attack'. We also tried the approach where each undesirable $p_{(x,y,z)}^n = 0.5$ becomes 0 with probability 2^{-1}. However, we could not reach anything better than 5 rounds without exceeding the generic complexity.

4   Preimage Attacks on Round-Reduced KECCAK

First, we describe the preimage attack on 3-round KECCAK-512 which is based on the rotational distinguisher given in the previous section. Then we show how to extend the attack to 4 rounds. To have the attack working on KECCAK hash function, we have to consider padding and KECCAK parameters. Let us consider KECCAK-512 which has $r = 576$, $c = 1024$ and a hash length set to 512 bits. For the preimage attack we propose the following structure of the message. A message length is 574 bits, where first 8 lanes (512 bits) are unknown (to be determined by the attacker). Last 62 bits of the message are set to 1. The message is padded with two 1's giving a block of 576 bits. This way we fulfil a condition that all lanes (except first 8 lanes) have all 0's or 1's. We would use similar constraints on a message when attacking KECCAK with different parameters (including all KECCAK variants proposed as SHA-3 candidates).

4.1   3-Round Preimage Attack

The goal of our attack is to find a preimage for a given 512-bit hash h. In the structure of the message described above we have 512 unknown bits, then we can expect that among 2^{512} possible messages there is, on average, one with a given hash. The main idea of our attack is to find a rotational counterpart of the preimage and show that the workload for this task is below exhaustively trying all 2^{512} values. Once we have a rotational counterpart of the preimage, we simply rotate it back and get the preimage.

As stated in Remark 1, for a given state there are up to 64 possible rotational pairs (including the identity function). There are 512 unknown preimage bits in the state A, then the probability that we guess one of the rotational counterpart $A^{\leftarrow}$ is $2^{-512} \cdot 64 = 2^{-506}$. Thus we need 2^{506} guesses. There is a subtlety here which should be mentioned. There are some messages which have fewer than 64 rotations. These 'special' messages have a cyclic pattern. For example a message starting with four 0's then four 1's, then four 0's and so on. However, the number of 'special' messages is relatively small in comparison to 2^{512}. It can be shown there are 2^{256} such messages for our case. (See Appendix for detailed analysis.) For simplicity, we can start our attack with checking 2^{256} these special messages. Then there are still almost 2^{512} possibilities left, but at least we are sure that in this poll each state gives 64 rotational pairs.

To make our attack working, at the end of the 3rd round we need some $p^n_{(x,y,z)} = 0$ or $p^n_{(x,y,z)} = 1$ for each rotational number n. In the precomputation phase of the attack we generate 64 diagrams (the same as shown in Fig. 3), each with a different rotational number n. From these diagrams for each rotational number n we make a list of 10 sets of coordinates (x, y, z) for which $p^n_{(x,y,z)}$ equals 0 or 1 at the end of the 3rd round. Please note that we have to consider only (x, y, z) such that $64x + 320y + z < 512$ because the attacker knows only 512 bits of a hash (not the whole 1600-bit state).

Here is the main loop of the attack given in the following pseudo-code:

1. guess first 8 lanes (512 bits) of the state $A^{\leftarrow}$, the other bits are fixed according to the structure of the message given above.
2. run 3-round KECCAK-$f[1600]$ on the state $A^{\leftarrow}$.
3. **for** $n := 0$ to $n < 64$ **do**
   (a) *candidate* := **true**;
   (b) **for all** 10 sets of coordinates (x, y, z) being on the list created in precomputation **do**
       if $(p^n_{(x,y,z)} = 0)$ **and** $(A_{(x,y,z)} \neq A^{\leftarrow}_{(x,y,z+n)})$ **then** *candidate* := **false**;
       if $(p^n_{(x,y,z)} = 1)$ **and** $(A_{(x,y,z)} = A^{\leftarrow}_{(x,y,z+n)})$ **then** *candidate* := **false**;
   (c) **if** (*candidate* = **true**) **then** rotate back the guessed state by n bits and run 3-round KECCAK-512 on it to check whether the state is the preimage of a given hash.

The attacker compares the probabilities $p^n_{(x,y,z)}$ from the distinguisher with the actual values of A (the given hash) and $A^{\leftarrow}$ state (a result of 3-round KECCAK-512 on a guessed state). So, for example, if $p^n_{(2,3,1)} = 0$, then the bits $A_{(2,3,1)}$ and $A^{\leftarrow}_{(2,3,1+n)}$ have to be the same. If the bits are different, then the candidate is rejected as a potential rotational counterpart of the preimage. (It is the point in the pseudo-code where a variable *candidate* becomes false.)

As said earlier, running the main loop 2^{506} times, we should get one rotational counterpart of the preimage. It could be the case that our guess (candidate) of a rotational counterpart is not rejected, but in fact it is not a rotational counterpart. Let us call it a false positive candidate. There will be many such false positive candidates and the number of them is calculated as follows. For each rotational number n there is a list of 10 sets of (x, y, z) (created in precomputation) for which $p^n_{(x,y,z)}$ equals 0 or 1. A probability that we hit on a candidate for which all 10 values of $p^n_{(x,y,z)}$ are the same as on the list is 2^{-10}. Hence there will be around $2^{512}/2^{10} = 2^{502}$ false positive candidates to check.

Now let us analyze the workload of inner loops. For each candidate there are 64 rotational numbers n, and for each n there are 10 sets of coordinates to check. Checking one set of coordinates can be implemented with 3 bitwise XOR operations. So the workload of inner loops is roughly $64 \cdot 10 \cdot 3 = 1920$ XOR operations. This workload is negligibly small as in the single step θ (in a single round) there are 3200 bitwise XOR operations.

Summing up, the workload of the attack is 2^{256} (checking special messages) + 2^{506} (main loop) + 2^{502} (checking false positive candidates). Thus complexity of the attack is roughly 2^{506} Keccak-512 calls, 64 times better than the exhaustive search.

4.2   Extension to 4-Round Preimage Attack

A direct extension of the attack to 4 rounds is not possible since there are not any $p^n_{(x,y,z)} = 0$ or $p^n_{(x,y,z)} = 1$ at the end of the 4th round of the rotational distinguisher. (As said earlier, we need some $p^n_{(x,y,z)}$ equals 0 or 1 for mounting the attack.)

It is easy to notice from Fig. 3 that ι flips some $p^n_{(0,0,z)}$ and in consequence it leads to undesirable $p^n_{(x,y,z)} = 0.5$. Then if we could limit this effect, hopefully some $p^n_{(x,y,z)} = 0$ or $p^n_{(x,y,z)} = 1$ would be kept till the end of the 4th round and make the attack work for 4 rounds. To realize this, we do the following. We trace the rotational relations between A and $A^{\leftarrow}$ (as in previous sections), but this time $A^{\leftarrow}$ is run on the modified version of Keccak-$f[1600]$ — Keccak-$f[1600]$ without ι. Such a modification leads to the following observation.

Observation 2. In Example 1, Sect. 3 it was shown that application of ι to A and $A^{\leftarrow}$ states flips the value $p^n_{(x,y,z)}$ for some triples (x, y, z). Our point is that if we do not apply ι to an $A^{\leftarrow}$ state, there will be half as many flips. (It is not a general rule but for constants with very low Hamming weight there are roughly half as many flips.) Let us see a simple example.

Example 2. Let us consider two 8-bit lanes $A_{(0,0)}$ and $A^{\leftarrow}_{(0,0)}$ with the rotational number $n = 3$. The lanes have the following binary values: $A_{(0,0)} = 00000010$ and $A^{\leftarrow}_{(0,0)} = 00010000$. Now $A_{(0,0)}$ is xored with 8-bit constant $C = 00000001$ and $A^{\leftarrow}_{(0,0)}$ is left without changes. Then we have $A_{(0,0)} = 00000011$ and the unchanged $A^{\leftarrow}_{(0,0)} = 00010000$. Therefore a rotational relation has been spoilt at only one position so now $p^3_{(0,0,0)}$ is equal to 1. In Keccak-$f[1600]$ the constants are 64-bit long but the reasoning shown here stays the same.

Now is the key point. As stated earlier, fewer flips lead to fewer $p^n_{(x,y,z)}$ with undesirable 0.5 value. In consequence, now in the 4th round there are 9 triples (x, y, z) for which $p^n_{(x,y,z)} = 0$ or $p^n_{(x,y,z)} = 1$. These triples fulfil the condition $64x + 320y + z < 512$ as the attacker is given only 512 bits of a hash. In fact $p^n_{(x,y,z)} = 0$ or $p^n_{(x,y,z)} = 1$ are not at the end of the 4th round but before χ in the 4th round. (Step χ destroys these desirable probabilities.) Fortunately, we can invert ι and χ from the given hash as χ operates on the rows independently and can be inverted on a row-by-row basis. In Appendix we give a diagram showing how the probabilities $p^n_{(x,y,z)}$ evolve and propagate in the modified version of Keccak-$f[1600]$ without ι.

In precomputation phase we generate the list of sets of coordinates in the very similar way as described for the 3-round attack. The only difference is that now we use the diagram dedicated to the modified version of KECCAK-f[1600] (without ι). The diagram and exact positions where $p^n_{(x,y,z)}$ equals 0 or 1 is given in Appendix. Also in precomputation we invert ι and χ of the 4th round from the given hash (since these desirable $p^n_{(x,y,z)}$ are before χ in the 4th round, χ destroys them). The result of the inversion is now our state A to which we refer in the pseudo-code of the attack.

Here is the main loop of the attack given in the following pseudo-code:

1. guess first 8 lanes (512 bits) of the state $A^{\leftarrow}$, the other bits are fixed according to the structure of the message given above.
2. run 4-round modified KECCAK-f[1600] on the state $A^{\leftarrow}$.
3. **for** $n := 0$ **to** $n < 64$ **do**
   (a) *candidate* := **true**;
   (b) **for all** 9 sets of coordinates (x, y, z) being on the list created in precomputation **do**
       if $(p^n_{(x,y,z)} = 0)$ and $(A_{(x,y,z)} \neq A^{\leftarrow}_{(x,y,z+n)})$ **then** *candidate* := **false**;
       if $(p^n_{(x,y,z)} = 1)$ and $(A_{(x,y,z)} = A^{\leftarrow}_{(x,y,z+n)})$ **then** *candidate* := **false**;
   (c) **if** (candidate = **true**) **then** rotate back the guessed state by n bits and run 4-round KECCAK-512 on it to check whether the state is the preimage of a given hash.

The main loop of the 4-round preimage attack on KECCAK-512 is very similar to the 3-round variant, they differ only in a few places. In Step 2 of the pseudo-code instead of running a normal, full 4-round KECCAK-f[1600], we run the modified version without ι (in all 4 rounds) up to χ in the 4th round. Finally, there will two times more false positive candidates as there are only 9 triples (x, y, z) for which $p^n_{(x,y,z)} = 0$ or $p^n_{(x,y,z)} = 1$. The complexity of the attack stays the same as in the 3-round attack. That is 2^{256} (checking special messages) + 2^{506} (main loop) + 2^{503} (checking false positive candidates), which is amounts roughly to 2^{506} evaluations of the 4-round KECCAK-512.

For KECCAK-512, the preimage attack is better than the exhaustive search by a factor of 2^6. The same gain can be achieved in the attack on KECCAK-384. Our preimage attack works also on KECCAK-256 and KECCAK-224 but the gain is slightly smaller for these variants. The reason is that there are more false positive candidates to check. It is because an attacker knows fewer bits of a hash (a hash is shorter in these variants) and hence there are fewer triples (x, y, z) (fewer than in KECCAK-512 and KECCAK-384) for which $p^n_{(x,y,z)} = 0$ or $p^n_{(x,y,z)} = 1$. Consequently, the complexities of the preimage attacks on KECCAK-224 and KECCAK-256 are 2^{221} and 2^{252}, respectively.

Please also note that if we try to attack KECCAK variant with higher bitrate r (e.g. a variant with $r = 600$, $c = 1000$, and a hash length equals 512), the claimed security for this variant is $2^{c/2} = 2^{500}$. In such a case our attack would not be actually an attack as its complexity is higher than the claimed security provided by designers.

We could not extend the attack to 5 or more rounds because in the 5th round all $p_{(x,y,z)}^n = 0.5$, while for the attack we need some $p_{(x,y,z)}^n = 0$ or $p_{(x,y,z)}^n = 1$.

5   Conclusion

In this paper we have presented the rotational distinguisher for KECCAK-f[1600] permutation — the main building block of the KECCAK hash function. The distinguisher has been enhanced with the correlation analysis, allowing us to reach 5 rounds with the complexity of 2^{12}. We have implemented and verified the distinguisher and experimental results have been consistent with the theoretical model. A family of 4-round distinguishers helps us to mount the 4-round preimage attack on KECCAK-512 variant with the complexity of 2^{506}. All the presented attacks are valid for all the KECCAK variants submitted as SHA-3 candidates. As future work, it would be interesting to investigate whether the differential rebound attack could improve the rotational distinguishers. These two types of analysis (rebound and rotational) were combined in the attacks on Skein hash function [13].

Acknowledgement. We would like to thank the Keccak Team for useful comments and discussion. We also thank Dmitry Khovratovich, Thomas Peyrin and anonymous reviewers for improving the quality of the paper. The research was cofounded by the European Union from resources of the European Social Fund, Project PO KL Information technologies: Research and their interdisciplinary applications, Agreement UDA-POKL.04.01.01-00-051/10-00. Josef Pieprzyk was supported by the Australian Research Council grant DP0987734.

Appendix

Proof of Lemma 1

Analyzing the AND operation we consider two pairs of input bits. A pair from an A state and its counterpart from an $A^{\leftarrow}$ state. There are 16 possible combinations of pairs and we group them in fours. We assume that all pairs of bits inside the groups are uniformly distributed. It is shown in Fig. 5. Probabilities of getting the given group are also shown. The most inner circles represents pair of output bits (one bit from an A state and its counterpart from an $A^{\leftarrow}$ state). It is clear from Fig. 5 that four paths lead to a circle with output bits having opposite values (pairs (0,1) and (1,0)). Actually, one path has probability 0 thus a calculation of P_{out} (a probability that output bits have opposite values) comes down to adding probabilities of the three paths. We have:

$$P_{out} = p_a p_b \cdot \frac{1}{2} + (1 - p_a) p_b \cdot \frac{1}{2} + (1 - p_b) p_a \cdot \frac{1}{2} = \frac{1}{2}(p_a + p_b - p_a p_b)$$

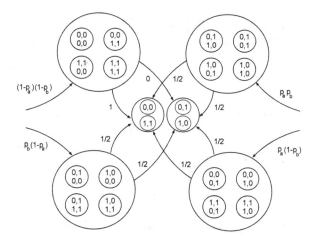

Fig. 5. All possible 'paths' for the bitwise AND operation for rotational pairs of bits.

Proof of Lemma 2

Proof of Lemma 2 is the same as for Lemma 1. The only difference is that now there are only two paths leading to a circle with output bits having opposite values. It is shown in Fig. 6. We have:

$$P_{out} = (1 - p_a)p_b \cdot 1 + (1 - p_b)p_a \cdot 1 = p_a + p_b - 2p_a p_b$$

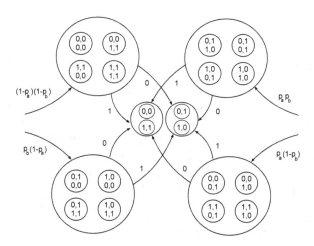

Fig. 6. All possible 'paths' for the bitwise XOR operation for rotational pairs of bits.

Probability of Relation Preservation by χ

We are given two pairs of bits $(A_{(1,2,43)}, A_{(1,2,44)}^{\leftarrow})$ and $(A_{(2,0,16)}, A_{(2,0,17)}^{\leftarrow})$. Each of these two pairs has the relation between its bits (that is bits have either the same or opposite values). We can also look at relation between pairs and there are two possibilities: either the same relation in both pairs or different relation in each pair. For example a pair $(0,1)$ and a pair $(1,0)$ means that relations in both pairs is the same (bits are different in pairs). We are interested in a probability that χ preserves the relation between pairs. χ changes the values of bits in the following way.

$$\left. \begin{aligned} A_{(1,2,43)} &:= A_{(1,2,43)} \text{ XOR } (A_{(2,2,43)} \text{ AND } A_{(3,2,43)}) \\ A_{(1,2,44)}^{\leftarrow} &:= A_{(1,2,44)}^{\leftarrow} \text{ XOR } (A_{(2,2,44)}^{\leftarrow} \text{ AND } A_{(3,2,44)}^{\leftarrow}) \end{aligned} \right\} \quad \text{first rotational pair}$$

$$\left. \begin{aligned} A_{(2,0,16)} &:= A_{(2,0,16)} \text{ XOR } (A_{(3,0,16)} \text{ AND } A_{(4,0,16)}) \\ A_{(2,0,17)}^{\leftarrow} &:= A_{(2,0,17)}^{\leftarrow} \text{ XOR } (A_{(3,0,17)}^{\leftarrow} \text{ AND } A_{(4,0,17)}^{\leftarrow}) \end{aligned} \right\} \quad \text{second rotational pair}$$

To keep the relation between bits $A_{(1,2,43)}$ and $A_{(1,2,44)}^{\leftarrow}$ from the first pair, the result of the AND operation has to be the same in both equations from the first pair. The probability of such event can be calculated from Fig. 5. We add probabilities (paths) leading to the left, inner circle. (This circle represents the output bits with the same values.) Then a probability is:

$$P = (1 - p_a)(1 - p_b) \cdot 1 + p_a p_b \cdot \frac{1}{2} + (1 - p_a)p_b \cdot \frac{1}{2} + (1 - p_b)p_a \cdot \frac{1}{2}$$

In the 5th round, after θ all $p_{(x,y,z)}^n = \frac{1}{2}$, then a numerical value of p is:

$$P = (1 - \frac{1}{2})(1 - \frac{1}{2})1 + \frac{1}{2}\frac{1}{2}\frac{1}{2} + (1 - \frac{1}{2})\frac{1}{2}\frac{1}{2} + (1 - \frac{1}{2})\frac{1}{2}\frac{1}{2} = \frac{5}{8}$$

For the second rotational pair calculations are exactly the same with the result of $\frac{5}{8}$. The event that χ preserves the relation between the first and second pair can happen either when the relation in each pair is preserved or the relation in each pair is spoilt. Thus the probability of this event is equal to:

$$P_{event} = \frac{5}{8} \cdot \frac{5}{8} + (1 - \frac{5}{8})(1 - \frac{5}{8}) = \frac{34}{64} = 0.53125$$

Values of Fixed Bits in the Distinguisher from Sect. 3.3

Bits given in tables below are set to 1. All other fixed bits which are not listed below (but are marked as fixed in Fig. 4) are set to 0.

Bit	Value
$A_{(4,4,50)}$	1
$A_{(4,4,51)}$	1
$A^{\leftarrow}_{(4,4,51)}$	1
$A^{\leftarrow}_{(0,2,21)}$	1
$A^{\leftarrow}_{(0,3,21)}$	1
$A^{\leftarrow}_{(0,0,22)}$	1
$A^{\leftarrow}_{(0,2,22)}$	1
$A^{\leftarrow}_{(0,3,22)}$	1
$A^{\leftarrow}_{(0,4,22)}$	1
$A^{\leftarrow}_{(2,0,20)}$	1
$A^{\leftarrow}_{(2,3,20)}$	1
$A^{\leftarrow}_{(2,2,21)}$	1

Bit	Value
$A^{\leftarrow}_{(2,3,21)}$	1
$A^{\leftarrow}_{(3,2,51)}$	1
$A^{\leftarrow}_{(3,3,51)}$	1
$A^{\leftarrow}_{(3,0,50)}$	1
$A^{\leftarrow}_{(3,3,50)}$	1
$A^{\leftarrow}_{(3,0,52)}$	1
$A^{\leftarrow}_{(3,2,52)}$	1
$A^{\leftarrow}_{(3,3,52)}$	1
$A^{\leftarrow}_{(3,4,52)}$	1
$A^{\leftarrow}_{(0,2,51)}$	1
$A^{\leftarrow}_{(0,3,51)}$	1

As a consequence of such settings, after π some bits have also fixed (known) values. Specifically, $A_{(1,0,0)}$ and $A_{(1,0,1)}$ with their rotational counterparts are equal to 0. Also $A_{(4,0,0)}$ and $A_{(4,0,1)}$ with their rotational counterparts are fixed, equal to 1. With this known values we are sure that the non-linear χ changes the states into the desirable rotational relation, as shown in Fig. 4.

Calculation of a Number of Special Messages

According to Definition 1 and Remark 1, for a given state A there are up to 64 possible rotational pairs (including an identity function). There are some messages which have fewer than 64 rotations. These special messages must have a cyclic pattern (e.g. alternating four 1's and four 0's) in all lanes. All 0's or all 1's in the given lane are also considered cyclic here. Please note that if at least one lane in a state A is not cyclic then there are exactly 64 possible rotational pairs $(A, A^{\leftarrow})$. It is because this non-cyclic lane is distinct for each rotational number n and consequently the whole $A^{\leftarrow}$ will be distinct.

For a 64-bit lane there are 2^{32} cyclic patterns. In our preimage attack there are 8 unknown lanes in the A state (remaining lanes are fixed and cyclic), so the number of combinations of cyclic patterns in these 8 lanes is: $\underbrace{2^{32} \cdot 2^{32} \dots \cdot 2^{32}}_{\text{8 factors}} =$ 2^{256}. And hence the number of special messages is 2^{256}.

Evolution of Probabilities $p^n_{(x,y,z)}$ in the Modified KECCAK Variant

Figure 7 shows how probabilities $p^n_{(x,y,z)}$ change in the modified KECCAK variant (without ι). The variant was used in 4-round preimage attack. Please note that in the 4th round, after θ, there are still $p^n_{(x,y,z)} = 0$ or $p^n_{(x,y,z)} = 1$ which is the key observation for the 4-round preimage attack.

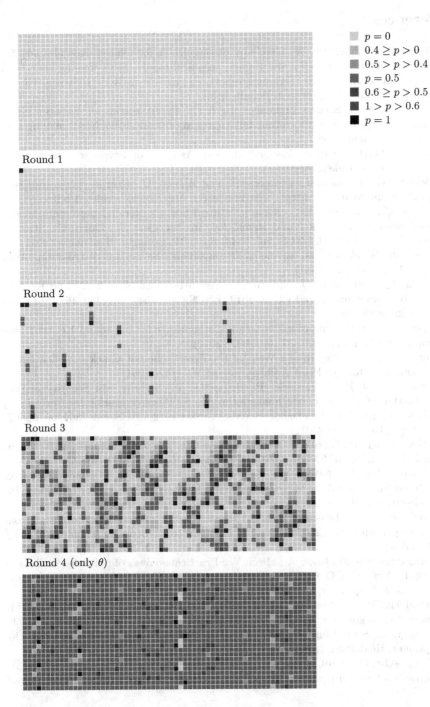

Fig. 7. Evolution of probabilities $p^n_{(x,y,z)}$ in the modified KECCAK variant.

References

1. Aumasson, J.P., Meier, W.: Zero-sum distinguishers for reduced Keccak-f and for the core functions of Luff a and Hamsi. Technical report, NIST mailing list (2009)
2. Bernstein, D.J.: Salsa20. Technical report, eSTREAM, ECRYPT Stream Cipher Project (2005). http://cr.yp.to/snuffle.html
3. Bernstein, D.J.: Second preimages for 6 (7? (8??)) rounds of Keccak? NIST mailing list (2010). http://ehash.iaik.tugraz.at/uploads/6/65/NIST-mailing-list_Bernstein-Daemen.txt
4. Bertoni, G., Daemen, J., Peeters, M., Van Assche, G.: Cryptographic sponges. http://sponge.noekeon.org
5. Bertoni, G., Daemen, J., Peeters, M., Van Assche, G.: Keccak sponge function family main document. http://keccak.noekeon.org/Keccak-main-2.1.pdf
6. Boura, C., Canteaut, A.: Zero-sum distinguishers for iterated permutations and application to KECCAK-f and Hamsi-256. In: Biryukov, A., Gong, G., Stinson, D.R. (eds.) SAC 2010. LNCS, vol. 6544, pp. 1–17. Springer, Heidelberg (2011)
7. Chernoff, H.: A note on an inequality involving the normal distribution. Ann. Probab. **9**, 533–535 (1981)
8. Dinur, I., Dunkelman, O., Shamir, A.: New attacks on Keccak-224 and Keccak-256. In: Canteaut, A. (ed.) FSE 2012. LNCS, vol. 7549, pp. 442–461. Springer, Heidelberg (2012)
9. Duan, M., Lai, X.: Improved zero-sum distinguisher for full round Keccak-f permutation. Chin. Sci. Bull. **57**, 694–697 (2012)
10. Duc, A., Guo, J., Peyrin, T., Wei, L.: Unaligned rebound attack - application to Keccak. Cryptology ePrint Archive, Report 2011/420 (2011)
11. Homsirikamol, E., Morawiecki, P., Rogawski, M., Srebrny, M.: Security margin evaluation of SHA-3 contest finalists through SAT-based attacks. In: Cortesi, A., Chaki, N., Saeed, K., Wierzchoń, S. (eds.) CISIM 2012. LNCS, vol. 7564, pp. 56–67. Springer, Heidelberg (2012)
12. Khovratovich, D., Nikolić, I.: Rotational cryptanalysis of ARX. In: Hong, S., Iwata, T. (eds.) FSE 2010. LNCS, vol. 6147, pp. 333–346. Springer, Heidelberg (2010)
13. Khovratovich, D., Nikolić, I., Rechberger, C.: Rotational rebound attacks on reduced Skein. In: Abe, M. (ed.) ASIACRYPT 2010. LNCS, vol. 6477, pp. 1–19. Springer, Heidelberg (2010)
14. Knudsen, L.R., Matusiewicz, K., Thomsen, S.S.: Observations on the Shabal keyed permutation (2009). http://www.mat.dtu.dk/people/S.Thomsen/shabal/shabal.pdf
15. Naya-Plasencia, M., Röck, A., Meier, W.: Practical analysis of reduced-round KECCAK. In: Bernstein, D.J., Chatterjee, S. (eds.) INDOCRYPT 2011. LNCS, vol. 7107, pp. 236–254. Springer, Heidelberg (2011)
16. Standaert, F.-X., Piret, G., Gershenfeld, N., Quisquater, J.-J.: SEA: a scalable encryption algorithm for small embedded applications. In: Domingo-Ferrer, J., Posegga, J., Schreckling, D. (eds.) CARDIS 2006. LNCS, vol. 3928, pp. 222–236. Springer, Heidelberg (2006)
17. Van Assche, G.: A rotational distinguisher on Shabal's keyed permutation and its impact on the security proofs. http://gva.noekeon.org/papers/ShabalRotation.pdf

Partial-Collision Attack on the Round-Reduced Compression Function of Skein-256

Hongbo Yu[1]([✉]), Jiazhe Chen[3], and Xiaoyun Wang[2,3]

[1] Department of Computer Science and Technology, Tsinghua University,
Beijing 100084, China
[2] Institute for Advanced Study, Tsinghua University, Beijing 100084, China
{yuhongbo,xiaoyunwang}@mail.tsinghua.edu.cn
[3] Key Laboratory of Cryptologic Technology and Information Security,
Ministry of Education, School of Mathematics,
Shandong University, Jinan 250100, China
jiazhechen@mail.sdu.edu.cn

Abstract. The hash function Skein is one of 5 finalists of the NIST SHA-3 competition. It is based on the block cipher Threefish which only uses three primitive operations: modular addition, rotation and bitwise XOR (ARX). This paper proposes a free-start partial-collision attack on round-reduced Skein-256 by combing the rebound attack with the modular differential techniques. The main idea of our attack is to connect two short differential paths into a long one with another differential characteristic that is complicated. Following our path, we give a free-start partial-collision attack on Skein-256 reduced to 32 rounds with Hamming distance 50 and complexity about 2^{85} hash computations. In particular, we provide practical near-collision examples for Skein-256 reduced to 24 rounds and 28 rounds in the fixed tweaks and choosing tweaks setting separately.

As far as we know, this is the first construction of a non-linear differential path for Skein which can lead to significantly improvement over previous analysis.

Keywords: Hash function · Near-collision · SHA-3 · Skein

1 Introduction

Cryptographic hash functions are very important in modern cryptology which provide integrity, authentication, etc. In 2005, as the most widely used hash functions MD5 and SHA-1 were broken by Wang *et al.* [15,16], the status of the hash functions becomes alarming. To deal with the undesirable situation, NIST

Supported by 973 program (No. 2013CB834205), the National Natural Science Foundation of China (No. 61133013 and 61373142), the Tsinghua University Initiative Scientific Research Program (No. 20111080970), and Tsinghua National Laboratory for Information Science and Technology.

S. Moriai (Ed.): FSE 2013, LNCS 8424, pp. 263–283, 2014.
DOI: 10.1007/978-3-662-43933-3_14, © Springer-Verlag Berlin Heidelberg 2014

started a hash competition for a new hash standard (SHA-3) in 2007. A total of 64 hash function proposals were submitted, and 51 of them advanced to the first round. After more than one-year's evaluation, 14 submissions have entered into the second round. By 2010, the competition came into the final round, and 5 out of the second round candidates were selected as finalists. Now NIST chooses Keccak [2] as the SHA-3 winner.

Skein [3] is one of the five finalists, which is a ARX-type hash function (based on modular addition, rotation and exclusive-OR). The core of Skein is a tweakable block cipher called Threefish, which is proposed with 256-, 512-, 1024-bit block sizes and 72, 72, 80 rounds respectively. During the competition, Skein has been attracting the attention of the cryptanalysts, and there are several cryptanalytic results on the security of the compression function of Skein. At Asiacrypt 2009 [1], Aumasson et al. proposed a free-start near-collision attack for 17-round Skein-512 compression function with the old constants. At CANS 2010 [14], Su et al. presented free-start near-collisions of Skein-256/-512 reduced to 20 rounds and Skein-1024 reduced to 24 rounds. At Asiacrypt 2010 [9], Khovratovich et al. combined the rotational attack with the rebound attack, and gave distinguishers for 53-round Skein-256 and 57-round Skein-512 respectively. When the algorithm was getting into the second round, the authors had changed the rotation constants to resist the rotational attack [8,9]. For the new version of Skein, Leurent and Roy [12] gave a boomerang distinguisher for 32-round compression function of Skein-256 and Yu et al. [17] provided a boomerang distinguisher for 36-round Skein-512. At FSE 2012 [10], Khovratovich et al. gave a pseudo-preimage attack on 22-round Skein-512 hash function and 37-round Skein-512 compression function by the biclique method, and their complexities of the attack are only marginally lower than exhaustive search.

Rebound attack for the ARX-type hash function. The rebound attack was presented by Mendel et al. at FSE 2009 [5] during the SHA-3 evaluation, it is used to analyze the hash functions based on the AES-like structure. Series of hash functions such as Whirlpool, Grøstl and JH [5–7,11] are vulnerable to the rebound attack. Its basic strategy is to match two short truncated differentials in the middle using freedom degrees of the chaining values and messages. As the matching part is the S-box layer, which has a good distribution for the input and output differences, i.e., the average probability for each input/output difference pair to pass the S-box is 1/2, one can search the differentials that can be connected with high probability.

However, when applying the rebound attack to the ARX-type hash functions, we have to find two specific differentials that can be matched. Furthermore, there aren't S-boxes in the connecting layer, and the distribution of the differences by applying the modular addition, rotation and XOR operations is harder to decided than that of S-boxes. As a result, it is far more difficult to apply the rebound attack to the ARX-type hash functions by connecting two differential paths into a long one.

Our contribution. This paper focuses on the cryptanalysis of Skein-256 compression function. We attempt to apply the rebound-type idea to the differential

Table 1. The main results of this paper.

Type	Rounds	Hamming distance	Complexity
Fixed-tweak free-start near-collision	24 (4–28)	2	2^{26}
Free-tweak free-start near-collision	28 (0–28)	34	2^{44}
Free-tweak free-start near-collision	28 (4–32)	28	2^{41}
Free-tweak free-start partial-collision	32 (0–32)	50	2^{85}

attack on the ARX-type algorithms. We first find two short differential paths by the modular differential techniques, then connect them to get a 32-round differential path. Finally, by applying the message modification techniques, we give a partial-collision attack on 32-round Skein-256 compression function. In order to verify the validity of our differential path, we provide examples of near-collision which follow our differential path for Skein-256 reduced to 24 and 28 rounds. The main results of this paper are shown in Table 1.

The rest of the paper is organized as follows. In Sect. 2, we give some notations and a brief description of Skein-256 compression function. The main idea of our attack is described in Sect. 3. In Sect. 4, we demonstrate the techniques of our attack in detail. Finally, a conclusion is given in Sect. 5.

2 Preliminaries

In this section, we first give some notations used through the paper, and then describe the compression function of Skein-256 briefly.

2.1 Notations

1. $\oplus$: exclusive-OR (XOR)
2. $+$ and $-$: addition and subtraction modular 2^{64}
3. Δa: the XOR difference of a and a'
4. $\Delta^+ a$: the modular subtraction difference of a and a' (modular 2^{64})
5. $\lll$: rotation to the left
6. $a_{i,j}$: the j-th bit of a_i, where a_i is a 64-bit word and $a_{i,64}$ is the most significant bit
7. $a_{i,j-k}$: the abbreviation of $a_{i,j}$, $a_{i,j+1}$,...,$a_{i,k}$

2.2 Near-Collision and Partial-Collision

The Handbook of Applied Cryptography [4] defines near-collision resistance by

Near-collision resistance. Let h be a hash function, it is hard to find any two inputs M, M' such that $h(M)$ and $h(M')$ differ in a small number of bits.

More specifically, h is a hash function that takes an n-bit initial value IV and an m-bit message block M as inputs, and outputs another n-bit chaining value.

A k-bit $(k < n)$ near-collision on h is obtained whenever two messages M_1 and M_2 satisfy:

$$HW(h(M_1, IV) \oplus h(M_2, IV)) = n - k,$$

where HW denotes the Hamming distance. Usually, we comprehend the "small number" as $n - k \leq n/3$.

- For a generic attack, it is expected to have a k-bit near-collision with complexity about $\sqrt{2^n/C_n^k}$. For $n = 256$ and $k = 206$, the complexity is only approximate to 2^{39} hash computations; for $n = 256$ and $k = 28$, the complexity is about $2^{66.5}$.
- However, if we fix the k-bit colliding positions, the complexity for finding a near-collision with Hamming distance $n - k$ is about $2^{k/2}$ by the birthday paradox. Previous works [13] have used the terms **partial-collision** for this notion. For $n = 256$ and $k = 206$, the complexity to find a 206-bit partial-collision is about 2^{103}.
- When we fix the k-bit colliding positions and keep the differences in the other positions being non-zero (actually, in this case the output difference is a given difference with k-bit zeroes), the complexity for finding a k-bit near-collision is about $2^{n/2}$ by the birthday paradox. For $n = 256$, the complexity is 2^{128} no matter what the value of k is.
- Furthermore, when input difference is also fixed, the generic complexity would be 2^n. In this paper, our attack belong to this case.

2.3   Brief Description of the Compression Function of Skein-256

The compression function of Skein is defined as $H = E(IV, T, M) \oplus M$, where $E(IV, T, M)$ is the block cipher Threefish, M is the message, IV is the initial value and T is the tweak value. Here E takes the message as plaintext and the IV as master key. The word size which Skein operates on is 64 bits. For Skein-256, both M and IV are 256 bits, and the length of T is 128 bits. Let us denote $h_i = (a_i, b_i, c_i, d_i)$ as the output value of the i-th round, where a_i, b_i, c_i and d_i are 64-bit words. Let $h_0 = M$ be the plaintext, the encryption procedure of Threefish-256 is carried out for $i = 1$ to 72 as follows.

If $(i - 1) \mod 4 = 0$, first compute $A_{i-1} = a_{i-1} + K_{(i-1)/4,a}$, $B_{i-1} = b_{i-1} + K_{(i-1)/4,b}$, $C_{i-1} = c_{i-1} + K_{(i-1)/4,c}$ and $D_{i-1} = d_{i-1} + K_{(i-1)/4,d}$, where $K_{(i-1)/4}$ are round subkeys which get involved every four rounds. Then carry out:

$$a_i = A_{i-1} + B_{i-1}, d_i = a_i \oplus (B_{i-1} \lll R_{i,1}),$$
$$c_i = C_{i-1} + D_{i-1}, b_i = c_i \oplus (D_{i-1} \lll R_{i,2}),$$

where $R_{i,1}$ and $R_{i,2}$ are rotation constants which can be found in [3]. For the sake of convenience, we denote $\overline{h_{i-1}} = (A_{i-1}, B_{i-1}, C_{i-1}, D_{i-1})$.

If $(i - 1) \mod 4 \neq 0$, compute:

$$a_i = a_{i-1} + b_{i-1}, d_i = a_i \oplus (b_{i-1} \lll R_{i,1}),$$
$$c_i = c_{i-1} + d_{i-1}, b_i = c_i \oplus (d_{i-1} \lll R_{i,2}).$$

After the last round, the ciphertext is computed as $\overline{h_{72}}$.

The key schedule starts with the master key $K = (k_0, k_1, k_2, k_3)$ and the tweak value $T = (t_0, t_1)$. First we compute:

$$k_4 := 0x1bd11bdaa9fc1a22 \oplus \bigoplus_{i=0}^{3} k_i \quad \text{and} \quad t_2 := t_0 \oplus t_1.$$

Then the subkeys are derived for $s = 0$ to 18:

$$K_{s,a} := k_{(s+0) \bmod 5}$$
$$K_{s,b} := k_{(s+1) \bmod 5} + t_{s \bmod 3}$$
$$K_{s,c} := k_{(s+2) \bmod 5} + t_{(s+1) \bmod 3}$$
$$K_{s,d} := k_{(s+3) \bmod 5} + s$$

3   Outline of Our Attack

Skein is one of the SHA-3 finalists which uses the operations modular addition, rotation and XOR. Because of the strong diffusion after several rounds, only short differential paths can be found for Skein. An easy way to get short differential path is to find a short local collision in the middle, and then extend the local collision forward and backward, see the left part of Fig. 1. After finding a differential path of this type, we try to modify the message of the first several rounds to enhance the efficiency. For Skein, by choosing proper differences in the messages, IVs and tweak values, we can get a local collision for 8 rounds. Then we can get differential paths with more rounds by extending the 8-round local collision forward and backward. But longer differential path is not easy to search as a single bit difference will propagate to a heavy weight difference after 4 rounds. A natural idea is raised to connect two short differential paths into a long one, and then cancel a vast number of conditions by using message modification techniques in the connecting layer, see the right part of Fig. 1. The most expensive part of this strategy is the connection of the two differential paths, which is described in Sect. 4. To solve this problem, we use the properties of both XOR difference and modular subtraction difference, and choose an optimal position for the connection. Then by the bit-carry technique (which is the key technique for the connection), we find a 8-round non-linear differential to connect two short differential paths with 16 and 8 rounds respectively. Consequently, a differential path with 32 rounds is constructed, which can be used to mount near-collision attack on 32-round Skein-256 by further applying message modification techniques to reduce the conditions. The details of our attack can be found in Sect. 4.

Actually, our method can be applied to the ARX-type hash functions that do not have complex message extensions, and the message words or IVs get involved every round (or every several rounds).

4   Partial Collisions for 32-Round Compression Function of Skein-256

As mentioned above, the basic idea of our near-collision attack is to connect two short differential paths into a long one. To achieve this purpose, there are several steps to be carried out. Firstly, proper difference in (K, T) should be chosen, which is the starting point of our attack. Secondly, we connect two short differential paths by the non-linear expansion in the middle rounds, and derive the sufficient conditions to guarantee the differential path to hold. Thirdly, the vast number of conditions in the intermediate rounds should be corrected by modifying the chaining variables, the key K and the tweak value T. Finally, after the message/IV modification, we search the remaining conditions by divide and conquer technique.

4.1   Finding Two Short Differential Paths

The differences of the master key $K = (k_0, k_1, k_2, k_3)$ and tweak value $T = (t_0, t_1)$ selected for our differential path are $\Delta k_3 = 2^{63}$ and $\Delta t_0 = 2^{63}$. According to the key schedule, the differences for the subkey $K_i = (K_{i,a}, K_{i,b}, K_{i,c}, K_{i,d})$ $(0 \leq i \leq 8)$ are shown in Table 2.

The first short differential path we used consists of 16 rounds. Because $\Delta K_1 = (0, 0, 0, 2^{63})$ and $\Delta K_2 = (0, 0, 0, 0)$, the intermediate values are selected to meet $\Delta h_4 = (0, 0, 0, 2^{63})$, resulting in an 8-round path with zero differential from rounds 5 to 12. By extending the difference Δh_4 in the backward direction for 4 rounds and the difference $\overline{\Delta h_{12}} = \Delta K_3$ in the forward direction for 4 rounds by the linear expansion, a 16-round differential path with high probability can be obtained.

The second differential path is shorter than the first one, as the number of zero-difference rounds in it is only 4. We choose Δh_{24} as $(0, 2^{63}, 2^{63}, 2^{63})$ to compensate the difference $\Delta K_6 = (0, 2^{63}, 2^{63}, 2^{63})$, which results in zero difference in rounds 25 to 28. As a consequence, a 8-round differential path with high probability can be obtained by linearly expanding the difference $\overline{\Delta h_{28}} = \Delta K_7$ in the forward direction for 4 rounds.

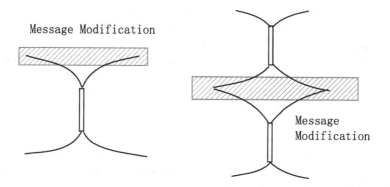

Fig. 1. Two attack models

Table 2. The subkey differences of 32-round Skein-256, given a difference $\delta = 2^{63}$ in k_3 and t_0.

i	Rd	$K_{i,a}$	$K_{i,b}$	$K_{i,c}$	$K_{i,d}$
0	0	k_0	$k_1 + t_0$	$k_2 + t_1$	k_3
		0	δ	0	δ
1	4	k_1	$k_2 + t_1$	$k_3 + t_2$	$k_4 + 1$
		0	0	0	δ
2	8	k_2	$k_3 + t_2$	$k_4 + t_0$	$k_0 + 2$
		0	0	0	0
3	12	k_3	$k_4 + t_0$	$k_0 + t_1$	$k_1 + 3$
		δ	0	0	0
4	16	k_4	$k_0 + t_1$	$k_1 + t_2$	$k_2 + 4$
		δ	0	δ	0
5	20	k_0	$k_1 + t_2$	$k_2 + t_0$	$k_3 + 5$
		0	δ	δ	δ
6	24	k_1	$k_2 + t_0$	$k_3 + t_1$	$k_4 + 6$
		0	δ	δ	δ
7	28	k_2	$k_3 + t_1$	$k_4 + t_2$	$k_0 + 7$
		0	δ	0	0
8	32	k_3	$k_4 + t_2$	$k_0 + t_0$	$k_1 + 8$
		δ	0	δ	0

4.2 Connecting the Two Short Differential Paths

The most difficult work in this paper is to connect the two short differential paths from rounds 16 to 24 by the non-linear difference expansion. We choose the 20-th round as the connecting point; the reason is that the 20-th round is the place where the subkeys is involved (in the form of integer modular addition), if we connect the two differential paths in this round, the only requirement is that the integer modular substraction differences $\Delta^+ h_{20}$ computed by the forward direction and the $\Delta^+ \overline{h_{20}}$ computed by the backward direction should satisfy the equation $\Delta^+ \overline{h_{20}} = \Delta^+ h_{20} + \Delta^+ K_5$. Otherwise, if we connect the two differential paths in the other rounds in which the subkeys do not intervene, both the integer modular substraction differences and the XOR differences computed by two directions must be equal. This will face more difficulties for connecting.

For example, let $\Delta a_i = 0x37$ be the XOR difference of round i computed in the forward direction, and $\Delta A_i = 0x11$ be the difference computed in the backward direction; the i-th round is the round where we want to match Δa_i and ΔA_i. If $i = 20$, it is easy to know that the difference $\Delta^+ a_i$ equals to $\Delta^+ A_i$ as long as $A_{i,1} = a_{i,1} \oplus 1$, $a_{i,1} = a_{i,2} = a_{i+3} \oplus 1$, $A_{i,5} = a_{i,5} \oplus 1$ and $a_{i,5} = a_{i,6} \oplus 1$.

Hence Δa_i and ΔA_i can be connected with probability 2^{-5}. Otherwise, if $i = 19$, it is obvious that Δa_i and ΔA_i can not be connected because $\Delta a_i \neq \Delta A_i$.

The major technique to connect two differential paths is the bit-carry technique; hundreds of bit equations need to be handled during the process of connection. Now we describe how to connect the two differential paths briefly.

For $16 < i \leq 20$, firstly we compute the modular difference $\Delta^+ a_{i+1} = \Delta^+ a_i + \Delta^+ b_i$ and $\Delta^+ c_{i+1} = \Delta^+ c_i + \Delta^+ d_i$, then we convert the modular differences into XOR differences so that Δa_i and Δc_i have the lowest Hamming weights respectively. Finally, the XOR differences Δb_{i+1} and Δd_{i+1} are computed as $\Delta b_{i+1} = \Delta c_{i+1} \oplus (\Delta d_i \lll R_{i,2})$ and $\Delta d_{i+1} = \Delta a_{i+1} \oplus (\Delta b_i \lll R_{i,1})$. In the same way, we can compute Δh_{24} to $\Delta \overline{h_{20}}$ by the backward direction so that the Hamming weights of Δa_i and Δc_i ($20 \leq i \leq 24$) are as low as possible (see Table 2).

What we have to do next is to match Δh_{20} and $\Delta \overline{h_{20}}$ so that their integer modular substraction difference is equal to $\Delta^+ K_5$. Generally, we first select $\Delta^+ a_{20}$ and $\Delta^+ c_{20}$ as the targets, and adjust the differences $\Delta^+ A_{20}$ and $\Delta^+ C_{20}$ to match $\Delta^+ a_{20}$ and $\Delta^+ c_{20}$ respectively by making a decision for the differences of $\Delta \overline{h_{20}}$ to Δh_{24}. Then we regard ΔB_{20} and ΔD_{20} as the targets again, and adjust the differences Δb_{20} and Δd_{20} to be consistent with ΔB_{20} and ΔD_{20} by modifying the differences Δh_{16} to Δh_{20}.

In the following, we demonstrate how to match the modular substraction differences of a_{20} and A_{20} as an example. Here $\Delta^+ a_{20}$ is the target, hence we would like to adjust the difference $\Delta^+ A_{20}$ by modifying the differences Δa_{21}, Δd_{21}, Δb_{22}, Δa_{23} and Δd_{23} so that $\Delta^+ a_{20} = \Delta^+ A_{20}$. From Table 3, we can express the modular differences of Δa_{20} and ΔA_{20} as

$$\Delta^+ a_{20} = \pm \mathbf{2^0} \pm 2^3 \pm 2^8 \pm \mathbf{2^{12}} \pm 2^{14} + \dots$$

$$\Delta^+ A_{20} = \pm \mathbf{2^0} \pm 2^2 \pm 2^4 \pm 2^6 \pm \mathbf{2^{12}} \pm 2^{24} + \dots$$

In order to match the 13 least significant bits of $\Delta^+ a_{20}$ and $\Delta^+ A_{20}$, we should eliminate the differences $\pm 2^2 \pm 2^4 \pm 2^6$ and produce the differences $\pm 2^3 \pm 2^8$ for $\Delta^+ A_{20}$. What has to be done is extending the bit differences in bold in Table 3. We first extend the differences $\Delta B_{20,1}$, $\Delta B_{20,3}$, $\Delta B_{20,5}$ and $\Delta B_{20,7}$ to be $\Delta B_{20,1-2}$, $\Delta B_{20,3-4}$, $\Delta B_{20,5-6}$ and $\Delta B_{20,7-9}$, respectively. And then, to obtain these extensions, differences $\Delta d_{21,26}$, $\Delta b_{22,38}$ and $\Delta a_{23,32}$ are modified for $\Delta B_{20,1}$; $\Delta a_{21,28}$ is modified for $\Delta B_{20,3}$; $d_{21,30}$ and $c_{22,42}$ are modified for $\Delta B_{20,5}$. In Table 3, we show the bit differences after extension in the brackets. Because $A_{20} = a_{21} - B_{20}$, we can produce the desired differences $\pm 2^3 \pm 2^8$ for A_{20} by further setting some conditions on B_{20} as follows:

$$B_{20,1} = B_{20,2} = B_{20,3} \oplus 1,$$

$$B_{20,4} = a_{20,4},$$

$$B_{20,4} = B_{20,5} = B_{20,6} = B_{20,7} = B_{20,8} \oplus 1,$$

$$B_{20,9} = a_{20,9} \oplus 1.$$

Table 3. Two differential paths for rounds $16 \sim 20$ and rounds $24 \sim \overline{20}$.

Round	shifts	Δa_i	Δb_i	Δc_i	Δd_i
16	32, 32	12, 22, 64	6, 12, 26, 38, 44, 58	6, 12, 58, 64	12, 22, 54
17	14, 16	6, 22, 26, 38, 44, 58, 64	22, 28, 38, 54, 58, 64	6, 22, 54, 58, 64	6, 8, 20, 22, 38, 40, 44, 52, 64
18	52, 57	6, 26, 28, 44, 54	1, 8, 13, 15, 20, 31, 33, 37, 38, 40, 44, 45, 52, 54, 57, 58, 63	8, 20, 38, 40, 44, 52, 54, 58	6, 10, 16, 28, 42, 44, 46, 52, 54
19	23, 40	1, 6, 8, 13, 15, 20, 26, 28, 31, 33, 37, 40, 52, 57, 63	4, 6, 8, 10, 16, 18, 22, 30, 38, 40, 42, 45, 46, 50, 56, 58	6, 8, 10, 16, 20, 28, 38, 40, 42, 45, 58	1, 3, 4, 6, 8, 11, 15, 16, 17, 20, 22, 24, 26, 28, 33, 36, 37, 38, 40, 43, 52, 54, 56, 57, 60, 61, 63
20	5, 37	1, 4, 9, 13, 15, 18, 20, 22, 26, 28, 30, 33, 37, 42, 45, 50, 52, 56, 63	3, 6, 8, 9, 11, 13, 15, 16, 22, 24, 25, 26, 27, 29, 30, 34, 38, 40, 43, 48, 53, 56, 57, 59, 60, 61	1, 3, 8, 10, 15, 22, 24, 26, 33, 36, 41, 45, 52, 54, 56, 60, 63	1, 4, 11, 18, 20, 21, 22, 23, 26, 27, 28, 30, 31, 33, 35, 37, 42, 43, 47, 51, 52, 55, 56, 61
$+\Delta K_5$		0	2^{63}	2^{63}	2^{63}
$\overline{20}$	5, 37	1, 3, 5, 7, 13, 25, 27, 31, 35, 37, 50, 56, 60	1(1-2), 3(3-4), 5(5-6), 7(7-9), 13, 25, 27, 31, 35, 37	9, 17, 19, 23, 26, 29, 41, 52, 57, 59, 61, 64	9, 17, 19, 23, 27, 29, 31, 41, 57, 59, 61
21	25, 33	**28**(28-29), **32** (32-34), 38, 50, 56, 60	28, 50, 56, 60	10, 26, 30, 42, 52, 62, 64	**26**(26-27), **30**(30-31), 52, 62
22	46, 12	32, 38	**38**(38-39)	10, **42**(42-43), 64	10, 42
23	58, 22	**32**(32-33)	32	64	0
24	32, 32	0	64	64	64

The entries of this Table indicate the positions of the difference bits of h_i.

Similarly, we can also match the other differences of a_{20} and A_{20}. That is, once an inconsistency occurs, we have to jump back to an earlier stage and make a different decision about the difference; this might result in changes of stages that are even earlier. Note that in this course, the following two requirements have to be considered.

1. For Skein-256, the subkeys (the IVs) intervene in the chaining values every 4 rounds, hence the degrees of freedom of four rounds between two subkeys are 256. As a result, the conditions deduced from guaranteeing the 4-round differential path to hold must be less than 256.
2. The conditions deduced from the 32-round differential path should be less than 640, because the degrees of the freedom of the M, K and T are 640.

The 32-round near-collision differential path is shown in Table 4. In Table 4, we use two kinds of difference: the XOR difference and the integer modular substraction difference. In the round $\overline{i}$ (the round after adding the subkey, $i = 0, 4, 8, ..., 28$), we express the difference in the positions a and c with the integer modular substraction difference, i.e., $\Delta^+A_i = \Delta^+a_i + \Delta^+K_{i,a}$ and $\Delta^+C_i = \Delta^+c_i + \Delta^+K_{i,c}$, because we only use the integer modular addition properties of A_i and C_i when computing the chaining value h_{i+1}). In the other positions of the differential path, we use the XOR difference (see Table 4).

Corresponding to the differential path in Table 4, we can compute the sufficient conditions in $h_{20} \sim h_0$ and $\overline{h_{20}} \sim \overline{h_{32}}$, which are shown in Tables 7 and 8 respectively.

4.3   Message/IV Modification

In order to fulfill the Message/IV modification, we replace the conditions $b_{i,j}$, $d_{i,j}$ $(\overline{16} \le i \le 19, 1 \le j \le 32)$ from the round 19 down to round $\overline{16}$ in Table 7 with

Table 4. Differential path used for the partial-collision of 32-round compression function of Skein-256, with a probability of 2^{-89} after the message/IV modification.

Round	Δa_i	Δb_i	Δc_i	Δd_i
0	0500900a50210840	8100100210210800	0040040082044204	8040000084004204
$\overline{0}{:}+K_0$	Δ^+a_0	0100100210210800	Δ^+c_0	0040000084004204
1	0400800840000040	0000800040000040	0000040002040000	0000040002000000
2	0400000800000000	0000000800000000	0000000000040000	0000000000040000
3	0400000000000000	0400000000000000	0000000000000000	0000000000000000
4	0000000000000000	0000000000000000	0000000000000000	8000000000000000
$\overline{4}{:}+K_1$	0000000000000000	0000000000000000	0000000000000000	0000000000000000
$5 - 12$	0000000000000000	0000000000000000	0000000000000000	0000000000000000
$\overline{12}{:}+K_3$	8000000000000000	0000000000000000	0000000000000000	0000000000000000
13	8000000000000000	0000000000000000	0000000000000000	8000000000000000
14	8000000000000000	8000000000000800	8000000000000000	8000000000000000
15	0000000000000800	0000000000200000	0000000000000000	0200000000000820
16	0000000000200800	0600082002000820	0600000000000820	0020000000200800
$\overline{16}{:}+K_4$	$\Delta^+a_{16} + 2^{63}$	0600182006000820	$\Delta^+c_{16} + 2^{63}$	0020000000600800
17	8600182002200020	8260006008200000	8260000000200020	800819a002801a0
18	08a0080006000020	4328099340d85f83	022819a000d80f80	08a82e0000008220
19	7898108fc7e9d4a1	0a4230a8a86980a0	0ac010a0004780a0	b1387ca0064840a5
20	d146001565005501	800001b6251fd503	4908150002104103	9900150068304100
$\overline{20}{:}+K_5$	Δ^+a_{20}	0000019fe700f703	$\Delta^+c_{20} + 2^{63}$	39001f01ebf3ff00
21	dfc601eff8000000	f7fe000008000000	2019fe007a003e03	e0080001fe000003
22	00003fff80000000	000001e000000000	80001e0000003e00	0000020000000200
23	0000000780000000	0000000080000000	8000000000000000	0000000000000000
24	0000000000000000	8000000000000000	8000000000000000	8000000000000000
$\overline{24}{:}+K_6$	0000000000000000	8000000000000000	8000000000000000	8000000000000000
25-28	0000000000000000	0000000000000000	0000000000000000	0000000000000000
$\overline{28}{:}+K_7$	0000000000000000	8000000000000000	0000000000000000	0000000000000000
29	8000000000000000	0000000000000000	0000000000000000	8000000001000000
30	8000000000000000	8000001001000800	8000000001000000	8000000000000000
31	0000001001000800	0000000001200000	0000000001000000	0200001041040820
32	0000001000200800	4304083042040830	0200001040040820	0120001000200800
$\overline{32}{:}+K_8$	8000001000200800	c104081042040810	8200001040040820	0120001000200800
Output Difference	8500901a50010040	4004181250250010	82400410c2004a24	8160001084204a04

$a_{i+1,((j+R_{i+1,0})\mod 64)} \oplus d_{i+1,((j+R_{i+1,0})\mod 64)}$ and $b_{i+1,((j+R_{i+1,1})\mod 64)} \oplus$ $c_{i+1,((j+R_{i+1,1})\mod 64)}$ respectively.

We divide the conditions in Tables 7 and 8 into three groups which are shown in Tables 9, 10, and 11 separately. The conditions in group-1 include all the conditions from round $\overline{16}$ to 20 which are determined by $h_{20}=(a_{20}, b_{20}, c_{20}$ and $d_{20})$. The conditions in group-2 consist of the conditions in $\overline{h}_{20}, h_{21}, ..., h_{24}$ and c_{16} that depend on h_{20} and K_5. All the other conditions are incorporated into group-3 which are decided by h_{20}, K_5, $K_{4,b}$ and $K_{4,d}$. The distribution of the conditions for 32-round Skein-256 is shown in Table 5.

There are 216 conditions in group-1, of which 174 conditions can be fulfilled by modifying the values of h_{20}. Most of conditions in group-2 can be corrected by modifying K_5 and only 18 conditions are left after message modification. The 15 conditions in a_{16}, b_{16}, d_{16} and a_{15} of group-3 can be modified by $K_{4,b}$ and $K_{4,d}$, and there are 89 conditions remaining after the message modification.

4.4 The Partial-Collision Attack on the Compression Function of 32-Round Skein-256

In our attack, we take the 256-bit value h_{20} and the 384-bit K_5, $K_{4,b}$ and $K_{4,d}$ as the random variables. As the chaining values h_{19}, h_{18}, h_{17} and $\overline{h}_{16}$ only depend on h_{20}, the search of the right h_{20} is independent of K_5 and K_4. Once h_{20} are fixed, the values of $\overline{h}_{20}$, h_{21}, h_{22}, h_{23}, h_{24} and c_{16} are only determined by K_5. Therefore, our near-collision search algorithm can be divided into three phases: the first phase is to find h_{20} that satisfies the conditions in group-1; the second phase is to find K_5 to ensure the conditions in group-2; the last phase is to find $K_{4,b}$ and $K_{4,d}$ so that the differential path in Table 4 holds.

The partial-collision search algorithm:

1. Select a 256-bit chaining value $h_{20} = (a_{20}, b_{20}, c_{20}, d_{20})$ which satisfies the 95 conditions in h_{20} in Table 9.
   - Compute the chaining value $h_{19} = (a_{19}, b_{19}, c_{19}, d_{19})$ from h_{20} and modify the 62 conditions in a_{19} and c_{19} in Table 9 by h_{20} using the message/IV modification techniques.
   - Calculate the chaining values $h_{18} = (a_{18}, b_{18}, c_{18}, d_{18})$, $h_{17} = (a_{17}, b_{17}, c_{17}, d_{17})$ and $\overline{h}_{16} = (A_{16}, B_{16}, C_{16}, D_{16})$ by h_{19} in the backward direction. Modify 17 out of the 59 conditions, and check whether the other 42 conditions hold. If so, goto step 2; otherwise, goto step 1.

Table 5. The conditions distribution for our attack of 32-round Skein-256.

Groups	Conditions	Modified conditions	Used message/IV
1	216	174	$a_{20}, b_{20}, c_{20}, d_{20}$
2	168	150	$K_{5,a}, K_{5,b}, K_{5,c}, K_{5,d}$
3	104	15	$K_{4,b}, K_{4,d}$

2. Choose the 256-bit subkey $K_5 = (K_{5,a}, K_{5,b}, K_{5,c}, K_{5,d})$ randomly.
   - Compute

$$\overline{h_{20}} = h_{20} + K_5 = (A_{20}, B_{20}, C_{20}, D_{20}),$$
$$c_{16} = C_{16} - K_{5,b}.$$

   Modify the 53 conditions in B_{20} and D_{20} by $K_{5,b}$ and $K_{5,d}$ respectively.
   - Compute h_{21}, h_{22}, h_{23} and h_{24} by $\overline{h_{20}}$ in the forward direction. Modify the 97 conditions in h_{21}, h_{22} and h_{23} by K_5. Then check whether the other 18 conditions are satisfied. If so, goto step 3; otherwise, goto step 2.
3. Select the 128-bit value $K_{4,b}$ and $K_{4,d}$ randomly.
   - According to the key schedule,

$$K_{5,a} = k_0, K_{5,b} = k_1 + t_2, K_{5,c} = k_2 + t_0, K_{5,d} = k_3 + 5,$$
$$K_{4,a} = k_4, K_{4,b} = k_0 + t_1, K_{4,c} = k_1 + t_2, K_{4,d} = k_2 + 4,$$

   where $k_4 = 0x1bd11bdaa9fc1a22 \oplus \bigoplus_{i=0}^{3} k_i$ and $t_2 = t_0 \oplus t_1$. Derive the key $K = (k_0, k_1, k_2, k_3)$ and the tweak value $T = (t_0, t_1)$:

$$k_0 = K_{5,a},$$
$$k_1 = K_{5,b} - ((K_{4,b} - K_{5,a}) \oplus (K_{5,c} - K_{4,d} + 4)),$$
$$k_2 = K_{4,d} - 4,$$
$$k_3 = K_{5,d} - 5,$$
$$t_0 = K_{5,c} - K_{4,d} + 4,$$
$$t_1 = K_{4,b} - K_{5,a}.$$

   Then further deduce:

$$K_{4,a} = 0x1bd11bdaa9fc1a22 \oplus K_{5,a} \oplus (K_{5,d} - 5) \oplus (K_{4,d} - 4) \oplus$$
$$(K_{5,b} - ((K_{4,b} - K_{5,a}) \oplus (K_{5,c} - K_{4,d} + 4))),$$
$$K_{4,c} = K_{5,b}.$$

   - Compute $b_{16} = B_{16} - K_{4,b}$, $d_{16} = D_{16} - K_{4,d}$ and $a_{16} = A_{16} - K_{4,a}$. Modify the 15 conditions in b_{16}, d_{16} and a_{16} by $K_{4,b}$ and $K_{4,d}$ respectively.
4. Compute $K_0, K_1, K_2, K_3, K_6, K_7, K_8$ by K and T, calculate $\overline{h_{24}}$ to $\overline{h_{32}}$ by h_{24}, K_6, K_7 and K_8 in the forward direction, and compute h_{15} to h_0 by h_{16}, K_0, K_1, K_2 and K_3 in the backward direction.
5. Let $h'_{20} = h_{20} \oplus \Delta h_{20}$, where Δh_{20} is the difference of round 20 in Table 4. Let $K' = (k_0, k_1, k_2, k_3 + 2^{63})$ and $T' = (t_0 + 2^{63}, t_1)$, compute $h'_{19} \sim h'_0$ and $\overline{h'_{20}} \sim \overline{h'_{32}}$ by h'_{20}, K' and T'. Then check whether $h_0 \oplus h'_0 = \Delta h_0$ and $\overline{h_{32}} \oplus \overline{h'_{32}} = \Delta \overline{h_{32}}$, where Δh_0 and $\Delta \overline{h_{32}}$ are the differences in round 0 and round 32 of Table 4. If so, output the message pair $(M = h_0, M' = h'_0)$, the master key $K = (k_0, k_1, k_2, k_3)$ and the tweak $T = (t_0, t_1)$; otherwise, goto step 3.

Degrees of freedom analysis: We consider the degrees of freedom from the following four inspects:

Table 6. Free-start near collisions examples for Skein-256.

Near-Collision 1: a near collision with Hamming distance 2 from rounds 4 to 28
Message of Round 4

$M^{(1)}$	e06dae5ef2a07f47 ab4a1eb0d3ca9657 2df69dff1cf902f7 <u>9</u>4f1d26c1640e047
$M^{(2)}$	e06dae5ef2a07f47 ab4a1eb0d3ca9657 2df69dff1cf902f7 <u>1</u>4f1d26c1640e047
Key	
$K^{(1)}$	276233eabba1aee6 66468bf4f9186874 4c1044cb8ebdb40 <u>7</u>1b6c3354128213a
$K^{(2)}$	276233eabba1aee6 66468bf4f9186874 4c1044cb8ebdb40 <u>f</u>1b6c3354128213a
Tweak	
$T^{(1)}$	<u>0</u>00000000000000 000000000000000
$T^{(2)}$	<u>8</u>00000000000000 000000000000000
Output: $a_4 \oplus \overline{a_{28}}$	
Output1	7d750ef8ccb0bbd0 <u>1</u>cc1e98ec9f9a18a eab66d1642a6c3f1 <u>f</u>a19cc4783700f1c
Output2	7d750ef8ccb0bbd0 <u>9</u>cc1e98ec9f9a18a eab66d1642a6c3f1 <u>7</u>a19cc4783700f1c

Near-Collision 2: a near collision with Hamming distance 34 from rounds 0 to 28
Message of Round 0

$M^{(1)}$	75<u>56</u>7a<u>6</u>7<u>22</u>e984c1 6aa7<u>4</u>b49<u>b</u>44a4b0e 8d<u>c</u>87<u>c2</u>2<u>35</u>f<u>e4944</u> 91<u>0</u>233d1a<u>5</u>628<u>f</u>29
$M^{(2)}$	70<u>56</u>ea6d<u>7</u>2c88c81; <u>e</u>ba7<u>5</u>b4<u>b</u>a46b4<u>3</u>0e 8d<u>8</u>87<u>822</u>b7<u>f</u>a0b4<u>0</u> 11<u>4</u>233d1<u>2</u>162c<u>d2</u>d
Key	
$K^{(1)}$	174b482acb8192de d581ea180039c605 6a83af6bc11fb1ca <u>7</u>3aaa3494528212f
$K^{(2)}$	174b482acb8192de d581ea180039c605 6a83af6bc11fb1ca <u>f</u>3aaa3494528212f
Tweak	
$T^{(1)}$	<u>2</u>04974d2f898e9cd 0085794e10264ba2
$T^{(2)}$	<u>a</u>04974d2f898e9cd 0085794e10264ba2
Output: $a_0 \oplus \overline{a_{28}}$	
Output1	9<u>b</u>a9ee2<u>0f</u>9e4d<u>b</u>f<u>b</u> d99ef6d<u>b</u>e7<u>0</u>3fd1b 567<u>0</u>33e4<u>7</u>cd85ebe b<u>f</u>a917f6<u>4</u>a5f8926
Output2	9<u>e</u>a97e2aa9<u>c</u>5d3bb d89ee6d9<u>f</u>722f<u>5</u>1b 563<u>0</u>37e4fedc1cba 3<u>f</u>e917f6<u>ce</u>5f<u>c</u>b22

Near-Collision 3: a near collision with Hamming distance 28 from rounds 4 to 32
Message of Round 4

$M^{(1)}$	7c4d70e0bb911686 126e7d70b549e195 687401fcfdda8a32 <u>7</u>4d4ba53d43c8f4b
$M^{(2)}$	7c4d70e0bb911686 126e7d70b549e195 687401fcfdda8a32 <u>f</u>4d4ba53d43c8f4b
Key	
$K^{(1)}$	174b482acb8192de f80431a5cb0dcdc8 43f0a9b602dfc4e2 <u>7</u>3aaa3494528212f
$K^{(2)}$	174b482acb8192de f80431a5cb0dcdc8 43f0a9b602dfc4e2 <u>f</u>3aaa3494528212f
Tweak	
$T^{(1)}$	<u>4</u>6dc7a88b6d8d6b5 b895bc87ab324c19
$T^{(2)}$	<u>c</u>6dc7a88b6d8d6b5 b895bc87ab324c19
Output: $a_4 \oplus \overline{a_{32}}$	
Output1	e5e0fd<u>7</u>e13<u>0</u>df9ae <u>c</u>d8<u>f</u>77d82<u>c</u>f7<u>0</u>926 <u>a</u>bd50d<u>6</u>73bc<u>9</u>f<u>a</u>b1 <u>f</u>eca27<u>3</u>55d<u>9</u>1f<u>4</u>5d
Output2	65e0fd<u>6</u>e13<u>2</u>df1ae <u>0</u>c8b<u>7</u>fc86ef3<u>0</u>136 <u>2</u>9d50d<u>7</u>77bcd<u>f</u>2<u>9</u>1 <u>7</u>fea27<u>2</u>55db1f<u>c</u>5d

- The total degrees of the freedom come from the message M, the master key K and the tweak value T. For skein-256, we have $256 + 256 + 128 = 640$ degrees of freedom to mount our attack. The number of conditions in our differentials is 488 (see Tables 7 and 8). Hence the degrees of freedom are sufficient to perform our attack.
- The local degrees of the freedom from rounds 20 down to $\overline{16}$ (group-1) are 256 which come from the chaining variables $h_{20} = (a_{20}, b_{20}, c_{20}, d_{20})$. The number of the conditions in these 5 rounds is 216. It is enough to find a pair h_{20} and h'_{20} so that the differential path of this part holds.
- The conditions in $\overline{h_{20}}$, h_{21}, ... , h_{24} and c_{16} (group-2) are determined by K_5 with 256-bit freedom degrees. While the number of conditions of this part is only 168, so it's enough to search a right K_5.
- The degrees of the freedom from rounds $\overline{24}$ to 32 and rounds 16 down to 0 are 128. The number of conditions of this part is 104. Consequently, it's enough to search a partial-collision after the message modifications.

The complexity computation: The complexity of our attack includes three parts:

- The first part is to find a right 256-bit chaining value h_{20} so that it satisfies the 216 conditions of h_{20}, h_{19}, h_{18}, h_{17} and $\overline{h_{16}}$ in Table 7. After the message modifications, there are 42 conditions remaining. Hence the complexity of this part is about 2^{42} 32-round Skein-256 compression function operations.
- The second part is to find a right 256-bit value K_5 that satisfies the 168 conditions in Table 10. After message modifications, the complexity for this part is about 2^{18}.
- The third part is to find a 128-bit value $K_{4,b}$ and $K_{4,d}$ that satisfies the 104 conditions in Table 11. After message modification, the complexity for this part is about 2^{89}.

As a result, the total complexity of our attack is about $2^{42} + 2^{18} + 2^{89} \approx 2^{89}$ 32-round Skein-256 compression function operations. The complexity can be reduced further when considering the impact of additional paths.

4.5   Near-Collisions Examples for Skein-256

In order to verify our differential path in Table 4, we give an example of 24-round (4–28) near-collision without choosing the tweak. The complexity is about 2^{26}, and the Hamming distance is only 2. We also give two near-collision examples for 28-round Skein-256 in the free tweak setting. The first example is a near collision from rounds 0 to 28 with Hamming distance 34, and the second is from rounds 4 to 32 with Hamming distance 28. Even though the complexities of the attacks for the two near collisions were estimated to be about 2^{46} and 2^{43} respectively according to our differential path, we expect they will be lower in practice due to the impact of additional paths. They are confirmed by our implementations, and the practical complexities are about 2^{44} and 2^{41} for the two near collisions respectively. This also deduces the complexity of the partial-collision attack on 32-round Skein-256 by a factor of $2^{2+2} = 2^4$ resulting in an attack complexity 2^{85}. The near collisions are shown in Table 6.

4.6   Discussions about the Application to Skein-512

Our techniques can be also applied to Skein-512 and Skein-1024. Since Skein-512 is the primary proposal of Skein by the authors, we will mainly discuss how to apply our techniques to Skein-512: By selecting the differences for the master key $K = (k_0, k_1, ..., k_7)$ and the tweak value $T = (t_0, t_1)$ as $\Delta k_7 = 2^{63}$ and $\Delta t_0 = 2^{63}$, we construct the first short differential path from rounds 37 to 52 with a 8-round zero-differential (from rounds 41 to 48) and the second short differential path from rounds 57 to 68 with a 4-round zero-differential in the middle. Similar to the attack on Skein-256, connecting the two differential paths (between round 53 and round 60) is also the most difficult part of the attack. Moreover, we consider the connection to be even harder than that of Skein-256 since now 512 bits have to be connected. By leveraging the strategy of Skein-256 on Skein-512 with more carefulness, we estimate that the complexity of the attack on Skein-512 reduced to 32 rounds with Hamming distance 55 is about 2^{88} 32-round Skein-512 computations.

5   Conclusions

In this paper, we apply the rebound-type idea to the differential attack of the ARX-type hash algorithms and connect two specific short differentials into a long one. Utilizing our technique, we give three near-collision examples for 24 and 28 rounds Skein-256 compression function. The complexity of partial-collision attack on 32-round Skein-256 compression function is about 2^{85}. Our method has potential application to other ARX-type hash functions.

Appendix

Table 7. The sufficient conditions for Round 20 down to 0 of the differential path in Table 4.

Round	Var	Conditions	Count
20	a_{20}	$a_{20,27} = a_{20,25} \oplus 1$, $a_{20,31} = a_{20,30}$, $a_{20,33} = a_{20,31}$, $a_{20,35} = a_{20,30}$, $a_{20,37} = a_{20,30} \oplus 1$, $a_{20,51} = a_{20,50}$, $a_{20,57} = a_{20,55}$	7
	b_{20}	$b_{20,1} = a_{20,1}$, $b_{20,2} = a_{20,1} \oplus 1$, $b_{20,9} = a_{20,9} \oplus 1$, $b_{20,11} = a_{20,11} \oplus 1$, $b_{20,13} = a_{20,13} \oplus 1$, $b_{20,15} = a_{20,15}$, $b_{20,16} = a_{20,15}$, $b_{20,17} = a_{20,15}$, $b_{20,18} = a_{20,15}$, $b_{20,19} = a_{20,15}$, $b_{20,20} = a_{20,15}$, $b_{20,21} = a_{20,15} \oplus 1$, $b_{20,25} = a_{20,25} \oplus 1$, $b_{20,27} = a_{20,27}$, $b_{20,30} = a_{20,30}$, $b_{20,34} = a_{20,30} \oplus 1$, $b_{20,35} = a_{20,35} \oplus 1$, $b_{20,37} = a_{20,37} \oplus 1$, $b_{20,38} = a_{20,37} \oplus 1$	19
	c_{20}	$c_{20,2} = c_{20,1}$, $c_{20,21} = c_{20,15} \oplus 1$, $c_{20,45} = c_{20,43}$, $c_{20,63} = c_{20,60}$	4
	d_{20}	$d_{20,9} = c_{20,9}$, $d_{20,15} = c_{20,15} \oplus 1$, $d_{20,21} = c_{20,21}$, $d_{20,22} = c_{20,21} \oplus 1$, $d_{20,41} = c_{20,41}$, $d_{20,43} = c_{20,43} \oplus 1$, $d_{20,45} = c_{20,45} \oplus 1$, $d_{20,57} = c_{20,57} \oplus 1$, $d_{20,60} = c_{20,60}$, $d_{20,61} = c_{20,61}$	10
19	a_{19}	$a_{19,1} = a_{20,1}$, $a_{19,6} = b_{19,6} \oplus 1$, $a_{19,8} = a_{20,9}$, $a_{19,11} = a_{20,11}$, $a_{19,13} = a_{20,13}$, $a_{19,15} = a_{20,15}$, $a_{19,16} = a_{20,15}$, $a_{19,17} = a_{20,15} \oplus 1$, $a_{19,20} = b_{19,20} \oplus 1$, $a_{19,22} = b_{19,22} \oplus 1$, $a_{19,23} = a_{20,25} \oplus 1$, $a_{19,24} = a_{20,25}$, $a_{19,25} = a_{20,25} \oplus 1$, $a_{19,26} = a_{20,25}$, $a_{19,27} = a_{20,25}$, $a_{19,31} = a_{20,30}$, $a_{19,32} = a_{19,31} \oplus 1$, $a_{19,33} = a_{20,30} \oplus 1$, $a_{19,34} = a_{20,30}$, $a_{19,35} = a_{20,30}$, $a_{19,36} = a_{20,30}$, $a_{19,40} = b_{19,40}$, $a_{19,45} = b_{19,45} \oplus 1$, $a_{19,52} = b_{19,50}$, $a_{19,53} = a_{19,52} \oplus 1$, $a_{19,56} = a_{20,55} \oplus 1$, $a_{19,60} = a_{20,61} \oplus 1$, $a_{19,61} = a_{20,61} \oplus 1$, $a_{19,62} = a_{20,61}$, $a_{19,63} = a_{20,63} \oplus 1$	30
	b_{19}	$b_{19,8} = a_{19,9}$, $b_{19,16} = a_{20,15} \oplus 1$, $b_{19,17} = a_{20,15}$, $b_{19,22} = b_{19,20} \oplus 1$, $b_{19,23} = a_{20,25} \oplus 1$, $b_{19,28} = a_{20,25} \oplus 1$, $b_{19,30} = a_{20,30}$, $b_{19,32} = a_{20,30}$, $b_{19,36} = a_{20,30}$, $b_{19,38} = a_{20,30} \oplus 1$, $b_{19,40} = a_{20,41}$, $b_{19,46} = b_{19,45} \oplus 1$, $b_{19,50} = a_{20,50} \oplus 1$, $b_{19,55} = a_{20,55} \oplus 1$, $b_{19,58} = a_{20,60}$, $b_{19,60} = a_{20,60} \oplus 1$	16
	c_{19}	$c_{19,6} = d_{19,6} \oplus 1$, $c_{19,8} = a_{19,9}$, $c_{19,16} = a_{20,15} \oplus 1$, $c_{19,17} = c_{19,16}$, $c_{19,18} = c_{19,17}$, $c_{19,19} = c_{19,18}$, $c_{19,23} = d_{20,23} \oplus 1$, $c_{19,38} = d_{19,38} \oplus 1$, $c_{19,40} = d_{19,40}$, $c_{19,45} = d_{19,45} \oplus 1$, $c_{19,55} = c_{20,52} \oplus 1$, $c_{19,56} = c_{20,52}$, $c_{19,58} = c_{20,57}$, $c_{19,60} = c_{20,60} \oplus 1$	14
	d_{19}	$d_{19,1} = c_{20,1} \oplus 1$, $d_{19,3} = c_{20,1}$, $d_{19,8} = c_{20,9}$, $d_{19,15} = c_{20,15} \oplus 1$, $d_{19,20} = c_{20,15} \oplus 1$, $d_{19,26} = c_{20,26} \oplus 1$, $d_{19,27} = c_{20,26}$, $d_{19,40} = c_{20,41}$, $d_{19,43} = c_{20,43} \oplus 1$, $d_{19,44} = d_{19,43}$, $d_{19,46} = d_{19,43}$, $d_{19,47} = d_{19,46} \oplus 1$, $d_{19,52} = c_{20,52} \oplus 1$, $d_{19,53} = d_{19,52}$, $d_{19,54} = d_{19,53}$, $d_{19,57} = c_{20,57} \oplus 1$, $d_{19,61} = c_{20,61} \oplus 1$, $d_{19,62} = c_{20,61} \oplus 1$	18
18	a_{18}	$a_{18,6} = a_{19,6}$, $a_{18,26} = a_{19,26}$, $a_{18,27} = a_{19,27}$, $a_{18,44} = b_{18,44}$, $a_{18,54} = b_{18,54} \oplus 1$, $a_{18,56} = a_{19,56} \oplus 1$, $a_{18,60} = a_{19,60} \oplus 1$	7
	b_{18}	$b_{18,1} = a_{19,1} \oplus 1$, $b_{18,2} = a_{19,1}$, $b_{18,8} = a_{19,8} \oplus 1$, $b_{18,9} = a_{19,8} \oplus 1$, $b_{18,10} = a_{19,8}$, $b_{18,11} = a_{19,11} \oplus 1$, $b_{18,12} = a_{19,11}$, $b_{18,13} = a_{19,13}$, $b_{18,15} = a_{19,15} \oplus 1$, $b_{18,20} = a_{19,20} \oplus 1$, $b_{18,21} = a_{19,20} \oplus 1$, $b_{18,23} = a_{19,23}$, $b_{18,24} = a_{19,23}$, $b_{18,31} = a_{19,31} \oplus 1$, $b_{18,33} = a_{19,33}$, $b_{18,34} = b_{18,33}$, $b_{18,37} = b_{18,33} \oplus 1$, $b_{18,40} = a_{19,40} \oplus 1$, $b_{18,41} = b_{18,40} \oplus 1$, $b_{18,44} = a_{19,45}$, $b_{18,52} = a_{19,52} \oplus 1$, $b_{18,54} = a_{19,56}$, $b_{18,57} = a_{19,56} \oplus 1$, $b_{18,58} = a_{19,56}$, $b_{18,63} = a_{19,63}$	25
	c_{18}	$c_{18,8} = c_{19,8} \oplus 1$, $c_{18,9} = c_{18,8} \oplus 1$, $c_{18,10} = d_{18,10}$, $c_{18,11} = d_{18,10}$, $c_{18,12} = d_{18,10} \oplus 1$, $c_{18,20} = d_{18,16}$, $c_{18,21} = c_{18,20} \oplus 1$, $c_{18,23} = c_{19,23}$, $c_{18,24} = c_{19,23}$, $c_{18,38} = c_{19,38}$, $c_{18,40} = c_{19,40} \oplus 1$, $c_{18,41} = c_{18,40} \oplus 1$, $c_{18,44} = d_{18,44} \oplus 1$, $c_{18,45} = c_{19,45} \oplus 1$, $c_{18,52} = d_{18,52} \oplus 1$, $c_{18,54} = d_{18,54}$, $c_{18,58} = c_{19,58}$	17
	d_{18}	$d_{18,6} = c_{19,6}$, $d_{18,10} = c_{19,8}$, $d_{18,16} = c_{19,16} \oplus 1$, $d_{18,42} = c_{19,40} \oplus 1$, $d_{18,43} = d_{18,42} \oplus 1$, $d_{18,46} = c_{19,45}$, $d_{18,54} = c_{19,55}$, $d_{18,56} = c_{19,56}$, $d_{18,60} = c_{19,60}$	9
17	a_{17}	$a_{17,6} = a_{18,6}$, $a_{17,22} = b_{17,22} \oplus 1$, $a_{17,26} = a_{18,26} \oplus 1$, $a_{17,38} = b_{17,38}$, $a_{17,44} = a_{18,44} \oplus 1$, $a_{17,45} = a_{18,44}$, $a_{17,58} = a_{18,60}$, $a_{18,59} = a_{18,60}$	8
	b_{17}	$b_{17,28} = a_{18,26}$, $b_{17,39} = b_{17,38}$, $b_{17,54} = a_{18,54}$, $b_{17,55} = a_{18,55}$, $b_{17,58} = a_{18,60}$	5
	c_{17}	$c_{17,6} = d_{17,6} \oplus 1$, $c_{17,22} = d_{17,22}$, $c_{17,54} = c_{18,54} \oplus 1$, $c_{17,55} = c_{18,55}$, $c_{17,58} = c_{18,58} \oplus 1$	5
	d_{17}	$d_{17,8} = c_{18,8}$, $d_{17,9} = d_{17,8}$, $d_{17,20} = c_{18,20} \oplus 1$, $d_{17,22} = c_{18,23} \oplus 1$, $d_{17,38} = c_{18,38} \oplus 1$, $d_{17,40} = c_{18,40}$, $d_{17,41} = c_{18,41}$, $d_{17,44} = c_{18,44}$, $d_{17,45} = c_{18,45}$, $d_{17,52} = c_{18,52}$	10
$\overline{16}$	B_{16}	$B_{16,6} = a_{17,6}$, $B_{16,26} = a_{17,26} \oplus 1$, $B_{16,27} = B_{16,26} \oplus 1$, $B_{16,38} = a_{17,38}$, $B_{16,44} = a_{17,44}$, $B_{16,45} = a_{17,45}$, $B_{16,58} = a_{17,58}$, $B_{16,59} = a_{17,59} \oplus 1$	8
	D_{16}	$D_{16,22} = c_{17,22} \oplus 1$, $D_{16,23} = D_{16,22} \oplus 1$, $D_{16,54} = c_{17,54} \oplus 1$	3
16	a_{16}	$a_{16,12} = B_{16,12} \oplus 1$, $a_{16,22} = a_{17,22}$	2
	b_{16}	$b_{16,6} = B_{16,6} \oplus 1$, $b_{16,12} = B_{16,12}$, $b_{16,26} = B_{16,26} \oplus 1$, $b_{16,38} = B_{16,38}$, $b_{16,44} = B_{16,44} \oplus 1$, $b_{16,58} = B_{16,58}$, $b_{16,59} = B_{16,59}$	7
	c_{16}	$c_{16,6} = c_{17,6}$, $c_{16,12} = D_{16,12} \oplus 1$, $c_{16,58} = c_{17,58} \oplus 1$, $c_{16,59} = c_{17,59}$	4
	d_{16}	$d_{16,12} = D_{16,12}$, $d_{16,22} = D_{16,22} \oplus 1$, $d_{16,54} = D_{16,54}$	3
15	a_{15}	$a_{15,12} = a_{16,12}$	1
	b_{15}	$b_{15,22} = a_{16,22}$	1
	d_{15}	$d_{15,6} = c_{16,6}$, $d_{15,12} = c_{16,12}$, $d_{15,58} = c_{16,58} \oplus 1$	3
14	b_{14}	$b_{14,12} = a_{15,12}$	1
3	a_3	$a_{3,59} = b_{3,59} \oplus 1$	1
2	a_2	$a_{2,59} = a_{3,59}$, $a_{2,36} = b_{2,36} \oplus 1$	2
	c_2	$c_{2,19} = d_{2,19} \oplus 1$	1
1	a_1	$a_{1,7} = b_{1,7} \oplus 1$, $a_{1,31} = b_{1,31} \oplus 1$, $a_{1,36} = a_{2,36}$, $a_{1,48} = b_{1,48} \oplus 1$, $a_{1,59} = a_{2,59}$	5
	c_1	$c_{1,19} = c_{2,19}$, $c_{1,26} = d_{1,26} \oplus 1$, $c_{1,43} = d_{1,43} \oplus 1$	3
0	a_0	$a_{0,7} = a_{1,7}$, $a_{0,12} = B_{0,12} \oplus 1$, $a_{0,17} = B_{0,17} \oplus 1$, $a_{0,22} = B_{0,22} \oplus 1$, $a_{0,29} = B_{0,29} \oplus 1$, $a_{0,31} = a_{1,31}$, $a_{0,34} = B_{0,34} \oplus 1$, $a_{0,36} = a_{1,36}$, $a_{0,45} = B_{0,45} \oplus 1$, $a_{0,57} = B_{0,57} \oplus 1$, $a_{0,59} = a_{1,59}$	12
	b_0	$b_{0,12} = B_{0,12}$, $b_{0,17} = B_{0,17}$, $b_{0,22} = B_{0,22}$, $b_{0,45} = B_{0,45}$, $b_{0,29} = B_{0,29}$, $b_{0,34} = B_{0,34}$, $b_{0,57} = B_{0,57}$	7
	c_0	$c_{0,3} = D_{0,3} \oplus 1$, $c_{0,10} = D_{0,10} \oplus 1$, $c_{0,15} = D_{0,15} \oplus 1$, $c_{0,19} = c_{1,19}$, $c_{0,26} = c_{1,26} \oplus 1$, $D_{0,27} = c_{1,26} \oplus 1$, $c_{0,32} = D_{0,32} \oplus 1$, $c_{0,43} = c_{1,43}$, $c_{0,55} = c_{1,55}$	9
	d_0	$d_{0,3} = D_{0,3}$, $d_{0,10} = D_{0,10}$, $d_{0,15} = D_{0,15}$, $d_{0,27} = D_{0,27}$, $d_{0,32} = D_{0,32}$, $d_{0,55} = D_{0,55}$	6

Table 8. The sufficient conditions for Round $\overline{20} \sim 32$ of the differential path in Table 4.

Round	Var	Conditions	#
20	B_{20}	$B_{20,1} = b_{20,1}$, $B_{20,2} = b_{20,2}$, $B_{20,9} = b_{20,9} \oplus 1$, $B_{20,10} = b_{20,9}$, $B_{20,11} = b_{20,11}$, $B_{20,13} = b_{20,13} \oplus 1$, $B_{20,14} = b_{20,13}$, $B_{20,15} = b_{20,15}$, $B_{20,16} = b_{20,15} \oplus 1$, $B_{20,25} = b_{20,25} \oplus 1$, $B_{20,26} = b_{20,25}$, $B_{20,27} = b_{20,27}$, $B_{20,30} = b_{20,30} \oplus 1$, $B_{20,31} = b_{20,30} \oplus 1$, $B_{20,32} = b_{20,30} \oplus 1$, $B_{20,33} = b_{20,30}$, $B_{20,34} = b_{20,34}$, $B_{20,35} = b_{20,35} \oplus 1$, $B_{20,36} = b_{20,35}$, $B_{20,37} = b_{20,37} \oplus 1$, $B_{20,39} = b_{20,37}$, $B_{20,40} = b_{20,40}$, $B_{20,41} = b_{20,41}$	23
	D_{20}	$D_{20,9} = d_{20,9} \oplus 1$, $D_{20,10} = d_{20,9} \oplus 1$, $D_{20,11} = d_{20,9} \oplus 1$, $D_{20,12} = d_{20,9} \oplus 1$, $D_{20,13} = d_{20,9} \oplus 1$, $D_{20,14} = d_{20,9}$, $D_{20,15} = d_{20,15} \oplus 1$, $D_{20,16} = d_{20,15} \oplus 1$, $D_{20,17} = d_{20,15} \oplus 1$, $D_{20,18} = d_{20,15}$, $D_{20,21} = d_{20,21}$, $D_{20,22} = d_{20,22} \oplus 1$, $D_{20,23} = d_{20,22} \oplus 1$, $D_{20,24} = d_{20,22} \oplus 1$, $D_{20,25} = d_{20,22} \oplus 1$, $D_{20,26} = d_{20,22}$, $D_{20,28} = d_{20,28}$, $D_{20,30} = d_{20,30}$, $D_{20,31} = d_{20,31} \oplus 1$, $D_{20,32} = d_{20,31} \oplus 1$, $D_{20,33} = d_{20,31}$, $D_{20,41} = d_{20,41} \oplus 1$, $D_{20,42} = d_{20,41}$, $D_{20,43} = d_{20,43} \oplus 1$, $D_{20,44} = d_{20,43}$, $D_{20,45} = d_{20,45}$, $D_{20,57} = d_{20,57}$, $D_{20,60} = d_{20,60}$, $D_{20,61} = d_{20,61} \oplus 1$, $D_{20,62} = d_{20,61}$	30
21	a_{21}	$a_{21,28} = b_{20,27} \oplus 1$, $a_{21,29} = a_{21,28}$, $a_{21,30} = a_{21,28}$, $a_{21,31} = a_{21,28} \oplus 1$, $a_{21,32} = a_{20,30}$, $a_{21,33} = a_{21,32}$, $a_{21,34} = a_{21,32}$, $a_{21,35} = a_{21,32}$, $a_{21,36} = a_{21,32} \oplus 1$, $a_{21,38} = b_{20,38} \oplus 1$, $a_{21,39} = b_{20,38}$, $a_{21,40} = b_{20,40}$, $a_{21,41} = b_{20,41}$, $a_{21,50} = a_{20,50}$, $a_{21,51} = a_{20,51}$, $a_{21,55} = a_{20,55} \oplus 1$, $a_{21,56} = a_{20,55}$, $a_{21,57} = a_{20,57} \oplus 1$, $a_{21,58} = a_{20,57} \oplus 1$, $a_{21,59} = a_{20,57} \oplus 1$, $a_{21,60} = a_{20,57}$, $a_{21,61} = a_{20,61}$, $a_{21,63} = a_{20,63}$	23
	b_{21}	$b_{21,28} = a_{21,28}$, $b_{21,50} = a_{21,50} \oplus 1$, $b_{21,51} = a_{21,51}$, $b_{21,52} = a_{21,51}$, $b_{21,53} = a_{21,51}$, $b_{21,54} = a_{21,51} \oplus 1$, $b_{21,55} = a_{21,55} \oplus 1$, $b_{21,56} = a_{21,55}$, $b_{21,57} = a_{21,57} \oplus 1$, $b_{21,58} = a_{21,58} \oplus 1$, $b_{21,59} = a_{21,59}$, $b_{21,61} = a_{21,61}$, $b_{21,62} = a_{21,62} \oplus 1$, $b_{21,63} = a_{21,63} \oplus 1$	14
	c_{21}	$c_{21,1} = c_{20,1}$, $c_{21,2} = c_{20,2}$, $c_{21,10} = c_{20,9} \oplus 1$, $c_{21,11} = c_{20,9} \oplus 1$, $c_{21,12} = c_{20,9} \oplus 1$, $c_{21,13} = c_{20,9} \oplus 1$, $c_{21,14} = c_{20,9}$, $c_{21,26} = c_{20,26}$, $c_{21,28} = D_{20,28} \oplus 1$, $c_{21,29} = D_{20,28}$, $c_{21,30} = d_{20,30}$, $c_{21,31} = d_{20,31}$, $c_{21,42} = c_{20,41} \oplus 1$, $c_{21,43} = c_{21,42}$, $c_{21,44} = c_{21,42}$, $c_{21,45} = c_{21,42}$, $c_{21,46} = c_{21,42}$, $c_{21,47} = c_{21,42}$, $c_{21,48} = c_{21,42}$, $c_{21,49} = c_{21,42} \oplus 1$, $c_{21,52} = c_{20,52} \oplus 1$, $c_{21,53} = c_{20,52}$, $c_{21,62} = c_{20,60} \oplus 1$	23
	d_{21}	$d_{21,1} = c_{21,1} \oplus 1$, $d_{21,2} = c_{21,2}$, $d_{21,26} = c_{21,26}$, $d_{21,27} = c_{21,26} \oplus 1$, $d_{21,28} = c_{21,28} \oplus 1$, $d_{21,29} = c_{21,29} \oplus 1$, $d_{21,30} = c_{21,30} \oplus 1$, $d_{21,31} = c_{21,31}$, $d_{21,32} = c_{21,31} \oplus 1$, $d_{21,33} = c_{21,31}$, $d_{21,52} = c_{21,52}$, $d_{21,62} = c_{21,62}$, $d_{21,63} = c_{21,62} \oplus 1$	13
22	a_{22}	$a_{22,32} = a_{21,32}$, $a_{22,33} = a_{22,32}$, $a_{22,34} = a_{22,32}$, $a_{22,35} = a_{22,32}$, $a_{22,36} = a_{22,32}$, $a_{22,37} = a_{22,32} \oplus 1$, $a_{22,38} = a_{21,38}$, $a_{22,39} = a_{21,39}$, $a_{22,40} = a_{21,40}$, $a_{22,41} = a_{21,41} \oplus 1$, $a_{22,42} = a_{22,41}$, $a_{22,43} = a_{22,41}$, $a_{22,44} = a_{22,41}$, $a_{22,45} = a_{22,41}$, $a_{22,46} = a_{22,41} \oplus 1$	15
	b_{22}	$b_{22,38} = a_{22,38} \oplus 1$, $b_{22,39} = a_{22,39} \oplus 1$, $b_{22,40} = a_{22,40} \oplus 1$, $b_{22,41} = a_{22,41}$	4
	c_{22}	$c_{22,10} = c_{21,10}$, $c_{22,11} = c_{21,11}$, $c_{22,12} = c_{21,12}$, $c_{22,13} = c_{21,13}$, $c_{22,14} = c_{21,14}$, $c_{22,42} = c_{21,42}$, $c_{22,43} = c_{21,43}$, $c_{22,44} = c_{21,44}$, $c_{22,45} = c_{21,45} \oplus 1$	9
	d_{22}	$d_{22,10} = c_{22,10}$, $d_{22,42} = c_{22,42}$	2
23	a_{23}	$a_{23,32} = a_{22,32}$, $a_{23,33} = a_{22,33}$, $a_{23,34} = a_{22,34}$, $a_{23,35} = a_{22,35} \oplus 1$	4
	b_{23}	$b_{23,32} = a_{23,32}$	1
30	c_{30}	$c_{30,25} = d_{29,25}$	1
31	a_{31}	$a_{31,12} = b_{30,12}$, $a_{31,25} = b_{30,25}$, $a_{31,37} = b_{30,37}$	3
	b_{31}	$b_{31,25} = a_{31,25} \oplus 1$	1
	c_{31}	$c_{31,25} = c_{30,25}$	1
	d_{31}	$d_{31,25} = c_{31,25} \oplus 1$	1
32	a_{32}	$a_{32,12} = a_{31,12}$, $a_{32,22} = b_{31,22}$, $a_{32,37} = a_{31,37}$	3
	b_{32}	$b_{32,6} = b_{32,5} \oplus 1$, $b_{32,38} = b_{32,37} \oplus 1$, $b_{32,58} = b_{32,57} \oplus 1$	3
	c_{32}	$c_{32,6} = d_{31,6}$, $c_{32,12} = d_{31,12}$, $c_{32,19} = d_{31,19}$, $c_{32,31} = d_{31,31}$, $c_{32,37} = d_{31,37}$, $c_{32,58} = d_{31,58}$	6
$\overline{32}$	A_{32}	$A_{32,12} = a_{32,12}$, $A_{32,22} = a_{32,22}$, $A_{32,37} = a_{32,37}$	3
	B_{32}	$B_{32,5} = b_{32,5} \oplus 1$, $B_{32,12} = b_{32,12}$, $B_{32,19} = b_{32,19}$, $B_{32,26} = b_{32,26}$, $B_{32,31} = b_{32,31}$, $B_{32,37} = b_{32,37} \oplus 1$, $B_{32,44} = b_{32,44}$, $B_{32,51} = b_{32,51}$, $B_{32,57} = b_{32,57} \oplus 1$, $B_{32,63} = b_{32,63} \oplus 1$	10
	C_{32}	$C_{32,6} = c_{32,6}$, $C_{32,12} = c_{32,12}$, $C_{32,19} = c_{32,19}$, $C_{32,31} = c_{32,31}$, $C_{32,37} = c_{32,37}$, $C_{32,58} = c_{32,58}$	6
	D_{32}	$D_{32,12} = d_{32,12}$, $D_{32,22} = d_{32,22}$, $D_{32,37} = d_{32,37}$, $D_{32,54} = d_{32,54}$, $D_{32,57} = d_{32,57}$	5

Table 9. The conditions in group-1.

20	a_{20}	$a_{20,22} = a_{20,21}$, $a_{20,27} = a_{20,25} \oplus 1$, $a_{20,31} = a_{20,30}$, $a_{20,33} = a_{20,30}$, $a_{20,35} = a_{20,30}$, $a_{20,37} = a_{20,30} \oplus 1$, $a_{20,45} = a_{20,30} \oplus a_{20,43} \oplus a_{20,41} \oplus 1$, $a_{20,51} = a_{20,50}$, $a_{20,55} = a_{20,30} \oplus a_{20,43} \oplus 1$, $a_{20,57} = a_{20,55}$	10
	b_{20}	$b_{20,1} = a_{20,1}$, $b_{20,2} = a_{20,1} \oplus 1$, $b_{20,9} = a_{20,9} \oplus 1$, $b_{20,11} = a_{20,11} \oplus 1$, $b_{20,13} = a_{20,13} \oplus 1$, $b_{20,15} = a_{20,15}$, $b_{20,16} = a_{20,15}$, $b_{20,17} = a_{20,15}$, $b_{20,18} = a_{20,15}$, $b_{20,19} = a_{20,15}$, $b_{20,20} = a_{20,15}$, $b_{20,21} = a_{20,15} \oplus 1$, $b_{20,25} = a_{20,25} \oplus 1$, $b_{20,27} = a_{20,27}$, $b_{20,30} = a_{20,30}$, $b_{20,34} = a_{20,30} \oplus 1$, $b_{20,35} = a_{20,35}$, $b_{20,37} = a_{20,37} \oplus 1$, $b_{20,45} = b_{20,9} \oplus a_{20,43} \oplus a_{20,13}$, $b_{20,52} = a_{20,61} \oplus a_{20,60} \oplus a_{20,55}$ $b_{20,63} = b_{20,52} \oplus a_{20,21} \oplus a_{20,15} \oplus a_{20,60} \oplus a_{20,55} \oplus b_{20,26}$	21
	c_{20}	$c_{20,2} = c_{20,1}$, $c_{20,4} = a_{20,30} \oplus b_{20,4} \oplus a_{20,9} \oplus 1$, $c_{20,5} = a_{20,30} \oplus b_{20,5} \oplus a_{20,9}$, $c_{20,6} = a_{20,30} \oplus b_{20,6} \oplus a_{20,9} \oplus 1$, $c_{20,7} = a_{20,30} \oplus b_{20,7} \oplus a_{20,11} \oplus 1$, $c_{20,8} = a_{20,11} \oplus a_{20,30} \oplus b_{20,8}$, $c_{20,9} = a_{20,30} \oplus a_{20,43} \oplus b_{20,45}$, $c_{20,13} = a_{20,41} \oplus b_{20,13} \oplus a_{20,30}$, $c_{20,15} = a_{20,21} \oplus a_{20,15}$, $c_{20,16} = a_{20,30} \oplus a_{20,43} \oplus b_{20,16} \oplus 1$, $c_{20,17} = c_{20,16} \oplus b_{20,16} \oplus b_{20,17}$, $c_{20,18} = a_{20,61} \oplus a_{20,60} \oplus a_{20,55} \oplus b_{20,11} \oplus c_{20,11} \oplus b_{20,18}$, $c_{20,19} = c_{20,16} \oplus b_{20,16} \oplus b_{20,19}$, $c_{20,20} = b_{20,20} \oplus c_{20,16} \oplus b_{20,16} \oplus 1$, $c_{20,21} = c_{20,15} \oplus 1$, $c_{20,25} = b_{20,52} \oplus c_{20,15} \oplus b_{20,25}$, $c_{20,26} = a_{20,60} \oplus a_{20,55} \oplus b_{20,26}$, $c_{20,28} = b_{20,28} \oplus b_{20,25} \oplus c_{20,25}$, $c_{20,29} = a_{20,30} \oplus a_{20,55} \oplus b_{20,29}$, $c_{20,30} = b_{20,57} \oplus c_{20,15} \oplus b_{20,30}$, $c_{20,33} = a_{20,61} \oplus b_{20,33} \oplus a_{20,30} \oplus 1$, $c_{20,34} = a_{20,60} \oplus a_{20,55} \oplus b_{20,34}$, $c_{20,35} = b_{20,35} \oplus a_{20,60} \oplus a_{20,55}$, $c_{20,36} = a_{20,30} \oplus a_{20,43} \oplus a_{20,63} \oplus b_{20,36} \oplus a_{20,45}$, $c_{20,38} = b_{20,38} \oplus c_{20,1} \oplus 1$, $c_{20,40} = b_{20,40} \oplus c_{20,1}$, $c_{20,41} = c_{20,13} \oplus b_{20,13}$, $c_{20,43} = a_{20,30} \oplus a_{20,43}$, $c_{20,45} = c_{20,43}$, $c_{20,48} = a_{20,11} \oplus b_{20,48} \oplus a_{20,50}$, $c_{20,50} = a_{20,13} \oplus b_{20,50} \oplus a_{20,55}$, $c_{20,52} = b_{20,52} \oplus c_{20,15} \oplus 1$, $c_{20,53} = a_{20,15} \oplus b_{20,53} \oplus a_{20,55}$, $c_{20,54} = a_{20,15} \oplus b_{20,54} \oplus a_{20,55}$, $c_{20,57} = b_{20,57} \oplus c_{20,15} \oplus 1$, $c_{20,60} = a_{20,60} \oplus a_{20,55} \oplus 1$, $c_{20,61} = a_{20,25} \oplus b_{20,61} \oplus a_{20,1} \oplus 1$, $c_{20,62} = a_{20,25} \oplus b_{20,62} \oplus a_{20,1} \oplus 1$, $c_{20,63} = c_{20,60}$, $c_{20,64} = c_{20,26} \oplus b_{20,64}$	41
	d_{20}	$d_{20,1} = a_{20,1} \oplus a_{20,61}$, $d_{20,9} = c_{20,9}$, $d_{20,13} = a_{20,9} \oplus a_{20,13}$, $d_{20,15} = c_{20,15} \oplus 1$, $d_{20,21} = c_{20,21}$, $d_{20,22} = c_{20,21} \oplus 1$, $d_{20,23} = c_{20,15} \oplus b_{20,13} \oplus c_{20,13}$, $d_{20,24} = a_{20,24} \oplus c_{20,15} \oplus c_{20,41} \oplus 1$, $d_{20,25} = a_{20,25} \oplus c_{20,59} \oplus b_{20,59} \oplus a_{20,63} \oplus 1$, $d_{20,27} = a_{20,27} \oplus a_{20,25} \oplus 1$, $d_{20,28} = a_{20,25} \oplus a_{20,28} \oplus 1$, $d_{20,33} = a_{20,25} \oplus a_{20,33} \oplus 1$, $d_{20,35} = a_{20,30} \oplus a_{20,35}$, $d_{20,37} = a_{20,30} \oplus a_{20,37}$, $d_{20,41} = c_{20,41}$, $d_{20,43} = c_{20,43} \oplus 1$, $d_{20,45} = c_{20,45}^1$, $d_{20,51} = a_{20,50} \oplus a_{20,51}$ $d_{20,50} \oplus 1$, $d_{20,55} = a_{20,50} \oplus a_{20,55} \oplus 1$, $d_{20,57} = c_{20,57} \oplus 1$, $d_{20,60} = c_{20,60}$, $d_{20,61} = c_{20,60}$, $d_{20,63} = a_{20,63} \oplus a_{20,55}$	23
19	a_{19}	$a_{19,1} = a_{20,1}$, $a_{19,3} = b_{20,40} \oplus c_{20,40} \oplus a_{20,50} \oplus c_{20,50} \oplus a_{20,50}$, $a_{19,4} = a_{20,61} \oplus b_{20,48} \oplus c_{20,48} \oplus b_{20,41} \oplus c_{20,41} \oplus b_{20,18} \oplus c_{20,18} \oplus a_{20,50} \oplus d_{20,50}$, $a_{19,6} = b_{19,6} \oplus 1$, $a_{19,8} = b_{19,8}$, $a_{19,11} = a_{20,11}$, $a_{19,13} = a_{20,13}$, $a_{19,15} = a_{20,15}$, $a_{19,16} = a_{20,15}$, $a_{19,17} = a_{20,15} \oplus 1$, $a_{19,20} = b_{19,20} \oplus 1$, $a_{19,22} = b_{19,22} \oplus 1$, $a_{19,23} = b_{19,23} = a_{20,25} \oplus 1$, $a_{19,24} = a_{20,25}$, $a_{19,25} = a_{20,25} \oplus 1$, $a_{19,26} = a_{20,25}$, $a_{19,27} = a_{20,25}$, $a_{19,28} = a_{19,4} \oplus d_{19,4} \oplus d_{19,45} \oplus d_{19,28} \oplus 1$ $a_{19,31} = a_{20,30}$, $a_{19,32} = a_{20,30} \oplus 1$, $a_{19,33} = a_{20,30} \oplus 1$, $a_{19,34} = a_{20,30}$, $a_{19,35} = a_{20,30}$, $a_{19,36} = a_{20,30}$, $a_{19,38} = b_{20,11} \oplus c_{20,11} \oplus a_{20,15} \oplus 1$, $a_{19,40} = b_{19,40} \oplus 1$, $a_{19,43} = b_{20,16} \oplus c_{20,16} \oplus a_{19,20} \oplus 1$, $a_{19,44} = b_{20,17} \oplus c_{20,17} \oplus a_{19,20} \oplus 1$, $a_{19,45} = b_{19,45}$, $a_{19,46} = b_{20,19} \oplus c_{20,19} \oplus a_{20,25} \oplus 1$, $a_{19,47} = b_{20,20} \oplus c_{20,20} \oplus a_{20,25} \oplus 1$, $a_{19,52} = a_{20,50} \oplus 1$, $a_{19,53} = a_{19,52} \oplus 1$, $a_{19,54} = b_{20,27} \oplus c_{20,27} \oplus a_{19,31} \oplus 1$, $a_{19,56} = a_{20,55} \oplus 1$, $a_{19,57} = b_{20,30} \oplus c_{20,30} \oplus a_{19,33}$, $a_{19,60} = a_{20,61} \oplus 1$, $a_{19,61} = a_{20,61} \oplus 1$ $a_{19,62} = a_{20,61}$, $a_{19,63} = a_{20,63} \oplus 1$, $a_{19,64} = b_{20,37} \oplus c_{20,37} \oplus a_{19,40}$	41
	c_{19}	$c_{19,3} = b_{19,3} \oplus b_{19,2} \oplus c_{19,2} \oplus 1$, $c_{19,6} = d_{19,6} \oplus 1$, $c_{19,8} = c_{20,9}$, $c_{19,18} = c_{20,9}$, $c_{19,19} = c_{20,15} \oplus 1$, $c_{19,22} = a_{20,27} \oplus b_{20,27} \oplus b_{20,18} \oplus c_{20,18} \oplus 1$, $c_{19,23} = d_{20,23} \oplus 1$, $c_{19,28} = a_{19,4} \oplus b_{20,41} \oplus c_{20,41} \oplus b_{20,18} \oplus c_{20,18} \oplus a_{20,33} \oplus d_{20,33} \oplus 1$, $c_{19,30} = a_{20,35} \oplus d_{20,35} \oplus c_{20,52} \oplus 1$, $c_{19,32} = a_{20,37} \oplus d_{20,37} \oplus c_{20,52}$, $c_{19,36} = a_{20,41} \oplus d_{20,41} \oplus c_{20,60} \oplus 1$, $c_{19,38} = d_{19,38} \oplus 1$, $c_{19,40} = c_{20,41}$, $c_{19,45} = d_{19,45} \oplus 1$, $c_{19,46} = a_{20,51} \oplus d_{20,51} \oplus c_{19,6}$, $c_{19,50} = c_{19,8} \oplus a_{20,55} \oplus d_{20,55}$, $c_{19,55} = c_{20,52} \oplus 1$, $c_{19,56} = c_{20,52}$, $c_{19,58} = c_{20,57}$, $c_{19,59} = c_{20,57}$, $c_{19,60} = c_{20,60} \oplus 1$	21
18	a_{18}	$a_{18,6} = a_{19,6}$, $a_{18,26} = a_{19,26}$, $a_{18,27} = a_{19,27}$, $a_{18,44} = b_{18,44}$, $a_{18,54} = b_{18,54} \oplus 1$, $a_{18,56} = a_{19,56} \oplus 1$, $a_{18,60} = a_{19,60} \oplus 1$, $a_{18,16} = a_{20,61} \oplus d_{20,61} \oplus c_{20,52} \oplus a_{20,25}$, $a_{18,42} = a_{20,23} \oplus d_{20,23} \oplus c_{20,15} \oplus a_{20,55} \oplus 1$, $a_{18,43} = a_{20,24} \oplus d_{20,24} \oplus c_{20,15} \oplus a_{20,55} \oplus 1$, $a_{18,46} = b_{20,18} \oplus c_{20,18} \oplus a_{20,61} \oplus 1$, $a_{18,58} = d_{18,58} \oplus d_{17,6} \oplus c_{18,54}$	12
	c_{18}	$c_{18,1} = a_{20,25} \oplus b_{20,61} \oplus c_{20,61} \oplus c_{20,9} \oplus 1$, $c_{18,2} = a_{19,25} \oplus b_{20,62} \oplus c_{20,62} \oplus c_{20,9} \oplus 1$, $c_{18,8} = c_{19,8} \oplus 1$, $c_{18,9} = c_{18,8} \oplus 1$, $c_{18,10} = d_{18,10}$, $c_{18,11} = d_{18,10}$, $c_{18,12} = d_{18,10} \oplus 1$, $c_{18,13} = a_{20,30} \oplus b_{20,9} \oplus c_{20,9} \oplus c_{20,15} \oplus 1$, $c_{18,15} = a_{20,15} \oplus b_{20,60} \oplus c_{20,60}$, $c_{18,20} = d_{18,16}$, $c_{18,21} = c_{18,20} \oplus 1$, $c_{18,23} = c_{19,23} \oplus 1$, $c_{18,24} = c_{19,23}$, $c_{18,31} = b_{20,11} \oplus c_{20,11} \oplus a_{20,30}$, $c_{18,33} = a_{20,55} \oplus b_{20,29} \oplus c_{20,29} \oplus c_{20,41}$, $c_{18,34} = a_{19,57} \oplus b_{20,30} \oplus c_{20,30} \oplus c_{20,41} \oplus 1$, $c_{18,37} = a_{20,61} \oplus b_{20,33} \oplus c_{20,33} \oplus a_{20,25} \oplus d_{20,25} \oplus c_{19,20}$, $c_{18,38} = c_{19,38}$, $c_{18,40} = c_{19,40} \oplus 1$, $c_{18,41} = c_{18,40} \oplus 1$, $c_{18,44} = d_{18,44} \oplus 1$, $c_{18,45} = c_{19,45} \oplus 1$, $c_{18,51} = a_{18,60} \oplus b_{18,51} \oplus a_{18,44} \oplus 1$, $c_{18,52} = d_{18,52} \oplus 1$, $c_{18,54} = d_{18,54}$, $c_{18,58} = c_{19,58}$	26
17	a_{17}	$a_{17,6} = a_{18,6}$, $a_{17,8} = d_{17,8} \oplus a_{18,60}$, $a_{17,9} = d_{17,9} \oplus a_{18,60}$ $a_{17,20} = a_{17,6} \oplus d_{17,20}$, $a_{17,22} = b_{17,22} \oplus 1$, $a_{17,26} = a_{18,26} \oplus 1$, $a_{17,38} = b_{17,38}$, $a_{17,40} = d_{17,40} \oplus a_{17,26}$, $a_{17,41} = d_{17,41} \oplus a_{17,26}$, $a_{17,44} = a_{18,44} \oplus 1$, $a_{17,45} = a_{18,44}$, $a_{17,52} = d_{17,52} \oplus a_{18,37}$, $a_{17,58} = a_{18,60}$, $a_{17,59} = a_{18,60}$	14
	c_{17}	$c_{17,6} = d_{17,6} \oplus 1$, $c_{17,22} = d_{17,22}$, $c_{17,38} = b_{17,38} \oplus c_{17,22} \oplus 1$ $c_{17,39} = b_{17,39} \oplus c_{17,22}$, $c_{17,54} = c_{18,54} \oplus 1$, $c_{17,55} = c_{18,55}$, $c_{17,58} = c_{18,58} \oplus 1$	7

Table 10. The conditions in group-2.

20	B_{20}	$B_{20,1} = b_{20,1}$, $B_{20,2} = b_{20,2}$, $B_{20,9} = b_{20,9} \oplus 1$, $B_{20,10} = b_{20,10}$, $B_{20,11} = b_{20,11}$, $B_{20,13} = b_{20,13} \oplus 1$, $B_{20,14} = b_{20,13}$, $B_{20,15} = b_{20,15}$, $B_{20,16} = b_{20,15}\oplus 1$, $B_{20,25} = b_{20,25}\oplus 1$, $B_{20,26} = b_{20,25}$, $B_{20,27} = b_{20,27}$, $B_{20,30} = b_{20,30} \oplus 1$, $B_{20,31} = b_{20,30} \oplus 1$, $B_{20,32} = b_{20,30} \oplus 1$, $B_{20,33} = b_{20,30}$, $B_{20,34} = b_{20,34}$, $B_{20,35} = b_{20,35}\oplus 1$, $B_{20,36} = b_{20,35}$, $B_{20,37} = b_{20,37}\oplus 1$, $B_{20,39} = b_{20,37}$, $B_{20,40} = b_{20,40}$, $B_{20,41} = b_{20,41}$	23
	D_{20}	$D_{20,9} = d_{20,9} \oplus 1$, $D_{20,10} = d_{20,9} \oplus 1$, $D_{20,11} = d_{20,9} \oplus 1$, $D_{20,12} = d_{20,9} \oplus 1$, $D_{20,13} = d_{20,9} \oplus 1$, $D_{20,14} = d_{20,9}$, $D_{20,15} = d_{20,15} \oplus 1$, $D_{20,16} = d_{20,15} \oplus 1$, $D_{20,17} = d_{20,15} \oplus 1$, $D_{20,18} = d_{20,15}$, $D_{20,21} = d_{20,21}$, $D_{20,22} = d_{20,22} \oplus 1$, $D_{20,23} = d_{20,22} \oplus 1$, $D_{20,24} = d_{20,22} \oplus 1$, $D_{20,25} = d_{20,22} \oplus 1$, $D_{20,26} = d_{20,22}$, $D_{20,28} = d_{20,28}$, $D_{20,30} = d_{20,30}$, $D_{20,31} = d_{20,31} \oplus 1$, $D_{20,32} = d_{20,31} \oplus 1$, $D_{20,33} = d_{20,31}$, $D_{20,41} = d_{20,41} \oplus 1$, $D_{20,42} = d_{20,41}$, $D_{20,43} = d_{20,43} \oplus 1$, $D_{20,45} = d_{20,45}$, $D_{20,57} = d_{20,57}$, $D_{20,60} = d_{20,60}$, $D_{20,61} = d_{20,61} \oplus 1$, $D_{20,62} = d_{20,61}$	30
21	a_{21}	$a_{21,28} = b_{20,27}\oplus 1$, $a_{21,29} = a_{21,28}$, $a_{21,30} = a_{21,28}$, $a_{21,31} = a_{21,28}\oplus 1$, $a_{21,32} = a_{20,30}$, $a_{21,33} = a_{21,32}$, $a_{21,34} = a_{21,32}$, $a_{21,35} = a_{21,32}$, $a_{21,36} = a_{21,32}\oplus 1$, $a_{21,38} = b_{20,38} \oplus 1$, $a_{21,39} = b_{20,38}$, $a_{21,40} = b_{20,40}$, $a_{21,41} = b_{20,41}$, $a_{21,50} = a_{20,50}$, $a_{21,51} = a_{20,51}$, $a_{21,55} = a_{20,55} \oplus 1$, $a_{21,56} = a_{20,55}$, $a_{21,57} = a_{20,57} \oplus 1$, $a_{21,58} = a_{20,57} \oplus 1$, $a_{21,59} = a_{20,57} \oplus 1$, $a_{21,60} = a_{20,57}$, $a_{21,61} = a_{20,61}$, $a_{21,63} = a_{20,63}$	23
	b_{21}	$b_{21,28} = a_{21,28}$, $b_{21,50} = a_{21,50} \oplus 1$, $b_{21,51} = a_{21,51}$, $b_{21,52} = a_{21,51}$, $b_{21,53} = a_{21,51}$, $b_{21,54} = a_{21,51} \oplus 1$, $b_{21,55} = a_{21,55}\oplus 1$, $b_{21,56} = a_{21,55}$, $b_{21,57} = a_{21,57}\oplus 1$, $b_{21,58} = a_{21,58}\oplus 1$, $b_{21,59} = a_{21,59}$, $b_{21,61} = a_{21,61}$, $b_{21,62} = a_{21,62} \oplus 1$, $b_{21,63} = a_{21,63} \oplus 1$	14
	c_{21}	$c_{21,1} = c_{20,1}$, $c_{21,2} = c_{20,2}$, $c_{21,10} = c_{20,9} \oplus 1$, $c_{21,11} = c_{20,9} \oplus 1$, $c_{21,12} = c_{20,9} \oplus 1$, $c_{21,13} = c_{20,9} \oplus 1$, $c_{21,14} = c_{20,9}$, $c_{21,26} = c_{20,26}$, $c_{21,28} = D_{20,28} \oplus 1$, $c_{21,29} = D_{20,28}$, $c_{21,30} = d_{20,30}$, $c_{21,31} = d_{20,31} \oplus 1$, $c_{21,42} = c_{20,41} \oplus 1$, $c_{21,43} = c_{21,42}$, $c_{21,44} = c_{21,42}$, $c_{21,45} = c_{21,42}$, $c_{21,46} = c_{21,42}$, $c_{21,47} = c_{21,42}$, $c_{21,48} = c_{21,42}$, $c_{21,49} = c_{21,42} \oplus 1$, $c_{21,52} = c_{20,52}$, $c_{21,53} = c_{20,52}$, $c_{21,62} = c_{20,60} \oplus 1$	23
	d_{21}	$d_{21,1} = c_{21,1} \oplus 1$, $d_{21,2} = c_{21,2} \oplus 1$, $d_{21,26} = c_{21,26}$, $d_{21,27} = c_{21,26} \oplus 1$, $d_{21,28} = c_{21,28} \oplus 1$, $d_{21,29} = c_{21,29} \oplus 1$, $d_{21,30} = c_{21,30} \oplus 1$, $d_{21,31} = c_{21,31}$, $d_{21,32} = c_{21,31} \oplus 1$, $d_{21,33} = c_{21,31}$, $d_{21,52} = c_{21,52}$, $d_{21,62} = c_{21,62}$, $d_{21,63} = c_{21,62} \oplus 1$	13
22	a_{22}	$a_{22,32} = a_{21,32}$, $a_{22,33} = a_{21,33}$, $a_{22,34} = a_{22,32}$, $a_{22,35} = a_{22,32}$, $a_{22,36} = a_{22,32}$, $a_{22,37} = a_{22,32} \oplus 1$, $a_{22,38} = a_{21,38}$, $a_{22,39} = a_{21,39}$, $a_{22,40} = a_{21,40}$, $a_{22,41} = a_{21,41} \oplus 1$, $a_{22,42} = a_{22,41}$, $a_{22,43} = a_{22,41}$, $a_{22,44} = a_{22,41}$, $a_{22,45} = a_{22,41}$, $a_{22,46} = a_{22,41} \oplus 1$	15
	b_{22}	$b_{22,38} = a_{22,38} \oplus 1$, $b_{22,39} = a_{22,39} \oplus 1$, $b_{22,40} = a_{22,40} \oplus 1$, $b_{22,41} = a_{22,41}$	4
	c_{22}	$c_{22,10} = c_{21,10}$, $c_{22,11} = c_{21,11}$, $c_{22,12} = c_{21,12}$, $c_{22,13} = c_{21,13}$, $c_{22,14} = c_{21,14}$, $c_{22,42} = c_{21,42}$, $c_{22,43} = c_{21,43}$, $c_{22,44} = c_{21,44}$, $c_{22,45} = c_{21,45} \oplus 1$,	9
	d_{22}	$d_{22,10} = c_{22,10}$, $d_{22,42} = c_{22,42}$,	2
23	a_{23}	$a_{23,32} = a_{22,32}$, $a_{23,33} = a_{22,33}$, $a_{23,34} = a_{22,34}$, $a_{23,35} = a_{22,35} \oplus 1$	4
	b_{23}	$b_{23,32} = a_{23,32}$	1
16	c_{16}	$c_{16,6} = c_{17,6}$, $c_{16,12} = D_{16,12} \oplus 1$, $c_{16,58} = c_{17,58}$, $c_{16,59} = c_{17,58} \oplus 1$ $c_{16,38} = B_{16,38} \oplus c_{17,6}$, $c_{16,44} = B_{16,44} \oplus D_{16,12}$, $c_{16,26} = B_{16,26} \oplus c_{17,58} \oplus 1$	7

Table 11. The conditions in group-3.

16	a_{16}	$a_{16,12} = B_{16,12} \oplus 1$, $a_{16,22} = a_{17,22}$, $a_{16,54} = D_{16,54} \oplus a_{17,22}$	3
	b_{16}	$b_{16,6} = B_{16,6} \oplus 1$, $b_{16,12} = B_{16,12}$, $b_{16,26} = B_{16,26} \oplus 1$, $b_{16,38} = B_{16,38}$, $b_{16,44} = B_{16,44}$, $b_{16,58} = B_{16,58}$, $b_{16,59} = B_{16,59}$	7
	d_{16}	$d_{16,12} = D_{16,12}$, $d_{16,22} = D_{16,22} \oplus 1$, $d_{16,54} = D_{16,54}$	3
15	a_{15}	$a_{15,6} = c_{16,6} \oplus a_{16,12}$, $a_{15,12} = a_{16,12}$	2
3	a_3	$a_{3,59} = b_{3,59} \oplus 1$	1
2	a_2	$a_{2,59} = a_{3,59}$, $a_{2,36} = b_{2,36} \oplus 1$	2
	c_2	$c_{2,19} = d_{2,19} \oplus 1$	1
1	a_1	$a_{1,7} = b_{1,7} \oplus 1$, $a_{1,31} = b_{1,31} \oplus 1$, $a_{1,36} = a_{2,36}$, $a_{1,48} = b_{1,48} \oplus 1$, $a_{1,59} = a_{2,59}$	5
	c_1	$c_{1,19} = c_{2,19}$, $c_{1,26} = d_{1,26} \oplus 1$, $c_{1,43} = d_{1,43} \oplus 1$	3
0	a_0	$a_{0,7} = a_{1,7}$, $a_{0,12} = B_{0,12} \oplus 1$, $a_{0,17} = B_{0,17} \oplus 1$, $a_{0,22} = B_{0,22} \oplus 1$, $a_{0,29} = B_{0,29} \oplus 1$, $a_{0,31} = a_{1,31}$, $a_{0,34} = B_{0,34} \oplus 1$, $a_{0,36} = a_{1,36}$, $a_{0,45} = B_{0,45} \oplus 1$, $a_{0,48} = a_{1,48}$, $a_{0,57} = B_{0,57} \oplus 1$, $a_{0,59} = a_{1,59}$	12
	b_0	$b_{0,12} = B_{0,12}$, $b_{0,17} = B_{0,17}$, $b_{0,22} = B_{0,22}$, $b_{0,45} = B_{0,45}$, $b_{0,29} = B_{0,29}$, $b_{0,34} = B_{0,34}$, $b_{0,57} = B_{0,57}$	7
	c_0	$c_{0,3} = D_{0,3} \oplus 1$, $c_{0,10} = D_{0,10} \oplus 1$, $c_{0,15} = D_{0,15} \oplus 1$, $c_{0,19} = c_{1,19}$, $c_{0,26} = c_{1,26} \oplus 1$, $c_{0,27} = c_{1,26} \oplus 1$, $c_{0,32} = D_{0,32} \oplus 1$, $c_{0,43} = c_{1,43}$, $c_{0,55} = c_{1,55}$	9
	d_0	$d_{0,3} = D_{0,3}$, $d_{0,10} = D_{0,10}$, $d_{0,15} = D_{0,15}$, $d_{0,27} = D_{0,27}$, $d_{0,32} = D_{0,32}$, $d_{0,55} = D_{0,55}$	6
30	c_{30}	$c_{30,25} = d_{29,25}$	1
31	a_{31}	$a_{31,12} = b_{30,12}$, $a_{31,25} = b_{30,25}$, $a_{31,37} = b_{30,37}$	3
	b_{31}	$b_{31,25} = a_{31,25} \oplus 1$	1
	c_{31}	$c_{31,25} = c_{30,25}$	1
	d_{31}	$d_{31,25} = c_{31,25} \oplus 1$	1
32	a_{32}	$a_{32,12} = a_{31,12}$, $a_{32,22} = b_{31,22}$, $a_{32,37} = a_{31,37}$	3
	b_{32}	$b_{32,6} = b_{32,5} \oplus 1$, $b_{32,38} = b_{32,37} \oplus 1$, $b_{32,58} = b_{32,57} \oplus 1$	3
	c_{32}	$c_{32,6} = d_{31,6}$, $c_{32,12} = d_{31,12}$, $c_{32,19} = d_{31,19}$, $c_{32,31} = d_{31,31}$, $c_{32,37} = d_{31,37}$, $c_{32,58} = d_{31,58}$	6
$\overline{32}$	A_{32}	$A_{32,12} = a_{32,12}$, $A_{32,22} = a_{32,22}$, $A_{32,37} = a_{32,37}$	3
	B_{32}	$B_{32,5} = b_{32,5} \oplus 1$, $B_{32,12} = b_{32,12}$, $B_{32,19} = b_{32,19}$, $B_{32,26} = b_{32,26}$, $B_{32,31} = b_{32,31}$, $B_{32,37} = b_{32,37} \oplus 1$, $B_{32,44} = b_{32,44}$, $B_{32,51} = b_{32,51}$, $B_{32,57} = b_{32,57} \oplus 1$, $B_{32,63} = b_{32,63} \oplus 1$	10
	C_{32}	$C_{32,6} = c_{32,6}$, $C_{32,12} = c_{32,12}$, $C_{32,19} = c_{32,19}$, $C_{32,31} = c_{32,31}$, $C_{32,37} = c_{32,37}$, $C_{32,58} = c_{32,58}$	6
	D_{32}	$D_{32,12} = d_{32,12}$, $D_{32,22} = d_{32,22}$, $D_{32,37} = d_{32,37}$, $D_{32,54} = d_{32,54}$, $D_{32,57} = d_{32,57}$	5

References

1. Aumasson, J.-P., Çalık, Ç., Meier, W., Özen, O., Phan, R.C.-W., Varıcı, K.: Improved cryptanalysis of skein. In: Matsui, M. (ed.) ASIACRYPT 2009. LNCS, vol. 5912, pp. 542–559. Springer, Heidelberg (2009)
2. Bertoni, G., Daemen, J., Peeters, M., Van Assche, G.: The KECCAK Reference. Submission to NIST (Round 3) (2011). http://keccak.noekeon.org/Keccak-reference-3.0.pdf
3. Ferguson, N., Lucks, S., Schneier, B., Whiting, D., Bellare, M., Kohno, T., Callas, J., Walker, J.: The Skein Hash Function Family. http://www.schneier.com/skein1.3.pdf
4. Menezes, A., van Oorschot, P., Vanstone, S.: Handbook of Applied Cryptography. CRC Press, Boca Raton (1996)
5. Mendel, F., Rechberger, C., Schläffer, M., Thomsen, S.S.: The rebound attack: cryptanalysis of reduced whirlpool and Grøstl. In: Dunkelman, O. (ed.) FSE 2009. LNCS, vol. 5665, pp. 260–276. Springer, Heidelberg (2009)
6. Mendel, F., Rechberger, C., Schläffer, M., Thomsen, S.S.: Rebound attacks on the reduced Grøstl hash function. In: Pieprzyk, J. (ed.) CT-RSA 2010. LNCS, vol. 5985, pp. 350–365. Springer, Heidelberg (2010)
7. Naya-Plasencia, M., Toz, D., Varici, K.: Rebound attack on JH42. In: Lee, D.H., Wang, X. (eds.) ASIACRYPT 2011. LNCS, vol. 7073, pp. 252–269. Springer, Heidelberg (2011)
8. Khovratovich, D., Nikolić, I.: Rotational cryptanalysis of ARX. In: Hong, S., Iwata, T. (eds.) FSE 2010. LNCS, vol. 6147, pp. 333–346. Springer, Heidelberg (2010)
9. Khovratovich, D., Nikolić, I., Rechberger, C.: Rotational rebound attacks on reduced skein. In: Abe, M. (ed.) ASIACRYPT 2010. LNCS, vol. 6477, pp. 1–19. Springer, Heidelberg (2010)
10. Khovratovich, D., Rechberger, C., Savelieva, A.: Bicliques for preimages: attacks on Skein-512 and the SHA-2 family. In: Canteaut, A. (ed.) FSE 2012. LNCS, vol. 7549, pp. 244–263. Springer, Heidelberg (2012)
11. Lamberger, M., Mendel, F., Rechberger, C., Rijmen, V., Schläffer, M.: Rebound distinguishers: results on the full whirlpool compression function. In: Matsui, M. (ed.) ASIACRYPT 2009. LNCS, vol. 5912, pp. 126–143. Springer, Heidelberg (2009)
12. Leurent, G., Roy, A.: Boomerang attacks on hash function using auxiliary differentials. In: Dunkelman, O. (ed.) CT-RSA 2012. LNCS, vol. 7178, pp. 215–230. Springer, Heidelberg (2012)
13. Leurent, G., Thomsen, S.S.: Practical near-collisions on the compression function of BMW. In: Joux, A. (ed.) FSE 2011. LNCS, vol. 6733, pp. 238–251. Springer, Heidelberg (2011)
14. Su, B., Wu, W., Wu, S., Dong, L.: Near-collisions on the reduced-round compression functions of skein and BLAKE. In: Heng, S.-H., Wright, R.N., Goi, B.-M. (eds.) CANS 2010. LNCS, vol. 6467, pp. 124–139. Springer, Heidelberg (2010)
15. Wang, X., Yu, H.: How to break MD5 and other hash functions. In: Cramer, R. (ed.) EUROCRYPT 2005. LNCS, vol. 3494, pp. 19–35. Springer, Heidelberg (2005)
16. Wang, X., Yin, Y.L., Yu, H.: Finding collisions in the full SHA-1. In: Shoup, V. (ed.) CRYPTO 2005. LNCS, vol. 3621, pp. 17–36. Springer, Heidelberg (2005)
17. Yu, H., Chen, J., Wang, X.: The boomerang attacks on the round-reduced Skein-512. In: Knudsen, L.R., Wu, H. (eds.) SAC 2012. LNCS, vol. 7707, pp. 287–303. Springer, Heidelberg (2013)

Message Authentication Codes

On Weak Keys and Forgery Attacks Against Polynomial-Based MAC Schemes

Gordon Procter[✉] and Carlos Cid

Information Security Group, Royal Holloway,
University of London, London, UK
{gordon.procter.2011,carlos.cid}@rhul.ac.uk

Abstract. Universal hash functions are commonly used primitives for fast and secure message authentication in the form of Message Authentication Codes (MACs) or Authenticated Encryption with Associated Data (AEAD) schemes. These schemes are widely used and standardised, the most well known being McGrew and Viega's Galois/Counter Mode (GCM). In this paper we identify some properties of hash functions based on polynomial evaluation that arise from the underlying algebraic structure. As a result we are able to describe a general forgery attack, of which Saarinen's cycling attack from FSE 2012 is a special case. Our attack removes the requirement for long messages and applies regardless of the field in which the hash function is evaluated. Furthermore we provide a common description of all published attacks against GCM, by showing that the existing attacks are the result of these algebraic properties of the polynomial-based hash function. Finally, we greatly expand the number of known weak GCM keys and show that almost every subset of the keyspace is a weak key class.

Keywords: Universal hashing · MAC · Galois/Counter Mode · Cycling attacks · Weak keys

1 Introduction

The study of information-theoretic message authentication codes and universal hashing was initiated by Gilbert et al. [14] and Carter and Wegman [10,11,38,39]. Universal hash functions can be used to construct message authentication codes in both the information-theoretically secure and computationally secure settings (see [9,39]). Simmons [33] provides a general summary of the theory of unconditionally secure message authentication. Bernstein [2,3] provides a thorough description of the geneology and more recent literature of unconditionally secure message authentication, including a description of the contributions of

The work described in this paper has been supported in part by the European Commission through the ICT programme under contract ICT-2007-216676 ECRYPT II.

S. Moriai (Ed.): FSE 2013, LNCS 8424, pp. 287–304, 2014.
DOI: 10.1007/978-3-662-43933-3_15, © Springer-Verlag Berlin Heidelberg 2014

Bierbrauer et al. [5], den Boer [12], and Taylor [36] to polynomial-based hashing. Bernstein [4] also gives an interesting overview of the security of universal hash function based MACs in the computationally secure setting. Shoup [32] describes several methods for realising universal hash function families that are related to polynomials including the evaluation hash [5, 12, 36] which is a variant of the division hash or cryptographic CRC of Krawczyk [21] (itself a variant of Rabin's fingerprinting codes [27]).

In this paper, we focus on message authentication codes constructed from universal hash functions that are realised by polynomial evaluation. These are widely used and standardised; for examples see [2, 13, 17, 20, 22, 31]. McGrew and Viega's Galois/Counter Mode (GCM) [26] is the most widely deployed polynomial-based scheme. The algorithm is generally assumed to be secure, with a small number of papers containing attacks against the authentication component via the universal hash function: Ferguson's attack against truncated GCM tags [15], demonstrating that the security of short tags is significantly lower than would be expected; Joux's 'forbidden attack' [19], illustrating the brittleness of GCM under nonce reuse; Handschuh and Preneel's [16] extension to Joux's attack [16]; and Saarinen's cycling attacks [29], which highlight a weakness due to the underlying algebraic structure of a hash function based on polynomial evaluation. Both Handschuh and Preneel [16] and Saarinen [29] have described classes of weak keys for polynomial evaluation based universal hash functions, with Saarinen particularly focusing on GCM.

Contributions. A motivation of this work was the observation that all existing attacks against GCM are algebraic in nature, and in fact seem to exploit a fundamental underlying algebraic structure of the polynomial-based hash function. The contributions of this paper are to identify and study some of the properties of hash functions based on polynomial evaluation that are the result of this underlying algebraic structure. As a result, we are able to describe a general forgery attack, of which Saarinen's cycling attack is a special case; our attack can however be used with short messages, applies regardless of the field in which the hash is evaluated, and facilitates length extension attacks against GCM. Furthermore, we provide a common description of all published attacks against GCM by showing that the existing attacks are the result of these algebraic properties of the polynomial-based hash function. Finally, we greatly expand the number of known weak GCM keys, and show that almost every subset of the keyspace is a weak key class. We note that the attacks presented in this paper do not in any way contradict the security bounds for GCM given by McGrew and Viega [24]. However the algebraic properties (and related attacks) discussed in this paper appear to be an inherent feature of polynomial-based authentication schemes and therefore should be considered in the security assessment of new schemes and extensions of existing ones.

Structure. This paper is structured as follows. In Sect. 2 we introduce the notation that will be used throughout this paper and provide a brief description of the syntax and security of message authentication codes. In Sect. 3 we give a basic overview of three schemes that use hash functions based on polynomial evaluation for message authentication, including GCM and SGCM. In Sect. 4 we describe the main technique used in this paper for the cryptanalysis of polynomial-based authentication schemes and discuss some features of the resulting attack that make it more interesting than cycling attacks. Section 5 contains a common description of the existing attacks against GCM. In Sect. 6 we show that there are many more weak key classes for hash functions based on polynomial evaluation than have previously been described and suggest a method to realise a key recovery attack against polynomial-based hash function schemes. Section 7 contains a discussion of the consequences of this attack.

2   Preliminaries

2.1   Notation

We consider a message M parsed as $M_1||\ldots||M_m$, where each M_i is n bits long and $||$ represents concatenation of strings. In the syntax of authenticated encryption with associated data [28], this message consists of associated data $A \in \mathcal{A}$ that is authenticated but not encrypted and plaintext $P \in \mathcal{P}$ that will be encrypted and authenticated.

A family of hash functions will be denoted $\mathcal{H} = \{h_H : \{0,1\}^\star \to \{0,1\}^n \mid H \in \mathcal{K}_\mathcal{H}\}$ with each hash function h_H indexed by a key $H \in \mathcal{K}_\mathcal{H}$. A block cipher E is a family of permutations on $\{0,1\}^n$, with each permutation indexed by a key $k \in \mathcal{K}_E$. The application of a block cipher to input $x \in \{0,1\}^n$ using key k will be denoted by $E_k(x)$. Where a nonce is used it will be denoted by N.

A finite field will be denoted by $\mathbb{K}$ unless the order of the field has particular relevance, in which case it will be denoted by $\mathbb{F}_{p^r}$ with $|\mathbb{F}| = p^r$. The multiplicative group of a field $\mathbb{K}$ will be denoted by $\mathbb{K}^\star$.

2.2   Universal Hash Functions

A family of hash functions is said to be $\epsilon\text{-}almost \oplus universal$ if for every $M, M' \in \{0,1\}^\star$ with $M \neq M'$ and for every $c \in \{0,1\}^n$, $\Pr_{H \in \mathcal{K}_\mathcal{H}}[h_H(M) \oplus h_H(M') = c] < \epsilon$. Throughout this paper ϵ–almost $\oplus$ universal will be abbreviated to ϵ–AXU. This condition was introduced by Krawczyk [21] under the name $\epsilon\text{-}OTP\text{-}Secure$ as it is a necessary and sufficient condition for unconditional MAC security when the output of the hash function is encrypted with the one time pad in a field of characteristic 2. In this paper we will generally refer to ϵ–AXU hash function families; however any remark made that requires an ϵ–AXU hash function family in characteristic 2 will also hold for an ϵ–almost strongly universal [34] or ϵ–almost Δ universal [35] hash function family in any finite field.

A polynomial based hash function family is a common way to realise an ϵ–AXU hash function family. Shoup [32] describes several examples of this type of construction; the main example of interest to this paper is the evaluation hash. In the case of the evaluation hash the message M determines a polynomial $g_M = \sum_{i=1}^{m} M_i x^i \in \mathbb{K}[x]$, where $M = M_1 || \ldots || M_m$ with each $M_i \in \mathbb{K}$. The hash key is an element $H \in \mathbb{K}$ and we define the hash function by $h_H(M) = g_M(H)$.

There are several methods for turning a universal hash function into a message authentication code (see [9,39] for early examples). The two most common methods are $E_k(N) + h_H(M)$ and $E_k(h_H(M))$.

2.3   Syntax

We will follow Black et al. [8] for a description of the syntax of nonce-based message authentication schemes. A message authentication scheme is a pair of algorithms, Gen and MAC, with four associated sets: $\mathcal{K}$, the set of possible keys; $\mathcal{M}$, the message space; $\mathcal{N}$, the set of nonces and $\mathcal{T}$, the set of possible authentication tags.

The key generation algorithm Gen takes as input the security parameter and probabilistically outputs the shared key $k \in \mathcal{K}$. The algorithm MAC takes as input a key $k \in \mathcal{K}$, a nonce $N \in \mathcal{N}$, and a message $M \in \mathcal{M}$ and outputs a tag $T \in \mathcal{T}$. The authenticity of a tuple (N, M, T) is verified by computing $\mathsf{MAC}(k, N, M)$: if $T = \mathsf{MAC}(k, N, M)$ then the tag is valid, otherwise it is invalid.

2.4   Security

An adversary attacking a message authentication scheme is given access to two oracles: a tag generation oracle $\mathcal{S}$ and a verification oracle $\mathcal{V}$. At the beginning of the experiment Gen is run to obtain k, then MAC takes queries (N, M) and returns $\mathsf{MAC}(k, N, M)$. The verification oracle takes queries (N, M, T) and returns 1 if $T = \mathsf{MAC}(k, N, M)$ or 0 otherwise. An adversary is said to successfully forge an authentication tag if they can produce a verification query (N, M, T) so that $\mathcal{V}$ returns 1 when (N, M) was not previously queried to $\mathcal{S}$.

A common restriction of this security notion is to nonce-respecting adversaries where, although the adversary can control the nonce, they never query $\mathcal{S}$ for (N, M') if they have previously queried $\mathcal{S}$ for (N, M).

McGrew and Viega [24], Ferguson [15], and Handschuh and Preneel [16] all assert that the probability of creating a valid (non-truncated) tag having seen a single valid (message, tag) pair is approximately $m/|\mathbb{K}|$ where the polynomial is evaluated in $\mathbb{K}$ and m is the length of message that the construction operates on. It is worth emphasising that in this context, m is the *maximum* permissable message length. This is included in the original paper [24] but is not made explicitly clear in the later papers [15,16]. In this paper we will demonstrate the importance of this distinction via a method of forging GCM tags using a longer message than the one that was given in the valid (message, tag) pair from the tag generation oracle.

Throughout this paper we will focus on GCM for concreteness however the majority of the comments apply equally to any other hash function based on polynomial evaluation. Most of the results in this paper apply equally to both common constructions of MACs from universal hash functions, either $T = E_k(N) + h_H(M)$ or $T = E_k(h_H(M))$, as our results are based on collisions in the hash function. Where necessary it will be made clear that a remark is dependent on one of these general constructions or the specific structure of GCM.

3 Polynomial-Based Authentication Schemes

We present below a brief description of some of the main authentication schemes based on polynomial evaluation hash functions that are of relevance to our work.

3.1 Galois/Counter Mode

Galois/Counter Mode (GCM) is an AEAD scheme submitted to NIST by McGrew and Viega in 2004, with the specification slightly revised in 2005 [26] (although the revision contained 'no normative changes [from the 2004 specification]'). GCM combines counter mode encryption with a polynomial evaluation based MAC following the Encrypt–then–MAC paradigm, although the authentication key is derived from the block cipher key.

AES–GCM encryption takes as input: a key k, an initialisation vector IV (the nonce), plaintext $P = P_1||\ldots||P_p$ and additional data $A = A_1||\ldots||A_a$. The key is 128, 192 or 256 bits long; the IV should preferably be 96 bits long although any length is supported (see [18]); and for each i, $|P_i| = |A_i| = 128$ except for perhaps a partial final block. With this input, AES–GCM returns a ciphertext $C = C_1||\ldots||C_p$ (the same length as the plaintext) and an authentication tag T.

The plaintext is encrypted using AES in counter mode, under key k with counter value starting at CTR_1. If the IV is 96 bits long the initial counter value (CTR_0) is $IV||0^{31}1$, otherwise it is a polynomial evaluation based hash of IV after zero padding (using the hash key described below). For each i, $CTR_i = \text{inc}(CTR_{i-1})$, where $\text{inc}(\cdot)$ increments the last 32 bits of its argument (modulo 2^{32}).

The authentication tag is computed from a polynomial evaluation hash (in $\mathbb{F}_{2^{128}}$). The message M is parsed as 128-bit blocks (with partial final blocks zero padded) and each block is interpreted as an element of $\mathbb{F}_{2^{128}}$. The first block M_1 encodes the length of the (unpadded) plaintext and additional data and will be referred to as the 'length field' throughout this paper. This is followed by blocks of additional data $M_2,\ldots,M_{a+1} = A_a,\ldots,A_1$ and then the encrypted plaintext $M_{a+2},\ldots,M_{a+p+1} = C_p,\ldots,C_1$. Note that in this description the labelling of the blocks M_i are reversed from those given in the original GCM specification as this gives a neater description of the polynomial used in evaluating the hash function. The hash key H is derived from the block cipher key: $H = E_k(0^{128})$. The hash function is then computed as $h_H(M) = \sum_{i=1}^{a+p+1} M_i H^i$ (where all operations are in $\mathbb{F}_{2^{128}}$). The authentication tag is given by:

$$T_M = E_k(CTR_0) \oplus h_H(M).$$

3.2 Sophie Germain Counter Mode

In 2012, Saarinen [29] observed cycling attacks against GCM and other polynomial MACs and hashes. Following this Saarinen proposed SGCM [30] as a variant of GCM; SGCM differs from GCM only by the choice of field in which the hash is computed. SGCM uses $\mathbb{F}_q$, where $q = 2^{128} + 12451$, rather than $\mathbb{F}_{2^{128}}$, as $\mathbb{F}_q^\star$ has significantly fewer subgroups than $\mathbb{F}_{2^{128}}^\star$. It was claimed that SGCM offers increased resistance to cycling attacks as a result of this change.

3.3 Poly1305–AES

Bernstein proposed Poly1305–AES in 2005 [2][1]. Poly1305–AES takes as input two 128-bit keys, one for AES and one for the hash (with some specific bits set to zero); a 128 bit nonce; and a message (a byte string). The output of Poly1305–AES is a 128-bit authentication tag.

The hash of a message is computed by evaluating a message-dependant polynomial at the secret key (in $\mathbb{F}_{2^{130}-5}$), and encrypting this by adding (in $\mathbb{F}_{2^{130}-5}$) the output of $\mathsf{AES}_k(N)$ before reducing modulo 2^{128}.

4 Algebraic Structure of Polynomial-Based Authentication Schemes

Let $\mathcal{H}$ be a family of hash functions $\mathcal{H} = \{h_H : \{0,1\}^\star \to \{0,1\}^n \mid H \in \mathcal{K}_\mathcal{H}\}$ based on polynomial evaluation and let M be an input string. Let $h_H(M) = g_M(H)$, where $g_M(x) = \sum_{i=1}^m M_i x^i \in \mathbb{K}[x]$ and $H \in \mathbb{K}$. Now let $q(x) = \sum_{i=1}^r q_i x^i \in \mathbb{K}[x]$ be a polynomial with constant term zero, such that $q(H) = 0$. Then it follows that

$$h_H(M) = g_M(H) = g_M(H) + q(H) = g_{M+Q}(H) = h_H(M+Q),$$

where $Q = q_1 \| q_2 \| \ldots \| q_r$ and the addition $M + Q$ is done block-wise (the shorter is zero-padded if required). Thus given a polynomial $q(x)$ satisfying these properties, it is straightforward to construct collisions for the hash function. It is trivial to see that one can use any polynomial $q(x) \in \langle x^2 - Hx \rangle \subseteq \mathbb{K}[x]$.

Collisions in the hash function correspond to MAC forgeries by substituting the original message for the one that yields a collision in the hash function. These forgeries arise from collisions in the hash function and hence the messages can be substituted without any dependence on the method or key used to encrypt the output of the hash function. This method allows an adversary to create forgeries when he has seen a tuple of (nonce, message, tag) by only modifying the message.

It should be noted that the polynomial defined by the message will always have a zero constant term and therefore the polynomial $q(x)$ that is used to forge will always have x as a factor. If this term were non-zero and the hash

---

[1] There is a preliminary version from 2004 on his website: http://cr.yp.to/mac.html.

of a message was encrypted additively (i.e. $T = E_k(N) + h_H(M)$), it would be possible to flip bits in the first message block and flip the same bits in the authentication tag to create a valid forgery. This is the major difference between Shoup's Cryptographic CRC [32] and Rabin's fingerprinting codes [27].

The main observation of this paper is that by working with polynomials in the ideal $\langle x^2 - Hx \rangle$, it is straightforward to produce forgeries for polynomial evaluation based authentication schemes. In [29], Saarinen proposed cycling attacks by working with particular polynomials, namely $x^n - x$ (for more detail, see Sect. 5.4). The forgery is successful if $(x - H)|(x^n - x)$ and therefore if $x^n - x \in \langle x^2 - Hx \rangle$. However, the forgery will be successful if *any* polynomial in this ideal is used to mount a similar attack. Furthermore, use of these polynomials also makes it possible to test for membership of large subsets of the keyspace with a single valid (message, tag) pair and a single verification query (see Sect. 6).

4.1   Malleability

In [29], Saarinen also describes 'targeted bit forgeries' against GCM where, rather than swapping the full blocks M_i and M_{i+jt}, corresponding bits in each ciphertext block are flipped. This can also be described by the more general attack, by using a multiple of $q(x)$.

If $q(H) = 0$, then $\alpha \cdot q(H) = 0$ for any $\alpha \in \mathbb{K}$ and

$$
\begin{aligned}
T_M &= E_k(N) + h_H(M) \\
&= E_k(N) + M_1 \cdot H + \cdots + M_m \cdot H^m \\
&= E_k(N) + (M_1 + \alpha q_1) \cdot H + \cdots + (M_m + \alpha q_m) \cdot H^m \\
&= T_{M+\alpha Q}
\end{aligned}
$$

where $T_{M+\alpha Q}$ is the authentication tag for the message $M_1 \oplus \alpha \cdot q_1 || \ldots || M_m \oplus \alpha \cdot q_m$ (recall that M contains the associated data, encrypted plaintext and the length of both).

If the plaintext is encrypted using a stream cipher (or a block cipher in counter mode) flipping bits in the ciphertext causes the same bits in the paintext to be flipped. This allows us to predict relations between the original plaintext and the forged plaintext (as $C_i \oplus \alpha q_i$ decrypts to $P_i \oplus \alpha q_i$). Because α can be chosen so as to set $C_i \oplus \alpha q_i$ equal to any value chosen by the adversary (for a single i), an adversary can choose a differential (in a single block) between the original message and the forged message.

If further control over the underlying plaintext in required, several forgery polynomials could be used. In the best case, using t polynomials permits the adversary control over t message blocks. The cost of this extra malleability is that the forgery is only successful if the authentication key is a root of the greatest common divisor of the two polynomials. This can be extended to give as much control over the plaintext as required, but for every extra malleable block the success probability is reduced by at least $\frac{1}{|\mathcal{K}_H|}$.

If the plaintext were encrypted using a block cipher (not in counter mode) then an adversary would not have this fine control over the plaintext, but would still be able to manipulate the ciphertext in this way.

This property also permits an adversary to create as many forgeries as there are non-zero elements in the field (see [7,25] for further discussion of multiple forgeries).

4.2 Length Extension

In the GCM specification, the last block input to the hash function (corresponding to the term $M_1 \cdot H$ in the MAC calculation) describes the length of the plaintext and additional data. The more general attack described in this paper allows an adversary to manipulate the length field (even though it does not explicitly appear in the sent message). If an adversary is given a valid tag for a message then the content of the length field is known, as it correctly encodes the length of the plaintext and additional data. It is therefore possible to choose a differential in the length field so that it corresponds to the length of the new message. In particular, forgeries can be created using high degree polynomial $q(x)$ regardless of the size of the message in the initial (message, tag) pair.

This is an important remark as it removes one significant limitation on the effectiveness of cycling attacks against GCM [29], which is the length of the message necessary to launch an attack. For a cycling attack to be attempted, an adversary requires as many blocks of correctly authenticated data as there are elements in the subgroup with which he wishes to forge, in order to swap the first and last blocks. By manipulating the length field any forgery probability can be realised starting with a valid authentication tag on a single message block.

A common criticism of GCM is that the maximum message length may be restrictive in the future as data rates increase [15]. However, it follows from our work (and the original security proofs [24]) that increasing the maximum permissible length would significantly decrease the security of the scheme.

4.3 Key Recovery

Saarinen suggests that once a weak key has been identified (by a successful cycling attack), the adversary would create many forgeries by further cycling attacks [29, Sect. 9]. Translating this to the more general polynomial root description: once a successful forgery occurs, the authentication key is known to be one of the roots of the 'forgery polynomial' q. Therefore rather than making repeated 'cycling forgeries' with guaranteed success but limited control of the plaintext, the adversary can aim to recover the authentication key and forge authentication tags for arbitrary messages. By attempting to forge using a subset of the roots of the forgery polynomial (and reducing the number of roots in the subset after each successful attempt), an adversary can gradually recover the authentication key using a method that is independent of encryption method or key used. This would give a forgery probability less than 1 at each stage, however the adversary can choose a trade-off between the forgery probability and the speed of recovering the authentication key. This is analogous to the key recovery attack described by Handschuh and Preneel [16] (where the subsets are chosen to realise a binary search of the keyspace). Note that in the case of GCM, recovery of the hash key H does not lead to the recovery of the encryption key k as $H = E_k(0)$.

4.4   Choosing Polynomials

To maximise the probability of a successful forgery it is important that the polynomial used to attempt a forgery has many distinct roots, as a root with multiplicities increases the degree of the polynomial (and hence the length of the attempted forgery) without increasing the probability of success. The naïve way to achieve this is to compute $q(x) = \prod_i (x - H_i)$ for as many H_i as is required to give the desired forgery probability.

Alternatively, if the polynomial defined by the hash function is evaluated in $\mathbb{F}_{p^r}$ and the irreducible factorisation of $x^{p^r} - x$ is computed in a subfield $\mathbb{F}_{p^d}$, a subset of these factors can be multiplied together (in $\mathbb{F}_{p^d}$). By choosing distinct irreducible factors, the roots of the product polynomial will be distinct. Cycling attacks [29] employ a variation on this method. The factorisation

$$2^{2^n} - 1 = \prod_{i=1}^{n} 2^{2^{i-1}} + 1$$

allows Saarinen to find factors of $x^{2^{128}} - x$ in $\mathbb{F}_2[x]$ which can be used in a cycling attack (although they are not necessarily irreducible):

$$x^{2^{128}} - x = x(x-1)\frac{(x^3 - 1)}{x-1}\frac{(x^5 - 1)}{x-1}\frac{(x^{17} - 1)}{x-1}\cdots$$
$$= x(x-1)(1 + x + x^2)(1 + x + \cdots + x^4)(1 + x + \cdots + x^{16})\cdots$$

To carry out a cycling attack using a subgroup of order t, the factors x, $(x-1)$ and $\frac{(x^t-1)}{x-1}$ are multiplied together to obtain the polynomial $x^{t+1} - x$. In general there is no requirement to select $(x - 1)$ or to use only three factors, for example the polynomial $x(1+x+x^2)(1+x+\ldots x^{16})$ could be used to give a forgery probability of $\frac{19}{2^{128}}$. This is not a cycling attack, as the polynomial used contains more than two terms so the forgery does not involve simply swapping two message blocks, but it does rely on the same underlying algebraic structure.

A third option is to use a randomly selected polynomial in $\mathbb{F}_{p^r}[x]$. One potential issue with this method is the presence of repeated factors. Square-free factorisation has been extensively studied as it is a common first step in many polynomial factorisation algorithms (for example, see [37, Ch. 14]). It may be feasible to sample polynomials from $\mathbb{F}_{p^r}[x]$ randomly and process this polynomial to make it more desirable by removing repeated factors. This method does not appear promising due to the large number of irreducible polynomials of any given degree in $\mathbb{F}_{p^r}[x]$ and the observation that a degree d polynomial that consists of a single linear factor and an irreducible polynomial of degree $d - 1$ is almost as bad as a degree d irreducible polynomial from a forgery probability perspective. Irreducible polynomials in $\mathbb{F}_p$ that are known to have a root in $\mathbb{F}_{p^r}$ would be good candidates for attempting forgeries as the normality of $\mathbb{F}_{p^r}/\mathbb{F}_p$ guarantees that these polynomials will split into linear factors. Unfortunately this does not appear to be a well studied area. A further disadvantage of choosing random polynomials is that, although the roots of a polynomial in $\mathbb{K}[x]$ can be identified efficiently (see [1] for example), it would be unlikely that a non-intersecting subset of the keyspace would be used for a second forgery attempt if the first was unsuccessful.

5   Existing Attacks Against GCM

We show below that the four known attacks on GCM can be described as special cases of the properties discussed in Sect. 4.

5.1   Ferguson's Short Tag Attack

Ferguson's attack against GCM when short tags are used [15] begins by attempting to forge using a particular class of polynomials (linearised polynomials). Linearised polynomials have the property that their roots form a linear subspace of the splitting field of the polynomial (see [23, Chap. 3.4] for an overview). Ferguson uses polynomials in $\mathbb{F}_2[x]$ that split over $\mathbb{F}_{2^{128}}$, so the roots correspond to possible authentication keys and it is possible to describe the roots of a linearised polynomial using a matrix over $\mathbb{F}_2$. Multiple successful forgeries reduce the dimension of the subspace of the keyspace that contains the authentication key and eventually an adversary can recover the key.

5.2   Joux's Forbidden Attack

Joux's 'forbidden attack' against GCM [19] is also a specific case of the properties discussed in this paper. This attack requires two messages, M and M', that are authenticated with the same (key, IV) pair. Reusing the (key, IV) pair in GCM has the effect of reusing H, k and N:

$$
\begin{aligned}
T_M \oplus T_{M'} &= (h_H(M) \oplus f_k(N)) \oplus (h_H(M') \oplus f_k(N)) \\
&= h_H(M) \oplus h_H(M') \\
&= h_H(M \oplus M')
\end{aligned}
$$

The adversary knows T_M, $T_{M'}$ and both messages so is able to derive a polynomial that is satisfied by the hash key. This attack is prevented if we only consider nonce-respecting adversaries.

5.3   Handschuh and Preneel

Handschuh and Preneel [16] describe a key recovery attack and a method to verify a guess for a key. They identify the key recovery attack as an extension of Joux's 'forbidden attack' which does not require nonce reuse. It consists of attempting to create a forgery and then searching through the roots of the polynomial defined by the difference betweeen the original message and the forged message. This was initially identified by Black and Cochran [6], but extended and generalised by Handschuh and Preneel. The method for verifying a key guess H corresponds precisely with attemping to forge using the polynomial $(x^2 - Hx)$.

Handschuh and Preneel consider their attack to be infeasible for GCM due to the blocksize of 128 bits, however it is precisely as feasible as Saarinen's cycling attacks.

5.4   Saarinen's Cycling Attacks

In 2012, Saarinen observed cycling attacks against GCM and other polynomial-based MACs and hashes [29]. If a hash key H lies in a subgroup of order t, then $H^t = 1 \in \mathbb{K}$ and (for any i, j) message blocks M_i and M_{i+jt} can be swapped without changing the value of the hash.

For example (ignoring GCM's length encoding), if $H^4 = H$ then blocks M_1 and M_4 can be swapped without changing the value of the hash:

$$
\begin{aligned}
h_H(M_1\|M_2\|M_3\|M_4) &= M_1 \cdot H \oplus M_2 \cdot H^2 \oplus M_3 \cdot H^3 \oplus M_4 \cdot H^4 \\
&= M_4 \cdot H \oplus M_2 \cdot H^2 \oplus M_3 \cdot H^3 \oplus M_1 \cdot H^4 \\
&= h_H(M_4\|M_2\|M_3\|M_1).
\end{aligned}
$$

It is more natural and general to consider the authentication keys that fall in low order subgroups as roots of a low degree polynomial. Cycling attacks correspond to the general attack introduced in this paper, using the polynomial

$$
q(x) = (M_i - M_{i+jt})(x^{t+1} - x),
$$

noting that in fields of characteristic 2 subtraction is the same as $\oplus$.

$$
\begin{aligned}
h_H(M_1\|M_2\|M_3\|M_4) =&M_1 \cdot H \oplus M_2 \cdot H^2 \oplus M_3 \cdot H^3 \oplus M_4 \cdot H^4 \\
=&M_1 \cdot H \oplus M_2 \cdot H^2 \oplus M_3 \cdot H^3 \oplus M_4 \cdot H^4 \\
&\oplus (M_1 \oplus M_4) \cdot H \oplus (M_1 \oplus M_4) \cdot H^4 \\
=&M_4 \cdot H \oplus M_2 \cdot H^2 \oplus M_3 \cdot H^3 \oplus M_1 \cdot H \\
=&h_H(M_4\|M_2\|M_3\|M_1)
\end{aligned}
$$

Using the more general 'polynomial roots' description it is possible to forge using any subset of the keyspace. If the authentication keys that we wish to attempt to forge with are the elements of a low order subgroup, for example the order three subgroup of $\mathbb{F}^{\star}_{2^{128}}$ (identified by Saarinen [29, Sect. 4.1]) plus the all zero key:

$$H_0 = \text{00 00 00 00 00 00 00 00 00 00 00 00 00 00 00 00}$$
$$H_1 = \text{80 00 00 00 00 00 00 00 00 00 00 00 00 00 00 00}$$
$$H_2 = \text{10 D0 4D 25 F9 35 56 E6 9F 58 CE 2F 8D 03 5A 94}$$
$$H_3 = \text{90 D0 4D 25 F9 35 56 E6 9F 58 CE 2F 8D 03 5A 94}$$

then the polynomial that is created corresponds precisely to Saarinen's cycling attack. In this case $(x - H_0)(x - H_1)(x - H_2)(x - H_3) = x^4 - x$.

6   Weak Keys for Polynomial-Based Authentication Schemes

For any cryptographic algorithm, a relevant question for its security assessment is whether it contains *weak keys*. Handschuh and Preneel [16, Sect. 3.1] give the following definition of weak keys:

> In symmetric cryptology, a class of keys [$\mathcal{D}$] is called a *weak key class* if for the members of that class the algorithm behaves in an unexpected way and if it is easy to detect whether a particular unknown key belongs to this class. For a MAC algorithm, the unexpected behavior can be that the forgery probability for this key is substantially larger than average. Moreover, if a weak key class [$\mathcal{D}$] is of size C, one requires that identifying that a key belongs to this class requires testing fewer than C keys by exhaustive search and fewer than C verification queries.

Handschuh and Preneel [16] identify 0 as a weak authentication key for GCM and other similar constructions as $h_0(M) = 0$ for every message M. Following the definition above and because $|\mathcal{D}| = 1$, an adversary is not allowed to test any key by exhaustive search, nor are they allowed any verification queries. For a single element subset of the keyspace $\mathcal{D} = \{H^{\star}\}$ to be a weak key class, a nonce-respecting adversary has to be able to identify whether or not $H = H^{\star}$ when they are given a number of (message, tag) pairs of their choosing (each created using a different IV). We note that a nonce-respecting adversary can detect whether $\mathcal{D} = \{0\}$ if $|\text{IV}| \neq 96$: in this case all IVs hash to give the same initial counter value and $h_0(M) = 0$ for every message M so all messages have the same authentication tag (as identified in [24, Sect. 5]). If $|\text{IV}| = 96$ a different initial counter value is used to encrypt the output of the hash function and so although the output of the hash function does not change this cannot be detected given the output of the MAC algorithm.

Saarinen [29] demonstrated that the situation is much worse than described by Handschuh and Preneel, as he was able to find classes of weak keys where the authentication key falls in a low order subgroup of $\mathbb{K}^{\star}$. It is then possible to create a valid forgery by swapping two message blocks of a valid (message, tag) pair without changing the authentication tag if the authentication key lies in a subgroup with order dividing the distance between the swapped message blocks.

This forgery will be successful if and only if the key is an element of such a subgroup and therefore this provides a simple method for identifying weak keys which requires one valid (message, tag) pair and one verification query. These classes of weak keys therefore meet Handschuh and Preneel's definition of weak keys.

For example, the subset of authentication keys corresponding zero and the elements of the subgroup of order 3 in $\mathbb{F}_{2^{128}}$ is a weak key class. Membership of this subset can be confirmed by a successful forgery if M_i and M_j are swapped and $i \equiv j \mod 3$. This is equivalent to attempting a forgery using (a multiple of) the polynomial $x^4 - x$.

However, it follows from the discussion in Sect. 4 that it is possible to derive comparable statements for any set of authentication keys in $\mathbb{F}_{2^{128}}$, except that rather than 'nice' binary descriptions, the polynomial description will involve elements of $\mathbb{F}_{2^{128}}$. In particular, for any set of authentication keys $\mathcal{D}$ we can use any polynomial in the ideal $\prod_{H \in \mathcal{D}} \langle x^2 - Hx \rangle$ to test for membership of that subset of the keyspace. It follows that *almost every* subset of the GCM keyspace is weak. We discuss this issue further in Sects. 6.1 and 7.

6.1 Keyspace Search

Based on the properties discussed in Sect. 4 it is possible to test for membership of any subset of the keyspace using at most two verification queries. Membership of subsets that include the zero key can be tested by setting $q(x) = \prod_{H \in \mathcal{D}} (x - H)$. This therefore requires one verification query, independent of the size of $\mathcal{D}$. To test for membership of a subset $\mathcal{D}$ that does not include zero, first test whether $H \in \mathcal{D} \cup \{0\}$ and then rule out $H = 0$ using the method described below. This therefore requires two verification queries, but again is independent of the size of $\mathcal{D}$. The distinction between subsets including zero or not including zero is a consequence of the constant term of $g_M(x)$ being zero to avoid predictable changes in the output of the hash from flipping low order bits.

Therefore, using Handschuh and Preneel's definition, a set $\mathcal{D}$ of GCM authentication keys is a weak key class if either: $|\mathcal{D}| \geq 3$ or $|\mathcal{D}| \geq 2$ and $0 \in \mathcal{D}$.

Given one valid (message, tag) pair for a single block message and one verification query it is easy to determine whether or not $H = 0$. If the adversary attempts to forge using any other single block message and the same tag, then the forgery is successful if and only if $H = 0$ as seen below.

If no length encoding is used:

$$T = E(\mathsf{CTR}_0) + (M \cdot H)$$
$$= E(\mathsf{CTR}_0) + (M' \cdot H)$$
$$\Leftrightarrow (M - M') \cdot H = 0$$
$$\Leftrightarrow M = M' \text{ or } H = 0$$

If a GCM style length encoding is used:

$$T = E(\mathsf{CTR}_0) + (\text{length} \cdot H) + (M \cdot H^2)$$
$$= E(\mathsf{CTR}_0) + (\text{length} \cdot H) + (M' \cdot H^2)$$
$$\Leftrightarrow (M - M') \cdot H^2 = 0$$
$$\Leftrightarrow M = M' \text{ or } H = 0$$

By testing for membership of subsets of the keyspace, it is plausible that an adversary could recover one bit of the authentication key with each forgery attempt. If $q(x) = \prod_{H \in \mathcal{Y}} (x - H)$, where $\mathcal{Y}$ is the set of authentication keys for which the first bit is zero, then a successful forgery confirms that the first bit of the authentication key is zero and a failure confirms that the first bit is one. Repeating this for each bit of the authentication key, the whole key could be recovered using 128 verification queries.

This would require unfeasibly large messages to be used in the forgery attempts in the case of authentication keys corresponding to elements of a field with $|\mathbb{K}| \approx 2^{128}$, but it is a strong argument against using a hash function based on polynomial evaluation in a field with $|\mathbb{K}| \ll 2^{128}$. This may be a direction taken by variants of GCM designed to improve the performance of GCM (see [40] for one such example), however we recommend extreme caution when considering these modifications. In the case of GCM the size of the subsets that can be tested is limited to around 2^{56} as the maximum message length is limited.

One advantage of being able to test for membership of arbitrary subsets is that it allows the adversary to use any partial knowledge of the authentication key that they may have.

7   Discussions and Conclusions

7.1   Choice of Fields

It is true that the security against cycling attacks, as presented in [29], can be increased by evaluating a hash function in a field with a multiplicative group, the order of which does not have many factors. However the attack introduced in this paper (of which cycling attacks is a special case) applies equally well in any finite field, so Saarinen's claim that 'The security of polynomial-evaluation MACs against attacks of this type of attack can be determined from the factorization of the group size in a straightforward manner' [29, Sect. 8] is somewhat misleading.

Saarinen's claim is valid in the sense that the factorisation of $|\mathbb{K}| - 1$ determines the extent to which the process of computing irreducible factors will succeed; however an attack using $\prod_{H \in \mathcal{D}} (x - H)$ will work equally well in every field. In particular, it follows from our work that the SGCM variant of GCM has the same inherent weaknesses regarding polynomial based forgery attacks.

7.2   Length Extension

It is unfortunate that including the length of the additional authenticated data and plaintext in the input to the hash function is not sufficient to prevent the length extension attack presented in this paper. In schemes that use a GCM–like length encoding, if the value of the length field were encrypted using a block cipher before being input to the hash function, it would not be possible to alter the message length as described in Sect. 4. However, one of the design goals of GCM was to take advantage of AES pipelining, which precludes the use of the block cipher to compute the authentication tag.

7.3   Malleability

Part of the reason that this weakness in the algebraic structure of polynomial hashing is problematic for GCM is that it allows an adversary to choose the changes that are made to the plaintext in a forged message. This is because addition in a field of characteristic 2 is used for both the counter mode encryption and the hash function evaluation.

One way to avoid this issue is to use different operations during encryption and MAC generation. This is one significant advantage that (CTR & Poly1305–AES) [2] has over GCM, as in this scheme the MAC is computed using addition in a prime order field while the message is encrypted using addition in a field of characteristic 2.

An alternative method to increase the difficulty for an adversary attempting to make meaningful manipulations of plaintext is to use a mode of operation other than CTR as this will prevent the 'targeted bit forgeries' described by Saarinen [29, Sect. 6] and the analogous forgeries in this paper.

GCM roughly follows the Encrypt–then–MAC paradigm, as is generally perceived to be best practice (although MAC–then–Encrypt has also been proved secure in the nonce-based AEAD setting [28]). Despite going against the perceived best practice, using a MAC–then–Encrypt approach (in addition to the proposed changes described above) would make it harder for an adversary to create ciphertexts that correctly decrypt to a plaintext known to be related to a (plaintext,ciphertext) pair obtained from a query. We note however that the introduction of other weaknesses caused by making these changes has not been ruled out.

7.4   Weak Keys

The weak key classes that are identified in Sect. 6 cause the forgery probability to be higher than expected because an adversary can detect whether the authentication key that is being used is a member of that class and can then forge with probability one.

The broader issue with polynomial evaluation based hashes is that it is possible to test for membership of large subsets of the keyspace with only one or two verification queries and once an adversary has successfully confirmed membership of a subset he can either continue to forge messages or conduct a search of a much reduced keyspace. This is an unusual and undesirable property of a cryptosystem.

It is interesting that the two-element subsets of the keyspace containing zero are weak key classes, while those that do not contain zero are not, yet any subset of the keyspace containing at least three elements is weak. This perhaps suggests a problem with the definition of a weak key class. In our opinion the definition is correct and the observations made in this paper are unavoidable properties of hash functions based on polynomial evaluation that result from the algebraic structure of the construction, so are not best described in terms of the number of weak keys.

The most important discussion around this issue is whether an algorithm in which almost every subset of the keyspace is a weak key class is a weak algorithm or whether this is a property of the construction that, although highly undesirable, is not considered to reduce the security of the scheme to an unacceptable level. We suggest that in the case of GCM it is the latter; in other polynomial-based MAC schemes with different parameters it may be the former and this property must be considered when designing and evaluating schemes.

References

1. Berlekamp, E.R.: Factoring polynomials over large finite fields. Math. Comput. **24**(111), 713–735 (1970)
2. Bernstein, D.J.: The Poly1305-AES message-authentication code. In: Gilbert, H., Handschuh, H. (eds.) FSE 2005. LNCS, vol. 3557, pp. 32–49. Springer, Heidelberg (2005)
3. Bernstein, D.J.: The Poly1305-AES message-authentication code. Slides from FSE (2005). http://cr.yp.to/talks/2005.02.21-1/slides.pdf
4. Bernstein, D.J.: Stronger security bounds for Wegman-Carter-Shoup authenticators. In: Cramer, R. (ed.) EUROCRYPT 2005. LNCS, vol. 3494, pp. 164–180. Springer, Heidelberg (2005)
5. Bierbrauer, J., Johansson, T., Kabatianskii, G., Smeets, B.: On families of hash functions via geometric codes and concatenation. In: Stinson, D.R. (ed.) CRYPTO 1993. LNCS, vol. 773, pp. 331–342. Springer, Heidelberg (1994)
6. Black, J., Cochran, M.: MAC reforgeability. Cryptology ePrint Archive, report 2006/095 (2006)
7. Black, J., Cochran, M.: MAC reforgeability. In: Dunkelman, O. (ed.) FSE 2009. LNCS, vol. 5665, pp. 345–362. Springer, Heidelberg (2009)
8. Black, J., Halevi, S., Krawczyk, H., Krovetz, T., Rogaway, P.: UMAC: fast and secure message authentication. In: Wiener, M. (ed.) CRYPTO 1999. LNCS, vol. 1666, pp. 216–233. Springer, Heidelberg (1999)
9. Brassard, G.: On computationally secure authentication tags requiring short secret shared keys. In: Chaum, D., Rivest, R.L., Sherman, A.T. (eds.) CRYPTO, pp. 79–86. Plenum Press, New York (1982)
10. Carter, L., Wegman, M.N.: Universal classes of hash functions (extended abstract). In: Hopcroft, J.E., Friedman, E.P., Harrison, M.A. (eds.) STOC, pp. 106–112. ACM (1977)

11. Carter, L., Wegman, M.N.: Universal classes of hash functions. J. Comput. Syst. Sci. **18**(2), 143–154 (1979)
12. den Boer, B.: A simple and key-economical unconditional authentication scheme. J. Comput. Secur. **2**, 65–72 (1993)
13. Dworkin, M.: Recommendation for block cipher modes of operation: Galois/Counter Mode (GCM) and GMAC. NIST Special Publication 800–38D, NIST, Nov 2007
14. MacWilliams, F.J., Gilbert, E.N., Sloane, N.J.A.: Codes which detect deception. Technical report 3, Bell Sys. Tech. J., Mar 1974
15. Ferguson, N.: Authentication weaknesses in GCM. Comments submitted to NIST Modes of Operation Process (2005)
16. Handschuh, H., Preneel, B.: Key-recovery attacks on universal hash function based MAC algorithms. In: Wagner, D. (ed.) CRYPTO 2008. LNCS, vol. 5157, pp. 144–161. Springer, Heidelberg (2008)
17. Igoe, K., Solinas, J.: AES Galois Counter Mode for the secure shell transport layer protocol. IETF Request for Comments 5647 (2009)
18. Iwata, T., Ohashi, K., Minematsu, K.: Breaking and repairing GCM security proofs. In: Safavi-Naini, R., Canetti, R. (eds.) CRYPTO 2012. LNCS, vol. 7417, pp. 31–49. Springer, Heidelberg (2012)
19. Joux, A.: Authentication failures in NIST version of GCM. Comments submitted to NIST Modes of Operation Process (2006)
20. Kohno, T., Viega, J., Whiting, D.: CWC: a high-performance conventional authenticated encryption mode. In: Roy, B., Meier, W. (eds.) FSE 2004. LNCS, vol. 3017, pp. 408–426. Springer, Heidelberg (2004)
21. Krawczyk, H.: LFSR-based hashing and authentication. In: Desmedt, Y.G. (ed.) CRYPTO 1994. LNCS, vol. 839, pp. 129–139. Springer, Heidelberg (1994)
22. Law, L., Solinas, J.: Suite B cryptographic suites for IPsec. IETF Request for Comments 6379 (2011)
23. Lidl, R., Neiderreiter, H.: Finite Fields, vol. 20, 2nd edn. Encylopedia of Mathematics and its Applications. Cambridge University Press, Cambridge (1997)
24. McGrew, D.A., Viega, J.: The security and performance of the Galois/Counter Mode (GCM) of operation. In: Canteaut, A., Viswanathan, K. (eds.) INDOCRYPT 2004. LNCS, vol. 3348, pp. 343–355. Springer, Heidelberg (2004)
25. McGrew, D.A., Fluhrer, S.R.: Multiple forgery attacks against message authentication codes. Comments submitted to NIST on the Choice Between CWC or GCM (2005)
26. McGrew, D.A., Viega, J.: The Galois/Counter Mode of operation (GCM). Submission to NIST Modes of Operation Process, May 2005
27. Rabin, M.O.: Fingerprinting with random polynomials. Technical report (1981)
28. Rogaway, P.: Authenticated-encryption with associated-data. In: Atluri, V. (ed.) ACM Conference on Computer and Communications Security, pp. 98–107. ACM (2002)
29. Saarinen, M.-J.O.: Cycling attacks on GCM, GHASH and other polynomial MACs and hashes. In: Canteaut, A. (ed.) FSE 2012. LNCS, vol. 7549, pp. 216–225. Springer, Heidelberg (2012)
30. Saarinen, M.-J.O.: SGCM: the Sophie Germain Counter Mode. Cryptology ePrint Archive, report 2012/326 (2012)
31. Salter, M., Housley, R.: Suite B profile for transport layer security (TLS). IETF Request for Comments 6460 (2011)

32. Shoup, V.: On fast and provably secure message authentication based on universal hashing. In: Koblitz, N. (ed.) CRYPTO 1996. LNCS, vol. 1109, pp. 313–328. Springer, Heidelberg (1996)
33. Simmons, G.J.: Contemporary Cryptology: The Science of Information Integrity. Institute of Electrical, and Electronics Engineers. IEEE Press, Piscataway (1992)
34. Stinson, D.R.: Universal hashing and authentication codes. Des. Codes Crypt. **4**(3), 369–380 (1994)
35. Stinson, D.R.: On the connections between universal hashing, combinatorial designs and error-correcting codes. Electron. Colloquium Comput. Complexity (ECCC) **2**(52), 1–24 (1995)
36. Taylor, R.: Near optimal unconditionally secure authentication. In: De Santis, A. (ed.) EUROCRYPT 1994. LNCS, vol. 950, pp. 244–253. Springer, Heidelberg (1995)
37. von zur Gathen, J., Gerhard, J.: Modern computer algebra, 2nd edn. Cambridge University Press, Cambridge (2003)
38. Wegman, M.N., Carter, L.: New classes and applications of hash functions. In: FOCS, pp. 175–182. IEEE Computer Society (1979)
39. Wegman, M.N., Carter, L.: New hash functions and their use in authentication and set equality. J. Comput. Syst. Sci. **22**(3), 265–279 (1981)
40. Aoki, K., Yasuda, K.: The security and performance of "GCM" when short multiplications are used instead. In: Kutyłowski, M., Yung, M. (eds.) Inscrypt 2012. LNCS, vol. 7763, pp. 225–245. Springer, Heidelberg (2013)

Secure Message Authentication Against Related-Key Attack

Rishiraj Bhattacharyya[1](✉) and Arnab Roy[2]

[1] ENS de Lyon/INRIA, Lyon, France
rishiraj.bhattacharyya@ens-lyon.fr
[2] SnT, Université du Luxembourg, Walferdange, Luxembourg
arnab.roy@uni.lu

Abstract. Security against related-key attacks is an important criteria for modern cryptographic constructions. In the related-key setting, the adversary has the ability to query the underlying function on the target key as well as on some related-keys. Although provable security against related-key attack has received considerable attention in recent years, most of the results in the literature aim to achieve pseudorandomness and semantic security and often lead to inefficient constructions.

In this paper, we formalize the notion of unpredictability in the related-key setting. We start with the definitions of related-key security of Message Authentication Codes and identify required properties of related-key derivation functions for provable security. We show that unlike PRFs, MACs can inherently tolerate related-key attacks against constant transformations. Next, we consider the construction of variable-input-length MACs from fixed-input-length related-key unpredictable functions. We present simple attacks against XCBC and TMAC. We present a general construction of related-key secure MACs. Our construction, instantiated with Enciphered CBC construction of Dodis, Pietrzak and Puniya (EUROCRYPT 2008), results into first provably secure domain extension of related-key secure unpredictable functions. Finally, we present two constructions of related-key secure MACs from DDH assumption. The first construction is extremely efficient and tolerates group-induced partial key transformations. The second construction achieves security against independent group-induced tranformations and is more efficient than the RK-PRFs achieved by Bellare and Cash (CRYPTO 2010).

Keywords: Message authentication · Related-key attack · Domain extension

1 Introduction

A series of cryptanalytic results have established the threat of related-key attacks as a mainstream cryptographic challenge. Introduced by Biham and Knudsen [6,16] for block ciphers, related-key cryptanalysis has led to high profile attacks,

S. Moriai (Ed.): FSE 2013, LNCS 8424, pp. 305–324, 2014.
DOI: 10.1007/978-3-662-43933-3_16, © Springer-Verlag Berlin Heidelberg 2014

ranging from key recovery [7] to distinguishers [8–10]. In a related-key setting, the secret key of a cryptosystem/primitive can be partially controlled by the adversary. Specifically, the adversary can apply key transformations to change the key and observe the outcome under the modified keys. A typical example of such transformation is fault injection attack.

Motivated by the cryptanalytic applications, Bellare and Kohno [5] initiated a theoretical study of related-key (RK) security of block ciphers, traditionally modelled as pseudorandom permutations (PRPs) and pseudorandom functions (PRFs). They defined related-key security with respect to a class of related-key-deriving (RKD) functions, Φ, which specifies the relations available to the adversary, and considered an adversary who can (adaptively) choose the relation from Φ during the attack. Although in some of the examples of [5], choice of RKD set makes the adversary quite powerful, they help to characterize the set of functions.

Despite of its importance in applied cryptography only a few positive results are known in the RK setting [2,4,5,17]. Bellare and Kohno [5], followed by Lucks [17] considered the construction of RK secure pseudorandom functions and permutations from the ideal primitives like ideal cipher. Lucks introduced the notion of group induced RKD class where, if the keyspace forms a group under some given operation, then the RKD functions may be chosen by an adversary using this group-operation. An obvious example of such operation is bit wise exclusive or (XOR) operation of a key with some known constant (of same bit length as the key). In a breakthrough result, Bellare and Cash [3] constructed RK secure PRPs based on hardness of DDH/DLIN assumptions. Although this construction proves an important feasibility result , the solution is quite inefficient and hard to use in practice.

On the other hand, related-key distinguishers have been found for widely used block-ciphers including AES [10]. Naturally, concerns are mounting over the security of the primitives, designed based on these ciphers [18]. Specifically, security of applications like message authentication codes, where block-ciphers are used heavily as the underlying primitive, needs to be revisited in light of the related-key attacks. Although, most of the popular MAC constructions were proven to be pseudorandom assuming pseudorandomness of the underlying block cipher, much weaker security notion, like unpredictability, is sufficient for MACs. As AES and some other block-ciphers are believed to remain unpredictable, even against related-key attacks, a natural question is what security guarantee we can prove from this assumption. Specifically, *Can we achieve an efficient construction of Message Authentication Code, secure against related-key attacks, if we only assume related-key unpredictability from the underlying block ciphers?*

Our Results. In this paper, we focus our attention to the security of message authentication codes against related-key attacks. Instead of modeling the block cipher as RK-PRP, we model underlying block cipher as only RK unpredictable. We reconsider several practical and popular constructions from the literature, and analyze them in the light of related-key attacks, towards their feasibility as related-key MACs. We also present two proofs of concept RK unpredictable functions, both based on DDH assumption. A more detailed description of our results follows.

Definitions. We start with presenting general definition of unpredictability against related-key attacks. We consider two types of security of unforgeability. In the first type (called Weak Related-Key Unforgeability), adversary's prediction has to be on a fresh message, i.e. she can not predict the output of the function (on the target key) on a message, which she has queried earlier even on a related-key. In the stronger type (called Related-Key Unforgeability), adversary can be more powerful. She is allowed to forge a message, even if she has queried it on a related-key (although, not on the target key).

Handling Constant Functions. We revisit the necessary conditions for the class of related-key transformations argued by Bellare and Kohno [5], specifically transformations mapping all keys to some constant. We present a simple proof that a general message authentication code is inherently secure against constant RKD functions. To the best of our knowledge, this results to a first symmetric key construction which can handle constant RKD transformations.

Cryptanalysis of Popular MAC Construction. Next, we show negative results on many popular constructions. We show simple attacks against XCBC and TMAC. We also prove that, if the key of the MAC construction is viewed as a single key, ECBC and FCBC constructions do not guarantee unforgeability, irrespective of the strength of underlying block ciphers.

A Related-Key Secure Domain Extension. The natural question that arises from the results of previous paragraph is whether any existing construction preserves unpredictability against a related-key adversary. For the general setting, most designs use the NI construction of [1]. The general idea behind the construction is a collision at the output would imply a collision at the compression function (by standard MD argument). Then one would try to design an efficient weak collision resistant compression function from unpredictable functions, and prove that a collision at the compression function output can be used to predict the output of the underlying functions. However, in the related-key scenario, this need not be the case. Indeed, the collision of the mode as well as the compression function may be with a related-key query. If the related key query was made later, then the previous approach will not work.

To solve this problem, we propose a Merkle-Damgård based construction (prefix-free NI) for related-key unpredictability. Specifically, our construction is a prefix free MD domain extension with an extra round at the end. Using this extra round, we prove that even if the collision is with a related-key query, input of the last round (during the evaluation of forgery output) is either new (hence can be used for prediction) or generates a collision with a previous query on the target key. Then one can extend the standard MD based arguments to find forgery on the underlying functions.

We instantiate this mode of operation by the enciphered CBC construction of Dodis, Pietrzak and Puniya [13], and prove that this gives a variable input length related-key unpredictable function from fixed input length related-key secure unpredictable functions and permutations.

A General Construction of RK Unpredictable Functions. Our final contribution is a provably secure construction of Related Key Unpredictable function in the standard model. We instantiate this construction by two recent constructions in [11]. Our basic construction, secure against partial key-transformations, is much efficient in terms of keysize. Specifically, the keysize in our case is linear as compared to quadratic keysize in [3]. Our second construction is fully secure against component-wise group induced transformations. The construction of Bellare and Cash [3] can be seen as a special case of our construction. Additionally, the concept of key homomorphism in this work avoids the complexity of key malleability faced in [3]. Compared to Bellare-Cash construction, this construction is efficient in terms of exponentiation.

2   Overview of Our Technique

CLAW-FREE RKD SETS. In this work, like most of the previous positive results, we focus on claw-free related-key deriving (RKD) functions. Roughly speaking, a set Φ of RKD functions is called claw-free if for all but negligible fraction of k, distinct functions ϕ_1 and ϕ_2 from Φ, $\phi_1(k) \neq \phi_2(k)$. We note that, Bellare, Cash, and Miller [4] have constructed related-key secure signature scheme where they could break this requirement. However, their construction heavily depends on the notion of ICR pseudorandom generator, which in turn depends on RK-secure pseudorandom functions. We stress that, no construction of RK-secure pseudorandom function against non-claw free RKD set is known till date, and constructions of [4] are not instantiable by current RK-secure PRFs. In such a situation, we consider the claw-free RKD sets as worthy target.

HANDLING MULTIPLE KEYS. The most popular paradigm to design variable-input-length (VIL) MAC (or PRF) is the Hash then MAC (or Hash then PRF) approach. The message is first hashed by applying a collision resistant hash function, and then passed through an independent fixed input length MAC (PRF). Naturally, the key of such a construction contains the key(s) of the hash function (or the underlying primitive) and an independently sampled key of the final transformation. The key of the variable input length MAC is simply the concatenation of these sampled keys. The question is, how will the adversary change this key, i.e. should she consider functions which work independently over the individual keys? Or we can allow her to consider any claw-free RKD transformation over the keyspace (Cartesian product of the keyspace of the hash function and the final transformation) of the variable input length MAC.

In Sect. 6, we show that if we allow any claw-free RKD transformation over the keyspace, then multi-key constructions have an inherent limitation. Specifically, we show attacks on ECBC and FCBC, where the related-key adversary can turn a three key construction into a two key construction, using a claw-free RKD class.

We identify an alternative yet natural class of RKD functions, called component-wise transformation as a feasible target. A component-wise transformation over the keyspace $\mathcal{K}^n$ is an n-element vector of RKD functions over $\mathcal{K}$. Let $\phi = (\phi_1, \phi_2, \cdots, \phi_n)$ be such a vector where each ϕ_i is a function over $\mathcal{K}$. For any key $k = (k_1, k_2, \cdots, k_n)$, $\phi(k)$ is defined by $(\phi_1(k_1), \phi_2(k_2), \cdots, \phi_n(k_n))$. We remark that this idea of component-induced transformation is not new. In fact, constructions of RK-PRFs [3] were shown essentially for such classes. However, we are the first to formalize such idea.

REMOVING UNKEYED COLLISION RESISTANCE ASSUMPTION. One of the most important tools of the related-key secure VIL-PRF of [3] is an unkeyed collision resistant hash function with carefully chosen range. Thus, security of this PRF is based on the assumption of existence of unkeyed collision resistant hash function. This assumption is very strong (in fact, stronger than existence of one-way function) and thus undesirable. However, the problem is, if we consider keyed hash function, then that key is also subject to related key attack. It is not clear from [3], how to tackle that problem.

We solve this problem by introducing the notion of identity collision resistance and target preimage resistance for keyed hash functions. Intuitively, against an identity collision resistant hash function H with key k, a related-key adversary (which makes adaptive queries serially) will not be able to output, with significant probability, a message m such that $H_k(m)$ matches with the output of the (related-key) queries she already made. We prove such a notion along with a notion of target preimage resistance (lifted to the RK setting) is enough for the Hash and MAC construction. We also show how to construct such an hash function from length preserving related-key secure MACs/permutations. Although we faced some technical challenges (mentioned in the previous section), we solve them with an elegant prefix-free padding and Merkle-Damgård mode of operation.

Independent Work

Independent to our work, Xagawa [19] also considered related key security of message authentication codes over additive rkd sets, extending the results of [12]. Some of his results are similar to our algebraic constructions in Sect. 10.

3   Notations and Security Definitions

NOTATIONS: If x is a string, $|x|$ denotes the length (number of characters) of the string, $x[i]$ denotes the ith character of x, and $x_1||x_2||..||x_t$ denotes concatenation of t strings. For a finite set X, $|X|$ denotes the size of the set. $x \leftarrow_R X$ means selecting an element x uniformly at random from the set X. $A \rightarrow x$ denotes that an algorithm A outputs x. $\mathsf{Func}(\mathcal{D}, \mathcal{R})$ denotes the set of all functions from $\mathcal{D}$ to $\mathcal{R}$. A family of functions $F : \mathcal{K} \times \mathcal{D} \rightarrow \mathcal{R}$ takes a key $k \in \mathcal{K}$ and an input $m \in \mathcal{D}$, and outputs $F(k, m)$. Throughout the paper F_k denotes the function $F(k, .)$. A block-cipher is a family of permutations $E : \mathcal{K} \times \mathcal{D} \rightarrow \mathcal{D}$ and E_k denotes the permutation $E(k, .)$ for $k \in \mathcal{K}$.

UNFORGEABILITY OF A FUNCTION FAMILY: The security of F as a MAC is expressed via the following security game, where $\mathcal{A}$ is an adversary with oracle access to F_k,

Game UF-CMA

- Setup: $k \leftarrow_R \mathcal{K}$.
- Query Phase: $\mathcal{A}$ makes a set of queries $\mathcal{Q}$ to the oracle F_k.
- Guess Phase: $\mathcal{A} \rightarrow (m, \sigma)$.
- Verify: If $m \notin \mathcal{Q}$ and $F_k(m) = \sigma$ then $\mathcal{A}$ wins, else $\mathcal{A}$ looses.

A family of function F is said to be (q, ℓ, ϵ) *unforgeable under chosen message attack* if for all adversary $\mathcal{A}$ who makes q queries with total size of the queries ℓ bits,

$$\mathbf{Adv}_F^{mac}(\mathcal{A}) \stackrel{def}{=} Prob[\mathcal{A} \text{ wins game UF-CMA}] \leq \epsilon.$$

We note that the notion of unforgeability is also known as the unpredictability.

FRAMEWORK FOR RELATED-KEY ATTACK. In the related-key setting, security of a function family $F(\mathcal{K}, \mathcal{D}, \mathcal{R})$ is defined against a *related-key adversary*. At the beginning of the corresponding security game the adversary outputs a set of functions $\Phi \subseteq \mathsf{Func}(\mathcal{K}, \mathcal{K})$, called related-key deriving (RKD) functions. Throughout the game, the adversary has access to a *related-key oracle* F_{RK}. The oracle takes an ordered pair (m, ϕ) as input ($m \in \mathcal{D}, \phi \in \Phi$) and returns $F(\phi(k), m)$, where $F_k \in F(\mathcal{K}, \mathcal{D}, \mathcal{R})$ for some $k(\leftarrow_R \mathcal{K})$ unknown to the adversary.

If Φ contains the identity function id then F_{RK} can also simulate the oracle $F(k, .)$. For the rest of the paper unless specified we will assume that Φ includes the function id.

In [17] Lucks described an elegant way of choosing Φ as a set of *group-induced transformations* when $(\mathcal{K}, *)$ is a group.

Definition 1 (Group Induced Transformations [17]). *Let $\mathcal{K}$ be a group under operation $\circ$. A group induced transformation is a set of functions, Φ, over $\mathcal{K}$ defined as*

$$\Phi \stackrel{def}{=} \{\phi : \mathcal{K} \rightarrow \mathcal{K} | \exists \delta \in \mathcal{K} : \phi(k) = k \circ \delta\}$$

Another important family of RKD functions, called *partial transformations*, is also used in [5,17]. Partial transformations restrict the adversary to choose a function which can change only a part of the entire key. For example if we have a family of functions with key space $\mathcal{K} \times \mathcal{K}$, then a partial key transformation ϕ' can be defined as $\phi'(k_1, k_2) = (k_1, \phi(k_2))$ where ϕ is an RKD function on $\mathcal{K}$.

Finally, we introduce the notion of component-induced key transformations for multiple-key constructions.

Definition 2 (Component-wise Transformations). *Let $\mathcal{K} = \mathcal{K}_1 \times \mathcal{K}_2 \times \cdots \mathcal{K}_n$ be a set of keys. A component-wise transformation is a set of functions Φ over $\mathcal{K}$ defined as*

$$\Phi \stackrel{def}{=} \{\phi = (\phi_1, \phi_2, \cdots, \phi_n) | \forall i, \phi_i : \mathcal{K}_i \rightarrow \mathcal{K}_i, \forall k = (k_1, k_2, \cdots, k_n) \in \mathcal{K}$$
$$\phi(k) = (\phi_1(k_1), \phi_2(k_2), \cdots, \phi_n(k_n))\}$$

We stress that, in case of component-wise transformations each ϕ_i is applied on k_i and is independent to other k_js.

4 Unforgeability Against Related-Key Attack

We start with a formal definition of the related-key security for MACs. Recall that, in the related-key setup, the adversary may query the oracle on a message and a related-key. The obvious way (analogous to [15], in the context of signature) to define the notion of related-key-unforgeability would be to ensure that the forgery m^* was never queried to the oracle with the relation id. However, the adversary may define the RKD function to be such that it agrees with id for all but negligable fraction of the keys. For such a function, the security gets broken trivially. In other words, such a restriction would force the RKD class to be claw-free. We present a general definition of related-key unforgeability through the following game between an adversary and the challenger. The adversary $\mathcal{A}$ has oracle access to F_{RK}.

Game RK–UF–CMA

- Setup: $k \leftarrow_R \mathcal{K}$, $\mathcal{A}$ gets the security parameter λ. $\mathcal{A}$ submits the description of the RKD class $\varPhi$. $\mathcal{Q} = \emptyset$.
- Query: $\mathcal{A}$ adaptively queries with (m, ϕ), the challenger returns $F(\phi(k), m)$. $\mathcal{Q} = \mathcal{Q} \cup (m, \phi)$.
- Guess: $\mathcal{A}$ outputs a forgery (m^*, σ^*).
- Verify: If $F(k, m^*) = \sigma^*$, and $\phi(k) \neq k$ for all $(m^*, \phi) \in \mathcal{Q}$ then $\mathcal{A}$ wins else $\mathcal{A}$ looses.

Definition 3 (Related-Key Unforgeability). *A family of functions F is said to be (q, ℓ, ϵ) unforgeable under chosen message related-key attack over the RKD set $\varPhi$ if for all adversary $\mathcal{A}$ who makes q queries with total size of the queries ℓ bits,*

$$\boldsymbol{Adv}_F^{rk-mac}(\mathcal{A}, \varPhi) \overset{def}{=} Prob[\mathcal{A} \text{ wins game } RK\text{-}UF\text{-}CMA \text{ with } RKD \text{ set} \varPhi] \leq \epsilon$$

where the probability is taken over the key k and the internal randomness of $\mathcal{A}$.

5 Properties of RKD Transformations

In this section, we analyze the necessary properties of $\varPhi$, the RKD transformation, necessary for related-key security of MAC. In [5], Bellare Kohno proposed two essential conditions, namely unpredictability and claw-free ness, for RKD functions for related-key security. Specifically, they proved that if $\varPhi$ contains a constant function, then no block cipher can be pseudorandom against related-key attack over $\varPhi$. In a sharp contrast, we now prove that, a general message authentication code is inherently *secure* against constant RKD functions.

Theorem 1. *Let* $F : \mathcal{K} \times \mathcal{D} \to \mathcal{R}$ *be a MAC. Let* $\Phi \stackrel{def}{=} \{\phi_c : c \in \mathcal{K}, \forall k \in \mathcal{K}, \phi_c(k) = c\}$ *be the set of constant RKD transformations. For all related-key adversary* $\mathcal{A}_{RK}$ *against related-key unforgeability of* F *over RKD set* Φ*, there exists adversary* $\mathcal{A}$ *such that*

$$\boldsymbol{Adv}_F^{rk-mac}(\mathcal{A}_{RK}, \Phi) \leq \boldsymbol{Adv}_F^{mac}(\mathcal{A})$$

Proof. The main idea of the proof is the following: the adversary $\mathcal{A}$ will simulate $\mathcal{A}_{RK}$. When $\mathcal{A}_{RK}$ queries with id, $\mathcal{A}$ will answer the queries by making query to its own oracle. However as the related-key functions are constant functions, $\mathcal{A}$ can answer any related-key query (m, ϕ_c) by computing $F(c, m)$ on its own[1]. Finally when $\mathcal{A}_{RK}$ outputs a forgery (m^*, σ^*), $\mathcal{A}$ outputs (m^*, σ^*). By the condition of the game RK-UF-CMA, (m^*, id) was never queried by $\mathcal{A}_{RK}$. Hence (m^*, id) was never queried by $\mathcal{A}$ as well. So, $\mathcal{A}$ succeeds whenever $\mathcal{A}_{RK}$ succeeds.

INSECURITY AGAINST COLLIDING FUNCTIONS. The claw-freeness condition, however, is essential for security of related-key security of MAC. The attack of [5], involving addition and xor over the keyspace, can indeed recover the secret key, resulting a forgery. For detailed description of this attack, we refer the reader to Proposition 4.3 of [5].

6   Related-Key Attacks Against Popular MAC Constructions

In this section we show examples of some simple related-key adversaries against some well known MAC constructions. We consider two popular variants of CBC-MAC, namely XCBC and TMAC. Constructions like ECBC and FCBC can also be attacked with a more aggressive class of transformations. Due to space constraint, the cryptanalysis of ECBC and FCBC are omitted in this proceedings version. All these constructions were proved to be secure under the assumption that underlying block cipher is PRP. Although our ultimate aim is to achieve a related-key secure MAC when the underlying primitive is related-key unforgeable, in the following examples we show that the XCBC and TMAC can be forged using related-key attack even if the underlying block ciphers are *related-key secure prp*.

Proposition 2. *XCBC is not related-key secure.*

Proof. The attack is extremely simple. Let n be the block length of the underlying block cipher. Consider a message $m = m_1 \| m_2$ such that $|m_1| = |m_2| = n$. Let the RKD set chosen by adversary be $\mathcal{A}_{RK}$. $\Phi = \{\phi_i(k_1, k_2, k_2) = (k_1, k_2 \oplus i, k_3) : 0 < i < 2^{|k_2|}\} \cup \text{id}$. $\mathcal{A}_{RK}$ makes a related-key query (m, ϕ_i) for any $i > 0$. Suppose σ be the answer. $\mathcal{A}_{RK}$ returns (m^*, σ) , where $m^* = m_1 \| m_2 \oplus i$.

---

[1] Note that, obvious description of ϕ_c leaks the constant c.

Let $y = E_{k_1}(m_1)$. Then the last block operation is $E_{k_1}(y \oplus m_2 \oplus k_2)$. We know that $E_{k_1}(y \oplus m_2 \oplus (k_2 \oplus i)) = E_{k_1}(y \oplus (m_2 \oplus i) \oplus k_2)$. Hence $XCBC_{\mathsf{RK}}(m, \phi_i) = XCBC(m^*) = \sigma$. This implies (m^*, σ) is a valid forgery and $\mathbf{Adv}_{XCBC}^{rk-mac}(\mathcal{A}_{XCBC}, \Phi) = 1$.

TMAC can be viewed as a variant of XCBC MAC and instead of using three keys it uses two keys in the construction. The last block operation of TMAC is given as $E_{k_1}(m' \oplus (k_2 \cdot u))$, where u is a constant polynomial in $GF(2^n)$ and the product is performed in the same field. The simplification of the product $x \cdot u$ is linear in x. Hence using a RKD set similar as above the adversary will be able to forge TMAC.

Corollary 1. *TMAC is not a secure MAC Against related-key attack.*

PREWHITENING KEY AND RKA: Both the attacks described above exploit the use of prewhitening key. Suppose a MAC construction involves an operation of the form $E_{k'}(k * x)$ (where x is a chaining value independent of k and $*$ is a commutative-group induced operation) and k is independent of k' and other keys used in the construction. Then it is always possible to mount similar related-key attack as above.

7   Technical Tools

In this section we introduce the tools we use in our construction. First we introduce the notion of weak unforgeability against related-key attack, which essentially bridges the notion of unforgeability between the standard and the related-key settings.

Weak Unforgeability against Related-Key Attack

Definition 4 (Key-Homomorphic MAC). *Let $F : \mathcal{K} \times \mathcal{D} \to \mathcal{R}$ be family of MACs. We say that F is key-homomorphic MAC if $\mathcal{K}$ and $\mathcal{R}$ are groups with efficient operations ($\circ$ and $*$ respectively) and for any fixed $m \in \mathcal{D}$, there is a group homomorphism form $\mathcal{K}$ to $\mathcal{R}$. Specifically, for any $k_1, k_2 \in \mathcal{K}$,*

$$F_{k_1 \circ k_2}(m) = F(k_1, m) * F(k_2, m)$$

Let F be a family of key-homomorphic MACs and Φ° a $(\mathcal{K}, \circ)$ group-induced RKD set. Essentially, for $\phi \in \Phi^\circ$, one can compute $F(\phi(k), m)$ by making queries to $F(k, m)$ and using the group homomorphism property of F. In the RK–UF–CMA game, the adversary is challenged to forge $F(k, .)$. Apparently, finding $F(\phi(k), .)$ from $F(k, .)$ does not directly help her. However, the adversary may first query the related-key oracle and get $F(\phi(k), m)$ for some m, then using the group homomorphism property, predict the value of $F(k, m)$. To see this, consider an adversary $\mathcal{A}$ who makes a query (m, ϕ) to F_{RK} for some $m \in \mathcal{D}$. Now, we know that $\phi(k) = k \circ \delta$ for $\delta \in \mathcal{K}$. So, $\mathcal{A}$ knows $\sigma_1 = F(\phi(k), m)$ and can compute

$\sigma_2 = F(\delta, m)$ on her own as the family F is public. Hence, $\mathcal{A}$ successfully forges $F(k, .)$ with (m, σ) where $\sigma = \sigma_1 * \sigma_2^{-1}$.

We observe that, previous adversary $\mathcal{A}$ is not a unique-message adversary. Against a unique-message adversary of the RK-UF-CMA game, a key-homomorphic MAC is related-key unforgeable over group induced Φ. Motivated by this observation, we introduce the notion of weak unforgeability against related-key attack. In this case, the adversary is not allowed to forge a message which she has queried even on some non-id RKD function.

Game WeakRK-UF-CMA

- Setup: $k \leftarrow_R K$, $\mathcal{A}$ gets the security parameter λ. $\mathcal{A}$ submits the description of the RKD class Φ. $\mathcal{Q} = \emptyset$.
- Query: $\mathcal{A}$ adaptively queries with (m, ϕ), the challenger returns $F(\phi(k), m)$. $\mathcal{Q} = \mathcal{Q} \cup (m, \phi)$.
- Guess: $\mathcal{A}$ outputs a forgery (m^*, σ^*).
- Verify: If $F(k, m^*) = \sigma^*$, and $(m^*, \phi) \notin \mathcal{Q}$ for any ϕ then $\mathcal{A}$ wins else $\mathcal{A}$ looses.

Definition 5 (Weak RK-Unforgeability). *A family of functions F is said to be (q, ℓ, ϵ) weakly unforgeable under chosen message related-key attack (WRK-UF) over the RKD set Φ if for all adversary $\mathcal{A}$ who makes q queries with total size of the queries ℓ bits,*

$$Adv_F^{wrk-mac}(\mathcal{A}, \Phi) \overset{def}{=} Prob[\mathcal{A} \; winsgame \; \texttt{WeakRK-UF-CMA} \; with \; RKD \; set \; \Phi] \leq \epsilon$$

where the probability is taken over the key k and the internal randomness of $\mathcal{A}$.

For a key homomorphic MAC the following lemma can be proved in a straightforward way.

Lemma 1 (Key Homomorphic MAC is WRK-UF). *Let $F : \mathcal{K} \times \mathcal{D} \to \mathcal{R}$ be a family of key-homomorphic MACs. Let Φ be a claw-free set of group induced RKD functions. $\mathcal{F}$ is a secure WRK-UF over Φ. Specifically, for every (q, ℓ) adversary $\mathcal{A}$, there exists a (q, ℓ) adversary $\mathcal{A}_F$ such that*

$$Adv_F^{wrk-mac}(\mathcal{A}, \Phi) \leq Adv_F^{mac}(\mathcal{A})$$

Identity Fingerprint. The main technical tool used in [3] in order to construct the RK secure PRF is the notion of *key fingerprint*. Informally, a key fingerprint (as defined in [3]) is a vector over the message space, such that under two different keys, outputs of the function will be different on at least one index. However, as observed in [4], this notion is too demanding and may not be achievable for some PRFs.

In this paper, we consider the following relaxed notion of key fingerprint.

Definition 6 (Identity Fingerprint). *Let $F : \mathcal{K} \times \mathcal{D} \to \mathcal{R}$ be family of functions and Φ be a set of RKD functions over $\mathcal{K}$. Let w be a d dimensional vector* *over $\mathcal{D}$. We call w an identity-fingerprint of F over Φ if*

$$Prob_{k \leftarrow_R \mathcal{K}}\left[\forall \phi \in \Phi : \Big(F(k, w_1), F(k, w_2), \cdots, F(k, w_d)\Big) \right.$$
$$\left. \neq \Big(F(\phi(k), w_1), F(\phi(k), w_2), \cdots, F(\phi(k), w_d)\Big)\right] > 1 - negl$$

where $d = \mathcal{O}(|k|)$, $negl$ is some negligible function in terms of $|k|$.

We remark that, the identity key fingerprint notion of [4] is similar. As argued in [4], few distinct points from the domain can be considered as a candidate identity fingerprint for any practical block-cipher. Although we cannot prove it formally, such an assumption seems to be consistent with the premise of crypt-analysis.

ICTPR Hash Function. In this paper we remove the collision resistant hash function assumption. In our framework, we encounter keyed hash function which is subject to tampering by the adversary. To achieve security even in such a scenario, we propose and use the notion of ICTPR hash functions.

An ICTPR hash function $H : \mathcal{K} \times \mathcal{D} \to \mathcal{R}$ has two properties: identity-collision (IC) resistance and target preimage (TP) resistance.

IDENTITY COLLISION RESISTANCE. Roughly, the identity collision resistance ensures that, for (related-key) adversary with oracle access to H_{RK}, output of a query on a message m and the secret key (i.e. query of the form (m, id)), does not collide with the output of some previous query (even on a related-key). The formal security game works in the following way.

Game ID-CR

- Setup: $k \leftarrow_R \mathcal{K}$, $\mathcal{A}$ gets the security parameter λ. $\mathcal{A}$ submits the description of the RKD class Φ. $\mathcal{Q} = \emptyset$.
- Query: $\mathcal{A}$ adaptively queries with (m, ϕ), the challenger returns $H(\phi(k), m)$. $\mathcal{Q} = \mathcal{Q} \cup (m, \phi)$.
- Collision: $\mathcal{A}$ outputs a message m^*.
- Verify: If for some $(m, \phi) \in \mathcal{Q}$, $H(\phi(k), m) = H(k, m^*)$ and $(m^*, \text{id}) \notin \mathcal{Q}$ then $\mathcal{A}$ wins else $\mathcal{A}$ looses.

Definition 7 (Identity Collision Resistant Hash Function). *Let $H : \mathcal{K} \times \mathcal{D} \to \mathcal{R}$ be family of hash functions and Φ be a set of RKD functions on $\mathcal{K}$. H is said to be (q, ℓ, ϵ) identity collision resistant (ICR) over the RKD set Φ if for all adversary $\mathcal{A}$ who makes q queries with total size of the queries ℓ bits,*

$$\boldsymbol{Adv}_H^{icr}(\mathcal{A}, \Phi) \overset{def}{=} Prob[\mathcal{A} \text{ wins game ID-CR with RKD set } \Phi] \leq \epsilon$$

where the probability is taken over the key k and the internal randomness of $\mathcal{A}$.

TARGET PREIMAGE RESISTANCE AGAINST RELATED-KEY ATTACK. In addition to the identity collision resistance, we also need a notion of everywhere preimage resistance against related-key attacks. The preimage resistance game between an adversary $\mathcal{A}$ and a challenger for a hash function $H : \mathcal{K} \times \mathcal{D} \to \mathcal{R}$ is described as following

Game RK-TPR

- Setup: $k \leftarrow_R \mathcal{K}$, $\mathcal{A}$ gets the security parameter λ. $\mathcal{A}$ submits t targets $z_1, \cdots, z_t \in \mathcal{R}$, and the description of the RKD class Φ. $\mathcal{Q} = \emptyset$.
- Query: $\mathcal{A}$ adaptively queries with (m, ϕ), the challenger returns $H(\phi(k), m)$. $\mathcal{Q} = \mathcal{Q} \cup (m, \phi)$.
- Preimage: $\mathcal{A}$ outputs a message m^*.
- Verify: If $H(k, m^*) = z_i$, for some i then $\mathcal{A}$ wins else $\mathcal{A}$ looses.

Definition 8 (Related-Key Target Preimage Resistant Hash Function).
Let $H : \mathcal{K} \times \mathcal{D} \to \mathcal{R}$ be family of hash functions and Φ be a set of RKD functions on $\mathcal{K}$. H is said to be (q, t, ℓ, ϵ) related-key target preimage resistant (RK-TPR) over the RKD set Φ if for all adversary $\mathcal{A}$ who submits t targets, makes q queries with total size of the queries ℓ bits,

$$\mathbf{Adv}_H^{rk-tpr}(\mathcal{A}, \Phi) \overset{def}{=} Prob[\mathcal{A} \text{ wins game RK-TPR with } RKD \text{ set } \Phi] \leq \epsilon$$

where the probability is taken over the key k and the internal randomness of $\mathcal{A}$.

We define ICTPR advantage of an adversary $\mathcal{A}$ against a hash function H as

$$\mathbf{Adv}_H^{ictpr} = \mathbf{Adv}_H^{rk-tpr} + \mathbf{Adv}_H^{icr}$$

8   Construction of Related-Key Secure MAC

In this section, we show a general construction of related-key secure MAC. The basic essence of our construction is essentially the Hash then MAC paradigm of An and Bellare [1], lifted to the related-key setting. In fact most of the proposed VIL-MAC constructions [13,14] have been proved secure in this paradigm. The intuitive approach while extending the arguments of [1] would be to show that a suitable hash function H followed by a FIL-*related-key unforgeable* MAC F will give us a VIL-related-key secure MAC G. However, in the following theorem, we prove that, for claw-free RKD sets, if the hash function is ICTPR, it is enough for F only to be *weak related-key unforgeable* (cf. Definition 5).

Theorem 3. *Let $F : \mathcal{K}_1 \times \mathcal{D} \to \mathcal{R}$ be a weak related-key unforgeable MAC over RKD set Φ_1 with identity fingerprint $\overline{w} = (w_1, w_2, \cdots, w_d)$. Let $H : \mathcal{K}_2 \times \{0,1\}^* \to \mathcal{D}$ be a ICTPR hash function over the RKD set Φ_2. Let $G : (\mathcal{K}_1 \times \mathcal{K}_2) \times \{0,1\}^* \to \mathcal{R}$ be a family of function defined as*

$$G(k_1, k_2, m) \overset{def}{=} F(k_1, H(k_2, m \| F(k_1, w_1) \| F(k_1, w_2) \| \cdots \| F(k_1, w_d)))$$

where $k_1 \in \mathcal{K}_1, k_2 \in \mathcal{K}_2$. G is related-key unforgeable against chosen message attack over the component-induced RKD set $\Phi \overset{def}{=} \Phi_1 \times \Phi_2$. Specifically if there *exists a (q, l) adversary $\mathcal{A}_G$ against G, then there exists a $(q, q \log |\mathcal{D}|)$ adversary $\mathcal{A}_F$ against F, and a (q, l) adversary $\mathcal{A}_H$ against H such that*

$$\mathbf{Adv}_F^{wrk-mac}(\mathcal{A}_F, \Phi_1) + \mathbf{Adv}_H^{ictpr}(\mathcal{A}_H, \Phi_2) \geq \mathbf{Adv}_G^{rk-mac}(\mathcal{A}_G, \Phi)$$

Proof. Let $\tau_{\text{id}} = F(k_1, w_1) \| F(k_1, w_2) \| \cdots \| F(k_1, w_d)$, and $\tau_{\phi_1} = F(\phi_1(k_1), w_1) \| F(\phi_1(k_1), w_2) \| \cdots \| F(\phi_1(k_1), w_d)$. The basic idea of the proof is the following. Let (m^*, σ) be a valid forgery. If $x^* = H(k_2, m^* \| \tau_{\text{id}})$ does not collide with any previous H query (including the related-key oracles, thus maintaining identity collision resistance), or one of the w_is of the identity fingerprint $\overline{w}$ (thus maintaining target preimage resistance), then the query to $F(k, .)$ is new and was not queried even to the related-key oracle F_{RK}. Hence (x^*, σ) is a valid forgery against weak related-key unforgeable F_k. Hence we need to show that against any related-key adversary if x^* collides with the output of some previous H_{RK} query or $x^* \in \{w_1, \cdots, w_d\}$, ICTPR property of H_{k_2} can be broken. The arguments for those cases are straightforward. We refer the reader to the full version for the formal proof.

Up to this point, our approach closely matched with the approach of Bellare and Cash, who also used similar arguments. The difference comes in while constructing a ICTPR hash function. While [3] assumes an unkeyed collision resistant function with tailor-made range, we present a mode of operation based on fixed-input length related-key secure MAC (to construct VIL-related key unforgeable MAC) in the next section. We mention that given a keyed collision resistant hash function $H(k, .)$, one can easily get an ICTPR hash function (against claw-free transformations), $\hat{H}(k, .)$ defined as $\hat{H}(k, m) = k \| H(k, m)$. However, when constructing from block ciphers (as done in practice), this construction is trivially insecure (as it gives away the key). Additionally, to use it in Theorem 3, the final transformation requires to have a larger domain. On the other hand, our construction can be instantiated with a single related-key unpredictable function with independently sampled keys.

9   ICTPR from FIL-RKUF

In this section, we propose a mode of operation to construct a ICTPR hash function from length preserving related-key unforgeable MACs. Such a mode along with Theorem 3 will give us a variable input length MAC. We stress that **the proof works for any RKD set, i.e. if one starts with a fixed-input-length related-key unpredictable function, secure without the claw-free assumption on the RKD set, the resulting MAC remains secure without the claw-free assumption.**

We will describe the mode in two steps. First we shall describe a domain extension of fixed-input-length ICTPR compression function. Then we shall show that the enciphered CBC compression function of Dodis, Pietrzak, and Puniya [13] can be used to construct a fixed-input-length ICTPR compression function from length preserving related-key unforgeable MACs.

9.1   VIL-ICTPR Hash Function from ICTPR Compression Function

We shall use a variant of prefix free Merkle-Damgård iteration. Let $\mathcal{D} = \{0,1\}^{2n}$, $\mathcal{R} = \{0,1\}^n$, and $H' : \mathcal{K} \times \mathcal{D} \to \mathcal{R}$ be a fixed-input-length ICTPR compression function.

PADDING RULE. Let m be input message. Let $len(m) = |m|$ be the length of the message. The message m is divided into blocks of $n-1$ bits. If $len(m)$ is not a multiple of $n-1$, the last block is padded with a bit 1 and sufficiently many 0s. After this padding let $m_1, m_2, \cdots, m_l$ be the blocks. The final padded message $\text{PAD}(m)$ will be the following

$$\text{PAD}(m) = y_1 \| y_2 \| \cdots \| y_l \| y,$$

where each $y_i = 0 \| m_i$, and $y = 1 \| len(m)$.

THE MODE. Our mode is essentially the Merkle-Damgård mode with an extra round at the end with $1\|0^{n-1}$ as the message block. Formal algorithm of the iteration is the following

---

Algorithm 1. pseudo-code for the pfNI mode of operation

> **function** $pfNI^{H'}(k, m)$
> $\quad h_0 \leftarrow 0^n$
> $\quad \text{PAD}(m) = y_1 \| y_2 \| \cdots \| y_l \| y$
> $\quad$ **for** $1 \leq i \leq l$ **do**
> $\quad\quad h_i \leftarrow H'(k, h_{i-1} \| y_i)$
> $\quad h_{l+1} \leftarrow H'(k, h_l \| y)$
> $\quad h \leftarrow H'(k, h_{l+1} \| 1 \| 0^{n-1})$
> $\quad$ **return** h

SECURITY. Now we show that the $pfNI$ mode is ICTPR preserving. Let $H' : \mathcal{K} \times \{0,1\}^{2n} \to \{0,1\}^n$ be a compression function. We shall prove that, if there exists an adversary $\mathcal{A}_H$ against $H \overset{def}{=} pfNI^{H'}$ breaking the ICTPR property, then there is an adversary $\mathcal{A}_{H'}$ against the ICTPR property of H'. To show this, we need to show reductions for both identity collision resistance and target preimage resistance (cf. Sect. 7).

Simulation of H. $\mathcal{A}_{H'}$ has access to the oracle H'_{RK}. Simulation of oracle H_{RK} will be performed by querying H'_{RK}. During the simulation, $\mathcal{A}_{H'}$ maintains a list Q containing the queries to H'_{RK} and the corresponding responses.

Reduction for Identity Collision Resistance: Suppose $\mathcal{A}_H$ breaks the identity collision resistance of H. Recall that, identity collision resistance requires that no query (m^*, id) generates a collision with a previous (m, ϕ) (ϕ may or may not be id) query. Hence, $\mathcal{A}_H$ makes a (m^*, id) query to H such that $H(k, m^*) = H(\phi(k), m)$ and (m, ϕ) query was made before (m^*, id) query.

Let h_{ℓ^*+1} be the penultimate chaining value during the computation of $H(k, m^*)$. The following two cases can happen depending on whether h_{ℓ^*+1}

was given as a response of some previous H'_{RK} query. Let $x = h_{\ell+1}\|10^{n-1}$ be the last H' query during the computation of $H(\phi(k), m)$.

1. $h_{\ell^*+1} = IV$: If h_{ℓ^*+1} is equal to IV, then we can show a reduction breaking the target preimage resistance of H'. We analyze it in the reduction for target preimage resistance.

2. $H'(k, h_{\ell^*+1}\|\omega)$ **was not queried during the simulation for any** $\omega \in \{0,1\}^n$: The padding ensures that 10^{n-1} is the last message block of all the queries. Hence $h_{\ell^*+1} \neq h_{\ell+1}$. Moreover, $H'(k, h_{\ell^*+1}\|10^{n-1})$ has been queried after $H'(\phi(k), h_{\ell+1}\|10^{n-1})$.

   As $H(k, m^*) = H(\phi(k), m)$, obviously

   $$H'(k, h_{\ell^*+1}\|10^{n-1}) = H'(\phi(k), h_{\ell+1}\|10^{n-1}).$$

   This collision breaks the identity collision resistance property of H'.

3. $H'(k, h_{\ell^*+1}\|\omega)$ **was queried during the simulation for some** ω: If h_{ℓ^*+1} is not equal to IV, then h_{ℓ^*+1} matches with some chaining value during the simulation of the $pfNI$ mode on some previous (m', id) query. As $m^* \neq m'$, by standard argument of prefix free padding and collision resistance of Merkle-Damgård iteration, we will find a collision with some previous $H'(k, .)$ query.

Reduction for Target Preimage resistance: When $\mathcal{A}_H$ submits the set of "target images" $\{z_1, \cdots, z_t\}$, $\mathcal{A}_{H'}$ submits $T = \{IV, z_1, \cdots, z_t\}$. For each $H_{\mathsf{RK}}(m, \phi)$ query, $\mathcal{A}_{H'}$, simulates the $pfNI^{H'_{\mathsf{RK}}}$ by making queries H'_{RK}. She checks whether during the simulation, output of some $H'(k, .)$ query is in T. In such a case, she wins trivially. Note that, this takes care of the left out case in the reduction of identity collision resistance.

If none of the outputs are in T, and $\mathcal{A}_H$ outputs m^*, $\mathcal{A}_{H'}$ simulates the $pfNI$ mode and outputs the last compression function input $(h_\ell^* + 1\|10^{n-1})$ as the output.

So in all the cases, if $\mathcal{A}_H$ breaks the ICTPR property of H, $\mathcal{A}_{H'}$ breaks the ICTPR property of H'.

Lemma 2. *Let* $H' : \mathcal{K} \times \{0,1\}^{2n} \rightarrow \{0,1\}^n$ *be a compression function. Let* $H : \mathcal{K} \times \{0,1\}^* \rightarrow \{0,1\}^n$ *be a hash function defined as*

$$H(k, m) \stackrel{def}{=} pfNI^{H'}(k, m).$$

For all adversary $\mathcal{A}_H$ *making* q *queries of total bit length* l, *there exists an adversary* $\mathcal{A}'_H$ *making* $\lceil ql/(n-1)\rceil + q$ *queries of total bit length* $n(\lceil ql/(n-1)\rceil + q)$, *such that*

$$\mathbf{Adv}_H^{ictpr}(\mathcal{A}_H, \Phi) \leq \mathbf{Adv}_{H'}^{ictpr}(\mathcal{A}_{H'}, \Phi)$$

9.2 Constructing ICTPR Hash Function Using Length Preserving RK-MAC

In this section we prove that the $pfNI$ mode instantiated with enciphered CBC-MAC compression function using a length-preserving, related-key-unforgeable function, gives a ICTPR hash function. Let $F : \mathcal{K} \times \{0,1\}^n \to \{0,1\}^n$ be a family of functions. The $EnCBC$ compression function based on length preserving function F is defined as $H'_{k_1,k_2}(x_1, x_2) = F(k_1, x_1) \oplus F(k_2, x_2)$.

Lemma 3. *Let $F : \mathcal{K} \times \{0,1\}^n \to \{0,1\}^n$ be a family of related-key unforgeable function over Φ with identity fingerprint $\overline{w} = \{w_1, \cdots, w_d\}$. Define $H' : (\mathcal{K} \times \mathcal{K}) \times \{0,1\}^{2n} \to \{0,1\}^n$ as*

$$H'_{k_1,k_2}(x_1, x_2) \overset{def}{=} F(k_1, x_1) \oplus F(k_2, x_2).$$

Define $H : (\mathcal{K} \times \mathcal{K}) \times \{0,1\}^* \to \{0,1\}^n$ as

$$H(k_1, k_2, m) \overset{def}{=} pfNI^{H'}(k_1, k_2, m)$$

Define $\Psi : \{0,1\}^{2\kappa} \to \{0,1\}^{2\kappa}$ as

$$((\Phi \setminus \{id\}) \times \Phi) \cup (id, id)$$

Then H is ICTPR against Related-Key Attack over the RKD set Ψ. For all adversary $\mathcal{A}_H$ making q queries of total bit length l, there exists an adversary $\mathcal{A}_F$ making $\lceil ql/(n-1) \rceil + q$ queries of total bit length $n(\lceil ql/(n-1) \rceil + q)$, such that

$$\mathbf{Adv}_H^{ictpr}(\mathcal{A}_H, \Psi) \leq \left(\frac{q^4}{2} + \frac{q^2 d}{2} \right) \mathbf{Adv}_F^{rk-mac}(\mathcal{A}_F, \Phi)$$

The most natural way to prove the above Lemma will be to show that $EnCBC$ construction, instantiated with RK-MAC gives an ICTPR compression function. However, there is an obstacle to prove such a claim. Recall that we want to show that when there is an ICTPR attack against the compression function, we can mount related-key forgery against the underlying RK-MAC. The general technique is to guess the colliding queries, and predict the output of chronologically last query. Unfortunately, the chronologically last query can indeed be on related-key(the target key of ICTPR attack may be derived from two separate target key queries made before the related-key query).

We give a direct proof the ICTPR security of the mode of operation, instantiated with EnCBC compression function. Specifically, we show that for both the conditions, described in the previous section, we can mount related-key forgery against the underlying MACs. We refer the reader to full version for the full proof.

10   Bellare-Cash Construction is MAC Preserving

Finally, as an application of Theorem 3, we show that the PRF construction of Bellare and Cash [3], can also be used to construct a related-key unforgeable MAC against chosen message attack. Note that, *this construction uses an unkeyed collision resistance hash function H.* Although, we focused on keyed hash function for all the previous results, we state this result to be complete in our analysis of related-key security of message authentication codes.

Theorem 4. *Let* $F : \mathcal{K} \times \mathcal{D} \to \mathcal{R}$ *be a weak related-key unforgeable MAC over RKD set* Φ *with identity fingerprint* $\overline{w} = (w_1, w_2, \cdots, w_d)$. *Let* $H : \{0,1\}^* \to \mathcal{D} \setminus \{w_1, \cdots, w_d\}$ *be a collision resistant hash function. Let* $G : \mathcal{K} \times \{0,1\}^* \to \mathcal{R}$ *be a family of functions defined as*

$$G(k, M) \overset{def}{=} F(k, H(M\|F(k,w_1)\|F(k,w_2)\| \cdots \|F(k,w_d))) \qquad k \in \mathcal{K}.$$

G is related-key unforgeable against chosen message attack over the RKD set Φ. *Specifically if there exists a* (q, l) *adversary* $\mathcal{A}_G$ *against* G, *then there exists a* $(q, q \log |D|)$ *adversary* $\mathcal{A}_F$ *against* F, *and a* (q, l) *adversary* $\mathcal{A}_H$ *against* H *such that*

$$\boldsymbol{Adv}_H^{cr}(\mathcal{A}_H) + \boldsymbol{Adv}_F^{wrk-mac}(\mathcal{A}_F, \Phi) \geq \boldsymbol{Adv}_G^{rk-mac}(\mathcal{A}_G, \Phi)$$

Proof (Proof Sketch). The proof is similar (infact, special case) to Theorem 3 and we skip the proof.

10.1 Security Against Partial Key Transformation from DDH Assumption

In this section, we give a concrete construction of a related-key secure MAC based on the following MAC construction, due to Dodis, Kiltz, Pietrzak, and Wichs [11] based on the hash proof system of Cramer and Shoup.

MAC_{HPS}

- **Setup.** p is a large prime. $\mathbb{G}$ is a group of order p. g is a random generator of $\mathbb{G}$. $\hat{H} : \mathbb{G}^2 \times \mathcal{D} \to \mathbb{Z}_p$ is a collision resistant hash function. $\mathcal{K} = \mathbb{Z}_p^3$, $\mathcal{R} = \mathbb{G}^3$.
- **Key Generation:** the secret key is $k = (k_1, k_2, k_3) \leftarrow_R \mathbb{Z}_p^3$.
- **MAC:** $F : \mathcal{K} \times \mathcal{D} \to \mathcal{R}$ is defined as

$$F(k_1, k_2, k_3, m) \overset{def}{=} (g \leftarrow_R \mathbb{G}, V = g^{k_1}, g^{k_2 \hat{H}(g, V, m) + k_3}) \qquad m \in \mathcal{D}, k_1, k_2, k_3 \in \mathbb{Z}_p.$$

For any element $k = (k_1, k_2, k_3) \in \mathcal{K}$ and $\Delta = (0, \delta_2, \delta_3) \in \mathbb{Z}_p^3$, define $k \circ \Delta = (k_1, k_2 + \delta_2, k_3 + \delta_3)$ where $+$ is addition modulo p. It is easy to check that $\mathcal{K}$ is a group under $\circ$. The group induced RKD class over $\mathcal{K}$ will be defined as $\Phi \overset{def}{=} \phi_\Delta(k) = (k \circ \Delta)$.

Although MAC_{HPS} is not key-homomorphic in general, but it is indeed key homomorphic over Φ. Hence, we get the following lemma.

Lemma 4. MAC_{HPS} *is weakly unforgeable against related-key attack over* Φ.

To use Theorem 4, it is now enough to prove the existence of a fingerprint for MAC_{HPS}. Due to space constraint we leave out the identity-fingerprint for MAC_{HPS} in this version.

Theorem 5. *Let* $\mathbb{G}$ *be a prime order group of* p *elements,* g_1, g_2 *be two random generators of* $\mathbb{G}$. *Let* w_1, w_2 *be two distinct elements from* $\mathcal{D}$. *Suppose*

$H : \mathcal{D} \times \mathbb{G} \to \mathcal{D} \setminus \{w_1, w_2\}$ and $\hat{H} : \mathbb{G}^2 \times \mathcal{D} \to \mathbb{Z}_p$ be two collision resistant hash functions. Define $\mathcal{K} = \mathbb{Z}_p^3$, $\mathcal{R} = \mathbb{G}^3$. Define $G_{HPS} : \mathcal{K} \times \mathcal{D} \to \mathcal{R}$ defined as

$$G_{HPS}(k_1, k_2, k_3, m) \overset{def}{=} MAC_{HPS}(k_1, k_2, k_3, H(m, \Gamma))$$

where

$$\Gamma = g_1, g_1^{k_1}, g_1^{k_2 \hat{H}(g_1, V, w_1) + k_3}, g_2, g_2^{k_1}, g_2^{k_2 \hat{H}(g_2, V, w_2) + k_3})$$

Let $\mathcal{A}_G$ be an adversary against the related-key unforgeability of G under chosen message attack over RKD set Φ, and $\mathcal{A}_G$ makes q queries. Then we can construct an adversary $\mathcal{A}_{DDH}$ against the DDH problem in $\mathbb{G}$, an adversary $\mathcal{A}_H$ against collision resistance of H, and an adversary $\mathcal{A}_{\hat{H}}$ against collision resistance of $\hat{H}$ such that

$$\mathbf{Adv}_G^{rk-mac}(\mathcal{A}_G, \Phi) \leq \mathbf{Adv}_{\mathbb{G}}^{ddh}(\mathcal{A}_{DDH}) + \mathbf{Adv}_H^{cr}(\mathcal{A}_H) + \mathbf{Adv}_{\hat{H}}^{cr}(\mathcal{A}_{\hat{H}})$$

10.2 Towards Full Security

Previous construction, although very efficient in terms of the keysize, is only secure against partial key transformation. Now, we construct a related-key unforgeable MAC against a full group induced key transformation. The weak unforgeable MAC is based on another construction of Dodis et al. [11] which is again based on weak PRF and arguments of Waters.

MAC_W

- **Setup.** p is a large prime. $\mathbb{G}$ is a group of order p. Message space is $\{0, 1\}^\lambda$. $\mathcal{K} = \mathbb{Z}_p^{\lambda+1}$, $\mathcal{R} = \mathbb{G}^3$.
- **Key Generation:** the secret key is $k = (k_0, k_1, \cdots, k_\lambda) \leftarrow_R \mathbb{Z}_p^{\lambda+1}$.
- **MAC:** $F : \mathcal{K} \times \mathcal{D} \to \mathcal{R}$ is defined as

$$F(k_0, k_1, \cdots, k_\lambda, m) \overset{def}{=} (g \leftarrow_R \mathbb{G}, g^{k_0 + \sum_{i=1}^\lambda m[i] k_i})$$

For any element $k = (k_0, k_1, \cdots, k_\lambda) \in \mathcal{K}$ and $\Delta = (\delta_0, \delta_1, \cdots, \delta_\lambda) \in \mathbb{Z}_p^{\lambda+1}$, define $k \circ \Delta = (k_0 + \delta_0, \cdots, k_\lambda + \delta_\lambda)$ where $+$ is addition modulo p. It is easy to check that $\mathcal{K}$ is a group under $\circ$. The group induced RKD class over $\mathcal{K}$ will be defined as $\Phi \overset{def}{=} \phi_\Delta(k) = (k \circ \Delta)$.

MAC_W is key-homomorphic in an obvious way. Using Lemma 1

Lemma 5. MAC_W is weakly unforgeable against related-key attack over Φ.

Using Theorem 4, we get the following theorem

Theorem 6. Let $\mathbb{G}$ be a prime order group of p elements. Let

$$\overline{w} = \{0^\lambda, 10^{\lambda-1}, 010^{\lambda-2}, \cdots, 0^{\lambda-1}1\}$$

Suppose $H : \mathcal{D} \times \mathbb{G}^{2(\lambda+1)} \to \mathcal{D} \setminus \{\overline{w}\}$ be a collision resistant hash functions. Define $\mathcal{K} = \mathbb{Z}_p^{\lambda+1}$, $\mathcal{R} = \mathbb{G}^2$. Define $G_W : \mathcal{K} \times \mathcal{D} \to \mathcal{R}$ as

$$G_W(k, m) \overset{def}{=} MAC_W(k, H(m, MAC_W(k, 0^\lambda), MAC_W(k, 10^{\lambda-1}), \cdots, MAC_W(k, 0^{\lambda-1}1)))$$

Let $\mathcal{A}_G$ be an adversary against the related-key unforgeability of G_W under chosen message attack over RKD set Φ, and $\mathcal{A}_G$ makes q queries. Then we can construct an adversary $\mathcal{A}_{DDH}$ against the DDH problem in $\mathbb{G}$, an adversary $\mathcal{A}_H$ against collision resistance of H such that

$$\mathbf{Adv}_G^{rk-mac}(\mathcal{A}_G, \Phi) \leq \mathbf{Adv}_{\mathbb{G}}^{ddh}(\mathcal{A}_{DDH}) + \mathbf{Adv}_H^{cr}(\mathcal{A}_H)$$

11   Conclusion

Security against related-key attacks is currently considered as a major challenge for symmetric key cryptography. In this paper, we considered security of message authentication codes against related-key attacks. We formalized the security definitions and identified feasible key transformations. We also presented the first security analysis for domain extension of related-key secure unpredictable functions(MAC). However our reduction for the Enciphered CBC construction achieves a reduction-factor of $\mathcal{O}(2^{n/4})$ queries (Lemma 3). Finding constructions with improved security bound is an interesting open problem. Specifically, analysis of related-key security of Dodis-Steinberger construction [14] will be very interesting.

Acknowledgements. We thank Mridul Nandi for useful discussions. We also thank Damien Stehlé for important feedback on the initial draft of the paper. We are grateful to the anonymous reviewers of FSE 2013 for insightful comments. Part of this work was done when Rishi was at the Centre of Excellence in Cryptology of Indian Statistical Institute, Kolkata.

References

1. An, J.H., Bellare, M.: Constructing VIL-MACs from FIL-MACs: message authentication under weakened assumptions. In: Wiener, M. (ed.) CRYPTO 1999. LNCS, vol. 1666, pp. 252–252. Springer, Heidelberg (1999)
2. Applebaum, B., Harnik, D., Ishai, Y.: Semantic security under related-key attacks and applications. In: ICS, pp. 45–60 (2011)
3. Bellare, M., Cash, D.: Pseudorandom functions and permutations provably secure against related-key attacks. In: Rabin, T. (ed.) CRYPTO 2010. LNCS, vol. 6223, pp. 666–684. Springer, Heidelberg (2010)
4. Bellare, M., Cash, D., Miller, R.: Cryptography secure against related-key attacks and tampering. In: Lee, D.H., Wang, X. (eds.) ASIACRYPT 2011. LNCS, vol. 7073, pp. 486–503. Springer, Heidelberg (2011)
5. Bellare, M., Kohno, T.: A theoretical treatment of related-key attacks: RKA-PRPs, RKA-PRFs, and applications. In: Biham, E. (ed.) EUROCRYPT 2003. LNCS, vol. 2656, pp. 491–506. Springer, Heidelberg (2003)
6. Biham, E.: New types of cryptanalytic attacks using related keys. J. Cryptol. **7**(4), 229–246 (1994)
7. Biham, E., Dunkelman, O., Keller, N.: Related-key boomerang and rectangle attacks. In: Cramer, R. (ed.) EUROCRYPT 2005. LNCS, vol. 3494, pp. 507–525. Springer, Heidelberg (2005)

8. Biham, E., Dunkelman, O., Keller, N.: A related-key rectangle attack on the full KASUMI. In: Roy, B. (ed.) ASIACRYPT 2005. LNCS, vol. 3788, pp. 443–461. Springer, Heidelberg (2005)

9. Biryukov, A., Dunkelman, O., Keller, N., Khovratovich, D., Shamir, A.: Key recovery attacks of practical complexity on AES-256 variants with up to 10 rounds. In: Gilbert, H. (ed.) EUROCRYPT 2010. LNCS, vol. 6110, pp. 299–319. Springer, Heidelberg (2010)

10. Biryukov, A., Khovratovich, D., Nikolić, I.: Distinguisher and related-key attack on the full AES-256. In: Halevi, S. (ed.) CRYPTO 2009. LNCS, vol. 5677, pp. 231–249. Springer, Heidelberg (2009)

11. Dodis, Y., Kiltz, E., Pietrzak, K., Wichs, D.: Message authentication, revisited. In Cryptology ePrint Archive (2012). http://eprint.iacr.org/2012/059

12. Dodis, Y., Kiltz, E., Pietrzak, K., Wichs, D.: Message authentication, revisited. In: Pointcheval, D., Johansson, T. (eds.) EUROCRYPT 2012. LNCS, vol. 7237, pp. 355–374. Springer, Heidelberg (2012)

13. Dodis, Y., Pietrzak, K., Puniya, P.: A new mode of operation for block ciphers and length-preserving MACs. In: Smart, N.P. (ed.) EUROCRYPT 2008. LNCS, vol. 4965, pp. 198–219. Springer, Heidelberg (2008)

14. Dodis, Y., Steinberger, J.: Message authentication codes from unpredictable block ciphers. In: Halevi, S. (ed.) CRYPTO 2009. LNCS, vol. 5677, pp. 267–285. Springer, Heidelberg (2009)

15. Goyal, V., O'Neill, A., Rao, V.: Correlated-input secure hash functions. In: Ishai, Y. (ed.) TCC 2011. LNCS, vol. 6597, pp. 182–200. Springer, Heidelberg (2011)

16. Knudsen, R.K.: Cryptanalysis of LOKI91. In: Zheng, Y., Seberry, J. (eds.) AUSCRYPT 1992. LNCS, vol. 718, pp. 196–208. Springer, Heidelberg (1993)

17. Lucks, S.: Ciphers secure against related-key attacks. In: Roy, B., Meier, W. (eds.) FSE 2004. LNCS, vol. 3017, pp. 359–370. Springer, Heidelberg (2004)

18. Peyrin, T., Sasaki, Y., Wang, L.: Generic related-key attacks for HMAC. In: Wang, X., Sako, K. (eds.) ASIACRYPT 2012. LNCS, vol. 7658, pp. 580–597. Springer, Heidelberg (2012)

19. Xagawa, K.: Message authentication codes secure against additively related-key attacks. Cryptology ePrint Archive, report 2013/111 (2013). http://eprint.iacr.org/2013/111

Provable Security

Attacks and Security Proofs of EAX-Prime

Kazuhiko Minematsu[1]([✉]), Stefan Lucks[2], Hiraku Morita[3], and Tetsu Iwata[3]

[1] NEC Corporation, Kawasaki-Shi, Japan
k-minematsu@ah.jp.nec.com
[2] Bauhaus-Universität Weimar, Weimar, Germany
stefan.lucks@uni-weimar.de
[3] Nagoya University, Nagoya, Japan
h_morita@echo.nuee.nagoya-u.ac.jp, iwata@cse.nagoya-u.ac.jp

Abstract. EAX′ (or EAX-prime) is an authenticated encryption (AE) specified by ANSI C12.22 as a standard security function for Smart Grid. EAX′ is based on EAX proposed by Bellare, Rogaway, and Wagner. While EAX has a proof of security based on the pseudorandomness of the internal blockcipher, no published security result is known for EAX′. This paper studies the security of EAX′ and shows that there is a sharp distinction in security of EAX′ depending on the input length. EAX′ encryption takes two inputs, called cleartext and plaintext, and we present various efficient attacks against EAX′ using single-block cleartext and plaintext. At the same time we prove that if cleartexts are always longer than one block, it is provably secure based on the pseudorandomness of the blockcipher.

Keywords: Authenticated encryption · EAX · EAX′ · Attack · Provable security

1 Introduction

ANSI C12.22 [3] specifies a blockcipher mode for authenticated encryption (AE) as the standard security function for Smart Grid. It is called EAX′ (or EAX-prime)[1]. As its name suggests, EAX′ is based on EAX proposed by Bellare, Rogaway, and Wagner at FSE 2004 [7]. Though EAX is already efficient with a small amount of precomputation, EAX′ aims at even reducing the amount of precomputation and memory, for making it suitable to the resource-constrained devices, typically smart meters. ANSI submitted EAX′ to NIST [13] and NIST called for the public comments on the proposal to approve EAX′. Following

---

A part of the result was presented at DIAC [12].

[1] The authors of [13] exchangeably use the three names, EAX′, EAX', and EAX-prime, to mean their proposal. To avoid any confusion by overlooking the tiny prime symbol or apostrophe, which could be misunderstood as claiming an attack on EAX, we prefer the longer name "EAX-prime" for the title. In the text we prefer the name EAX′.

S. Moriai (Ed.): FSE 2013, LNCS 8424, pp. 327–347, 2014.
DOI: 10.1007/978-3-662-43933-3_17, © Springer-Verlag Berlin Heidelberg 2014

ANSI C12.22, IEEE 1703 [6] and MC1222 [4] included EAX'. There is also an RFC [5] related to ANSI C12.22.

Though EAX' is similar to EAX, to the best of our knowledge, its formal security analysis has not been published to date. In this paper, we investigate the security of EAX' and show that there is a sharp distinction depending on the input length. The encryption algorithm of EAX' takes two inputs, called cleartext and plaintext. In the standard AE terminology, the cleartext serves as a nonce, or a combination of nonce and associated data (the latter is also called header).

First, we show that if the lengths of cleartext and plaintext are not exceeding one block, there exist attacks against EAX' for both privacy and authenticity. Specifically, we present

- *forgeries*, i.e., cleartext/ciphertext pairs with valid authentication tags,
- *chosen-plaintext distinguishers*, distinguishing the EAX' encryption from a random encryption process, and
- *chosen-ciphertext plaintext recovery attacks*, decrypting ciphertexts by asking for the decryption of another ciphertext with a valid authentication tag.

Our attacks are simple and efficient as they require only one or two queries. The simplest one even produces a successful forgery without observing any valid plaintext/ciphertext pair. Our forgery and distinguishing attacks strictly require the target system to accept one-block cleartext and plaintext. The plaintext recovery attacks relax this condition, and given any ciphertext with one-block cleartext it works for any circumstance where ciphertext is decrypted without checking the cleartext length. This makes the possibility of attack even larger. Our attacks imply that, while the original EAX has a proof of security, the security of EAX' has totally collapsed as a general-purpose AE.

Next, we show that if the cleartext is always longer than one block, it recovers the provable security based on the pseudorandomness of the blockcipher for both privacy and authenticity notions. The security proof is obtained by combining previous proof techniques of EAX by Bellare, Rogaway, and Wagner [7] with some non-trivial extensions, such as Iwata and Kurosawa's one used for proving the security of OMAC [9].

One may naturally wonder if our attacks are applicable to ANSI C12.22. Unfortunately we do not know if ANCI C12.22 protocols exclude one-block cleartexts or not, hence we have no clear answer. Still, considering the effect of our attacks, we conclude that EAX' must be used with cleartext length check mechanisms at both ends of encryption and decryption.

2   Preliminaries

Basic Notations. Let $\mathbb{N} = \{0, 1, \dots\}$. Let $\{0,1\}^*$ be the set of all finite-length binary strings, including the empty string ε. The bit length of a binary string X is written as $|X|$, and let $|X|_n \stackrel{\text{def}}{=} \lceil |X|/n \rceil$. Here $|\varepsilon| = 0$. A concatenation of $X, Y \in \{0,1\}^*$ is written as $X\|Y$ or simply XY. A sequence of a zeros (ones) is denoted by 0^a (1^a). For $k \geq 0$, let $\{0,1\}^{>k} \stackrel{\text{def}}{=} \bigcup_{i=k+1,\ldots} \{0,1\}^i$ and $(\{0,1\}^n)^{>k} \stackrel{\text{def}}{=} \bigcup_{j=k+1,\ldots} (\{0,1\}^n)^j$, and $(\{0,1\}^n)^+ \stackrel{\text{def}}{=} (\{0,1\}^n)^{>0}$. We also define $\{0,1\}^{\geq k}$, $(\{0,1\}^n)^{\geq k}$, $\{0,1\}^{<k}$, $(\{0,1\}^n)^{<k}$, $\{0,1\}^{\leq k}$, and $(\{0,1\}^n)^{\leq k}$ analogously. For $X, Y \in \{0,1\}^n$, $X + Y$ or $X - Y$ is considered as an addition or a subtraction modulo 2^n.

For $X \in \{0,1\}^*$, let $X[1] \| X[2] \| \ldots \| X[m] \stackrel{n}{\leftarrow} X$ denote the n-bit block partitioning of X, i.e., $X[1] \| X[2] \| \ldots \| X[m] = X$ where $m = |X|_n$, and $|X[i]| = n$ for $i < m$ and $|X[m]| \leq n$. For $X, Y \in \{0,1\}^*$, let $X \oplus_{\text{end}} Y$ be the XOR of X into the end of Y if $|X| \leq |Y|$, i.e. $X \oplus_{\text{end}} Y = (0^{|Y|-|X|} \| X) \oplus Y$. Otherwise $X \oplus_{\text{end}} Y = X \oplus (0^{|X|-|Y|} \| Y)$.

For a finite set $\mathcal{X}$, if X is uniformly chosen from $\mathcal{X}$ we write $X \stackrel{\$}{\leftarrow} \mathcal{X}$.

Random Function and Random Permutation. Let $\text{Func}(n, m)$ be the set of all functions $\{0,1\}^n \to \{0,1\}^m$. We may abbreviate $\text{Func}(n, n)$ to $\text{Func}(n)$. In addition, let $\text{Perm}(n)$ be the set of all permutations over $\{0,1\}^n$. A uniform random function (URF) having n-bit input and m-bit output is the set $\text{Func}(n, m)$ with uniform distribution over $\text{Func}(n, m)$. It is denoted by R, and the corresponding sampling is written as $\mathsf{R} \stackrel{\$}{\leftarrow} \text{Func}(n, m)$. An n-bit uniform random permutation (URP) is the set $\text{Perm}(n)$ with uniform distribution over $\text{Perm}(n)$. It is denoted by P, and the corresponding sampling is written as $\mathsf{P} \stackrel{\$}{\leftarrow} \text{Perm}(n)$.

Galois Field. Following [7], an n-bit string X may be viewed as an element of $\text{GF}(2^n)$ by taking X as a coefficient vector of the polynomial in $\text{GF}(2^n)$. We write $2X$ to denote the multiplication of 2 and X over $\text{GF}(2^n)$, where 2 denotes the generator of the field $\text{GF}(2^n)$. This operation is called *doubling*. We also write $4L$ to denote $2(2L)$. The doubling is efficiently implemented by one-bit shift with conditional XOR of a constant, see e.g. [9].

3   Specification of EAX-Prime

We describe the encryption and decryption algorithms of EAX'. We changed the original notations of EAX' [3,13] following those of EAX [7]. This illustrates the similarities and the differences of EAX and EAX' (See also the last part of this section).

EAX' is a mode of operation based on an n-bit blockcipher, E. Here we typically assume $(n, E) = (128, \text{AES-128})$, however other choice is possible [13]. The key of E is written as K. Formally, the encryption function of EAX' accepts a cleartext, $N \in \{0,1\}^*$ with $N \neq \varepsilon$, a plaintext, $M \in \{0,1\}^*$, and a secret key, K, to produce the ciphertext, $C \in \{0,1\}^*$, with $|C| = |M|$ and the tag $T \in \{0,1\}^{32}$. The decryption function, which we also call the verification function, accepts N, C, T, and K and generates the decrypted plaintext M if (N, C, T) is valid, or the flag $\perp$ if invalid. Cleartext N contains information that needs to be authenticated, but not encrypted. ANSI document requires that N must be unique for all encryptions using the same key[2]. Hence N can be seen as a combination of a nonce and associated data in the standard terminology of AE (e.g., see [7]). The plaintext M can be the empty string ε, corresponding to the null string in [13], and in this case EAX$'$ works as a message authentication code for N.

For generality we assume that the tag length is specified by a predetermined parameter, $\tau \in \{1, \dots, n\}$. The original definition employs $\tau = 32$. Let EAX$'[E, \tau]$ be EAX$'$ using n-bit blockcipher E with τ-bit tag. The corresponding encryption and decryption algorithms are written as EAX$'$-$\mathcal{E}_{K,\tau}$ and EAX$'$-$\mathcal{D}_{K,\tau}$. If τ is clear from the context we may write EAX$'[E]$ and EAX$'$-$\mathcal{E}_K$ and EAX$'$-$\mathcal{D}_K$. These algorithms and their components are shown in Fig. 1. The encryption algorithm of EAX$'$ is depicted in Fig. 2. In Fig. 1, α denotes an n-bit constant, $(1^{n-32}\|01^{15}\|01^{15})$. Note that CBC'$_K(0^n, M)$ is equivalent to the standard CBC-MAC using E_K with input M, denoted by CBC$_K(M)$. In our description, we fixed an apparent error in line 72 of the original definition of EAX$'$.encrypt$_K$ in [3,13]. Some editorial errors of [13] were also pointed out by [1].

EAX$'$ and the Original EAX. The major differences between EAX$'$ and the original EAX are summarized as follows. For other minor differences, see Section 3 of [13]. For the definition of EAX, see [7].

1. Role of N. Inputs to EAX$'$-$\mathcal{E}_K$ consist of a cleartext N and a plaintext M, whereas those to the original EAX consist of a nonce N, a header (or associated data) H, and a plaintext M. EAX$'$ requires N to be unique, hence it works as a nonce. EAX$'$ does not explicitly define a header H; information corresponding to the header is included in the cleartext N.
2. Tweaking method for CMAC. For input M, CMAC [2] using E_K is defined as CMAC$_K(M) = $ CBC$_K(\mathrm{pad}(M; D, Q))$. The original EAX uses the tweaked CMAC having an n-bit tweak t, defined as CMAC$_K(t\|M)$, for $t \in \{0^n, 0^{n-1}1, 0^{n-2}10\}$, to process N, H, and C. For fast operation we need to precompute $E_K(t)$ for all t and store them to RAM. EAX$'$ employs a different way to tweak CMAC accepting two tweak values ($i = 0, 1$) to generate CMAC$'^{(0)}_K$ and CMAC$'^{(1)}_K$ for processing N and C. For fast operation we can precompute $L = E_K(0^n)$. This reduces the precomputation time and RAM consumption from the original EAX.
3. Counter mode incrementation. The original EAX uses CMAC$_K(0^n\|N)$ as an initial counter block for CTR mode, while that of EAX$'$ is CMAC$'^{(0)}_K(N) \wedge \alpha$ to set some bits to zero. One can find a similar zeroing-out in the deterministic authenticated encryption called SIV [15]. As explained by [15], this contributes to a slight simpler operation.

---

[2] In ANSI C12.22, the uniqueness of N is guaranteed by including time information with a specific format.

Algorithm EAX'-$\mathcal{E}_{K,\tau}(N,M)$	Algorithm EAX'-$\mathcal{D}_{K,\tau}(N,C,T)$
1. $\underline{N} \leftarrow \text{CMAC}'^{(0)}_K(N)$ 2. $C \leftarrow \text{CTR}'_K(\underline{N}, M)$ 3. $\underline{T} \leftarrow \underline{N} \oplus \text{CMAC}'^{(1)}_K(C)$ 4. $T \leftarrow \text{msb}_\tau(\underline{T})$ 5. **return** (C, T)	1. $\underline{N} \leftarrow \text{CMAC}'^{(0)}_K(N)$ 2. $\underline{T} \leftarrow \underline{N} \oplus \text{CMAC}'^{(1)}_K(C)$ 3. $\widehat{T} \leftarrow \text{msb}_\tau(\underline{T})$ 4. **if** $\widehat{T} \neq T$ **return** $\perp$ 5. $M \leftarrow \text{CTR}'_K(\underline{N}, C)$ 6. **return** M

Algorithm $\text{CMAC}'^{(i)}_K(M)$ (for $i \in \{0,1\}$)	Algorithm $\text{CBC}'_K(I, M)$ (for $M \in (\{0,1\}^n)^+$)
1. $L \leftarrow E_K(0^n)$ 2. $D \leftarrow 2L, Q \leftarrow 4L$ 3. **if** $i = 0$ **then** 4. **return** $\text{CBC}'_K(D, \text{pad}(M; D, Q))$ 5. **if** $i = 1$ **then** 6. **return** $\text{CBC}'_K(Q, \text{pad}(M; D, Q))$	1. $M[1]\|M[2]\| \ldots \|M[m] \xleftarrow{n} M$ 2. $C[0] \leftarrow I$ 3. **for** $i \leftarrow 1$ to m **do** 4. $\quad C[i] \leftarrow E_K(M[i] \oplus C[i-1])$ 5. **return** $C[m]$

Algorithm $\text{CTR}'_K(\underline{N}, M)$	Algorithm $\text{pad}(M; B_1, B_2)$
1. $m \leftarrow |M|_n$ 2. $\underline{N}^\wedge \leftarrow \underline{N} \wedge \alpha$ 3. $S \leftarrow E_K(\underline{N}^\wedge)\| \cdots \|E_K(\underline{N}^\wedge + m - 1)$ 4. $C \leftarrow M \oplus \text{msb}_{|M|}(S)$ 5. **return** C	1. **if** $|M| \in \{n, 2n, 3n, \ldots, \}$ 2. **then return** $M \oplus_{\text{end}} B_1$ 3. **else** 4. **return** $(M\|10^{n-1-(|M| \bmod n)}) \oplus_{\text{end}} B_2$

Fig. 1. (Upper) The encryption and decryption algorithms of EAX'$[E, \tau]$, originally with $\tau = 32$. (Lower) Component algorithms of EAX'$[E, \tau]$. Here, $\alpha = (1^{n-32}\|01^{15}\|01^{15})$.

4   Attacks Based on One-Block Cleartext

4.1   Chosen-Message Forgeries

We first describe forgery attacks against EAX'$[E, \tau]$. Throughout the section D and Q denote $2L$ and $4L$ with $L = E_K(0^n)$. The adversary $\mathcal{A}$ we consider here can access both encryption and decryption (verification) oracles, namely EAX'-$\mathcal{E}_K$ and EAX'-$\mathcal{D}_K$. Suppose $\mathcal{A}$ (possibly adaptively) asks q queries to the encryption oracle, $(N_1, M_1), \ldots, (N_q, M_q)$, and receives $(C_1, T_1), \ldots, (C_q, T_q)$, and then asks (N, C, T) to the decryption oracle. We say $\mathcal{A}$ is successful if $\mathcal{A}$ receives a string other than $\perp$ and $(N, C, T) \neq (N_i, C_i, T_i)$ for any $1 \leq i \leq q$ (see also Sect. 5). Here we assume the nonce-respecting adversary [14]; it is allowed to query any (N_i, M_i) to the encryption oracle as long as N_i is unique.

Suppose $M \in \{0,1\}^{\leq n}$. Then $\text{pad}(M; D, Q) = M \oplus_{\text{end}} D = M \oplus D$ when $|M| = n$ and $\text{pad}(M; D, Q) = M\|10^{n-1-|M|} \oplus_{\text{end}} Q = M\|10^{n-1-|M|} \oplus Q$ when $0 \leq |M| < n$. Therefore, the definition of $\text{CMAC}'^{(i)}_K$ in the previous section

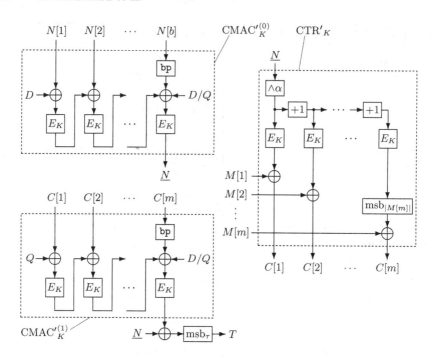

Fig. 2. The encryption algorithm of EAX'. In the figure, $|N|_n = b$ and $|M|_n = m$. $\mathtt{bp}(x) = x$ if $|x| = n$ and $\mathtt{bp}(x) = x\|10^{n-1-(|x| \bmod n)}$ if $|x| < n$.

conforms to that

$$\mathrm{CMAC'}_K^{(0)}(M) = \begin{cases} E_K(M) & \text{if } |M| = n \\ E_K(M\|10^{n-1-|M|} \oplus D \oplus Q) & \text{if } 0 \le |M| < n \end{cases}$$

$$\mathrm{CMAC'}_K^{(1)}(M) = \begin{cases} E_K(M \oplus D \oplus Q) & \text{if } |M| = n \\ E_K(M\|10^{n-1-|M|}) & \text{if } 0 \le |M| < n \end{cases}$$

The above observation immediately gives the following attacks:

Forgery attack 1 ($|N| = n$ and $|C| < n$).

1. Prepare (N, C) such that $|N| = n$ and $|C| < n$ and $C\|10^{n-1-|C|} = N$.
2. Query (N, C, T) to the verification oracle, where $T = 0^\tau$.

This attack always succeeds as the "valid" tag for (N, C) is $\mathrm{msb}_\tau(E_K(N) \oplus E_K(C\|10^{n-1-|C|})) = 0^\tau$.

Forgery attack 2 ($|N| < n$ and $|C| = n$).

1. Prepare (N, C) such that $|N| < n$, $|C| = n$, and $N\|10^{n-1-|N|} = C$.
2. Query (N, C, T) to the verification oracle, where $T = 0^\tau$.

The attack is again successful as the valid tag for (N, C) is $\mathrm{msb}_\tau(E_K(D \oplus Q \oplus N \| 10^{n-1-|N|}) \oplus E_K(Q \oplus D \oplus C)) = 0^\tau$. These attacks use only one forgery attempt and no encryption query. By using one encryption query the forgery attack is possible even when $|N| = n$ and $|C| = n$:

Forgery attack 3 ($|N| = |M| = n$).

1. Query (N, M) with $|N| = |M| = n$ and $N \neq 0^n$ to the encryption oracle.
2. Obtain (C, T) (where $|C| = n$) from the oracle and see if $C \neq 0^n$ (quit if $C = 0^n$).
3. Query $(\tilde{N}, \tilde{C}, \tilde{T})$ to the verification oracle, where $|\tilde{N}| < n$, $\tilde{N} \| 10^{n-1-|\tilde{N}|} = C$, $|\tilde{C}| < n$, $\tilde{C} \| 10^{n-1-|\tilde{C}|} = N$, and $\tilde{T} = T$.

The above attack is almost always successful; unless $C = 0^n$ we have $T = \mathrm{msb}_\tau(E_K(N) \oplus E_K(Q \oplus D \oplus C))$ and the valid tag for $(\tilde{N}, \tilde{C})$ is

$$
\mathrm{msb}_\tau(E_K(D \oplus Q \oplus \tilde{N} \| 10^{n-1-|\tilde{N}|}) \oplus E_K(Q \oplus Q \oplus \tilde{C} \| 10^{n-1-|\tilde{C}|}))
$$
$$
= \mathrm{msb}_\tau(E_K(D \oplus Q \oplus C) \oplus E_K(N)),
$$

thus equals to T. The converse of Forgery attack 3 is also possible for $|N| < n$ and $|M| < n$:

Forgery attack 4 ($|N| < n$ and $|M| < n$).

1. Query (N, M) with $|N| < n$ and $|M| < n$ to the encryption oracle.
2. Obtain (C, T) (where $|C| = |M| < n$) from the oracle.
3. Query $(\tilde{N}, \tilde{C}, \tilde{T})$ to the verification oracle, where $|\tilde{N}| = |\tilde{C}| = n$, $\tilde{N} = C \| 10^{n-1-|C|}$, $\tilde{C} = N \| 10^{n-1-|N|}$, and $\tilde{T} = T$.

We have $T = \mathrm{msb}_\tau(E_K(D \oplus Q \oplus N \| 10^{n-1-|N|}) \oplus E_K(Q \oplus Q \oplus C \| 10^{n-1-|C|}))$ and the valid tag for $(\tilde{N}, \tilde{C})$ is

$$
\mathrm{msb}_\tau(E_K(D \oplus D \oplus \tilde{N}) \oplus E_K(Q \oplus D \oplus \tilde{C}))
$$
$$
= \mathrm{msb}_\tau(E_K(C \| 10^{n-1-|C|}) \oplus E_K(Q \oplus D \oplus N \| 10^{n-1-|N|})) = T.
$$

Partially Selective Forgeries. A forgery is *selective* instead of *existential*, if the adversary can determine the content of the message to be forged. Since EAX′ provides *authenticated encryption with associated data* (AEAD), the content of the message consists of both the confidential plaintext M and the non-confidential associated data (or cleartext) N. While the above attacks do not allow to choose M, the adversary can arbitrarily choose N (restricted to $|N| \leq n$ and, for $|N| = n$, $N \neq 0^n$). In this sense, the forgery attacks above are *partially selective*.

4.2   Chosen-Plaintext Distinguishers

The forgery attacks above are based on the idea of generating (N, C) that makes the tag $T = 0^\tau$. To distinguish EAX′-$\mathcal{E}_K$ from a random encryption process, which produces $(|M| + \tau)$-bit random sequence on receiving (N, M), one can similarly make (N, M) so that EAX'-$\mathcal{E}_K$ will generate (C, T) with $T = 0^\tau$.

Distinguishing attack 1 ($|N| = n$ and $|M| = 0$).

1. Query (N, M) to the encryption oracle, where $N = 10^{n-1}$ and $M = \varepsilon$.
2. Obtain (C, T) from the oracle with $C = \varepsilon$.
3. If $T = 0^\tau$ then return 1, otherwise return 0.

As EAX'-$\mathcal{E}_K$ returns $T = 0^\tau$ with probability 1 while the same event occurs with probability $1/2^\tau$ with a random encryption process, this enables us to easily distinguish T from random with the distinguishing advantage almost 1, using only one encryption query.

Distinguishing attack 2 ($|N| = n$, $1 \le |M| < n$, and fixed i for $1 \le i \le n-1$).

1. Fix $M \in \{0, 1\}^i$, and query (N, M) to the encryption oracle with $N = M\|10^{n-1-|M|}$.
2. Obtain (C, T) from the oracle.
3. If $C = M$ and $T = 0^\tau$ then return 1, otherwise return 0.

In this case, we have $C = M$ with probability $1/2^i$ for both EAX'-$\mathcal{E}_K$ and a random encryption process. Given the event $C = M$, we have

$$T = \text{msb}_\tau(E_K(N) \oplus E_K(C\|10^{n-1-|C|})) = 0^\tau$$

with probability 1 for EAX'-$\mathcal{E}_K$, while $T = 0^\tau$ occurs with probability $1/2^\tau$ for the random encryption process. Thus, with probability $1/2^i$ the distinguisher succeeds with a high probability, which is non-negligible when i is small.

4.3   Chosen-Ciphertext Plaintext Recovery Attacks

Consider a triple (N^*, C^*, T^*) of cleartext N^*, ciphertext C^* and tag T^*. The corresponding plaintext M^* is unknown. The adversary can ask a decryption oracle, for the decryption of any (N, C, T) under its choice, except for $(N, C, T) = (N^*, C^*, T^*)$ (otherwise, finding M^* would be trivial). The adversary receives either $\perp$ (if verification fails) or the decryption M of C. This is the setting in a *chosen ciphertext attack*. Below, we focus on *plaintext recovery attacks*, where the adversary actually finds (a part of) M^*. We describe two attacks: the first for $|N^*| = n$, the second for $|N^*| < n$.

Plaintext recovery attack 1 ($|N^*| = n$).

1. Obtain (N^*, C^*, T^*) for unknown plaintext M^*.
2. Prepare C with $|C| < n$ and $C\|10^{n-1-|C|} = N^*$ and $T = 0^\tau$.
3. Query (N^*, C, T) to the decryption oracle. Let M be the answer.
4. Compute the keystream $KS = C \oplus M \in \{0, 1\}^{|C|}$.

Since the decryption of (N^*, C^*, T^*) uses the same keystream KS, we now can compute the first $|C|$ bits of M^*, or the full M^* if $|M^*| \le |C|$. It succeeds for the same reason as Forgery attack 1 (unless $N^* = 0^n$, in which case there is no C in Step 2, or $C^*\|10^{n-1-|C^*|} = N^*$ and $T^* = 0^\tau$, in which case the decryption query in Step 3 makes the attack trivial).

Plaintext recovery attack 2 $(|N^*| < n)$.

1. Obtain (N^*, C^*, T^*) for unknown plaintext M^*.
2. Prepare C with $|C| = n$ and $N^* \| 10^{n-1-|N^*|} = C$ and $T = 0^\tau$.
3. Query (N^*, C, T) to the decryption oracle. Let M be the answer.
4. Compute the keystream $KS = C \oplus M \in \{0,1\}^n$.

Unless $N^* \| 10^{n-1-|N^*|} = C^*$ and $T^* = 0^\tau$, the attack succeeds for the same reason as Forgery attack 2.

4.4 Remarks

The Source of Attacks. Not to mention, our attacks cannot be applied on the original EAX having the proof of security. Our attacks exploit the wrong tweaking method of CMAC in EAX$'$. While the tweaking method in the original EAX provides a set of computationally independent PRFs, the tweaking method of EAX$'$ fails to do this. For instance $\mathrm{CMAC}'^{(0)}_K(M) = \mathrm{CMAC}'^{(1)}_K(M')$ holds with probability 1 for any (M, M') such that $|M| = n$ and $|M'| < n$ and $M' \| 10^{n-1-|M'|} = M$, which is unlikely to occur if $\mathrm{CMAC}'^{(0)}_K$ and $\mathrm{CMAC}'^{(1)}_K$ were computationally independent. The SIV-like counter incrementation also increases the collision probability of counter blocks, however this only leads to a small degradation in security, as mentioned by [3], hence our attacks do not rely on this fact.

Applicability to ANSI C12.22 Protocols. All our attacks require $|N| \leq n$. The forgery and distinguishing attacks also require $|M|, |C| \leq n$, and the plaintext recovery attacks actually require at most the first n bits of the ciphertext. In addition, the forgery and plaintext recovery attacks could not be prevented by restricting the input length at encryption: one must implement the input length check at decryption as well.

One can find some examples that have $|M| = n$ or $|M| = 0$ (i.e. the authentication of N) with $n = 128$ in communication examples of ANSI C12.22 (Annex G of [3]) or test vectors[3] of EAX$'$ (Section V of [13]). At the same time, we do not know[4] whether $|N| > n$ holds for ANSI C12.22 protocols, even though the specification [13] does not, at least explicitly, regulate the length of cleartext. The reference code of EAX$'$ given by [3,6] has no restriction on input lengths, and we verified our attacks with that code.

A natural question arises from the above observation: whether EAX$'$ is provably secure under the restriction $|N| > n$. In the next section we provide a positive answer to this question.

---

[3] One can find test vectors with n-bit cleartexts in [13]. However, they seem to contain an editorial error; the cleartext may mean the plaintext and vice versa.

[4] In [13], "Justification" of Issue 6 (in page 3) states that "The CMAC$'$ computations here always involve CBC of at least two blocks". This looks odd since M or C can be null (as stated by ANSI) and CMAC$'$ taking the empty string certainly operates on the single-block CBC, but it may be a hint that $|N| > n$ would hold for any legitimate ANSI C12.22 messages.

5 Provable Security for More-Than-One-Block Cleartext

Now we are going to prove that EAX$'$ provides the provable security when the cleartext N is always more than n bits for both encryption and decryption. Combined with the attacks described in the previous section, the result of this section draws a sharp distinction on the security between the case $|N| > n$ and the case $|N| \leq n$.

Security Notions. Following [7,14], we introduce two security notions, privacy and authenticity, to model the security of EAX$'$. For c oracles, $O_1, O_2, \ldots, O_c$, we write $\mathcal{A}^{O_1, O_2, \ldots, O_c}$ to represent the adversary $\mathcal{A}$ accessing these c oracles in an arbitrarily order. If F and G are oracles having the same input and output domains, we say they are compatible.

A CPA-adversary $\mathcal{A}$ against EAX$'[E, \tau]$ accesses EAX$'$-$\mathcal{E}_{K,\tau}$. The encryption queries made by $\mathcal{A}$ are denoted by $(N_1, M_1), \ldots, (N_q, M_q)$. We define $\mathcal{A}$'s parameter list as (q, σ_N, σ_M), where $\sigma_N \overset{\text{def}}{=} \sum_{i=1}^{q} |N_i|_n$ and $\sigma_M \overset{\text{def}}{=} \sum_{i=1}^{q} |M_i|_n$ if all $|M_i|_n > 0$. For convention, if $|M_i| = 0$ for some $i \leq q$, $\sigma_M \overset{\text{def}}{=} (\sum_{i=1}^{q} |M_i|_n) + 1$. We also define random-bit oracle, \$, which takes $(N, M) \in \{0,1\}^* \times \{0,1\}^*$ and returns $(C, T) \overset{\$}{\leftarrow} \{0,1\}^{|M|} \times \{0,1\}^\tau$. The privacy notion for CPA-adversary $\mathcal{A}$ is defined as

$$\mathsf{Adv}^{\mathrm{priv}}_{\mathrm{EAX}'[E,\tau]}(\mathcal{A}) \overset{\text{def}}{=} \Pr[K \overset{\$}{\leftarrow} \mathcal{K} : \mathcal{A}^{\mathrm{EAX}'\text{-}\mathcal{E}_K} \Rightarrow 1] - \Pr[\mathcal{A}^{\$} \Rightarrow 1]. \tag{1}$$

We assume $\mathcal{A}$ in the privacy notion is nonce-respecting, i.e., all N_is are distinct. Similarly, a CCA-adversary $\mathcal{A}$ against EAX$'[E, \tau]$ accesses EAX$'$-$\mathcal{E}_{K,\tau}$ and EAX$'$-$\mathcal{D}_{K,\tau}$. The encryption and decryption queries made by $\mathcal{A}$ are denoted by $(N_1, M_1), \ldots, (N_q, M_q)$ and $(\widetilde{N}_1, \widetilde{C}_1, \widetilde{T}_1), \ldots, (\widetilde{N}_{q_v}, \widetilde{C}_{q_v}, \widetilde{T}_{q_v})$. We define $\mathcal{A}$'s parameter list as $(q, q_v, \sigma_N, \sigma_M, \sigma_{\widetilde{N}}, \sigma_{\widetilde{C}})$, where $\sigma_{\widetilde{N}} \overset{\text{def}}{=} \sum_{i=1}^{q_v} |\widetilde{N}_i|_n$, $\sigma_{\widetilde{C}} \overset{\text{def}}{=} \sum_{i=1}^{q_v} |\widetilde{C}_i|_n$ when all $|\widetilde{C}_i|_n > 0$ and $\sigma_{\widetilde{C}} \overset{\text{def}}{=} (\sum_{i=1}^{q_v} |\widetilde{C}_i|_n) + 1$ otherwise. The definitions of σ_N and σ_M are the same as above. The authenticity notion for a CCA-adversary $\mathcal{A}$ is defined as

$$\mathsf{Adv}^{\mathrm{auth}}_{\mathrm{EAX}'[E,\tau]}(\mathcal{A}) \overset{\text{def}}{=} \Pr[K \overset{\$}{\leftarrow} \mathcal{K} : \mathcal{A}^{\mathrm{EAX}'\text{-}\mathcal{E}_K, \mathrm{EAX}'\text{-}\mathcal{D}_K} \text{ forges}], \tag{2}$$

where $\mathcal{A}$ forges if EAX$'$-$\mathcal{D}_K$ returns a bit string (other than $\perp$) for a query $(\widetilde{N}_i, \widetilde{C}_i, \widetilde{T}_i)$ for some $1 \leq i \leq q_v$ such that $(\widetilde{N}_i, \widetilde{C}_i, \widetilde{T}_i) \neq (N_j, C_j, T_j)$ for all $1 \leq j \leq q$. We assume $\mathcal{A}$ in the authenticity notion is always nonce-respecting with respect to encryption queries; using the same N for encryption and decryption queries is allowed, and the same N can be repeated within decryption queries, i.e. N_i is different from N_j for any $j \neq i$ but $\widetilde{N}_i$ may be equal to N_j or $\widetilde{N}_{i'}$ for some j and $i' \neq i$.

Bounds. We denote EAX$'$ with an n-bit URP being used as a blockcipher by EAX$'[\mathrm{Perm}(n), \tau]$ and the corresponding encryption and decryption functions by EAX$'$-$\mathcal{E}_{\mathsf{P}}$ and EAX$'$-$\mathcal{D}_{\mathsf{P}}$. Similarly, the subscript K in the component algorithms is substituted with P, e.g. CMAC$'^{(i)}_{\mathsf{P}}$. We here provide the security bounds for

EAX$'$[Perm$(n), \tau$]; the computational counterpart for EAX$'$[E, τ] is trivial. The security bound for the privacy notion is as follows.

Theorem 1. *Let $\mathcal{A}$ be the CPA-adversary against EAX$'$[Perm$(n), \tau$] who does not query cleartexts of n bits or shorter and has parameter list (q, σ_N, σ_M). Let $\sigma_{\mathrm{priv}} = \sigma_N + \sigma_M$. Then we have*

$$\mathrm{Adv}^{\mathrm{priv}}_{\mathrm{EAX}'[\mathrm{Perm}(n), \tau]}(\mathcal{A}) \leq \frac{18\sigma^2_{\mathrm{priv}}}{2^n}.$$

The security bound for the authenticity notion is as follows.

Theorem 2. *Let $\mathcal{A}$ be the CCA-adversary against EAX$'$[Perm$(n), \tau$] who does not query cleartexts of n bits or shorter for both encryption and decryption oracles, and has parameter list $(q, q_v, \sigma_N, \sigma_M, \sigma_{\widetilde{N}}, \sigma_{\widetilde{C}})$. Let $\sigma_{\mathrm{auth}} = \sigma_N + \sigma_M + \sigma_{\widetilde{N}} + \sigma_{\widetilde{C}}$. Then we have*

$$\mathrm{Adv}^{\mathrm{auth}}_{\mathrm{EAX}'[\mathrm{Perm}(n), \tau]}(\mathcal{A}) \leq \frac{18\sigma^2_{\mathrm{auth}}}{2^n} + \frac{q_v}{2^\tau}.$$

6 Proofs of Theorem 1 and Theorem 2

6.1 Overview

The proofs of Theorems 1 and 2 are bit long, hence we first provide the overview. The basic strategy follows from the proof of the original EAX [7] with some extensions taken from OMAC proofs [9,10]. We first break down the algorithm of EAX$'$[Perm$(n), \tau$] into a pair of functions, which we call OMAC-extension, OMAC-e[P] = (OMAC-e[P]$^{(0)}$, OMAC-e[P]$^{(1)}$), where OMAC-e[P]$^{(0)}$: $\{0,1\}^{>n} \times \mathbb{N} \to (\{0,1\}^n)^{>0}$ and OMAC-e[P]$^{(1)}$: $\{0,1\}^* \to \{0,1\}^n$. It uses an n-bit random permutation P and an additional independent and random value, $U \in \{0,1\}^n$. Intuitively, OMAC-e[P]$^{(0)}$ is a function that takes (N, d), where $d = |M|_n$ $(d = |C|_n)$ for encryption (decryption), and produces $\underline{N} \oplus U$ and the d-block keystream before truncation, i.e., S of Fig. 1 (See also Fig. 2). Similarly, OMAC-e[P]$^{(1)}$ takes a ciphertext, C, and produces CMAC$'^{(1)}_{\mathsf{P}}(C) \oplus U$. Since $(\underline{N} \oplus U) \oplus (\mathrm{CMAC}'^{(1)}_{\mathsf{P}}(C) \oplus U) = \underline{N} \oplus \mathrm{CMAC}'^{(1)}_{\mathsf{P}}(C)$, such a function pair can perfectly simulate EAX$'$[Perm$(n), \tau$]. We introduce U to make the remaining analysis less involved. Then, the bound evaluation for EAX$'$[Perm$(n), \tau$] is mostly reduced to that of the indistinguishability between OMAC-e[P] and a random function pair $\mathbb{RND} = (\mathbb{RND}^{(0)}, \mathbb{RND}^{(1)})$. Here $\mathbb{RND}^{(0)}$ takes (N, d) and samples $Y \xleftarrow{\$} (\{0,1\}^n)^{d_{\max}+1}$ if N is new, and outputs the first $(d+1)$ blocks of Y, where $d_{\max}$ is the maximum possible value of d implied by the game we consider. Similarly $\mathbb{RND}^{(1)}$ takes $C \in \{0,1\}^*$ and outputs $Y' \xleftarrow{\$} \{0,1\}^n$ if C is new. To bound the indistinguishability between OMAC-e[P] and $\mathbb{RND}$, we further break down OMAC-e[P] into a set of ten small functions, $\mathbf{Q} = \{\mathbf{Q}_i\}_{i=1,\dots,10}$, following the proof of OMAC [9]. Using two random values in addition to U, these functions are built so that they behave close to a set of independent URFs or URPs, and at the same time have the capability to perfectly simulate OMAC-e[P] (hence EAX'[Perm(n)]). The indistinguishability of $\mathbf{Q}$ from the set of URPs/URFs is relatively easy to derive, and as a result the following analysis becomes much easier.

6.2 Proof

Setup. Without loss of generality and for simplicity this section assumes that the space of valid cleartexts of EAX' is $\{0,1\}^{>n}$, rather than restricting the adversary's strategy.

For convenience we introduce the following notions. Let $F_K : \mathcal{X} \to \mathcal{Y}$ and $G_{K'} : \mathcal{X} \to \mathcal{Y}$ be two keyed functions with $K \in \mathcal{K}$ and $K' \in \mathcal{K}'$, and let $\mathcal{A}$ be the CPA-adversary. We define

$$\mathrm{Adv}_{F,G}^{\mathrm{cpa}}(\mathcal{A}) \overset{\mathrm{def}}{=} \Pr[K \overset{\$}{\leftarrow} \mathcal{K} : \mathcal{A}^{F_K} \Rightarrow 1] - \Pr[K' \overset{\$}{\leftarrow} \mathcal{K}' : \mathcal{A}^{G_{K'}} \Rightarrow 1]. \quad (3)$$

Note that this definition can be naturally extended when $G_{K'}$ is substituted with the random-bit oracle compatible with F_K. Moreover, when F_K and $G_{K'}$ are compatible with EAX'-$\mathcal{E}_K$, we define $\mathrm{Adv}_{F,G}^{\mathrm{cpa-nr}}(\mathcal{A})$ as the same function as $\mathrm{Adv}_{F,G}^{\mathrm{cpa}}(\mathcal{A})$ but CPA-adversary $\mathcal{A}$ is restricted to be nonce-respecting. Let $\mathbf{F} = (F_K^e, F_K^d)$ and $\mathbf{G} = (G_{K'}^e, G_{K'}^d)$ be the pairs of functions that are compatible with $(\mathrm{EAX'}\text{-}\mathcal{E}_K, \mathrm{EAX'}\text{-}\mathcal{D}_K)$. We define

$$\mathrm{Adv}_{\mathbf{F},\mathbf{G}}^{\mathrm{cca-nr}}(\mathcal{A}) \overset{\mathrm{def}}{=} \Pr[K \overset{\$}{\leftarrow} \mathcal{K} : \mathcal{A}^{F_K^e, F_K^d} \Rightarrow 1] - \Pr[K' \overset{\$}{\leftarrow} \mathcal{K}' : \mathcal{A}^{G_{K'}^e, G_{K'}^d} \Rightarrow 1], \quad (4)$$

where the underlying $\mathcal{A}$ is assumed to be nonce-respecting for encryption queries. Note that we have $\mathrm{Adv}_{\mathrm{EAX'}[E,\tau]}^{\mathrm{priv}}(\mathcal{A}) = \mathrm{Adv}_{\mathrm{EAX'}\text{-}\mathcal{E}_K,\$}^{\mathrm{cpa-nr}}(\mathcal{A})$ for any nonce-respecting CPA-adversary $\mathcal{A}$.

Step 1: OMAC-extension. For $x \in \{0,1\}^{\leq n}$, let $\mathtt{bp}(x) = x$ if $|x| = n$ and $\mathtt{bp}(x) = x\|10^{n-1-(|x| \bmod n)}$ if $|x| < n$. If $x = \varepsilon$ then $\mathtt{bp}(x) = 10^{n-1}$. We first define OMAC-extension using an n-bit URP, denoted by OMAC-e[P] : $\{0,1\} \times \{0,1\}^* \times \mathbb{N} \to (\{0,1\}^n)^{>0}$. The definition is given in Fig. 3. See also Fig. 4. Actually it consists of two functions, written as

$$\mathrm{OMAC}\text{-}\mathrm{e}[\mathsf{P}]^{(0)} : \{0,1\}^{>n} \times \mathbb{N} \to (\{0,1\}^n)^{>0}, \text{ and} \quad (5)$$

$$\mathrm{OMAC}\text{-}\mathrm{e}[\mathsf{P}]^{(1)} : \{0,1\}^* \to \{0,1\}^n, \quad (6)$$

where the first argument to OMAC-e[P], $t \in \{0,1\}$, specifies which function to be used, i.e., OMAC-e[P]$(0, X, d) = $ OMAC-e[P]$^{(0)}(X, d)$ and OMAC-e[P]$(1, X, d) = $ OMAC-e[P]$^{(1)}(X)$ (d is discarded). Here $|\mathrm{OMAC}\text{-}\mathrm{e}[\mathsf{P}]^{(0)}(X, d)| = (d + 1)n$. For simplicity we assume the input domain of OMAC-e[P] is a set of $(t, X, d) \in \{0,1\} \times \{0,1\}^* \times \mathbb{N}$ that is acceptable for OMAC-e[P]$^{(t)}$. More formally, when $t = 0$ we assume $|X| > n$ and $d \in \mathbb{N}$, and when $t = 1$ we assume d is fixed (say 0). As described in Sect. 6.1, OMAC-e[P] enables us to simulate EAX'-$\mathcal{E}_\mathsf{P}$ and EAX'-$\mathcal{D}_\mathsf{P}$; note that the simulator only needs to compute the sum of two outputs from

$\text{CMAC}'^{(0)}_\mathsf{P}$ and $\text{CMAC}'^{(1)}_\mathsf{P}$, and not to compute the output itself. For instance, if we want to perform EAX'-$\mathcal{E}_\mathsf{P}$ for $N = (N[1]\|N[2])$ and $M = (M[1]\|M[2])$ with $|N[1]| = |N[2]| = |M[1]| = n$ and $|M[2]| = n - 2$, then the procedure is (1) $Y\|S[1]S[2] \leftarrow \text{OMAC-e}[\mathsf{P}](0, N, 2)$, (2) $C \leftarrow \text{msb}_{2n-2}(S[1]S[2]) \oplus M$, (3) $Y' \leftarrow \text{OMAC-e}[\mathsf{P}](1, C, 0)$, where the last argument is arbitrary, (4) $T \leftarrow \text{msb}_\tau(Y \oplus Y')$, and (5) output (C, T). The following proposition is easy to check.

Proposition 1. *There exist deterministic procedures, $f_e(\cdot)$ and $f_d(\cdot)$, that use OMAC-e$[\mathsf{P}]$ as a black box and perfectly simulate EAX'-$\mathcal{E}_\mathsf{P}$ and EAX'-$\mathcal{D}_\mathsf{P}$. That is, we have[5] EAX'-$\mathcal{E}_\mathsf{P} \equiv f_e(\text{OMAC-e}[\mathsf{P}])$ and EAX'-$\mathcal{D}_\mathsf{P} \equiv f_d(\text{OMAC-e}[\mathsf{P}])$.*

A keyed function F compatible with OMAC-e$[\mathsf{P}]$ is said to have OMAC-e profile, and we denote $F(t, X, d)$ by $F^{(t)}(X, d)$. Suppose an adversary querying F of OMAC-e profile has q queries $(t_1, X_1, d_1), \ldots, (t_q, X_q, d_q)$ and corresponding answers are $Y_1, \ldots, Y_q$. Such an adversary is called to be with parameter list $(q, \sigma_{\text{in}}, \sigma_{\text{out}})$ where $\sigma_{\text{in}} \stackrel{\text{def}}{=} \sum_{i=1,\ldots,q} |X_i|_n$ and $\sigma_{\text{out}} \stackrel{\text{def}}{=} \sum_{i=1,\ldots,q; t_i=0} |Y_i|_n$.

Algorithm OMAC-e$[\mathsf{P}]$:
Initialization
00      $L \leftarrow \mathsf{P}(0^n), U \stackrel{\$}{\leftarrow} \{0,1\}^n$
On query $(t, X, d) \in \{0,1\} \times \{0,1\}^* \times \mathbb{N}$
10      $X[1]\|X[2]\|\ldots\|X[m] \stackrel{n}{\leftarrow} X$
11   if $|X| \bmod n \neq 0$ or $X = \varepsilon$ then $w \leftarrow 1$, else $w \leftarrow 0$ (note: $w \leftarrow w(X)$)
12   if $t = 0$ (note: $m \geq 2$ holds for valid queries)
13          $Y[1] \leftarrow \mathsf{P}(2L \oplus X[1])$
14   for $i = 1$ to $m - 2$ do $Y[i+1] \leftarrow \mathsf{P}(Y[i] \oplus X[i+1])$
15          $V \leftarrow \mathsf{P}(Y[m-1] \oplus \text{bp}(X[m]) \oplus 2^{w+1}L)$
15          $Y \leftarrow V \oplus U$
16   if $d = 0$ return Y
17   else $V^\wedge \leftarrow V \wedge \alpha$
18   for $j = 0$ to $d - 1$ do $S[j+1] \leftarrow \mathsf{P}(V^\wedge + j)$
19   return $Y\|S[1]S[2]\ldots S[d]$
20   if $t = 1$
21   if $|X| \leq n$ then $Y' \leftarrow \mathsf{P}(\text{bp}(X) \oplus 4L \oplus 2^{w+1}L) \oplus U$; return Y'
22   else $Y'[1] \leftarrow \mathsf{P}(4L \oplus X[1])$
23   for $i = 1$ to $m - 2$ do $Y'[i+1] \leftarrow \mathsf{P}(Y'[i] \oplus X[i+1])$
24          $Y' \leftarrow \mathsf{P}(Y'[m-1] \oplus \text{bp}(X[m]) \oplus 2^{w+1}L) \oplus U$
25   return Y'

Fig. 3. OMAC-extension using an n-bit URP, P.

---

[5] Here $F \equiv G$ means the equivalence of the output probability distribution functions, i.e. $\Pr[F(x_1) = y_1, \ldots, F(x_q) = y_q] = \Pr[G(x_1) = y_1, \ldots, G(x_q) = y_q]$ for any fixed possible $x_1, \ldots, x_q$ and $y_1, \ldots, y_q$. The probabilities are defined over F and G's randomness.

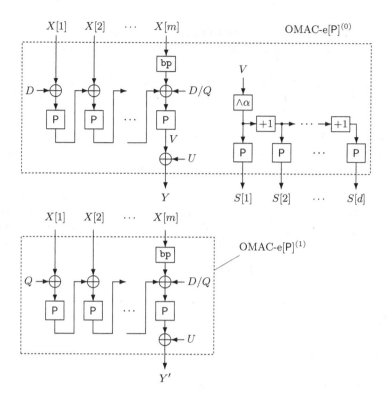

Fig. 4. Component functions of OMAC-extension. Here D and Q denote $2L$ and $4L$ with $L = \mathsf{P}(0^n)$, and U is uniformly random over n bits.

To further analyze OMAC-e[P], we introduce a set of ten functions, $\mathbf{Q} = \{\mathbf{Q}_i\}_{i=1,\dots,10}$.

Definition 1. *Let* $\mathbf{Q}_i : \{0,1\}^n \to \{0,1\}^n$ *for* $i = 1,2,3,4,7,8,9$ *and let* $\mathbf{Q}_j : \{0,1\}^n \times \mathbb{N} \to (\{0,1\}^n)^{>0}$ *for* $j = 5,6$, *and let* $\mathbf{Q}_{10} : \{0,1\}^n \setminus \{0^n\} \to \{0,1\}^n$. *These functions are defined as*

$$\mathbf{Q}_1(x) \overset{\text{def}}{=} \mathsf{P}(2L \oplus x) \oplus \mathrm{Rnd}_1, \qquad \mathbf{Q}_2(x) \overset{\text{def}}{=} \mathsf{P}(4L \oplus x) \oplus \mathrm{Rnd}_2,$$

$$\mathbf{Q}_3(x) \overset{\text{def}}{=} \mathsf{P}(\mathrm{Rnd}_1 \oplus x) \oplus \mathrm{Rnd}_1, \qquad \mathbf{Q}_4(x) \overset{\text{def}}{=} \mathsf{P}(\mathrm{Rnd}_2 \oplus x) \oplus \mathrm{Rnd}_2,$$

$$\mathbf{Q}_5(x,d) \overset{\text{def}}{=} G_{\mathsf{P},U}(\mathsf{P}(2L \oplus \mathrm{Rnd}_1 \oplus x), d), \quad \mathbf{Q}_6(x,d) \overset{\text{def}}{=} G_{\mathsf{P},U}(\mathsf{P}(4L \oplus \mathrm{Rnd}_1 \oplus x), d)$$

$$\mathbf{Q}_7(x) \overset{\text{def}}{=} \mathsf{P}(2L \oplus \mathrm{Rnd}_2 \oplus x) \oplus U, \qquad \mathbf{Q}_8(x) \overset{\text{def}}{=} \mathsf{P}(4L \oplus \mathrm{Rnd}_2 \oplus x) \oplus U,$$

$$\mathbf{Q}_9(x) \overset{\text{def}}{=} \mathsf{P}(2L \oplus 4L \oplus x) \oplus U, \qquad \mathbf{Q}_{10}(x) \overset{\text{def}}{=} \mathsf{P}(x) \oplus U,$$

where P *is an* n-*bit URP, and* $L = \mathsf{P}(0^n)$, *and* Rnd_1 *and* Rnd_2 *are independent* n-*bit random sequences, and* U *is another random* n-*bit value. Here,* $G_{\mathsf{P},U}(v,d)$ *is* $v \oplus U$ *if* $d = 0$ *and* $(v \oplus U \| \mathsf{P}(v \wedge \alpha) \| \mathsf{P}((v \wedge \alpha) + 1) \| \dots \| \mathsf{P}((v \wedge \alpha) + (d-1)))$ *if* $d > 0$. *The sampling procedures for* $\mathsf{P}, \mathrm{Rnd}_1, \mathrm{Rnd}_2,$ *and* U *are shared by all* $\mathbf{Q}_i s$.

We also treat $\mathbf{Q}$ as a tweakable function with tweak $t \in \{1, \ldots, 10\}$ by writing $\mathbf{Q}(t, x, d) = \mathbf{Q}_t(x, d)$ when $t \in \{5, 6\}$ and otherwise $\mathbf{Q}(t, x, d) = \mathbf{Q}_t(x)$. We can easily see that OMAC-e[P] can be simulated with black-box access to $\mathbf{Q}$, just the same as Q functions appeared in the proof of OMAC [9] that simulate OMAC.

We next define $\widetilde{\mathbf{Q}} = \{\widetilde{\mathbf{Q}}_i\}_{i=1,\ldots,10}$. For all $i = 1, \ldots, 10$, $\widetilde{\mathbf{Q}}_i$ is compatible with $\mathbf{Q}_i$.

Definition 2. *Let* $\mathsf{P}_1, \ldots, \mathsf{P}_4$ *be four independent* n*-bit URPs. Let* $\mathsf{R}_7, \ldots, \mathsf{R}_{10}$ *be four independent* n*-bit URFs, and let* R_5 *and* R_6 *be two independent URFs with* n*-bit input and* $(d_{\max} + 1)n$*-bit output. Using them we define*

$$\widetilde{\mathbf{Q}}_1(x) \stackrel{\text{def}}{=} \mathsf{P}_1(x), \qquad\qquad \widetilde{\mathbf{Q}}_2(x) \stackrel{\text{def}}{=} \mathsf{P}_2(x),$$

$$\widetilde{\mathbf{Q}}_3(x) \stackrel{\text{def}}{=} \mathsf{P}_3(x), \qquad\qquad \widetilde{\mathbf{Q}}_4(x) \stackrel{\text{def}}{=} \mathsf{P}_4(x),$$

$$\widetilde{\mathbf{Q}}_5(x, d) \stackrel{\text{def}}{=} \mathsf{R}_5^{d+1}(x), \qquad\qquad \widetilde{\mathbf{Q}}_6(x, d) \stackrel{\text{def}}{=} \mathsf{R}_6^{d+1}(x)$$

$$\widetilde{\mathbf{Q}}_7(x) \stackrel{\text{def}}{=} \mathsf{R}_7(x), \qquad\qquad \widetilde{\mathbf{Q}}_8(x) \stackrel{\text{def}}{=} \mathsf{R}_8(x),$$

$$\widetilde{\mathbf{Q}}_9(x) \stackrel{\text{def}}{=} \mathsf{R}_9(x), \qquad\qquad \widetilde{\mathbf{Q}}_{10}(x) \stackrel{\text{def}}{=} \mathsf{R}_{10}(x),$$

where $\mathsf{R}_i^{d+1}(x) = \mathrm{msb}_{n(d+1)}(\mathsf{R}_i(x))$ *for* $i = 5, 6$. *Here* $d_{\max}$ *is the maximum possible value of queried* d, *which will be determined by the underlying game and the adversary's parameter.*

We say a function compatible with $\mathbf{Q}$ is said to have $\mathbf{Q}$ profile. An adversary querying a function of $\mathbf{Q}$ profile is characterized by the number of queries, q, and the total sum of output n-bit blocks for $t \in \{5, 6\}$, σ_{out}. The next lemma shows the CPA-advantage in distinguishing $\mathbf{Q}$ and $\widetilde{\mathbf{Q}}$.

Lemma 1. *Let* $\mathcal{A}$ *be the adversary querying a function of* $\mathbf{Q}$ *profile with parameter list* (q, σ_{out}). *Then we have* $\mathrm{Adv}_{\mathbf{Q},\widetilde{\mathbf{Q}}}^{\mathrm{cpa}}(\mathcal{A}) \le (3.5q^2 + 10\sigma_{\text{out}}q + 2.5\sigma_{\text{out}}^2)/2^n$.

The proof is given in the full-version.

Step 2: Modified CBC-MAC. For any n-bit (keyed) permutations, G and G', let $\mathrm{CBC}_{G,G'} : (\{0,1\}^n)^{>0} \to \{0,1\}^n$ be defined as

$$\mathrm{CBC}_{G,G'}(X[1]\|\ldots\|X[m]) = \begin{cases} G(X[1]) & \text{if } m = 1 \\ \mathrm{CBC}_{G'}(G(X[1])\|X[2]\|\ldots\|X[m]) & \text{if } m \ge 2, \end{cases}$$

where $\mathrm{CBC}_{G'}$ is the standard CBC-MAC using G'. We then define a function compatible with OMAC-e[P], denoted by $\mathbb{CBC}$. For any $X \in \{0,1\}^*$, let $w(X) = 1$ if $|X| \bmod n \ne 0$ or $X = \varepsilon$ and otherwise $w(X) = 0$. For $|X| > n$, $\mathbb{CBC}^{(0)}(X, d)$ is computed as follows.

1. $X[1]\|X[2]\|\ldots\|X[m] \stackrel{n}{\leftarrow} X$ and $w \leftarrow w(X)$
2. $Z \leftarrow \mathrm{CBC}_{\mathsf{P}_1,\mathsf{P}_3}(X[1]\|\ldots\|X[m-1])$
3. Output $Y\|S[1]\|\ldots\|S[d] \leftarrow \mathsf{R}_{5+w}^{d+1}(Z \oplus \mathrm{bp}(X[m]))$

Here, if $d = 0$ the output is Y. Similarly, for $X \in \{0,1\}^*$, $\mathbb{CBC}^{(1)}(X)$ is computed as follows.

1. $X[1]\|X[2]\|\ldots\|X[m] \overset{n}{\leftarrow} X$ and $w \leftarrow w(X)$
2. If $|X| \le n$ output $Y' \leftarrow \mathsf{R}_{9+w}(\mathsf{bp}(X))$,
3. Otherwise $Z' \leftarrow \mathrm{CBC}_{\mathsf{P}_2,\mathsf{P}_4}(X[1]\|\ldots\|X[m-1])$, and output $Y' \leftarrow \mathsf{R}_{7+w}(Z' \oplus \mathsf{bp}(X[m]))$.

The pseudo-code of $\mathbb{CBC}$ (combining $\mathbb{CBC}^{(0)}$ and $\mathbb{CBC}^{(1)}$) is presented in Fig. 5. Here, $\mathsf{R}_j^i(X)$ for $j = 5,6$ denotes $\mathrm{msb}_{ni}(\mathsf{R}_j(X))$. One can simulate OMAC-e[P] via black-box accesses to $\mathbf{Q}$, including the final mask by U. For example, to simulate OMAC-e[P]$(0,N,2)$ for $|N| = 3n$, we first perform a partition, $N[1]\|N[2]\|N[3] \overset{n}{\leftarrow} N$, and then proceed as (1) $Y[1] \leftarrow \mathbf{Q}_1(N[1])$, (2) $Y[2] \leftarrow \mathbf{Q}_3(N[2] \oplus Y[1])$, and (3) $Y[3]\|S[1]S[2] \leftarrow \mathbf{Q}_5(N[3] \oplus Y[2])$. If $|N[3]| = n-2$ then $\mathbf{Q}_5(N[3]\oplus Y[2])$ is replaced with $\mathbf{Q}_6(N[3]\|10\oplus Y[2])$. For more examples, OMAC-e[P]$(1,C,0)$ for $|C| = n$ can be simulated via calling $\mathbf{Q}_9(C)$. For $|C| < n$, OMAC-e[P]$(1,C,0)$ can be simulated via calling $\mathbf{Q}_{10}(\mathsf{bp}(C)) = \mathbf{Q}_{10}(C\|10\ldots0)$. Formally, we have the following proposition.

Proposition 2. *There exists a procedure $h(\cdot)$ that uses $\mathbf{Q}$ as a black box and perfectly simulates OMAC-e[P], i.e. $h(\mathbf{Q}) \equiv$ OMAC-e[P]. Moreover, we have $h(\widetilde{\mathbf{Q}}) \equiv \mathbb{CBC}$ for this $h(\cdot)$.*

Let $\mathbb{RND}^{(0)}$ and $\mathbb{RND}^{(1)}$ be the independent random functions compatible with OMAC-e[P]$^{(0)}$ and OMAC-e[P]$^{(1)}$. Here, $\mathbb{RND}^{(0)}$ takes $(N,d) \in \{0,1\}^{>n} \times \mathbb{N}$ and samples $Y \overset{\$}{\leftarrow} (\{0,1\}^n)^{d_{\max}+1}$ if N is new, and outputs $\mathrm{msb}_{n(d+1)}(Y)$, where $d_{\max}$ is the same as $\mathbb{CBC}$. Similarly $\mathbb{RND}^{(1)}$ takes $C \in \{0,1\}^*$ and outputs $Y' \overset{\$}{\leftarrow} \{0,1\}^n$ if C is new. We define $\mathbb{RND}$ as a function consisting of $\mathbb{RND}^{(0)}$ and $\mathbb{RND}^{(1)}$ and taking $t = 0,1$ as a tweak. Then, we have the following lemma. The proof is given in the full-version.

Lemma 2. *Let $\mathcal{A}$ be an adversary querying a function of OMAC-e profile with parameter list $(q, \sigma_{in}, \sigma_{out})$. Then, $\mathrm{Adv}^{\mathrm{cpa}}_{\mathbb{CBC},\mathbb{RND}}(\mathcal{A}) \le 2\sigma_{in}^2/2^n$.*

Step 3: Derivation of PRIV Bound. Combining the above lemmas and propositions, our PRIV bound is derived. Let $\mathcal{A}$ be the CPA-adversary against AE with parameter list (q, σ_N, σ_M). Then there exist adversary $\mathcal{B}$ querying to a function of OMAC-e profile with $2q$ queries, $\sigma_{\mathrm{in}} = \sigma_N + \sigma_M$ input blocks, and $\sigma_{\mathrm{out}} = \sigma_M + 2q$ output blocks, and adversary $\mathcal{C}$ querying to a set of ten functions with $\mathbf{Q}$ profile, using $\sigma_N + \sigma_M$ queries and $\sigma_M + q$ output n-bit blocks for queries with $t = 5,6$, such that

$$\mathrm{Adv}^{\mathrm{priv}}_{\mathrm{EAX}'[\mathrm{Perm}(n)]}(\mathcal{A}) = \mathrm{Adv}^{\mathrm{cpa-nr}}_{\mathrm{EAX}'\text{-}\mathcal{E}_\mathsf{P},\$}(\mathcal{A}) = \mathrm{Adv}^{\mathrm{cpa-nr}}_{f_e(\mathrm{OMAC\text{-}e[P]}),\$}(\mathcal{A}) \quad (7)$$

$$\le \mathrm{Adv}^{\mathrm{cpa-nr}}_{f_e(\mathrm{OMAC\text{-}e[P]}),f_e(\mathbb{CBC})}(\mathcal{A}) + \mathrm{Adv}^{\mathrm{cpa-nr}}_{f_e(\mathbb{CBC}),f_e(\mathbb{RND})}(\mathcal{A}) + \underbrace{\mathrm{Adv}^{\mathrm{cpa-nr}}_{f_e(\mathbb{RND}),\$}(\mathcal{A})}_{=0} \quad (8)$$

$$\le \mathrm{Adv}^{\mathrm{cpa}}_{\mathrm{OMAC\text{-}e[P]},\mathbb{CBC}}(\mathcal{B}) + \mathrm{Adv}^{\mathrm{cpa}}_{\mathbb{CBC},\mathbb{RND}}(\mathcal{B}) \quad (9)$$

$$= \mathrm{Adv}^{\mathrm{cpa}}_{h(\mathbf{Q}),h(\widetilde{\mathbf{Q}})}(\mathcal{B}) + \mathrm{Adv}^{\mathrm{cpa}}_{\mathrm{CBC},\mathrm{RND}}(\mathcal{B}) \tag{10}$$

$$\leq \mathrm{Adv}^{\mathrm{cpa}}_{\mathbf{Q},\widetilde{\mathbf{Q}}}(\mathcal{C}) + \frac{2(\sigma_N + \sigma_M)^2}{2^n} \tag{11}$$

$$\leq \frac{3.5(\sigma_N + \sigma_M)^2 + 10(\sigma_M + q)(\sigma_N + \sigma_M) + 2.5(\sigma_M + q)^2}{2^n} + \frac{2(\sigma_N + \sigma_M)^2}{2^n} \tag{12}$$

$$\leq \frac{18(\sigma_N + \sigma_M)^2}{2^n} = \frac{18\sigma^2_{\mathrm{priv}}}{2^n}, \tag{13}$$

as $q \leq \sigma_N$. Here, the second equality in Eq. (7) follows from Proposition 1, Eq. (10) follows from Proposition 2, Eq. (11) follows from Lemma 2, and Eq. (12) follows from Lemma 1. In addition, $\mathrm{Adv}^{\mathrm{cpa\text{-}nr}}_{f_e(\mathrm{RND}),}(\mathcal{A}) = 0$ holds because when $\mathcal{A}$ queries (N, M) to $f_e(\mathrm{RND})$ the output is a subsequence of $\mathrm{RND}^{(0)}(N, |M|_n)$ with the first n bits XORed by the output of $\mathrm{RND}^{(1)}$ (whose input is a part of $\mathrm{RND}^{(0)}(N, |M|_n)$). As N is always fresh, the output is always random. This concludes the proof of Theorem 1.

Step 4: Derivation of AUTH Bound. The AUTH bound is derived in a similar way. Let EAX' be the AE algorithm compatible with $\mathrm{EAX}'[\mathrm{Perm}(n)]$ using $f_e(\mathrm{RND})$ and $f_d(\mathrm{RND})$ for the encryption and decryption algorithms. We let $\mathcal{A}$ be the CCA-adversary against AE with parameter list $(q, q_v, \sigma_N, \sigma_M, \sigma_{\widetilde{N}}, \sigma_{\widetilde{C}})$. Then we have the following bound.

$$\mathrm{Adv}^{\mathrm{auth}}_{\mathrm{EAX}'}(\mathcal{A}) \leq q_v/2^\tau. \tag{14}$$

The proof of Eq. (14) is given in the full-version. Then, there exist adversary $\mathcal{B}$ querying to a function of OMAC-e profile with $2(q + q_v)$ queries with $\sigma_{\mathrm{in}} = \sigma_N + \sigma_M + \sigma_{\widetilde{N}} + \sigma_{\widetilde{C}}$ and $\sigma_{\mathrm{out}} = \sigma_M + 2q + \sigma_{\widetilde{C}} + 2q_v$, and adversary $\mathcal{C}$ querying to a function of $\mathbf{Q}$ profile with $\sigma_N + \sigma_M + \sigma_{\widetilde{N}} + \sigma_{\widetilde{C}}$ queries and $\sigma_M + q + \sigma_{\widetilde{C}} + q_v$ output blocks for queries with $t = 5, 6$, such that

$$\mathrm{Adv}^{\mathrm{auth}}_{\mathrm{EAX}'[\mathrm{Perm}(n)]}(\mathcal{A})$$

$$\leq \mathrm{Adv}^{\mathrm{cca\text{-}nr}}_{(\mathrm{EAX}'\text{-}\mathcal{E}_\mathrm{P},\mathrm{EAX}'\text{-}\mathcal{D}_\mathrm{P}),(f_e(\mathrm{RND}),f_d(\mathrm{RND}))}(\mathcal{A}) + \mathrm{Adv}^{\mathrm{auth}}_{\mathrm{EAX}'}(\mathcal{A}) \tag{15}$$

$$\leq \mathrm{Adv}^{\mathrm{cca\text{-}nr}}_{(f_e(\mathrm{OMAC\text{-}e}[\mathrm{P}]),f_d(\mathrm{OMAC\text{-}e}[\mathrm{P}])),(f_e(\mathrm{RND}),f_d(\mathrm{RND}))}(\mathcal{A}) + \frac{q_v}{2^\tau} \tag{16}$$

$$\leq \mathrm{Adv}^{\mathrm{cpa}}_{\mathrm{OMAC\text{-}e}[\mathrm{P}],\mathrm{RND}}(\mathcal{B}) + \frac{q_v}{2^\tau} \tag{17}$$

$$\leq \mathrm{Adv}^{\mathrm{cpa}}_{\mathrm{OMAC\text{-}e}[\mathrm{P}],\mathrm{CBC}}(\mathcal{B}) + \mathrm{Adv}^{\mathrm{cpa}}_{\mathrm{CBC},\mathrm{RND}}(\mathcal{B}) + \frac{q_v}{2^\tau} \tag{18}$$

$$= \mathrm{Adv}^{\mathrm{cpa}}_{h(\mathbf{Q}),h(\widetilde{\mathbf{Q}})}(\mathcal{B}) + \mathrm{Adv}^{\mathrm{cpa}}_{\mathrm{CBC},\mathrm{RND}}(\mathcal{B}) + \frac{q_v}{2^\tau} \tag{19}$$

$$\leq \mathrm{Adv}^{\mathrm{cpa}}_{\mathbf{Q},\widetilde{\mathbf{Q}}}(\mathcal{C}) + \frac{2(\sigma_N + \sigma_M + \sigma_{\widetilde{N}} + \sigma_{\widetilde{C}})^2}{2^n} + \frac{q_v}{2^\tau} \tag{20}$$

$$\leq \frac{3.5(\sigma_N + \sigma_M + \sigma_{\widetilde{N}} + \sigma_{\widetilde{C}})^2 + 10(\sigma_M + q + \sigma_{\widetilde{C}} + q_v)(\sigma_N + \sigma_M + \sigma_{\widetilde{N}} + \sigma_{\widetilde{C}})}{2^n}$$

$$+ \frac{2.5(\sigma_M + q + \sigma_{\widetilde{C}} + q_v)^2}{2^n} + \frac{2(\sigma_N + \sigma_M + \sigma_{\widetilde{N}} + \sigma_{\widetilde{C}})^2}{2^n} + \frac{q_v}{2^\tau} \tag{21}$$

$$\leq \frac{18\sigma_{\text{auth}}^2}{2^n} + \frac{q_v}{2^\tau}, \tag{22}$$

since $q \leq \sigma_N$ and $q_v \leq \sigma_{\widetilde{N}}$. Here, Eq. (16) follows from Proposition 1 and Eqs. (14), (19) follows from Proposition 2, Eq. (20) follows from Lemma 2, and Eq. (21) follows from Lemma 1. This concludes the proof of Theorem 2.

7   Fixing the Flaw

There would be ways to fix the flaw of EAX′ to make it as a secure general-purpose AE accepting cleartexts of any length. Below, we provide some of them, naming it to EAX″. The concept here is not to touch the inside of EAX′, instead using it as a black box. We only propose the fixes for encryption, as the corresponding decryptions are fairly straightforward.

Method 1: EAX″$_1$-$\mathcal{E}_K(N, M) \stackrel{\text{def}}{=}$ EAX′-$\mathcal{E}_K(0^n \| N, M)$.

Algorithm $\mathbb{CBC}$ (given $d_{\max}$):
Initialization
00   for $i = 1$ to 4 do $\mathsf{P}_i \stackrel{\$}{\leftarrow} \text{Perm}(n)$
01      $\mathsf{R}_5 \stackrel{\$}{\leftarrow} \text{Func}(n, d_{\max})$, $\mathsf{R}_6 \stackrel{\$}{\leftarrow} \text{Func}(n, d_{\max})$
02   for $j = 7$ to 10 do $\mathsf{R}_j \stackrel{\$}{\leftarrow} \text{Func}(n)$ (note: R_{10}'s actual input is in $\{0,1\}^n \setminus \{0^n\}$)
On query $(t, X, d) \in \{0, 1\} \times \{0, 1\}^* \times \mathbb{N}$
10      $X[1]\|X[2]\|\dots\|X[m] \stackrel{n}{\leftarrow} X$
11   if $|X| \bmod n \neq 0$ or $X = \varepsilon$ then $w \leftarrow 1$, else $w \leftarrow 0$ (note: $w \leftarrow w(X)$)
12   if $t = 0$ (note: $m \geq 2$ holds for valid queries)
13          $Y[1] \leftarrow \mathsf{P}_1(X[1])$
14   for $i = 1$ to $m - 2$ do $Y[i + 1] \leftarrow \mathsf{P}_3(Y[i] \oplus X[i + 1])$
15   if $d = 0$ then $Y \leftarrow \mathsf{R}_{5+w}^1(Y[m - 1] \oplus \mathsf{bp}(X[m]))$; return Y
16   else $Y\|S[1]\|S[2]\|\dots\|S[d] \leftarrow \mathsf{R}_{5+w}^{d+1}(Y[m - 1] \oplus \mathsf{bp}(X[m]))$
17   return $Y\|S[1]\|S[2]\|\dots\|S[d]$
18   if $t = 1$
19   if $|X| \leq n$ then $Y' \leftarrow \mathsf{R}_{9+w}(\mathsf{bp}(X))$; return Y'
20   else $Y'[1] \leftarrow \mathsf{P}_2(X[1])$
21   for $i = 1$ to $m - 2$ do $Y'[i + 1] \leftarrow \mathsf{P}_4(Y'[i] \oplus X[i + 1])$
22          $Y' \leftarrow \mathsf{R}_{7+w}(Y'[m - 1] \oplus \mathsf{bp}(X[m]))$
23   return Y'

Fig. 5. $\mathbb{CBC}$ using four n-bit URPs, four n-bit URFs, and two n-bit input, $(d_{\max} + 1)n$-bit output URFs.

Method 2: Use two keys for E, K and K', and let

$$\text{EAX}''_2\text{-}\mathcal{E}_{K,K'}(N, M) \stackrel{\text{def}}{=} \begin{cases} \text{EAX}'\text{-}\mathcal{E}_K(N, M) & \text{if } |N| > n, \\ \text{EAX}'\text{-}\mathcal{E}_{K'}(0^n \| N, M) & \text{if } |N| \leq n, \end{cases}$$

where K and K' are independent or $K' = K \oplus \text{cst}$ for a non-zero constant cst. The choice of cst must be done with care to avoid related-key attacks. For instance, letting $\text{cst} = 1^{|K|}$ seems natural while this is problematic with DES due to the complementary property of the key schedule. One option is to use a random-looking constant, say the first few digits of π.

Method 3: Use a key for E, K, and an independent n-bit key, L, and let

$$\text{EAX}''_3\text{-}\mathcal{E}_{K,L}(N, M) \stackrel{\text{def}}{=} \begin{cases} \text{EAX}'\text{-}\mathcal{E}_K(N, M) & \text{if } |N| > n, \\ \text{EAX}'\text{-}\mathcal{E}^{\oplus}_{K,L}(0^n \| N, M) & \text{if } |N| \leq n, \end{cases}$$

where $\text{EAX}'\text{-}\mathcal{E}^{\oplus}_{K,L}$ is EAX' encryption with blockcipher $\widetilde{E}_{K,L}$ defined as $\widetilde{E}_{K,L}(X) = E_K(X \oplus L)$.

The security bounds of the above methods are easily derived from the results of Theorems 1 and 2. For the latter option of Method 2 we also need a very restricted form of related-key security of E, and for Method 3 we need the theory of tweakable blockcipher [11]. Each method has its own pros and cons: Method 1 is the simplest but needs additional blockcipher calls irrespective of $|N|$. Methods 2 and 3 keep the original operation for $|N| > n$, but need additional key or a stronger security requirement on E. We also warn that Method 3 allows a partial key recovery attack with birthday complexity.

8 Concluding Remarks

Practical Implications. Attacks as those described in the current paper are often turned down by non-cryptographers as "only theoretical" or "don't apply in practice". Indeed, none of our attacks is applicable if the cleartext size exceeds n bits. But even if ANSI C12.22 prohibited any cleartexts of size $n = 128$ bits or shorter, including EAX' in the standard would be like an unexploded bomb – waiting to go off any time in the future. Remember that EAX' is intended for Smart Grid, i.e., for the use in dedicated industrial systems such as electrical meters, controllers and appliances. It hardly seems reasonable to assume that *every* device will *always* carefully check cleartexts and plaintexts for validity and plausibility. Also, vendors may be tempted to implement their own nonstandard extensions avoiding "unnecessarily long" texts.

For a non-cryptographer, assuming a "decryption oracle" may seem strange – if there were such an oracle, why bother with message recovery attacks at all? However, experience shows that such theoretical attacks are often practically exploitable. For example, some error messages return the input that caused the error: "Syntax error in 'xyzgarble'." Even if the error message does not transmit the entire fake plaintext, any error message telling the attacker whether the fake message followed some syntactic conventions or not is potentially useful for the attacker. See [8] for an early example.

Also note that our forgery attacks allow a malicious attacker to create a large number of messages with given single-block cleartexts and random single-block plaintexts, that appear to come from a trusted source, because the authentication succeeded. What the actual devices will do when presented with apparently valid random commands is a source of great speculation.

Our Recommendation. Whenever possible, avoid adopting EAX′ in new applications. If EAX′ cannot be avoided, then this has to be carefully implemented to exclude one-block cleartexts. We note that specifying the minimum data length in standard documents does not necessarily prevent the adversary from using short cleartexts. Therefore, the cleartext length checking mechanisms are needed at both ends of encryption and decryption. Instead, one can safely use EAX″ which allows the re-use of EAX′ implementations. Other provably secure authenticated encryptions, including the original EAX, are also safe options.

Acknowledgments. The authors thank the anonymous FSE 2013 reviewers for helpful comments. This paper is based on the collaboration started at Dagstuhl Seminar 12031, Symmetric Cryptography. We thank participants of the seminar for useful comments, and discussions with Greg Rose were invaluable for writing Sect. 8. We also thank Mihir Bellare and Jeffrey Walton for feedback. The work by Tetsu Iwata was supported by MEXT KAKENHI, Grant-in-Aid for Young Scientists (A), 22680001.

References

1. Comment for EAX Cipher Mode (by Toshiba Corporation). http://csrc.nist.gov/groups/ST/toolkit/BCM/documents/comments/EAX%27/Toshiba_Report2NIST_rev051.pdf
2. Recommendation for Block Cipher Modes of Operation: The CMAC Mode for Authentication. NIST Special Publication 800-38B (2005)
3. American National Standard Protocol Specification For Interfacing to Data Communication Networks. ANSI C12.22-2008 (2008)
4. Measurement Canada, Specification for Local Area Network/Wide Area Network (LAN/WAN) Node Communication Protocol to Complement the Utility Industry End Device Data Tables. MC1222, 2009 (2009)
5. ANSI C12.22, IEEE 1703, and MC12.22 Transport Over IP. RFC 6142 (2011)
6. IEEE Standard for Local Area Network/Wide Area Network (LAN/WAN) Node Communication Protocol to Complement the Utility Industry End Device Data Tables. IEEE 1703–2012 (2012)
7. Bellare, M., Rogaway, P., Wagner, D.: The EAX mode of operation. In: Roy, Meier: [16], pp. 389–407
8. Bleichenbacher, D.: Chosen ciphertext attacks against protocols based on the RSA encryption standard PKCS #1. In: Krawczyk, H. (ed.) CRYPTO 1998. LNCS, vol. 1462, pp. 1–12. Springer, Heidelberg (1998)
9. Iwata, T., Kurosawa, K.: OMAC: one-key CBC MAC. In: Johansson, T. (ed.) FSE 2003. LNCS, vol. 2887, pp. 129–153. Springer, Heidelberg (2003)

10. Iwata, T., Kurosawa, K.: Stronger security bounds for OMAC, TMAC, and XCBC. In: Johansson, T., Maitra, S. (eds.) INDOCRYPT 2003. LNCS, vol. 2904, pp. 402–415. Springer, Heidelberg (2003)

11. Liskov, M., Rivest, R.L., Wagner, D.: Tweakable block ciphers. J. Cryptology **24**(3), 588–613 (2011)

12. Minematsu, K., Lucks, S., Morita, H., Iwata, T.: Cryptanalysis of EAX-Prime. DIAC - Directions in Authenticated Ciphers (2012). http://hyperelliptic.org/DIAC/

13. Moise, A., Beroset, E., Phinney, T., Burns, M.: EAX' cipher mode. NIST Submission, May 2011. http://csrc.nist.gov/groups/ST/toolkit/BCM/documents/proposedmodes/eax-prime/eax-prime-spec.pdf

14. Rogaway, P.: Nonce-based symmetric encryption. In: Roy, Meier: [16], pp. 348–359

15. Rogaway, P., Shrimpton, T.: A provable-security treatment of the key-wrap problem. In: Vaudenay, S. (ed.) EUROCRYPT 2006. LNCS, vol. 4004, pp. 373–390. Springer, Heidelberg (2006)

16. Roy, B., Meier, W. (eds.): FSE 2004. LNCS, vol. 3017. Springer, Heidelberg (2004)

Towards Understanding the Known-Key Security of Block Ciphers

Elena Andreeva[1,2], Andrey Bogdanov[3], and Bart Mennink[1,2](✉)

[1] Department of Electrical Engineering, ESAT/COSIC, KU Leuven, Leuven, Belgium
{elena.andreeva,bart.mennink}@esat.kuleuven.be
[2] iMinds, Leuven, Belgium
[3] Technical University of Denmark, Kongens Lyngby, Denmark
anbog@dtu.dk

Abstract. Known-key distinguishers for block ciphers were proposed by Knudsen and Rijmen at ASIACRYPT 2007 and have been a major research topic in cryptanalysis since then. A formalization of known-key attacks in general is known to be difficult. In this paper, we tackle this problem for the case of block ciphers based on ideal components such as random permutations and random functions as well as propose new generic known-key attacks on generalized Feistel ciphers. We introduce the notion of known-key indifferentiability to capture the security of such block ciphers under a known key. To show its meaningfulness, we prove that the known-key attacks on block ciphers with ideal primitives to date violate security under known-key indifferentiability. On the other hand, to demonstrate its constructiveness, we prove the balanced Feistel cipher with random functions and the multiple Even-Mansour cipher with random permutations known-key indifferentiable for a sufficient number of rounds. We note that known-key indifferentiability is more quickly and tightly attained by multiple Even-Mansour which puts it forward as a construction provably secure against known-key attacks.

Keywords: Block ciphers · Known-key security · Known-key distinguishers · Indifferentiability

1 Introduction

Known-Key Attacks and Our Approach. *Known-key distinguishers* for block ciphers were introduced by Lars Knudsen and Vincent Rijmen at ASIACRYPT 2007 [25]. In the classical single secret-key setting, the attacker does not know the randomly generated key and aims to recover it or build another distinguisher for the cipher. The security model in known-key attacks is quite different though: the attacker knows the randomly drawn key the block cipher operates with and aims to find a structural property for the cipher under the known key – a property which an ideal cipher (a permutation drawn at random) would not have. An example of such a structural property from [25] is

S. Moriai (Ed.): FSE 2013, LNCS 8424, pp. 348–366, 2014.
DOI: 10.1007/978-3-662-43933-3_18, © Springer-Verlag Berlin Heidelberg 2014

as follows. For an n-bit block cipher with a known key, the goal is to find a plaintext/ciphertext pair with the least $s < n/2$ significant bits zero. For the ideal cipher, the adversary needs to invest about 2^s encryptions. A cipher that allows one to find such a pair with much less effort than 2^s encryptions is considered insecure in the known-key model. The seminal work [25] proposes a distinguisher for a permutation-based 7-round Feistel cipher and for 7 rounds of AES.

Since their introduction, known-key attacks have been a major research topic in the symmetric-key community. In explicit terms, there has been a great deal of effort towards refining and extending the distinguishers proposed by Knudsen and Rijmen, including generalizations to Rijndael [34,44], SP-based Feistel ciphers [45–47] and some other constructions [17,35,37]. More importantly though, implicitly, known-key attacks have drawn attention to the security of block ciphers in the *open key model* where the adversary knows or even chooses keys. We think it is to some extent this renewed attention that eventually has given rise to a recent line of cryptanalytic results for the full AES: chosen-key distinguishers [7], related-key attacks [5–7] and single-key biclique meet-in-the-middle attacks [8] — all essentially exploiting the weaknesses of AES in the open key model.

Despite this cumulative impact in the symmetric-key community over the last years, known-key attacks have been known to be difficult to formalize since, formally speaking, it is not clear what an exploitable structural property of a block cipher under a known key is. There have been several attempts to solve the problem in general but we are not aware of any published results here. In this work, we take a slightly different approach to the problem: we focus on known-key distinguishers for *block ciphers based on idealized primitives* such as randomly drawn functions or permutations (examples of such constructions are balanced Feistel ciphers, generalized Feistel ciphers, and (multiple) Even-Mansour ciphers). For such block ciphers, we formulate the new notion of *known-key indifferentiability* which we believe captures the known-key security. To demonstrate its meaningfulness, we prove that the existing known-key attacks on block ciphers with idealized primitives actually lead to the violation of this notion. To demonstrate its constructiveness, we prove Feistel and Even-Mansour known-key indifferentiable for a sufficient number of rounds.

Indifferentiability Framework. Traditionally, block ciphers have been examined under the classical notion of indistinguishability. In that setting a block cipher $\mathcal{C}$ is claimed secure if it is (computationally) indistinguishable from a fixed random permutation $\mathcal{R}$ with the same domain and range as $\mathcal{C}$. In other words, an attacker has to distinguish between $\mathcal{C}$ and $\mathcal{R}$ when placed in either *real* or *ideal* worlds, respectively. The seminal paper [27] of Luby and Rackoff showed that three (four) rounds of the Feistel construction, with independent pseudorandom functions in each round, yield a pseudorandom permutation (strong pseudorandom permutation) where the distinguisher does not have access to the internal functions. This result was followed by a number of works [21,30,36,38–41,52].

On the other hand, the indistinguishability of Even-Mansour cipher was only analyzed by [9,18,51]. Indistinguishability has been established as the *de facto* security notion for block ciphers because in the encryption setting the intended use of the cipher key is in a secret manner; a fact comfortably accommodated by the notion of indistinguishability.

However, block ciphers find numerous and important uses beyond encryption. Block ciphers have been used as a building block for hash functions [19,23,26,31,33,42,50].[1] Here, the block cipher should work towards achieving the desired property of the higher level structure, and the cipher key is not necessarily secret, but known or easy to manipulate by a distinguisher. Clearly, indistinguishability cannot provide strong security guarantees in the open key model: a distinguisher's task becomes trivial once the key is known or chosen. Even more, if for example we decide to examine the indistinguishability "security" of a block cipher built out of an ideal underlying primitive (by explicitly giving to the distinguisher additional access to the internal primitive) in the open key setting, then again the notion indistinguishability falls short. A straightforward distinguishability attack here is possible in only two queries: one (K, M) query to the cipher $\mathcal{C}$ to obtain Y and one message and/or public key dependant x input to the underlying primitive $\mathcal{P}$ to help him compute Y' as a function of $\mathcal{C}_K$. The distinguisher needs to only verify if Y equals Y', which is true for the real construction $\mathcal{C}$ and false with high probability for a random permutation $\mathcal{R}$. The weakness of such an indistinguishability notion that allows access to the internal primitives lays in the fact that there is an obvious "constructive" gap in the ideal world where no communication between $\mathcal{R}$ and $\mathcal{P}$ is provided (as opposed to the real world where $\mathcal{C}$ evaluates on $\mathcal{P}$).

It is here where the notion of *indifferentiability* of Maurer et al. [29] comes into use to allow for: (i) arguing security in the open key model and (ii) enabling the distinguisher to gain access to the input/output behavior of the underlying primitive. The notion of indifferentiability argues the security of an idealized system built upon ideal underlying components, such as random functions or permutations. Initially, indifferentiability was used to analyze hash functions [1–4,11,20], more recently results for block ciphers have also appeared. In [15], Dodis and Puniya proved that the Feistel construction with a super-logarithmic number of rounds (random functions) is *indifferentiable* from an ideal permutation in the *honest-but-curious indifferentiability* model, where the adversary can only query the global Feistel construction and get all the intermediate results. The work of Coron et al. [10] attempted an indifferentiability proof for the Feistel construction with 6 rounds to obtain a fixed random permutation. But it were Holenstein et al. [22] who succeeded in proving a 14 round Feistel construction indifferentiable from a fixed random permutation. Weaker variants of the indifferentiability notion have appeared also in [16,28,53].

In its essence, indifferentiability, similarly to indistinguishability, aims at estimating the adversarial distinguishing advantage between the cipher $\mathcal{C}$ and $\mathcal{R}$ in

---

[1] Many hash functions based on a fixed-key block cipher (also called permutation based hash functions) have also been proposed [32,43,48].

the real and ideal worlds, respectively. Indifferentiability allows the adversary to access the underlying primitive(s) where the underlying ideal primitive(s) in the ideal world is replaced by a simulator $\mathcal{S}$, which aims to both mimic the behavior of the ideal primitive(s) and provide for responses that evaluate correctly when computed under the cipher composition. To fulfill the latter task the simulator is given access to the idealized system $\mathcal{R}$. That functionality of $\mathcal{S}$ allows for overcoming the existing "constructive" gap in the indistinguishability definition.

In fact, indifferentiability was introduced as the right notion to argue security of a block cipher as an ideal cipher, where each key names a new randomly chosen permutation. This theoretical treatment of block ciphers allows one to argue security results in a setting where the adversary freely chooses the key and each chosen key namely fixes a new random permutation. But while this interpretation might accommodate the analysis of block ciphers in the chosen key setting, it appears to be too strong for the case when the key is actually fixed but publicly known and thus the permutation is fixed. This brings us to our newly proposed notion of known-key indifferentiability (iff-KK), which examines the security of a block cipher as a composition from ideal primitives under a known key. Notice that an indifferentiability related view was already taken in the work of Mandal, Patarin and Seurin [28], who introduced the notion sequential indifferentiability and then relate it to that of correlation intractability in the ideal model to argue known key security. Our iff-KK notion is however more general and differs by the fact that it does not limit the adversary to make queries first to the underlying primitive and then to the cipher. Moreover, iff-KK explicitly provides the distinguisher with a public key which directly influences the queries to the block cipher and potentially the ones to the underlying primitives (whenever that is required by composition).

Our Contributions. The contributions of this paper are as follows:

Known-key attacks on type-I generalized Feistel networks. Knudsen-Rijmen [25] proposed known-key distinguishers on 7 rounds of the 2-line (balanced) Feistel network: $\text{GFN}_{(2,7)}$ with any permutations and explicit key addition at the beginning of the round function. We propose a known-key attack on $4\ell - 1$ rounds of an ℓ-line permutation-based type-I generalized Feistel network: $\text{GFN}_{(\ell, 4\ell-1)}$ also with explicit key addition at the beginning of the round function. See Sect. 3.

Known-key indifferentiability. We propose a way to formalize the known-key security of block ciphers based on ideal primitives via the indifferentiability framework and put forward the notion of *known-key indifferentiability* in Sect. 4. By no means we claim to have formalized what a known-key attack is for all block ciphers and all existing attacks, but we do believe to have found an appropriate notion when the underlying components of the cipher are ideal (e.g. random permutations or random functions).

Meaningfulness of known-key indifferentiability. To show that our notion of known-key indifferentiability is useful and meaningful, we prove that the known-key attacks proposed to date on block ciphers with ideal components and explicit key input (namely, the attack by Knudsen-Rijmen on 7-round Feistel with permutations, our attack on $(4\ell - 1)$-round ℓ-line type-I Generalized Feistel construction, and an attack by Coron et al. and Mandal et al. [10,28]) imply the known-key differentiability bound computed in Sect. 5.

Constructiveness of known-key indifferentiability. To demonstrate the constructiveness of our known-key indifferentiability notion, we prove two popular generic block cipher constructions known-key indifferentiable in Sect. 6. First, regarding the general indifferentiability result of [22], we prove that 14 rounds of balanced Feistel with random functions are known-key indifferentiable with a security bounds of $O(q^{16}/2^{n/2})$. Second, we prove that the multiple Even-Mansour construction instantiated with random permutations is perfectly known-key indifferentiable for any number of rounds starting from 1. As opposed to Feistel ciphers, this puts forward the Even-Mansour construction as particularly suitable for building known-key resistant ciphers.

2   Block Cipher Constructions

In this work, we mainly focus on known-key security of generalized Feistel networks and multiple Even-Mansour constructions.

2.1   Generalized Feistel Networks

Feistel networks are very common block cipher designs, dating back to the design of Lucifer [49], and many generalizations of this design appeared in literature. In our work, we focus on type-I networks, as described by Zheng, Matsumoto and Imai [54], simply referring to it as generalized Feistel networks.

The generalized Feistel network $\mathrm{GFN}_{(\ell,r)} : \{0,1\}^k \times \{0,1\}^n \rightarrow \{0,1\}^n$ consists of r evaluations of a fixed random permutation π on n/ℓ bits, and it uses ℓ lines. For $i \in \{1,\ldots,r\}$, the i-th round ψ_i of $\mathrm{GFN}_{(\ell,r)}$ is defined as

$$\psi_i(p_1,\ldots,p_\ell) = (p_2 \oplus \pi(p_1 \oplus k_i), p_3,\ldots,p_\ell,p_1),$$

where $k_1,\ldots,k_r$ denote the round keys derived from the master key K using some key schedule. The function ψ_i is depicted in Fig. 1. In this work, we also consider a slightly modified variant of $\mathrm{GFN}_{(\ell,r)}$, where no keys are XORed with the inputs to the primitive, but instead, r *different* random functions $f_1,\ldots,f_r$ are employed. We refer to this construction as $\mathrm{GFNR}_{(\ell,r)}$, where the i-th round is defined as $\psi_i(p_1,\ldots,p_\ell) = (p_2 \oplus f_i(p_i), p_3,\ldots,p_\ell,p_1)$. Note that by construction, $\mathrm{GFNR}_{(\ell,r)}$ does not have an explicit key input. However, one can append an n-bit subkey to the input of function f_i if explicit key input is needed. In this case, random function f_i maps $(1 + 1/\ell)n$ bits to n/ℓ bits.

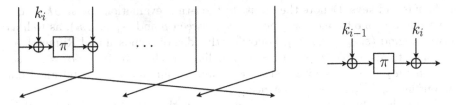

Fig. 1. For $1 \leq i \leq r$, round i of $\text{GFN}_{(\ell,r)}$ with ℓ input lines (left) and EM_r (right, with XOR of previous key additionally included).

Luby and Rackoff showed in the setting where independent pseudorandom functions are used, three (four) rounds of the balanced Feistel construction (that is, $\text{GFNR}_{(2,3)}$ and $\text{GFNR}_{(2,4)}$) yield a pseudorandom permutation (strong pseudorandom permutation) where the distinguisher does not have access to the internal functions. This research line was followed up by a number of works [21, 30, 36, 38–41, 52].

2.2 Multiple Even-Mansour

The multiple Even-Mansour construction relates to the notion of key-alternating ciphers, which itself goes back to Daemen [12–14] and was used in the design of AES. However, it was Knudsen [24] who proposed to instantiate multiple-round key-alternating ciphers with randomly drawn, fixed and public permutations. The single-round key-alternating construction or EM_1 was proposed by Even-Mansour [18].

Multiple Even-Mansour constructions $\text{EM}_r : \{0,1\}^k \times \{0,1\}^n \rightarrow \{0,1\}^n$ consist of r evaluations of a fixed permutation π on n bits, which are separated by key addition. In other words,

$$\text{EM}_r(K, p) = k_r \oplus \pi(\cdots \pi(k_1 \oplus \pi(k_0 \oplus p)) \cdots),$$

where $k_0, \ldots, k_r$ denote the round keys derived from the master key K using some key schedule. For $i \in \{1, \ldots, r\}$, round i of EM_r (together with the addition of the previous key) is depicted in Fig. 1.

In the setting where the r permutations are distinct and the round keys are independently generated and secret, Bogdanov et al. [9] recently proved that EM_r is indistinguishable from a randomly drawn permutation with less than $2^{2n/3}$ queries for $r \geq 2$, and Steinberger [51] improved this result to indistinguishability up to $2^{3n/4}$ queries for $r \geq 3$.

3   Known-Key Attacks on $\text{GFN}_{(\ell,r)}$

Consider $\text{GFN}_{(\ell,4\ell-1)}$ based on $r = 4\ell - 1$ calls to a random invertible function π. Label the incoming lines as $p = (p_1, \ldots, p_\ell)$ and the outgoing ones as $c = (c_1, \ldots, c_\ell)$. Denote by K the random, but known, master key, and let $k_1, \ldots, k_r$

be the r round keys. Denote the inputs to the i-th π-evaluations by $s_i \oplus k_i$. Note that there is a one-to-one correspondence between p and $(s_1, \ldots, s_\ell)$, as well as between c and $(s_{r-\ell+1}, \ldots, s_r)$. Following the idea of Knudsen and Rijmen [25], the goal is to find tuples p, p' with corresponding c, c' that satisfy $p_1 \oplus c_2 = p_1' \oplus c_2'$. Note that $c_2 = s_{r-\ell+2}$ by construction, and in our analysis we refrain from computing $(s_{r-\ell+3}, \ldots, s_r)$ if not needed.

Before describing the inputs p, p' chosen by the attacker, we first explain the attack. Let x be an arbitrary value, and consider $z, \alpha, \beta, \gamma, \delta$ variables to be determined later. Distinguisher D aims at the following intermediate state values

$$s_{\ell+1} = x \oplus k_{\ell+1} \qquad\qquad s_{\ell+1}' = x \oplus \alpha \oplus k_{\ell+1}$$
$$s_{\ell+2} = x \oplus k_{\ell+2} \qquad\qquad s_{\ell+2}' = x \oplus \beta \oplus k_{\ell+2}$$
$$s_{\ell+3} = x \oplus k_{\ell+3} \qquad\qquad s_{\ell+3}' = x \oplus k_{\ell+3}$$
$$\vdots \qquad\qquad\qquad\qquad \vdots$$
$$s_{2\ell-1} = x \oplus k_{2\ell-1} \qquad\qquad s_{2\ell-1}' = x \oplus k_{2\ell-1}$$
$$s_{2\ell} = z \oplus k_{2\ell} \qquad\qquad s_{2\ell}' = z \oplus \gamma \oplus k_{2\ell}$$
$$s_{2\ell+1} = x \oplus \delta \oplus k_{2\ell+1} \qquad\qquad s_{2\ell+1}' = x \oplus k_{2\ell+1} \, .$$

Here, we point out two exceptions from this general (otherwise) description of the attack. Firstly, for $\ell = 2$, s_4 and s_4' adapt the value of $s_{2\ell}$ and $s_{2\ell}'$, and similarly for s_5 and s_5'. Secondly, for $\ell = 3$, s_6 and s_6' follow the notation of $s_{2\ell}$ and $s_{2\ell}'$, and similarly for later state values. For $\ell > 3$ the description is non-ambiguous. Then, $s_\ell, \ldots, s_1$ and $s_{2\ell+2}, \ldots, s_r$ are computed in the straightforward way (i.e. using $s_i = s_{i+\ell} \oplus f(s_{i+\ell-1} \oplus k_{i+\ell-1})$), and similar for the s'-values. For $\ell > 3$, the general attack is depicted in Fig. 2. By construction, z and γ need to be such that $\pi(z) = \delta \oplus k_{\ell+1} \oplus k_{2\ell+1}$ (from $s_{\ell+1}$, $s_{2\ell}$, and $s_{2\ell+1}$) and $\pi(z \oplus \gamma) = \alpha \oplus k_{\ell+1} \oplus k_{2\ell+1}$ (from $s_{\ell+1}'$, $s_{2\ell}'$, and $s_{2\ell+1}'$). For the rest of the attack, we distinguish among $\ell = 2$, $\ell = 3$, and $\ell > 3$.

$\ell = 2$. Starting with $\ell = 2$ (this is in fact the attack of Knudsen and Rijmen [25]). Note that β does not occur in the analysis. We simply set $\gamma = 0$, and thus $\delta = \alpha$ and we require $\pi(z) = \alpha \oplus k_3 \oplus k_5$. It remains to determine the value α. We have:

$$p_1 = s_1 = x \oplus k_3 \oplus \pi(z \oplus k_2 \oplus k_4 \oplus \pi(x))$$
$$c_2 = s_7 = x \oplus \alpha \oplus k_5 \oplus \pi(z \oplus k_4 \oplus k_6 \oplus \pi(x \oplus \alpha))$$
$$p_1' = s_1' = x \oplus \alpha \oplus k_3 \oplus \pi(z \oplus k_2 \oplus k_4 \oplus \pi(x \oplus \alpha))$$
$$c_2' = s_7' = x \oplus k_5 \oplus \pi(z \oplus k_4 \oplus k_6 \oplus \pi(x)) \, .$$

As demonstrated in [25], $p_1 \oplus c_2 = p_1' \oplus c_2'$ holds if $\alpha = x \oplus \pi^{-1}(\pi(x) \oplus k_2 \oplus k_6)$. The tuples p and p' queried by D are easily derivable and not discussed.

$\ell = 3$. Next we consider $\ell = 3$. This case turns out to require a special treatment. We have:

$$p_1 = s_1 = x \oplus k_4 \oplus \pi(z \oplus k_3 \oplus k_6 \oplus \pi(x))$$
$$c_2 = s_{10} = x \oplus \delta \oplus k_7 \oplus \pi(z \oplus k_6 \oplus k_9 \oplus \pi(x \oplus k_5 \oplus k_8 \oplus \pi(x \oplus \delta)))$$
$$p_1' = s_1' = x \oplus \alpha \oplus k_4 \oplus \pi(z \oplus \gamma \oplus k_3 \oplus k_6 \oplus \pi(x \oplus \beta))$$
$$c_2' = s_{10}' = x \oplus k_7 \oplus \pi(z \oplus \gamma \oplus k_6 \oplus k_9 \oplus \pi(x \oplus \beta \oplus k_5 \oplus k_8 \oplus \pi(x))) \,.$$

Note that

$$p_1 \oplus c_2 = \pi(z) \oplus \pi(z \oplus k_3 \oplus k_6 \oplus \pi(x)) \oplus$$
$$\pi(z \oplus k_6 \oplus k_9 \oplus \pi(x \oplus k_5 \oplus k_8 \oplus \pi(x \oplus \delta)))$$
$$p_1' \oplus c_2' = \pi(z \oplus \gamma) \oplus \pi(z \oplus \gamma \oplus k_3 \oplus k_6 \oplus \pi(x \oplus \beta)) \oplus$$
$$\pi(z \oplus \gamma \oplus k_6 \oplus k_9 \oplus \pi(x \oplus \beta \oplus k_5 \oplus k_8 \oplus \pi(x))) \,.$$

Our goal is these values to satisfy $p_1 \oplus c_2 = p_1' \oplus c_2'$, but the same approach as for $\ell = 2$ (and [25]) does not work here. However, if we take δ such that $\pi(x \oplus k_5 \oplus k_8 \oplus \pi(x \oplus \delta)) = k_6 \oplus k_9$, and β such that $\pi(x \oplus \beta \oplus k_5 \oplus k_8 \oplus \pi(x)) = k_6 \oplus k_9$, and $\gamma = \pi(x) \oplus \pi(x \oplus \beta)$, the desired equation is satisfied. Then, by construction, $z = \pi^{-1}(\delta \oplus k_4 \oplus k_7)$ and $\alpha = \pi(z \oplus \gamma) \oplus k_4 \oplus k_7$. The tuples p and p' queried by D are easily derivable and not discussed.

$\ell > 3$. Remains to consider the general case, $\ell > 3$. This attack is visualized in Fig. 2. In this case, we simply set $\gamma = 0$, and thus $\delta = \alpha$ and we require $\pi(z) = \alpha \oplus k_{\ell+1} \oplus k_{2\ell+1}$. It remains to determine the values α and β. We find:

$$p_1 = s_1 = x \oplus k_{\ell+1} \oplus \pi(z \oplus k_\ell \oplus k_{2\ell} \oplus \pi(x))$$
$$c_2 = s_{3\ell+1} = x \oplus \alpha \oplus k_{2\ell+1} \oplus \pi(z \oplus k_{2\ell} \oplus k_{3\ell} \oplus \tilde{\pi}(K, x, \alpha))$$
$$p_1' = s_1' = x \oplus \alpha \oplus k_{\ell+1} \oplus \pi(z \oplus k_\ell \oplus k_{2\ell} \oplus \pi(x))$$
$$c_2' = s_{3\ell+1}' = x \oplus k_{2\ell+1} \oplus \pi(z \oplus k_{2\ell} \oplus k_{3\ell} \oplus \tilde{\pi}'(K, x, \alpha, \beta)) \,,$$

where

$$\tilde{\pi}(K, x, \alpha) = \pi(x \oplus k_{2\ell-1} \oplus k_{3\ell-1} \oplus \cdots \pi(x \oplus k_{\ell+2} \oplus k_{2\ell+2} \oplus$$
$$\pi(x \oplus k_{\ell+1} \oplus k_{2\ell+1} \oplus \pi(x \oplus \alpha))) \cdots)$$
$$\tilde{\pi}'(K, x, \alpha, \beta) = \pi(x \oplus k_{2\ell-1} \oplus k_{3\ell-1} \oplus \cdots \pi(x \oplus \beta \oplus k_{\ell+2} \oplus k_{2\ell+2} \oplus$$
$$\pi(x \oplus \alpha \oplus k_{\ell+1} \oplus k_{2\ell+1} \oplus \pi(x))) \cdots) \,.$$

Note that

$$p_1 \oplus c_2 \oplus p_1' \oplus c_2' = \pi(z \oplus k_{2\ell} \oplus k_{3\ell} \oplus \tilde{\pi}(K, x, \alpha)) \oplus$$
$$\pi(z \oplus k_{2\ell} \oplus k_{3\ell} \oplus \tilde{\pi}'(K, x, \alpha, \beta)) \,.$$

We now put α to satisfy $\tilde{\pi}(K, x, \alpha) = k_{2\ell} \oplus k_{3\ell}$ (note that by the construction of $\tilde{\pi}$ this is really possible), and β to satisfy $\tilde{\pi}'(K, x, \alpha, \beta) = k_{2\ell} \oplus k_{3\ell}$ for this given

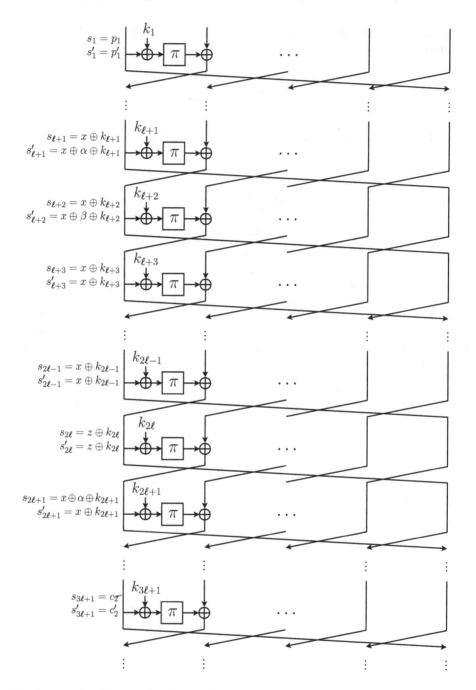

Fig. 2. Attack of Sect. 3 for $\ell > 3$. Parameter x can be freely chosen, parameters $\alpha\ (= \beta)$, γ, and z depend on x and the round keys, and are explained in the text.

α. This choice is well-defined: α is defined as a function of K and x, while β and z are a function of K, x, and α. The tuples p and p' queried by D are easily derivable and not discussed.

Conclusion of the attack. Once x is arbitrarily chosen, $z, \alpha, \beta, \gamma, \delta$ are easily computable from K and x. For $\mathrm{GFN}_{(\ell, 4\ell-1)}$, the resulting plaintexts and ciphertexts satisfy $p_1 \oplus c_2 = p'_1 \oplus c'_2$ with probability 1. This equation is, however, satisfied by an ideal cipher $\mathcal{R}$ with probability at most $1/2^{n/\ell}$. This completes the attack.

4   Known-Key Indifferentiability for Block Ciphers

Consider a composed system $\mathcal{C} : \{0,1\}^k \times \{0,1\}^n \to \{0,1\}^n$ based on an underlying idealized primitive $\mathcal{P} : \{0,1\}^\kappa \times \{0,1\}^x \to \{0,1\}^y$. Here, $\mathcal{C}$ is always a keyed primitive (i.e., a block cipher), but $\mathcal{P}$ may or may not be keyed, and the key space may differ from that of $\mathcal{C}$. Furthermore, depending on $\mathcal{C}$, $\mathcal{P}$ denotes either a single or a composition of multiple idealized primitives $\mathcal{P}_i$.

Where the classical notion of indistinguishability is established to provide strong security guarantees in the *secret* key setting, this is not true in the *open* key model where chosen or known keys come into play. In the latter setting, one can benefit from the known indifferentiability definition introduced in the work of Maurer et al. [29] and adapted for the case of hash functions by Coron et al. [11]. Building upon these results, we propose a new definition of known-key security. Our definition differs from earlier weaker versions of indifferentiability [11,16,28,53] by its generality and the fact that it explicitly provides the distinguishing adversary with a public key under which it queries both the block cipher and potentially the underlying primitives (if that is required by composition). It moreover, does not limit the adversary's type of queries, as is the case for leaky, public, and sequential indifferentiability.

We thus propose the following formalization:

Definition 1. *Let $\mathcal{C}$ be a composed primitive with oracle access to an ideal primitive $\mathcal{P}$. Let $\mathcal{R}$ be an ideal primitive with the same domain and range as $\mathcal{C}$. Let $\mathcal{S}$ be a simulator with the same domain and range as $\mathcal{P}$ with oracle access to $\mathcal{R}$ and making at most $q_\mathcal{S}$ queries, and let D be a distinguisher making at most q_D queries. The known-key indifferentiability advantage $\mathbf{Adv}_{\mathcal{C},\mathcal{S}}^{\text{iff-KK}}(D)$ of D is defined as*

$$\left| \Pr\left(K \xleftarrow{\$} \{0,1\}^k; \mathsf{D}^{\mathcal{C}^\mathcal{P},\mathcal{P}}(K) = 1 \right) - \Pr\left(K \xleftarrow{\$} \{0,1\}^k; \mathsf{D}^{\mathcal{R},\mathcal{S}^\mathcal{R}}(K) = 1 \right) \right|.$$

By $\mathbf{Adv}_{\mathcal{C},\mathcal{S}}^{\text{iff-KK}}(q_D)$ we denote the maximum advantage of any distinguisher making at most q_D queries to its oracles. Primitive $\mathcal{C}$ is said to be $(q_D; q_\mathcal{S}; \varepsilon)$ indifferentiable from $\mathcal{R}$ if $\mathbf{Adv}_{\mathcal{C},\mathcal{S}}^{\text{iff-KK}}(q_D) < \varepsilon$.

In this indifferentiability experiment, the distinguisher is provided with access to either of two worlds: *left (real)* and *right (ideal)*. In the *left* world the distinguisher D has a query access to the composed construction $\mathcal{C}$ and the primitive $\mathcal{P}$, while in the *right* world D accesses the ideal primitive $\mathcal{R}$ and the simulator $\mathcal{S}$,

Table 1. Interface of D with the composed oracle $\mathcal{O}_1$ ($\mathcal{C}$ in the left world, $\mathcal{R}$ in the right world) in the standard indifferentiability setting and in Definition 1. For both security definitions, the interface with the right oracle $\mathcal{O}_2$ is the same: D has full access to $\mathcal{O}_2$.

Indifferentiability	Forward O_1 query	Inverse O_1 query
Indifferentiability (iff)	$(K, M) \longrightarrow C = \mathcal{O}_1(K, M)$	$(K, C) \longrightarrow M = \mathcal{O}_1^{-1}(K, C)$
Known-key indiff. (iff-KK) $(K \xleftarrow{\$} \{0,1\}^k$ fixed, public)	$M \longrightarrow C = \mathcal{O}_1(K, M)$	$C \longrightarrow M = \mathcal{O}_1^{-1}(K, C)$

respectively. In case the composed primitive $\mathcal{C}$ is invertible, D obtains access to it in both forward and backward (inverse) direction. We refer to $\mathcal{C}$ and $\mathcal{R}$ as the "composed" oracles $\mathcal{O}_1$, and these oracles always respond under the known-key K. Hence, D can forward query a message input M to receive $C = \mathcal{C}(K, M)$ in the left world and $C = \mathcal{R}(M)$ in the right world (here the randomly chosen key K implicitly fixes an instance of $\mathcal{R}$), or D can also backward query C to receive $M = \mathcal{C}^{-1}(K, C)$ and $M = \mathcal{R}^{-1}(M)$ in the left and right worlds, respectively. We refer to $\mathcal{P}$ and $\mathcal{S}$ as the "small" oracles $\mathcal{O}_2$, to which D has full access (i.e., even if $\mathcal{C}$ is designed to query $\mathcal{P}$ only on the key K), but we note that $\mathcal{S}$ knows this public key K. From a practical point of view, the full access to the small oracles makes perfect sense, as the original idea of indifferentiability is that the distinguisher may know the underlying structure, and thus, use the underlying primitive as it wishes.

The particular way of allowing the key input to the composed primitive to be always the known key K but the key input to the small primitive to be anything, sets this known-key indifferentiability definition apart from existing versions of indifferentiability like [11,16,28,53]. In more detail, in Table 1, we compare the interfaces in Definition 1 with the ones used in the indifferentiability definition (see [10,22] for its block cipher instantiation). As it turns out, this change makes our definition particularly suitable for analyzing known-key security. In Proposition 1, we prove that iff implies iff-KK. Moreover, in Sect. 6 we also show a counterexample that an implication in the opposite direction does not hold.

Proposition 1. *If $\mathcal{C}$ is $(q_D; q_S; \varepsilon)$ iff-secure block cipher, then it is $(q_D; q_S; \varepsilon)$ iff-KK-secure.*

Proof. Let $\mathcal{S}$ be a simulator such that for any distinguisher D making at most q_D queries, the iff advantage is at most ε. We define $\mathcal{S}' = \mathcal{S}$ to be the simulator for the iff-KK security. We prove that for any iff-KK distinguisher D' making at most q_D queries, we have $\mathbf{Adv}_{\mathcal{C},\mathcal{S}'}^{\text{iff-KK}}(D') < \varepsilon$.

Let D' be any such distinguisher. We build an iff distinguisher D using D' that has the same advantage in breaking $\mathcal{C}$. Distinguisher D simulates the environment for D' as follows: firstly, it selects uniformly at random a key $K \xleftarrow{\$} \{0,1\}^k$ and runs D' on input K; then it forwards all queries by D' to its own oracles. If D' succeeds in distinguishing the left and right worlds, D succeeds as well. In particular, we have $\mathbf{Adv}_{C,S'}^{\text{iff-KK}}(D') = \mathbf{Adv}_{C,S}^{\text{iff}}(D) < \varepsilon$.

5   Known-Key Indifferentiability is Meaningful

Consider any known-key distinguishing attack on a block cipher C with idealized primitive P. Let $K \in \{0,1\}^k$ be a known key. A classical known-key distinguisher for a function $C(K, \cdot)$ based on ideal primitive P operates as follows: it makes q queries to its primitives, and then it outputs 1 if the queries show some "unexpected" relation, which means that such relation should not hold for a random primitive R with the same domain and range of C. We formalize and translate such known-key distinguisher D to a distinguisher for the indifferentiability notion iff-KK as follows. Let S be a simulator. In advance of making any queries, this distinguisher fixes a predicate $\varphi(Q)$, where Q is a list of query tuples. Then, the distinguisher makes q_D queries to its left and right oracles, to obtain a query history Q_{q_D} of size q_D. If $\varphi(Q_{q_D})$ holds, it outputs 1, and otherwise it outputs 0. Clearly, D bases its decision solely on the predicate $\varphi(Q_{q_D})$, and by Definition 1:

$$\mathbf{Adv}_{C,S}^{\text{iff-KK}}(q_D) \geq \mathbf{Adv}_{C,S}^{\text{iff-KK}}(D)$$
$$= \left| \Pr\left(\varphi(Q_{q_D}) \text{ for } C^P, P \right) - \Pr\left(\varphi(Q_{q_D}) \text{ for } R, S^R \right) \right|. \quad (1)$$

Now, in classical known-key distinguishing attacks, the first probability is (close to) 1, while the second probability is significantly smaller. Note that for the second probability, the distinguisher may ask queries to the simulator S, but in order for S to be successful, it will try to consult R as often as possible and queries to S can consequently be seen as indirect queries to R.

We demonstrate this approach using the attack of Sect. 3 on $GFN_{(\ell, 4\ell-1)}$ and an attack on $GFNR_{(2,5)}$ by Coron et al. and Mandal et al. [10, 28], therewith demonstrating that this approach applies to *any* known-key distinguishing attack known in literature.

Theorem 1. *Let C be $GFN_{(\ell, r)} : \{0,1\}^k \times \{0,1\}^n \to \{0,1\}^n$ for $r = 4\ell - 1$ with oracle access to an ideal primitive $P = \pi : \{0,1\}^{n/\ell} \to \{0,1\}^{n/\ell}$ (cf. Sect. 3). Let R denote an ideal cipher with the same domain and range as C. For any simulator S that makes at most $q_S \leq 2^{n-1} - 1$ queries to R, there exists a distinguisher D that makes at most $2r + 2$ queries to its oracles, such that*

$$\mathbf{Adv}_{C,S}^{\text{iff-KK}}(D) \geq 1 - \frac{q_S^2 + 2}{2^{n/\ell}}.$$

Proof. Let S be any simulator making at most q_S queries to R. Let $K \xleftarrow{\$} \{0,1\}^k$ be the given key, and $k_1, \ldots, k_r$ be the round keys. We construct a distinguisher D that differentiates (C, P) from (R, S) with high probability. Define predicate $\varphi(Q)$ as follows:

$$\exists\, (p_1 \ldots p_\ell; c_1 \ldots c_\ell), (p_1' \ldots p_\ell'; c_1' \ldots c_\ell') \in Q \text{ such that } p_1 \oplus c_2 = p_1' \oplus c_2'. \quad (2)$$

The distinguisher makes $2r$ queries to $\mathcal{P}$ as explained in Sect. 3. Then, it makes its two corresponding queries to the left oracle, which results in $\mathcal{Q}_{2r+2}$ containing exactly two left oracle queries. By construction,

$$\Pr\left(\varphi(\mathcal{Q}_{2r+2}) \text{ for } \mathrm{GFN}^{\mathcal{P}}_{(\ell,r)}, \mathcal{P}\right) = 1.$$

Remains to consider the probability $\varphi(\mathcal{Q}_{2r+2})$ holds in the other game. Suppose the simulator makes $q_{\mathcal{S}}$ queries, denote by $\mathcal{Q}^{\mathcal{S}}$ the query history of $\mathcal{S}$ to $\mathcal{R}$. By basic probability theory:

$$\Pr\left(\varphi(\mathcal{Q}_{2r+2}) \text{ for } \mathcal{R}, \mathcal{S}^{\mathcal{R}}\right) = \Pr\left(\varphi(\mathcal{Q}_{2r+2}) \text{ for } \mathcal{R}, \mathcal{S}^{\mathcal{R}} \mid \varphi(\mathcal{Q}^{\mathcal{S}})\right) \Pr\left(\varphi(\mathcal{Q}^{\mathcal{S}})\right) +$$
$$\Pr\left(\varphi(\mathcal{Q}_{2r+2}) \text{ for } \mathcal{R}, \mathcal{S}^{\mathcal{R}} \mid \neg\varphi(\mathcal{Q}^{\mathcal{S}})\right) \Pr\left(\neg\varphi(\mathcal{Q}^{\mathcal{S}})\right)$$
$$\le \Pr\left(\varphi(\mathcal{Q}^{\mathcal{S}})\right) + \Pr\left(\varphi(\mathcal{Q}_{2r+2}) \text{ for } \mathcal{R}, \mathcal{S}^{\mathcal{R}} \mid \neg\varphi(\mathcal{Q}^{\mathcal{S}})\right).$$

We first consider $\Pr\left(\varphi(\mathcal{Q}^{\mathcal{S}})\right)$. Any two queries the simulator makes to $\mathcal{R}$ satisfy $p_1 \oplus c_2 = p'_1 \oplus c'_2$ with probability at most $\frac{2^{n-n/\ell}}{2^n-q_{\mathcal{S}}}$, as any query is randomly drawn from a set of size at least $2^n - q_{\mathcal{S}}$. Consequently, as the simulator makes $q_{\mathcal{S}}$ queries, and any couple may result in a collision,

$$\Pr\left(\varphi(\mathcal{Q}^{\mathcal{S}})\right) \le \binom{q_{\mathcal{S}}}{2} \frac{2^{n-n/\ell}}{2^n - q_{\mathcal{S}}}.$$

Regarding the second probability: conditioned on $\neg\varphi(\mathcal{Q}^{\mathcal{S}})$, (2) may still hold if the two queries the distinguisher makes to $\mathcal{R}$ accidentally satisfy it. As the second oracle query is drawn from a set of size at least $2^n - (q_{\mathcal{S}}+1)$, the queries satisfy $p_1 \oplus c_2 = p'_1 \oplus c'_2$ with probability at most $\frac{2^{n-n/\ell}}{2^n-(q_{\mathcal{S}}+1)}$. Concluding, we find

$$\Pr\left(\varphi(\mathcal{Q}_{2r+2}) \text{ for } \mathcal{R}, \mathcal{S}^{\mathcal{R}}\right) \le \left(\binom{q_{\mathcal{S}}}{2}+1\right)\frac{2^{n-n/\ell}}{2^n-(q_{\mathcal{S}}+1)} \le \frac{q_{\mathcal{S}}^2+2}{2^{n/\ell}}.$$

where we use that $2^n - (q_{\mathcal{S}}+1) \ge 2^{n-1}$ for $q_{\mathcal{S}} + 1 \le 2^{n-1}$. Hence, we find $\mathbf{Adv}^{\text{iff-KK}}_{\mathcal{C},\mathcal{S}}(2r+2) \ge 1 - \frac{q_{\mathcal{S}}^2+2}{2^{n/\ell}}.$ □

Next we consider a distinguishing attack described in [10] and [28, Appendix C].

Theorem 2. *Let $\mathcal{C}$ be $\mathrm{GFNR}_{(2,5)} : \{0,1\}^n \to \{0,1\}^n$ with oracle access to 5 ideal primitives $\mathcal{P} = (f_1,\ldots,f_5)$ with $f_i : \{0,1\}^{n/2} \to \{0,1\}^{n/2}$ (see Fig. 3).*

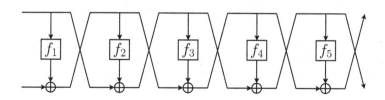

Fig. 3. $\mathrm{GFNR}_{(2,5)}$ (see Theorem 2)

Let $\mathcal{R}$ denote an ideal permutation with the same domain and range as $\mathcal{C}$. For any simulator $\mathcal{S}$ that makes at most $q_S \leq 2^{n-1} - 1$ queries to $\mathcal{R}$, there exists a distinguisher D that makes at most 24 queries to its oracles, such that

$$\mathbf{Adv}^{\text{iff-KK}}_{\mathcal{C},\mathcal{S}}(D) \geq 1 - \frac{q_S^4 + 2}{2^{n/2}}.$$

Proof. Denote the inputs of a $\text{GFNR}_{(2,5)}$ evaluation by (p, r) and the outputs by (c, d). The attack of [10] and [28, Appendix C] describes a way to find 4 plaintext-ciphertext pairs that satisfy $p_1 \oplus p_2 \oplus p_3 \oplus p_4 = d_1 \oplus d_2 \oplus d_3 \oplus d_4 = 0$. As in Theorem 1, predicate $\varphi(\mathcal{Q})$ is defined as follows:

$$\exists (p_1, r_1; c_1, d_1), \ldots, (p_4, r_4; c_4, d_4) \in \mathcal{Q} \text{ such that}$$
$$p_1 \oplus p_2 \oplus p_3 \oplus p_4 = d_1 \oplus d_2 \oplus d_3 \oplus d_4 = 0. \quad (3)$$

The distinguisher makes 20 queries to $\mathcal{P}$ (as in the proof of Theorem 1), and the four corresponding queries to the left oracle, which results in $\mathcal{Q}_{24}$. By construction, $\varphi(\mathcal{Q}_{24})$ holds for $\text{GFN}^{\mathcal{P}}_{(2,5)}, \mathcal{P}$ with probability 1, and it remains to consider the probability $\varphi(\mathcal{Q}_{24})$ holds in the other game. Similar to the proof of Theorem 1, we find

$$\Pr\left(\varphi(\mathcal{Q}_{24}) \text{ for } \mathcal{R}, \mathcal{S}^{\mathcal{R}}\right) \leq \binom{q_S}{4} \frac{2^{n/2}}{2^n - q_S} + \frac{2^{n/2}}{2^n - (q_S + 1)},$$

and hence we obtain $\mathbf{Adv}^{\text{iff-KK}}_{\mathcal{C},\mathcal{S}}(24) \geq 1 - \frac{q_S^4 + 2}{2^{n/2}}$, for $q_S + 1 \leq 2^{n-1}$. $\square$

6   Known-Key Indifferentiability is Constructive

The next obvious question then is, whether there exist block cipher constructions that are known-key indifferentiable from an ideal cipher. In this section, we prove that this is indeed the case.

First, we consider generalized Feistel networks. In [22], Holenstein et al. considered $\text{GFNR}_{(2,14)}$, a variant of $\text{GFN}_{(2,14)}$ where the keys are not XORed to get the input to the primitives, but are used to obtain 14 different random functions (see also Sect. 2), and proved that this construction has indifferentiable advantage from an ideal cipher of $O(q^{16}/2^{n/2})$. Here, we refer to standard indifferentiability (see Table 1 for the interfaces in this notion). Using this result, we obtain the following theorem.

Theorem 3. *Let $\mathcal{C}$ be $\text{GFNR}_{(2,14)}$ with oracle access to an ideal primitive $\mathcal{P}$ consisting of 14 random functions (and where no round keys are XORed). Let D be an arbitrary distinguisher making at most q queries. Then there exists a simulator $\mathcal{S}$ such that*

$$\mathbf{Adv}^{\text{iff-KK}}_{\mathcal{C},\mathcal{S}}(D) = O(q^{16}/2^{n/2}),$$

where $\mathcal{S}$ makes at most $1400q^8$ queries to $\mathcal{R}$ and runs in time $O(q^8)$.

Proof. Holenstein et al. [22] proved that for $\mathcal{C}$ being $\mathrm{GFN}_{(2,14)}$ any distinguisher making at most q queries, has indifferentiability an advantage of $\mathbf{Adv}^{\mathrm{iff}}_{\mathcal{C},\mathcal{S}}(\mathsf{D}) = O(q^{16}/2^{n/2})$. Their simulator makes at most $1400q^8$ queries to $\mathcal{R}$ and runs in time $O(q^8)$. From Proposition 1, we conclude that the same bound holds for the iff-KK-security of $\mathrm{GFN}_{(2,14)}$, which completes the proof. $\qquad\square$

Next, we consider multiple Even-Mansour, and show that already with one round, this construction turns out to be optimally known-key indifferentiable secure.

Theorem 4. *Let for $r \geq 1$, $\mathcal{C}_r$ be EM_r with oracle access to an ideal primitive $\mathcal{P}$ consisting of r random permutations. Let D be an arbitrary distinguisher making at most q queries. Then there exists a simulator $\mathcal{S}$ such that*

$$\mathbf{Adv}^{\mathrm{iff\text{-}KK}}_{\mathcal{C},\mathcal{S}}(\mathsf{D}) = 0\,,$$

where $\mathcal{S}$ makes at most q queries to $\mathcal{R}$ and runs in time $O(q)$.

Proof. First, consider $r = 1$. Let $k_0 \| k_1 \xleftarrow{\$} \{0,1\}^{2n}$ be the public key. Intuitively, as soon as $k_0 \| k_1$ is fixed, $\mathcal{C}$ behaves perfectly as a random permutation as $\mathcal{P}$ is. Formally, simulator $\mathcal{S}$ uses oracle $\mathcal{R}$ to respond with $Y = \mathcal{R}(X \oplus k_0) \oplus k_1$ on a forward query X; and uses its oracle $\mathcal{R}$ to respond with $X = \mathcal{R}^{-1}(Y \oplus k_1) \oplus k_0$ on an inverse query Y. By construction, all queries made by the distinguisher to $\mathcal{S}$ are exactly in correspondence with the random primitive $\mathcal{R}$ and D cannot distinguish.

Now, for $r > 1$, the proof is not much different, although the simulator needs to do some more bookkeeping. It responds randomly at every query, except when it completes a chain, an evaluation $EM_r(K, p)$, in which case it adapts its response to fit the random oracle. Note that, as the key is fixed, it can be considered constant, and different EM_r evaluations never collide somewhere in the middle. In other words, for any $i \in \{1, \dots, r\}$ the following holds: if π_i denotes the permutation in the i-th round, then one input-output-tuple of π_i corresponds to exactly one $\mathcal{C}(K, \cdot)$ evaluation, and vice versa. $\qquad\square$

We note that EM_1 is *not* iff-secure. Briefly, let $\mathcal{S}$ be any simulator making at most $q_{\mathcal{S}}$ queries. We construct a distinguisher D as follows. Here, $\mathcal{O}_1$ denotes its composed oracle ($\mathcal{C}$ or $\mathcal{R}$) and $\mathcal{O}_2$ its primitive oracle ($\mathcal{P}$ or $\mathcal{S}$). Firstly, D chooses arbitrary key $k_0 \| k_1$ and message M, and queries $Y \leftarrow \mathcal{O}_2(M \oplus k_0)$ and $C \leftarrow \mathcal{O}_1(k_0 \| k_1, M)$. Then, if $C = Y \oplus k_1$, then D outputs 1, otherwise it outputs 0. Note that $C = Y \oplus k_1$ holds with probability 1 in the real world, and with probability $1/2^n$ in the ideal world (as in this setting the simulator does not know k_1). Using Theorem 4, this renders a separation between iff-KK and iff, as already mentioned in Sect. 4.

Acknowledgments. This work has been funded in part by the IAP Program P6/26 BCRYPT of the Belgian State (Belgian Science Policy), in part by the European Commission through the ICT program under contract ICT-2007-216676 ECRYPT II, and in part by the Research Council K.U.Leuven: GOA TENSE. Elena Andreeva is supported by a Postdoctoral Fellowship from the Flemish Research Foundation (FWO-Vlaanderen). Bart Mennink is supported by a Ph.D. Fellowship from the Institute for the Promotion of Innovation through Science and Technology in Flanders (IWT-Vlaanderen).

References

1. Andreeva, E., Mennink, B., Preneel, B.: On the indifferentiability of the Grøstl hash function. In: Garay, J.A., De Prisco, R. (eds.) SCN 2010. LNCS, vol. 6280, pp. 88–105. Springer, Heidelberg (2010)
2. Bellare, M., Ristenpart, T.: Multi-property-preserving hash domain extension and the EMD transform. In: Lai, X., Chen, K. (eds.) ASIACRYPT 2006. LNCS, vol. 4284, pp. 299–314. Springer, Heidelberg (2006)
3. Bertoni, G., Daemen, J., Peeters, M., Van Assche, G.: On the indifferentiability of the sponge construction. In: Smart, N.P. (ed.) EUROCRYPT 2008. LNCS, vol. 4965, pp. 181–197. Springer, Heidelberg (2008)
4. Bhattacharyya, R., Mandal, A., Nandi, M.: Security analysis of the mode of JH hash function. In: Hong, S., Iwata, T. (eds.) FSE 2010. LNCS, vol. 6147, pp. 168–191. Springer, Heidelberg (2010)
5. Biryukov, A., Dunkelman, O., Keller, N., Khovratovich, D., Shamir, A.: Key recovery attacks of practical complexity on AES-256 variants with up to 10 rounds. In: Gilbert, H. (ed.) EUROCRYPT 2010. LNCS, vol. 6110, pp. 299–319. Springer, Heidelberg (2010)
6. Biryukov, A., Khovratovich, D.: Related-key cryptanalysis of the full AES-192 and AES-256. In: Matsui, M. (ed.) ASIACRYPT 2009. LNCS, vol. 5912, pp. 1–18. Springer, Heidelberg (2009)
7. Biryukov, A., Khovratovich, D., Nikolić, I.: Distinguisher and related-key attack on the full AES-256. In: Halevi, S. (ed.) CRYPTO 2009. LNCS, vol. 5677, pp. 231–249. Springer, Heidelberg (2009)
8. Bogdanov, A., Khovratovich, D., Rechberger, C.: Biclique cryptanalysis of the full AES. In: Lee, D.H., Wang, X. (eds.) ASIACRYPT 2011. LNCS, vol. 7073, pp. 344–371. Springer, Heidelberg (2011)
9. Bogdanov, A., Knudsen, L.R., Leander, G., Standaert, F.-X., Steinberger, J., Tischhauser, E.: Key-alternating ciphers in a provable setting: encryption using a small number of public permutations. In: Pointcheval, D., Johansson, T. (eds.) EUROCRYPT 2012. LNCS, vol. 7237, pp. 45–62. Springer, Heidelberg (2012)
10. Coron, J.-S., Patarin, J., Seurin, Y.: The random oracle model and the ideal cipher model are equivalent. In: Wagner, D. (ed.) CRYPTO 2008. LNCS, vol. 5157, pp. 1–20. Springer, Heidelberg (2008)
11. Coron, J.-S., Dodis, Y., Malinaud, C., Puniya, P.: Merkle-Damgård revisited: how to construct a hash function. In: Shoup, V. (ed.) CRYPTO 2005. LNCS, vol. 3621, pp. 430–448. Springer, Heidelberg (2005)
12. Daemen, J., Govaerts, R., Vandewalle, J.: Correlation matrices. In: Preneel, B. (ed.) FSE 1994. LNCS, vol. 1008, pp. 275–285. Springer, Heidelberg (1995)
13. Daemen, J., Rijmen, V.: The wide trail design strategy. In: Honary, B. (ed.) Cryptography and Coding 2001. LNCS, vol. 2260, pp. 222–238. Springer, Heidelberg (2001)
14. Daemen, J.: The Design of Rijndael: AES - The Advanced Encryption Standard. Springer, Heidelberg (2002)

15. Dodis, Y., Puniya, P.: On the relation between the ideal cipher and the random oracle models. In: Halevi, S., Rabin, T. (eds.) TCC 2006. LNCS, vol. 3876, pp. 184–206. Springer, Heidelberg (2006)
16. Dodis, Y., Ristenpart, T., Shrimpton, T.: Salvaging Merkle-Damgård for practical applications. In: Joux, A. (ed.) EUROCRYPT 2009. LNCS, vol. 5479, pp. 371–388. Springer, Heidelberg (2009)
17. Dong, L., Wu, W., Wu, S., Zou, J.: Known-key distinguisher on round-reduced 3D block cipher. In: Jung, S., Yung, M. (eds.) WISA 2011. LNCS, vol. 7115, pp. 55–69. Springer, Heidelberg (2012)
18. Even, S., Mansour, Y.: A construction of a cipher from a single pseudorandom permutation. In: Matsumoto, T., Imai, H., Rivest, R.L. (eds.) ASIACRYPT 1991. LNCS, vol. 739. Springer, Heidelberg (1993)
19. Hirose, S.: Some plausible constructions of double-block-length hash functions. In: Robshaw, M. (ed.) FSE 2006. LNCS, vol. 4047, pp. 210–225. Springer, Heidelberg (2006)
20. Hirose, S., Park, J.H., Yun, A.: A Simple variant of the Merkle-Damgård scheme with a permutation. In: Kurosawa, K. (ed.) ASIACRYPT 2007. LNCS, vol. 4833, pp. 113–129. Springer, Heidelberg (2007)
21. Hoang, V.T., Rogaway, P.: On generalized Feistel networks. In: Rabin, T. (ed.) CRYPTO 2010. LNCS, vol. 6223, pp. 613–630. Springer, Heidelberg (2010)
22. Holenstein, T., Künzler, R., Tessaro, S.: The equivalence of the random oracle model and the ideal cipher model, revisited. In: ACM Symposium on Theory of Computing, STOC, San Jose, CA, USA, pp. 89–98. ACM (2011)
23. Jetchev, D., Özen, O., Stam, M.: Collisions are not incidental: a compression function exploiting discrete geometry. In: Cramer, R. (ed.) TCC 2012. LNCS, vol. 7194, pp. 303–320. Springer, Heidelberg (2012)
24. Knudsen, L.: Block ciphers - the basics. ECRYPT II Summer School on Design and Security of Cryptographic Algorithms and Devices. Invited talk, Albena, Bulgaria (2011)
25. Knudsen, L.R., Rijmen, V.: Known-key distinguishers for some block ciphers. In: Kurosawa, K. (ed.) ASIACRYPT 2007. LNCS, vol. 4833, pp. 315–324. Springer, Heidelberg (2007)
26. Lai, X., Massey, J.L.: Hash functions based on block ciphers. In: Rueppel, R.A. (ed.) EUROCRYPT 1992. LNCS, vol. 658, pp. 55–70. Springer, Heidelberg (1993)
27. Luby, M., Rackoff, C.: How to construct pseudorandom permutations from pseudorandom functions. SIAM J. Comput. 17(2), 373–386 (1988)
28. Mandal, A., Patarin, J., Seurin, Y.: On the public indifferentiability and correlation intractability of the 6-round Feistel construction. In: Cramer, R. (ed.) TCC 2012. LNCS, vol. 7194, pp. 285–302. Springer, Heidelberg (2012)
29. Maurer, U.M., Renner, R.S., Holenstein, C.: Indifferentiability, impossibility results on reductions, and applications to the random oracle methodology. In: Naor, M. (ed.) TCC 2004. LNCS, vol. 2951, pp. 21–39. Springer, Heidelberg (2004)
30. Maurer, U.M.: A simplified and generalized treatment of Luby-Rackoff pseudorandom permutation generators. In: Rueppel, R.A. (ed.) EUROCRYPT 1992. LNCS, vol. 658, pp. 239–255. Springer, Heidelberg (1993)
31. Mennink, B.: Optimal collision security in double block length hashing with single length key. In: Wang, X., Sako, K. (eds.) ASIACRYPT 2012. LNCS, vol. 7658, pp. 526–543. Springer, Heidelberg (2012)
32. Mennink, B., Preneel, B.: Hash functions based on three permutations: a generic security analysis. In: Safavi-Naini, R., Canetti, R. (eds.) CRYPTO 2012. LNCS, vol. 7417, pp. 330–347. Springer, Heidelberg (2012)

33. Meyer, C., Schilling, M.: Secure program load with manipulation detection code. In: Proceedings of Securicom, pp. 111–130 (1988)

34. Minier, M., Phan, R.C.-W., Pousse, B.: Distinguishers for ciphers and known key attack against Rijndael with large blocks. In: Preneel, B. (ed.) AFRICACRYPT 2009. LNCS, vol. 5580, pp. 60–76. Springer, Heidelberg (2009)

35. Nakahara Jr, J.: New impossible differential and known-key distinguishers for the 3D cipher. In: Bao, F., Weng, J. (eds.) ISPEC 2011. LNCS, vol. 6672, pp. 208–221. Springer, Heidelberg (2011)

36. Naor, M., Reingold, O.: On the construction of pseudorandom permutations: Luby-Rackoff revisited. J. Cryptol. **12**(1), 2966 (1999)

37. Nikolić, I., Pieprzyk, J., Sokołowski, P., Steinfeld, R.: Known and chosen key differential distinguishers for block ciphers. In: Rhee, K.-H., Nyang, D.H. (eds.) ICISC 2010. LNCS, vol. 6829, pp. 29–48. Springer, Heidelberg (2011)

38. Patarin, J.: Pseudorandom permutations based on the DES scheme. In: Charpin, P., Cohen, G. (eds.) EUROCODE 1990. LNCS, vol. 514. Springer, Heidelberg (1991)

39. Patarin, J.: New results on pseudorandom permutation generators based on the DES scheme. In: Feigenbaum, J. (ed.) CRYPTO 1991. LNCS, vol. 576, pp. 301–312. Springer, Heidelberg (1992)

40. Patarin, J.: About Feistel schemes with six (or more) rounds. In: Vaudenay, S. (ed.) FSE 1998. LNCS, vol. 1372, p. 103. Springer, Heidelberg (1998)

41. Patarin, J.: Security of random Feistel schemes with 5 or more rounds. In: Franklin, M. (ed.) CRYPTO 2004. LNCS, vol. 3152, pp. 106–122. Springer, Heidelberg (2004)

42. Preneel, B., Govaerts, R., Vandewalle, J.: Hash functions based on block ciphers: a synthetic approach. In: Stinson, D.R. (ed.) CRYPTO 1993. LNCS, vol. 773, pp. 368–378. Springer, Heidelberg (1994)

43. Rogaway, P., Steinberger, J.P.: Constructing cryptographic hash functions from fixed-key blockciphers. In: Wagner, D. (ed.) CRYPTO 2008. LNCS, vol. 5157, pp. 433–450. Springer, Heidelberg (2008)

44. Sasaki, Y.: Known-key attacks on Rijndael with large blocks and strengthening *ShiftRow* parameter. In: Echizen, I., Kunihiro, N., Sasaki, R. (eds.) IWSEC 2010. LNCS, vol. 6434, pp. 301–315. Springer, Heidelberg (2010)

45. Sasaki, Y.: Known-key attacks on Rijndael with large blocks and strengthening *ShiftRow* parameter. IEICE Trans. **95**–**A**(1), 21–28 (2012)

46. Sasaki, Y., Emami, S., Hong, D., Kumar, A.: Improved known-key distinguishers on Feistel-SP ciphers and application to camellia. In: Susilo, W., Mu, Y., Seberry, J. (eds.) ACISP 2012. LNCS, vol. 7372, pp. 87–100. Springer, Heidelberg (2012)

47. Sasaki, Y., Yasuda, K.: Known-key distinguishers on 11-round Feistel and collision attacks on its hashing modes. In: Joux, A. (ed.) FSE 2011. LNCS, vol. 6733, pp. 397–415. Springer, Heidelberg (2011)

48. Shrimpton, T., Stam, M.: Building a collision-resistant compression function from non-compressing primitives. In: Aceto, L., Damgård, I., Goldberg, L.A., Halldórsson, M.M., Ingólfsdóttir, A., Walukiewicz, I. (eds.) ICALP 2008, Part II. LNCS, vol. 5126, pp. 643–654. Springer, Heidelberg (2008)

49. Smith, J.: The design of Lucifer: a cryptographic device for data communications. IBM Research Report RC 3326 (1971)

50. Stam, M.: Blockcipher-based hashing revisited. In: Dunkelman, O. (ed.) FSE 2009. LNCS, vol. 5665, pp. 67–83. Springer, Heidelberg (2009)

51. Steinberger, J.: Improved security bounds for key-alternating ciphers via Hellinger distance. Cryptology ePrint Archive, Report 2012/481 (2012)

52. Vaudenay, S.: Decorrelation: a theory for block cipher security. J. Cryptol. **16**(1), 249–286 (2003)
53. Yoneyama, K., Miyagawa, S., Ohta, K.: Leaky random oracle. IEICE Trans. **92–A**(1), 1795–1807 (2009)
54. Zheng, Y., Matsumoto, T., Imai, H.: On the construction of block ciphers provably secure and not relying on any unproved hypotheses. In: Brassard, G. (ed.) CRYPTO 1989. LNCS, vol. 435, pp. 461–480. Springer, Heidelberg (1990)

On Symmetric Encryption with Distinguishable Decryption Failures

Alexandra Boldyreva[1], Jean Paul Degabriele[2], Kenneth G. Paterson[2]([✉]),
and Martijn Stam[3]

[1] Georgia Institute of Technology, Atlanta, USA
[2] Royal Holloway, University of London, London, UK
kenny.paterson@rhul.ac.uk
[3] University of Bristol, Bristol, UK

Abstract. We propose to relax the assumption that decryption failures are indistinguishable in security models for symmetric encryption. Our main purpose is to build models that better reflect the reality of cryptographic implementations, and to surface the security issues that arise from doing so. We systematically explore the consequences of this relaxation, with some surprising consequences for our understanding of this basic cryptographic primitive. Our results should be useful to practitioners who wish to build accurate models of their implementations and then analyse them. They should also be of value to more theoretical cryptographers proposing new encryption schemes, who, in an ideal world, would be compelled by this work to consider the possibility that their schemes might leak more than simple decryption failures.

1 Introduction

ATTACKS BASED ON DECRYPTION FAILURES. Encryption schemes meeting strong notions of security typically introduce redundancy into their ciphertexts, and as a consequence ciphertexts may be deemed invalid during decryption. A scheme's correctness ensures that honestly generated ciphertexts will always decrypt correctly, hence we expect decryption to 'fail' only for ciphertexts that are corrupted during transmission or are adversarially generated. Typically, protocols making use of an encryption scheme report decryption failures to the sender through error messages, and thus the fact that a decryption failure has occurred becomes known to the adversary. After Bleichenbacher's attack on RSA PKCS#1 [9], it became recognised in the academic community that these decryption failures (and the attendant error messages) may leak significant information to an adversary, undermining schemes' confidentiality properties. Other examples in the asymmetric setting were subsequently discovered [16,21] and called *reaction attacks*. Vaudenay then showed that similar issues can arise in the symmetric setting [27], and his ideas were extended to produce significant attacks against (among others) SSL/TLS [11,23], IPsec [12,13], ASP.NET [14], XML encryption [19] and DTLS [2]. Analysis of error messages in the symmetric setting was also crucial to the success of attacks against the SSH Binary Packet Protocol [1].

S. Moriai (Ed.): FSE 2013, LNCS 8424, pp. 367–390, 2014.
DOI: 10.1007/978-3-662-43933-3_19, © Springer-Verlag Berlin Heidelberg 2014

THE RELATION BETWEEN ATTACKS AND SECURITY DEFINITIONS. At a very high level the above-mentioned attacks on symmetric schemes have the common feature that during decryption some information about the plaintext is leaked, due to error messages, their timing, or some other aspect of the implementation. The leaked information is normally quite small, and the power of these attacks really comes from the adversary's ability to amplify this leakage through iteration. That is, given a target ciphertext, an adversary is able to produce a sequence of related ciphertexts which when decrypted will leak more information about the target plaintext. If we now compare this to the IND-CCA security model, it appears that such attacks should be fully accounted for and prevented, given the very conservative approach adopted in this model. Indeed, in the IND-CCA model, the adversary is given full access to a decryption oracle for any ciphertext except the target ciphertext, from which he learns either the corresponding plaintext or the fact that decryption fails; and yet this should not leak any information about the target plaintext. Furthermore, several of the attacks above do not even make full use of the decryption oracle, but only consider ciphertexts which result in decryption failures.

Why then are the attacks possible at all? Are the underlying encryption schemes actually IND-CCA secure? Is the IND-CCA model the right one for capturing these classes of attack?

SSL/TLS makes an instructive case study for answering these questions. At a high level, SSL/TLS most commonly uses a Mac-then-Encrypt (MtE) construction, with either a stream cipher or CBC-mode encryption of a block cipher as the encryption scheme. Thus SSL/TLS is covered by Krawczyk's result [20], and one might reasonably conclude that its symmetric encryption scheme is IND-CCA secure. Yet Canvel et al. [11] presented plaintext-recovering attacks against the OpenSSL implementation of SSL/TLS when CBC-mode is used, in which the attacker does nothing other than submit certain ciphertexts for decryption and analyse the results (i.e. the attacker ostensibly operates within the IND-CCA model). The key point, however, is that at the time of Canvel et al.'s attacks in 2003, it was possible to infer more from SSL/TLS decryption failures than the simple fact that decryption had failed: decryption could fail either because either the underlying padding needed by CBC-mode was incorrectly formatted or because of a MAC failure, and it was possible to tell these conditions apart (either because they were indicated by different error messages or because the error messages were produced at different times during decryption processing). This additional information was sufficient to realise a padding oracle attack, in the style of [27]. Furthermore, this attack is technically *outside* the IND-CCA security model, because this model only ever provides a single decryption failure symbol $\perp$ to the adversary. Thus, while SSL/TLS may be provably IND-CCA secure in theory, it turned out not to be in practice. Suitable countermeasures involve making it hard for an attacker to learn the cause of decryption failures and were incorporated into the TLS specification from version 1.1 onwards. Meanwhile, building an accurate model of SSL/TLS's symmetric encryption scheme and proving its security has turned out to be a complex task that was only recently completed in [23]. Even there, however, it was necessary to assume that all decryption failures are indistinguishable (since, otherwise, attacks like those of [2,3,11,27] are possible). A similar story could be told for MAC-then-encryption configurations of IPsec, to which the theory in [20] and the attacks of [13] both apply.

So the answers to our questions above are, respectively, yes and no. Yes, the underlying encryption schemes *are* provably IND-CCA secure. However, this is for some description of the schemes that may not accurately reflect how they are actually implemented. And no, the standard model for IND-CCA security is not the right one for capturing these attacks: in the current formalism, more specifically the basic syntax adopted for encryption schemes, it is assumed that decryption failures are indistinguishable and that each decryption failure will return the same error symbol $\perp$. This creates a *gap* in the effective power conferred by a decryption oracle between the IND-CCA model and practical attack scenarios (where decryption failures are often distinguishable). In short, knowing *why* decryption failed may be more informative to the adversary than the mere fact that decryption has failed.

OUR CONTRIBUTIONS. We propose to strengthen the existing security definitions for symmetric encryption by letting the adversary distinguish various possible decryption errors. Our main purpose is to build models that better reflect the reality of cryptographic implementations, and to surface the security issues that arise from doing so. We are not the first to make this relaxation (see, for example, [22,24]), but we are the first to systematically explore its consequences, with some surprising consequences for our understanding of this basic cryptographic primitive. Our results should be useful to practitioners who wish to build accurate models of their implementations and then analyse them. They should also be of value to more theoretical cryptographers proposing new encryption schemes, who, in an ideal world, would be compelled by this work to consider the possibility that their schemes might leak more than simple decryption failures. (Of course, an alternative reaction by the latter group would be to cast this as an implementation issue and simply assume indistinguishable errors as usual; however, the history of attacks tells us that this is hard to guarantee in practice and therefore a dangerous assumption to make.)

Our approach requires the adoption of a slightly different syntax for encryption schemes to the standard one. Now, our decryption algorithm will either return a message from the message space, or an error message from a predetermined finite set of values which we refer to as the *error space*. Technically, then, encryption schemes with multiple errors are a slightly different object from single-error schemes. This approach allows us to handle schemes that can fail in a finite number of distinguishable ways that will be indicated in practice by different error messages. It also enables us to treat attacks in which indistinguishable error messages are returned (perhaps because they are all encrypted, as is the case in SSL/TLS), but in which the errors are returned at a discrete set of times. We note that our approach is equally applicable to the asymmetric setting; here we will restrict our scope to the symmetric setting only.

With this new syntax in hand, we re-examine the statement due to Bellare and Namprempre [10] that semantic (IND-CPA) security in combination with integrity of ciphertexts (INT-CTXT) is sufficient to imply chosen ciphertext (IND-CCA) security. One consequence of their results is that 'IND-CPA + INT-CTXT' has come to be seen as the 'right' security notion to aim for in the symmetric case, with this combined notion now being referred to as *authenticated-encryption security*. This seems to be mostly because it implies IND-CCA security, and because that is by now the accepted notion in the asymmetric setting. We show, through separations, that this important relation no longer holds for multiple error symmetric encryption schemes. Indeed, it is easy to see where the proof of this relation in [10] breaks down: in the passage from the INT-CTXT security game to the IND-CPA security game, the simulation in [10] simply replies to all decryption queries with the error message ⊥; only if an adversary forges a ciphertext does this simulation go awry. But this is not an accurate response in the multiple error setting, since one of several possible error messages should be returned, and the simulation does not necessarily know which.

We then go on to establish relations that are similar in spirit to the classic relations, in that they combine a weak form of confidentiality with some form of ciphertext integrity to obtain strong confidentiality. An interesting aspect that emerges in our analysis is that it is not at all obvious how the notion of ciphertext integrity should be extended to the multiple-error setting. We identify two candidate definitions for ciphertext integrity, one being strictly stronger than the other. We compare and contrast the two, and provide evidence (by means of a rather non-trivial counterexample) for requiring the stronger variant in our relations.

We also provide a natural extension of the IND-CCA3 security notion to the multiple-error setting. This notion, due to Rogaway and Shrimpton [26], is an elegant combination of semantic security and ciphertext integrity into a single equivalent security notion. We show that it serves as a good security notion for symmetric encryption with multiple errors. More specifically we show that our extension to IND-CCA3 security does imply chosen-ciphertext security in the multiple error setting.

We conclude by showing that the encode-then-encrypt-then-MAC (EEM) construction is IND-CCA secure for any encoding scheme, any IND-CPA secure encryption scheme with arbitrary error messages, and any SUF-CMA MAC. Following the works of Bellare and Namprempre [10] and Krawczyk [20], this result provides further formal grounds for preferring the EEM composition over other generic constructions, for example MAC-then-encrypt.

In addition to the standard symmetric encryption notions, we provide equivalent results for security definitions involving indistinguishability from random bits introduced by Rogaway [25], and for the stateful setting introduced by Bellare et al. [8]. Many of these additional results follow rather straightforwardly, but we consider it valuable to include them for completeness.

For reasons of space, all proofs are deferred to the full version [6].

2 Preliminaries

2.1 Notation

Unless otherwise stated, an algorithm may be randomized. An adversary is an algorithm. For any algorithm $\mathcal{A}$ we use $y \leftarrow \mathcal{A}(x_1, x_2, \ldots)$ to denote executing $\mathcal{A}$ with fresh coins on inputs $x_1, x_2, \ldots$ and assigning its output to y. If $\mathcal{S}$ is a set then $|\mathcal{S}|$ denotes its size, and $y \leftarrow_{\$} \mathcal{S}$ denotes the process of selecting an element from $\mathcal{S}$ uniformly at random and assigning it to y. The set of all finite binary strings is denoted by $\{0,1\}^*$, for any positive integer n and bit b, we denote by b^n the string of n consecutive b's and $\{0,1\}^n$ represents the set of all binary strings of length n. The empty string is represented by ε. For any two strings w and z and a positive integer i, $w \parallel z$ denotes their concatenation, $w \oplus z$ denotes their bitwise XOR, $|w|$ denotes the length of w, and $w[i]$ denotes the ith bit of w. If j is a non-negative integer, then $\langle j \rangle_\ell$ denotes the unsigned ℓ-bit binary representation of j. Accordingly $\langle \cdot \rangle^{-1}$ represents the inverse mapping which maps strings of any length to $\mathbb{N}$. If w is an ℓ-bit string and i is an integer we use $w + i$ as shorthand for $\langle \langle w \rangle^{-1} + i \mod 2^\ell \rangle_\ell$. We use $\text{Func}(\mathcal{X}, \mathcal{Y})$ to denote the set of all functions with domain $\mathcal{X}$ and codomain $\mathcal{Y}$. We will often have that $\mathcal{X} = \{0,1\}^\ell$ or $\mathcal{X} = \{0,1\}^*$, and $\mathcal{Y} = \{0,1\}^n$ for some positive integers ℓ and n. Accordingly we abbreviate notation for the corresponding sets of functions to $\text{Func}(\ell, n)$ and $\text{Func}(*, n)$ respectively.

2.2 Building Blocks

PSEUDORANDOM FUNCTIONS. A *function family* is a map $F : \mathcal{K} \times \mathcal{X} \to \mathcal{Y}$. We refer to $\mathcal{K}$ as the key space of F, $\mathcal{X}$ as the domain of F, and $\mathcal{Y}$ as the codomain of F. In this paper $\mathcal{K}$, $\mathcal{X}$, and $\mathcal{Y}$ will be sets of bit-strings. For eack $K \in \mathcal{K}$ we define the map $F_K : \mathcal{X} \to \mathcal{Y}$ by $F_K(x) = F(K, x)$ for all $x \in \mathcal{X}$. Thus F can be seen as a collection of maps from $\mathcal{X}$ to $\mathcal{Y}$, each identified by some key in $\mathcal{K}$. We will refer to F_K as an instance of F. We will often make use of function families that are *pseudorandom*.

Definition 1 (Pseudorandom functions). *Let $F : \mathcal{K} \times \mathcal{X} \to \mathcal{Y}$ be a function family. Consider an adversary $\mathcal{A}$ with oracle access to some function with domain $\mathcal{X}$ and codomain $\mathcal{Y}$, that returns a single bit as its output. We define the prf-advantage of adversary $\mathcal{A}$ with respect to the function family F as:*

$$\mathbf{Adv}_F^{\text{prf}}(\mathcal{A}) = \mathbf{Pr}\left[K \leftarrow_{\$} \mathcal{K} : \mathcal{A}^{F_K(\cdot)} = 1 \right] - \mathbf{Pr}\left[f \leftarrow_{\$} \text{Func}(\mathcal{X}, \mathcal{Y}) : \mathcal{A}^{f(\cdot)} = 1 \right].$$

F is said to be a pseudorandom function (PRF), if for every adversary $\mathcal{A}$ with reasonable resources its prf-advantage $\mathbf{Adv}_F^{\text{prf}}(\mathcal{A})$ is small.

MACs. A *message authentication code (MAC)* $\mathcal{MA} = (\mathcal{K}, \mathcal{T}, \mathcal{V})$ with associated error space $\mathcal{Q}_\perp$ consists of three algorithms. The randomized *key-generation* algorithm $\mathcal{K}$ takes no input and returns a secret key K. We will sometimes abuse notation and regard $\mathcal{K}$ as a set of keys. The *tagging* algorithm $\mathcal{T}$ may be randomized or stateful. It takes as input the secret key K and a message $m \in \{0,1\}^*$ to return a tag τ. The *verification* algorithm $\mathcal{V}$ is deterministic and stateless. It takes the secret key K, a message $m \in \{0,1\}^*$ and a candidate tag τ, and returns either 1 or an error message in $\mathcal{Q}_\perp$. We require that for all K that can be output by $\mathcal{K}$ and all $m \in \{0,1\}^*$, it hold (with probability 1) that if $\tau \leftarrow \mathcal{T}_K(m)$ then $\mathcal{V}_K(m,\tau) = 1$. Here, we allow multiple possible error messages for $\mathcal{MA}$ in order to be able to model certain types of attack, e.g. that in [3].

The standard security notion for MACs is existential unforgeability under chosen message attacks (UF-CMA). We will however require a stronger variant of this notion SUF-CMA which is defined below.

Definition 2 (SUF-CMA). *Let* $\mathcal{MA} = (\mathcal{K}, \mathcal{T}, \mathcal{V})$ *be a message authentication code with associated error space* $\mathcal{Q}_\perp$. *For an adversary* $\mathcal{A}$, *define experiment* $\mathbf{Exp}^{\text{suf-cma}}_{\mathcal{MA}}(\mathcal{A})$ *as shown in Fig. 1. A key K is first generated by calling $\mathcal{K}$. The adversary $\mathcal{A}$ is then given access to a tagging oracle* $\mathsf{Tag}(\cdot)$ *and a verification oracle* $\mathsf{Ver}(\cdot, \cdot)$. *The adversary wins if it queries a valid message-tag pair that was not previously returned by the tagging oracle. We define the adversary's advantage as:*

$$\mathbf{Adv}^{\text{suf-cma}}_{\mathcal{MA}}(\mathcal{A}) = \Pr\left[\mathbf{Exp}^{\text{suf-cma}}_{\mathcal{MA}}(\mathcal{A})\right].$$

The scheme $\mathcal{MA}$ *is said to be* SUF-CMA *secure if, for every adversary $\mathcal{A}$ consuming reasonable resources its advantage* $\mathbf{Adv}^{\text{suf-cma}}_{\mathcal{MA}}(\mathcal{A})$ *is small.*

The standard UF-CMA notion is defined analogously but the adversary is only granted a win if it forges a tag for a message that was not previously queried to the tagging oracle.

ENCODING SCHEMES. When constructing symmetric encryption schemes from other components it is common to perform some form of preprocessing on the message. Its purpose may be to map messages to the message space of the encryption scheme, or as an attempt to extend the scheme's functionality, such as masking the message length. Generally such transformations are unkeyed, but may be randomized. We model such transformations by encoding schemes.

An *encoding scheme* $\mathcal{ES} = (\mathcal{EC}, \mathcal{DC})$ consists of two algorithms and associated domain, codomain, and an error space. The *encoding* algorithm $\mathcal{EC}$ which may be randomized, takes as input an element from its domain and maps it to some

$\mathbf{Exp}^{\text{suf-cma}}_{\mathcal{SE}}(\mathcal{A})$	$\underline{\mathsf{Tag}(m)}$	$\underline{\mathsf{Ver}(m,\tau)}$
$K \leftarrow \mathcal{K}$	$\tau \leftarrow \mathcal{T}_K(m)$	$v \leftarrow \mathcal{V}_K(m,\tau)$
$\mathsf{L} \leftarrow \emptyset, \text{win} \leftarrow 0$	$\mathsf{L} \leftarrow \mathsf{L} \cup (m,\tau)$	if $v \notin \mathcal{Q}_\perp$ and $(m,\tau) \notin \mathsf{L}$
$\mathcal{A}^{\mathsf{Tag}(\cdot),\mathsf{Ver}(\cdot,\cdot)}$	**return** τ	**then** win $\leftarrow 1$
return win		**return** v

Fig. 1. SUF-CMA experiment for message authentication codes.

element in its codomain. The *decoding* algorithm $\mathcal{DC}$ is deterministic and takes an element from its codomain and returns either an element in its domain or an error symbol from its error space. The scheme must be correct, i.e. for every element m in its domain it holds with probability 1 that $\mathcal{DC}(\mathcal{EC}(m)) = m$.

3 Symmetric Encryption with Multiple Errors: Definitions

SYNTAX. A *symmetric encryption scheme* $\mathcal{SE} = (\mathcal{K}, \mathcal{E}, \mathcal{D})$ with associated message space $\mathcal{M} \subseteq \{0,1\}^*$, ciphertext space $\mathcal{C} \subseteq \{0,1\}^*$, and error space $\mathcal{S}_\perp$ consists of three algorithms. The randomized *key-generation* algorithm $\mathcal{K}$ takes no input and returns a secret key K, an initial encryption state σ_0, and an initial decryption state ϱ_0. We will sometimes abuse notation and regard $\mathcal{K}$ as a set of keys. The randomized and stateful *encryption* algorithm $\mathcal{E} : \mathcal{K} \times \mathcal{M} \times \Sigma \to \mathcal{C} \times \Sigma$ takes as input the secret key $K \in \mathcal{K}$, a plaintext $m \in \mathcal{M}$, and the current encryption state $\sigma \in \Sigma$, and returns a ciphertext in $\mathcal{C}$ together with an updated state. The deterministic and stateful *decryption* algorithm $\mathcal{D} : \mathcal{K} \times \mathcal{C} \times \Sigma \to (\mathcal{M} \cup \mathcal{S}_\perp) \times \Sigma$ takes as input the secret key K, a ciphertext $c \in \mathcal{C}$, and the current decryption state ϱ to return the corresponding plaintext $m \in \mathcal{M}$ or a special symbol from $\mathcal{S}_\perp$ (indicating that the ciphertext is invalid) and an updated state.

Our syntax of symmetric encryption schemes differs in two main ways from the more conventional way of modelling symmetric encryption schemes. Firstly it allows the decryption algorithm to indicate invalid ciphertexts with distinct error messages within the error space. We will assume the error space be a set of symbols $\{\perp_1, \perp_2, \ldots, \perp_n\}$ for some positive integer n. The symbol $\perp$ will be used interchangeably to denote a specific error symbol or a variable assuming values from the error space. We will use the term *multiple-error encryption scheme* to indicate schemes with an error space of size strictly greater than one. Secondly we adopt a stateful syntax for both encryption and decryption. This is without loss of generality. Both encryption and decryption can be made stateless by defining $\mathcal{K}$ to always return the empty string for the corresponding initial state, and having $\mathcal{E}, \mathcal{D}$ ignore (i.e. never update) the state.

For any $\ell \in \mathbb{N}$ and any $\mathbf{m} = [m_1, \ldots, m_\ell] \in \mathcal{M}^\ell$, we write $(\mathbf{c}, \sigma) \leftarrow \mathcal{E}_K(\mathbf{m}, \sigma_0)$ as shorthand for $(c_1, \sigma_1) \leftarrow \mathcal{E}_K(m_1, \sigma_0)$, $(c_2, \sigma_2) \leftarrow \mathcal{E}_K(m_2, \sigma_1), \ldots (c_\ell, \sigma_\ell) \leftarrow \mathcal{E}_K(m_\ell, \sigma_{\ell-1})$, where $\mathbf{c} = [c_1, \ldots, c_\ell]$ and $\sigma = \sigma_\ell$. Similarly we use $(\mathbf{m}', \varrho) \leftarrow \mathcal{D}_K(\mathbf{c}, \varrho_0)$ to denote the analogous process for decryption. Finally, we require that a symmetric encryption scheme satisfy *correctness* which is defined as follows:

Definition 3 (Correctness of $\mathcal{SE}$). *For all (K, σ_0, ϱ_0) that can be output by $\mathcal{K}$, all $\ell \in \mathbb{N}$, and all $\mathbf{m} \in \mathcal{M}^\ell$, it holds (with probability 1) that if $(\mathbf{c}, \sigma) \leftarrow \mathcal{E}_K(\mathbf{m}, \sigma_0)$ and $(\mathbf{m}', \varrho) \leftarrow \mathcal{D}_K(\mathbf{c}, \varrho_0)$, then $\mathbf{m}' = \mathbf{m}$.*

INDISTINGUISHABILITY NOTIONS. We adopt the 'left-or-right' model of indistinguishability from Bellare et al. [5] to define three notions of confidentiality for symmetric encryption. Indistinguishability under chosen-plaintext attack (IND-CPA), and indistinguishability under chosen-ciphertext attack (IND-CCA) are fairly standard, except for the fact that for multiple-error schemes the decryption oracle will now return one of many possible error messages. We introduce the notion of indistinguishability under ciphertext-validity attack (IND-CVA), which can be seen as a *strengthened* adaption of a similar notion defined by Bauer et al. [4] to the symmetric setting. Here, in addition to an encryption oracle the adversary is given access to a *ciphertext-validity* oracle which indicates whether a ciphertext is valid or not, and if not, *returns the exact error message* output by the decryption algorithm.

Definition 4 (IND-ATK security). *Let* $\mathcal{SE} = (\mathcal{K}, \mathcal{E}, \mathcal{D})$ *be a symmetric encryption scheme. For an adversary $\mathcal{A}$ and a bit b, define the experiments* $\mathbf{Exp}_{\mathcal{SE}}^{\text{ind-atk-}b}(\mathcal{A})$ *where* atk $\in$ {cpa, cva, cca} *as shown in Fig. 2. In all three experiments, a key K is first generated by calling $\mathcal{K}$. The adversary $\mathcal{A}$ is then given access to a left-or-right encryption oracle* LoR$(\cdot)$*, and possibly a ciphertext-validity oracle* Val$(\cdot)$ *or a decryption oracle* Dec$(\cdot)$*. No restriction is imposed on the adversary's queries, rather if it queries a pair of messages of unequal length to* LoR$(\cdot)$*, or if it queries a ciphertext to* Dec$(\cdot)$ *previously returned by* LoR$(\cdot)$*, the $\notin$ symbol is returned. In the* Val$(\cdot)$ *oracle the $\notin$ symbol indicates that the queried ciphertext was valid.*

The adversary's goal is to output a bit b', as its guess of the challenge bit b, and the experiment returns b' as well. For each of these three experiments we define the corresponding advantages of an adversary $\mathcal{A}$ as:

$$\mathbf{Adv}_{\mathcal{SE}}^{\text{ind-atk}}(\mathcal{A}) = \Pr\left[\mathbf{Exp}_{\mathcal{SE}}^{\text{ind-atk-1}}(\mathcal{A}) = 1\right] - \Pr\left[\mathbf{Exp}_{\mathcal{SE}}^{\text{ind-atk-0}}(\mathcal{A}) = 1\right].$$

The scheme $\mathcal{SE}$ is said to be IND-ATK *secure, if for every adversary $\mathcal{A}$ with reasonable resources its advantage* $\mathbf{Adv}_{\mathcal{SE}}^{\text{ind-atk}}(\mathcal{A})$ *is small.*

INDISTINGUISHABILITY FROM RANDOM BITS. We can recast the above three security notions in terms of indistinguishability from random bits as introduced

$\mathbf{Exp}_{\mathcal{SE}}^{\text{ind-cpa-}b}(\mathcal{A})$	$\mathbf{Exp}_{\mathcal{SE}}^{\text{ind-cva-}b}(\mathcal{A})$	$\mathbf{Exp}_{\mathcal{SE}}^{\text{ind-cca-}b}(\mathcal{A})$
$(K, \sigma, \varrho) \leftarrow \mathcal{K}$	$(K, \sigma, \varrho) \leftarrow \mathcal{K}$	$(K, \sigma, \varrho) \leftarrow \mathcal{K}$
$i \leftarrow 0, \mathsf{C} \leftarrow ()$	$i \leftarrow 0, \mathsf{C} \leftarrow ()$	$i \leftarrow 0, \mathsf{C} \leftarrow ()$
$b' \leftarrow \mathcal{A}^{\text{LoR}(\cdot)}$	$b' \leftarrow \mathcal{A}^{\text{LoR}(\cdot),\text{Val}(\cdot)}$	$b' \leftarrow \mathcal{A}^{\text{LoR}(\cdot),\text{Dec}(\cdot)}$
return b'	**return** b'	**return** b'
$\underline{\text{LoR}((m_0, m_1))}$	$\underline{\text{Val}(c)}$	$\underline{\text{Dec}(c)}$
if $\|m_0\| \neq \|m_1\|$	$(m, \varrho) \leftarrow \mathcal{D}_K(c, \varrho)$	$(m, \varrho) \leftarrow \mathcal{D}_K(c, \varrho)$
then return $\notin$	**if** $m \in \mathcal{M}$ **then** $m \leftarrow \notin$	**if** $c \in \mathsf{C}$ **then** $m \leftarrow \notin$
$(c, \sigma) \leftarrow \mathcal{E}_K(m_b, \sigma)$	**return** m	**return** m
$i \leftarrow i + 1, \mathsf{C}_i \leftarrow c$		
return c		

Fig. 2. IND-ATK experiments for symmetric encryption schemes.

by Rogaway [25]. Here the adversarial goal is to distinguish encrypted messages from random bit-strings of the same length.

Definition 5 (IND$-ATK security). *Let* $\mathcal{SE} = (\mathcal{K}, \mathcal{E}, \mathcal{D})$ *be a symmetric encryption scheme. For an adversary* $\mathcal{A}$ *and a bit* b, *define the experiments* $\mathbf{Exp}_{\mathcal{SE}}^{\text{ind\$-atk-b}}(\mathcal{A})$ *where* atk $\in \{\text{cpa}, \text{cva}, \text{cca}\}$ *as shown in Fig. 3. In all three experiments, a key* K *is first generated by calling* $\mathcal{K}$. *The adversary* $\mathcal{A}$ *is then given access to a special encryption oracle* Enc$(\cdot)$, *if* $b = 1$ *the oracle returns the encrypted message, otherwise it returns a uniformly-random bit-string of the same length. In the* ind\$-cva *and* ind\$-cca *experiments, the adversary is additionally given access to a ciphertext-validity oracle* Val$(\cdot)$ *and a decryption oracle* Dec$(\cdot)$ *respectively. Trivial-win conditions are avoided by having the decryption oracle return* ↯ *in response to any ciphertext that was previously output by the encryption oracle. The ciphertext-validity oracle uses* ↯ *to indicate that the queried ciphertext was valid or has been previously output by the encryption oracle.*

The adversary's goal is to output a bit b', *as its guess of the challenge bit* b, *and the experiment returns* b' *as well. For each of these three experiments we define the corresponding advantages of an adversary* $\mathcal{A}$ *as:*

$$\mathbf{Adv}_{\mathcal{SE}}^{\text{ind\$-atk}}(\mathcal{A}) = \Pr\left[\mathbf{Exp}_{\mathcal{SE}}^{\text{ind\$-atk-1}}(\mathcal{A}) = 1\right] - \Pr\left[\mathbf{Exp}_{\mathcal{SE}}^{\text{ind\$-atk-0}}(\mathcal{A}) = 1\right].$$

The scheme $\mathcal{SE}$ *is said to be* IND$-ATK *secure, if for every adversary* $\mathcal{A}$ *with reasonable resources its advantage* $\mathbf{Adv}_{\mathcal{SE}}^{\text{ind\$-atk}}(\mathcal{A})$ *is small.*

STATEFUL INDISTINGUISHABILITY NOTIONS. Secure protocols like SSH, SSL/TLS and IPsec aim to protect against replay and reordering of ciphertexts. These security goals are not captured by any of the above security notions. Bellare et al. [8] introduced a notion called IND-sfCCA. This notion implies IND-CCA security and additionally protects against replay and reordering of ciphertexts. We recall

$\mathbf{Exp}_{\mathcal{SE}}^{\text{ind\$-cpa-b}}(\mathcal{A})$	$\mathbf{Exp}_{\mathcal{SE}}^{\text{ind\$-cva-b}}(\mathcal{A})$	$\mathbf{Exp}_{\mathcal{SE}}^{\text{ind\$-cca-b}}(\mathcal{A})$
$(K, \sigma, \varrho) \leftarrow \mathcal{K}$	$(K, \sigma, \varrho) \leftarrow \mathcal{K}$	$(K, \sigma, \varrho) \leftarrow \mathcal{K}$
$b' \leftarrow \mathcal{A}^{\text{Enc\$}(\cdot)}$	$i \leftarrow 0, \mathsf{C} \leftarrow ()$	$i \leftarrow 0, \mathsf{C} \leftarrow ()$
return b'	$b' \leftarrow \mathcal{A}^{\text{Enc\$}(\cdot), \text{Val}(\cdot)}$	$b' \leftarrow \mathcal{A}^{\text{Enc\$}(\cdot), \text{Dec}(\cdot)}$
	return b'	**return** b'
$\underline{\text{Enc\$}(m)}$	$\underline{\text{Val}(c)}$	$\underline{\text{Dec}(c)}$
$(c, \sigma) \leftarrow \mathcal{E}_K(m, \sigma)$	$(m, \varrho) \leftarrow \mathcal{D}_K(c, \varrho)$	$(m, \varrho) \leftarrow \mathcal{D}_K(c, \varrho)$
if $b = 0$	**if** $m \in \mathcal{M}$ **or** $c \in \mathsf{C}$	**if** $c \in \mathsf{C}$ **then** $m \leftarrow$ ↯
then $c \leftarrow_\$ \{0,1\}^{|c|}$	**then** $m \leftarrow$ ↯	**return** m
$i \leftarrow i + 1, \mathsf{C}_i \leftarrow c$	**return** m	
return c		

Fig. 3. IND$-ATK experiments for symmetric encryption schemes.

this notion and introduce natural variants in terms of indistinguishability from random bits and ciphertext-validity attacks. Of course, our definitions are also for the setting of multiple errors. In what follows we will classify the adversary's decryption queries to be *in-sync*, if the sequence of queried ciphertexts is a prefix of the sequence of ciphertexts returned by the encryption oracle. Accordingly we refer to the first decryption query (and any subsequent one) for which this is no longer true as an *out-of-sync* query.

Definition 6 (Stateful indistinguishability). *Let* $\mathcal{SE} = (\mathcal{K}, \mathcal{E}, \mathcal{D})$ *be a symmetric encryption scheme. For an adversary* $\mathcal{A}$ *and a bit* b, *define experiments* $\mathbf{Exp}_{\mathcal{SE}}^{\text{ind-sfcca-}b}(\mathcal{A})$ *and* $\mathbf{Exp}_{\mathcal{SE}}^{\text{ind\$-atk-}b}(\mathcal{A})$ *where* atk $\in \{\text{sfcva}, \text{sfcca}\}$ *as shown in Fig. 4. In all three experiments, a key* K *is first generated by calling* $\mathcal{K}$. *In the* ind-sfcca *experiment the adversary is given access to a left-or-right encryption oracle* $\text{LoR}(\cdot)$, *and a stateful decryption oracle* $\text{sfDec}(\cdot)$. *The stateful decryption oracle returns the decrypted ciphertexts only for out-of-sync queries, and returns* $\natural$ *otherwise. Similarly in the* ind\$-atk *experiments the adversary is given access to the special encryption oracle* $\text{Enc}\$(\cdot)$, *and either a stateful ciphertext-validity oracle* $\text{sfVal}(\cdot)$ *or a stateful decryption oracle* $\text{sfDec}(\cdot)$.

The adversary's goal is to output a bit b', *as its guess of the challenge bit* b, *and the experiment returns* b' *as well. For each of these three experiments we define the corresponding advantages of an adversary* $\mathcal{A}$ *as:*

$$\mathbf{Adv}_{\mathcal{SE}}^{\text{ind-sfcca}}(\mathcal{A}) = \Pr\left[\mathbf{Exp}_{\mathcal{SE}}^{\text{ind-sfcca-1}}(\mathcal{A}) = 1\right] - \Pr\left[\mathbf{Exp}_{\mathcal{SE}}^{\text{ind-sfcca-0}}(\mathcal{A}) = 1\right]$$

$$\mathbf{Adv}_{\mathcal{SE}}^{\text{ind\$-atk}}(\mathcal{A}) = \Pr\left[\mathbf{Exp}_{\mathcal{SE}}^{\text{ind\$-atk-1}}(\mathcal{A}) = 1\right] - \Pr\left[\mathbf{Exp}_{\mathcal{SE}}^{\text{ind\$-atk-0}}(\mathcal{A}) = 1\right].$$

The scheme $\mathcal{SE}$ *is said to be* IND-sfCCA *or* IND\$-ATK *secure, if for every adversary* $\mathcal{A}$ *with reasonable resources its respective advantage* $\mathbf{Adv}_{\mathcal{SE}}^{\text{ind-sfcca}}(\mathcal{A})$ *or* $\mathbf{Adv}_{\mathcal{SE}}^{\text{ind\$-atk}}(\mathcal{A})$ *is small.*

The naming of these notions is partly justified by the fact that the decryption and ciphertext-validity oracles are stateful. In addition, it is easy to see that for an encryption scheme to be IND-sfCCA or IND\$-sfCCA secure, its decryption algorithm must be stateful. However, a scheme need not have a stateful decryption algorithm to be IND\$-sfCVA secure. As the reader may have noticed, we did not define an IND-sfCVA notion. This is because in the presence of a left-or-right encryption oracle, the $\text{sfVal}(\cdot)$ oracle reduces to a $\text{Val}(\cdot)$ oracle, and therefore IND-sfCVA (defined in the obvious way) is equivalent to IND-CVA.

CIPHERTEXT INTEGRITY. We define ciphertext integrity analogously to Bellare and Namprempre [10], and we also consider its stateful variant [8] which additionally protects against replay and reordering attacks. Here an adversary trying to forge a ciphertext is granted multiple attempts by giving it access to a verification oracle $\text{Try}(\cdot)$, in addition to a standard encryption oracle. When extending these notions to schemes with multiple errors, it is not clear how to interpret the verification oracle's functionality. That is, should the verification oracle indicate only whether a ciphertext is valid or not, or should it additionally return

$\underline{\mathbf{Exp}_{\mathcal{SE}}^{\text{ind-sfcca-}b}(\mathcal{A})}$

$(K, \sigma, \varrho) \leftarrow \mathcal{K}$
$i \leftarrow 0, j \leftarrow 0$
$\mathsf{C} \leftarrow ()$, $\mathsf{sync} \leftarrow 1$
$b' \leftarrow \mathcal{A}^{\text{LoR}(\cdot), \text{sfDec}(\cdot)}$
return b'

$\underline{\text{LoR}((m_0, m_1))}$

if $|m_0| \neq |m_1|$
   then return $\lightning$
$(c, \sigma) \leftarrow \mathcal{E}_K(m_b, \sigma)$
$i \leftarrow i + 1, \mathsf{C}_i \leftarrow c$
return c

$\underline{\text{sfDec}(c)}$

$j \leftarrow j + 1$
$(m, \varrho) \leftarrow \mathcal{D}_K(c, \varrho)$
if $j > i$ **or** $c \neq \mathsf{C}_j$
   then $\mathsf{sync} \leftarrow 0$
if $\mathsf{sync} = 1$ **then** $m \leftarrow \lightning$
return m

$\underline{\mathbf{Exp}_{\mathcal{SE}}^{\text{ind\$-sfcva-}b}(\mathcal{A})}$

$(K, \sigma, \varrho) \leftarrow \mathcal{K}$
$i \leftarrow 0, j \leftarrow 0$
$\mathsf{C} \leftarrow ()$, $\mathsf{sync} \leftarrow 1$
$b' \leftarrow \mathcal{A}^{\text{Enc\$}(\cdot), \text{sfVal}(\cdot)}$
return b'

$\underline{\text{Enc\$}(m)}$

$(c, \sigma) \leftarrow \mathcal{E}_K(m, \sigma)$
if $b = 0$
   then $c \leftarrow^{\$} \{0, 1\}^{|c|}$
$i \leftarrow i + 1, \mathsf{C}_i \leftarrow c$
return c

$\underline{\mathbf{Exp}_{\mathcal{SE}}^{\text{ind\$-sfcca-}b}(\mathcal{A})}$

$(K, \sigma, \varrho) \leftarrow \mathcal{K}$
$i \leftarrow 0, j \leftarrow 0$
$\mathsf{C} \leftarrow ()$, $\mathsf{sync} \leftarrow 1$
$b' \leftarrow \mathcal{A}^{\text{Enc\$}(\cdot), \text{sfDec}(\cdot)}$
return b'

$\underline{\text{sfVal}(c)}$

$j \leftarrow j + 1$
$(m, \varrho) \leftarrow \mathcal{D}_K(c, \varrho)$
if $j > i$ **or** $c \neq \mathsf{C}_j$
   then $\mathsf{sync} \leftarrow 0$
if $\mathsf{sync} = 1$ **or** $m \in \mathcal{M}$
   then $m \leftarrow \lightning$
return m

Fig. 4. Stateful indistinguishability experiments for symmetric encryption schemes.

the exact error message output by the decryption algorithm if the ciphertext is invalid? For single-error schemes the two interpretations are equivalent, but this does not hold in general (see Sect. 4). For each of the standard and stateful notions we consider both variants and we denote the weaker variant (i.e. the one that is less informative to the adversary) with '∗'. In what follows we classify verification queries to be in-sync or out-of-sync in an analogous manner as we did for decryption.

Definition 7 (Ciphertext Integrity). *Let* $\mathcal{SE} = (\mathcal{K}, \mathcal{E}, \mathcal{D})$ *be a symmetric encryption scheme. For an adversary* $\mathcal{A}$ *define the experiments* $\mathbf{Exp}_{\mathcal{SE}}^{\text{int-atk}}(\mathcal{A})$ *where* atk $\in \{\text{ctxt}, \text{ctxt∗}, \text{sfctxt}, \text{sfctxt∗}\}$ *as shown in Fig. 5. In all experiments, a key* K *is first generated by calling* $\mathcal{K}$. *The adversary* $\mathcal{A}$ *is then given access to an encryption oracle* Enc$(\cdot)$, *and one of the following verification oracles* Try$(\cdot)$, Try∗$(\cdot)$, sfTry$(\cdot)$, *or* sfTry∗$(\cdot)$. *The* Try∗$(\cdot)$ *oracle (and similarly the* sfTry∗$(\cdot)$ *oracle) returns* $\lightning$ *if the queried ciphertext is valid, or if the ciphertext has been previously output by the encryption oracle (respectively: if the verification query is in-sync), and returns* $\perp$ *if the ciphertext is invalid. The* Try$(\cdot)$ *and* sfTry$(\cdot)$ *oracles operate analogously but return the exact error message output by the decryption oracle when a ciphertext is invalid.*

In the int-ctxt *and* int-ctxt∗ *experiments the adversary's goal is to make a valid verification query not previously output by the encryption oracle. In the*

$\mathbf{Exp}_{\mathcal{SE}}^{\text{int-ctxt}}(\mathcal{A})$

$(K, \sigma, \varrho) \leftarrow \mathcal{K}$
$i \leftarrow 0, \mathsf{C} \leftarrow (), \text{win} \leftarrow 0$
$\mathcal{A}^{\text{Enc}(\cdot), \text{Try}(\cdot)}$
return win

$\mathbf{Exp}_{\mathcal{SE}}^{\text{int-sfctxt}}(\mathcal{A})$

$(K, \sigma, \varrho) \leftarrow \mathcal{K}$
$i \leftarrow 0, j \leftarrow 0, \mathsf{C} \leftarrow ()$
sync $\leftarrow 1$, win $\leftarrow 0$
$\mathcal{A}^{\text{Enc}(\cdot), \text{sfTry}(\cdot)}$
return win

$\mathbf{Exp}_{\mathcal{SE}}^{\text{int-ctxt*}}(\mathcal{A})$

$(K, \sigma, \varrho) \leftarrow \mathcal{K}$
$i \leftarrow 0, \mathsf{C} \leftarrow (), \text{win} \leftarrow 0$
$\mathcal{A}^{\text{Enc}(\cdot), \text{Try}^*(\cdot)}$
return win

$\mathbf{Exp}_{\mathcal{SE}}^{\text{int-sfctxt*}}(\mathcal{A})$

$(K, \sigma, \varrho) \leftarrow \mathcal{K}$
$i \leftarrow 0, j \leftarrow 0, \mathsf{C} \leftarrow ()$
sync $\leftarrow 1$, win $\leftarrow 0$
$\mathcal{A}^{\text{Enc}(\cdot), \text{sfTry}^*(\cdot)}$
return win

$\underline{\text{Enc}(m)}$

$(c, \sigma) \leftarrow \mathcal{E}_K(m, \sigma)$
$i \leftarrow i + 1, \mathsf{C}_i \leftarrow c$
return c

$\underline{\text{Try}(c)}$

$(m, \varrho) \leftarrow \mathcal{D}_K(c, \varrho)$
if $c \notin \mathsf{C}$ and $m \notin \mathcal{S}_\perp$
    then win $\leftarrow 1$
if $m \notin \mathcal{S}_\perp$ then $m \leftarrow \not\xi$
return m

$\underline{\text{sfTry}(c)}$

$j \leftarrow j + 1$
$(m, \varrho) \leftarrow \mathcal{D}_K(c, \varrho)$
if $j > i$ or $c \neq \mathsf{C}_j$
    then sync $\leftarrow 0$
if sync $= 0$ and $m \notin \mathcal{S}_\perp$
    then win $\leftarrow 1$
if $m \notin \mathcal{S}_\perp$ then $m \leftarrow \not\xi$
return m

$\underline{\text{Try}^*(c)}$

$(m, \varrho) \leftarrow \mathcal{D}_K(c, \varrho)$
if $c \notin \mathsf{C}$ and $m \notin \mathcal{S}_\perp$
    then win $\leftarrow 1$
if $m \in \mathcal{S}_\perp$ then $m \leftarrow \perp$
else $m \leftarrow \not\xi$
return m

$\underline{\text{sfTry}^*(c)}$

$j \leftarrow j + 1$
$(m, \varrho) \leftarrow \mathcal{D}_K(c, \varrho)$
if $j > i$ or $c \neq \mathsf{C}_j$
    then sync $\leftarrow 0$
if sync $= 0$ and $m \notin \mathcal{S}_\perp$
    then win $\leftarrow 1$
if $m \in \mathcal{S}_\perp$ then $m \leftarrow \perp$
else $m \leftarrow \not\xi$
return m

Fig. 5. Ciphertext integrity experiments for symmetric encryption schemes.

int-sfctxt *and* int-sfctxt* *experiments the adversary's goal is to make a valid out-of-sync verification query. In all cases the experiment outputs a bit indicating the adversary's success. For each experiment we define the advantage of an adversary* $\mathcal{A}$ *as:*

$$\mathbf{Adv}_{\mathcal{SE}}^{\text{int-atk}}(\mathcal{A}) = \Pr\left[\mathbf{Exp}_{\mathcal{SE}}^{\text{int-atk}}(\mathcal{A}) = 1\right].$$

The scheme $\mathcal{SE}$ *is said to be* INT-ATK *secure, if for every adversary* $\mathcal{A}$ *with reasonable resources its advantage* $\mathbf{Adv}_{\mathcal{SE}}^{\text{int-atk}}(\mathcal{A})$ *is small.*

ERROR INVARIANCE. Although an encryption scheme may have multiple error messages, not all error messages may be 'available' to the adversary. In particular an adversary may not be able to produce (invalid) ciphertexts that generate all possible error messages. We introduce a simple security notion that captures exactly this situation. Informally an encryption scheme is *error-invariant* if no efficient adversary can generate more than one of the possible error messages. Of course any single-error scheme is trivially error invariant.

Definition 8 (INV-ERR **security**). *Let* $\mathcal{SE} = (\mathcal{K}, \mathcal{E}, \mathcal{D})$ *be a symmetric encryption scheme with error space* $\mathcal{S}_\perp$. *For any* $\perp \in \mathcal{S}_\perp$ *and an adversary* $\mathcal{A}$,

$\mathbf{Exp}_{\mathcal{SE},\perp}^{\text{inv-err}}(\mathcal{A})$	$\mathsf{Enc}(m)$	$\mathsf{Dec}(c)$
$(K, \sigma, \varrho) \leftarrow \mathcal{K}$	$(c, \sigma) \leftarrow \mathcal{E}_K(m, \sigma)$	$(m, \varrho) \leftarrow \mathcal{D}_K(c, \varrho)$
win $\leftarrow 0$	**return** c	**if** $m \in \mathcal{S}_\perp$ **and** $m \neq \perp$
$\mathcal{A}^{\mathsf{Enc}(\cdot),\mathsf{Dec}(\cdot)}$		**then** win $\leftarrow 1$
return win		**return** m

Fig. 6. INV-ERR experiment for symmetric encryption schemes.

define the experiment $\mathbf{Exp}_{\mathcal{SE},\perp}^{\text{inv-err}}(\mathcal{A})$ as shown in Fig. 6. A key K is first generated by calling $\mathcal{K}$. The adversary $\mathcal{A}$ is then given access to an encryption oracle $\mathsf{Enc}(\cdot)$ and a decryption oracle $\mathsf{Dec}(\cdot)$.

The adversary's goal is to submit a ciphertext to the decryption oracle which results in an error message not equal to $\perp$. The experiment outputs a bit indicating the adversary's success. We define the advantage of an adversary $\mathcal{A}$ with respect to $\perp$ as:

$$\mathbf{Adv}_{\mathcal{SE},\perp}^{\text{inv-err}}(\mathcal{A}) = \Pr\left[\,\mathbf{Exp}_{\mathcal{SE},\perp}^{\text{inv-err}}(\mathcal{A}) = 1\,\right].$$

The scheme $\mathcal{SE}$ is said to be INV-ERR secure if there exists a unique $\perp \in \mathcal{S}_\perp$ such that for every adversary $\mathcal{A}$ with reasonable resources its advantage $\mathbf{Adv}_{\mathcal{SE},\perp}^{\text{inv-err}}(\mathcal{A})$ is small.

ADDITIONAL NOTES. The reader may be wondering how exactly to interpret the $\frac{1}{\ell}$ symbol, given that we assign to it different meanings in our security definitions. In general we use it to 'suppress' certain outputs from an oracle, and hence limit the information conveyed by the oracle to the adversary. We use it to avoid trivial win conditions by suppressing the output of in-sync decryption queries, or left-or-right queries containing messages of different lengths. We also use it to define ciphertext-validity and verification oracles by suppressing any plaintext that is output by the decryption algorithm.

For each security definition we have defined the corresponding advantage of an adversary with respect to some cryptographic scheme. We will sometimes refer to the *maximum* advantage with respect to a cryptographic scheme over all adversaries consuming reasonable resources. Any advantage not parametrized by an adversary is to be interpreted this way.

4   Relations and Separations

INTERPRETING OUR IMPLICATIONS AND SEPARATIONS. An implication from security notion X to security notion Y, indicated by X $\longrightarrow$ Y, means that any scheme which is X-secure is also Y-secure. More formally there exists a constant $\kappa > 0$ such that for any symmetric encryption scheme $\mathcal{SE}$ and any Y adversary $\mathcal{A}_y$ there exists a X adversary $\mathcal{A}_x$ (with similar resources) such that:

$$\mathbf{Adv}_{\mathcal{SE}}^{\text{y}}(\mathcal{A}_y) \leq \kappa \cdot \mathbf{Adv}_{\mathcal{SE}}^{\text{x}}(\mathcal{A}_x)$$

A separation from security notion X to security notion Y indicated by X $\nrightarrow$ Y, means that there exists a symmetric encryption scheme which meets notion X but for which we can exhibit an attack showing that it does not meet notion Y. The separation is interesting only if there exists some scheme which meets security notion X, as otherwise the implication X $\longrightarrow$ Y is vacuously true. Our separations can be categorised into two types. In the former we will assume that there exists some scheme $\mathcal{SE}$ which meets notion X, and use it to construct a scheme $\overline{\mathcal{SE}}$ which meets notion X but is insecure in the Y sense. From the foregoing discussion, such an assumption is in some sense minimal. In the second type of separations we will assume the existence of pseudorandom functions and UF-CMA MACs to construct a scheme which meets notion X but not notion Y. In this paper for all separations of the latter type we will have that X $\longrightarrow$ IND-CPA. It is a well-known result that the existence of IND-CPA-secure symmetric encryption implies the existence of pseudorandom functions [15,17,18]. In addition a pseudorandom function can be combined with an almost-universal hash function to obtain a variable-input-length pseudorandom function, which in turn yields a UF-CMA MAC. Thus from a theoretical viewpoint the underlying assumptions for either type of separation are equivalent.

Note that when proving a separation we do not require the scheme to have distinct error messages, as we are interested solely in the *existence* of a counterexample showing that the relation under question cannot be established. Secondly any multiple-error scheme which is secure under some notion X implies the existence of a single-error scheme which is also secure under notion X (simply by mapping all error messages to a single error message). Consequently it is best to prove separations using schemes with an error space of *minimal cardinality*. It then follows that the separation also holds for all schemes of higher error-space cardinality.

STRAIGHTFORWARD RELATIONS. The following set of relations are self-evident. We state them here for the sake of completeness without proofs.

Proposition 1

$$\text{IND} - \text{sfCCA} \longrightarrow \text{IND} - \text{CCA} \longrightarrow \text{IND} - \text{CVA} \longrightarrow \text{IND} - \text{CPA}$$

$$\text{IND\$} - \text{sfCCA} \longrightarrow \text{IND\$} - \text{CCA} \longrightarrow \text{IND\$} - \text{CVA} \longrightarrow \text{IND\$} - \text{CPA}$$
$$\text{IND\$} - \text{sfCVA}$$

$$\text{INT} - \text{sfCTXT} \longrightarrow \text{INT} - \text{CTXT} \longrightarrow \text{INT} - \text{CTXT}^*$$
$$\text{INT} - \text{sfCTXT}^*$$

REVISITING CLASSIC RELATIONS. If a symmetric encryption scheme that only supports a single possible error symbol satisfies both passive confidentiality

(IND-CPA) and integrity of ciphertexts, then it offers confidentiality against chosen-ciphertext attacks [8,10]. Often, when analysing a particular scheme, its chosen-plaintext security and ciphertext integrity are proven first, and then the results of [8,10] are used to guarantee chosen-ciphertext security. Indeed, the combination of IND-CPA and INT-sfCTXT (or their stateful versions) has come to be the accepted security notion for symmetric encryption. We proceed to re-examine the classic relations from [8,10] in the context of encryption schemes with multiple error messages.

The following theorem serves as the basis for the two separations in Corollaries 1 and 2, showing that the classic relations no longer hold for multiple-error schemes.

We point out that in proving the separations, we adopt the stronger interpretations of ciphertext integrity so as to avoid any ambiguity in the results.

Theorem 1 (IND-CPA $\wedge$ INT-sfCTXT$\not\rightarrow$ IND-CCA). *Let $F : \mathcal{K}_e \times \{0,1\}^\ell \rightarrow \{0,1\}^n$ be a pseudorandom function, and let $\mathcal{MA} = (\mathcal{K}_m, \mathcal{T}, \mathcal{V})$ be a UF-CMA secure MAC with tag length $\ell_{tag} < n$. Consider the stateful symmetric encryption scheme $\overline{\mathcal{SE}}_1$ having message space $\{0,1\}^{n-\ell_{tag}}$ and error space $\{\perp_0, \perp_1\}$ shown in Fig. 7. For any IND-CPA adversary $\mathcal{A}_{cpa}$ and any INT-sfCTXT adversary $\mathcal{A}_{int}$ against $\overline{\mathcal{SE}}_1$, both making at most $2^\ell - 1$ encryption queries, there exist two corresponding adversaries $\mathcal{A}_{prf}$ and $\mathcal{A}_{uf}$ using roughly the same resources as $\mathcal{A}_{cpa}$ and $\mathcal{A}_{int}$, respectively, such that:*

$$\mathbf{Adv}^{\text{ind-cpa}}_{\overline{\mathcal{SE}}_1}(\mathcal{A}_{cpa}) \leq 2 \cdot \mathbf{Adv}^{\text{prf}}_F(\mathcal{A}_{prf}), \tag{1a}$$

$$\mathbf{Adv}^{\text{int-sfctxt}}_{\overline{\mathcal{SE}}_1}(\mathcal{A}_{int}) \leq \mathbf{Adv}^{\text{uf-cma}}_{\mathcal{MA}}(\mathcal{A}_{uf}). \tag{1b}$$

Moreover there exist efficient adversaries $\mathcal{A}_{cca}$ and $\mathcal{A}'_{uf}$ such that:

$$\mathbf{Adv}^{\text{ind-cca}}_{\overline{\mathcal{SE}}_1}(\mathcal{A}_{cca}) = 1 - \mathbf{Adv}^{\text{uf-cma}}_{\mathcal{MA}}(\mathcal{A}'_{uf}). \tag{1c}$$

Combining Theorem 1 and Proposition 1 yields the following two separations corresponding to the aforementioned relations from [10] and [8].

Corollary 1 (IND-CPA $\wedge$ INT-CTXT$\not\rightarrow$ IND-CCA). *Let $F : \mathcal{K}_e \times \{0,1\}^\ell \rightarrow \{0,1\}^n$ be a pseudorandom function, and let $\mathcal{MA} = (\mathcal{K}_m, \mathcal{T}, \mathcal{V})$ be a UF-CMA secure MAC with tag length $\ell_{tag} < n$. Then there exists a symmetric encryption scheme that is both IND-CPA secure and INT-CTXT secure but that is not secure in the IND-CCA sense.*

Corollary 2 (IND-CPA $\wedge$ INT-sfCTXT$\not\rightarrow$ IND-sfCCA). *Let $F : \mathcal{K}_e \times \{0,1\}^\ell \rightarrow \{0,1\}^n$ be a pseudorandom function, and let $\mathcal{MA} = (\mathcal{K}_m, \mathcal{T}, \mathcal{V})$ be a UF-CMA secure MAC with tag length $\ell_{tag} < n$. Then there exists a symmetric encryption scheme that is both IND-CPA secure and INT-sfCTXT secure but that is not secure in the IND-sfCCA sense.*

Note that in proving Theorem 1 we resorted to a stateful scheme. Only a stateful scheme can be INT-sfCTXT secure, and therefore the counterexample

Algorithm $\overline{\mathcal{K}}$	Algorithm $\overline{\mathcal{E}}_K(m,\sigma)$	Algorithm $\overline{\mathcal{D}}_K(c,\varrho)$

$K_e \leftarrow^\$ \mathcal{K}_e$
 $K_m \leftarrow \mathcal{K}_m$
 $\sigma \leftarrow 1,\varrho \leftarrow 1$
 $K \leftarrow K_e \parallel K_m$
 return (K,σ,ϱ)
	$\tau \leftarrow \mathcal{T}_{K_m}(\langle\sigma\rangle_\ell \parallel m)$
	 $c \leftarrow F_{K_e}(\langle\sigma\rangle_\ell) \oplus (m \parallel \tau)$
	 $\sigma \leftarrow \sigma + 1 \bmod 2^\ell$
	 return (c,σ)
		if $\|c\| \neq n$ **then** $\varrho \leftarrow 0$
		 if $\varrho = 0$ **then**
		    return $(\perp_0,\varrho)$
		 $w \leftarrow F_{K_e}(\langle\varrho\rangle_\ell) \oplus c$
		 parse w **as** $m \parallel \tau$
		 $v \leftarrow \mathcal{V}_{K_m}(\langle\varrho\rangle_\ell \parallel m,\tau)$
		 if $v = 1$
		    then $\varrho \leftarrow \varrho + 1 \bmod 2^\ell$
		 else
		    $\varrho \leftarrow 0$
		    if $m[1] = 0$ **then** $m \leftarrow \perp_0$
		    else $m \leftarrow \perp_1$
		 return (m,ϱ)

Fig. 7. The scheme $\overline{\mathcal{SE}}_1$ of Theorem 1.

used to prove Corollary 2 needs to be stateful. The same cannot be said however about the separation in Corollary 1, and in fact it can be proven more generally using a stateless scheme, but we omit the details for the sake of brevity.

NEW RELATIONS. We now go on to investigate how chosen-ciphertext security can be obtained in the multiple-error setting. Given how useful the relations of [10] and [8] have turned out to be, it would make sense to attempt to derive analogous relations that hold more generally. The following theorem extends the relation of [10] to schemes with multiple errors.

Theorem 2 (IND-CVA $\wedge$ INT-CTXT $\longrightarrow$ IND-CCA). *Let* $\mathcal{SE} = (\mathcal{K},\mathcal{E},\mathcal{D})$ *be a symmetric encryption scheme. For any* IND-CCA *adversary* $\mathcal{A}_{cca}$ *there exist adversaries* $\mathcal{A}_{cva}$ *and* $\mathcal{A}_{int}$ *consuming similar resources to* $\mathcal{A}_{cca}$ *such that:*

$$\mathbf{Adv}_{\mathcal{SE}}^{\text{ind-cca}}(\mathcal{A}_{cca}) \leq \mathbf{Adv}_{\mathcal{SE}}^{\text{ind-cva}}(\mathcal{A}_{cva}) + 2 \cdot \mathbf{Adv}_{\mathcal{SE}}^{\text{int-ctxt}}(\mathcal{A}_{int}). \qquad (2)$$

A similar relation can be established for stateful chosen-ciphertext security, and each of these relations can be re-proven for security notions involving indistinguishability from random bits. We state these relations below.

Proposition 2

$$\text{IND-CVA} \ \wedge \ \text{INT-sfCTXT} \ \longrightarrow \ \text{IND-sfCCA}$$
$$\text{IND\$-CVA} \ \wedge \ \text{INT-CTXT} \ \longrightarrow \ \text{IND\$-CCA}$$
$$\text{IND\$-sfCVA} \ \wedge \ \text{INT-sfCTXT} \ \longrightarrow \ \text{IND\$-sfCCA}$$

NECESSITY OF STRONG CIPHERTEXT INTEGRITY. The above relations can be seen as strengthened variants of the relations from [10] and [8], where we replaced CPA security with CVA security and adopted the stronger notions of ciphertext integrity. It is natural to ask whether the left-hand side of each relation can be somehow relaxed. We have seen in Corollaries 1 and 2 that reverting from CVA security to CPA security is not an option. However it is not evident whether it is necessary to require the stronger variants of ciphertext integrity. Theorem 3 answers this question by means of a separation, proving that strong ciphertext integrity is necessary for Theorem 2 to hold.

Theorem 3 (IND-CVA $\wedge$ INT-CTXT* $\not\rightarrow$ IND-CCA). *Let $\mathcal{SE} = (\mathcal{K}, \mathcal{E}, \mathcal{D})$ be a symmetric encryption scheme with a large message space $\mathcal{M}$ and an error space $\{\bot_0\}$, such that it is both IND-CVA secure and INT-CTXT* secure. Let the length of its ciphertexts be bounded above by 2^ℓ for some integer ℓ. Consider the scheme $\overline{\mathcal{SE}}_2$ having message space $\mathcal{M}$ and error space $\{\bot_0, \bot_1\}$ shown in Fig. 8. For any IND-CVA adversary $\mathcal{A}_{cva}$ making q_e left-or-right queries, and any INT-CTXT* adversary $\mathcal{A}_{int}$ making q_t verification queries, there exist adversaries $\mathcal{A}_{cva}^1$, $\mathcal{A}_{cva}^2$, and $\mathcal{A}_{int}^1$ (consuming similar resources to $\mathcal{A}_{cva}$ and $\mathcal{A}_{int}$) such that:*

$$\mathbf{Adv}_{\overline{\mathcal{SE}}_2}^{\text{ind-cva}}(\mathcal{A}_{cva}) \leq \mathbf{Adv}_{\mathcal{SE}}^{\text{ind-cva}}(\mathcal{A}_{cva}^1) + \frac{1}{2} \cdot \mathbf{Adv}_{\mathcal{SE}}^{\text{ind-cva}}(\mathcal{A}_{cva}^2) + \frac{q_e}{|\mathcal{M}|}, \quad (3a)$$

$$\mathbf{Adv}_{\overline{\mathcal{SE}}_2}^{\text{int-ctxt*}}(\mathcal{A}_{int}) \leq \mathbf{Adv}_{\mathcal{SE}}^{\text{int-ctxt*}}(\mathcal{A}_{int}^1) + \frac{q_t}{|\mathcal{M}|}. \quad (3b)$$

Moreover there exists an adversary $\mathcal{A}_{cca}$, making at most $(\ell + \max_{m \in \mathcal{M}}(|m|) + 1)$ decryption queries and one left-or-right query such that:

$$\mathbf{Adv}_{\overline{\mathcal{SE}}_2}^{\text{ind-cca}}(\mathcal{A}_{cca}) = 1. \quad (3c)$$

Theorem 3 also serves as a separation between INT-CTXT* and INT-CTXT, showing that the latter is strictly stronger. Separations similar to that of Theorem 3 corresponding to the relations of Proposition 2 can also be established.

Proposition 3

$$2\text{IND} - \text{CVA} \wedge \text{INT} - \text{sfCTXT*} \not\rightarrow \text{IND} - \text{sfCCA}$$

$$\text{IND\$} - \text{CVA} \wedge \text{INT} - \text{CTXT*} \not\rightarrow \text{IND\$} - \text{CCA}$$

$$\text{IND\$} - \text{sfCVA} \wedge \text{INT} - \text{sfCTXT*} \not\rightarrow \text{IND\$} - \text{sfCCA}$$

Algorithm $\overline{\mathcal{K}}$	Algorithm $\overline{\mathcal{E}}_{K_0}(m, \sigma)$	Algorithm $\overline{\mathcal{D}}_{K_0}(c, \varrho)$

$(K, \sigma, \varrho) \leftarrow \mathcal{K}$
 $m^* \leftarrow_\$ \mathcal{M}$
 $(c^*, \sigma) \leftarrow \mathcal{E}_K(m^*, \sigma)$
 $K_0 \leftarrow (K, m^*, c^*)$
 return (K_0, σ, ϱ)
	if $(m = m^*)$ **then** $c \leftarrow c^*$
	 else $(c, \sigma) \leftarrow \mathcal{E}_K(m, \sigma)$
	 return $(0 \parallel c, \sigma)$
		parse c as $b \parallel c'$
		 if $(b = 0)$ **then**
		   if $(c' = c^*)$ **then** $m \leftarrow m^*$
		   else $(m, \varrho) \leftarrow \mathcal{D}_K(c', \varrho)$
		 else $\psi \leftarrow \langle |c^*| \rangle_\ell \parallel c^*$
		   if $\langle c' \rangle^{-1} \leq |\psi|$ **then**
		     $d \leftarrow \psi[\langle c' \rangle^{-1}], m \leftarrow \bot_d$
		   else $m \leftarrow \bot_0$
		 return (m, ϱ)

Fig. 8. The scheme $\overline{\mathcal{SE}}_2$ of Theorem 3.

5   Further Relations and the IND\$-CCA3 Notion

AUTHENTICATED-ENCRYPTION SECURITY. Following the work of Bellare and Namprempre [10], chosen-plaintext security and ciphertext integrity were identified as the two security goals for symmetric encryption. Rogaway and Shrimpton [26] presented a *single* security notion, sometimes referred to as IND\$-CCA3 and more commonly called authenticated-encryption security, that is equivalent to the combination of chosen plaintext security and ciphertext integrity. We now present a natural extension of this notion to the multiple error setting. Then in Theorem 4 we show that this characterisation is equivalent to the combination of chosen-plaintext security, weak chosen ciphertext integrity, and error invariance.

Definition 9 (IND\$-CCA3 notion for multiple-error symmetric encryption). *Let $\mathcal{SE} = (\mathcal{K}, \mathcal{E}, \mathcal{D})$ be a multiple-error symmetric encryption scheme with error space $\mathcal{S}_\perp$. For an adversary $\mathcal{A}$, an error $\perp \in \mathcal{S}_\perp$ and a bit b, define experiment $\mathbf{Exp}_{\mathcal{SE},\perp}^{\mathrm{ind\$-cca3-}b}(\mathcal{A})$ as shown in Fig. 9. First $\mathcal{K}$ is called to generate a key K, an initial encryption state σ, and an initial decryption state ϱ. The adversary $\mathcal{A}$ is then given access to a special encryption oracle $\mathsf{Enc\$}(\cdot)$ and a special decryption oracle $\mathsf{Dec}\varnothing(\cdot)$. When b = 1 both oracles behave as normal encryption and decryption oracles. When b = 0 then $\mathsf{Enc\$}(\cdot)$ will return a random bit string (of the same length as an actual ciphertext would have been), and $\mathsf{Dec}\varnothing(\cdot)$ will always return $\perp$ (unless the queried ciphertext was output by $\mathsf{Enc\$}(\cdot)$, in which case it will return $\not\downarrow$).*

The adversary's goal is to output a bit b', as its guess of the challenge bit b. The experiment returns b' as well and, for $\perp \in \mathcal{S}_\perp$ and an adversary $\mathcal{A}$, the advantage is defined as:

$$\mathbf{Adv}_{\mathcal{SE},\perp}^{\mathrm{ind\$-cca3}}(\mathcal{A}) = \Pr\left[\mathbf{Exp}_{\mathcal{SE},\perp}^{\mathrm{ind\$-cca3-1}}(\mathcal{A}) = 1\right] - \Pr\left[\mathbf{Exp}_{\mathcal{SE},\perp}^{\mathrm{ind\$-cca3-0}}(\mathcal{A}) = 1\right].$$

The scheme $\mathcal{SE}$ is said to be IND\$-CCA3 secure if there exists $\perp \in \mathcal{S}_\perp$ such that for every adversary $\mathcal{A}$ with reasonable resources its advantage $\mathbf{Adv}_{\mathcal{SE},\perp}^{\mathrm{ind\$-cca3}}(\mathcal{A})$ is small.

Note: An IND-CCA3 notion can be defined by replacing the $\mathsf{Enc\$}(\cdot)$ oracle with a *real-or-random* encryption oracle (cf. [5]). Such an oracle returns either an encryption of the queried message or an encryption of a random message of the same length.

Theorem 4 (IND\$-CPA $\wedge$ INT-CTXT* $\wedge$ INV-ERR $\rightleftarrows$ IND\$-CCA3). *Let $\mathcal{SE} = (\mathcal{K}, \mathcal{E}, \mathcal{D})$ be a symmetric encryption scheme with error space $\mathcal{S}_\perp$.*

– *For any $\perp \in \mathcal{S}_\perp$ and any adversary $\mathcal{A}_{cca3}$ there exist adversaries $\mathcal{A}_{cpa}$, $\mathcal{A}_{int}$ and $\mathcal{A}_{err}$ (consuming similar resources to $\mathcal{A}_{cca3}$) such that:*

$$\mathbf{Adv}_{\mathcal{SE},\perp}^{\mathrm{ind\$-cca3}}(\mathcal{A}_{cca3}) \leq \mathbf{Adv}_{\mathcal{SE}}^{\mathrm{ind\$-cpa}}(\mathcal{A}_{cpa}) + \mathbf{Adv}_{\mathcal{SE}}^{\mathrm{int-ctxt*}}(\mathcal{A}_{int}) + \mathbf{Adv}_{\mathcal{SE},\perp}^{\mathrm{inv-err}}(\mathcal{A}_{err}).$$

$$\tag{4}$$

$\mathbf{Exp}_{\mathcal{SE},\perp}^{\mathsf{ind\$-cca3}-b}(\mathcal{A})$	$\mathsf{Enc\$}(m)$	$\mathsf{Dec}\varnothing(c)$
$(K, \sigma, \varrho) \leftarrow \mathcal{K}$	$(c, \sigma) \leftarrow \mathcal{E}_K(m, \sigma)$	$(m, \varrho) \leftarrow \mathcal{D}_K(c, \varrho)$
$i \leftarrow 0, \mathsf{C} \leftarrow ()$	if $b = 0$ then $c \leftarrow \{0,1\}^{|c|}$	if $b = 0$ then $m \leftarrow \perp$
$b' \leftarrow \mathcal{A}^{\mathsf{Enc\$}(\cdot),\mathsf{Dec}\varnothing(\cdot)}$	$i \leftarrow i + 1, \mathsf{C}_i \leftarrow c$	if $c \in \mathsf{C}$ then $m \leftarrow \between$
return (b')	return c	return m

Fig. 9. IND\$-CCA3 experiment for multiple-error symmetric encryption schemes.

– *For any* $\perp \in \mathcal{S}_\perp$ *and any three adversaries* $\mathcal{A}'_{cpa}$, $\mathcal{A}'_{int}$ *and* $\mathcal{A}'_{err}$ *there exist three corresponding adversaries* $\mathcal{A}^1_{cca3}$, $\mathcal{A}^2_{cca3}$ *and* $\mathcal{A}^3_{cca3}$ *(consuming similar resources to* $\mathcal{A}'_{cpa}$, $\mathcal{A}'_{int}$ *and* $\mathcal{A}'_{err}$, *respectively) such that:*

$$\mathbf{Adv}_{\mathcal{SE}}^{\mathsf{ind\$-cpa}}(\mathcal{A}'_{cpa}) \leq \mathbf{Adv}_{\mathcal{SE},\perp}^{\mathsf{ind\$-cca3}}(\mathcal{A}^1_{cca3}), \tag{5a}$$

$$\mathbf{Adv}_{\mathcal{SE}}^{\mathsf{int-ctxt*}}(\mathcal{A}'_{int}) \leq 2 \cdot \mathbf{Adv}_{\mathcal{SE},\perp}^{\mathsf{ind\$-cca3}}(\mathcal{A}^2_{cca3}), \tag{5b}$$

$$\mathbf{Adv}_{\mathcal{SE},\perp}^{\mathsf{inv-err}}(\mathcal{A}'_{err}) \leq 2 \cdot \mathbf{Adv}_{\mathcal{SE},\perp}^{\mathsf{ind\$-cca3}}(\mathcal{A}^3_{cca3}). \tag{5c}$$

It can be similarly shown that:

Proposition 4 IND-CPA $\wedge$ INT-CTXT* $\wedge$ INV-ERR $\rightleftharpoons$ IND-CCA3.

The question remains whether IND\$-CCA3 security guarantees IND\$-CCA security in the multiple error setting, which is the ultimate target security notion. Proposition 5 tells us that this is indeed the case. In fact it says something stronger, in that it relates IND\$-CCA3 to the security notions from Proposition 2.

Proposition 5 IND\$-CCA3 $\longrightarrow$ IND\$-CVA $\wedge$ INT-CTXT $\longrightarrow$ IND\$-CCA.

6   The Security of Encode-Then-Encrypt-Then-MAC

The works of Bellare and Namprempre [10] and Krawczyk [20] provide formal evidence for preferring Encrypt-then-MAC (EtM) over other generic compositions like MAC-then-encrypt (MtE). However we believe that the merits of EtM as a generic composition technique go beyond the implications of their work. By combining results from [20] and [7], we know that MtE is actually IND-CCA secure when instantiated with CBC or counter-mode encryption. Thus the analysis of [10,20] does not explain why EtM should be more secure than MtE when both are instantiated with CBC or counter-mode encryption. Nonetheless practical cryptosystems (employing CBC and counter-mode encryption) based on EtM have so far proved themselves less vulnerable to attack than ones based on MtE. For example, the attacks in [2,3,11,13] exploit features of the encoding schemes used in specific MtE constructions and the fact that an adversary can distinguish among distinct decryption failures. Neither of these aspects were considered in [10]. Reconsidering the generic compositions in the light of

Algorithm $\overline{\mathcal{K}}$	Algorithm $\overline{\mathcal{E}}_K(m, \sigma)$	Algorithm $\overline{\mathcal{D}}_K(\psi, \varrho)$

$(K_e, \sigma, \varrho) \leftarrow \mathcal{K}_e$
 $K_m \leftarrow \mathcal{K}_m$
 $K \leftarrow K_e \parallel K_m$
 return (K, σ, ϱ)
	$w \leftarrow \mathcal{EC}(m)$
	 $(c, \sigma) \leftarrow \mathcal{E}_{K_e}(w, \sigma)$
	 $\tau \leftarrow \mathcal{T}_{K_m}(c)$
	 return $(c \parallel \tau, \sigma)$
		if $\lvert\psi\rvert < \ell_{tag} + 1$ **then**
		     return $(\perp_0, \varrho)$
		 parse ψ **as** $c \parallel \tau$
		 $v \leftarrow \mathcal{V}_{K_m}(c, \tau)$
		 if $v \in \mathcal{Q}_\perp$ **then**
		     return (v, ϱ)
		 $(w, \varrho) \leftarrow \mathcal{D}_{K_e}(c, \varrho)$
		 if $w \in \mathcal{S}_\perp$ **then**
		     return (w, ϱ)
		 $m \leftarrow \mathcal{DC}(w)$
		 return (m, ϱ)

Fig. 10. The generic Encode-then-Encypt-then-MAC composition $\overline{\mathcal{SE}}_{EEM}$ with distinguishable decryption failures.

multiple-error messages (or equivalently distinguishable decryption failures) provides new formal grounds for preferring the EtM composition. More specifically we consider an encode-then-encrypt-then-MAC (EEM) composition to account for the pre-processing (such as padding) that is common in practical schemes. The EEM composition is specified in Fig. 10. Theorem 5 shows that EEM is a *robust* composition, in the sense that it provides IND-CVA and INT-CTXT security, and therefore IND-CCA security, in the multiple-error setting, irrespective of the encoding scheme used (and the error messages it returns) and the error messages that the encryption component may return, as long as the encryption component is IND-CPA and the MAC is SUF-CMA. In fact, we can prove that EEM provides IND-CCA3 security if its MAC component only has a single error message.

Theorem 5 (EEM provides IND-CVA+INT-CTXT). *Suppose* $\mathcal{SE} = (\mathcal{K}_e, \mathcal{E}, \mathcal{D})$ *is a symmetric encryption scheme with message space* $\mathcal{M}$ *and error space* $\mathcal{S}_\perp$. *Let* $\mathcal{MA} = (\mathcal{K}_m, \mathcal{T}, \mathcal{V})$ *be a MAC with error space* $\mathcal{Q}_\perp$ *producing tags of length* ℓ_{tag}. *Let* $\mathcal{ES} = (\mathcal{EC}, \mathcal{DC})$ *be a length-regular encoding scheme with domain* $\overline{\mathcal{M}}$, *codomain* $\mathcal{M}$, *and error space* $\mathcal{U}_\perp$. *Figure 10 then defines a symmetric encryption scheme* $\overline{\mathcal{SE}}_{EEM}$ *with message space* $\overline{\mathcal{M}}$ *and error space* $\overline{\mathcal{S}_\perp} = \mathcal{S}_\perp \cup \mathcal{Q}_\perp \cup \mathcal{U}_\perp \cup \{\perp_0\}$, *for some* $\perp_0 \notin \mathcal{S}_\perp \cup \mathcal{Q}_\perp \cup \mathcal{U}_\perp$. *For any* IND-CVA *adversary* $\mathcal{A}_{cva}$ *and any* INT-CTXT *adversary* $\mathcal{A}_{int}$ *against* $\overline{\mathcal{SE}}_{EEM}$, *there exist adversaries* $\mathcal{A}_{cpa}$, $\mathcal{A}^1_{suf}$, *and* $\mathcal{A}^2_{suf}$ *such that:*

$$\mathbf{Adv}^{\text{ind-cva}}_{\overline{\mathcal{SE}}_{EEM}}(\mathcal{A}_{cva}) \leq \mathbf{Adv}^{\text{ind-cpa}}_{\mathcal{SE}}(\mathcal{A}_{cpa}) + \mathbf{Adv}^{\text{suf-cma}}_{\mathcal{MA}}(\mathcal{A}^1_{suf}), \qquad (6)$$

$$\mathbf{Adv}^{\text{int-ctxt}}_{\overline{\mathcal{SE}}_{EEM}}(\mathcal{A}_{int}) \leq \mathbf{Adv}^{\text{suf-cma}}_{\mathcal{MA}}(\mathcal{A}^2_{suf}). \qquad (7)$$

Moreover, these adversaries consume similar resources to $\mathcal{A}_{cva}$ *and* $\mathcal{A}_{int}$.

It is instructive to consider some distinguishable decryption failure attacks that have been discovered on instantiations of the MAC-then-Encode-then-Ecrypt

(MEE) composition, in order to see how such implementation flaws are captured by our treatment. The attacks on TLS [11] and on DTLS [2] use timing differences to distinguish a MAC failure from a padding failure. In the case of IPsec [13], the encoding includes a padding portion as well as a header portion, and it is the ability to discern between malformed padding and a malformed header that gives rise to the attack. The recent Lucky 13 attack on TLS [3] exploits timing differences in the verification algorithm of HMAC. More specifically each compression function evaluation in HMAC results in additional processing time during decryption that can be detected by the adversary from the time delay in returning TLS's MAC failure message; the size of the delay relates to the amount of TLS padding previously removed and can be used to infer plaintext in an extension of Vaudenay's padding oracle attack [27]. This timing channel can be modelled in our framework by transforming HMAC into a multiple-error MAC. Then the error messages that HMAC returns can be easily predicted from the length of the string on which the tag is to be verified. It follows from this observation that any proof of SUF-CMA security for the usual single-error HMAC can be extended to this multiple-error version of HMAC. So, while this multiple-error HMAC is still SUF-CMA secure, its interaction with the TLS padding renders the MEE composition used in TLS insecure. By contrast, as established in Theorem 5, an EEM composition would not be compromised by such an implementation flaw.

7 More Separations

We now present a separation showing that IND-CVA is strictly stronger than IND-CPA. We actually show something slightly stronger, in that the separation also holds for schemes which are error invariant. This separation further serves to point out that, even for single-error schemes, Theorem 2 does not reduce to the relation of Bellare and Namprempre from [10].

Theorem 6 (IND-CPA $\wedge$ INV-ERR $\not\rightarrow$ IND-CVA). *Let* $F : \mathcal{K}_e \times \{0,1\}^\ell \rightarrow \{0,1\}^n$ *be a pseudorandom function, where* ℓ *is sufficiently large. Then the symmetric encryption scheme* $\overline{\mathcal{SE}}_3$ *having message space* $\cup_{k\geq 1}\{0,1\}^{nk}$ *and error space* $\{\perp\}$ *shown in Fig. 11 is such that, for any* IND-CPA *adversary* $\mathcal{A}_{cpa}$ *making* q *encryption queries totalling* μ *bits of plaintext, there exists a corresponding adversary* $\mathcal{A}_{prf}$ *(consuming similar resources to* $\mathcal{A}_{cpa}$*) with:*

$$\mathbf{Adv}^{\text{ind-cpa}}_{\overline{\mathcal{SE}}_3}(\mathcal{A}_{cpa}) \leq 2 \cdot \mathbf{Adv}^{\text{prf}}_F(\mathcal{A}_{prf}) + \left(\frac{\mu}{n} + q\right)\left(\frac{q-1}{2^\ell}\right). \tag{8a}$$

Moreover there exists an efficient adversary $\mathcal{A}_{cva}$ *such that:*

$$\mathbf{Adv}^{\text{ind-cva}}_{\overline{\mathcal{SE}}_3}(\mathcal{A}_{cva}) = 1. \tag{8b}$$

In Sect. 3 it was noted that if the IND-sfCVA experiment is defined in the obvious way, it would be syntactically equivalent to the IND-CVA experiment. In the case of indistinguishability from random bits, an analogous equivalence is not evident from the syntax. Theorem 7 settles this in the negative.

Algorithm $\overline{\mathcal{K}}$	Algorithm $\overline{\mathcal{E}}_K(m, \sigma)$	Algorithm $\overline{\mathcal{D}}_K(c, \varrho)$
$K \leftarrow_\$ \mathcal{K}_e$	**if** $|m| \notin \{\alpha n : \alpha \geq 1\}$ **then**	**if** $|c| \notin \{\ell + \alpha n : \alpha \geq 2\}$ **then**
$\sigma \leftarrow \varepsilon, \varrho \leftarrow \varepsilon$	$\quad$ **return** $\perp$	$\quad$ **return** $\perp$
return (K, σ, ϱ)	$p \leftarrow |m|/n$	$q \leftarrow (|c| - \ell)/n$
	parse m **as** $m_1 \parallel \ldots \parallel m_p$	**parse** c **as** $c_0 \parallel \ldots \parallel c_q$
	$m_{p+1} \leftarrow 0^n, c_0 \leftarrow_\$ \{0,1\}^\ell$	**for** $i \leftarrow 1$ **to** q **do**
	for $i \leftarrow 1$ **to** $p+1$ **do**	$\quad m_i \leftarrow F_K(c_0 + i) \oplus c_i$
	$\quad c_i \leftarrow F_K(c_0 + i) \oplus m_i$	**if** $m_q \neq 0^n$ **then** $m \leftarrow \perp$
	$c \leftarrow c_0 \parallel c_1 \parallel \ldots \parallel c_{p+1}$	**else** $m \leftarrow m_1 \parallel \ldots \parallel m_{q-1}$
	return (c, σ)	**return** (m, ϱ)

Fig. 11. The scheme $\overline{\mathcal{SE}}_3$ of Theorem 6.

Theorem 7 (IND\$-CVA $\wedge$ INV-ERR$\nrightarrow$ IND\$-sfCVA). *Let* $F : \mathcal{K}_e \times \{0,1\}^\ell \rightarrow \{0,1\}^n$ *be a pseudorandom function, where ℓ is sufficiently large. Let* $\mathcal{MA} = (\mathcal{K}_m, \mathcal{T}, \mathcal{V})$ *be a single-error MAC where* $\mathcal{T} : \mathcal{K}_m \times \{0,1\}^* \rightarrow \{0,1\}^{\ell_{tag}}$ *is pseudo-random. Consider the symmetric encryption scheme* $\overline{\mathcal{SE}}_4$ *having message space* $\cup_{k \geq 1}\{0,1\}^{nk}$ *and error space* $\{\perp\}$ *shown in Fig. 12. For any* IND\$-CVA *adversary* $\mathcal{A}_{cva}$ *making q encryption queries totalling μ bits of plaintext, there exist three adversaries* $\mathcal{A}^1_{prf}$, $\mathcal{A}^2_{prf}$, *and* $\mathcal{A}_{uf}$ *with:*

$$\mathbf{Adv}^{\text{ind\$-cva}}_{\overline{\mathcal{SE}}_4}(\mathcal{A}_{cva}) \leq \mathbf{Adv}^{\text{prf}}_F(\mathcal{A}^1_{prf}) + \mathbf{Adv}^{\text{prf}}_\mathcal{T}(\mathcal{A}^2_{prf}) + \mathbf{Adv}^{\text{uf-cma}}_{\mathcal{MA}}(\mathcal{A}_{uf})$$

$$+ \frac{\mu}{n} \cdot \left(\frac{q-1}{2^\ell}\right) + \frac{q(q-1)}{2^{\ell+n+1}} \,.$$

Moreover there exist efficient adversaries $\mathcal{A}_{sfcva}$ *and* $\mathcal{A}'_{uf}$ *such that:*

$$\mathbf{Adv}^{\text{ind\$-sfcva}}_{\overline{\mathcal{SE}}_4}(\mathcal{A}_{sfcva}) = 1 - \mathbf{Adv}^{\text{uf-cma}}_{\mathcal{MA}}(\mathcal{A}'_{uf}) \,. \tag{9a}$$

Algorithm $\overline{\mathcal{K}}$	Algorithm $\overline{\mathcal{E}}_K(m, \sigma)$	Algorithm $\overline{\mathcal{D}}_K(\psi, \varrho)$
$K_e \leftarrow_\$ \mathcal{K}_e$	**if** $|m| \notin \{\alpha n : \alpha \geq 1\}$ **then**	**if** $|\psi| \notin \{\ell + \ell_{tag} + \alpha n : \alpha \geq 1\}$ **then**
$K_m \leftarrow_\$ \mathcal{K}_m$	$\quad$ **return** $\perp$	$\quad$ **return** $(\perp, \varrho)$
$K \leftarrow K_e \parallel K_m$	$p \leftarrow |m|/n$	**parse** ψ **as** $c \parallel \tau$
$\sigma \leftarrow \varepsilon, \varrho \leftarrow \varepsilon$	**parse** m **as** $m_1 \parallel \ldots \parallel m_p$	$v \leftarrow \mathcal{V}_{K_m}(c, \tau)$
return (K, σ, ϱ)	$c_0 \leftarrow_\$ \{0,1\}^\ell$	**if** $(v \neq 1)$ **then**
	for $i \leftarrow 1$ **to** p **do**	$\quad$ **return** $(\perp, \varrho)$
	$\quad c_i \leftarrow F_K(c_0 + i) \oplus m_i$	$q \leftarrow (|c| - \ell)/n$
	$c \leftarrow c_0 \parallel c_1 \parallel \ldots \parallel c_p$	**parse** c **as** $c_0 \parallel \ldots \parallel c_q$
	$\tau \leftarrow \mathcal{T}_{K_m}(c)$	**for** $i \leftarrow 1$ **to** q **do**
	return $(c \parallel \tau, \sigma)$	$\quad m_i \leftarrow F_K(c_0 + i) \oplus c_i$
		$m \leftarrow m_1 \parallel \ldots \parallel m_q$
		return (m, ϱ)

Fig. 12. The scheme $\overline{\mathcal{SE}}_4$ of Theorem 7.

Acknowledgements. This work has been supported in part by the European Commission through the ICT programme under contract ICT-2007-216676 ECRYPT II. Alexandra Boldyreva is supported by NSF: CT-ISG 36566D3. Jean Paul Degabriele is supported by Vodafone Group Services Limited, a Thomas Holloway Research Studentship, and the Strategic Educational Pathways Scholarship Scheme (Malta), part-financed by the European Union European Social Fund. Kenneth Paterson is supported by EPSRC Leadership Fellowship EP/H005455/1.

References

1. Albrecht, M.R., Paterson, K.G., Watson, G.J.: Plaintext recovery attacks against SSH. In: IEEE Symposium on Security and Privacy, pp. 16–26. IEEE Computer Society (2009)
2. AlFardan, N.J., Paterson, K.G.: Plaintext-recovery attacks against datagram TLS. In: Proceedings of the 19th Annual Network and Distributed System Security Symposium (NDSS 2012)
3. AlFardan, N.J., Paterson, K.G.: Lucky thirteen: breaking the TLS and DTLS record protocols. In: IEEE Symposium on Security and Privacy 2013. http://www.isg.rhul.ac.uk/tls/TLStiming.pdf (To appear)
4. Bauer, A., Coron, J.-S., Naccache, D., Tibouchi, M., Vergnaud, D.: On the broadcast and validity-checking security of PKCS#1 v1.5 encryption. In: Zhou, J., Yung, M. (eds.) ACNS 2010. LNCS, vol. 6123, pp. 1–18. Springer, Heidelberg (2010)
5. Bellare, M., Desai, A., Jokipii, E., Rogaway. P.: A concrete security treatment of symmetric encryption. In: Proceedings of 38th Annual Symposium on Foundations of Computer Science (FOCS 1997), pp. 394–403. IEEE (1997)
6. Boldyreva, A., Degabriele, J.P., Paterson, K.G., Stam, M.: On symmetric encryption with distinguishable decryption failures. IACR Cryptology ePrint Archive. http://eprint.iacr.org (full version of this paper)
7. Bellare, M., Goldreich, O., Mityagin, A.: The power of verification queries in message authentication and authenticated encryption. IACR Cryptology ePrint Archive. http://eprint.iacr.org/2004/309
8. Bellare, M., Kohno, T., Namprempre, C.: Breaking and provably repairing the SSH authenticated encryption scheme: a case study of the encode-then-encrypt-and-MAC paradigm. ACM Trans. Inf. Syst. Secur. **7**(2), 206–241 (2004)
9. Bleichenbacher, D.: Chosen ciphertext attacks against protocols based on the RSA encryption standard PKCS #1. In: Krawczyk, H. (ed.) CRYPTO 1998. LNCS, vol. 1462, pp. 1–12. Springer, Heidelberg (1998)
10. Bellare, M., Namprempre, C.: Authenticated encryption: relations among notions and analysis of the generic composition paradigm. In: Okamoto, T. (ed.) ASIACRYPT 2000. LNCS, vol. 1976, pp. 531–545. Springer, Heidelberg (2000)
11. Canvel, B., Hiltgen, A.P., Vaudenay, S., Vuagnoux, M.: Password interception in a SSL/TLS channel. In: Boneh, D. (ed.) CRYPTO 2003. LNCS, vol. 2729, pp. 583–599. Springer, Heidelberg (2003)
12. Degabriele, J.P., Paterson, K.G.: Attacking the IPsec standards in encryption-only configurations. In: IEEE Symposium on Security and Privacy, pp. 335–349. IEEE Computer Society (2007)
13. Degabriele, J.P., Paterson, K.G.: On the (in)security of IPsec in MAC-then-encrypt configurations. In: Al-Shaer, E., Keromytis, A.D., Shmatikov, V. (eds.) ACM Conference on Computer and Communications Security, pp. 493–504. ACM (2010)

14. Duong, T., Rizzo, J.: Cryptography in the web: the case of cryptographic design flaws in ASP.NET. In: IEEE Symposium on Security and Privacy, pp. 481–489. IEEE Computer Society (2011)
15. Goldreich, O., Goldwasser, S., Micali, S.: How to construct random functions. J. ACM **33**(4), 792–807 (1986)
16. Hall, C., Goldberg, I., Schneier, B.: Reaction attacks against several public-key cryptosystem. In: Varadharajan, V., Mu, Y. (eds.) ICICS 1999. LNCS, vol. 1726, pp. 2–12. Springer, Heidelberg (1999)
17. Håstad, J., Impagliazzo, R., Levin, L.A., Luby, M.: A pseudorandom generator from any one-way function. SIAM J. Comput. **28**(4), 1364–1396 (1999)
18. Impagliazzo, R., Luby, M.: One-way functions are essential for complexity based cryptography (extended abstract). In: Proceedings of 30th Annual Symposium on Foundations of Computer Science (FOCS 1989), pp. 230–235. IEEE (1989)
19. Jager, T., Somorovsky, J.: How to break XML encryption. In: Chen, Y., Danezis, G., Shmatikov, V. (eds.) ACM Conference on Computer and Communications Security, pp. 413–422. ACM (2011)
20. Krawczyk, H.: The order of encryption and authentication for protecting communications (or: how secure is SSL?). In: Kilian, J. (ed.) CRYPTO 2001. LNCS, vol. 2139, pp. 310–331. Springer, Heidelberg (2001)
21. Manger, J.: A chosen ciphertext attack on RSA optimal asymmetric encryption padding (OAEP) as standardized in PKCS #1 v2.0. In: Kilian, J. (ed.) CRYPTO 2001. LNCS, vol. 2139, pp. 230–238. Springer, Heidelberg (2001)
22. Paterson, K.G., Watson, G.J.: Plaintext-dependent decryption: a formal security treatment of SSH-CTR. In: Gilbert, H. (ed.) EUROCRYPT 2010. LNCS, vol. 6110, pp. 345–361. Springer, Heidelberg (2010)
23. Paterson, K.G., Ristenpart, T., Shrimpton, T.: Tag size *does* matter: attacks and proofs for the TLS record protocol. In: Lee, D.H., Wang, X. (eds.) ASIACRYPT 2011. LNCS, vol. 7073, pp. 372–389. Springer, Heidelberg (2011)
24. Paterson, K.G., Watson, G.J.: Authenticated-encryption with padding: a formal security treatment. In: Naccache, D. (ed.) Cryphtography and Security: From Theory to Applications. LNCS, vol. 6805, pp. 83–107. Springer, Heidelberg (2012)
25. Rogaway, P.: Nonce-based symmetric encryption. In: Roy, B., Meier, W. (eds.) FSE 2004. LNCS, vol. 3017, pp. 348–359. Springer, Heidelberg (2004)
26. Rogaway, P., Shrimpton, T.: A provable-security treatment of the key-wrap problem. In: Vaudenay, S. (ed.) EUROCRYPT 2006. LNCS, vol. 4004, pp. 373–390. Springer, Heidelberg (2006)
27. Vaudenay, S.: Security flaws induced by CBC padding - applications to SSL, IPSEC, WTLS. In: Knudsen, L.R. (ed.) EUROCRYPT 2002. LNCS, vol. 2332, pp. 534–546. Springer, Heidelberg (2002)

Implementation Aspects

Minimalism of Software Implementation

Extensive Performance Analysis of Symmetric Primitives on the RL78 Microcontroller

Mitsuru Matsui and Yumiko Murakami[✉]

Information Technology R&D Center,
Mitsubishi Electric Corporation,
5-1-1 Ofuna, Kamakura, Kanagawa, Japan
Murakami.Yumiko@cw.MitsubishiElectric.co.jp,
Matsui.Mitsuru@ab.MitsubishiElectric.co.jp

Abstract. This paper studies state-of-the-art software implementation of lightweight symmetric primitives from embedded system programmer's standpoint. In embedded environments, due to many possible variations of ROM/RAM-size combinations, it is not always easy to obtain an entire performance picture of a given primitive and to create a fair benchmark from top speed records.

In this study we classify these size combinations into several categories and optimize operation speed in each category. We implemented on Renesas' RL78 microcontroller - a typical CISC embedded processor, four block ciphers and seven hash functions with various combinations of ROM and RAM sizes to make performance characteristics of these primitives clearer. We also discuss how to create an interface and measure size and speed of a given primitive from a practical point of view.

As a result, our AES encryption codes run at as fast as 3,855 cycles/block in the ROM-1KB RAM-64B category, and 6,622 cycles/block in the ROM-512B RAM-128B category. For another examples aiming at minimizing a ROM size, we have achieved 453-byte Keccak, 396-byte Skein-256 and 210-byte PRESENT encryption codes on this processor.

1 Introduction

Lightweight crypto has become one of hot topics in cryptography, with increasing market requirements of embedded security as a background. In the SHA-3 project, suitability to embedded applications was regarded as an important metric for selection, and ISO/IEC 29192 is standardizing lightweight cipher primitives. Lightweight crypto has been more often discussed in hardware contexts, such as low area and low power consumption, but some of recent studies focus on software implementation on low resource processors, which is, we believe, equally important since it is rather common in embedded systems that encryption is carried out in hardware, but decryption is done in software.

One of such activities is ECRYPT II block cipher and hash function projects [1,2], which have published performance evaluation results of many symmetric

S. Moriai (Ed.): FSE 2013, LNCS 8424, pp. 393–409, 2014.
DOI: 10.1007/978-3-662-43933-3_20, © Springer-Verlag Berlin Heidelberg 2014

primitives on the ATtiny45 processor. All codes were written in an assembly language, aiming at low-cost implementation. These works are effectively the first extensive benchmarking on a low-end microprocessor.

The paper also deals with assembly language programming of symmetric primitives on a low-end embedded processor, but takes different approaches. First of all, our target processor RL78 has an accumulator-based CISC architecture with 8 registers and read-modify instructions, while ATtiny is a RISC processor with 32 registers and a fixed instruction length. Looking at implementations of the same algorithm on different processor architectures will be of independent interest.

Secondly we aim at demonstrating various ROM/RAM-size and speed trade-offs for each primitive, not only pursuing pin-point top speed records. Embedded system programmers often deal with a crypto routine as an almost black box and want to know beforehand whether given size and speed can be achieved or not on a target processor. One of our purposes is to give them information about what ROM/RAM-size combinations are possible or **impossible** to implement on this processor. To do this, we first classify the size combinations into several categories and optimize each primitive in each category. Additionally we show a code toward a fastest speed and another code focusing on a smallest ROM size, accepting (very) slow computation speed.

Also we discuss interface and metric issues of symmetric primitives for embedded applications. In particular we point out that currently there is no consensus of how to count a RAM size of a given program. We here again take embedded programmers' viewpoint. What they are interested in is the amount of resources that they must allocate for a primitive. In this regard, we count the entire temporary area internally used in the primitive as RAM bytes, say, argument area and stack consumption including callee save register storage with a standard subroutine interface.

Our target primitives are AES [3], Camellia [4] and Clefia [5] with 128-bit key and Present [6] with 80-bit key for block ciphers. Note that AES and Camellia are included in ISO/IEC 18033-3, and Clefia and Present have been recently adopted as ISO/IEC 29192-2, a standard of lightweight block ciphers. For hash functions, our choices are SHA-256, SHA-512 [7], Keccak-256 [8], Skein-256, Skein-512 [9] Grøstl-256 and Grøstl-512 [10], where Keccak-256, Skein-256 and Skein-512 denote Keccak[r = 1088,c = 512], Skein-256-256 and Skein-512-512, respectively.

As a result, it is shown that AES achieves excellent size-speed balances for all ROM/RAM combinations on this processor. It runs at the speed of 3,855 cycles/block in the ROM-1KB RAM-64B category. Its ROM size was able to be reduced down to 486 bytes. Camellia outperforms AES in decryption. It is also demonstrated that the key scheduling of Clefia is a bottleneck for minimizing a code and Present is slow due to its harware-oriented nature, but its simple structure contributes to creating a very small program; we were able to write its encryption code with 210 ROM bytes.

For hash functions, it is shown that SHA-256 and SHA-512 are still good choices from a performance point of view. For 256-bit hash functions SHA-256 is fastest if 1 KB or more ROM is given, and for 512-bit hash functions Skein-512 is the only option if only 256-byte RAM is given. It is also demonstrated that Keccak and Skein can be implemented in a very compact way; our smallest codes of Keccak-256/Skein-256 had 453/396 ROM bytes, respectively.

2   The RL78 Microcontroller

RL78 is Renesas Electronics' next-generation low-power microcontroller family combining advanced features from both the 78 K and R8C families [11] which have been widely used in embedded applications such as in-vehicle controlling and mobile communication systems. It supports a wide range of pin, package and memory size combinations, currently covering Flash-ROM/RAM size variations of low-end 2KB/256B up to 512KB/32KB.

RL78 has a typical CISC architecture with an 8-bit accumulator-based instruction set including a small number of 16-bit instructions. It has eight 8-bit general registers a,x,b,c,d,e,h,l, which can be also used as register pairs ax,bc,de,hl. Most instructions allow only register a as a destination register, and only register pair hl as a general address pointer. For instance, xor a,[hl] is a valid instruction, but xor b,[hl] and xor a,[de] are not. This often causes size and speed penalties in programming symmetric primitives.

On the other hand, an advantage of this architecture is that it supports read-modify instructions and its average instruction length is short. Most instructions of RL78 used in a small model i.e. all segments are within 64 KB, are one- to three-byte long. For instance, xor a,[hl] is a read-modify one-cycle instruction whose length is one byte.

As for the memory access speed, reading from internal RAM takes only one cycle, but reading from ROM takes four cycles. Moreover when an address register is modified in the preceding instruction, an additional one-cycle delay happens due to an address generation interlock stall. Hence a table lookup can be costly on this processor.

Table 1 shows some of the instructions essential in our programming:

Table 1. Key instructions on RL78 in symmetric programming.

Instruction	Length (byte)	Latency	Comment
addw ax,[hl+byte]	3	1 cycle	16-bit add without carry-in (with carry-out)
sknc	2	1 cycle	skip next instruction if non-carry
xor/and/or reg1,reg2	1	1 cycle	reg1 or reg2 must be register a
shl/shr a/b/c,cnt	2	1 cycle	8-bit left/right shift; shr accepts only a
shlw/shrw ax/bc,cnt	2	1 cycle	16-bit left/right shift; shrw accepts only ax
rolc/rorc a,1	2	1 cycle	8-bit rotate shift with carry
rolwc ax/bc,1	2	1 cycle	16-bit rotate shift with carry; left shift only
push/pop regpair	1	1 cycle	push/pop a register pair to/from stack
call 16bit-adrs	3	3 cycles	stack pointer is subtracted by 4 bytes
ret	1	6 cycles	stack pointer is added by 4 bytes

The 16-bit add instruction `addw` is convenient but unfortunately only works without carry-in (its result affects the carry bit, though). Using `sknc`, however, a memory-to-memory 32-bit addition can be implemented as shown below, which is slightly shorter and faster than using an 8-bit add-with-carry instruction:

```
movw    ax,[mem1+2]
addw    ax,[mem2+2]
movw    [mem3+2],ax
movw    ax,[mem1]
sknc                        ; skip next instruction if no carry
incw    ax                  ; ax = ax + 1
addw    ax,[mem2]
movw    [mem3],ax
```

On the other hand, no 16-bit operations are supported in logical instructions such as `xor,or,and`, and these instructions accept only register pair `hl` as an address pointer. Also note that a subroutine call is quite expensive in this processor. A `call/ret` pair takes a total of nine cycles, and consumes stack by four bytes. For comparison, AVR's `rcall/ret` pair (short call) takes seven cycles with two stack bytes [12]. A programmer must try to minimize the number of subroutine calls if aiming at a speed record on RL78. Interestingly, however, a `push/pop` pair is inexpensive and handy for avoiding register starvation.

3 Interface and Metrics

3.1 Interface

First of all, we have adopted a commonly accepted program interface in embedded systems; i.e. we implemented a target primitive as a subroutine callable from C language, which we believe is a portable and small-overhead choice. In the following we use the calling conventions described in [13]: (1) the first argument is passed by `ax`, (2) other arguments are passed through stack, and (3) `hl` must be recovered at the end of the subroutine (callee-save register).

To reduce register pressure, we use only the first argument, and `ax` points to the RAM area prepared by a caller, which includes a message block to be encrypted or hashed, secret key (if any), a flag indicating first/middle/last block, and temporary buffer for internal use. For instance, one of our AES encryption routines has the following argument format that consists of a total of 50 bytes:

```
Bytes 00-15: plaintext/ciphertext
Bytes 16-31: secret key
Bytes 32-33: flag (bit 0/1: active in the first/last block)
Bytes 34-49: buffer for internal use
```

The first 16-byte plaintext is replaced by its correspondent ciphertext after encryption. It is allowed to overwrite this area during encryption to minimize RAM usage. The secret key can be also destroyed, but our codes were designed so that a caller does not have to rewrite the same secret key every block when encrypting a multiple number of blocks. Note that this does not always mean that the secret key area remains unchanged.

Our routines process one block in a single call. A caller is responsible for creating a block format from a target message and calling a routine block-by-block. This looks common in block cipher setting, but it is not obvious which side (caller or callee) should be responsible for formatting the last block including a padding in hash functions from performance point of view. In fact, in embedded applications message size is often fixed or at most varies within a small range and in such a case a fully general interface supporting an arbitrary length in the callee side could simply lead to an overhead. Therefore in this paper we have decided that, from a minimalist point of view, rather than pursuing a full black box design, the interface policy of hash functions should be the same as that of block ciphers.

3.2 ROM/RAM Count

There does not seem to exist a consensus of how to count ROM/RAM size of a given crypto subroutine, especially RAM bytes on an embedded processor. Since RAM is much more expensive than ROM, it is important to give unambiguous information about RAM consumption to an embedded system programmer.

For instance, out of three implementation papers on the AVR processor [14–16], the first one does not count mandatory parameters such as plaintext and key areas as RAM bytes, the first and second papers seem to have excluded stack consumption from the RAM count, and the second and third papers introduce an uncommon subroutine calling convention where a callee can destroy any register without restoration.

For another example, a code of Grøstl designed by Feichtner on the same processor [10] pushes/pops 20 callee-save registers out of a total of 32 registers at the beginning and end of the routine, which agrees with our code design policy. In our metric, the ROM/RAM size should indicate the entire resource consumption of a target subroutine, and hence, for example, we count the size of RAM that the following sample code consumes as (at least) twelve bytes:

```
_Encryption_Routine:     ; 4 bytes for calling this routine itself
     push hl             ; 2 bytes for storing hl, callee-save register
     movw hl,ax

     call _Leaf_Routine  ; 4 bytes for calling this function
     ..
     pop  hl             ; restoring hl
     ret

_Leaf_Routine:
     push bc             ; 2 bytes for pushing bc
     ..
     pop  bc
     ret
```

Table 2. Portfolio of a primitive (an example).

	ROM-Min (400B)	ROM-512B	ROM-1024B	ROM-2048B
RAM-128B	20,000	9,000	3,000	-
RAM-64B	x	x	4,000	3,500

A consequence of this is that 64-byte RAM is very restrictive for most 128-bit block ciphers with 128-bit key, because 32-byte RAM is a must (plaintext+key) and often we need additional 16 bytes for keeping temporary data. Moreover, as mentioned above, if we call an internal subroutine, 12-byte stack is needed. At this stage we have only four free RAM bytes.

3.3   Categorization as to Resources

One of the purposes of this paper is to give a system programmer practical information on size and speed trade-offs for each algorithm, not only pin-point record data. We expect that this approach will make performance characteristics of each algorithm much clearer, and in addition, will reveal that a specific size-speed combination is **impossible** to implement on this processor, which is also important information for a programmer.

On the other hand, it is not realistic to write codes for too many possible ROM/RAM size combinations. Hence in this paper, we introduce several categories as to given memory size. Specifically, we categorize ROM size variations into 512B, 1024B and 2048B and RAM size variations into 64B, 128B, 256B, 512B (first two are for block ciphers and latter two are for hash functions). Our interest is to find out in which category i.e. in which ROM/RAM combination, a target primitive is implementable or not, and if yes, what performance it can achieve within the amount of resources specified in the category (Table 2).

Our complete implementation results are given in Appendix, but in the next section, we use the following type of diagram to illustrate a performance portfolio of each algorithm:

This table shows five different implementations for the target algorithm, one of which runs at 3,000 cycles/block with less than 1024 ROM bytes and 128 RAM bytes. If the given RAM resource is reduced down to 64 bytes, then its speed also goes down to 4,000 cycles/block. Also if only 512 ROM bytes is available, then its speed penalty becomes serious, 9,000 cycles/block. 'x' means that it is (or seems) impossible to implement in this category, and '-' denotes "satiated", i.e. already reached enough resource for achieving high speed and having further resource does not lead to significant speed-up as compared with other implementations (left or down whichever faster; 3,000 cycles/block in this case). From this table, we can deliver important messages to an application programmer such as:

- 1024B/128B are most reasonable ROM/RAM resources for this primitive.
- If ROM size is less than 1024 bytes, its speed rapidly worsens.
- If only 512B/64B are available, using this primitive should be given up.

In the next section, we skip rows and columns that contain only '-' or 'x' entries. A special case is the left-most column, which is a ROM-minimum implementation concentrating on minimizing ROM memory, lowering priority of speed. We believe that this information is also practically important. In fact, in some industrial systems, speed is not an issue since mechanical motion is usually far more time-consuming than cryptographic applications.

3.4 Portability

All of our codes were written in assembly language in the small model, but we tried them to be as portable as possible. Our codes are relocatable, i.e. independent of the address where the code/data are located in physical memory.

Also we took into consideration that our codes should not conflict with other modules, and therefore avoided to access system memory area. We used only a single bank (RL78 has four register banks, each of which has an independent register memory), and also we did not access 256-byte short address RAM, which is a special area where a fast and short instruction is available. This area is shared with system programs and use of this area could affect portability.

4 Implementations

4.1 Block Ciphers

AES: We implemented encryption-only and encryption-decryption versions separately for all block ciphers. For AES, all of our RAM-64B programs are based on "flat" implementation, i.e. its round function including a key scheduling step (due to the on-the-fly implementation) does not contain any loop/subroutine inside. These flat programs required 1 KB ROM for encryption-only version and 2 KB ROM for encryption-decryption version, respectively. To reduce the ROM size to 512B and 1 KB, we introduced a loop inside MixColumns, having a single vector-matrix multiplication code, instead of having the entire matrix-matrix multiplication. As a result, the RAM size of these codes exceeded 64B (Table 3).

On RL78, multiplying {02} can be done with the following simple sequence of instructions without a branch:

```
shl   a,1
sknc
xor   a,#01bh
```

In Table 4, the first number of each entry denotes encryption cycles, and the second/third number shows decryption cycles for first/second (and later) block, respectively. Note that in decryption, the second and later blocks can be faster than the first block by skipping part of its key scheduling. The right most column is another implementation for aiming at maximum speed by unrolling non-critical parts, which exceeded 2048 ROM bytes.

It looks that around 3,800 and 5,700 cycles/block is the fastest speed of AES encryption and decryption on this processor, respectively.

Table 3. AES128 encryption-only portfolio.

	ROM-Min (486B)	ROM-512B	ROM-1024B
RAM-128B	7,288	6,622	-
RAM-64B	x	x	3,855

Table 4. AES128 encryption-decryption portfolio.

	ROM-Min (970B)	ROM-1024B	ROM-2048B	Fast (2380B)
RAM-128B	7,743:12,683/10,862	7,339:10,636/9,106	-	-
RAM-64B	x	x	3,917:6,804/5,911	3,865:6,541/5,706

Camellia: The key scheduling part of Camellia has rotate shifts on 128-bit data whose shift counts are irregular. This irregularity and its FL functions lead to a penalty in terms of ROM size. However since Camellia has Feistel structure, its decryption is as fast as encryption and is faster than AES decryption. Main ROM-size and speed trade-offs come from the number of different S-boxes that the code contains, which can vary from one (256B) to four (1 KB), and the number of independent rotate shift routines. Its speed converges to around 4,000 cycles/block for both encryption and decryption.

Several efforts were made to create ROM-minimum codes (800B for encryption-only and 1024B for encryption-decryption): The P matrix is stored in an 8-byte ROM table and its computation is done bit-by-bit. Also having only one rotate shift routine that shifts 128-bit data by one bit, an n-bit rotate shift is done by running the routine n times. Obviously these methods resulted in heavy performance penalty, but it should be again noted that we focused on minimizing ROM size, and hence this is a forget-the-speed option, unlike other categories.

Clefia: Clefia has two independent 256-byte S-boxes, two 4x4 Matrices and a 240-byte constant value used in its key scheduling part, which causes a heavy

Table 5. Camellia128 encryption-only portfolio.

	ROM-Min (800B)	ROM-1024B	ROM-2048B
RAM-128B	43,182/39,358	5,539/4,631	4,738/3,966
RAM-64B		5,733/4,820	4,918/4,125

Table 6. Camellia128 encryption-Decryption portfolio.

	ROM-1024B	ROM-2048B
RAM-128B	43,190/39,357:175,417/152,023	4,978/4,125:5,255/4,244
RAM-64B	x	5,126/4,337:5,512/4,477

Table 7. Clefia128 encryption-only portfolio.

	ROM-Min (961B)	ROM-1024B	ROM-2048B
RAM-128B	17,434	12,367	8,208/5,302
RAM-64B	x	x	9,142/6,194

Table 8. Clefia128 encryption-decryption portfolio.

	ROM-Min (1,309B)	ROM-2048B
RAM-128B	18,062:18,759	9,399/6,208:9,931/6,740
RAM-64B		11,388/7,768:11,419/7,799

ROM size penalty. However the constant value can be generated on-the-fly. All implementations except ROM-2048B versions used this technique to reduce their code size (Tables 5 and 6).

The methodology for implementing Clefia is basically the same as that for AES. RAM-128B versions are a bit faster than RAM-64B version, which is mainly because the former codes were able to allocate more and enough memory for on-the-fly subkey. The ROM-2048B versions have unrolled their most critical parts but are not still flat programs. We have not written a fastest possible flat code by accepting more ROM bytes, but it looks that around 5,000 cycles/block is a maximal performance of this primitive (Tables 7 and 8).

Present: Present is a 64-bit block cipher with 80-bit key, and a 64-byte memory is enough for its RAM size. On the other hand, this algorithm is heavily optimized for hardware and in software we have to compute its round function bit-by-bit. Main design trade-offs come from a 4-bit S-box v.s. an 8-bit S-box. Our ROM-1024B version for encryption-only and ROM-2048B version for encryption-decryption have a latter choice. Once an 8-bit output of the S-box is stored on register x, then the pLayer of Present can be implemented basically by a repetition of the following simple code:

Table 9. Present80 encryption-only portfolio.

	ROM-Min (210B)	ROM-512B	ROM-1024B
RAM-64B	144,879	122,00	9,007

Table 10. Present80 encryption-decryption portfolio.

	ROM-512B	ROM-1024B	ROM-2048B
RAM-64B	61,634:104,902/60,834	13,883:16,046/14,014	9,007:10,823/8,920

```
mov    a,reg1
addw   ax,ax     (shrw ax,1  in decryption)
mov    reg2,a
```

As seen below, its fastest speed is around 9,000 cycles/block, significantly slower than other lightweight block ciphers. On the other hand, since the structure of Present is very simple, further reduction of code size is possible at the cost of speed. Our ROM-minimum implementation requires only 210 ROM bytes (encryption only), which runs at the speed of 144,879 cycles/block (Tables 9 and 10).

4.2   Hash Functions

SHA: It is obvious that SHA-256/SHA-512 cannot be implemented within 128/256 RAM bytes and we assume that 256/512-byte RAM is given. Then we have room for storing intermediate message words $W_i(0 \leq i \leq 15)$ doubly. This makes the message scheduling part simpler by arranging the double-size message buffer as $W_0||W_1||...||W_{15}||W_0||W_1||...||W_{15}$ where the first W_i and the second W_i always the same. All of our codes of SHA-256/SHA-512 use this method.

For SHA256, our ROM-2048B version has achieved a flat code - its step function is fully unrolled -, which actually needed only 1,239 ROM bytes. This ROM size was able to be reduced to 1024B by introducing a byte-wise loop within the Ch and Maj functions and making frequent xor-to-memory operations a subroutine. The ROM-minimum version has a single rotate shift routine that rotates by one bit (as that of Camellia). For SHA512, 2048 ROM bytes were not enough for creating a flat code and 2,499 bytes were needed. The implementation method for the ROM-2048B/ROM-minimum version of SHA-512 is the same as that for the ROM-1024B/ROM-minimum version of SHA-256, respectively (Tables 11 and 12).

Keccak: Keccak can be implemented within 256 RAM bytes only if a message size is always within a single block. Hence we assume that 512-byte RAM is given. Our flat code slightly exceeded 2048B, and in order to create a smaller code, we had to deal with reduction of a total of 24 different rotate shift operations in the ρ function. Our ROM-1024B code has a 1-bit rotate shift routine and m-byte

Table 11. Portfolio of SHA-256.

	ROM-Min (796B)	ROM-1024B	ROM-2048B
RAM-256B	216,775/216,393	41,175/40,793	25,265/25,143

Table 12. Portfolio of SHA-512.

	ROM-Min (1,285B)	ROM-2048B	Fast (2499B)
RAM-512B	819,034/818,268	81,610/80,844	66,008/65,562

Table 13. Portfolio of Keccak.

	ROM-Min (453B)	ROM-512B	ROM-1024B	ROM-2048B
RAM-512B	516,528/517,022	237,960/238,454	155,209/155,703	118,705/119,171
	Fast (2,214B)			
RAM-512B	110,185/110,651			

rotate shift routines ($1 \leq m \leq 7$) independently, and a given $n = 8n_1 + n_2$-bit rotate shift is done by carrying out the n_1-byte shift routine and an n_2-time repetition of the 1-bit shift routine. Similarly our ROM-512B routine has a 1-byte rotate routine and a 1-bit rotate routine, and an n-bit shift is made by an n_1-time repetition of the former and an n_2-time repetition of the latter. The ROM-minimum version has a 1-bit rotate routine only and repeating it n times creates an n-bit rotate shift (Tables 13, 14 and 15).

Skein: An advantage of Skein is that it allows a very compact ROM/RAM implementation. 2048 ROM bytes and 256 RAM bytes are enough for creating a flat implementation of Skein-256. The methodology for reducing its ROM size is basically the same as that of Keccak. Our ROM-1024B/512B/Min versions correspond to Keccak's ROM-1024B/512B/Min versions, respectively.

For Skein-512, our ROM-2048B code contains n_1-byte rotate routines ($1 \leq n_1 \leq 7$) and n_2-bit rotate routines ($1 \leq n_2 \leq 7$) independently, and our ROM-1024B code uses four rotate routines (1-byte, 3-byte, 1-bit and 5-bit shifts) to create a given n-bit rotation. The ROM-512B version has a 1-byte rotate routine and a 1-bit rotate routine.

Grøstl: The most time-consuming part of Grøstl is obviously a computation of MixBytes. To minimize speed penalty, reducing this part must be the last option. Most of our ROM-2048B/1024B programs have an unrolled 8-dimensional vector-matrix multiplication code and ROM size reduction comes from AddRoundConst. Special implementations were made for the RAM-512B versions Grøstl-256. In these programs, the 256-byte S-box is copied from ROM to RAM before

Table 14. Portfolio of Skein-256.

	ROM-Min (457B)	ROM-512B	ROM-1024B	ROM-2048B
RAM-256B	823,806/823,038	121,590/120,822	66,834/66,066	46,747/46,299

Table 15. Portfolio of Skein-512.

	ROM-Min (457B)	ROM-512B	ROM-1024B	ROM-2048B
RAM-256B	823,806/823,038	121,590/120,822	66,834/66,066	46,747/46,299

Table 16. Portfolio of Grøstl-256.

	ROM-Min (615B)	ROM-1024B	ROM-2048B
RAM-512B		95,271/63,286	73,011/47,746
RAM-256B	164,664/111,349	99,625/67,126	77,365/51,586

Table 17. Portfolio of Grøstl-512.

	ROM-Min (672B)	ROM-1024B	ROM-2048B
RAM-512B	452,122/306,713	277,626/188,889	215,634/144,159

starting the first block for better performance, since reading from RAM is faster than reading from ROM. As a result, we achieved a small gain of performance (Tables 16 and 17).

In the following table, the cycle count of the output transformation Ω is included in that of the first block.

5   Comparative Figures

This section briefly discusses performance comparison of our target algorithms. Throughout this section, left and right graphs correspond to low and high resources (1024 ROM bytes or less/2048 ROM bytes), respectively. The horizontal axis denotes message length (bytes) and the vertical axis shows speed (cycles/byte). We have excluded ROM-minimum implementations since they are not optimized for operation speed. Note that only points make sense as performance data. Lines are added only for visibility of these graphs.

Figure 1 shows performance comparison of encryption-only programs of block ciphers. Since AES and Present have reached their maximal speed with 1 KB

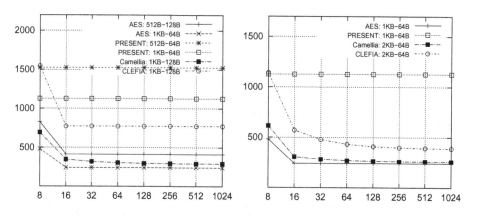

Fig. 1. Block ciphers (encryption-only)

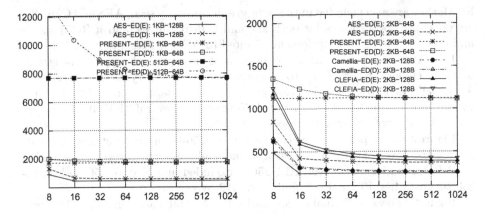

Fig. 2. Block ciphers (encryption-decryption)

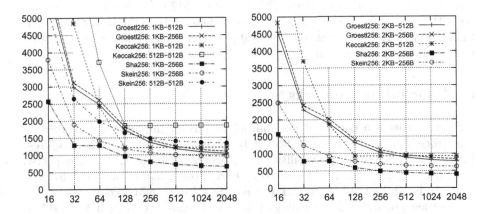

Fig. 3. 256-bit hash functions

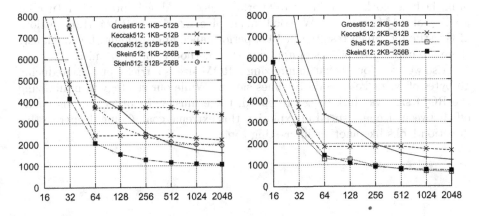

Fig. 4. 512-bit hash functions

ROM, they are also included in the right graph. As easily seen, AES and Camellia are generally good choices for both low and high resources, and if ROM size is limited to 512 bytes, our options are limited to AES or Present.

Figure 2 shows performance comparison of encryption-decryption programs of block ciphers, where (E)/(D) denotes encryption/decryption, respectively. Again AES achieves a good performance. In this case, if a given ROM size is 1 KB, Camellia and Clefia are excluded. Note that however if 2 KB ROM is given, Camellia's decryption speed outperforms AES.

Figure 3 shows performance comparison of 256-bit hash functions. Interestingly, SHA-256 is fastest for both low and high resource categories assuming 1 KB ROM is given. However SHA-256 is excluded and Keccak-256 and Skein-256 survive when ROM size is limited to 512 bytes.

Figure 4 shows performance comparison of 512-bit hash functions. The performance of Keccak-512 (Keccak[$r = 576, c = 1024$]) was derived from that of Keccak-256 (Keccak[$r = 1088, c = 512$]), since these codes can be almost the same except for input block sizes. This case Skein-512 is fastest on low resources but SHA-512 again remains a good choice when 2 KB ROM is available. The SHA-3 winner Keccak is not a high speed primitive, but is a low memory option with Skein on this processor.

6   Concluding Remarks

We here mention a couple of possibilities to further improve performance on this processor. As described in Sect. 3.4, we did not access any short address RAM area to maintain portability of our programs. In general it is expected that utilizing this area could lead to a shorter code, but in our case, its gain seems to be limited unless we aim at a new ROM-minimum record.

Another possibility for speeding-up is to copy constant ROM data to RAM. RL78 takes one cycle to read a RAM byte/word to register, but takes four cycles to read from ROM. So if we copy ROM data to RAM before starting the routine or in the first block, then the overall performance could be improved in return for additional RAM resources. We tried this implementation in RAM-512B versions of Grøstl only, which resulted in 10 % performance improvement, but obviously there are many possibilities of applying this method to other primitives.

Also we have found that minimizing a ROM size is a tricky puzzle. Reducing 10 bytes often makes a code 10 times slower. While our strategy in minimizing the ROM size was just to ignore speed, there must exist other various trade-offs between size and speed in exploring this extreme goal. Going deeper to this direction looks like another interesting topic.

Appendix: Summary of Our Implementation Results

Block Ciphers

Category ROM RAM	AES128 Enc-only ROM RAM cycles/block			AES128 Enc,Dec ROM RAM cycles/block		
1 KB 128B	-	-	-	1,024	84	7,339 : 10,636/9,106
512B 128B	510	78	6,622	x	x	x
Min 128B	486	78	7,288	970	84	7,743 : 12,683/10,862
Fast 64B	-	-	-	2,380	64	3,865 : 6,541/5,706
2 KB 64B	-	-	-	1,989	64	3,917 : 6,804/5,911
1 KB 64B	1,021	60	3,855	x	x	x

Category ROM RAM	Camellia128 Enc-only ROM RAM cycles/block			Camellia128 Enc,Dec ROM RAM cycles/block		
2 KB 128B	2,004	70	4,738/3,966	2,047	74	4,978/4,125 : 5,255/4,244
1 KB 128B	1,023	70	5,539/4,631	1,020	78	43,190/39,357 : 175,417/152,023
Min 128B	800	74	43,182/39,358	x	x	x
2 KB 64B	2,037	64	4,918/4,125	2,033	64	5,216/4,337 : 5,512/4,477
1 KB 64B	1,024	64	5,733/4,820	x	x	x

Category ROM RAM	Clefia128 Enc-only ROM RAM cycles/block			Clefia128 Enc,Dec ROM RAM cycles/block		
2 KB 128B	2,006	94	8,208/5,302	2,040	86	9,399/6,208 : 9,931/6,740
1 KB 128B	1,024	74	12,367	x	x	x
Min 128B	961	76	17,434	1,309	76	18,062 : 18,759
2 KB 64B	2,037	64	9,142/6,194	2,026	64	11,388/7,768 : 11,419/7,799

Category ROM RAM	Present80 Enc-only ROM RAM cycles/block			Present80 Enc,Dec ROM RAM cycles/block		
2 KB 64B	-	-	-	1,855	48	9,007 : 10,823/8,920
1 KB 64B	897	42	9,007	1,009	54	13,883 : 16,046/14,014
512B 64B	510	46	12,200	512,	62	61,634 : 104,902/60,834
Min 64B	210	54	144,879			

Hash functions

Category ROM RAM	SHA256 ROM RAM cycles/block			SHA512 ROM RAM cycles/block		
Fast 512B	-	-	-	2,499	420	66,008/65,562
2 KB 512B	-	-	-	2,034	428	81,610/80,844
Min 512B	-	-	-	1,285	430	819,034/818,268
2 KB 256B	1,239	216	25,265/25,143	x	x	x
1 KB 256B	1,016	224	41,175/40,793	x	x	x
Min 256B	796	224	216,775/216,393	x	x	x

Category	Keccak256		
ROM RAM	ROM	RAM	cycles/block
Fast 512B	2,214	392	110,185/110,651
2 KB 512B	2,017	392	118,705/119,171
1 KB 512B	1,024	392	155,209/155,703
512B 512B	512	392	237,960/238,454
Min 512B	453	392	516,528/517,022

Category	Skein256			Skein512		
ROM RAM	ROM	RAM	cycles/block	ROM	RAM	cycles/block
2 KB 256B	1,615	166	20,156/19,772	1,921	254	46,747/46,299
1 KB 256B	1,015	166	30,524/30,140	1,024	252	66,834/66,066
512B 256B	502	144	42,566/42,182	509	252	121,590/120,822
Min 256B	396	144	122,348/121,964	457	252	823,806/823,038

Category	Grøstl256			Grøstl512		
ROM RAM	ROM	RAM	cycles/block	ROM	RAM	cycles/block
2 KB 512B	1,481	476	73,011/47,746	2,044	412	215,634/144,159
1 KB 512B	1,023	476	95,271/63,286	1,015	412	277,627/188,889
Min 512B				672	412	452,122/306,713
2 KB 256B	1,471	220	77,365/51,586	x	x	x
1 KB 256B	1,019	220	99,625/67,126	x	x	x
Min 256B	615	230	164,664/111,349	x	x	x

References

1. Ecrypt, II, Implementations of low cost block ciphers in Atmel AVR devices, http://perso.uclouvain.be/fstandae/source_codes/lightweight_ciphers/
2. ECRYPT II, Implementations of hash functions in Atmel AVR devices. http://perso.uclouvain.be/fstandae/source_codes/hash_atmel/
3. Advanced Encryption Standard (AES), Federal Information Processing Standards Publication 197, NIST (2001)
4. Aoki, K., Ichikawa, T., Kanda, M., Matsui, M., Moriai, S., Nakajima, J., Tokita, T.: The 128-Bit block cipher camellia. IEICE Trans. Fundam. E85–A(1), 11–24 (2002)
5. Shirai, T., Shibutani, K., Akishita, T., Moriai, S., Iwata, T.: The 128-Bit blockcipher CLEFIA (extended abstract). In: Biryukov, A. (ed.) FSE 2007. LNCS, vol. 4593, pp. 181–195. Springer, Heidelberg (2007)
6. Bogdanov, A.A., Knudsen, L.R., Leander, G., Paar, C., Poschmann, A., Robshaw, M., Seurin, Y., Vikkelsoe, C.: PRESENT: an ultra-lightweight block cipher. In: Paillier, P., Verbauwhede, I. (eds.) CHES 2007. LNCS, vol. 4727, pp. 450–466. Springer, Heidelberg (2007)
7. Secure Hash Standard (SHS), Federal Information Processing Standards Publication 180–3, NIST (2008)
8. Bertoni, G., Daemen, J., Peeters, M., Assche, G.V.: The Keccak sponge function family. http://keccak.noekeon.org/

9. Ferguson, N., Lucks, S., Schneier, B., Whiting, D., Bellare, M., Kohno, T., Callas, J., Walker, J.: The skein hash function family. http://www.skein-hash.info/
10. Gauravaram1, P., Knudsen, L.R., Matusiewicz, K., Mendel, F., Rechberger, C., Schläffer, M., Thomsen, S.S.: Grøstl - a SHA-3 candidate. http://www.groestl.info/
11. RL78 Family, Resesas Electronics. http://www.renesas.com/products/mpumcu/rl78/index.jsp
12. AVR Instruction Set, Atmel Corporation. http://www.atmel.com/images/doc0856.pdf
13. CodeSuite+ V1.02.00 Integrated Development Environment User's Manual: RL78,78K0R Coding. http://documentation.renesas.com/doc/products/tool/doc/+r20ut0977ej0100_qscd78.pdf
14. Eisenbarth, T., Kumar, S.S., Paar, C., Poschmann, A., Uhsadel, L.: A survey of lightweight-cryptography implementations. IEEE Des. Test Comput. **24**(6), 522–533 (2007)
15. Eisenbarth, T., et al.: Compact implementation and performance evaluation of block ciphers in attiny devices. In: Mitrokotsa, A., Vaudenay, S. (eds.) AFRICACRYPT 2012. LNCS, vol. 7374, pp. 172–187. Springer, Heidelberg (2012)
16. Balasch, J., Ege, B., Eisenbarth, T., Gerard, B., Gong, Z., Guneysu, T., Heyse, S., Kerckhof, S., Koeune, F., Plos, T., Poppelmann, T., Regazzoni, F., Standaert, F.-X., Assche, G.V., Keer, R.V., van Oldeneel tot Oldenzeel, L., von Maurich, I.: Compact Implementation and Performance Evaluation of Hash Functions in ATtiny Devices, cryptology e-Print archive, report 2012/507

Higher-Order Side Channel Security and Mask Refreshing

Jean-Sébastien Coron[1], Emmanuel Prouff[2], Matthieu Rivain[3]([✉]),
and Thomas Roche[2]

[1] Tranef, Paris, France
jscoron@tranef.com
[2] ANSSI, Paris, France
{emmanuel.prouff,thomas.roche}@ssi.gouv.fr
[3] CryptoExperts, Paris, France
matthieu.rivain@cryptoexperts.com

Abstract. Masking is a widely used countermeasure to protect block
cipher implementations against side-channel attacks. The principle is to
split every sensitive intermediate variable occurring in the computation
into $d + 1$ shares, where d is called the *masking order* and plays the
role of a security parameter. A masked implementation is then said to
achieve d^{th}-order security if any set of d (or less) intermediate variables
does not reveal key-dependent information. At CHES 2010, Rivain and
Prouff have proposed a higher-order masking scheme for AES that works
for any arbitrary order d. This scheme, and its subsequent extensions,
are based on an improved version of the shared multiplication processing
published by Ishai *et al.* at CRYPTO 2003. This improvement enables
better memory/timing performances but its security relies on the refreshing of the masks at some points in the algorithm. In this paper, we show
that the method proposed at CHES 2010 to do such mask refreshing
introduces a security flaw in the overall masking scheme. Specifically, we
show that it is vulnerable to an attack of order $\lceil d/2 \rceil + 1$ whereas the
scheme is supposed to achieve d^{th}-order security. After exhibiting and
analyzing the flaw, we propose a new solution which avoids the use of
mask refreshing, and we prove its security. We also provide some implementation trick that makes our proposed solution, not only secure, but
also faster than the original scheme.

1 Introduction

In the late nineties, attacks called *Side Channel Analysis* (SCA for short) have
been exhibited against cryptosystems implemented in embedded devices. Since
the seminal works [7,8], they have been refined and, in particular, the initial principle has been generalized in order to exploit several leakage points
simultaneously. This led to the introduction of the *higher-order SCA* concept.

S. Moriai (Ed.): FSE 2013, LNCS 8424, pp. 410–424, 2014.
DOI: 10.1007/978-3-662-43933-3_21, © Springer-Verlag Berlin Heidelberg 2014

Those attacks are based on leakage observations resulting from the handling of several (say d) intermediate variables during the cryptosystem processing. One way to make them ineffective is to randomize the algorithm such that the probability distribution of any vector of less than d observations is independent of the key. To perform this randomization, a standard technique is to apply Boolean masking [2]. It consists in replacing the manipulation of every secret-dependent intermediate variable x (called *sensitive variable*) by that of $d+1$ *shares* $x_0, \ldots,$ x_d satisfying $x_0 \oplus x_1 \oplus \cdots \oplus x_d = x$. Usually, the d shares $x_1, \ldots, x_d$ (called *the masks*) are randomly picked up and the last one x_0 (called *the masked variable*) is processed such that it satisfies the previous equality. When d random masks are involved per sensitive variable, the masking is said to be *of order d* and every d-tuple of intermediate variables of the computation is statistically independent of any sensitive variable. In fact, only attacks exploiting the leakages related to $d+1$ intermediate variables may succeed in retrieving sensitive information. Since the efficiency of such an attack becomes impractical as d increases [2], the masking order is usually considered as a sound criterion to refer to the robustness against SCA.

When applying the principle of masking to secure a block cipher implementation, a so-called *masking scheme* must be designed to operate on the masks and the masked data. It must ensure that the final shares enable the recovery of the expected ciphertext, while satisfying the dth-order *security property* for the chosen order d. When satisfied, the latter property guarantees that no attack of order lower than or equal to d is possible. The main difficulty in designing a Boolean masking scheme lies in masking the non-linear parts of the cipher, the so-called s-boxes.

The first scheme achieving d^{th}-order security for an arbitrary chosen d has been designed by Ishai, Sahai and Wagner in [5]. The here called *ISW scheme* consists in masking the Boolean representation of an algorithm which is composed of logical operations NOT and AND. Securing a NOT for any order d is straightforward since $x = \bigoplus_i x_i$ implies $\text{NOT}(x) = \text{NOT}(x_0) \oplus x_1 \cdots \oplus x_d$. The main contribution of [5] is a method to secure the AND operation for any arbitrary order d (the description of this scheme is recalled in Sect. 2). A direct application of ISW scheme to secure an s-box in software would consist in taking the Boolean representation of the s-box and to process every logical operation successively in a masked way. Since the Boolean representation of common s-boxes involves a huge number of logical operations, a direct application of [5] is often not possible in practice. A solution to deal with this efficiency issue has first been proposed by Rivain and Prouff in [10] for the AES (it will be called RP Scheme in the sequel), and then extended to any block cipher by Carlet *et al.* in [1]. Those works start from the observation that the ISW scheme can be extended to secure a multiplication over any finite field. The core idea is then to represent the s-box to protect as a polynomial function over a finite field and to secure the polynomial evaluation thanks to the ISW scheme.

Since the processing of affine transformations is performed by operating on each share separately, proving its dth-order security is straightforward as noticed in [5,10]. Actually, only the secure processing of the multiplication $a \times b$ from the sharings $(a_0, a_1, \cdots, a_d)$ and $(b_0, b_1, \cdots, b_d)$ is challenging. In [5], the ISW scheme is shown to be secure at the order $d/2$, meaning that a dth-order security is obtained from a masking of order $2d$. As the complexity of ISW is quadratic in the number of shares, such a doubling of the masking order makes the resulting implementation roughly 4 times slower. To avoid such a penalty, the authors of [10] additionally assume that the multiplication operands sharings involve mutually independent random masks and they prove that ISW scheme is actually d^{th}-order secure under the latter condition.[1] To satisfy this independence when a multiplication of the form $a \times g(a)$ occurs in a secure s-box processing, with g being a linear function, the authors of [10] suggest to refresh the mask of $g(a)$ before performing the secure multiplication $a \times g(a)$. To do so, they use a so-called *mask-refreshing* procedure which from the sharing of $g(a)$, computes a new sharing of with fresh random values. Such a procedure is mandatory in [10] as well as in the subsequent schemes [1,6] to deduce the dth-order security of the whole s-box processing from that of the secure multiplications.

Our Contribution. In this paper, we show that the actual proposal of mask-refreshing procedure in [10] fails in reaching its goal and introduces a security flaw in the overall masking scheme. In fact, even if both the mask-refreshing procedure and the ISW multiplication are secure at order d, their composition is insecure and it is defeated by an attack of order $\lceil d/2 \rceil + 1$. After exhibiting and analyzing the flaw, we propose a secure solution which avoids the use of mask refreshing, and we prove its dth-order security. Our solution consists in adapting ISW scheme to directly process, from a sharing of a, the multiplications of the form $a \times g(a)$ with g being a linear function. We also provide an improvement that allows to avoid costly multiplications over $\mathbb{F}_{2^n}$ in this context. As a consequence, the resulting shared multiplication for $a \times g(a)$ is not only secure but also more efficient than the original scheme proposed in [10].

Paper Organisation. In Sect. 2, we recall the ISW scheme and the existing solutions to mask a full s-box computation at any order d. The flaw from the composition of the mask-refreshing procedure and the secure multiplication is exhibited and analyzed in Sect. 3. Then, we describe our new algorithm and prove its dth-order security in Sect. 4. Eventually, implementation results are provided in Sect. 5 to report on the efficiency of our improved algorithm when plugged in RP Scheme.

2   Higher-Order Masking Schemes for S-Boxes

This section presents the different schemes published in the literature to mask an s-box processing at any order d. We first recall the ISW scheme [5] which is the starting point of the different solutions. Then we detail the RP Scheme for

---

[1] Specifically [10] requires that every $2d$-tuple composed of d elements from $(a_i)_i$ and of d elements from $(b_i)_i$ is uniformly distributed and independent of any sensitive variable.

the AES s-box [10]. Eventually, we briefly recall the improvement proposed by Kim *et al.* [6], and the extension put forward by Carlet *et al.* [1].

Ishai-Sahai-Wagner's Scheme. Let a and b be binary values from $\mathbb{F}_2$ and let $(a_i)_{0 \leqslant i \leqslant d}$ and $(b_i)_{0 \leqslant i \leqslant d}$ be d^{th}-order sharings of a and b respectively. To securely compute a sharing of $c = a \times b$ from $(a_i)_i$ and $(b_i)_i$, the ISW method works as follows:[2]

1. For every $0 \leqslant i < j \leqslant d$, pick up a random bit $r_{i,j}$.
2. For every $0 \leqslant i < j \leqslant d$, compute $r_{j,i} = (r_{i,j} \oplus a_i b_j) \oplus a_j b_i$.
3. For every $0 \leqslant i \leqslant d$, compute $c_i = a_i b_i \oplus \bigoplus_{j \neq i} r_{i,j}$.

It can be checked that the obtained shares form a sound encoding of c. Namely, we have: $\bigoplus_{i=0}^{d} c_i = \left(\bigoplus_{i=0}^{d} a_i \right) \left(\bigoplus_{i=0}^{d} b_i \right) = ab = c$. In [5] it is moreover shown that the above computation achieves security at order $d/2$.

Rivain and Prouff's Scheme. In [10], the authors proposed to use the ISW scheme to secure a multiplication $c = a \times b$ over $\mathbb{F}_{2^n}$ for any n greater than 1. For completeness sake, we recall the obtained algorithm hereafter, where the multiplication over $\mathbb{F}_{2^n}$ is denoted $\odot$.

Algorithm 1. SecMult

Input: shares a_i satisfying $\bigoplus_i a_i = a$, shares b_i satisfying $\bigoplus_i b_i = b$
Output: shares c_i satisfying $\bigoplus_i c_i = a \odot b$
1: **for** $i = 0$ **to** d **do**
2:    **for** $j = i+1$ **to** d **do**
3:       $r_{i,j} \xleftarrow{\$} \mathbb{F}_{2^n}$
4:       $r_{j,i} \leftarrow (r_{i,j} \oplus a_i \odot b_j) \oplus a_j \odot b_i$
5:    **end for**
6: **end for**
7: **for** $i = 0$ **to** d **do**
8:    $c_i \leftarrow a_i \odot b_i$
9:    **for** $j = 0$ **to** d, $j \neq i$ **do** $c_i \leftarrow c_i \oplus r_{i,j}$
10: **end for**
11: **return** $(c_0, c_1, \ldots, c_d)$

As shown in [10], for Algorithm 1 to be secure at order d, the masks $(a_i)_{i \geqslant 1}$ and $(b_i)_{i \geqslant 1}$ in input must be mutually independent. When this condition is not satisfied, the authors suggest to refresh the masks of one of the operands prior to the secure multiplication processing. For such a purpose, they suggest to apply the following mask-refreshing procedure.

---

[2] The use of brackets indicates the order in which the operations are performed, which is mandatory for security of the scheme.

Algorithm 2. RefreshMasks

Input: shares $(z_i)_i$ satisfying $\bigoplus_i z_i = z$
Output: shares $(z'_i)_i$ satisfying $\bigoplus_i z'_i = z$
1: $(z'_0, z'_1, \ldots, z'_d) \leftarrow (z_0, z_1, \ldots, z_d)$
2: **for** $i = 1$ **to** d **do**
3: $\quad r_i \xleftarrow{\$} \mathbb{F}_{2^n}$
4: $\quad z'_0 \leftarrow z'_0 \oplus r_i$
5: $\quad z'_i \leftarrow z'_i \oplus r_i$
6: **end for**
7: **return** $(z'_0, z'_1, \ldots, z'_d)$

In [10], Algorithms 1 and 2 are eventually involved to secure the whole exponentiation to the power 254 over $\mathbb{F}_{256}$ (that is the non-linear part of the AES s-box). We recall the complete exponentiation algorithm hereafter:

Algorithm 3. SecExp254

Input: shares x_i satisfying $\bigoplus_i x_i = x$
Output: shares y_i satisfying $\bigoplus_i y_i = x^{254}$
1: **for** $i = 0$ **to** d **do** $z_i \leftarrow x_i^2$ $// \bigoplus_i z_i = x^2$
2: $(z_0, z_1, \ldots, z_d) \leftarrow \mathsf{RefreshMasks}(z_0, z_1, \ldots, z_d)$
3: $(y_0, y_1, \ldots, y_d) \leftarrow \mathsf{SecMult}((x_0, x_1, \ldots, x_d), (z_0, z_1, \ldots, z_d))$ $// \bigoplus_i y_i = x^3$
4: **for** $i = 0$ **to** d **do** $w_i \leftarrow y_i^4$ $// \bigoplus_i w_i = x^{12}$
5: $(w_0, w_1, \ldots, w_d) \leftarrow \mathsf{RefreshMasks}(w_0, w_1, \ldots, w_d)$
6: $(y_0, y_1, \ldots, y_d) \leftarrow \mathsf{SecMult}((y_0, y_1, \ldots, y_d), (w_0, w_1, \ldots, w_d))$ $// \bigoplus_i y_i = x^{15}$
7: **for** $i = 0$ **to** d **do** $y_i \leftarrow y_i^{16}$ $// \bigoplus_i y_i = x^{240}$
8: $(y_0, y_1, \ldots, y_d) \leftarrow \mathsf{SecMult}((y_0, y_1, \ldots, y_d), (w_0, w_1, \ldots, w_d))$ $// \bigoplus_i y_i = x^{252}$
9: $(y_0, y_1, \ldots, y_d) \leftarrow \mathsf{SecMult}((y_0, y_1, \ldots, y_d), (z_0, z_1, \ldots, z_d))$ $// \bigoplus_i y_i = x^{254}$

Kim-Hong-Lim's Improvement. In [6], Kim *et al.* propose an alternative to Rivain-Prouff's scheme based on the so-called *tower-field representation* of the AES s-box from [11]. The exponentiation is performed by representing the field $\mathbb{F}_{256}$ as a quadratic extension of $\mathbb{F}_{16}$. In such a way, the AES s-box can be computed with 5 multiplications over $\mathbb{F}_{16}$ rather than 4 multiplications over $\mathbb{F}_{256}$. Even if the number of field multiplications is greater than in the orginal scheme, multiplications over $\mathbb{F}_{16}$ can be tabulated, which eventually leads to a significant timing improvement.

Carlet-Goubin-Prouff-Quisquater-Rivain's Scheme. In [1], Carlet *et al.* extend [10] to design a higher-order masking scheme for any nonlinear function from $\{0,1\}^n$ to $\{0,1\}^m$ with $m \leqslant n$ and n small (typically $n \in \{4,6,8\}$). Their approach is to express such an s-box as a sequence of affine functions over $\mathbb{F}_2^n$ and multiplications over $\mathbb{F}_{2^n}$. Such a strategy is always possible since any function from $\{0,1\}^n$ to $\{0,1\}^m$ (with $m \leqslant n$) can be represented by a polynomial $\bigoplus_{i=0}^{2^n-1} \alpha_i x^i$ in $\mathbb{F}_{2^n}[x]$ and the α_i can be obtained from the s-box look-up table by applying Lagrange Interpolation Theorem. As for the secure exponentiation (Algorithm 3), the secure evaluation algorithms proposed in [1] involve a mask-refreshing procedure to change the sharing of some intermediate results before applying the multiplication scheme. Once again, each sub-routine of the evaluation procedure (affine transformation, multiplication processing and mask refreshing) is provably d^{th}-order secure and the security of the whole function evaluation is essentially deduced from those local securities.

3 A Flaw from the Mask-Refreshing Procedure

Even though Algorithms 1 and 2 are both secure against d^{th}-order SCA when considered separately, we show hereafter that their sequential application, as done in Steps 2–3 and Steps 5–6 of Algorithm 3, is not. Namely, we exhibit a tuple of $\lceil d/2 \rceil + 1$ intermediate variables that jointly depend on the sensitive input. Hence, for $d > 1$, this flaw invalidates the claim that the schemes proposed in [1,6,10] achieve d^{th}-order security.

To exhibit the flaw, we assume that the attacked s-box evaluation procedure contains the following sequence:

$$(z_0, z_1, \cdots, z_d) \leftarrow (g(x_0), g(x_1), \ldots, g(x_d)),$$
$$(z'_0, z'_1, \cdots, z'_d) \leftarrow \text{RefreshMasks}((z_0, z_1, \cdots, z_d)),$$
$$(y_0, y_1, \cdots, y_d) \leftarrow \text{SecMult}((x_0, x_1, \cdots, x_d), (z'_0, z'_1, \cdots, z'_d)),$$

with $(x_i)_i$, being a sharing of some sensitive variable x and with g being some $\mathbb{F}_2$-linear function. Two examples of occurrence of this sequence can be found in Algorithm 3: from Step 1 to Step 3 (with the function g corresponding to a squaring over $\mathbb{F}_{256}$), and from Step 4 to Step 6 (with the function g corresponding to a raising to the 4 over $\mathbb{F}_{256}$). The sequence above also occurs in the schemes proposed in [1,6]

For the sake of clarity, we only consider the case where d is even (in the odd case an extra intermediate variable would be needed). The flaw arises from a particular intermediate variable of the mask refreshing combined with $d/2$ intermediate variables of the multiplication. Namely, the targeted intermediate variables are:

– the variable z'_0 just after the fourth step during the $(d/2)^{\text{th}}$ iteration of the loop in RefreshMasks (Algorithm 2), denoted ℓ_0 hereafter, and which satisfies

$$\begin{aligned}
\ell_0 &= z_0 \oplus \bigoplus_{i=1}^{d/2} r_i \\
&= z \oplus \bigoplus_{i=1}^{d} z_i \oplus \bigoplus_{i=1}^{d/2} r_i \\
&= z \oplus \bigoplus_{i=1}^{d/2} (z_i \oplus r_i \oplus z_{d/2+i}) \\
&= g(x) \oplus \bigoplus_{i=1}^{d/2} (g(x_i) \oplus r_i \oplus g(x_{d/2+i})),
\end{aligned} \tag{1}$$

- the product $z_i' \odot x_j$ arising at Step 4 of SecMult (Algorithm 1 called on $(x_i)_i$ and $(z_i')_i$) for every $i \in \{1, 2, \ldots, d/2\}$ and $j = i + d/2$, denoted ℓ_i hereafter, and which satisfies

$$\ell_i = z_i' \odot x_{d/2+i} = (z_i \oplus r_i) \odot x_{d/2+i} = (g(x_i) \oplus r_i) \odot x_{d/2+i}. \quad (2)$$

In a nutshell, the intermediate variable $\ell_i = (g(x_i) \oplus r_i) \odot x_{d/2+i}$ is statistically dependent on the sum $g(x_i) \oplus r_i \oplus g(x_{d/2+i})$ involved to mask $z = g(x)$ in the expression of ℓ_0 (see (1)). Therefore, the $(d/2)$-tuple $(\ell_i)_i$ defined in (2) provides information on the $d/2$ masks $g(x_i) \oplus r_i \oplus g(x_{d/2+i})$ and this information can be used to partially unmask ℓ_0. In other terms, the family of $d/2 + 1$ intermediate variables $\ell_0, \ell_1, \ldots, \ell_{d/2}$ depends on the sensitive variable x.

In the context of side-channel attacks, the physical leakage of an implementation does not reveal the exact values of the intermediate variables but a noisy function of them. That is why, and according to the methodology described in [12], we analyze hereafter the quantity of information about x that an attacker can expect to retrieve from noisy leakages on the ℓ_i, and we report the results of some standard side-channel attack simulations in this context.

Information Theoretic Evaluation. To estimate the sensitive information leakage corresponding to the identified flaw, we conduct hereafter an information theoretic analysis for $d = 2$ (i.e. data are split in 3 shares). For comparison purpose, we also conduct it for the sensitive information leakage corresponding to a first-order and second-order Boolean masking. To this purpose we consider that the leakage related to a variable manipulation corresponds to the Hamming weight of the variable (denoted $\mathrm{HW}(\cdot)$) affected by an independent Gaussian noise.

Let $(B_i)_{i=1,2,3}$, denote three mutually independent random variables with zero mean and standard deviation σ and let $(M_i)_{i=1,2,3}$ be three mutually independent random variables with uniform distribution over $\mathbb{F}_{256}$. For the three considered cases, we computed the mutual information $I(X; L)$ between the targeted sensitive variable $X \in \mathbb{F}_{256}$ and the vector of leakages $\boldsymbol{L} = (L_i)_i$ defined as follows depending on the case:

1. For the flaw described in this paper with $d = 2$ and g being the squaring in $\mathbb{F}_{256}$, we have $\boldsymbol{L} = (L_1, L_2)$ such that:

$$L_1 = \mathrm{HW}(X^2 \oplus M_1^2 \oplus M_2^2 \oplus M_3) + B_1,$$
$$L_2 = \mathrm{HW}(M_2 \odot (M_1^2 \oplus M_3)) + B_2.$$

2. For the classical third-order leakage on a second-order Boolean masking, we have $\boldsymbol{L} = (L_1, L_2, L_3)$ where

$$L_1 = \mathrm{HW}(X \oplus M_1 \oplus M_2) + B_1,$$
$$L_2 = \mathrm{HW}(M_1) + B_2,$$
$$L_3 = \mathrm{HW}(M_2) + B_3.$$

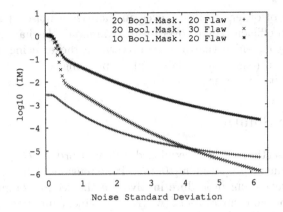

Fig. 1. Mutual information $I(X; L)$ over an increasing σ.

3. For the classical second-order leakage on a first-order Boolean masking, we have $L = (L_1, L_2)$ where

$$L_1 = \mathrm{HW}(X \oplus M_1) + B_1,$$
$$L_2 = \mathrm{HW}(M_1) + B_2.$$

The results are given in Fig. 1. We see that, for $d = 2$ and $g = (\cdot)^2$, the flaw described in this paper delivers only small information about the sensitive variable. This can be explained by the algebraic complexity of the relation between the sensitive variable and the two leakages. However, the progression of the information leakage as σ grows is comparable to that of the classical second-order leakage. This means that the security of the flawed second-order masking scheme tends towards the security of a first-order masking scheme as the amount of noise increases.

Attack Simulations. We have analyzed above the information leakage resulting from the exhibited flaw in comparison to unflawed first-order masking and second-order masking. However, we did not discuss the capacity of an attacker to exploit this information leakage using classical side-channel attack techniques. To fill this gap we applied two classical side-channel distinguishers on simulated traces using the introduced leakage model for different values of noise standard deviations. Specifically we launched a second-order Correlation Power Analysis (CPA for short) and a second-order Mutual Information Analysis (MIA for short). The second-order CPA was performed by means of the centered product combining function and its associated optimal prediction function as described in [9], whereas the second-order MIA used an histogram-based bivariate pdf estimation [4]. None of these attacks reached a success rate greater than 20 % when applied on the exhibited second-order flaw for a number of leakage measurements up to one million, even when the noise component was null (i.e. $\sigma = 0$). These results show that although the information leakage is comparable to a classical leakage of order $\lceil d/2 \rceil + 1$ over an increasing noise, it seems difficult to turn it into an efficient key-recovery using common side-channel attack tools. It is however not excluded that a more powerful attacker using advanced side-channel techniques (e.g. multivariate and/or profiling attacks) could properly exploit the exhibited information leakage.

4   A Secure Solution

In the previous section we have exhibited a flaw of order $\lceil d/2 \rceil + 1$ in the dth-order masking scheme proposed in [10] (and its extensions [1,6]). This flaw arises from the mask-refreshing procedure involved in the secure computation of the multiplications of the form $x \odot g(x)$ (where g is a linear function). Although the resulting information leakage is small and seems difficult to exploit by standard side-channel attack techniques, it is asymptotically stronger than the information from a proper d^{th}-order secure masking scheme. In order to avoid such a security flaw, we propose in this section a new solution for the secure masked processing of multiplications of the form $x \odot g(x)$.

Let a and b be two sensitive variables such that $b = g(a)$ for a $\mathbb{F}_2$-linear function g. When such a relation stands for a and b in Algorithm 3, their corresponding sharings $(a_i)_i$ and $(b_i)_i$ before the call to the mask-refreshing procedure satisfy $b_i = g(a_i)$ for every $i \in [0; d]$. By exploiting this property, the idea is to modify the secure multiplication algorithm in such a way that the masks refreshing is not longer needed.

Before introducing our solution, let us introduce the function f defined from $\mathbb{F}_{2^n} \times \mathbb{F}_{2^n}$ to $\mathbb{F}_{2^n}$ by

$$f(x, y) = x \odot g(y) \oplus g(x) \odot y,$$

where $\odot$ denotes the multiplication over $\mathbb{F}_{2^n}$. It can be checked that the $\mathbb{F}_2$-linearity of g implies the $\mathbb{F}_2$-bilinearity of f. That is, for every $x, y, r \in \mathbb{F}_{2^n}$, f satisfies:

$$f(x, y) = f(x \oplus r, y) \oplus f(r, y) = f(x, y \oplus r) \oplus f(x, r). \tag{3}$$

When b_i equals $g(a_i)$ for every i, the value $r_{j,i}$ computed at Step 4 of the ISW Scheme (Algorithm 1) satisfies:

$$r_{j,i} = a_i b_j \oplus a_j b_i \oplus r_{i,j} = f(a_i, a_j) \oplus r_{i,j},$$

where $r_{i,j}$ is a freshly generated random value. One can then compute $r_{j,i}$ by evaluating f on (a_i, a_j) and by adding the random value $r_{i,j}$. However, $f(a_i, a_j)$ cannot be directly computed since it would leak on two different shares of a at the same time. To avoid such a leakage we use an additional fresh random value, denoted $r'_{i,j}$, to split the computation of $f(a_i, a_j)$ into the computation of $f(a_i, a_j \oplus r'_{i,j})$ and $f(a_i, r'_{i,j})$. That is, the variable $r_{j,i}$ is computed as:

$$r_{j,i} = \left(r_{i,j} \oplus f(a_i, r'_{i,j}) \right) \oplus f(a_i, a_j \oplus r'_{i,j}),$$

where the brackets indicate the order in which the operations are processed. Doing so, we avoid any joint leakage on a_i and a_j. We give hereafter the algorithmic description of our solution.

Algorithm 4. Secure evaluation of $h : x \mapsto x \odot g(x)$

Input: shares $(a_i)_i$ such that $\bigoplus_i a_i = a$
Output: shares c_i satisfying $\bigoplus_i c_i = a \odot g(a)$ for some $\mathbb{F}_2$-linear function g

```
 1: for i = 0 to d do
 2:     for j = i + 1 to d do
 3:         r_{i,j} ←$ F_{2^n}
 4:         r'_{i,j} ←$ F_{2^n}
 5:         t ← r_{i,j} ⊕ a_i ⊙ g(r'_{i,j})
 6:         t ← t ⊕ (r'_{i,j} ⊙ g(a_i))        // t = r_{i,j} ⊕ f(a_i, r'_{i,j})
 7:         t ← t ⊕ (a_i ⊙ g(a_j ⊕ r'_{i,j}))
 8:         t ← t ⊕ ((a_j ⊕ r'_{i,j}) ⊙ g(a_i))    // t = r_{i,j} ⊕ f(a_i, a_j)
 9:         r_{j,i} ← t
10:     end for
11: end for
12: for i = 0 to d do
13:     c_i ← a_i ⊙ g(a_i)
14:     for j = 0 to d, j ≠ i do c_i ← c_i ⊕ r_{i,j}
15: end for
```

In Algorithm 4, the computation of $r_{j,i}$ involves four additions and four multiplications over $\mathbb{F}_{2^n}$. When n is small enough (e.g. $n = 4$), the multiplication over $\mathbb{F}_{2^n}$ can be tabulated in a look-up table with 2^{2n} n-bit elements. However for greater values of n (e.g. $n = 6$, $n = 8$), the size of such a table becomes prohibitive and other strategies must be considered to implement the multiplication. A typical choice is to use so-called log/alog tables (see for instance [3]), but the resulting multiplication is less efficient. We show hereafter how the bilinearity of f can be exploited to prevent such an efficiency loss.

Let us first introduce the function h mapping $\mathbb{F}_{2^n}$ to $\mathbb{F}_{2^n}$ and satisfying $h(x) = x \odot g(x)$. The $\mathbb{F}_2$-linearity of g then implies the following relation between f and h:

$$f(x, y) = h(x \oplus y) \oplus h(x) \oplus h(y),$$

for every $x, y \in \mathbb{F}_{2^n}$. Then (3) gives:

$$f(x, y) = h(x \oplus r \oplus y) \oplus h(x \oplus r) \oplus h(y \oplus r) \oplus h(r),$$

for every $x, y, r \in \mathbb{F}_{2^n}$. Our approach is then to store a look-up table for h and to compute $r_{j,i}$ as:

$$r_{j,i} = \left(\left(\left(r_{i,j} \oplus h(a_i \oplus r'_{i,j})\right) \oplus h(r'_{i,j} \oplus a_j)\right) \oplus h(a_i \oplus r'_{i,j} \oplus a_j)\right) \oplus h(r'_{i,j}).$$

We give the algorithmic description of our improved solution in Algorithm 5. Note that the use of brackets in Step 8 indicates the order in which the operations are processed.

Algorithm 5. Secure evaluation of $h : x \mapsto x \odot g(x)$

Input: shares $(a_i)_i$ such that $\bigoplus_i a_i = a$, a look-up table for $h : x \mapsto x \odot g(x)$
Output: shares c_i satisfying $\bigoplus_i c_i = a \odot g(a)$ for some $\mathbb{F}_2$-linear function g

1: **for** $i = 0$ **to** d **do**
2:      **for** $j = i + 1$ **to** d **do**
3:          $r_{i,j} \xleftarrow{\$} \mathbb{F}_{2^n}$
4:          $r'_{i,j} \xleftarrow{\$} \mathbb{F}_{2^n}$
5:          $t \leftarrow r_{i,j}$
6:          $t \leftarrow t \oplus h(a_i \oplus r'_{i,j})$
7:          $t \leftarrow t \oplus h(a_j \oplus r'_{i,j})$
8:          $t \leftarrow t \oplus h\big((a_i \oplus r'_{i,j}) \oplus a_j\big)$
9:          $t \leftarrow t \oplus h(r'_{i,j})$ $// \ t = f(a_i, a_j) \oplus r_{i,j}$
10:         $r_{j,i} \leftarrow t$
11:     **end for**
12: **end for**
13: **for** $i = 0$ **to** d **do**
14:     $c_i \leftarrow h(a_i)$
15:     **for** $j = 0$ **to** $d, \ j \neq i$ **do** $c_i \leftarrow c_i \oplus r_{i,j}$
16: **end for**

In Sect. 5, we provide implementation results to compare the above solution when plugged in the RP Scheme (Steps 1 to 3 and Steps 4 to 6 in Algorithm 3) to the original scheme using mask refreshing. We see that the scheme using our new solution is not only secure, but also faster than the original scheme.

The only drawback of the new scheme is to require more random generations. Specifically it needs $d(d + 1)$ random field elements *versus* d (mask refreshing) plus $d(d+1)/2$ (secure multiplication) for the original scheme. However, the mask refreshing procedure involved in the original scheme is flawed and it is not clear whether it could be patched with less than $d(d + 1)/2$ random field elements.

Security Proof. We prove hereafter that our solution achieves d^{th}-order security. Namely we show that any d-tuple of intermediate variables of Algorithm 4 is independent of the sensitive variable a. The (very similar) proof for Algorithm 5 is given in appendix.

Our proof consists in constructing a strict subset I of indices in $[0; d]$ such that the distribution of any d-tuple $(v_1, v_2, \dots, v_d)$ of intermediate variables of Algorithm 4 can be perfectly simulated from $a_{|I} := (a_i)_{i \in I}$. This will prove the dth-order security since, by definition, $a_{|I}$ is independent of a as long as the cardinality of I is strictly smaller than d.

By construction, it can first be checked that an intermediate variable v_h of Algorithm 4 necessarily belongs to one of the five following categories:

1. a_i, $g(a_i)$ and $a_i \odot g(a_i)$
2. $r'_{i,j}$, $g(r'_{i,j})$, $a_i \odot g(r'_{i,j})$ and $r'_{i,j} \odot g(a_i)$,
3. $a_j \oplus r'_{i,j}$, $g(a_j \oplus r'_{i,j})$, $a_i \odot g(a_j \oplus r'_{i,j})$ and $(a_j \oplus r'_{i,j}) \odot g(a_i)$

4. $r_{i,j}$, $f(a_i, r'_{i,j}) \oplus r_{i,j}$, $f(a_i, r'_{i,j}) \oplus a_i \odot g(a_j \oplus r'_{i,j}) \oplus r_{i,j}$ and $f(a_i, a_j) \oplus r_{i,j}$

5. $a_i \odot g(a_i) \oplus \bigoplus_{j=0}^{j_0}(f(a_j, a_i) \oplus r_{j,i})$ with $j_0 \leqslant i - 1$ and

   $a_i \odot g(a_i) \oplus \bigoplus_{j=0}^{i-1}(f(a_j, a_i) \oplus r_{j,i}) \oplus \bigoplus_{j=i+1}^{j_0} r_{i,j}$ with $i < j_0 \leqslant d$

For the sake of clarity we use the notations $r_{i,j}$ and $r_{j,i}$ in the above list only for fresh random values (i.e. the $r_{i,j}$ are always such that $i < j$ and the $r_{j,i}$ are always such that $j < i$).

To construct the set I, we proceed as follows. Initially, I is empty. First, for every v_h in category 1 or 5, we add i to I. Then, for the remaining v_h (in categories 2, 3 and 4), we add j to I if i is already in I and we add i to I otherwise.

Now that the set I has been determined – and note that since there are at most d intermediate variables v_h, the cardinality of I can be at most d – we show how to perfectly simulate the d-tuple $(v_1, v_2, \ldots, v_d)$ using only the components of $a_{|I}$. First, we assign a random value to every $r_{i,j}$ and $r'_{i,j}$ entering in the computation of any v_h (as done in Steps 3 and 4 of Algorithm 4). Then every intermediate variable v_h is simulated as follows.

1. If v_h is in category 1, then $i \in I$ and v_h is directly computed from a_i.
2. If v_h is in category 2, then $i \in I$ and v_h is directly computed from a_i and $r'_{i,j}$.
3. If v_h is in category 3, then $i \in I$ and two possible cases occur:
   – if $j \in I$, then v_h can be directly assigned from a_i, a_j and $r'_{i,j}$,
   – if $j \notin I$, then $r'_{i,j}$ does not enter in the expression of any other v_h (otherwise j would be in I), and $a_j \oplus r'_{i,j}$ is randomly distributed and mutually independent of the variables in $\{v_1, v_2, \ldots, v_d\}\backslash\{v_h\}$. Hence v_h can be assigned to either r, $g(r)$, $a_i \odot g(r)$, or $r \odot g(a_i)$, where r is a fresh random value (and $r'_{i,j}$ does not need to be assigned to a random value at the beginning of the simulation).
4. If v_h is in category 4, then $i \in I$ and two possible cases occur:
   – if $j \in I$, then v_h can be directly assigned from a_i, a_j, $r_{i,j}$ and $r'_{i,j}$,
   – if $j \notin I$, then $r_{i,j}$ does not enter in the expression of any other v_h (otherwise j would be in I), and v_h is randomly distributed and mutually independent of the variables in $\{v_1, v_2, \ldots, v_d\}\backslash\{v_h\}$. Hence v_h can be assigned to a fresh random value (and $r_{i,j}$ does not need to be assigned to a random value at the beginning of the simulation).
5. If v_h is in category 5, then $i \in I$ and the firm term $a_i \odot g(a_i)$ is hence directly computed from a_i, whereas the second term $\bigoplus_{j=i+1}^{j_0} r_{i,j}$ is directly deduced from the $r_{i,j}$'s. Eventually, every element $f(a_j, a_i) \oplus r_{j,i}$ in the sum $\bigoplus_{j=0}^{i-1}(f(a_j, a_i) \oplus r_{j,i})$ is assigned as follows:
   – if $j \in I$ then $f(a_j, a_i) \oplus r_{j,i}$ is directly assigned from a_j, a_i and $r_{i,j}$,
   – if $j \notin I$ then $r_{j,i}$ does not enter in the expression of any other v_h (otherwise j would be in I), and $f(a_j, a_i) \oplus r_{j,i}$ is randomly distributed and mutually independent of the variables in the set $\{v_1, v_2, \ldots, v_d\}\backslash\{v_h\}$. Hence $f(a_j, a_i) \oplus r_{j,i}$ can be assigned to a fresh random value (and $r_{j,i}$ does not need to be assigned to a random value at the beginning of the simulation).

Table 1. Timings (clock cycles) for a masked implementation of the AES s-box w.r.t. the masking order d.

	d = 1	d = 2	d = 3
Rivain and Prouff scheme [10]	533	832	1905
Improved scheme (this paper)	407	622	1237

Table 2. Timings (clock cycles) for a masked implementation of a multiplication of the form $x \odot g(x)$ where g is $\mathbb{F}_2$-linear and with masking order $d \in \{1, 2, 3\}$.

	d = 1	d = 2	d = 3
Algorithm 1	110	252	346
Algorithm 5	41	107	204

5   Implementation Results

In this section, we give implementation results to compare, the original RP Scheme with our new proposal. We implemented the RP scheme (Algorithm 3) using Algorithm 5 for multiplications of the form $x \odot g(x)$ (i.e. for Steps 2–3 and Steps 4–6 in Algorithm 3) with the appropriate look-up tables (for h being $x \mapsto x \odot x^2$ and $x \mapsto x \odot x^4$ respectively). Codes were written in assembly language for an 8051 based 8-bit architecture with bit-addressable memory. Table 1 lists the timing performances of the two versions of the scheme for $d \in \{1, 2, 3\}$. In Table 2, we also report on the timing performances of a secure multiplication of the form $x \odot g(x)$ when processed either with our new algorithm (Algorithm 5) or with the original ISW scheme (Algorithm 1). We see that our improved method achieves a significant gain in timings. Regarding memory, the RAM consumption is similar for both implementations, while our new secure multiplication requires more ROM for the storage of the look-up table. For the RP scheme, our new solution implies a 600-byte overhead in ROM to store the two look-up tables ($x \mapsto x \odot x^2$ and $x \mapsto x \odot x^4$) and for Algorithm 5 source code.

A   Security Proof for Algorithm 5

Similarly to what has been done in Sect. 4 for Algorithm 4, we show here that any d-tuple of intermediate variables of Algorithm 5 is independent of the sensitive variable a.

Our proof consists in constructing a set I of indices in $[0; d]$ with cardinality lower than or equal to d and such that the distribution of any d-tuple $(v_1, v_2, \ldots, v_d)$ of intermediate variables of Algorithm 5 can be perfectly simulated from $a_{|I} := (a_i)_{i \in I}$. This will prove the dth-order security, by definition, since $a_{|I}$ is independent of a as long as the cardinality of I is strictly smaller than d.

Let us first enumerate five possible categories for the intermediate variables of Algorithm 5:

1. a_i or $h(a_i)$;
2. $r'_{i,j}$, $a_i \oplus r'_{i,j}$, $h(r'_{i,j})$ or $h(a_i \oplus r'_{i,j})$;
3. $a_j \oplus r'_{i,j}$, $a_i \oplus r'_{i,j} \oplus a_j$, $h(a_j \oplus r'_{i,j})$ or $h(a_i \oplus r'_{i,j} \oplus a_j)$;
4. $r_{i,j}$, $r_{i,j} \oplus h(a_i \oplus r'_{i,j})$, $r_{i,j} \oplus h(a_i \oplus r'_{i,j}) \oplus h(a_j \oplus r'_{i,j})$,
   $r_{i,j} \oplus h(a_i \oplus r'_{i,j}) \oplus h(a_j \oplus r'_{i,j}) \oplus h(a_i \oplus r'_{i,j} \oplus a_j)$,
   or $r_{i,j} \oplus h(a_i \oplus r'_{i,j}) \oplus h(a_j \oplus r'_{i,j}) \oplus h(a_i \oplus r'_{i,j} \oplus a_j) \oplus h(r'_{i,j})$;
5. $h(a_i) \oplus \bigoplus_{j=0}^{j_0} (f(a_j, a_i) \oplus r_{j,i})$ with $j_0 \leqslant i - 1$, or
   $h(a_i) \oplus \bigoplus_{j=0}^{i-1} (f(a_j, a_i) \oplus r_{j,i}) \oplus \bigoplus_{j=i+1}^{j_0} r_{i,j}$ with $j_0 \leqslant d$

For the sake of clarity we use the notations $r_{i,j}$ and $r_{j,i}$ in the above list only for fresh random values (i.e. the $r_{i,j}$ are always such that $i < j$ and the $r_{j,i}$ are always such that $j < i$).

To construct the set I, we proceed as follows. Initially, I is empty and all the v_h's are unassigned. First, for every v_h of category 1 or 5, we add i to I. Then, for every v_h of category 2, 3 or 4, if i is already in I, then we add j to I, otherwise we add i to I.

Now that the set I has been determined – and note that since there are at most d intermediate variables v_h, the cardinality of I can be at most d – we show how to complete a perfect simulation of the d-tuple $(v_1, v_2, \ldots, v_d)$ using only the values of $a_{|I}$. First, we assign a random value to every $r_{i,j}$ and $r'_{i,j}$ entering in the computation of any v_h (as done in steps 3 and 4 of Algorithm 5). Then every intermediate variable v_h is simulated as follows.

1. If v_h is of category 1, then $i \in I$ and v_h is directly assigned from a_i.
2. If v_h is of category 2, then $i \in I$ and v_h is directly assigned from a_i and $r'_{i,j}$.
3. If v_h is of category 3, then $i \in I$ and two possible cases occur:
   - if $j \in I$, then v_h can be directly assigned from a_i, a_j and $r'_{i,j}$,
   - if $j \notin I$, then $r'_{i,j}$ does not enter in the expression of any other v_h (otherwise j would be in I). Therefore $a_j \oplus r'_{i,j}$ (or $a_i \oplus r'_{i,j} \oplus a_j$) is randomly distributed and mutually independent of variables in $\{v_1, v_2, \ldots, v_d\} \backslash \{v_h\}$. Hence v_h can be assigned to either r or $h(r)$, where r is a fresh random value (and $r'_{i,j}$ does not need to be assigned to a random value at the beginning of the simulation).
4. If v_h is of category 4, then $i \in I$ and two possible cases occur:
   - if $j \in I$, then v_h can be directly assigned from a_i, a_j, $r_{i,j}$ and $r'_{i,j}$,
   - if $j \notin I$, then $r_{i,j}$ does not enter in the expression of any other v_h (otherwise j would be in I), and v_h is randomly distributed and mutually independent of variables in $\{v_1, v_2, \ldots, v_d\} \backslash \{v_h\}$. Hence v_h can be assigned to a fresh random value (and $r_{i,j}$ does not need to be assigned to a random value at the beginning of the simulation).
5. If v_h is of category 5, then $i \in I$, $h(a_i)$ is directly assigned from a_i, and $\bigoplus_{j=i+1}^{j_0} r_{i,j}$ is directly assigned from the $r_{i,j}$'s. Then for the sum $\bigoplus_{j=0}^{i-1} (f(a_j, a_i) \oplus r_{j,i})$, every $f(a_j, a_i) \oplus r_{j,i}$ is assigned as follows:

- if $j \in I$, then $f(a_j, a_i) \oplus r_{j,i}$ is directly assigned from a_j, a_i and $r_{i,j}$,
- if $j \notin I$, then $r_{j,i}$ does not enter in the expression of any other v_h (otherwise $j \in I$), and $f(a_j, a_i) \oplus r_{j,i}$ is randomly distributed and mutually independent of variables in $\{v_1, v_2, \ldots, v_d\} \setminus \{v_h\}$. Hence $f(a_j, a_i) \oplus r_{j,i}$ can be assigned to a fresh random value (and $r_{j,i}$ does not need to be assigned to a random value at the beginning of the simulation).

References

1. Carlet, C., Goubin, L., Prouff, E., Quisquater, M., Rivain, M.: Higher-order masking schemes for S-Boxes. In: Canteaut, A. (ed.) FSE 2012. LNCS, vol. 7549, pp. 366–384. Springer, Heidelberg (2012)
2. Chari, S., Jutla, C.S., Rao, J.R., Rohatgi, P.: Towards sound approaches to counteract power-analysis attacks. In: Wiener, M. (ed.) CRYPTO 1999. LNCS, vol. 1666, pp. 398–412. Springer, Heidelberg (1999)
3. Daemen, J., Rijmen, V.: The Design of Rijndael. Springer, Heidelberg (2002)
4. Gierlichs, B., Batina, L., Preneel, B., Verbauwhede, I.: Revisiting Higher-Order DPA Attacks: Multivariate Mutual Information Analysis. Cryptology ePrint Archive, report 2009/228 (2009). http://eprint.iacr.org/
5. Ishai, Y., Sahai, A., Wagner, D.: Private circuits: securing hardware against probing attacks. In: Boneh, D. (ed.) CRYPTO 2003. LNCS, vol. 2729, pp. 463–481. Springer, Heidelberg (2003)
6. Kim, H., Hong, S., Lim, J.: A fast and provably secure higher-order masking of AES S-Box. In: Preneel, B., Takagi, T. (eds.) CHES 2011. LNCS, vol. 6917, pp. 95–107. Springer, Heidelberg (2011)
7. Kocher, P.C.: Timing attacks on implementations of Diffie-Hellman, RSA, DSS, and other systems. In: Koblitz, N. (ed.) CRYPTO 1996. LNCS, vol. 1109, pp. 104–113. Springer, Heidelberg (1996)
8. Kocher, P., Jaffe, J., Jun, B.: Differential power analysis. In: Wiener, M. (ed.) CRYPTO 1999. LNCS, vol. 1666, pp. 388–397. Springer, Heidelberg (1999)
9. Prouff, E., Rivain, M., Bévan, R.: Statistical analysis of second order differential power analysis. IEEE Trans. Comput. **58**(6), 799–811 (2009)
10. Rivain, M., Prouff, E.: Provably secure higher-order masking of AES. In: Mangard, S., Standaert, F.-X. (eds.) CHES 2010. LNCS, vol. 6225, pp. 413–427. Springer, Heidelberg (2010)
11. Satoh, A., Morioka, S., Takano, K., Munetoh, S.: A compact rijndael hardware architecture with S-Box optimization. In: Boyd, C. (ed.) ASIACRYPT 2001. LNCS, vol. 2248, pp. 239–254. Springer, Heidelberg (2001)
12. Standaert, F.-X., Malkin, T.G., Yung, M.: A unified framework for the analysis of side-channel key recovery attacks. In: Joux, A. (ed.) EUROCRYPT 2009. LNCS, vol. 5479, pp. 443–461. Springer, Heidelberg (2009)

Masking Tables—An Underestimated Security Risk

Michael Tunstall[✉], Carolyn Whitnall, and Elisabeth Oswald

Department of Computer Science, University of Bristol,
Merchant Venturers Building, Woodland Road,
Bristol BS8 1UB, UK
{michael.tunstall,carolyn.whitnall,elisabeth.oswald}@bristol.ac.uk

Abstract. The literature on side-channel analysis describes numerous masking schemes designed to protect block ciphers at the implementation level. Such masking schemes typically require the computation of masked tables prior to the execution of an encryption function. In this paper we revisit an attack which directly exploits this computation in such a way as to *recover* all or some of the masks used. We show that securely implementing masking schemes is only possible where one has access to a significant amount of random numbers.

Keywords: Side-channel analysis · Secure implementations · Block ciphers

1 Introduction

In recent years a wide range of (higher-order) masking schemes have appeared in the literature. A few of these works are dedicated hardware implementations but the majority are designed to be implemented in embedded software (e.g. as described by Akkar and Giraud [1]), which will be the focus of this article. For instance, Rivain et al. [2] showed how to achieve resistance to second-order DPA (using a table re-masking method). Recent work has discussed affine masking [3], and a hardware-oriented masking scheme proposed by Ishai et al. [4–6].

First- and higher-order masking schemes (i.e. schemes which use one or several random values as masks) are attractive because they (in theory) provide provable security against differential power analysis (DPA) attacks and do not require any specific alterations to a device. In other words, they seem (together with hiding countermeasures) the panacea when it comes to securely implementing ciphers such as AES and DES on otherwise leaky devices (i.e. devices not resistant to DPA).

In this paper we focus on the precomputation based on a rather simple observation: if masks could be extracted by attacking the precomputation, there would be no security at all in the masked encryption rounds. An attacker could simply first extract the masks and use them to correctly predict the masked intermediate

S. Moriai (Ed.): FSE 2013, LNCS 8424, pp. 425–444, 2014.
DOI: 10.1007/978-3-662-43933-3_22, © Springer-Verlag Berlin Heidelberg 2014

values, which would then make a standard DPA attack trivial. Even if an implementation were to use on-the-fly computations of masked S-box tables, if these were vulnerable, then an attack would succeed, as demonstrated by Pan et al. [7].

In this paper we set out to provide a thorough analysis of the application of this type of attack to a variety of state-of-the-art masking approaches when the precomputation is implemented using hiding strategies. We give a thorough theoretical analysis using the evaluation approach suggested by Whitnall and Oswald [8]. This enables us to show, independently of a specific device, how well such attacks work by giving a number of key figures for varying signal-to-noise ratios (SNR, as defined by Mangard et al. [9]), such as the magnitude of resulting correlation coefficients, success probabilities for deriving masks, and the number of traces required for the subsequent key recovery step.

Furthermore, we describe some practical results of attacks on real devices for two representative platforms (an 8-bit and a 32-bit microprocessor). Our results serve as both warning and guidance: they show that the attacks work even with strong hiding countermeasures, and provide information about what SNR is required such that hiding begins to effectively mitigate our attacks.

We have structured our work as follows. We begin by briefly recalling the necessary background with regards to Boolean and affine masking, hiding countermeasures, and the working principle of standard DPA attacks in Sect. 2. Then we explain our attacks against precomputation, including how we model them for our theoretic analysis in Sect. 3. Results of this analysis are provided for all combinations of masking schemes and hiding strategies, for different SNRs. Following on from that we describe our practical processors and setups and report on practical attack outcomes in Sect. 4. We conclude in the last section of the article. After providing references we also use an appendix to collect those tables that are too unwieldy to be included in the main body of this work.

2   Background to Masking, Hiding, and DPA

The masking of intermediate values is a popular software countermeasure in practice (evidence for this is provided by the large number of articles and patents with industrial co-authors [1,3,10,11]). Boolean masking fits well to symmetric encryption schemes (such as AES) and variants such as higher-order masking or affine masking have been the topic of many recent publications. The simple underlying principle of any masking scheme is that, rather than processing the intermediate values (e.g. a key byte, plaintext byte, output of an S-box look-up) directly, one conceals these values with some random value. The hope is that the intermediate value will no longer be predictable and hence the implementation will be secure with regard to (first-order) DPA attacks.

To complicate the adversary's task even further one may also employ hiding techniques. In software this typically means using dummy (or sequences of) instructions (i.e. additional sequences of instructions operating on dummy data, which are indistinguishable from the flow of the actual algorithm) and randomising the sequence of instructions in various ways. Adding dummy instructions is simple but can be costly, moreover recent work points to the inherent difficulty of achieving indistinguishability in practice [12].

In the following sections we introduce details of Boolean and affine masking that are relevant for DPA attacks on the precomputation that we concentrate on. Further, we explain three randomization strategies which are relatively cheap to implement, and to the best of our knowledge are relevant in practice. We complete the necessary background by very briefly explaining Differential Power Analysis (DPA).

2.1 Masking

We now explain the general principle of masking schemes based on Boolean masks. Thereafter we explain how other schemes such as second-order Boolean masking and affine masking are different.

Boolean masks are random values that are exclusive-ored (short XORed) with intermediate values. In the case of AES, this implies that every state byte is masked in this way (whether or not different masks are used for different state bytes depends on efficiency considerations and on the order of DPA attacks one wants to prevent). Similarly, all keys bytes are masked (the decision for different or equal masks again depends on security and efficiency considerations). For example, Herbst et al. [13] give a full explanation of a first-order masking scheme for a typical software implementation of AES[1]. To keep this paper self-contained we briefly summarise how the masked round functions are implemented:

AddRoundKey remains the same but operates on masked inputs. We assume key and plaintext mask are different.
SubBytes is replaced by a masked table which is precomputed at the beginning of each encryption round using Algorithm 1. There are two random values involved in this precomputation: r, the *address mask* and s, the *data mask*.
ShiftRows remains unchanged.
The MixColumns function is implemented to ensure that all intermediate values remain masked throughout.
KeySchedule remains the same but works on masked data using the same masked substitution table as the masked SubBytes function.

Second-order Boolean Masking: Second-order masking extends first-order masking by applying a second mask to each intermediate value, i.e. a value is represented by three shares ($x = (x_1, x_2, x_3)$, such that $x = x_1 \oplus x_2 \oplus x_3$). A masking scheme for AES following this principle has been described by Rivain et al. [2]. As for Boolean masking, the majority of the round functions remain largely unchanged. However, conducting a SubBytes operation becomes problematic because, unlike in first-order masking, it is not possible to 're-use' a

---

[1] Herbst et al. describe how to mask AES and randomise the flow within rounds (the S-box precomputation is not randomised).

Algorithm 1. Masking a Substitution Table for Boolean Masking.

Input: S a 256-byte substitution table, random values $r, s \in \{0, \ldots, 255\}$.
Output: S' a 256-byte masked substitution table.

1 **for** $i \leftarrow 0$ **to** 255 **do**
2 $\quad | \quad S'[i] = S[i \oplus r] \oplus s$;
3 **end**

4 **return** S'

---

precomputed table (re-using a table with the same set of masks two or more times would produce a second-order leakage). Consequently, the entire masked S-box needs to be produced when required during the round function. Algorithm 2 shows how to securely compute such an S-box.

Algorithm 2. Masking a Substitution Table for Second-Order Boolean masking [2].

Input: S a 256-byte substitution table, random values
$\qquad r_1, r_2, r_3, s_1, s_2 \in \{0, \ldots, 255\}$, and x' where $x = x' \oplus r_1 \oplus r_2$
Output: $S(x) \oplus s_1 \oplus s_2$.

1 $r' = (r_1 \oplus r_2) \oplus r_3$;
2 **for** $i \leftarrow 0$ **to** 255 **do**
3 $\quad | \quad a = i \oplus r'$;
4 $\quad | \quad S'[i] = (S[a \oplus x'] \oplus s_1) \oplus s_2$;
5 **end**

6 **return** $S'[r_3]$

Affine Masking: Fumaroli et al. proposed an alternative masking scheme that uses an affine transformation G rather than a Boolean mask [3]. Hence to mask a value x ones applies G where

$$G : \mathbb{F}_{2^8} \longrightarrow \mathbb{F}_{2^8} : x \longmapsto r \cdot x \oplus r' \ ,$$

with randomly chosen mask bytes $r \in \mathbb{F}_{2^8} \setminus \{0\}$ and $r' \in \mathbb{F}_{2^8}$.

Affine masking can be applied to all round functions by adapting the functions accordingly (see Fumaroli et al. [3] for details). As we focus our attacks on those operations relating to the computation required to produce a masked substitution table we only give the algorithm required to generate such a table, see Algorithm 3.

Algorithm 3. Masking a Substitution Table for Affine Masking.

Input: S a 256-byte substitution table, r, r' two random values used as masks.
Output: S a 256-byte masked substitution table.

1 **for** $i \leftarrow 0$ **to** 255 **do**
2 | $G[i] = r \cdot i \oplus r'$;
3 **end**

4 **for** $i \leftarrow 0$ **to** 255 **do**
5 | $S'[i] = G[S[G[i]]]$;
6 **end**

7 **return** G, S'

2.2   Hiding

Our focus is on how to generate a masked (S-box) table prior to an encryption run in some random order. Randomly going through the loop indices can be achieved in various ways, and we list the three most generic strategies in order of increasing complexity. Using Algorithm 1 as an example, line 2 would be replaced by

$$S'[f(i)] = S[f(i) \oplus r] \oplus s$$

for some function f.

Random start index. One method to introduce some randomness into the indexing (when looking at multiple runs of the loop as in multiple traces) is to randomly choose the start index. That is

$$f : \{0, \dots, 255\} \longrightarrow \{0, \dots, 255\} : x \longmapsto x + k \quad \mod 256 \ ,$$

where a fresh $k \in \{0, \dots, 255\}$ is generated for each instance of the algorithm. This is also the method that was suggested by Herbst et al. [13].

Random walk. Another simple method, defined by Naccache et al. [14], uses an LFSR to generate a (pseudo)random walk through the indices. That is,

$$f : \{0, \dots, 255\} \longrightarrow \{0, \dots, 255\} : x \longmapsto (((x \oplus w) \times u) + y) \oplus z \quad \mod 256 \ ,$$

where a fresh $w, y, z \in \{0, \dots, 255\}$ and $u \in \{1, 3, \dots, 255\}$ are generated for each instance of the algorithm.

Random permutation. To go through all the indices one could generate a random permutation of the 256 elements in $\{0, \dots, 255\}$. However, creating such a random permutation requires the generation of 256 random numbers [15]. Random number generation is costly and one approach to make this more practical is to generate a shorter sequence of random numbers and apply the same sequence repeatedly to the 256 elements. That is,

$$f : \{0, \ldots, 255\} \longrightarrow \{0, \ldots, 255\} : x \longmapsto g_{x \bmod n} + m \left\lfloor \frac{x}{n} \right\rfloor \bmod 256 \ ,$$

where g is a random sequence of length m given $m | 256$ and $n = 256/m$. As previously, a fresh random sequence is generated for each instance of the algorithm. Intuitively, the larger m is, the closer one gets to a truly random permutation.

2.3 Differential Power Analysis

We consider a 'standard' Differential Power Analysis (DPA) scenario as defined by Mangard et al. [16]. That is, we assume that the power consumption T of a cryptographic device depends on some internal value (or state) $F_{k^*}(X)$ which we call the *intermediate value*: a function $F_{k^*} : \mathcal{X} \to \mathcal{Z}$ of some part of the known plaintext (a random variable $X \in \mathcal{X}$) which is dependent on some part of a secret key $k^* \in \mathcal{K}$. Consequently, we have $T = L \circ F_{k^*}(X) + \varepsilon$, where $L : \mathcal{Z} \longrightarrow \mathbb{R}$ describes the data-dependent component and ε contains the remaining power consumption which can be modelled as independent random noise. We consider an attacker who acquires N power measurements corresponding to encryptions of N known plaintexts $x_i \in \mathcal{X}$, $i = 1, \ldots, N$ and wishes to recover the secret key k^*. The attacker can accurately compute the internal values as they would be under each key hypothesis $\{F_k(x_i)\}_{i=1}^{N}$, $k \in \mathcal{K}$ and uses whatever information available about the true leakage function L to construct a prediction model $M : \mathcal{Z} \to \mathcal{M}$.

DPA is based on the assumption that the power model values corresponding to the correct key hypothesis should have a closer resemblance to true trace measurements than the power model values corresponding to incorrect key hypotheses. This similarity can be measured using the correlation coefficient:

$$D_{\rho,T}(k) = \rho(T, M_k) = \frac{\operatorname{cov}(T, M_k)}{\sqrt{\operatorname{var}(T)} \sqrt{\operatorname{var}(M_k)}} \ . \tag{1}$$

Whitnall and Oswald [8] note that the *nearest rival margin* (i.e., the distance between the correct key and the closest rival hypothesis when the theoretic distinguishing vector[2] is ranked) has a substantial bearing on practical outcomes, because the number of needed power traces (NNT) that are required to detect a statistically significant difference increases as the actual magnitude of the true difference decreases. By defining practically relevant scenarios, it is hence possible to derive true correlation coefficients, examine the resulting margins and then conclude on the number of needed traces (as explained in Chaps. 4 and

---

[2] The theoretic distinguishing vector represents the underlying values which an attack seeks to estimate, and is computed from known distributions rather than estimated on sampled data.

6 of [9]). The correlation coefficient in an ideal (noise-free) setting scales with the SNR as shown in (2) (which corresponds to (6.5) Chap. 6 of [9]). Given the correlation coefficient corresponding to the correct key ρ_{ck} and the correlation coefficient of the nearest rival ρ_{nr} we can use (3) (which corresponds to (4.43) in [9]) to calculate the NNT. In this equation we choose $\alpha = 0.05$ according to the usual statistical practice).

$$\rho(T, M_k) = \frac{\rho(L \circ F_{k^*}(X), M_k)}{\sqrt{1 + \frac{1}{SNR}}} \tag{2}$$

$$NNT = 3 + 8 \cdot \frac{z^2{}_{1-\alpha}}{\left(\ln \frac{1+\rho_{ck}}{1-\rho_{ck}} - \ln \frac{1+\rho_{nr}}{1-\rho_{nr}}\right)^2} \tag{3}$$

3   Mask Recovery Attacks

In an attack on the precomputation we take a single power consumption trace for one encryption run and extract the part of the trace that corresponds to the precomputation. This trace is then divided up into 256 portions that are then used as a set of traces to conduct a standard DPA. The message is the index i used to control the loop, and the unknowns that we wish to derive are the masks used.

3.1   Boolean Masking

To attack an implementation of Boolean masking (see Algorithm 1) one proceeds by determining the mask r used to blind the address of the S-box table followed by the mask s used to mask the data elements in the table. Note that the application of this strategy does not change when applying it to second-order Boolean masking: in order to target the masked S-box outputs it is sufficient to extract $r_1 \oplus r_2$ and $s_1 \oplus s_2$ as they occur in Algorithm 2—which, in *practice*, is no different to extracting r and s from Algorithm 1. Wherever we present tables and results labelled 'Boolean masking' it should be understood that they relate equally to second- and first-order outcomes.

Masking only. We now explain in more detail how the above description translates into a model that can be used to predict attack outcomes. As per our description, we first attempt to extract r. The attack outcome here is a distinguishing vector that allows us to 'rank' our hypotheses for r. We then use r to determine s. Looking at this differently: we can actually test several values of r and examine the attack outcomes for s in each case (intuitively for incorrect r the recovery of s will completely fail). In our work we settled on allowing a certain number of the best, denoted h, hypotheses for r to be tested with s. Consequently, to model the mask recovery attack for our theoretic analysis we define the $K_{x,h}$ to represent the h highest ranking hypotheses for the variable x. We can then consider the probability of complete mask recovery to be

$$\Pr(r \in K_{r,h}) \cdot \Pr(s \in K_{s,1} | r \text{ is known})$$

We also take into account the probability of *partially* uncovering the masks, by which we mean that our guess at r is correct and our guess at s is incorrect but close (i.e. a short Hamming distance from the correct s)—which is reasonable because the nearest rivals in an attack against an XOR operation *are* of this form. These probabilities can be computed, for any *given number of observations* (i.e., in our case the $N = 256$ trace-segments relating to the loops of the S-box masking procedure), via a formula related to Eqn. (3):

$$\Pr(\rho_{cm} \text{ distinguished from } \rho_{alt}) = 1 - \Phi \left[z_{1-\alpha} - \frac{\left(\ln \frac{1+\rho_{cm}}{1-\rho_{cm}} - \ln \frac{1+\rho_{alt}}{1-\rho_{alt}} \right)}{2 \cdot \sqrt{2/(N-3)}} \right] \quad (4)$$

where ρ_{cm} denotes the correct-hypothesis correlation and ρ_{alt} denotes the correlation produced by the relevant alternative (for example, the h-th ranked candidate for r). The values ρ_{cm} and ρ_{alt} are taken directly from theoretic distinguishing vector. As (4) shows we use the statistical power related to the correct-hypothesis correlation and the relevant alternative to approximate the probabilities for recovering r, and having r ranked among the first $K_{r,h}$ hypotheses respectively. Our method of retaining and confirming h hypotheses means that we are not so concerned with minimising 'false positives'—which corresponds (implicitly) with relaxing the significance criteria. For our theoretic analysis to be meaningful we need to choose, for these computations, a value of α which reflects an attacker's approach in practice, rather than obey typical statistical conventions which impose strong decision criteria as protection against false positives.[3] We settle on $\alpha = 0.2$, which we were able to experimentally confirm *does* align well with the apparent workings of our attack strategy in practice.

Based on these probabilities we can model the success of the subsequent key recovery step carried out in a practical attack. The probabilities for (partial) mask recovery describe how, in effect, an adversary would bias the masks (either remove them if masks are recovered without error, or correctly predict most of the bits effectively leaving only a small bias due to the remaining unknown bits). With this information we can compute theoretic outcomes for the key recovery

---

[3] Note that in many typical applications of *formal* hypothesis testing—medical treatment evaluation, for example—false positives have serious consequences. Competent analysts will opt to increase their sample sizes rather than weaken their decision criteria in order to get conclusive results. Since the unmasking phase of a mask recovery attack is constrained to a sample size of 256 an attacker does not have this option, nor are the consequences of a false positive so 'expensive'.

step and use the nearest rival margins to obtain the number of needed traces (for the entire attack) in practice for a given SNR[4].

Table 1 lists the outcomes of these theoretic, modelled attacks for different SNRs (where $h = 10$). The top line states the SNR level, increasing from high noise at the left, towards no noise on the right. The second table line then lists the percentage of masks fully recovered, and the third line lists the percentage of masks partially recovered (a single-bit error). The numbers show that, up to an SNR of two, full mask recovery is possible, but afterwards only partial recovery is possible. The precise cut-off point for full recovery is 1.897 as we determined in our theoretic model. The fourth and fifth line list then the values of the correct key correlation and the margin to the nearest rival in the key recovery step. This margin actually translates into the number of needed power traces. As the values show up to an SNR of 2^{-1} the attack is basically equally effective as would be a standard DPA attack on an unprotected device.

Table 1. Data complexity of mask recovery attacks against a Boolean masked AES S-box (straightforward pre-computation phase).

	2^{-5}	2^{-3}	2^{-1}	2^1	2^3	2^5	2^7	Pure signal
S-box unmasked	29.4	56.9	91.2	100.0	100.0	100.0	100.0	100.0
S-box partially unmasked	55.0	42.7	8.8	0.0	0.0	0.0	0.0	0.0
Correct key correlation	0.123	0.296	0.565	0.816	0.943	0.985	0.996	1.000
Nearest rival margin	0.100	0.241	0.459	0.663	0.766	0.800	0.809	0.812
Traces needed	538	90	22	8	5	4	4	3

Masking and hiding. We now investigate how the three hiding strategies we listed before impact on the effectiveness of the mask recovery attacks. We briefly describe how the countermeasures change the model we detailed before. When the starting index for the precomputation is chosen randomly, the first step of the unmasking procedure attempts to recover the index i *and* the address mask r, by trying each pair. In fact there is irresolvable ambiguity between two equally ranked hypotheses—the correct pair (r, i) and the shifted pair $(r + 128 \mod 256, i + 128 \mod 256)$. Fortunately, this does not pose an obstacle to recovering the mask on the S-box output, as either pair will produce the same unmasked address

---

[4] Throughout this paper we assume in our models that the device leaks the Hamming weight and that the adversary uses this as power model. This is not a shortcoming for several reasons. Firstly, the numbers we provide are independent of the actual power model; they do however depend on the fact that we assume that the adversary's model effectively matches the leakage model of the device. If an adversary were to use an imprecise model, this would change the outcomes and the analysis would need to be done accounting for the imprecision. Secondly, leakages observed in practice from software implementations on small processors originate typically from transfers of intermediate data or address values over buses. These components typically leak the Hamming weight or the Hamming distance from some fixed value.

and therefore provide the predicted values for the second stage mask recovery attack.

When the pre-computation is performed according to the ordering given by an LFSR, the LFSR function itself must be recovered, which requires more attack steps and leads to a larger aggregate loss of precision. However, it is still feasible. If the index function is of the form

$$f : \{0, \ldots, 255\} \longrightarrow \{0, \ldots, 255\} : x \longmapsto (((x \oplus w) \times u) + y) \oplus z \quad \mod 256 \ ,$$

then, by retaining the top h hypotheses at every step (which in practice is usually smaller than for the standard attack—we take $h = 4$ in our analysis, to represent an attacker's response to the increased computational complexity), and using the following step as confirmation, we estimate the proportion unmasked as:

$$\Pr(w \in K_{w,h}) \cdot \Pr(x \in K_{x,h}|w \text{ is known}) \cdot \Pr(y \in K_{y,h}|w, x \text{ are known})$$
$$\cdot \Pr(z \oplus r \in K_{z\oplus r,h}|w, x, y \text{ are known}) \cdot \Pr(s \in K_{s,1}|w, x, y, z \oplus r \text{ are known}),$$

noting that we are unable to recover r as distinct from z, but that, for the purposes of unmasking the address, it is sufficient to recover the XOR between the two.

The theoretic analysis for attacks against the implementation which permutes the indices in aligned blocks before precomputing the masked table is slightly more complicated because one must take into account the probability of uncovering only a proportion of the columns (see Sect. 2.2 for notation). Additionally, as with the random start index variant, there remains ambiguity over the correct column and mask pair: each column hypothesis will result in a maximal peak for a certain hypothesis on the mask (From an information theoretic perspective, it is clear that we cannot expect to recover 10 bits of information from an 8-bit target value). However, all of these pairs reproduce the *same* (correct) 8-bit unmasked address value, and since this is what we need for the second stage output unmasking the ambiguity does not matter.

The proportion unmasked is estimated (via the Law of Total Probability[5]) as:

$$\sum_{c=1}^{n} \Pr(c \text{ columns are unmasked}) \cdot \Pr(s \in K_{s,1}|c \text{ columns are unmasked})$$
$$= \sum_{c=1}^{n} \binom{n}{c} \cdot \Pr(\text{column unmasked})^c \cdot (1 - \Pr(\text{column unmasked}))^{n-c}$$
$$\cdot \Pr(s \in K_{s,1}|c \text{ columns are unmasked})$$

Table 2 (which is laid out similarly to Table 1) presents the theoretic mask recovery rates and subsequent key recovery performance for the hiding countermeasures. The attack remains (theoretically) successful against all countermeasures,

---

[5] Law of Total Probability states that if $\{B_n : n = 1, 2, 3, \ldots\}$ is a finite or countably infinite partition of a sample space and each event B_n is measurable, then for any event A, $\Pr(A) = \sum_n \Pr(A \cap B_n) = \sum_n \Pr(A|B_n) \Pr(B_n)$.

Table 2. Data complexity of mask recovery attacks against a Boolean masked AES S-box with hiding countermeasures.

	2^{-5}	2^{-3}	2^{-1}	2^1	2^3	2^5	2^7	Pure signal
Randomised start index								
S-box unmasked	20.5	50.1	91.1	100.0	100.0	100.0	100.0	100.0
S-box partially unmasked	41.1	41.3	8.9	0.0	0.0	0.0	0.0	0.0
Correct key correlation	0.089	0.270	0.564	0.816	0.943	0.985	0.996	1.000
Nearest rival margin	0.073	0.220	0.459	0.663	0.766	0.800	0.809	0.812
Traces needed	1024	109	22	8	5	4	4	3
Random walk (LFSR)								
S-box unmasked	1.1	8.6	50.9	97.6	100.0	100.0	100.0	100.0
S-box partially unmasked	3.9	21.0	40.2	2.4	0.0	0.0	0.0	0.0
Correct key correlation	0.01	0.08	0.47	0.81	0.94	0.98	1.00	1.00
Nearest rival margin	0.01	0.07	0.38	0.66	0.77	0.80	0.81	0.81
Traces needed	169275	1249	34	9	5	4	4	3
Permuted in 4 columns								
S-box unmasked	24.1	42.7	87.4	100.0	100.0	100.0	100.0	100.0
S-box partially unmasked	31.7	38.1	12.0	0.0	0.0	0.0	0.0	0.0
Correct key correlation	0.083	0.237	0.557	0.816	0.943	0.985	0.996	1.000
Nearest rival margin	0.068	0.193	0.452	0.663	0.766	0.800	0.809	0.812
Traces needed	1175	142	23	8	5	4	4	3
Permuted in 8 columns								
S-box unmasked	23.3	33.0	65.6	99.5	100.0	100.0	100.0	100.0
S-box partially unmasked	23.0	28.1	23.2	0.5	0.0	0.0	0.0	0.0
Correct key correlation	0.071	0.180	0.479	0.815	0.943	0.985	0.996	1.000
Nearest rival margin	0.057	0.146	0.389	0.662	0.766	0.800	0.809	0.812
Traces needed	1644	249	32	9	5	4	4	3
Permuted in 16 columns								
S-box unmasked	23.3	28.7	45.3	86.9	100.0	100.0	100.0	100.0
S-box partially unmasked	18.7	21.0	22.9	9.0	0.0	0.0	0.0	0.0
Correct key correlation	0.065	0.148	0.361	0.765	0.943	0.985	0.996	1.000
Nearest rival margin	0.053	0.121	0.293	0.621	0.766	0.800	0.809	0.812
Traces needed	1933	369	59	10	5	4	4	3
Permuted in 32 columns								
S-box unmasked	22.9	26.2	33.1	47.2	75.3	96.7	99.4	99.4
S-box partially unmasked	15.9	16.0	16.2	16.5	12.2	2.5	0.6	0.6
Correct key correlation	0.061	0.127	0.261	0.487	0.797	0.971	0.994	0.998
Nearest rival margin	0.049	0.103	0.212	0.395	0.647	0.789	0.808	0.811
Traces needed	2223	502	117	31	9	4	4	3

although the noise threshold at which mask recovery begins to deteriorate varies. For the randomised start index this threshold is 1.897, for the random walk it is 9.409, for the column-wise permutations it is 3.959, 9.029, and 25.260 for the 4-, 8- and 16-column variants respectively, whilst for the 32-column variant irresolvable ambiguity on some of the columns means that the masks can never be perfectly recovered, even from noise-free leakage.

3.2   Affine Masking

The attack on the affine masking scheme requires the recovery of a multiplicative and a Boolean mask. As is clear from Algorithm 3, we cannot recover the Boolean mask r' without having first recovered the multiplicative mask r. But once we have recovered the Boolean mask r' we can use it to 'confirm' the correctness of the multiplicative mask r.

Masking only. The strategy for recovering the multiplicative and additive components of an affine-masked S-box output is slightly different. By retaining the top $h = 10$ (say) candidates on the multiplicative mask, then looking at the highest peak produced by the additive hypotheses for each of the 10, we hope to confirm the correct multiplicative mask at the same time as discovering the correct additive hypothesis. Because the input and output are masked with the same values we only need recover the two, e.g. by attacking the pre-computation of the affine transformation look-up table. If the outputs in the masked S-box pre-computation can be identified and targeted then the nonlinearity of the S-box improves the recovery of the second, additive mask—otherwise the margin between the correct mask and the incorrect alternatives will be small, as always when attacking a Boolean addition. We have produced two versions of the analysis accordingly—one where we suppose the S-box structure may be exploited, one where we suppose it cannot. These are presented in Table 3, from which we see that, when the S-box nonlinearity is exploited, the affine masked table precomputation is more vulnerable to mask recovery than the Boolean masked table pre-computation (the SNR thresholds at which the mask recovery begins to degrade are 0.500 when the S-box is exploited in the mask recovery stage, and 1.897—the same as for the Boolean masking—when it is not). However, the more complex nature of the mask application means that any imperfection in the mask recovery incurs a greater penalty on the number of traces needed for the *key recovery* stage (compared to the attacks on Boolean masking), so that in noisy scenarios the affine scheme is the more resilient to the *overall* attack strategy.

Masking and hiding. For the deliberately-complicated versions of the masking schemes, different problems are associated with recovering the affine transformations to those which are associated with recovering the Boolean transformations. In particular, there are far more cases where ambiguity prevents recovering the correct pairs with any confidence. In the analysis, we have generally adopted the approach that, where c candidate pairs are equally theoretically ranked, the probability of recovering the correct one is taken to be $\frac{1}{c}$-times the probability that the c will stand out together. That is, we cannot, except by chance, distinguish it from the others, but will be able to unmask a proportion $(\frac{1}{c} \times \Pr(\text{top set correctly identified}))$ which will still help us in the key-recovery phase of the attack.

The permuted columns variant requires particular adaptation, as there is increasing ambiguity as the size of the permutation increases, with some even producing constant leakage by virtue of the form of the affine transformation

Table 3. Data complexity of mask recovery attacks against an affine masked AES S-box.

	2^{-5}	2^{-3}	2^{-1}	2^1	2^3	2^5	2^7	Pure signal
Exploiting the S-box								
Both masks recovered	57.7	97.4	100.0	100.0	100.0	100.0	100.0	100.0
Multiplicative mask recovered	19.6	2.0	0.0	0.0	0.0	0.0	0.0	0.0
Correct key correlation	0.101	0.325	0.577	0.816	0.943	0.985	0.996	1.000
Nearest rival margin	0.082	0.264	0.469	0.663	0.766	0.800	0.809	0.812
Traces needed	804	74	21	8	5	4	4	3
Not exploiting the S-box								
Both masks recovered	27.2	56.3	91.2	100.0	100.0	100.0	100.0	100.0
Multiplicative mask recovered	33.7	32.8	8.8	0.0	0.0	0.0	0.0	0.0
Correct key correlation	0.048	0.188	0.526	0.816	0.943	0.985	0.996	1.000
Nearest rival margin	0.037	0.151	0.430	0.663	0.766	0.800	0.809	0.812
Traces needed	3911	233	26	9	5	4	4	3

(this does not happen with the Boolean masking). For a theoretic analysis, it is tricky in places to approximate the *best* that can be achieved by a canny attacker because different ways of combining the information and confirming candidate hypotheses will inevitably produce different outcomes, and it is not possible to explore and evaluate them all. We propose a strategy whereby each column is attacked separately (searching over the column index space as well as the mask space) and then the recovered affine transformation candidates are compared over the columns to find the most likely. Accordingly, the proportion unmasked for the key-recovery stage is computed as the probability of the correct transformation achieving a majority vote.

The results corresponding to the modelling of these attacks can be found in Tables 6 and 7 of Appendix A. Essentially, they show that the attacks are less efficient than on the Boolean scheme, but that we can still expect them to succeed for realistic platforms (they work for very low SNRs).

4   Theory Put to Practice

To gain some insight into the practical effectiveness of such attacks we performed some of them on two platforms, an 8-bit and a 32-bit microprocessor. The 8-bit microprocessor was an AT89S5253, which has an 8051 architecture. In this case acquisitions were taken with a sampling rate of 500 MS/s and a clock speed of 11 MHz. No filtering was conducted since this did not have any impact on the SNR. The 32-bit microprocessor was an ARM7TDMI microprocessor, where acquisitions were taken with a sampling rate of 200 MS/s and a clock speed of 7.3728 MHz. These acquisitions were filtered using a low-pass filter with a corner frequency at 7.3728 MHz to improved the SNR.

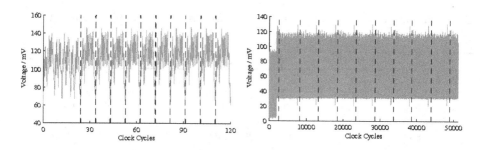

Fig. 1. The above traces show the instantaneous power consumption during the first ten rounds of Algorithm 1. The left trace corresponds to the AT89 microprocessor and the right traces to the ARM microprocessor. The power consumption showing the individual rounds are delimited by dashed lines.

The SNR (as defined by Mangard et al. [9]) of these two setups is rather different: the 8-bit controller features a very strong signal such that the overall SNR is about 22, whereas the 32-bit processor only delivers an SNR of 0.54.

Boolean masking requires a simple precomputation as described in Algorithm 1 and Algorithm 2 resp. As these algorithms suggest, one can see distinct patterns corresponding to the 256 loops when inspecting power traces corresponding to the execution of these algorithm on a device[6]. This is demonstrated in Fig. 1 where the rounds of Algorithm 1 are clearly visible.

Our experiments showed that on both platforms mask recovery worked almost perfectly. To provide some meaningful and statistically sound numbers we repeated the experiment 1000 times with different masks and produced the results shown in Table 4. These numbers give the error rates for recovering the masks r and s in Algorithm 1, and show clearly that for both platforms the fact that we have 256 traces available is sufficient to recover the masks even with the relatively poor SNR of the 32-bit platform. Note that proportions of data masks recovered with zero-bit errors correspond to the first row of Table 1 ("S-box un-masked"), while the proportions recovered with one-bit errors relate to the second row ("S-box partially un-masked"). The SNRs of the two devices mean that both can be expected to lead to almost perfect mask recovery (as indicated by the first two rows in Table 1), which is reflected in our practical experiments. Some results of the AT89 attacks are somewhat peculiar: we consistently observed a single bit error in the recovered data masks (but not always for the same bit). We are currently unable to explain this behavior in any satisfying way.

The introduction of simple hiding strategies has almost no impact, only a sufficiently strong permutation starts to degrade the attack performance in practice. We show some more results giving the error rates for data mask recovery for the ARM7 platform in Table 5. The numbers indicate that, as the size of the permutation increases, the distribution of the error rate approaches a binomial

---

[6] The practical attacks applied to an implementation of second-order Boolean masking.

Table 4. The error rates for identifying masks for implementations of Boolean masking.

Error (bits)	Address mask					Data mask				
	0	1	2	3	4+	0	1	2	3	4+
ARM	0.99	0.0012	0.0020	0.00075	0.00020	0.92	0.075	0.0030	0.00075	0.0029
AT89	0.98	0.0081	0.0079	0.0067	0.00010	0	0.98	0.0027	0.0047	0.015

distribution where one would not be able to conduct an attack. All the permutation lengths tested would lead to a viable attack, we refer the reader to Mangard et al. [9] for a description of how to compute the number of traces required to conduct an attack.

Table 5. Error rates for Boolean masking using different hiding strategies.

Error (bits)	Data mask, ARM								
	0	1	2	3	4	5	6	7	8
RSI	0.94	0.035	0.0040	0.0060	0.0080	0.0030	0	0.0010	0
Random walk	0.35	0.52	0.11	0.011	0.0070	0.0040	0.0020	0.0010	0
Random permutation:									
$n = 4$	0.84	0.093	0.017	0.016	0.013	0.012	0.0070	0	0
$n = 8$	0.47	0.15	0.11	0.066	0.10	0.061	0.030	0.0070	0
$n = 16$	0.064	0.11	0.19	0.23	0.21	0.12	0.065	0.015	0.0020
$n = 32$	0.011	0.052	0.13	0.25	0.27	0.19	0.081	0.015	0.0020

5 Conclusion

Masking schemes are popular in the literature, as indicated by the large number of publications in this area. Claims about the security of these schemes are typically supported by evaluation with regards to what (higher) order DPA attacks they can resist, but no focus has yet been put on scrutinising the practically inevitable precomputation of masked tables.

After explaining, for the most common and practically relevant masking approaches, how to randomize the precomputation step, we analyze the security of the resulting implementations using both a theoretic approach and practical implementations. For the theoretic analysis we explain how to model our attacks and what this allows us to conclude about the percentage of masks recovered, nearest rival margins and hence the number of needed power traces for different SNRs. This analysis is generic and to some extent independent of the power model (it can be adapted to incorporate other models).

These theoretic results indicate that our attacks are likely to work in practice, since we see good theoretic results even for low SNRs (with the exception of the largest permutation). In the penultimate section of this paper we showed results of actual attacks on two platforms. They tally with our theoretic outcomes and hence confirm that our attacks are indeed highly relevant and applicable to practice. Without much effort we can break any of the implementations employing masking and hiding in the precomputation.

Our results provide both a warning and some guidance. The warning is that, without substantial extra effort to secure the computation of masked tables, this operation will most likely leak the masks and hence render the masking of the round function pointless. The guidance that we can give is with regards to the SNR that needs to be achieved for the discussed randomisation strategies to have some impact. Even if the device SNR itself is fixed, one can attempt to use dummy instructions (bearing recent results in mind [12]) to lower the SNR by desynchronising the loops in the precomputation. Given that the discussed randomisation strategies themselves lead to a significant performance penalty (more randomness required, increased effort in computing data and address values), a further performance loss might however be unacceptable in practical applications. Our final conclusion is hence rather pessimistic: precisely for the devices in which masking seems an inescapable necessity, the computation of masked tables will most likely render the scheme insecure.

Acknowledgments. The work described in this paper has also been supported in part the European Commission through the ICT Programme under Contract ICT-2007-216676 ECRYPT II and the EPSRC via grant EP/I005226/1.

A   Tables

Table 6. Data complexity of mask recovery attacks against an affine masked AES S-box with hiding countermeasures, when the nonlinearity of the S-box is exploited in the mask-recovery stage. (SNR thresholds of degradation—where applicable—in parentheses).

	2^{-5}	2^{-3}	2^{-1}	2^1	2^3	2^5	2^7	Pure signal
Randomised start index (0.73)								
Both masks recovered	42.3	85.1	99.9	100.0	100.0	100.0	100.0	100.0
Multiplicative mask recovered	26.7	11.2	0.111	$2.36e-010$	0.000	0.000	0.000	0.000
Correct key correlation	0.0743	0.284	0.577	0.816	0.943	0.985	0.996	1.00
Nearest rival margin	0.0594	0.232	0.469	0.663	0.766	0.800	0.809	0.812
Traces needed	$1.53e+003$	96.8	21.0	8.50	5.16	4.07	3.63	3.02
Random walk (LFSR) (4.49)								
Both masks recovered	0.380	4.81	46.5	97.6	100.0	100.0	100.0	100.0
Multiplicative mask recovered	0.632	5.02	24.9	2.39	$3.30e-007$	0.000	0.000	0.000
Correct key correlation	0.00149	0.0286	0.376	0.811	0.943	0.985	0.996	1.00
Nearest rival margin	0.00121	0.0232	0.306	0.659	0.766	0.800	0.809	0.812
Traces needed	$3.71e+006$	$1.00e+004$	54.2	8.67	5.16	4.07	3.63	3.02
Permuted in 4 columns (NA)								
Both masks recovered	8.86	39.2	92.6	98.4	98.4	98.4	98.4	98.4
Multiplicative mask uncovered	32.3	35.4	6.85	1.58	1.57	1.57	1.57	1.57
Correct key correlation	0.0576	0.219	0.564	0.813	0.939	0.981	0.992	0.996
Nearest rival margin	0.0468	0.178	0.458	0.661	0.763	0.797	0.806	0.809
Traces needed	$2.47e+003$	167	22.1	8.6	5.24	4.19	3.81	3.63
Permuted in 8 columns (NA)								
Both masks recovered	0.125	1.29	24.2	89.5	95.6	95.7	95.7	95.7
Multiplicative mask uncovered	12.3	24.3	47.8	10.3	4.35	4.32	4.32	4.32
Correct key correlation	0.0162	0.0651	0.347	0.794	0.933	0.974	0.985	0.989
Nearest rival margin	0.0132	0.0529	0.282	0.646	0.758	0.791	0.801	0.804
Traces needed	$3.12e+004$	$1.93e+003$	64.6	9.21	5.4	4.38	4.05	3.92
Permuted in 16 columns (NA)								
Both masks recovered	$1.16e-005$	0.000135	0.0116	4.96	81	96.1	96.4	96.4
Multiplicative mask uncovered	0.857	1.66	6.05	41.5	18.8	3.95	3.61	3.61

Table 6. (*Continued*)

Correct key correlation	0.00112	0.00414	0.0263	0.294	0.897	0.975	0.987	0.991
Nearest rival margin	0.000909	0.00337	0.0214	0.239	0.728	0.792	0.802	0.805
Traces needed	6.55e+006	4.78e+005	1.19e+004	90.9	6.28	4.35	3.99	3.86
Permuted in 32 columns (NA)								
Both masks recovered	1.49e−014	7.11e−014	1.99e−012	2.1e−009	7.97e−005	0.775	35.7	76.1
Multiplicative mask uncovered	0.000117	0.000145	0.000248	0.00111	0.0443	4.98	29	17
Correct key correlation	1.52e−007	3.64e−007	1.07e−006	6.79e−006	0.000314	0.0444	0.572	0.889
Nearest rival margin	1.24e−007	2.96e−007	8.72e−007	5.52e−006	0.000255	0.0361	0.465	0.722
Traces needed	3.54e+014	6.2e+013	7.11e+012	1.78e+011	8.32e+007	4.16e+003	21.3	6.47

Table 7. Data complexity of mask recovery attacks against an affine masked AES S-box with hiding countermeasures, when the nonlinearity of the S-box is *not* exploited in the mask-recovery stage. (SNR thresholds of degradation—where applicable—in parentheses).

	2^{-5}	2^{-3}	2^{-1}	2^{1}	2^{3}	2^{5}	2^{7}	Pure signal
Randomised start index (1.90)								
Both masks recovered	19.9	49.2	91.1	100.0	100.0	100.0	100.0	100.0
Multiplicative mask recovered	37.1	38.2	8.86	0.00274	0.000	0.000	0.000	0.000
Correct key correlation	0.0355	0.165	0.526	0.816	0.943	0.985	0.996	1.00
Nearest rival margin	0.0245	0.131	0.430	0.663	0.766	0.800	0.809	0.812
Traces needed	8.99e+003	312.0	25.7	8.50	5.16	4.07	3.63	3.02
Random walk (LFSR) (4.49)								
Both masks recovered	0.176	1.97	28.9	95.2	100.0	100.0	100.0	100.0
Multiplicative mask recovered	0.633	5.17	33.1	4.71	6.59e−007	0.000	0.000	0.000
Correct key correlation	0.00113	0.0195	0.310	0.806	0.943	0.985	0.996	1.00
Nearest rival margin	0.000919	0.0158	0.252	0.655	0.766	0.800	0.809	0.812
Traces needed	6.41e+006	2.16e+004	81.6	8.84	5.16	4.07	3.63	3.02

Table 7. (*Continued*)

Permuted in 4 columns (NA)								
Both masks recovered	4.35	14.9	51.2	87.4	92.3	92.4	92.4	92.4
Multiplicative mask uncovered	33.9	49.5	45	12.6	7.68	7.64	7.64	7.64
Correct key correlation	0.0519	0.173	0.49	0.791	0.925	0.966	0.977	0.981
Nearest rival margin	0.0421	0.141	0.398	0.643	0.751	0.785	0.794	0.797
Traces needed	$3.04e+003$	269	30.4	9.34	5.59	4.59	4.3	4.19
Permuted in 8 columns (NA)								
Both masks recovered	0.0339	0.254	4.63	47	79.7	81.7	81.8	81.8
Multiplicative mask uncovered	12.3	24.6	60.1	52.5	20.3	18.3	18.2	18.2
Correct key correlation	0.0161	0.0623	0.287	0.705	0.895	0.94	0.951	0.954
Nearest rival margin	0.0131	0.0506	0.233	0.573	0.727	0.764	0.772	0.775
Traces needed	$3.17e+004$	$2.11e+003$	95.8	12.8	6.32	5.23	4.97	4.88
Permuted in 16 columns (NA)								
Both masks recovered	$1.82e-006$	$1.42e-005$	0.000619	0.16	9.35	26.1	28.2	28.2
Multiplicative mask uncovered	0.857	1.66	6.05	43.6	89.7	73.9	71.8	71.8
Correct key correlation	0.00112	0.00414	0.0262	0.268	0.723	0.803	0.817	0.821
Nearest rival margin	0.000909	0.00337	0.0213	0.218	0.587	0.652	0.664	0.667
Traces needed	$6.55e+006$	$4.78e+005$	$1.19e+004$	110	12	8.94	8.47	8.37
Permuted in 32 columns (NA)								
Both masks recovered	$8.73e-019$	$4.03e-018$	$1.03e-016$	$7.99e-014$	$1.36e-009$	$6.57e-006$	0.000549	0.00234
Multiplicative mask uncovered	0.000117	0.000145	0.000248	0.00111	0.0443	5.01	45.2	71.3
Correct key correlation	$1.52e-007$	$3.64e-007$	$1.07e-006$	$6.79e-006$	0.000313	0.037	0.337	0.535
Nearest rival margin	$1.24e-007$	$2.96e-007$	$8.72e-007$	$5.52e-006$	0.000254	0.0301	0.274	0.435
Traces needed	$3.54e+014$	$6.2e+013$	$7.11e+012$	$1.78e+011$	$8.36e+007$	$5.97e+003$	68.4	25

References

1. Akkar, M.-L., Giraud, C.: An implementation of DES and AES, secure against some attacks. In: Koç, Ç.K., Naccache, D., Paar, C. (eds.) CHES 2001. LNCS, vol. 2162, pp. 309–318. Springer, Heidelberg (2001)
2. Rivain, M., Dottax, E., Prouff, E.: Block ciphers implementations provably secure against second order side channel analysis. In: Nyberg, K. (ed.) FSE 2008. LNCS, vol. 5086, pp. 127–143. Springer, Heidelberg (2008)
3. Fumaroli, G., Martinelli, A., Prouff, E., Rivain, M.: Affine masking against higher-order side channel analysis. In: Biryukov, A., Gong, G., Stinson, D.R. (eds.) SAC 2010. LNCS, vol. 6544, pp. 262–280. Springer, Heidelberg (2011)
4. Ishai, Y., Sahai, A., Wagner, D.: Private circuits: securing hardware against probing attacks. In: Boneh, D. (ed.) CRYPTO 2003. LNCS, vol. 2729, pp. 463–481. Springer, Heidelberg (2003)
5. Rivain, M., Prouff, E.: Provably secure higher-order masking of AES. In: Mangard, S., Standaert, F.-X. (eds.) CHES 2010. LNCS, vol. 6225, pp. 413–427. Springer, Heidelberg (2010)
6. Kim, H.S., Hong, S., Lim, J.: A fast and provably secure higher-order masking of AES S-box. In: Preneel, B., Takagi, T. (eds.) CHES 2011. LNCS, vol. 6917, pp. 95–107. Springer, Heidelberg (2011)
7. Pan, J., den Hartog, J.I., Lu, J.: You cannot hide behind the mask: power analysis on a provably secure S-box implementation. In: Youm, H.Y., Yung, M. (eds.) WISA 2009. LNCS, vol. 5932, pp. 178–192. Springer, Heidelberg (2009)
8. Whitnall, C., Oswald, E.: A fair evaluation framework for comparing side-channel distinguishers. J. Cryptogr. Eng. 1(2), 145–160 (2011)
9. Mangard, S., Oswald, E., Popp, T.: Power Analysis Attacks: Revealing the Secrets of Smart Cards. Springer, New York (2007)
10. Chari, S., Jutla, C.S., Rao, J.R., Rohatgi, P.: Towards sound approaches to counteract power-analysis attacks. In: Wiener, M. (ed.) CRYPTO 1999. LNCS, vol. 1666, pp. 398–412. Springer, Heidelberg (1999)
11. Genelle, L., Prouff, E., Quisquater, M.: Thwarting higher-order side channel analysis with additive and multiplicative maskings. In: Preneel, B., Takagi, T. (eds.) CHES 2011. LNCS, vol. 6917, pp. 240–255. Springer, Heidelberg (2011)
12. Durvaux, F., Renauld, M., Standaert, F.-X., van Oldeneel tot Oldenzeel, L., Veyrat-Charvillon, N.: Efficient removal of random delays from embedded software implementations using hidden Markov models. In: Mangard, S. (ed.) CARDIS 2012. LNCS, vol. 7771, pp. 123–140. Springer, Heidelberg (2013)
13. Herbst, C., Oswald, E., Mangard, S.: An AES smart card implementation resistant to power analysis attacks. In: Zhou, J., Yung, M., Bao, F. (eds.) ACNS 2006. LNCS, vol. 3989, pp. 239–252. Springer, Heidelberg (2006)
14. Naccache, D., Nguyên, P.Q., Tunstall, M., Whelan, C.: Experimenting with faults, lattices and the DSA. In: Vaudenay, S. (ed.) PKC 2005. LNCS, vol. 3386, pp. 16–28. Springer, Heidelberg (2005)
15. Knuth, D.: The Art of Computer Programming, vol. 2, 3rd edn. Addison-Wesley, Reading (1998)
16. Mangard, S., Oswald, E., Standaert, F.X.: One for all–all for one: unifying standard DPA attacks. IET Inf. Secur. 5(2), 100–119 (2011)

Lightweight Authenticated Encryption

ALE: AES-Based Lightweight Authenticated Encryption

Andrey Bogdanov[1], Florian Mendel[2]($\boxtimes$), Francesco Regazzoni[3,4],
Vincent Rijmen[5], and Elmar Tischhauser[5]

[1] Technical University of Denmark, Kongens Lyngby, Denmark
[2] IAIK, Graz University of Technology, Graz, Austria
florian.mendel@iaik.tugraz.at
[3] ALaRI - USI, Lugano, Switzerland
[4] Delft University of Technology, Delft, Netherlands
[5] Department of ESAT/COSIC,
KU Leuven and iMinds, Leuven, Belgium

Abstract. In this paper, we propose a new *A*uthenticated *L*ightweight *E*ncryption algorithm coined *ALE*. The basic operation of ALE is the AES round transformation and the AES-128 key schedule. ALE is an online single-pass authenticated encryption algorithm that supports optional associated data. Its security relies on using nonces.

We provide an optimized low-area implementation of ALE in ASIC hardware and demonstrate that its area is about 2.5 kGE which is almost two times smaller than that of the lightweight implementations for AES-OCB and ASC-1 using the same lightweight AES engine. At the same time, it is at least 2.5 times more performant than the alternatives in their smallest implementations by requiring only about 4 AES rounds to both encrypt and authenticate a 128-bit data block for longer messages. When using the AES-NI instructions, ALE outperforms AES-GCM, AES-CCM and ASC-1 by a considerable margin, providing a throughput of 1.19 cpb close that of AES-OCB, which is a patented scheme. Its area- and time-efficiency in hardware as well as high performance in high-speed parallel software make ALE a promising all-around AEAD primitive.

Keywords: Authenticated encryption · Lightweight cryptography · AES

1 Introduction

Motivation. As essential security applications go ubiquitous, the demand for cryptographic protection in low-cost embedded systems (such as RFID and sensor networks) is drastically growing. This necessitates secure yet efficiently implementable cryptographic schemes. In such use cases, the area and power consumptions of a primitive in hardware are usually of paramount importance and standard solutions are often prohibitively costly to deploy.

S. Moriai (Ed.): FSE 2013, LNCS 8424, pp. 447–466, 2014.
DOI: 10.1007/978-3-662-43933-3_23, © Springer-Verlag Berlin Heidelberg 2014

Once this problem was recognized, the cryptographic community was fast to address it by proposing a great deal of specialized lightweight cryptographic algorithms, which include stream ciphers like Trivium [17], Grain [25], and Mickey [5], block ciphers like SEA [41], DESL, DESXL [30], HIGHT [26], mCrypton [31], KATAN/KTANTAN [16], and PRESENT [10], and hash functions like Quark [4], Photon [24], and Spongent [9] — to mention only some fraction of them. We note that the latter hash functions are following the overall design strategy of a permutation-based sponge construction [6], similarly to Keccak [7], which also provides competitive lightweight properties [29].

However, when it comes to *authenticated encryption* — the fundamental security functionality in most real-world security systems — one has to establish that, rather surprisingly, only a few lightweight schemes have been proposed so far, examples are Grain-128a [2] and Hummingbird-2 [21]. At the same time, message secrecy – as provided by plain encryption – is often of limited value in practice if not accompanied by message authentication. This stipulates the acute need for authenticated encryption in the field which is reflected in NIST [20] and ISO/IEC [1] documents on modes of operation for block ciphers.

In the context of lightweight cryptography though, these standard modes of operation have significant practical limitations. First, the lightweight block ciphers are usually designed to save on state bits, so that the block size and key size are usually kept at the edge of the reasonable minimum (it is rather typical in lightweight cryptography to propose a block cipher with a 64-bit block and a 80-bit key). This significantly confines the security level of modes of operation theoretically attainable due to generic attacks. Second, the standard authenticated-encryption modes of operation traditionally aim at high-speed implementations by minimizing the number of block cipher calls and other operations one has to perform per data block processed. For example, OCB [39], which clearly outperforms such wide-spread schemes as AES-GCM and AES-CCM in standard software, requires essentially a single AES call per data block at bulk encryption only. However, such modes usually do not pay too much attention to the amount of memory and the circuit size one needs in a lightweight hardware implementation. For instance, AES-OCB requires at least four 128-bit registers and both AES-encryption and -decryption engines for both encryption/authentication and decryption/verification. Besides, OCB is a patented scheme which hampers its wide deployment in the field.

A straightforward solution would be to address the first limitation (small state) by raising the total internal state size of the lightweight primitives, for instance, to 256 bits to avoid generic attacks up to a bound of 2^{128} operations. However, this would in turn take away their major source of advantage and make their area occupation comparable to that of AES-128. That is why we feel that a dedicated authenticated-encryption design can also be based on AES when 128-bit level of security is desired.

In an attempt to mitigate the second limitation (additional memory requirements imposed by modes) one might choose to go for encrypt-then-mac or mac-then-encrypt. However, not only would it jeopardize the highly relevant implementation goal for the scheme to be online but also require double message input (being essentially two-pass) and twice more operations per data block than e.g. OCB. In general, there appear to be no single-pass authentication encryption modes of operation for block ciphers preserving the minimal state size required. This emphasizes the demand for a dedicated lightweight authenticated-encryption design.

Moreover, we also want to make this new design fast in software, as opposed to some bit-oriented lightweight ciphers (such as Grain, Trivium, KATAN, PRESENT, etc.) which succeed in attaining a low area in hardware but whose performance in software is not even comparable to that of AES, especially in the presence of the Intel AES-NI instructions. We feel that not much efficiency can be gained by designing a slightly more efficient *generic* authenticated-encryption mode of operation for block ciphers since the bottleneck will remain the one block cipher call per data block. This is not only true for authenticated encryption modes but also for MAC-only and encryption-only modes.

The situation is, however, essentially different if the designer is allowed to look inside the specific underlying block cipher such as AES and to construct a dedicated mode of operation which only uses exactly as many operations of the underlying block cipher as needed. This is the approach taken in the designs of the stream cipher LEX [8] and the message authentication algorithm Pelican [14]. Lately, similar reasoning was applied to the setting of authenticated encryption resulting in the design of ASC-1 [28].

ALE. This paper proposes a lightweight authenticated encryption algorithm based on AES called *ALE* (*A*uthenticated *L*ightweight *E*ncryption) which is efficient both in hardware and software. It is a single-pass nonce-based online scheme that preserves the memory alignment of data. The design of ALE combines some ideas of Pelican, LEX and ASC-1 in a lightweight manner. In a nutshell, the algorithm uses Pelican keyed in all rounds (similarly to PC-MAC [34]) for computing the authentication tag and leaks bytes of the state in every round in a LEX-type way for encryption/decryption. It has a 256-bit secret internal state dependent on both key and nonce.

By requiring only 2.5 kGE of area in lightweight ASIC hardware, which is less than 100 GE overhead compared to plain AES-ECB in the smallest implementation available [35], ALE is about half the size of AES-OCB and ASC-1. In terms of speed in the lightweight implementation for medium-size messages and longer, ALE is about 2.5 times faster than AES-OCB and about 4.5 times faster than ASC-1 in its smallest implementation. When using the parallel AES-NI instructions, ALE outperforms AES-GCM, AES-CCM and ASC-1 by a considerable margin, providing a throughput close to that of AES-OCB, which is a patented scheme.

At a first glance, the overall design philosophy of ALE might seem similar to that of ASC-1. However, as the numbers of relative area and speed above already strikingly suggest, ASC-1 has several crucial shortcomings in the way of practical implementation. First, ASC-1 needs an internal state which is twice larger than that of ALE, which accounts to the significant difference in area requirements. Second, the non-sequential order in which the AES-256 subkeys are used in ASC-1 (e.g. subkey 11 is needed already in the first round) combined with its serial nature, has a considerable impact on its performance. In lightweight hardware, the engine in adjacent operations has to have subkeys which are many rounds apart which can be done either by computing a key state back and forth (which costs time) or by storing some values high-speed software (which costs area). In high-performance parallel software implementations, the subkeys have to be computed on the fly (since the key state is evolving) beforehand and stored in registers to avoid additional memory accesses, which contains the advantage of using AES-NI instructions a lot. Finally, ASC-1 does not accept associated data that can be vital in some networking settings while ALE explicitly deals with it.

The remainder of the paper is organized as follows. Section 2 gives a specification of the algorithm. Section 3 introduces some elements of its cryptanalysis. Section 4 provides lightweight implementation numbers of the algorithm in ASIC hardware. Section 5 implements ALE in software using AES-NI instructions on a SandyBridge Intel processor. We conclude in Sect. 6.

2   The Authenticated Lightweight Encryption (ALE) Algorithm

In this section, we describe ALE – our new authenticated lightweight encryption algorithm. The basic operation of ALE is the AES round transformation and the AES-128 key schedule. In all the following, we assume that the reader is familiar with AES.

2.1   Specification

ALE is an online single-pass nonce-based authenticated encryption algorithm with associated data. Its encryption/authentication procedure accepts a 128-bit master key κ, a message μ, associated data α and a 128-bit nonce $\nu \neq 0$. An equivalent of at most 2^{48} bits are allowed to be authenticated or both authenticated and encrypted with the same master key. The encryption/authentication procedure outputs the ciphertext γ of exactly the same bit length as the message μ and the authentication tag τ of 128 bits for both the message μ and associated data α. Its decryption/verification procedure accepts key κ, ciphertext γ, associated data α, nonce ν and tag τ. It returns the decrypted message μ if tag is correct or $\perp$ otherwise.

The encryption/authentication operation can be described in five steps:

Padding: The padding of ALE is similar to the one of the MD4 hash function. First a "1" is appended to the message μ, followed by ℓ "0" bits (with $\ell = 128 - (|\mu| + 1 + 64 \pmod{128}))$, and finally the message length $|\mu|$ coded on 64 bits is appended. The resulting padded message M is split into t blocks

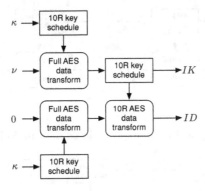

Fig. 1. Initialization of ALE.

of 128 bits each, $M = m_1 \| \cdots \| m_t$. Note that for associated data the same padding method is used and the padded associated data is split into r blocks of 128 bit each, $A = a_1 \| \cdots \| a_r$.

Initialization: The internal state consists of two 128-bit states: the key state (upper line in Fig. 1) and the data state (lower line in Fig. 1). The key state is initialized with nonce ν encrypted with AES[1] under the master key κ. The data state is initialized in two steps, First, it is initialized with 0 encrypted with AES under the user-supplied key κ. Second, the result $\text{AES}_\kappa(0)$ is AES-encrypted using the initialized key state as key. After that, the final subkey of the last AES encryption is updated one more time using the AES round key schedule with byte round constant x^{10} in $\mathbb{F}_{2^8}$. This value is stored in the key state. Now both states are initialized.

Processing associated data: If there is only one padded associated data block, then a_1 is xored to the data state and one proceeds with processing message immediately. Otherwise, if there are at least two padded associated data blocks, A is processed block by block: The data state is encrypted with 4 rounds of AES using the key state as key. The final round subkey is updated one more time using the AES round key schedule with byte round constant x^4 in $\mathbb{F}_{2^8}$. This value is stored in the key state. The next block of A is xored to the data state (Fig. 2).

Processing message: M is processed block by block: The data state is encrypted with 4 rounds of AES using the key state as key. 16 bytes are leaked from the data state in the 4 rounds of AES in accordance with the LEX specification (Fig. 3).

This leak is xored to the current block of M. The final round subkey is updated one more time using the AES round key schedule with byte round constant x^4 in $\mathbb{F}_{2^8}$. This value is stored in the key state. The current block of M is xored to the data state.

---

[1] Here and further in the paper, we imply AES-128 whenever we write AES.

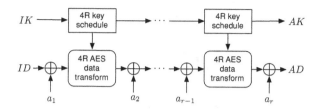

Fig. 2. Processing associated data in ALE.

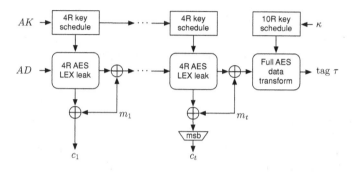

Fig. 3. Processing message and finalization in ALE.

For the last block of M the exact required number of most significant bits are taken from the leak and xored to the last block (without padding) to produce the last bits of ciphertext, and m_t is xored to the data state.

Finalization: The data state is encrypted with the full AES using the master key κ. The output of this encryption is returned as the authentication tag τ for the message and associated data (Fig. 3).

The decryption/verification procedure is defined correspondingly. The only two differences are that one works with the ciphertext $\gamma = c_1 || \cdots || c_t$ instead of the message μ while xoring with the stream and that the supplied tag value τ is compared to the one computed by the algorithm. We want to stress that only if the tag is correct the decrypted message is returned.

2.2   Security Assumptions and Claims

The security analysis of the algorithm starts from the following two assumptions.

Assumption 1 (Nonce-respecting adversary). *A nonce value is only used once with the same master key for encryption.*

This assumption is quite common among nonce-based designs. Note that on most platforms, this assumption can be easily satisfied by implementing the nonce as a counter.

Assumption 2 (Abort on verification failure). *If the verification step of the algorithm reveals that the ciphertext has been tampered with, then the algorithm returns no information beyond the verification failure. In particular, no plaintext blocks are returned.*

This assumption significantly reduces the impact of chosen-ciphertext attacks, since the adversary obtains very little information from a chosen-ciphertext query. We feel that this assumption is quite natural for authenticated encryption modes. After all, when the verification fails, we know that the integrity of the plaintext has been jeopardised, and there is no reason to output it. The assumption does, however, exclude implementations where decryption is done in a streaming mode, since all plaintext blocks need to be kept inside until the verification has completed successfully.

Under these assumptions, the security claims for the algorithm are as follows.

Claim 1 (Resistance against state recovery). *Any internal state recovery with complexity equivalent to processing N data blocks has a success probability at most $N2^{-128}$.*

Claim 2 (Resistance against key recovery). *Any key recovery with complexity equivalent to processing N data blocks has a success probability at most $N2^{-128}$, even if the internal state has been recovered.*

Claim 3 (Resistance against forgery w/o state recovery). *Any forgery attack not involving key recovery/internal state recovery has a success probability at most 2^{-128}.*

2.3 Properties

Here we list some of ALE's merits in terms of implementation. Since ALE is based on similar design principles as Pelican MAC and LEX, it also shares many strong properties of these two designs.

- Security analysis benefits from existing analysis on AES as well as Pelican MAC and LEX.
- AES hardware/software implementations might be reused with only a few simple modifications, including the usage of Intel AES instructions.
- Side-channel attack countermeasures developed for the AES will be useful for ALE as well, including threshold implementations in hardware to thwart first-order power- and EM-based differential attacks and bitsliced implementations to mitigate cache-timing leakage.
- For long messages, ALE needs only about 4 AES rounds to both encrypt and authenticate a block of message, which is similar to ASC-1. However, about 10 AES rounds are needed by AES-OCB and 20 AES rounds are required by AES-CCM to process a data block.

– The overhead of ALE per message amounts to 3 AES calls. This is less than the overhead of ASC-1 which is 4 AES calls but more than the overhead of AES-OCB of 2 AES calls. AES-CCM has virtually no overhead but has an excessive cost per block.

However, in terms of the number of AES rounds, AES-OCB becomes less efficient already for messages longer than 128 bits and ASC-1 is always inferior to ALE. Note that AES-OCB contains a nonce stretching mechanism that effectively saves one AES call overhead if multiple messages are encrypted with the same key and with adjacent counter values as nonces. However, implementing this mechanism in lightweight hardware requires an additional 128-bit state which increases the area requirement by another 700–800 GE.

– Only two 128-bit states are needed by ALE to implement encryption, which makes it lightweight-friendly. At the same time, 4 states needed for AES-OCB and ASC-1. AES-CCM requires 3 states. In fact, 2 states needed by ALE are even less than the encryption-only AES-CTR occupies, where some space needs to be allocated for the counter.

– Only the AES encryption engine is needed by ALE for both the encryption/authentication and decryption/verification procedures. AES-OCB requires both encryption and decryption engines for supporting those operations.

– ALE is an online scheme meaning it is single-pass and does not have to know message length before the last message block is input. AES-CCM is off-line. Additionally AES-CCM is two-pass. AES-OCB and ASC-1 are also online schema.

– ALE accepts associated data while ASC-1 does not. AES-CCM and AES-OCB can both work with associated data. AES-OCB is additionally capable of accepting static associated data (which does not require any recomputation for a new nonce).

3   Security Analysis

Since ALE combines some ideas of Pelican MAC [14] and LEX [8] it benefits from existing security analysis. In the following, we briefly recall existing security analysis on these two primitives and discuss their relevance to ALE with respect to its Claims 1,2 and 3.

3.1   Forgery Without State Recovery

Like any MAC derived from the ALRED construction [15] also Pelican MAC enjoys some level of provable security. It is shown that, in the absence of internal collisions, the security of the construction can be reduced to the security of the n-bit underlying block cipher [15, Theorems 1 and 2]. In other words, Pelican cannot be broken with less than $2^{n/2}$ queries unless the adversary also breaks the block cipher itself. However, the security proofs of Pelican MAC rely on the fact that the iteration function is unkeyed. Therefore, they don't carry over to ALE. PC-MAC is another MAC function derived from the original design [34]. PC-MAC uses a keyed iteration function and has a proof of security in the indistinguishability framework.

For the Pelican MAC two approaches to exploit knowledge of the (unkeyed) iteration function are described by the designers to generate internal collisions and hence forgeries.

Fixed Points. Since the iteration function is known in Pelican MAC, one may compute the number of state values that are resulting in fixed points for a given message block m_i. Assume the number of fixed points is x, then the probability that inserting the message block m_i in a message will not impact its tag and hence result in a forgery is $x \cdot 2^{-n}$.

However, if the iteration function can be modeled as a random permutation, then the number of fixed points has a Poisson distribution and is expected to be small [15]. Moreover, in ALE the iteration function is keyed with a nonce dependent session key. Since this key changes for every iteration function, one needs a fixed point in both the key state and data state rendering the attack inefficient.

Extinguishing Differentials. Extinguishing differentials are very similar to differential cryptanalysis for block ciphers. The main idea is to find pairs of messages (or in our case also ciphertexts) with a certain difference that may result in a zero difference in the state with a high probability after the difference has been injected.

However, in the case of Pelican MAC the iteration function consists of 4 rounds of Rijndael implementing the wide trail design strategy [13], which allows to prove good bounds against differential attacks. In more detail, any differential characteristic spanning over 4 rounds has at least 25 active S-boxes resulting in an upper bound for the differential probability of 2^{-150}. Moreover, the differential probability of any differential can be upper bounded by 2^{-114} [27]. Note that this is not far away from the theoretically optimal bound of $2 \cdot 2^{-128}$. In other words, Pelican MAC and hence also ALE provides good upper bounds for the probability of extinguishing differentials.

Moreover, we want to note that in ALE the iteration function is keyed with a nonce dependent session key, which is changed for every encryption/authentication procedure, complicating the application of differential cryptanalysis to ALE, since an attacker also needs to predict the differences in the session key. However, since this session key is generated by encrypting the nonce with the master key using 10 rounds of AES, this seems to be a very difficult task.

3.2   State Recovery

All published attacks [11, 19, 43] on Pelican MAC so far are forgery attacks making use of (generic) internal collisions on the internal state. Note that due to the small state size of Pelican MAC of 128 bits, internal collisions can be found with complexity of 2^{64} due to the birthday paradox. However, in ALE a nonce dependent session key is used making it difficult to detect internal collisions on the state unless the session key collides as well, basically doubling the internal state size and giving some reinsurance in the design.

Most attacks on LEX published so far use the fact that LEX uses the same round keys repeatedly. For instance the main idea of the key-recovery attack in [11,18] is to find a pair of internal states after different numbers of encryptions that partially collides after 4 rounds. Since the round keys are reused in LEX, the adversary can easily locate two states that collide in the part of the state which contains the round key. Hence, the complexity of a brute-force search for (partial) internal collisions is determined by the size of the part of the state that contains the ciphertext, i.e. 128 bits.

In ALE however, the round keys are not reused. Hence, the complexity of a brute-force search for (partial) internal collisions is determined by the size of the full internal state, i.e. 256 bits. It follows that finding (partial) internal collisions becomes more difficult rendering the attack infeasible. Note that even if the attack would be applicable, it might only be used to recover the internal state, but not the master key.

If Assumption 1 is not satisfied, i.e. if nonce values are used repeatedly, then the round keys are repeated. In that case, the attacks on Pelican and LEX can be extended and applied to ALE. Because ALE combines injection and extraction, the attacks become more powerful, and security is lost.

3.3   Key-Recovery

To recover the master key κ in ALE an attacker needs to break the initialization of ALE. However, even though assuming that the full internal sate after the initialization is known to the attacker, he still needs to break full (10 rounds) of AES to recover the master key.

3.4   Additional Security Analysis

Distinguishing Attacks. The encryption component of ALE is inspired by the stream cipher LEX. The keystream bits in LEX are generated by extracting 32 bits from each round of AES in the OFB mode. In [22], Englund et al. describe a distinguishing attack that is applicable to block ciphers in the OFB mode in general. To be more precise, whenever the part of the state that depends on both the key and the IV is smaller than twice the key size (as it is the case for instance in LEX) the attack theoretically succeeds. However, in LEX the attack is thwart by limiting the number of keystream bits that can generated from one master key. In ALE we have a similar restriction but more important the internal state is larger due to the session key (depending on the nonce and the master key) used to key the iteration function.

Slide Attack. A slide attack for an earlier version of LEX has been found by Wu and Preneel in [42] and fixed later by Biryukov in a new version of LEX. To avoid slide attacks two different functions for the initialization and the encryption/authentication should be used. Even a very small difference between the two is sufficient. For instance, the new version of LEX uses the full AES with the XOR of the last subkey for the initialization and AES without the XOR of this subkey for the encryption.

However, ALE uses the full AES (10 rounds without the application of Mix-Columns in the last round) in the initialization, but only 4 rounds of AES for the encryption/authentication. We think that this is sufficient to break the similarities used by slide attacks.

4 Lightweight ASIC Hardware Implementation

This section presents a lightweight ASIC hardware implementation of ALE, and compares it to the existing authentication encryption schemes such as AES-OCB, AES-CCM and ASC-1. In this section, we did not include the results obtained with AES-GCM as this schema is not particularly suitable for low cost hardware. In fact, it requires an extra module for implementing the Galois field multiplication which, additionally, has to be invoked several times.

4.1 Hardware Architecture

ALE was implemented targeting the lowest ASIC area occupation possible. For this reason, our hardware architecture is based on the most compact AES implementation published so far [35]. The original AES implementation has a mixed data-path: it instantiate a single S-box following the proposal of Canright [12] but performs the MixColumn on all the 32 bit in parallel.

The overall design is depicted in Fig. 4. The base AES design was extended to support our authenticated encryption proposal. A more complex control unit was developed to handle the padding, the initialization and finalization, the LEX-type leak, and the xor of the state with the input message. Also, a number of multiplexers where added to the architecture to correctly select the inputs of the AES accelerator. Our implementation requires to load two times the key and one time the nonce and the null vector. The nonce is loaded in the first execution of AES, while the null vector is loaded in the second. The key is loaded once during the first execution of the AES and once during the last execution of AES. Also, the input and output values should be maintained in the respective wires and synchronized with the operations of the accelerator on order to correctly perform the additions with the message and the additional data.

4.2 Comparison

We implemented all the designs having the same design goals and using the same lightweight AES engine in their core. All the considered schemes were described

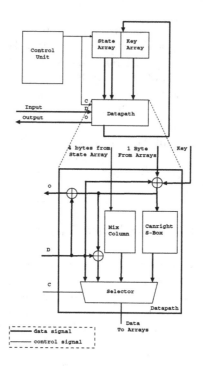

Fig. 4. The lightweight implementation of ALE.

in VHDL and then synthesized using the tool Synopsys design compiler 2009.06. We performed a number of synthesis targeting different technologies (90 nm, 65 nm, and 45 nm), frequencies, and optimization parameters of the synthesis tool.

Table 1 summarizes the implementation numbers (including area and timing) of ALE as compared to the reference designs. These results were obtained setting the clock frequency to 20 MHz and using the STMicroelectronics 65 nm CMOS technology and the corresponding standard cell library characterized for LP-HVT (low power high Vt) process. This technology was the one which exhibits the best trade off between area and power consumption, thus the one which resulted more suitable for lightweight applications. The clock frequency was set to 20 MHz as usually, in low-cost hardware applications, the speed constraint is very relaxed (contrary to the area and power consumption). However, during the whole set of experiments, we successfully synthesized our designs with a clock frequency of up to 200 MHz.

As we were targetting low-cost hardware, we also report clocks per byte and provide a graph for different message lengths in Table 2 and Fig. 5. The cycle count does not consider the overhead for loading and offloading of the data. As indication, Table 1 reports also the power consumption of each algorithm. The estimation was carried out with Synopsys power compiler 2009.06, using the standard tool parameters for the switching activity.

Table 1. Lightweight ASIC implementation numbers for ALE compared to AES-OCB2, AES-CCM and ASC-1. Overhead indicates the number of cycles needed for the initial setup and the finalization of the authenticated encryption. The net per block provides the number of clock cycles required to process each block of data, on top of the overhead per message. The designs marked with 'e/d' incorporate both encryption/authentication and decryption/verification functionalities.

Design	Area (GE)	Net per 128-bit block (clock cycles)	Overhead per message (clock cycles)	Power (uW)
AES-ECB	2,435	226	-	87.84
AES-OCB2	4,612	226	452	171.23
AES-OCB2 e/d	5,916	226	452	211.01
ASC-1 A	4,793	370	904	169.11
ASC-1 A e/d	4,964	370	904	193.71
ASC-1 B	5,517	235	904	199.02
ASC-1 B e/d	5,632	235	904	207.13
AES-CCM	3,472	452	-	128.31
AES-CCM e/d	3,765	452	-	162.15
ALE	**2,579**	**105**	678	94.87
ALE e/d	**2,700**	**105**	678	102.32

Table 2. Lightweight ASIC implementation numbers for ALE compared to AES-OCB2, AES-CCM and ASC-1 (in clocks per byte)

Algorithm	Message length (bytes)									
	16	32	64	128	256	512	1024	2048	4096	8192
ECB	14.12	14.12	14.12	14.12	14.12	14.12	14.12	14.12	14.12	14.12
OCB2	42.38	28.25	21.19	17.66	15.89	15.01	14.57	14.35	14.24	14.18
ASC-1 A	79.62	51.38	37.25	30.19	26.66	24.89	24.01	23.57	23.35	23.24
ASC-1 B	71.19	42.94	28.81	21.75	18.22	16.45	15.57	15.13	14.91	14.80
CCM	28.25	28.25	28.25	28.25	28.25	28.25	28.25	28.25	28.25	28.25
ALE	48.93	27.75	17.15	11.85	9.21	7.88	6.20	6.89	6.72	6.64

ALE occupies 2,581 GE, and requires 783 clock cycles to authenticate and encrypt one block of 128 bits. This cycle count includes the overhead of 678 cycles, which is caused by the three invocation of the AES algorithm needed for initialization and finalization. Thus, only 105 clock cycles are needed to process each further 128-bit block of data.

As comparison, we report in Table 1 also the performances of the AES core used as starting point (AES-ECB) of our implementation and the ones of AES-OCB, ASC-1, and AES-CCM authentication encryption schema. All the algorithms were implemented using the same lightweight AES engine [35] and the same experimental setup as ALE.

In its most compact implementation, ASC-1 is especially slow due to its complex non-serial key schedule which has a high overhead (for instance, one

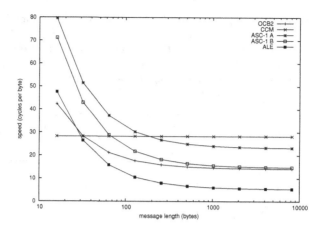

Fig. 5. Hardware performance of ALE with respect to other AES-based authenticated encryption schemes for different message lengths in lightweight ASIC implementations

has to know the 11th key of the AES-256 expanded key to compute the first round and the first key again to compute the 5th round) which makes backward and forward computations necessary. This implementation is given in Table 1 as ASC-1 A. However, The key schedule overhead can be reduced if an additional 128-bit register is introduced. This implementation is given referred to as ASC-1 B in the table.

It can be observed that the overhead for the support of both the encryption/authentication and decryption/verification functionalities (those implementations are marked as 'e/d' in Table 1) is fairly small for ALE and ASC-1. At the same time, since AES-OCB additionally requires an AES decryption engine for decryption, the overhead is much more significant there.

ALE occupies an area which is approximately two times lower than those of AES-OCB and ASC-1, while providing an overall speed at least two times higher, being particularly suitable for lightweight applications. ALE also nicely compares with the results reported in literature for Hummingbird-2 [21], which in its smallest version has an area of approximately 2,159 (estimated using a different technological library), and Grain-128a with authentication [2] which occupies approximately 2,770 gates (estimated by the designers).

5   High-Performance Software Implementation

In this section, we evaluate the software performance of ALE and compare it to other authenticated encryption schemes based on the AES. We propose such evaluation because, as pointed out by Matsuda and Moriai [32], lightweight algorithms will be used in the sensors which will populate the internet of things. After the collection, the data will be forwarded to the servers of the cloud, where the same algorithm, this time implemented to achieve high performances, will be used for decryption.

5.1   The Setting

First, we need to establish a common setting for the performance evaluation of all algorithms in order to have a fair platform for comparison. We base our scenario on the following assumptions.

Message lengths. In most communication protocols, typical messages are relatively short, rarely exceeding 1024 bytes [33]. It is therefore of great importance to include initialisation overhead and take measurements for messages consisting of only one or a few blocks. At the same time, performance usually starts to saturate with messages of two or four kilobytes. We therefore provide data for $16 \cdot 2^b$ bytes, with $0 \le b \le 10$. Furthermore, we assume that these 2^b blocks encompass the already padded message.

Parallel processing of messages. The fact that most processed messages are rather short suggests that many of them will typically be encrypted under the same key, but with a different nonce. This implies that a high-performance software implementation can benefit from processing multiple messages for different nonces in parallel. Note that the processing of messages with several different keys and different nonces can be parallelised in the same way.

AES-NI and pipelining. Since we deal with AES-based ciphers, high performance software implementations means using the AES-NI instructions [23]. The most critical factor in achieving good performance with AES-NI is to fully utilise the pipeline, which is 8 cycles for the Sandy Bridge microarchitecture, for which our implementations are optimised.

5.2   Implementation

According to this common scenario, we have implemented the following authenticated encryption schemes: CCM, GCM and OCB3 with AES as the underlying block cipher; ASC-1, and ALE. As a base line, we also include the unauthenticated modes ECB and CTR. The used OCB3 implementation is the most recent reference implementation from [40], the GCM implementation is the one of OpenSSL v1.0.1c.

Those algorithms that are not inherently parallelisable (CCM and ALE) were implemented following the paradigm of processing multiple messages with different nonces in parallel, with CCM processing two independent messages in parallel, and ALE four. ASC-1 was found not to benefit from this, since the overhead introduced by its key schedule already requires storing key material in cache memory due to the limited number of 128-bit registers. As an example, its key scheduling requires the use of the 11th key already in the first round, and the first key again in the 5th, and so forth. For OCB3, we include the overhead introduced by calculating the initial key- and nonce-dependent values. However, we do employ nonce-spreading to avoid the initial block cipher call most of the time.

For the implementation of ALE, we only have four AES rounds per message block instead of ten for the authenticated modes. However, this also means that in order to fill the 8 pipeline stages, we would have to calculate 8 key schedule updates. Using the native AESKEYGENASSIST instruction for this purpose actually decreases the performance, since it not pipelined in the same way as the AES round functions.

With four messages processed in parallel, we can however avoid using AESKEYGENASSIST by using AESENCLAST for the S-box step for the four AES keys, and doing the key schedule's LFSR manually, but in parallel on 128 bits. This implies that we can at most issue 5 AES round instructions every 8 cycles. See the pseudocode below:

```
loop:
    # ... combine 4*32 bits from key1, ..., key4 in keyblock
    aesenclast keyblock, 0
    aesenc     state1, key1
    aesenc     state2, key2
    aesenc     state3, key3
    aesenc     state4, key4
    # ... LEX leaks
    # ... inverse ShiftRows on keyblock
    # ... spread keyblock to key1, ..., key4
    # ... key schedule LFSR parallel on key1, ..., key4
    goto loop
```

We also note that in a serial (as opposed to high-performance) implementation, ALE has the distinct advantage over OCB3 by only requiring 4 AES round plus key scheduling per block, in contrast to full 10 AES rounds.

5.3   Results

All measurements were taken on a single core of an Intel Core i5-2400 CPU at 3100 MHz, and averaged over 100000 repetitions. Our findings are summarised in Table 3 and illustrated in Fig. 6.

One can see that while the initialisation overhead generally has a huge impact on the performance, this effect starts to fade out already at messages of around 256–512 bytes. Due to the parallel processing used for CCM, it almost ties with GCM for medium-size and larger messages. OCB3 achieves nearly optimal performance starting from 512 byte message length due to its parallelisability which enables it to fully utilise the eight pipeline stages and compensates for its initialisation overhead. ASC-1 generally performs slower, mostly due to its non-sequential use of the AES-256 key schedule which requires additional storage of key material, exceeding the available 128-bit registers.

The experimental findings can be summarised as follows: When implemented for multiple message processing, ALE provides software performance quite close to OCB3-AES, and significantly better performance than CCM, GCM or ASC-1. In [33], McGrew estimates that for high-speed data links, authenticated encryption with a throughput of up to 100 GBit/s would be desirable. In view of the results of [3], AES-NI instructions benefit from a practically linear speed-up on multiple cores. At the moment, standard Sandy Bridge desktop processors are

Table 3. Software performance of authenticated encryption schemes based on the AES. The platform is Intel Sandy Bridge (AES-NI). All numbers are given in cycles per byte (cpb). A star (*) indicates that this implementation is processing multiple messages in parallel (for inherently serial algorithms for which this results in a performance increase).

Algorithm	Message length (bytes)						
	128	256	512	1024	2048	4096	8192
ECB	1.53	1.16	0.93	0.81	0.75	0.72	0.71
CTR	1.61	1.22	0.99	0.87	0.80	0.77	0.76
CCM*	3.97	3.49	3.31	3.22	3.18	3.15	3.15
GCM	4.95	3.88	3.33	3.05	2.93	2.90	2.89
OCB3	2.69	1.79	1.34	1.12	1.00	0.88	0.86
ASC-1	7.74	4.80	3.69	2.88	2.78	2.64	2.61
ALE*	3.55	2.34	1.74	1.44	1.31	1.23	1.19

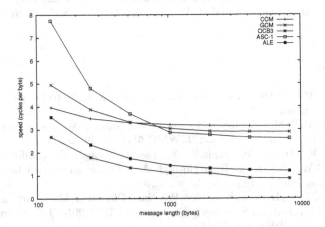

Fig. 6. Software performance of AES-based authenticated encryption schemes for different message lengths on Intel Sandy Bridge (AES-NI).

available with 6 cores at a frequency of 3.1 GHz. For messages of 1 KB length, this implies a throughput of 103.3 GBit/s with ALE, and 132.8 GBit/s with OCB3. This means that the above-mentioned performance requirement can be fulfilled with either ALE or OCB3 using only one standard desktop CPU, with ALE having the advantage of not being patented.

6 Conclusion

In this paper, we have proposed ALE – a new Authenticated Lightweight Encryption algorithm based on AES. It is a single-pass nonce-based online scheme that combines some ideas of Pelican MAC, LEX and ASC-1 in a highly lightweight manner. ALE is about half the size of ASC-1 and in terms of speed in the lightweight implementation, it is about 4.5 times faster than ASC-1 in its smallest implementation.

By requiring only 2.5 kGE of area in lightweight ASIC hardware ALE is actually significantly smaller than most other authentication encryption modes including the popular modes AES-OCB and AES-CCM. In terms of speed in the lightweight implementation, ALE is about 2.5 times faster than AES-OCB and about 5 times faster than AES-CCM. When using the parallel AES-NI instructions, ALE outperforms AES-GCM, AES-CCM and ASC-1 by a considerable margin, providing a throughput close to that of AES-OCB, which is a patented scheme.

Acknowledgments. The authors thank Axel Poschmann for providing the reference implementation of the AES algorithm. Part of this work was done while Andrey Bogdanov and Florian Mendel were with KU Leuven. The work has been supported in part by the Austrian Science Fund (FWF), project TRP 251-N23 and by the Research Fund KU Leuven, OT/08/027.

References

1. ISO/IEC 19772:2009. Information Technology - Security techniques - Authenticated Encryption (2009)
2. Ågren, M., Hell, M., Johansson, T., Meier, W.: Grain-128a: a new version of Grain-128 with optional authentication. IJWMC **5**(1), 48–59 (2011)
3. Akdemir, K., Dixon, M., Feghali, W., Fay, P., Gopal, V., Guilford, J., Erdinc Ozturk, G.W., Zohar, R.: Breakthrough AES Performance with Intel AES New Instructions. Intel white paper, January 2010
4. Aumasson, J.-P., Henzen, L., Meier, W., Naya-Plasencia, M.: Quark: a lightweight hash. In: Mangard, S., Standaert, F.-X. (eds.) CHES 2010. LNCS, vol. 6225, pp. 1–15. Springer, Heidelberg (2010)
5. Babbage, S., Dodd, M.: The MICKEY stream ciphers. In: Robshaw and Billet [37], pp. 191–209
6. Bertoni, G., Daemen, J., Peeters, M., Van Assche, G.: On the indifferentiability of the sponge construction. In: Smart, N.P. (ed.) EUROCRYPT 2008. LNCS, vol. 4965, pp. 181–197. Springer, Heidelberg (2008)
7. Bertoni, G., Daemen, J., Peeters, M., Van Assche, G.: The Keccak reference. Submission to NIST (Round 3), January 2011. http://keccak.noekeon.org
8. Biryukov, A.: design of a new stream cipher-LEX. In: Robshaw and Billet [37], pp. 48–56
9. Bogdanov, A., Knežević, M., Leander, G., Toz, D., Varıcı, K., Verbauwhede, I.: Spongent: a lightweight hash function. In: Preneel, B., Takagi, T. (eds.) CHES 2011. LNCS, vol. 6917, pp. 312–325. Springer, Heidelberg (2011)
10. Bogdanov, A.A., Knudsen, L.R., Leander, G., Paar, C., Poschmann, A., Robshaw, M., Seurin, Y., Vikkelsoe, C.: PRESENT: an ultra-lightweight block cipher. In: Paillier, P., Verbauwhede, I. (eds.) CHES 2007. LNCS, vol. 4727, pp. 450–466. Springer, Heidelberg (2007)
11. Bouillaguet, C., Derbez, P., Fouque, P.A.: Automatic search of attacks on round-reduced AES and applications. In: Rogaway [38], pp. 169–187

12. Canright, D.: A very compact S-box for AES. In: Rao, J.R., Sunar, B. (eds.) CHES 2005. LNCS, vol. 3659, pp. 441–455. Springer, Heidelberg (2005)
13. Daemen, J., Rijmen, V.: The wide trail design strategy. In: Honary, B. (ed.) Cryptography and Coding 2001. LNCS, vol. 2260, pp. 222–238. Springer, Heidelberg (2001)
14. Daemen, J., Rijmen, V.: The Pelican MAC Function. Cryptology ePrint Archive, Report 2005/088 (2005)
15. Daemen, J., Rijmen, V.: Refinements of the ALRED construction and MAC security claims. IET Inf. Secur. 4(3), 149–157 (2010)
16. De Cannière, C., Dunkelman, O., Knežević, M.: KATAN and KTANTAN — a family of small and efficient hardware-oriented block ciphers. In: Clavier, Ch., Gaj, K. (eds.) CHES 2009. LNCS, vol. 5747, pp. 272–288. Springer, Heidelberg (2009)
17. De Cannière, C., Preneel, B.: Trivium. In: Robshaw and Billet [37], pp. 244–266
18. Dunkelman, O., Keller, N.: An improved impossible differential attack on MISTY1. In: Pieprzyk, J. (ed.) ASIACRYPT 2008. LNCS, vol. 5350, pp. 441–454. Springer, Heidelberg (2008)
19. Dunkelman, O., Keller, N., Shamir, A.: ALRED Blues: New Attacks on AES-Based MAC's. Cryptology ePrint Archive, Report 2011/095 (2011)
20. Dworkin, M.: Recommendation for Block Cipher Modes of Operation: Methods and Techniques. NIST Special Publication, Gaithersburg (2001)
21. Engels, D., Saarinen, M.-J.O., Schweitzer, P., Smith, E.M.: The Hummingbird-2 lightweight authenticated encryption algorithm. In: Juels, A., Paar, C. (eds.) RFIDSec 2011. LNCS, vol. 7055, pp. 19–31. Springer, Heidelberg (2012)
22. Englund, H., Hell, M., Johansson, T.: A note on distinguishing attacks. In: Pre-proceedings of State of the Art of Stream Ciphers workshop (SASC 2007), Bochum, Germany, pp. 73–78 (2007)
23. Gueron, S.: Intel Advanced Encryption Standard (AES) Instructions Set. Intel white paper, January 2010
24. Guo, J., Peyrin, T., Poschmann, A.: The PHOTON family of lightweight hash functions. In: Rogaway [38], pp. 222–239
25. Hell, M., Johansson, T., Maximov, A., Meier, W.: The Grain family of stream ciphers. In: Robshaw and Billet [37], pp. 179–190
26. Hong, D., Sung, J., Hong, S.H., Lim, J.-I., Lee, S.-J., Koo, B.-S., Lee, C.-H., Chang, D., Lee, J., Jeong, K., Kim, H., Kim, J.-S., Chee, S.: HIGHT: a new block cipher suitable for low-resource device. In: Goubin, L., Matsui, M. (eds.) CHES 2006. LNCS, vol. 4249, pp. 46–59. Springer, Heidelberg (2006)
27. Hong, S.H., Lee, S.-J., Lim, J.-I., Sung, J., Cheon, D.H., Cho, I.: Provable security against differential and linear cryptanalysis for the SPN structure. In: Schneier, B. (ed.) FSE 2000. LNCS, vol. 1978, pp. 273–283. Springer, Heidelberg (2001)
28. Jakimoski, G., Khajuria, S.: ASC-1: an authenticated encryption stream cipher. In: Miri, A., Vaudenay, S. (eds.) SAC 2011. LNCS, vol. 7118, pp. 356–372. Springer, Heidelberg (2012)
29. Kavun, E.B., Yalcin, T.: A lightweight implementation of Keccak hash function for radio-frequency identification applications. In: Ors Yalcin, S.B. (ed.) RFIDSec 2010. LNCS, vol. 6370, pp. 258–269. Springer, Heidelberg (2010)
30. Leander, G., Paar, C., Poschmann, A., Schramm, K.: New lightweight DES variants. In: Biryukov, A. (ed.) FSE 2007. LNCS, vol. 4593, pp. 196–210. Springer, Heidelberg (2007)
31. Lim, C.H., Korkishko, T.: mCrypton – a lightweight block cipher for security of low-cost RFID tags and sensors. In: Song, J.-S., Kwon, T., Yung, M. (eds.) WISA 2005. LNCS, vol. 3786, pp. 243–258. Springer, Heidelberg (2006)

32. Matsuda, S., Moriai, S.: Lightweight cryptography for the cloud: exploit the power of bitslice implementation. In: Prouff, E., Schaumont, P. (eds.) CHES 2012. LNCS, vol. 7428, pp. 408–425. Springer, Heidelberg (2012)
33. McGrew, D.: Authenticated Encryption in Practice. DIAC – Directions in Authenticated Ciphers, July 2012
34. Minematsu, K., Tsunoo, Y.: Provably secure MACs from differentially-uniform permutations and AES-based implementations. In: Robshaw [36], pp. 226–241
35. Moradi, A., Poschmann, A., Ling, S., Paar, C., Wang, H.: Pushing the limits: a very compact and a threshold implementation of AES. In: Paterson, K.G. (ed.) EUROCRYPT 2011. LNCS, vol. 6632, pp. 69–88. Springer, Heidelberg (2011)
36. Robshaw, M. (ed.): FSE 2006. LNCS, vol. 4047. Springer, Heidelberg (2006)
37. Robshaw, M., Billet, O. (eds.): New Stream Cipher Designs. LNCS, vol. 4986. Springer, Heidelberg (2008)
38. Rogaway, P. (ed.): CRYPTO 2011. LNCS, vol. 6841. Springer, Heidelberg (2011)
39. Rogaway, P., Bellare, M., Black, J., Krovetz, T.: OCB: a block-cipher mode of operation for efficient authenticated encryption. In: Reiter, M.K., Samarati, P. (eds.) Computer and Communications Security, pp. 196–205. ACM, New York (2001)
40. Rogaway, P., Krovetz, T.: OCB Latest Code and News. http://www.cs.ucdavis.edu/~rogaway/ocb/news/
41. Standaert, F.-X., Piret, G., Gershenfeld, N., Quisquater, J.-J.: SEA: a scalable encryption algorithm for small embedded applications. In: Domingo-Ferrer, J., Posegga, J., Schreckling, D. (eds.) CARDIS 2006. LNCS, vol. 3928, pp. 222–236. Springer, Heidelberg (2006)
42. Wu, H., Preneel, B.: Cryptanalysis of the stream cipher DECIM. In: Robshaw [36], pp. 30–40
43. Yuan, Z., Wang, W., Jia, K., Xu, G., Wang, X.: New birthday attacks on some MACs based on block ciphers. In: Halevi, S. (ed.) CRYPTO 2009. LNCS, vol. 5677, pp. 209–230. Springer, Heidelberg (2009)

Related-Key Attacks Against Full Hummingbird-2

Markku-Juhani O. Saarinen$^{(\boxtimes)}$

Revere Security (now defunct), Helsinki, Finland
mjos@iki.fi

Abstract. We present attacks on full Hummingbird-2 which are able to recover the 128-bit secret keys of two black box cipher instances that have a certain type of low-weight XOR difference in their keys. We call these highly correlated keys as they produce the same ciphertext with a significant probability. The complexity of our main chosen-IV key-recovery attack is 2^{64}. The first 64 bits of the key can be independently recovered with only 2^{36} effort. This is the first sub-exhaustive attack on the full cipher under two related keys. Our attacks use some novel tricks and techniques which are made possible by Hummingbird-2's unique word-based structure. We have verified the correctness and complexity of our attacks by fully implementing them. We also discuss enabling factors of these attacks and describe an alternative design for the WD16 nonlinear keyed function which is resistant to attacks of this type. The new experimental function replaces S-boxes with simple χ functions.

Keywords: Hummingbird-2 · Related-key cryptanalysis · Lightweight cryptography · Authenticated encryption · Hummingbird-2nu

1 Introduction

Hummingbird-2 is a light-weight authenticated encryption primitive designed by a team led by Eric Smith of Revere Security and presented in RFIDSec '11 [1]. Hummingbird-2 has been proposed for standardization in RFID use within ISO [2].

Hummingbird-2 was created largely in response to an effective FSE '11 attack by Saarinen [3] against the original Hummingbird algorithm [4–6]. Saarinen's single-key attack broke the 256-bit Hummingbird-1 with 2^{64} effort.

Some independent analysis on Hummingbird-2 has been published. In [7] a "differential sequence attack" is described, but the total complexity of the attack is higher than exhaustive search and therefore it is "of theoretical interest only". The same is said of the side channel cube attack presented in [8]. An even more far-fetched attack is described in [9], requiring 2^{240} memory.

IACR ePrint [10] described an attack simultaneously using dozens of related keys. Unfortunately the attack, as described, had some errors and the authors subsequently withdrew the paper. However, some observations contained in it

S. Moriai (Ed.): FSE 2013, LNCS 8424, pp. 467–482, 2014.
DOI: 10.1007/978-3-662-43933-3_24, © Springer-Verlag Berlin Heidelberg 2014

inspired our research that led to the discovery of high-probability correlated keys described in Sect. 2.1.

The structure of this paper is as follows. In Sect. 2 we describe the relevant components of the Hummingbird-2 algorithm and make a number of observations about its various features. In Sect. 3 we describe an effective key-recovery attack that uses a single key relation. We discuss enabling factors of the attack in Sect. 3.7, followed by conclusions in Sect. 4.

Appendix A contains a full specification for a new variant which is resistant to these attacks and is based on novel χ functions (rather than traditional S-boxes).

2   Examining the Hummingbird-2 Algorithm

Hummingbird-2 is neither a block cipher nor a stream cipher in the traditional sense but combines some of the features of both. In this it resembles other integrated authenticated encryption proposals such as Helix [11] and Phelix [12].

The "Hummingbird structure" uses 16-bit data paths throughout as it was originally targeted towards low-end microcontrollers such as the TI MSP430 family. Data is always encrypted or decrypted in 16-bit increments. The cipher accepts a 64-bit initialization vector IV, a 128-bit secret key K, and maintains a 128-bit state in registers R. A method for deriving message authentication tags from the internal state is also given in the specification [1].

We use the following symbols and notation:

$x \oplus y$: Exclusive-or operation between x and y.

$x \boxplus y$: Modular addition $x + y \bmod 2^{16}$.

$x \boxminus y$: Modular subtraction $x - y \bmod 2^{16}$.

$x \lll n$: Left circular shift (rotation) of x by n bits.

$x \ggg n$: Right circular shift (rotation) of x by n bits.

S_i : A 4×4 - bit nonlinear substitution box, $i \in \{1,2,3,4\}$.

IV_i : Word i of the 64-bit initialization vector, $i \in \{1,2,3,4\}$.

K_i : Word i of the 128-bit secret key, $i \in \{1,2,\cdots,8\}$.

R_i^r : Word i of the 128-bit state at position r, $i \in \{1,2,\cdots,8\}$.

P^r, C^r : Plaintext and ciphertext words at position r.

$t_i^{(r)}$: Used to mark temporary, internal quantities.

In the following sections, we will describe the various algorithm components and present observations that will be used in the final overall attack. These cryptanalytic observations may also be useful in attacks of other types than the one described in this work. For a complete specification of Hummingbird-2, we refer the reader to [1].

2.1   WD16 (and High-Correlation Related Keys)

Hummingbird-2 draws almost all of its nonlinearity from the WD16 function. WD16 uses four keying words (total 64 bits) which define a permutation on a 16-bit input value. One may see WD16 as a 16-bit block cipher with a 64-bit key.

WD16 is a four-round substitution-permutation network. In each round, a 16-bit subkey is XORed to the state, four 4×4 - bit S-boxes are applied in parallel, followed by a linear mixing step. The structure is shown in Fig. 1.

We use $S(x)$ to denote the parallel application of the 4-bit S-boxes S_1, S_2, S_3, S_4 on the 16-bit word x. The linear operation is $L(x) = x \oplus (x \lll 6) \oplus (x \ggg 6)$. If we shorten their compound operation to $LS(x) = L(S(x))$ then WD16 can be written as:

$$WD16(x, k_1, k_2, k_3, k_4) = LS(LS(LS(LS(x \oplus k_1) \oplus k_2) \oplus k_3) \oplus k_4). \quad (1)$$

We occasionally also use LS^{-1} and $WD16^{-1}$ to denote the inverses of respective functions. We fist observe that the WD16 can produce closely correlated output with some distinct but related keys.

Observation 1. *Consider two 64-bit WD16 keys* (k_1, k_2, k_3, k_4) *and* (k_1', k_2', k_3', k_4') *that for some* $i \in \{1, 2, 3\}$ *are related by* $\delta = k_i \oplus k_i'$ *and* $\Delta = k_{i+1} \oplus k_{i+1}'$, *with the other two key words equivalent. There are such pairs that will yield equivalent WD16 encryption and decryption for approximately 1/4 for input and output values.*

In a differential attack we only want to have a single active S-box to maximize the probability. As with any 4×4 S-box, each one of S_1, S_2, S_3 and S_4 must have differentials that work for at least four of the 16 input values, leading to the given probability 1/4.

Looking at Fig. 1 we can see how after the $\delta = k_i \oplus k_i'$ difference is introduced at position i, it is then subjected to a S-box substitution and a linear transformation before the $\Delta = k_{i+1} \oplus k_{i+1}'$ key difference cancels it out at $i+1$ with the given probability 1/4.

Table 1 gives a list of all of such pairs that have the optimum probability of exactly 1/4. This table was created via an exhaustive search.

We give some examples of WD16 key pairs for which $WD16_A(x) = WD16_B(x)$ with probability 1/4:

```
A = 0001 0000 0000 0000    B = 0000 3B8E 0000 0000
A = FFFF FFFF F000 6198    B = FFFF FFFF 0000 0000
A = 1234 5000 6090 1234    B = 1234 A000 0108 1234
```

The last two examples use the F000 → 6198 relation which was (randomly) chosen for the main attack described in Sect. 3 of this paper. There is a wide spectrum of variations of a more general attack methodology that is represented by that specific case; picking some other relation leads to a different attack.

2.2 Initialization and State Collisions

The initialization phase of Hummingbird-2 creates a 128-bit initial state from the 64-bit IV using the secret key and the WD16 function.

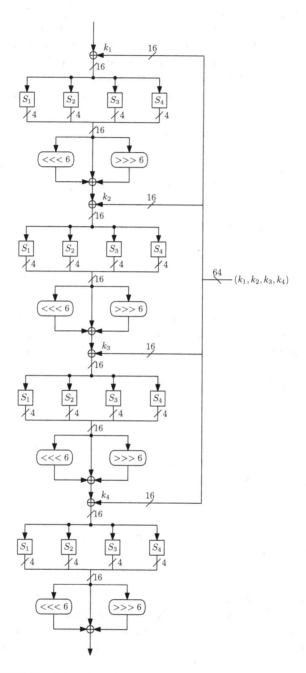

Fig. 1. The "WD16" mixing function is a 16-bit substitution-permutation network with four rounds and a 64-bit subkey (k_1, k_2, k_3, k_4). It is used in both initialization and encryption phases.

Table 1. All $4 \times 18 = 72$ high-probability related key word pairs where $\delta = k_i \oplus k'_i$ is canceled by $\Delta = k_{i+1} \oplus k'_{i+1}$ in the WD16 nonlinear function with probability $1/4$.

$\delta \to \Delta$	$\delta \to \Delta$	$\delta \to \Delta$	$\delta \to \Delta$
0001 → 3B8E	0010 → 74D3	0100 → C30C	1000 → D374
0002 → 2A8A	0010 → DC71	0100 → C71D	2000 → 6198
0002 → 2ECB	0020 → 30C3	0200 → 4D37	2000 → E3B8
0003 → 0441	0020 → B8E3	0300 → 8208	3000 → 2088
0007 → 0441	0030 → CC30	0300 → 8E3B	3000 → B2EC
0007 → 3B8E	0040 → CC30	0400 → 4515	5000 → E3B8
0008 → 1545	0050 → 1041	0400 → 8619	6000 → 8220
0008 → 3FCF	0060 → DC71	0600 → 4926	7000 → 8220
0009 → 330C	0060 → FCF3	0700 → 0822	8000 → 9264
000A → 1104	0070 → 1041	0700 → 8E3B	8000 → C330
000A → 3FCF	0080 → 5451	0A00 → 8208	9000 → 5154
000B → 0882	00A0 → 4410	0B00 → 0411	B000 → 1044
000C → 0CC3	00B0 → FCF3	0B00 → 4926	B000 → B2EC
000C → 2208	00C0 → 6492	0C00 → 4104	C000 → 4110
000E → 0882	00D0 → 2082	0D00 → 4D37	E000 → 1044
000E → 2649	00D0 → B8E3	0E00 → 0411	E000 → F3FC
000F → 1DC7	00F0 → 4410	0E00 → CF3F	F000 → 4110
000F → 2649	00F0 → 5451	0F00 → 4104	F000 → 6198

Initialization is a four-round process. Figure 2 shows a single initialization round. The state is first set as $R = IV \mid IV$. In each round, there are four invocations of WD16 together with some mod 2^{16} additive mixing, followed by cyclic rotations of the first four registers and linear exclusive-or "accumulation" mixing of the first four registers with the last four. The round counter $i = 0, 1, 2, 3$ is also used in the mix at the very beginning. The input keys to WD16 alter between the two halves of the master key (K_1, K_2, K_3, K_4) and (K_4, K_5, K_7, K_8).

Observation 2. *For each key K, there is a family of 432 related keys K' that yield the same state R after four initialization rounds with probability $P = 2^{-16}$ over all IV values.*

There are six possible positions i for $\delta = K_i \oplus K'_i$ and $\Delta = K_{i+1} \oplus K'_{i+1}$ that maximize the probability; $i \in \{1, 2, 3, 5, 6, 7\}$. Since there are two S-box activations in each round and four initialization rounds, the total probability of arriving at the same initial state for two such related keys is $(1/4)^{2 \times 4} = 2^{-16}$. As there are 72 suitable (δ, Δ) pairs (see Table 1), for each 128-bit key K there are at least $6 \times 72 = 432$ related keys that will give the same initial state with the given 2^{-16} probability. This observation has been experimentally verified.

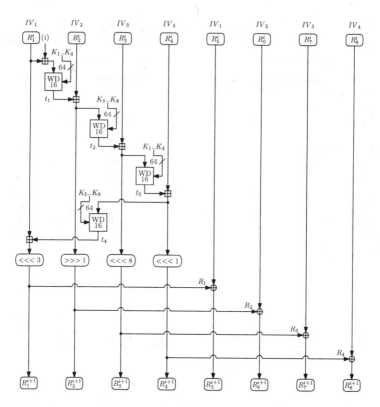

Fig. 2. Initialization round. There are four initialization rounds with a counter stepping through $i = 0, 1, 2, 3$.

2.3   Encryption

Hummingbird-2 encrypts and decrypts data in 16-bit increments, as shown in Fig. 3. The 128-bit state R^i and key K define a permutation from the plaintext word P^i to the ciphertext word C^i or vice versa. To encrypt plaintext word P^i into a ciphertext word C^i, the following steps are taken:

$$t_0^i = P^i \boxplus R_1^i$$
$$t_1^i = \mathrm{WD16}(t_0^i, K_1, K_2, K_3, K_4)$$
$$t_2^i = \mathrm{WD16}(t_1^i \boxplus R_2^i, K_5 \oplus R_5^i, K_6 \oplus R_6^i, K_7 \oplus R_7^i, K_8 \oplus R_8^i)$$
$$t_3^i = \mathrm{WD16}(t_2^i \boxplus R_3^i, K_1 \oplus R_5^i, K_2 \oplus R_6^i, K_3 \oplus R_7^i, K_4 \oplus R_8^i)$$
$$t_4^i = \mathrm{WD16}(t_3^i \boxplus R_4^i, K_5, K_6, K_7, K_8)$$
$$C^i = t_4^i \boxplus R_1^i.$$

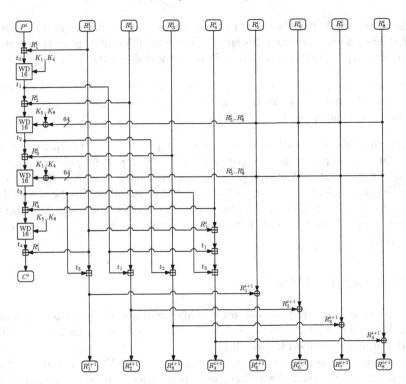

Fig. 3. Encryption of plaintext word P^i to ciphertext word C^i and update of state R. The "temporary" variables $t_0 \cdots t_4$ are used in the description of the attack.

After each encrypted word is processed, the state is updated:

$$R_1^{i+1} = R_1^i \boxplus t_3^i$$
$$R_2^{i+1} = R_2^i \boxplus t_1^i$$
$$R_3^{i+1} = R_3^i \boxplus t_2^i$$
$$R_4^{i+1} = R_4^i \boxplus R_1^i \boxplus t_3^i \boxplus t_1^i$$
$$R_5^{i+1} = R_5^i \oplus (R_1^i \boxplus t_3^i)$$
$$R_6^{i+1} = R_6^i \oplus (R_2^i \boxplus t_1^i)$$
$$R_7^{i+1} = R_7^i \oplus (R_3^i \boxplus t_2^i)$$
$$R_8^{i+1} = R_8^i \oplus (R_4^i \boxplus R_1^i \boxplus t_3^i \boxplus t_1^i).$$

For decryption, an inverse of WD16 function is required and the t quantities are computed in reverse order. The update function remains the same.

2.4   Related-Key Progression in Encryption

We see that there are four invocations of WD16 in each encryption operation and that key halves $K_1..K_4$ and $K_5..K_8$ are used twice each. In the middle two WD16 rounds the key is XORed with four of the higher "accumulator" state registers, but that has no effect on the differential. Since the differential is activated twice, there is a $(1/4)^2 = 1/16$ probability of matching ciphertexts.

Observation 3. *There is a 1/16 probability that for a matching state R the related keys K and K' (as defined in Sect. 2.1) will encrypt the same plaintext word to the equivalent ciphertext word.*

Note that if the key difference is in $K_5..K_8$, there is a 1/4 probability of equivalent state update as the last WD16 invocation only affects ciphertext output, not the state. Conversely, if the key difference is in $K_1..K_4$, the state update will be equivalent in decryption with 1/4 probability. Furthermore, if the (δ, Δ) difference is in (K_1, K_2) as the first WD16 does not affect the state in decryption and at least 12 bits of the plaintext will be equivalent as there is only one active S-box.

3   Crafting an Attack

There are many ways that one can use the high-probability correlated keys in an attack. We will describe the one that we implemented, which uses only a single related key pair described in Sect. 3.1.

The attack proceeds in a number of distinct stages. We first find a suitable IV values for the attack (Sect. 3.2), and then proceed to solve various internal quantities (Sects. 3.3 and 3.4) and finally parts of the secret key (Sects. 3.5 and 3.6).

3.1   Attack Model

We assume that the attacker has access to two "black box" oracles whose keys are related by

$$K \oplus K' = (\text{F000 6198 0000 0000 0000 0000 0000 0000}). \tag{2}$$

The choice of this particular key relation is almost arbitrary in the set of admissible key differences. Many of the differentials in Table 1 could be used as well.

In our model the attacking algorithm may perform chosen-IV initializations and query encryptions and decryptions from the oracles. For an ideal cipher the most effective way to recover the secret key K (and K') would be to through brute force with expected complexity of 2^{128} trials. Therefore we will use the estimated time required for a single trial, consisting of initialization and encryption/decryption of a single word as the "unit complexity" $c = 2^0$.

We note that in a brute force attack eight words need to be encrypted in order to be reasonably sure that the correct key has been found, but with the probability $65535/65536$ the incorrect ones can be rejected after encryption of a single word. Hence we use this as the unit complexity.

3.2   Finding a State Collision

The first stage of the attack is to find an IV value that produces a matching state R after the four-round initialization procedure for both K and K'. As indicated by Observation 2 in Sect. 2.2, one expects to find such a collision after searching through 2^{16} different IV values. Detection of a collision can be made by trial decryptions. If we decrypt a word x immediately after initialization, then there is a 1/4 probability that 12 bits of the corresponding plaintext words will match as discussed in Sect. 2.4. The overall complexity of this step is no more than 2^{20} to find an IV collision that holds with overwhelming probability.

Note that subsequent collisions may be found faster (for this K_1, K_2 relation) if we first search using words (IV_1, IV_2, IV_3) and for consecutive searches keep those words constant and loop through values of IV_4. The two initial round collisions are therefore guaranteed and consecutive collisions can be found with probability 2^{-12}.

Our attack requires only a single initialization state collision, henceforth denoted simply as IV.

3.3   Attacking R_1^i with Carry Bits

It is important to note that in HB2 encryption we can also have state and ciphertext word collisions when the plaintext words P (for K instance) and P' (for K' instance) are not equal.

The next stage involves the recovery of R_1^i. We can generate full codebooks $P^i \leftrightarrow C^i$ and $P'^i \leftrightarrow C'^i$ that depend on the IV and previous P^j, $j < i$ values with roughly 2^{17} effort if i is small. We fix $C^j = C'^j$ for $j < i$ and the states R^i do not diverge. Looking at Figures 1 and 3 we note the following.

Observation 4. *The first (δ, Δ) collision in the encryption operation works when*

$$S((P^i \boxplus R_1^i) \oplus K_1) \oplus S((P'^i \boxplus R_1^i) \oplus K_1') = L^{-1}(\Delta). \qquad (3)$$

Here we use S to denote the four parallel S-box lookups and L^{-1} to denote the inverse of the shift/XOR linear step in WD16, as in Eq. 1.

The δ and Δ values dictate which values the input differential $P^i \oplus P'^i$ can take. Since the input differential $\delta = K_1 \oplus K_1' = \text{F000}$ is in the high nibble, only the high nibbles $N = ((P^i \boxplus R_1^i) \oplus K_1)) >> 12$ and $N' = ((P'^i \boxplus R_1^i) \oplus K_1') >> 12$ really matter. We can tabulate successful pairs; see Table 2.

We see that Table 2 has only one entry per each horizontal and vertical line; N' can be given as a function of N and vice versa. If the N and N' entries are shifted by one position the collision at that point becomes impossible.

As we only want to have a single active S-box, may choose the high nibbles of P^i and P'^i arbitrarily, but we have to keep the low 12 bits the same.

Observation 5. *The probability of the carry shift depends solely on the value of plaintext low bits and the low bits of R_1^i. The shift will occur only when*

$$(P^i \wedge \text{0FFF}) + (R_1^i \wedge \text{0FFF}) \geq 1000. \qquad (4)$$

Table 2. High nibbles of intermediate values $N = ((P^i \boxplus R_1^i) \oplus K_1)) >> 12$ and $N' = ((P'^i \boxplus R_1^i) \oplus K_1') >> 12$ in WD16 that will provide a collision. These are the pairs for which $S_1(N) \oplus S_1(N' \oplus \texttt{0xF}) = \texttt{0x6}$. Note that in the diagonal there are four entries as expected; if $N = N'$ there is a $1/4$ probability of a collision.

$N \backslash N'$	0	1	2	3	4	5	6	7	8	9	A	B	C	D	E	F
0	-	-	-	-	-	-	-	-	-	-	A	-	-	-	-	-
1	-	1	-	-	-	-	-	-	-	-	-	-	-	-	-	-
2	-	-	2	-	-	-	-	-	-	-	-	-	-	-	-	-
3	-	-	-	-	-	-	-	-	8	-	-	-	-	-	-	-
4	-	-	-	3	-	-	-	-	-	-	-	-	-	-	-	-
5	-	-	-	-	-	-	-	-	-	-	-	-	-	-	-	F
6	0	-	-	-	-	-	-	-	-	-	-	-	-	-	-	-
7	-	-	-	-	-	-	-	-	-	-	-	-	C	-	-	-
8	-	-	-	-	-	5	-	-	-	-	-	-	-	-	-	-
9	-	-	-	-	4	-	-	-	-	-	-	-	-	-	-	-
A	-	-	-	-	-	-	7	-	-	-	-	-	-	-	-	-
B	-	-	-	-	-	-	6	-	-	-	-	-	-	-	-	-
C	-	-	-	-	-	-	-	-	-	-	-	B	-	-	-	-
D	-	-	-	-	-	-	-	-	-	-	-	-	-	D	-	-
E	-	-	-	-	-	-	-	-	-	-	-	-	-	-	E	-
F	-	-	-	-	-	-	-	-	-	9	-	-	-	-	-	-

Since we have created a codebook of $P^i \leftrightarrow C^i$, we may effectively loop through the low 12 bits of $p = P^i \wedge \texttt{0FFF} = P'^i \wedge \texttt{0FFF}$ and until the carry-over "shift" occurs and the pattern changes from $p = \texttt{0000}$. This will give us the low bits of R_1^i. This process isn't entirely foolproof as there are is a second collision that is required in the encryption process, but due to abundance of trials we may accurately pinpoint the p carry transition point with a good probability.

For each p value we may test $16 \times 16 = 256$ high nibble pairs for a matching ciphertext collision. Those collisions must occur at the points with an entry in Table 2. We may loop from low values of p towards higher values and see the lowest p value which starts to give different "grid". The algorithm we use is therefore essentially based on elimination of impossible combinations.

Note that the K_1 keying XOR in Eq. 3 also affects this step and the actual shift that occurs. However, we have found that if we guess the highest bit of K_1 (and hence K_1' which has the inverse high bit), we can actually determine all 16 bits of R_1^i with high probability with roughly 2^{17} total complexity and one guessed bit.

3.4 Deriving Additional Quantities for an Attack

From Sect. 2.3 we see that R_1 is updated as $R_1^{i+1} = R_1^i \boxplus t_3^i$. If we have derived two consecutive R_1 values using the technique outlined in Sect. 3.3, we obtain the value of t_3 at round i:

$$t_3^i = R_1^{i+1} \boxminus R_1^i. \tag{5}$$

Furthermore, since $C^i = t_4^i \boxplus R_1^i$, we obtain

$$t_4^i = C^i \boxminus R_1^i. \tag{6}$$

This stage proceeds by attempting to create a sequence where $t_4^i = t_4^{i+1}$ holds with a high probability. To do this, for $i = 1, 2, 3 \cdots 2^7$ process each full 16-bit codebook as discussed in Sect. 3.3 and choose C_i to be the smallest value after R_1^i such that corresponding P_i and P_i' form a state collision.

For those pairs where $t_4^i = t_4^{i+1}$, the following relation holds since WD16 is a permutation and matching output words imply matching input words:

$$t_3^i \boxplus R_4^i = t_3^{i+1} \boxplus R_4^{i+1}. \tag{7}$$

We manipulate Eq. 7 into $t_3^i = t_3^{i+1} \boxplus R_4^{i+1} \boxminus R_4^i$ and substitute that into the R_4 update function

$$R_4^{i+1} = R_4^i \boxplus R_1^i \boxplus t_3^i \boxplus t_1^i \tag{8}$$

to obtain

$$t_1^i = \boxminus R_1^i \boxminus t_3^{i+1}. \tag{9}$$

Since R_1^i and t_3^{i+1} are known quantities, as is $t_0^i = P^i \boxplus R_1^i$, we now can attack the first half of the keywords:

$$t_1^i = \text{WD16}(t_0^i, K_1, K_2, K_3, K_4). \tag{10}$$

Note that due to the probabilistic nature of our R_1 derivation method, not all of these candidate pairs are valid. However, we have experimentally verified that in practice a sufficient number is valid and the key search algorithm (described in Sect. 3.5) is designed in a way that accounts for false pairs.

3.5 A Time-Memory Trade-off for $K_1 \cdots K_4$ Search

The information obtained in Sects. 3.3 and 3.4 – especially Eq. 10 – already allow the keyspace of Hummingbird-2 to be split in half and a 2^{64} attack can be mounted via exhaustive search. We will describe a simple time-memory tradeoff attack that allows further square root reduction for the first half of the key words.

In this step, we are given n values (x_i, y_i), $1 \leq i \leq n$, that satisfy

$$\text{WD16}(x_i, K_1, K_2, K_3, K_4) = y_i \tag{11}$$

with a reasonable probability (see Eq. 10).

We've experimentally discovered that if we perform the search for matching consecutive t_4 pairs discussed in Sect. 3.4 up to a limit of 2^7 plaintext / ciphertext words, we are typically left with $n = 2^4$ candidates. Out of these, about 2^3 will be "right pairs" that actually satisfy Eq. 11 for the correct subkeys. This is a sufficient fraction for a time-memory trade-off technique.

To eliminate one of the keys, we pair the values and investigate (x_i, y_i) and (x_j, y_j), $1 \leq i \leq j \leq n$. There are $n(n-1)/2$ pairs, quarter of which will be right pairs. This will help to cancel out K_3 in the computation.

Table Generation. For each i, j pair, we first construct a lookup table for subkey K_4. For each guessed $0 \le K_4 < 2^{16}$ we compute the middle value h and build a table $T()$:

$$h = \mathrm{LS}^{-1}(\mathrm{LS}^{-1}(y_i) \oplus K_4) \oplus \mathrm{LS}^{-1}(\mathrm{LS}^{-1}(y_j) \oplus K_4)$$
$$T(h) = K_4.$$

Here a candidate for K_4 can be obtained from the h value by building an appropriate data structure that takes care of collisions.

Key Search. Approaching the WD16 from the other direction, we then loop through the 2^{32} values of K_1 and K_2 and look for a match in

$$h' = \mathrm{LS}(\mathrm{LS}(x_i \oplus K_1) \oplus K_2) \oplus \mathrm{LS}(\mathrm{LS}(x_j \oplus K_1) \oplus K_2) \tag{12}$$

Here $T(h')$ gives a candidate for K_4 with $O(1)$ effort. Then we check for *all* $1 \le k \le n$ pairs (x_k, y_k) how many of those yield the same K_3 value

$$K_3 \stackrel{?}{=} \mathrm{LS}(\mathrm{LS}(x_k \oplus K_1) \oplus K_2) \oplus \mathrm{LS}^{-1}(\mathrm{LS}^{-1}(y_k) \oplus T(h')). \tag{13}$$

If five or six of those K_3 values agree, then there is a significant probability that we have found the correct 64-bit quartet (K_1, K_2, K_3, K_4) of the secret key words.

Complexity. Since about 2^4 lookup key searches of 2^{32} primitive operations (and a total of 2^{16} memory) is required, we estimate that the total complexity of this step is less than 2^{36} when adjusted to the scale of the complexity of brute force key search as discussed in the beginning of Sect. 3.

3.6 Finding the Rest: $K_5 \cdots K_8$ Search

After the first half of the keying material has been discovered, it is a simple matter to brute force the rest. We have not found a time-memory tradeoff or other simple shortcut for the recovery of this part. Hence the total complexity is dominated by the second half, giving the total complexity of 2^{64} processing and about 2^{16} data.

It is quite easy to see that the last WD16 instance could be used to speed up key recovery if the difference between two keys would be at the right half of the key. However, in the beginning of Sect. 3 we chose a specific difference which lies at the first words. If we adopt the nonstandard setting of [10] where more than two "black boxes" with specific key relations can be accessed, then it the overall complexity of key recovery can be pushed down to the 2^{36} range. However, this attack model is rather unrealistic.

3.7 Discussion

Our attacks are specific to the Hummingbird structure as they do not purely follow any clear classical attack path such as linear or differential cryptanalysis. One may create a number of different attacks based on the same observations.

We developed the attack described in this paper while we were implementing it. One discovery led to the next. Our attack implementation used clear black box insulation and therefore we have a high degree of confidence that it works. We have tested it with various subsets of key space.

Design Issues. The attacks are made possible by a combination of factors. Lessons were perhaps not fully learned from the attacks of [3] which exploited the simplistic key schedule and algebraic properties of the Hummingbird structure. However, a simple and fast key schedule is partly dictated by the timing constraints of the RFID environment and protocols for which Hummingbird was designed. It can also be argued that having 16-bit datapaths with additive mixing has certain advantages when a cipher is specifically to be used with a 16-bit embedded CPU, even though the particular structure of Hummingbird may not fully utilize the potential.

Fixing WD16: Hummingbird-2ν. The main enabler of the attacks is the WD16 function and the way it is keyed. Furthermore WD16 has a linear mixing stage $L(x)$ that has suboptimal diffusion and does not allow effective use of lookup tables to speed up decryption of data like the MDS [13] matrices of SHARK [14] and AES [15] do.

To mitigate both security and efficiency issues, we propose an alternative where WD16(x, k_1, k_2, k_3, k_4) has been replaced with "S-boxless" $\chi_\nu(x, k_1, k_2, k_3, k_4)$ to produce a variant called Hummingbird-2ν. Hummingbird-2ν is described in more detail in Appendix A. This variant is geared towards hardware implementation. We note that that the estimated implementation footprint for a 32-cycle version of HB2 is only 500 GE and an implementation that can perform both encryption and decryption is around 700 GE. More accurate implementation results will be reported separately.

4 Conclusions

We have discovered and demonstrated large related key classes which produce closely correlated output for any given input. The weak key classes penetrate both the initialization and actual ciphering stages of Hummingbird-2.

We have developed a full key recovery related-key attack algorithm which effectively halves the cipher's key size. This attack allows the secret key can to be recovered with only 2^{64} time and 2^{16} data in a two-key setting. The attack has been implemented and verified to work. Furthermore, the first half of the key can be recovered with only 2^{36} effort. Other types of attacks may be derived from the same observations.

Even though it may be tempting to derive multiple keys from a single one (e.g. one for each communication direction or medium), Hummingbird-2 should only be used with strictly random keys. This approach is taken in the ISO protocol proposal [2]. System designs where the secret keys of tags are related or shortened should be avoided. Key bits must never be used to denote access / product categories or other information.

Appendix

A Hummingbird-2ν

The new experimental variant Hummingbird-2ν is the same as Hummingbird-2, expect that the WD16 substitution-permutation network has been replaced with a new function, $\chi_\nu(x, k_1, k_2, k_3, k_4)$. The new variant is geared towards hardware implementation and has a lower gate count than Hummingbird-2. Due to space constraints, we can only give a brief description of the new variant here and leave more detailed analysis for a separate report.

The new construction is based on χ functions, which are simple shift-invariant transformations that were first characterized by Daemen in [16]. The SHA3 algorithm Keccak uses a χ function as it's sole nonlinear component [17]. This selection was done in part to inspire research on functions of this type. The S-Boxes of the Hummingbird-2 WD16 design were selected based on extensive research [18].

We define two nonlinear functions f and g that operate on 16-bit words:

$$f(x) = \big((x \lll 2) \wedge \neg(x \lll 1) \wedge (x \ggg 1)\big) \oplus x$$
$$g(x) = \big(\neg x \wedge (x \lll 4) \wedge \neg(x \lll 12)\big) \oplus (x \lll 8)$$

The steps required to compute $y = \chi_\nu(x, k_1, k_2, k_3, k_4)$ are

$$
\begin{aligned}
t_1 &= f(g(x \oplus k_1) \oplus \text{4D71}) & t_2 &= f(g(t_1 \oplus k_2) \oplus \text{0F65}) \\
t_3 &= f(g(t_2 \oplus k_3) \oplus \text{2746}) & t_4 &= f(g(t_3 \oplus k_4) \oplus \text{0B7C}) \\
t_5 &= f(g(t_4 \oplus k_1) \oplus \text{CFD5}) & t_6 &= f(g(t_5 \oplus k_3) \oplus \text{8E45}) \\
t_7 &= f(g(t_6 \oplus k_2) \oplus \text{40DA}) & y &= f(g(t_7 \oplus k_4) \oplus \text{62F0})
\end{aligned}
$$

We acknowledge that one could use more of the keying material in each χ_ν function to make divide-and-conquer attacks more difficult. We decided not to change the overall structure outside the nonlinear component at all, however.

The "magic constants" 4D710F6527.. are derived from the Ehrenfeucht-Mycielski sequence [19,20]. The inverse function $x = \chi_\nu^{-1}(y, k_1, k_2, k_3, k_4)$ is easy to derive when we note that f and g are involutions: $f(f(x)) = x$ and $g(g(x)) = x$. The steps are simple performed in reverse order. In a hardware implementation the decryption circuitry closely matches the encryption circuit.

Here are some test vectors for χ_ν and a trace of execution for the last entry:

$$\chi_\nu(0000, 0000, 0000, 0000, 0000) = \text{FECB}$$
$$\chi_\nu(1234, 5555, 5555, 5555, 5555) = \text{18E6}$$
$$\chi_\nu(0000, 0123, 4567, 89\text{AB}, \text{CDEF}) = 3286$$

```
x=0000   t: 4C70 D80E 8857 2DB9 169D B89A 39B7   y=3286
```

Note that Hummingbird byte-word conversions are little-endian. Here's a test vector for Hummingbird-2ν encryption of 16 bytes and the resulting MAC:

```
KEY = 01 23 45 67 89 AB CD EF FE DC BA 98 76 54 32 10
IV  = 12 34 56 78 9A BC DE F0


PT  = 00 11 22 33 44 55 66 77 88 99 AA BB CC DD EE FF
CT  = 63 66 F6 CB 60 0F A4 CE 52 78 D8 A8 5B 39 E2 B3


MAC = E8 50 64 50 68 CA 49 04 9C E8 6A 54 55 F0 00 F0
```

References

1. Engels, D., Saarinen, M.-J.O., Schweitzer, P., Smith, E.M.: The hummingbird-2 lightweight authenticated encryption algorithm. In: Juels, A., Paar, C. (eds.) RFIDSec 2011. LNCS, vol. 7055, pp. 19–31. Springer, Heidelberg (2012)
2. Engels, D.: HB2-128 crypto-suite proposal. Technical report, Revere Security, December 2011 Version 1.1
3. Saarinen, M.-J.O.: Cryptanalysis of hummingbird-1. In: Joux, A. (ed.) FSE 2011. LNCS, vol. 6733, pp. 328–341. Springer, Heidelberg (2011)
4. Engels, D., Fan, X., Gong, G., Hu, H., Smith, E.M.: Ultra-lightweight cryptography for low-cost RFID tags: hummingbird algorithm and protocol. Technical report CACR-2009-29, University of Waterloo (2009). http://www.cacr.math.uwaterloo.ca/techreports/2009/cacr2009-29.pdf
5. Engels, D., Fan, X., Gong, G., Hu, H., Smith, E.M.: Hummingbird: Ultra-Lightweight Cryptography for Resource-Constrained Devices. In: Sion, R., Curtmola, R., Dietrich, S., Kiayias, A., Miret, J.M., Sako, K., Sebé, F. (eds.) FC 2010 Workshops. LNCS, vol. 6054, pp. 3–18. Springer, Heidelberg (2010)
6. Fan, X., Hu, H., Gong, G., Smith, E.M., Engels, D.: Lightweight implementation of Hummingbird cryptographic algorithm on 4-bit microcontroller. In: The 1st International Workshop on RFID Security and Cryptography (RISC'09), pp. 838–844 (2009)
7. Chai, Q., Gong, G.: A cryptanalysis of hummingbird-2: the differential sequence analysis. IACR ePrint 2012/233, April 2012. http://eprint.iacr.org/2012/233
8. Fan, X., Gong, G.: On the security of hummingbird − 2 against side channel cube attacks. In: Armknecht, F., Lucks, S. (eds.) WEWoRC 2011. LNCS, vol. 7242, pp. 18–29. Springer, Heidelberg (2012)
9. Zhu, B., Gong, G.: Multidimensional meet-in-the-middle attack and its applications to GOST, KTANTAN and Hummingbird-2. IACR ePrint 2011/619, November 2011. http://eprint.iacr.org/2011/619

10. Zhang, K., Ding, L., Guan, J.: Cryptanalysis of hummingbird-2. IACR ePrint 2012/207, April 2012. http://eprint.iacr.org/2012/207

11. Ferguson, N., Whiting, D., Schneier, B., Kelsey, J., Lucks, S., Kohno, T.: Helix: fast encryption and authentication in a single cryptographic primitive. In: Johansson, T. (ed.) FSE 2003. LNCS, vol. 2887, pp. 330–346. Springer, Heidelberg (2003)

12. Whiting, D., Schneier, B., Lucks, S., Muller, F.: Phelix - fast encryption and authentication in a single cryptographic primitive. ECRYPT Stream Cipher Project Report 2005/027 (2005). http://www.schneier.com/paper-phelix.html

13. Vaudenay, S.: On the need for multipermutations: cryptanalysis of MD4 and SAFER. In: Preneel, B. (ed.) FSE 1994. LNCS, vol. 1008, pp. 286–297. Springer, Heidelberg (1995)

14. Rijmen, V., Daemen, J., Preneel, B., Bosselaers, A., Win, E.D.: The cipher SHARK. In: Gollmann, D. (ed.) FSE 1996. LNCS, vol. 1039, pp. 99–111. Springer, Heidelberg (1996)

15. NIST: Advanced Encryption Standard (AES). Federal Information Processing Standards 197 (2001)

16. Daemen, J.: Cipher and hash function design strategies based on linear and differential cryptanalysis. Ph.D. thesis (1995)

17. Bertoni, G., Daemen, J., Peeters, M., Assche, G.V.: The Keccak reference, version 3.0. NIST SHA3 Submission Document, January 2011

18. Saarinen, M.-J.O.: Cryptographic analysis of all 4 × 4-bit S-boxes. In: Miri, A., Vaudenay, S. (eds.) SAC 2011. LNCS, vol. 7118, pp. 118–133. Springer, Heidelberg (2012)

19. Ehrenfeucht, A., Mycielski, J.: A pseudorandom sequence - how random is it. Amer. Math. Mon. **99**, 373–375 (1992)

20. Sutner, K.: The Ehrenfeucht-Mycielski sequence. In: Ibarra, O.H., Dang, Z. (eds.) CIAA 2003. LNCS, vol. 2759, pp. 282–293. Springer, Heidelberg (2003)

Stream Ciphers II

A Low Data Complexity Attack on the GMR-2 Cipher Used in the Satellite Phones

Ruilin Li[1]([✉]), Heng Li[2], Chao Li[2], and Bing Sun[2]

[1] College of Electronic Science and Engineering,
National University of Defense Technology, Changsha 410073,
Hunan, People's Republic of China
securitylrl@gmail.com
[2] College of Science, National University of Defence Technology,
Changsha 410073, Hunan, People's Republic of China
lihlsm1989@gmail.com,
lichao_nudt@sina.com,
happy_come@163.com

Abstract. The GMR-1 and GMR-2 stream ciphers, which are used in the satellite phones, have been reconstructed by Driessen et al. recently. The GMR-1 cipher is shown to be a proprietary variant of the GSM A5/2 algorithm, thus it could be cracked using the previous known method. For the newly designed GMR-2 cipher, by observing a non-uniform behavior of its component, Driessen et al. proposed an efficient known plaintext attack to recover the encryption key (a session key with 64-bit) with approximately 5–6 frames (50–65 bytes) of keystream.

In this paper, we first revisit the properties of each component of the GMR-2 cipher, and then present a low data complexity attack on it by adopting the strategy of guess-and-determine. We call this kind of attack the *dynamic guess and determine attack*, since the evolution of the guessing part of the internal state of the attack is changed dynamically according to the intermediate process. Our theoretical analysis demonstrates that, using the proposed attack, the 64-bit encryption key could be recovered by guessing no more than 32 bits when 15 bytes (1 frame) of the keystream is available. Some experimental results are also performed on a single PC to confirm our analysis, and the number of candidates for exhaustive search is about 2^{28} on average.

Keywords: Satellite phone · Stream cipher · GMR-2 · Guess-and-determine

1 Introduction

1.1 Backgrounds and the GMR-2 Cipher

Nowadays, mobile communication systems have revolutionized the way we interact with each other, and there have been built many cellular mobile network such

S. Moriai (Ed.): FSE 2013, LNCS 8424, pp. 485–501, 2014.
DOI: 10.1007/978-3-662-43933-3_25, © Springer-Verlag Berlin Heidelberg 2014

as GSM, UMTS, CDMA2000, or 3GPP LTE. These cellular mobile networks all require a so called cell site to create a cell within the network, which provides all the necessary equipment for transmitting and receiving radio signals from mobile handsets and the radio network. However, in some cases, such as the crew on oil rig or ships on open sea, researchers on a field trip in a desert, or people living in remote areas or areas that are affected by a natural disaster, it is not always to be close to a mobile phone cellular network, then these residents, military and government systems need to use satellite phones to communicate.

Satellite phone is a type of mobile phone that connects to orbiting satellites instead of terrestrial cell sites. They provide similar functionality to terrestrial mobile telephones such as the voice, short messaging service etc. Currently, there are two major satellite phone standards both developed by ETSI, namely the GMR-1 standard and the GMR-2 (aka GMR-2+) standard. For instance, Thuraya phone implements the GMR-1 standard, while the GMR-2 standard is mainly used by Inmarsat[1].

As we all know, security plays a significant role for satellite phones, yet from ETSI, we can only obtain the specifications of those two standards without any information about implementation details of security aspects. In fact, these two standards employ two different encryption algorithms called GMR-1 cipher and GMR-2 cipher, whose details had not been publicly known until [7] was reported in January 2012.

According to [7], the GMR-1 cipher is an improved version of A5/2 which belongs to the GSM encryption standard. Thus the methods of analyzing A5/2 as introduced in [3,5] can almost be applied to the GMR-1 cipher [8]. The GMR-2 cipher is a newly designed stream cipher, and at present, only [7] presents a known plaintext attack against GMR-2 cipher which is based on the read-collision technique. This method needs approximately 50–65 bytes (5–6 frames) of the keystream to recover the full key, and the computational complexity is about 2^{18}.

1.2   Main Contribution and the Outline

In this paper, we propose a low data complexity attack on the GMR-2 cipher using the guess and determine approach. Guess-and-determine attack is a common cryptanalytic approach against stream ciphers [1,2,4,6,9–12,15]. Its basic idea is to guess some parts of the internal state and derive other part through the relationship between the keystream and the internal state introduced by the keystream generation process. The validity of a guessed and determined internal state is checked by running the cipher forward from that state. If the generated keystream matches the intercepted keystream, we accept it. Otherwise, we discard the current candidate and try the attack again.

---

[1] Recently, the work in [13] shows that they can modify the firmware of a Inmarsat IsatPhonePro satellite phone using only a USB cable, which allows to read and write frames directly to any layer of the GMR-2 communication system, or even allows users to inject and/or sniff frames without the need of any additional equipment.

The general guess-and-determine attack assumes that the guessed part and the corresponding determined part of the internal state are known to the adversary prior to mounting the attack procedure. However, this approach cannot directly applied to the GMR-2 cipher due to its special structure. Considering this, we present a new strategy for guess-and-determine attack which we call *the dynamic guess-and-determine*. In this strategy, the evolution of guessing part of the internal state is changed dynamically according to the intermediate process, i.e., the new guessing part depends on both the previous guessed and determined parts of the internal state. We show how this kind of attack can be used to analyze the GMR-2 stream cipher. Our theoretical analysis demonstrates that, using the proposed attack, the 64-bit session key could be recovered by guessing no more than 32 bits when 15 bytes (1 frame) of the keystream are available. The experimental results also confirm our analysis, and the number of candidates for exhaustive search is about 2^{28} on average.

The rest of this paper is organized as follows: In Sect. 2, we recall the GMR-2 cipher briefly. Section 3 gives some properties of the components of the cipher and Sect. 4 gives basic analysis of the cipher. Section 5 presents our low data complexity attack on GMR-2 cipher in detail and finally Sect. 6 concludes this paper.

2   Description of the GMR-2 Cipher

2.1   Overall Structure of the GMR-2 Cipher

The GMR-2 cipher uses a 64-bit encryption-key, denoted as $K = \{K_7, K_6, \cdots, K_0\}$ and operates on bytes. When the cipher is clocked, it generates one byte of the keystream denoted by Z_l, where l represents the number of clockings. The cipher exhibits an 8-byte state register $S = (S_7, S_6, \cdots, S_0)$, three major components $\mathcal{F}$, $\mathcal{G}$, $\mathcal{H}$, a 3-bit counter $c \in \{0, 1, \cdots, 7\}$ and a toggle-bit $t \in \{0, 1\}$. A schematic overview of the overall structure is depicted in Fig. 1.

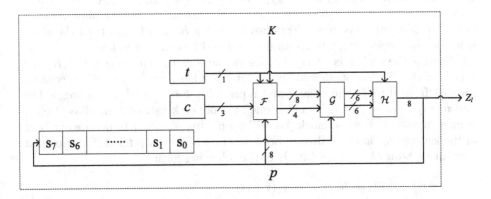

Fig. 1. Overall structure of the GMR-2 cipher

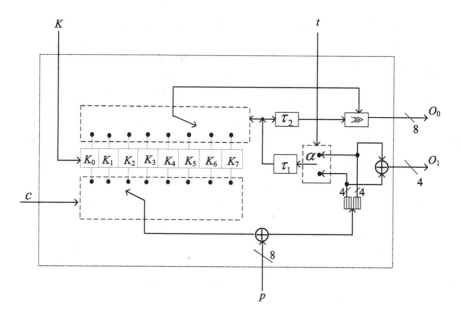

Fig. 2. The structure of $\mathcal{F}$-component

The $\mathcal{F}$-component combines two bytes of the encryption-key with the previous output (a keystream byte), the $\mathcal{G}$-component is a linear function for mixing purpose, and the $\mathcal{H}$-component consists of two DES S-boxes as a nonlinear filter. In the following subsections, we will describe the three major components in detail.

2.2 $\mathcal{F}$-Component

The $\mathcal{F}$-component is the most interesting part of the cipher, and Fig. 2 shows its internal structure. The 64-bit encryption-key $K=(K_7, K_6, \cdots, K_0)$ is fed into a 64-bit resister and it is unchanged during the execution of the cipher. At each clock, the $\mathcal{F}$-component just selects two key bytes K_c and $K_{\tau_1(\alpha)}$ from the lower side and the upper side, which can be described formally as follows.

Assume the cipher is at the l-th clock, besides the encryption-key K, the inputs of the $\mathcal{F}$-component contain t, c and p, where $c = l \mod 8$ is a counter ranging from 0 to 7 sequentially and repeatedly, $t = c \mod 2$ is a toggle bit, and $p = (p_7, p_6, \cdots, p_0) \in \{0,1\}^8$ is one byte of the keystream that has already been generated in the last clock. We will simply use $p = Z_{l-1}$ to denote one byte of the keystream that has already been generated. The outputs of $\mathcal{F}$-component contain an 8-bit O_0 and a 4-bit O_1 of the following form

$$\begin{cases} O_0 = (K_{\tau_1(\alpha)} \ggg \tau_2(\tau_1(\alpha)))_8; \\ O_1 = ((((K_c \oplus p) \gg 4)\&0\mathsf{xF}) \oplus ((K_c \oplus p)\&0\mathsf{xF}))_4. \end{cases} \quad (1)$$

Table 1. Definition of τ_1 and τ_2

α	$\tau_1(\alpha)$	$\tau_2(\tau_1(\alpha))$	α	$\tau_1(\alpha)$	$\tau_2(\tau_1(\alpha))$
(0,0,0,0)	2	6	(1,0,0,0)	3	7
(0,0,0,1)	5	3	(1,0,0,1)	0	4
(0,0,1,0)	0	4	(1,0,1,0)	6	2
(0,0,1,1)	6	2	(1,0,1,1)	1	5
(0,1,0,0)	3	7	(1,1,0,0)	5	3
(0,1,0,1)	7	1	(1,1,0,1)	7	1
(0,1,1,0)	4	4	(1,1,1,0)	4	4
(0,1,1,1)	1	5	(1,1,1,1)	2	6

where $\tau_1 : \{0,1\}^4 \longrightarrow \{0,1\}^3$ and $\tau_2 : \{0,1\}^3 \longrightarrow \{0,1\}^3$ are defined by table-lookups as shown in Table 1, and α is defined as

$$\alpha = \mathcal{N}(t, K_c \oplus P) = \begin{cases} ((K_c \oplus p)\&0\mathrm{xF}))_4, & \text{if } t = 0; \\ (((K_c \oplus p) \gg 4)\&0\mathrm{xF})_4, & \text{if } t = 1, \end{cases} \quad (2)$$

which can also be expressed using the following simple form

$$\alpha = [(K_c \oplus p) \gg 4 \times (c \bmod 2)] \,\&\, 0\mathrm{xF}.$$

2.3 $\mathcal{G}$-Component

As demonstrated in Fig. 3, the $\mathcal{G}$-component gets the output of the $\mathcal{F}$-component and one byte S_0 of the state as its input. It employs three sub-components, denoted by $\mathcal{B}_1$, $\mathcal{B}_2$, $\mathcal{B}_3$, all work on 4-bit input and returns 4-bit output with the

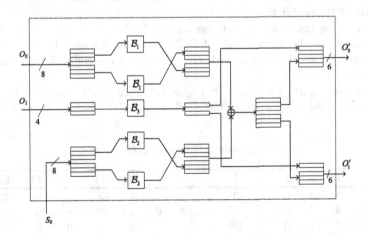

Fig. 3. The structure of $\mathcal{G}$-component (the upper lines indicates lower bits)

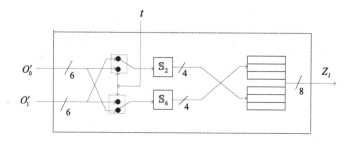

Fig. 4. The structure of $\mathcal{H}$-component

following definitions

$$
\begin{cases}
\mathcal{B}_1 : (x_3, x_2, x_1, x_0) \mapsto (x_3 \oplus x_0, x_3 \oplus x_2 \oplus x_0, x_3, x_1); \\
\mathcal{B}_2 : (x_3, x_2, x_1, x_0) \mapsto (x_1, x_3, x_0, x_2); \\
\mathcal{B}_3 : (x_3, x_2, x_1, x_0) \mapsto (x_2, x_0, x_3 \oplus x_1 \oplus x_0, x_3 \oplus x_0).
\end{cases}
$$

Since each $\mathcal{B}_i$ is linear, and all the other operations are just transposition or XOR, the $\mathcal{G}$-component is an entirely linear transformation, and we can express the two 6-bit outputs O_0' and O_1' as linear functions of the input by Eq. (3)

$$
\begin{cases}
O_0' = (O_{0,7} \oplus O_{0,4} \oplus S_{0,5},\ O_{0,7} \oplus O_{0,6} \oplus O_{0,4} \oplus S_{0,7},\ O_{0,7} \oplus S_{0,4}, \\
\qquad O_{0,5} \oplus S_{0,6},\ O_{1,3} \oplus O_{1,1} \oplus O_{1,0},\ O_{1,3} \oplus O_{1,0}) \\
O_1' = (O_{0,3} \oplus O_{0,0} \oplus S_{0,1},\ O_{0,3} \oplus O_{0,2} \oplus O_{0,0} \oplus S_{0,3},\ O_{0,3} \oplus S_{0,0}, \\
\qquad O_{0,1} \oplus S_{0,2},\ O_{1,2},\ O_{1,0}).
\end{cases}
\tag{3}
$$

2.4 $\mathcal{H}$-Component

The input of the $\mathcal{H}$-component as shown in Fig. 4, is the outputs of $\mathcal{G}$-component O_0', O_1' and a toggle-bit t.

$\mathcal{H}$-component contains two S-boxes $\mathbb{S}_2$ and $\mathbb{S}_6$, where $\mathbb{S}_2$ is the second S-box of DES and $\mathbb{S}_6$ is the sixth S-box of DES. See Tables 2 and 3 for a reference. However, these two S-boxes have been reordered to account for the different addressing.

Assume the input of S-box is $(x_6, x_5, x_4, x_3, x_2, x_1)$, then in this cipher, the least-significant bits (x_2, x_1) select the S-box row and the four most-significant

Table 2. The S-box $\mathbb{S}_2$

	0	1	2	3	4	5	6	7	8	9	10	11	12	13	14	15
0	15	1	8	14	6	11	3	4	9	7	2	13	12	0	5	10
1	3	13	4	7	15	2	8	14	12	0	1	10	6	9	11	5
2	0	14	7	11	10	4	13	1	5	8	12	6	9	3	2	15
3	13	8	10	1	3	15	4	2	11	6	7	12	0	5	14	9

Table 3. The S-box $\mathbb{S}_6$

	0	1	2	3	4	5	6	7	8	9	10	11	12	13	14	15
0	12	1	10	15	**9**	2	6	8	0	13	3	4	14	7	5	11
1	10	15	4	2	7	12	9	5	6	1	13	14	0	11	3	8
2	9	14	15	5	2	8	12	3	7	0	4	10	1	13	11	6
3	4	3	2	12	**9**	5	15	10	11	14	1	7	6	0	8	13

bits (x_6, x_5, x_4, x_3) select the S-box column. Now depending on the value of t, the output of $\mathcal{H}$-component, which is the l-th byte of the keystream, can be defined by

$$Z_l = \begin{cases} (\mathbb{S}_2(O_1'), \mathbb{S}_6(O_0'))_8, & \text{if } t = 0; \\ (\mathbb{S}_2(O_0'), \mathbb{S}_6(O_1'))_8, & \text{if } t = 1. \end{cases} \tag{4}$$

2.5   Mode of Operation

Now, we can describe the mode of operation [7] for the GMR-2 cipher. When the cipher is clocked for the l-th time, the following happens:

- Based on the current state of the state-register S, the counter c, and the toggle-bit t, the cipher generates one byte Z_l of keystream.
- The counter c is incremented by one and the toggle-bit is computed as $t = c \bmod 2$. When 8 is reached for c, then c is reset to 0.
- The state-register S is shifted by 8 bits to the right: $S_i = S_{i+1}$, $i = 0, 1, \ldots, 6$, and $S_7 = Z_l$. Meanwhile, $p = Z_l$ is also passed to the $\mathcal{F}$-component as input for the next iteration (the $(l+1)$-th clock).

The cipher is operated in two modes, the initialization mode and the generation mode.

Initialization Mode. In the initialization phase, the following steps are performed:

- The counter $c = 0$ and the toggle-bit $t = 0$.
- The 64-bit encryption-key is written into the resister in the $\mathcal{F}$-component.
- The state-register S is initialized with the 22-bit frame-number N, and this procedure is not detailed here as it is irrelevant with our attack. After c, t, S have been initialized, the cipher is clocked eight times, but the resulting keystream is *discarded*.

Generation Mode.[2] After the initialization is finished, the cipher is clocked to generate and output actual keystream bytes. We use $Z_l^{(N)}$ to denote the l-th $(l \geq 0)$ byte of keystream generated after initialization with frame-number N.

---

[2] There is a slight difference between the notation of [7] and ours in the generation mode, in this paper, we always assume that $Z_0^{(N)}$ is the first output byte of the keystream after the cipher is clocked eight times in the initialization phase.

The frame-number is always incremented after 15 bytes of keystream, which forces a re-initialization of the cipher. Therefore the keystream Z' that is actually used for $N \in \{0, 1, \cdots\}$ is made up of blocks of 15 bytes that are concatenated as follows:

$$Z' = (Z_0^{(0)}, Z_1^{(0)}, \cdots, Z_{14}^{(0)}, Z_0^{(1)}, Z_1^{(1)}, \cdots, Z_{14}^{(1)}, \cdots).$$

3   Properties of the Components of the GMR-2 Cipher

In this section, we carefully study the characteristic of the GMR-2 cipher and propose several properties of its components which are related to our later analysis.

3.1   Property of the $\mathcal{F}$-Component

We first note that after the 64-bit encryption key K is fed into the $\mathcal{F}$-component, it remains unchanged not only in the phase of the initialization, but also in the phrase of the keystream generation. Since the $\mathcal{F}$-component is used to select two key bytes K_c and $K_{\tau_1(\alpha)}$ from K, and the counter c is changed sequentially from 0–7, we only need to know how $K_{\tau_1(\alpha)}$ is selected.

Property of α. By Eq. (2), α can be expressed as:

$$\alpha = \mathcal{N}(t, K_c \oplus p)$$
$$= \begin{cases} (K_{c,3} \oplus p_3, \ K_{c,2} \oplus p_2, \ K_{c,1} \oplus p_1, \ K_{c,0} \oplus p_0)_4, & \text{if} \quad t = 0; \\ (K_{c,7} \oplus p_7, \ K_{c,6} \oplus p_6, \ K_{c,5} \oplus p_5, \ K_{c,4} \oplus p_4)_4, & \text{if} \quad t = 1. \end{cases}$$

This tells us that if p is known, then at each clock, we can get the value of α only by the four least-significant bits of K_c when $t = 0$ (c is even) or the four most-significant bits of K_c when $t = 1$ (c is odd). Thus, the key byte $K_{\tau_1(\alpha)}$ selected by the upper side can be determined by the value of the most (least) significant 4-bit of K_c provided p is known.

Properties of τ_1 **and** τ_2. From Table 1, we know that τ_1 maps 4-bit to 3-bit, thus a collision always exists. For instance, $\tau_1(0, 0, 1, 0) = \tau_1(1, 0, 0, 1) = 0$, and $\tau_1(0, 1, 1, 0) = \tau_1(1, 1, 1, 0) = 4$, this observation combined with $\tau_2(0) = \tau_2(4) = 4$ lead to the efficient read-collision based attack in [7]. Note that $\tau_2(\cdot)$ maps 3-bit to 3-bit, but it is non-surjective. Since one of the output of $\mathcal{F}$-component is $O_0 = K_{\tau_1(\alpha)} \ggg \tau_2(\tau_1(\alpha))$, we guess the reason why the designers choose a non-surjective table for $\tau_2(\cdot)$, he just want to make the right rotation parameter always being non-zero. Currently, we do not know whether this kind of non-uniformity could lead to some other potential attacks.

3.2 Property of the $\mathcal{G}$-Component

According to Eq. (3), the link between the input and output of the $\mathcal{G}$-component can be expressed by

$$
\begin{pmatrix} O'_{0,5} \\ O'_{0,4} \\ O'_{0,3} \\ O'_{0,2} \\ O'_{1,5} \\ O'_{1,4} \\ O'_{1,3} \\ O'_{1,2} \\ O'_{0,1} \\ O'_{0,0} \\ O'_{1,1} \\ O'_{1,0} \end{pmatrix}
=
\begin{pmatrix}
1\,0\,0\,1\,0\,0\,0\,0\,0\,0\,0\,0 \\
1\,1\,0\,1\,0\,0\,0\,0\,0\,0\,0\,0 \\
1\,0\,0\,0\,0\,0\,0\,0\,0\,0\,0\,0 \\
0\,0\,1\,0\,0\,0\,0\,0\,0\,0\,0\,0 \\
0\,0\,0\,0\,1\,0\,0\,1\,0\,0\,0\,0 \\
0\,0\,0\,0\,1\,1\,0\,1\,0\,0\,0\,0 \\
0\,0\,0\,0\,1\,0\,0\,0\,0\,0\,0\,0 \\
0\,0\,0\,0\,0\,0\,1\,0\,0\,0\,0\,0 \\
0\,0\,0\,0\,0\,0\,0\,1\,0\,1\,1 \\
0\,0\,0\,0\,0\,0\,0\,1\,0\,0\,1 \\
0\,0\,0\,0\,0\,0\,0\,0\,1\,0\,0 \\
0\,0\,0\,0\,0\,0\,0\,0\,0\,0\,1
\end{pmatrix}
\cdot
\begin{pmatrix} O_{0,7} \\ O_{0,6} \\ O_{0,5} \\ O_{0,4} \\ O_{0,3} \\ O_{0,2} \\ O_{0,1} \\ O_{0,0} \\ O_{1,3} \\ O_{1,2} \\ O_{1,1} \\ O_{1,0} \end{pmatrix}
\oplus
\begin{pmatrix} S_{0,5} \\ S_{0,7} \\ S_{0,4} \\ S_{0,6} \\ S_{0,1} \\ S_{0,3} \\ S_{0,0} \\ S_{0,2} \\ 0 \\ 0 \\ 0 \\ 0 \end{pmatrix},
\tag{5}
$$

based on which we can obtain the following three linear equation systems:

$$ \mathbf{y} = \mathbf{W} \cdot \mathbf{x} \oplus \mathbf{v}, \tag{6} $$

$$ \mathbf{y_1} = \mathbf{W_1} \cdot \mathbf{x_1} \oplus \mathbf{v_1}, \tag{7} $$

$$ \mathbf{y_2} = \mathbf{W_2} \cdot \mathbf{x_2} \oplus \mathbf{v_2}, \tag{8} $$

where

$$
\mathbf{W} = \begin{pmatrix} A & 0 & 0 \\ 0 & A & 0 \\ 0 & 0 & B \end{pmatrix}, \quad
\mathbf{W_1} = \begin{pmatrix} A & 0 \\ 0 & A \end{pmatrix}, \quad
\mathbf{W_2} = (B),
$$

$$
A = \begin{pmatrix} 1\,0\,0\,1 \\ 1\,1\,0\,1 \\ 1\,0\,0\,0 \\ 0\,0\,1\,0 \end{pmatrix}, \quad
B = \begin{pmatrix} 1\,0\,1\,1 \\ 1\,0\,0\,1 \\ 0\,1\,0\,0 \\ 0\,0\,0\,1 \end{pmatrix}, \quad
0 = \begin{pmatrix} 0\,0\,0\,0 \\ 0\,0\,0\,0 \\ 0\,0\,0\,0 \\ 0\,0\,0\,0 \end{pmatrix},
$$

and

$$
\begin{cases}
\mathbf{y_1} = (O'_{0,5}, O'_{0,4}, O'_{0,3}, O'_{0,2}, O'_{1,5}, O'_{1,4}, O'_{1,3}, O'_{1,2})^T \\
\mathbf{y_2} = (O'_{0,1}, O'_{0,0}, O'_{1,1}, O'_{1,0})^T \\
\mathbf{y} \ = (\mathbf{y_1}, \mathbf{y_2})
\end{cases},
$$

$$
\begin{cases}
\mathbf{x_1} = (O_{0,7}, O_{0,6}, O_{0,5}, O_{0,4}, O_{0,3}, O_{0,2}, O_{0,1}, O_{0,0})^T \\
\mathbf{x_2} = (O_{1,3}, O_{1,2}, O_{1,1}, O_{1,0})^T \\
\mathbf{x} \ = (\mathbf{x_1}, \mathbf{x_2})
\end{cases},
$$

$$
\begin{cases}
\mathbf{v_1} = (S_{0,5}, S_{0,7}, S_{0,4}, S_{0,6}, S_{0,1}, S_{0,3}, S_{0,0}, S_{0,2})^T \\
\mathbf{v_2} = (0, 0, 0, 0)^T \\
\mathbf{v} \ = (\mathbf{v_1}, \mathbf{v_2})
\end{cases}.
$$

Further, let $K_c = (\mathbf{k_h}, \mathbf{k_l})$, where $\mathbf{k_h} = (K_{c,7}, K_{c,6}, K_{c,5}, K_{c,4})^T$ denotes the most significant 4-bit of K_c, and $\mathbf{k_l} = (K_{c,3}, K_{c,2}, K_{c,1}, K_{c,0})^T$ denotes the least significant 4-bit of K_c. Similarly let $p = (\mathbf{p_h}, \mathbf{p_l})$, where $\mathbf{p_h} = (p_7, p_6, p_5, p_4)^T$, $\mathbf{p_l} = (p_3, p_2, p_1, p_0)^T$, and define $\mathbf{u} = \mathbf{p_h} \oplus \mathbf{p_l}$, then Eq. (1) implies the following two linear systems

$$\mathbf{x_1} = K_{\tau_1(\alpha)} \ggg \tau_2(\tau_1(\alpha)) \tag{9}$$

$$\mathbf{x_2} = \mathbf{k_h} \oplus \mathbf{k_l} \oplus \mathbf{u} \tag{10}$$

In the following attack on the GMR-2 cipher, we will always use one of the above linear systems, and we can guarantee that both the exact values of $\mathbf{u}$ and $\mathbf{v}$ are known to us. We have the following observations:

Observation 1. Since $\mathbf{A}$ and $\mathbf{B}$ are invertible, so are $\mathbf{W}$, $\mathbf{W_1}$ and $\mathbf{W_2}$, then from Eqs. (6)–(8), we can obtain the value of $\mathbf{y}$ ($\mathbf{y_i}$) from $\mathbf{x}$ ($\mathbf{x_i}$) easily, and vice vera.

Observation 2. If both $\mathbf{y_1}$ and α are known, then from observation 1, we can get the value of $\mathbf{x_1}$, and further from Eq. (9), we can calculate $K_{\tau_1(\alpha)} = \mathbf{x_1} \lll \tau_2(\tau_1(\alpha))$.

Observation 3. If both $\mathbf{y_2}$ and $\mathbf{k_h}$ ($\mathbf{k_l}$) are known, then from observation 1, we can get the value of $\mathbf{x_2}$, and further from Eq. (10), we can calculate $\mathbf{k_l} = \mathbf{x_2} \oplus \mathbf{k_h} \oplus \mathbf{u}$ ($\mathbf{k_h} = \mathbf{x_2} \oplus \mathbf{k_l} \oplus \mathbf{u}$).

Observation 4. The column indices of the two S-boxes $\mathbb{S}_2$ and $\mathbb{S}_6$ are selected by $\mathbf{y_1}$, and the row indices are selected by $\mathbf{y_2}$. This relationship is depicted in Fig. 5.

3.3   Property of the $\mathcal{H}$-Component

According to Eq. (4) and the definition of the two S-boxes, we have the following three results:

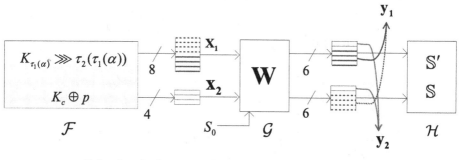

———————   Related to the four most-significant bits of $K_{\tau_1(\alpha)} \ggg \tau_2(\tau_1(\alpha))$ and S_0

·············   Related to the four least-significant bits of $K_{\tau_1(\alpha)} \ggg \tau_2(\tau_1(\alpha))$ and S_0

———————   Related to $K_c \oplus p$

Fig. 5. The links between the input and output of the $\mathcal{G}$-component (the upper lines indicates lower bits). Note that $\alpha = [(K_c \oplus p) \gg 4 \times (c \mod 2)]\ \&\ \mathtt{0xF}$

- If the row index and the output of an S-box are known, then we will get the column index uniquely.
- If the column index and the output of an S-box are known, then we will also get the row index uniquely except for $\mathbb{S}_6$ when the column index is 4 and the output is 9, in this situation, the row index can be either 0 or 3.
- If only the outputs of both S-boxes are known, then we will get $4 \times 4 = 16$ possible inputs for $\mathcal{H}$-component.

The above three results indicate that by intercepting the keystream of the GMR-2 cipher (the output of the two S-boxes) and combining the guessed/determined values of the row or column indices, we can "invert" these two S-boxes to obtain the corresponding (partial) input candidates.

4   Basic Analysis of the GMR-2 Cipher

The previous section presents some properties of the three components of the GMR-2 cipher. In this section, we show how these components interact with each other.

Given the frame number N, let $S_i^{(l)}$ denote the state of S_i at the l-th ($0 \leq l \leq 14$) clock in the keystream generation phrase, then for $8 \leq l \leq 14$ we have

$$S_0^{(l)} = Z_{l-8}^{(N)} \quad \text{and} \quad p = S_7^{(l)} = Z_{l-1}^{(N)},$$

which indicates that for $8 \leq l \leq 14$, both $S_0^{(l)}$ and p are known to us, thus the vectors $\mathbf{v}$, $\mathbf{v_1}$, $\mathbf{v_2}$ and $\mathbf{u}$ as defined in the previous section are also known to us. To simply our analysis, in the following of this section, we only focus on the cipher at the $(c+8)$-th clock with $0 \leq c \leq 6$.

Note that at the $(c+8)$-th clock, the $\mathcal{F}$-component just selects two key bytes K_c and $K_{\tau_1(\alpha)}$ from the lower side and the upper side. According to the property of the $\mathcal{F}$-component, just by guessing the half value of $K_c = (\mathbf{k_h}, \mathbf{k_l})$, we can determine the value of α and then know which key byte the $\mathcal{F}$-component will select.

Now, based on the fact that the link between the input and output of the $\mathcal{G}$-component can be expressed by a well-structured matrix $\mathbf{W}$, we present the following four rules for the guessing strategy when applying the dynamic guess-and-determine attack as described in the next section.

Rule 1. Let $K_c = (\mathbf{k_h}, \mathbf{k_l})$, assume c is odd, and given a guessed value for $\mathbf{k_h}$, if $\tau_1(\alpha) = c$, then from $Z_{c+8}^{(N)}$, either the guessed value of $\mathbf{k_h}$ is wrong or the candidate value of $\mathbf{k_l}$ can be determined; Similarly, assume c is even, and given a guessed value for $\mathbf{k_l}$, if $\tau_1(\alpha) = c$, then from $Z_{c+8}^{(N)}$, either the guessed value of $\mathbf{k_l}$ is wrong or the candidate value of $\mathbf{k_h}$ can be determined.

Proof. We only give the proof for the first case, the other case is similar, and thus the detail is omitted.

From $\tau_1(\alpha) = c$, we have $K_{\tau_1(\alpha)} = K_c$, thus

$$\mathbf{x_1} = K_{\tau_1(\alpha)} \ggg \tau_2(\tau_1(\alpha)) = (\mathbf{k_h}, \mathbf{k_l}) \ggg \tau_2(\tau_1(\alpha)).$$

Noting that

$$\mathbf{x_2} = \mathbf{k_h} \oplus \mathbf{k_l} \oplus \mathbf{u} \quad \text{and} \quad \mathbf{x} = (\mathbf{x_1}, \mathbf{x_2}),$$

thus if $\mathbf{k_h}$ is known, then for each possible $\mathbf{y}$ (whose value is calculated later), Eq. (6) can be converted into another linear equation system (which is related to the guessed value of $\mathbf{k_h}$) with 12 equations and 4 indeterminate variables representing $\mathbf{k_l}$.

According to the properties of the $\mathcal{H}$-component, there will be 16 different values for $\mathbf{y} = (\mathbf{y_1}, \mathbf{y_2})$ from $Z_{c+8}^{(N)}$. Thus, in total, 16 linear equation systems for $\mathbf{k_l}$ can be obtained.

If the guessed value of $\mathbf{k_h}$ is the actual value, at least one of the above 16 linear systems will have a solution that can be find through Gaussian elimination method. While if $\mathbf{k_h}$ is a random guessed value, then based on the theory of *Linear Consistency Test* [14], the probability that each linear equation system has solutions is no more than

$$\frac{1}{2^{12-4}} \times \left(1 + \frac{1}{2^{12+1}}\right)^4 \approx 2^{-8}.$$

Thus, the probability that the above 16 linear equation systems have solutions is upper bounded by $16 \times 2^{-8} = 2^{-4}$. In other words, this indicates that the number of candidates for $\mathbf{k_l}$ is small. □

Rule 2. Let $K_c = (\mathbf{k_h}, \mathbf{k_l})$, assume c is odd (even), and given a guessed value for $\mathbf{k_h}$ ($\mathbf{k_l}$), if $\tau_1(\alpha) \neq c$, we further guess the value of $\mathbf{k_l}$ ($\mathbf{k_h}$), in this situation, we have a guessed value for K_c, and then $K_{\tau_1(\alpha)}$ can be determined by $Z_{c+8}^{(N)}$.

Proof. Since $K_c = (\mathbf{k_h}, \mathbf{k_l})$ is known by guess, $\mathbf{x_2} = \mathbf{k_h} \oplus \mathbf{k_l} \oplus \mathbf{u}$ is known, according to observation 1, $\mathbf{y_2}$ can be calculated. By observation 4, the row indices for the two S-boxes are known, then from $Z_{c+8}^{(N)}$, the value of $\mathbf{y_1}$ which corresponds to the column indices for the two S-boxes can be uniquely determined. By observation 2, the value of $K_{\tau_1(\alpha)}$ can be obtained. □

Rule 3. Let $K_c = (\mathbf{k_h}, \mathbf{k_l})$, assume c is odd, and given guessed value for $\mathbf{k_h}$, if $K_{\tau_1(\alpha)}$ had already been guessed or determined previously, then $\mathbf{k_l}$ can be determined by $Z_{c+8}^{(N)}$; Similarly, assume c is even, and given guessed value for $\mathbf{k_l}$, if $K_{\tau_1(\alpha)}$ had already been guessed or determined previously, then $\mathbf{k_h}$ can be determined by $Z_{c+8}^{(N)}$.

Proof. Since $K_{\tau_1(\alpha)}$ is known, $\mathbf{x_1}$ is known, by observation 1, the value of $\mathbf{y_1}$ can be obtained. Noting that $\mathbf{y_1}$ corresponds to the column indices for S-boxes, thus $\mathbf{y_2}$ which represents the row indices for S-boxes can be obtained from $Z_{c+8}^{(N)}$. According to observation 3, $\mathbf{k_h}$ ($\mathbf{k_l}$) can be calculated with known $\mathbf{k_l}$ ($\mathbf{k_h}$). □

Remark 1. We remind here that, from $\mathbf{y_1}$ and $Z_{c+8}^{(N)}$, we cannot always uniquely deduce $\mathbf{y_2}$ as explained in Sect. 3.3, thus we will sometimes obtain two candidates for $\mathbf{y_2}$.

Rule 4. Assume that the values for K_c and $K_{\tau_1(\alpha)}$ had already been guessed or determined previously, then we can judge whether those guessed or determined values are wrong by $Z_{c+8}^{(N)}$.

Proof. Since K_c and $K_{\tau_1(\alpha)}$ are known, they can pass through the three components to generate a keystream byte at the $(c+8)$-th clock, then we can compare it with $Z_{c+8}^{(N)}$. If they are not matched, the guessed values for K_c and $K_{\tau_1(\alpha)}$ are wrong.   □

Remark 2. When applying dynamic guess-and-determine attack on the GMR-2 cipher in the next section, in fact, at each step, we just adopt Rule 1–Rule 3 to guess or determine some parts of K, or adopt Rule 4 to verify whether the guessed or determined value is wrong. If Rule 4 indicates some inconsistency at the current clock, then the guessed value for the nearest clock is wrong, in this situation, we must *backtrack* to this position, and try another guessed value.

5   Low Data Complexity Attack on the GMR-2 Cipher

As discussed in the introduction, the general guess-and-determine attack assumes that both the guessed part and the corresponding determined part of the internal state are known to the adversary prior to mounting the attack. However, considering the mechanism of the GMR-2 cipher, we cannot directly applied the general guess-and-determine attack on it. Thus, we introduce a new strategy for guess-and-determine attack which we call *the Dynamic Guess-and-Determine*. The main feature is that we cannot decide which parts must be guessed and which parts have to be determined in prior, what we can do is just *dynamically* guessing some parts of the internal state. The idea can be further described as follows.

First, we guess some part of the internal state of the target cipher, and then according to the guessed value, we determine some other parts of the internal state through the intercepted keystream. Next, we continue to guess some new part of the internal state, but this time the guessed part depends on both the previous guessed and determined parts. Do this process until all parts of the internal state are deduced. This indicates that we need to dynamically build the candidates for K by *backtracking*.

Now we can adopt the above strategy to present a low data complexity attack on the GMR-2 cipher. Our attack only needs one frame (15-byte) of the keystream, and without loss of generality, we assume $N = 0$. The attack contains the following two major steps[3]:

---

[3] We point out here that although we describe our attack in two separate steps, in fact, the second step (the exhaustive search step) can be incorporated in the first step: if a candidate is obtained from the dynamic guess-and-determine phase, it can be quickly tested to decide whether it is the right key.

- In the first step, from the known keystream $Z_0^{(0)} \sim Z_{14}^{(0)}$, we adopt the dynamic guess-and-determine method to analyze the cipher at the $(c+8)$-th clock, where $0 \le c \le 6$, and this can reduce the candidates for the 64-bit encryption-key K from 2^{64} to no more than 2^{32}.
- In the second step, we test the candidates for K from the first step by comparing the keystream generated from these candidates with the exact keystream $Z_0^{(0)} \sim Z_7^{(0)}$, thus we obtain the unique value for K.

Since the second step of our attack is just doing exhaustive search operations for the candidate set, we only discuss the first step in detail in the following subsection.

5.1 The Attack Procedure

As explained before, to guarantee that the values of p and $S_0^{(l)}$ are known for us at the l-th clock, we should analyze the cipher at the $(c+8)$-th clock with $0 \le c \le 6$.

Before introducing the proposed attack, we first define an index set

$$\Gamma \subseteq \{0, 1, \cdots, 7\}$$

to save the byte indices for the encryption key K that had already been known by guessing or determining before the $(c+8)$-th clock. Γ is initialized with $\varnothing$ at the 8th clock, and is changed during the attack process.

Now let's analyze the GMR-2 cipher at the $(c+8)$-th clock with $0 \le c \le 6$. At each clock, we calculate the following values:

$$c, \ t, \ p = Z_{c+7}^{(0)}, \ S_0^{(c+8)} = Z_c^{(0)}, \ \text{and} \ \Gamma,$$

and judge whether $c \in \Gamma$:

- If $c \in \Gamma$, then K_c had been known, we could calculate α and judge whether $\tau_1(\alpha) \in \Gamma$:
  - If $\tau_1(\alpha) \in \Gamma$, then $K_{\tau_1(\alpha)}$ had been known, thus we can adopt Rule 4 to determine whether K_c and $K_{\tau_1(\alpha)}$ are wrong. If they are incorrect (i.e., the guessed and determined values are wrong), then we trace back to the nearest clock (at which the guessed value indicates such inconsistency) to re-analyze the cipher.
  - If $\tau_1(\alpha) \notin \Gamma$, then $K_{\tau_1(\alpha)}$ had not been known, we can adopt Rule 2 to obtain $K_{\tau_1(\alpha)}$, and meanwhile set $\Gamma \leftarrow \Gamma \cup \{\tau_1(\alpha)\}$.
- If $c \notin \Gamma$, then $K_c = (\mathbf{k_h}, \mathbf{k_l})$ had not been known, now we decide to guess $\mathbf{k_l}$ if c is even, and $\mathbf{k_h}$ if c is odd. Next, we calculate α and judge whether $\tau_1(\alpha) \in \Gamma$:
  - If $\tau_1(\alpha) \in \Gamma$, then $K_{\tau_1(\alpha)}$ had been known, we can adopt Rule 3 to get $\mathbf{k_h}$ if c is even, and $\mathbf{k_l}$, if c is odd, and meanwhile set $\Gamma \leftarrow \Gamma \cup \{c\}$.
  - If $\tau_1(\alpha) \notin \Gamma$, then $K_{\tau_1(\alpha)}$ had not been known. We further judge whether $c = \tau_1(\alpha)$:

If $c = \tau_1(\alpha)$, then we can adopt Rule 1 to either get the rest bits of K_c, and set $\Gamma \leftarrow \Gamma \cup \{c\}$, or deduce that the guessed value of $\mathbf{k_l}$ ($\mathbf{k_h}$) is wrong if c is even (odd), and then we guess another value for $\mathbf{k_l}$ ($\mathbf{k_h}$).

If $c \neq \tau_1(\alpha)$, then we guess the other four bits of K_c, and we can adopt Rule 2 to get $K_{\tau_1(\alpha)}$, and meanwhile set $\Gamma \leftarrow \Gamma \cup \{c, \tau_1(\alpha)\}$.

The above process sequentially executes on the GMR-2 cipher from the 8th clock to the 14th clock. When it is finished, there will be a candidate for the 64-bit K, then we test whether it is the right key by $Z_0^{(0)} \sim Z_7^{(0)}$. If not, we discard this candidate, and then we modify the guessed values to obtain another candidate. This process is repeated until the right key is found at last.

5.2   Complexity Analysis and Experimental Results

From the attack procedure, especially from Rule 1– Rule 3, it is shown that if we guess 8 bits, then we will obtain other 8 bits; while if we guess 4 bits, then we will also deduce other 4 bits. Furthermore, Rule 4 can be further used to filter the wrong guessed values. We thus conclude that for a 64-bit key K, we only need to guess at most 32 bits on average, and the other 32 bits can be determined. This estimation is rough, however, it seems difficult and even impossible to calculate the exact time complexity of our attack in theory. So we do some experiments for different frames and random keys. Our experimental results almost confirm our analysis, and the number of candidates is a little better, it is about 2^{28} on average.

More specifically, we perform a *non-optimized*[4] realization of the above attack 1000 times on a 3.2 GHz PC, and the result demonstrates that the 64-bit encryption-key can be obtained in around 700 seconds on average, where 580 seconds are consumed to deduce the 2^{28} candidates, and 120 seconds are consumed to exhaustively search the candidates. Figure 6 is the frequence distribution of the exhaustive bits (the logarithm of the number of candidates) from 1000 experimental results.

The data complexity of the attack is just a frame of the keystream, i.e., 15-byte keystream. The dynamic guess-and-determine phase only analyze 8th~14th clock, because $S_7, S_6, \ldots, S_0$ must be known in this phase. While for the exhaustive search phase, $Z_0^{(0)} \sim Z_7^{(0)}$ can be used to distinguish the right key from the 2^{28} candidates.

---

[4] As described in Sect. 5.1, in the dynamic guess-and-determine attack, if we detect some inconsistency at the $(c+8)$-th clock, we should backtrack to the nearest clock. However, for easy programming with the recursive method, in our "non-optimized" realization, we just trace back to the $(c+7)$-th clock, thus there maybe exist many redundant computations. We believe that using the original realization, the time complexity of the attack can be further reduced quickly.

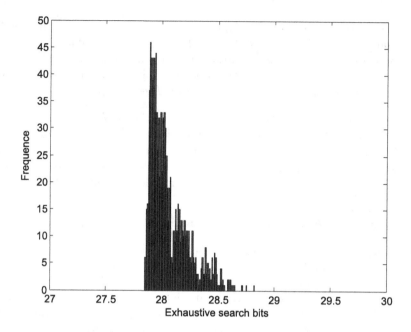

Fig. 6. The frequence distribution of exhaustive bits from 1000 experimental results

Table 4. Cryptanalytic results on the GMR-2 cipher

Method	Data	Time	Source
Read-Collision Based Technique	15–20 frames	2^{10}	[7]
Read-Collision Based Technique	5–6 frames (50–65 bytes)	2^{18}	[7]
Dynamic Guess-and-Determine	1 frames (15 bytes)	2^{28}	Sect. 5

6 Conclusion

The GMR-2 cipher has been widely used in the satellite phones communications, and thus it is of special significant to analyze its security. The design methodology of GMR-2 cipher seems new and more complex, yet an efficient low data complexity attack based on the strategy of dynamic guess-and-determine could be mounted. This kind of attack needs only 1 frame (15-byte) of the keystream, and it can recover the 64-bit session key by testing about 2^{28} candidates on average. Table 4 is the comparison between the known cryptanalytic result and ours. Our proposed attack can also be implemented on a single PC, which again demonstrates that the design methodology of the GMR-2 cipher is really far from what is "state of the art" in stream ciphers.

Acknowledgments. The authors wish to thank the anonymous reviewers of FSE 2013 for their valuable suggestions and comments, which greatly improve the presentation and quality of this paper. The work in this paper is supported by the National Natural Science Foundation of China (No: 61070215, 61103192).

References

1. Abdelraheem, M.A., Borghoff, J., Zenner, E., David, M.: Cryptanalysis of the light-weight cipher A2U2. In: Chen, L. (ed.) IMACC 2011. LNCS, vol. 7089, pp. 375–390. Springer, Heidelberg (2011)

2. Anderson R, Roe M. A5 (1994). http://jya.com/crack-a5.htm

3. Barkan, P., Biham, E., Keller, N.: Instant ciphertext-only cryptanalysis of GSM encrypted communication. J. Cryptol. (Springer) **21**(3), 392–429 (2008)

4. Biham, E., Dunkelman, O.: Cryptanalysis of the A5/1 GSM stream cipher. In: Roy, B., Okamoto, E. (eds.) INDOCRYPT 2000. LNCS, vol. 1977, pp. 43–51. Springer, Heidelberg (2000)

5. Bogdanov, A., Eisenbarth, T., Rupp, A.: A hardware-assisted realtime attack on A5/2 without precomputations. In: Paillier, P., Verbauwhede, I. (eds.) CHES 2007. LNCS, vol. 4727, pp. 394–412. Springer, Heidelberg (2007)

6. Debraize, B., Goubin, L.: Guess-and-determine algebraic attack on the self-shrinking generator. In: Nyberg, K. (ed.) FSE 2008. LNCS, vol. 5086, pp. 235–252. Springer, Heidelberg (2008)

7. Driessen, B., Hund, R., Willems, C., Parr, C., Holz, T.: Don't trust satellite phones: a security analysis of two satphone standards. In: IEEE Security and Privacy 2012, pp. 128–142 (2012)

8. Driessen B. Eavesdropping on satellite telecommunication system. Cryptology ePrint Archive, Report 2012/051. http://eprint.iacr.org/2012/051

9. Golić, J.D.: Cryptanalysis of alleged A5 stream cipher. In: Fumy, W. (ed.) EURO-CRYPT 1997. LNCS, vol. 1233, pp. 239–255. Springer, Heidelberg (1997)

10. Shah, J., Mahalanobis, A.: A new guess-and-determine attack on the A5/1 stream cipher. Cryptology ePrint Archive, Report 2012/208. http://eprint.iacr.org/2012/208

11. Feng, X., Liu, J., Zhou, Z., Wu, Ch., Feng, D.: A byte-based guess and determine attack on sosemanuk. In: Abe, M. (ed.) ASIACRYPT 2010. LNCS, vol. 6477, pp. 146–157. Springer, Heidelberg (2010)

12. Philip, H., Gregory, G.: Guess-and-determine attack on SNOW. In: Nyberg, K., Heys, H. (eds.) SAC 2002. LNCS, vol. 2595, pp. 37–46. Springer, Heidelberg (2003)

13. Sebastian, M., Alfredo, O.: Satellite Baseband firmware modifications. In: Ekoparty Security Conference, 2012. http://www.groundworkstech.com/blog/ekoparty2012satellitebasebandmods

14. Zeng, K., Yang, C.H., Rao, T.R.N.: On the linear consistency test (LCT) in cryptanalysis with applications. In: Brassard, G. (ed.) CRYPTO 1989. LNCS, vol. 435, pp. 164–174. Springer, Heidelberg (1990)

15. Zhang, B., Feng, D.: New guess-and-determine attack on the self-shrinking generator. In: Lai, X., Chen, K. (eds.) ASIACRYPT 2006. LNCS, vol. 4284, pp. 54–68. Springer, Heidelberg (2006)

Improving Key Recovery to 784 and 799 Rounds of Trivium Using Optimized Cube Attacks

Pierre-Alain Fouque[1]($\boxtimes$) and Thomas Vannet[2]

[1] Rennes 1 University, Rennes, France
pierre-alain.fouque@ens.fr
[2] NTT Secure Platform Laboratories, Tokyo, Japan
thomas.vannet@lab.ntt.co.jp

Abstract. Dinur and Shamir have described cube attacks at EURO-CRYPT '09 and they have shown how efficient they are on the stream cipher Trivium up to 767 rounds. These attacks have been extended to distinguishers but since this seminal work, no better results on the complexity of key recovery attacks on Trivium have been presented. It appears that the time complexity to compute cubes is expensive and the discovery of linear superpoly also requires the computation of many cubes. In this paper, we increase the number of attacked initialization rounds by improving the time complexity of computing cube and we show attacks that go beyond this bound. We were able to find linear superpoly up to 784 rounds, which leads to an attack requiring 2^{39} queries. Using quadratic superpoly, we were also able to provide another attack up to 799 rounds which complexity is 2^{40} queries and 2^{62} for the exhaustive search part. To achieve such results, we find a way to reduce the density of the polynomials, we look for quadratic relations and we extensively use the Moebius transform to speed up computations for various purposes.

Keywords: Trivium · Cube attacks · Cryptanalysis · Moebius transform

1 Introduction

After every stream cipher submitted to the NESSIE project in 2000 was successfully broken, a new European project called eSTREAM was started in 2004 in order to build new secure stream ciphers. One of the ciphers submitted, Trivium, has a very simple design and yet no attack was discovered on its full version, which uses 1152 initialization rounds.

There have been various attempts to attack reduced variants of Trivium. In [12], Vielhaber managed to recover 47 bits of the key after 576 rounds using an algebraic method. Afterwards, Dinur and Shamir described a full key recovery in less than 2^{30} requests to Trivium limited to 735 rounds and recovered 35 key bits after 767 rounds in about 2^{36} requests using the so-called cube attacks in [7].

S. Moriai (Ed.): FSE 2013, LNCS 8424, pp. 502–517, 2014.
DOI: 10.1007/978-3-662-43933-3_26, © Springer-Verlag Berlin Heidelberg 2014

Consequently, the on-line attack requires an exhaustive search of 2^{45}. With the introduction of cube testers, Aumasson *et al.* were able to build a distinguisher on Trivium after 790 rounds and detect non-randomness properties after up to 885 rounds in [2]. Independently, in [10], Knellwolf, Meier and Naya-Plasencia built a distinguisher up to 806 rounds for all keys and up to 961 rounds for some very specific keys.

Despite a warning suggesting that the cube attack may be applied on stronger versions of Trivium, no such results were obtained since 2009. In this paper, we investigate how far the cube attack can realistically be applied to Trivium. Cube attacks usually are composed of an online and an offline phase. During the offline phase, the adversary is looking for linear relations and once the number of such relations are high enough, the on-line phase requires to compute cube using chosen public variables. In [7], only the complexity of the online phase is given. The only information regarding the offline phase is that it lasted "several weeks" for the strongest version, i.e. the attack on 767 rounds of Trivium. However, this phase of the attack is the most interesting if we try to extend the previous attacks. We were able to reproduce this phase in a matter of hours and a stronger version in a couple of days worth of computation. The online phase has a low-enough complexity to be feasible in practice.

Our Contributions. First of all, we develop efficient implementations and optimizations to compute large cubes and for instance, we can compute a cube of size 27 in less than a second on a standard computer. Using fast implementation of the Moebius Transform, we realize many interesting computations such as polynomial density measurements, degree testing or interpolation. In addition, we used a different method than the one suggested in [7] to test many different parameters at once. Thanks to this, over 90,000 computations which should each require 2^{36} operations can be computed in merely 2 hours where this would have required about 13,000 hours with the classical method, offering an average computing time of 80ms for every cube of size 36.

Furthermore, we investigated ways to smartly select the parameters with an empirical filter which greatly improved the rate at which linear key bits relations were established. This preselection technique is the main ingredient we propose and we use to push the attack further with little increase in complexity. Indeed, we were able to recover 42 key bits after 784 rounds of initialization for the first time with less than 2^{38} cipher requests in the online phase. Adding a phase of brute-force, the 80-bit key can be fully recovered in less than 2^{39} requests. After 799 rounds, 12 key bits can be recovered directly, which leads to an attack. Besides, studying the polynomials of degree 2 found after 784 rounds, we experimentally interpolated several quadratic polynomials which reveal information for a very large amount of keys after up to 799 initialization rounds. This phase of the attack has a complexity about 2^{39}. This in turn allows a full key recovery attack in 2^{68} requests, then reduced to about 2^{62}.

Organization of the Paper. In Sect. 2, we describe the Trivium stream cipher, recall how cube attacks work and we present the Moebius transform. In Sect. 3, we show that this transformation can be used in many places to improve the complexity of Cube attacks and then, we explain how we can reduce empirically the density of the polynomial in Trivium. This technique allows to look for linear relations more easily and increases the number of initialization rounds we can attack. Finally, we present our result on Trivium using 784 rounds. In Sect. 4, we present an attack on 799 initialization rounds. To extend the attack further, we need to look for quadratic relations and we show that we have to look for specific relations, otherwise the search would not be possible. We also use the previous technique to reduce the density and then, we show that we obtain quadratic and linear relations.

2   Backgrounds

2.1   Trivium Description

The stream cipher Trivium [4] has an internal state of 288 bit registers $s_1, \ldots, s_{288}$ and works with a 80-bit key $x_1, \ldots, x_{80}$ using a 80-bit initialization vector $v_1, \ldots, v_{80}$.

It has three non-linear feedback shift registers (NLFSR) which are updated in the following way after each of the 1152 rounds of initialization:

$$t_1 \leftarrow s_{66} + s_{93}$$
$$t_2 \leftarrow s_{162} + s_{177}$$
$$t_3 \leftarrow s_{243} + s_{288}$$
$$z_i \leftarrow t_1 + t_2 + t_3$$
$$t_1 \leftarrow t_1 + s_{91} \cdot s_{92} + s_{171}$$
$$t_2 \leftarrow t_2 + s_{175} \cdot s_{176} + s_{264}$$
$$t_3 \leftarrow t_3 + s_{286} \cdot s_{287} + s_{69}$$
$$(s_1, s_2, \ldots, s_{93}) \leftarrow (t_3, s_1, \ldots, s_{92})$$
$$(s_{94}, s_{95}, \ldots, s_{177}) \leftarrow (t_1, s_{94}, \ldots, s_{176})$$
$$(s_{178}, s_{279}, \ldots, s_{288}) \leftarrow (t_2, s_{178}, \ldots, s_{287})$$

During the initialization phase, the output bit z_i is discarded. Once this phase is over, $(z_i)_i$ is the generated stream of bits which will be added to the plaintext (Fig. 1).

Furthermore, we denote by *recursive expression of Trivium* the following equations:

$$\begin{cases} s_{1,r+1} = s_{243,r} + s_{288,r} + s_{286,r} \cdot s_{287,r} + s_{69,r} \\ s_{94,r+1} = s_{66,r} + s_{93,r} + s_{91,r} \cdot s_{92,r} + s_{171,r} \\ s_{178,r+1} = s_{162,r} + s_{177,r} + s_{175,r} \cdot s_{176,r} + s_{264,r} \end{cases}$$

Trivium was a candidate for the hardware profile of the eSTREAM competition. As such, it is designed to be implemented with a small number of gates and was not designed to be efficiently used in software applications. Even then, the

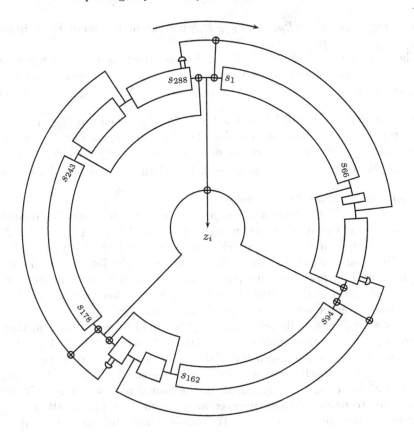

Fig. 1. The Trivium cipher.

standard software implementation is very efficient. Indeed, after being generated by the feedback function, a bit will not be used again for at least 64 rounds. This is used to compute 64 initialization rounds at once. As such, the registers only have to be updated $1152/64 = 18$ times during the initialization phase.

2.2 Cube Attacks

Given a cipher on secret bits and public bits, the cube attack, introduced by Shamir and Dinur in [7], allows one to find linear or low degree relations between key bits. Then using simple linear algebra or Grobner basis techniques, it is possible to recover the bit values. The following method is used, in particular in the easier case of linear relations:

Let $x_1, \ldots, x_n$ be the secret key bits and $v_1, \ldots, v_p$ the public bits (plaintext or initialization vector) under the attacker's control. In the ring $\mathcal{R} = \mathbb{F}_2[x_1, \ldots, x_n, v_1, \ldots, v_p]$, we consider the polynomial representation of the first output bit of the cipher as the polynomial $P(x_1, \ldots, x_n, v_1, \ldots, v_p)$ in $\mathcal{R}$. Given a subset ("cube") of the public variables $C = \{v_{c_1}, \ldots, v_{c_k}\}$ of size k, we write

P as $P = v_{c_1} \ldots v_{c_k} P_C + P_R$, $P_C, P_R \in R$, where no monomial of P_R is divisible by $v_{c_1} \ldots v_{c_k}$.

Then, given an assignment of the variables outside of C, summing P over every possible assignment of the variables of C will give the evaluation of the polynomial P_C on this assignment. In other words, $\sum_C P = P_C$ in $\mathcal{R}$. Indeed, every monomial of P_R will be summed with itself an even number of times in the process because at least one variable of C does not appear in said monomial. Meanwhile, $v_{c_1} \ldots v_{c_k}$ will be non-zero only once, when every variable of the cube is set to 1. We call P_C the *superpoly* yielded by C and $\prod_{i \in C} v_i$ is called a *maxterm* if the superpoly yielded by C is *linear*.

Therefore, if P has a *low-enough degree* d, even though it has a large number of variables, linear relations between key bits can be obtained by summing 2^{d-1} evaluations of the cipher. Once sufficient such linear relations have been found in an offline phase which has to be done only once, the linear system can be partially solved during the online phase. All it requires is the evaluation of all the cubes obtained in the offline phase for a specific unknown key. Finally, the full key can be recovered with a phase of offline brute-force.

However, if P is a uniformly random polynomial of high degree d, then it is extremely unlikely that there exists maxterms of size $k < d - 1$. Indeed, this would require every single monomial of degree at most $d - k$ to be linear.

Because the feedback function of Trivium as described in Sect. 2.1 has a single monomial of degree 2, the polynomials in the formal representation of Trivium are expected to retain a low degree even after hundreds of initialization rounds. Furthermore, the output function of Trivium is simply the sum of the values of 6 registers, which does not affect the degree at all.

This makes reduced versions of this cipher suitable targets for the cube attack. Indeed, even though the theoretical maximum degree is 160 (since there are 160 variables), linear expressions were yielded by cubes of size only 29 after 767 rounds. In the same fashion we have found cubes of size 30 yielding linear superpolys after 784 rounds and of size 32 after 799 rounds.

2.3   Moebius Transformation

In [8], Dinur and Shamir suggest using the Moebius transform as described in [9] to compute every single subcube of a large cube at once. Because this is such a powerful tool, we describe it and show some of the ways we used it to study the cube attacks on Trivium.

Let us consider the algebraic normal form of a polynomial $P \in \mathbb{F}_2[X]$, where $X = X_1, \ldots, X_n : P = \sum_{\sigma \in \{0,1\}^n} \alpha_\sigma X^\sigma$ with for all σ, $\alpha_\sigma \in \mathbb{F}_2$ and where $X^{\sigma_1 \ldots \sigma_n} = X_1^{\sigma_1} \ldots X_n^{\sigma_n}$.

Now the Moebius transform of P is the function $P^m : \begin{matrix} \{0,1\}^n \to \mathbb{F}_2 \\ \sigma \to \alpha_\sigma \end{matrix}$.

In other words, given the truth table of a boolean polynomial, the Moebius transform returns the truth table of a function indicating whether a given monomial is part of the polynomial. It is computed with the following simple algorithm (proof is provided in [9]).

The innermost loop is executed $\sum_{i=0}^{k-1} \frac{2^k}{2 \cdot 2^i} \cdot \sum_{j=0}^{2^i-1} 1 = \sum_{i=0}^{k-1} 2^{k-1} = k \cdot 2^{k-1}$ times,

yet it consists of a single assignment and an exclusive or operation. Besides, the 32-bit implementation presented in [9] performs roughly 32 times less operations. Similarly, we implemented a 128-bit version with a complexity of the order of $k \cdot 2^{k-7}$ operations.

Require: Input Truth table S of Boolean function P, with 2^k entries
    Variable Sz is the small table size
    Variable Pos is the small table position
    for $i = 0$ to $k - 1$ **do**
      Let $Sz \leftarrow 2^i$, $Pos \leftarrow 0$
      while $Pos < 2^k$ **do**
        for $j = 0$ to $Sz - 1$ **do**
          $S[Pos + Sz + j] \leftarrow S[Pos + j] \oplus S[Pos + Sz + j]$
        Let $Pos \leftarrow Pos + 2 \cdot Sz$
Output overwritten content of S containing Moebius transform

Now if we consider a cube $C = \{v_{c_1}, \ldots, v_{c_k}\}$ and the polynomial representation of a cipher $P(x_1, \ldots, x_n, v_1, \ldots, v_p) \in \mathcal{R}$, by fixing every variable outside C to some constant, we obtain a polynomial on the variables of C which we may call Q. Now $Q^m(\sigma_1, \ldots, \sigma_k)$ is the value of the superpoly yielded by $D = \{v_{c_i} | \sigma_i = 1\}$ when every variable of $C \setminus D$ is set to 0.

As it happens, a 128-bit implementation of the attack on r rounds can compute a cube of size k in $r \cdot 2^{k-7}$ calls to Trivium's round function, where $r \approx 800$ and $k \approx 40$. In this regard the computation of the Moebius transform, while still non-negligible, remained much faster than the computation of a single cube. Of course, because the full truth table has to be stored, a lot of memory may be required. Indeed, the computation of all subcubes of a cube of size k requires 2^k bits of memory.

3 An Attack on 784 Rounds of Trivium

In this section, we will describe a cube attack on Trivium up to 784 rounds. We will mainly explain how we manage to compute linear superpoly in an efficient manner.

3.1 Using the Moebius Transform to Improve the Cube Attack

In this section, we will describe how the Moebius Transform may improve the complexity of the cube search phase in the cube attacks.

Moebius Transform Is Interesting to Compute Polynomial Density.
An interesting application of the Moebius transform is the ability it gives us
to empirically measure the density of a black-box polynomial. Mainly we are
interested in checking up to which degree the polynomial can be considered
random (every monomial appears with probability $1/2$). However testing the
presence of a given monomial is an NP-hard problem [5]. With the Moebius
transform, we can however test many monomials at once and get an approximate
result with a single exponential computation.

We can choose a large cube of size k and create the truth table of the boolean
function of the k variables in the cube and returning the first bit produced by the
cipher. Applying the Moebius transform on this truth table, one can check how
many monomials of every degree less than k appear in this restricted polynomial.
Because $\binom{k}{d}$ becomes very large when d decreases (for $d \geq k/2$), this method
provides an accurate result. Of course since we restrict the polynomial to a
fraction of its variables (in Trivium's case, likely no more than 40 out of 160),
there is no guarantee that the full polynomial P would follow the same density
distribution. Still, a low density observed on monomials of a given degree on
those variables is a clear indicator that the polynomial can not be considered
random at this degree.

Tables 1, 2, 3 and 4 show some of the results obtained with this method for
randomly selected cubes.

Table 1. Observed polynomial density after 732 rounds

Monomial size	23	24	25	26	27	28
Density (%)	41.21	30.19	16.14	5.47	1.01	0

Table 2. Observed polynomial density after 768 rounds

Monomial size	25	26	27	28	29	30	31
Density (%)	49.14	46.95	42.34	34.49	21.84	6.21	0

Table 3. Observed polynomial density after 784 rounds

Monomial size	30	31	32	33	34	35	36	37	38
Density (%)	48.74	47.09	42.38	35.57	25.38	15.07	6.90	1.60	0

Table 4. Observed polynomial density after 799 rounds

Monomial size	33	34	35	36	37	38	39
Density for random cube (%)	49.89	49.55	48.25	44.19	34.07	16.47	3.66
Density for selected cube (%)	38.44	28.36	16.82	7.31	1.84	0.15	0

As can be observed, the degree up to which the cipher behaves like a random polynomial increases very quickly until it reaches the point where neither measurements nor cube computations can be done efficiently.

Moebius Transform Is Interesting to Test Polynomial Degree. Another obvious application of the transform is to simply realize the constant /linearity /degree 2 testing required in the attack and described in Sect. 4.1 on many cubes at once. Doing this, every linearity or degree 2 test has to be fully computed on the large cube before the test is applied. Because of this, it is not possible to optimize by aborting the computations on cubes that are clearly not linear. Still, using 2^{40} bits of memory (128 GB), one can compute $\binom{40}{35} = 658,008$ cubes of size 35 and $\binom{40}{36} = 91,390$ cubes of size 36 in only 2^{40} calls to Trivium, compared to about $658,008 \cdot 2^{35} + 91,390 \cdot 2^{36} > 2^{54}$ calls with straight up cube computations. Using a computer with 16 cores running at 2.67 GHz, the full computation takes about two hours.

Because one will naturally try to use a large cube as large as can fit in the computer's memory (the method gets considerably much better results when the large cube is much larger than the target size), it is not possible to store the cube values for every key needed for the test (over 50 keys, most likely). This is not likely to be an issue as there is little reason to store the values of subcubes with a small size. For instance, when computing on a large cube of size 40 after 800 rounds, the probability of finding a linear superpoly from a subcube of size 30 or less is negligible and $\sum_{i=31}^{40} \binom{40}{i} < 2^{29} \ll 2^{40}$.

Moebius Transform Is Interesting to Interpolate Polynomials. Once a maxterm has been found, the polynomial in question has to be interpolated. For Trivium, this typically requires 80 additional cube computations. If the search for maxterms was done through a Moebius transform, it is likely several cubes have been found at once. Depending on the number of cubes found and their sizes, it can be more profitable to interpolate them all at once through yet another Moebius transform on the smallest cube containing every maxterm studied. In most cases, this will be the original large cube.

3.2   Empirical Reduction of Density

The cube attacks described in [7] rely on the fact that the studied black-box polynomial has a low degree. However, as explained previously, even though the degree of polynomials in Trivium grows slowly, it is very likely it reaches 160 by the end of the 1152 initialization rounds. Studying the size of cubes required to find linear maxterms also shows that the degree reaches well over 40 after 800 initialization rounds and is likely to reach 80 by 900 initialization rounds, at which point the attack would be no better than brute force.

However, for a sparse enough polynomial, one can hope to find linear combinations of key bits even when monomials of much higher degree remain. This brings us to wonder how dense the polynomial representation of Trivium is. First, looking at the results presented in [7], one can see Trivium should not be considered a random polynomial. For such a polynomial, one would expect about half of the key bits to be present in linear terms, however most of them contain a single key bit, and none more than four. This leads us to believe that specific cubes of small size yielding very sparse low-degree polynomials coexist with large cubes yielding high-degree or dense polynomials. While the random walk described in [7] will detect the latter, we would be more interested in discovering the former.

To achieve this, let us look at the formal expression of the output bit of Trivium. It is the sum of 6 registers $s_{66} + s_{93} + s_{162} + s_{177} + s_{243} + s_{288}$ where each of these registers can be recursively expressed as a polynomial with a single degree 2 monomial. As such there are 12 registers involved in the high-degree part of the polynomial expression of the output bit.

Now we are looking for a maxterm c in the output polynomial P. Let us assume c has a size greater than the degree of the monomials outside the high-degree part of P. Then the polynomial yielded by c out of P is the sum of the 6 polynomials yielded by c out of the terms of degree 2, $P_{1,1}P_{1,2}, \ldots, P_{6,1}P_{6,2}$, in the recursive expression of P. If these polynomials are independent, it is unlikely their non linear monomials will cancel each other during the sum. As such, we also assume c is a maxterm for every $P_{i,1}P_{i,2}$. A sufficient condition for this property is that every partition $\{c_1, c_2\}$ of c is such that for all i the product of the polynomials yielded by c_1 out of $P_{i,1}$ and by c_2 out of $P_{i,2}$ when every variable of c is set to 1 is linear or constant.

This is the property we want to satisfy. Since in practice the maxterms tend to yield polynomials with only a couple monomials, it is to be expected that many such partitions will yield the zero polynomial on all 12 registers involved. Looking at it another way, this is an empirical reduction of the output polynomial's density by checking that its high-degree part is the product of low-density polynomials.

Once again, the search can be achieved with the Moebius transform [9]. After picking two disjoint large cubes, one can find many subcubes yielding the zero polynomial on all 12 coefficients. Now the disjoint union of two such subcubes is a candidate for the cube c.

This method does not directly produce very satisfying results, but the large number of cube candidates allows for further restrictions. The natural next step is to pick disjoint cubes c_1 and c_2 both of which have as many subcubes yielding the zero polynomial as possible. In practice, it is usually possible to find two disjoint cubes of size k such that each of their subcubes of size at least $k - 3$ yields the zero polynomial on all twelve registers involved. The union of c_1 and c_2 gives us a large cube on which to apply the Moebius transform to study its subcubes, many of which are candidates. As can be observed in Table 4, the reduction in density is notable and in return the number of maxterms detected in a single transform increased from an average of 83 to an average of 916 after

784 rounds. Similarly, after 799 rounds, the only way maxterms have been found was using this method and its drastic reduction of density.

3.3   Results on 784 Rounds

Using the heuristic explained in Sect. 3.2, notable reductions in polynomial density have been observed in practice. Mainly tests have been conducted on the version reduced to 784 rounds since a large cube of size 38 is sufficient to find linear superpoly and takes reasonable time to be computed. In such a situation, filtering the cubes only takes about 5 min while actual computation of a cube of size 38 takes about 30 min (28 h to fully complete a linearity test). Doing this, the density of monomials of size 34 falls from over 25 % to less than 10 %.

The Annex A contains the list of all 42 distinct key bits ("superpoly") which have been recovered after 784 rounds, along with the cubes yielding them. As can be observed, they are made of 30 to 33 indices and a lot of them are subsets of the same cube of size 38. One can also notice that every bit between x_{49} and x_{69} has been recovered, while none were found between x_{70} and x_{80}, suggesting that the mixing is not applied uniformly on the key. This is the same in the cubes found by Dinur and Shamir: they have all the bits between 54 and 67 and none between 70 and 80 for 735 rounds.

4   An Attack on 799 Rounds of Trivium

4.1   Testing Properties of Boolean Functions in a Black-Box Manner

Testing Constant and Linearity. The most common linearity test for polynomials is the Blum Luby Rubinfeld (BLR) test [3]. Given a black-box polynomial P on n variables one wants to test for linearity, the BLR test requires the computation on random inputs X_1 and X_2, two vectors of n bits, on the 0 vector and on $X_1 + X_2$. One then simply checks whether $P(X_1) + P(X_2) + P(0) = P(X_1 + X_2)$. The value of $P(0)$ can be computed once at the start but every subsequent test will require another 3 queries, each query in turn being the result of a cube computation in time 2^k where k is the size of the cube (in pratice, at least 30). What is more, most polynomials tested are very far from being linear and a weaker and faster version of the test could be used and still effectively detect non linear polynomials.

To achieve this, we simply pick at random r vector of bits $K_1, \ldots, K_r$ representing the keys, and test for every $r(r-1)/2$ pair of keys $\{K_i, K_j\}$ if the black-box polynomial yielded by a cube is such that $P(K_i) + P(K_j) + P(0) = P(K_i + K_j)$. This way, $r(r-1)/2$ linearity tests are done in merely $1 + r + r(r-1)/2 = r(r+1)/2 + 1$ queries instead of $1 + 3r(r-1)/2$. In practice, we chose $r = 10$ which brought the total number of queries to 56 instead of 136. To discard the non linear polynomials as soon as possible, linearity tests are conducted right when they become available. In other words, we test $P(0), P(K_1), P(K_2), P(K_1 + K_2), P(K_3), P(K_1 + K_3), P(K_2 + K_3)$, etc.

However most polynomials tested which are not of degree at least two are actually constant polynomials. As such, they would pass every single linearity test and waste a lot of time. We then arbitrarily decided to stop the tests if the polynomial returns the same value 20 times. In this case however, it is important to test all 10 different keys by the time the 20 tests are done. Otherwise, only 6 different random keys would be tested and with probability $1/64$ a linear, non constant superpoly would be discarded. Since we hope to find about 80 such superpolys, 10 independent random keys seem sufficient.

It is worth noting that there exist other linearity tests besides BLR which can detect with greater precision if a polynomial is not quite linear. However they are usually based on machine learning techniques and require a number of queries too high to be applied to cube attacks where a single query can take several hours of computation. Besides, an almost-linear superpoly is sufficient for the attack as it will return the correct value of a key bit in almost every case.

Testing Degree 2. The special case of testing for quadratic polynomials is a very interesting one. First, it is not very costly. The classical test consists in independently picking 3 random keys k_1, k_2 and k_3 and checking whether $P(0)+P(k_1)+P(k_2)+P(k_3)+P(k_1+k_2)+P(k_1+k_3)+P(k_2+k_3)+P(k_1+k_2+k_3) = 0$. However, because we have already queried on every sum of 2 random keys while testing the polynomial for linearity, the only unknown expression is $P(k_1 + k_2 + k_3)$. Thus we get a test for degree 2 with a single extra cube computation over the linearity test. Since the keys are not chosen independently, the test is a bit weaker than the theoretical one, but once again it is sufficient to discard most polynomials of higher degree.

In practice, with r initially picked random keys, it is then theoretically possible to realize $r(r-1)(r-2)/6$ tests of degree 2. For $r = 10$, this is 120 tests. Because this would be quite long, we decided to stop after 56 tests, mimicking the number of queries for the linearity test. In addition, polynomials of degree 2 are easy to exploit to directly obtain key bits values. Because of the general sparseness of the polynomials interpolated we can hope to find isolated monomials of degree 2 among monomials of lower degree. This would reveal two keys bits for a fourth of all keys, which is non negligible. Furthermore, if one of the two bits happens to be known through a linear expression, the value of the other one can be deduced for half of all possible keys.

Besides, when particular shapes arise (see Sect. 4.2 for details), it can become easy to find additional linear relations between the key bits. For instance, if $x_i \cdot x_{i+1} + x_{i+2} = \alpha$ and $x_{i+1} \cdot x_{i+2} + x_{i+3} = \beta$, $\alpha, \beta \in \mathbb{F}_2$, then $x_{i+1} \cdot x_i + \alpha x_{i+1} + x_{i+3} = \beta$ which yields $\alpha x_{i+1} + x_{i+2} + x_{i+3} = \alpha + \beta$.

4.2 Empirical Interpolation of Degree 2 Polynomials

First let us mention that there exist 2^n distinct polynomials on a given set of n monomials. Since every query to the black-box returns a binary information (0 or 1), one cannot hope to exactly interpolate a polynomial in less than n queries.

Thus, when trying to interpolate a polynomial P known to be linear on 80 variables, the best method should require no more than 81 requests. This is easily achieved by first querying the polynomial on the 0 key (thus getting the coefficient of the 1 monomial) and then on the key whose only non-zero value is x_i, for $i \in \{1, \ldots, 80\}$. If $P(0, \ldots, 0) = P(0, \ldots, 0, x_i, 0, \ldots, 0)$ then x_i's coefficient is 0 in P and 1 otherwise.

Similarly, one can interpolate a polynomial of degree 2 in $\sum_{i=0}^{2} \binom{80}{i} = 3241$ requests, which is optimal. The process simply consists in first checking the presence of all linear monomials as described before and then checking for every pair $\{x_i, x_j\}$ if $P(\{x_i, x_j\}) + P(x_i) + P(x_j) = P(0)$. The process can also be done for a higher degree d, but the number of queries grows exponentially and quickly becomes impractical.

It has however been observed in every single cube attack result brought forth so far that the interpolated linear polynomials tend to be very sparse, most of them containing a single key bit and none of them more than 5. If we make the assumption that a linear black-box polynomial is actually a dictator (a single key bit), it can easily be found in about $1 + \lceil log_2(80) \rceil = 7$ queries. However this is not very accurate and because 81 queries is still reasonable, it is better to avoid doing this.

Yet this becomes incredibly useful when interpolating polynomials of degree 2. In theory, interpolating a polynomial of degree 2 over 80 variables would require $80 \times 81/2 = 3240$ cube computations. This can still be achieved in reasonable time for cubes of size 30 (obtained after 784 rounds), and allowed us to formally interpolate dozens of them but becomes unreasonable for polynomials of size 34 and more (obtained after 800 rounds).

However, every such polynomial interpolated so far had a very specific shape. It contains a single monomial of degree 2 which is of the form $x_i \cdot x_{i+1}$ accompanied by the monomial of degree 1 x_{i+2}, and possibly some other monomials of degree 1. The same result can be observed on the polynomials obtained in [11] after 704 rounds. This behavior can easily be explained by noticing that polynomials of this shape appear in the very first rounds of Trivium (they are part of the feedback function). It then does not come as a surprise that they are the most likely candidates to appear in the sparsest part of the polynomial representation of the cipher.

Now if we assume the quadratic polynomial detected has this shape, we can easily interpolate it. Indeed, it suffices to test the presence of every linear monomial (81 cubes need to be computed) and for every one detected, test the presence of the associated monomial of degree 2 as described earlier (most likely less than 10 extra cube computations). Then one can check whether the interpolated polynomial actually matches the behavior of the superpoly on the already computed cubes during the linearity and degree 2 tests. This works very well in practice and out of dozens of such polynomials interpolated after 799 rounds, this process only failed on one of them.

4.3   Results on 799 Rounds

Annex B lists all the linear and quadratic polynomials yielded after 799 rounds. The 6 quadratic polynomials, which were chronologically found first as subcubes of a large cube of size 40, have themselves a size between 34 and 37. The 12 linear polynomials, which were found later in a low-density large cube also of size 40, have a size between 32 and 33. As 12 key bits can be directly recovered thanks to the maxterms in less than 2^{37} queries, a full key recovery is possible by adding a phase of 2^{68} brute-force queries. Furthermore, due to the simplistic nature of the 6 quadratic polynomials, which can be evaluated in less than 2^{40} queries, the key space to be brute-forced can be reduced to 2^{62} elements. Indeed, by choosing an assignment for every variable appearing in a quadratic expression but a linear one, the value of this linear variable becomes immediately known. Because all of the 6 quadratic polynomials discovered have at least one such distinct linear variable, the complexity is reduced by a factor of 2^6. In this regard, up to a certain point, quadratic polynomials provide as much information as linear ones.

5   Conclusion

We have used the Moebius transform to analyze the off-line complexity of cube attacks on Trivium. We propose a new technique to decrease the density of the polynomials in Trivium and using this technique we were able to find 42 linear relations between key bits after 784 rounds for the first time, providing the first full key recovery attack at 784 rounds, feasible in about 15 min on a regular computer. Besides, we have recovered 12 key bits and 6 quadratic relations after 799 rounds of initialization of Trivium. We also provided a method to empirically select cubes yielding low degree polynomials.

A   Key Bits Recovered After 784 Rounds

Cube indices	Superpoly
2,5,6,9,10,13,21,23,25,27,29,32,34,36,38,40,42,44,45,48,51,53,55,57,59,63,65,68,73,78	x_2
2,5,6,9,13,16,19,21,23,25,27,29,30,32,34,36,38,40,42,44,45,48,53,57,59,61,65,68,73,75,78	x_4
2,3,4,6,8,9,10,14,16,19,21,22,23,25,28,30,32,36,37,39,41,49,51,56,59,64,68,71,74,76,79	x_7+1
2,4,6,8,10,13,15,19,24,28,29,31,32,34,37,38,40,41,44,47,49,51,53,55,57,59,62,68,70,73,76,78	x_9
1,3,6,8,11,14,15,18,22,25,27,29,34,37,40,42,46,48,50,52,55,57,59,61,66,68,69,71,74,79	x_{11}
1,6,8,10,15,19,20,22,24,26,29,31,34,37,38,40,42,44,47,49,51,53,55,57,59,62,68,70,76,78	x_{19}
2,4,6,8,10,13,15,19,22,24,28,29,32,34,37,38,40,41,44,47,49,51,53,55,57,59,62,70,73,78	x_{20}
2,3,4,6,8,9,10,14,16,19,21,22,23,25,28,29,30,34,36,37,39,41,46,47,48,51,56,59,64,68,71,74,79	x_{21}
2,5,6,9,11,13,16,19,21,23,24,25,27,29,30,32,34,36,38,40,42,44,45,48,51,53,55,57,59,68,73	x_{22}
2,3,6,8,11,13,14,16,17,20,22,24,27,30,32,35,37,39,42,44,46,47,48,49,50,53,55,59,64,68,70,72,78	$x_{23}+x_{68}$

Cube indices	Expression
2,4,6,8,10,12,14,16,19,21,22,23,25,29,30,32,34,39,41,46,47,48,49,51,56,59,64,67,68,71,79	x_{24}
1,3,6,11,14,16,20,22,24,27,30,32,35,37,39,42,44,46,47,48,49,50,53,55,59,64,68,70,72,78	x_{25}
2,5,6,9,11,13,16,19,21,23,25,27,29,32,34,36,38,40,42,44,45,48,51,55,57,65,68,70,75,78	x_{26}
1,3,6,8,11,13,14,17,20,22,24,27,30,32,34,37,39,42,44,46,47,49,50,53,55,57,59,62,68,70,72,78	x_{35}
1,2,3,6,8,11,14,17,20,22,24,27,32,34,37,39,42,44,46,47,48,50,53,55,57,59,62,64,68,70,72	$x_{37}+1$
2,3,6,8,11,13,14,16,20,22,24,27,30,32,34,35,37,39,42,44,46,48,50,53,55,57,59,62,68,72,78	x_{38}
2,4,6,8,10,12,14,16,21,23,25,30,32,34,36,37,39,41,46,47,48,49,51,56,59,64,67,68,71,79	$x_{39}+1$
2,5,6,10,13,16,21,23,25,27,29,34,36,38,40,42,44,45,48,51,53,55,59,61,65,68,70,73,75,78	$x_{41}+1$
2,4,6,8,10,12,13,15,19,20,22,24,26,31,34,37,38,42,44,47,49,53,55,57,59,68,70,73,76,78	x_{43}
4,6,8,10,13,15,19,20,24,26,28,31,34,37,38,40,41,42,44,47,49,51,53,55,57,59,68,70,73,76,78	x_{44}
1,4,6,8,10,13,15,19,20,22,24,26,28,29,32,34,38,40,41,42,49,51,53,55,57,59,62,68,70,76,78	x_{47}
2,4,6,8,10,13,15,19,20,22,24,26,28,29,31,34,37,38,40,42,44,47,49,51,53,55,57,59,62,68,70,76,78	x_{49}
2,4,6,8,13,15,19,20,22,24,26,28,32,34,37,38,40,42,47,49,51,53,55,57,59,62,70,73,76,78	x_{50}
2,5,9,10,13,16,21,23,25,27,29,30,32,34,36,38,40,42,44,45,48,53,55,57,59,63,65,68,75,78	x_{51}
2,4,6,8,10,13,15,19,20,24,26,31,34,37,38,40,42,44,47,49,51,53,55,57,59,68,70,73,76,78	x_{52}
2,5,6,9,13,16,23,25,27,29,30,34,36,38,40,42,44,45,48,51,53,55,57,59,61,63,65,68,70,78	x_{53}
1,4,6,8,10,12,13,15,19,20,22,24,26,28,31,34,38,40,41,42,44,47,49,55,57,59,68,70,73,76,78	x_{54}
2,4,6,8,10,13,15,19,20,22,24,26,31,32,37,38,40,42,44,47,49,51,53,55,57,59,68,70,73,76,78	x_{55}
2,4,6,8,10,13,15,20,22,24,26,28,31,34,37,38,40,42,44,47,49,51,53,55,57,59,62,68,70,73,78	x_{56}
2,4,6,8,10,13,15,19,20,22,24,26,28,29,31,32,34,37,38,40,42,44,47,51,53,57,59,62,70,73,76,78	x_{57}
1,4,6,8,10,13,15,20,22,24,26,28,31,32,34,37,38,41,42,47,49,53,55,57,59,68,70,73,76,78	x_{58}
2,4,6,8,10,12,14,16,19,21,22,23,25,28,29,30,34,36,37,39,41,46,48,51,56,59,64,71,76,79	x_{59}
1,4,6,8,10,13,15,19,20,22,24,26,28,29,31,34,38,40,42,44,47,49,51,53,55,57,59,68,70,76,78	x_{60}
1,4,6,8,10,12,13,15,19,22,24,26,29,31,34,37,38,42,44,47,49,51,53,55,57,59,68,70,73,78	x_{61}
2,4,6,8,15,19,20,22,24,26,29,31,32,34,37,38,40,42,44,47,49,51,53,55,57,59,68,70,76,78	x_{62}
2,4,6,8,13,15,19,20,22,24,26,28,31,32,34,40,41,42,47,49,51,53,55,57,59,68,70,73,76,78	x_{63}
2,4,6,8,10,13,15,19,20,22,24,26,28,29,31,32,34,40,42,44,47,49,53,55,57,59,68,70,76,78	x_{64}
2,4,6,8,10,12,15,19,20,22,24,26,28,29,32,34,37,40,42,44,47,49,51,53,55,57,59,62,68,70,78	x_{65}
2,4,6,8,10,13,15,19,20,22,24,26,28,29,32,34,37,42,44,47,49,51,53,55,57,59,68,70,76,78	x_{66}
2,3,4,6,8,10,14,16,19,21,22,23,25,28,30,32,34,36,37,39,41,46,51,56,59,64,68,71,74,76,79	x_{67}
2,6,8,10,13,15,19,20,22,24,26,28,29,31,32,34,37,38,40,41,42,44,51,53,55,57,59,68,70,76,78	$x_{68}+1$
1,2,6,8,11,13,14,17,20,22,24,27,32,34,37,39,42,44,46,47,48,50,53,55,57,59,62,64,68,70,78	x_{69}

B   TExpressions Recovered After 799 Rounds

Cube indices	Expression
0,2,4,5,6,7,9,11,13,14,15,18,20,22,24,26,32,35,37, 39,42,44,46,48,53,55,57,61,68,70,72,79	x_{25}
0,2,4,5,6,7,9,11,13,14,15,18,20,22,24,26,32,35,39, 42,44,46,48,52,55,57,62,68,70,74,76,79	$x_{25}+x_{40}$
0,2,4,5,6,7,9,11,13,14,15,18,20,22,24,26,32,35,37, 39,42,44,46,48,52,53,55,57,61,62,68,70,79	x_{36}
0,2,4,5,7,9,11,13,14,15,18,20,24,26,30,32,35,37,39, 40,42,44,46,48,52,53,55,62,68,70,74,79	x_{38}
0,4,5,6,7,9,11,13,14,15,18,20,22,24,26,30,32,35,37, 39,40,44,46,48,52,55,57,62,68,70,74,79	x_{42}
0,4,5,6,7,9,11,13,14,18,20,22,24,26,30,35,37,39,40, 44,46,48,52,55,57,62,68,70,72,74,76,79	x_{53}
0,2,4,5,6,9,11,13,14,15,17,18,19,20,22,24,26,30,32, 35,39,40,44,48,53,55,57,61,62,70,74,76,79	x_{58}

0,5,6,7,9,11,13,17,19,22,24,26,30,32,35,37,39,42, 44,46,48,52,53,55,57,61,62,68,72,74,76,79	x_{60}
0,2,4,5,6,7,9,11,13,15,17,18,19,22,24,26,30,32,37, 39,42,44,46,52,53,57,61,62,68,74,76,79	x_{62}
0,4,5,7,9,11,13,14,15,17,18,19,20,22,24,26,30,32, 35,37,39,40,44,48,53,55,61,68,72,74,76,79	x_{64}
0,4,5,6,7,9,11,13,15,18,20,22,24,26,30,32,35,37,39, 40,42,44,46,48,55,57,62,68,70,72,76,79	x_{66}
0,4,5,6,7,9,11,13,14,15,17,19,22,24,26,32,35,37,39, 40,42,46,48,52,55,57,62,68,70,74,76,79	x_{67}
0,2,4,6,8,11,13,16,19,21,23,26,28,30,32,34,36,38,40, 42,44,46,49,50,53,56,62,64,69,72,74,75,77,79	$x_9 + x_{34}x_{35} + x_{36}$
0,2,4,6,8,11,13,16,19,21,23,26,28,30,32,34,36,38,40, 42,44,46,50,53,56,58,62,64,69,72,74,75,77,79	$x_{22} + x_{47}x_{48} + x_{49}$
0,2,4,6,8,11,13,16,19,21,23,26,28,30,32,34,36,38,40, 42,44,46,49,50,53,56,58,59,62,69,71,74,75,79	$x_{24} + x_{49}x_{50} + x_{51}$
0,2,4,6,8,11,13,16,19,21,23,28,30,32,34,36,38,40,42, 44,46,49,50,53,56,59,62,64,66,69,72,74,75,77,79	$x_{11} + x_{36}x_{37} + x_{38}$
0,2,4,6,8,11,13,16,19,21,23,26,28,32,34,36,38,40,42, 44,46,50,53,56,58,59,62,64,66,69,71,72,74,75,77,79	$x_{52} + x_{77}x_{78} + x_{79}$
0,2,4,6,8,11,13,16,19,21,23,26,28,32,34,36,38,40,42, 44,46,48,50,52,53,56,58,59,62,66,69,71,72,74,75,77,79	$x_9 + x_{34}x_{35} + x_{36} +$ $x_{61} + x_{17}x_{18} + x_{19}$

References

1. Alon, N., Kaufman, T., Krivelevich, M., Litsyn, S.N., Ron, D.: Testing low-degree polynomials over $GF(2)$. In: Arora, S., Jansen, K., Rolim, J.D.P., Sahai, A. (eds.) APPROX 2003 and RANDOM 2003. LNCS, vol. 2764, pp. 188–199. Springer, Heidelberg (2003)

2. Aumasson, J.-P., Dinur, I., Meier, W., Shamir, A.: Cube testers and key recovery attacks on reduced-round MD6 and trivium. In: Dunkelman, O. (ed.) FSE 2009. LNCS, vol. 5665, pp. 1–22. Springer, Heidelberg (2009)

3. Blum, M., Luby, M., Rubinfeld, R.: Self-testing/correcting with applications to numerical problems. In: Proceedings of the Twenty-Second Annual ACM Symposium on Theory of Computing, STOC '90, pp. 73–83. ACM, New York (1990)

4. De Cannière, C.: TRIVIUM: a stream cipher construction inspired by block cipher design principles. In: Katsikas, S.K., López, J., Backes, M., Gritzalis, S., Preneel, B. (eds.) ISC 2006. LNCS, vol. 4176, pp. 171–186. Springer, Heidelberg (2006)

5. Chen, Z., Fu, B.: The complexity of testing monomials in multivariate polynomials. In: Wang, W., Zhu, X., Du, D.-Z. (eds.) COCOA 2011. LNCS, vol. 6831, pp. 1–15. Springer, Heidelberg (2011)

6. Crowley, P.: Trivium, sse2, corepy, and the gcube attackh (2008)

7. Dinur, I., Shamir, A.: Cube attacks on tweakable black box polynomials. In: Joux, A. (ed.) EUROCRYPT 2009. LNCS, vol. 5479, pp. 278–299. Springer, Heidelberg (2009)

8. Dinur, I., Shamir, A.: Breaking grain-128 with dynamic cube attacks. In: Joux, A. (ed.) FSE 2011. LNCS, vol. 6733, pp. 167–187. Springer, Heidelberg (2011)

9. Joux, A.: Algorithmic Cryptanalysis, 1st edn. Chapman & Hall/CRC, Boca Raton (2009)

10. Knellwolf, S., Meier, W., Naya-Plasencia, M.: Conditional differential cryptanalysis of NLFSR-based cryptosystems. In: Abe, M. (ed.) ASIACRYPT 2010. LNCS, vol. 6477, pp. 130–145. Springer, Heidelberg (2010)
11. Mroczkowski, P., Szmidt, J.: The cube attack on stream cipher trivium and quadraticity tests. Fundam. Inform. 114(3–4), 309–318 (2012)
12. Vielhaber, M.: Breaking one.fivium by aida an algebraic iv differential attack. Cryptology ePrint Archive, Report 2007/413, (2007). http://eprint.iacr.org/

Near Collision Attack on the Grain v1 Stream Cipher

Bin Zhang[1]($\boxtimes$), Zhenqi Li[2]($\boxtimes$), Dengguo Feng[2], and Dongdai Lin[1]

[1] State Key Laboratory of Information Security, IIE,
Chinese Academy of Sciences, Beijing 100093, China
[2] IOS, Chinese Academy of Sciences, Beijing 100190, China
{zhangbin,lizhenqi}@is.iscas.ac.cn

Abstract. Grain v1 is one of the 7 finalists selected in the final portfolio by the eSTREAM project. It has an elegant and compact structure, especially suitable for a constrained hardware environment. Though a number of potential weaknesses have been identified, no key recovery attack on the original design in the single key model has been found yet. In this paper, we propose a key recovery attack, called near collision attack, on Grain v1. The attack utilizes the compact NFSR-LFSR combined structure of Grain v1 and works even if all of the previous identified weaknesses have been sewed and if a perfect key/IV initialization algorithm is adopted. Our idea is to identify near collisions of the internal states at different time instants and restore the states accordingly. Combined with the BSW sampling and the non-uniform distribution of internal state differences for a fixed keystream difference, our attack has been verified on a reduced version of Grain v1 in experiments. An extrapolation of the results under some assumption indicates an attack on Grain v1 for any fixed IV in $2^{71.4}$ cipher ticks after the pre-computation of $2^{73.1}$ ticks, given $2^{62.8}$-bit memory and $2^{67.8}$ keystream bits, which is the best key recovery attack against Grain v1 so far. Hopefully, it provides some new insights on such compact stream ciphers.

Keywords: Stream ciphers · Cryptanalysis · Grain · Near collision

1 Introduction

Grain v1, designed by Hell et al. [13], is a stream cipher for restricted hardware environments. It uses 80-bit key and 64-bit IV and consists of two combined registers, one NFSR and one LFSR, filtered together by a non-linear function.

This work was supported by the National Grand Fundamental Research 973 Program of China (Grant No. 2013CB338002), the Strategic Priority Research Program of the Chinese Academy of Sciences (Grant No. XDA06010701), IIE's Research Project on Cryptography (Grant No. Y3Z0016102) and the programs of the National Natural Science Foundation of China (Grant No. 60833008, 60603018, 61173134, 91118006, 61272476).

S. Moriai (Ed.): FSE 2013, LNCS 8424, pp. 518–538, 2014.
DOI: 10.1007/978-3-662-43933-3_27, © Springer-Verlag Berlin Heidelberg 2014

During the eSTREAM competition, Grain v1 has successfully withstood huge cryptanalytic efforts and in April 2008, it was selected into the final portfolio by the eSTREAM project, as it has pushed the state of the art of stream ciphers in terms of compact implementation [10].

Grain v1 has a compact structure with carefully chosen tap positions, feedback functions and output function. The feedback function of NFSR and the filter function are chosen in such a way that the correlation [3] and distinguishing attacks [16] on the former version, Grain v0, have been made impossible in time faster than exhaustive search. The companion cipher, Grain-128 [14], is designed in a similar way except that the feedback function is of low algebraic degree (a property not in Grain v1), which results in distinguishing attacks [2,18], an algebraic attack of a modified version [4] and a dynamic cube attack of full initialization rounds [8,9] and a new version, Grain-128a [15], with optional authentication. In [7], a slide property in the initialization phase was discovered, which can be used to reduce by half the cost of exhaustive key search for a fixed IV and to mount related-key chosen IV attacks [7,17] against Grain v1 and Grain-128.

In this paper, we propose a new key recovery attack, called near collision attack, on Grain v1. The attack utilizes the compact NFSR-LFSR combined structure of Grain v1 and works even if all of the previous identified weaknesses have been sewed and if a perfect key/IV initialization algorithm is adopted, e.g., the slide property does not exist any more and there are a sufficiently large number of initialization rounds. It is observed that the NFSR and LFSR are of length exactly 80-bit (the same as the key length, with no redundancy) and the LFSR updates independently in the keystream generation phase. Further, if the 160-bit internal states at two different time instants differ in only a small number of positions, the output keystreams they generate will be similar to each other. In fact, the keystream segment differences in this case can not take all the possible values, i.e., there are lots of impossible keystream segment differences and even for the possible differences, the distribution is heavily non-uniform. Some differences occur with very high probability, while others do not. This is due to the fact that for some keystream segment differences, there are many low weight internal state differences that can cause them. Based on the near match generalization of the birthday paradox, such near collisions of the internal states do exist given enough keystream and the problem is how to explicitly and efficiently identify them.

We develop an approach to detect such near collision internal states and the basic attack is called NCA-1.0[1]. Combined with BSW sampling, an enhanced attack, NCA-2.0, is proposed and it can reduce the attack complexity compared to NCA-1.0. We further improve it to NCA-3.0 by utilizing the heavily non-uniform distribution of the internal state differences for a fixed keystream difference. Then our attack has been launched and verified on a reduced version of Grain v1 with 32-bit LFSR and 32-bit NFSR. An extrapolation of the results under some reasonable assumption indicates an attack on Grain v1 for any fixed

---

[1] Near collision attack version 1.0.

Table 1. The attack complexity

Attack model	Pre-computation time	Data	Memory	Time
NCA-1.0	$2^{95.7}$	$2^{45.8}$	$2^{78.6}$	$2^{85.9}$
NCA-2.0	$2^{83.4}$	2^{62}	$2^{65.9}$	$2^{76.1}$
NCA-3.0	$2^{73.1}$	$2^{67.8}$	$2^{62.8}$	$2^{71.4}$

IV in $2^{71.4}$ cipher ticks after the pre-computation of $2^{73.1}$ ticks, given $2^{62.8}$-bit memory and $2^{67.8}$ keystream bits. This is the best key recovery attack against Grain v1 so far[2]. The results of all the NCA attacks are summarized in the following table. Our attack is just a starting point for further analysis of Grain-like stream ciphers and hopefully it provides some new insights on the design of such compact stream ciphers.

This paper is structured as follows. Some notations and preliminaries are given in Sect. 2. Then, some key observations used in our attack and the description of Grain v1 are presented in Sect. 3. The general attack model and its complexity analysis are formalized in Sect. 4. The NCA-2.0 based on BSW sampling resistance is given in Sect. 5 and the NCA-3.0 based on the non-uniform distribution of keystream segment differences is presented in Sect. 6, respectively. The basis simulation results on the reduced version of Grain is provided in Sect. 7. Finally, we conclude in Sect. 8.

2   Notations and Preliminaries

In this section, we give a brief description of Grain[3] and propose some lemmas that we will use. The following notations are used throughout the paper.

- $w_H(\cdot)$: the Hamming weight function, output the number of 1s in the binary representation of the input argument.
- d: the maximum Hamming weight of the internal state difference.
- l: the length of the keystream segment, measured in bit.
- n: the length of the internal state, measured in bit.
- Δs: the internal state difference.
- $V(n, d)$: the total number of the internal state differences with $w_H(\Delta s) \le d$.
- $Q(n, d, l)$: the total number of all the possible keystream segment differences, while traversing all the $V(n, d)$ internal state differences.
- $R(n, d, l)$: the average number of the internal state differences, corresponding to a fixed keystream segment difference.
- B_d: the set of the internal state differences with $\Delta s \in B_d$ and $w_H(\Delta s) \le d$.
- $I_{\Delta s}$: the set of the difference position indexes of Δs. The difference position indexes range from 0 to 159, corresponding to $n_0, n_1, \ldots, n_{79}, l_0, l_1, \ldots, l_{79}$.
- P: the pre-computation time complexity.

---

[2] We give a rigorous analysis on the time complexity of the brute force attack on Grain v1 in Sect. 3.3 and find that the actual complexity is $2^{87.4}$ cipher ticks, which is higher than 2^{80} ticks.

[3] We use Grain to denote Grain v1 hereafter.

- T: the on-line time complexity.
- M: the memory requirement.
- D: the data complexity.
- Ω: the number of CPU clock cycles to generate one bit keystream in software.

It is easy to see that[4] $B_d = \{\Delta s \in \mathbb{F}_2^n | w_H(\Delta s) \le d\} = \{\Delta s_1, \Delta s_2, \dots, \Delta s_{V(n,d)}\}$ and $|B_d| = V(n,d) = \sum_{i=0}^{d} \binom{n}{i}$. The definition of d-near-collision for two binary strings is as follows.

Definition 1. *Two n-bit strings s, s' are d-near-collision, if $w_H(s \oplus s') \le d$.*

Similar to the birthday paradox, which states that two random subsets of a space with 2^n elements are expected to intersect when the product of their sizes exceeds 2^n, we present the following lemma of d-near-collision.

Lemma 1. *Given two random subsets A, B of a space with 2^n elements, then there exists a pair (a, b) with $a \in A$ and $b \in B$ that is an d-near-collision if*

$$|A| \cdot |B| \ge \frac{2^n}{V(n,d)} \tag{1}$$

holds, where $|A|$ and $|B|$ are the size of A and B respectively.

Proof. Let $A = \{a_1, a_2, \dots, a_{|A|}\}$ and $B = \{b_1, b_2, \dots, b_{|B|}\}$. Each $a_i \in A$, $b_j \in B$ are uniformly random variables with values in $\mathbb{F}_2^n$. Consider the random variables $w_H(a_i \oplus b_j)$ and let ϕ be the characteristic function of the event $w_H(a_i \oplus b_j) \le d$, that is,

$$\phi(w_H(a_i \oplus b_j) \le d) = \begin{cases} 1 & \text{if } w_H(a_i \oplus b_j) \le d \\ 0 & \text{otherwise.} \end{cases}$$

For $1 \le i \le |A|$, $1 \le j \le |B|$, we consider the number $N_{A,B}(d)$ of pairs (a_i, b_j) satisfying $w_H(a_i \oplus b_j) \le d$ (the number of d-near-collisions): $N_{A,B}(d) = \sum_{i=1}^{|A|} \sum_{j=1}^{|B|} \phi(w_H(a_i \oplus b_j) \le d)$. The expected value of $N_{A,B}(d)$ of pairwise-independent random variables can be computed as $E(N_{A,B}(d)) = |A| \cdot |B| \cdot \frac{V(n,d)}{2^n}$. Therefore, if we choose the size of A and B satisfying Eq. (1), the expected number of d-near-collisions pairs is at least 1. □

If $d = 0$, then $V(n, d) = 1$ and Lemma 1 reduces to the common collision, otherwise the data required of finding a d-near-collision is much less than that of finding a complete collision. If $|A| \cdot |B| = 2^n / V(n, d)$, then the probability to find a d-near-collision is about 50 %. If $|A| \cdot |B| = 3 \cdot 2^n / V(n, d)$, then the probability to find a d-near-collision is larger than 98 %.

2.1   Grain-v1

Grain-v1 is one of the 7 finalists selected in the final portfolio by the eSTREAM project. It is a bit-oriented stream cipher taking an 80-bit key and a 64-bit IV.

---

[4] $|\cdot|$ denotes the cardinality of a set.

The cipher consists of a pair of linked 80-bit shift registers, one is linear feedback shift register (LFSR) and another is non-linear feedback shift register (NFSR), denoted as $\{l_i, l_{i+1}, \ldots, l_{i+79}\}$ and $\{n_i, n_{i+1}, \ldots, n_{i+79}\}$ respectively. The update function of the LFSR is $l_{i+80} = l_{i+62} + l_{i+51} + l_{i+38} + l_{i+23} + l_{i+13} + l_i$ and the update function of the NFSR is

$$
\begin{aligned}
n_{i+80} = {} & l_i + n_{i+62} + n_{i+60} + n_{i+52} + n_{i+45} + n_{i+37} + n_{i+33} + n_{i+28} + n_{i+21} \\
& + n_{i+14} + n_{i+9} + n_i + n_{i+63}n_{i+60} + n_{i+37}n_{i+33} + n_{i+15}n_{i+9} \\
& + n_{i+60}n_{i+52}n_{i+45} + n_{i+33}n_{i+28}n_{i+21} + n_{i+63}n_{i+45}n_{i+28}n_{i+9} \\
& + n_{i+60}n_{i+52}n_{i+37}n_{i+33} + n_{i+63}n_{i+60}n_{i+21}n_{i+15} \\
& + n_{i+63}n_{i+60}n_{i+52}n_{i+45}n_{i+37} + n_{i+33}n_{i+28}n_{i+21}n_{i+15}n_{i+9} \\
& + n_{i+52}n_{i+45}n_{i+37}n_{i+33}n_{i+28}n_{i+21}.
\end{aligned}
$$

During keystream generation phase, shown in Fig. 1, the output bit z_i is filtered by a non-linear function $h(x)$, which is balanced and correlation immune of the first order, defined as follows.

$$
\begin{aligned}
h(x) = {} & x_1 + x_4 + x_0x_3 + x_2x_3 + x_3x_4 + x_0x_1x_2 + x_0x_2x_3 + x_0x_2x_4 \\
& + x_1x_2x_4 + x_2x_3x_4,
\end{aligned}
$$

where the variables x_0, x_1, x_2, x_3 and x_4 correspond to the tap positions l_{i+3}, $l_{i+25}, l_{i+46}, l_{i+64}$ and n_{i+63} respectively. The output function is taken as $z_i = \sum_{k\in\mathcal{A}} n_{i+k} + h(l_{i+3}, l_{i+25}, l_{i+46}, l_{i+64}, n_{i+63})$, where $\mathcal{A} = \{1, 2, 4, 10, 31, 43, 56\}$.

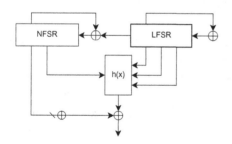   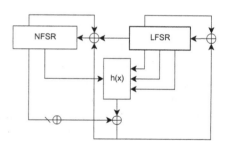

Fig. 1. Keystream generation mode   **Fig. 2.** Initialization mode

Let the bits of the key be k_i, $0 \le i \le 79$ and the bits of the IV be IV_i, $0 \le i \le 63$. In the initialization phase, shown in Fig. 2, first load the NFSR with the key bits, $n_i = k_i$, $0 \le i \le 79$, then load the first 64 bits of the LFSR with the IV, $s_i = IV_i$, $0 \le i \le 63$. The remaining bits of the LFSR are filled with ones, i.e., $s_i = 1$, $64 \le i \le 79$. Then the cipher is clocked 160 times without producing any keystream bit. Instead the output function is fed back and xored with the input, both to the LFSR and to the NFSR.

3   Some Key Observations

We start with some key observations used in our attacks. More technical descriptions of the various steps will be provided in the next sections.

3.1   State Recovery with Known State Difference

According to NFSR-LFSR combined structure of Grain, the internal states at two different time instants can be recovered in a reasonable time if we know the state difference. More precisely, during the keystream generation phase, we denote the LFSR state as $L^{t_1} = (l_0^{t_1}, l_1^{t_1}, \ldots, l_{79}^{t_1})$ at time t_1 and $L^{t_2} = (l_0^{t_2}, l_1^{t_2}, \ldots, l_{79}^{t_2})$ at time t_2 $(0 \leq t_1 < t_2)$.

Suppose that we know the difference $\Delta L = (l_0^{t_1} \oplus l_0^{t_2}, \ldots, l_{79}^{t_1} \oplus l_{79}^{t_2}) = (\Delta l_0, \Delta l_1, \ldots, \Delta l_{79})$ with the time interval $\Delta t = t_2 - t_1$. Since the LFSR is clocked independently (never affected by the NFSR or the keystream bits) in the keystream generation phase of Grain, each $l_i^{t_2}$ in L^{t_2} can thus be linearly expressed by the variables in L^{t_1}:

$$\begin{cases} l_0^{t_2} = c_0^0 l_0^{t_1} + c_1^0 l_1^{t_1} + \cdots + c_{79}^0 l_{79}^{t_1} \\ l_1^{t_2} = c_0^1 l_0^{t_1} + c_1^1 l_1^{t_1} + \cdots + c_{79}^1 l_{79}^{t_1} \\ \quad \vdots \\ l_{79}^{t_2} = c_0^{79} l_0^{t_1} + c_1^{79} l_1^{t_1} + \cdots + c_{79}^{79} l_{79}^{t_1}, \end{cases}$$

where c_i^j, $0 \leq i, j \leq 79$ can be pre-computed according to Δt and the update function of the LFSR, not depending on t_1 and t_2. Combined with ΔL, we can easily derive the following linear system.

$$\begin{cases} \Delta l_0 = l_0^{t_2} \oplus l_0^{t_1} = (c_0^0 + 1) l_0^{t_1} + c_1^0 l_1^{t_1} + \cdots + c_{79}^0 l_{79}^{t_1} \\ \Delta l_1 = l_1^{t_2} \oplus l_1^{t_1} = c_0^1 l_0^{t_1} + (c_1^1 + 1) l_1^{t_1} + \cdots + c_{79}^1 l_{79}^{t_1} \\ \quad \vdots \\ \Delta l_{79} = l_{79}^{t_2} \oplus l_{79}^{t_1} = c_0^{79} l_0^{t_1} + c_1^{79} l_1^{t_1} + \cdots + (c_{79}^{79} + 1) l_{79}^{t_1}. \end{cases} \quad (2)$$

Variables in L^{t_1} can then be determined by solving (2), which means that we can obtain the internal state of LFSR at t_1. The time complexity of this step is upper bounded by $T_L \approx 2^{18.9}$ basic operations [19]. Suppose one basic operation needs one CPU cycle, then according to Appendix C that one tick of Grain needs $2^{10.4}$ CPU clock cycles, hence $T_L = 2^{18.9}/2^{10.4} = 2^{8.5}$ cipher ticks in software.

The next step is to recover the NFSR state at t_1. This process can be found in Appendix A. The time complexity of this phase is upper bounded by $T_N = 2^{20.3}$ cipher ticks. The key can then be easily recovered by the running internal state at t_1 backward. To sum up, given the internal state difference with the time interval, the time complexity to retrieve the internal state is $T_K = T_L + T_N = 2^{20.3}$ cipher ticks.

3.2   The Distribution of the Keystream Segment Differences

The second observation is that the distribution of keystream segment differences (KSDs) is heavily biased, given a specific internal state differential (ISD).

Table 2. The distribution of KSDs

ISD	KSD	Proportion (%)	ISD	KSD	Proportion (%)
Δs_1	0xa120	49.4	Δs_4	0x0000	52.0
	0xe120	50.6		0x0080	48.0
Δs_2	0x0000	12.9	Δs_3	0x0001	13.2
	0x0001	13.8		0x0201	12.1
	0x2000	38.3		0x0801	37.2
	0x2001	35.1		0x0a01	37.5

For instance, we choose $d = 4$, $l = 16$, $I_{\Delta s_1} = \{9, 31, 39, 69\}$[5], $I_{\Delta s_2} = \{99, 121, 134, 149\}$[6], $I_{\Delta s_3} = \{29, 64, 101, 147\}$[7] and $I_{\Delta s_4} = \{20, 26, 53, 141\}$[8]. Then we randomly choose 10^4 internal states, calculate the companion states by adding Δs_1, Δs_2, Δs_3, Δs_4 and generate the corresponding KSDs for Δs_1, Δs_2, Δs_3 and Δs_4 in Table 2.

From Table 2, there are only 2 values of KSD, each occurred with proportion close to $1/2$ for Δs_1 and Δs_4 respectively. There are 4 values of KSD with varying proportions for Δs_2 and Δs_3 respectively, e.g., if the ISD is Δs_2, then 38.3% KSDs are 0x2000. We also test other ISDs with different d and l, the results are similar to Table 2.

In many cases, there exists some impossible KSDs when d and l are fixed. To illustrate this, given $1 \leq d \leq 4, l \in \{8, 16, 24, 32\}$, we enumerated each $\Delta s \in B_d$ and count the number of $Q(n, d, l)$ for all the possible ISDs in B_d. The results show that there exists some impossible differences for most of (d, l) pairs. Thus the value of $Q(n, d, l)$ can be estimated as $2^{l-\gamma}$ where 2^γ is the number of impossible differences, e.g., for $(d, l) = (3, 24)$, $\gamma = 4.7$. Even for the possible differences, the distribution is non-uniform, which causes some entropy leakage as well. These features can be further utilized to enhance our attack.

3.3   Complexity of the Brute Force Attack

The third observation is that the complexity of brute force attack is higher than 2^{80} ticks and such an attack can only be mounted for each fixed IV, while our attack can be applied to the scenario with arbitrary IVs.

As a baseline, we analyzed the time complexity of the brute force attack on Grain. Given a known fixed IV and a 80-bit keystream segment w, generated by (K, IV) pair, the goal is to recover K using the exhaustive search strategy.

For each enumerated k_i, $1 \leq i \leq 2^{80} - 1$, the attacker first needs to proceed the initialization phase which needs 160 ticks. During the keystream generation phase, once a keystream bit is generated, the attacker compares it to the corresponding bit in w. If they are equal, the attacker continue to generate the

---

[5] $\Delta s_1 = $ 0x0002008080000000200000000000000000000000.

[6] $\Delta s_2 = $ 0x0000000000000000000000080000000240002000.

[7] $\Delta s_3 = $ 0x0000002000000000001000000200000000000800.

[8] $\Delta s_4 = $ 0x0000100400002000000000000000000000200000.

next keystream bit and do the comparison. If not, the attacker search another key and repeat the previous steps. If each keystream bit is treated as a random independent variable, then for each k_i, the probability that the attacker need to generate l $(1 \leq l \leq 80)$ bits keystream is 1 for $l = 1$ and $2^{-(l-1)}$ for $l > 1$, which means that the previous $l - 1$ bits are equal to the counter bits in w. Let N_w be the expected number of bits needed to generate for each enumerated key, which is $N_w = \sum_{l=1}^{80} l \cdot P_l = \sum_{l=1}^{80} l \cdot 2^{-(l-1)} \approx 4$. Then, the total time complexity is $(2^{80} - 1) \cdot (160 + 4) \approx 2^{87.4}$ cipher ticks.

4 The General Attack Model

In this section, we will give a general description of our attack model. From Sect. 3.1, it is easy to recover the internal state by utilizing the known ISD and the time interval, thus the main concern is to retrieve the ISD derived from the two d-near-collision internal states. Our attack consists of two phases, i.e., an off-line stage only performed once followed by an on-line stage.

4.1 Off-line Stage

In the off-line stage, some well structured differential tables are pre-computed. Given l and d, we enumerated the $V(n, d)$ different ISDs in B_d and generate their corresponding KSDs with proportions. In total, $Q(n, d, l)$ different tables will be constructed and indexed with KSD. The ISDs with the proportions, which will generate the indexed KSD, will be stored in each KSD table. For example, following Table 2 in Sect. 3.2, Δs_2 together with the proportion 12.9 % will be stored in one line of table-0x0000 and Δs_4 together with the proportion 52.0 % will also be saved in another line of table-0x0000. The table structure can be illustrated as follows.

$$\text{table} - \text{0x0000} \begin{cases} \Delta s_4 & 52.0\,\% \\ \Delta s_2 & 12.9\,\% \\ \vdots \end{cases} \quad \text{table} - \text{0x0001} \begin{cases} \Delta s_2 & 13.8\,\% \\ \Delta s_3 & 13.2\,\% \\ \vdots \end{cases} \quad \dots$$

$$\text{table} - \text{0x0080} \begin{cases} \Delta s_4 & 48.0\,\% \\ \vdots \end{cases} \quad \dots$$

The total number of tables is $Q(n, d, l)$ and the average number of rows in each table is $R(n, d, l)$. Due to the non-uniform distribution of the KSDs for a fixed ISD, we only consider at most 100 KSDs whose proportions are the first 100 largest among all the KSDs, then each ISD will be stored in at most 100 different KSD tables. Hence $R(n, d, l)$ is upper bounded by $100 \cdot V(n, d)/Q(n, d, l)$. The memory requirement is thus $M_1 = Q(n, d, l) \cdot R(n, d, l) = V(n, d) \cdot 2^{6.6}$ entries, each containing $n + \delta$ bits where δ is used to store the proportion and $\delta = 7$ bits[9].

---

[9] We use a 7-bit string to store the percentage number, e.g., for 67 %, we only store binary representation of 67 (67 < 128).

We sort each table with respect to the values of those proportions so that the ISD with the maximum proportion will appear in the first row. All the tables will be sorted with respect to their KSD indexes. Let N be the sampling number of the random internal states when determining the projection from ISD to KSD, then we have $P = 2 \cdot N \cdot V(n, d) \cdot l$ cipher ticks.

4.2   On-line Stage

Now we discuss how to obtain the ISD by utilizing the pre-computed tables and the truncated keystreams. Let the length of the keystream segment be $\hat{l} = l + \beta$, where β is the length of the keystream suffix used for verification. The on-line stage contains the following steps:

Step 1. We randomly collect two keystream segments sets A and B, each element $a_i \in A$, $b_j \in B$ of which is $\hat{l}$-bit. Let $a_i^{[l]}$ and $b_j^{[l]}$ denote the first l bits of the keystream segments and the time instants for each $a_i^{[l]}$ and $b_j^{[l]}$ are also recorded. Let s_i^A and s_j^B be the internal states corresponding to $a_i^{[l]}$ and $b_j^{[l]}$ respectively, from Lemma 1, in order to assure that there exists at least one pair (s_i^A, s_j^B) so that $s_i^A \oplus s_j^B \in B_d$, it is required that $|A| \cdot |B| \geq 2^n / V(n, d)$.

Step 2. We sort A and B with respect to the value of the first l bits and divide A, B into m different groups $G_1^A, G_2^A, \ldots, G_m^A$ and $G_1^B, G_2^B, \ldots, G_m^B$ respectively. The keysream segments in A (B) with the same $a_i^{[l]}$ ($b_j^{[l]}$) will be put into the same group with the index $a_i^{[l]}$ ($b_j^{[l]}$). The size of each group can be estimated as $|G_i^A| = |A|/2^l$, $|G_i^B| = |B|/2^l$, $1 \leq i \leq m$. Note that if $|A| \geq 2^l$, then $m = 2^l$. If $|A| < 2^l$, then there may be some empty groups and we define $m = |A|$. The sorting time is $T_1 = |A| \cdot \log |A| + |B| \cdot \log |B|$ comparisons.

Step 3. Now we need to identify the candidate (s_i^A, s_j^B) pairs that is d-near-collision. Denote the $Q(n, d, l)$ different KSDs in the off-line stage by $W = \{w_1, w_2, \ldots, w_{Q(n,d,l)}\}$ where each w_k, $1 \leq k \leq Q(n, d, l)$ is of l-bit lengths. For each $w_k \in W$, we need to find all the pairs $(a_i^{[l]}, b_j^{[l]})$ satisfying $a_i^{[l]} \oplus b_j^{[l]} = w_k$. There are two strategies to achieve this goal:

Strategy I. For each $w_k \in W$, we xor it to each group index of G_i^A in A and get A^*. If there is one group $G_i^{A^*}$ with the group index same as the index of another group G_i^B in B, then we get $a_p^{[l]} \oplus b_q^{[l]} = w_k$ for any $1 \leq p \leq |G_i^{A^*}|$ and $1 \leq q \leq |G_i^B|$, for if we xor w_k to each $a_p^{[l]} \in G_j^{A^*}$ and get $a_p^{[l]^*} = a_p^{[l]} \oplus w_k$, then any $(a_p^{[l]^*}, b_q^{[l]})$ pair is a match satisfying $a_p^{[l]^*} = a_p^{[l]} \oplus w_k = b_q^{[l]}$, see Fig. 3. The time complexity is $T_2^I = Q(n, d, l) \cdot m \cdot \log m$ comparisons.

Strategy II. For each G_i^A in A, we xor its index to each index of G_j^B in B (get B^*) and search a match in the sorted $W = \{w_1, w_2, \ldots, w_{Q(n,d,l)}\}$. If a match $w_k \in W$ is found, then we have $(a_p^{[l]}, b_q^{[l]})$ satisfying $a_p^{[l]} \oplus b_q^{[l]} = w_k$ with $a_p^{[l]} \in G_i^A, b_q^{[l]} \in G_j^B$, see Fig. 4. The time complexity is $T_2^{II} = m \cdot m \cdot \log Q(n, d, l)$ comparisons.

The time complexity of Step 3 is $T_2 = min\{T_2^I, T_2^{II}\}$.

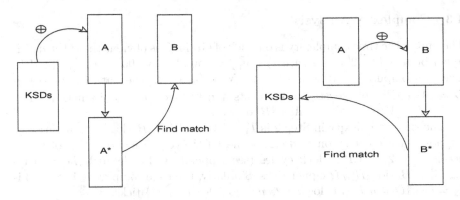

Fig. 3. Strategy I   **Fig. 4.** Strategy II

Step 4. From the previous steps, if we choose Strategy I in step 3, then for each w_i, there are at most $C_{w_i} = 2^l \cdot |G_j^A| \cdot |G_j^B| = |A| \cdot |B|/2^l$ matches, thus the total number of matches is at most $C = C_{w_i} \cdot Q(n,d,l) = Q(n,d,l) \cdot |A| \cdot |B|/2^l = |A| \cdot |B|$ (Strategy II get at most C=$|A| \cdot |B|$ matches), among which there are many pseudo-collisions[10]. This step is to filter out these pseudo-collisions and find the real one. Precisely, for each pair $(a_p^{[l]}, b_q^{[l]})$, we look for the table with the index $a_p^{[l]} \oplus b_q^{[l]} = w_i$, read the corresponding ISD list $B_d^{w_i}$ and for each $\Delta s \in B_d^{w_i}$, we can derive the internal state by using the method described in Sect. 3.1. Finally, we can easily verify the correctness of the state by running the cipher forward and compare the generated keystream with those β bits collected in A and B. The average size of the table is $R(n,d,l) = 100 \cdot V(n,d)/Q(n,d,l)$. The time complexity is $T_3 = C \cdot R(n,d,l) \cdot T_K = |A| \cdot |B| \cdot V(n,d) \cdot 2^{6.6} \cdot T_K/2^l$ cipher ticks[11] (for strategy II, $T_3 = |A| \cdot |B| \cdot V(n,d) \cdot 2^{6.6} \cdot T_K/Q(n,d,l)$).

The total online complexity of the on-line state is thus $T = T_1 + T_2 + T_3$ and the memory complexity is $M_2 = |A| + |B|$ entries, each containing $\hat{l}$ bits.

Table 3. The attack complexity with various l

l	P	T_1	T_2	T_3	T
102	$2^{95.7}$	$2^{40.9}$	$2^{85.8}$	$2^{86.4}$	$2^{86.4}$
104	$2^{95.7}$	$2^{40.9}$	$2^{85.9}$	$2^{84.4}$	$2^{85.9}$
106	$2^{95.7}$	$2^{40.9}$	$2^{85.9}$	$2^{72.4}$	$2^{85.9}$

$n = 160$, $d = 16$, $D = 2^{45.8}$, $M = 2^{78.6}$.
Strategy II is chosen in Step 3.

---

[10] Pseudo-collision indicates the case that $a_i^{[l]} \oplus b_j^{[l]}$ matches to a KSD, but the internal state recovered from the ISD found in the table indexed with the KSD is not correct.

[11] We ignore the cost for verifying the correctness of the state, since it does not make significant change in T_3.

4.3   Complexity Analysis

The unit of the time complexity is one tick of Grain. It is obvious that $Q(n, d, l)$ is upper bounded by 2^l and $R(n, d, l)$ is upper bounded by $100 \cdot V(n, d)/Q(n, d, l)$. The pre-computation time is $P = 2 \cdot N \cdot V(n, d) \cdot l$. The data complexity is $D = |A| + |B|$ $\hat{l}$-bit keystream segments and the memory requirement is $M = M_1 + M_2 = V(n, d) \cdot 2^{6.6} + |A| + |B|$ entries.

The time complexity in Step 2 is $T_1 = |A| \cdot \log |A| + |B| \cdot \log |B|$ comparisons. Suppose each comparison is done in one CPU cycle. Since one tick of Grain needs $\Omega = 2^{10.4}$ CPU clock cycles (see Appendix C for details), $T_1 = (|A| \cdot \log |A| + |B| \cdot \log |B|)/\Omega$ cipher ticks. Similarly, the time complexity in Step 3 is $T_2 = min\{Q(n, d, l) \cdot m \cdot \log m/\Omega, \ m^2 \cdot \log Q(n, d, l)/\Omega\}$ ticks.

For Grain $n = 160$ and $d = 16$, then $V(n, d) \approx 2^{72}$. If we choose $|A| = |B| = \sqrt{3} * 2^{n/2}/\sqrt{V(n, d)} \approx 2^{44.8}$ and the sample size $N = 2^{16}$, then the data complexity is thus $D = |A| + |B| = 2^{45.8}$, the memory requirement is $M = 2^{78.6}$ 167-bit entries and the time complexity of pre-computation is $P = 2^{89} \cdot l$. The complexities varying with l are shown in Table 3. From Table 3, our attack has a rather uniform complexity tradeoff. Besides, from $|A| \cdot |B| = 3 \cdot 2^n/V(n, d)$, the estimated success probability is about 98 %. We name this basic attack as NCA-1.0. However, the pre-computation complexity $P = 2^{95.7}$ exceeds the brute force attack complexity of $2^{87.4}$. In the following sections, we will propose some enhanced attacks.

5   Improvement I

The first improvement is designated by combining the sampling resistance property of Grain with NCA-1.0. Biryukov and Shamir proposed the concept of sampling resistance in [5], named BSW-sampling. It can be used to obtain larger choices of tradeoff parameters on the Biryukov-Shamir tradeoff curve.

5.1   Sampling Resistance of Grain

The main idea is to find an efficient way to generate and enumerate special states, from which some subsequent generated keystream bits have a fixed pattern (e.g., a string of zeros). If the length of the fixed pattern is k, then the sampling resistance of the cipher is $R = 2^{-k}$. In [6], it was proved that the sampling resistance of Grain is 2^{-21} by guess and determine strategy. We use a simple method to derive the sampling resistance of Grain which has lower complexity than the guess and determine strategy in [6]. Here comes our Lemma 2, proved in Appendix B.

Lemma 2. *Given the value of 139 particular state bits of Grain and the first 21 keystream bits produced from that state, another 21 internal state bits can be deduced directly.*

Table 4. The attack complexities with various l based on sampling resistance

l	P^*	T_1	T_2	T_3	T
92	$2^{83.4}$	$2^{35.9}$	$2^{76.1}$	$2^{75.4}$	$2^{76.1}$
94	$2^{83.4}$	$2^{35.9}$	$2^{76.2}$	$2^{73.4}$	$2^{76.2}$
96	$2^{83.4}$	$2^{35.9}$	$2^{76.2}$	$2^{71.4}$	$2^{76.2}$

$n^* = 139$, $d = 13$, $D = 2^{62}$, $M = 2^{65.9}$.
Strategy II is chosen in Step 3.

The 139 particular state bits contained 60 bits of the NFSR state and 79 bits of the LFSR state. From Lemma 2, the sampling resistance of Grain is $R = 2^{-21}$. Thus, we define a restricted one-way function $\tau : \{0,1\}^{139} \to \{0,1\}^{139}$ by choosing a prefix of 0^{21}.

1. For each 139-bit input value x, the remaining 21-bit internal state can be determined by Lemma 2 and the prefix of 0^{21}.
2. Run the cipher forward for 160 ticks, generate an 160-bit segment $0^{21}\|y$ and output y.

Now, the searching space is reduced to a special subset of the internal states.

5.2   Complexity Analysis Based on Sampling Resistance

Now, the goal is to recover the $n^* = 139$ bits ISD which contains 60 NFSR state bits and 79 LFSR state bits, instead of the $n = 160$ bits ISD. Note that if we observe l-bit keystream from the output y of τ, we need additional 42 ticks, 21 ticks to compute the remaining 21-bit internal state and 21 ticks to generate the prefix keystream. The pre-computation time complexity is thus $P^* = 2 \cdot N \cdot V(n^*, d) \cdot (l + 42)$ ticks. In the on-line stage, we need to collect those keystream segments with the prefix pattern 0^{21}, which can ensure that the corresponding internal state existed in the reduced searching space. Hence, the data complexity is $D = (|A| + |B|) \cdot 2^{21}$. Given $d = 13$, then $V(n^*, d) \approx 2^{59.3}$ and $|A| = |B| = \sqrt{3} \cdot 2^{n^*/2} / \sqrt{V(n^*, d)} \approx 2^{40}$. Thus, the data complexity is $D = (|A| + |B|) \cdot 2^{21} = 2^{62}$, the memory complexity is $M = V(n^*, d) \cdot 2^{6.6} + |A| + |B| = 2^{65.9}$ entries, each containing $n^* + \delta$ bits instead of $n + \delta$ bits. The pre-computation time is $P^* = 2 \cdot N \cdot V(n^*, d) \cdot (l + 42) = 2^{76.3} \cdot (l + 42)$. The time complexities with various l are summarized in Table 4. From Table 4, compared to NCA-1.0, our improved attack reduces P by a factor of $2^{12.3}$ and it saves 10-bit storage for each entry in A and B. All the complexities are under the brute force attack complexity of $2^{87.4}$. We name this combined attack as NCA-2.0.

6   Improvement II

The second improvement is based on NCA-2.0 by utilizing the non-uniform distribution of KSDs among all the tables.

Table 5. The attack complexity on Grain with various l based on special tables

l	P^*	T_1	T_2	T_3	T
92	$2^{73.1}$	$2^{41.9}$	$2^{60.5}$	$2^{75.4}$	$2^{75.4}$
94	$2^{73.1}$	$2^{41.9}$	$2^{60.6}$	$2^{73.4}$	$2^{73.4}$
96	$2^{73.1}$	$2^{41.9}$	$2^{60.7}$	$2^{71.4}$	$2^{71.4}$

$n^* = 139$, $d = 10$, $M = 2^{62.8}$ bits, $D = 2^{67.8}$.
Strategy I is chosen in Step 3.

6.1   Special Tables

As we have observed in Sect. 3.2, the distribution of the table size for each (d, l) are non-uniform. For $(d, l) = (4, 16)$, there are altogether $Q(160, 4, 16) = 2^{15.5}$ tables among which some tables like table-0x0000, table-0x0008, table-0x0004 contains 10 times more rows than those like table-0x0012 and table-0x0048. Table-0x0000 contains the most rows among all the tables. Furthermore, most tables like table-0xfe00, table-0xfd68 and table-0xfad1 only contain a single row. Those tables with low Hamming weight indexes contains most of the ISD. The distributions among other (d, l) pairs are similar.

For each (d, l) pair that $1 \le d \le 4, l \in \{8, 16, 24, 32\}$, we found that the tables with low Hamming weight indexes satisfying $w_H(\text{KSD}) \le 3$ contain about 80 % of all the $V(n, d)$ different ISDs. We call these tables special tables. In general, we make the following assumption which is verified in random experiments.

Assumption 1. *On average, the special tables can cover 50 % of all the $V(n^*, d)$ different ISDs, when d and l becomes larger.*

The assumption indicates that in the off-line stage, we only need to construct those special tables.

6.2   Complexity Analysis Based on Special Tables

All the complexities remain unchanged except $T_2 = min\{l^3 \cdot m \cdot \log m, \ m^2 \cdot \log l^3\}$. In NCA-2.0, $n^* = 139$, then given $d = 10$, $V(n^*, d) \approx 2^{49}$. If we choose $|A| = |B| = \sqrt{3} \cdot 2^{n^*/2}/\sqrt{V(n^*, d)} \approx 2^{45.8}$ and the sample size $N = 2^{16}$, then the pre-computation time complexity is $P^* = 2^{66} \cdot (l + 42)$ and the data complexity is $D = (|A| + |B|) \cdot 2^{21} = 2^{67.8}$ entries[12], each containing $\hat{l}$ bits. The memory complexity is $M = V(n, d) \cdot 2^{6.6} + |A| + |B| = 2^{55.6}$ entries, each containing $n^* + \delta = 146$ bits. The time complexities with various l are summarized in Table 5. From it, we can obtain an attack of $T = 2^{71.4}$, $M = 2^{62.8}$ and $D = 2^{67.8}$ with the pre-computation complexity $P = 2^{73.1}$. We name this enhanced attack as NCA-3.0.

---

[12] In the on-line stage, the data can be collected in an overlapping way, thus to get $2^{67.8}$ keysream segments, each containing $\hat{l}$ bits, we only need $\hat{l} + 2^{67.8} - 1 \approx 2^{67.8}$ keystream bits.

7   Simulations and Results

In this section, we validate our attacks by simulating a reduced version of Grain v1 stream cipher. We first give a brief description of the reduced version and then verify the Assumption 1 under various parameters. Finally, we apply NCA-2.0 and NCA-3.0 to the reduced cipher.

7.1   Reduced Version

The reduced version of Grain v1 cipher consists of an LFSR of 32 bits and an NFSR of 32 bits. $f'(x) = 1 + x^2 + x^7 + x^{16} + x^{32}$ is a primitive polynomial of degree 32. The update function of LFSR is defined as $l'_{i+32} = l'_{i+30} + l'_{i+25} + l'_{i+16} + l'_i$. The feedback polynomial of the NFSR, $g'(x)$ is defined as

$$g'(x) = 1 + x^7 + x^9 + x^{17} + x^{24} + x^{32} + x^7 x^9 + x^{17} x^{24}$$
$$+ x^7 x^9 x^{17} + x^9 x^{17} x^{24} + x^7 x^9 x^{17} x^{24},$$

which is a balanced function of degree 4. Similar to Grain, the update function of NFSR with the bit l'_i masked to the input is

$$n'_{i+32} = l'_i + n'_{i+25} + n'_{i+23} + n'_{i+15} + n'_{i+8} + n'_i + n'_{i+25}n'_{i+23} + n'_{i+15}n'_{i+8}$$
$$+ n'_{i+25}n'_{i+23}n'_{i+15} + n'_{i+23}n'_{i+15}n'_{i+8} + n'_{i+25}n'_{i+23}n'_{i+15}n'_{i+8}.$$

We use the same non-linear filter function $h(x)$ as in Grain v1 and take the output function as $z'_i = \sum_{k \in \mathcal{A}'} n'_{i+k} + h(l'_{i+3}, l'_{i+11}, l'_{i+21}, l'_{i+25}, n'_{i+24})$, where $\mathcal{A} = \{1, 4, 10, 21\}$. The key initialization is similar to Grain-v1. First, load the NFSR with the 32-bit key, then load the first 24 bits of LFSR with the 24-bit IV. The remaining bits of the LFSR are filled with ones. Then the cipher is clocked 64 times without producing any keystream. Instead the output function is feedback and xored with the input, both to the LFSR and to the NFSR. The actual complexity of the brute force attack on the reduced version is $2^{38.1}$ cipher ticks. By using the same strategy in Appendix B, given the value of 53 particular state bits of the reduced Grain (including 32 bits LFSR and 21 bits NFSR) and the first 11 keystream bits produced from that state, another 11 internal state bits can be deduced directly. Then the sampling resistance is $R' = 2^{-11}$.

7.2   Verification of Assumption 1

Recall that the special tables are those with low Hamming weight indexes satisfying $w_H(\text{KSD}) \leq 3$. We first verify Assumption 1 in a random experiment. More precisely, we randomly chose 10^4 ISDs in B_d and generate their corresponding KSDs with the proportions. For each ISD, N random internal states were generated to determine the projection from ISD to KSD. Only those KSDs satisfying

Table 6. Verification of Assumption 1

η	l	No. of ISDs	Proportion (%)
50	24	9842	98.4
1000	24	9851	98.5
50	32	9202	92.0
1000	32	9153	91.5

$n = 53$, $d = 4$.

$w_H(\text{KSD}) \leq 3$ will be recorded and their corresponding ISDs will be stored in a text file named with KSD. Similar to the process of the off-line stage, we only consider at most η KSDs whose proportions are the first η largest among all the KSDs. Finally, we count the number of different ISDs in these special tables. For the reduced version of Grain, the length of the internal state is $n = 53$ and we set $d = 4$, $N = 2^{12}$. thus we randomly chose 10^4 ISDs, each of which has Hamming weight at most 4. The number of different ISDs in the special tables under various l and η are summarized in the following Table. From it, we can see that when $\eta = 50$ and $l = 32$, the special tables can cover more than 90 % of all the ISDs, which corroborate our theoretical assumption very well. Under this configuration, we will apply NCA-2.0 and NCA-3.0 to the reduced version in the following section.

7.3   Simulations

In the off-line stage, we set $\eta = 50$, $N = 2^{12}$ and $d = 4$. The theoretical complexity with various l are given in the following table. The contents of a table will be stored in a text file named with the corresponding KSD. The pre-computation time under various keystream length l are summarized in the follow table. From Table 8, the table construction of NCA-2.0 takes more time than that of NCA-3.0, since NCA-3.0 only need to construct those special tables and the number of text files is much less than that of NCA-2.0, which indicates a lower cost of table look-up. In the on-line stage, we collected $|A| = |B| = \sqrt{3} \cdot 2^{n^*/2} / \sqrt{V(n^*, d)} \approx 2^{18}$ keystream segments. We apply NCA-2.0 and NCA-3.0 to the reduced version of Grain respectively for 140 randomly generated (K, IV) pairs. The average time for each attack and the experimental success probability are summarized in Table 9. For both NCA-2.0 and NCA-3.0, the experimental time is based on running an non-optimized C++ program on a 1.83 GHz CPU with 2 GB RAM and 1 TB harddisk. The success probability is given in the last column of Table 10. It is the proportion of the number of the correct internal state difference stored in the KSD tables.

We also conducted an experiment to analyze all those randomly collected keystream segments in the on-line stage of NCA-3.0. We attempt to find all those keystream segment pairs satisfying $w_H(\text{KSD}) \leq 3$ and $w_H(\text{ISD}) \leq d$, but get no results. We then repeat the experiment by increasing the maximum Hamming weight of the special indexes from 3 to 5, we finally get an average

Table 7. Theoretical complexity on reduced version of Grain

Attack	l	P	D	M	T
NCA-2.0	24	$2^{36.3}$	$2^{29.2}$	$2^{23.9}$	$2^{36.2}$
NCA-3.0	24	$2^{36.3}$	$2^{29.2}$	$2^{23.9}$	$2^{36.2}$
NCA-2.0	32	$2^{36.7}$	$2^{29.2}$	$2^{23.9}$	$2^{31.4}$
NCA-3.0	32	$2^{36.7}$	$2^{29.2}$	$2^{23.9}$	$2^{28.2}$

$\eta = 50$, $N = 2^{12}$, $d = 4$.

Table 8. Pre-computation time of NCA-2.0 and NCA-3.0

Attack	l	Time	Memory	No. of tables
NCA-2.0	24	9 h, 50 min	643 MB	8192
NCA-3.0	24	6 h, 35 min	216 MB	378
NCA-2.0	32	27 h, 41 min	4.45 GB	2097152
NCA-3.0	32	6 h, 37 min	11.6 MB	1562

$\eta = 50$, $N = 2^{12}$, $d = 4$.

Table 9. The simulation results on reduced version of Grain

Attack	l	Average attack time[a]	Success probability (%)
NCA-2.0	24	1 h, 53 min	9
NCA-3.0	24	1 h, 31 min	7
NCA-2.0	32	2 h, 12 min	6
NCA-3.0	32	41 min	4

[a] This is the average time for each on-line attack.

success rate of 10 %, i.e., 1 qualified keystream segment pair out of 10 simulations. These experimental results suggest that we can not ensure a very stable success probability of NCA-3.0 on the full version currently. It need to be refined further and we indeed get some improvements by reducing the complexity of recovering the NFSR given the LFSR and the state difference by a factor of about 2^9. We will provide the details in the upcoming papers.

From Table 9, we can also see that the experimental success probability of NCA-2.0 is lower than estimated in theory. The reason is that we choose a restricted value of η and N. These two parameters directly influence the size and the number of the pre-computed tables, hence affect the success probability. How to theoretically derive the relationship between the success probability and these two parameters is our future work.

8   Further Explanations and Discussions

To link the reduced version results with the full version analysis, the following assumption is used in our analysis.

Assumption 2. *The attack parameters in the full version analysis are chosen based on a linear extrapolation according to the state length ratio.*

Precisely, the sampling size of $N = 2^{16}$ in the full version of our attack is chosen as follows. For the reduced version, we have a non-negligible success probability when $N = 2^{12}$. The proportion of the state length for the full version and the reduced version is $160/64 \approx 3$. Similarly, the KSD length proportions are $106/32 \approx 4$ and $96/32 = 3$. This indicates that $N = 2^{12} \cdot 4 = 2^{14}$ is an appropriate choice for the full version. To further enhance the success probability, we choose the sampling size $N = 2^{16}$. The theoretical relationship between N and the success probability is not easy to determine analytically, but we will try to pursue this issue in our future work.

In our simulations, we also tested the time of one tick for the reduced version on our PC. One tick needs approximately 2^9 CPU clocks (about $0.24 * 10^{-6}$ seconds to generate one keystream bit). When $l = 32$, the cost for NCA-2.0 is about 2 h and 12 min, which contains a number of I/O operations for table look-ups (access to hard disk). The size of the pre-computed tables is about 4 GB, which contains millions of txt files (This can be replaced by binary file, which is faster for read and write operations). These hard disk operations will add some burden to the running time our non-optimized C++ program. Therefore, there exist some gaps between the time complexity of Tables 7, 8 and 9. We will further optimized our experimental code in the future. We can actually improve the running time by loading all the tables into CPU memory before the on-line attack, then the I/O operation costs can be reduced in the on-line phase.

9   Conclusion

In this paper, we have proposed a key recovery attack, called near collision attack on Grain v1. Based on some key observations, we have presented the basic attack called NCA-1.0 and further enhance it to NCA-2.0 and NCA-3.0 by combining the sampling resistance of Grain v1 and the non-uniform distribution of the KSD table size respectively. Our attack has been verified on a reduced version of Grain v1. Under some assumption, an extrapolation of the results indicates an attack on the original Grain v1 for any fixed IV in $2^{71.4}$ cipher ticks after the pre-computation of $2^{73.1}$ ticks, given $2^{62.8}$-bit memory and $2^{67.8}$ keystream bits, while the brute force attack can only be mounted for a fixed IV. Our attack is just a starting point for further analysis of Grain-like stream ciphers and hopefully it provides some new insights on the design of such compact stream ciphers.

A   Recovering the NFSR Initial State

We will discuss how to recover the NFSR state at t_1, once the LFSR state at t_1 has been recovered. In [1], Afzal et al. conducted several experiments to retrieve the maximum number of bits that can be obtained when the other bits are guessed. Results show that no more than 77 bits can be recovered out of 160 bits, while guessing the remaining 83 bits (including all 80 bits LFSR and 3 bits of NFSR). The method is to solve an equation system containing the 77 unknown NFSR state bits. Furthermore, they also generate algebraic equations of Grain-v1 in Maple 10, and solved the equations with Magma V 2.13-5 [11] on a PC with CPU at 1.73 GHz and 1 GB RAM. This method was also utilized in a weak Key-IVs attack [20]. The results are summarized in the following table.

Table 10. Simulation results of algebraic analysis of Grain

Version	No. of bits guessed[a]	No. of bits recovered	Time to find solution	Keystream bits used
Grain-v1	3	77	0.204 s	150

[a]Since the LFSR state is known, only 3 NFSR need to be guessed.

From Table 10, suppose that one operation (basic operation for solving the non-linear equation) acts in one clock cycle of the CPU, then $1.73 \cdot 10^9 \approx 2^{29.9}$ operations are executed per second for 1.73 GHz PC. Therefore, we need $2^{29.9} \cdot 0.204 \cdot 2^3 \approx 2^{30.7}$ operations (or CPU clock cycles) and 150 bits keystream to retrieve all the 80 NFSR state at t_1. Now we need to convert this time complexity to one tick of Grain. According to Appendix C, one tick of Grain needs $\Omega = 2^{10.4}$ CPU clock cycles. Therefore, the complexity to recover the NFSR state is $T_N = 2^{30.7}/\Omega = 2^{20.3}$ cipher ticks.

B Proof of Lemma 2

Proof. The listing strategy is same to the proof of the Lemma 1 in [6]. However, we extend the steps from 18 to 21. From the output function of Grain $z_i = \sum_{k \in A} n_{i+k} + h(l_{i+3}, l_{i+25}, l_{i+46}, l_{i+64}, n_{i+63},)$ where $A = \{1, 2, 4, 10, 31, 43, 56\}$. We attempt to enumerate all the NFSR bits from n_{i+10} to n_{i+31}. It is important to know that the non-linear feedback of Grain does not affect the output function until the cipher has been clocked 18 times. Thus, we can easily derive the following 17 steps

$$n_{10} = z_0 + n_1 + n_2 + n_4 + n_{31} + n_{43} + n_{56} + h(l_3, l_{25}, l_{46}, l_{64}, n_{63}),$$
$$\vdots$$
$$n_{25} = z_{15} + n_{16} + n_{17} + n_{19} + n_{46} + n_{58} + n_{71} + h(l_{18}, l_{40}, l_{61}, l_{79}, n_{78}),$$
$$n_{26} = z_{16} + n_{17} + n_{18} + n_{20} + n_{47} + n_{59} + n_{72} + h(l_{19}, l_{41}, l_{62}, l_{80}, n_{79}),$$

In step 1, the value of n_{10} can be determined by fixing 4 LFSR bits and 7 NFSR bits. We continue this procedure to derive the following values of $n_{11}, n_{12}, \ldots, n_{25}$. At this point, we have fixed 57 NFSR bits, 64 LFSR bits and deduced 16 NFSR bits. In step 17, l_{80} is involved in the computation of n_{26}, according to the linear feedback function, we need to fix 5 LFSR bits and 1 NFSR bit.

In step 18, n_{80} and l_{81} exist in the expression of n_{27}, we have to fix 5 LFSR bits and 2 NFSR bits (n_{28} and n_0) to deduce n_{27}. In the step 19, we can not deduce n_{28} in this step, since it was fixed in the last step. However, n_{29} exists in the expression of z_{18}, we can thus derive the value of n_{29} by fixing 3 LFSR bits. In step 20, n_{30} can be obtained by fixing 2 LFSR bits. In the last step (step 21), l_{45} can be deduced directly without fixing any state bit. All the state bits are known from step 22. The number of the fixed state bits are summarized in Table 11. To sum up, we have recovered the 20 NFSR state bits and 1 LFSR state bit using 60 bits of the NFSR state and 79 bits of the LFSR state (Altogether 139 bits of internal state).   □

C   How Can We Measure One-clock Cycle of Grain

The goal of this section is to measure the CPU clock cycle cost by one tick of Grain in software. The source code of Grain we used here is written by the designers [12]. We performed the testing several times on a PC with 2.83 GHz CPU and the average time to generate one keystream bit is $0.475 \cdot 10^{-6}$ s. Thus, one tick of Grain is $\Omega = 0.475 \cdot 10^{-6} \cdot 2.83 \cdot 10^9 \approx 2^{10.4}$ CPU cycles. The testing codes is in Fig. 5 (This program should run with the source code of Grain).

Table 11. The fixed state bits in each step

Step	Deduced bit	Fixed LFSR	Fixed NFSR bits
1	n_{10}	$l_3, l_{25}, l_{46}, l_{64}$	$n_1, n_2, n_4, n_{31}, n_{43}, n_{56}, n_{63}$
2	n_{11}	$l_4, l_{26}, l_{47}, l_{65}$	$n_3, n_5, n_{32}, n_{44}, n_{57}, n_{64}$
3	n_{12}	$l_5, l_{27}, l_{48}, l_{66}$	$n_6, n_{33}, n_{45}, n_{58}, n_{65}$
4	n_{13}	$l_6, l_{28}, l_{49}, l_{67}$	$n_7, n_{34}, n_{46}, n_{59}, n_{66}$
5	n_{14}	$l_7, l_{29}, l_{50}, l_{68}$	$n_8, n_{35}, n_{47}, n_{60}, n_{67}$
6	n_{15}	$l_8, l_{30}, l_{51}, l_{69}$	$n_9, n_{36}, n_{48}, n_{61}, n_{68}$
7	n_{16}	$l_9, l_{31}, l_{52}, l_{70}$	$n_{37}, n_{49}, n_{62}, n_{69}$
8	n_{17}	$l_{10}, l_{32}, l_{53}, l_{71}$	n_{38}, n_{50}, n_{70}
9	n_{18}	$l_{11}, l_{33}, l_{54}, l_{72}$	n_{39}, n_{51}, n_{71}
10	n_{19}	$l_{12}, l_{34}, l_{55}, l_{73}$	n_{40}, n_{52}, n_{72}
11	n_{20}	$l_{13}, l_{35}, l_{56}, l_{74}$	n_{41}, n_{53}, n_{73}
12	n_{21}	$l_{14}, l_{36}, l_{57}, l_{75}$	n_{42}, n_{54}, n_{74}
13	n_{22}	$l_{15}, l_{37}, l_{58}, l_{76}$	n_{55}, n_{75}
14	n_{23}	$l_{16}, l_{38}, l_{59}, l_{77}$	n_{76}
15	n_{24}	$l_{17}, l_{39}, l_{60}, l_{78}$	n_{77}
16	n_{25}	$l_{18}, l_{40}, l_{61}, l_{79}$	n_{78}
17	n_{26}	$l_{19}, l_{41}, l_{62}, l_0, l_{23}$	n_{79}
18	n_{27}	$l_{20}, l_{42}, l_{63}, l_1, l_{24}$	n_{28}, n_0
19	n_{29}	l_{21}, l_{43}, l_2	-
20	n_{30}	l_{22}, l_{44}	-
21	l_{45}	-	-

```
ECRYPT_ctx* ctx=new ECRYPT_ctx;
u32 KSLen=2000;
u8 key[10],IV[8],keyStream[KSLen];
ECRYPT_keysetup(ctx,key,80,64);
ECRYPT_ivsetup(ctx,IV);
clock_t start, finish;
double duration, speed;
start=clock();
ECRYPT_keystream_bytes(ctx,keyStream,KSLen);
finish=clock();
duration=((double)finish-start)/CLOCKS_PER_SEC;
speed=duration*2.83*1000*1000*1000/((double)KSLen*8);
printf("time%4.4f sec\n"
"The encryption speed is %3.4f cycles/bit \n",duration,speed);
```

Fig. 5. Code of testing.

References

1. Afzal, M., Masood, A.: Algebraic cryptanalysis of A NLFSR based stream cipher. In: The 3rd International conference on Information and Communication Technologies: From Theory to Applications, ICTTA 2008, pp. 1–6 (2008)
2. Aumasson, J.-P., Dinur, I., Henzen, L., Meier, W., Shamir, A.: Efficient FPGA implementations of high-dimensional cube testers on the stream cipher Grain-128, In: Special Purpose Hardware for Attacking Cryptographic Systems-SHARCS'09 (2009)
3. Berbain, C., Gilbert, H., Maximov, A.: Cryptanalysis of Grain. In: Robshaw, M. (ed.) FSE 2006. LNCS, vol. 4047, pp. 15–29. Springer, Heidelberg (2006)
4. Berbain, C., Gilbert, H., Joux, A.: Algebraic and correlation attacks against linearly filtered non linear feedback shift registers. In: Avanzi, R.M., Keliher, L., Sica, F. (eds.) SAC 2008. LNCS, vol. 5381, pp. 184–198. Springer, Heidelberg (2009)
5. Biryukov, A., Shamir, A.: Cryptanalytic time/memory/data tradeoffs for stream ciphers. In: Okamoto, T. (ed.) ASIACRYPT 2000. LNCS, vol. 1976, p. 1. Springer, Heidelberg (2000)
6. Bjorstad, TE.: Cryptanalysis of Grain using Time/Memory/Data Tradeoffs (2006). http://www.ecrypt.eu.org/
7. De Cannière, C., Küçük, Ö., Preneel, B.: Analysis of Grain's initialization algorithm. In: Vaudenay, S. (ed.) AFRICACRYPT 2008. LNCS, vol. 5023, pp. 276–289. Springer, Heidelberg (2008)
8. Dinur, I., Güneysu, T., Paar, C., Shamir, A., Zimmermann, R.: An experimentally verified attack on full Grain-128 using dedicated reconfigurable hardware. In: Lee, D.H., Wang, X. (eds.) ASIACRYPT 2011. LNCS, vol. 7073, pp. 327–343. Springer, Heidelberg (2011)
9. Dinur, I., Shamir, A.: Breaking Grain-128 with dynamic cube attacks. In: Joux, A. (ed.) FSE 2011. LNCS, vol. 6733, pp. 167–187. Springer, Heidelberg (2011)
10. http://www.ecrypt.eu.org/stream/e2-grain.html
11. Magma Computational Algebra System. http://magma.maths.usyd.edu.au/

12. Grain-v1 Software Implementation using C. http://www.ecrypt.eu.org/stream/e2-grain.html/
13. Hell, M., Johansson, T., Meier, W.: Grain: a stream cipher for constrained environments. Int. J. Wirel. Mob. Comput. (IJWMC) **2**(1), 86–93 (2007)
14. Hell, M., Johansson, T., Maximov, A., Meier, W.: A stream cipher proposal: Grain-128. In: IEEE International Symposium on Information Theory-ISIT'2006, pp. 1614–1618 (2006)
15. Agren, M., Hell, M., Johansson, T., Meier, W.: Grain-128a: a new version of Grain-128 with optional authentication. Int. J. Wirel. Mob. Comput. (IJWMC) **5**(1), 48–59 (2011)
16. Khazaei, S., Hassanzadeh, M., Kiaei., M.: Distinguishing attack on Grain. ECRYPT Stream Cipher Project Report 2005/071 (2005). http://www.ecrypt.eu.org/stream
17. Lee, Y., Jeong, K., Sung, J., Hong, S.H.: Related-key chosen IV attacks on Grain-v1 and Grain-128. In: Mu, Y., Susilo, W., Seberry, J. (eds.) ACISP 2008. LNCS, vol. 5107, pp. 321–335. Springer, Heidelberg (2008)
18. Stankovski, P.: Greedy distinguishers and nonrandomness detectors. In: Gong, G., Gupta, K.C. (eds.) INDOCRYPT 2010. LNCS, vol. 6498, pp. 210–226. Springer, Heidelberg (2010)
19. Strassen, V.: Gaussian elimination is not optimal. Nume. Math. **13**, 354–356 (1969)
20. Zhang, H., Wang, X.: Cryptanalysis of stream cipher Grain family, Cryptology ePrint Archive, Report 2009/109 (2009). http://eprint.iacr.org/

Automated Cryptanalysis

Exhausting Demirci-Selçuk Meet-in-the-Middle Attacks Against Reduced-Round AES

Patrick Derbez[1(✉)] and Pierre-Alain Fouque[1,2]

[1] École Normale Supérieure, 45 Rue d'Ulm, 75005 Paris, France
[2] Université de Rennes 1, INRIA Rennes, Rennes, France
{Patrick.Derbez,Pierre-Alain.Fouque}@ens.fr

Abstract. In this paper, we revisit Demirci and Selçuk meet-in-the-middle attacks on AES. We find a way to automatically model SPN block cipher and meet-in-the-middle attacks that allows to perform exhaustive search of this kind of attacks. This search uses the tool developed by Bouillaguet, Derbez and Fouque at CRYPTO 2011 as a subroutine to solve specific systems. We also take into account ideas introduced by Dunkelman, Keller and Shamir at ASIACRYPT 2010 which can be seen as a new tradeoff of the classical time/memory tradeoff used by Demirci and Selçuk. As a result, we automatically recover all the recent improved attacks of Derbez, Fouque and Jean on AES and we show new improved attacks against 8-rounds of AES-192 and AES-256.

1 Introduction

The AES encryption scheme [18] has been developed in the late nineties and has been specifically designed to resist against differential and linear cryptanalysis. Since 2008, the best attack for the 128-bit version was an impossible differential attacks by Lu *et al.* in [16] going back to a remark of Biham and Keller [1] improved by Bahrak and Aref in 2007. For the 192-bit and 256-bit versions, Demirci and Selçuk have described generalization of the Gilbert-Minier attack [15] which has also been discovered during the AES competition. During almost 10 years, there was no new cryptanalytic result and the first successful direction to analyze the AES encryption function comes from differential attacks in *the related-key setting* in 2009. This is a very powerful adversarial model in theory and it has recently been studied due to its applications in the analysis of hash functions. In this model, many other interesting results have been obtained by carefully studying the key schedule algorithms of AES-192 and AES-256 [2–5].

Despite important work on side-channel analysis on the AES, no real theoretical improvement on the first analysis performed during the AES competition [1,9,14,15] has been made. In this paper we turn our attention to the standard *single-key model* using meet-in-the-middle attack since these attacks are very efficient and are now the most efficient on all version of AES [11]. The first new theoretical result has been shown by Demirci and Selçuk at FSE 2008 using the old Meet-in-the-Middle cryptanalysis technique [10]. They improve the

S. Moriai (Ed.): FSE 2013, LNCS 8424, pp. 541–560, 2014.
DOI: 10.1007/978-3-662-43933-3_28, © Springer-Verlag Berlin Heidelberg 2014

Gilbert and Minier attack using meet-in-the-middle technique instead of collision ideas. These results at that time use a very small data complexity 2^{34} but require high precomputation and memory in 2^{216}. They need a hash table parameterized by 24 byte values. These attacks only work for the 256-bit and 192-bit versions thanks to a time/memory tradeoff which significantly increases the data and time complexity. They have been improved by Dunkelman et al. in [13] and more recently by Derbez et al. in [11]. Finally, recent biclique attacks [6] have been able to attack the full number of rounds of the AES at the price of using an exhaustive loop on all the key bits.

Meet-in-the-Middle Attacks on AES. At Asiacrypt 2010, Dunkelman, Keller and Shamir improve Demirci and Selçuk attacks on AES-192 and AES-256 using many interesting new ideas in [13]. They introduce the idea of multisets, a clever differential enumeration technique and a remark on the AES-192 key schedule to present attacks whose complexity is better than [10]. The main technique is the differential enumeration which allows to reduce the high memory complexity. This is mainly the bottleneck of the previous attacks with the precomputation phase. The attack can be seen as a new time/memory tradeoff, while Demirci and Selçuk one was very simple. Indeed, in this latter basic attack the memory is greater than the time. Consequently, they reduce the data in memory by repeating the attack as many times as the inverse of the probability of being in the table. Dunkelman et al. tradeoff uses a specific differential path to reduce the memory. This saving allows to consider a new attack on 7 rounds of AES-128 with basically the same complexity as the impossible differential attack, which is the best attack on this version. They also improve the attacks on the two other versions. However, since these attacks rely on a differential technique, they require a huge amount of data. Basically, they show that the number of parameters can be reduced from 24 to 16 while the time complexity is constant. These attacks have been recently improved by Derbez et al. in [11] by showing that the table can be reduced since many sequences in the table are never reached. They exactly compute the size of the memory needed and show that the table can be described by 10 parameters. This leads to the best attack for 7 rounds of AES-128 and also to the other versions.

Finally, Bouillaguet et al. in [7] study low data complexity attacks in reduce-round AES and in [8], some the authors build a computer-aided tool to look for the best meet-in-the-middle attacks in this model. A software has been developed allowing to solve linear systems of equations in $\mathbb{F}_{256}$ in the variables $x, S(x)$ where S is the AES S-box. This algorithm has been able to find attacks up to 5 rounds, but its complexity is exponential in the number of S-boxes. It is very versatile and has been used to solve systems for other cryptosystems such as the LEX stream cipher, the Pelican-MAC or fault attacks on AES [8,12].

Our Results. In this paper, we consider another direction to improve on Demirci and Selçuk (DS) attack using only meet-in-the-middle techniques. Here, we generalize DS attack using DS or DKS time/memory tradeoffs and we automatize the search of these attacks to find the best ones. We discover many efficient attacks and we also rediscovered the recent improved attacks on all the versions of AES presented in [11]. To perform this search, we use the tool of Bouillaguet, Derbez and Fouque, but only on the keyschedule equations instead of the system of equations describing the AES. These equations are sparse in the number of Sbox and consequently, the complexity of the search is very low. In particular, we have been able to improve the complexity on AES-192 and AES-256 by a factor 2^{32} and 2^{40} respectively as it is summarized in Table 1. Finally, some of the attacks we discovered have a small data complexity such as the basic DS attack. This leads us to increase the number of rounds attacked using small data complexity as in [7,8]. For instance, we present on AES-128 an attack on up to 6 rounds using 256 data complexity and 2^{106} in time and memory whereas Bouillaguet et al. were able to find attack on 5 rounds with complexity 2^{120}. It is possible to extend this last attack to 7 rounds with a marginal improvement over exhaustive search. We refer the reader to Table 1 for all the attacks.

Organization of the Paper. In Sect. 2, we describe the AES cipher and some properties useful to analyze its security for meet-in-the-middle techniques. Then, we present the previous attacks and ideas in Sect. 3 before showing our ideas in Sect. 4. In Sect. 5, we discuss on the results and describe some of our new attacks requiring at most 2^{32} chosen plaintexts. The Sect. 6 is dedicated to the differential enumeration technique introduced by Dunkelman et al. and contains the description of new attacks on AES-192 requiring 2^{104} data, 2^{138} in memory and 2^{140} in time and on AES-256 requiring 2^{103} in data, 2^{140} in memory and 2^{156} in time.

2 AES and Observations

2.1 Description of the AES

The Advanced Encryption Standard [18] is a Substitution-Permutation Network that can be instantiated using three different key sizes: 128, 192, and 256. The 128-bit plaintext initializes the internal state viewed as a 4×4 matrix of bytes as values in the finite field $\mathbb{F}_{256}$, which is defined using the irreducible polynomial $x^8 + x^4 + x^3 + x + 1$ over $\mathbb{F}_2$. Depending on the version of the AES, N_r rounds are applied to that state: $N_r = 10$ for AES-128, $N_r = 12$ for AES-192 and $N_r = 14$ for AES-256. Each of the N_r AES round (Fig. 1) applies four operations to the state matrix (except in the last round where the **MixColumns** operation is missing):

- **AddRoundKey** (AK) adds a 128-bit subkey to the state.
- **SubBytes** (SB) applies the same 8-bit to 8-bit invertible S-Box S 16 times in parallel on each byte of the state,
- **ShiftRows** (SR) shifts the i-th row left by i positions,

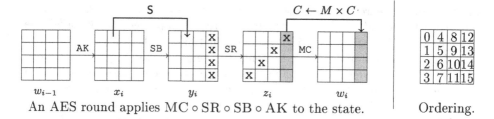

An AES round applies MC ∘ SR ∘ SB ∘ AK to the state.   Ordering.

Fig. 1. Description of one AES round and the ordering of bytes in an internal state.

--- **MixColumns** (MC) replaces each of the four column C of the state by $M \times C$ where M is a constant 4×4 maximum distance separable matrix over $\mathbb{F}_{256}$,

After the N_r-th round has been applied, a final subkey is added to the internal state to produce the ciphertext. We refer to the original publication [18] for the key expansion algorithms.

Notations. In this paper, we count the AES rounds from 0 and we refer to a particular byte of an internal state x by $x[i]$, as depicted in Fig. 1. Moreover, in the ith round, we denote the internal state after **AddRoundKey** by x_i, after **SubBytes** by y_i, after **ShiftRows** by z_i and after **MixColumns** by w_i. To refer to the difference in a state x, we use the notation Δx. The first added subkey is the master key k_{-1}, and the one added after round i is denoted k_i.

In some cases, we are interested in swapping the order of the **MixColumns** and **AddRoundKey** operations. As these operations are linear they can be interchanged, by first XORing the data with an equivalent key and only then applying the **MixColumns** operation. We denote the equivalent subkey for the altered version by:

$$u_i = MC^{-1}(k_i) = \begin{pmatrix} 0e\ 0b\ 0d\ 09 \\ 09\ 0e\ 0b\ 0d \\ 0d\ 09\ 0e\ 0b \\ 0b\ 0d\ 09\ 0e \end{pmatrix} \times k_i$$

2.2   Observations on the Structure of AES

In this section we recall two well-known observations on the structure of AES, that will be used later in our attacks. We first consider the propagation of differences through **SubBytes** layer.

Property 1. (the **SubBytes** *property*) Consider pairs $(\alpha \neq 0, \beta)$ of input/output differences for a single S-box in the **SubBytes** operation. For $129/256$ of such pairs, the differential transition is impossible, i.e., there is no pair (x, y) such that $x \oplus y = \alpha$ and $S(x) \oplus S(y) = \beta$. For $126/256$ of the pairs (α, β), there exist two ordered pairs (x, y) such that $x \oplus y = \alpha$ and $S(x) \oplus S(y) = \beta$, and for the remaining $1/256$ of the pairs (α, β) there exist four ordered pairs (x, y) that

Table 1. Current cryptanalysis of AES variants in the single-key model

Version	Rounds	Data (CP)	Memory	Time	Technique	Reference
128	6	2^8	$2^{106.17}$	$2^{106.17}$	MITM	Sect. 5.2
	7	2^{32}	$2^{126.47}$	$2^{126.47}$	MITM	Full ver.
	7	$2^{90.4}$	2^{106}	$2^{117.2}$ MA	ID	[17]
	7	2^{97}	2^{98}	2^{99}	MITM	[11]
	8	2^{88}	2^8	$2^{125.3}$	Bicliques	[6]
	10 (full)	2^{88}	2^8	$2^{126.2}$	Bicliques	[6]
192	6	2^8	$2^{109.67}$	$2^{109.67}$	MITM	Full ver.
	7	2^8	$2^{153.34}$	2^{163}	MITM	Full ver.
	7	2^{32}	$2^{129.67}$	$2^{129.67}$	MITM	Sect. 5.4
	7	$19 \cdot 2^{32}$	$19 \cdot 2^{32}$	2^{155}	Square	[14]
	7	$2^{91.2}$	$2^{139.2}$	2^{101}	ID	[16]
	7	2^{95}	2^{143}	2^{143}	MITM	[10]
	7	2^{97}	2^{98}	2^{99}	MITM	[11]
	8	2^{32}	$2^{182.17}$	$2^{182.17}$	MITM	Full ver.
	8	2^{41}	2^{186}	$2^{187.63}$	MITM	[19]
	8	$\mathbf{2^{104.83}}$	$\mathbf{2^{138.17}}$	$\mathbf{2^{140}}$	**MITM**	Sect. 6.1
	8	2^{107}	2^{96}	2^{172}	MITM	[11]
	8	$\mathbf{2^{113}}$	$\mathbf{2^{130}}$	$\mathbf{2^{140}}$	**MITM**	Sect. 6.1
	8	2^{113}	2^{82}	2^{172}	MITM	[11]
	9	2^{80}	2^8	$2^{188.8}$	Bicliques	[6]
	12 (full)	2^{80}	2^8	$2^{189.4}$	Bicliques	[6]
256	6	2^8	$2^{114.34}$	2^{122}	MITM	Full ver.
	7	2^8	2^{186}	$2^{170.34}$	MITM	Full ver.
	7	2^{16}	$2^{153.34}$	2^{178}	MITM	Sect. 5.3
	7	2^{32}	$2^{133.67}$	$2^{133.67}$	MITM	Full ver.
	7	$21 \cdot 2^{32}$	$21 \cdot 2^{32}$	2^{172}	Square	[14]
	7	2^{95}	2^{143}	2^{143}	MITM	[10]
	7	2^{97}	2^{98}	2^{99}	MITM	[11]
	8	2^8	$2^{234.17}$	$2^{234.17}$	MITM	Full ver.
	8	2^{32}	$2^{193.34}$	2^{195}	MITM	Full ver.
	8	$2^{34.2}$	$2^{205.8}$	$2^{205.8}$	MITM	[10]
	8	$\mathbf{2^{102.83}}$	$\mathbf{2^{140.17}}$	$\mathbf{2^{156}}$	**MITM**	Sect. 6.1
	8	2^{107}	2^{96}	2^{196}	MITM	[11]
	8	$\mathbf{2^{113}}$	$\mathbf{2^{130}}$	$\mathbf{2^{156}}$	**MITM**	Sect. 6.1
	8	2^{113}	2^{82}	2^{196}	MITM	[11]
	9	2^{32}	$2^{254.17}$	$2^{254.17}$	MITM	Full ver.
	9	2^{120}	2^{203}	2^{203}	MITM	[11]
	9	2^{120}	2^8	$2^{251.9}$	Bicliques	[6]
	14 (full)	2^{40}	2^8	$2^{254.4}$	Bicliques	[6]

CP: Chosen-plaintext.   ID: Impossible Differential.   MITM: Meet-in-the-Middle.

satisfy the input/output differences. Moreover, the pairs (x, y) of input values corresponding to a given difference pattern (α, β) can be found instantly from the difference distribution table of the Sbox.

Property 1 means that given the input and output difference of an S-box, we can find in constant time the possible absolute values of the input, and there is only a single one on average.

The second observation is a necessary and sufficient condition for a matrix to be MDS applied to the matrix MC used in the **MixColumns** operation.

Property 2. (**MixColumns** *property*) Consider a pair (a, b) of 4-byte vectors, such that $a = MC(b)$, *i.e.* the input and the output of a **MixColumns** operation applied to one column. Denote $a = (a_0, a_1, a_2, a_3)$ and $b = (b_0, b_1, b_2, b_3)$ where a_i and b_j are elements of $\mathbb{F}_{256}$. Then there is no equation involving less than five bytes and for each choice of five bytes among the eight bytes $(a_0, a_1, a_2, a_3, b_0, b_1, b_2, b_3)$ there is a linear equation between them.

Finally, in our attacks we consider the encryption of structured sets of 256 plaintexts in which one active byte takes each one of the 256 possible values exactly once, and each one of the other 15 bytes is a (possibly different) constant. Such a structure is called a δ-set.

3   Related Results from Previous Work

In this section, we remind Demirci and Selçuk attack together with its improvements which are the main results used in our attack. We refer the reader to [10] and [13] for details.

3.1   The Demirci and Selçuk Attack

At FSE 2008, Demirci and Selçuk described the following 4-round property for AES.

Property 3. Consider the encryption of a δ-set through four full AES rounds. For each of the 16 bytes of the state, the ordered sequence of 256 values of that byte in the corresponding ciphertexts is fully determined by just 25 byte parameters. Consequently, for any fixed byte position, there are at most $(2^8)^{25} = 2^{200}$ possible sequences when we consider all the possible choices of keys and δ-sets (out of the $(2^8)^{256} = 2^{2048}$ theoretically possible 256-byte sequences).

The 25 parameters are intermediate state bytes for any message of the δ-set and their positions depend on the active byte of the δ-set and on which byte we want to build values. As depicted on Fig. 2, if there are both at position 0 then the 25 parameters are the first column of x_{i+1}, the full state x_{i+2}, the first column of z_{i+3} and $x_{i+4}[0]$. Indeed, if those bytes are known for one of the messages, we can compute the value of $x_{i+4}[0]$ for each message of the δ-set as follows:

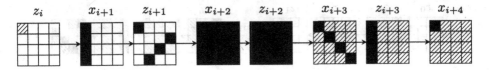

$$z_i \qquad x_{i+1} \qquad z_{i+1} \qquad x_{i+2} \qquad z_{i+2} \qquad x_{i+3} \qquad z_{i+3} \qquad x_{i+4}$$

Fig. 2. 4 AES-rounds. The 25 black bytes are the parameters of Property 3. Hatched bytes play no role. The differences are null in white squares

1. Knowing the 256 differences in the full state z_i we can compute the 256 differences in the full state x_{i+1} because $\Delta x_{j+1} = \mathrm{MC}.\Delta z_j$ for any round number j, where MC is the matrix used in the **MixColumns** operation.
2. Knowing the value of the first column of x_{i+1} for one message we can now compute the value of this column for all messages.
3. Then we apply the Sbox on those bytes and get the value of $z_{i+1}[0]$, $z_{i+1}[7]$, $z_{i+1}[10]$ and $z_{i+1}[13]$ for each message of the δ-set.
4. The differences are null in all the other bytes of z_{i+1} so we know the 256 differences in the full state z_{i+1}.
5. In the same way we obtain the 256 differences in the full state z_{i+2} and then in the first column of z_{i+3} to finally compute the 256 values of $x_{i+4}[0]$

They first use this property to mount a basic meet-in-the-middle attack on 7 rounds **AES-256** depicted on Fig. 3 and its procedure is roughly as follows:

- **Preprocessing phase:** Compute all the 2^{200} possible sequences according to Property 3, and store them in a hash table.
- **Online phase:**
  1. Ask for a structure of 2^{32} chosen plaintexts such that the main *diagonal* can take the 2^{32} possible values and the remaining bytes are constant.
  2. Choose one plaintext and guess the first column of its intermediate state z_0 and byte $z_1[0]$.
  3. For each of the 255 non-zero values of Δz_1 compute the corresponding difference in the plaintext using the guessed bytes.
  4. Order the obtained δ-set according to the value of the state byte $z_1[0]$.
  5. Guess the first column of x_6 and the byte $x_5[0]$ for one of the message and deduce those state bytes for the 256 ciphertexts.
  6. Build the sequence and check whether it exists in the hash table. If not, discard the guess.

Note that the parameters of both the online and offline phases are state bytes which we shall refer in the sequel as respectively $\mathcal{B}_{on}$ and $\mathcal{B}_{off}$. The complexity of the attack depends directly on how many values can assume those state bytes and how fast can we enumerate them. Indeed, bytes of $\mathcal{B}_{off}$ (resp. $\mathcal{B}_{on} \cup P \cup C$) are related by the **AES** equations and thus lead to the knowledge of some linear combinations of the (sub)keys bytes. Then it may exist some relations derived from the key-schedule between them, allowing to reduce the number of assumed values. In the sequel, we will denote by $\mathcal{K}_{off}$ (resp. $\mathcal{K}_{on}$) the vector space generated from these linear combinations. For instance, in the case of the described attack and if the last **MixColumns** is omitted,

Fig. 3. Online phase of Demirci and Selçuk attack. $\mathcal{B}_{on}$ is composed by gray and black bytes. Gray bytes are used to identify a δ-set and to order it. Black bytes are used to build the sequence from ciphertexts. Hatched bytes play no role. The differences are null in white squares.

- $\{k_{-1}[0,5,10,15], k_0[0], u_5[0], k_6[0,7,10,13]\}$ is a basis of $\mathcal{K}_{on}$,
- $\{u_1[0], u_2[0,7,10,13], k_3[0,5,10,15], k_4[0]\}$ is a basis of $\mathcal{K}_{off}$.

All in all, this attack has a data complexity of 2^{32} chosen plaintexts, a time complexity of $2^{80} \times 2^8$ partial encryptions/decryptions, and a memory requirement of 2^{200} 256-byte sequences. The memory complexity of this attack is too high to apply it on the 128 and 192-bit versions. But its time complexity is low enough to mount an attack from it on 8 rounds AES-256. This is done by fully guessing the last subkey, decrypting the last round and applying the 7-round attack, which increases the time complexity by a factor 2^{128}.

3.2 Previous Improvements of the Original Attack

We summarize the main improvements to the original attack of Demirci and Selçuk.

Difference Instead of Value. Demirci and Selçuk showed that the number of parameters can be reduced to 24 in Property 3 by considering the sequence of the differences instead of values because in that case $x_{i+4}[0]$ is not needed.

Data/Time/Memory Trade-Off. They also showed that one can do a classical trade-off by storing in the hash table only a fraction of the possible sequences. Then the attacker has to repeat the online phase many times to compensate the probability of failure if the sequence is not present in the table which will increase the data and time complexities. In other word, if the attack has a complexity (D, T, M) (D for the data, T for the time complexity of the online phase and M for the memory) then it is possible to modify it to reach a complexity equal to $(D \times N, T \times N, M/N)$ for any positive N such that $D \times N$ is smaller than the size of the codebook. This trade-off allows to adapt the attack on 7 rounds of AES-256 to attack the 192-bit version.

Data Recycling. The structure of 2^{32} plaintexts used in the attack contains 2^{24} δ-sets. Thus the data may be reused 2^{24} times in the Data/Time/Memory Trade-Off.

Time/Memory Trade-Off. Kara observed that considering the sequence of the differences instead of values allows to remove $x_5[0]$ from $\mathcal{B}_{off}$ (as Demirci and Selçuk did) or from $\mathcal{B}_{on}$.

Multiset. A multiset is an unordered set in which elements can occur many times. Dunkelman *et al.* introduce them to replace the functional concept used in the DS attack and propose to store in the hash table unordered sequences of 256 bytes instead of ordered sequences. Moreover, they claim that a multiset still contains enough information to make the attack possible. Indeed they showed that given two random functions $f, g : \mathbb{F}_{256} \longrightarrow \mathbb{F}_{256}$, the multisets $[f(0), \ldots, f(255)]$ and $[g(0), \ldots, g(255)]$ are equal with a probability smaller than $2^{-467,6}$. Combined to the fact that the Sbox is a bijection, the main gain is to remove $z_1[0]$ from $\mathcal{B}_{on}$ since it was used only to ordered the δ-set, and thus the time complexity is decreased by a factor 2^8. Finally, we note that a multiset contains about 512 bits of information and its representation can be easily compressed into 512 bits of space while an ordered sequence needs $256 \times 8 = 2048$ bits.

Differential Enumeration. In [13], Dunkelman *et al.* introduce a more sophisticated trade-off which reduces the memory without increasing the time complexity. The main idea is to add restrictions on the parameters used to build the table such that those restrictions can be checked (at least partially) during the online phase. More precisely, they impose that sequences stored come from a δ-set containing a message m which belongs to a pair (m, m') that follows a well-chosen differential path. Then the attacker first focus on finding such pair before to identify a δ-set and build the sequence. Sect. 6 is dedicated to this technique.

4   Generalization of the Demirci and Selçuk Attack

The basic attack of Demirci and Selçuk requires a huge memory and a relatively small time complexity. The classical data/time/memory trade-off allows to *balance* these complexities by increasing the data complexity and randomizing the attack. In this section we present new improvements to reduce the data complexity increase which leads to almost 2^{16} variants of the Demirci and Selçuk attack and we explain how to find the best ones between them.

4.1   New Improvements of the Original Attack

In this section we summarized our new improvements that allow us to reduce the increase of the data complexity and, sometimes, to keep the deterministic nature of the original attack.

Difference Instead of Value. The sequences stored in the table have the form $[f(0) + f(0), \ldots, f(0) + f(255)]$ where f is a function that maps the value of $z_i[0]$ to the value of $x_{i+4}[0] + k_{i+3}[0]$. But, as shown Sect. 3.1, the procedure used to build the table produces functions that map the value of $\Delta z_{i+4}[0]$ to the value of $\Delta x_{i+4}[0]$ and then the only effect of mapping the value of $z_i[0]$ is to set the value of the subkey byte $u_i[0]$ (i.e. $u_i[0] \in \mathcal{K}_{off}$). In another hand, if we store in the table sequences of the form $[f(0), \ldots, f(255)]$ where f is a function that maps the value of $\Delta z_i[0]$ to the value of $\Delta x_{i+4}[0]$, then each δ-set can be ordered in 256 ways, saving data in the classical data/time/memory trade-off described Sect. 3.2. Furthermore, in the case of a δ-set encryption, each byte of the first columns of x_{i+1} assumes the 256 values. As a consequence, to set one of those bytes to 0 when building the hash table can be compensated by trying the 256 orders of a δ-set without randomizing the attack.

Multiset. Note that, given a sequence of 256 bytes $b_0, \ldots, b_{255}$, $b_i = b_j$ implies that the multisets $[b_i + b_0, \ldots, b_i + b_{255}]$ and $[b_j + b_0, \ldots, b_j + b_{255}]$ are equal too. But Dunkelman et al. shown that given a random function $f : \mathbb{F}_{256} \longrightarrow \mathbb{F}_{256}$, the multiset $[f(0) + f(1), \ldots, f(0) + f(255)]$ contains on average 162 different values out of 256. Thus we conclude that a δ-set can be reused $162 \approx 2^{7.34}$ times on average. This remark holds on for the multisets stored in the hash table during the precomputation phase and so the memory requirement must be corrected by a factor $2^{-0.66}$.

Time/Memory Trade-Off. To improve the attack of Demirci and Selçuk our idea is to store in the sequences the 256 differences in a linear combinations of bytes of x_5 instead of the 256 differences in a byte of x_5. Thanks to Property 2, minimal equations involving Δz_i and Δx_{i+1} contains exactly 5 variables such that k are on a column c of Δz_i and $5 - k$ are on the column c of Δx_{i+1}, with $1 \leq k \leq 4$ for any round number i. We emphase that Demirci and Selçuk only consider cases $k = 1$ and $k = 4$. The size of the set $\mathcal{B}_{on}$ (resp. $\mathcal{B}_{off}$) is determined by k and it decreases (resp. increases) when k is increased. Thus we can trade time by memory and vice-versa without affecting the data complexity. Furthermore, contrary to the other data/time/memory trade-offs, the attack need not to be randomized. Attacks taking advantage of this trade-off are described Sects. 5.2 and 5.4.

New Data/Time/Memory Trade-Off. The idea of the previous trade-off can be applied to the δ-set. Instead of considering sets of 256 plaintexts such that one byte assumes the 256 values and the others are constant, we consider set of 256 plaintexts such that exactly 5 bytes of z_i and x_{i+1} are active. We still call such a set a δ-set. The consequences on the attack are the same as the previous trade-off but it now affects the size of the structure needed and bytes of z_i must be guessed in the online phase despite the use of unordered sequences. An attack taking advantage of this trade-off is described Sect. 5.3.

4.2   Finding the Best Attack

Once the round-reduced AES is split into three parts, the new improvements allow to mount $(4 \times \binom{8}{5})^2 \approx 2^{15.6}$ different attacks but there are only $(4 \times (\binom{4}{1} + \binom{4}{2} + \binom{4}{3} + \binom{4}{4}))^2 \approx 2^{11.8}$ possible sets $\mathcal{B}_{on}$ (resp. $\mathcal{B}_{off}$) to study. To exhaust all of them and find the best attacks we decide to automatize the search. Thus for each set we need to answer to the two following questions:

- How many values can assume those state bytes?
- How fast can we enumerate them?

A priori, this is not an easy task because S-boxes are involved in the keyschedule. To perform it we used the tool developed in [8], originally designed to find the best solver for an AES-like system of equations among a particular class of solvers based on the meet-in-the-middle technique.

Algorithm 1. OriginalTool
Data: System of equations E in variables X involving some S-boxes.
Result: An optimal algorithm to enumerate all the solutions of E with predictable time and memory complexities.

The problem we seek to solve is very close to the problem solved by this tool but is still different and so we have slightly tweaked it.

Algorithm 2. TweakedTool (naive implementation)
Data: System of equations E in variables X involving some S-boxes and a subset $Y \subseteq X$.
Result: A list of optimal algorithms to enumerate all the possible values of Y according to the system of equations E with predictable time and memory complexities.
$L \leftarrow \emptyset$;
foreach $Y \subseteq Z \subseteq X$ **do**
$\quad F \leftarrow$ the biggest subspace of E in variables Z;
$\quad \mathcal{A} \leftarrow$ OriginalTool(F);
$\quad L \leftarrow$ best algorithms from $L \cup \{A\}$;
end
return L

The output of our tweaked tool is a list because the number of possible values of Y enumerated by considered algorithms is not necessary constant and if an algorithm is slower than an other but finds less possible values for Y than it then both of them must be studied. Note that the tweaked tool can be applied directly to the set $\mathcal{B}_{off}$ (resp. $\mathcal{B}_{on}$) and the system of equations describing the AES but it is faster to apply it on a basis of $\mathcal{K}_{off}$ (resp. $\mathcal{K}_{on}$) and the keyschedule equations since the complexity of the original tool is exponential in the number of S-box.

Finally we were able to perform an exhaustive search over all the parameters for all round-reduced versions of AES for the three key lengths in less than an hour on a personal computer.

5   Results

In this section we present the results obtained by exhausting the variants of the attack of Demirci and Selçuk. We give an overview of the complexities reached and describe three new attacks requiring at most 2^{32} chosen plaintexts and minimizing the maximum between the time complexity (counted in AES encryption) and the memory complexity (counted in 128-bit block).

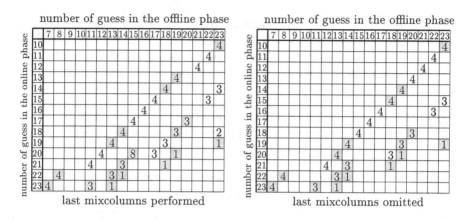

Fig. 4. Best variants on 7 rounds AES-192.

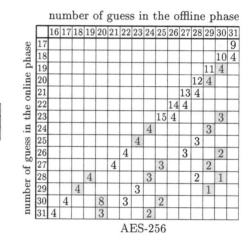

Fig. 5. Best variants on 8 rounds.

5.1 Overview of the Results

Some of our best results on 7 and 8 rounds are summarized on Figs. 4 and 5. They give the ($\log_{256}$ of) data complexity reached as a function of the number of guess to perform in the online phase and in the offline phase. A gray cell means that the corresponding attack is deterministic while the other attacks are obtained by applying the classical data/time/memory trade-off.

We observe that almost all the best attacks work with only 2^{32} chosen-plaintexts. For comparison, to reach balanced complexities on seven rounds from the original attack by using the classical data/time/memory trade-off, the amount of data needed will be approximately 2^{71} chosen plaintexts. Furthermore, we have been able to increase by one the number of rounds attacked with 2^{32} chosen-plaintexts for the three key length but with time and memory

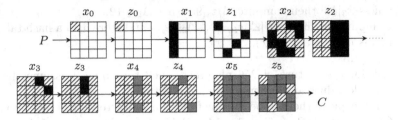

Fig. 6. Attack on 6 AES rounds. Bytes of $\mathcal{B}_{off}$ are in black. Bytes of $\mathcal{B}_{on}$ are in gray. Hatched bytes play no role. The differences are null in white squares

complexities very close to the natural bound of the exhaustive search. We also obtained competitive results in the very low data complexity league with, for instance, attacks on 8 rounds of AES-256 requiring only 2^8 chosen plaintexts.

5.2 Attack on Six Rounds AES-128 with 2^8 Chosen-Plaintexts

If the data available is limited to 2^8 chosen-plaintexts, the best attack found is based on the attack depicted on Fig. 6 and the meet-in-the-middle is performed on the equation

$$03.\Delta z_3[8] + \Delta z_3[9] = 07.\Delta x_4[8] + 07.\Delta x_4[9] + 02.\Delta x_4[11].$$

Let be $e_{in} = 03.z_3[8] + z_3[9]$ and $e_{out} = 07.x_4[8] + 07.x_4[9] + 02.x_4[11]$.

The bytes of $\mathcal{B}_{off}$ are the first column of x_1, the two last columns of z_2, and bytes 8 and 9 of z_3. They can assume $2^{8 \times 14}$ different values and so the memory requirement is $2^{112-0,66} = 2^{111,34}$ multisets on average according to the remark made in Sect. 4.1.

As the S-box is a bijection and as we consider a δ-set in which only one byte is active, we do not need to guess $x_0[0]$ in order to identify the corresponding set of 256 plaintexts to build the multiset. As a consequence, the bytes of $\mathcal{B}_{on}$ are the entire state x_5 except the first column, and the third column of x_4 except byte 10. Thanks to the keyschedule equations, they can take only $2^{8 \times 12}$ values instead of $2^{8 \times 15}$ since we have the three equations $u_4[5] = u_5[1] + u_5[5]$, $u_4[8] = u_5[4] + u_5[8]$ and $u_4[15] = u_5[11] + u_5[15]$.

All in all this leads to the following attack:

- **Preprocessing phase:**
  1. Set $\Delta_i z_0[0]$ to i for $0 \leq i \leq 255$. Then $\Delta_i z_0$ is known since the other differences are null.
  2. Guess $x_1[0..3]$ (for one of the 256 messages) and use $\Delta_i z_0$ to compute $\Delta_i z_1[0]$, $\Delta_i z_1[7]$, $\Delta_i z_1[10]$ and $\Delta_i z_1[13]$. Then $\Delta_i z_1$ is known since the other differences are null.
  3. Guess bytes 1, 2, 6, 7, 8, 11, 12 and 13 of x_2. Use them with $\Delta_i z_1$ to compute $\Delta_i z_2[8..15]$.
  4. Guess $x_3[8]$ then compute $\Delta_i z_3[8]$ using $\Delta_i z_2[8..11]$.

5. Guess $x_3[13]$ then compute $\Delta_i z_3[9]$ using $\Delta_i z_2[12..15]$.
6. Compute the multiset $[\Delta_0 e_{in}, \ldots, \Delta_{255} e_{in}]$ and store it in a hash table (if it was not already in it).

- **Online phase:**
  1. Ask for a structure of 256 plaintexts such that byte 0 assume the 256 possible values and others bytes are constant.
  2. Choose one of them to be the one from which difference will be computed.
  3. Guess bytes 1, 2, 4, 5, 8, 11, 14 and 15 of u_5. Compute $u_4[5]$ and $u_4[8]$ and then partially decrypt the ciphertexts to obtain $\Delta_i x_4[8]$ and $\Delta_i x_4[9]$ for $0 \leq i \leq 255$.
  4. Guess bytes 3, 6 and 9 of u_5, and continue to partially decrypt the ciphertexts.
  5. Guess byte 12 of u_5. Compute $u_4[15]$ and then partially decrypt the ciphertexts to obtain $\Delta_i x_4[11]$.
  6. Build the multiset $[\Delta_0 e_{out}, \ldots, \Delta_{255} e_{out}]$ and check whether the multiset exists in the hash table. If not, discard the key guess.

Finally, the time complexity is equivalent to $2 \times 2^{-6} \times 2^8 \times 2^{96} = 2^{99}$ encryptions and the memory requirement is $2^{113,34}$ AES-blocks. The probability for a wrong guess to succeed is approximatively $2^{111,34} \times 2^{-467,6} = 2^{-356,26}$ and, as we try 2^{96} key guess, we expect that only the right value remains after the last step.

Trade-Off. Since the memory is higher than the time complexity, the data/time/memory trade-off presented Sect. 3.2 is possible. This leads to an attack using 2^8 chosen plaintexts (as the data is reused $2^{7,17}$ times), with a time complexity equivalent to $2^{106,17}$ encryptions and requiring $2^{106,17}$ 128-bit blocks.

Key Recovery. This attack retrieves the right value of u_5 except on bytes 0, 7, 10 and 13 and so can easily be turned into a key-recovery attack. The attacker guesses the four missing bytes of u_5 to retrieve the master key and try it. This step has a negligible complexity compared to the previous one.

5.3   Attack on 7 Rounds AES-256 with 2^{16} Chosen-Plaintexts

The best attack on seven rounds AES-256 with 2^{16} chosen-plaintexts is depicted on Fig. 7.

The bytes of $\mathcal{B}_{off}$ are bytes 0,2 and 3 of x_1, the three first columns of x_2 and the third column of z_3. The bytes of $\mathcal{B}_{on}$ are bytes 0 and 15 of x_0, the entire state x_6, the second column of x_5 and byte 9 of x_4. The number of values assumed by the bytes of $\mathcal{B}_{on}$ is reduced by a factor 2^8 using the equation $u_4[5] = u_6[1] + u_6[5]$. The time complexity is equivalent to 2^{178} encryptions and the memory is $2^{153,34}$ AES-blocks.

Key Recovery. This attack can easily be turned into a key-recovery attack without increasing the complexity since only 12 key bytes are sufficient to recover the master key.

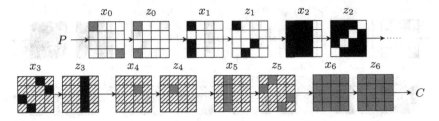

Fig. 7. Attack on 7 AES rounds (key length: 128 bits). Bytes of $\mathcal{B}_{off}$ are in black. Bytes of $\mathcal{B}_{on}$ are in gray. Hatched bytes play no role. The differences are null in white squares

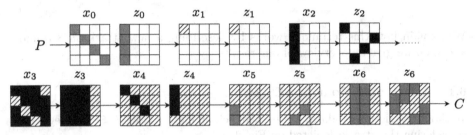

Fig. 8. Attack on 7 AES rounds (key length: 192 bits). Bytes of $\mathcal{B}_{off}$ are in black. Bytes of $\mathcal{B}_{on}$ are in gray. Hatched bytes play no role. The differences are null in white squares

5.4 Attack on 7 Rounds AES-192 with 2^{32} Chosen-Plaintexts

The best attack on seven rounds AES-192 with 2^{32} chosen-plaintexts is depicted on Fig. 8.

The bytes of $\mathcal{B}_{off}$ are the first column of x_2, the three first columns of z_3, and bytes 0, 1 and 2 of z_4. The bytes of $\mathcal{B}_{on}$ are the first column of z_0, the second and third columns of x_6 and bytes 2 and 3 of x_5. Thanks to the keyschedule equations, we can reduce the number of possible values assumed by them by a factor 2^8 since $u_5[7] = u_6[11] + u_6[15]$. The time complexity is equivalent to 2^{106} encryptions and the memory requirement is $2^{153,34}$ AES-blocks.

Trade-Off. Applying the classical data/time/memory trade-off leads to an attack using 2^{32} chosen plaintexts, with a time complexity equivalent to $2^{129,67}$ encryptions and a memory requirement of $2^{129,67}$ AES-blocks. Note that the data complexity remains 2^{32} because the structure may be divided into 2^{24} δ-sets and each of them may be reused $2^{7,34}$ times on average.

Key Recovery. This attack can easily be turned into a key-recovery attack without increasing the complexity since only 15 key bytes are sufficient to recover the master key.

6 The Differential Enumeration Technique

We present here our results using the differential enumeration technique first introduced by Dunkelman *et al.* in [13] and improved by Derbez *et al.* in [11].

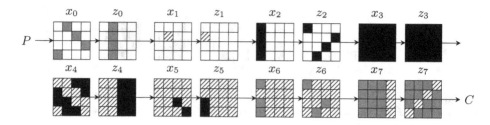

Fig. 9. Attack on 8 AES rounds. Bytes of $\mathcal{B}_{off}$ are in black. Bytes of $\mathcal{B}_{on}$ are in gray. Hatched bytes play no role. The differences are null in white squares

We explain how this technique works by describing a new attack on 8 rounds and then we give an overview of our results.

6.1   Attack on 8 Rounds AES-192

Without restriction on data, the best attack on eight rounds AES-192 begins by considering the attack depicted on Fig. 9.

The bytes of $\mathcal{B}_{off}$ are the first column of x_2, the entire state x_3, the two last columns of z_4 and bytes 2 and 3 of z_5. The bytes of $\mathcal{B}_{on}$ are the second column of z_0, the three first columns of x_7, and the first column of x_6 excepted byte 1. Thanks to the Keyschedule of AES-192 they take only $2^{8 \times 17} = 2^{136}$ values because $u_6[0] = u_7[4] + u_7[8]$ and $u_6[7] = u_7[11] + u_7[15]$. Finally, the time complexity is equivalent to 2^{138} encryptions and the memory requirement is $2^{241,34}$ AES-blocks.

Differential Enumeration. The idea of Dunkelman *et al.* is to store in the hash table only the multisets built from a δ-set containing a message m that belongs to a pair (m, m') following a well-chosen differential path. In our case this is the truncated differential $4 \to 1 \to 4 \to 16 \to 8 \to 2 \to 3 \to 12$ depicted on Fig. 10. Then the bytes of $\mathcal{B}_{off}$ can take only $2^{16 \times 8}$ values for such a pair. Indeed, if we guess the differences in circled bytes then we obtain the difference before and after the S-box for each bytes of $\mathcal{B}_{off}$ and thus we can derive their absolute value

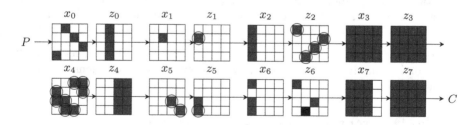

Fig. 10. Differential characteristic on 8 AES rounds. The differences are null in white squares. The value of bytes of $\mathcal{B}_{off}$ can be derived from the differences in circled bytes.

thanks to Property 1. As a consequence, the memory requirement is decreased by a factor 2^{112}. However, we now need to find a pair that follows this truncated differential path and so the procedure of the online phase becomes:

1. Ask for a structure of 2^{32} plaintexts such that the second *diagonal* assume the 2^{32} possible values and others bytes are constant.
2. Store the corresponding ciphertexts in a hash table to identify the pairs that have a non-zero probability to follow the differential path.
3. For each of these pairs:
   (a) Guess $\Delta z_6[0]$, $\Delta z_6[7]$ and $\Delta z_6[10]$ and compute the difference in the three first columns of x_7.
   (b) Deduce the value of the three first columns of x_7 using Δz_7.
   (c) Deduce $u_6[0]$ and $u_6[7]$ using $u_7[4]$, $u_7[8]$, $u_7[11]$ and $u_7[15]$.
   (d) Deduce $z_6[0]$ and $z_6[7]$ and compute $\Delta x_6[0]$ and $\Delta x_6[3]$.
   (e) Check if the equation between $\Delta x_6[0]$ and $\Delta x_6[3]$ is satisfied.
   (f) Deduce $\Delta x_6[2]$ and then compute $x_6[2]$ using $\Delta z_6[10]$.
   (g) Guess $\Delta x_1[5]$ and compute the difference in the second column of z_0.
   (h) Deduce the value of the second column of z_0 using Δx_0.
   (i) Get the δ-set associated to one of the message of the pair and build the multiset from the corresponding ciphertexts.
   (j) Check whether the multiset exists in the hash table. If not, discard the key guess.
4. Restart with a new structure if no check found.

As each structure contains 2^{63} pairs and each of these pairs follows the differential with probability 2^{-144}, we need 2^{81} structures on average. Then, for each structure we have to study only $2^{63-32} = 2^{31}$ pairs and for each of them we have to perform $2^{24} \times 2^8$ partial encryptions that is equivalent to 2^{28} encryptions. All in all, this leads to an attack with 2^{113} chosen plaintexts, a time complexity equivalent to 2^{140} encryptions and a memory requirement of 2^{130} AES-blocks.

Reducing the data complexity. Note that for each possible choice of the active *diagonal* in the plaintext we found 96 attacks with the same complexity. As the corresponding differential paths are different it is possible to perform many attacks in parallel to save data in exchange of memory. For instance, if we use structure with three active *diagonals*, it is possible to reach a complexity of $2^{104,83}$ chosen plaintexts and $2^{138,17}$ AES-blocks, the time remaining unchanged.

Key Recovery. This attack can easily be turned into a key-recovery attack without increasing the complexity since only 9 key bytes are sufficient to recover the master key.

AES-256. This attack can be applied to the AES-256 excepted that the keyschedule does not allow us to reduce the time complexity anymore. This leads to an attack with 2^{113} chosen plaintexts, a time complexity equivalent to 2^{156} encryptions and a memory requirement of 2^{130} AES-blocks. For each possible choice of the active *diagonal* in the plaintext we found 384 attacks with the same complexity so it is possible to save more data than previously. For instance, if we use structure with three active *diagonals*, it is possible to reach a complexity of $2^{102,83}$ chosen plaintexts and $2^{140,17}$ AES-blocks, the time remaining unchanged.

number of guess in the offline phase

number of guess in the online phase (left table — last mixcolumn performed)

	10	11	12	13	14	15	16	17	18	19	20	21	22
12												6.0	
13												7.0	
14												10.9	9.9
15											9.2	9.9	
16											6.6	7.6	11.0
17							8.6				6.6	7.6	11.0
18							9.6				7.6	10.2	13.6
19						10.7	10.5		6.2	8.0	8.5	8.5	
20					4.2	7.7	13.3	10.0		7.6	8.6	10.0	8.5
21	6.6	8.0			5.2	6.5	10.9	8.4		6.9	6.9	10.1	
22	7.3	10.8			3.3	4.3	12.2				8.0		
23		13.4					11.9						

last mixcolumn performed

number of guess in the offline phase

number of guess in the online phase (right table — last mixcolumn omitted)

	10	11	12	13	14	15	16	17	18	19	20	21	22
14												11.1	9.9
15											9.2	9.9	
16													
17											6.2	7.2	10.6
18							8.6				8.3	10.4	13.9
19						10.3	10.5		6.2	8.0	8.5	8.5	
20					4.2	7.7	13.4	10.0		7.6	8.6	10.0	8.5
21	6.6	8.0			5.2	6.5	10.9	8.4		6.9	6.9	10.1	
22	7.3	11.0			3.3	4.3	12.2				8.0		
23		13.3					11.9						

last mixcolumn omitted

Fig. 11. Differential Enumeration: results on 8 rounds AES-192. All attacks have a data complexity of 2^{113} chosen plaintexts. Numbers in cells are the $\log_2$ of the numbers of attacks found with the same complexity.

6.2 Results

As in the previous section, we have exhausted the almost 2^{16} variants to find the best attacks. For instance our results on the AES-192 reduced to 8 rounds are summarized on Fig. 11. As expected we have automatically rediscovered the attacks found by Dunkelman et al. and the ones found by Derbez et al., but we have also obtained many new attacks including the best known attacks on 8 rounds for both AES-192 and AES-256 described Sect. 6.1.

Limitations. To save more data, Dunkelman et al. propose to consider differential paths with a bigger probability. We have exhausted the simple case where the new differential paths do not have active new bytes in the middle rounds. However, we did not try interesting cases where the active bytes of the pair and bytes of $\mathcal{B}_{on}$ and $\mathcal{B}_{off}$ are *desynchronized* since, besides the number of cases to handle, the complexity of our tweaked tool tends to explode as we cannot apply it to the keyschedule only.

7 Conclusion

We have presented new attacks on AES by generalizing Demirci and Selçuk meet-in-the-middle attacks. We took into account various time/memory tradeoffs including more advanced techniques introduced by Dunkelman et al. in [13]. We automatized the search of the best attacks of this kind using the tool developed by Bouillaguet et al. in [8] solving linear systems of equations involving S-boxes. As a result, we recovered all best attacks on AES-128, including the recent one of Derbez et al. in [11] and found new more efficient attacks for AES-192 and AES-256.

References

1. Biham, E., Keller, N.: Cryptanalysis of Reduced Variants of Rijndael. Technical report, Computer Science Department, Technion - Israel Institute of Technology (2000)
2. Biryukov, A., Dunkelman, O., Keller, N., Khovratovich, D., Shamir, A.: Key recovery attacks of practical complexity on AES-256 variants with up to 10 rounds. In: Gilbert, H. (ed.) EUROCRYPT 2010. LNCS, vol. 6110, pp. 299–319. Springer, Heidelberg (2010)
3. Biryukov, A., Khovratovich, D.: Related-key cryptanalysis of the full AES-192 and AES-256. In: Matsui, M. (ed.) ASIACRYPT 2009. LNCS, vol. 5912, pp. 1–18. Springer, Heidelberg (2009)
4. Biryukov, A., Khovratovich, D., Nikolić, I.: Distinguisher and related-key attack on the full AES-256. In: Halevi, S. (ed.) CRYPTO 2009. LNCS, vol. 5677, pp. 231–249. Springer, Heidelberg (2009)
5. Biryukov, A., Nikolić, I.: Automatic search for related-key differential characteristics in byte-oriented block ciphers: application to AES, camellia, khazad and others. In: Gilbert, H. (ed.) EUROCRYPT 2010. LNCS, vol. 6110, pp. 322–344. Springer, Heidelberg (2010)
6. Bogdanov, A., Khovratovich, D., Rechberger, C.: Biclique cryptanalysis of the full AES. In: Lee, D.H., Wang, X. (eds.) ASIACRYPT 2011. LNCS, vol. 7073, pp. 344–371. Springer, Heidelberg (2011)
7. Bouillaguet, C., Derbez, P., Dunkelman, O., Fouque, P.A., Keller, N., Rijmen, V.: Low-data complexity attacks on AES. IEEE Trans. Inf. Theor. **58**(11), 7002–7017 (2012)
8. Bouillaguet, C., Derbez, P., Fouque, P.-A.: Automatic search of attacks on round-reduced AES and applications. In: Rogaway, P. (ed.) CRYPTO 2011. LNCS, vol. 6841, pp. 169–187. Springer, Heidelberg (2011)
9. Daemen, J., Rijmen, V.: AES proposal: Rijndael (1998)
10. Demirci, H., Selçuk, A.A.: A meet-in-the-middle attack on 8-round AES. In: Nyberg, K. (ed.) FSE 2008. LNCS, vol. 5086, pp. 116–126. Springer, Heidelberg (2008)
11. Derbez, P., Fouque, P.A., Jean, J.: Improved Key Recovery Attacks on Reduced-Round AES in the Single-Key Setting (2013) (To appear). http://eprint.iacr.org/
12. Derbez, P., Fouque, P.-A., Leresteux, D.: Meet-in-the-middle and impossible differential fault analysis on AES. In: Preneel, B., Takagi, T. (eds.) CHES 2011. LNCS, vol. 6917, pp. 274–291. Springer, Heidelberg (2011)
13. Dunkelman, O., Keller, N., Shamir, A.: Improved single-key attacks on 8-round AES-192 and AES-256. In: Abe, M. (ed.) ASIACRYPT 2010. LNCS, vol. 6477, pp. 158–176. Springer, Heidelberg (2010)
14. Ferguson, N., Kelsey, J., Lucks, S., Schneier, B., Stay, M., Wagner, D., Whiting, D.L.: Improved cryptanalysis of rijndael. In: Schneier, B. (ed.) FSE 2000. LNCS, vol. 1978, pp. 213–230. Springer, Heidelberg (2001)
15. Gilbert, H., Minier, M.: A collision attack on 7 rounds of Rijndael. In: AES Candidate Conference, pp. 230–241 (2000)
16. Lu, J., Dunkelman, O., Keller, N., Kim, J.-S.: New impossible differential attacks on AES. In: Chowdhury, D.R., Rijmen, V., Das, A. (eds.) INDOCRYPT 2008. LNCS, vol. 5365, pp. 279–293. Springer, Heidelberg (2008)
17. Mala, H., Dakhilalian, M., Rijmen, V., Modarres-Hashemi, M.: Improved impossible differential cryptanalysis of 7-round AES-128. In: Gong, G., Gupta, C.K. (eds.) INDOCRYPT 2010. LNCS, vol. 6498, pp. 282–291. Springer, Heidelberg (2010)

18. NIST: Advanced Encryption Standard (AES), FIPS 197. Technical report, NIST, November 2001
19. Wei, Y., Lu, J., Hu, Y.: Meet-in-the-middle attack on 8 rounds of the AES block cipher under 192 key bits. In: Bao, F., Weng, J. (eds.) ISPEC 2011. LNCS, vol. 6672, pp. 222–232. Springer, Heidelberg (2011)

A Framework for Automated
Independent-Biclique Cryptanalysis

Farzaneh Abed, Christian Forler, Eik List[(✉)],
Stefan Lucks, and Jakob Wenzel

Bauhaus-Universität Weimar, Weimar, Germany
{farzaneh.abed,christian.forler,eik.list,
stefan.lucks,jakob.wenzel}@uni-weimar.de

Abstract. In this paper we introduce **Janus**, a software framework – written in Java – which is built to provide assistance in finding independent-biclique attacks for a user-chosen set of parameters, e.g., the number of rounds and dimension of the biclique. Given a certain cipher, **Janus** not only finds an optimal bipartite graph (biclique), but also provides an all-round carefree package of finding an optimal matching-with-precomputation step, rendering the found biclique, and determining the computational complexity of the attack.

We have used the **Janus** framework to verify existing results on ARIA and the AES. Additionally, by using this framework, we could find the first full-round biclique attacks on all versions of the AES-like cipher BKSQ.

Keywords: Automated cryptanalysis · Biclique · BKSQ

1 Introduction

Overview. Biclique cryptanalysis was first introduced by Khovratovich *et al.* in 2011 [17] and presented at the FSE 2012 [18]. The authors used this approach to find preimages for reduced-round versions of the block cipher based hash functions Skein [12] and SHA-2 [21]. Bicliques represent an improvement of the splice-and-cut approach [4,22,23], which itself is a variant of meet-in-the-middle attacks. More detailed, biclique cryptanalysis uses a complete bipartite graph (biclique), which can be constructed over a part of a primitive, to extend an existing meet-in-the-middle or similar attack. While the splice-and-cut approach was intentionally designed to target hash functions, Wei *et al.* presented the first splice-and-cut attacks on the block cipher KTANTAN [28]. Bogdanov *et al.* then adapted biclique-based attacks on the AES [5]. Their work obtained a high level of attention, since they demonstrated the first single-key attacks on all full versions of the AES with a significant advantage over exhaustive search. Since then, biclique attacks have become a well-known technique and attacks on several further ciphers have been published in [1–3,7,8,13–15,20,24,26,27].

S. Moriai (Ed.): FSE 2013, LNCS 8424, pp. 561–581, 2014.
DOI: 10.1007/978-3-662-43933-3_29, © Springer-Verlag Berlin Heidelberg 2014

Finding good (independent) bicliques over a given number of rounds is a time-consuming task which requires in-depth knowledge of the investigated cipher to find well-suited differentials. Thus, it is adequate to think about using a computer to find such bicliques. Usually, implementations of common block cipher APIs are not designed to provide a sufficiently fine granularity, e.g., access to single steps and the basic operations of the cipher is not supported, but required to find good bicliques.

Our Contribution. A unified API is needed to reduce the effort of modifying a block-cipher implementation for the biclique search. In addition, such an API would allow applying one single biclique-searching framework that fits all. In this paper, we present such a framework, called Janus, which is open source and free to use[1]. The main feature of Janus is to find a complete and independent bipartite graph for a certain number of given rounds. In addition, it computes the corresponding step of matching with precomputations, and the overall complexity. Finally, it supports rendering a graphical illustration of the found biclique and the matching part.

Janus provides a highly modular and flexible API, i.e., it allows the user to determine parameters like the used cryptographic primitive, the starting/ending round, the dimension of the biclique, the starting difference, etc.

First, we used our framework to verify and validate published attacks on variants of the AES and ARIA (see Sect. 4). Thereby, we detected a flaw in the complexity computation of the attack on AES-192. Thus, we were not able to verify the claim made for this attack. But secondly, further analysis revealed that the authors just forgot to include one round during the matching-with-precomputation phase. This example points out the importance of an automated framework to validate claims for existing attacks.

Additionally, we used Janus to find the first full-round attacks on variants of the AES-like cipher BKSQ [10]. Results of our work can be found in Sect. 4 in Table 1.

Related Work. There are several published tools and frameworks which support certain cryptanalytic techniques. Though, these frameworks are mostly limited to a very specific area of application. For example, the work of Daemen and Van Assche[2] concentrates only on analyzing their SHA-3 winner Keccak [9]. They provide, among other things, a computation of linear and differential trails. Another framework was introduced by Leurent [19] to analyze ARX-based hash functions (like Skein or Blake) with the goal to assist in finding good differential trails. Further, Stankovski implemented an automated algebraic cryptanalysis framework [25], which uses the Maximum-Degree-Monomial (MDM) test to launch algebraic attacks against stream and block ciphers. Currently, it supports more than 20 stream and block ciphers, and provides a possibility to produce TeX code for graphs.

---

[1] https://github.com/janus-framework/janus

[2] http://keccak.noekeon.org/KeccakTools-doc/ [April 2013]

Outline. In Sect. 2 we will provide a brief introduction of biclique cryptanalysis. In Sect. 3 we introduce Janus – containing the search for bicliques, the matching phase, and the rendering option. We used our framework to verify existing attacks on the AES and ARIA, as well as to mount new attacks on BKSQ. Our results are shown in Sect. 4. Section 5 concludes the paper.

2   Independent-Biclique Cryptanalysis

In this section we review the basics of independent-biclique cryptanalysis following the work of [17]. A biclique is a complete bipartite graph which covers some steps of a given cipher. It connects every element in a set of starting states S with every element in a set of ending states C. We enumerate the elements in S by S_j and the elements in C by C_i, where a path from S_j to C_i represents the encryption under a key $K[i,j]$. More formally, the 3-tuple of sets $[\{S_j\}, \{C_i\}, \{K[i,j]\}]$ is called a *d-dimensional biclique*, if

$$\forall i,j \in \{0,\ldots,2^d-1\}: \quad S_j \xrightarrow[\mathcal{B}]{K[i,j]} C_i,$$

where $\mathcal{B}$ denotes the steps of the cipher covered by the biclique. The basic idea is to divide the key space into 2^{k-2d} groups of 2^{2d} keys, where k denotes the length of the secret key and d is the dimension of the biclique. A biclique can then be defined for one such group of keys $K[i,j]$, where the individual keys are represented relative to a so-called *base key* of the group, $K[0,0]$, and two differences Δ_i^K and ∇_j^K:

$$K[i,j] = K[0,0] \oplus \Delta_i \oplus \nabla_j.$$

An adversary can construct a biclique over one part of a cipher and apply then a meet-in-the-middle or similar attack over the remaining parts.

2.1   Independent Bicliques

In [5,16,17], Khovratovich *et al.* proposed two different paradigms for biclique attacks: *bicliques from independent differential trails* (or *independent bicliques*) and *bicliques from interleaving differential trails* (or *long bicliques*). Independent bicliques allow the construction of bicliques from two sets of differentials:

1. In the beginning, the adversary chooses a so-called *base computation*, i.e., a 3-tupel $\{S_0, C_0, K[0,0]\}$, where the key $K[0,0]$ maps the internal state S_0 to the state C_0 over $\mathcal{B}$:

$$S_0 \xrightarrow[\mathcal{B}]{K[0,0]} C_0.$$

2. Then, it chooses 2^d differences Δ_i^K, derives new keys $K[i,0] = K[0,0] \oplus \Delta_i^K$, perfoms 2^d computations from the state S_0 in forward direction and arrives at 2^d states C_i:

$$S_0 \xrightarrow[\mathcal{B}]{K[0,0]\oplus\Delta_i^K} C_0 \oplus \Delta_i = C_i \quad \forall i \in \{0,\ldots,2^d-1\}.$$

These are called the Δ_i-differentials.

3. Similarly, it chooses 2^d further differences ∇_j^K, again derives new keys $K[0,j]$ $= K[0,0] \oplus \nabla_j^K$, computes 2^d times from the state C_0 in backward direction, and arrives at 2^d states S_j:

$$S_j = S_0 \oplus \nabla_j \xleftarrow[\mathcal{B}-1]{K[0,0] \oplus \nabla_j^K} C_0 \quad \forall j \in \{0, \ldots, 2^d - 1\}.$$

These are called the ∇_j-differentials.

If all Δ_i-differentials *do not share any active non-linear operations* with the ∇_j-differentials, then every state S_j can be connected with every state C_i by encrypting S_j under the key $K[i,j] = K[0,0] \oplus \Delta_i^K \oplus \nabla_j^K$. Thus, one obtains a set of 2^{2d} *independent* (Δ_i, ∇_j)-*differential trails*:

$$S_0 \oplus \nabla_j \xrightarrow[\mathcal{B}]{K[0,0] \oplus \Delta_i^K \oplus \nabla_j^K} C_0 \oplus \Delta_i \quad \forall i,j \in \{0, \ldots, 2^d - 1\}.$$

The length of the biclique differentials is limited by two full diffusions of the cipher. An adversary can potentially create bicliques over more rounds by using the long-biclique approach. Though, the construction of long bicliques is quite sophisticated and requires a significantly higher computational effort. More importantly, the requirement for independent differentials is a very clear and well-understood criterion that allows us to test it by using an automated approach. Therefore, we focus on the independent-biclique approach in this work.

2.2   Matching-with-Precomputations

If a constructed biclique is quite short and the matching part needs to cover too many rounds, then a meet-in-the-middle attack may no longer be applicable. In such cases, [5] proposed an alternative procedure called *matching-with-precomputations*.

Assume an adversary is given a cipher E which can be split into three parts $E = \mathcal{B} \circ E_2 \circ E_1$, where E_1 is the subcipher that maps a plaintext P to an internal state V, E_2 maps V to another internal state S, and $\mathcal{B}$ maps the state S to the ciphertext C:

$$P \xrightarrow{E_1} V \xrightarrow{E_2} S \xrightarrow{\mathcal{B}} C.$$

After constructing a biclique over $\mathcal{B}$, the adversary is given 2^d states C_i, and obtains the corresponding plaintexts P_i from a decryption oracle. Then, it performs 2^d forward computations from the plaintexts P_i to $\overrightarrow{V_{i,0}}$,

$$P_i \xrightarrow[E_1]{K[i,0]} \overrightarrow{V_{i,0}},$$

and stores the 2^d values $\overrightarrow{V_{i,0}}$. Similarly, it performs 2^d backward computations from the states S_j to $\overleftarrow{V_{0,j}}$,

$$\overleftarrow{V_{0,j}} \xleftarrow[E_2^{-1}]{K[0,j]} S_j,$$

and stores the 2^d values $\overleftarrow{V_{0,j}}$. These two steps are called the *precomputations*. In the following, the adversary re-uses the stored values for the remaining $2^{2d} - 2^d$ computations

$$P_i \xrightarrow[E_1]{K[i,j]} \overrightarrow{V_{i,j}}, \quad \text{and} \quad \overleftarrow{V_{i,j}} \xleftarrow[E_2^{-1}]{K[i,j]} S_j,$$

where it recomputes only those parts of the key schedule and the round transformation that differ from the stored values. By using this method, one can reduce the computational effort significantly even if no attacks are known to cover the remaining parts of the cipher. The recomputation costs can be further reduced by only matching in a part of V (*partial matching*).

2.3 Complexity Calculation

For every biclique, the adversary tests 2^{2d} keys. Hence, it needs to construct 2^{k-2d} bicliques to cover the full key space. For the time complexity, [5] proposed the equation:

$$C_{full} = 2^{k-2d} \left(C_{biclique} + C_{decrypt} + C_{precomp} + C_{recomp} + C_{falsepos} \right), \quad (1)$$

where

- $C_{biclique}$ denotes the costs for computing $2 \cdot 2^d$ trails over $\mathcal{B}$,
- $C_{decrypt}$ is the complexity of the oracle to decrypt 2^d ciphertexts,
- $C_{precomp}$ represents the effort for 2^d computations of E_1 to determine $\overleftarrow{V_{0,j}}$ and 2^d computations of E_2^{-1} to determine $\overrightarrow{V_{i,0}}$,
- C_{recomp} describes the costs of recomputing 2^{2d} values $\overleftarrow{V_{i,j}}$ and $\overrightarrow{V_{i,j}}$, and
- $C_{falsepos}$ is the complexity to eliminate false positives.

The full computational effort of the attack is dominated by the recomputations. The memory requirements are upper bounded by storing 2^d intermediate states $V_{i,j}$.

3 Framework Design

Our current implementation consists of four components:

1. The `biclique search` subsystem is responsible for searching for independent differential trails over some sub-cipher $\mathcal{B}$ of a given primitive E.
2. Given a found biclique, the `matching` subsystem analyzes the remaining parts of the cipher to find a matching which leads to an attack with a minimal computational effort.

3. The `rendering` subsystem can visualize bicliques as well as matching phase differentials in PDF format, using the community version 5.3.0 of the open-source library iText [6].
4. Moreover, the framework contains a number of common components, such as cipher implementations, serialization and utility classes, as well as cipher-dependent helper classes which generate and compare differentials.

In this work we concentrate on describing the two major components in detail.

3.1 Biclique Search

The task of finding independent bicliques can be transformed into the task of finding pairs of independent differentials (Δ^f, ∇^b). In advance, the user needs to specify:

- a target cipher E,
- the round range of the sub-cipher $\mathcal{B}$,
- the dimension of bicliques d,
- a strategy to test the independency of differentials,
- and a strategy to define and generate round key differences.

The general biclique search follows the steps from Sect. 2.1. Assume that $\mathcal{B}$ covers the rounds $[r, s]$ with $1 \leq r \leq s \leq N_r$ of a given cipher E, where N_r is the total number of rounds in E. We denote

- by $N_r^{\mathcal{B}} = s - r + 1$ the number of rounds covered by $\mathcal{B}$,
- by T_i the state after Round i,
- by U_i the intermediate state after the non-linear operation in Round i,
- and by K_i the round key of Round i.

We further call the state of the cipher's key register, which contains the key for Round r, the starting key, and the state which contains the key for Round s the ending key.

First, we fix $K[0,0]$ and S_0 to and derive C_0. This base computation is computed only once for a given cipher and round interval. We then create a trail Δ^f which will store all state values T_i, all intermediate state values U_i, as well as all round keys K_i which are used in $\mathcal{B}$. At the beginning, we initialize them with all-zero values. Then, we choose a starting key difference Δ^{K^f} with d bits set. In the following, we iterate over all 2^d possible values for the d set bits in Δ^{K^f}, and compute $2^d - 1$ differential trails

$$S_0 \xrightarrow[\mathcal{B}]{K[0,0] \oplus \Delta_i^{K^f}} C_i^f, \quad \forall\, i \in \{1, \ldots, 2^d - 1\}.$$

We denote by Δ_i^f the resulting differences between the corresponding states, intermediate states and round keys of the trail Δ^f and the base computation:

$$\Delta_i^f = \left(S_0 \xrightarrow[\mathcal{B}]{K[0,0]} C_0 \right) \oplus \left(S_0 \xrightarrow[\mathcal{B}]{K[0,0] \oplus \Delta_i^{K^f}} C_i^f \right).$$

Bits which are active in any of the 2^{d-1} differential trails Δ_i^f should remain active in the differential Δ^f. Thus, the Δ_i^f-trails are accumulated to Δ^f by applying the logical OR pair-wise to all corresponding state and round key differences of all differentials Δ_i^f:

$$\Delta^f \leftarrow \bigvee_{i=1}^{2^d-1} \Delta_i^f.$$

This procedure is repeated for in total N_d unique starting key differences Δ^{K^f}, $\forall f \in \{1, \ldots, N_d\}$. All N_d accumulated forward trails Δ^f are stored in a list. The N_d backward trails ∇^b are computed similarly afterwards.

For every pair of differentials (Δ^f, ∇^b), we check if any of their corresponding states or round keys share active parts in non-linear operations. If not, the current pair yields an independent biclique. Since any identified biclique can be used to mount an attack, we provide an option for the early abort as soon as the first such pair has been found. The time complexity of the biclique search process is given by

$$C_{time} = C_{forward} + C_{backward} + C_{testing},$$

where

- $C_{forward}$ is given by constructing N_d Δ-differentials,
- $C_{backward}$ denotes the effort of constructing N_d ∇-differentials,
- and $C_{testing}$ represents the costs for comparing N_d^2 pairs of differentials (Δ, ∇).

The complexity is dominated by the effort for testing N_d^2 pairs of differentials. We have to store the states and round keys of N_d forward differentials, where every differential holds $N_r^{\mathcal{B}} + 1$ (from $r-1$ to s) state differences, $N_r^{\mathcal{B}}$ (from r to s) intermediate state differences, and a cipher-dependent number of N_k round key differences, since E may employ pre- and post-whitening keys. Hence, we need to store

$$C_{memory} = N_d \cdot (2N_r^{\mathcal{B}} + 1) \cdot n + N_k \cdot k$$

bits, where n and k denote the state and round-key size, respectively. In the case when the available memory is not sufficient to store all forward differentials, the biclique search is performed in iterations.

Ciphers. Throughout the framework we employ a unified interface for cipher implementations. Standard implementations allow the client to specify only the plaintext, the used key and, in some cases, a tweak. The implementations in our framework have to provide access also to internal values, such as intermediate states to allow the comparison of state differences.

In addition, they have to provide access to the values of round keys as well as to their internal key register. To obtain the longest possible independent bicliques, one should not minimize the number of active bits with respect to the secret key. Since the key schedule of most ciphers provides a significant diffusion, it would increase the number of affected bits in the round-key differences Δ_i^K or ∇_j^K and hence, would increase the number of active bits in the differential trails. Instead, one should choose key differences which have a minimum number of active bits in the round keys at the beginning (for Δ-differentials) or at the end (for ∇-differentials) of $\mathcal{B}$, respectively. This minimizes the number of active bits in non-linear operations of the differential trails through $\mathcal{B}$. Thus, the starting point for choosing key differences should be an intermediate state of the cipher's key register, from where one can derive the differences for all further round keys. The ciphers we are interested in utilize a key register which is updated in an iterated reversible procedure, with the consequence that the secret key can be reconstructed from any given register state. Our implementations specify if the key schedule of a cipher is reversible. In this case – which applies to most AES-like primitives and modern lightweight ciphers – they provide a method which allows to invert the key schedule given an arbitrary k-bit state of the key register at a certain number of iterations. In the opposite case, the starting key differences are injected in the secret key as a fallback solution.

Starting Key Differences. The number of tested differentials, N_d, depends on the dimension of the biclique d and the size of the key register k. Given k and d, one could potentially generate $N_d = \binom{k}{d}$ forward and backward differentials, which becomes infeasible for $k \geq 64$. Though, this effort can be reduced significantly for byte- and nibble-wise operating ciphers. In the following, we consider three strategies to generate key differences for such primitives, which are illustrated in Fig. 1.

1. Firstly, one can set only a minimum number of d active bits in the starting key difference. Then, for byte-wise operating primitives, there are only $\frac{k}{\lceil d/8 \rceil}$

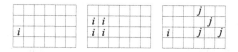

Fig. 1. Approaches to iterate over key differences for byte-wise/nibble-wise operating ciphers: iterate over a minimum number of active bytes/nibbles (left), over multiple bytes/nibbles with equal value (middle), or choose user-defined differences over a part of the key to cancel out results of the round transformation (right).

active bytes in the difference. As a consequence, for byte- and nibble-wise primitives the number of possible differences which can be tested reduces to

$$N_d = \binom{k/8}{\lceil d/8 \rceil} \quad \text{and} \quad N_d = \binom{k/4}{\lceil d/4 \rceil}$$

differentials, respectively. For bit-wise operating primitives, one can limit the number of generated key differences to a user-definable number.

2. Secondly, one can set the same difference for multiple nibbles/bytes in the starting key difference. At the first sight, these will produce additional active bytes in the state after a key injection, making it harder for the differential to be independent in a pair. At second sight, the additional active bytes may cancel out byte differences in the key schedule and/or the round transformation of AES-like ciphers, as we can learn from the attack on SQUARE by Mala [20]. Though, this strategy increases the number of tested keys to $N_d = 2^{k/8}$ for byte-wise and $N_d = 2^{k/4}$ for nibble-wise primitives, respectively.

3. Alternatively, one can employ custom rules to generate round-key differences. In their attack on AES-192, Bogdanov *et al.* employed the inverse result of a MixColumns operation as a part of the round key difference [5]. And in their attack on ARIA-256 [8], the authors used dedicated differences in which the right half of the 256-bit key canceled the difference injected by the left half. One can learn from those examples that cipher-specific key differences can result in longer bicliques for AES-like ciphers. Since testing all custom differences in the key space is infeasible, the task of choosing "good" custom starting key differentials can be left to the user.

3.2 Matching

A matching-with-precomputations step is supposed to be applied to the sub-ciphers not covered by a given biclique (here $E_2 \circ E_1$). Our framework can help to identify a well-suited matching by investigating two aspects: first, it tests all possible rounds which can be used to locate V:

$$P \xrightarrow{E_1} V \xleftarrow{E_2^{-1}} S,$$

and second, it tests all possible nibbles or bytes in V which can be used for a partial matching. For every round r that can be used to locate V, we perform four steps:

1. First, we compute differentials from the start and the end of the matching part to the middle:

$$P \xrightarrow[E_1]{K[0,0] \oplus \nabla_j^K} V_r \oplus \nabla_j^V \quad \text{and} \quad V_r \oplus \Delta_i^V \xleftarrow[E_2^{-1}]{K[0,0] \oplus \Delta_i^K} S.$$

Note that these differential trails result from injecting differences in the round keys.

2. Then, for every nibble/byte in V, we create a new difference δ^V in which the bits that are used for a partial matching are set. We compute the differentials from V to start and end:

$$P \oplus \delta^P \xleftarrow[E_1^{-1}]{K[0,0]} V_r \oplus \delta^V \quad \text{and} \quad V_r \oplus \delta^V \xrightarrow[E_2]{K[0,0]} S \oplus \delta^S.$$

These active bits in these trails represent the parts of the states and round keys that have to be known in order to apply the partial matching.

3. For the recomputation effort of an attack, one has to consider only those parts of the states and round keys that are active in both differential trails: $0 \rightarrow \nabla_j^V$ and $\delta^P \leftarrow \delta^V$. Therefore, we apply the logical AND ($\wedge$) between the active bits/nibbles/bytes (depending on the cipher) of all corresponding states and round keys and obtain the accumulated differential Δ_j^P by

$$\Delta_j^P = (0 \rightarrow \delta^V) \wedge (\delta^P \leftarrow V_r).$$

Similarly, we compute the accumulated differential ∇_i^S

$$\nabla_i^S = (\delta V_r \leftarrow 0) \wedge (\delta_r^V \rightarrow \delta S).$$

4. As the final step, the number of active bits/nibbles/bytes in keys, states, and intermediate states is counted in both Δ_j^P and ∇_i^S to have a single number which refers to the recomputational effort.

4   Applications

We used our implementation to validate existing biclique attacks on the AES and ARIA from [5,8], and to mount new attacks on the three versions of the cipher BKSQ. Table 1 summarizes our results and compares them with previous attacks.

4.1   Verifications

AES. In our experiments on the AES we could construct bicliques on up to three rounds for the 128-bit, and on up to four rounds for the 192-bit and 256-bit versions. Hence, our results confirm to the findings of Bogdanov *et al.* in terms of maximal biclique lengths. In their independent-biclique attacks, Bogdanov *et al.* pointed out that the round key differences are a linear function of the indices i and j. Thus, the authors could neglect the effort for recomputing the S-boxes in the key schedule. We did not employ this optimization, since we searched for a more general approach in our implementation. Additionally, we detected a minor flaw in the complexity calculation for the independent-biclique attack on the 192-bit version. There, the authors forgot to consider either the round 6 or 7 with 16 active S-boxes which increases the number of SubByte operations from 2.8125 to 3.8125, and the total complexity from $2^{189.74}$ to $2^{190.16}$.

Table 1. Independent-biclique attacks constructed by automated search in comparison with previously published attacks. CP: chosen plaintexts, $(*)$: the computational complexity should be $2^{190.16}$ (cf. Sect. 4.1).

Primitive	Rounds	Comp. complexity	Data complexity (CP)	Memory complexity	Ref.
AES					
AES-128	10 (full)	$2^{126.72}$	2^{72}	2^8	This work
AES-128	10 (full)	$2^{126.18}$	2^{88}	2^8	[5]
AES-192	12 (full)	$2^{190.28}$	2^{48}	2^8	This work
AES-192	12 (full)	$2^{189.74}(*)$	2^{80}	2^8	[5]
AES-256	14 (full)	$2^{254.53}$	2^{64}	2^8	This work
AES-256	14 (full)	$2^{254.42}$	2^{40}	2^8	[5]
ARIA					
ARIA-256	16 (full)	$2^{255.20}$	2^{80}	2^8	[8]
BKSQ					
BKSQ-96	10 (full)	$2^{94.47}$	2^{80}	2^8	This work
BKSQ-144	14 (full)	$2^{142.63}$	2^{96}	2^8	This work
BKSQ-192	18 (full)	$2^{190.78}$	2^{96}	2^8	This work

ARIA. ARIA is a Korean variant of the AES. Its round transformation provides a significant diffusion, where every input byte is involved in the computation of seven output bytes. In the key schedule of ARIA, the input key is transformed in a four-round Feistel structure to create four intermediate key words W_0, W_1, W_2, W_3. All round keys are then extracted from these words using rotations and XORs. Chen and Xu [8] injected one-byte differences for the Δ_i- and ∇_j-differentials in the leftmost 128 bits of the key, and used the rightmost 128 bits to cancel the resulting seven-byte difference. We have implemented and verified the attack on ARIA-256. However, the Feistel preparation in the key schedule refused more efficient attacks.

4.2 Independent-Biclique Attack on the Full AES-128 and AES-192

While the time complexities of the previous works on the AES are better than our results for them, we could decrease the data complexity for the 128-bit and 192-bit versions. In the biclique for the 128-bit version, the ciphertexts C_i differ in only 11 out of 16 bytes, as can be seen on the left side of Fig. 2 in Appendix A. The bytes $0, 8, 12$ (from left: the first, third and fourth byte in the uppermost row) are active in the ciphertexts only after the key injection in the final round. Due to the key schedule of the AES, these bytes in the final round key always have an equal difference. As a consequence, since the ciphertexts can only take $(2^8)^9$ values, the data complexity is upper bounded by 2^{72}.

Similarly, in the biclique for the 192-bit version, the ciphertexts C_i differ in only five out of 16 bytes before the final key addition, as illustrated on the right side of Fig. 2 in Appendix A.

Due to the key schedule, the bytes $1, 5, 9$ (from left: the first, third and fourth byte in the second row) in the round key for the final round always have an equal difference. The ciphertexts for this biclique can take only $(2^8)^6$ values. Thus, the data complexity of an attack using this biclique is upper bounded by 2^{48}.

4.3   Specification of BKSQ

BKSQ is a substitution-permutation network that was proposed by Daemen and Rijmen in [10]. The cipher represents a generalization of Rijndael, in which the state has a rectangular $m \times n$-structure (cf. [11]). There are three different versions of BKSQ which all have a state size of 96 and individual key lengths of 96, 144, or 192 bits. The internal state is represented by a 3×4- and the secret key is represented as a 3×4-, 6×4-, or 9×4-byte matrix. The plaintext is transformed in $10/14/18$ rounds using the four operations:

- *MixColumns*/θ: The internal state is multiplied column-wise by a circulant MDS-matrix in the Galois-Field $GF(2^8)$.
- *SubBytes*/γ: Each byte in the internal state is replaced using an 8×8-bit S-box.
- *ShiftRows*/π: The i-th row of the internal state for $i \in \{0, 1, 2\}$ is rotated by i bytes to the left.
- *AddRoundKey*/$\sigma[k_i]$: The internal state is XORed byte-wise with the subkey k_i for round i.

Before the first round, an inverse θ-operation is applied to the plaintext and an additional key k_0 is XORed with the state.

4.4   Independent-Biclique Attack on Full BKSQ-96

This subsection explains our independent-biclique attack on full BKSQ-96. The attack includes three steps: partitioning the key space, constructing a biclique, and matching over the remaining parts of the cipher. The complexity of the attack is described at the end.

Key Space Partitioning. We partition the key space in 2^{80} sets with respect to the round key for Round 8, k_8. The base keys $K[0, 0]$ of the sets are the 2^{80} 12-byte values with two bytes fixed to zero, where the ten remaining bytes run over all possible values. The 2^{16} keys $K[i, j]$ in a set are defined by applying the key differences Δ_i^K and ∇_j^K to the base key, where $i, j \in \{0, \ldots, 255\}$.

$$K[0,0] = \boxed{\begin{matrix} & & & \\ & & 0 & 0 \\ & & & \end{matrix}} \qquad \Delta_i^K(k_8) = \boxed{\begin{matrix} & & & \\ & & & i \\ & & & \end{matrix}} \qquad \nabla_j^K(k_8) = \boxed{\begin{matrix} & & & I \ I \\ & & & j \\ & & & \end{matrix}}$$

Note that the key schedule of BKSQ-96 performs a bijective mapping where every value for the secret key is mapped uniquely to one value of each round key. Thus, our splitting of the key space covers the full secret key space.

3-Round Biclique of Dimension 8. We construct a biclique of dimension eight over the rounds 8-10. Fig. 3 in Appendix B shows the base computation as well as the Δ_i- and ∇_j-differentials. It can be seen from there that all Δ_i- and ∇_j-differentials are independent, i.e., their keys and states do not share active bytes which are used as inputs to the non-linear S-box. From Fig. 3 in Appendix B one can see that the Δ_i-differentials affect the ciphertexts C_i in only 10 bytes. By fixing C_0 for all bicliques, we can upper bound the data complexity of this attack by 2^{80} ciphertexts.

Matching Over 7 Rounds. The matching part covers the first seven rounds of the cipher, as illustrated in Fig. 4 in Appendix B. We choose the first byte of the state after Round 3 for the partial matching. The bytes which have to be recomputed are darkened in Fig. 4.

Similar to the attacks on the AES in [5], we have to be accurate concerning the recomputation effort. In all attacks on BKSQ we follow the argumentation of [5] and focus on the number of S-boxes which require recomputation in order to have a single value which refers best to the total effort, since the number of S-box lookups is the dominant summand compared to the number of recomputed θ- and σ- operations.

As we can see from Fig. 4 in Appendix B, we need to consider nine S-boxes in the first, three S-boxes in the second, and one additional S-box in the third round. Hence, we have $9 + 3 + 1 = 13$ S-boxes in the forward part of the round transformation. In backward direction (covering rounds 4 to 7) we need to consider $3 + 9 + 7 + 3 = 22$ S-boxes in the round transformation. Additionally, we have to take into account the S-boxes that require recomputation in the key schedule. BKSQ uses the S-box for the rightmost column of each of its round keys. There are $3 + 3 + 3 + 3 + 1 + 1 + 0 + 1 = 15$ such active S-boxes in the last column of the round keys. These sum up to $13 + 22 + 15 = 50$ S-boxes for one group of keys.

Complexity of the Attack. In the full BKSQ-96, there are $10 \cdot 12 = 120$ S-boxes in all γ-operations of the full cipher and 30 S-boxes in the key schedule. Thus, for 2^{16} keys in one key group, C_{recomp} is equivalent to $2^{16} \cdot \frac{50}{150} = 2^{14.42}$ full encryptions. In all of our attacks on BKSQ we use bicliques of dimension eight. Therefore, the decryption oracle needs 2^8 decryptions per biclique. Since we match in eight bits in the state v, we can expect to have 2^{16-8} false positive key candidates per key group in average, which have to be tested in a brute-force stage.

For BKSQ-96, the effort to construct a biclique, $C_{biclique}$, is given by computing $2 \cdot 2^8$ times three out of 10 rounds, which is equal to $2^{7.26}$ full encryptions. The precomputations costs are given by computing 2^8 times three rounds in forward direction from P to V and 2^8 times four rounds in backward direction from S to V. Hence, $C_{precomp}$ is equal to $2^{7.49}$ encryptions. The full computational complexity is given by

$$2^{80} \cdot (2^{7.26} + 2^8 + 2^{7.49} + 2^{14.42} + 2^8) = 2^{94.48}$$

encryptions. This attack requires 2^{80} chosen plaintexts, and memory to store 2^8 96-bit states at a time.

4.5   Independent-Biclique Attack on Full BKSQ-144

Key Space Partitioning. In the attack on the 144-bit version of BKSQ we partition the key space in 2^{128} sets with respect to the block $(k_{12}\|k_{13}^L)$, which contains the full round key k_{12} and the leftmost two columns of k_{13}. The base keys of the sets, $K[0,0]$, are the 2^{128} 18-byte values, where two bytes are fixed to zero and the remaining 16 bytes run over all possible values. The 2^{16} keys $K[i,j]$ in a set are defined by applying the key differences Δ_i^K and ∇_j^K to the base key, where $i, j \in \{0, \ldots, 255\}$.

$$K[0,0] = \boxed{} \qquad \Delta_i^K(k_{12}\|k_{13}^L) = \boxed{} \qquad \nabla_j^K(k_{12}\|k_{13}^L) = \boxed{}$$

Note that the key schedule of BKSQ-144 maps every value of the secret key uniquely to one value of each 18-byte block of the key register. Thus, our splitting of the key space with respect to $(k_{12}\|k_{13}^L)$ covers the full secret-key space.

4-Round Biclique of Dimension 8. We construct a four-round biclique which covers the rounds 11 to 14, as shown in Fig. 5 in Appendix C. This time, the ciphertexts C_i are affected in all bytes. Thus, the attack can potentially include the full codebook.

Matching Over 9 Rounds. We match in the first byte of the state after Round 3. Figure 6 in Appendix C shows the active bytes in the matching phase. We consider $9 + 3 + 1 = 13$ S-boxes in forward and $3 + 9 + 12 + 12 + 12 + 6 + 2 = 56$ active S-boxes in the backward part of the matching. Moreover, in the key schedule, we have to recompute one active S-box in each of the round keys k_1, k_4, k_7, and k_{10}. Hence, there are in total $13 + 56 + 4 = 73$ active S-boxes in the matching phase.

Complexity of the Attack. In the full cipher, there are $14 \cdot 12 = 168$ S-boxes in the γ-operations and 27 S-boxes in the key schedule. Thus, for 2^{16} keys in one key group, C_{recomp} is equivalent to $2^{16} \cdot \frac{73}{195} = 2^{14.58}$ full encryptions. $C_{biclique}$ is given by computing $2 \cdot 2^8$ times four out of 14 rounds, which is equivalent to $2^{7.19}$ full encryptions. Considering $C_{precomp}$, one has to compute 2^8 times ten out of 14 rounds, which is equivalent to $2^{7.51}$ full computations. The total time complexity is given by

$$2^{128} \cdot (2^{7.19} + 2^8 + 2^{7.51} + 2^{14.58} + 2^8) = 2^{142.63}$$

full encryptions. The data complexity of this attack is 2^{96}, and we need memory to store 2^8 states.

4.6 New Independent-Biclique Attack on Full BKSQ-192

Key Space Partitioning. For this attack we divide the key space into 2^{176} sets with respect to the block $(k_{16}\|k_{17})$, which contains the keys for rounds 16 and 17. The base keys $K[0,0]$ are the 2^{176} 24-byte values with two bytes fixed to zero, where all other bytes run over all possible values. The 2^{16} keys $K[i,j]$ in a set are defined by applying the key differences Δ_i^K and ∇_j^K to the base key, where $i, j \in \{0, \ldots, 255\}$.

$$K[0,0] = \boxed{\genfrac{}{}{0pt}{}{0}{0}} \quad \Delta_i^K(k_{16}\|k_{17}) = \boxed{\;i\;|\;i\;} \quad \nabla_j^K(k_{16}\|k_{17}) = \boxed{\;j\;}$$

Note, that the key schedule of BKSQ-192 maps every value of the secret key uniquely to one value of each 24-byte block of the key register. Thus, our splitting of the key space with respect to $(k_{16}\|k_{17})$ covers the full secret-key space.

5-Round Biclique of Dimension 8. We construct a 5-round biclique which covers the rounds 14 to 18, as shown in Fig. 7 in Appendix D. For this attack, the Δ_i-differentials affect all bytes in the ciphertexts C_i. Hence, this attack may require the full codebook.

Matching Over 13 Rounds. We match in the first byte of the state after Round 5, as shown in Fig. 8, Appendix D. There, an adversary should recompute $12 + 12 + 9 + 3 + 1 = 37$ S-boxes in the forward direction, $3 + 9 + 4 \cdot 12 + 6 + 2 = 68$ S-boxes in backward direction and six S-boxes in the key schedule. Hence, $37 + 68 + 6 = 111$ S-boxes need to be recomputed in total.

Complexity of the Attack. In BKSQ-192, there are $18 \cdot 12 = 216$ S-boxes in the γ-operations and 51 bytes in the key schedule. Thus, for 2^{16} keys in one key group, C_{recomp} results in $2^{16} \cdot \frac{111}{267} = 2^{14.73}$ full encryptions. $C_{biclique}$ is given by computing $2 \cdot 2^8$ times five out of 18 rounds, which is equivalent to $2^{7.15}$ full encryptions. $C_{precomp}$ is given by computing 2^8 times 13 out of 18 rounds or $2^{7.53}$ computations. The full time complexity is given by

$$2^{176} \cdot (2^{7.15} + 2^8 + 2^{7.53} + 2^{14.73} + 2^8) = 2^{190.78}$$

full encryptions. Again, the data complexity is 2^{96} and the memory complexity is 2^8.

5 Conclusion and Outlook

With Janus, we have introduced a user-friendly, highly flexible, and expandable framework for cryptanalysts which supports automated biclique cryptanalysis of a user-specified cryptographic algorithm. With this framework, we found the first full-round attacks on BKSQ-96, BKSQ-144, and BKSQ-192. It is planned to increase the number of supported primitives, e.g., the AES and SHA-3 finalists to analyze the resistance against biclique attacks.

A   Bicliques from the Attack on Full AES-128 and AES-192

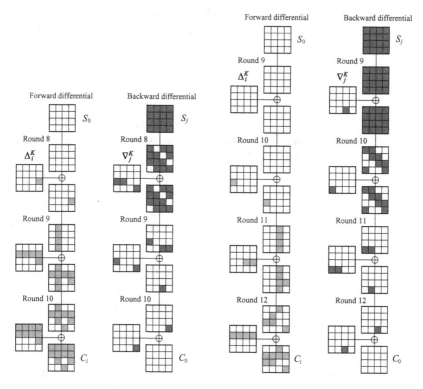

Fig. 2. Δ_i- and ∇_j-differentials of the bicliques for the AES-128 (left) over the rounds 8 - 10 and the AES-192 (right) over the rounds 9 - 12.

B   Independent-Biclique Attack on Full BKSQ-96

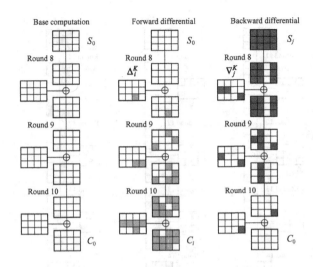

Fig. 3. Biclique for BKSQ-96 over the rounds 8 - 10 with Δ_i- and ∇_j-differentials.

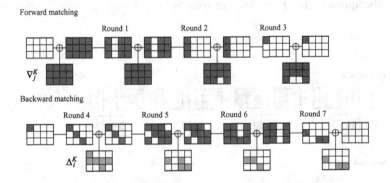

Fig. 4. Recomputations for BKSQ-96 in forward and backward direction.

C   Independent-Biclique Attack on Full BKSQ-144

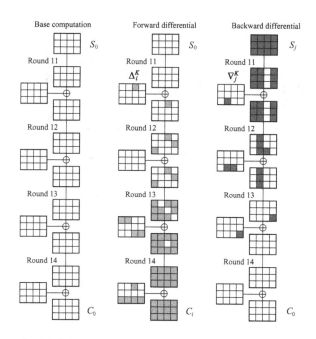

Fig. 5. Biclique for BKSQ-144 over the rounds 11 - 14 with Δ_i- and ∇_j-differentials.

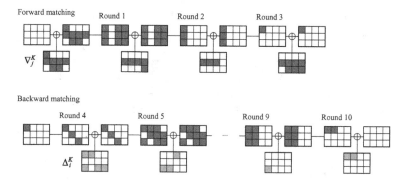

Fig. 6. Recomputations for BKSQ-144 in forward and backward direction.

D   Independent-Biclique Attack on Full BKSQ-192

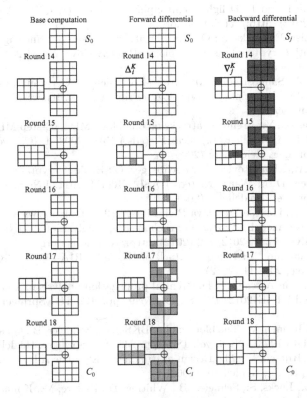

Fig. 7. Biclique for BKSQ-192 over the rounds 14 - 18 with Δ_i- and ∇_j-differentials.

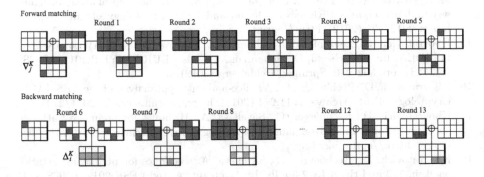

Fig. 8. Recomputations for BKSQ-192 in forward and backward direction.

References

1. Abed, F., Forler, C., List, E., Lucks, S., Wenzel, J.: Biclique Cryptanalysis of the PRESENT and LED lightweight ciphers. Cryptology ePrint Archive, report 2012/591 (2012). http://eprint.iacr.org/
2. Abed, F., List, E., Lucks, S.: On the security of the core of prince against biclique and differential cryptanalysis. Cryptology ePrint Archive, report 2012/712 (2012). http://eprint.iacr.org/
3. Ahmadian, Z., Salmasizadeh, M., Aref, M.R.: Biclique Cryptanalysis of the Full-Round KLEIN block cipher. Cryptology ePrint Archive, report 2013/097 (2013). http://eprint.iacr.org/
4. Aoki, K., Sasaki, Y.: Preimage attacks on one-block MD4, 63-step MD5 and more. In: Avanzi, R.M., Keliher, L., Sica, F. (eds.) SAC 2008. LNCS, vol. 5381, pp. 103–119. Springer, Heidelberg (2009)
5. Bogdanov, A., Khovratovich, D., Rechberger, C.: Biclique cryptanalysis of the full AES. In: Lee, D.H., Wang, X. (eds.) ASIACRYPT 2011. LNCS, vol. 7073, pp. 344–371. Springer, Heidelberg (2011)
6. 1T3XT BVBA. iText, a Free Java-PDF Library (2012). http://www.itextpdf.com/
7. Çoban, M., Karakoç, F., Boztaş, Ö.: Biclique cryptanalysis of TWINE. Cryptology ePrint Archive, report 2012/422 (2012). http://eprint.iacr.org/
8. Chen, S., Tianmin, X.: Biclique attack of the full ARIA-256. IACR Cryptology ePrint Archive, 2012:11 (2012)
9. Daemen, J., Van Assche, G.: Differential propagation analysis of keccak. In: Canteaut, A. (ed.) FSE 2012. LNCS, vol. 7549, pp. 422–441. Springer, Heidelberg (2012)
10. Daemen, J., Rijmen, V.: The block cipher BKSQ. In: Schneier, B., Quisquater, J.-J. (eds.) CARDIS 1998. LNCS, vol. 1820, pp. 236–245. Springer, Heidelberg (2000)
11. Daemen, J., Rijmen, V.: The Design of Rijndael: AES - The Advanced Encryption Standard. Springer, Heidelberg (2002)
12. Ferguson, N., Lucks, S., Schneier, B., Whiting, D., Bellare, M., Kohno, T., Callas, J., Walker, J.: The skein hash function family. Submission to NIST (Round 3) (2010)
13. Hong, D., Koo, B., Kwon, D.: Biclique attack on the full HIGHT. In: Kim, H. (ed.) ICISC 2011. LNCS, vol. 7259, pp. 365–374. Springer, Heidelberg (2012)
14. Jeong, K., Kang, H., Lee, C., Sung, J., Hong, S.: Biclique cryptanalysis of lightweight block ciphers PRESENT, piccolo and LED. Cryptology ePrint Archive, report 2012/621 (2012). http://eprint.iacr.org/
15. Khovratovich, D., Leurent, G., Rechberger, C.: Narrow-Bicliques: cryptanalysis of full IDEA. In: Pointcheval, D., Johansson, T. (eds.) EUROCRYPT 2012. LNCS, vol. 7237, pp. 392–410. Springer, Heidelberg (2012)
16. Khovratovich, D., Rechberger, C.: A splice-and-cut cryptanalysis of the AES. IACR Cryptology ePrint Archive, 2011:274 (2011). http://eprint.iacr.org/2011/274
17. Khovratovich, D., Rechberger, C., Savelieva, A.: Bicliques for preimages: attacks on skein-512 and the SHA-2 family. Cryptology ePrint Archive, report 2011/286 (2011). http://eprint.iacr.org/
18. Khovratovich, D., Rechberger, C., Savelieva, A.: Bicliques for preimages: attacks on skein-512 and the SHA-2 family. In: Canteaut, A. (ed.) FSE 2012. LNCS, vol. 7549, pp. 244–263. Springer, Heidelberg (2012)
19. Leurent, G.: ARXtools: a toolkit for ARX analysis. University of Luxembourg, Technical report (2012)

20. Mala, H.: Biclique cryptanalysis of the block cipher SQUARE. Cryptology ePrint Archive, report 2011/500 (2011). http://eprint.iacr.org/
21. NIST National Institute of Standards and Technology. FIPS 180–2: Secure Hash Standard. April 1995. http://csrc.nist.gov
22. Sasaki, Y., Aoki, K.: Preimage attacks on step-reduced MD5. In: Mu, Y., Susilo, W., Seberry, J. (eds.) ACISP 2008. LNCS, vol. 5107, pp. 282–296. Springer, Heidelberg (2008)
23. Sasaki, Y., Wang, L., Aoki, K.: Preimage attacks on 41-step SHA-256 and 46-step SHA-512. Cryptology ePrint Archive, report 2009/479 (2009). http://eprint.iacr.org/
24. Shakiba, M., Dakhilalian, M., Mala, H.: Non-isomorphic biclique cryptanalysis and its application to full-round mCrypton. Cryptology ePrint Archive, report 2013/141 (2013). http://eprint.iacr.org/
25. Stankovski, P.: Automated algebraic cryptanalysis. Department of Electrical and Information Technology. Technical report, Department of Electrical and Information Technology, Lund University (2010)
26. Wang, Y., Wu, W., Yu, X.: Biclique cryptanalysis of reduced-round piccolo block cipher. In: Ryan, M.D., Smyth, B., Wang, G. (eds.) ISPEC 2012. LNCS, vol. 7232, pp. 337–352. Springer, Heidelberg (2012)
27. Wang, Y., Wu, W., Yu, X., Zhang, L.: Security on LBlock against biclique cryptanalysis. In: Lee, D.H., Yung, M. (eds.) WISA 2012. LNCS, vol. 7690, pp. 1–14. Springer, Heidelberg (2012)
28. Wei, L., Rechberger, C., Guo, J., Wu, H., Wang, H., Ling, S.: Improved meet-in-the-middle cryptanalysis of KTANTAN (poster). In: Parampalli, U., Hawkes, P. (eds.) ACISP 2011. LNCS, vol. 6812, pp. 433–438. Springer, Heidelberg (2011)

Boolean Functions

A New Criterion for Avoiding the Propagation of Linear Relations Through an Sbox

Christina Boura[1,2]([✉]) and Anne Canteaut[1]

[1] SECRET Project-Team - INRIA Paris-Rocquencourt, B.P. 105,
78153 Le Chesnay Cedex, France
[2] Gemalto, 6, Rue de la Verrerie, 92190 Meudon, France
{Christina.Boura,Anne.Canteaut}@inria.fr

Abstract. In several cryptographic primitives, Sboxes of small size are used to provide nonlinearity. After several iterations, all the output bits of the primitive are ideally supposed to depend in a nonlinear way on all of the input variables. However, in some cases, it is possible to find some output bits that depend in an affine way on a small number of input bits if the other input bits are fixed to a well-chosen value. Such situations are for example exploited in cube attacks or in attacks like the one presented by Fuhr against the hash function Hamsi. Here, we define a new property for nonlinear Sboxes, named (v, w)-linearity, which means that 2^w components of an Sbox are affine on all cosets of a v-dimensional subspace. This property is related to the generalization of the so-called Maiorana-McFarland construction for Boolean functions. We show that this concept quantifies the ability of an Sbox to propagate affine relations. As a proof of concept, we exploit this new notion for analyzing and slightly improving Fuhr's attack against Hamsi and we show that its success strongly depends on the (v, w)-linearity of the involved Sbox.

Keywords: Sbox · Boolean function · Linear relations · Maiorana-McFarland construction · Hash functions

1 Introduction

In the construction of symmetric primitives such as block ciphers and hash functions, nonlinear functions are iterated to provide confusion. In particular, it is required that all the outputs of the primitive depend in a nonlinear way on the inputs. However, it might happen that some output bits can be expressed in an affine way as a function of a small number of input bits, when the other input bits are fixed to some well-chosen values. Clearly, the sizes of the corresponding sets of inputs and outputs provide a measure of the induced weaknesses: such a property always holds for any input set of size 1, but it should be avoided for larger sets. Actually, in such a situation, an attacker would be able to derive some

Partially supported by the French Agence Nationale de la Recherche through the BLOC project under Contract ANR-11-INS-011.

S. Moriai (Ed.): FSE 2013, LNCS 8424, pp. 585–604, 2014.
DOI: 10.1007/978-3-662-43933-3_30, © Springer-Verlag Berlin Heidelberg 2014

conditional relations of algebraic degree 1 between some inputs and some outputs of the primitive and to exploit them in a cryptanalysis, like a cube attack [9] or an attack similar to the one presented by Fuhr on Hamsi [12]. However, it is often difficult to determine whether such affine relations exist and even more difficult to find them. Furthermore, from the designer's point of view, it is not easy to understand how such relations can be avoided at a low implementation cost, especially without increasing the number of rounds.

Our Contributions. In this paper, we show that the number of affine relations between input bits and output bits after several rounds of an SPN construction depends on a new linearity measure of the Sbox, that we call (v, w)-*linearity*. The parameters (v, w) quantify the ability of the Sbox to propagate affine relations. More precisely, a vectorial function S from $\mathbf{F}_2^n$ into $\mathbf{F}_2^m$ is (v, w)-linear, if there exist a subspace $V \subset \mathbf{F}_2^n$ with $\dim V = v$ and a subspace $W \subset \mathbf{F}_2^m$ with $\dim W = w$ such that all Boolean functions $x \mapsto \lambda \cdot S(x)$, for $\lambda \in W$, have degree at most 1 on all cosets of V. We show that the (v, w)-linear functions correspond to the functions which follow the generalized Maiorana-McFarland construction [18] applied to vectorial functions. In other words, the use of Sboxes obtained by this construction, which have been extensively studied for instance in [6,14,19, 21], introduces some weaknesses into a cryptographic primitive, which might be exploited by a cube attack or by an attack like [12].

As a proof of concept, we analyze and slightly improve Fuhr's attack against Hamsi with the new insights brought by this notion. Most notably, we show that the feasibility of this attack mainly depends on the (v, w)-linearity of the Hamsi Sbox. By classifying 4-bit Sboxes in terms of (v, w)-linearity, we exhibit the families of Sboxes which considerably reduce the success of the attack.

The rest of the paper is organized as follows. In Sect. 2 we introduce the notion of (v, w)-linearity and present some general properties. We characterize, in this same section, the (v, w)-linear functions for certain values of (v, w) and we exhibit a classification of 4-bit Sboxes with respect to this new criterion. In Sect. 3, we recall the principle of the second preimage attack by Fuhr against the hash function Hamsi. Section 4 points out that the notion of (v, w)-linearity for the involved Sbox brings a new insight on Fuhr's attack. In particular, a more extensive use of this notion enables us to slightly improve the attack against Hamsi. We also investigate the feasibility of the attack for all possible choices of the 4-bit Sbox. We refer to [2] for further details, especially on the classification of 4-bit Sboxes and on the algorithms we used for finding affine relations for Hamsi-256.

2   The Notion of (v, w)-linearity

When we consider an Sbox, i.e., a vectorial function with several output coordinates, some of its cryptographic properties are derived from the properties of its components, in the following sense.

Definition 1. *[20] Let S be a function from $\mathbf{F}_2^n$ into $\mathbf{F}_2^m$. The components of S are the linear combinations of its coordinates, i.e., the Boolean functions of n variables $S_\lambda : x \mapsto \lambda \cdot S(x)$, where $\lambda \in \mathbf{F}_2^m$ and S_0 is the null function.*

In the following, we often consider the *restriction* of S to an (affine) subspace $a + V$ of $\mathbf{F}_2^n$. This restriction corresponds to the function $x \in V \mapsto S(a + x)$, and it can be identified with a function of $\dim V$ variables.

2.1 Definition and Link with the Maiorana-McFarland Construction

Definition 2. *Let S be a function from $\mathbf{F}_2^n$ into $\mathbf{F}_2^m$. Then, S is said to be (v, w)-linear if there exist two linear subspaces $V \subset \mathbf{F}_2^n$ and $W \subset \mathbf{F}_2^m$ with $\dim V = v$ and $\dim W = w$ such that, for all $\lambda \in W$, S_λ has degree at most 1 on all cosets of V.*

Obviously, a function S that is (v, w)-linear is equally (v, i)-linear for every $1 \le i < w$. Similarly, it is (i, w)-linear for every $1 \le i < v$.

Any Boolean function f which is linear on all cosets of a v-dimensional subspace V can be written as

$$f(x, y) = \pi(x) \cdot y + h(x) \text{ with } (x, y) \in U \times V,$$

where U is a supplementary subspace of V, π is a function from U to $\mathbf{F}_2^v$ and h is a Boolean function from U to $\mathbf{F}_2$. This construction is a well-known generalization of the so-called Maiorana-McFarland construction of bent functions [18]. This class has been generalized to vectorial functions in [19] and studied by several authors, e.g. [6,14,21]. Then, it follows that an Sbox is (v, w)-linear if and only if its 2^w components corresponding to W define a function which is equivalent to a vectorial Maiorana-McFarland function, in the sense of the following proposition.

Proposition 1. *Let S be a function from $\mathbf{F}_2^n$ into $\mathbf{F}_2^m$, and V and W two linear subspaces $V \subset \mathbf{F}_2^n$ and $W \subset \mathbf{F}_2^m$ with $\dim V = v$ and $\dim W = w$. Then, S is (v, w)-linear w.r.t. (V, W) if and only if the function S_W corresponding to all components $S_\lambda, \lambda \in W$, can be written as*

$$S_W(x, y) = M(x)y + G(x)$$

where $\mathbf{F}_2^n$ is the direct sum of U and V, G is a function from U to $\mathbf{F}_2^w$ and $M(x)$ is a $w \times v$ binary matrix whose coefficients are Boolean functions defined on U.

Proof. Let $(\lambda_1, \ldots, \lambda_w)$ be a basis of W. Clearly, S is (v, w)-linear w.r.t. (V, W) if and only if, for any $1 \le i \le w$, S_{λ_i} can be written as

$$S_{\lambda_i}(x, y) = \pi_i(x) \cdot y + g_i(x) .$$

Let G denote the function from U to $\mathbf{F}_2^w$ whose w coordinates correspond to g_i, $1 \le i \le w$, and let $M(x)$ denote the $w \times v$ matrix whose i-th row corresponds to the v coordinates of $\pi_i(x)$. Then, the previous condition can be equivalently written as

$$S_W(x, y) = M(x)y + G(x) .$$

$\square$

2.2   General Properties

It directly follows from the definition that (v, w)-linear functions have some weaknesses with respect to the usual cryptographic properties. In particular, the algebraic degree and the nonlinearity of some components of the Sbox both decrease when v increases. Indeed, an upper bound on the degree of the components of S can be directly deduced from Proposition 1.

Proposition 2. *Let S be a function from $\mathbf{F}_2^n$ into $\mathbf{F}_2^m$. If S is (v, w)-linear w.r.t. (V, W), then all its components S_λ, $\lambda \in W$ have degree at most $n + 1 - v$.*

We now show that the (v, w)-linearity provides an upper bound on the nonlinearity of the function, i.e., on its distance to the set of all affine functions. The following notation will be extensively used. For any Boolean function f of n variables, we denote by $\mathcal{F}(f)$ the following value related to the Hamming weight of f:

$$\mathcal{F}(f) = \sum_{x \in \mathbf{F}_2^n} (-1)^{f(x)} = 2^n - 2wt(f) .$$

This quantity is just the discrete Fourier transform (aka., Walsh transform) at point 0 of the sign function $(-1)^f$.

Definition 3. *The Walsh spectrum of an Sbox S from $\mathbf{F}_2^n$ into $\mathbf{F}_2^m$ is the multiset*

$$\mathcal{W}(\mathcal{S}) = \{\mathcal{F}(S_\lambda + \varphi_\alpha), \alpha \in \mathbf{F}_2^n, \lambda \in \mathbf{F}_2^m \setminus \{0\}\} ,$$

where φ_α denotes the n-variable linear function $x \mapsto \alpha \cdot x$. The nonlinearity of S is the Hamming distance between the set of its nontrivial components $\{S_\lambda, \lambda \neq 0\}$ and the set of all affine functions. It is given by

$$2^{n-1} - \frac{1}{2}\mathcal{L}(S) \quad where \quad \mathcal{L}(S) = \max_{\alpha \in \mathbf{F}_2^n, \lambda \neq 0} |\mathcal{F}(S_\lambda + \varphi_\alpha)| .$$

Proposition 3. *Let S be a function from $\mathbf{F}_2^n$ into $\mathbf{F}_2^m$. If S is (v, w)-linear, then $\mathcal{L}(S) \geq 2^v$.*

Proof. The result comes from the fact that the linearity of a Boolean function f, $\mathcal{L}(f)$, is lower-bounded by the linearity of any of its restrictions to a subspace (see e.g. Corollary V.3 in [4]). Since the restriction of S_λ, $\lambda \in W$, to V is affine, it has linearity 2^v. $\square$

The notion of (v, w)-linearity is also related to the notion of *normality* introduced by Dobbertin [11], and then generalized by Charpin [7] as follows: a Boolean function f of n variables is said to be *weakly v-normal*, if it is affine on an (affine) subspace V of dimension v. However, $(v, 1)$-linearity is a stronger requirement than weak v-normality since the component of S needs to have degree at most 1 on all cosets of V while weak normality requires this property on a single coset.

It is worth noticing that the two conditions derived from Propositions 2 and 3, i.e., $\deg f \leq n + 1 - v$ and $\mathcal{L}(f) \geq 2^v$ are not sufficient for guaranteeing that f is

$(v,1)$-linear. For instance, it has been shown in [5] that the Boolean function of 14 variables, $f(x) = \text{Tr}(\alpha x^{57})$ with $\alpha \in \mathbf{F}_4 \setminus \mathbf{F}_2$, is not 7-weakly normal. Then, this function is not $(7,1)$-linear while it has degree 4 and satisfies $\mathcal{L}(f) = 2^7$.

It is known that the Boolean functions which are affinely equivalent to a Maiorana-McFarland bent function can be characterized by their second-order derivatives [8]. The situation is similar for vectorial functions. In the following, we denote by $D_a S$ the derivative of a function from $\mathbf{F}_2^n$ into $\mathbf{F}_2^m$, i.e., $D_a S$ is the function from $\mathbf{F}_2^n$ into $\mathbf{F}_2^m$ defined by $D_a S(x) = S(x+a) + S(x)$.

Proposition 4. *Let S be a function from $\mathbf{F}_2^n$ into $\mathbf{F}_2^m$. Then, S is (v,w)-linear w.r.t. (V,W) if and only if the function S_W corresponding to all components $S_\lambda, \lambda \in W$ is such that all its second-order derivatives, $D_\alpha D_\beta S_W$ with $\alpha, \beta \in V$ vanish.*

Proof. Let U denote a supplementary subspace of V.

– If S is (v,w)-linear w.r.t. (V,W), then for any $x \in U$,

$$S_W(x,y) = M(x)y + G(x),$$

where $M(x)$ is a $w \times v$ matrix and G a function from U to $\mathbf{F}_2^w$. It follows that, for any $\alpha, \beta \in V$, we have

$$D_\alpha D_\beta S_W(x,y) = S_W(x,y) + S_W(x,y+\alpha) + S_W(x,y+\beta) + S_W(x,y+\alpha+\beta) = 0 .$$

– Conversely, if the second-order derivatives of S_W, $D_\alpha D_\beta S_W$ with $\alpha, \beta \in V$, vanish, then for any $x \in U$, the function F_x from V to $\mathbf{F}_2^v$ defined by $F_x(y) = S_W(x,y)$ is such that all its second-order derivatives vanish. However, if a function has degree at least 2, then it has at least one second-order derivative which does not vanish. It follows that, for any $x \in U$, S_W has degree at most 1 on $x + V$.   □

2.3 $(v,1)$-linear Functions

In the following, we focus on $(v,1)$-linear functions since the highest value of v such that S is $(v,1)$-linear is a relevant parameter. Actually, as seen in Propositions 2 and 3, this value provides bounds on the degree and on the nonlinearity of the corresponding component: $\deg f \leq n + 1 - v$ and $\mathcal{L}(f) \geq 2^v$. Obviously, any function is $(1,1)$-linear. Then, we first consider $(2,1)$-linear functions. From Proposition 4, a Boolean function is $(2,1)$-linear if and only if one of its second-order derivatives vanishes. We now give a sufficient condition for this property.

Proposition 5. *Let f be a balanced Boolean function of n variables, n even, with $\deg(f) \leq 3$. Then f is $(2,1)$-linear.*

Proof. Since f is balanced, it is obviously not bent. Then, by definition, f has at least one derivative, say $D_\alpha f$, that is not balanced. Since $\deg(f) \leq 3$, we have that $\deg(D_\alpha f) \leq 2$. If $\deg(D_\alpha f) < 2$, then $D_\beta D_\alpha f$ vanishes for at least all values of β in a (affine) hyperplane. Thus, we deduce from Proposition 4 that f is $(2,1)$-linear. Suppose now that $\deg(D_\alpha f) = 2$ and consider its restriction to a hyperplane H such that $\alpha \notin H$. Let g denote this restriction, i.e. $g = D_\alpha f_{|H}$. This restriction is a quadratic function of $(n-1)$ variables that is not balanced (since its Hamming weight is half of the Hamming weight of $D_\alpha f$). Since n is even, $n-1$ is odd and thus g cannot be bent. Therefore, g has at least one derivative that is constant. That is, there exists some $\beta \in \mathbf{F}_2^n$ such that $D_\beta D_\alpha f$ is constant. Though, a quadratic function is balanced if and only if it has a derivative equal to 1. Therefore, $D_\beta D_\alpha f$ is the all-zero function.   □

Most notably, it follows that all nontrivial components of a permutation of $\mathbf{F}_2^4$ are $(2,1)$-linear.

The other extremal case of $(n-1,1)$-linear Boolean functions can be completely characterized. Indeed, it can be shown that the necessary conditions on the degree and nonlinearity of an $(n-1,1)$-linear Boolean function (Propositions 2 and 3) are sufficient.

Proposition 6. *Let f be a Boolean function of n variables. Then, f is $(n-1,1)$-linear if and only if $\deg f \leq 2$ and $\mathcal{L}(f) \geq 2^{n-1}$. Moreover, if $\deg(f) = 2$ and $\mathcal{L}(f) \geq 2^{n-1}$, there exist exactly three distinct hyperplanes H such that f has degree at most 1 on both H and $\bar{H}$.*

Proof. The fact that any $(n-1,1)$-linear function has degree at most 2 and linearity greater than or equal to 2^{n-1} is derived from the previous propositions. Conversely, let us consider a quadratic Boolean function f (we assume that $\deg f = 2$ since the result is trivial for affine or constant functions). Any quadratic function f satisfies $\mathcal{L}(f) = 2^{\frac{n+h}{2}}$ where $0 \leq h < n$ is the dimension of the linear space of f, $LS(f)$ (see e.g. [4, Appendix 1]):

$$LS(f) = \{a \in \mathbf{F}_2^n \; : \; D_a f : x \mapsto f(x+a) + f(x) \text{ is constant}\} \, .$$

Moreover, the set

$$LS^0(f) = \{a \in \mathbf{F}_2^n \; : \; D_a f = 0\}$$

is a subspace of $LS(f)$ of dimension either $\dim LS(f)$ or $(\dim LS(f) - 1)$. Since $\mathcal{L}(f) = 2^{n-1}$, there are exactly 4 values of α such that $|\mathcal{F}(f + \varphi_\alpha)| = 2^{n-1}$, and exactly three among these four have the same sign. Now, we will prove that these four values are the elements of $\beta + LS(f)^\perp$, where $\beta = 0$ if $\dim LS^0(f) = \dim LS(f)$, and $\beta \in LS^0(f)^\perp \setminus LS(f)^\perp$ otherwise. We get from Lemma V.2 in [4] that

$$\sum_{\alpha \in LS(f)^\perp} \mathcal{F}^2(f + \varphi_{\alpha+\beta}) = 2^2 \sum_{e \in LS(f)} (-1)^{\beta \cdot e} \mathcal{F}(D_e f)$$

$$= 2^2 \left(\sum_{e \in LS^0(f)} \mathcal{F}(D_e f) - \sum_{e \in LS(f) \setminus LS^0(f)} \mathcal{F}(D_e f) \right) = 2^{2n} \, .$$

Therefore, all four $\mathcal{F}^2(f + \varphi_{\alpha+\beta})$, $\alpha \in LS(f)^\perp$, are equal to 2^{2n-2}. Now, since

$$2\mathcal{F}((f + \varphi_\beta)|_{H_a}) = \mathcal{F}(f + \varphi_\beta) + \mathcal{F}(f + \varphi_{\beta+a})$$

and

$$2\mathcal{F}((f + \varphi_\beta)|_{\bar{H}_a}) = \mathcal{F}(f + \varphi_\beta) - \mathcal{F}(f + \varphi_{\beta+a})$$

we deduce that f is linear both on H_a and $\bar{H}_a$ for some $a \neq 0$, if and only if there exist some u_1, u_2, u_3 such that

$$\mathcal{F}(f + \varphi_{u_1}) = \mathcal{F}(f + \varphi_{u_2}) = \mathcal{F}(f + \varphi_{u_3}) = (-1)^b 2^{n-1}$$

and

$$\mathcal{F}(f + \varphi_{u_1+u_2+u_3})(-1)^{b+1} 2^{n-1} \, .$$

Moreover, a can be any element in $\{u_1 + u_2, u_1 + u_3, u_2 + u_3\}$. Therefore, we get that f is linear both on H_a and $\bar{H}_a$ if and only if a is a nonzero element of $LS(f)^\perp$. □

If we focus on Sboxes which guarantee the best resistance to linear attacks, i.e., on permutations S of $\mathbf{F}_2^n$ with $\mathcal{L}(S) \leq 2^{\lceil \frac{n+1}{2} \rceil}$, then, for $n = 4$, we deduce from the previous propositions that any 4-bit permutation is $(2,1)$-linear, and that it is $(3,1)$-linear if and only if it has maximal nonlinearity and a quadratic component. For larger values of n, the situation is different. For instance, we can prove the following.

Corollary 1. *Let S be a permutation of $\mathbf{F}_2^n$ with the best known nonlinearity, that is $\mathcal{L}(S) \leq 2^{\lceil \frac{n+1}{2} \rceil}$. Then, if $n \geq 5$, S is not $(n-1,1)$-linear.*

Proof. If S has a component that is $(n-1,1)$-linear, then we deduce from Proposition 3 that

$$n - 1 \leq \left\lceil \frac{n+1}{2} \right\rceil \leq \frac{n}{2} + 1.$$

Consequently, $\frac{n}{2} \leq 2$ and thus $n \leq 4$. □

2.4   Classification of 4-bit Sboxes

Many symmetric primitives are based on 4-bit balanced Sboxes. Several classifications of these Sboxes have been previously provided. We can for example mention the classification by De Cannière [3], the one provided by Leander and Poschmann [17] and another one by Saarinen [22]. In particular in [17], the authors have proved that, for affine equivalence, there are exactly 16 classes of 4-bit permutations which are *optimal* in terms of resistance against both linear and differential attacks. Here, we go one step further in this classification, and consider the notion of (v, w)-linearity for those 16 classes. Actually, the number of pairs (V, W) such that an Sbox is (v, w)-linear w.r.t (V, W) is invariant under affine equivalence.

The previous result shows that the number of quadratic components of the Sbox plays an important role for $(n-1, w)$-linearity. For instance, for a permutation of $\mathbf{F}_2^4$ which is optimal for linear cryptanalysis, we have proved that the number of pairs (V, W) with $\dim V = 3$ and $\dim W = 1$ such that S is $(3, 1)$-linear w.r.t to (V, W) is equal to $3Q$, where Q is the number of quadratic components of S. Therefore, we first focus on the number of quadratic components for a permutation of $\mathbf{F}_2^4$.

All classes of 5-variable Boolean functions for affine equivalence have been exhibited in [1]. From this classification, since the 4-variable Boolean functions can be seen as a subset of the functions in 5 variables, it can be deduced that any of the 2^{15} possible Boolean functions of four variables with degree at most 3 is equivalent to one of the five functions given in Table 1. This table also provides the corresponding Walsh spectra since affine equivalence preserves the multiset composed of the magnitudes of all Walsh coefficients, i.e. functions belonging to the same equivalence class, have the same multiset $\mathcal{W}(f) = \{|\mathcal{F}(f + \varphi_a)|, a \in \mathbf{F}_2^n\}$.

Table 1. Number of occurrences of each value in the Walsh spectrum of any of the five equivalence classes for the 4-variable Boolean functions of degree at most 3.

| Class | Representative | Walsh spectrum | | | | |
		± 16	± 12	± 8	± 4	0
I	$x_1 x_2 x_3$	1			7	8
II	$x_1 x_2 x_3 + x_1 x_4$			2	8	6
III	$x_1 x_2$			4		12
IV	$x_1 x_2 + x_3 x_4$				16	0
V	0		1			15

Proposition 7. *Let S be a permutation of $\mathbf{F}_2^4$ having no affine or constant component. Then, S has c_I components of the class I, c_{II} components of the class II and c_{III} components of the class III, with*

$$c_I + c_{II} + c_{III} = 15.$$

Moreover, the number Q of quadratic components of S (i.e., of components of degree exactly 2) is equal to c_{III} and is of the form $Q = 2^r - 1$, $0 \le r \le 4$. It is characterized by the Walsh spectrum of S (see Definition 3):

$$Q = W_{12} + \frac{1}{2}W_8 - 15,$$

where W_i denotes the number of occurrences of i in $\mathcal{W}(S)$. Most notably, S and S^{-1} have the same number of quadratic components.

Proof. As S is a permutation, all of its components are of degree at most 3 and are equivalent to one of the five above classes. By hypothesis, as S does not have any constant or affine component, S has no component of the class V. Moreover, the number of components of degree 2 is equal to the number of components of degree at most 2. Similarly, as all the non-trivial components of a permutation are balanced, S has no component of the class IV. The number of non-trivial components of the permutation S is equal to 15. Therefore, $c_I + c_{II} + c_{III} = 15$. The class III corresponds to quadratic functions. Consequently, c_{III} represents the number of quadratic components Q of S. As the values of λ such that $\deg S_\lambda \leq 2$ form a vectorial subspace of $\mathbf{F}_2^4$, Q has the form $2^r - 1$. According to Table 1 we have that

$$W_{12} = c_I$$
$$W_8 = 2c_{II} + 4c_{III} = 30 - 2c_I + 2c_{III}$$

implying that the number of quadratic components of S is given by $c_{III} = W_{12} + \frac{1}{2}W_8 - 15$. Finally, as the inverse permutation of S has the same set $(W_i)_{0 \leq i \leq 16}$ as S, the two permutations have the same number of quadratic components. $\square$

We have carried out an exhaustive search among all the permutations of $\mathbf{F}_2^4$ in order to determine all possible 4-tuples $(c_I, c_{II}, c_{III}, c_V)$. All possible configurations can be found in Appendix A of [2]. Then, we have exhibited some permutations with $Q \in \{0, 1, 3, 7, 15\}$. But, permutations with $Q = 15$ satisfy $c_V = 1$, i.e., every quadratic permutation of $\mathbf{F}_2^4$ has one non-trivial component of degree 1. There exist permutations with 7 quadratic components and optimal nonlinearity, but they do not guarantee optimal resistance to differential attacks.

(v,w)-linearity of Optimal 4-bit Sboxes

We concentrate now on *optimal* permutations of $\mathbf{F}_2^4$, i.e., permutations which guarantee an optimal resistance against linear and differential attacks. The exhaustive search over all 16 classes of such Sboxes in [17] shows that there are 8 classes of optimal Sboxes with $Q = 0$, 4 with $Q = 1$, and 4 with $Q = 3$. For each of the 16 classes of optimal Sboxes, Table 2 gives, for each pair (v, w), the number $N_{(v,w)}$ of subspaces V such that the Sbox is (v, w)-linear w.r.t. (V, W).

Since all optimal Sboxes have at most 3 quadratic components, we deduce from Proposition 6 that they cannot be $(3,3)$-linear, i.e. $N_{(3,3)} = 0$.

The fact that, for all these Sboxes, $N_{(2,1)} = 35$ comes from the following result.

Proposition 8. *Let S be a function from $\mathbf{F}_2^n$ into $\mathbf{F}_2^n$ of degree at most 3. Then, for any pair (a, b) of elements in $\mathbf{F}_2^n$, there exists some nonzero $\lambda \in \mathbf{F}_2^n$ such that $D_a D_b S_\lambda = 0$.*

Equivalently, for any 2-dimensional subspace $V \subset \mathbf{F}_2^n$, there exists at least one nonzero $\lambda \in \mathbf{F}_2^n$ such that S is $(2,1)$-linear w.r.t $(V, \{0, \lambda\})$.

Proof. The first statement is proved by contradiction as follows. Suppose that there exists a pair (a, b) such that $D_a D_b S_\lambda \neq 0$ for all $\lambda \neq 0$. This situation

Table 2. Number $N_{(v,w)}$ of subspaces V of dimension v for which there exists a w-dimensional W such that G_i is (v,w)-linear with respect to (V,W), for the 16 optimal Sboxes G_i described in [17].

		(v,w)							
	Q	(2,1)	(2,2)	(2,3)	(2,4)	(3,1)	(3,2)	(3,3)	(3,4)
G_0	3	35	19	5	0	7	1	0	0
G_1	3	35	23	3	0	7	1	0	0
G_2	3	35	23	3	0	7	1	0	0
G_3	0	35	5	0	0	0	0	0	0
G_4	0	35	5	0	0	0	0	0	0
G_5	0	35	5	0	0	0	0	0	0
G_6	0	35	5	0	0	0	0	0	0
G_7	0	35	5	0	0	0	0	0	0
G_8	3	35	19	5	0	7	1	0	0
G_9	1	35	13	0	0	3	0	0	0
G_{10}	1	35	13	0	0	3	0	0	0
G_{11}	0	35	5	0	0	0	0	0	0
G_{12}	0	35	5	0	0	0	0	0	0
G_{13}	0	35	5	0	0	0	0	0	0
G_{14}	1	35	13	0	0	3	0	0	0
G_{15}	1	35	11	1	0	3	0	0	0

can occur only if $\langle a,b \rangle$ has dimension 2. Obviously, all the $(2^n - 1)$ functions $D_a D_b S_\lambda$, $\lambda \neq 0$, are distinct since $D_a D_b S_{\lambda_1} + D_a D_b S_{\lambda_2} = D_a D_b S_{\lambda_1 + \lambda_2}$. Let U be a supplementary subspace of $\langle a,b \rangle$. Then, the whole function $D_a D_b S_\lambda$ is determined by its restriction to U since $D_a D_b S_\lambda(x) = D_a D_b S_\lambda(x + v)$ for any $v \in \langle a,b \rangle$. Then, because $\deg D_a D_b S_\lambda \leq 1$, the number of distinct and nonzero $D_a D_b S_\lambda$ corresponds to the number of nonzero affine functions of $(n - 2)$ variables, which is equal to $(2^{n-1} - 1)$. This leads to a contradiction since the $(2^n - 1)$ functions $D_a D_b S_\lambda$ are all distinct. The equivalent formulation in terms of $(2,1)$-linearity is a direct consequence of Proposition 4. □

The next proposition explains why $N_{(2,3)} = 0$ when $Q = 0$.

Proposition 9. *Let S be a function from $\mathbf{F}_2^n$ into $\mathbf{F}_2^n$ such that all its non trivial components have degree exactly $(n - 1)$. Then, S is not $(2, n - 1)$-linear.*

Proof. Suppose that there exist a hyperplane H and two nonzero distinct elements a and b in $\mathbf{F}_2^n$ such that $D_a D_b S_\lambda = 0$ for all $\lambda \in H$. Let L be a linear permutation which maps a and b to the first two elements of the canonical basis e_1 and e_2. Then, $D_a D_b S(x) = D_{e_1} D_{e_2}(S \circ L^{-1})(L(x))$, implying that $D_{e_1} D_{e_2}(S \circ L^{-1})_\lambda = 0$ for all $\lambda \in H$. Let $\mathcal{M}$ denote the set of all monomials of degree $(n - 1)$ of n variables whose second derivative with respect to e_1 and e_2 vanishes. Then, $|\mathcal{M}| = n - 2$. Since all $(S \circ L^{-1})_\lambda$, $\lambda \in H \setminus \{0\}$ have degree $(n - 1)$, all their ANF contain a sum of monomials of $\mathcal{M}$, and all these $(2^{n-1} - 1)$ sums must be distinct. However, this situation cannot occur since there are only $2^{|\mathcal{M}|} - 1 = 2^{n-2} - 1$ such sums. □

Moreover, a counting argument shows that for 4-bit permutations with optimal nonlinearity,

$$N_{(2,2)} + 2N_{(2,3)} + 4N_{(2,4)} = 5 + 8Q \text{ and } N_{(3,1)} + 2N_{(3,2)} + 4N_{(3,3)} + 8N_{(3,4)} = 3Q .$$

Indeed, let us denote by A_w (resp. B_w) the number of subspaces V of dimension 2 (resp. dimension 3) such that w is the highest dimension such that S is (v, w)-linear w.r.t. (V, W) for some W of dimension w. Then,

$$N_{(2,i)} = \sum_{w=i}^{4} A_w \text{ and } N_{(3,i)} = \sum_{w=i}^{4} B_w .$$

On the other hand, if S_λ is quadratic, it belongs to Class III identified in Table 1, implying that it is $(2, 1)$-linear w.r.t. 19 subspaces of dimension 2, and $(3, 1)$-linear w.r.t. 3 hyperplanes. If S_λ has degree 3, then it belongs to Class II, and has three zero second-order derivatives. Then,

$$A_1 + 3A_2 + 7A_3 + 15A_4 = 3(15 - Q) + 19Q \text{ and } B_1 + 3B_2 + 7B_3 + 15B_4 = 3Q .$$

Since $N_{(2,1)} = 35$ from Proposition 8, we deduce that

$$35 + 2N_{(2,2)} + 4N_{(2,3)} + 8N_{(2,4)} = 45 + 16Q$$

and

$$N_{(3,1)} + 2N_{(3,2)} + 4N_{(3,3)} + 8N_{(3,4)} = 3Q .$$

It is also worth noticing that $N_{(3,2)} \in \{0, 1, 3\}$. Actually, we have proved in Proposition 6 that S is $(3, 2)$-linear w.r.t. $(H_a, \langle \lambda_1, \lambda_2 \rangle)$ if and only if a belongs to all three sets $LS(S_\lambda)^\perp$, $\lambda \in \{\lambda_1, \lambda_2, \lambda_1 + \lambda_2\}$. Therefore, either all these three $LS(S_\lambda)^\perp$ are distinct, or they share one nonzero element or they are all equal.

From these results, we can deduce the values of $N_{(v,w)}$ in most cases for all 4-bit optimal Sboxes. All these values are provided in Table 2. In particular, all figures for $Q \in \{0, 1\}$ can be deduced from the previous propositions. For $Q \geq 3$, the weighted sum of $N_{(3,1)}$ and $N_{(3,2)}$ (resp. of $N_{(2,2)}$, $N_{(2,3)}$ and $N_{(2,4)}$) can be explained theoretically, but a theoretical explanation of their exact individual values remains open. Most notably, Table 2 shows that there are five different behaviours of 4-bit optimal Sboxes with respect to (v, w)-linearity. It is worth noticing here that an Sbox and its inverse do not always have the same behaviour. Indeed, as pointed out in [17], any optimal Sbox G_i belongs to the same equivalence class as its inverse except G_0, G_2, G_{14} and G_{15} which are such that G_0^{-1} belongs to the same class as G_2 and G_{14}^{-1} belongs to the same class as G_{15}. Then, we deduce that, for all Sboxes S in the four classes defined by G_0, G_2, G_{14} and G_{15}, S and S^{-1} do not have the same behaviour regarding (v, w)-linearity.

3   Fuhr's Attack Against Hamsi-256

The hash family Hamsi was designed by Küçük [15] in 2008 for the SHA-3 competition. It was among the 14 algorithms that were chosen by the NIST for the second round of the contest. A special feature of this function is that its compression function consists of a small number of rounds of a permutation with a particularly low algebraic degree. These weaknesses have been exploited by Fuhr [12] and by Dinur and Shamir [10] in order to find second preimages for the entire hash function. We show here that Fuhr's attack is related to the (v, w)-linearity of the Sbox used in Hamsi. More precisely, we use this notion for formalizing an important part of the attack in [12], that is the search for affine relations between some input and output bits of the compression function of Hamsi-256. This enables us to slightly improve Fuhr's result and to analyse the influence of the choice of the Sbox on this type of attack.

3.1   Description of Hamsi-256

We start by describing the most important parts of the design of Hamsi-256, the instance of the hash function outputting 256-bit digests. The Hamsi hash function follows the Davies-Meyer construction. In Hamsi-256, the message is padded and cut into 32-bit blocks. A linear code over $\mathbf{F}_4$ is used to expand each 32-bit message block to a 256-bit value $(m_0, \ldots, m_7)$, where every m_i is a 32-bit word. Then, the 256-bit expanded message is combined together with the 256-bit chaining value h_{i-1} and provides a 512-bit state. The inner permutation P is then applied to this 512-bit state, seen as a 4×4 matrix of 32-bit words.

Concatenation: The chaining value $(c_0, \ldots, c_7)$ is concatenated to the message words $(m_0, \ldots, m_7)$ to form a 512-bit state $s = (s_0, \ldots, s_{15})$, seen as a 4×4 matrix. The state s as also the way that the message and the chaining value words are arranged within it are illustrated in Fig. 1.

The nonlinear permutation P of $\mathbf{F}_2^{512}$ is then applied to this concatenated state. It is composed of three rounds of a permutation R, called the round function. This round function is made up of three different layers of operations. First, some constant values are added to the state. Then, a nonlinear layer corresponding to 128 parallel applications of a 4-bit Sbox S is applied. Finally, the bits of the state are mixed by a linear application L.

The *substitution layer* is based on a 4-bit Sbox S. S is one of the Sboxes used in **Serpent** and is given by

$$S[16] = \{8, 6, 7, 9, 3, 12, 10, 15, 13, 1, 14, 4, 0, 11, 5, 2\}.$$

s_0	s_1	s_2	s_3	m_0	m_1	c_0	c_1
s_4	s_5	s_6	s_7	c_2	c_3	m_2	m_3
s_8	s_9	s_{10}	s_{11}	m_4	m_5	c_4	c_5
s_{12}	s_{13}	s_{14}	s_{15}	c_6	c_7	m_6	m_7

Fig. 1. Input state of the inner permutation P in Hamsi-256.

The algebraic normal forms of its coordinates are

$$y_0 = x_0 x_2 + x_1 + x_2 + x_3$$
$$y_1 = x_0 x_1 x_2 + x_0 x_1 x_3 + x_0 x_2 x_3 + x_1 x_2 + x_0 x_3 + x_2 x_3 + x_0 + x_1 + x_2$$
$$y_2 = x_0 x_1 x_3 + x_0 x_2 x_3 + x_1 x_2 + x_1 x_3 + x_2 x_3 + x_0 + x_1 + x_3$$
$$y_3 = x_0 x_1 x_2 + x_1 x_3 + x_0 + x_1 + x_2 + 1.$$

This Sbox is applied in parallel to the 128 columns of the state. In the first round, due to the way that the state is obtained by concatenation, every Sbox mixes two message bits with two bits coming from the chaining value.

The *diffusion layer* of Hamsi-256 is based on the linear function $L : \mathbf{F}_2^{128} \rightarrow \mathbf{F}_2^{128}$ that operates on 32-bit words. In the case of Hamsi-256, this function is called four times in total in every round, one time for every diagonal of the state. The function $L(a, b, c, d)$, with $a, b, c, d \in \mathbf{F}_2^{32}$ can be described as follows:

$a := a \lll 13$	$d := (d \oplus c \oplus (a \ll 3)) \lll 7$
$c := c \lll 3$	$a := (a \oplus b \oplus d) \lll 5$
$b := (b \oplus a \oplus c) \lll 1$	$c := (c \oplus d \oplus (b \ll 7)) \lll 22$

Truncation and Feed-forward: The truncation $T : \mathbf{F}_2^{512} \rightarrow \mathbf{F}_2^{256}$ eliminates the second and the last row of the state:

$$T(s_0, s_1, s_2, \ldots, s_{14}, s_{15}) = (s_0, s_1, s_2, s_3, s_8, s_9, s_{10}, s_{11}).$$

The truncated 256-bit state is then XORed to the previous chaining value h_{i-1} to form h_i.

Notations: Table 3 describes how we have numbered the 512 bits of the state. According to the representation of the Hamsi state seen in Fig. 1, we will say that the bit 0 of the state, is the leftmost bit of s_0, 31 is the rightmost bit of s_0, 32 the leftmost bit of s_1, 128 the leftmost bit of s_4, etc.

3.2   Description of Fuhr's Attack

Fuhr described in [12] a method for finding second preimages for Hamsi-256. This cryptanalysis, of complexity equal to $2^{251.3}$ evaluations of the compression function, was the first attack on this candidate that had a lower complexity

Table 3. Enumeration of the bits of the state.

0......31	32.....63	64.....95	96......127
128...159	160...191	192...223	224...255
256...287	288...319	320...351	352...383
384...415	416...447	448...479	480...511

than the generic attack when treating small messages. The key idea in this cryptanalysis consists in finding affine relations between some input bits and some output bits of the compression function, when the other input bits are fixed to a constant value. These relations lead to preimages for the compression function of Hamsi-256. These pseudo-preimages for the hash function are then transformed into second preimages by using a meet-in-the-middle approach.

In order to find affine relations between some input and output bits of the compression function, Fuhr noticed that, for the Hamsi Sbox S,

$$S(1, x, 0, 1 + x) = (1, 0, 0, x), \text{ for every } x \in \mathbf{F}_2, \tag{1}$$

where the least significant bit is the leftmost bit.

With this property in mind, it is possible to choose a set of variables in the following way. If $y \in \mathbf{F}_2^{32}$, we will denote by y^j the j-th bit of y. If the message block after the constant addition in the first round is such that $s_0^j = 1$ and $s_8^j = 0$, then we can define a variable bit $x^j \in \mathbf{F}_2$ and set $s_4^j = x^j$ and $s_{12}^j = 1 + x^j$. Due to relation (1), after the application of the first nonlinear layer, only s_{12}^j will depend on x^j. This has a particular interest as s_{12}^j will be part of the input word d of the linear function L, which has a relatively slow diffusion, much slower than the words a or c. The same applies for the neighboring column of the state, i.e. the words s_1, s_5, s_9, s_{13}. If $s_1^j = 1$ and $s_9^j = 0$, we define the variable bit $y^j \in \mathbf{F}_2$ and set $s_5^j = y^j$ and $s_{13}^j = 1 + y^j$.

For mounting the attack, a message block is randomly picked. The first step is to choose the set of variables $\mathcal{I} = X \cup Y$. For this, the values of s_0, s_1, s_8 and s_9 before the first Sbox layer are computed. If $s_0^j = 1$ and $s_8^j = 0$ then the variable x^j is added to X. In the same way, if $s_1^j = 1$ and $s_9^j = 0$, the variable y^j is added to Y. Once the variable set has been chosen, one has to search for a set of output bits of the compression function $\mathcal{O}$ such that each bit of this set can be expressed as an affine function of the variables of $\mathcal{I}$.

Suppose that such a set has been found and denote $N_\mathcal{O} = \#\mathcal{O}$ and $N_\mathcal{I} = \#\mathcal{I}$. Let $x_0, \ldots, x_{N_\mathcal{I}-1}$ be the elements of $\mathcal{I}$ and $z_0, \ldots, z_{N_\mathcal{O}-1}$ the elements of $\mathcal{O}$. Then, if we are given a chaining value h^* it is possible to find preimages for the compression function, i.e. a message block m and a chaining value h, such that $f(h, m) = h^*$, where f is the compression function of Hamsi-256, with the following simple algorithm, described in [12].

1. Choose a message m such that the conditions required by Eq. (1) for the positions indicated by the variables of $\mathcal{I}$ are satisfied.
2. Choose a chaining value h such that the conditions required by Eq. (1) for the positions indicated by the variables of $\mathcal{I}$ are satisfied.
3. Compute the bits $z_0, \ldots, z_{N_\mathcal{O}-1}$. Compute the coefficients of the affine system.
5. Solve the affine system. If the system has no solution then choose other values for the constant part of h (without modifying the part of h imposed by the conditions (1)) and go to Step 3. If there is still no solution, choose another message m that fulfills the same constraints and go to Step 2.
6. If the affine system has a solution, check whether $f(h, m) = h^*$. This equation has a solution with probability $2^{N_\mathcal{O}-256}$.

The overall complexity of the attack, corresponding to $2^{251.3}$ evaluations of the compression function, has been estimated in [12] by a very precise estimation of the number of binary operations performed during each step of the algorithm.

Searching for Affine Relations for the Compression Function. A very important part of the attack in [12] is the search for affine relations between some input and some output bits of the compression function of Hamsi-256.

Due to Relation (1), after one round of computation all the bits of the state depend affinely on the variable bits. However, this is not the case after the second and the third round of the computation, since the initial variables pass through the Sboxes of the last two rounds. Under some conditions though, some output bits of an Sbox can still be expressed as a linear combination of the input variables. The conditions identified in [12] are the following.

1. All but one input bits of the Sbox are constant. If this bit is some affine combination of the initial variables, then this will also be the case for all the four outputs of the Sbox.
2. If all the inputs of the Sbox depend on at most one initial variable, then all the output bits of the Sbox will depend affinely on this variable.
3. If none of the first two situations occurs, this means that there exist at least two inputs to the Sbox that depend in an affine way on at least two different variables. However, by looking at the ANF of the four outputs of the Sbox, it is possible to do the following two observations. The only nonlinear term of the first output bit y_0 is x_0x_2. Thus if this term is an affine combination of the initial variables, this will also be the case for y_0. Equally, if $x_0x_1x_2$ and x_1x_3 are affine in the initial variables, this will also be the case for y_3.

These properties were used by Fuhr in the search for a set of variable bits $\mathcal{I}$ and a set of output bits $\mathcal{O}$ which affinely depend on the variable bits $\mathcal{I}$. In his first paper [12], the number of variable bits $N_{\mathcal{I}}$ was fixed and then an automated search was launched in order to determine the variable set that would give the largest number $N_{\mathcal{O}}$ of such output bits. These results could then be used in order to generate the largest possible set of affine relations. By using this method, Fuhr found for some $\mathcal{I}$ of size $N_{\mathcal{I}} = 7$, $N_{\mathcal{O}} = 14$ affine equations in $\mathcal{I}$ and for $N_{\mathcal{I}} = 8, 11$ affine equations for the compression function. Later, in [13] he improved these results, by finding for $N_{\mathcal{I}} = 8$, 16 affine equations and for $N_{\mathcal{I}} = 9, 11$ affine equations.

4   Analysis and Improvement of Fuhr's Attack

We show in this section how to make the search for affine relations between the input and the output bits of the compression function more efficient. Besides the improvement on Hamsi, our approach can similarly be applied to the search for affine relations for any SPN construction using small Sboxes. The success of this part of the work depends, to a large extend, on the quality of the used Sboxes.

Our improvements are based on two different directions. The first one concerns the way that the propagation through the Sboxes of the second and the third round is treated. For this, we use the concept introduced in Sect. 2.

The second direction is related to the way we determine which Sboxes of the first round should be affected and how. Furthermore, another differential property of the Hamsi Sbox is used together with Relation (1) to go through the Sbox layer of the first round.

4.1   Propagation of Affine Relations Through the Hamsi Sbox

Let $x = (x_0, x_1, x_2, x_3)$ denote the input to an Sbox and $y = (y_0, y_1, y_2, y_3)$ its output. As described in Sect. 3.2, Fuhr exploited the following two algebraic properties of the Hamsi Sbox in order to treat the case when at least two input variables of an Sbox are affected by at least two different variables in the second and third round.

- y_0 has degree at most 1 if $x_0 x_2$ has degree at most 1.
- y_3 has degree at most 1 if $x_1 x_3$ and $x_0 x_1 x_2$ have degree at most 1.

These two properties can be reformulated in the following way (where each vector x of $\mathbf{F}_2^4$ is represented by the integer $(\sum_{i=0}^3 x_i 2^i)$).

- S_1 is $(3, 1)$-linear w.r.t. $(H_\alpha, \langle 1 \rangle)$ where H_α denotes the hyperplane $\langle \alpha \rangle^\perp$ for $\alpha \in \{1, 4, 5\}$.
- S_8 is $(2, 1)$-linear w.r.t. $(V, \langle 8 \rangle)$ for the three 2-dimensional subspaces $V = \langle 1, 8 \rangle$, $V = \langle 4, 8 \rangle$ and $V = \langle 5, 8 \rangle$.

With the notation used in [17] and in Table 2, the Hamsi Sbox is affinely equivalent to G_1. Therefore, there exist 23 subspaces V of dimension 2 for which the Sbox is $(2, 2)$-linear and 3 subspaces of dimension 2 on which it is $(2, 3)$-linear. For the Hamsi Sbox, all corresponding pairs (V, W) can be deduced from Table 4.

Table 4. List of all $\lambda \in \mathbf{F}_2^4$ such that S is $(2, 1)$-linear w.r.t. $(V, \langle \lambda \rangle)$, for each subspace V of dimension 2.

V	List of λ	V	List of λ	V	List of λ	V	List of λ
$\langle 1, 2 \rangle$	$\{1, e, f\}$	$\langle 2, 8 \rangle$	$\{1, e, f\}$	$\langle 3, d \rangle$	$\{3, c, f\}$	$\langle 6, 8 \rangle$	$\{1, 4, 5, a, b, e, f\}$
$\langle 1, 4 \rangle$	$\{e\}$	$\langle 2, 9 \rangle$	$\{1, e, f\}$	$\langle 4, 8 \rangle$	$\{1, 6, 7, 8, 9, e, f\}$	$\langle 6, 9 \rangle$	$\{4, a, e\}$
$\langle 1, 6 \rangle$	$\{4, a, e\}$	$\langle 2, c \rangle$	$\{1, e, f\}$	$\langle 4, 9 \rangle$	$\{e\}$	$\langle 6, a \rangle$	$\{1, e, f\}$
$\langle 1, 8 \rangle$	$\{1, 8, 9\}$	$\langle 2, d \rangle$	$\{1, e, f\}$	$\langle 4, a \rangle$	$\{1, 2, 3, c, d, e, f\}$	$\langle 6, b \rangle$	$\{5, b, e\}$
$\langle 1, a \rangle$	$\{1\}$	$\langle 3, 4 \rangle$	$\{e\}$	$\langle 4, b \rangle$	$\{e\}$	$\langle 7, 8 \rangle$	$\{1, 6, 7\}$
$\langle 1, c \rangle$	$\{f\}$	$\langle 3, 5 \rangle$	$\{5, b, e\}$	$\langle 5, 8 \rangle$	$\{1, 8, 9\}$	$\langle 7, 9 \rangle$	$\{3, e, f\}$
$\langle 1, e \rangle$	$\{2, d, f\}$	$\langle 3, 8 \rangle$	$\{1, 6, 7\}$	$\langle 5, 9 \rangle$	$\{f\}$	$\langle 7, a \rangle$	$\{1\}$
$\langle 2, 4 \rangle$	$\{1, e, f\}$	$\langle 3, 9 \rangle$	$\{1\}$	$\langle 5, a \rangle$	$\{1\}$	$\langle 7, b \rangle$	$\{f\}$
$\langle 2, 5 \rangle$	$\{1, e, f\}$	$\langle 3, c \rangle$	$\{f\}$	$\langle 5, b \rangle$	$\{2, d, f\}$		

From this table, we can check that, for $\lambda = 1$ (resp. for $\lambda = 8$), the properties given by Fuhr describe the whole list of subspaces V such that S is $(3,1)$-linear (resp. $(2,1)$-linear) w.r.t. to $(V, \langle \lambda \rangle)$. Nevertheless, it appears that S is also $(3,2)$-linear, and $(2,2)$-linear with respect to many other subspaces. In particular, we can see that it is possible to identify other components of S which have also degree at most 1 on the same subspaces. This is very useful in practice, as by using this table we can now guarantee the affine propagation of some components of S that we would have rejected before. For example we can observe that y_1 and y_2 are $(2,1)$-linear with respect to three different subspaces of dimension 2 each. These cases that are not treated at all in [12] can now be used to search for a possible affine propagation of the initial variables through the second and the third round.

4.2   Searching for the Input Variables

In [12], Relation (1) is used in order to ensure the affine propagation through the nonlinear layer of the first round. As we have already mentioned, this property guarantees that after the Sbox layer of the first round, there is at most one variable per *active* Sbox. We name *active* an Sbox that takes at least one variable as input. In the contrary, we call an Sbox *non-active* if its input vector is constant. Moreover, Relation (1) ensures that this unique variable belongs to a word corresponding to the d-input of the linear function L (see Sect. 3.1). It is easy to see from the description of L that the variables that belong to a word d of the state propagate much slower than the variables in the words a and c. In particular, each variable of a word d affects at most three bits of the state after the application of the linear part. However, the variables of the words b have the same slow propagation as the words d and this property was not exploited in [12]. In this sense, the following property of the Hamsi Sbox appears to be very useful:

$$S(1, x, 0, x) = (0, x, 1, 0), \text{ for every } x \in \mathbf{F}_2. \tag{2}$$

Our aim is to find a set of input variables $\mathcal{I}$ such that the set of output bits $\mathcal{O}$ that are affine in $\mathcal{I}$, is maximized. Then, the most difficult problem is to choose which Sboxes of the state during the first round will be active. We have used the following approach to solve this problem.

First, we restrict the search to the first 64 Sboxes of the state for the following reason. Equally with the approach in [12], we are searching for a preimage h of a given chaining value h^*. This is why the chosen variable bits of the internal state must be assigned to positions that, after the concatenation, contain variables coming out from the chaining value. By using Relation (1) or Relation (2), this constraint is verified for the first half of the state. On the contrary, this does not hold anymore for the second half, because the positions of the message bits and the chaining value bits are interchanged.

However, it is obvious that we cannot test all the possible pairs $(\mathcal{I}, \mathcal{O})$ because of the high complexity of such a search. For this reason we have adopted a heuristic strategy, that can be found in Appendix B of [2]. This heuristic method exploits the low diffusion through the three rounds of the function for finding good candidates for the input and output sets. An algorithm for obtaining such candidate sets is equally described in [2] (Algorithm 1). Once such candidate sets have been obtained, we launch an automated search, to see which combination of $N_\mathcal{I}$ of the input bits in the candidate set gives the largest number of affine output bits. For each test, we check the propagation through the last two rounds by using the relations identified by Table 4. These techniques have led to the following results.

4.3   Results

For $N_\mathcal{I} = 9$ input variables. For the 9 Sboxes $\{0, 7, 24, 30, 35, 37, 51, 59, 61\}$, we are fixing the inputs as required by Relation (1) for the Sboxes $\{0, 30, 35, 37\}$ and by Relation (2) for the others. Then the 13 output bits

$$\{6, 8, 43, 78, 262, 278, 313, 320, 343, 345, 350, 355, 380\}$$

depend in an affine way on the 9 input variables. In particular, we are able to find two more affine relations than in [12] for $N_\mathcal{I} = 9$ variables.

For $N_\mathcal{I} = 10$ input variables. For the 10 Sboxes $\{0, 7, 12, 16, 30, 35, 37, 51, 59, 61\}$, we are fixing the inputs as required by Relation (1) for the Sboxes $\{0, 16, 30, 35, 37\}$ and by Relation (2) for the others. Then the 11 output bits

$$\{6, 8, 43, 78, 278, 313, 320, 343, 345, 350, 380\}$$

depend affinely on the 10 input variables. Here again we find two more output bits than Fuhr in [12].

As we were able to find in both cases a higher number of affine equations than those of the original paper, the overall complexity of the attack should slightly decrease. However a complete complexity evaluation of our attack is a very complex task since it requires to count down the performed number of bitwise operations during all the steps of the attack. This procedure exceeds the scope of this work.

5   Conclusions

We have introduced a new cryptographic property for vectorial Boolean functions, that we call the (v, w)-linearity. This notion can be used as a new measure of linearity for Sboxes and is related to the number of linear relations that propagate through them. As the 4-bit balanced Sboxes are among the most used building-blocks in symmetric primitives, we classify them according to this new criterion. In particular, we analyse the (v, w)-linearity of "optimal" 4-bit permutations, according to the classification of Leander and Poschmann in [17].

For instance, our analysis points out that the Sbox used in Hamsi does not guarantee the best resistance to Fuhr's attack. Indeed, if an Sbox belonging to one of the classes $G_3, G_4, G_5, G_6, G_7, G_{11}, G_{12}$ or G_{13} was used, the good linear and differential properties of the Sbox would still be preserved, but the function would be (v, w)-linear for a smaller value of w. In other words, the Sbox would have fewer components which may remain affine with respect to the input variables. Moreover, the number of 2-dimensional subspaces V such that S is $(2, w)$-linear w.r.t. (V, W) for some W is quite large. This increases the degrees of freedom in the cryptanalysis introduced by Fuhr, while the attack would probably have failed for an Sbox without any quadratic component. In order to verify this in practice, we implemented the same attack on the variant of Hamsi based on some other Sbox. More precisely, we first used the representative Sbox of the class G_3, as this is given in [17] and then, the Sbox S_0 of the finalist of the SHA-3 competition, JH [23]. Indeed, we noticed that in both cases Fuhr's attack failed.

A future line of work would be to determine how the new notion of (v, w)-linearity is related to some other recent attacks. For instance, the invariant subspace attack [16] exploits a similar but stronger property of the 3×3 Sbox used in PRINTcipher: two outputs of this Sbox are constant on a subspace of dimension 1 and on all its cosets (the coset is here determined by the key). Some relation to the resistance to first-order DPA could also be investigated.

Acknowledgments. We would like to thank María Naya Plasencia for her valuable advices, and Christian Rechberger for very interesting discussions.

References

1. Berlekamp, E.R., Welch, L.R.: Weight distributions of the cosets of the (32,6) Reed-Muller code. IEEE Trans. Inf. Theor. **18**(1), 203–207 (1972)
2. Boura, C., Canteaut, A.: A new criterion for avoiding the propagation of linear relations through an Sbox (Full version). IACR ePrint Report 2013/211, April 2013. http://eprint.iacr.org/2013/211
3. De Cannière, C.: Analysis and Design of Symmetric Encryption Algorithms. Ph.D. thesis, Katholieke Universiteit Leuven (2007)
4. Canteaut, A., Carlet, C., Charpin, P., Fontaine, C.: On cryptographic properties of the cosets of $R(1, m)$. IEEE Trans. Inf. Theor. **47**(4), 1494–1513 (2001)
5. Canteaut, A., Daum, M., Dobbertin, H., Leander, G.: Finding nonnormal bent functions. Discret. Appl. Math. **154**(2), 202–218 (2006)
6. Carlet, C., Prouff, E.: Vectorial functions and covering sequences. In: Mullen, G.L., Poli, A., Stichtenoth, H. (eds.) Fq7 2003. LNCS, vol. 2948, pp. 215–248. Springer, Heidelberg (2004)
7. Charpin, P.: Normal Boolean functions. J. Complex. **20**(2–3), 245–265 (2004)
8. Dillon, J.F.: Elementary Hadamard Difference Sets. Ph.D. thesis, University of Maryland (1974)
9. Dinur, I., Shamir, A.: Cube attacks on tweakable black box polynomials. In: Joux, A. (ed.) EUROCRYPT 2009. LNCS, vol. 5479, pp. 278–299. Springer, Heidelberg (2009)
10. Dinur, I., Shamir, A.: An improved algebraic attack on Hamsi-256. In: Joux, A. (ed.) FSE 2011. LNCS, vol. 6733, pp. 88–106. Springer, Heidelberg (2011)

11. Dobbertin, H.: Construction of bent functions and balanced Boolean functions with high nonlinearity. In: Preneel, B. (ed.) FSE 1994. LNCS, vol. 1008, pp. 61–74. Springer, Heidelberg (1995)
12. Fuhr, T.: Finding second preimages of short messages for Hamsi-256. In: Abe, M. (ed.) ASIACRYPT 2010. LNCS, vol. 6477, pp. 20–37. Springer, Heidelberg (2010)
13. Fuhr, T.: Conception, preuves et analyse de fonctions de hachage cryptographiques. Ph.D. thesis, Télécom ParisTech (2011)
14. Gupta, C.K., Sarkar, P.: Improved construction of nonlinear resilient S-boxes. In: Zheng, Y. (ed.) ASIACRYPT 2002. LNCS, vol. 2501, pp. 466–483. Springer, Heidelberg (2002)
15. Küçük, Ö: The Hash Function Hamsi. Submission to NIST (Round 2) (2009)
16. Leander, G., Abdelraheem, M.A., AlKhzaimi, H., Zenner, E.: A cryptanalysis of PRINTCIPHER: the invariant subspace attack. In: Rogaway, P. (ed.) CRYPTO 2011. LNCS, vol. 6841, pp. 206–221. Springer, Heidelberg (2011)
17. Leander, G., Poschmann, A.: On the classification of 4 Bit S-boxes. In: Carlet, C., Sunar, B. (eds.) WAIFI 2007. LNCS, vol. 4547, pp. 159–176. Springer, Heidelberg (2007)
18. McFarland, R.L.: A family of noncyclic difference sets. J. Comb. Theor. Ser. A **15**, 1–10 (1973)
19. Nyberg, K.: Perfect nonlinear S-boxes. In: Davies, D.W. (ed.) EUROCRYPT 1991. LNCS, vol. 547, pp. 378–386. Springer, Heidelberg (1991)
20. Nyberg, K.: S-boxes and round functions with controllable linearity and differential uniformity. In: Preneel, B. (ed.) FSE 1994. LNCS, vol. 1008, pp. 111–130. Springer, Heidelberg (1995)
21. Pasalic, E., Maitra, S.: Linear codes in generalized construction of resilient functions with very high nonlinearity. IEEE Trans. Inf. Theor. **48**(8), 2182–2191 (2002)
22. Saarinen, M.-J.O.: Cryptographic analysis of all 4×4-Bit S-boxes. In: Miri, A., Vaudenay, S. (eds.) SAC 2011. LNCS, vol. 7118, pp. 118–133. Springer, Heidelberg (2012)
23. Wu, H.: The Hash Function JH. Submission to NIST (Round 3) (2011)

Author Index

Printed in the United States
By Bookmasters

Printed in the United States
By Bookmasters